MIRRORS & WINDOWS

Connecting with Literature

American Tradition

EMC
Publishing

ST. PAUL • LOS ANGELES • INDIANAPOLIS

Staff Credits

Senior Editor: Brenda Owens
Editor: Susan Freese
Associate Editors: Carley Bomstad, Stephanie Djock, Keri Henkel Stifter
Assistant Editors: Brendan Curran, Julie Nelson
Editorial Assistants: Lindsay Ryan, Erin Saladin
Teacher's Edition Editors: Sheila Anderson, Stephanie Djock, Cheryl Drivdahl, Nancy Papsin
Permissions Coordinator: Valerie Murphy
Proofreader: Carol Rogers
Photo Researchers: Brendan Curran, Julie Nelson
Marketing Managers: Bruce Ayscue, Laurie Skiba
Production Editor: Bob Dreas
Cover Designer: Leslie Anderson
Page Layout Designers: Matthias Frasch, Jack Ross
Production Specialist: Petrina Nyhan
Production Services: Shepherd, Inc.

Literary Acknowledgments: Literary Acknowledgments appear following the Glossary of Vocabulary Words. We have made every effort to trace the ownership of all copyrighted material and to secure permission from copyright holders. In the event of any question arising as to the use of any material, we will be pleased to make the necessary corrections in future printings. Thanks are due to the authors, publishers, and agents for permission to use the materials indicated.

Art and Photo Credits: Art and Photo Credits appear following the Literary Acknowledgments.

ISBN 978-0-82193-189-9 (Student Edition Text)
ISBN 978-0-82193-191-2 (Annotated Teacher's Edition Text)

© 2009 by EMC Publishing, LLC
875 Montreal Way
St. Paul, MN 55102
E-mail: educate@emcp.com
Web site: www.emcp.com

Consultants, Reviewers, and Focus Group Participants

Jean Martorana
Reading Specialist/English Teacher
Desert Vista High School
Phoenix, Arizona

Tracy Pulido
Language Arts Instructor
West Valley High School
Fairbanks, Alaska

Cindy Johnston
English Teacher
Argus High School
Ceres, California

Susan Stoehr
Language Arts Instructor
Aragon High School
San Mateo, California

John Owens
Reading Specialist
St. Vrain Valley Schools
Longmont, Colorado

Fred Smith
Language Arts Instructor
St. Bernard High School
Uncasville, Connecticut

Penny Austin-Richardson
English Department Chair
Seaford Senior High School
Seaford, Delaware

Cecilia Lewis
Language Arts Instructor
Mariner High School
Cape Coral, Florida

Jane Feber
Teacher
Mandarin Middle School
Jacksonville, Florida

Dorothy Fletcher
Language Arts Instructor
Wolfson Senior High School
Jacksonville, Florida

Tamara Doehring
English/Reading Teacher
Melbourne High School
Melbourne, Florida

Patti Magee
English Instructor
Timber Creek High School
Orlando, Florida

Margaret J. Graham
Language Arts/Reading Teacher
Elizabeth Cobb Middle School
Tallahassee, Florida

Elizabeth Steinman
English Instructor
Vero Beach High School
Vero Beach, Florida

Wanda Bagwell
Language Arts Department Chair
Commerce High School
Commerce, Georgia

Betty Deriso
Language Department Chairperson
Crisp County High School
Cordele, Georgia

Dr. Peggy Leland
English Instructor
Chestatee High School
Gainsville, Georgia

Matthew Boedy
Language Arts Instructor
Harlem High School
Harlem, Georgia

Patty Bradshaw
English Department Chair
Harlem High School
Harlem, Georgia

Dawn Faulkner
English Department Chair
Rome High School
Rome, Georgia

Carolyn C. Coleman
AKS Continuous Improvement
  Director
Gwinnett County Public Schools
Suwanee, Georgia

Elisabeth Blumer Thompson
Language Arts Instructor
Swainsboro High School
Swainsboro, Georgia

Toi Walker
English Instructor
Northeast Tifton County High
  School
Tifton, Georgia

Jeanette Rogers
English Instructor
Potlatch Jr.-Sr. High School
Potlatch, Idaho

Gail Taylor
Language Arts Instructor
Rigby High School
Rigby, Idaho

Carey Robin
Language Arts Instructor
St. Francis College Prep
Brookfield, Illinois

Patricia Meyer
English Department Chair
Glenbard East High School
Lombard, Illinois

Liz Rebmann
Language Arts Instructor
Morton High School
Morton, Illinois

Helen Gallagher
English Department Chair
Main East High School
Park Ridge, Illinois

Rosemary Ryan
Dean of Students
Schaumburg High School
Schaumburg, Illinois

Donna Cracraft
English Department Co-Chair/IB
  Coordinator
Pike High School
Indianapolis, Indiana

Consultants, Reviewers, and Focus Group Participants (cont.)

K. C. Salter
Language Arts Instructor
Knightstown High School
Knightstown, Indiana

Lisa Broxterman
Language Arts Instructor
Axtell High School
Axtell, Kansas

Shirley Wells
Language Arts Instructor
Derby High School
Derby, Kansas

Karen Ann Stous
Speech & Drama Teacher
Holton High School
Holton, Kansas

Martha-Jean Rockey
Language Arts Instructor
Troy High School
Troy, Kansas

Shelia Penick
Language Arts Instructor
Yates Center High School
Yates Center, Kansas

John Ermilio
English Teacher
St. Johns High School
Shrewsbury, Massachusetts

James York
English Teacher
Waverly High School
Lansing, Michigan

Mary Spychalla
Gifted Education Coordinator
Valley Middle School
Apple Valley, Minnesota

Shari K. Carlson
Advanced ILA Teacher
Coon Rapids Middle School
Coon Rapids, Minnesota

Rebecca Benz
English Instructor
St. Thomas Academy
Mendota Heights, Minnesota

Michael F. Graves
Professor Emeritus
University of Minnesota
330A Peik Hall
Minneapolis, Minnesota

Kathleen Nelson
English Instructor
New Ulm High School
New Ulm, Minnesota

Adonna Gaspar
Language Arts Teacher
Cooper High School
Robbinsdale, Minnesota

Sara L. Nystuen
English Department Chair; AP
Instructor
Concordia Academy
Roseville, Minnesota

Tom Backen
English Teacher
Benilde-St. Margaret's School
St. Louis Park, Minnesota

Daniel Sylvester
Jr. High English & American
Experience Teacher
Benilde-St. Margaret's School
St. Louis Park, Minnesota

Jean Borax
Literacy Coach
Harding High School
St. Paul, Minnesota

Erik Brandt
English Teacher
Harding High School
St. Paul, Minnesota

Kevin Brennan
High School English Teacher
Cretin-Derham Hall
St. Paul, Minnesota

Anna Newcombe
English Instructor
Harding High School
St. Paul, Minnesota

Rosemary Ruffenach
Language Arts Teacher, Consultant,
and Writer
St. Paul, Minnesota

Nancy Papsin
English Teacher/Educational
Consultant
White Bear Lake, Minnesota

Shannon Umfleet
Communication Arts Instructor
Northwest High School
Cedar Hill, Missouri

Ken Girard
Language Arts Instructor
Bishop LeBlond High School
St. Joseph, Missouri

Jessica Gall
Language Arts Instructor
Fremont High School
Fremont, Nebraska

Michael Davis
Language Arts Instructor
Millard West High School
Omaha, Nebraska

Lisa Larnerd
English Teacher
Basic High School
Henderson, Nevada

Jo Paulson
Title I Reading Teacher
Camino Real Middle School
Las Cruces, New Mexico

Stacy Biss
Language Arts Instructor
Hackensack High School
Hackensack, New Jersey

J. M. Winchock
Reading Specialist, Adult Literacy
Instructor
Hillsborough High School
Hillsborough, New Jersey

Consultants, Reviewers, and Focus Group Participants (cont.)

Matthew Cahn
Department of English & Related
Arts Supervisor
River Dell High School
Oradell, New Jersey

Jean Mullooly
Language Arts Instructor
Holy Angels High School
Trenton, New Jersey

Fenice Boyd
Assistant Professor, Learning and
Instruction
State University of New York at
Buffalo
Buffalo, New York

Michael Fedorchuk
Assistant Principal
Auburn High School
Auburn, New York

Robert Balch
English Instructor
Beacon High School
Beacon, New York

Rene A. Roberge
Secondary English/AP English
Instructor
Hudson Falls High School
Hudson Falls, New York

Melissa Hedt
Literacy Coach
Asheville Middle School
Asheville, North Carolina

Jane Shoaf
Educational Consultant
Durham, North Carolina

Kimberly Tufts
Department Chair for ELA
Cranberry Middle School
Elk Park, North Carolina

Cheryl Gackle
English Instructor
Kulm High School
Kulm, North Dakota

Barbara Stroh
English Department Chair
Aurora High School
Aurora, Ohio

Mary Jo Bish
Language Arts Instructor
Lake Middle School
Millbury, Ohio

Judy Ellsesser-Painter
Language Arts Instructor
South Webster High School
South Webster, Ohio

Adele Dahlin
English Department Chair
Central Catholic High School
Toledo, Ohio

Joshua Singer
English Instructor
Central Catholic High School
Toledo, Ohio

Debbie Orendorf
Language Arts Instructor
Berlin Brothers Valley High School
Berlin, Pennsylvania

Dona Italiano
English Teacher/Language Arts
Coordinator
Souderton Area High School
Souderton, Pennsylvania

Tina Parlier
Secondary English Instructor
Elizabethton High School
Elizabethton, Tennessee

Wayne Luellen
English Instructor
Houston High School
Germantown, Tennessee

Ed Farrell
Senior Consultant
Emeritus Professor of English
Education
University of Texas at Austin
Austin, Texas

Terry Ross
Secondary Language Arts
Supervisor
Austin Independent School District
Austin, Texas

Angelia Greiner
English Department Chair
Big Sandy High School
Big Sandy, Texas

Sharon Kremer
Educational Consultant
Denton, Texas

E. J. Brletich
Supervisor of English/Language
Arts
Spotsylvania City School
Fredericksburg, Virginia

Jeffrey Golub
Educational Consultant
Bothell, Washington

Clifford Aziz
Language Arts Instructor
Washington High School
Tacoma, Washington

Becky Palmer
Reading Teacher
Madison Middle School
Appleton, Wisconsin

Mary Hoppe
English Teacher
Bonduel High School
Bonduel, Wisconsin

Lou Wappel
English, Humanities & Guidance
Instructor
St. Lawrence Seminary High School
Mount Calvary, Wisconsin

Gregory R. Keir
Language Arts Instructor
East Elementary School
New Richmond, Wisconsin

CONTENTS IN BRIEF

Language Arts Resources

LANGUAGE ARTS WORKSHOPS

Grammar & Style

Vocabulary & Spelling

Speaking & Listening

Writing

Test Practice

> ## "The whole purpose of education is to turn mirrors into windows."
>
> — Sydney J. Harris

Think about when you were young and about to start school for the first time. When you stood in front of the mirror, your view was focused on your own reflection and limited by your own experience. Then the windows of learning began to open your mind to new ideas and new experiences, broadening both your awareness and your curiosity.

As you discovered reading, you learned to connect with what you read and to examine your own ideas and experiences. And the more you read, the more you learned to connect with the ideas and experiences of other people from other times and other places. Great literature provides *mirrors* that help you reflect on your own world and *windows* that lead you into new worlds. This metaphor for the reading experience expresses the power of words to engage and transform you.

EMC's literature program, *Mirrors & Windows: Connecting with Literature,* provides opportunities for you to explore new worlds full of people, cultures, and perspectives different from your own. This book contains stories, essays, plays, and poems by outstanding authors from around the globe. Reading these selections will expand your appreciation of literature and your world view. Studying them will help you examine universal themes such as honesty, integrity, and justice and common emotions such as fear, pride, and belonging. You may already have thought about some of these ideas and feelings yourself.

As you read the selections in this book, try to see yourself in the characters, stories, and themes. Also try to see yourself as a citizen of the world—a world from which you have much to learn and to which you have much to offer.

DeSoto's Discovery of the Mississippi River, 1853.
William Henry Powell. New York Public Library, New York.

Origins of the American

Unit 1

PART 1

Native American Traditions

"O our Mother the Earth,
O our Father the Sky,
Your children are we."

—FROM TEWA TRIBAL SONG

PART 2

Shaping the New World

"Everything of worth is found full of difficulties."

—JOHN SMITH

PART 3

The American Revolution

"Give me liberty or give me death!"

—PATRICK HENRY

Tradition to 1800

Origins of the American Tradition to 1800

BCE–1500s   1600

AMERICAN LITERATURE

1400s–1500s CE
The Iroquois Constitution is created, joining the peoples of the Iroquois League

1552 CE
Bartolomé de Las Casas publishes *A Brief Account of the Destruction of the Indies*

1568 CE
Bernal Diaz del Castillo writes *The True History of the Conquest of New Spain*

DE LAS CASAS

1588 CE
Thomas Harriot writes *A Brief and True Report of the New Found Land of Virginia*

1624
John Smith of Jamestown publishes *The General History of Virginia*

1640
The *Bay Psalm Book* is printed, the first book printed in New England

1663
John Eliot translates the Bible into Algonquin; its printing makes it the first Bible published in North America

1682
Mary Rowlandson publishes a narrative about being held captive by Native Americans

1693
Cotton Mather's *The Wonders of the Invisible World* is published

AMERICAN HISTORY

14,000 BCE
Siberian peoples migrate across the Bering Strait to North America

5000 BCE
Civilization begins among the native peoples of North America

1000 CE
Leif Ericson makes contact with North America

1325 CE
The capital of the Aztec Empire, Tenochtitlan, Mexico, is founded

1492 CE
Christopher Columbus lands in the modern-day Bahamas

1565 CE
Spanish explorers establish St. Augustine in Florida

VIRGINIA

1607
John Smith founds the Jamestown Colony in modern-day Virginia

1619
Slavery begins when twenty Africans are brought to Jamestown for sale as indentured servants

1620
William Bradford founds the Plymouth Colony in modern-day Massachusetts

1635
The first public school, Boston Latin, is established

1692
During the Salem witch trials, 150 people are accused of practicing witchcraft and 20 are executed

WORLD HISTORY

8000 BCE
The Egyptians settle the Nile River Valley

2205 BCE
The Xia Dynasty begins in China

509 BCE
The Romans establish the Roman Republic

1517 CE
Martin Luther initiates the Reformation in Europe

1545 CE
Portuguese merchants begin capturing Africans and transporting them for slave labor

1600
The East India Company is established and ensured favorable trading privileges by Great Britain

1603
Tokugawa Ieyasu unifies Japan as its new Shogun

1610
Galileo sees the moons of Jupiter through a telescope

1665
The Great Plague of London kills 75,000

1685
Protestantism is outlawed in France

1689
Peter the Great becomes Czar of Russia

Note: Eras are designated as BCE ("before the common era"; formerly BC) and CE ("of the common era"; formerly AD).

AMERICAN LITERATURE AMERICAN LITERATURE AMERICAN LITERATURE AMERICAN LITERATURE AMERICAN

1700
Samuel Sewall publishes "The Selling of Joseph," an antislavery article

1704
The first successful American newspaper, the *News-Letter,* is published in Boston

1732
Benjamin Franklin circulates *Poor Richard's Almanack*

1741
Jonathan Edwards delivers "Sinners in the Hands of an Angry God"

1755
Dr. Richard Schuckburgh, a British surgeon, writes the lyrics to "Yankee Doodle Dandy"

1773
Phillis Wheatley publishes her first volume of poetry

1776
Thomas Paine argues against British rule in his pamphlet *Common Sense*

1776
Thomas Jefferson writes the Declaration of Independence

1787
Alexander Hamilton, James Madison, and John Jay publish *The Federalist Papers*

JEFFERSON

1789
William H. Brown writes *The Power of Sympathy,* sometimes considered the first American novel

AMERICAN HISTORY AMERICAN HISTORY AMERICAN HISTORY AMERICAN HISTORY AMERICAN H

1731
Ben Franklin founds the first public library in Philadelphia

1741
Vitus Bering discovers Alaska

1754
The French and Indian War erupts between English and French colonists over territory disputes

1765
Great Britain passes the Stamp Act, imposing taxation on the American colonies

1774
The First Continental Congress meets in Philadelphia

1775
The Revolutionary War begins

1776
The colonies declare independence from Great Britain

1783
The Treaty of Paris is signed, ending the Revolutionary War and granting independence to the American colonies

1787
The U.S. Constitution is adopted

WASHINGTON

1789
George Washington becomes the first president

1791
The Bill of Rights becomes law

WORLD HISTORY WORLD HISTORY WORLD HISTORY WORLD HISTORY WORLD HISTORY WO

1707
The United Kingdom of Great Britain is formed, joining England, Scotland, and Wales

1709
Great Britain passes the world's first copyright law

1755
An earthquake in Lisbon, Portugal, kills 60,000

1757
The British Empire colonizes India

1763
The Treaty of Paris cedes Canada to Great Britain

1772
Poland is divided among Russia, Prussia, and Austria

1783
The first hot air balloon with passengers takes flight in Paris

1788
Great Britain establishes the penal colony of New South Wales in Australia

AUSTRALIA

1789
The French Revolution begins

1794
Haiti establishes independence from France

1799
Napoleon stages a coup d'etat and becomes dictator of France

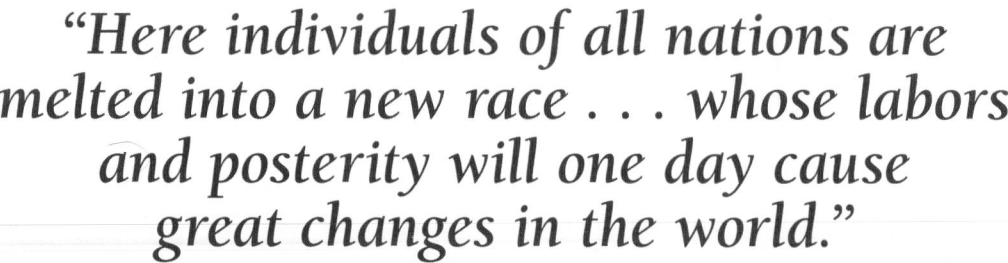

"Here individuals of all nations are melted into a new race . . . whose labors and posterity will one day cause great changes in the world."

—J. HECTOR ST. JEAN DE CRÈVECOEUR

The First Americans

When Europeans arrived on the North American continent, it had been inhabited for somewhere between twenty thousand and fifty thousand years, with the first peoples likely traveling from Asia across a land bridge spanning the Bering Strait. Although Viking explorers established a short-lived settlement in what is now Newfoundland about 1000 CE, it wasn't until 1492, when Christopher Columbus landed on San Salvador, that Europeans returned to the Americas and stayed. At that time, about 240 distinct Native American cultures flourished in North America alone, boasting a population of between one million and two million.

Thinking that he had reached India, Columbus called the Arawak natives whom he met "Indians" and, on his return, suggested to the Spanish monarchs that they would make good slaves. Soon European powers were competing to seize the opportunities they imagined this New World offered, with the Spanish, Dutch, French, and English all establishing colonies in North America. However, for the native population of the Americas, the arrival of the Europeans spelled disaster. Millions died as a result of European diseases, to which they had no natural immunities, and millions more were enslaved or driven from their ancestral lands.

"Broken spears lie in the roads;
we have torn our hair in our grief.
The houses are roofless now, and
their walls are red with blood."

—AZTEC LEADER

Jamestown and the Origins of the Plantation System

The earliest European-founded settlements in the continental United States were in Florida, beginning as early as 1559. The first one to survive was St. Augustine, settled by the Spanish in 1565. The first European born in what would become the United States was born in St. Augustine one year later.

In 1587, a group of 117 English settlers, led by Sir Walter Raleigh and John White, founded a colony on Roanoke Island off the coast of what is now North Carolina. Within three years, however, its people had disappeared, so Jamestown, Virginia, settled in 1607, became the first English colony to survive. Its colonists hoped to

---

NOTABLE NUMBERS

1/3 Fraction of the 25,000 Native Americans in New England who died in the plague of 1616–1618

4 Women who arrived on the *Mayflower* and survived the first year (out of 18)

Over 50% Colonists who came to America as indentured servants, committed to five to seven years of free service for their passage

300 British troops killed or wounded at Concord and Lexington; 100 colonial troops were killed or wounded

21% Slave population of the American colonies in 1776, rising from 8% in 1700

100 Number of U.S. newspapers in 1790

establish a self-sustaining community but faced great hardship because they knew little of the new land.

The story of leader John Smith's rescue by Pocahontas may or may not be true, but it contains a symbolic truth: Only with the assistance of native peoples were the colonists able to survive. Native Americans taught the colonists how to build adequate shelters and how to cultivate crops such as corn and tobacco for food and export. Soon the Jamestown colonists had created large tobacco plantations and imported first indentured servants and then slaves to do the work. Thus developed the plantation system and slave trade that would have a dramatic effect on the course of North American history.

New England Colonization and the Puritan Era

Two other settlements established in the early colonial years played a decisive role in North American history. The Plymouth Colony, founded in 1620, and the Massachusetts Bay Colony, founded in 1630, were both Puritan settlements. The Plymouth colonists arrived at Cape Cod on the *Mayflower* in 1620 and established the terms of their settlement by means of the Mayflower Compact. After a difficult winter, the colonists learned from native peoples how to plant indigenous crops, and under the direction of Governor William Bradford, the colony flourished. The Massachusetts

Bay colonists saw their enterprise as divinely guided. Their governor, John Winthrop, would write that they were about the business of building, as described in the New Testament, a "city upon a hill" in the new land.

Puritan communities functioned as *theocracies,* or societies guided by religious law, and their early leaders were largely intolerant of opposition. When Roger Williams objected to the Puritans' arrogant intolerance of diversity and the taking of lands from the Native Americans in 1635, he was banished from Massachusetts. He went on to found the colony of Rhode Island, which became the first place in America where people of all faiths could worship freely. In 1637, when Anne Hutchinson bypassed the official church and began teaching home Bible classes, she was accused of threatening the religion and of being more a "husband than a wife." Also banished, she founded a settlement at Portsmouth, Rhode Island.

Even though pressures from progressive elements led to relaxing old rules, tensions remained. Some saw the decline of orthodoxy as a sign of weakness and came to believe that Satan had infiltrated the town of Salem and nearby communities. The ensuing witch trials, followed by embarrassment and recanting, further diminished the Puritan hold on New England. By 1692, their colonies no longer required voters to be church members.

Meanwhile, William Penn, having received a tract of land from the English king, decided to put Quaker ideals into practice. He paid the Native Americans for what would become Pennsylvania and then welcomed people of all religious faiths and offered them the privilege of self-government.

The European Enlightenment and the Great Awakening

The scientific and empirical thinking that emerged in England in 1660 had a significant effect on later Puritan intellectuals such as Cotton Mather and Jonathan Edwards. Enlightenment thinkers John Locke and Isaac Newton believed that the study of human experience

> *"Remember, all men would be tyrants if they could. If particular care and attention are not paid to the ladies, we are determined to foment a rebellion."*
>
> —ABIGAIL ADAMS

and the natural world was the proper means of arriving at true knowledge. Such inquiry did not, in their opinion, challenge religious faith.

This emphasis on empirical evidence and human experience gave rise to Jonathan Edwards's claim that a person must feel or experience God, not just intellectually assent to the existence of God from a belief system or reading the Bible. Such emotional experiences, or *awakenings* as they came to be called, formed the basis for a religious revival called the Great Awakening.

The Emergence of American Diversity

During the colonial period, New England remained relatively homogeneous, populated largely by Puritans of British descent. However, the mid-Atlantic and southern regions saw rapid changes driven by the arrival of other peoples, who brought their religions and ways of life with them. By the time of the American Revolution, the colonies had achieved a great deal of social diversity.

In the colony of Pennsylvania, Quakers established a community based on equality and religious tolerance. In other parts of the mid-Atlantic region, such as New York, New Jersey, and Delaware, the arrival of Jewish, German, and Irish immigrants brought a more individualistic, capitalist approach to the life of their communities. There, on the many middle-sized farms that were cleared, labor often was performed by slaves and indentured servants. In the Southern colonies, the economy was based largely on produce grown for sale, such as cotton and tobacco, and relied largely on slave labor.

Rebellion Against Great Britian and a New Nation

The diverse and growing population of the American colonies came to resent domination by Great Britain. In 1763, after the French and Indian War, Britain imposed the Stamp Act on the colonies, the first of a series of heavy taxes that became the focus of the colonies' resentment. A tax on tea followed in 1773, resulting in the Boston Tea Party. The British then passed the Intolerable Acts, which restricted colonists' meetings and required them to house and supply more British soldiers.

The colonists had had enough. They sent representatives to the First Continental Congress, held in Philadelphia in 1774. There, delegates approved a letter of protest to King George III along with a boycott of British goods and the organization of a militia.

In April 1775, British troops moved toward Concord, Massachusetts, hoping to capture rebel leaders and weapons. But the rebels had been warned. When they blocked the roadway, there was a momentary standoff—until a shot was fired. That shot marked the beginning of the American Revolutionary War.

The Second Continental Congress, meeting in Philadelphia in May 1775, organized an army under General George Washington. In June, after the Battle of Bunker Hill near Boston, King George officially declared the colonies in rebellion. In June 1776, the Congress voted in favor of independence and later adopted Thomas Jefferson's draft of the Declaration of Independence.

In 1777, Congress adopted the Articles of Confederation, creating a weak central government and reserving most powers for the individual colonies. When British troops were defeated at Yorktown in 1781, the war effectively ended. Under the terms of the Treaty of Paris, the British gave up their claim to the colonies. Subsequently, a new Constitution was adopted in 1787. Although institutionalizing the "more perfect union" promised by the Constitution would prove challenging in the years to come, the diversity of the union would also be its greatest strength.

The origins of American literature lie in the traditional myths, legends, tales, songs, and other orally transmitted works of the Native American peoples. No written literature existed among the more than 240 distinct tribal peoples who lived in North America before the arrival of the first Europeans.

The diversity of these native peoples is reflected in their oral literature, where distinct regional and cultural differences can be identified. The narratives of the Ojibwa, who lived in the wooded region around the western Great Lakes, are quite different from those of such desert tribes as the Hopi. Even among tribal groups within the same region, as in what is now the U.S. Southwest, the traditional literature reflects differences in lifestyle, such as the nomadic hunting lifestyle of the Apache versus the more settled agricultural lifestyle of the Navajo and the Pueblo.

Religious diversity also characterized the Native American peoples and thus their literature. Various tribes worshipped their own gods, animals, plants, and sacred individuals. The consistent thread running among these various religions, however, was a reverence for nature, which often was viewed as a spiritual as well as a physical mother.

The oral tradition also was the means by which Native Americans recorded and transmitted their philosophies and systems of government. The Iroquois Constitution, created to preserve peace among the Iroquois League of Nations in New York State, expresses clear democratic values. Other tribal groups functioned as autocracies (in which a single individual had primary or exclusive power) or were governed by councils of elders.

Newspaper Rock petroglyph panel, c. 500–1500 CE. Newspaper Rock State Historical Monument, Utah.

The Oral Tradition Defined

Myths, folk tales, legends, and songs are all forms of oral literature, or what is called the **oral tradition.** The narratives in this form were handed down through many generations by word of mouth and only recorded in detail within the last hundred years. Although long familiar to the specific cultures that produced them, these tales did not yet belong to world literature.

In North America, the task of collecting oral stories has been complicated by language and cultural barriers. To help overcome these barriers, cultural anthropologists pioneered the theory of *cultural relativism,* which recognizes that the elements that hold meaning for one culture may hold little or no meaning for another.

Remember that the selections that follow come from an oral tradition, where the stories were not written down. When dealing with an oral text from a foreign culture, the storyteller must first transcribe the spoken word and then translate the richness of a language and belief system into a written text. It has taken the efforts of anthropologists, linguists, and native speakers to bring us the literary works collected here.

Reading Oral Literature

The work that originates in the oral tradition comprises little more than action and theme, with the plot serving as the vehicle of a moral and a theme or two. To some, the characters of myths and folk tales may seem two dimensional and flat, and little may seem to be going on below the surface meaning.

In fact, there is an entire universe of meaning, but we have to alter our approach to investigate the text. We can appreciate the subtle humor of a trickster tale, in which a character such as Coyote prevails because and in spite of his brashness and pride. There is psychology at work in "Coyote and the Earth Monster," when the trickster is first tricked and then turns the trick around. In reading the Osage creation myth, we get a glimpse of how the Osage originally envisioned the cosmos and their place within it.

Types of Oral Literature

Works commonly found in the oral tradition include folk tales, fables, fairy tales, tall tales, proverbs, legends, myths, parables, and ballads. The selections you will read include creation myths, a trickster tale, a tribal song, and a piece by contemporary author Leslie Marmon Silko. These works are what Silko, the first Native American woman novelist, refers to as "a collective effort in the recollection" of tribal wisdom. Her own poem "Prayer to the Pacific" is a retelling of the myth of how the tribal peoples reached North America from Asia. Rich in natural imagery, the poem draws on traditional Native American symbols.

"The oral tradition stays in the human brain and then it is a collective effort in the recollection. . . . It is a collective memory and depends upon the whole community."

—LESLIE MARMON SILKO,
POET, NOVELIST, AND STORYTELLER

Myth

A **myth** is a traditional story, rooted in a particular culture, that deals with gods, goddesses, and other supernatural beings, as well as human heroes. Myths often embody religious beliefs and values and explain natural phenomena. An example of a myth is the explanation of the sky as a piece of weaving in "Song of the Sky Loom."

Creation myths explain how the world came about. In Native American mythology, creation can take place from a hole in the sky, as it does in the Osage myth. Or it can begin in a hole in the earth, as in the Navajo account, where Begochiddy, one of the First Beings, plays the role of Creator.

The Trickster Tale

The *trickster* is a familiar character in Native American storytelling. He challenges the established order of things, bending others to his will. In the story you will read, Coyote creates disorder and change that is ultimately beneficial. Like other trickster figures such

as Rabbit, Raven, and Spider, Coyote represents the comic principle in the midst of tragedy.

Song

A *tribal song* is another form of cultural expression that contains the wisdom of a people compressed into a lyrical performance. Each singer brings meaning to the song, performing it in a unique way. You can find contemporary recordings of "Song of the Sky Loom" that evoke the original spirit of the verses.

Elements of Oral Literature

Performance and Audience

Because traditional tales and songs are intended to be spoken or sung, the relationship between teller and listener must be attentive and respectful. The tribal audience knows the context for each work and can readily supply the associations necessary for full understanding. The performer tells the story with particular gestures and vocal tone, acting out the events for the audience. As in a theater, the role of the audience is to listen attentively and engage with the narrative.

Narrative Voice

A **narrative** is a story told in fiction, nonfiction, poetry, or drama. A narrative is usually told in the order in which events occurred, or **chronological order.** The **voice** that tells the story determines the point of view from which events are told. In Native American oral literature, the narrative voice is that of a tribal elder, the source of wisdom and knowledge.

Theme

A **theme** is a central message or perception about life that is revealed through a literary work. Themes may be stated or implied. A *stated theme* is presented directly, whereas an *implied theme* must be inferred. A *universal theme* is a message about life that can be understood by people of most cultures.

The myth of creation, central to every culture, establishes the centrality of the people and explains why things are as they are. The number four runs throughout traditional Navajo beliefs; the Navajo believe in four worlds, four directions, four seasons, and so on. Physical transformation and emergence are also strong themes in Native American narratives. For example, in the Osage myth, Elk, whose majesty inspires all other living things to follow him, makes the land fruitful by rolling over the soft earth.

In reading the myths, notice how the maintenance of order and harmony depends on the relationship of earth, sky, water, animal, and human being. The human does not assert superiority over these other elements and creatures.

HOW TO READ

Oral Literature

Connect to prior knowledge. Works in the oral tradition belong to specific cultures. Consider what you know about the culture to which the work belongs. Also consider what you may need to know more about to understand the language and belief system of the culture from which the work originated.

Identify the sequence of events. Many works of oral literature are narratives and thus follow chronological order. To ensure you understand the sequence of events, create a timeline or map.

Read the work aloud. Remember that works in the oral tradition were intended to be spoken or sung. To hear the language and sense the tone of voice and gestures a speaker might have used in sharing a story or song, read it aloud.

The Osage Creation Account
The Navajo Creation Myth
Creation Myths

Build Background

Cultural Context **"The Osage Creation Account"**
emphasizes the relationship between nature and people.
The Osage, who called themselves the "Children of the
Middle Waters," migrated from the Atlantic coast to the
woodlands of present-day Missouri and the Great Plains
beyond. In religious ceremonies, Osage members were chosen to represent the sky, dry land, or water. The creation
myth explores the interweaving of these elements and
their role in the origin of the universe.

    "The Navajo Creation Myth" also reflects the inter-
dependence between Native Americans and their environment. In the Navajo religion, there are four worlds, with
our current world being the fourth "Glittering World." At each earlier level, the
beings were combinations of gods and animals before becoming more human-
like, but in each world, there was conflict, requiring removal to a higher world.
In the excerpt here, Begochiddy, the Great God, is helping the people move
from the third world to the fourth.

Reader's Context Think back to your earliest childhood memories of the
natural world. What explanations did you create to explain natural occurrences
such as rainbows and the changing phases of the moon?

Tatanka—The Story of the Bison, c. 2003. Peggy Detmer.
This sculpture is located near Deadwood, South Dakota.

Analyze Literature

Myth and Chronological Order
A **myth** is a story that explains
objects or events in the natural
world as resulting from the
action of some supernatural
force or entity, most often
a god.

Chronological order is the
arrangement of details in order
of their occurrence. It is the
primary method of organization
used in narrative writing.

Set Purpose

Explaining how the world came
to be is part of the oral tradition of most native cultures. As
you read the creation myths of
the Osage and Navajo, make a
chronological list of the events
that occur in each myth. Look
for similarities in how the two
peoples explain the natural
forces that both create and
sustain their world.

Preview Vocabulary

abode, 11
petrified, 12

THE *Osage Creation Account*

Hunting Elk, c. 1837. Alfred Jacob Miller.
Buffalo Bill Historical Center, Cody, Wyoming.
(See detail on page 10.)

Way beyond, a part of the Wazha'zhe[1] lived in the sky. They desired to know their origin, the source from which they came into existence. They went to the sun. He told them that they were his children. Then they wandered still farther and came to the moon. She told them that she gave birth to them, and that the sun was their father. She told them that they must leave their present <u>abode</u> and go down to the earth and dwell there. They came to the earth, but found it covered with water. They could not return to the place they had left, so they wept, but no answer came to them from anywhere. They floated about in the air, seeking in every direction for help from some god; but they found none. The animals were with them, and of all these the elk was the finest and most stately, and inspired all the creatures with confidence; so they appealed to the elk for help. He dropped into the water and began to sink. Then he called to the winds, and the winds came from all quarters and blew until the waters went upward as in a mist.

At first rocks only were exposed, and the people traveled on the rocky places that produced no plants, and there was nothing to eat. Then the waters began to go down until the soft earth was exposed. When this happened, the elk in his joy rolled over and over on the soft earth, and all his loose hairs clung to the soil. The hairs grew, and from them sprang beans, corns, potatoes, and wild turnips, and then all the grasses and trees. ❖

---

1. **Wazha'zhe.** One of the names by which the Osage were known

abode (ä bōd′) *n.,* where one lives or stays; home

MIRRORS & WINDOWS

Why do people want "to know their origin, the source from which they came into existence"? What do you know about your origin?

The Navajo Creation Myth

Begochiddy went back to the Lukatso, bamboo, and found the people much excited, and they were very glad to see Begochiddy, and when he came back to them they called him Sechai (Grandfather). He told them that he had met many people above, and that the world was good. They were very glad to hear that, and then Begochiddy sent Badger up to see the world. When he reached the hole, he tried to jump onto the crust but he broke through, and that is the reason why his paws are black to this day.

Begochiddy asked how the wet earth could be dried, and they sent up to the fourth world white thunder (Iknee-lakai) from the white mountain, also white cyclone (Niholtso-lakai) and white hail (N'dlohe-lakai), and black, blue and yellow cyclones. When the hail and thunder and cyclones hit the <u>petrified</u> wood and the mud columns which stuck up out of the mud, they were broken into pieces. Then the cyclones blew until they had dried the mud. And they sent five dust-devils, Nastoldisse, to trim up the rock pillars and make holes in them. After that five little whirlwinds were sent up, and they spread the tiny stones about smoothly.

Then the storms all went below to the third world from which they came, and the Lukatso began to grow again. And the people came up into this world led by the ants, with the turkey people coming last. Begochiddy pulled the bamboo up by the tassel on top and then threw the tassel back into the hole, which is why Lukatso, the bamboo, has no tassel now. This fourth world they called Hahjeenah. ❖

pet • ri • fied (peˊtrə fīd) *adj.,* turned to stone

MIRRORS & WINDOWS

What does your culture or religion teach you to expect from life? Do you believe the past dictates the future? What is and is not under your control?

Refer to Text ▶ ▶ ▶ ▶ ▶ Reason with Text

1a. In "The Navajo Creation Myth," what did the Badger do to get black paws?	**1b.** Explain why Badger was sent to see the new world.	**Understand** Find meaning
2a. In "The Osage Creation Account," what problems did the Wazha'zhe encounter once they left their home?	**2b.** Based on this creation myth, what did the Osage value?	**Apply** Use information
3a. According to the Navajo myth, how do the people come up into the Fourth World?	**3b.** Analyze the role Lukatso plays in this part of the creation.	**Analyze** Take things apart
4a. In "The Osage Creation Account," how do the Wazha'zhe feel about their new home?	**4b.** What effect might this creation myth have on the young Osage who listened to it? Support your answer with details from the myth.	**Evaluate** Make judgments
5a. In "The Navajo Creation Myth," how is the Fourth World made habitable for the people?	**5b.** Consider the elements involved in the creation of the world. Summarize how the Navajo seem to view these aspects of nature.	**Create** Bring ideas together

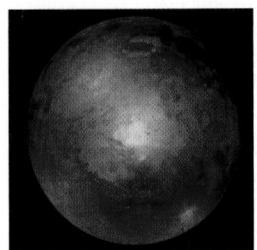

Analyze Literature

Myth and Chronological Order

These two creation myths start in distinctly opposite places: one in the sky, and the other in worlds below. What does this origin suggest about how each culture views its connection to the natural world? Use examples to support your answer.

Compare the lists you compiled of the chronological order of events that occur in the Osage and Navajo myths. How similar are the two narratives? Explain.

Extend the Text

Writing Options

Creative Writing Imagine that you have traveled back in time and want to explain to the Osage or Navajo an element of modern life, such as wireless communication or the Internet. Write a narrative paragraph in which you describe the origin of this element using a supernatural explanation, as in a myth.

Expository Writing Write a comparison-and-contrast paragraph about the similarities and differences in the Osage and Navajo peoples' views of the natural world, the gods, and human relationships with both.

Critical Literacy

Communicate in a New Way When the Native Americans and Europeans first communicated with each other, they often had to use sign language. In a small group, develop a sign-language version of "The Osage Creation Account," and have one person present it to the class. Then discuss how using sign language could be helpful in other activities or places, such as scuba diving or in a hospital room.

Lifelong Learning

Learn More About the Osage or Navajo As a class, develop a list of aspects of Navajo or Osage life about which you want to learn more, such as what happened to the Osage or Navajo once they encountered European settlers or how they governed themselves. Assign topics to small groups; have each group research its topic and deliver an oral presentation to the class.

 Go to **www.mirrorsandwindows.com** for more.

1. Which of the following is the best description of the relationship between the Osage and Navajo peoples and the natural world?
   A. The Osage and Navajo view the natural world as frightening and filled with dangerous forces beyond their control.
   B. The Osage and Navajo feel conflicted about the natural world. While they are thankful for the natural gifts provided by the gods, they also are concerned that the gods will punish them and take away these gifts.
   C. The Osage and Navajo have different views of the natural world. The Navajo revere the natural world, and the Osage fear it.
   D. The Osage and Navajo feel a close kinship with nature and celebrate its gifts.
   E. None of the above

2. What problem do the early peoples have with the world in both creation accounts?
   A. The animals have taken over.
   B. There is too much wind.
   C. There isn't any food.
   D. The earth is too wet.
   E. The land is too rocky.

3. What does "The Osage Creation Account" suggest is the origin of people?
   A. People came from the sky; the sun is their father, and the moon is their mother.
   B. People came from Begochiddy in the third world.
   C. The elk created people out of the soft earth.
   D. The ants and the whirlwinds worked together to create people.
   E. The mist that blew off the water created people.

4. How do the Osage regard the sun, moon, and wind, as shown in their story of creation?
   A. as animals
   B. as enemies
   C. as scary beings
   D. as forces of nature
   E. as humanlike gods

5. Find the phrase "and the winds came from all quarters" near the end of the first paragraph of "The Osage Creation Account." Which definition of *quarters* is correct in this phrase?
   A. coins
   B. divisions
   C. directions
   D. four equal periods
   E. living accommodations

6. What does "The Navajo Creation Myth" suggest is the origin of people?
   A. People are from the bamboo.
   B. Badger created people.
   C. The sun and moon made people.
   D. The white thunder, white cyclone, and white hail made people.
   E. People came from out of the land in the world below.

7. In the second paragraph of the Navajo myth, what does the word *petrified* mean?
   A. frightened
   B. layered
   C. turned to stone
   D. historic
   E. in full leaf

8. Why does the bamboo no longer have a tassel, according to the Navajo myth?
   A. Badger scratched it off when he tried to climb up to the fourth world.
   B. The cyclones blew the tassels off.
   C. The elk rolled over on the bamboo and broke it off.
   D. Begochiddy pulled the bamboo up by the tassel and threw it in the hole.
   E. None of the above

9. **Constructed Response:** Compare and contrast the role that animals play in each creation myth. What role might animals play in the culture of the Osage and Navajo? Explain.

10. **Constructed Response:** In the Navajo myth, the current world is the fourth world. What might the concept of multiple worlds indicate about the world view of the Navajo people? Support your ideas with evidence from the text.

Song of the Sky Loom

Tribal Song of the Tewa

Build Background

Cultural Context The Tewa are a Pueblo people of the southwestern United States who live in multilevel, multi-unit adobe structures that are often built into the hard desert mesas. Like other Pueblo peoples, the Tewa have a vital interdependence with the natural world and often perform rituals and ceremonies related to nature, especially to bring much-needed rain.

   "Song of the Sky Loom" is a traditional tribal song that uses the language of weaving to reflect on the natural world on which the Tewa depend. This song also describes the role of the earth and the sky as the weavers, or creators, of the natural world.

   The Tewa are known as accomplished artisans who create intricately decorated pottery and elaborate baskets in addition to richly woven fabrics. They passed on the art of weaving to the Navajo, another southwestern tribe, who today are renowned weavers of rugs and blankets.

Reader's Context If you could describe yourself only in terms of an art form, such as a painting, a sculpture, or a musical work, which would you choose? Why?

Analyze Literature

Metaphor and Repetition Songs often use **metaphors** to create pictures in the mind of the reader or listener. The actual subject of the metaphor, called the *tenor,* is expressed through another idea or image, called the *vehicle.*

Repetition is the intentional reuse of a sound, word, phrase, or sentence; writers often use repetition to emphasize ideas or create a musical effect, especially in poetry.

Set Purpose

As you read this traditional tribal song, notice how the language of weaving is used to describe the natural world. In a simple two-column chart, record the tenor of each metaphor along with its corresponding vehicle. For example, "white light of morning" is a tenor, and "warp" is its vehicle. Also identify the repeated words and phrases, and consider what effect they have on your reading of the song.

Preview Vocabulary

garment, 16

Tewa Dancers of the North perform the Eagle Dance at the Eight Northern Indian Pueblos Arts & Crafts Show in San Juan Pueblo, New Mexico. Native Americans consider the eagle the connecting link between heaven and earth.

Song *of the* Sky Loom

O our Mother the Earth, O our Father the Sky,
Your children are we, and with tired backs
We bring you the gifts you love.
Then weave for us a <u>garment</u> of brightness;
5   May the warp[1] be the white light of morning,
May the weft[2] be the red light of evening,
May the fringes be the falling rain,
May the border be the standing rainbow.
Thus weave for us a garment of brightness,
10 That we may walk fittingly where birds sing,
That we may walk fittingly where grass is green,
O our Mother the Earth, O our Father the Sky. ❖

---

1. **warp.** Threads in a loom that run lengthwise
2. **weft.** Horizontal threads in a loom. The weft crosses the warp to make a woven fabric.

> **gar • ment** (gär′ mənt) *n.,* any article of clothing

 **MIRRORS & WINDOWS**   When do you feel that you "walk fittingly" on the earth?

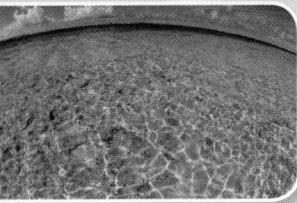

Literature Connection

The writing of **Leslie Marmon Silko** (b. 1948) reflects themes from her Native American heritage, including the relationship between humans and nature and the tensions of living within different cultures. In her poem **"Prayer to the Pacific,"** Silko celebrates nature and tells a myth that explains Native American migration to America. A poet, novelist, and short story writer, Silko grew up on the Laguna Pueblo Reservation in New Mexico. She attended Bureau of Indian Affairs elementary schools, a Catholic high school, and the University of New Mexico. After leaving law school to work on her writing, Silko published her first story in 1969; "Prayer to the Pacific" was published in 1974 in *Laguna Woman,* a collection of poetry.

Prayer to the Pacific
by Leslie Marmon Silko

I traveled to the ocean
        distant
                from my southwest land of sandrock
                to the moving blue water
5   Big as the myth of origin.

Pale
pale water in the yellow-white light of
                sun   floating west
                to China
10   where ocean herself was born.
Clouds that blow across the sand are wet.

Squat in the wet sand and speak to the Ocean:
   I return to you   turquoise   the red coral you sent us,
                sister spirit of Earth.
15 Four round stones in my pocket I carry back the ocean
                to suck and to taste.

Thirty thousand years ago
            Indians came riding across the ocean
            carried by giant sea turtles.

20   Waves were high that day
            great sea turtles waded   slowly out
                        from the gray sundown sea.

Grandfather Turtle rolled in the sand four times
            and disappeared
25   swimming into the sun.

And so   from that time
    immemorial,[1]
                        as the old people say,
rain clouds drift from the west
30   gift from the ocean.

Green leaves in the wind
Wet earth on my feet
            swallowing raindrops
                        clear from China. ❖

_____

1. **immemorial.** Extending or existing since beyond the reach of memory

Review Questions

1. What does the speaker take from the ocean? Explain why the speaker intends "to suck and to taste" the stones.

2. Describe how Native Americans arrived in this land. What evidence demonstrates the speaker's understanding of and feelings toward her culture?

3. Where does the speaker live? How does the speaker appreciate nature: intellectually or physically? Give evidence to support your answer.

TEXT ᵀᴼ TEXT CONNECTION

Make a list of the natural elements in this poem, and compare them to those from "Song of the Sky Loom." What elements do the two works have in common? What elements have a revered position in each culture? Why? Consider the landscape in the area where each tribe lived.

Refer to Text ▶ ▶ ▶ ▶ ▶   Reason with Text

1a. In "Song of the Sky Loom," what do the speakers ask for in return for their gifts?	**1b.** What do the speakers really want when they ask for "a garment of brightness"?	**Understand** Find meaning
2a. Identify to whom "Song of the Sky Loom" is addressed.	**2b.** Based on this song, infer what attitude the Tewa people have toward their gods.	**Apply** Use information
3a. Name the elements of nature described in the song.	**3b.** The speakers repeat that they want to walk on the earth "fittingly." What does this word choice suggest about the Tewa people?	**Analyze** Take things apart
4a. What do the speakers call themselves?	**4b.** How might this song be used to instill values in children? What values would it teach?	**Evaluate** Make judgments
5a. Where do the speakers want to walk?	**5b.** Based on the evidence in this song, describe the life of the Tewa people.	**Create** Bring ideas together

Analyze Literature

Metaphor and Repetition

Review the chart you created. What natural events, or *tenors,* are described? What ideas and images, or *vehicles,* are used to describe them? What is the overall metaphor used to portray the natural world? Discuss what it suggests about Tewa culture and values.

What examples of repetition did you identify? What is the effect of repeating these words and phrases? Read the song aloud and consider how repetition contributes to its musical nature.

Extend the Text

Writing Options

Creative Writing Write a brief *hymn* that praises or offers thanks for some aspect of the natural world. Model your hymn on "Song of the Sky Loom," using repetition and unrhymed lines to express your thoughts and feelings.

Expository Writing Write a one-paragraph analysis of what you can infer about Tewa culture from this song. For instance, what items, natural elements, and activities do they seem to value? Cite evidence from the song to support your answer.

Lifelong Learning

Explore a Day in the Life of the Tewa With a small group, prepare and deliver an oral report in which you describe a day in the life of a Tewa character. The character will be fictional, but the information you present should be based on facts. Conduct library and Internet research about Tewa culture; divide topics among members of your group. Then compile your information to prepare the oral report.

Media Literacy

Create a Collection of Nature Songs Collect lyrics of songs about nature, including Native American songs, folk songs from other cultures, and even pop ballads. To preserve your collection of lyrics, either bind the pages in a folder or create a digital collection using MP3s. Include a written introduction or analysis of each song.

 Go to **www.mirrorsandwindows.com** for more.

1. Which of the following is *not* something the speakers ask of Mother Earth and Father Sky in the "Song of the Sky Loom"?
   A. They ask for their crops of beans, corn, potatoes, and wild turnips to thrive.
   B. They ask for the white light of morning and the red light of evening.
   C. They ask for rain to fall and rainbows to form.
   D. They ask for a garment of brightness to be woven.
   E. The speakers ask for all these things.

2. Suppose the poet were to add another line before the last line of "Song of the Sky Loom." Which of the following would best fit with "a garment of brightness," "where birds sing" and "where grass is green" and the structure of the preceding two lines (lines 10 and 11)?
   A. We will go quietly into the bright light
   B. Let us live in a land where rain gently falls
   C. That we may walk fittingly where the sun shines
   D. O let us stride into the brightness of the day
   E. That we may walk fittingly while war rages

3. What does it likely mean to "walk fittingly" on the earth?
   A. to live in harmony with nature
   B. to wear shoes that fit
   C. to be proud and rule wisely
   D. to go where food is most abundant
   E. None of the above

4. What seems the best reason for the physical appearance of "Prayer to the Pacific," with the widely varying line lengths and unusual spacing?
   A. It fits the rhythm, or meter, of the poem.
   B. It is typical of poems written during this time period.
   C. It is meant to resemble the waves of the ocean.
   D. It makes some lines less important than others in meaning.
   E. The poet wants the text to seem like a poem, even though it has no poetic elements.

5. In line 13 of "Prayer to the Pacific"—"I return to you"—the poet is addressing
   A. Earth.
   B. herself.
   C. the reader.
   D. the ocean.
   E. the turquoise.

6. Why might the speaker in "Prayer to the Pacific" want to "carry back the ocean"?
   A. There is not enough water in her land.
   B. She wants to connect with her origins.
   C. She wants a souvenir for her family and friends.
   D. It is proof of the existence of the ocean.
   E. The saltwater will flavor her traditional dishes.

7. What is the significance of the "gifts" in the two poems?
   A. By giving gifts, the receivers expect something in return.
   B. The gift giving marks the anniversary of an important event in each culture.
   C. The givers have too much; they give gifts to avoid wasting what they have.
   D. The gifts show gratitude to or blessings from the ancestors.
   E. All of the above

8. **Constructed Response:** Identify the features of "Prayer to the Pacific" that make it a prayer. Compare and contrast this poem with "Song of the Sky Loom" or another prayer you know.

9. **Constructed Response:** Analyze the images of nature in these two poems. How are the two poems similar to other early Native American literature? How are they unique in their representations of nature? Use examples from the poems to support your answers.

> **TEST-TAKING TIP**
>
> In some tests, the directions tell you to choose the *best* answer for each question. This means that more than one answer could be correct but that one always will be a better choice than the others. Pay close attention to the phrasing of every question, and always read every available option before deciding on an answer.

COYOTE AND THE EARTH MONSTER

So-called trickster tales, such as **"Coyote and the Earth Monster,"** abound in mythologies from around the world. In Native American cultures, the trickster is often Coyote, who is clever but not always reliable. In some trickster tales, Coyote helps humans without intending to do so; in other tales, he tricks a more powerful being into helping people.

This tale comes from the Flathead (Salish) tribe, who resided primarily in western Montana. They were never a large tribe, but they were known for their bravery, honesty, and generally peaceful nature, except in their historical conflict with the powerful Blackfeet. The name *Flathead* was attributed to the Salish people by early white traders, who observed that members of neighboring tribes had pointed heads due to the practice of skull compression whereas the Salish had naturally shaped but somewhat flat heads in comparison.

It was a fine day. Coyote was strolling along, humming a little tune.

"Where are you going?" a voice chirruped. It was Titmouse, perched on the branch of a tree.

"Here and there, this way and that," replied Coyote.

"Well, take care where you walk. To the north there lives a giant monster who swallows up anyone who comes along."

"How will I know him?"

"He is very big."

"As big as a boulder?"

"Bigger."

"As big as a hill?"

"Bigger."

"As big as a mountain?"

"Bigger."

"Tsch! Well, I'm not afraid of him. I won't fall into his trap—no, not me!"

But—just in case—as soon as he was out of sight, Coyote pulled up a tree by its roots and slung it over his shoulders (he was very strong). "Hah! Just let him try it—he won't be so hungry when I jam his mouth open with this trunk. Swallow me, indeed!" And he continued, hummingly, on his way.

He soon found himself in a vast canyon—or was it a cave? Tall red cliffs towered above him on either side. Their tops were so close together that not even a sliver of sky could be seen between them. And the canyon seemed to stretch forever. Coyote could not see where it ended.

And then his feet crunched on something. He looked down. The whole of the canyon floor was littered with bones. Human bones. What was this place—the valley of the dead?

"Help me," cried a faint voice. "Give me food. I'm starving to death."

Coyote saw an old woman, as wasted as a skeleton. "Here," he said, offering her a piece of *pemmican*—dried meat pounded with fat and berries—which he kept on him.

The woman gulped the food down. "Thank you," she said. "But tell me: why are you carrying a tree over your shoulders?"

THE WHOLE OF THE CANYON FLOOR WAS LITTERED WITH BONES. HUMAN BONES.

"Aah," said Coyote, "that is to stop the monster swallowing me. I'll just wedge it into his mouth and he won't be able to shut it."

"It's too late!" wailed the woman. "He has already swallowed you. You are in his belly. He has closed his mouth, and there is no way out. No one ever leaves here. We are going to die, we are all going to die . . ." And her wailing alerted hundreds of other souls who came crawling and dragging themselves along the canyon floor, too weak to stand—the cadaverous, skeletal, living dead.

Coyote looked back to the entrance of the canyon. What the old woman had said was true: the opening was sealed.

"Well," he said. "I don't know what you're all complaining about. This place is full of food! If we are inside the monster's belly, then the sides of the canyon must be his flesh." And he sliced off some of the lining of the monster's stomach and shared it out. "How about some liver? Or a little kidney?"

The starving people gorged themselves on the monster's body. Its blood quenched their thirst. Its meat made them strong.

Far away, Coyote could hear a drumming sound. *Thrumm, thrumm*, it went. He decided to investigate. He began to explore. *Thrumm, thrumm*. The drumming was getting louder: he must be getting closer.

And then Coyote saw it. A vast, throbbing, pulsating thing as big as a mountain.

It was the monster's heart.

Coyote took out the knife he carried in his belt. He plunged it deep into the heart. Again he plunged it and again, slicing and slashing and hacking.

With a mighty explosion that shook the universe, the heart burst, disgorging a torrent of thick, treacly, red-hot liquid, like lava from a volcano.

"Quick!" screamed Coyote, "run!"

As the earth monster writhed and shuddered in its death throes and the whole world trembled, the people made for its mouth, which was now opening and shutting wildly as it gasped for air.

"Quick! This way!"

At last, everyone was out. Except, that is, for one small creature, which had become stuck in the dying monster's closing mouth. It was Woodtick.

"Come on," said Coyote, "I'll pull you out." And he took hold of Woodtick's front legs and pulled. *Ooh, aah,* just one more time . . . what a tight squeeze . . . now breathe in . . . that's it, nearly done.

At last! Woodtick was free. But all the pulling and the squashing and the squeezing had changed his shape. Where once he had been round, now he was flat. Woodtick went off to hide in the mountain woods where he has lived ever since, waiting to suck the blood of the animals and people that pass by.

Perhaps Coyote should have left him behind. ❖

The narrator questions whether Coyote should have saved Woodtick or left him behind. In what other circumstances might doing a good deed be a bad idea?

Refer and Reason

1. Why was Coyote able to enter the belly of the monster without realizing it? Infer what this suggests about Coyote's initial assumption about the Earth Monster.

2. Identify the passages that describe the monster's death in detail. Why was such a level of detail used in the story? What effect does it have?

3. Describe Coyote's relationship to the people. What word would you use to describe Coyote's actions?

Writing Options

1. Write your own trickster tale about how a certain animal came to be the way it is through its interactions with a trickster. Use one of the traditional Native American animals as the trickster character, such as a coyote, rabbit, or spider.

2. Write a one-paragraph analysis of the symbolism that underlies the Earth Monster. Consider that the creatures trapped inside the monster are able to eat it. Speculate on what this portrayal of the earth may indicate about the Flathead tribe's relationship to nature.

 Go to **www.mirrorsandwindows.com** for more.

FROM THE
Iroquois
CONSTITUTION

The **Iroquois Constitution,** dating from the fifteenth or sixteenth century, joined several peoples who lived on the shores of the Great Lakes into the Iroquois League, or Iroquois Confederacy. Initially, the Iroquois League included the Mohawk, Oneida, Onondaga, Cayuga, and Seneca. In the 1700s, the Tuscarora joined the confederacy, making it the League of Six Nations.

Tradition holds that the league was begun by **Dekanawidah,** a Huron man who was known as "The Great Peacemaker" and by Hiawatha, an Onondaga who lived among the Mohawks. The goal of the league was to put an end to war among its members, and the Iroquois Constitution established rules to keep the peace.

The constitution was not written down but became a part of the Iroquois' oral tradition. The words of the Iroquois Constitution are ascribed to Dekanawidah, a visionary diplomat about whom little is known. People remembered the constitution with the aid of small beads made of shell, known as *wampum.*

I am Dekanawidah and with the Five Nations[1] confederate lords I plant the Tree of the Great Peace. I name the tree the Tree of the Great Long Leaves. Under the shade of this Tree of the Great Peace we spread the soft white feathery down of the globe thistle[2] as seats for you, Adodarhoh,[3] and your cousin lords.

We place you upon those seats, spread soft with the feathery down of the globe thistle, there beneath the shade of the spreading branches of the Tree of Peace. There shall you sit and watch the council fire of the confederacy[4] of the Five Nations, and all the affairs of the Five Nations shall be transacted at this place before you.

Roots have spread out from the Tree of the Great Peace, one to the north, one to the east, one to the south, and one to the west. The name of these roots is the Great White Roots and their nature is peace and strength.

If any man or any nation outside the Five Nations shall obey the laws of the Great Peace and make known their disposition[5] to the lords of the confederacy, they may trace the roots to the tree and if their minds are clean and they are obedient and promise to obey the wishes of the confederate council, they shall be welcomed[6] to take shelter beneath the Tree of the Long Leaves.

We place at the top of the Tree of the Long Leaves an eagle who is able to see afar.

If he sees in the distance any evil approaching or any danger threatening he will at once warn the people of the confederacy.

---

1. **Five Nations.** The Mohawk, Oneida, Onondaga, Cayuga, and Seneca tribes. These tribes formed the Iroquois Confederacy.
2. **globe thistle.** Plant that grows round, blue or white flower heads
3. **Adodarhoh.** Chief confederate lord of the Onondaga, on whose land the council fire was lit
4. **confederacy.** People or groups united for a common purpose
5. **disposition.** State of mind; general nature
6. **they shall be welcomed.** The Tuscarora tribe joined the Confederacy in 1722.

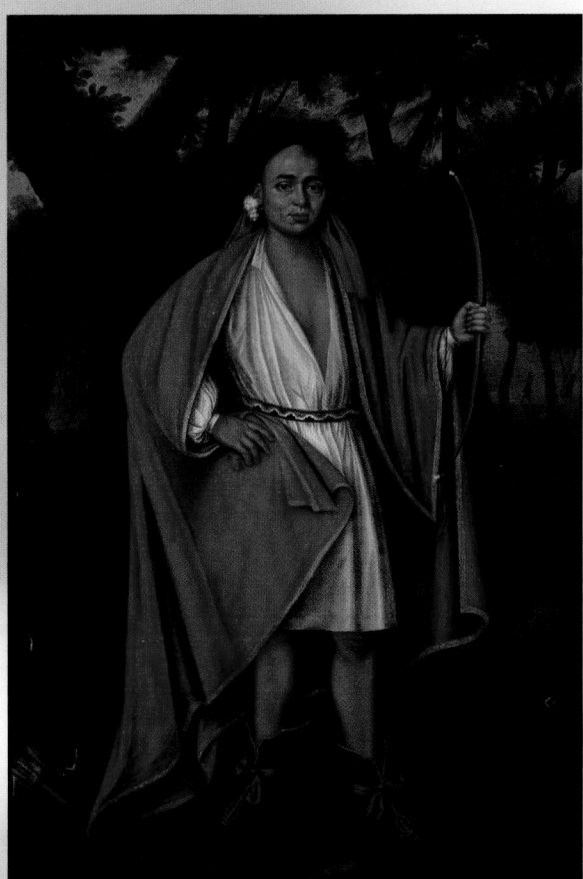

No Nee Yeath Tan No Ton, King of the Generath,
1710. Johannes Verelst. Private collection.

The smoke of the confederate council fire shall ever ascend and pierce the sky so that other nations who may be allies may see the council fire of the Great Peace. . . .

Whenever the confederate lords shall assemble for the purpose of holding a council, the Onondaga lords shall open it by expressing their gratitude to their cousin lords and greeting them, and they shall make an address and offer thanks to the earth where men dwell, to the streams of water, the pools, the springs and the lakes, to the maize and the fruits, to the medicinal herbs and trees, to the forest trees for their usefulness, to the animals that serve as food and give their pelts for clothing, to the great winds and the lesser winds, to the thunderers, to the sun, the mighty warrior, to the moon, to the messengers of the Creator

The smoke of the confederate council fire shall ever ascend and pierce the sky so that other nations who may be allies may see the council fire of the Great Peace.

who reveal his wishes and to the Great Creator who dwells in the heavens above, who gives all the things useful to men, and who is the source and the ruler of health and life.

Then shall the Onondaga lords declare the council open. . . .

All lords of the Five Nations' Confederacy must be honest in all things. . . . It shall be a serious wrong for anyone to lead a lord into trivial[7] affairs, for the people must ever hold their lords high in estimation[8] out of respect to their honorable positions.

When a candidate lord is to be installed he shall furnish[9] four strings of shells (or wampum) one span in length bound together at one end. Such will constitute the evidence of his pledge to the confederate lords that he will live according to the constitution of the Great Peace and exercise justice in all affairs.

When the pledge is furnished the speaker of the council must hold the shell strings in his hand and address the opposite side of the

---

7. **trivial.** Unimportant
8. **estimation.** Respect; value
9. **furnish.** Supply or provide

council fire and he shall commence his address saying: "Now behold him. He has now become a confederate lord. See how splendid he looks." An address may then follow. At the end of it he shall send the bunch of shell strings to the opposite side and they shall be received as evidence of the pledge. Then shall the opposite side say:

"We now do crown you with the sacred emblem of the deer's antlers, the emblem of your lordship. You shall now become a mentor of the people of the Five Nations. The thickness of your skin shall be seven spans—which is to say that you shall be proof against anger, offensive actions and criticism. Your heart shall be filled with peace and good will and your mind filled with a yearning for the welfare of the people of the confederacy. With endless patience you shall carry out your duty and your firmness shall be tempered with tender-ness for your people. Neither anger nor fury shall find lodgement in your mind and all your words and actions shall be marked with calm deliberation.[10] In all of your deliberations in the confederate council, in your efforts at law making, in all your official acts, self-interest shall be cast into oblivion. Cast not over your shoulder behind you the warnings of the nephews and nieces should they chide you for any error or wrong you may do, but return to the way of the Great Law which is just and right. Look and listen for the welfare of the whole people and have always in view not only the present but also the coming generations, even those whose faces are the ground—the unborn of the future nation." ❖

---

10. **deliberation.** Consideration and discussion of alternatives before reaching a decision

If you were forming a new country, which elements of the Iroquois Constitution would you incorporate into your government?

Refer and Reason

1. Identify all the references to nature in the Iroquois Constitution. What do these descriptions reveal about the Iroquois people's relationship with nature?

2. List the rules Dekanawidah presents in this excerpt. Analyze whether he established a *confederacy,* or group of nations, that had the means necessary to keep the peace.

3. What qualities are Iroquois leaders expected to have? Evaluate whether these qualities are still considered important to leadership.

Writing Options

1. The writer of the Iroquois Constitution uses the symbol of a tree to describe the original five nations of the confederacy. Write a descriptive paragraph to share with the class in which you describe the current U.S. government with a symbol of your own design. You might compare the government to another form of nature, or you might choose a metaphor from your surroundings.

2. In an essay, compare and contrast the ideas in the Iroquois Constitution with those of the Constitution of the United States. How might the Iroquois Constitution have influenced the creation of the U.S. Constitution?

 Go to **www.mirrorsandwindows.com** for more.

PART 2

Shaping the New World

The writing that comes down to us from the explorers and early settlers had several purposes. The first was to describe the new land and encourage Europeans to look westward. Another purpose of early American writing was to influence political decision making in the mother countries, since the governing authorities were far away and had little understanding of conditions in these new lands. A third purpose was to record what was actually occurring for future readers. This category of writing includes descriptions of the impact of settlement on native peoples and the growing self-understanding of the colonists.

Because many of these early settlers came to the New World in pursuit of religious freedom, much of early colonial literature is identified with religious groups. The writing of the Puritans holds a unique place in American literature, even though the Puritans are not representative of the large number of colonists who came to North America because of their strong separatist views. Nonetheless, the Puritans' story and worldview is deeply engrained in our national consciousness. In sermons, colonial histories, personal diaries, and devotional poems, Puritan writers often explored the story of spiritual struggles in personal and public life.

In contrast to the Puritans, the Quakers espoused religious tolerance and equality. The "Friends," as they were known, believed in the sacredness of the individual and his or her obligation to do good works in this life. Early Quaker writing addressed individual morality as the basis for social order and humanitarianism. The Quakers nurtured relationships with local Native American communities, demonstrating respect for these peoples' knowledge and customs, and Quaker writers were among the first in America to denounce slavery.

Penn's Treaty with the Indians, 1840. Edward Hicks. Museum of Fine Arts, Houston, Texas.

A Journey through Texas
A Travel Narrative by Álvar Núñez Cabeza de Vaca

Build Background

Historical Context "A Journey through Texas" recounts the experiences of Álvar Núñez Cabeza de Vaca and three companions, who were the sole survivors of a large party of Spanish explorers that set out from Tampa Bay, Florida, in the summer of 1528. Over a period of more than six years, Cabeza de Vaca and his men traveled on foot from present-day Louisiana through Texas, New Mexico, and Arizona to Sinaloa, Mexico, in colonized New Spain.

The first natives encountered by Cabeza de Vaca's party treated them harshly, stripping them of their clothes, starving them, and enslaving them. Eventually, Cabeza de Vaca's knowledge of Western medicine earned him respect and even awe from his captors. He, in turn, came to respect his captors and their customs; he was elevated to the status of trader and aided in his journey to the South Sea, or Gulf of Mexico.

Cabeza de Vaca's descriptions of the settlements he encountered and the stories he heard about prosperous cities to the north prompted a fevered search by subsequent explorers for Eldorado, the Seven Golden Cities of Cíbola.

Reader's Context Imagine that you are alone in a strange land and encounter people who want to enslave you. What could you do to earn their respect and to gain your freedom?

Meet the Author

Álvar Núñez Cabeza de Vaca (c.1490–c.1559) was a Spanish explorer who wrote an account that inspired the exploration and conquest of the American Southwest. Despite his bravery, Cabeza de Vaca felt his accomplishments were less than those of his courageous ancestors, who had served the king of Spain in defeating the Moors. This seeming humility contrasts with his refusal to aid a subsequent expedition to Florida when he was offered the position of second in command.

From 1540 to 1545, Cabeza de Vaca served as governor of present-day Argentina. In this capacity of leadership, he displayed the empathy for Native American peoples and their cultures that readers can find in "A Journey through Texas." Most of all, Cabeza de Vaca emerges as a dauntless and skilled leader who could write, "Our resolution was not shaken by the fear of great starvation."

Analyze Literature

Narrative and Abridgment
A **narrative** is a story told in fiction, nonfiction, poetry, or drama; the events are usually told in *chronological order*, or the order in which they occurred.

An **abridgment** is a shortened version of a work. The editor who alters the work attempts to preserve the most significant elements of the original.

Set Purpose

"A Journey through Texas" opens with the lines "The same Indians led us to a plain. . . . By those, we were treated in the same manner as before." With these words, we know we are reading an abridgment of a narrative. As you read, judge whether this abridgment adequately explains the events that befall Cabeza de Vaca and his men.

Preview Vocabulary

feign, 30
singular, 30
procure, 30
subsist, 31

A JOURNEY THROUGH
Texas

by Álvar Núñez Cabeza de Vaca

They besought us not to be angry nor to procure the death of any more of their number, for they were convinced that we killed them by merely thinking of it.

The same Indians led us to a plain beyond the chain of mountains, where people came to meet us from a long distance. By those we were treated in the same manner as before, and they made so many presents to the Indians who came with us that, unable to carry all, they left half of it. . . . We told these people our route was towards sunset, and they replied that in that direction people lived very far away.

So we ordered them to send there and inform the inhabitants that we were coming and how. From this they begged to be excused, because the others were their enemies, and they did not want us to go to them. Yet they did not venture to disobey in the end, and sent two women, one of their own and the other a captive. They selected women because these can trade everywhere, even if there be war.

We followed the women to a place where it had been agreed we should wait for them. After five days they had not yet returned, and the Indians explained that it might be because they had not found anybody. So we told them to take us north, and they repeated that there were no people, except very far away, and neither food nor water. Nevertheless we insisted, saying that we wanted to go there, and they still excused themselves as best they could, until at last we became angry.

> All over the country, where it was known, they became so afraid that it seemed as if the mere sight of us would kill them.

One night I went away to sleep out in the field apart from them; but they soon came to where I was, and remained awake all night in great alarm, talking to me, saying how frightened they were. They entreated us not to be angry any longer, because, even if it was their death, they would take us where we chose. We <u>feigned</u> to be angry still, so as to keep them in suspense, and then a <u>singular</u> thing happened.

On that same day many fell sick, and on the next day eight of them died! All over the country, where it was known, they became so afraid that it seemed as if the mere sight of us would kill them. They besought[1] us not to be angry nor to <u>procure</u> the death of any more of their number, for they were convinced that we killed them by merely thinking of it. In truth, we were very much concerned about it, for, seeing the great mortality, we dreaded that all of them might die or forsake us in their terror, while those further on, upon learning of it, would get out of our way hereafter. We prayed to God our Lord to assist us, and the sick began to get well. Then we saw something that astonished us very much, and it was that, while the parents, brothers and wives of the dead had shown deep grief at their illness, from the moment they died the survivors made no demonstration whatsoever, and showed not the slightest feeling; nor did they dare to go near the bodies until we ordered their burial. . . .

The sick being on the way of recovery, when we had been there already three days, the women whom we had sent out returned, saying that they had met very few people, nearly all having gone after the cows, as it was the season. So we ordered those who had been sick to remain, and those who were well to accompany us, and that, two days' travel from there, the same women should go with us and get people to come to meet us on the trail for our reception.

The next morning all those who were strong enough came along, and at the end of three journeys we halted. Alonso del Castillo and Estevanico,[2] the negro, left with the women as guides, and the woman who was a captive took them to a river that flows between mountains, where there was a village, in which her father lived, and these were the first abodes we saw that were like unto real houses. Castillo and Estevanico went to these and, after holding parley[3] with the Indians, at the end of three days Castillo returned to where he had left us, bringing with him five or six of the Indians. He told how he had found permanent houses, inhabited, the people of which ate beans and squashes, and that he had also seen maize.

---

1. **besought.** Pleaded with
2. **Estevanico.** He was a former slave, and his Moorish heritage made him the first African to visit Texas.
3. **holding parley.** Talking or conferring

feign (fān) *v.*, pretend; dissemble
sin • gu • lar (siŋ´ gyü lər) *adj.*, unusual; strange
pro • cure (prō kyür´) *v.*, obtain by any means; acquire

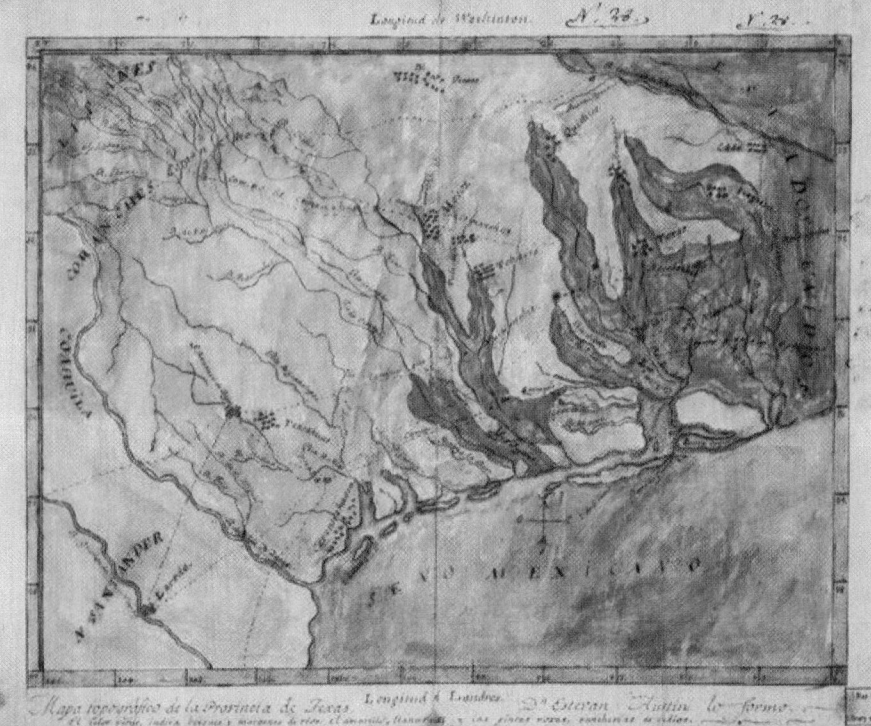

This map was drawn on cloth and labeled in Spanish by Stephen F. Austin in 1822. Both he and Cabeza de Vaca were outsiders to Texas and had to explore its rugged terrain with limited information and insight about what lay ahead.

The people who heard of our approach did not, as before, come out to meet us on the way, but we found them at their homes, and they had other houses ready for us. . . . There was nothing they would not give us. They are the best formed people we have seen, the liveliest and most capable; who best understood us and answered our questions. We called them "of the cows," because most of the cows die near there, and because for more than fifty leagues up that stream they go to kill many of them. Those people go completely naked, after the manner of the first we met. The women are covered with deerskins, also some men, especially the old ones, who are of no use any more in war.

The country is well settled. We asked them why they did not raise maize, and they replied that they were afraid of losing the crops, since for two successive years it had not rained, and the seasons were so dry that the moles had eaten the corn, so that they did not dare to plant any more until it should have rained very hard. And they also begged us to ask Heaven for rain, which we promised to do. We also wanted to know from where they brought their maize, and they said it came from where the sun sets, and that it was found all over that country, and the shortest way to it was in that

Of all things upon earth this caused us the greatest pleasure, and we gave endless thanks to our Lord for this news. Castillo also said that the negro was coming to meet us on the way, near by, with all the people of the houses. For that reason we started, and after going a league and a half met the negro and the people that came to receive us, who gave us beans and many squashes to eat, gourds to carry water in, robes of cowhide, and other things. As those people and the Indians of our company were enemies, and did not understand each other, we took leave of the latter, leaving them all that had been given to us, while we went on with the former and, six leagues beyond, when night was already approaching, reached their houses, where they received us with great ceremonies. Here we remained one day, and left on the next, taking them with us to other permanent houses, where they <u>subsisted</u> on the same food also, and thence on we found a new custom.

sub · sist (sub sist´) v., maintain with food and clothing; live

direction. We asked them to tell us how to go, as they did not want to go themselves, to tell us about the way.

> ## It seemed to them that we ought not to take that road.

They said we should travel up the river towards the north, on which trail for seventeen days we would not find a thing to eat, except a fruit called *chacan,* which they grind between stones; but even then it cannot be eaten, being so coarse and dry; and so it was, for they showed it to us and we could not eat it. But they also said that, going upstream, we could always travel among people who were their enemies, although speaking the same language, and who could give us no food, but would receive us very willingly, and give us many cotton blankets, hides and other things; but that it seemed to them that we ought not to take that road.

In doubt as to what should be done, and which was the best and most advantageous road to take, we remained with them for two days. They gave us beans, squashes, and cala-bashes.[4] Their way of cooking them is so new and strange that I felt like describing it here, in order to show how different and queer are the devices and industries of human beings. They have no pots. In order to cook their food they fill a middle-sized gourd with water, and place into a fire such stones as easily become heated, and when they are hot to scorch they take them out with wooden tongs, thrusting them into the water of the gourd, until it boils. As soon as it boils they put into it what they want to cook, always taking out the stones as they cool off and throwing in hot ones to keep the water steadily boiling. This is their way of cooking.

After two days were past we determined to go in search of maize, and not to follow the road to the cows, since the latter carried us to the north, which meant a very great circuit, as we held it always certain that by going towards sunset we should reach the goal of our wishes.

So we went on our way and traversed the whole country to the South Sea,[5] and our resolution was not shaken by the fear of great starvation, which the Indians said we should suffer (and indeed suffered) during the first seventeen days of travel. All along the river, and in the course of these seventeen days we received plenty of cowhides, and did not eat of their famous fruit (*chacan*), but our food consisted (for each day) of a handful of deer-tallow, which for that purpose we always sought to keep, and so endured these seventeen days, at the end of which we crossed the river and marched for seventeen days more. At sunset, on a plain between very high mountains, we met people who, for one-third of the year, eat but powdered straw, and as we went by just at that time, had to eat it also, until, at the end of that journey we found some permanent houses, with plenty of harvested maize, of which and of its meal they gave us great quantities, also squashes and beans, and blankets of cotton. ❖

---

4. **calabashes.** Gourds whose hard shells are used for making drinking utensils
5. **South Sea.** Gulf of Mexico

MIRRORS & WINDOWS

After reading Cabeza de Vaca's account, what can you infer about the future of Native American and European relationships?

Refer to Text ▷ ▷ ▷ ▷ ▷ **Reason with Text**

1a. Recall what happened to the Indians immediately after the Spaniards pretended to be angry with them. What did the Indians believe was the reason for this?	**1b.** Why did Cabeza de Vaca and his men pretend to be angry with the Indians?	**Understand** Find meaning
2a. What was the "new and strange" cooking custom that Cabeza de Vaca felt compelled to describe?	**2b.** Find examples from the text that show why Cabeza de Vaca might have believed stories about advanced civilizations and wealth.	**Apply** Use information
3a. Identify whom the Indians send to inform the next people who live on the Spaniards' route that they will have guests. Why do they send these people?	**3b.** How does Cabeza de Vaca avoid the potential clash between the natives who accompany him and the new people who can advance his journey? What does this show about his leadership style?	**Analyze** Take things apart
4a. For what did the Indians ask Cabeza de Vaca and his men to pray?	**4b.** Determine what events in this narrative support the Spaniards' belief that God was assisting them on this difficult journey.	**Evaluate** Make judgments
5a. How did the Indians react to the sickness and death of their family members?	**5b.** If you were a Native American who had helped Cabeza de Vaca, what would you tell your children about your experiences? What would be your attitude toward the Spaniards?	**Create** Bring ideas together

Analyze Literature

Narrative and Abridgment
Would an abridgment of the narrative that includes Cabeza de Vaca's first encounter with natives who told tales of Cíbola be more interesting than one that does not? Defend or criticize the passage selected.

Extend the Text

Writing Options
Creative Writing Pretend that you are Estevanico, the former slave who accompanies Cabeza de Vaca. Write a diary entry for either the time you were left alone to secure the aid of the natives or the day on which you finally encounter people from the colony of New Spain.

Persuasive Writing Write a letter to the King of Spain recommending or opposing appointment of Cabeza de Vaca to a governorship in South America. Your primary concern is the advancement of Spain. Before writing, consider the pros and cons of the appointment.

Collaborative Learning
Form a Group Consensus In groups of three, discuss the following statement: The Native Americans' lack of understanding of cause-and-effect relationships aided Cabeza de Vaca and probably was the key to his group's ultimate survival. Appoint one group member to try to obtain consensus among your members, one to record your findings, and one to report to the class.

Critical Literacy
Role-Play an Interview With a partner, research what happened in Cabeza de Vaca's life after his experiences in Texas. Then prepare an interview with him. Write out both the interviewer's questions and Cabeza de Vaca's answers, and role-play the interview.

 Go to **www.mirrorsandwindows.com** for more.

from The General History of Virginia
A Nonfiction Account by John Smith

from Of Plymouth Plantation
A Nonfiction Account by William Bradford

Build Background

Historical Context In *The General History of Virginia,* John Smith presents a detailed and often exciting account of events in the Virginia Colony from 1607, the year of its founding, to 1609, the year Smith left. In 1606, Smith was hired by the Virginia Company of London to assist in a project that would return great profit for great risk. Smith clashed immediately with the leaders of the colonists "that understood not at all what they undertook."

William Bradford began writing *Of Plymouth Plantation* in 1630, ten years after settlement of Plymouth Colony. While the colonists hoped that life in the New World would be profitable, their primary motive for leaving England was to escape religious persecution. They were sometimes discouraged by the hardships they endured, but they persevered, sustained by their belief that "God's providence" would protect them.

Reader's Context Could you move to a strange land and survive hostile conditions? What would you need to believe to keep going and not give up?

Meet the Authors

John Smith (1580–1631) was born in Willoughby, England. In 1606, he joined a group of about one hundred people and set sail for the New World. There, on the Chesapeake Bay, he helped to found Jamestown, the first permanent English colony in America. A year later, he was captured by Powhatan, chief of one of the area's native peoples. In later writings, he claimed to have been saved from execution by the chief's young daughter, known to history by her nickname, Pocahontas. Smith served as governor of the Jamestown Colony from 1608 to 1609 and then returned to England.

William Bradford (1590–1657) was a farmer from Yorkshire, England. After fleeing England, Bradford and a group of fellow Separatists were granted land in the New World and sailed across the Atlantic on the *Mayflower,* landing at Plymouth, Massachusetts, in 1620. Bradford was elected governor, a position he held for more than thirty years, and his tolerance for diverse beliefs was in part responsible for the success of the Plymouth Colony. While governor, Bradford wrote a history of the founding of the Plymouth Colony, *Of Plymouth Plantation;* the excerpt presented here describes a portion of the voyage of the *Mayflower.*

Compare Literature

Point of View
Point of view is the vantage point from which a story is told. Stories are typically written from a *first-person* point of view, in which the narrator uses words such as *I* and *we;* from a *second-person* point of view, in which the narrator uses *you;* or from a *third-person* point of view, in which the narrator uses words such as *he, she, it,* and *they.*

Set Purpose

John Smith and William Bradford undertook similar journeys but with quite different purposes and results. As you read each man's account of his experiences, trace the use of point of view. Consider how the use of point of view affects the telling of the story.

Preview Vocabulary

pilfer, 36
gluttony, 36
extremity, 36
conceit, 36
ensue, 37
entreaty, 38
doleful, 39
mollify, 39
profane, 41
haughty, 41

Map of Virginia, 1622. John Smith. British Library, London, England. (See detail on page 34.)

from *The General History of Virginia*

by John Smith

The fault of our going was our own.

What Happened Till the First Supply

Being thus left to our fortunes, it fortuned[1] that within ten days, scarce ten amongst us could either go[2] or well stand, such extreme weakness and sickness oppressed us. And

thereat none need marvel if they consider the cause and reason, which was this: While the ships stayed, our allowance was somewhat

---

1. **fortuned.** Happened
2. **go.** Go about; walk

bettered by a daily proportion of biscuit which the sailors would <u>pilfer</u> to sell, give, or exchange with us for money, sassafras,[3] or furs. But when they departed, there remained neither tavern, beer house, nor place of relief but the common kettle.[4] Had we been as free from all sins as <u>gluttony</u> and drunkenness we might have been canonized for saints, but our President[5] would never have been admitted for engrossing to his private,[6] oatmeal, sack,[7] oil, aqua vitae,[8] beef, eggs, or what not but the kettle: that indeed he allowed equally to be distributed, and that was half a pint of wheat and as much barley boiled with water for a man a day, and this, having fried some twenty-six weeks in the ship's hold, contained as many worms as grains so that we might truly call it rather so much bran than corn; our drink was water, our lodgings castles in the air.

With this lodging and diet, our extreme toil in bearing and planting palisades[9] so strained and bruised us and our continual labor in the <u>extremity</u> of the heat had so weakened us, as were cause sufficient to have made us as miserable in our native country or any other place in the world.

From May to September, those that escaped lived upon sturgeon[10] and sea crabs. Fifty in this time we buried: the rest seeing the President's projects to escape these miseries in our pinnace[11] by flight (who all this time had neither felt want nor sickness) so moved our dead spirits as we deposed him and established Ratcliffe in his place. . . .

But now was all our provision spent, the sturgeon gone, all helps abandoned, each hour expecting the fury of the savages; when God, the patron of all good endeavors, in that desperate extremity so changed the hearts of the savages that they brought such plenty of their fruits and provision as no man wanted.

And now where some affirmed it was ill done of the Council[12] to send forth men so badly provided, this incontradictable reason will show them plainly they are too ill advised to nourish such ill <u>conceits</u>: First, the fault of our going was our own: what could be thought fitting or necessary we had, but what we should find, or want, or where we should be, we were all ignorant and supposing to make our passage in two months, with victual to live and the advantage of the spring to work; we were at sea five months where we both spent our victual and lost the opportunity of the time and season to plant, by the unskillful presumption of our ignorant transporters that understood not at all what they undertook.

> Some affirmed it was ill done of the Council to send forth men so badly provided.

Such actions have ever since the world's beginning been subject to such accidents, and everything of worth is found full of difficulties, but nothing so difficult as to establish a commonwealth so far remote from men

---

3. **sassafras.** Tree with aromatic bark, the root of which was valued for its supposed medicinal qualities
4. **common kettle.** Public or general supplies or cooking pot
5. **President.** Edward Maria Wingfield (c. 1560–1613), first president of Virginia colony
6. **private.** Private or personal stock
7. **sack.** Dry Spanish white wine, popular in England during the sixteenth and seventeenth centuries
8. **aqua vitae.** [Latin] Brandy
9. **palisades.** Pointed stakes set in the ground to form a fence for fortification or defense
10. **sturgeon.** Large, edible, bony fish
11. **pinnace.** Small sailing ship
12. **Council.** Group in charge of the Virginia experiment

---

pil • fer (pil′ fʉr) v., steal
glut • tony (glut′ tən ē) n., habit or act of eating too much
ex • trem • i • ty (eks trem′ ə tē) n., state of extreme necessity or danger
con • ceit (kən sēt′) n., idea, thought; personal opinion

and means and where men's minds are so untoward[13] as neither do well themselves nor suffer others. But to proceed.

The new President and Martin, being little beloved, of weak judgment in dangers, and less industry in peace, committed the managing of all things abroad[14] to Captain Smith, who, by his own example, good words, and fair promises set some to mow, others to bind thatch, some to build houses, others to thatch them, himself always bearing the greatest task for his own share, so that in short time he provided most of them lodgings, neglecting any for himself. . . .

Leading an expedition on the Chickahominy River, Captain Smith and his men are attacked by Indians, and Smith is taken prisoner.

When this news came to Jamestown, much was their sorrow for his loss, few expecting what <u>ensued</u>.

Six or seven weeks those barbarians kept him prisoner, many strange triumphs and conjurations[15] they made of him, yet he so demeaned himself amongst them, as he not only diverted them from surprising the fort, but procured his own liberty, and got himself and his company such estimation amongst them, that those savages admired him.

The manner how they used and delivered him is as followeth:

The savages having drawn from George Cassen whither Captain Smith was gone, prosecuting[16] that opportunity they followed him with three hundred bowmen, conducted by the King of Pamunkee, who in divisions searching the turnings of the river found Robinson and Emry by the fireside; those they shot full of arrows and slew. Then finding the Captain, as is said, that used the savage that was his guide as his shield (three of them being slain and

---

13. **untoward.** Stubborn
14. **abroad.** Outside the enclosed camp
15. **conjuration.** Magic; sorcery
16. **prosecuting.** Following up or pursuing

en • sue (en sü´) v., come afterward; follow immediately

The Lost Colony of Roanoke Island

In 1587, a group of 117 English settlers, led by Sir Walter Raleigh and John White, landed on Roanoke Island off the coast of North Carolina. Shortly after arriving, White's daughter, Eleanor, gave birth to the first English person born on American soil, a girl named Virginia Dare.

Conditions were rough for the colonists, and the native peoples in the area were largely unwilling to help them, recalling poor treatment from Englishmen who earlier had established an outpost on the island. When the colonists ran short of supplies, White reluctantly left them to return to England and bring back more. Unfortunately, his return was delayed by several years due to bad weather and England's battle with the Spanish armada.

In 1590, White returned to Roanoke Island to find the colony abandoned. He could find no trace of the hundred-some people he had left behind. Moreover, he found no signs of battle and no bodies, skeletons, or burial areas. The fate of the Roanoke colonists remains a mystery to this day.

WHITE

divers[17] others so galled),[18] all the rest would not come near him. Thinking thus to have returned to his boat, regarding them, as he marched, more than his way, slipped up to the middle in an oozy creek and his savage with him; yet dared they not come to him till being near dead with cold he threw away his arms. Then according to their composition[19] they drew him forth and led him to the fire where his men were slain. Diligently they chafed his benumbed limbs.

He demanding for their captain, they showed him Opechancanough, King of Pamunkee, to whom he gave a round ivory double compass dial. Much they marveled at the playing of the fly and needle,[20] which they could see so plainly and yet not touch it because of the glass that covered them. But when he demonstrated by that globe-like jewel the roundness of the earth and skies, the sphere of the sun, moon, and stars, and how the sun did chase the night round about the world continually, the greatness of the land and sea, the diversity of nations, variety of complexions, and how we were to them antipodes[21] and many other such like matters, they all stood as amazed with admiration.

Notwithstanding, within an hour after, they tied him to a tree, and as many as could stand about him prepared to shoot him, but the King holding up the compass in his hand, they all laid down their bows and arrows and in a triumphant manner led him to Orapaks where he was after their manner kindly feasted and well used. . . .

At last they brought him to Werowocomoco, where was Powhatan, their Emperor. Here more than two hundred of those grim courtiers stood wondering at him, as he had been a monster, till Powhatan and his train had put themselves in their greatest braveries. Before a fire upon a seat like a bedstead, he sat covered with a great robe made of raccoon skins and all the tails hanging by. On either hand did sit a young wench of sixteen or eighteen years and along on each side the house, two rows of men and behind them as many women, with all their heads and shoulders painted red, many of their heads bedecked with the white down of birds, but every one with something, and a great chain of white beads about their necks.

> *Within an hour after, they tied him to a tree, and as many as could stand about him prepared to shoot him.*

At his entrance before the King, all the people gave a great shout. The Queen of Appomattoc was appointed to bring him water to wash his hands, and another brought him a bunch of feathers, instead of a towel, to dry them; having feasted him after their best barbarous manner they could, a long consultation was held, but the conclusion was, two great stones were brought before Powhatan; then as many as could, laid hands on him, dragged him to them, and thereon laid his head and being ready with their clubs to beat out his brains, Pocahontas, the King's dearest daughter, when no <u>entreaty</u> could prevail, got his head in her arms and laid her own upon his to save him from death; whereat the Emperor was contented he should live to make him hatchets, and her bells, beads, and copper, for they thought him as well of all occupations as

---

17. **divers.** Several
18. **galled.** Wounded
19. **composition.** Habits; customary manners
20. **fly and needle.** Parts of a compass
21. **antipodes.** On opposite sides of the earth

---

en • treaty (en trē´ tē) *n.*, earnest request

themselves.[22] For the King himself will make his own robes, shoes, bows, arrows, pots; plant, hunt, or do anything so well as the rest.

Two days after, Powhatan, having disguised himself in the most fearfulest manner he could, caused Captain Smith to be brought forth to a great house in the woods and there upon a mat by the fire to be left alone. Not long after, from behind a mat that divided the house, was made the most <u>dolefulest</u> noise he ever heard; then Powhatan more like a devil than a man, with some two hundred more as black as himself, came unto him and told him now they were friends, and presently he should go to Jamestown to send him two great guns and a grindstone for which he would give him the country of Capahowasic and forever esteem him as his son Nantaquond.

So to Jamestown with twelve guides Powhatan sent him. That night they quartered in the woods, he still expecting (as he had done all this long time of his imprisonment) every hour to be put to one death or other, for all their feasting. But almighty God (by His divine providence) had <u>mollified</u> the hearts of those stern barbarians with compassion. The next morning betimes[23] they came to the fort, where Smith having used the savages with what kindness he could, he showed Rawhunt, Powhatan's trusty servant, two demiculverins[24] and a millstone to carry Powhatan: they found them somewhat too heavy, but when they did see him discharge them, being loaded with stones, among the boughs of a great tree loaded with icicles, the ice and branches came so tumbling down that the poor savages ran away half dead with fear. But at last we regained some conference with them and gave them such toys and sent to Powhatan, his

women, and children such presents as gave them in general full content.

Now in Jamestown they were all in combustion, the strongest preparing once more to run away with the pinnace; which, with the hazard of his life, with saker falcon[25] and musket shot, Smith forced now the third time to stay or sink.

Some, no better than they should be, had plotted with the President the next day to have him put to death by the Levitical law,[26] for the lives of Robinson and Emry; pretending the fault was his that had led them to their ends; but he quickly took such order with such lawyers that he laid them by their heels till he sent some of them prisoners for England.

Now every once in four or five days, Pocahontas with her attendants brought him so much provision that saved many of their lives, that else for all this had starved with hunger. His relation of the plenty he had seen, especially at Werowocomoco, and of the state and bounty of Powhatan (which till that time was unknown), so revived their dead spirits (especially the love of Pocahontas) as all men's fear was abandoned.

Thus you may see what difficulties still crossed any good endeavor; and the good success of the business being thus oft brought to the very period of destruction: yet you see by what strange means God hath still delivered it. ❖

---

22. **him as well . . . as themselves.** He had as much capability as they did.
23. **betimes.** Early
24. **demiculverins.** Large cannon
25. **saker falcon.** Small cannon
26. **Levitical law.** Biblical law from the Old Testament that states "He that killeth any man shall surely be put to death" (Leviticus 24:17)

---

dole • ful (dōl′ fəl) *adj.,* full of or causing sorrow or sadness
mol • li • fy (môl′ ə fī) *v.,* soothe the temper of

MIRRORS & WINDOWS   Smith states that "everything of worth is found full of difficulties." What in your life has been hard to achieve but worth the effort?

The Pilgrims at Plymouth: The First Sermon Ashore, 1621, c. 1800s. Jean Leon Gerome Ferris.

from # Of Plymouth Plantation

by William Bradford

So they committed themselves to the will
of God and resolved to proceed.

Book I, Chapter IX. Of Their Voyage and How They Passed the Sea; and of Their Safe Arrival at Cape Cod

September 6. These troubles[1] being blown over, and now all being compact together in one ship, they put to sea again with a prosperous wind, which continued divers days together, which was some encouragement unto them; yet, according to the usual manner, many were afflicted with seasickness. And I may not omit here a special work of God's providence. There was a proud and very profane young man, one of the seamen, of a lusty,[2] able body, which made him the more haughty; he would always be condemning the poor people in their sickness and cursing them daily with grievous execrations;[3] and did not let[4] to tell them that he hoped to help to cast half of them overboard before they came to their journey's end, and to make merry with what they had; and if he were by any gently reproved, he would curse and swear most bitterly. But it pleased God before they came half seas over, to smite this young man with a grievous disease, of which he died in a desperate manner, and so was himself the first that was thrown overboard. Thus his curses light on his own head, and it was an astonishment to all his fellows for they noted it to be the just hand of God upon him.

After they had enjoyed fair winds and weather for a season, they were encountered many times with cross winds and met with many fierce storms with which the ship was shroudly[5] shaken, and her upper works made very leaky; and one of the main beams in the midships was bowed and cracked, which put them in some fear that the ship could not be able to perform the voyage. So some of the chief of the company, perceiving the mariners to fear the sufficiency of the ship as appeared by their mutterings, they entered into serious consultation with the master and other officers of the ship, to consider in time of the danger, and rather to return than to cast themselves into a desperate and inevitable peril. And truly there was great distraction and difference of opinion amongst the mariners themselves; fain[6] would they do what could be done for their wages' sake (being now near half the seas over) and on the other hand they were loath to hazard their lives too desperately. But in examining of all opinions, the master and others affirmed they knew the ship to be strong and firm under water; and for the buckling of the main beam, there was a great iron screw the passengers brought out of Holland, which would raise the beam into his place; the which being done, the carpenter and master affirmed that with a post put under it, set firm in the lower deck and otherways bound, he would make it sufficient. And as for the decks and upper works, they would caulk them as well as they could, and though with the working of the ship they would not long keep staunch,[7] yet there would otherwise be no great danger, if they did not overpress her with sails. So they committed themselves to the will of God and resolved to proceed. In sundry of these storms the winds were so fierce and the seas so high, as they could not bear a knot of sail, but were forced to hull[8] for divers days together. And in one of them, as they thus lay at hull in a mighty storm, a lusty young man called John Howland, coming upon some occasion

---

1. **troubles.** Another vessel, the *Speedwell,* had proved unseaworthy and everything was transferred to the *Mayflower.*
2. **lusty.** Strong; energetic
3. **execrations.** Curses
4. **let.** Hesitate
5. **shroudly.** Shrewdly, meaning wickedly
6. **fain.** Gladly
7. **staunch.** Watertight
8. **hull.** Drift with the wind with short sails

---

pro • fane (prō fān´) *adj.,* blasphemous, irreverent; not devoted to religion or religious ends
haugh • ty (hô´ tē) *adj.,* disdainfully or contemptuously proud

which was William Butten, a youth, servant to Samuel Fuller, when they drew near the coast.

But to omit other things (that I may be brief) after long beating at sea they fell with that land which is called Cape Cod; the which being made and certainly known to be it, they were not a little joyful. After some deliberation had amongst themselves and with the master of the ship, they tacked[11] about and resolved to stand for the southward (the wind and weather being fair) to find some place about Hudson's River for their habitation. But after they had sailed that course about half the day, they fell amongst dangerous shoals and roaring breakers, and they were so far entangled therewith as they conceived themselves in great danger; and the wind shrinking upon them withal, they resolved to bear up again for the Cape and thought themselves happy to get out of those dangers before night overtook them, as by God's good providence they did. And the next day they got into Cape Harbor[12] where they rid in safety. ❖

above the gratings was, with a seele[9] of the ship, thrown into sea; but it pleased God that he caught hold of the topsail halyards[10] which hung overboard and ran out at length. Yet he held his hold (though he was sundry fathoms under water) till he was hauled up by the same rope to the brim of the water, and then with a boat hook and other means got into the ship again and his life saved. And though he was something ill with it, yet he lived many years after and became a profitable member both in church and commonwealth. In all this voyage there died but one of the passengers,

---

9. **seele.** Roll
10. **halyards.** Rope for raising and lowering a sail
11. **tacked.** Change course against the wind
12. **Cape Harbor.** The ship arrived in Cape Harbor, now known as Provincetown Harbor, on November 11, 1620, sixty-five days after leaving England.

MIRRORS & WINDOWS

Bradford states that it was "the just hand of God" that struck and killed a young bully with disease. Do you believe that people get what they deserve?

Refer to Text ▶ ▶ ▶ ▶ ▶ Reason with Text

1a. Who is present at Werowocomoco when John Smith is brought there, as described in "The General History of Virginia"?	**1b.** Why does Powhatan dress in his "greatest braveries" to speak with John Smith? Why does Smith feel the courtiers treat him "as if he had been a monster"?	**Understand** Find meaning
2a. In Bradford's account, where did the colonists first find land? Where did they decide to go from that point, and why did they turn back?	**2b.** Predict how the colonists will react to the difficulties they encounter in establishing a colony.	**Apply** Use information
3a. In Smith's account, what hardships did the colonists face in getting to Virginia and starting a colony?	**3b.** Outline what qualities were needed to succeed as an early colonist in Virginia.	**Analyze** Take things apart
4a. Who ordered John Smith's execution? Who saved him from death? How did this person save him?	**4b.** It is possible that Smith misunderstood a native custom and mistakenly assumed Powhatan wanted to harm him. Why might he have told this story repeatedly and included it in his history?	**Evaluate** Make judgments
5a. Based on these two accounts, identify what qualities were needed to be a successful leader in early colonial America.	**5b.** Smith and Bradford never met. What might have happened if they had? Support your answer with examples from the accounts.	**Create** Bring ideas together

Compare Literature

Point of View
What point or points of view does each writer use? What effect does the writer's choice have on the telling of the story? Consider which story seems more real or compelling.

Extend the Text

Writing Options
Creative Writing Design a leaflet that could be distributed at the docks at any English port to attract colonists to sail for the New World. You may write using modern English or emulate the language of the period.

Expository Writing Although both John Smith and William Bradford can be considered successful leaders, Smith left Virginia while Bradford stayed in Plymouth. Write a paragraph about each man that explains how his choice can be seen as a result of his character and the motivation that drew him to the New World.

Collaborative Learning
Map the New World As a class, create a map of North America, showing where various European countries had established North American colonies by 1620. Discuss what nations had a presence in North America and what areas likely posed conflict between them.

Media Literacy
Explore William Bradford's Journal To learn more about William Bradford's account of Plymouth Colony, visit the website of the Pilgrim Hall Museum. Read the introduction and several excerpts from Bradford's journal. In a small group, discuss what you learned at this site and any difficulties you had reading the excerpts.

 Go to **www.mirrorsandwindows.com** for more.

1. Which of the following statements best explains why Powhatan dresses himself in his "greatest braveries," as described by John Smith in "The General History of Virginia"?
   A. He wants to impress and intimidate Smith.
   B. He wants to appear handsome for his queen.
   C. He wants to demonstrate his wealth to Smith.
   D. He is preparing to engage in battle.
   E. He is going to participate in a tribal ceremony he wants Smith to observe.

2. In *The General History of Virginia,* Smith describes the men being fed a mixture of wheat and barley that "contained as many worms as grains so that we might truly call it rather so much bran than corn." Given the tone of the selection, how did Smith likely mean for this to be interpreted?
   A. as humorous
   B. as persuasive
   C. as exaggerated
   D. as strictly factual
   E. as poetically descriptive

3. In this line from *The General History of Virginia*—"our President would never have been admitted for engrossing to his private"—what does the word *engrossing* mean?
   A. absorbing
   B. collecting
   C. largely copying
   D. preparing a document
   E. taking one's whole attention

4. Which of the following phrases from *The General History of Virginia* means the same as "after their manner," as used near the end of the second complete paragraph on page 38?
   A. "according to their composition"
   B. "notwithstanding, within an hour after"
   C. "in a triumphant manner"
   D. "when no entreaty could prevail"
   E. "by His divine providence"

5. Smith and the other colonists were miserable after the ships left them in Virginia for all the following reasons *except* which one?
   A. They did not have enough good food.
   B. They had only water to drink.
   C. They slept outside.
   D. They were not prepared for the summer heat.
   E. They had hard work to do.

6. Which of the following is a *true* statement about events aboard the *Mayflower,* as described by William Bradford in the excerpt from "Of Plymouth Plantation"?
   A. Unlike the colonists in Jamestown, the passengers on the Mayflower never tried to convince others to sail back to England.
   B. Starvation and scurvy resulted in several deaths among the passengers.
   C. The majority of the passengers actually wanted to head for the Hudson River.
   D. John Howland was saved when he fell overboard but died later in a tragic accident while landing near Plymouth Rock.
   E. The passengers threw overboard a rude young man who taunted them when they were ill.

7. Which of the following events is *not* something Bradford attributes to "God's providence"?
   A. The "profane young man" comes down with a fatal disease.
   B. John Howland is saved.
   C. The ship avoids the dangerous shoals and makes its way back to Cape Harbor.
   D. The "great iron screw" helps the carpenter to raise the beam.
   E. The *Mayflower* is substituted for the *Speedwell.*

8. What point or points of view are used in these selections?
   A. first-person in both
   B. second-person in both
   C. third-person in both
   D. first-person and third-person in *The General History of Virginia* and primarily third-person in *Of Plymouth Plantation*
   E. third-person in *The General History of Virginia* and primarily first-person in *Of Plymouth Plantation*

9. **Constructed Response:** The details of John Smith's capture by the Native Americans are not entirely clear. What evidence in the excerpt suggests that the Native Americans might have singled out Smith for capture? Why might they have done this?

10. **Constructed Response:** Compare and contrast the hardships suffered by the colonists of Jamestown and Plymouth. How did the leadership provided by Smith and Bradford affect the outcome for their respective groups?

Understand the Concept

When you write a sentence, be sure that the subject and the verb **agree.** If the subject is **singular** (referring to one person or thing), then the verb must also be singular. If the subject is **plural** (two or more), then the verb must also be plural. (The **subject** tells who or what the sentence is about; the **verb** indicates what the subject is or does.)

To check for agreement in your sentences, first identify the subject and the verb. A phrase between these two sentence parts does not affect agreement, as shown in these examples:

EXAMPLES

According to Smith, the *gluttony* of sinners *prevents* them from becoming saints. [Both the subject and the verb are singular.]

Eggs kept in the ship hold for a long time *are* certain to rot. [Both the subject and the verb are plural.]

A subject that contains two or more parts is called a **compound subject.** If the parts of a compound subject are joined by *and,* the verb must be plural. If the items are joined by *or* or *nor,* the verb must agree with the subject closer to it, whether singular or plural.

EXAMPLES

Law, ordinances, and *acts* passed by an official body *create* civil order in a nation.

Either *Myles Standish,* the military commander, or *William Brewster,* a respected elder, *is* the subject of her report.

Neither the *wind* nor the dangerous *shoals were* able to keep the voyagers from landing.

Neither the dangerous *shoals* nor the *wind was* able to keep the voyagers from landing.

Collective nouns, such as *family, committee,* and *class,* refer to groups and may be either singular or plural, depending on the context.

EXAMPLES

The *audience,* seated in the auditorium, *watches* the play enthusiastically. [A singular verb with the collective noun *audience* indicates that the members of the group act as a unit.]

The *audience,* assembled in the TV studio, *express* a variety of reactions to the speakers. [Here a plural verb, *express,* used with a singular collective noun indicates that the members of the group act individually.]

Apply the Skill

Identify Agreement

In each of the following sentences, identify the form of the verb, singular or plural, that agrees with the subject.

1. In William Bradford's account, the curses of the profane young man (cause/causes) his downfall.
2. Neither the hazards at sea nor the condition of the ship (represent/represents) a reason to abandon the journey, Bradford suggests.
3. Either drifting at sea or facing fierce storms (endanger/endangers) the lives of passengers and crew.
4. Today, ships such as *Queen Elizabeth II* (stand/stands) as monuments to the achievements of marine engineering.
5. Which name, Cape Harbor or Provincetown, better (reflect/reflects) the Pilgrims' joy at finding a safe landing?

Revise to Create Agreement

Revise the following paragraph to create agreement between subject and verb.

Modern-day readers of John Smith's work probably responds according to their cultural background. For instance, either a deep faith or an interest in Native American history influence some readers. Neither the teacher nor students uneasy with a word like *savages* is likely to accept Smith's account without some reflection. What has scholars learned, over the generations, about the impact of language on education?

To My Dear and Loving Husband

A Lyric Poem by Anne Bradstreet

Build Background

Cultural Context Written in a time when most marriages were arranged based on financial or other practical concerns, **"To My Dear and Loving Husband"** remains a noble expression of the sustaining and transforming power of love. Anne Bradstreet often wrote about her love for her husband and family and her strong, though at times conflicted, Puritan faith. Puritan society frowned on women who did not follow the feminine ideal of being silent and modest, but some of Bradstreet's poems seem to question this ideal.

Literary Context Because women were discouraged from intellectual pursuits such as writing, Bradstreet distributed her writings privately. For that reason, the date of composition of "To My Dear and Loving Husband" is unknown. After Bradstreet's brother-in-law had a volume of her poetry published in England without her consent, she decided to put out a second, authorized edition. That second edition, which contained "To My Dear and Loving Husband," was not published in Boston until 1678, six years after her death.

Reader's Context Think about a time you felt very connected to someone. Did you ever feel that you and this person could complete each other's sentences or that the two of you were almost like one person?

Meet the Author

Anne Bradstreet (c. 1612–1672) was the first resident of the American colonies to have her writing published. Born in England, she had the advantage of an education, unusual for a woman of her time, and she began writing poetry as a child. She married Simon Bradstreet, a graduate of Cambridge University and an associate of her father, when she was only sixteen.

A year after their marriage, Simon was appointed to assist in establishment of the Massachusetts Bay Company, and the Bradstreets sailed to the New World. Life there was hard, especially for Anne, who had been weakened by a childhood illness; she described colonial life as having a "rough and fearsome aspect." When Simon became governor of the Massachusetts Bay Colony, Anne's duties increased.

Yet despite raising eight children and having ill health, Anne Bradstreet found time to continue writing poetry. She addressed those who were critical of female poets in the prologue to one of her collections, writing, "I am obnoxious to each carping tongue / Who says my hand a needle better fits. / A poet's pen all scorn I should thus wrong, / For such despite they cast on female wits. / If what I do prove well, it won't advance, / They'll say it's stol'n, or else it was by chance."

Analyze Literature

Hyperbole and Paradox
A **hyperbole** is a deliberate exaggeration made for effect.

A **paradox** is a seemingly contradictory statement, idea, or event that may actually be true. Some paradoxes present unresolvable contradictory ideas.

Set Purpose

Anne Bradstreet was not a traditional Puritan woman in several respects. For instance, in writing about her love for her husband, she uses hyperbole to express her passion. Look for examples of overstatement and exaggeration as you read. Also look for a paradoxical statement. Think about how its placement affects your reading of the poem.

Preview Vocabulary

recompense, 47
manifold, 47
persevere, 47

To My Dear and Loving Husband

by Anne Bradstreet

Elizabeth Freake and Baby Mary, c. 1671–1674. Artist unknown.
Worcester Art Museum, Worcester, Massachusetts.
(See detail on page 46.)

If ever two were one, then surely we.
If ever man were loved by wife, then thee;
If ever wife was happy in a man,
Compare with me, ye women, if you can.
5   I prize thy love more than whole mines of gold
Or all the riches that the East doth hold.
My love is such that rivers cannot quench,
Nor ought[1] but love from thee, give <u>recompense</u>.
Thy love is such I can no way repay,
10   The heavens reward thee <u>manifold</u>, I pray.
Then while we live, in love let's so <u>persevere</u>
That when we live no more, we may live ever. ❖

---

1. **ought.** Anything

> **rec • om • pense** (rek´ əm pens) *n.,* reward; payment
> **man • i • fold** (man´ i fōld) *adv.,* many times; a great deal
> **per • se • vere** (pʉr sə vēr´) *v.,* continue in spite of difficulty;
> persist

MIRRORS & WINDOWS

Bradstreet says she can never "repay the heavens" for her loving relationship with her husband. What enables people to develop this sort of relationship? How many people ever achieve it?

Refer to Text 	**Reason with Text**	
1a. The speaker prizes her husband's "love more than" what? What is the speaker's love "such that"?	**1b.** What does the speaker see as more valuable: her own love for her husband or his love for her? Explain your answer.	**Understand** Find meaning
2a. What can give the speaker recompense for her love for her husband?	**2b.** Based on this poem, infer what Anne Bradstreet valued.	**Apply** Use information
3a. Identify the only way the speaker's husband can be repaid for his love.	**3b.** Is the speaker's love for her husband reciprocated? Support your answer.	**Analyze** Take things apart
4a. What does the speaker believe about the afterlife and about the consequences of being, in this life, someone who perseveres in love despite its difficulties?	**4b.** Using evidence from the poem, argue whether it is an accurate or idealized picture of the relationship between the speaker and her husband.	**Evaluate** Make judgments
5a. In lines 11 and 12 of the poem, what does the speaker want to do while she lives? What does the speaker say this will enable the couple to do?	**5b.** This poem can be seen as part of a literary tradition of talking about love as if it had the power to overcome death. Why might this be a recurring theme in literature?	**Create** Bring ideas together

Analyze Literature

Hyperbole and Paradox

Review Bradstreet's use of hyperbole in this poem. What examples did you find? Why does she use hyperbole? How does it affect your reading and understanding of her poem?

What paradoxical statement appears in this poem? What does this seemingly contradictory statement mean? Consider why Bradstreet uses this technique, particularly at the place in the poem where the statement is made.

Extend the Text

Writing Options

Creative Writing Choose a holiday or special occasion, and write a greeting card message for it. Include at least one example of hyperbole. Use creative language to make your message unique.

Expository Writing Write an essay that explains what made Anne Bradstreet both typical and atypical for her time and place. You can use the "Before Reading" information as a starting point, but also consult other sources to research Bradstreet's life.

Collaborative Learning

Role-Play an Interview With another classmate, role-play a television interview with Anne Bradstreet, in which one of you plays a modern-day marriage counselor on a talk show and the other plays Bradstreet. The person playing the counselor should ask questions about what makes Bradstreet's relationship with her husband successful. Share your best question-and-answer segments with the class.

Lifelong Learning

Research the Muses The title of Anne Bradstreet's first volume of poetry refers to her as "the tenth muse." In Greek mythology, the muses were the nine daughters of Mnemosyne and Zeus, and each one presided over a different art or science. As a class, form nine groups, assigning a muse to each group and having them prepare a brief oral presentation on what a muse represents, using an example from art or science.

 Go to **www.mirrorsandwindows.com** for more.

Understand the Concept

New words constantly are being invented and added to the English language. Some become popular and their use becomes widespread; these words eventually are added to the dictionary. For example, *spyware* and *supersize* recently were added to *Webster's*. Other words never become popular or gradually fall out of favor.

Many of the new words added to the English language can be characterized as **slang:** colorful, informal speech made up of invented words or old words given new meanings. Few slang terms have staying power; most ultimately become archaic or obsolete.

Archaic words are those that were once common but are now used rarely, such as in poetry. Anne Bradstreet's "To My Dear and Loving Husband," written during the seventeenth century, uses a number of what are now considered archaic words. Both *thee* and *ye* are archaic forms of the word *you,* and *thy* is an archaic form of *your.* In addition, the poem uses the word *doth,* an archaic form of the verb *do.*

Such words also are known as *obsolete words,* meaning that they are no longer in use. Some dictionaries classify as obsolete any word that has not been seen in print since 1750.

Encountering archaic words in reading can be challenging, especially if a word has a contemporary meaning quite different from its old one. Approach archaic words as you would other unfamiliar words. Use context clues and footnotes, or consult the dictionary.

Apply the Skill

Exercise A

Work with a partner to identify the modern meanings of the archaic words in the sentences below. Each sentence is taken from a selection in this unit, and the archaic word you should identify appears in italic type.

1. He would always be condemning the poor people in their sickness and cursing them daily with grievous *execrations.*
2. *Fain* would they do what could be done for their wages' sake.
3. In *sundry* of these storms the winds were so fierce and the seas so high.
4. But when we came to lie down they *bade* me to go out, and lie somewhere else.
5. For whom the Lord loveth he *chasteneth.*
6. And the world would spew you out, if it were not for the sovereign hand of Him who *hath* subjected it in hope.
7. My love is such that rivers cannot quench, / Nor *ought* but love from thee, give recompense.
8. He that *lieth* down with dogs shall rise up with fleas.
9. It *fortuned* that within ten days, scarce ten amongst us could either go or well stand.
10. Our little ones . . . shall not be deficient in virtue or *probity.*

Exercise B

Write a brief diary entry describing a typical day in your life, but use archaic language in place of modern English. For example, instead of writing "She told me to tell her the truth about her new haircut," you might write, "She camest to me and beseecheth, 'Speaketh to me plain and verily. What thinkest thou of mine newest adornment of hair?'"

SPELLING PRACTICE

Vowel Combinations

Vowel combinations can be tricky to spell because the same pair of letters can be pronounced in different ways. Review this list of spelling words from the lesson for "To My Dear and Loving Husband" to see different vowel combinations. Identify the sounds made by the various vowel combinations.

appointed		
associate	marriage	sustaining
discouraged	pursuits	weakened
intellectual	society	

Huswifery
A Lyric Poem by Edward Taylor

Build Background

Literary Context Although Edward Taylor is known today as one of colonial America's best poets, his work was not published during his lifetime. In fact, his work became known only in the 1930s after a collection of his poetry was found in the Yale University Library in one of the most significant literary discoveries of the twentieth century. Some of his poetry was published in 1937, but the entire collection was not published until 1960.

Not a lot is known about Taylor's life except that he was a minister, which has led scholars to speculate that he did not seek publicity because his exuberant, confessional poetic style ran contrary to his strong Puritan values. In the poem **"Huswifery,"** whose title means "housekeeping," Taylor examines God's relationship to humans.

Reader's Context To what object or process would you compare your primary relationships? Why?

Meet the Author

Edward Taylor (1642–1729) was born in Sketchley, Leicestershire, England, and, according to some accounts, studied at Cambridge University. He decided to emigrate to New England at age twenty-six after refusing to sign an oath of loyalty to the Church of England; that refusal would have prevented him from being a teacher or minister.

Within weeks after arriving in the Massachusetts Bay Colony, Taylor was admitted to Harvard College, where he studied theology. After graduating, he served as a physician and pastor in Westfield, Massachusetts, the westernmost settlement in the colony. There, Taylor experienced the many challenges of frontier life, facing occasional skirmishes with Native Americans as well as enduring the deaths from illness of his first wife, Elizabeth, and five infant children.

Taylor's reflections on premature death can be found in some of his poems, which are elegiac in nature. Other of his poems can be tied to themes from his sermons or preaching notes; these works are more meditative in nature and seem to be self-examinations. An ardent Puritan, Taylor was a penitent sinner and considered himself unworthy of receiving God's grace.

Analyze Literature

Plain Style and Extended Metaphor
The **plain style** of writing uses uncomplicated sentences and precise words to produce clear, simple statements.

An **extended metaphor** is a point-by-point presentation of one thing as though it were another. The description is meant as an implied comparison, inviting the reader to associate the thing being described with something that is quite different from it.

Set Purpose

The work of Puritan writers reflects their opposition to unnecessary ornamentation in both the religious and secular aspects of life. Taylor's poem, however, contains many examples of vivid and complex language. As you read, note what about the poem is and is not typical of the plain style. In particular, analyze the extended metaphor Taylor creates. What items are meant to be representative, and what do they represent?

Preview Vocabulary

affections, 51
varnished, 51
apparel, 52

Huswifery

by Edward Taylor

Make me, O Lord, Thy Spinning Wheel complete.
Thy Holy Word my Distaff[1] make for me.
Make mine <u>Affections</u> Thy Swift Flyers[2] neat
And make my Soul thy holy Spool[3] to be.
5   My conversation make to be Thy Reel[4]
And reel the yarn thereon spun of Thy Wheel.

Make me Thy Loom then, knit therein this Twine:
And make Thy Holy Spirit, Lord, wind quills:
Then weave the Web Thyself. The yarn is fine.
10 Thine Ordinances make my Fulling Mills.[5]
Then dye the same in Heavenly Colors Choice,
All pinked[6] with <u>Varnished</u> Flowers of Paradise.

---

1. **Distaff.** Tool that holds the raw wool
2. **Flyers.** Parts that regulate the spinning
3. **Spool.** Part on which yarn is wound
4. **Reel.** Part that takes up the finished thread
5. **Fulling Mills.** Machines that beat and clean cloth
6. **pinked.** Adorned

af • fec • tions (ä fek´ shənz) *n.*, emotions
var • nished (vär´ nisht) *adj.*, decorated; adorned

Then clothe therewith mine Understanding, Will,
Affections, Judgment, Conscience, Memory,
15 My Words, and Actions, that their shine may fill
My ways with glory and Thee glorify.
Then mine <u>apparel</u> shall display before Ye
That I am Clothed in Holy robes for glory. ❖

ap • par • el (ä pār´ 'l) *n.*, clothing

M̲IRRORS & W̲INDOWS

The metaphor of a spinning wheel would not make sense to a modern audience.
What modern machine or device would you choose to update Taylor's poem?

EDUCATION CONNECTION

The New England Primer

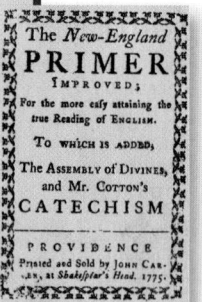

The New England Primer was the first textbook produced in America to teach reading. Evidence places publication of the first edition between 1687 and 1690.

Since the New England colonies were founded for religious reasons, it was only natural that religion formed the basis of all education and therefore dominated the book. Its contents included the Lord's Prayer, the Apostles' Creed, a series of moral and instructive sentences from the Bible, and an illustrated alphabet.

The *Primer* was popular throughout the English colonies and was sold in the United States until the nineteenth century. The excerpt here is the alphabet from the 1727 edition of the *Primer*.

Refer to Text ▶ ▶ ▶ ▶ ▶   Reason with Text

1a. In the first stanza of the poem, what household items does the speaker ask to be?	**1b.** Describe the type of relationship with God that is suggested by these items.	**Understand** Find meaning
2a. State what the cloth being woven looks like.	**2b.** Based on what you know about plain style, how does the appearance of the cloth go against Puritan values?	**Apply** Use information
3a. In the second stanza, what is the speaker asking to be?	**3b.** Compare the making of the garment from the first to the last stanza to the speaker's relationship with God. How does it change?	**Analyze** Take things apart
4a. What does the speaker become in the final stanza?	**4b.** Judge whether the speaker is glorifying himself or God. What are the different ways in which one might glorify God?	**Evaluate** Make judgments
5a. How is this poem representative of the religious ideals of the day?	**5b.** Propose how this poem might be written differently today. What common objects could be used?	**Create** Bring ideas together

Analyze Literature

Plain Style and Extended Metaphor

Go back through the poem and compile a list of the household items that are mentioned. How do they fit with the sense of plain style that was fundamental to Puritan values? What aspects of this poem run contrary to plain style and Puritan values?

Refer again to your list. What do the items have in common? How does Taylor use them to create an extended metaphor? What is the overall comparison being made?

Extend the Text

Writing Options

Creative Writing Write an extended metaphor about an important relationship you have with, say, a parent, sibling, or friend. Choose a *vehicle* (the image expressing the relationship) that can show a process, just as Taylor does. You can write either a poem or prose.

Expository Writing Write a one-paragraph analysis of this poem that examines the progression in the relationship between the speaker and God from the first stanza to the last. What is the speaker's ultimate hope? In what ways do his hopes align with Puritan thought, and in what ways do they differ?

Collaborative Learning

Deliver a Presentation With a small group, research the Puritan lifestyle. Assign each group member specific topic, such as religion, school, clothing, or education. Compile your findings and prepare a report or presentation, including visual aids as appropriate. Deliver the presentation to the whole class.

Critical Literacy

Analyze Language Conventions In Taylor's time, rules of capitalization, punctuation, and other conventions of language were not fixed, so the writer decided how best to convey his or her work. Find a copy of the original version of "Huswifery," and examine the use of capitalization. Determine whether the capitalization style used in the original version alters the meaning or emphasis of the poem. Also find other poems by Edward Taylor and compare them to "Huswifery" in terms of subject and style.

 Go to **www.mirrorsandwindows.com** for more.

from Sinners in the Hands of an Angry God

A Sermon by Jonathan Edwards

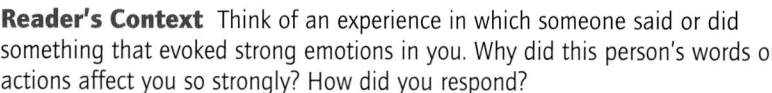

Build Background

Historical Context The following excerpt is from **"Sinners in the Hands of an Angry God,"** a sermon that the Reverend Jonathan Edwards delivered in Enfield, Connecticut, on Sunday, July 8, 1741. Another minister who was present reported that Edwards spoke with calm dignity, yet the effect on Edwards's audience was highly emotional, with "such a breathing of distress, and weeping, that the preacher was obliged to speak to the people and desire silence, that he might be heard."

Edwards was one of several ministers who led an evangelical religious movement called the Great Awakening, which spread throughout colonial America during the 1730s and 1740s (see Cultural Connection on page 58). The text of the sermon was published more than eighty years later (1829–1830) in a multivolume edition of Edwards's works.

Reader's Context Think of an experience in which someone said or did something that evoked strong emotions in you. Why did this person's words or actions affect you so strongly? How did you respond?

Meet the Author

Jonathan Edwards (1703–1758) was born in East Windsor, Connecticut. He was a dedicated scholar even as a child and was admitted to Yale College when he was only thirteen. Edwards flourished in the rigorous academic setting and devoted himself to the study of theology. Having come from a line of noteworthy ministers, Edwards was determined to carry on his family's tradition. He moved to Northampton, Massachusetts, where he succeeded his grandfather as minister of the local church and also married and raised a family.

Edwards's goals as a minister were not only to heighten his followers' commitment to religion but also to enrich their religious experience. Known for his vivid and fiery sermons, Edwards tried to make religion so moving and real that it was almost a physical experience. His religious views gained great popularity during the Great Awakening, and he attracted a large following. But when he decided to single out prestigious members of the clergy who were not expressing the proper devotion and tried to reinstate the rite of communion, he was dismissed from his church. Edwards then served as a missionary to the Housatonic native tribe and was elected president of the College of New Jersey (now Princeton).

Analyze Literature

Analogy and Repetition
An **analogy** is a comparison of two things that are alike in some respects but otherwise different. Often an analogy explains or describes something unfamiliar by comparing it to something more familiar.

Repetition is a writer's intentional reuse of a sound, word, phrase, or sentence, often for the purpose of emphasis.

Set Purpose

Like other evangelical ministers of the Great Awakening, Jonathan Edwards was a dynamic speaker who evoked strong emotions in his listeners. He achieved this, in large part, by using literary techniques such as analogy and repetition. Identify the analogies he uses to give his listeners clear, concrete pictures of the abstract ideas he presents. Also identify the words and phrases he repeats throughout the sermon.

Preview Vocabulary

constitution, 55
avail, 55
prudence, 56
contrivance, 56
sovereign, 56
loathsome, 57
abhor, 57
provoke, 57
ascribe, 57
incense, 57
induce, 57

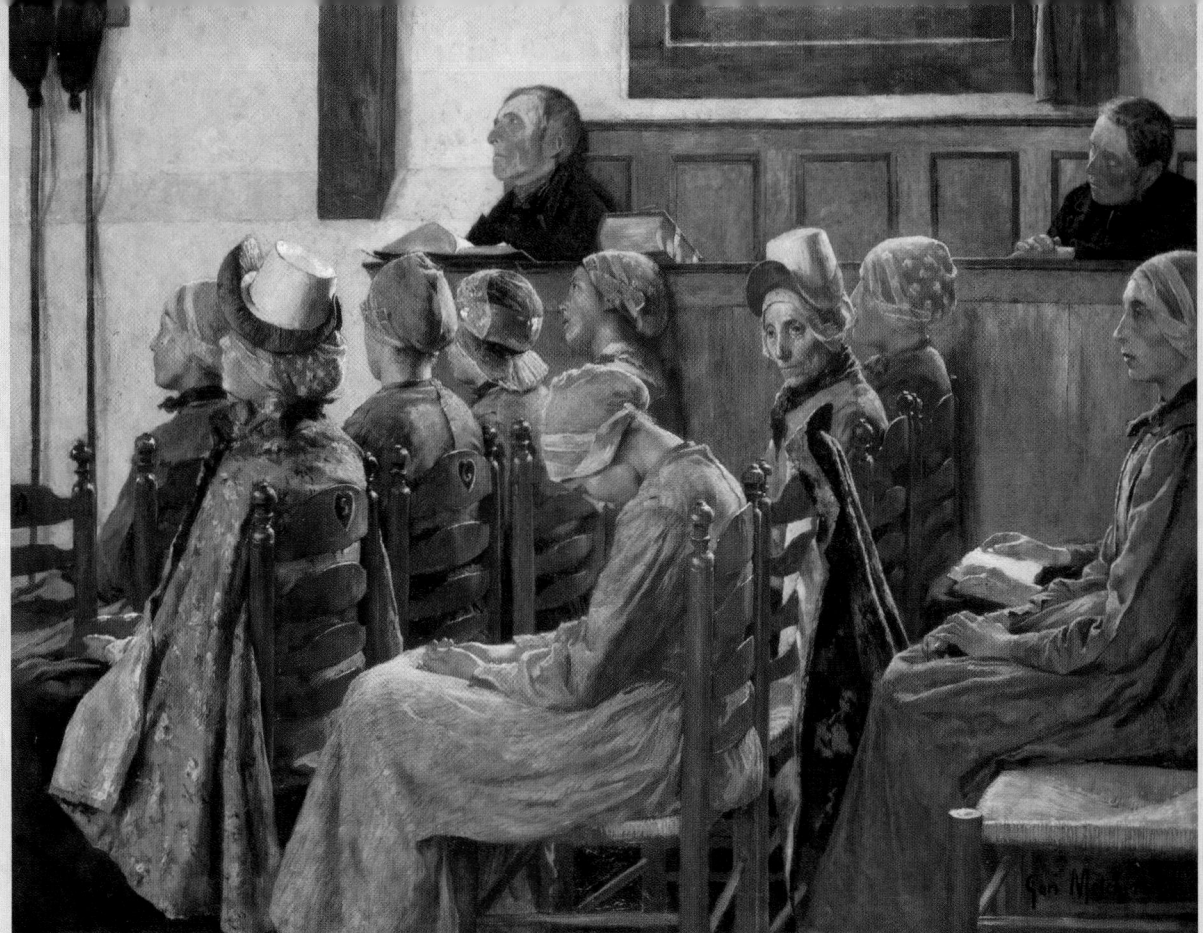

The Sermon, 1886. Gari Melchers.
Smithsonian American Art Museum, Washington, DC.

from Sinners in the Hands of an Angry God

by Jonathan Edwards

The God that holds you over the pit of hell, much as one holds a spider or some loathsome insect over the fire, abhors you, and is dreadfully provoked.

You probably are not sensible[1] of this; you find you are kept out of hell, but do not see the hand of God in it; but look at other things, as the good state of your bodily constitution, your care of your own life, and the means you use for your own preservation. But indeed these things are nothing; if God should withdraw His hand, they would avail no more to keep you from falling, than the thin air to hold up a person that is suspended in it.

---

1. **sensible.** Aware

con • sti • tu • tion (kän′ stə tū′ shən) *n.*, physical makeup of a person
avail (ä vāl′) *v.*, be of use or advantage

Your wickedness makes you as it were heavy as lead, and to tend downwards with great weight and pressure towards hell; and if God should let you go, you would immediately sink and swiftly descend and plunge into the bottomless gulf, and your healthy constitution, and your own care and <u>prudence</u>, and best <u>contrivance</u>, and all your righteousness, would have no more influence to uphold you and keep you out of hell, than a spider's web would have to stop a fallen rock. Were it not for the <u>sovereign</u> pleasure of God, the earth would not bear you one moment; for you are a burden to it; the creation groans with you; the creature is made subject to the bondage of your corruption, not willingly; the sun does not willingly shine upon you to give you light to serve sin and Satan; the earth does not willingly yield her increase[2] to satisfy your lusts; nor is it willingly a stage for your wickedness to be acted upon; the air does not willingly serve you for breath to maintain the flame of life in your vitals,[3] while you spend your life in the service of God's enemies. God's creatures are good, and were made for men to serve God with, and do not willingly subserve[4] to any other purpose, and groan when they are abused to purposes so directly contrary to their nature and end. And the world would spew you out, were it not for the sovereign hand of Him who hath subjected it in hope. There are black clouds of God's wrath now hanging directly over your heads, full of the dreadful storm, and big with thunder; and were it not for the restraining hand of God, it would immediately burst forth upon you. The sovereign pleasure of God, for the present, stays His rough wind; otherwise it would come with fury, and your destruction would come like a whirlwind, and you would be like the chaff of the summer threshing floor.[5] . . .

The bow of God's wrath is bent, and the arrow made ready on the string, and justice bends the arrow at your heart, and strains the bow, and it is nothing but the mere

It is nothing but His mere pleasure that keeps you from being this moment swallowed up in everlasting destruction.

pleasure of God, and that of an angry God, without any promise or obligation at all, that keeps the arrow one moment from being made drunk with your blood. Thus all you that never passed under a great change of heart, by the mighty power of the Spirit of God upon your souls, all you that were never born again, and made new creatures, and raised from being dead in sin, to a state of new, and before altogether unexperienced light and life, are in the hands of an angry God. However you may have reformed your life in many things, and may have had religious affections,[6] and may keep up a form of religion in your families and closets,[7] and in the house of God, it is nothing but His mere pleasure that keeps you from being this moment swallowed up in everlasting destruction. However unconvinced you may now be of the truth of what you hear, by and by you will be fully convinced of it. Those that are gone from being in the like circumstances with you see that it was so with them; for destruction came suddenly upon most of them; when they expected nothing of it and while they were saying, peace and safety: now they see that those things on which they depended for peace and safety, were nothing but thin air and empty shadows.

---

2. **increase.** Harvest
3. **vitals.** Necessary organs
4. **subserve.** Serve
5. **chaff . . . threshing floor.** *Chaff*—husks of wheat that are left behind; *threshing floor*—place where grain is separated from husks
6. **affections.** Feelings
7. **closets.** Studies; meditations

> pru • dence (prü´ dəns) *n.*, sense; care; caution
> con • triv • ance (kən trī´ vəns) *n.*, invention; clever plan
> sov • er • eign (sô´ vʉr ən) *adj.*, above or superior to all others

The God that holds you over the pit of hell, much as one holds a spider or some <u>loathsome</u> insect over the fire, <u>abhors</u> you, and is dreadfully <u>provoked</u>: His wrath towards you burns like fire; He looks upon you as worthy of nothing else but to be cast into the fire; He is of purer eyes than to bear to have you in His sight; you are ten thousand times more abominable in His eyes than the most hateful venomous serpent is in ours. You have offended Him infinitely more than ever a stubborn rebel did his prince; and yet it is nothing but His hand that holds you from falling into the fire every moment. It is to be <u>ascribed</u> to nothing else, that you did not go to hell the last night; that you was suffered to awake again in this world, after you closed your eyes to sleep. And there is no other reason to be given, why you have not dropped into hell since you arose in the morning, but that God's hand has held you up. There is no other reason to be given why you have not gone to hell, since you have sat here in the house of God, provoking His pure eyes by your sinful wicked manner of attending His solemn worship. Yea, there is nothing else that is to be given as a reason why you do not this very moment drop down into hell.

O sinner! Consider the fearful danger you are in: it is a great furnace of wrath, a wide and bottomless pit, full of the fire of wrath, that you are held over in the hand of that God, whose wrath is provoked and <u>incensed</u> as much against you, as against many of the damned in hell. You hang by a slender thread, with the flames of divine wrath flashing about

O sinner! Consider the fearful danger you are in: it is a great furnace of wrath, a wide and bottomless pit, full of the fire of wrath, that you are held over in the hand of that God.

it, and ready every moment to singe it, and burn it asunder; and you have no interest in any Mediator, and nothing to lay hold of to save yourself, nothing to keep off the flames of wrath, nothing of your own, nothing that you have done, nothing that you can do, to <u>induce</u> God to spare you one moment. ❖

---

loath • some (lō<u>th</u>´ səm) *adj.*, disgusting
ab • hor (äb hōr´) *v.*, shrink from in disgust
pro • voked (prə vōkt´) *adj.*, made very angry; irritated; annoyed
as • cribe (ə skrīb´) *v.*, assign; attribute
in • cense (in sens´) *v.*, make very angry
in • duce (in düs´) *v.*, persuade

MIRRORS & WINDOWS

Put yourself in the place of one of Edwards's followers. How would hearing his sermon make you feel about yourself? How would it make you feel about people in general?

The Great Awakening

During the 1730s and 1740s, the American colonies were swept by a religious revival known as the *Great Awakening.* A similar movement took place in Europe, particularly in England, Scotland, and Germany. This revival, which occurred among Protestant groups, promoted an intensely personal and emotional involvement in religion, or *evangelism.* Religious services were characterized by fiery sermons about the power of faith and redemption but also the sinful nature of humanity and the terrors of hell.

The Great Awakening developed in response to a worldwide movement known as the *Age of Reason* or *Enlightenment.* Revolutionary scientific discoveries made during the late 1600s and early 1700s had encouraged people to apply reason and logic to other areas of human activity, including government, ethics, and education. Leaders of the Great Awakening hoped to counter that thinking, encouraging people to rely on God and the Bible for direction, not human reason.

In America, three preachers were known as the leaders of the Great Awakening. The first was William Tennent, a Presbyterian minister. Beginning in the 1730s, Tennent and his four sons, all ministers, held religious revivals throughout New Jersey and Pennsylvania. They also established a seminary to train preachers who could deliver highly charged sermons and draw people to their church; that seminary, originally called "the Log College," would later become Princeton University.

The success of the Tennent family was quickly recognized, and evangelism spread to the Congregationalists (Puritans) and Baptists of New England. A Congregationalist minister from Massachusetts, Jonathan Edwards, became a powerful force in the Great Awakening, attracting a large following. Edwards was known for instilling fear and guilt in his followers; "Sinners in the Hands of an Angry God" (1741) is his most famous sermon.

The third major figure in the Great Awakening was actually an English preacher who traveled throughout the American colonies from 1739 to 1741. George Whitefield, a Methodist minister, was a dramatic, even theatrical speaker; he drew such large audiences that he often had to conduct his services outdoors. His popularity throughout the colonies helped unite the various denominations and strengthen the evangelical cause.

The Great Awakening reached the southern colonies in the late 1740s, in large part because of the missionary activities of northern preachers. As the movement took hold, some missionaries attempted to spread their faith among African-American slaves and Native Americans, which created conflict among followers. Criticism also came from outside the movement, as moderate and conservative religious groups, such as the Quakers and the Anglicans, took issue with the revival's excesses. The methods of traveling preachers, such as Whitefield—who often came to an area, criticized the efforts of local clergy, and then moved on—were especially condemned.

Despite these conflicts, the Great Awakening is generally credited with bringing about several important developments in colonial America. Followers of this movement made the first real efforts to abolish slavery and to initiate other humanitarian causes, many of which would be pursued during subsequent "awakenings" in the 1820s and 1880s. Followers of the Great Awakening also founded a number of colleges and academies, including Princeton, Brown, Rutgers, and Dartmouth.

Princeton University (c. 1764).

Refer to Text ▶ ▶ ▶ ▶ ▶ **Reason with Text**

Refer to Text	Reason with Text	
1a. According to Edwards, what does the average person think keeps him or her alive? To what does Edwards give complete credit?	**1b.** What emotions was Edwards's sermon designed to evoke in a listener? Describe what he wanted listeners to do.	**Understand** Find meaning
2a. In paragraph 2 of the sermon, how do the various elements of nature regard humans, according to Edwards?	**2b.** To what extent does this sermon make sinners fear punishment but still hope for God's grace?	**Apply** Use information
3a. In the beginning of paragraph 4, to what does Edwards compare his listeners?	**3b.** In paragraph 4, what progression does Edwards trace in speaking of the threat to the sinner's existence? Outline how doing so might be effective in arousing listeners.	**Analyze** Take things apart
4a. To what is God's wrath compared in paragraph 3?	**4b.** Argue whether Edwards's sermon could inspire listeners to throw themselves on the mercy of an angry God.	**Evaluate** Make judgments
5a. Identify what Edwards claims is required to take a person out of the "sinner" classification.	**5b.** How might Edwards respond to someone who is confident of being rewarded in the afterlife because of living a good life on Earth?	**Create** Bring ideas together

Analyze Literature

Analogy and Repetition

Identify some of the analogies Edwards uses. How does each create a clear, concrete picture of an abstract idea?

What are some of the words and phrases Edwards repeats throughout this sermon? What is the effect of this use of repetition? Why might the use of both these techniques be particularly effective in a sermon?

Extend the Text

Writing Options

Creative Writing Write a radio advertisement for a modern-day church headed by a minister like Jonathan Edwards, who warns of the dangers of sin and explains that salvation is possible through this church. Try to emulate Edwards's style, but make sure your advertisement will connect with modern listeners.

Expository Writing Read Portia's speech in Act IV, Scene i of Shakespeare's *The Merchant of Venice*, which begins "The quality of mercy is not strain'd." Then write a paragraph in which you compare and contrast the view of God presented in this speech with that presented in Edwards's sermon.

Collaborative Learning

Define a Good Person Regardless of whether you agree with him, Jonathan Edwards had a well-defined view of what it means to be a good person. As a class, discuss what that concept means, and create a list of characteristics that you agree make a person good.

Lifelong Learning

Compare Sermons As a class, create a list of other famous sermons, whether from Edwards's contemporaries or modern-day religious leaders. Form small groups, and have each group focus on one sermon, summarizing its content, language, theme, and purpose in a presentation.

 Go to **www.mirrorsandwindows.com** for more.

1. Which of the following statements best summarizes the relationship between humans and God described in "Sinners in the Hands of an Angry God"?
   A. "The God that holds you over the pit of hell, much as one holds a spider or some loathsome insect over the fire, abhors you, and is dreadfully provoked."
   B. "You probably are not sensible of this; you find you are kept out of hell, but do not see the hand of God in it."
   C. "If God should let you go, you would immediately sink and swiftly descend and plunge into the bottomless gulf."
   D. "God's creatures are good, and were made for men to serve God with."
   E. "There is no other reason to be given why you have not gone to hell, since you have sat here in the house of God, provoking His pure eyes by your sinful wicked manner of attending His solemn worship."

2. According to Jonathan Edwards, what is the sinner's only hope?
   A. To have "religious affections" and "keep up a form of religion in your families and closets."
   B. To undergo "a great change of heart, by the mighty power of the Spirit of God upon your soul."
   C. To take stock of the "good state of your bodily constitution, [and] your care of your own life."
   D. To stop attending worship services, of which the sinner is not worthy.
   E. According to Edwards, there is no hope at all for sinners.

3. What are Edwards's main purposes in "Sinners in the Hands of an Angry God"?
   A. to reflect and entertain
   B. to describe and tell a story
   C. to inform and reflect
   D. to entertain and remind
   E. to explain and persuade

4. Which of the following statements is an example of an analogy?
   A. "You may have reformed your life in many things, and may have had religious affections, and may keep up a form of religion in your families and closets."
   B. "You probably are not sensible of this; you find you are kept out of hell, but do not see the hand of God in it."

C. "He looks upon you as worthy of nothing else but to be cast into the fire."
   D. "All your righteousness, would have no more influence to uphold you and keep you out of hell, than a spider's web would have to stop a fallen rock."
   E. "Those that are gone from being in the like circumstances with you see that it was so with them; for destruction came suddenly upon most of them."

5. Which of the following words is a synonym for *induce?*
   A. persuade
   B. create
   C. start
   D. discourage
   E. threaten

6. Which of the following best sums up Edwards's view of the earth's attitude toward people?
   A. ". . . for you are a burden to it . . ."
   B. ". . . and the earth serves your wicked ways . . ."
   C. ". . . full of the dreadful storm, and big with thunder . . ."
   D. ". . . those things they depended on for peace and safety . . ."
   E. None of the above

7. **Constructed Response:** In "Sinners in the Hands of an Angry God," Edwards writes the following: "The sovereign pleasure of God, for the present, stays His rough wind; otherwise it would come with fury, and your destruction would come like a whirlwind, and you would be like the chaff of the summer threshing floor." What comparisons does Edwards make in this passage? What does this passage reveal about Edwards's view of the relationship between humans and God?

8. **Constructed Response:** According to a witness, Edwards's sermon caused "such a breathing of distress, and weeping, that the preacher was obliged to speak to the people and desire silence, that he might be heard." Why did Edwards's sermon have this effect on his listeners? What literary techniques did he use to create this reaction?

Understand the Concept

A **verb tense** conveys a sense of time and tells when an action takes place. The use of tense establishes a sequence of events. In everyday writing and speaking, the most commonly used verb tenses are present tense, past tense, and future tense.

The **present tense** denotes an action that is happening now or that is ongoing or consistent:

EXAMPLES

Rachel *reads* the selections assigned for her English class. [Action is happening now]

George *wears* a wool coat in the winter to keep warm. [Action is ongoing or consistent]

The present tense also is used when discussing or writing about literature:

EXAMPLE

In "Sinners in the Hands of an Angry God," Jonathan Edwards *shows* no pity for his listeners.

The **past tense** indicates that an action happened at some prior time. The past tense of a regular verb is formed by adding *-d* or *-ed* to the present verb form:

EXAMPLES

Edwards *began* preaching in his native England and later emigrated to the United States.

The Great Awakening *spread* throughout colonial America during the 1730s and 1740s.

The **future tense** denotes that an action will happen at some future point. The future tense is formed by adding the word *will* or *shall* before the present verb form:

EXAMPLE

Alanna *will present* an oral report on Edwards's sermon tomorrow.

As a general rule, you should maintain the same tense in writing. However, sometimes a shift in tense is necessary to indicate a difference in time:

EXAMPLES

Edwards, who *lived* from 1703 to 1758, *is known* for writing sermons that *arouse* fear and guilt among listeners. [*Lived* refers to a specific event in Edwards's life; *is known* and *arouse* refer to an ongoing or consistent situation]

Efforts to bring the Great Awakening to slaves in the southern colonies *caused* tensions, but the movement often *is praised* for its help in abolishing slavery. [*Caused* refers to past events; *is praised* states an ongoing or consistent situation]

Using verb tenses accurately is essential to good writing. Errors and unnecessary switches in tense are both confusing and distracting to readers, who cannot make sense of the sequence of events.

Apply the Skill

Identify the Correct Tense

In each of the following sentences, identify the correct tense from the choices in parentheses.

1. In which paragraph of the sermon (does/did) Edwards say that humans (are/were) as powerless to prevent sin as spiders (are/were) to stop a falling rock?
2. The insects that (appear/appeared) in "Sinners in the Hands of an Angry God" (are/were) also mentioned in an essay that Edwards (writes/wrote) when he (is/was) still a teenager.
3. What characteristics of this creature, which to Edwards (seem/seemed) so repulsive, (make/made) this member of the class Arachnida such a target of scorn?
4. To present-day readers, the preacher's sermons probably (sound/sounded) harsh. How (do/did) you think his parishioners (react/reacted) to these fiery talks?
5. Edwards's style as a speaker (will be studied/is studied) by generations to come.

Revise to Create Agreement

Revise the following paragraph to create consistency of tenses.

If you were interested in the link between readers' responses to literature and their cultural background, you can look for research that had been done on the topic. In a study conducted last year, for example, students are asked to read a passage by Edwards. Do students who have a religious upbringing react differently from classmates who came from nonreligious homes?

from
The Interesting Narrative of the Life of Olaudah Equiano,
or Gustavus Vassa, the African, Written by Himself

by Olaudah Equiano

Olaudah Equiano (1745–1797) claimed that he was born in what is now Nigeria. As a child, he was sold into slavery and eventually shipped across the Atlantic Ocean to the West Indies. He was later sold to a Quaker merchant from Philadelphia. On trading ventures in the Caribbean, Equiano witnessed some of the most horrific abuses of plantation slavery. While helping to manage his owner's shipping business, Equiano was able to raise enough money from his own trading activities to buy his freedom at age twenty-one.

After he was freed, Equiano became an outspoken opponent of the British slave trade. He also secured sponsors to help him publish his autobiography, which he hoped would influence the debate about slavery. In 1807, ten years after Equiano's death, the English slave trade was finally outlawed. Published in 1789, **The Interesting Narrative of the Life of Olaudah Equiano** was a best seller in England and the United States.

The small account in which the life of a negro is held in the West Indies is so universally known, that it might seem impertinent to quote the following extract, if some people had not been hardy enough of late to assert that negroes are on the same footing in that respect as Europeans. By the 329th Act, page 125, of the Assembly of Barbadoes, it is enacted 'That if any negro, or other slave, under punishment by his master, or his order, for running away, or any other crime or misdemeanor towards his said master, unfortunately shall suffer in life or member, no person whatsoever shall be liable to a fine; but if any man shall out of *wantonness,*[1] *or only of bloody-mindedness, or cruel intention, willfully kill a negro, or other slave, of his own, he shall pay into the public treasury fifteen pounds sterling.'* And it is the same in most, if not all, of the West India islands. Is not this one of the many acts of the islands which call loudly for redress? And do not the assembly which enacted it deserve the appellation[2] of savages and brutes rather than of Christians and men? It is an act at once unmerciful, unjust, and unwise; which for cruelty would disgrace an assembly of those who are called barbarians; and for its injustice and *insanity* would shock the morality and common sense of a Samaide or a Hottentot.[3] . . .

---

1. **wantonness.** Cruelty; having no just provocation
2. **appellation.** Name or designation
3. **a Samaide or a Hottentot.** Hottentots come from South Africa; Samaide (Samoyeds) are Mongolians.

I have often seen slaves, particularly those who were meagre,[4] in different islands, put into scales and weighed; and then sold from three pence to six pence or nine pence a pound. My master, however, whose humanity was shocked at this mode, used to sell such by the lump. And at or after a sale it was not uncommon to see negroes taken from their wives, wives taken from their husbands, and children from their parents, and sent off to other islands, and wherever else their merciless lords chose; and probably never more during life to see each other! Oftentimes my heart has bled at these partings; when the friends of the departed have been at the water side, and, with sighs and tears, have kept their eyes fixed on the vessel till it went out of sight.

A poor Creole negro I knew well, who, after having been often thus transported from island to island, at last resided in Montserrat. This man used to tell me many melancholy[5] tales of himself. Generally, after he had done working for his master, he used to employ his few leisure moments to go a fishing. When he had caught any fish, his master would fre-

quently take them from him without paying him; and at other times some other white people would serve him in the same manner. One day he said to me, very movingly, 'Sometimes when a white man take away my fish I go to my maser, and he get me my right; and when my maser by strength take away my fishes, what me must do? I can't go to any body to be righted': then said the poor man, looking up above, 'I must look up to God Mighty in the top for right.' This artless tale moved me much, and I could not help feeling the just cause Moses had in redressing his brother against the Egyptian.[6] I exhorted[7] the man to look up still to the God on the top, since there was no redress below. Though I little thought then that I myself should more than once experience such imposition, and read the same exhortation hereafter, in my own transactions in the islands; and that even this poor man and I

> ## I have often seen slaves ... put into scales and weighed; and then sold from three pence to six pence or nine pence a pound.

---

4. **meagre.** Thin or lacking in flesh
5. **melancholy.** Sad, depressing, or dismal
6. **Egyptian.** From the Bible, Exodus 2:11–12: "And it came to pass in those days, when Moses was grown, that he went out unto his brethren, and looked on their burdens: and he spied an Egyptian smiting a Hebrew, one of his brethren. And he looked this way and that way, and when he saw that there was no man, he slew the Egyptian, and hid him in the sand."
7. **exhorted.** Advised; encouraged

should some time after suffer together in the same manner. . . .

Nor was such usage as this confined to particular places or individuals; for, in all the different islands in which I have been (and I have visited no less than fifteen) the treatment of the slaves was nearly the same; so nearly indeed, that the history of an island, or even a plantation, with a few such exceptions as I have mentioned, might serve for a history of the whole. Such a tendency has the slave-trade to debauch[8] men's minds, and harden them to every feeling of humanity! For I will not suppose that the dealers in slaves are born worse than other men—No; it is the fatality of this mistaken avarice,[9] that it corrupts the milk of human kindness and turns it into gall.[10] And, had the pursuits of those men been different, they might have been as generous, as tender-hearted and just, as they are unfeeling, rapacious[11] and cruel. Surely this traffic cannot be good, which spreads like a pestilence, and taints what it touches! which violates that first natural right of mankind, equality and independency, and gives one man a dominion over his fellows which God could never intend! For it raises the owner to a state as far above man as it depresses the slave below it; and, with all the presumption of human pride, sets

a distinction between them, immeasurable in extent, and endless in duration! Yet how mistaken is the avarice even of the planters? Are slaves more useful by being thus humbled to the condition of brutes, than they would be if suffered to enjoy the privileges of men? The freedom which diffuses health and prosperity throughout Britain answers you—No. When you make men slaves you deprive them of half their virtue, you set them in your own conduct an example of fraud, rapine, and cruelty, and compel them to live with you in a state of war; and yet you complain that they are not honest or faithful! You stupify them with stripes,[12] and think it necessary to keep them in a state of ignorance; and yet you assert that they are incapable of learning; that their minds are such a barren soil or moor, that culture would be lost

> ## Surely this traffic cannot be good, which spreads like a pestilence, and taints what it touches!

---

8. **debauch.** Corrupt; lead away from virtue or excellence
9. **avarice.** Greed; inordinate desire for wealth
10. **gall.** From William Shakespeare's *Macbeth. Gall* here means bitterness of human spirit.
11. **rapacious.** Excessively grasping or covetous
12. **stupify . . . with stripes.** Make senseless by beating or lashing

on them; and that they come from a climate, where nature, though prodigal of her bounties in a degree unknown to yourselves, has left man alone scant and unfinished, and incapable of enjoying the treasures she has poured out for him!—An assertion at once impious[13] and absurd. Why do you use those instruments of torture? Are they fit to be applied by one rational being to another? And are ye not struck with shame and mortification,[14] to see the partakers of your nature reduced so low? But, above all, are there no dangers attending this mode of treatment? Are you not hourly in dread of an insurrection? Nor would it be surprising: for when

> ————No peace is given
> To us enslav'd, but custody severe;
> And stripes and arbitrary punishment
> Inflicted—What peace can we return?

But to our power, hostility and hate;
> Untam'd reluctance, and revenge,
>   though flow.
> Yet ever plotting how the conqueror least
> May reap his conquest, and may least
>   rejoice
> In doing what we most in suffering feel.[15]

But by changing your conduct, and treating your slaves as men, every cause of fear would be banished. They would be faithful, honest, intelligent and vigorous; and peace, prosperity, and happiness would attend you. ❖

---

13. **impious.** Irreverent; profane
14. **mortification.** Humiliation; chagrin; extreme embarrassment
15. **No peace is given . . . what we most in suffering feel.** From John Milton's *Paradise Lost*

Some scholars question whether Equiano relates only his own experiences or incorporates the experiences of others into his narrative. Does it matter to you whether these events were a blending of several slaves' experiences or Equiano's own?

Refer and Reason

1. State the meaning of the excerpt from John Milton's *Paradise Lost.* How does it reinforce the point that Equiano is trying to make?

2. Examine the last two sentences in this excerpt. Explain whether you think that Equiano really believes this.

3. Predict the reactions of eighteenth-century readers to Equiano's narrative. What might different groups of people in both England and the United States have felt or thought when they read this work?

Writing Options

1. Travel back in time to join forces with the English abolitionists. Imagine that you have asked Olaudah Equiano to speak at your next public meeting. Prepare a flyer to be distributed in the hope of attracting a wide audience for this event. Before writing your flyer, think about the following questions: Why would anyone want to hear Equiano speak? What will attendees gain by hearing Equiano speak and attending your meeting?

2. Write a one-paragraph character sketch of Olaudah Equiano based on what you infer about him from his writing.

 Go to **www.mirrorsandwindows.com** for more.

Born in West Africa, **Phillis Wheatley** (c. 1753–1784) was kidnapped at eight years old and brought on a slave ship to Boston. John Wheatley, a wealthy tailor, purchased Phillis as a servant for his wife, who taught her to read and write. By age fourteen, Phillis was beginning to write poetry. Her first poem was published in 1770. In 1773, Phillis Wheatley traveled to London, where she received assistance in publishing her first book, *Poems on Various Subjects, Religious and Moral.* With this publication, Wheatley became widely known in both Europe and America.

Wheatley seldom wrote poems about herself, so **"On Being Brought from Africa to America"** offers the reader a rare opportunity to determine what she thought about herself and her circumstances. In **"To S. M., a Young African Painter, on Seeing His Works,"** Wheatley celebrates the artistry of Scipio Moorhead, a servant to the Reverend John Moorhead of Boston.

Wheatley gained her freedom in 1778, after both John Wheatley and his wife had died. When Wheatley died at thirty-one, her uncompleted second volume of poems was lost.

On Being Brought from Africa to America

by Phillis Wheatley

'Twas mercy[1] brought me from Pagan land,
Taught my benighted[2] soul to understand
That there's a God, that there's a Saviour too:
Once I redemption neither sought nor knew.
Some view our sable[3] race with scornful eye,
"Their colour is a diabolic die."[4]
Remember, Christians, Negros, black as Cain,[5]
May be refin'd, and join th' angelic train. ❖

---

1. **mercy.** Any circumstance thought to be providential, or guided by God
2. **benighted.** Involved in or due to moral darkness or ignorance
3. **sable.** Black in color; dark
4. **diabolic die.** Color associated with the devil or devils
5. **black as Cain.** Biblical reference both to the sin of Cain, who killed his brother, and to the belief that black Africans can trace their ancestry back to Cain

Wheatley says that "mercy" brought her from Africa to America. What is ironic about this statement?

The Last Sale of Slaves in St. Louis, 1870. Thomas Satterwhite Noble.

To S. M., a Young African Painter, on Seeing His Works

by Phillis Wheatley

To show the laboring bosom's deep intent,
And thought in living characters to paint,
When first thy pencil did those beauties
    give,
And breathing figures learnt from thee to
    live,
5 How did those prospects give my soul
    delight,
A new creation rushing on my sight?
Still, wond'rous youth! each noble path
    pursue,

On deathless glories fix thine ardent[1] view:
Still may the painter's and the poet's fire
10 To aid thy pencil, and thy verse conspire!
And may the charms of each seraphic[2]
    theme
Conduct thy footsteps to immortal fame!
High to the blissful wonders of the skies
Elate[3] thy soul, and raise thy wishful eyes.

---

1. **ardent.** Intensely enthusiastic or devoted
2. **seraphic.** Angelic
3. **Elate.** Raise the spirits of

15 Thrice[4] happy, when exalted to survey
 That splendid city, crowned with endless
  day,
 Whose twice six gates[5] on radiant hinges
  ring:
 Celestial Salem[6] blooms in endless spring.

 Calm and serene thy moments glide along,
20 And may the muse[7] inspire each future song!
 Still, with the sweets of contemplation[8]
  blest,
 May peace with balmy[9] wings your soul
  invest!
 But when these shades of time are chased
  away,
 And darkness ends in everlasting day,
25 On what seraphic pinions[10] shall we move,
 And view the landscape in the realms above?
 There shall thy tongue in heavenly
  murmurs flow,

 And there my muse with heavenly
  transport[11] glow:
 No more to tell of Damon's[12] tender sighs,
30 Or rising radiance of Aurora's[13] eyes,
 For nobler themes demand a nobler strain,
 And purer language on the ethereal[14] plain.
 Cease, gentle muse! the solemn gloom of
  night
 Now seals the fair creation from my sight. ❖

---

4. **Thrice.** Triple (extremely)
5. **twice six gates.** Twelve gates to heaven
6. **Salem.** Jerusalem
7. **muse.** Any of the nine goddesses who preside over litera-ture and the arts in Greek mythology
8. **contemplation.** Thoughtful inspection, study, or meditation
9. **balmy.** Soothing, mild, or pleasant
10. **pinions.** Wings
11. **transport.** Strong emotion; rapture
12. **Damon.** Mythical hero and loyal friend (to Pythias)
13. **Aurora.** Mythical goddess of dawn
14. **ethereal.** Not earthly; heavenly, celestial

 **MIRRORS & WINDOWS**   Do you agree with Wheatley's ideas about the importance of art and the nature of inspiration?

Refer and Reason

1. In "To S. M., a Young African Painter," what is the speaker's underlying assumption about inspiration? How does Wheatley follow her own advice in writing this poem?

2. In "On Being Brought from Africa to America," how does Wheatley describe her personal experiences? Argue whether her description likely would have convinced a late-eighteenth-century audience that black people and white people are equal.

3. What if Phillis Wheatley had been a teenager when she was kidnapped and forced into the slave trade? How might her attitude toward herself, her homeland, and her masters be different?

Writing Options

1. Imagine that it is 1783, and you are a reporter for a Boston newspaper. You are planning to interview Phillis Wheatley, who is working as a servant, on the tenth anniversary of the publication in England of her *Poems on Various Subjects*. Create a list of the questions you would ask, and then provide the answers you think Wheatley might give.

2. In the 1800s, abolitionists rediscovered Phillis Wheatley's poems and used her work and her life to pro-mote their cause. Write an editorial for an abolitionist newspaper using examples from both Wheatley's poems and her life to advocate the abolition of slavery.

 Go to **www.mirrorsandwindows.com** for more.

PART 3

The American Revolution

The American Revolution served not just as a political revolt against English rule but also as a call for the new nation to define itself. Even though many well-known Americans were writing during this time, such as Benjamin Franklin and Thomas Jefferson, there were few recognized writers of literature until around the 1820s.

Several reasons explain this lack of literary output. First of all, publishing was largely an activity for people from wealthy backgrounds, since most writers had to pay to have their works printed. Second, readers of the day preferred European writers, who were considered more sophisticated. Additionally, women and minorities were rarely given the opportunity to write more than letters and journals. A final difficulty was the lack of copyright protection; published works were easily pirated, such that authors were not paid for their work.

The founders of the new nation wanted to engage citizens in forming a viable political system. To do so, they needed voters to be educated and informed. Consequently, the literature that marks the American Revolutionary period is largely nonfiction. Newspapers and political pamphlets flourished during this period. In works such as Thomas Paine's pamphlets and Benjamin Franklin's autobiography, the writing is clear and direct, making it accessible to the widest range of readers.

Eventually, a strong sense of nationalism pushed citizens of the new nation to forge an identity and develop a national culture that was uniquely American. The next generation of writers would establish the body of American literature, but they would be indebted to the earlier writers who helped form the nation.

The Death of General Mercer at the Battle of Princeton, January 3, 1777, c. 1800. John Trumbull.

Benjamin Franklin

> ## *"An investment in knowledge always pays the best interest."*

Benjamin Franklin (1706–1790) was a writer, scientist, inventor, and statesman. The tenth son of a soap and candle maker, Franklin entered the printing trade as his brother's apprentice at age twelve. At age sixteen, he submitted a series of clever essays to his brother James's newspaper. Written under the name Mrs. Silence Dogood, who was presumed to be a middle-aged widow, the essays drew public acclaim. In that same year, Franklin assumed responsibility for running his brother's paper while James was temporarily imprisoned for offending local authorities.

As a young man, Benjamin Franklin developed his writing skills by studying the masterful essays from The Spectator, a popular British periodical of the early 1700s. The periodical aimed to "enliven morality with wit, and to temper wit with morality" while making astute observations about social life and politics, thus reflecting the Neoclassical spirit that permeated European thinking and culture.

At seventeen, Franklin moved to Philadelphia, where he eventually set up a printing business of his own. He produced a successful newspaper, the Pennsylvania Gazette, as well as paper currency for the Pennsylvania colony. For twenty-five years, he also printed the wildly popular Poor Richard's Almanack. Franklin's publishing enterprises helped to make him quite a wealthy man.

Franklin was also a public-spirited person of many talents and interests. Having a particular passion for science, he conducted experiments with electricity and invented, among other things, the lightning rod (see the Informational Text Connection on pages 76–77). He also founded the first American subscription library and was instrumental in founding the University of Pennsylvania.

In the 1750s, Franklin became active in politics. He spent eighteen years in England as an unofficial ambassador, seeking to protect the rights of the American colonies while keeping them within the British empire. After the Revolutionary War began, Franklin helped to draft the Declaration of Independence and secured military and financial support from the French. As minister to France from 1776 to 1785, he helped to draft the treaty that ended the Revolutionary War. His last act of public service, at age eighty-one, was to attend the Constitutional Convention as a delegate from Pennsylvania.

Noted Works

Autobiography of Benjamin Franklin (1791; 1868)

Experiments and Observations on Electricity (1751)

Father Abraham's Sermon (1758)

Poor Richard's Almanack (1733–1758)

from The Autobiography of Benjamin Franklin

from Poor Richard's Almanack

An Autobiography and an Almanac by Benjamin Franklin

Build Background

Literary Context Benjamin Franklin wrote *The Autobiography of Benjamin Franklin* over a period of twenty years, beginning in 1771 and completing the final two sections between 1788 and 1790, when illness forced him to put the work aside. The first part of the book was published in 1791, but the entire work was not published until 1868.

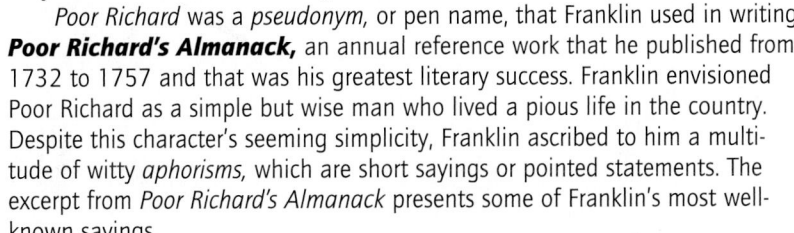

Interestingly, Franklin's autobiography covers his life only until 1758, when he was fifty-two years old (he would live to be eighty-four), at which time he embarked on a career as a diplomat. In this excerpt, the author describes the time during his youth when he was becoming established as a writer and printer.

Poor Richard was a *pseudonym,* or pen name, that Franklin used in writing *Poor Richard's Almanack,* an annual reference work that he published from 1732 to 1757 and that was his greatest literary success. Franklin envisioned Poor Richard as a simple but wise man who lived a pious life in the country. Despite this character's seeming simplicity, Franklin ascribed to him a multitude of witty *aphorisms,* which are short sayings or pointed statements. The excerpt from *Poor Richard's Almanack* presents some of Franklin's most well-known sayings.

Together, the selections from *The Autobiography of Benjamin Franklin* and *Poor Richard's Almanack* show Franklin's skill at writing two very different genres of literature.

Reader's Context Benjamin Franklin was remarkably accomplished in many areas. Think about your own personal goals. What actions have you taken or might you take to help you meet these goals?

Benjamin Franklin drew this political cartoon and published it in his newspaper, *The Pennsylvania Gazette*—one of many American "firsts" for his newspaper. With the cartoon, Franklin hoped to urge the American colonies to unite during the French and Indian War.

Analyze Literature

Autobiography and Neoclassicism

An **autobiography** is the story of a person's life written by that person.

Neoclassicism was the revival of Greek and Roman ideals of art and literature that occurred in Europe during the eighteenth-century Enlightenment. Those ideals included respect for authority and tradition, reason and order, and moderation and simplicity.

Set Purpose

The selections in this Author Focus grouping reveal the varied interests and experiences of Benjamin Franklin. As you read, record the facts you learn about Franklin's life and then infer what they reveal about his character. Consider how Franklin's life and work reflect the Neoclassical spirit.

Preview Vocabulary

ingenious, 72
indulgence, 73
admonish, 73
consultation, 73
evade, 73
venture, 74

from
THE AUTOBIOGRAPHY OF
Benjamin Franklin

by Benjamin Franklin

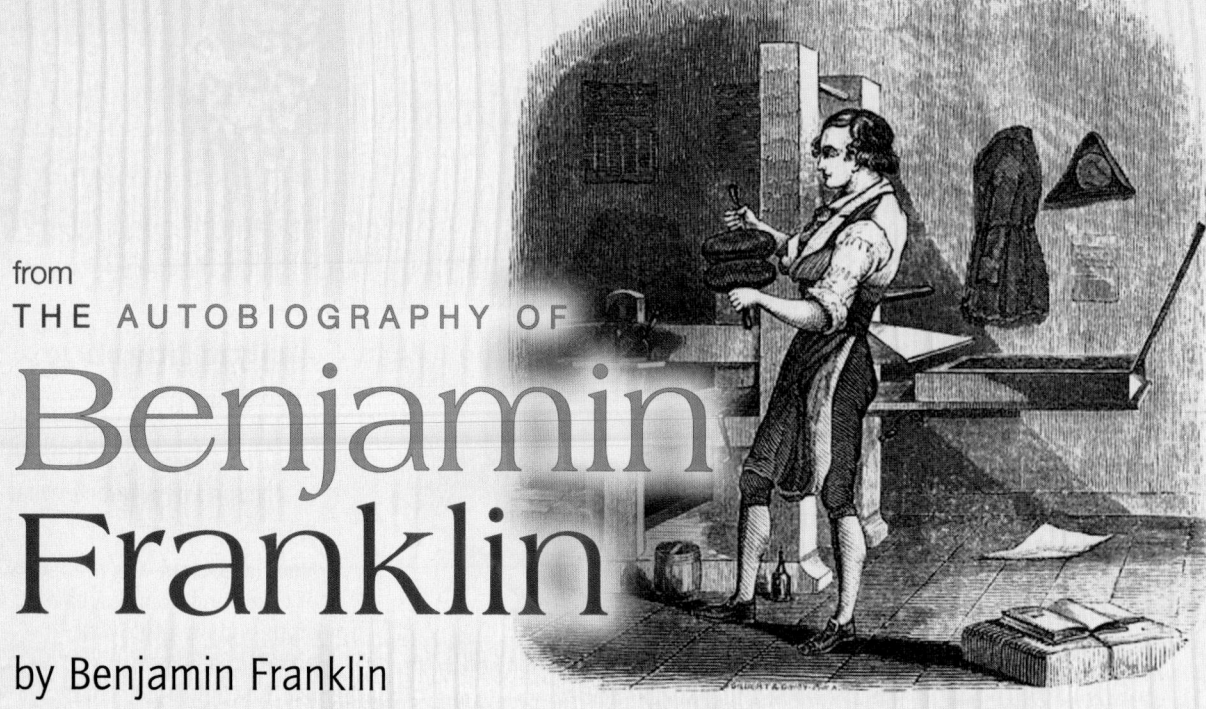

*I contrived to disguise my Hand,
and writing an anonymous Paper,
I put it in at Night under the Door
of the Printing-House.*

My Brother had in 1720 or '21, begun to print a Newspaper. It was the second that appeared in America and was called the *New England Courant.*[1] The only one before it was *The Boston News Letter.* I remember his being dissuaded by some of his Friends from the Undertaking, as not likely to succeed, one Newspaper being in their Judgment enough for America. At this time (1771) there are not less than five-and-twenty. He went on, however, with the Undertaking, and after having worked in composing the Types and printing off the Sheets, I was employed to carry the Papers through the Streets to the Customers. He had some <u>ingenious</u> Men among his Friends who amused themselves by writing little Pieces for this Paper, which gained it Credit and made it more in Demand, and these Gentlemen often visited us. Hearing their Conversations and their Accounts of the Approbation[2] their Papers were received with, I was excited to try my Hand among them. But being still a Boy, and suspecting that my Brother would object to printing any Thing of mine in his Paper if he knew it to be mine, I contrived to disguise my Hand, and writing an anonymous Paper, I put it in at Night under the Door of the Printing-House.

---

1. **It was . . . *New England Courant.*** James Franklin's paper was actually the fifth American paper.
2. **Approbation.** Approval or commendation

in • ge • nious (in jēn´ yəs) *adj.,* having great mental ability

It was found in the Morning and communicated to his Writing Friends when they called in as Usual. They read it, commented on it in my Hearing, and I had the exquisite Pleasure of finding it met with their Approbation, and that, in their different Guesses at the Author, none were named but Men of some Character among us for Learning and Ingenuity. I suppose now that I was rather lucky in my Judges, and that perhaps they were not really so very good ones as I then esteemed them. Encouraged however by this, I wrote and conveyed in the same Way to the Press several more Papers, which were equally approved, and I kept my Secret till my small Fund of Sense for such Performances was pretty well exhausted, and then I discovered[3] it, when I began to be considered a little more by my Brother's Acquaintance, and in a manner that did not quite please him, as he thought, probably with reason, that it tended to make me too vain. And perhaps this might be one Occasion of the Differences that we began to have about this Time. Though a Brother, he considered himself as my Master, and me as his Apprentice, and accordingly expected the same Services from me as he would from another; while I thought he demeaned me too much in some he required of me, who from a Brother expected more Indulgence. Our Disputes were often brought before our Father, and I fancy I was either generally in the right or else a better Pleader, because the Judgment was generally in my favor. But my Brother was passionate and had often beaten me, which I took extremely amiss; and, thinking my Apprenticeship very tedious, I was continually wishing for some Opportunity of shortening it, which at length offered in a manner unexpected.

One of the Pieces in our Newspaper, on some political Point which I have now forgotten, gave Offense to the Assembly. He was taken up, censured, and imprisoned for a Month by the Speaker's Warrant. I suppose

because he would not discover his Author. I too was taken up and examined before the Council; but though I did not give them any Satisfaction, they contented themselves with admonishing me, and dismissed me, considering me perhaps as an Apprentice who was bound to keep his Master's Secrets. During my Brother's Confinement, which I resented a good deal, notwithstanding our private Differences, I had the Management of the Paper, and I made bold to give our Rulers some Rubs in it, which my Brother took very kindly, while others began to consider me in an unfavorable Light, as a young Genius that had a Turn for Libeling and Satire. My Brother's Discharge was accompanied with an Order of the House (a very odd one) "that James Franklin should no longer print the paper called the *New England Courant.*" There was a Consultation held in our Printing-House among his Friends what he should do in this Case. Some proposed to evade the Order by changing the Name of the Paper; but my Brother seeing Inconveniences in that, it was finally concluded on as a better Way to let it be printed for the future under the Name of Benjamin Franklin. And to avoid the Censure of the Assembly that might fall on him as still printing it by his Apprentice, the Contrivance was that my old Indenture should

---

3. **discovered.** Revealed

in • dul • gence (in dul´ jents) *n.,* favor or privilege
ad • mon • ish (ad män´ ish) *v.,* caution or advise of one's responsibilities or behavior
con • sul • ta • tion (kän' səl tā´ shən) *n.,* meeting to discuss, decide, or plan something
evade (ē vād´) *v.,* avoid or escape from by deceit or cleverness

Protecting Anonymous Sources

In 1722, James Franklin published fourteen articles in his *New England Courant* anonymously, without an author's name. Because of the controversial ideas in the articles, New England's censorship committee demanded that Franklin reveal who wrote them. When he refused, the committee shut down his newspaper and put him in prison.

The nation's founders realized the effect such practices would have on journalists' ability to report all the news. In response, they established a free-press clause within the First Amendment, granting journalists the right to protect the names of confidential sources. Doing so has brought to the public a wellspring of information that otherwise would have gone unreported.

One of the most famous examples of this occurred in 1972, when an anonymous government insider nicknamed "Deepthroat" provided *Washington Post* reporters Bob Woodward and Carl Bernstein with information that linked President Richard Nixon to the Watergate scandal

WOODWARD & BERNSTEIN

and ultimately brought about his resignation. In 2005, *New York Times* reporter Judith Miller spent twelve weeks in jail for refusing to name a confidential source she used in writing about the investigation of who leaked the identity of a Central Intelligence Agency (CIA) operative.

Despite the protection provided by the First Amendment, most journalists treat anonymous sources with great caution. They almost always dismiss tipsters who refuse to reveal their names and positions. Journalists also try to verify the facts of a story through other means if they have any doubts about the source. In addition, most news organizations require journalists to disclose the identity of an anonymous source to a senior editor.

Using information from anonymous sources still can be problematic. In 2002, *New York Times* editors discovered that correspondent Jayson Blair repeatedly had fabricated information from so-called unnamed sources and also plagiarized materials. Upon reporting Blair's resignation, the *Times* commented, "The widespread fabrication and plagiarism represent a profound betrayal of trust and a low point in the 152-year history of the newspaper."

---

be returned to me with a full Discharge on the Back of it, to be shown on Occasion; but to secure to him the Benefit of my Service, I was to sign new Indentures for the Remainder of the Term, which were to be kept private. A very flimsy Scheme it was; but however, it was immediately executed, and the Paper went on accordingly under my Name for several Months. At length a fresh Difference arising between my Brother and me, I took upon me to assert my Freedom, presuming that he would not <u>venture</u> to produce the new Indentures. It was not fair in me to take this

Advantage, and this I therefore reckon one of the first Errata[4] of my Life; but the Unfairness of it weighed little with me, when under the Impressions of Resentment, for the Blows his Passion too often urged him to bestow upon me. Though he was otherwise not an ill-natured Man: perhaps I was too saucy and provoking. ❖

---

4. **Errata.** [Latin] Printer's term for *errors*

ven • ture (ven´ chʉr) *v.*, undertake the risk of

M**IRRORS** & **WINDOWS**   What are some of the problems and benefits of working for a relative? How might Franklin's account be different if his master had been someone other than his brother?

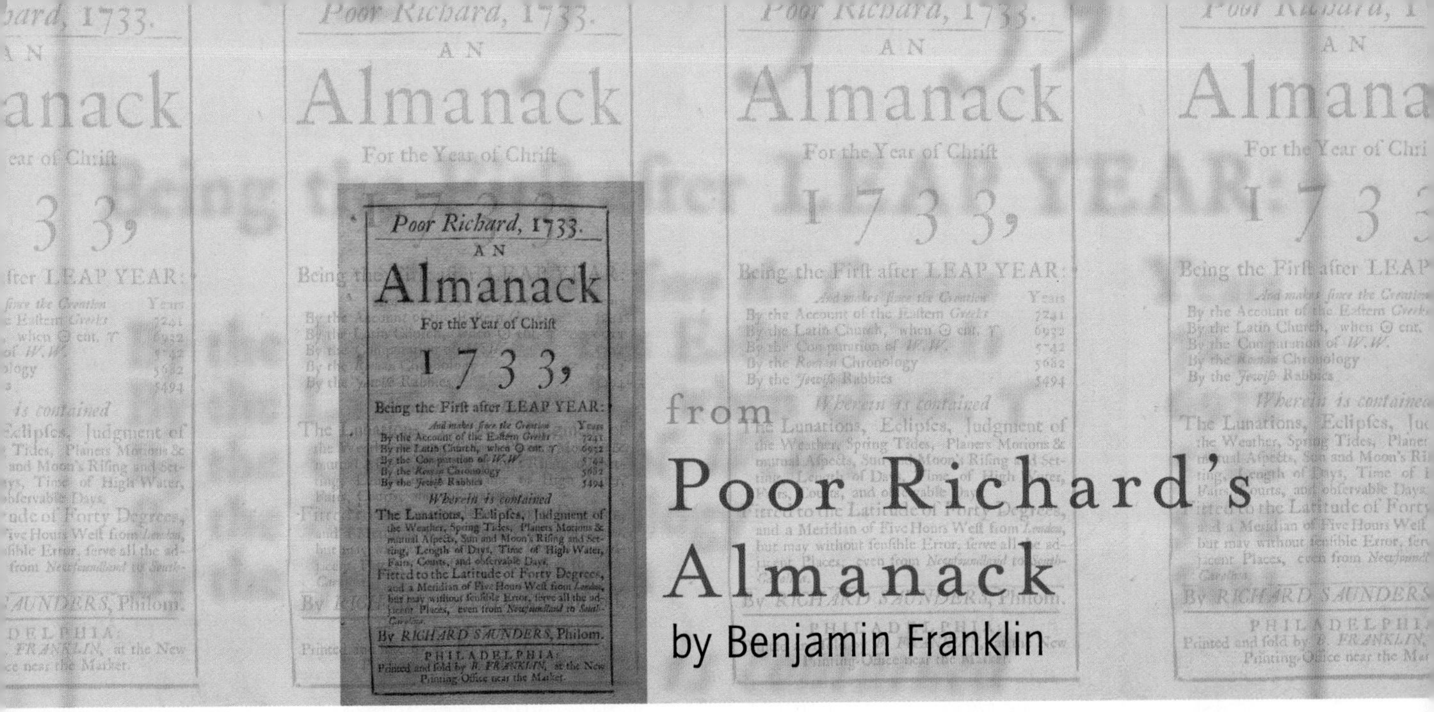

from Poor Richard's Almanack

by Benjamin Franklin

1. A penny saved is a penny earned.
2. If a man empties his purse into his head, no man can take it away from him. An investment in knowledge always pays the best interest.
3. There never was a good war or a bad peace.
4. Tart words make no friends; a spoonful of honey will catch more flies than a gallon of vinegar.
5. He that falls in love with himself shall have no rivals.
6. Fish and visitors smell in three days.
7. He that lieth down with dogs shall rise up with fleas.
8. One today is worth two tomorrows.
9. A truly great man will neither trample on a worm nor sneak to an emperor.
10. In this world nothing can be certain except death and taxes.
11. If you would know the value of money, go and try to borrow some; he that goes a-borrowing goes a-sorrowing.
12. If you would not be forgotten as soon as you are dead, either write things worth reading or do things worth writing.
13. He that is of the opinion that money will do every thing may well be suspected of doing everything for money.
14. If a man could have half his wishes, he would double his troubles.
15. The early bird catches the worm.
16. A small leak will sink a great ship.
17. A plowman on his legs is higher than a gentleman on his knees.
18. If you will not hear reason, she will surely rap your knuckles.
19. We must indeed all hang together, or, most assuredly, we will all hang separately.
20. Time is money. ❖

MIRRORS & WINDOWS

Which of these sayings has the most relevance to your life?

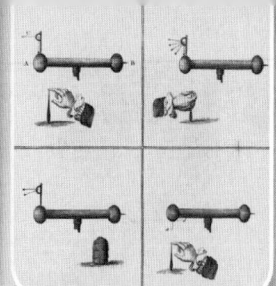

Fig.2

Informational Text Connection

Among **Benjamin Franklin's** many interests were science and technology. He was a prolific and wide-ranging inventor, creating everything from musical instruments and swim fins to more practical devices and concepts such as the odometer, a map of the Gulf Stream, a heat-efficient stove, the lightning rod, bifocals, and Daylight Saving Time. In 1743, Franklin founded the American Philosophical Society to provide scientists with a forum in which to discuss their discoveries. Franklin's own success as a businessman allowed him the time and money to pursue these interests, and his discoveries established him as a scientific genius worldwide. He refused to take out patents on his many inventions, however, preferring instead to work for the public good.

Ben Franklin: Scientist and Inventor

Many of Ben Franklin's inventions were motivated by his desire to try to improve or enrich people's everyday lives. In 1743, he invented a stove to provide an efficient, clean, and safe means of heating a home. The Franklin stove was enclosed in the front, which prevented sparks from flying out into the room, and it had an airbox in the back, which provided good ventilation and thus made the fire burn more efficiently. In fact, this stove burned about one-quarter as much wood and produced twice as much heat as a traditional fireplace.

In 1750, Franklin set out to prove that lightning was electricity. He conducted a successful trial of his now-famous kite-flying experiment on June 15, 1752, drawing electrical sparks to a kite from a cloud. Other scientists around the world were conducting similar experiments, some with fatal results. Franklin clearly had found a way to insulate himself from the electrical charge.

Franklin's experiments with electricity led to his inventing the lightning rod. He had dis-covered that objects with sharp points were better conductors of electricity than those with smooth points. He also had considered the possibility of protecting a building from lightning by placing an upright rod on its roof and connecting it via cable to the ground. (House fires from lightning strikes were common in the 1700s.) Experimenting on his own house, Franklin proved that lightning would hit the rod instead of the building. After this discovery, lightning rods were installed in 1752 on the Pennsylvania State House (what would become Independence Hall, the home of the Liberty Bell) and the Academy of Philadelphia (later renamed the University of Pennsylvania).

Although Franklin's creative spirit often was motivated by practicality, he also created devices for leisurely activities. In 1762, he designed the *armonica* (or glass harmonica), a musical instrument that produced sound from a series of graduated glass bowls. The bowls were arranged horizontally on a spinning iron rod, which was controlled by a large foot pedal.

The musician created a melody by lightly stroking the rims of the bowls with his or her moistened fingertips. As the first musical instrument created by an American, the armonica won Franklin widespread recognition in Europe. Composers Wolfgang Amadeus Mozart, Ludwig van Beethoven, and Richard Strauss all wrote material specifically for this instrument.

In 1784, Franklin invented something that he needed for himself: bifocal glasses. At seventy-eight years old, he was having difficulty seeing both up close and at a distance. Switching between two types of glasses had become tiresome, so Franklin decided to create a single pair of glasses containing both types of lenses. He placed the distance lens in the top of the glasses and the magnifying lens in the bottom—the format that is still used in modern-day eyewear.

Also in 1784, Franklin proposed the concept of Daylight Saving Time for the practical purpose of conserving energy. In a visit to France, he noted that Parisians stayed up late at night and slept until early afternoon, making poor use of the daylight hours, in his view. To demonstrate this point, he devised a formula proving that if every French person started the day at the break of dawn, the entire country could save sixty-four million pounds of candle wax in six months. Franklin never lobbied the U.S. government to establish an official Daylight Saving Time, but he was the first person to point out the logic of using daylight to conserve energy. Congress finally did establish Daylight Saving Time in 1918, when excessive energy consumption became a national defense issue during World War I. ❖

Review Questions

1. What features made the Franklin stove different from other stoves at the time? Explain how these differences made for a safer, more efficient heating system.

2. What risk did Franklin face in experimenting with lightning? Infer what his risk taking suggests about his character.

3. From Franklin's view, what was the logic underlying the concept of Daylight Saving Time? How was Franklin ahead of his time in proposing this concept? How are many of his ideas still relevant?

TEXT $\xleftarrow{\text{TO}}$ TEXT CONNECTION

What parallels do you see between Benjamin Franklin's role as a scientist and inventor and his roles as writer, publisher, and statesman? What seemed to motivate Franklin to try new things on both personal and professional levels?

Refer to Text ▷ ▷ ▶ ▶ ▶   Reason with Text

1a. As described in his autobiography, what was Benjamin Franklin excited to try? Why? What was his one worry? How did he accomplish his goal?

1b. Describe how Benjamin Franklin felt after his work was published. Why did he feel this way?

Understand
Find meaning

2a. Why was James Franklin imprisoned? Recall how the newspaper come to be published under Franklin's name.

2b. If Benjamin and James were not brothers, would there have been less tension between the master and his apprentice? Explain.

Apply
Use information

3a. Examine the twenty maxims from *Poor Richard's Almanack*. What topics or themes do they address?

3b. Identify two maxims that could apply to Franklin's time as an apprentice or his thoughts about leaving his job. Explain how each applies.

Analyze
Take things apart

4a. What led Franklin to leave the newspaper and his job as apprentice?

4b. Judge whether Franklin was justified in leaving his apprenticeship.

Evaluate
Make judgments

5a. How did Benjamin Franklin feel when he left his brother's employ?

5b. Have you ever broken an agreement because you thought you were treated unfairly? What happened?

Create
Bring ideas together

Analyze Literature

Autobiography and Neoclassicism

Review the facts you recorded in reading the selections by and about Franklin. Based on this information, how would you describe him? What general qualities can you infer about his character? In particular, what qualities made him successful in so many areas?

What Neoclassical ideals run throughout Franklin's life and work? In particular, how do the sayings from *Poor Richard's Almanack* reflect these ideals? How did Franklin use wit (dry humor) to make these lessons more appealing to readers?

Extend the Text

Writing Options

Creative Writing Imagine that you are James Franklin. Write a want ad for the position of apprentice at the *New England Courant*, detailing the desired qualifications for and duties of the position.

Narrative Writing Suppose you are beginning an autobiography that you will work on throughout your life. Write one chapter about a specific period in your life so far. Relate your experiences in a way that will help others in the future understand you.

Collaborative Learning

Conduct a Talk-Show Interview With a partner, conduct a talk-show interview, in which one of you plays the role of Franklin late in life and the other plays the talk-show host. The host should prepare a list of questions to ask Franklin, and the person playing Franklin should be prepared to give detailed responses to the questions.

Lifelong Learning

Find a Modern-Day Apprenticeship An *internship*, whether paid or unpaid, helps introduce a worker to a particular business or industry and can lead to a full-time position. Spend some time thinking about your career goals, and research internships that will help you learn more about a career in which you are interested. Then write a brief résumé and cover letter to apply for an internship.

 Go to **www.mirrorsandwindows.com** for more.

1. Which statement best identifies the mistake that Franklin calls "the first Errata of my Life"?
   A. He trusts that his brother will treat him fairly under the terms of their new agreement.
   B. He allows his brother to make a secret agreement.
   C. He breaks the terms of apprenticeship.
   D. He is "saucy and provoking" to his brother.
   E. He secretly writes papers and submits them to his brother's newspaper.

2. Which statement best identifies the meaning of the saying "He that composes himself is wiser than he that composes books"?
   A. Book learning is not as important as practical learning.
   B. A person who creates a successful business knows more than a person who creates books about life.
   C. People learn more by writing than by reading other people's writing.
   D. A self-made person who learns to stay calm and composed has knowledge more valuable than that necessary to write books.
   E. Taking care of your person, such as your appearance, will get you further in life than arranging your possessions.

3. In the first paragraph of *The Autobiography of Benjamin Franklin,* the author describes how his brother's friends tried to discourage him from starting a newspaper. What is the author's attitude toward the friends' advice?
   A. excited
   B. surprised
   C. insincere
   D. strictly impartial
   E. gently critical

4. Franklin describes his brother James beating him, saying that he felt "extremely amiss" about it. What other phrase from the selection has the same meaning?
   A. "contrived to disguise"
   B. "did not quite please him"
   C. "tended to make me too vain"
   D. "resented a good deal"
   E. "took very kindly"

5. Which of the following is most nearly opposite in meaning of the word *evade?*
   A. face directly
   B. flee an area
   C. defy
   D. confuse
   E. celebrate

6. Which of the following aphorisms from *Poor Richard's Almanack* warns against the influence of negative friends and associates?
   A. "He that lieth down with dogs shall rise up with fleas."
   B. "A truly great man will neither trample on a worm nor sneak to an emperor."
   C. "A plowman on his legs is higher than a gentleman on his knees."
   D. "If you will not hear reason, she will surely rap your knuckles.
   E. "We must indeed all hang together, or, most assuredly, we will all hang separately."

7. From the following, choose the best paraphrase of the aphorism "He that falls in love with himself will have no rivals."
   A. Being in love with yourself will give you power to defeat your enemies.
   B. If you love yourself, you will be loved by anyone you desire.
   C. Loving yourself to the point of selfishness and vanity will alienate others.
   D. Thinking highly of yourself will make you the best person.
   E. None of the above

8. What concept underlies the aphorism "We must indeed all hang together, or, most assuredly, we will all hang separately"?
   A. teamwork
   B. capital punishment
   C. individuality
   D. honesty
   E. None of the above

9. **Constructed Response:** Benjamin Franklin is considered the most notable example of an American Neoclassicist. What from the excerpts from his autobiography and *Poor Richard's Almanack* supports this assertion? Are any of Franklin's actions inappropriate for a true Neoclassicist? Explain.

10. **Constructed Response:** Consider the character Franklin shows in his autobiography. After reading the Author Focus on page 70 and "Ben Franklin: Scientist and Inventor" on pages 76–77, determine how the character he demonstrated early in life was evident in his later life. Use evidence from the texts to support your answer.

Speech in the Virginia Convention

A Speech by Patrick Henry

Build Backgroud

Historical Context The **Speech in the Virginia Convention** was delivered on March 23, 1775, during a time of growing political tension in the thirteen colonies. Resentment at the British Parliament's attempts to tax the American colonies had led to increasingly violent protests. These protests culminated in the Boston Tea Party in 1773, an action that prompted Parliament to place two thousand British troops in Boston. At the same time, Parliament shut down all shipping from the port and restricted self-government in Massachusetts.

In addressing the Virginia Convention, Patrick Henry argued that war was the inevitable outcome of "the noble struggle in which we have been so long engaged." Less than a month later, the first shots of the American Revolution were fired at Lexington and Concord, Massachusetts. Although more than 230 years have passed since Henry addressed the Virginia Convention, his speech remains a stirring example of political rhetoric. His fierce declaration "Give me liberty or give me death!" was a powerful call to action.

Reader's Context When have a friend's or relative's words motivated you to take action? Why did these words motivate you? What action did you take?

Meet the Author

Patrick Henry (1736–1799) was a distinguished political leader during the American Revolution. Born in Hanover County, Virginia, Henry was educated at home by his father. As a young man, he failed as a storekeeper and farmer but eventually found success after training himself to practice law.

Known for his courtroom eloquence and skill in composing an argument, Henry soon became a member of the Virginia legislature. In this role, he argued aggressively for American defiance of Great Britain. Notably, in 1765, he used his fiery oratory skills to persuade the Virginia House of Burgesses to pass five resolutions against the Stamp Act, a tax measure enacted by Parliament. Henry's passionate words at first brought cries of treason from his conservative colleagues, but he succeeded in winning them to the cause of liberty. In the following decade, he continued to be a tireless and influential spokesperson for the independence movement.

From 1776 on, Henry remained active in public life. He helped to draft Virginia's first state constitution and served as its governor during the Revolutionary War. In the 1780s, he again served as a member of the state legislature and as governor. Henry died at his home on Red Hill Plantation in 1799 at age sixty-three.

Analyze Literature

Rhetorical Question and the Enlightenment
A **rhetorical question** is one asked for effect but not meant to be answered because the answer is clear from the context.

The **Enlightenment** was an eighteenth-century philosophical movement characterized by belief in reason, the scientific method, and the perfectibility of people and society.

Set Purpose

A skilled speaker, Patrick Henry effectively used both emotion and reason in developing an argument. While reading his speech, write down four rhetorical questions Henry asks to appeal to people's hearts and minds. Also look for evidence of his knowledge of classical *rhetoric,* or persuasive communication, and other Enlightenment principles.

Preview Vocabulary

insidious, 82
subjugation, 82
martial, 82
submission, 82
avert, 82
remonstrate, 82
inviolate, 82
inestimable, 82
formidable, 83
effectual, 83

Speech in the *Virginia Convention*

by Patrick Henry

Patrick Henry Speaking in the Virginia House of Burgesses, c. 1800s. Peter Frederick Rothermel. (See detail on page 80.)

I know not what course others may take; but as for me, give me liberty or give me death!

Mr. President:[1] No man thinks more highly than I do of the patriotism, as well as abilities, of the very worthy gentlemen who have just addressed the house. But different men often see the same subject in different lights: and, therefore, I hope it will not be thought disrespectful to those gentlemen, if, entertaining, as I do, opinions of a character very opposite to theirs, I shall speak forth my sentiments freely and without reserve. This is no time for ceremony. The question before the house is one of awful moment to this country. For my own part, I consider it as nothing less than a question of freedom or slavery. And in proportion to the magnitude of the subject ought to be the freedom of the debate. It is only in this way that we can hope to arrive at truth, and fulfill the great responsibility which we hold to God and our country. Should I keep back my opinions at such a time, through fear of giving offense, I should consider myself as guilty of treason toward my country, and of an act of disloyalty toward the Majesty of Heaven, which I revere above all earthly kings.

Mr. President, it is natural to man to indulge in the illusions of hope. We are apt to shut our eyes against a painful truth, and listen to the song of that siren[2] till she transforms us into beasts. Is this the part of wise men, engaged in a great and arduous struggle for liberty? Are we disposed to be of the number of

---

1. **Mr. President.** The president of the Virginia Convention
2. **siren.** In Greek mythology, one of a group of female part-human creatures who lured sailors to their destruction with their singing

those who having eyes see not, and having ears hear not, the things which so nearly concern their temporal[3] salvation? For my part, whatever anguish of spirit it may cost, I am willing to know the whole truth; to know the worst and to provide for it.

I have but one lamp by which my feet are guided, and that is the lamp of experience. I know of no way of judging of the future but by the past. And judging by the past, I wish to know what there has been in the conduct of the British ministry for the last ten years to justify those hopes with which gentlemen have been pleased to solace[4] themselves and the house? Is it that <u>insidious</u> smile with which our petition[5] has been lately received? Trust it not, sir: it will prove a snare to your feet. Suffer not yourselves to be betrayed with a kiss. Ask yourselves how this gracious reception of our petition comports[6] with those warlike preparations which cover our waters and darken our land. Are fleets and armies necessary to a work of love and reconciliation? Have we shown ourselves so unwilling to be reconciled that force must be called in to win back our love? Let us not deceive ourselves, sir. These are the implements of war and <u>subjugation</u>—the last arguments to which kings resort.

Suffer not yourselves to be betrayed with a kiss.

I ask gentlemen, sir, what means this <u>martial</u> array,[7] if its purpose be not to force us to <u>submission</u>? Can gentlemen assign any other possible motive for it? Has Great Britain any enemy in this quarter of the world, to call for all this accumulation of navies and armies? No, sir, she has none. They are meant for us: they can be meant for no other. They are sent over to bind and rivet upon us those chains which the British ministry have been so long forging.

And what have we to oppose to them? Shall we try argument? Sir, we have been trying that for the last ten years. Have we anything new to offer upon the subject? Nothing. We have held the subject up in every light of which is capable; but it has been all in vain. Shall we resort to entreaty and humble supplication?[8] What terms shall we find which have not been already exhausted? Let us not, I beseech[9] you, sir, deceive ourselves longer. Sir, we have done everything that could be done to <u>avert</u> the storm which is now coming on. We have petitioned; we have <u>remonstrated</u>; we have supplicated; we have prostrated[10] ourselves before the throne, and have implored its interposition[11] to arrest the tyrannical hands of the ministry and Parliament. Our petitions have been slighted; our remonstrances have produced additional violence and insult; our supplications have been disregarded; and we have been spurned with contempt from the foot of the throne! In vain, after these things, may we indulge the fond[12] hope of peace and reconciliation. There is no longer any room for hope. If we wish to be free, if we mean to preserve <u>inviolate</u> those <u>inestimable</u> privileges for which we

---

3. **temporal.** Lasting only for a time; temporary
4. **solace.** Comfort; relieve
5. **petition.** "Olive Branch Petition," in which the king was asked to intercede between Parliament and the colonies
6. **comports.** Agrees; goes along
7. **array.** Display; assembly
8. **supplication.** Instance of begging
9. **beseech.** Beg; plead
10. **prostrated.** Bowed down
11. **interposition.** Intervention
12. **fond.** Foolish

in • sid • i • ous (in sid´ ē əs) *adj.*, sly; crafty
sub • ju • ga • tion (sub jə gā´ shən) *n.*, takeover; enslavement
mar • tial (mär´ shəl) *adj.*, warlike; relating to the military
sub • mis • sion (sub mi´ shən) *n.*, act of yielding; surrendering
avert (ä vʉrt´) *v.*, turn away; prevent
re • mon • strate (rə män´ strāt) *v.*, demonstrate
in • vi • o • late (in vī´ ə lət) *adj.*, sacred
in • es • ti • ma • ble (in es´ tə mə bəl) *adj.*, too great to be measured

have been so long contending, if we mean not basely to abandon the noble struggle in which we have been so long engaged, and which we have pledged ourselves never to abandon until the glorious object of our contest shall be obtained—we must fight! I repeat it, sir, we must fight! An appeal to arms and to the God of Hosts is all that is left us!

> *The battle, sir, is not to the strong alone; it is to the vigilant, the active, the brave.*

They tell us, sir, that we are weak—unable to cope with so <u>formidable</u> an adversary. But when shall we be stronger? Will it be the next week, or the next year? Will it be when we are totally disarmed, and when a British guard shall be stationed in every house? Shall we gather strength by irresolution and inaction? Shall we acquire the means of <u>effectual</u> resistance by lying supinely[13] on our backs and hugging the delusive phantom of hope until our enemies shall have bound us hand and foot? Sir, we are not weak, if we make a proper use of those means which the God of nature hath placed in our power. Three millions of people, armed in the holy cause of liberty, and in such a country as that which we possess, are invincible by any force which our enemy can send against us. Besides, sir, we shall not fight our battles alone. There is a just God who presides over the destinies of nations and who will raise up friends to fight our battles for us. The battle, sir, is not to the strong alone; it is to the vigilant, the active, the brave. Besides, sir, we have no election.[14] If we were base enough to desire it, it is now too late to retire from the contest. There is no retreat but in submission and slavery! Our chains are forged! Their clanging may be heard on the plains of Boston! The war is inevitable—and let it come! I repeat it, sir, let it come![15]

It is in vain, sir, to extenuate the matter. Gentlemen may cry, "Peace, peace"—but there is no peace. The war is actually begun! The next gale that sweeps from the north will bring to our ears the clash of resounding arms! Our brethren are already in the field! Why stand we here idle? What is it that gentlemen wish? What would they have? Is life so dear, or peace so sweet, as to be purchased at the price of chains and slavery? Forbid it, Almighty God! I know not what course others may take; but as for me, give me liberty or give me death! ❖

---

13. **supinely.** Passively
14. **election.** Choice
15. **The war . . . come!** Boston had recently been occupied by British troops under the leadership of General Howe.

---

for • mi • da • ble (fōr mid′ ə b'l) *adj.,* overwhelming
ef • fec • tu • al (i fek′ chə[wə]l) *adj.,* effective

MIRRORS & WINDOWS

This speech by Patrick Henry contains several famous patriotic expressions, including "Give me liberty or give me death!" Why have Henry's words endured?

Refer to Text ▶ ▶ ▶ ▶ ▶ **Reason with Text**

1a. Recall what Henry says is the only way of the judging the future.	**1b.** What can you infer about the opinions of the speakers who addressed the convention before Henry? For Henry, what is the unthinkable alternative to war?	**Understand** Find meaning
2a. What evidence suggests to Henry that Great Britain means to wage war?	**2b.** What actions could the British have taken that might have appeased Henry so that he would not have called for war?	**Apply** Use information
3a. How had the colonists' petition to the king been received?	**3b.** Compare and contrast the colonists' and the British authorities' attempts to resolve the conflict in the colonies.	**Analyze** Take things apart
4a. Identify who is favored in battle, according to Henry.	**4b.** Do you agree with Patrick Henry that the colonists in 1775 were facing a choice between "freedom and slavery"? Explain.	**Evaluate** Make judgments
5a. What does Henry say is the "purchase price" of life and peace?	**5b.** What people in the world today seem to agree with Henry's declaration that death is preferable to a life without liberty?	**Create** Bring ideas together

Analyze Literature

Rhetorical Question and the Enlightenment

Review the four rhetorical questions you wrote down from Henry's speech. Next to each, write down the answer that Henry assumes his listeners will infer. What is effective about letting people answer these questions for themselves, rather than telling them the information directly?

What indications did you find that Patrick Henry was familiar with classical *rhetoric*, or persuasive communication? Where does he support the importance of using reason as a guide to action? What prediction does he make based on observable phenomena?

Extend the Text

Writing Options

Creative Writing Imagine that you are a loyalist who wants Great Britain to retain control of the colonies. Write your own speech to loyalist sympathizers, detailing Henry's treasonous remarks.

Descriptive Writing You are a newspaper reporter who attended the Virginia Convention the day that Patrick Henry gave his speech. Write an article summarizing the speech and describing the audience's reaction.

Collaborative Learning

Develop a Television Commercial With two classmates, write a television commercial to arouse support from the American colonists for Britain's King George III. Draw a storyboard to show the text and visuals to be used.

Media Literacy

Analyze a Significant Speech Select another historically significant speech from American history. Read it carefully, both silently and aloud. Then analyze the rhetorical features that make it memorable. Identify the passages from the speech that illustrate your points. Share your findings with a small group, and discuss how form and content work together in an effective speech.

 Go to **www.mirrorsandwindows.com** for more.

Understand the Concept

Reading literature from early time periods can be challenging because of the use of unfamiliar words. When you come across such a word, try analyzing its parts. You may be able to determine the meaning of the word if you recognize its root and affixes.

A **word root** is a central word part that cannot stand alone. In the word *mortal,* for instance, *mort* is the word root. In Latin, *mort* means "death."

An **affix** is added to a root to change its meaning. There are two kinds of affixes: **prefixes,** which are added to the beginnings of words, and **suffixes,** which are added to the ends of words. In the word *mortal,* the suffix *-al* has been added to the root *mort.* This suffix means "of" or "related to." The word *mortal,* which is an adjective, therefore means "related to death." Adding the prefix *im-,* which means "not," creates *immortal,* which means "not related to death."

Although neither word roots nor affixes can stand alone, they all have meanings. Here are some of the most commonly used prefixes and suffixes and examples of words that contain them:

Word Part	Meaning	Examples
Prefixes		
pre-	"before"	preview, precaution
post-	"after"	postgame, postmortem
non-	"not"	nonbreakable, nonsurgical
dis-	"opposite of"	disagree, discomfort
re-	"again"	revisit, remember
Suffixes		
-sion, -tion	"action" or "process"	submission, intention
-able	"capable of "	understandable, reasonable
-ance, -ence	"quality" or "state of"	performance, confidence
-ant, -ante	"one that does"	attendant, confidante
-ally, -ly	"in the manner of"	logically, quickly

The more meanings of prefixes, suffixes, and word roots you know, the more easily you will be able to determine the meanings of unfamiliar words in your reading.

Apply the Skill

Exercise A

Write a definition for one of the example words in each row of the chart above. Use a dictionary to help you. Then use each word in a sentence in which the word's meaning is clear from the context.

Exercise B

Locate words beginning with these prefixes: *mal-, ante-, poly-, con-, col-,* and *cor-.* Then locate words ending with these suffixes: *-ization, -hood, -ify, -ment,* and *-dom.* For each word, give the meaning of the prefix or the suffix and of the word itself. Your answers can include both prefixes and suffixes.

SPELLING PRACTICE

Words with Prefixes and Suffixes

Being able to recognize common prefixes and suffixes will help to make you a better speller because you will know how to spell these affixes when you hear them. Some affixes are recognized immediately, such as adding *-s* or *-es* to the end of a noun to make it plural; others are less common. Review this list of words from "Speech in the Virginia Convention" and determine which affixes have been used.

accumulation	disrespectful	invincible
additional	effectual	irresolution
argument	formidable	reconciliation
delusive	glorious	responsibility
destinies	gracious	supinely
disloyalty	inestimable	tyrannical

from **Common Sense**

from **The Crisis, No. 1**

An Essay and a Pamphlet by Thomas Paine

Build Background

Historical Context "A government of our own is our natural right," wrote Thomas Paine in **Common Sense**, an essay called the most influential ever written because it galvanized the American colonists' opinion in favor of independence from Great Britain. Published anonymously in 1776, *Common Sense* was the first publication to call for independence. It rapidly sold more than 100,000 copies and eventually sold almost 500,000 copies. At the time of its publication, the Second Continental Congress was meeting in Philadelphia, and the British were attacking Boston.

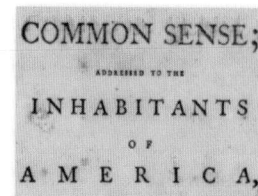

COMMON SENSE;
ADDRESSED TO THE
INHABITANTS
OF
AMERICA,

The Crisis, No. 1, was the first in a series of sixteen pamphlets published from 1776 to 1783. When the first *Crisis* pamphlet appeared in December 1776, General George Washington and his troops had just retreated to Trenton, New Jersey, and Americans were wavering in their support for the revolution. The rebels welcomed Paine's words of encouragement and inspiration, and Washington immediately read the pamphlet to his troops to lift their morale. Because the sentiments Paine expressed in his pamphlets were clearly treasonous, he tried to conceal his identity by signing his pamphlets "Common Sense" instead of using his own name; however, the identity of the author soon became common knowledge.

Reader's Context Think back to a time when you felt panic in a crisis. How did the feeling of panic affect your thoughts and actions? Did you feel stronger or weaker for having experienced the crisis?

Meet the Author

Perhaps more than any other person, **Thomas Paine** (1737–1809) fueled the fire that led to American independence. He had a gift for expressing lofty ideas in simple language. Yet the man who crafted such lines as "What we obtain too cheap, we esteem too lightly" received little formal education and worked in various jobs with little success until his midthirties.

In London in the early 1770s, Paine met Benjamin Franklin, who provided contacts in Philadelphia that led to a job editing the new *Pennsylvania Magazine*. In the decades following his arrival in America in 1775, Paine became one of the most influential political writers in history. In addition to denouncing the African slave trade in print, he was an ardent supporter of the American and French Revolutions. He also wrote the highly influential book *The Rights of Man*, which analyzed and offered remedies to many forms of social injustice and inequality.

Analyze Literature

Argument and Tone

An **argument** is a form of persuasion that makes a case to an audience for accepting or rejecting a proposition or course of action.

Tone is the emotional attitude toward the reader or toward the subject implied by a literary work—for instance, familiar, ironic, playful, sarcastic, serious, or sincere. Word choice, or *diction,* determines tone.

Set Purpose

When Thomas Paine wrote in *Common Sense* "The period of debate is closed," he was beginning an argument to convince the American colonists of the need for immediate revolution. Evaluate how Paine makes the case for revolution as you read both selections. Pay particular attention to Paine's tone and the words he chooses to create it.

Preview Vocabulary

divest, 87
ineffectual, 87
precariousness, 87
apparition, 89

from *Common Sense*

by Thomas Paine

From III. Thoughts on the Present State of American Affairs

In the following pages I offer nothing more than simple facts, plain arguments, and common sense: and have no other preliminaries to settle with the reader, than that he will <u>divest</u> himself of prejudice and prepossession, and suffer his reason and his feelings to determine for themselves: that he will put on, or rather that he will not put off, the true character of a man, and generously enlarge his views beyond the present day.

Volumes have been written on the subject of the struggle between England and America. Men of all ranks have embarked in the controversy, from different motives, and with various designs; but all have been <u>ineffectual</u>, and the period of debate is closed. Arms as the last resource decide the contest; the appeal was the choice of the King, and the continent has accepted the challenge.

◆ ◆ ◆

A government of our own is our natural right: and when a man seriously reflects on the <u>precariousness</u> of human affairs, he will become convinced that it is infinitely wiser and safer to form a constitution of our own in a cool deliberate manner, while we have it in our power, than to trust such an interesting event to time and chance. If we omit it now, some Massanello[1] may hereafter arise, who, laying hold of popular disquietudes, may collect together the desperate and the discontented,

and by assuming to themselves the powers of government, finally sweep away the liberties of the continent like a deluge. Should the government of America return again into the hands of Britain, the tottering situation of things will be a temptation for some desperate adventurer to try his fortune; and in such a case, what relief can Britain give? Ere she could hear the news, the fatal business might be done; and ourselves suffering like the wretched Britons under the oppression of the conqueror. Ye that oppose independence now, ye know not what ye do: ye are opening a door to eternal tyranny by keeping vacant the seat of government. There are thousands and tens of thousands, who would think it glorious to expel from the continent that barbarous and hellish power. ❖

---

1. **Massanello.** Thomas Anello, or Massanello, a fisherman, became king for a day after inciting a revolt against the Spanish who were occupying the city of Naples.

---

di • vest (dī vest´) *v.*, strip; cast off
in • ef • fec • tu • al (i nə fek´ chə[wə]l) *adj.*, not powerful enough to achieve the desired effect; inadequate
pre • car • i • ous • ness (prə kār´ ē əs nəs) *n.*, uncertainty; danger

When is the best time to take action? Is it best to jump in and work out the details later or to form a plan and follow it step by step?

from The Crisis, No 1

by Thomas Paine

We have none to blame but ourselves.

These are the times that try men's souls. The summer soldier and the sunshine patriot will, in this crisis, shrink from the service of their country, but he that stands it now, deserves the love and thanks of man and woman. Tyranny, like hell, is not easily conquered; yet we have this consolation with us, that the harder the conflict, the more glorious the triumph. What we obtain too cheap, we esteem too lightly: it is dearness only that gives everything its value. Heaven knows how to put a proper price upon its goods; and it would be strange indeed if so celestial an article as freedom should not be highly rated. Britain, with an army to enforce her tyranny, has declared that she has a right (not only to tax) but "to bind us in all cases whatsoever,"[1] and if being bound in that manner is not slavery, then is there not such a thing as slavery upon earth. Even the expression is impious; for so unlimited a power can belong only to God.

Whether the independence of the continent was declared too soon, or delayed too long, I will not now enter into as an argument; my own simple opinion is, that had it been eight months earlier, it would have been much better. We did not make a proper use of last winter, neither could we, while we were in a dependent state. However, the fault, if it were one, was all our own;[2] we have none to blame but ourselves. But no great deal is lost yet. All that Howe[3] has been doing for this month past is rather a ravage than a conquest, which the spirit of the Jerseys,[4] a year ago, would have quickly repulsed, and which time and a little resolution will soon recover.

I have as little superstition in me as any man living, but my secret opinion has ever been, and still is, that God Almighty will not give up a people to military destruction, or leave them unsupportedly to perish, who have so earnestly and so repeatedly sought to avoid the calamities of war, by every decent method which wisdom could invent. Neither have I so much of the infidel[5] in me as to suppose that He has relinquished the government of the world, and given us up to the

---

1. **"to bind us in all cases whatsoever."** On February 24, 1776, the Declaratory Act of Parliament established British authority over the American colonies.
2. **own.** Paine wanted an immediate declaration of independence uniting the colonies.
3. **Howe.** Lord William Howe was commander of the British army in America from 1775 to 1778.
4. **Jerseys.** East and West Jersey were separate colonies.
5. **infidel.** Person who does not accept some particular theory or belief; used derogatorily

care of devils; and as I do not, I cannot see on what grounds the King of Britain can look up to heaven for help against us: a common murderer, a highwayman, or a housebreaker has as good a pretense as he.

'Tis surprising to see how rapidly a panic will sometimes run through a country. All nations and ages have been subject to them: Britain has trembled like an ague[6] at the report of a French fleet of flat-bottomed boats, and in the fourteenth century[7] the whole English army, after ravaging the kingdom of France, was driven back like men petrified with fear; and this brave exploit was performed by a few broken forces collected and headed by a woman, Joan of Arc. Would that heaven might inspire some Jersey maid to spirit up her countrymen, and save her fair fellow sufferers from ravage and ravishment! Yet panics, in some cases, have their uses; they produce as much good as hurt. Their duration is always short; the mind soon grows through them, and acquires a firmer habit than before. But their peculiar advantage is that they are the touchstones[8] of sincerity and hypocrisy, and bring things and men to light, which might otherwise have lain forever undiscovered. In fact, they have the same effect on secret traitors, which an imaginary <u>apparition</u> would have upon a private murderer. They sift out the hidden thoughts of man, and hold them up in public to the world. Many a disguised tory[9] has lately shown his head, that shall penitentially solemnize with curses the day on which Howe arrived upon the Delaware. . . .

The far and the near, the home counties and the back,[10] the rich and poor will suffer or rejoice alike. The heart that feels not now is dead: the blood of his children will curse his cowardice who shrinks back at a time when a little might have saved the whole, and made them happy. I love the man that can smile in trouble, that can gather strength from distress, and grow brave by reflection. 'Tis the business of little minds to shrink; but he whose heart is firm, and whose conscience approves his conduct, will pursue his principles unto death. My own line of reasoning is to myself as straight and clear as a ray of light. Not all the treasures of the world, so far as I believe, could have induced me to support an offensive war, for I think it murder; but if a thief breaks into my house, burns and destroys my property, and kills or threatens to kill me, or those that are in it, and to "bind me in all cases whatsoever" to his absolute will, am I to suffer it? What signifies it to me, whether he who does it is a king or a common man; my countryman or not my countryman; whether it be done by an individual villain, or an army of them? If we reason to the root of things we shall find no difference; neither can any just cause be assigned why we should punish in the one case and pardon in the other. Let them call me rebel, and welcome, I feel no concern from it; but I should suffer the misery of devils were I to make a whore of my soul by swearing allegiance to one whose character is that of a sottish, stupid, stubborn, worthless, brutish man. I conceive likewise a horrid idea in receiving mercy from a being, who at the last day shall be shrieking to the rocks and mountains to cover him, and fleeing with terror from the orphan, the widow, and the slain of America. ❖

---

6. **ague.** Chill; fit of shivering
7. **fourteenth century.** Actually the fifteenth; Joan of Arc triumphed over the English in 1429.
8. **touchstones.** Types of stone formerly used to test the purity of gold or silver; hence, any test for determining genuineness or value
9. **tory.** Someone who continues to show allegiance to Great Britain
10. **the back.** Backwoods

> **ap • pa • ri • tion** (a pə ri´ shən) *n.*, ghost, specter, or phantom

MIRRORS & WINDOWS

If you were alive in Paine's day and were an ardent supporter of the movement for American independence, how would reading this essay make you feel? How might you feel if you were a British loyalist?

Refer to Text ▶ ▶ ▶ ▶ ▶   Reason with Text

1a. Identify the reason Paine gives in *The Crisis, No. 1*, for believing that God is on the side of the colonists.	**1b.** Infer why Paine starts his argument by assuring his readers that God is on their side.	**Understand** Find meaning
2a. In *Common Sense*, when does Paine argue is the best time for a country to form a constitution?	**2b.** What present-day world events reflect the danger posed when a country has a "vacant seat of government"?	**Apply** Use information
3a. What does Paine believe will happen if Great Britain regains control of the government of America, as stated in *Common Sense?*	**3b.** Why does Paine write that even if Britain again takes control of the American colonies, it would not be able to give "relief" to Americans who may be abused by a tyrant?	**Analyze** Take things apart
4a. In *The Crisis, No. 1*, what rights does Britain claim that Paine contends constitute "slavery"? Why does Paine believe this?	**4b.** Determine Paine's strongest reason for fighting for independence. Where does he state it?	**Evaluate** Make judgments
5a. In *Common Sense*, what does Paine say he is offering the reader?	**5b.** Reread the first paragraph. Suggest how it could be reworded to get the attention of a modern audience—say, the audience of a talk show.	**Create** Bring ideas together

Analyze Literature

Argument and Tone
How logical is the case Paine makes for revolution in each selection? Identify the emotional elements in his argument, as well. How successfully does he lead readers to his position?

Examine Paine's word choices in *Common Sense* and *The Crisis, No. 1*. What is the tone of each selection? Give examples of word choices that create this tone.

Extend the Text

Writing Options
Creative Writing You are an officer under the command of General George Washington at Valley Forge. He has just finished reading to the troops Paine's words from *The Crisis, No. 1*. Now it is your turn to tell them why you are grateful that they are not "sunshine soldiers and summer patriots" and that they continue to fight for independence. Write the speech you would deliver.

Persuasive Writing Imagine that you are Thomas Paine's publisher. Write a paragraph either supporting his decision to write anonymously or encouraging him to publish his writing under his own name.

Collaborative Learning
Evaluate Media Coverage Form a small group and have each member select a news story about a current event. Evaluate the coverage of this event in three media: a printed newspaper, a television or radio newscast, and an online source. Then participate in a panel discussion on how effectively various media cover the news.

Media Literacy
Investigate Propaganda Find a printed brochure or online source that reflects the views of an organization with a specific political agenda. Prepare an outline of the organization's philosophy and activities, and use it to create a poster that informs others about the group's agenda.

 Go to **www.mirrorsandwindows.com** for more.

Understand the Concept

A **pronoun** is a word that takes the place of a noun or that stands in for an unidentified noun. The noun that the pronoun replaces is called the **antecedent.** A pronoun should agree with, or match, its antecedent in *gender* (*he, she, it*) and *number* (singular or plural).

EXAMPLE

The "summer *soldier*" shrinks from serving *his* country. True *patriots,* in contrast, do what is asked of *them* for the common good. [*Soldier* is the antecedent of *his; patriots* is the antecedent of *them.*]

When you use a pronoun to refer to a noun, make sure your readers can easily tell to which noun the pronoun refers.

EXAMPLES

Not clear Thomas Paine met Benjamin Franklin in London in the early 1770s. *He* provided *him* with contacts in the United States that led to a job editing a new magazine.

Clear Thomas Paine met Benjamin Franklin in London in the early 1770s. Franklin provided Paine with contacts in the United States that led to a job editing a new magazine.

When referring to a singular noun such as *person* or *student,* the correct pronoun is *he or she* (or *his or her*) together. Using *they* or *them* is grammatically incorrect because both are plural pronouns. Because using *he or she* repeatedly makes writing awkward, the best solution often is to make both the noun and the pronoun plural.

EXAMPLES

Incorrect Every *citizen* should decide how *they* can do the most good for the nation.

Correct (singular) Every *citizen* should decide how *he or she* can do the most good for the nation.

Correct (plural) *Citizens* should decide how *they* can do the most good for the nation.

Apply the Skill

Identify the Correct Pronoun
For each of the following items, identify the pronoun that correctly refers to its antecedent.

1. The phrases "summer soldier" and "sunshine patriot" are examples of figures of speech. (It is/They are) meant to be understood imaginatively, rather than literally.
2. The colonists resented Britain when (it/they) decided that Parliament could "bind" (it/them) "in all cases whatsoever."
3. In Paine's opinion, the American government should be praised for (its/their) efforts to avoid war.
4. In 1429, the French defeated the British in a historic battle. (It/They) represented one of the few times a European woman commanded an army.
5. Paine wishes that Joan of Arc would inspire "some Jersey maid" to lead (her/their) soldiers in an uprising against the British.

Revise for Clear Pronoun References
Revise the following paragraph so that all pronoun-antecedent references are clear.

In *Common Sense,* Paine says that volumes have been written on the struggle between England and America. Because debates have not resolved them, arms have become necessary. The government of America must establish laws of their own. If the people rely on chance to shape their future, it may not be as they had hoped. War cannot provide independence; it will be possible only if they write a constitution.

Declaration of Independence

A Government Document by Thomas Jefferson

Build Background

Historical Context The **Declaration of Independence** contains a proclamation that has reso-nated across centuries and around the world: "We hold these truths to be self-evident:—that all men are created equal; that they are endowed by their

Creator with certain unalienable rights; that among these are life, liberty, and the pursuit of happiness." Although many generations have been inspired by Thomas Jefferson's words, the Declaration of Independence was, in fact, written in just a few days.

In June 1776, Richard Henry Lee, a delegate from Virginia, brought before the Continental Congress two resolutions: one calling for the American colonies' separation from Great Britain and the other calling for formation of a new government. After much debate, the Congress decided to accept the resolutions and, on June 11, set up a committee to draft a declaration of independence. Jefferson wrote much of the document, and the committee then took three days to discuss and amend the draft. When it was passed in July, "The Unanimous Declaration of the Thirteen United States of America," which later became known as the Declaration of Independence, announced to the world that a new kind of nation had been born.

Reader's Context What rights do you have at home, at school, and at work? How do you know you have these rights?

Meet the Author

Thomas Jefferson (1743–1826) was born into a wealthy land-owning family in Virginia. After attending the College of William and Mary, he practiced law and was elected to the Virginia House of Burgesses. In 1775, he was sent as a delegate to the Second Continental Congress, where he drafted the Declaration of Independence with input from Benjamin Franklin, John Adams, and others. Jefferson then returned to the Virginia legislature, where he wrote a bill that established religious freedom. He was governor of the state from 1779 to 1781.

In the 1780s, Jefferson's political career shifted to the national level. After serving as the first secretary of state under President George Washington and as vice president under John Adams, Jefferson was elected the third president of the United States in 1800, a position he held until 1809. During his time in office, Jefferson more than doubled the size of the country through acquisition of the Louisiana Purchase. After his presidency, Jefferson retired to Monticello, his plantation in Virginia. He died there on the Fourth of July, fifty years after the signing of the Declaration of Independence.

Analyze Literature

Thesis and Parallelism
A **thesis** is the main idea presented and supported in a work of nonfiction.

Parallelism is a rhetorical technique in which a writer emphasizes the equal value or weight of two or more ideas by expressing them in the same grammatical form.

Set Purpose

Although the Declaration of Independence was created by a committee of legislators, scholars have established that much of the draft was written by Thomas Jefferson. As you read, determine the thesis that underlies this historical document. Also determine how Jefferson uses parallelism in his writing. Consider why he uses this technique to present the colonists' grievances against the British king.

Preview Vocabulary

transient, 94
usurpation, 94
evince, 94
assent, 94
inestimable, 94
abdicate, 95
insurrection, 96
redress, 96
magnanimity, 96
acquiesce, 96

The Drafting of the Declaration of Independence, c. 1900.
Jean Leon Jerome Ferris. Private collection. (See detail on page 92.)

Declaration *of* INDEPENDENCE

by Thomas Jefferson

*Governments are instituted among men, deriving
their just powers from the consent of the governed.*

*[handwritten: 1. Rights that God has given every person
2. Purpose of gov: protect rights]*

IN CONGRESS, JULY 4, 1776

[handwritten margin: INTRO]

[handwritten margin: FOUNDATION]

When in the course of human events, it becomes necessary for one people to dissolve the political bands which have connected them with another, and to assume, among the powers of the earth, the separate and equal station to which the laws of nature and of nature's God entitle them, a decent respect to the opinions of mankind requires that they should declare the causes which impel them to the separation.

We hold these truths to be self-evident:— that all men are created equal; that they are endowed by their Creator with certain unalienable[1] rights; that among these are life, liberty, and the pursuit of happiness. That, to secure these rights, governments are instituted among men, deriving their just powers from the consent of the governed; that, whenever any form of government becomes destructive of these ends, it is the right of the people to alter or to abolish it, and to institute a new government, laying its foundation on such principles, and organizing its powers in such form, as to them shall seem most likely to effect their safety and happiness. Prudence, indeed, will dictate that governments long established should not be

---

1. **unalienable.** That which may not be taken away

changed for light and <u>transient</u> causes; and, accordingly, all experience hath shown that mankind are more disposed to suffer, while evils are sufferable, than to right themselves by abolishing the forms to which they are accustomed. But, when a long train of abuses and <u>usurpations</u>, pursuing invariably the same object, <u>evinces</u> a design to reduce them under absolute despotism,[2] it is their right, it is their duty, to throw off such government, and to provide new guards for their future security. Such has been the patient sufferance of these colonies; and such is now the necessity that constrains them to alter their former systems of government. The history of the present King of Great Britain[3] is a history of repeated injuries and usurpations, all having, in direct object, the establishment of an absolute tyranny over these States. To prove this, let facts be submitted to a candid world.

He has refused his <u>assent</u> to laws the most wholesome and necessary for the public good.

He has forbidden his Governors to pass laws of immediate and pressing importance, unless suspended in their operation till his assent should be obtained; and when so suspended, he has utterly neglected to attend to them.

He has refused to pass other laws for the accommodation of large districts of people, unless these people would relinquish the right of representation in the legislature—a right <u>inestimable</u> to them, and formidable to tyrants only.

He has called together legislative bodies at places unusual, uncomfortable, and distant from the depository of their public records, for the sole purpose of fatiguing them into compliance with his measure.

He has dissolved representative houses repeatedly, for opposing, with manly firmness, his invasions on the rights of the people.

> The history of the present King of Great Britain is a history of repeated injuries and usurpations, all having, in direct object, the establishment of an absolute tyranny over these States.

He has refused, for a long time after such dissolutions, to cause others to be elected; whereby the legislative powers, incapable of annihilation, have returned to the people at large for their exercise; the State remaining, in the meantime, exposed to all dangers of invasion from without, and convulsions within.

He has endeavored to prevent the population of these States; for that purpose obstructing the laws for the naturalization[4] of foreigners; refusing to pass others to encourage their migration hither, and raising the conditions of new appropriations of lands.

He has obstructed the administration of justice, by refusing his assent to laws for establishing judiciary powers.

He has made judges dependent on his will alone for the tenure of their offices, and the amount and payment of their salaries.

He has erected a multitude of new offices, and sent hither swarms of officers to harass our people and eat out their substance.

He has kept among us in times of peace, standing armies, without the consent of our legislatures.

He has affected to render the military independent of, and superior to, the civil power.

He has combined with others to subject us to a jurisdiction foreign to our constitutions,

---

2. **despotism.** Government by a tyrant
3. **present King of Great Britain.** King George III (1760–1820)
4. **naturalization.** Bestowal of the rights of citizenship

---

tran • si • ent (tran´ zē ənt) *adj.*, not permanent; temporary
usur • pa • tion (yü´ sɹr pā´ shən) *n.*, unlawful or violent taking of power
evince (ē vins´) *v.*, show plainly
as • sent (ə sent´) *n.*, agreement
in • es • ti • ma • ble (in es´ tə mä b'l) *adj.*, that which cannot be measured

The Declaration of Independence is on display in the rotunda of the National Archives Building in Washington, DC. It is referred to as the *engrossed* version of the document, which means it was recopied from an earlier draft in large-hand writing and on a sizable piece of parchment (about 30 x 24 inches). Although the order to create the engrossed document stipulated that every member of Congress was to sign it, only fifty-six actually did. Not all the members were present on August 2, 1776, the day of the signing.

and acknowledged by our laws; giving his assent to their acts of pretended legislation:

For quartering large bodies of armed troops among us;

For protecting them, by a mock trial, from punishment for any murders which they should commit on the inhabitants of these States;

For cutting off our trade with all parts of the world;

For imposing taxes on us without our consent;

For depriving us, in many cases, of the benefits of trial by jury;

For transporting us beyond the seas, to be tried for pretended offences;

For abolishing the free system of English laws in a neighboring province, establishing there an arbitrary government, and enlarging its boundaries, so as to render it at once an example and fit instrument for introducing the same absolute rule into these colonies;

For taking away our charters, abolishing our most valuable laws, and altering, fundamentally, the forms of our governments;

For suspending our own legislatures, and declaring themselves invested with power to legislate for us in all cases whatsoever.

He has <u>abdicated</u> government here, by declaring us out of his protection, and waging war against us.

He has plundered our seas, ravaged our coasts, burnt our towns, and destroyed the lives of our people.

He is at this time transporting large armies of foreign mercenaries[5] to complete the works of death, desolation, and tyranny, already begun with circumstances of cruelty and perfidy[6] scarcely paralleled in the

---

5. **mercenaries.** Hired soldiers
6. **perfidy.** Betrayal of trust

ab • di • cate (abʹ də kāt) *v.*, give up a right or a responsibility

most barbarous ages, and totally unworthy the head of a civilized nation.

He has constrained our fellow-citizens, taken captive on the high seas, to bear arms against their country, to become the executioners of their friends and brethren, or to fall themselves by their hands.

He has excited domestic <u>insurrection</u> amongst us, and has endeavored to bring on the inhabitants of our frontiers the merciless Indian savages, whose known rule of warfare is an undistinguished destruction of all ages, sexes, and conditions.

In every state of these oppressions we have petitioned for <u>redress</u>, in the most humble terms; our repeated petitions have been answered only by repeated injury. A prince whose character is thus marked by every act which may define a tyrant is unfit to be the ruler of a free people.

Nor have we been wanting in our attentions to our British brethren. We have warned them, from time to time, of attempts by their legislature to extend an unwarrantable jurisdiction over us. We have reminded them of the circumstances of our emigration and settlement here. We have appealed to their native justice and <u>magnanimity</u>; and we have conjured them, by the ties of our common kindred, to disavow these usurpations, which would inevitably interrupt our connections and correspondence. They, too, have been deaf to the voice of justice and of consanguinity.[7] We must, therefore, <u>acquiesce</u> in the necessity which denounces our separation; and hold them, as we hold the rest of mankind, enemies in war, in peace friends.

WE, THEREFORE, THE REPRESENTATIVES OF THE UNITED STATES OF AMERICA, in General Congress assembled, appealing to the Supreme Judge of the world for the rectitude[8] of our intentions, do, in the name and by the authority of the good people of these colonies, solemnly publish and declare, That these United Colonies are, and of right ought to be, FREE AND INDEPENDENT STATES; that they are absolved from all allegiance to the British crown, and that all political connection between them and the state of Great Britain is, and ought to be, totally dissolved; and that, as free and independent states, they have full power to levy war, conclude peace, contract alliances, establish commerce, and to do all other acts and things which independent states may of right do. And, for the support of this declaration, with a firm reliance on the protection of Divine Providence, we mutually pledge to each other our lives, our fortunes, and our sacred honor. ❖

Declares U.S. as country

---

7. **consanguinity.** Close association or connection
8. **rectitude.** Correctness

---

in • sur • rec • tion (in sʉr rek´ shən) *n.*, uprising, rebellion
re • dress (rə dres´) *n.*, compensation or satisfaction, as for a wrong done
mag • na • nim • i • ty (mag' nə nim´ ə tē) *n.*, state of being above pettiness
ac • qui • esce (a kwē es´) *v.*, agree without protest

MIRRORS & WINDOWS

Do Americans take for granted the ideals stated in the Declaration of Independence and the freedoms they ensure?

Informational Text Connection

During the debate on adoption of the U.S. Constitution, a group of people known as the *Anti-Federalists* opposed the Constitution on the grounds that it called for a strong federal government. The Anti-Federalists, who included well-known leaders of the Revolutionary period such as Patrick Henry, claimed that the Constitution, as it was originally drafted, could lead to tyranny. What was needed, they argued, was a guarantee that certain individual basic rights would be protected. To ensure that the Constitution would be ratified by all thirteen states, Congress agreed to add a "bill of rights," spelling out limits on the power of the federal government. Passed by Congress in 1789 and ratified by the states in 1791, the **Bill of Rights** contains the first ten amendments to the U.S. Constitution.

Bill of Rights

Amendment 1

Congress shall make no law respecting an establishment of religion, or prohibiting the free exercise thereof; or abridging the freedom of speech, or of the press; or the right of the people peaceably to assemble, and to petition the Government for a redress of grievances.

Amendment 2

A well-regulated militia, being necessary to the security of a free State, the right of the people to keep and bear arms shall not be infringed.

Amendment 3

No soldier shall, in time of peace, be quartered in any house, without the consent of the owner, nor in time of war, but in a manner to be prescribed by law.

Amendment 4

The right of the people to be secure in their persons, houses, papers, and effects, against unreasonable searches and seizures, shall not be violated, and no warrants shall issue, but upon probable cause, supported by oath or affirmation, and particularly describing the place to be searched, and the persons or things to be seized.

Amendment 5

No person shall be held to answer for a capital, or otherwise infamous crime, unless on a presentment or indictment of a Grand Jury, except in cases arising in the land or naval forces, or in the militia, when in actual service in time of war or public danger; nor shall any person be subject for the same offense to be twice put in jeopardy of life or limb; nor shall be compelled in any criminal case to be a witness against himself, nor be deprived of life, liberty, or property, without due process of law; nor shall private property be taken for public use without just compensation.

Amendment 6

In all criminal prosecutions, the accused shall enjoy the right to a speedy and public trial, by an impartial jury of the State and district wherein the crime shall have been committed, which district shall have been previously ascertained by law, and to be informed of the nature and cause of the accusation; to be confronted with the witnesses against him; to have compulsory process for obtaining witnesses in his favor, and to have the assistance of counsel for his defense.

Amendment 7

In suits at common law, where the value in controversy shall exceed twenty dollars, the right of trial by jury shall be preserved, and no fact tried by a jury shall be otherwise reexamined in any court of the United States, than according to the rules of the common law.

Amendment 8

Excessive bail shall not be required, nor excessive fines imposed, nor cruel and unusual punishments inflicted.

Amendment 9

The enumeration in the Constitution, of certain rights, shall not be construed to deny or disparage others retained by the people.

Amendment 10

The powers not delegated to the United States by the Constitution, nor prohibited by it to the States, are reserved to the States respectively, or to the people.

Review Questions

1. What rights are guaranteed by the First Amendment? Evaluate whether it is the most important amendment in terms of the freedoms it guarantees.

2. What rights are guaranteed by the Second Amendment? Is this amendment as relevant today as it was when it was written in 1789? Suggest how the purpose of this amendment might be interpreted differently in modern times.

3. What does the Tenth Amendment guarantee? Infer what this amendment reveals about the fears of the new nation's founders. What kind of country did they not want to create?

TEXT $\xleftrightarrow{\text{TO}}$ TEXT CONNECTION

Does the Bill of Rights guarantee the unalienable rights described in the Declaration of Independence: life, liberty, and the pursuit of happiness? Try to name a specific amendment from the Bill of Rights that supports each of these three unalienable rights, or explain which of these unalienable rights is not addressed in the Bill of Rights.

Refer to Text ▶ ▶ ▶ ▶ ▶	**Reason with Text**	
1a. Define the term *unalienable right*. What rights does Jefferson consider as being unalienable?	**1b.** According to the Declaration of Independence, why are governments created? What are people entitled to do when their government takes away their rights?	**Understand** Find meaning
2a. What language in the Declaration seems to condemn slavery without specifically mentioning it?	**2b.** How do you reconcile the fact that Jefferson owned slaves with what you know about his beliefs about personal liberty?	**Apply** Use information
3a. With what personal statement do the signers of the Declaration conclude the document?	**3b.** Using evidence from the text, analyze to what extent ideas about human reason and natural laws influenced Jefferson in writing the Declaration of Independence.	**Analyze** Take things apart
4a. What declaration does Jefferson make about the United Colonies? What does he say that the colonies no longer owe?	**4b.** Evaluate whether Jefferson makes an adequate argument that the colonies had the right to fight for their independence.	**Evaluate** Make judgments
5a. List some of the specific grievances that the colonists had against the British monarch.	**5b.** Some of the grievances Jefferson lists against the king were committed after the American Revolution had started. Given this, suggest how King George III might have reacted to the Declaration.	**Create** Bring ideas together

Analyze Literature

Thesis and Parallelism

In your own words, state the thesis of the Declaration of Independence. Into how many sections is the Declaration divided? How does each section support the thesis?

How does Jefferson use parallelism in his presentation of grievances against King George? What effect does this parallelism have on the reader?

Extend the Text

Writing Options

Creative Writing Imagine that you are a colonial printer. Write a one-page flyer that explains to your fellow colonists how their lives will be different after declaring independence from Great Britain.

Persuasive Writing Write an essay to give to President Thomas Jefferson that argues for outlawing slavery. Remember that Jefferson valued evidence and reason, so make your argument a logical one, not an emotional one.

Media Literacy

Analyze a Documentary Locate and view a documentary film about the Declaration of Independence. In a small group, analyze the techniques and sources the filmmaker used, such as reenactments, readings from the document, and so on. Does the documentary cover its topic in an interesting and informative way? Summarize your observations.

Lifelong Learning

Investigate a Document The original draft of the Declaration contained a passage condemning slavery. Find out how this passage was worded and why it was removed. Also find out what other changes were made to the document. Write a short essay explaining what you learned.

 Go to **www.mirrorsandwindows.com** for more.

1. Which of the following statements best explains why the Continental Congress felt it had to write the Declaration of Independence?
   A. "When in the course of human events, it becomes necessary for one people to dissolve the political bands which have connected them with another . . . a decent respect to the opinions of mankind requires that they should declare the causes which impel them to the separation."
   B. "We hold these truths to be self-evident:—that all men are created equal; that they are endowed by their Creator with certain unalienable rights."
   C. "Whenever any form of government becomes destructive of these ends, it is the right of the people to alter or to abolish it, and to institute a new government."
   D. "The history of the present King of Great Britain is a history of repeated injuries and usurpations, all having, in direct object, the establishment of an absolute tyranny over these States. To prove this, let facts be submitted to a candid world."
   E. "He has plundered our seas, ravaged our coasts, burnt our towns, and destroyed the lives of our people."

2. Which of the following is *not* one of the rights guaranteed by the First Amendment in the Bill of Rights?
   A. freedom of the press
   B. freedom of religion
   C. the right to bear arms
   D. the right to assemble peaceably
   E. the freedom of speech

3. What does the statement "Prudence, indeed, will dictate that governments long established should not be changed for light and transient causes" suggest about the colonists' efforts?
   A. They do not want to answer to the king of England.
   B. They are willing to negotiate with the king.
   C. They are having reservations about their actions.
   D. They have given a lot of thought to their decision.
   E. They regret that some of their actions have been hasty.

4. As used in the Declaration of Independence, the word *transient* means
   A. unusual
   B. permanent
   C. undeniable
   D. superficial
   E. temporary

5. Which of the following statements best summarizes the relationship between the colonists and their "British brethren" in the Declaration of Independence?
   A. The colonists feel that their British brethren are tyrants and unfit to be leaders.
   B. The colonists feel that their British brethren are friends in times of peace.
   C. The colonists are jealous of their British brethren because they have the unalienable rights that the colonists lack.
   D. The colonists have appealed to their British brethren to consider their common heritage and recognize that they have been unjust in usurping the colonists' rights.
   E. None of the above

6. What is the main idea in Amendment 10 of the Bill of Rights?
   A. Powers not specifically assigned to the federal government belong to the states or the people.
   B. The states, the people, and the federal government have equal powers.
   C. Neither the states nor the federal government may inflict cruel and unusual punishment for a crime.
   D. Powers not specifically assigned to individuals belong to the federal government.
   E. The people or the states may ignore the federal laws they disagree with.

7. Which of the following is opposite in meaning to the word *acquiesce?*
   A. protest
   B. surrender
   C. disagree
   D. compensate
   E. show plainly

8. **Constructed Response:** Although the Declaration of Independence and Bill of Rights were written at different times and for different purposes, in what ways can they be seen as complementary, or balancing one another? Use examples from the texts to support your answer.

Letter to *John Adams*

May 7, 1776

by Abigail Adams

Braintree [Massachusetts]

Abigail Adams (1744–1818) was born in Weymouth, Massachusetts. She did not receive a traditional education, but her father had an extensive library and encouraged his daughter to read widely. Although largely self-taught, Abigail developed a reputation for being witty and intelligent. At the age of twenty, she married John Adams, a Boston lawyer who played an important role in the founding of the United States and later served as its second president.

Abigail Adams's **letter to John Adams** provides an intimate look at how the wife of a leading American statesman of the Revolutionary period felt about and was affected by the events leading up to the signing of the Declaration of Independence. More important, it shows that politics and the shape the new nation might take were issues that concerned women of the period, too, not just men.

How many are the solitary hours I spend, ruminating upon the past and anticipating the future whilst you, overwhelmed with the cares of state, have but few moments you can devote to any individual. All domestic pleasures and enjoyments are absorbed in the great and important duty you owe your country "for our country is, as it were, a secondary god and the first and greatest parent. It is to be preferred to parents, wives, children, friends and all things; the gods only excepted. For if our country perishes, it is as impossible to save an individual as to preserve one of the fingers of a mortified[1] hand." Thus do I suppress every wish and silence every murmur, acquiescing in a painful separation from the companion of my youth and the friend of my heart.

I believe it is near ten days since I wrote you a line. I have not felt in a humor to entertain you. If I had taken up my pen, perhaps some unbecoming invective might have fallen from it; the eyes of our rulers have been closed and a lethargy[2] has seized almost every member. I fear a fatal security has taken possession of them. Whilst the building is in flame, they tremble at the expense of water to quench it. In short, two months have elapsed since the evacuation of Boston and very little has been done in that time to secure it or the harbor from future invasion until the people are all in a flame, and no one among us that I have heard of even mentions expense. They think universally that there has been an amazing neglect somewhere. Many have turned out as volunteers to work upon Nodles Island, and many more would go upon Nantasket if it was once set on foot. "It is a maxim of state that power and liberty are like heat and moisture; where they are well mixed everything prospers; where they are single, they are destructive."

---

1. **mortified.** Decayed or gangrenous
2. **lethargy.** Sluggishness or indifference

John Adams, 1826. Gilbert Stuart.
Smithsonian American Art Museum, Washington, DC.

A government of more stability is much wanted in this colony, and they are ready to receive it from the hands of the Congress, and since I have begun with maxims[3] of state, I will add another: A people may let a king fall, yet still remain a people, but if a king lets his people slip from him, he is no longer a king. And as this is most certainly our case, why not proclaim to the world in decisive terms your own importance?

Shall we not be despised by foreign powers for hesitating so long at a word?

I cannot say that I think you very generous to the ladies, for whilst you are proclaiming peace and good will to men, emancipating all nations, you insist upon retaining an absolute power over wives. But you must remember that arbitrary[4] power is like most other things which are very hard, very liable to be broken—and notwithstanding all your wise laws and

3. **maxim.** Concisely expressed principle or rule of conduct
4. **arbitrary.** Occurring at random or without reason

ART CONNECTION

Gilbert Stuart

If asked to describe George Washington, most people would refer to the image that appears on the American dollar bill. In fact, that image is from a famous portrait of Washington rendered by early American painter Gilbert Stuart. Stuart created this familiar portrait, along with approximately one hundred more of Washington, at the end of the eighteenth century. Stuart also created over one thousand portraits of America's founders, including the portrait of John Adams shown above.

Gilbert Stuart (1755–1828) was born in Saunderstown, Rhode Island. As a young man, he was mentored by a Scottish artist named Cosmo Alexander. Stuart left for London at the start of the Revolutionary War, afraid the ensuing turbulence would threaten his budding artistic career. In England, art critics praised his work, prompting the Royal Academy of Arts to exhibit his paintings in 1777.

Notoriously bad at managing his finances, Stuart fled England in 1793 to escape debtor's prison.

He returned to the United States and founded a studio in Philadelphia, which was then the nation's capital and thus the center of political and economic activity. Many of the individuals who had led the American Revolution and forged the new government were based in Philadelphia.

Stuart realized that because of the recent revolution, portraits of the nation's founders would become extremely valuable. He also knew that many of these individuals would want their portraits painted to perpetuate their legacy. Making this shrewd calculation helped establish Stuart's own legacy as the United States' first famous artist.

Critical Viewing As you look at the portrait of John Adams, imagine what he was like. What qualities of the painting might offer clues to his personality? Does the information in Abigail Adams's letter reinforce or contradict what you infer from the painting? Explain.

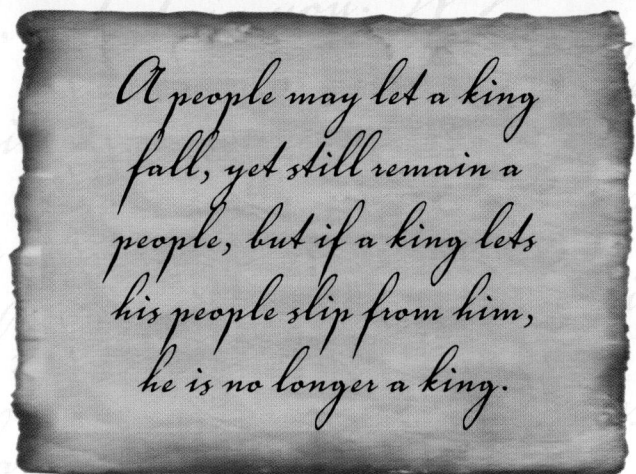

A people may let a king fall, yet still remain a people, but if a king lets his people slip from him, he is no longer a king.

maxims, we have it in our power not only to free ourselves but to subdue our masters, and without violence throw both your natural and legal authority at our feet—

Charm by accepting, by submitting sway
Yet have our humor most when we obey.

I thank you for several letters which I have received since I wrote last. They alleviate a tedious absence, and I long earnestly for a Saturday evening and experience a similar pleasure to that which I used to find in the return of my friend upon that day after a week's absence. Our little ones, whom you so often recommend to my care and instruction, shall not be deficient in virtue or probity[5] if the precepts[6] of a mother have their desired effect, but they would be doubly enforced could they be indulged with the example of a father constantly before them; I often point them to their sire

Engaged in a corrupted state
Wrestling with vice and faction. ❖

---

5. **probity.** Integrity
6. **precept.** Command or principle

 **MIRRORS & WINDOWS**

Abigail Adams suggests that women will find ways to have equal rights, whether men support them or not. What have you accomplished on your own, without the support of others?

Refer and Reason

1. Identify the argument that Abigail Adams makes in the paragraph of her letter that begins "I cannot say that I think you very generous." Then analyze how each paragraph of her letter contributes to this argument or lends support to it.

2. At the end of the same paragraph, Adams quotes two lines from "Of the Characters of Women: An Epistle to a Lady," a poem by British writer Alexander Pope: "Charm by accepting, by submitting sway / Yet have our humor most when we obey." What point is Adams trying to make in this part of the letter? How does using this quotation help her achieve the desired effect?

3. Imagine what John Adams might have thought and felt about his wife's letter. Would his response likely have been different if he had lived in modern times? Explain.

Writing Options

1. Play the role of John Adams, and write a personal letter in response to the one you received from your wife. In it, acknowledge her thoughts and experiences. Try to emulate some of the archaic language of the period in writing this personal letter.

2. Locate one or more letters written by Deborah Read Franklin, wife of Benjamin Franklin, and conduct research about her education and life experiences. Then write a comparison-and-contrast essay in which you discuss the two women's backgrounds and experiences during the events leading up to the revolution.

 Go to **www.mirrorsandwindows.com** for more.

from
Letters from an
AMERICAN FARMER

by J. Hector St. Jean de Crèvecoeur

J. Hector St. Jean de Crève-coeur (1735–1813) was, at one time, the most widely read commentator on America. He was born in France but moved to the American colonies as a young man, settling on a farm in New York State and becoming a citizen in 1769. When the American Revolution broke out, Crèvecoeur was torn between the two sides and opted to return to Europe with one of his sons. There, he wrote his famous essay collection, *Letters from an American Farmer,* and published it in both English (1782) and French (1784).

When Crèvecoeur returned to the United States after the Revolutionary War, he found his home burned, his wife killed, and his other two children living with strangers. Despite this adversity, Crèvecoeur continued to both celebrate and criticize the America he found in his travels and in his daily life.

I wish I could be acquainted with the feelings and thoughts which must agitate the heart and present themselves to the mind of an enlightened[1] Englishman, when he first lands on this continent. He must greatly rejoice that he lived at a time to see this fair country discovered and settled; he must necessarily feel a share of national pride, when he views the chain of settlements which embellishes these extended shores. When he says to himself, this is the work of my countrymen, who, when convulsed by factions,[2] afflicted by a variety of miseries and wants, restless and impatient, took refuge here. They brought along with them their national genius, to which they principally owe what liberty they enjoy, and what substance they possess. Here he sees the industry of his native country displayed in a new manner, and traces in their works the embryos of all the arts, sciences, and ingenuity which flourish in Europe. Here he beholds fair cities, substantial villages, extensive fields, an immense country filled with decent houses, good roads, orchards, meadows, and bridges, where an hundred years ago all was wild, woody, and uncultivated! What a train of pleasing ideas this fair spectacle must suggest; it is a prospect which must inspire a good citizen with the most heartfelt pleasure. The difficulty consists in the manner of viewing so extensive a scene. He is arrived on a new continent; a modern society offers itself to his contemplation, different from what he had hitherto seen. It is not composed, as in Europe, of great lords who possess everything, and of a herd of people who have nothing. Here are no aristocratical families, no courts, no kings, no bishops, no ecclesiastical dominion,[3] no

---

1. **enlightened.** Knowledgeable; full of understanding
2. **convulsed by factions.** Upset by disagreement among groups of citizens
3. **ecclesiastical dominion.** Religious authority over a state

The Ploughman, c. 1800. Theodore Rousseau.
The Hermitage, St. Petersburg, Russia.

invisible power giving to a few a very visible one; no great manufacturers employing thousands, no great refinements of luxury. The rich and the poor are not so far removed from each other as they are in Europe. Some few towns excepted,[4] we are all tillers of the earth, from Nova Scotia to West Florida. We are a people of cultivators, scattered over an immense territory, communicating with each other by means of good roads and navigable rivers, united by the silken bands of mild government, all respecting the laws, without dreading their power, because they are equitable. We are all animated with the spirit of an industry which is unfettered and unrestrained, because each person works for himself. If he travels through our rural districts he views not the hostile castle, and the haughty mansion, contrasted with the clay-built hut and miserable cabin, where cattle and men help to keep each other warm, and dwell in meanness, smoke, and indigence.[5] A pleasing uniformity of decent competence appears throughout our habitations. The meanest of our log-houses is a dry and comfortable habitation. Lawyer or merchant are the fairest titles our towns afford; that of a farmer is the only appellation of the rural inhabitants of our country. It must take some time ere he can reconcile himself to our dictionary, which is but short in words of dignity, and names of honor. There, on a Sunday, he sees a congregation of respectable farmers and their wives, all clad in neat homespun, well mounted, or

---

4. **excepted.** Excluded
5. **indigence.** Poverty

Watching Father Work, c. 1800s. Albert Neuhuijs.

riding in their own humble wagons. There is not among them an esquire, saving the unlettered[6] magistrate. There he sees a parson as simple as his flock, a farmer who does not riot on the labor of others. We have no princes, for whom we toil, starve, and bleed; we are the most perfect society now existing in the world. Here man is free as he ought to be; nor is this pleasing equality so transitory as many others are. Many ages will not see the shores of our great lakes replenished with inland nations, nor the unknown bounds of North America entirely peopled. Who can tell how far it extends? Who can tell the millions of men whom it will feed and contain? for no European foot has as yet traveled half the extent of this mighty continent!

WE ARE THE MOST PERFECT SOCIETY NOW EXISTING IN THE WORLD.

The next wish of this traveler will be to know whence[7] came all these people? They are a mixture of English, Scotch, Irish, French, Dutch, Germans and Swedes. From this promiscuous breed, that race now called Americans have arisen. The eastern provinces[8] must indeed be excepted, as being the unmixed descendants of Englishmen. I have heard many wish that they had been more intermixed also: for my part, I am no wisher, and think it much better as it has happened. They exhibit a most conspicuous figure in this great and variegated picture; they too enter for a great share in the pleasing perspective displayed in these thirteen provinces. I know it is fashionable to reflect on them, but respect them for what they have done; for the accuracy and wisdom with which they have settled their territory; for the decency of their manners; for their early love of letters; their ancient college,[9] the first in this hemisphere; for their industry, which to me who am but a farmer is the criterion of everything. There never was a people, situated as they are, who with so ungrateful a soil have done more in so short a time. ❖

---

6. **unlettered.** Uneducated
7. **whence.** From where
8. **provinces.** Colonies
9. **college.** Harvard College (founded in 1636) in Cambridge, Massachusetts

MIRRORS & WINDOWS How would you describe your family and life to a stranger? What details would you include? What details would you leave out?

Refer and Reason

1. Why does Crèvecoeur emphasize that he is writing as an "American farmer"? What significance does this term have for him?

2. Which statements about Americans seem to be exaggerated to contrast with conditions that Crèvecoeur finds intolerable in Europe? How do these statements relate to his opinions about Europe?

3. Based on evidence in this essay and in the background material, why did Crèvecoeur leave America during the revolution rather than join the rebels or the Tories? Suggest which side he would have joined had he stayed. Explain your answer.

Writing Options

1. Imagine that you are Crèvecoeur, living in Europe away from your wife and two children during the Revolutionary War. Compose a letter to them in which you evaluate your decision to return to Europe and leave them behind in America.

2. Write a one-paragraph analysis of Crèvecoeur's essay to determine where he might stand on modern immigration policy. Support your main idea using the words and ideas expressed in *Letters from an American Farmer*.

 Go to **www.mirrorsandwindows.com** for more.

HISTORY CONNECTION

Loyalists in the American Revolution

When the American Revolution began, many colonists were torn over which side to take in the struggle. Although most of them aligned with the Patriots, who were in favor of American independence, historians estimate that 20 to 25 percent of the population (roughly one-half million people) remained loyal to the British crown during the war.

These so-called Loyalists cited a number of reasons for siding with the British during the revolution. Many still considered themselves members of England's Anglican Church and were slow to break with its traditions. Colonial merchants who had close business ties with the British Empire were reluctant to jeopardize their livelihood by siding with the less wealthy colonies. Those colonists who had just recently emigrated from England, Scotland, and Ireland felt more loyal to the place of their birth than their new home.

Still other colonists were nervous about severing ties with a mother nation that could ensure military and financial protection against the increasing presence of other European nations in North America. Finally, the high levels of incompetence and oppression that many colonists saw in local Patriot governments before the war caused them to believe the colonies could not govern themselves.

Most Native Americans supported the British during the war. In the prewar years, native peoples preferred negotiating with British officials and remained distrustful of the colonists. The British government honored many (though not all) of its promises to uphold peace treaties and territorial boundaries, while the colonists and settlers rarely did so.

Surprisingly few slaves and freedmen joined the Loyalists. The likely explanation for this is that many slave owners threatened their slaves with torture and death if they were caught trying to escape to the British army. Freedmen knew that if they were captured while fighting for the British, they immediately would be thrown back into slavery.

When the Revolutionary War ended, the new American government allowed Loyalists to leave the country without reprimand. Approximately twenty percent of the Loyalist population, or an estimated seventy thousand people, moved to Canada, England, or the English colonies in the Caribbean.

Founding Mothers: The Women Who Raised Our Nation by Cokie Roberts

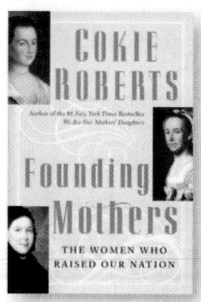

The women of the American Revolution were equally as heroic as the men. Eliza Pinckney was left in charge of three plantations at age sixteen, and Deborah Read Franklin managed several businesses so husband Ben could represent the colonies abroad. Journalist Cokie Roberts shares their stories and others in a suspenseful narrative.

A People's History of the American Revolution: How Common People Shaped the Fight for Independence by Ray Raphael

The American Revolution was won by the common people, argues author Ray Raphael: farmers, laborers, and soldiers, as well as women, Native Americans, and free and enslaved African Americans. Before the war, they supported the revolution by protesting British abuses. Later, many died in America's longest war.

Dearest Friend: A Life of Abigail Adams by Lynne Withey

Abigail Adams understood the implications of the American Revolution for slaves and women. Rich with excerpts from her letters, this biography of the most influential woman in revolutionary America shows her battling loneliness, managing the family farm and four children, and keeping her husband informed of the political mood at home.

The Interesting Narrative of the Life of Olaudah Equiano, or Gustavus Vassa, the African by Olaudah Equiano, edited by Werner Sollors

Olaudah Equiano spent most of his life a slave. Before managing to purchase his freedom, he traveled the seas for his owner and participated in naval battles and expeditions. Settling in England, Equiano wrote his best-selling account, the first slave narrative written in English, and bolstered the abolitionist cause.

The Four Voyages: Being His Own Log-Book, Letters and Dispatches with Connecting Narrative by Christopher Columbus, translated by J. M. Cohen

This collection of primary source documents provides an authentic, detailed account of Columbus's exploration of the New World. Reading the explorer's own words, along with those of his son and several others, gives insight into the man as well as his voyages. Cohen has masterfully interpreted Columbus's writings without editorializing.

American Indian Myths and Legends by Richard Erdoes and Alfonso Ortiz

Erdoes and Ortiz have collected 160 tales from over 80 different Native American tribes in this fascinating collection of creation myths, trickster tales, and apocalyptic visions of the future. Anyone seeking to learn more about Native American oral and spiritual traditions will find this collection invaluable.

Many people enjoy listening to readings of poems or brief works of prose, such as stories and essays. Presenting a poem or brief work of prose to an audience can be enjoyable, as well. Reciting a work of literature is known as *oral interpretation.* Following the steps outlined here will help you make the most of an opportunity to present a favorite work of literature to an audience.

1. Select a Work

You can present a poem or a work of prose, such as a short story, a brief chapter from a novel, or an essay. The oral interpretation will probably take about five minutes (check with your teacher), so look for a work you can recite within that time. Choosing a work you enjoy will make it easier to communicate your enthusiasm to your audience. A short piece of literature also will be easier to present than a long one.

To recite a poem, you can choose a *lyric poem,* which expresses an emotion or sudden insight, or a *narrative poem,* which tells a story. If you prefer to recite prose, such as a short story or novel, select an *excerpt,* or a part of the complete work. The excerpt should not need a lot of explanation for the audience to understand it, and it should be complete and satisfying in itself. If you decide to recite all or part or an essay, choose one that is about a topic of interest to your listeners and that is written in a clear, lively style.

2. Familiarize Yourself with the Work

To give an effective oral interpretation, you must have a good understanding of and appreciation for the work. To prepare, read the work carefully several times, until you can identify the following elements: the speaker in a lyric poem; the speaker, characters, and action in a narrative poem; the characters and action in a short story or chapter; or the main idea in an essay.

Also determine the *mood* and *tone* of the work: Is the poem intended to amuse? Is the story suspenseful? Is the essay meant to persuade? Plan to recite the work in the most appropriate way, given the mood and tone.

3. Practice Reading the Work Aloud

After becoming familiar with the work, practice reading it aloud. As you read, pay attention to your *delivery,* or presentation. Consider which tone of voice, facial expression, gestures, pace (speed) of speaking, and volume (loudness or softness) are most suitable for each part of the work.

To get feedback on your presentation, rehearse in front of a mirror, or ask a family member or friend to be your practice audience. If you can, audiotape or videotape your presentation, and use the replay to help you make improvements.

4. Memorize the Work, If You Are Asked To

If your assignment is to recite the work from memory, start by memorizing one passage at a time. Speak each passage aloud until you have committed it to memory. If the assignment does not ask you to memorize the work, practice reading it aloud. Use index cards, printing or writing a single passage on each card using easily readable type. Reciting your selection from cards, one passage at a time, will be more manageable than reading the entire thing from one or two printed pages.

5. Present the Oral Interpretation

When the time comes, try to remain calm as you recite the work. Take several deep breaths before you start. As you recite, make eye contact with your listeners, and use facial expressions appropriate for the selection.

SPEAKING & LISTENING RUBRIC

Your oral presentation will be evaluated on these elements:

Content

- ❏ The literary work is appropriate for the audience.
- ❏ The length of the work meets the assignment.

Delivery & Presentation

- ❏ The volume, pace, and enunciation (clarity of speech) fit the selection.
- ❏ The facial expressions and gestures fit the selection.
- ❏ The tone (emotional quality) and emphasis of delivery are effective.

Whether it's John F. Kennedy's "Ask not what your country can do for you" or, as you read in this unit, Patrick Henry's fervent "Give me liberty or give me death!" passionate addresses inspire audiences, persuading them to change their viewpoint or rise to action.

While few of us will be called on to deliver a speech that will effect national change, we still use words to persuade others, perhaps by convincing a friend to watch a certain movie or challenging our community to change a policy. Writing a persuasive essay is, then, merely an extension of what we do naturally in everyday life.

In this assignment, you will write a persuasive essay, defending a viewpoint that expresses an informed opinion about a topic that interests you. Support your opinion with information gathered from research on the topic.

> **Assignment** Plan, write, and revise an essay that supports your opinion on an arguable topic
>
> **Purpose** To persuade readers to your point of view
>
> **Audience** Someone who disagrees with your standpoint or is undecided about the topic

1 Prewrite

Select a Topic

The best topics for a persuasive essay are those that have two or more clear factions and are perhaps controversial. Generate a list of four to six such topics. Choose the topic that most interests you.

Gather Information

The Internet is a great place to begin your search, as it provides a wide range of avenues to investigate, but don't limit yourself to it. Scour news media, including television and radio news shows, newspapers, and news magazines, for additional insights and data. If your topic is not as current, search back issues of newspapers and magazines. If your topic is not of national concern—for example, changing a school policy—consider

interviewing the individuals involved; they can offer what they know and point you to additional sources.

Create a chart of at least five arguments and counterarguments like the one shown on page 111. Try to come up with a counterargument for each point you make. Remember that often the most convincing argument is made in debunking a counterargument.

Organize Ideas

Review your chart. Do you have at least five distinct points of argument? Does every argument have a balanced counterargument? Do you disprove the counterargument in a convincing way?

Circle your three most convincing arguments. Then number them in the order you want them to appear in the essay. In a persuasive argument, it is often best to lead with the most common argument and to end with the strongest argument.

Write a Thesis Statement

Based on the points you have chosen, write a one-sentence argument. This is your **thesis statement.** Using information from the Argument Chart, one student, Meghan, wrote this thesis statement about fining people whose cell phones ring during a movie or play:

> *A patron whose cell phone rings during a performance should be fined.*

> **WRITING RUBRIC**
>
> A successful persuasive essay has these qualities:
> - ❏ an introduction that captures the reader's interest and identifies the topic
> - ❏ a clear thesis statement that expresses the argument the author plans to make
> - ❏ a body that provides evidence gathered from research to support the argument and acknowledges and refutes possible counterarguments
> - ❏ a conclusion that reemphasizes the main point and provides closure

Argument Chart

My Argument	The Counterargument	Why I'm Still Right
It's not fair to pay for a movie or play and have it ruined by a cell phone	Cell phones are needed so people can be reached	The phone can be put on silent or vibrate
Money made from fines can be put into theater maintenance	Patrons already pay for maintenance in the price of their tickets	Fines could bring more money in; any extra could be put back into the community
Paying a fine will teach people a lesson	Fines are too extreme	There has to be some consequence for the person to change
People need to be taught etiquette	It's a free country—you should be able to use cell phones whenever	People need to be taught general respect and not to be selfish
People need to learn to be less dependent on their cell phones	Cell phones are a part of our culture and aren't going away	Like some of the less desirable aspects of culture, cell phones need to be put in check

❷ Draft

Write your essay by following the three-part framework described at right: introduction, body, and conclusion.

Draft the Introduction

In a persuasive essay, the introduction begins by capturing the reader's attention and by giving the argument a context. You can do this by introducing your argument with a statistic, an interesting fact, an anecdote, or a *rhetorical question* (a question that is not meant to be answered but rather meant to get readers to think about your topic). The introduction also states the thesis, establishing the main idea or point of the essay. Finally, a good introduction generates interest by insinuating the importance of your topic.

The introduction that Meghan wrote during the draft stage is shown in the first column on page 113. In the first two sentences, Meghan creates a context for her argument. In the last sentence, she states her thesis. She hasn't provided motive, though. What could Meghan include to get her readers invested in her argument?

Introduction Start by "hooking" your readers. Include your thesis statement and the points you plan to make.

Body Write one paragraph for each main point of your argument. Support each point with information from your research. Include a counterargument as well as a refutation for each point.

Conclusion Re-emphasize the thesis, and give your essay closure.

Draft the Body

In the body, state each point you want to make about the argument you are presenting and then support or prove it using research you have gathered. Use the counterargument points you listed in the Argument Chart, making sure you include your refutation to each counterargument. This is information that you already mapped out in the Prewrite stage.

Meghan decided to begin her essay using the most common argument—that cell phones ringing

What Great Writers Do

As Robin McKinley, contemporary fantasy fiction author, notes, "If you are excited by what you are writing, you have a much better chance of putting that excitement over to a reader." How can you tell Patrick Henry is passionate about his topic in "Speech in the Virginia Convention"?

HENRY

- He acknowledges the validity of his opponents' arguments but stands firmly by his belief that "The question before the house is one of awful moment to this country. . . . I consider it as nothing less than a question of freedom or slavery."
- He chooses words that portray his convictions: *truth, treason, arduous, salvation, insidious, pledged, formidable, liberty, submission.*
- He ends with a rousing line: "Give me liberty or give me death!"

during a performance create a disturbance. Look at the draft of her first body paragraph in the left-hand column of the chart on page 113. Meghan also wrote two more body paragraph drafts. She proved her thesis by providing specific examples and by effectively refuting the counterargument.

Review the three statements you circled on your Argument Chart and the order in which you planned to present them. Develop each statement into a paragraph by adding evidence you gathered from research.

Draft the Conclusion

Finally, write the conclusion for your persuasive essay. A good conclusion does two things: (1) it summarizes the main point made in the body of the essay, re-emphasizing the thesis without merely restating it, and (2) it brings the discussion to a close, often ending with a warning or call to action.

Does Meghan do both these things in her conclusion? Look at the draft of her conclusion in the chart on page 113.

❸ Revise

Evaluate the Draft

You can evaluate your own writing or exchange essays with a classmate and evaluate each other's work. Either way, think carefully about what works well and what can be improved.

Start by looking at the content and organization. Make sure that the three parts of the essay—the introduction, body, and conclusion—work together to prove the thesis. Every paragraph should relate clearly back to that main argument, and each paragraph should logically connect to the next. Use the Revision Checklist on page 114 to help you evaluate. Make notes directly on the essay about what changes need to be made.

Next, check the language for errors. Go back through your draft to make sure you have correctly applied the guidelines in the Grammar & Style workshops in this unit. Again, use the Revision Checklist to evaluate the writing. Consider how the writing can be clarified or be made more engaging.

Maintaining a consistent point of view (first, second, or third person, singular or plural) is challenging for many novice writers. However, doing so is essential, as shifting viewpoints within a sentence sounds sloppy and confuses readers. Note how Meghan is able to sharpen her sentences by changing to a consistent viewpoint in her final draft.

What Great Writers Do

Writing an effective conclusion that reminds readers of your thesis without merely restating it can be a difficult but important task. You don't want to end an otherwise strong essay with a weak finish. As Henry Wadsworth Longfellow, the famous nineteenth-century American poet, once said, "Great is the art of beginning, but greater is the art of ending."

LONGFELLOW

DRAFT STAGE		REVISE STAGE	
Introduction People have become very dependent on their cell phones. Everywhere you go, you are almost guaranteed to see people talking on a cell phone. It's really annoying when someone's phone rings during a movie or play. A patron whose cell phone rings during a performance should be fined.	Provides a context for the argument States thesis	People have become very dependent on their cell phones. Everywhere you go, you are almost guaranteed to see people talking on ~~a~~ cell phones. Is there a point where cell phones become more annoying than useful? ~~It's really annoying when someone's phone rings during a movie or play.~~ When does one person's convenience interfere with another person's enjoyment of something like a movie or play? A patron whose cell phone rings during a performance should be fined.	Corrects agreement error Inserts motive Sets up thesis with another question, rather than a statement
Body Paragraph When you are paying money to see a movie or play you don't expect any disturbances. If every couple of minutes you hear the ringing or buzzing of a cell phone, your experience will be ruined. It's not fair to disrupt everyone because you are not willing to turn your cell phone off. There are certain instances when having a cell phone on is a necessity. If this is the case, then you should turn your phone on silent or vibrate.	Gives specific example Acknowledges counter-argument Refutes counter-argument	When you are paying money to see a movie or play, you don't expect any disturbances. If every couple of minutes, you hear the ringing or buzzing of a cell phone, your experience will be ruined. It's not fair for one person to disrupt everyone else because ~~you are~~ he or she is not willing to turn off ~~your~~ his or her cell phone ~~off~~. ~~There are certain instances when~~ If having a cell phone on is necessary, ~~a necessity. If this is the case, then you should turn your phone~~ then it should be set on silent or vibrate.	Adds comma Corrects point of view Moves preposition Avoids passive voice; streamlines language
Conclusion Overall, I think that everyone would benefit from fining patrons for leaving their cell phones turned on during performances. Offenders would learn to respect the people around them. If they didn't, they would literally pay the price. Enforcing this policy would make going to a play or movie a relaxing and enjoyable experience again.	Re-emphasizes thesis without restating it Restates main points made in body Gives some closure	Overall, ~~I think that~~ everyone would benefit from fining patrons for leaving their cell phones turned on during performances. Offenders would learn to respect the people around them ~~If they didn't, they would~~ or literally pay the price. Enforcing this policy would make going to a play or movie a relaxing and enjoyable experience again. Ignoring the problem will encourage people's rude behavior.	Eliminates unnecessary "I" Combines two sentences Adds greater sense of closure; provides a warning

Revise for Content, Organization, and Style

Meghan evaluated her essay and noted a number of things that could be improved. Look at the chart on page 113 (this time, the right-hand column) to see how she revised the draft of her three paragraphs:

- **Introduction:** Meghan corrected some minor errors and added a rhetorical question, giving her essay motive.
- **Body:** Meghan improved the language by correcting some point-of-view issues and a homophone issue. She also clarified one of her points by adjusting her wording.
- **Conclusion:** By eliminating an off-topic sentence and tightening the prose, Meghan was able to give her conclusion a more polished feel. She also added a few final words to further give her essay a sense of closure.

REVISION CHECKLIST

Content & Organization

- ❏ Does the introduction give the argument a context and captivate readers?
- ❏ Does the introduction present a clear thesis statement?
- ❏ Does each paragraph in the body clearly relate back to the thesis?
- ❏ Does each body paragraph provide enough relevant evidence gathered from research to back up its point? Is there a counterargument given for each argument made? Is the counterargument refuted in a convincing way?
- ❏ Does the conclusion summarize the essay by reemphasizing the thesis? Does it provide a warning or call for action that helps bring the essay to a close?

Grammar & Style

- ❏ Do all of your subjects and verbs agree? (page 45)
- ❏ Do you use correct tenses of verbs? (page 61)
- ❏ Do you use correct pronouns throughout? Do your pronouns agree with their antecedents? (page 91)

Review the notes you or your partner made as you evaluated your draft. Then apply each comment in effectively revising your draft.

Proofread for Errors

The purpose of proofreading is to check for any remaining errors. While you can look for errors as you evaluate your essay, you should really focus on those you might have missed or introduced in new material you added. Use proofreader's symbols to mark any errors you find.

To complete the assignment, print out a final draft and read it aloud once before submitting it. Reading your draft aloud will help you slow down and catch errors you might otherwise miss.

Take a look at Meghan's final draft on the next page. Review how she worked through the three stages of the writing process: Prewrite, Draft, and Revise.

Writing Follow-Up

Publish and Present

- Find out whether your school has a magazine, journal, or newspaper that publishes students' writing. If it does, consider submitting your persuasive essay as an editorial piece. If it doesn't, see if your teacher will compile a "book" of the persuasive essays written by you and your classmates.
- If your essay focused on a community decision, consider presenting your argument at a public meeting on the topic.

Reflect

- Does the topic you chose seem more or less pressing now that you have researched it and written this persuasive essay? Explain your answer.
- What have you learned about effective arguments from having compiled your own? Think about arguments you have heard for other contemporary issues. Of the arguments you have read, seen, or heard, who makes the most convincing case? Why?

STUDENT MODEL

Cell Phone Fines
by Meghan Casey

People have become very dependent on their cell phones. Everywhere you go, you are almost guaranteed to see people talking on cell phones. Is there a point where cell phones become more annoying than useful? When does one person's convenience interfere with another person's enjoyment of something like a movie or play? A patron whose cell phone rings during a performance should be fined.

When you are paying money to see a movie or play, you don't expect any disturbances. If every couple of minutes, you hear the ringing or buzzing of a cell phone, your experience will be ruined. It's not fair for one person to disrupt everyone else because he or she is not willing to turn off his or her cell phone. If having the phone on is necessary, then it should be set on silent or vibrate.

Fining someone whose cell phone goes off during a performance would also help teach him or her proper cell phone etiquette. Using a cell phone just isn't appropriate in places where the ringing and talking will disturb other people. Places such as hospitals, libraries, theaters, and even restaurants have posted signs stating their policy of "No cell phone use." If you make the decision to go to one of these places, then you should not plan on taking or making calls. Some people argue that they should be able to use their phones wherever they choose, but that's selfish and disrespectful of others. Paying a penalty may be the only way for them to learn to recognize the feeings and rights of the people around them.

Furthermore, if someone is fined once, he or she will be less likely to cause a disturbance again. Not only paying the fine but also being singled out in a theater full of people might make someone reconsider using his or her cell phone during another performance. While charging a fine might seem extreme, it would definitely teach people a lesson. If there are no consequences to using cell phones in inappropriate places, then people will continue to do so.

Overall, everyone would benefit from fining patrons for leaving their cell phones turned on during performances. Offenders would learn to respect the people around them or literally pay the price. Enforcing this policy would make going to a play or movie a relaxing and enjoyable experience again. Ignoring the problem will encourage people's rude behavior.

How does the writer provide context for the argument?

What is the writer's thesis statement?

Point 1: cell phones ringing during a performance create a disturbance. What is the counter-argument? How does the writer refute it?

What is the writer's second argument? How does she convince you that her argument is solid?

Why would enforcing fines teach people a lesson?

Besides re-emphasizing her thesis, how does the writer bring the essay to a close?

Reading Skills

Use Context Clues

You often can figure out the meaning of an unfamiliar word by using context clues. In most cases, **context clues** are words and phrases near a difficult word that provide hints about its meaning. Learn how to use these types of context clues:

- A *comparison clue* shows how the unfamiliar word is like something else. Words that signal a comparison include *and, like,* and *as.*
- A *contrast clue* shows that something differs from something else by using such words as *but, nevertheless, on the other hand, however, although,* and *in spite of.*
- A *restatement clue* (also called an *apposition clue*) uses different words to express the same idea. This type of clue is signaled by *that is, in other words,* or *namely.*
- An *illustrative clue* uses a word such as *including, such as, for example,* or *for instance* to indicate that an example is being provided to show the meaning of something.

Sentence structure also can provide clues. Read the following sentence from Bartolomé de las Casas's *A Brief Account of the Destruction of the Indies:*

> And it is a great sorrow and heartbreak to see this coastal land which was so flourishing, now a depopulated desert.

If you do not know the meaning of the word *flourishing,* you can determine from the structure of the sentence that it means the opposite of *depopulated.*

Another use of sentence structure to determine the meaning of an unknown word is to identify what part of speech the word is. Knowing that a word is, for instance, a verb will help you figure out its function in the sentence and perhaps its meaning. In the preceding example, the word *flourishing* is an adjective describing the word *land.* Many *-ing* words are adjectives, as are many words ending in *-ed,* such as *depopulated* in the above example. Learn clues to other parts of speech, as well. For instance, many adverbs end in *-ly,* such as *quickly* and *silently.* Singular nouns often are preceded by an article, such as *a, an,* or *the,* as in *an accident* and *the island.* Plural nouns typically end in *-s,* such as *captives* and *ships.*

Context clues also can come from the tone of the section. For example, an author who is being sarcastic or ironic may use a particular word to mean the opposite of its real definition. Consider someone who says "That's just *great!*" when something bad happens. You understand that *great,* in this context, actually means "awful."

TEST-TAKING TIP

What is an effective test-taking strategy for using context clues to determine the meaning of a word? Start by looking at nearby words and phrases for hints to meaning. Then identify what part of speech the word is. Finally, consider the tone of the passage for additional clues.

Practice

Directions: Read the following passage. The questions that come after it will ask you to use context clues to figure out the meanings of words that are difficult or used in unfamiliar ways.

NONFICTION: This passage is from Bartolomé de Las Casas's travel narrative *A Brief Account of the Destruction of the Indies.*

1   [The Spaniards] have brought to the island of Hispaniola and the island of San Juan more than two million souls taken captive, and have sent them to do hard labor in
5   the mines, labors that caused many of them to die. And it is a great sorrow and heartbreak to see this coastal land which was so flourishing, now a depopulated desert.
    This is truth that can be verified, for
10 no more do they bring ships loaded with

Indians that have been thus attacked and captured as I have related. No more do they cast overboard into the sea the third part of the numerous Indians they stow
15 on their vessels, these dead being added to those they have killed in their native lands, the captives crowded into the holds of their ships, without food or water, or with very little, so as not to deprive the Spanish
20 tyrants who call themselves ship owners and who carry enough food for themselves on their voyages of attack. And for the pitiful Indians who died of hunger and thirst, there is no remedy but to cast them into the
25 sea. And verily, as a Spaniard told me, their

ships in these regions could voyage without compass or chart, merely by following for the distance between the Lucayos Islands and Hispaniola, which is sixty or seventy
30 leagues, the trace of those Indian corpses floating in the sea, corpses that had been cast overboard by earlier ships.

Afterward, when they disembark on the island of Hispaniola, it is heartbreaking to
35 see those naked Indians, heartbreaking for anyone with a vestige of piety, the famished state they are in, fainting and falling down, weak from hunger, men, women, old people, and children.

Multiple Choice

1. What is the definition of *souls,* as used in line 3–4?
   A. spirits
   B. people
   C. laborers
   D. personifications

2. Which is a synonym for *verily,* which is found in line 25?
   F. truly
   G. extremely
   H. confirm
   J. alas

3. In this context, the word *holds* in line 17 means
   A. has in one's possession.
   B. prevents from some action.
   C. below-deck cargo compartments.
   D. nonphysical bonds that affect someone.

4. In line 33, what part of speech is *disembark?*
   F. noun
   G. verb
   H. adverb
   J. adjective

Constructed Response

5. Using your own words (not quotations from the passage), write a detailed description of the ship owners.

Writing Skills

Plan Your Time

For the ACT, you will have thirty minutes to complete the writing test. Plan your time to allow reading and considering the prompt and then outlining, writing, and revising your essay. If you know how much time to spend on each step, you will feel more in control of your writing and produce a better response.

To help manage your time, use these estimates of minutes to spend on each step:

- *Read and consider the prompt:* Spend three to five minutes evaluating the prompt. Make certain you understand what you are supposed to do.
- *Outline your response:* Take another three to five minutes to plan your response. What main points do you want to make in the essay, and in what order do you want to present them?
- *Write your response:* Start writing at about the nine- or ten-minute mark, and give yourself about fifteen minutes overall to write your response. Spend the first five minutes on the introduction. This is an important part of your essay; if it is clearly thought

out and well written, the remainder of your essay will come more easily. Write the remainder of your essay in ten minutes or so.

- *Revise your response:* Allow at least five minutes to review what you have written and make changes. Cross out unnecessary words and add new ones as neatly as possible.

> **TEST-TAKING TIP**
>
> Don't let the thought of being timed upset you. To stay focused, follow the steps of the writing process (prewrite, draft, and revise), just as you would in writing any other essay or paper. Monitor how much time you spend on each step, but don't constantly look at your watch or check the clock. To prepare for this kind of testing situation, practice writing in timed situations.

Practice

Timed Writing: 30 minutes

Literature and film are quite different media. Each has certain advantages and disadvantages. Watching a movie that is based on a book you are supposed to read for class can never replace the reading of the book. But sometimes viewing the movie in addition to reading the book will give you new understanding or insight into the story. In these cases, some people like to watch the movie before reading the book, while others prefer to watch the movie after reading the book. In your opinion, is it better to read the book first and then watch the movie or to watch the movie first and then read the book?

In your essay, take a position on this question. You may write about one of the two perspectives given, or you may present a different perspective on this question. Use specific reasons and examples to support your position.

Revising and Editing Skills

Some standardized tests ask you to read a draft of an essay and answer questions about how to improve it. As you read the draft, watch for errors such as these:

- Incorrect spellings
- Disagreement between subject and verb; inconsistent verb tense; incorrect forms for irregular verbs; sentence fragments and run-ons; double negatives; and incorrect use of frequently confused words (such as *affect* and *effect*)

- Missing end marks, incorrect comma use, and lowercase proper nouns and proper adjectives
- Unclear purpose, unclear main ideas, and lack of supporting details
- Confusing order of ideas and missing transitions
- Language and mood that are inappropriate to the audience and purpose

After checking for errors, read each test question and decide which answer is best.

Practice

Directions: In the passage that follows, certain words and phrases are numbered and underlined. In the questions below the passage, there are alternatives for each underlined word or phrase. In each case, choose the alternative that best expresses the idea, that is worded most consistently with the style and tone of the rest of the passage, or that makes the text correct according to the conventions of standard written English.

If you think the original version is best, choose the first alternative, No CHANGE. To indicate your answer, circle the letter of the chosen alternative.

(1) The novel "The Great Gatsby" is a good example of this. (2) I couldn't get interested in the book at all because the characters and there lives seemed so outdated and unreal to me. (3) Then I watched the DVD, which I found very interesting. (4) I started reading the book again and was able to get alot more out of it.

Multiple Choice

1. A. No CHANGE.
    B. novel, "The Great Gatsby",
    C. novel *The Great Gatsby*
    D. novel, "The Great Gatsby,"

2. F. No CHANGE.
    G. they're lives
    H. there lifes
    J. their lives

3. A. No CHANGE.
    B. dvd, which
    C. DVD which
    D. DVD that

4. F. No CHANGE.
    G. again, and was able to get alot
    H. again and was able to get allot
    J. again and was able to get a lot

Owl's Head, Penobscot Bay, Maine, 1862. Fitz H. Lane.

New England Renaissance

Unit 2

1800–1850

New England Renaissance 1800–1850

1800

1820

AMERICAN LITERATURE

1800
The Library of Congress is created

1806
Noah Webster publishes his first English dictionary

WEBSTER

1807
Henry Wadsworth Longfellow is born

1815
The North American Review makes its debut

1819
Walt Whitman and Herman Melville are born

1819
Washington Irving publishes "Rip Van Winkle"

1821
Atkinson & Alexander first publish the *Saturday Evening Post*

1826
James Fenimore Cooper publishes *The Last of the Mohicans*

1827
Freedom's Journal, the first African-American-owned newspaper in the United States, is founded in New York

1827
John James Audubon publishes the first of his ten-volume work *The Birds of America*

AMERICAN HISTORY

1803
Under the direction of President Thomas Jefferson, the U.S. government purchases the Louisiana Territory from France for $15 million

1804
Lewis and Clark begin their famous expedition into the American West

1808
The United States bans the slave trade

1812
The War of 1812 breaks out between the Americans and the British

1821
The United States purchases Florida from Spain

1823
The Monroe Doctrine proclaims that European countries should no longer interfere with American affairs

1825
The Erie Canal opens passage from Albany, New York, to Lake Erie

1826
Thomas Jefferson and John Adams both die on July 4

1826
The American Temperance Society is founded

1828
Andrew Jackson is elected president

WORLD HISTORY

c. 1800
The Industrial Revolution transforms Great Britain's cultural and physical landscape

1804
Napoleon crowns himself Emperor of France

NAPOLEON

1804
Haiti wins independence from France

1808
Ludwig van Beethoven premieres his Fifth Symphony

1809
French scientist Nicolas Appert invents canning, revolutionizing food preparation and storage

1821
Napoleon dies in exile

1822
Black American settlers establish the colony of Liberia in West Africa

1825
A small group of noblemen in Russia attempt unsuccessfully to overthrow Tsar Nicholas I in the Decembrist Revolt

1825
Brazil gains independence from Portugal

1828
Shaka Zulu is assassinated

1829
Greece receives autonomy from the Ottoman Empire

1830

1840

1830
Joseph Smith publishes *The Book of Mormon*

1831
William Lloyd Garrison begins printing *The Liberator*, an abolitionist periodical

GARRISON

1836
Ralph Waldo Emerson inspires the Transcendentalism movement through his nonfiction work *Nature*

1837
The Little, Brown and Company publishing house opens its doors

1837
Nathaniel Hawthorne publishes a collection of short stories called *Twice-Told Tales*

1841
Ralph Waldo Emerson publishes "Self-Reliance"

1845
Edgar Allan Poe publishes *The Raven*

1845
Henry David Thoreau embarks on a two-year excursion into the outdoors at Walden Pond

1849
Edgar Allan Poe dies under mysterious circumstances

1850
Nathaniel Hawthorne publishes *The Scarlet Letter*

HAWTHORNE

1831
Nat Turner stages a slave rebellion in Virginia

1833
Three hundred fifty settlers found the city of Chicago

1835
Texas secedes from Mexico

1835
Richard Lawrence unsuccessfully attempts to shoot President Andrew Jackson, marking the first presidential assassination attempt in U.S. history

1838
The Underground Railroad begins

1838
The Cherokee are forcibly relocated in the Trail of Tears march

1841
William Henry Harrison delivers the longest inaugural address in presidential history on a very cold day; he catches pneumonia and dies thirty days later

1844
Samuel Morse sends the first electrical telegraph, from Baltimore to Washington, DC

1845
President John Tyler authorizes the annexation of Texas, instigating the Mexican-American War

1849
The first gold rush begins in California

1830
Egba refugees, fleeing the Yoruba civil wars, found the city of Abeokuta in southwest Nigeria

1834
Slavery is abolished in the British Empire

1837
Queen Victoria becomes monarch of Great Britain at age eighteen; she would reign for almost sixty-four years

1839
African slaves aboard the slave ship *La Amistad* overthrow their captors

1839
The First Opium War begins between the Chinese and the British

VICTORIA

1842
The Treaty of Nanking cedes Hong Kong to the British

1845
The great potato famine starts in Ireland, prompting a wave of emigration

1847
The British Parliament passes legislation to limit the working hours of women and children to ten hours a day

1848
Karl Marx publishes *The Communist Manifesto*

> *"If a man does not keep pace with his companions, perhaps it is because he hears a different drummer."*
>
> —HENRY DAVID THOREAU

Territorial Expansion

After his 1803 purchase of the Louisiana Territory from France doubled the size of the new nation, President Thomas Jefferson wanted to know more about the lands west of the Mississippi and persuaded Congress to authorize the Corps of Discovery. The findings of the expedition inspired the westward movement. However, as settlers began to move west and create new states, the country became embroiled in a series of wars.

In 1811, General William Henry Harrison attacked a Native American Confederacy in the Northwest led by the Shawnee Tecumseh at Tippecanoe. Harrison's victory forced Tecumseh to join the British side in the War of 1812, declared by President James Madison because the British were seizing American ships. That war saw the British burn the nation's capitol and president's mansion before their defeat at Lake Champlain.

> *"They have driven us from the sea to the lakes—we can go no farther."*
>
> —TECUMSEH

New territories were added to the nation's boundaries by often questionable means. Instructed to stop Seminole raids on American territory from bases in Florida, Andrew Jackson simply invaded the Spanish territory. Not wanting a war, the Spanish agreed to sell the territory if the United States gave up claims to Texas. By 1836, the original thirteen colonies had grown into twenty-five states, stretching as far west as Arkansas, and the Texas settlers had demanded and won independence from Mexico.

When Mexico announced in 1845 that it intended to reclaim Texas, hostilities erupted again. President James Polk, determined to carve a clear passage to the Pacific Ocean, sent troops into disputed territory. This time the prize for the victorious United States was not only Texas but also

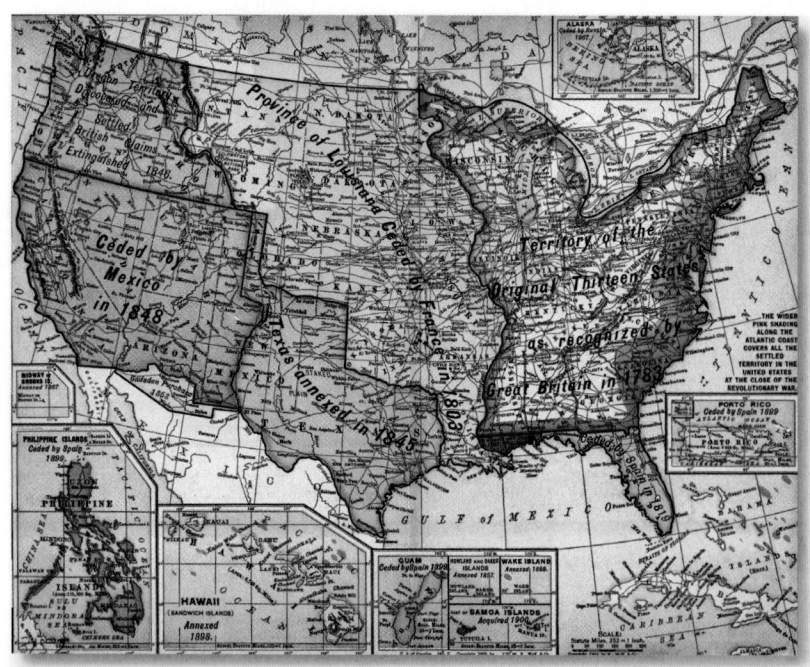

New Mexico and California, where gold had been discovered in 1846. A compromise that same year with Great Britain over the boundary of the Oregon territory allowed the United States to accomplish its *manifest destiny:* to occupy the whole continent.

Industrialization

Meanwhile, technological innovations and capital investments brought about an Industrial Revolution in New England. The inventions of the spinning jenny, which spun cotton into thread; the power loom, which wove thread into cloth; and interchangeable parts spurred the growth of towns and cities and brought about the development of the factory system. All operations involved with turning cotton into cloth could be done under one roof by a mostly female workforce, who often worked a sixteen-hour day for twenty-five cents. These harsh labor practices led to ongoing strikes for better conditions; some of the earliest occurred in the 1830s in these textile mills.

Two important technological developments helped to make U.S. expansion across the continent less daunting. The invention of the telegraph by

Samuel Morse in 1838 made it possible to communicate across distances instantly, and the introduction of the steam locomotive by John Stephens in 1825 made possible the development of a railway system to connect towns and cities across vast areas. By the 1850s, rails connected the East Coast to the western side of the Mississippi River. However, while the industrial transformation was well under way in the East, the rest of the country remained predominantly agricultural, with small farms springing up in the new territories.

Democratization

With the election of Andrew Jackson as president in 1828, a shift toward recognizing the importance of common people was under way. Many states granted voting rights to all free men, whereas previously voting had been restricted to wealthy property owners, like those who had framed the U.S. Constitution. For the first time, factory workers and sharecroppers could vote. The political system also was made more democratic, replacing a system in which members of Congress chose major political candidates with one in which nominating conventions composed of states' delegates did so. Jackson also initiated the so-called *spoils system,* replacing federal workers with his own political supporters.

The focus on common people also resulted in increased concern about cultural and educational life. Horace Mann undertook studies in the 1830s that would eventually lead to developing more systematic methods for public education throughout the North. Many states, beginning with Massachusetts, started to offer free public education at the primary and secondary levels; by 1850, free education was widespread in the North.

Outsiders

The concern for ordinary people did not extend beyond white males, however. In 1830, Congress passed the Indian Removal Act, which forced the

NOTABLE NUMBERS

- **$2,500** Funding authorized by Congress in 1803 to support the Corps of Discovery in exploring the unmapped U.S. West

- **2,000 to 20,000** Population growth of San Francisco in the first six months of 1849 due to the discovery of gold

- **50%** Nation's workforce in 1850 that were women: 333,000 were domestic servants, 55,000 were teachers, 181,000 worked in factories (half of them in textile mills)

- **31%** Increase in the number of American voters between 1824 and 1828

- **100,000** Native Americans forced to move from their traditional homelands to territory west of the Mississippi between 1830 and 1850

> *"Nothing is at last sacred, but the integrity of our own mind."*
>
> —HENRY DAVID THOREAU

eastern tribal nations to move west of the Mississippi under desperate conditions so their lands could be claimed by speculators. Those who resisted were slaughtered. In the most notorious of these removals, which came to be known as the Trail of Tears, the U.S. Army removed the Cherokee from their homelands in Georgia and North Carolina to Oklahoma in 1838. Four thousand Cherokee died en route. By 1842, only a few Native American groups were left east of the Mississippi.

Meanwhile, African Americans rebelled against their enslavement in a number of states. The most well-known uprising was that led by Nat Turner in 1831. Calls for emancipation were increasingly frequent, as Northern support for the abolitionist movement grew. Among its most effective voices was that of freed slave Frederick Douglass.

Faced with an ideology of a "women's sphere" within the home and the need for some women to enter the workforce, women joined movements that increased their solidarity: for health reform, for the welfare of prisoners and the insane, and for the emancipation of slaves. Middle-class women came to monopolize teaching in primary schools, reading and writing more and, consequently, subverting older ways of thinking.

Thus, when a feminist movement emerged in the 1840s, demanding that women have a voice in public affairs and voting rights, many women already had become effective orators and organizers. Women were ready for reform in 1848, when Elizabeth Cady Stanton and Lucretia Mott called the Seneca Falls Convention, the first American gathering in support of voting rights for women.

A Literary Renaissance

In Europe, the cultural and political era known as the Enlightenment was superseded by Romanticism. Whereas the Enlightenment thinkers of the eighteenth century had stressed objectivity and the power of reason as the means to understand the laws of the universe, the Romantics praised the natural over the artificial, the emotional over the rational, and the individual will and conscience over external authority and control.

European Romanticism had a profound impact on American literature. By the first decades of the nineteenth century, American writers had begun to turn their attention toward nature, both as a source of beauty and inspiration and as a vehicle for self-exploration and personal growth. Social and political topics were explored, as well, including the ethic of material success and social advancement advanced by writers in the postrevolutionary years.

Several milestones mark the Renaissance of American literature that occurred in the first half of the nineteenth century. For the first time, American writers were recognized in Europe. The historical novels of James Fennimore Cooper and the tales of adventure told by writers such as Herman Melville were favored by Europeans. A second milestone was the emergence of the short story. Nathaniel Hawthorne, Washington Irving, and Edgar Allan Poe all contributed to the development and popularity of this form.

Nonetheless, few American writers were able to support themselves by writing full time. The economics of publishing still made it difficult for writers of limited wealth to get their works into print. The lack of copyright protection was another issue. The United States had enacted copyright laws in 1790, but international copyright protection was not provided until 1891. American books could be sold legally in England without paying royalties to American authors, and English books could be sold legally in America without paying royalties to English authors. To get published, American authors often agreed to sell their books without any claim to royalties.

PART 1

Fireside Poets

The group of writers known as the **Fireside poets** were the first Americans to receive the same literary recognition and popularity enjoyed by European poets of the day. Both Americans and Europeans praised the work of such poets as Henry Wadsworth Longfellow, William Cullen Bryant, Oliver Wendell Holmes, James Russell Lowell, and John Greenleaf Whittier. The label *Fireside* described readers sitting in front of the family hearth, enjoying an evening of reading.

The writing of the Fireside poets generally was conventional in form, meter, and rhyme, a quality that made it suitable for memorization and recitation. Several of the most popular of these authors' works were long narratives, such as Longfellow's "Hiawatha" and "Evangeline" and Whittier's "Snow-Bound."

In terms of subjects, the Fireside poets wrote primarily about American domestic life, mythology and legends, and history and politics. Highly educated and socially involved, these writers also addressed some of the critical issues of their time. Whittier and Lowell, in particular, were active in the movement to abolish slavery. By today's standards, the tone of these writers may seem overly sentimental and moralistic, but audiences of the day found it pleasant, even compelling.

The Fireside poets sometimes were called the *Schoolroom poets* because students were required to memorize and recite their works. Generations of Americans learned lines from such poems as Longfellow's "Paul Revere's Ride": "Listen my children and you shall hear / Of the midnight ride of Paul Revere."

Romantic Novel, 1892. Santiago Rusiñol y Prats.

Thanatopsis

A Lyric Poem by William Cullen Bryant

Build Background

Literary Context William Cullen Bryant probably began **"Thanatopsis"** in 1811, when he was only sixteen. The first version of the poem consisted of the present poem's lines 18–66. Bryant's father submitted this poem and another on the subject of death to the *North American Review* in 1817, and the two were mistakenly published as a single work. In 1821, Bryant completed "Thanatopsis," framing the original lines with an introduction (lines 1–17) and a conclusion (lines 66–82). In the earlier version, the central lines had been in the poet's own voice; in the later version, the speaker is a romanticized and personified Nature.

The ideas in the three parts of the poem reveal the shifts in Bryant's thinking over the ten years of its composition. The beauty of the poem's language and the grandeur of its images immediately established Bryant's literary reputation and helped create pride in the ability of American writers to equal the literary creations of the British Romantic poets.

Reader's Context If you were to comfort someone facing his or her own death or the death of a friend or family member, what might you say?

Meet the Author

William Cullen Bryant (1794–1878), born in rural Massachusetts, had an enduring love for nature and became interested in poetry as a boy. Although he wanted to earn a living as a poet, he realized that goal was unrealistic. Bryant studied law and became an attorney in his early twenties. In 1820, he became justice of the peace in Great Barrington.

Even while working as a government official, Bryant wrote poetry. In 1821, his book *Poems* won him recognition. Within a few years, he gave up the practice of law and became a magazine and newspaper editor in New York. As editor-in-chief of the *Evening Post,* he acquired wealth, fame, and influence. He became so important to the newspaper, in fact, that he was known as "the grand old man of the *Post.*"

Bryant championed humanitarian causes, including the abolition of slavery and debtors' prisons. As a key figure in American politics, he helped form the Republican Party and promoted the election of both Andrew Jackson and Abraham Lincoln to the White House. From the 1830s on, Bryant published a few more volumes of poetry and was considered a major American writer during his lifetime.

Analyze Literature

Blank Verse and Elaboration
Blank verse is unrhymed poetry written in iambic pentameter. An *iambic pentameter* line consists of five metric units, or *feet,* each containing two syllables. The first is weakly stressed, and the second is strongly stressed.)

Elaboration is a writing technique in which a subject is introduced and then expanded on through repetition with minor changes, the addition of details, or similar methods.

Set Purpose

The word *Thanatopsis* has come to mean "a meditation upon death." Bryant created this title by joining the Greek word *thanatos,* which means "death," and the suffix *-opsis,* which means "resembling." As you read this poem, think about how it is meditative. Observe its regular rhythm, which creates a prayerful quality. Also observe Bryant's use of elaboration, as demonstrated by his listing of details.

Preview Vocabulary

communion, 129
blight, 130
insensible, 130
clod, 130
patriarch, 130
hoary, 130
sepulcher, 130
pensive, 131
venerable, 131
lapse, 131

Thanatopsis[1]

by William Cullen Bryant

Kindred Spirits, 1849. Asher Brown Durand.
New York Public Library, New York. (See detail on page 128.)

> To him who in the love of Nature holds
> <u>Communion</u> with her visible forms, she speaks
> A various language; for his gayer hours
> She has a voice of gladness, and a smile
> 5   And eloquence of beauty, and she glides

---

1. **Thanatopsis.** This word, coined by Bryant, means "views and thoughts on death."

com • mun • ion (kə myū´ nyən) *n.,* act of sharing thoughts and actions

Into his darker musings, with a mild
And gentle sympathy, that steals away
Their sharpness, ere he is aware. When thoughts
Of the last bitter hour come like a blight
10 Over thy spirit, and sad images
Of the stern agony, and shroud, and pall,
And breathless darkness, and the narrow house,[2]
Make thee to shudder, and grow sick at heart,—
Go forth under the open sky, and list[3]
15 To Nature's teachings, while from all around—
Earth and her waters, and the depths of air,—
Comes a still voice—Yet a few days, and thee
The all-beholding sun shall see no more
In all his course; nor yet in the cold ground,
20 Where thy pale form was laid, with many tears,
Nor in the embrace of ocean shall exist
Thy image. Earth, that nourished thee, shall claim
Thy growth, to be resolv'd to earth again;
And, lost each human trace, surrend'ring up
25 Thine individual being, shalt thou go
To mix forever with the elements,
To be a brother to th' insensible rock
And to the sluggish clod, which the rude swain
Turns with his share,[4] and treads upon. The oak
30 Shall send his roots abroad, and pierce thy mould.[5]
Yet not to thy eternal resting place
Shalt thou retire alone—nor couldst thou wish
Couch more magnificent. Thou shalt lie down
With patriarchs of the infant world—with kings
35 The powerful of the earth—the wise, the good,
Fair forms, and hoary seers of ages past,
All in one mighty sepulcher.—The hills
Rock-ribb'd and ancient as the sun,—the vales

---

2. **shroud . . . narrow house.** *Shroud*—cloth used to wrap a corpse for burial; *pall*—cloth draped over a coffin; *narrow house*—grave
3. **list.** Listen
4. **share.** Plow
5. **mould.** Form or body

blight (blīt) *n.,* anything that destroys or prevents growth
in • sen • si • ble (in sen′ sə bəl) *adj.,* lacking sensation; unaware
clod (kläd) *n.,* lump, often of earth or clay
pa • tri • arch (pā′ trē ärk) *n.,* father; ruler; founder
hoar • y (hōr′ ē) *adj.,* having white or gray hair
sep • ul • cher (sep′ əl kʉr) *n.,* vault for burial

DURAND

The Hudson River School

Trends in literature often parallel those in the visual arts. In the mid-1800s, a group of American painters believed in the spiritual power of nature, as did many writers of the New England Renaissance. These painters, who became known as the *Hudson River School,* re-created American landscapes, striving to replicate nature with painstaking detail. However, like their literary contemporaries, these painters also tended to romanticize the natural world. Their paintings were infused with color and light, generally creating a peaceful, pastoral quality and sometimes exaggerating specific elements. In addition, some of their paintings were composites, in which distinct natural settings were combined or people were added to wilderness scenes.

The founder of the Hudson River School was Thomas Cole (1801–1848), whose work did feature the Hudson River Valley. As the movement grew, painters such as Frederic Edwin Church (1826–1900) portrayed the Catskill, Berkshire, and White Mountains, and with the westward expansion of the United States, more rugged landscapes became the focus of artists such as Albert Bierstadt (1830–1902).

The Hudson River painters established the first truly American fine art. In its day, their work was so popular that it drew large crowds of paying admirers. In the long term, these painters' reverence for nature fostered an attitude of respect for the American wilderness that persists today.

Critical Viewing One year after the death of Thomas Cole, fellow painter and close friend Asher Brown Durand (1796–1886) created *Kindred Spirits* (see page 129), in which he placed Cole and poet William Cullen Bryant in a scene from the Catskill Mountains. What is suggested by the title of the painting? What words and phrases in Bryant's poem capture the mood in Durand's painting? Do you share these individuals' idealized view of nature? Explain.

Stretching in <u>pensive</u> quietness between;
40 The <u>venerable</u> woods—rivers that move
In majesty, and the complaining brooks
That make the meadows green; and pour'd round all,
Old ocean's grey and melancholy waste,—
Are but the solemn decorations all
45 Of the great tomb of man. The golden sun,
The planets, all the infinite host of heaven,
Are shining on the sad abodes of death,
Through the still <u>lapse</u> of ages. All that tread

---

pen • sive (pen´ səv) *adj.,* expressing deep thoughtfulness, often mixed with sadness
ven • er • a • ble (ven´ ʉr ə b´l) *adj.,* worthy of respect by reason of age and dignity
lapse (laps) *n.,* discontinuation; passing away

The globe are but a handful to the tribes
50   That slumber in its bosom.—Take the wings
Of morning—and the Barcan desert[6] pierce,
Or lose thyself in the continuous woods
Where rolls the Oregan,[7] and hears no sound,
Save his own dashings—yet—the dead are there,
55   And millions in those solitudes, since first
The flight of years begin, have laid them down
In their last sleep—the dead reign there alone.—
So shalt thou rest—and what if thou shalt fall
Unnoticed by the living—and no friend
60   Take note of thy departure? All that breathe
Will share thy destiny. The gay will laugh
When thou art gone, the solemn brood of care
Plod on, and each one as before will chase
His favorite phantom; yet all these shall leave
65   Their mirth and their employments, and shall come,
And make their bed with thee. As the long train
Of ages glide away, the sons of men,
The youth in life's green spring, and he who goes
In the full strength of years, matron, and maid,
70   The bow'd with age, the infant in the smiles
And beauty of its innocent age cut off,—
Shall one by one be gathered to thy side,
By those, who in their turn shall follow them.
So live, that when thy summons comes to join
75   The innumerable caravan, that moves
To the pale realms of shade, where each shall take
His chamber in the silent halls of death,
Thou go not, like the quarry-slave at night,
Scourged to his dungeon, but sustain'd and sooth'd
80   By an unfaltering trust, approach thy grave,
Like one who wraps the drapery of his couch
About him, and lies down to pleasant dreams. ❖

---

6. **Barcan desert.** Desert in northeast Libya
7. **Oregan.** Early spelling of *Oregon*

MIRRORS & WINDOWS

In reading "Thanatopsis," we can see how Bryant's view of death changed over a period of ten years, starting when he was sixteen. How have your views of, say, a social or political topic changed over even the last three or four years?

Refer to Text ▶ ▶ ▶ ▶ ▶   Reason with Text

1a. Identify the people included in the lists of those who have died (lines 33–37) and of those who will die (lines 67–70).	**1b.** Determine what each list suggests about death. What effect do both lists have?	**Understand** Find meaning
2a. According to the speaker, what should be the feelings of someone approaching death (lines 74–82)?	**2b.** A *lyric poem* expresses the speaker's emotions. What other feelings does the speaker of "Thanatopsis" convey?	**Apply** Use information
3a. Identify the two attitudes toward death presented in lines 24–37.	**3b.** Determine which of these two views of death the speaker stresses later in the poem. How can you tell?	**Analyze** Take things apart
4a. What elaboration occurs in lines 37–45?	**4b.** Do you agree with the speaker that Nature provides the "solemn decorations" of "the great tomb of man"? Explain your response.	**Evaluate** Make judgments
5a. In lines 8–17, which words indicate who the speaker is addressing?	**5b.** Explain how a work of literature like "Thanatopsis" can influence or affect readers.	**Create** Bring ideas together

Analyze Literature

Blank Verse and Elaboration

How does the steady rhythm of iambic pentameter, which characterizes blank verse, contribute to the effect of the poem? How might the poem be different if it had a different type of rhythm or no rhythm?

What might have been the speaker's reason for using elaboration, as shown by the number of long lists in the poem? Other than being shorter, how would the poem be different without the lists?

Extend the Text

Writing Options

Creative Writing Imagine that an elderly person has died and you are writing his or her *epitaph,* or message on a tombstone. Create an epitaph with words and phrases that describe the person.

Expository Writing In a one-paragraph literary analysis to be presented to members of a reading club, discuss the theme, or central idea, of "Thanatopsis." To make your analysis credible, give evidence from the poem that supports your choice of theme.

Collaborative Learning

Hold an Interview You are one of several journalists who have traveled back to the 1820s to interview William Cullen Bryant. After briefly explaining to Bryant how life has changed, you ask him what he thinks about modern life and what kind of poems he would write if he were alive today. As a small group, write out the interview: what you would tell Bryant about modern life, what questions you would ask him, and what responses he would give.

Media Literacy

Create an Art Exhibit As explained in the Art Connection on page 131, the painting shown at the start of this selection is an example of the Hudson River School of painting. On the Internet, locate a few other paintings done in this style; if possible, print them. For each painting, give the name of the artist and the dates of his or her life; then provide a brief description of the painting.

 Go to **www.mirrorsandwindows.com** for more.

1. To whom does Nature speak with "a various language"?
   A. a man on his deathbed
   B. a lover of nature
   C. a poet
   D. God
   E. the powerful of the earth

2. Which of the following phrases best defines the word *pensiveness?*
   A. quiet reflection
   B. desperate struggle
   C. intense yearning
   D. sad thoughtfulness
   E. anxious waiting

3. According to the poem, what happens to someone's friends and family after his or her death?
   A. They gain a better understanding of death.
   B. They celebrate the soul's ascension to heaven.
   C. They mourn for the rest of their lives.
   D. They erect a memorial appropriate to the deceased person's life.
   E. They go on living.

4. Which of the following literary quotations most agrees with the theme of "Thanatopsis"?
   A. "Do not go gentle into that good night. / . . . Rage, rage against the dying of the light." —Dylan Thomas
   B. "Death is an endless night so awful to contemplate that it can make us love life and value it with such passion that it may be the ultimate cause of all joy and all art." —Paul Theroux
   C. "But what is all this fear of and opposition to Oblivion? What is the matter with the soft Darkness, the Dreamless Sleep?" —James Thurber
   D. "He that dies pays all debts." —William Shakespeare
   E. None of the above

5. Which of the following phrases best defines the word *venerable?*
   A. sharing thoughts and actions
   B. lacking sensation
   C. susceptible to attack
   D. having white or gray hair
   E. respectable due to age

6. Which of these lines from "Thanatopsis" best expresses the concern someone might have of dying alone or being separated from loved ones after death?
   A. "All that tread / The globe are but a handful to the tribes / That slumber in its bosom."
   B. "Yet a few days, and thee / The all-beholding sun shall see no more / In all his course; not yet in the cold ground, / Where they pale form was laid, with many tears."
   C. "And, lost each human trace, surrend'ring up / Thine individual being, shalt thou go / To mix forever with the elements, / To be a brother to th' insensible rock / And to the sluggish clod."
   D. "The golden sun, / The planets, all the infinite host of heaven, / Are shining on the sad abodes of death, / Through the still lapse of ages."
   E. "—and what if thou shalt fall / Unnoticed by the living—and friend take note of thy departure?"

7. **Constructed Response:** Consider how the biblical expression "ashes to ashes, dust to dust" relates to the view of death expressed by William Cullen Bryant in "Thanatopsis." Cite specific lines of the poem to support your response.

8. **Constructed Response:** In "Thanatopsis," Bryant uses the common theme *memento mori,* which warns that death comes quickly and unexpectedly. However, he blends this theme with his own notion that death is not to be dreaded because it is part of the natural order. Using examples from the poem, explain how these two themes are used in "Thanatopsis."

TEST-TAKING TIP

Avoid second-guessing yourself in selecting responses. If you consider all the possible answers carefully before choosing one, your first impression usually will be correct. Don't change that initial response unless you are absolutely sure it is wrong. Follow this guideline especially when you review your answers at the end of the test-taking session.

Understand the Concept

The origins of many English words can be traced to ancient Greece, and numerous words used today are derived from Latin, the language of the ancient Romans. As noted earlier, the word *Thanatopsis* is based on the Greek word *thanatos,* meaning "death."

The study of word origins, called **etymology,** involves examining both printed works and cultural history to identify how language changes across time. Specifically, etymologists trace the use of a given word as far back as possible, determining from what language the word derived and when and in what form the word entered the English vocabulary. Dates of origin before 1700, when printed materials became widely distributed, must be considered approximate. Many words likely were used for centuries in conversation before they were recorded in printed works.

Most dictionaries, both print and online, provide etymological information in addition to current conventions of pronunciation, usage, and meaning. The etymology of a word often appears in brackets after the pronunciation near the start of the dictionary entry. If you look up the word *etymology,* you will find that it is Greek in origin, coming from the words *etymon,* meaning "true," and *logia* or *logos,* meaning "word."

Understanding word etymologies can be helpful in several ways. First, recognizing word parts can help you determine the meanings of unfamiliar English words. For instance, knowing that the Latin *mors* or *mort* means "death" would help you infer the meanings of such English words as *mortuary, mortician, morbid,* and *mortal.*

In addition, understanding word histories can help you make connections among related words. The Latin *mare,* meaning "sea," is the root of such English words as *marina, marine,* and *maritime.* And in fact, all these words are related to the word *marinara,* an Italian word that originally meant "to cook in sailor style," using tomatoes, onions, garlic, and other spices. Although we no longer associate the word *marinara* with sailors, we still use it to describe a kind of tomato sauce.

Apply the Skill

Exercise A

Identify an English word that comes from each of the following Greek or Latin word parts. For each word, also identify the part of speech. Use a dictionary to help you.

Words from Greek
1. *-logy* ("word" or "study of")
2. *penta-* ("five")
3. *-graphein* ("to write")
4. *demos-* ("people")
5. *-meton* ("to measure")

Words from Latin
6. *fidere* ("to trust")
7. *capit* ("head")
8. *prosequi* ("to pursue")
9. *sedere* ("to sit")
10. *ventus* ("the wind")

Exercise B

Write a sentence using each of the English words you identified in Exercise A. Be sure to use the word correctly given its part of speech.

SPELLING PRACTICE

Greek and Latin Words and Word Parts

Recognizing Greek and Latin words and word parts will not only help you determine the meanings of words but will also help you spell them correctly. For example, the word *patriarch* is from the Latin word *pater,* which means "father," and the Latin suffix *-arch,* which means "ruler" or "leader." Knowing how to spell *patriarch* may also help you spell words such as *matriarch* and *monarch.* Examine these words from "Thanatopsis" to determine their Greek and Latin word parts and meanings.

communion	eternal	pensive
cycle	individual	solitudes
decorations	infinite	sustained
describe	insensible	sympathy
eloquence	melancholy	venerable

Old Ironsides

A Lyric Poem by Oliver Wendell Holmes

Build Background

Historical Context The poem **"Old Ironsides"** was written as a tribute to the U.S.S. *Constitution,* a forty-four-gun warship, one of six commissioned by the Naval Act of 1794. Launched in 1797, the *Constitution* was central in defeating the British during the War of 1812. The ship earned the name "Old Ironsides" for several impressive victories, after which British sailors described cannonballs bouncing off the hull of the sturdy ship.

In 1828, the U.S. government announced plans to destroy the *Constitution,* whose heroic service had left her battered and broken. Like many other Americans, Oliver Wendell Holmes was angry about the upcoming demolition. His outrage inspired him to write the poem in 1830, and it turned into a battle cry for all those who did not want the ship destroyed. The government was forced to give up its plan, and the *Constitution* was saved.

Ongoing renovation has kept the *Constitution* afloat, and it is now the oldest commissioned vessel afloat in the world. Currently on display in Boston Harbor, the ship is maintained by a crew of fifty-five sailors and visited by millions of tourists year-round.

Reader's Context Why is there value in preserving reminders of a nation's history? Why do people sometimes oppose the preservation of such memorials?

Meet the Author

Oliver Wendell Holmes (1809–1894) was born in Cambridge, Massachusetts, and was class poet at Harvard in 1829. In 1836, the year his book *Poems* was published, he received his medical degree from Harvard.

After serving briefly as a professor of anatomy at Dartmouth College, in Hanover, New Hampshire, Holmes moved to Boston. There, he published professional articles about health care and, from 1847 to 1882, was a professor of anatomy at Harvard. In the late 1850s, the *Atlantic Monthly* magazine, which he had helped establish, published his humorous essays and poems.

Beginning in the 1860s, Holmes wrote volumes of poetry and essays, as well as a biography of Ralph Waldo Emerson. His best-known collection of essays is *The Autocrat at the Breakfast Table* (1858); it was followed by *The Professor at the Breakfast Table* (1860) and then *The Poet at the Breakfast Table* (1872). The titles of these works suggest that Holmes, despite his high standing on the social scale, did not take himself too seriously. That likely explains why he was a popular dinner companion, appreciated for his humor and generosity.

Analyze Literature

Description and Meter
A **description** is a picture in words. Descriptions include *sensory details*—words and phrases that describe how things look, sound, smell, taste, or feel.

Meter is the regular rhythmic pattern in poetry, which is determined by the number of beats, or stresses, in each line. Stressed and unstressed syllables are divided into rhythmical units called *feet.* An *iambic foot* consists of an unstressed syllable and a stressed syllable, as in "be-NEATH" (line 5 of "Old Ironsides").

Set Purpose

Holmes's passion for the *Constitution* resonates throughout this poem, which celebrates her proud history and condemns those who want to destroy her. Trace the details Holmes provides in this vivid description of the warship. Also read the poem aloud to observe how the steady beat, or meter, contributes to the sense of passion. Note how "Old Ironsides" goes back and forth between lines of four iambic feet and lines of three iambic feet, with occasional variations.

Preview Vocabulary

vanquished, 137
foe, 137

USS Constitution vs. HMS Guerriere, 1813. Thomas Birch.
U.S. Naval Academy Museum, Annapolis, Maryland. (See detail on page 136.)

OLD IRONSIDES

by Oliver Wendell Holmes

Ay, tear her tattered ensign[1] down!
   Long has it waved on high,
And many an eye has danced to see
   That banner in the sky;
5 Beneath it rung the battle shout,
   And burst the cannons roar;—
The meteor of the ocean air
   Shall sweep the clouds no more.

Her deck, once red with heroes' blood,
10   Where knelt the <u>vanquished</u> <u>foe</u>,
When winds were hurrying o'er the flood,
   And waves were white below,
No more shall feel the victors tread,
   Or know the conquered knee;—
15 The harpies[2] of the shore shall pluck
   The eagle of the sea!

Oh, better that her shattered hulk
   Should sink beneath the wave;
Her thunders shook the mighty deep,
20   And there should be her grave;
Nail to the mast her holy flag.
   Set every threadbare sail,
And give her to the god of storms,
   The lightning and the gale! ❖

---

1. **ensign.** Flag flown by a ship to signify its nationality
2. **harpies.** In Greek mythology, winged monsters with the head and trunk of a woman and the tail, legs, and talons of a bird. Here, the word applies to people who would destroy the ship.

van • quished (vaŋ′ kwish) *adj.,* conquered or defeated
foe (fō) *n.,* enemy or adversary

MIRRORS & WINDOWS

What would Holmes likely have thought of the ship's current status as the oldest commissioned vessel afloat in the world? How would he have felt about its popularity as a tourist attraction?

Refer to Text ▶ ▶ ▶ ▶ ▶ **Reason with Text**

1a. What rings out beneath the "banner in the sky," or flag?

1b. To which two of the five senses (taste, sight, smell, hearing, and touch) do the first eight lines of the poem primarily appeal? Identify words and phrases that support your response.

Understand
Find meaning

2a. The poem has a distinct meter, or rhythm. In every two-syllable iambic foot, indicate which syllable is stressed and which is unstressed.

2b. Is the steady beat appropriate to the subject? Explain.

Apply
Use information

3a. According to the speaker, to whom should the ship be given?

3b. Infer the verbal irony in line 1 of the poem. Why does Holmes uses this literary device?

Analyze
Take things apart

4a. What does the speaker say should happen to the ship rather than let it be destroyed?

4b. Argue whether the ship would be better off sinking or being scrapped by the U.S. Navy.

Evaluate
Make judgments

5a. The "eagle of the sea" (line 16) is a *metaphor*, or comparison between unlike things. Explain what the eagle represents. What creatures will prey on it?

5b. In Holmes's day, poetry was more widely read than it is today, so writing a poem was a good way to sway opinion. What strategies might have greater impact today?

Create
Bring ideas together

Analyze Literature

Description and Meter
Identify details in the poem that appeal to the senses. How do these vivid descriptions increase the reader's appreciation of the poem?

How might "Old Ironsides" sound if it did not have a steady beat, or meter? To see or hear for yourself, write down two or three lines of the poem but break the lines in different places so the rhythm shifts. As you read the lines aloud, listen for the effect of the new rhythm.

Extend the Text

Writing Options

Creative Writing Select one of the three eight-line stanzas of "Old Ironsides," and create a less formal version. You can omit the meter and the rhyme of the original poem, but keep the subject and the ideas.

Persuasive Writing Write an editorial to submit to the school or local newspaper on a topic of controversy in your school or community—for instance, that students cannot leave the school grounds during the day. Your purpose is to persuade readers to accept your viewpoint.

Collaborative Learning

Give a Presentation Working with a small group, do research on sunken ships and the efforts made to find and salvage them. Then prepare a presentation in which group members discuss the research findings. Display photographs and other illustrations that you find or create yourself.

Media Literacy

Conduct a Survey Imagine that leaders in two neighboring cities are planning to discontinue bus service between the locations. Although most people have cars, you think that many youths and senior citizens rely on the bus service. Conduct a survey by asking friends and family members if they think public transportation is important. Keep careful records of the responses. Then prepare a report of your findings. Compare your findings with those of classmates.

 Go to **www.mirrorsandwindows.com** for more.

Stanzas on Freedom

A Lyric Poem by James Russell Lowell

Build Background

Historical Context Although an early draft of the U.S. Constitution prohibited slavery, the final version did not establish a federal policy, instead allowing individual states to decide the matter. Massachusetts was the first state to ban slavery outright in 1780, and the other New England states soon followed. This region later became the center of the abolitionist movement.

Starting in the 1820s, a variety of abolitionist literature was distributed to inform people about the depravation that slavery brought both to slaves and their masters. The most influential of these publications was *The Liberator,* a weekly newspaper published by William Lloyd Garrison. In the first issue, which was distributed in 1831 to about four hundred readers, Garrison wrote, "On this subject, I do not wish to think, or to speak, or write, with moderation." Although Garrison called for an immediate end to slavery, he advocated peaceful resistance, not violence. He reached a large national audience with *The Liberator,* publishing nearly two thousand issues over the next thirty-four years.

Many established authors were passionate about banning slavery and wrote poems, essays, articles, speeches, and even children's books in support of this cause. Among them was James Russell Lowell, who wrote some fifty poems and prose selections about abolition. In **"Stanzas on Freedom,"** published in 1843, Lowell pleads with his fellow citizens to recognize the horrors of slavery and the necessity of eliminating it.

Reader's Context What is meant by the expression "If one person is not free, no one is free"? How does the saying apply today?

Meet the Author

James Russell Lowell (1819–1891) was an idealist who devoted himself to a number of causes, including women's rights, temperance (or avoidance of alcohol), and abolition. He attended Harvard College, where he earned bachelor's and law degrees and wrote for college publications. Upon graduation, he started a career as a lawyer but soon abandoned it to pursue writing.

Between 1844 and 1848, Lowell became a nationally recognized literary figure with the publication of several works, including *Poems* (two collections), *A Fable for Critics,* the first series of *The Bigelow Papers,* and *The Vision of Sir Launfal.* Within a few years, Lowell was appointed editor of the *Atlantic Monthly* and later served as coeditor of the *North American Review.*

During the Civil War, in which he lost a number of friends and family members, Lowell used the magazines to promote the Union (Northern) cause. Some of Lowell's poems remain popular today, but his lasting literary influence was as a critic and editor.

Analyze Literature

Rhetorical Question, Rhyme, and Couplet
A **rhetorical question** is one asked for effect but not meant to be answered because the answer is clear from the context.

Rhyme is the repetition of sounds at the ends of words.

A **couplet** is two lines of verse that rhyme.

Set Purpose

Written almost twenty years before the Civil War, "Stanzas on Freedom" is representative of the literature created to raise people's awareness of slavery and build support for the abolitionist cause. In reading this poem, examine Lowell's use of rhetorical questions, in which he asks men and women to think about their place in a nation that allows slavery. Also examine how he uses rhyme to provide unity and create a musical quality in this poem.

Preview Vocabulary

base, 140
scoffing, 140

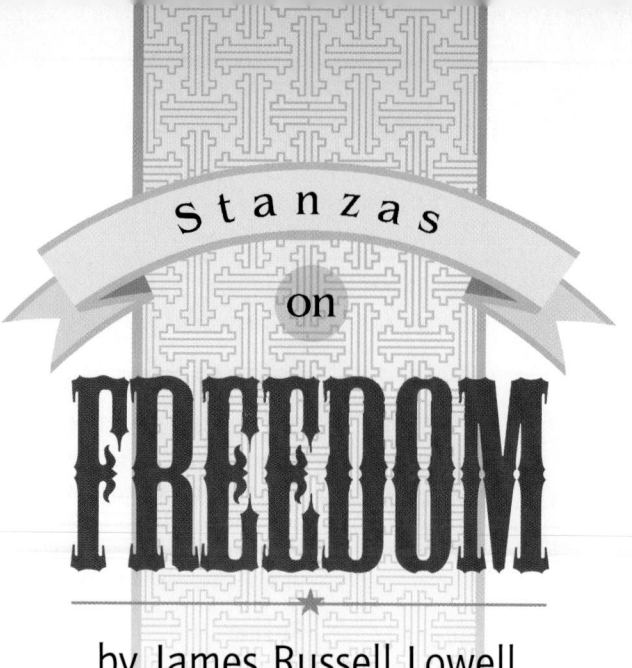

Stanzas on FREEDOM

by James Russell Lowell

Men! whose boast it is that ye
Come of fathers brave and free,
If there breathe on earth a slave,
Are ye truly free and brave?
5 If ye do not feel the chain,
When it works a brother's pain,
Are ye not <u>base</u> slaves indeed,
Slaves unworthy to be freed?

Women! who shall one day bear
10 Sons to breathe New England air,
If ye hear, without blush,
Deeds to make the roused blood rush
Like red lava through your veins,
For your sisters now in chains—
15 Answer! are ye fit to be
Mothers of the brave and free?

Is true freedom but to break
Fetters[1] for our own dear sake,
And, with leathern[2] hearts, forget
20 That we owe mankind a debt?
No! true freedom is to share
All the chains our brothers wear,
And, with heart and hand, to be
Earnest to make others free!

25 They are slaves who fear to speak
For the fallen and the weak;
They are slaves who will not choose
Hatred, <u>scoffing</u>, and abuse,
Rather than in silence shrink
30 From the truth they needs must think;
They are slaves who dare not be
In the right with two or three. ❖

---

1. **fetters.** Chains or shackles
2. **leathern.** Leathery; tough, hard

base (bās) *adj.,* of low place or position
scoff • ing (skäf´ iŋ) *n.,* showing disrespect; mocking

A Ride for Freedom—The Fugitive Slaves, 1862. Eastman Johnson. Brooklyn Museum of Art, Brooklyn, New York. (See detail on page 139.)

MIRRORS & WINDOWS Lowell suggests that citizens who do not protest against slavery are "unworthy to be free." Do you agree or disagree?

Refer to Text ▶ ▶ ▶ ▶ ▶ ▶ Reason with Text

1a. According to the speaker, when would a truly free person feel "the chain" (line 5)?	**1b.** Describe the debt that free men and women owe humankind.	**Understand** Find meaning
2a. What should caring people be willing to suffer, rather than remain silent, when they hear about injustice?	**2b.** Why is the poem addressed to men and women of New England, even though many Northerners were opposed to slavery?	**Apply** Use information
3a. In the last eight lines of the poem, the speaker gives three examples of "slaves" among his readers. What are the examples?	**3b.** Analyze what the last two lines of the poem mean.	**Analyze** Take things apart
4a. According to the speaker, when should "the roused blood" rush through readers' veins?	**4b.** The speaker addresses readers bluntly, without social niceties. Judge whether a more polite approach would be more or less effective.	**Evaluate** Make judgments
5a. How does the speaker characterize "true freedom" (lines 21–22)?	**5b.** Summarize the measures governments take to prevent or punish dissent, or disagreement with their policies. What may be the result of efforts to silence dissent?	**Create** Bring ideas together

Analyze Literature

Rhetorical Question, Rhyme, and Couplet
How many rhetorical questions does Lowell ask in "Stanzas on Freedom"? How would this poem be different if it contained statements, rather than questions?

What is the effect of the rhyme in this poem—specifically, the use of rhyming couplets? How might the poem differ if in every stanza, only alternating lines rhymed?

Extend the Text

Writing Options
Creative Writing Imagine that you are one of the New Englanders the speaker addresses in "Stanzas on Freedom." Write a brief personal essay in which you respond to the challenges raised in the poem.

Expository Writing Poetry often uses formal language, but "Stanzas on Freedom" contains many single-syllable words. Write a one-paragraph literary analysis that examines the effect of the *diction,* or word choice, in the poem.

Collaborative Learning
Compare Poems Working with a partner, locate one or two poems that protest unjust conditions. Consider both historical and contemporary works. Then discuss how the poems you have found are similar to and different from Lowell's. Also compare the rhyme, meter, diction, and other poetic elements.

Media Literacy
Create a Public Relations Campaign Select an issue of concern in your school or community, such as recycling or traffic congestion. Then develop a public relations campaign to promote your stand on the issue. Consider the strategies you can use—preparing and distributing posters, for example—and decide which ones will be most effective.

 Go to **www.mirrorsandwindows.com** for more.

The Tide Rises, the Tide Falls
A Psalm of Life

Lyric Poems by Henry Wadsworth Longfellow

Build Background

Literary Context Tides, the cyclical rising and falling of the ocean's surface, are caused by the gravitational pull of the moon or the sun and occur on a regular schedule. Henry Wadsworth Longfellow's poem **"The Tide Rises, the Tide Falls"** is characterized by the repetition of the title within the poem itself. As you read the poem, consider whether the traveler refers to a particular person or is a symbol of people in general. Do the events in the poem take place from evening to the next morning, or should the action be read as occurring over a longer span of time? What might have happened to the traveler?

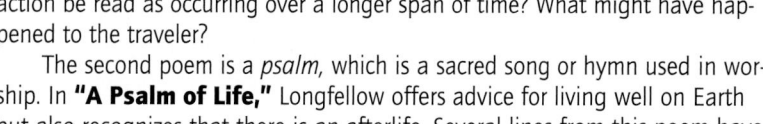

The second poem is a *psalm,* which is a sacred song or hymn used in worship. In **"A Psalm of Life,"** Longfellow offers advice for living well on Earth but also recognizes that there is an afterlife. Several lines from this poem have become *aphorisms,* short sayings that make poignant observations about life. For instance, the line "Art is long, and Time is fleeting" often is used to describe the ability of art, including literature, to speak to generations of people.

Reader's Context Why is the sea a frequent *symbol,* or representation, of nature's permanence and lack of concern for human beings?

Meet the Author

Henry Wadsworth Longfellow (1807–1882) was born in Portland, Maine, and attended Bowdoin College there. After graduating and then studying in Europe, he taught foreign languages at Bowdoin and then at Harvard.

Longfellow's most famous poems were retellings of stories from history or legend. These poems were generally romantic, didactic, and occasionally gripping and so appealed greatly to readers' tastes of the day. The two best loved of Longfellow's works are "Song of Hiawatha," a long poem about a sixteenth-century leader of the Iroquois Confederation, and "Paul Revere's Ride," a dramatic narrative poem that has brought to life, for generations of readers, the first shot in the American Revolution.

As famous in Great Britain as in the United States, Longfellow received honorary degrees from Oxford and Cambridge, two prestigious British universities, and was given a private audience with Queen Victoria. After his death, a statue of Longfellow was placed in the Poet's Corner of Westminster Abbey. The New Englander is the only American poet to be memorialized in this centuries-old London church.

Analyze Literature

Mood and Personification
Mood, or atmosphere, is the emotion created in the reader by a literary work. Mood is expressed by word choice, details, repetition, and symbols.

Personification is a type of figurative language in which an animal, force of nature, or idea is described as if it were human.

Set Purpose

Longfellow wrote "A Psalm of Life" in 1838, when he was just thirty-one years old, and he wrote "The Tide Rises, the Tide Falls" in 1879, just a few years before he died. As you read these two poems, think about how the passage of forty-some years may have altered Longfellow's perspective on life. Determine the primary mood each poem conveys. As you read "The Tide Rises, the Tide Falls," also look for examples of personification.

Preview Vocabulary

efface, 143
sublime, 145
forlorn, 145

The Beach at Low Tide, c.1800s. Louis Timmermans. Private collection. (See detail on page 142.)

The Tide Rises, the Tide Falls

by Henry Wadsworth Longfellow

The tide rises, the tide falls.
The twilight darkens, the curlew[1] calls;
Along the sea sands damp and brown
The traveler hastens toward the town,
5   And the tide rises, the tide falls.

Darkness settles on roofs and walls,
But the sea, the sea in the darkness calls:
The little waves, with their soft, white hands,
<u>Efface</u> the footprints in the sands,
10   And the tide rises, the tide falls.

The morning breaks; the steeds in their stalls
Stamp and neigh, as the hostler[2] calls:
The day returns, but nevermore
Returns the traveler to the shore,
15   And the tide rises, the tide falls. ❖

---

1. **curlew.** Seashore bird
2. **hostler.** Person who takes care of horses or mules

ef • face (i fās´) *v.,* erase; eliminate

MIRRORS & WINDOWS Many authors have written about the power of nature over human life, often in a negative sense, depicting nature as harsh and unyielding and humans as temporary and frail. What might be positive about this relationship?

The Lonely Cross, c. 1800s. Thomas Cole.
Musée d'Orsay, Paris, France.

A Psalm of Life

by Henry Wadsworth Longfellow

WHAT THE HEART OF THE YOUNG MAN
SAID TO THE PSALMIST

Tell me not, in mournful numbers,
  Life is but an empty dream!—
For the soul is dead that slumbers,
  And things are not what they seem.

5 Life is real! Life is earnest!
  And the grave is not its goal;
Dust thou art, to dust returnest,
  Was not spoken of the soul.

Not enjoyment, and not sorrow,
10   Is our destined end or way;
But to act, that each to-morrow
     Find us farther than to-day.

Art is long, and Time is fleeting,
     And our hearts, though stout and brave,
15 Still, like muffled drums, are beating
     Funeral marches to the grave.

In the world's broad field of battle,
     In the bivouac[1] of Life,
Be not like dumb, driven cattle!
20   Be a hero in the strife!

Trust no Future, howe'er pleasant!
     Let the dead Past bury its dead!
Act,—act in the living Present!
     Heart within, and God o'erhead!

25 Lives of great men all remind us
     We can make our lives <u>sublime</u>,
And, departing, leave behind us
     Footprints on the sands of time;

Footprints, that perhaps another,
30   Sailing o'er life's solemn main,
A <u>forlorn</u> and shipwrecked brother,
     Seeing, shall take heart again.

Let us, then, be up and doing,
     With a heart for any fate;
35 Still achieving, still pursuing,
     Learn to labor and to wait. ❖

---

1. **bivouac.** Temporary camp or shelter

sub • lime (sə blīm´) *adj.,* grand or exalted
for • lorn (fər lôrn´) *adj.,* sad and lonely due to isolation
   or desertion

There is a saying that "Time waits for no man." What does it mean? Do you agree
with this idea?

Refer to Text ▶ ▶ ▶ ▶ ▶ **Reason with Text**

1a. In which lines of "The Tide Rises, the Tide Falls" is the title repeated?

1b. Describe the effect of repeating the title line.

Understand
Find meaning

2a. Which action does the sea perform in "The Tide Rises, the Tide Falls" and when? What function do the footprints in the sand serve in "A Psalm of Life"?

2b. What difference might the poet's age make in how he uses the image of footprints in the sand?

Apply
Use information

3a. How does the speaker describe the traveler's actions in the first poem?

3b. Identify contrast described in lines 10–15. What does it suggest about the traveler?

Analyze
Take things apart

4a. Indicate what the speaker encourages the reader to do in the last stanza of "A Psalm of Life."

4b. Consider how both poems can be read as stories of a journey through life.

Evaluate
Make judgments

5a. What does the speaker in "A Psalm of Life" say our hearts are doing in the fourth stanza? What does the speaker in "The Tide Rises, the Tide Falls" say the traveler does not do in the last stanza?

5b. Propose how works of literature about the cycle of life and death can be both cheerful and mournful.

Create
Bring ideas together

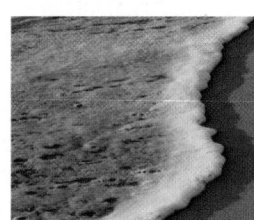

Analyze Literature

Mood and Personification

What is the primary mood, or emotional element, of each poem? How does Longfellow create this emotional response in the reader? Give details to support your response.

In lines 8–9 of "The Tide Rises, the Tide Falls," the waves are said to have "soft, white hands" that wash over footprints in the sand. What is the personification, and what is its effect?

Extend the Text

Writing Options

Creative Writing Design a line of greeting cards that are uplifting in tone. Find photos and drawings in magazines (or create your own) that portray the images in Longfellow's poems, and use them to illustrate your cards. Select several lines of poetry to go with each illustration.

Expository Writing In the poem "Autumn Within," Longfellow writes, "Youth and spring are all about; / It is I that have grown old." Write an essay discussing the similarities and differences between the theme suggested by these lines and the themes in "The Tide Rises, the Tide Falls" and "A Psalm of Life."

Collaborative Learning

Create a Mood Working in a small group, prepare a list of moods (such as happiness, sadness, worry, and relief).

Have each student choose a mood and write a brief passage, in poetry or prose, about it. Read your work aloud and ask classmates to identify the mood.

Lifelong Learning

Research Life Expectancy Conduct research on life expectancy in the United States to determine trends over the last two hundred years and to project trends into the near future. Also identify factors such as gender, race/ethnicity, disease, and lifestyle that affect individual life expectancy. Summarize this information in a newsletter intended for someone your age. Offer recommendations for living a long, healthy life.

 Go to **www.mirrorsandwindows.com** for more.

1. Which of the following best expresses the theme shared by the two poems?
   A. The death of one person is insignificant in the grand scheme of nature.
   B. Each person has only a limited amount of time on Earth.
   C. People should make good use of the time they have.
   D. The body is fated to die, but the soul is eternal.
   E. Nature can be a cruel force that devastates human life.

2. Why does Longfellow repeat the line "The tide rises, the tide falls" in the poem of the same name?
   A. Using this line completes the rhyme scheme in each stanza.
   B. Doing so helps create the setting of the poem.
   C. The poet couldn't think of what else to say.
   D. Repeating this line mimics the regular movement of the tides.
   E. All of the above

3. In "The Tide Rises, the Tide Falls," what does the word *efface* mean?
   A. trace, outline
   B. characterize
   C. erase
   D. follow
   E. cleanse

4. Which of the following lines best summarizes "A Psalm of Life"?
   A. "Life is real! Life is earnest! / And the grave is not its goal."
   B. "Life is but an empty dream!"
   C. "In the world's broad field of battle, / In the bivouac of Life, / Be not like dumb, driven cattle!"
   D. "Lives of great men all remind us / We can make our lives sublime."
   E. "Trust no Future, howe'er pleasant! / Let the dead Past bury its dead!"

5. In "A Psalm of Life," the word *forlorn* in line 31 means
   A. grand or exalted.
   B. poor.
   C. foreign.
   D. in a ragged, disheveled state.
   E. sad and lonely.

6. What is the main idea of "A Psalm of Life"?
   A. No one can escape death; therefore, everyone should prepare for it.
   B. The idea of dying is not frightening to someone who believes in an afterlife.
   C. An individual's life will be meaningless unless he or she performs grand actions for which to be remembered.
   D. What happens to a person's soul after death is not as important as what he or she does while alive.
   E. People should not think about the past or the future, only the present.

7. **Constructed Response:** Both "The Tide Rises, the Tide Falls" and "A Psalm of Life" contain the image of footprints in the sand. Compare and contrast the use and meaning of this image in the poems.

8. **Constructed Response:** Both "The Tide Rises, the Tide Falls" and "A Psalm of Life" examine the idea of human mortality. However, "The Tide Rises" seems to focus more on nature, whereas "A Psalm of Life" seems to focus more on spirituality. What perspectives do the two poems present, and what conclusions do they reach?

TEST-TAKING TIP

Multiple-choice tests sometimes provide answer options such as "None of the above" and "All of the above." Before marking either of these as the correct response, double-check all the other answers. Review each answer individually to verify its accuracy. Don't choose the "none" or "all" response based on your initial reaction to one or two items.

from
Snow-Bound
by John Greenleaf Whittier

John Greenleaf Whittier (1807–1892) was born to devout Quaker parents and raised on his family's homestead in Haverhill, Massachusetts. At the age of nineteen, he had his first poem published in the *Newburyport Free Press.*

William Lloyd Garrison, a well-known abolitionist, was editor of the paper at that time; his influence, along with Whittier's Quaker beliefs, led to Whittier's becoming an active participant in the abolitionist cause. He wrote for and edited several abolitionist newspapers and magazines—work that put his life in danger on several occasions. In addition, Whittier served in the Massachusetts legislature during 1834–1835, ran for the U.S. Congress in 1842 (but lost), and was a founding member of the Republican Party.

Whittier wrote and published throughout his life and helped found the *Atlantic Monthly* magazine in 1857. He turned to writing full time after the Civil War, publishing **"Snow-Bound: A Winter Idyll"** in 1866. This long poem of 759 lines (excerpted here), which was an instant success when published, is representative of Whittier's later work, centering on nature, rural life, and the family.

The sun that brief December day
Rose cheerless over hills of gray,
And, darkly circled, gave at noon
A sadder light than waning moon.
5   Slow tracing down the thickening sky
Its mute and ominous prophecy,
A portent seeming less than threat,
It sank from sight before it set.
A chill no coat, however stout,
10 Of homespun stuff could quite, shut out,
A hard, dull bitterness of cold,
That checked, mid-vein, the circling race
Of life-blood in the sharpened face,
The coming of the snow-storm told.
15 The wind blew east; we heard the roar
Of Ocean on his wintry shore,
And felt the strong pulse throbbing there
Beat with low rhythm our inland air.
Meanwhile we did our nightly chores,—
20 Brought in the wood from out of doors,
Littered the stalls, and from the mows
Raked down the herd's-grass for the cows
Heard the horse whinnying for his corn;
And, sharply clashing horn on horn,
25 Impatient down the stanchion rows
The cattle shake their walnut bows;
While, peering from his early perch
Upon the scaffold's pole of birch,
The cock his crested helmet bent
30 And down his querulous challenge sent.

Unwarmed by any sunset light
The gray day darkened into night,
A night made hoary with the swarm,

A Winter Landscape, c. 1900. Peder Monsted.
Galerie Mensing, Berlin, Germany.

And whirl-dance of the blinding storm,
35 As zigzag, wavering to and fro,
Crossed and recrossed the winged snow
And ere the early bedtime came
The white drift piled the window-frame,
And through the glass the clothes-line posts
40 Looked in like tall and sheeted ghosts.
So all night long the storm roared on
The morning broke without a sun;
In tiny spherule traced with lines
Of Nature's geometric signs,
45 In starry flake, and pellicle,[1]
All day the hoary meteor fell;
And, when the second morning shone,
We looked upon a world unknown,
On nothing we could call our own.
50 Around the glistening wonder bent
The blue walls of the firmament,[2]
No cloud above, no earth below,—
A universe of sky and snow
The old familiar sights of ours
55 Took marvellous shapes; strange domes
        and towers
Rose up where sty or corn-crib stood,
Or garden-wall, or belt of wood;
A smooth white mound the brush-pile showed,
A fenceless drift what once was road;

60 The bridle-post an old man sat
With loose-flung coat and high cocked hat;
The well-curb had a Chinese roof;
And even the long sweep, high aloof,
In its slant splendor, seemed to tell
65 Of Pisa's leaning miracle.[3]

A prompt, decisive man, no breath
Our father wasted: "Boys, a path!"
Well pleased, (for when did farmer boy
Count such a summons less than joy?)
70 Our buskins[4] on our feet we drew;
With mittened hands, and caps drawn low,
To guard our necks and ears from snow,
We cut the solid whiteness through.
And, where the drift was deepest, made
75 A tunnel walled and overlaid
With dazzling crystal: we had read
Of rare Aladdin's wondrous cave,[5]
And to our own his name we gave,
With many a wish the luck were ours
80 To test his lamp's supernal powers.

---

1. **pellicle.** Thin film that reflects light
2. **firmament.** Heavens
3. **Pisa's leaning miracle.** Leaning Tower of Pisa in Italy
4. **buskins.** Laced boots reaching midcalf or higher
5. **Aladdin's wondrous cave.** In *The Book of One Thousand and One Nights,* Aladdin finds the djinn's (genie's) lamp in a magical cave.

Marsden Hartley

Marsden Hartley (1877–1943) was born in Lewiston, Maine, during the winter of 1877. He left home at age fifteen to attend the Cleveland Art Institute, and in his early twenties, he moved to New York City to attend the National Academy of Design. In New York, he associated with some of the leading writers and artists of the early twentieth century and soon established himself as one of the United States' foremost painters.

As an artist, Hartley had a nomadic, roving lifestyle. Always longing for a permanent home, he continued to identify strongly with Maine, aspiring to one day be considered "the painter of Maine." As a result, much of his work, such as the painting *Winter Chaos—Blizzard* on the next page, depicts the state's rugged, sometimes harsh landscape.

Hartley participated in two artistic movements during his life. He began as a *Regionalist* painter, portraying the common people and settings of his native Maine. Then as a young man, he embraced *Modernism,* a movement that abandoned traditional forms and explored new, often abstract modes of expression. He later returned to his Regionalist roots, painting rugged landscapes.

Critical Viewing Hartley hoped to capture in his painting the spiritual power of nature, as expressed by Transcendentalist writers Ralph Waldo Emerson and Henry David Thoreau (see Part 2 of this unit). What does the painting *Winter Chaos—Blizzard* suggest about Hartley's view of winter? What ideas and feelings come to mind when you look at this painting?

We reached the barn with merry din,
And roused the prisoned brutes within.
The old horse thrust his long head out,
And grave with wonder gazed about;
85 The cock his lusty greeting said,
And forth his speckled harem led;
The oxen lashed their tails, and hooked,
And mild reproach of hunger looked;
The horned patriarch of the sheep,
90 Like Egypt's Amun[6] roused from sleep,
Shook his sage head with gesture mute,
And emphasized with stamp of foot.

All day the gusty north-wind bore
The loosening drift its breath before;
95 Low circling round its southern zone,
The sun through dazzling snow-mist shone.
No church-bell lent its Christian tone
To the savage air, no social smoke
Curled over woods of snow-hung oak.
100 A solitude made more intense
By dreary-voiced elements,
The shrieking of the mindless wind,
The moaning tree-boughs swaying blind,
And on the glass the unmeaning beat

105 Of ghostly finger-tips of sleet.
Beyond the circle of our hearth
No welcome sound of toil or mirth
Unbound the spell, and testified
Of human life and thought outside.
110 We minded that the sharpest ear
The buried brooklet could not hear,
The music of whose liquid lip
Had been to us companionship,
And, in our lonely life, had grown
115 To have an almost human tone.

As night drew on, and, from the crest
Of wooded knolls that ridged the west,
The sun, a snow-blown traveller, sank
From sight beneath the smothering bank,
120 We piled, with care, our nightly stack
Of wood against the chimney-back,—
The oaken log, green, huge, and thick,
And on its top the stout back-stick;
The knotty forestick laid apart,
125 And filled between with curious art

---

6. **Egypt's Amun.** Most powerful of the ancient Egyptian gods, often depicted with the head of a ram

Winter Chaos—Blizzard, c. 1909–1911. Marsden Hartley.
Philadelphia Museum of Art, Philadelphia, Pennsylvania.

Dead white, save where some sharp
    ravine
Took shadow, or the sombre green
Of hemlocks turned to pitchy black
Against the whiteness at their back.
For such a world and such a night
Most fitting that unwarming light,
Which only seemed where'er it fell
To make the coldness visible.

Shut in from all the world without,
We sat the clean-winged hearth
    about,
Content to let the north-wind roar
In baffled rage at pane and door,
While the red logs before us beat
The frost-line back with tropic heat;
And ever, when a louder blast
Shook beam and rafter as it passed,
The merrier up its roaring draught
The great throat of the chimney
    laughed;
The house-dog on his paws
    outspread

The ragged brush; then, hovering near,
We watched the first red blaze appear,
Heard the sharp crackle, caught the gleam
On whitewashed wall and sagging beam,
130 Until the old, rude-furnished room
Burst, flower-like, into rosy bloom;
While radiant with a mimic flame
Outside the sparkling drift became,
And through the bare-boughed lilac-tree
135 Our own warm hearth seemed blazing free.
The crane and pendent trammels[7] showed,
The Turks' heads on the andirons glowed;
While childish fancy, prompt to tell
The meaning of the miracle,
140 Whispered the old rhyme: *"Under the tree,*
When fire outdoors burns merrily,
There the witches are making tea."
The moon above the eastern wood
Shone at its full; the hill-range stood
145 Transfigured in the silver flood,
Its blown snows flashing cold and keen,

Laid to the fire his drowsy head,
The cat's dark silhouette on the wall
A couchant tiger's seemed to fall;
And, for the winter fireside meet,
170 Between the andirons' straddling feet,
The mug of cider simmered slow,
The apples sputtered in a row,
And, close at hand, the basket stood
With nuts from brown October's wood.

. . .

175 So days went on: a week had passed
Since the great world was heard from last.
The Almanac we studied o'er,
Read and reread our little store,
Of books and pamphlets, scarce a score;
180 One harmless novel, mostly hid
From younger eyes, a book forbid,
And poetry, (or good or bad,
A single book was all we had,)

---

7. **trammels.** Adjustable pothooks on a fireplace crane

Where Ellwood's[8] meek, drab-skirted Muse,
185 A stranger to the heathen Nine,[9]
     Sang, with a somewhat nasal whine,
The wars of David and the Jews.
At last the floundering carrier bore
The village paper to our door.
190 Lo! broadening outward as we read,
To warmer zones the horizon spread;
In panoramic length unrolled
We saw the marvels that it told.
Before us passed the painted Creeks,
195   And daft McGregor on his raids
         In Costa Rica's everglades.
And up Taygetos winding slow
Rode Ypsilanti's Mainote Greeks,[10]
A Turk's head at each saddle-bow
200 Welcome to us its week-old news,
Its corner for the rustic Muse,
     Its monthly gauge of snow and rain,
Its record, mingling in a breath

The wedding bell and dirge of death;
205 Jest, anecdote, and love-lorn tale,
The latest culprit sent to jail;
Its hue and cry of stolen and lost,
Its vendue sales and goods at cost,
     And traffic calling loud for gain.
210 We felt the stir of hall and street,
The pulse of life that round us beat;
The chill embargo of the snow
Was melted in the genial glow;
Wide swung again our ice-locked door,
215 And all the world was ours once more! ❖

---

8. **Ellwood's.** Thomas Ellwood (1639–1714), an English Quaker poet who wrote religious poetry, most famously *Davideis* about the life of King David
9. **Muse . . . Nine.** Nine Greek muses, goddesses of the arts. The "drab-skirted Muse" here implies that Ellwood's poetry was rather conventional or boring.
10. **Ypsilanti's Mainote Greeks.** In the early 1800s, Prince Alexander Ypsilanti attempted to liberate Greece from the Ottoman Empire (Turkey).

 **MIRRORS & WINDOWS** Have you ever been snowbound or otherwise forced to stay indoors by the weather? If so, what was your experience like? If not, what would you imagine such an experience to be like?

Refer and Reason

1. In lines 1–18, what is revealed about the weather? At this point, how does the weather affect the speaker and his family?

2. How is the snow described? Identify the descriptions that give the impression of the snow being supernatural, magical, or otherworldly.

3. What do the speaker and his family do while they are trapped indoors? How might such a scene be different in modern times? Explain.

Writing Options

1. Write a paragraph describing a scene in a modern home where the family members cannot leave due to bad weather. Choose your tone for the description; it can be warmly sentimental, like Whittier's poem, or it can be humorous or frightening. Be sure to include sensory details so your reader can picture the scene.

2. Select two of the allusions to other stories or historical events that Whittier makes in his poem. Research the allusions to learn more about them; then write an essay explaining what they are and how they pertain to the poem.

 Go to **www.mirrorsandwindows.com** for more.

The real flowering of Romanticism in American literature came in the New England literary movement called **Transcendentalism.** At the core of Transcendentalism was the belief in a realm of spiritual or transcendent truths beyond what humans can know through their senses. These truths could be apprehended in moments of heightened contemplation or by living close to nature.

Because the Transcendentalists believed each person capable of intuiting truths directly, they opposed any authority beyond that of the individual conscience, including cultural and social conventions. For the first time in America, "the self" became something to celebrate rather than deny. By studying the self, a person could know the universe.

The Transcendentalist movement attracted many of the leading intellectuals of the day, including Ralph Waldo Emerson, Henry David Thoreau, Bronson Alcott, Margaret Fuller, and Elizabeth Palmer Peabody. While the movement lacked an official leader, Emerson and Thoreau emerged as its most prominent voices.

Ralph Waldo Emerson wanted to change how people thought, advising them to trust their own better natures. In his essay "Self-Reliance," he stated, "Nothing is at last sacred, but the integrity of our own mind." Henry David Thoreau, a protégé of Emerson, carried out an experiment in self-reliance, building a small cabin in the woods near Walden Pond to live simply and in close contact with nature. *Walden,* a record of this experience, was a clear statement of American individualism and later became an inspiration to environmentalists.

A Catskill Stream, 1867. Asher Brown Durand. Brooklyn Museum of Art, Brooklyn, New York.

The Essay Defined

An **essay** is a short nonfiction work that presents a single main idea, or *thesis,* about a particular topic. The essay is uniquely designed for reflection because it is free of the limitations that shape other literary forms.

It is fitting that Ralph Waldo Emerson and Henry David Thoreau became masters of this literary form. During a time of rapid industrial growth and social change in the United States, intellectuals turned inward to examine their values and beliefs. Reaction gave rise to the philosophical movements such as Transcendentalism, which resisted the materialism and expansionism of the age. The introspective, spiritual nature of this movement provided fertile ground for the flowering of the essay form.

Over time, the essay has become increasingly popular and accessible to the general reader. Most of us are comfortable with the first-person voice that seems to echo our own thoughts or speak to us in instructive tones. For the writer, the essay is a way of trying on a more intimate, unconstrained voice: many novelists, poets, and dramatists are also accomplished essayists.

Types of Essays

Essays are as varied as the people who write them. If you have ever read the editorial section of a newspaper or a magazine article with a markedly personal tone, you have already encountered the essay form. The essay writer asks What do I think about this matter? and Why?

There are three broad categories of essay, and they may overlap in some instances. The type of essay is determined by what the author hopes to accomplish through the essay, or the writer's **purpose.**

An *expository,* or *informative, essay* explores a topic with the goal of informing or enlightening the reader. Emerson's "Nature" is an example of an expository essay. The author's formal tone is compatible with his philosophical bent. Consider such broad statements as "Nature always wears the colors of the spirit" and "The reason why the world lacks unity, and

lies broken and in heaps, is because man is disunited with himself." The narrative voice is easily identified with Emerson the man and minister. It is an authoritative voice; the writer's aim is to transmute his personal experience and observations into universal truths.

> *"The essayist is a self-liberated man, sustained by the childish belief that everything he thinks about, everything that happens to him, is of general interest."*
>
> —E. B. WHITE, AWARD-WINNING ESSAYIST AND NOVELIST

A *persuasive essay* aims to convince the reader to accept a certain point of view. Such essays are often weighted with **abstract language,** words or phrases that cannot be directly perceived by the senses: *government, power, conscience.* The writer shows his or her colors through bold declarations. For instance, Thoreau begins his "Civil Disobedience" with the proclamation "That government is best which governs not at all," a thesis developed throughout the essay. Hoping to persuade, Thoreau advances his argument, marshalling charged words and phrases meant to move readers to accept his main idea and even to take positive action, as he did when refusing to pay the poll tax.

A *personal essay* explores a topic related to the life or interests of the writer. Personal essays are characterized by an intimate and informal style and tone. The writer makes no pretense that his or her experience or viewpoint is universal. You can find many examples of the personal essay in magazines, on the Internet, and in anthologies.

Elements of the Essay

Introduction

Whether an essay is formal or informal, it includes an *introduction.* The introductory paragraph or paragraphs catch the reader's attention, state the topic, and establish the background for the discussion. It is here that the author usually states the thesis of the essay.

Thesis Statement

The **thesis** is the main idea that is supported in a work of nonfiction. It contains the kernel of the essay and tells the reader the writer's planned focus. The thesis of the literary work may be implied or directly stated. A writer typically plants this central statement within the first two paragraphs of the essay, but you may have to look elsewhere for the sentence that best states the main idea. Sometimes, you will find variations on the thesis.

In "Civil Disobedience," having established his position on government—"That government is best which governs not at all"—Thoreau later comments, "A government in which the majority rule in all cases cannot be based on justice, even as far as men understand it." He asks for "a better government," if we must have one at all. The examples he presents all serve to develop his thesis about government versus autonomy, while modifying his initial sweeping statement.

Argument

An **argument** is a form of **persuasion** that makes a case to the audience for accepting or rejecting a proposition or course of action. The writer appeals to readers by citing authorities and statistics, using logic, and referring to personal experience. In analyzing the author's viewpoint, you look at the language and the content of the essay. You identify opinions, facts, and possible bias in the argument. When you understand the argument, you can then formulate your own response to it.

Rhetoric

The author may also employ a **rhetorical device,** a technique used by a speaker or writer to achieve a particular effect, especially to persuade or influence. Common rhetorical devices include **parallelism, repetition,** and **rhetorical questions.**

Emerson uses the first two of these when he asks "What is a day? What is a year? What is summer?" Thoreau is posing a rhetorical question when he asks "Can there not be a government in which majorities do not virtually decide right and wrong, but conscience?" He does not expect an answer; he phrases his argument as a question, hoping to strike a sympathetic chord in the reader.

Conclusion

The *conclusion* of the essay returns to the thesis. The writer uses this final section of the essay to underscore the significance of the argument. It is an opportunity to summarize the main points and deliver some powerful remarks upon which the reader may reflect. The conclusion may even be designed to startle readers and force them to reconsider the entire topic from a new vantage point.

HOW TO READ

An Essay

Find the main idea. Ask yourself what the writer wants you to know, think, or feel after reading the essay. Then look for details to support what the writer says. Evaluate the details to see if they make sense.

Distinguish fact from opinion. The details that support a writer's main idea are facts and opinions. A *fact* is a statement that can be proven either true or false. An *opinion* expresses an attitude or desire. You can agree or disagree with an opinion but not prove it true or false.

Recognize bias. *Bias* is a personal judgment about something, a mental leaning in one direction or the other. Bias can be evident in what the writer says directly or in the details he or she leaves out—the things left unsaid.

Question the author. If you do not understand something the writer is telling you, ask questions such as these: What does the writer mean? Why does the writer say this? What support does the writer give for this statement? Record your questions in a notebook or question log.

Ralph Waldo Emerson

> *"Finish each day and be done with it. You have done what you could."*

Ralph Waldo Emerson (1803–1882) was considered the greatest American thinker of his time. Born in Boston, he attended Boston Latin School as a child, where he received a classical education; at the age of fourteen, he entered Harvard, graduating with honors in 1821. After teaching school and studying for the ministry, he was ordained a Unitarian minister in 1829 and served as junior pastor of Boston's Second Church. That same year, he married Ellen Tucker, who died of tuberculosis just eighteen months later.

Ellen's death brought about a religious crisis for Emerson, prompting him to resign from Second Church. He traveled to England in 1832 and developed relationships with such great thinkers and writers as economist John Stuart Mill, essayist Thomas Carlyle, and poets Samuel Taylor Coleridge and William Wordsworth. With these individuals, Emerson explored human's relationship to nature and society and the perfectibility of the human spirit.

Emerson returned to the United States in 1834, ready to begin a new career as a lecturer. In Boston, he surrounded himself with a circle of poets, artists, and philosophers, including Henry David Thoreau, Nathaniel Hawthorne, Margaret Fuller, and Bronson Alcott and his daughter Louisa May. With these individuals, Emerson founded the Transcendentalist Club, a group who believed in the deep spiritual connection between humanity and nature. By concentrating on their innermost thoughts and feelings, Emerson said, individuals could glimpse the spirit of the universe. With his literary friends, Emerson founded a magazine called *The Dial,* which became an important vehicle for Transcendentalist thought.

Although Emerson was criticized for leaving the ministry, he held strongly to his belief in personal intuition and flexibility. His views led him to develop a profound respect for the individualism that helped shape the American spirit. "To believe your own thought," he said, "to believe that what is true for you in your private heart is true for all men,—that is genius."

In 1835, Emerson moved to Concord, Massachusetts, the first rural artist's colony and the first community to offer a spiritual and cultural alternative to American materialism. There he married Lydia Jackson, and the two raised four children. During their fifty-year marriage, the Emersons entertained many of the leading intellectuals of the day. Today, Emerson is considered a symbol of optimism and independent thinking. He influenced a long line of American poets, including Emily Dickinson, Walt Whitman, Edwin Arlington Robinson, Wallace Stevens, and Robert Frost.

Noted Works

Nature (1836)

"The American Scholar" (speech, 1837)

"The Divinity School Address" (speech, 1838)

"Self-Reliance," in *Essays: First Series* (1841)

"Experience" and "Politics," in *Essays: Second Series* (1844)

The Conduct of Life (1860)

from Nature

An Essay by Ralph Waldo Emerson

The Rhodora

A Lyric Poem by Ralph Waldo Emerson

Build Background

Literary Context In 1836, Emerson published a short book (just ninety-five pages) called *Nature,* in which he expressed the basic principles of the Transcendentalist movement. Never considering himself a philosopher, Emerson felt his purpose in writing was to relate what he had experienced in the world: what he had seen, thought, and felt. He preferred to think of his essays as offering "revelations," from which others would infer meaning.

In the excerpts presented here, Emerson describes the thoughts and feelings triggered by a walk through the fields and woods. In the first section, the forest renews his reason and his faith, and he senses a unity with earth's bounty. In the second section, Emerson notes that humans have distanced themselves from the natural environment by relating to it mostly through the intellect. In the third section, the writer explores ways in which human beings can renew their ties to nature.

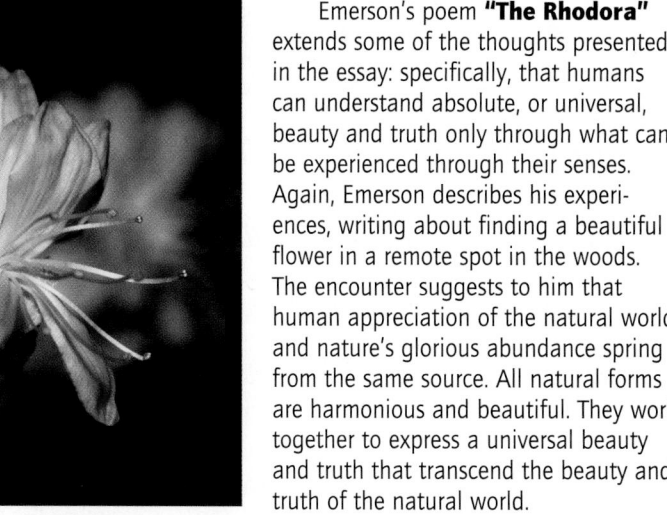

Emerson's poem **"The Rhodora"** extends some of the thoughts presented in the essay: specifically, that humans can understand absolute, or universal, beauty and truth only through what can be experienced through their senses. Again, Emerson describes his experiences, writing about finding a beautiful flower in a remote spot in the woods. The encounter suggests to him that human appreciation of the natural world and nature's glorious abundance spring from the same source. All natural forms are harmonious and beautiful. They work together to express a universal beauty and truth that transcend the beauty and truth of the natural world.

Reader's Context How can an activity as simple as walking in the woods change your perspective on life?

Analyze Literature

Argument and Theme
An **argument** is a form of persuasion that makes a case to an audience for accepting or rejecting a proposition or course of action.

A **theme** is a central message or perception about life that is revealed through a literary work. The theme may be *stated,* or presented directly, or it may be *implied,* leaving the reader to infer it.

Set Purpose

In his roles as teacher, minister, lecturer, philosopher, and poet, Emerson seemed intent on leading others to self-discovery. As a writer, he believed sharing his own experiences would help others find truth and meaning in life. As you read the excerpts from *Nature,* write down the arguments Emerson makes and what evidence he uses to support them. Then consider how these arguments relate to the themes that run through both the essay and the poem.

Preview Vocabulary

exhilaration, 159
sanctity, 159
perennial, 159
calamity, 159
blithe, 159
temperance, 159
contempt, 159

Springtime, c. 1875. Christian Zacho.

from *Nature*

by Ralph Waldo Emerson

Standing on the bare ground,—my head bathed by the blithe air and uplifted into infinite space,—all mean egotism vanishes.

To speak truly, few adult persons can see nature. Most persons do not see the sun. At least they have a very superficial seeing. The sun illuminates only the eye of the man, but shines into the eye and the heart of the child. The lover of nature is he whose inward and outward senses are still truly adjusted to each other; who has retained the spirit of infancy even into the era of manhood. His intercourse with heaven and earth, becomes part of his daily food. In the presence of nature, a wild delight runs through the man, in spite of real sorrows. Nature says,—he is my creature, and maugre all his impertinent griefs,[1] he shall be glad with me. Not the sun or the summer

---

1. **maugre . . . griefs.** Despite all his unrelated griefs

alone, but every hour and season yields its tribute of delight; for every hour and change corresponds to and authorizes a different state of the mind, from breathless noon to grimmest midnight. Nature is a setting that fits equally well a comic or a mourning piece. In good health, the air is a cordial[2] of incredible virtue. Crossing a bare common, in snow puddles, at twilight, under a clouded sky, without having in my thoughts any occurrence of special good fortune, I have enjoyed a perfect <u>exhilaration</u>. I am glad to the brink of fear. In the woods too, a man casts off his years, as the snake his slough, and at what period soever of life, is always a child. In the woods, is perpetual youth. Within these plantations of God, a decorum and <u>sanctity</u> reign, a <u>perennial</u> festival is dressed, and the guest sees not how he should tire of them in a thousand years. In the woods, we return to reason and faith. There I feel that nothing can befall me in life,—no disgrace, no <u>calamity</u>, (leaving me my eyes,) which nature cannot repair. Standing on the bare ground,—my head bathed by the <u>blithe</u> air, and uplifted into infinite space,—all mean egotism vanishes. I become a transparent eyeball; I am nothing; I see all; the currents of the Universal Being circulate through me; I am part or particle of God. The name of the nearest friend sounds then foreign and accidental: to be brothers, to be acquaintances,—master or servant, is then a trifle and a disturbance. I am the lover of uncontained and immortal beauty. In the wilderness, I find something more dear and connate[3] than in streets or villages. In the tranquil landscape, and especially in the distant line of the horizon, man beholds somewhat as beautiful as his own nature.

The greatest delight which the fields and woods minister, is the suggestion of an occult relation between man and the vegetable. I am not alone and unacknowledged. They nod to me, and I to them. The waving of the boughs in the storm, is new to me and old. It takes me by surprise, and yet is not unknown. Its effect is like that of a higher thought or a better emotion coming over me, when I deemed I was thinking justly or doing right.

Yet it is certain that the power to produce this delight, does not reside in nature, but in man, or in a harmony of both. It is necessary to use these pleasures with great <u>temperance</u>. For, nature is not always tricked[4] in holiday attire, but the same scene which yesterday breathed perfume and glittered as for the frolic of the nymphs, is overspread with melancholy today. Nature always wears the colors of the spirit. To a man laboring under calamity, the heat of his own fire hath sadness in it. Then, there is a kind of <u>contempt</u> of the landscape felt by him who has just lost by death a dear friend. The sky is less grand as it shuts down over less worth in the population. . . .

> *The power to produce this delight, does not reside in nature, but in man, or in a harmony of both.*

I shall therefore conclude this essay with some traditions of man and nature, which a certain poet sang to me; and which, as they have always been in the world, and perhaps reappear to every bard, may be both history and prophecy. . . .

"A man is a god in ruins. When men are innocent, life shall be longer, and shall pass into the immortal, as gently as we awake from dreams. Now, the world would be insane and

---

2. **cordial.** Stimulating drink
3. **connate.** Kindred; similar
4. **tricked.** Dressed

---

ex • hil • a • ra • tion (eks il′ ə rā′ shən) *n.*, joy and excitement
sanc • ti • ty (sāŋk′ tə tē) *n.*, holiness
per • en • ni • al (pʉr en′ ē 'l) *adj.*, repeated every year
ca • lam • i • ty (kə lam′ ə tē) *n.*, disaster
blithe (blī<u>th</u>) *adj.*, happy; blissful
tem • per • ance (tem′ pʉr əns) *n.*, moderation; restraint
con • tempt (kən tempt′) *n.*, strong dislike; lack of respect

rabid, if these disorganizations should last for hundreds of years. It is kept in check by death and infancy. Infancy is the perpetual Messiah,[5] which comes into the arms of fallen men, and pleads with them to return to paradise.

"Man is the dwarf of himself. Once he was permeated[6] and dissolved by spirit. He filled nature with his overflowing currents. Out from him sprang the sun and moon; from man, the sun; from woman, the moon. The laws of his mind, the periods of his actions externized themselves into day and night, into the year and the seasons. But, having made for himself this huge shell, his waters retired; he no longer fills the veins and veinlets; he is shrunk to a drop. He sees, that the structure still fits him, but fits him colossally. Say, rather, once it fitted him, now it corresponds to him from far and on high. He adores timidly his own work. Now is man the follower of the sun, and woman the follower of the moon. Yet sometimes he starts in his slumber, and wonders at himself and his house, and muses strangely at the resemblance betwixt him and it. He perceives that if his law is still paramount, if still he have elemental power, if his word is sterling yet in nature, it is not conscious power, it is not inferior but superior to his will. It is Instinct." Thus my Orphic poet[7] sang.

> *At present, man applies to nature but half his force. He works on the world with his understanding alone.*

At present, man applies to nature but half his force. He works on the world with his understanding alone. He lives in it, and masters it by a penny-wisdom; and he that works most in it, is but a half-man, and whilst his arms are strong and his digestion good, his mind is imbruted, and he is a selfish savage. His relation to nature, his power over it, is through the understanding; as by manure; the economic use of fire, wind, water, and the mariner's needle; steam, coal, chemical agriculture; the repairs of the human body by the dentist and the surgeon. This is such a resumption of power, as if a banished king should buy his territories inch by inch, instead of vaulting at once into his throne. . . .

The problem of restoring to the world original and eternal beauty, is solved by the redemption of the soul. The ruin or the blank, that we see when we look at nature, is in our own eye. The axis of vision is not coincident with the axis of things, and so they appear not transparent but opaque. The reason why the world lacks unity, and lies broken and in heaps, is, because man is disunited with himself. He cannot be a naturalist, until he satisfies all the demands of the spirit. Love is as much its demand, as perception. Indeed, neither can be perfect without the other. In the uttermost meaning of the words, thought is devout, and devotion is thought. Deep calls unto deep. But in actual life, the marriage is not celebrated. There are innocent men who worship God after the tradition of their fathers, but their sense of duty has not yet extended to the use of all their faculties. And there are patient naturalists, but they freeze their subject under the wintry light of the understanding. Is not prayer also a study of truth,—a sally of the soul into the unfound infinite? No man ever prayed heartily, without learning something. But when a faithful thinker, resolute to detach every object from personal relations, and see it in the light of thought, shall, at the same time, kindle science with the fire of the holiest affections, then will God go forth anew into the creation.

It will not need, when the mind is prepared for study, to search for objects. The invariable

---

5. **Messiah.** Jesus
6. **permeated.** Filled with
7. **my Orphic poet.** Affectionate reference to A. Bronson Alcott, a fellow Transcendentalist, whose philosophy on the decline of humanity is presented in this final section; *Orphic* is derived from *Orpheus,* a poet and musician in Greek mythology.

mark of wisdom is to see the miraculous in the common. What is a day? What is a year? What is summer? What is woman? What is a child? What is sleep? To our blindness, these things seem unaffecting. We make fables to hide the baldness of the fact and conform it, as we say, to the higher law of the mind. But when the fact is seen under the light of an idea, the gaudy fable fades and shrivels. We behold the real higher law. To the wise, therefore, a fact is true poetry, and the most beautiful of fables. These wonders are brought to our own door. You also are a man. Man and woman, and their social life, poverty, labor, sleep, fear, fortune, are known to you. Learn that none of these things is superficial, but that each phenomenon has its roots in the faculties and affections of the mind. Whilst the abstract question occupies your intellect, nature brings it in the concrete to be solved by your hands. It were a wise inquiry for the closet, to compare, point by point, especially at remarkable crises in life, our daily history, with the rise and progress of ideas in the mind.

> *The invariable mark of wisdom is to see the miraculous in the common.*

So shall we come to look at the world with new eyes. It shall answer the endless inquiry of the intellect,—What is truth? and of the affections,—What is good? by yielding itself passive to the educated Will. Then shall come to pass what my poet said; "Nature is not fixed but fluid. Spirit alters, moulds, makes it. The immobility or bruteness of nature, is the absence of spirit; to pure spirit, it is fluid, it is volatile, it is obedient. Every spirit builds itself a house; and beyond its house a world; and beyond its world, a heaven. Know then, that the world exists for you. For you is the phenomenon perfect. What we are, that only can we see. All that Adam[8] had, all that Caesar[9] could, you have and can do. Adam called his house, heaven and earth; Caesar called his house, Rome; you perhaps call yours, a cobler's trade; a hundred acres of ploughed land; or a scholar's garret. Yet line for line and point for point, your dominion is as great as theirs, though without fine names. Build, therefore, your own world. As fast as you conform your life to the pure idea in your mind, that will unfold its great proportions. A correspondent revolution in things will attend the influx of the spirit. So fast will disagreeable appearances, swine, spiders, snakes, pests, madhouses, prisons, enemies, vanish; they are temporary and shall be no more seen. The sordor and filths of nature, the sun shall dry up, and the wind exhale. As when the summer comes from the south; the snow-banks melt, and the face of the earth becomes green before it, so shall the advancing spirit create its ornaments along its path, and carry with it the beauty it visits, and the song which enchants it; it shall draw beautiful faces, warm hearts, wise discourse, and heroic acts, around its way, until evil is no more seen. The kingdom of man over nature, which cometh not with observation,— a dominion such as now is beyond his dream of God,—he shall enter without more wonder than the blind man feels who is gradually restored to sight." ❖

---

8. **Adam.** In the Bible, the first man
9. **Caesar.** Julius Caesar, famous emperor of the Roman Empire

MIRRORS & WINDOWS

Emerson wrote, "Nature always wears the colors of the spirit." When have you felt that nature has reflected your mood? Do the changing seasons affect your outlook on life?

The Rhodora
by Ralph Waldo Emerson

On Being Asked, Whence[1] Is the Flower?

In May, when sea-winds pierced our solitudes,
I found the fresh Rhodora[2] in the woods,
Spreading its leafless blooms in a damp nook,
To please the desert and the sluggish brook.
5   The purple petals, fallen in the pool,
Made the black water with their beauty gay;
Here might the red-bird come his plumes
    to cool,
And court the flower that cheapens his array.

Rhodora! if the sages[3] ask thee why
10   This charm is wasted on the earth and sky,
Tell them, dear, that if eyes were made
    for seeing,
Then Beauty is its own excuse for being:
Why thou wert there,[4] O rival of the rose!
I never thought to ask, I never knew;
15   But, in my simple ignorance, suppose
The self-same Power that brought me there
    brought you. ❖

---

1. **Whence.** From where
2. **Rhodora.** Deciduous plant, native to northeastern United States, that bears pink flowers in spring
3. **sages.** Wise older people
4. **thou wert there.** You were there

MIRRORS & WINDOWS Why is it important for human beings to reflect on their relation to the natural world? Considering today's world, how may that bond have changed since Emerson's time?

Refer to Text ▷ ▷ ▷ ▷ ▷ Reason with Text

1a. According to Emerson, where does the power to delight in nature dwell (paragraph 3 of the essay)?

1b. Emerson says that, in the distance, "man beholds" his own nature. Suggest why people look toward the far horizon to find something that comes from within them (paragraph 1).

Understand
Find meaning

2a. In "The Rhodora," to whom does the speaker address lines 9–16? List the words that are clues to this.

2b. Which flower would the speaker probably find more pleasing: the rhodora blooming alone in the woods or an orchid blossoming in a greenhouse? Explain.

Apply
Use information

3a. In the poem, for whose benefit does the plant spread its blossoms?

3b. Determine whether the speaker agrees with the sages that the flower's charm is wasted because of its isolated spot.

Analyze
Take things apart

4a. In the essay, identify what Emerson says will happen when humans adapt their lives to the "the pure idea" in their minds.

4b. Do you agree that when humans renew their spiritual link to the natural world, evil will disappear? Explain your response.

Evaluate
Make judgments

5a. How does Emerson describe a "lover of nature" (paragraph 1 of the essay)?

5b. Imagine that you are in a natural setting, such as a forest, seashore, or park. Summarize how the surroundings or sensations might influence your inner feelings.

Create
Bring ideas together

Analyze Literature

Argument and Theme

What is the primary argument Emerson makes in these excerpts from *Nature?* What evidence does he provide to support the argument? Is his argument convincing? Why or why not?

Themes relating to humans' relationship with nature run throughout Emerson's writing. What themes does *Nature* contain? What is the theme of "The Rhodora"? Are these themes stated or implied?

Extend the Text

Writing Options

Creative Writing Who is the speaker in "The Rhodora"? Write a brief character sketch of the voice behind the poem. Use details from the poem to create your portrait.

Expository Writing Write a comparison-and-contrast essay in which you point out the differences and similarities between *Nature* and "The Rhodora." Use examples from each selection to support your ideas.

Collaborative Learning

Teach a Lesson Suppose that a middle school class studying American history and noted American writers needs some help in appreciating Emerson's essay *Nature*. With a partner or in a group, create an outline of the main ideas in the essay, showing how they relate to each other.

Critical Literacy

Act as an Interpreter Imagine that Ralph Waldo Emerson has agreed to be interviewed on TV. Since he still has a nineteenth-century perspective on life, you have been asked to interpret his ideas, making his responses clear to his present-day audience. Prepare a transcript that includes the interviewer's questions, Emerson's responses, and your interpretations.

 Go to **www.mirrorsandwindows.com** for more.

Understand the Concept

Writing that does too much of one thing often loses the attention of readers. For instance, a passage in which most of the sentences are **simple sentences,** following the subject-predicate model, may sound stiff or stilted when read. On the other hand, a passage of mostly **complex** or **compound sentences,** which have multiple independent and dependent clauses, may become difficult and tiresome to read.

Consider the following pairs of examples. In each pair, the *a* sentences (1a, 2a, and 3a) are simple sentences, following the subject-predicate form. Each of the *b* sentences (1b, 2b, and 3b) provides the same information but is written in another sentence structure, either compound or complex. In each pair, which sentence, *a* or *b*, seems more readable?

EXAMPLES

1a. Emerson wrote his thoughts in his journal. They provided ideas for many of his lectures. [Two *simple sentences,* each an independent clause]

1b. Emerson wrote his thoughts in his journal, and they provided ideas for many of his lectures. [One *compound sentence,* containing two independent clauses joined by a coordinating conjunction (*and*)]

2a. *Nature* is a significant example of Transcendentalist literature. It remains influential today. [Two *simple sentences*]

2b. *Nature* is a significant example of Transcendentalist literature that remains influential today. [One *complex sentence,* containing an independent clause and a relative clause (introduced by *that*)]

3a. Emerson and Thoreau had similar views on important matters. Emerson was recognized during his lifetime. Thoreau was not. [Three *simple sentences*]

3b. Although Emerson and Thoreau had similar views on important matters, Emerson was recognized during his lifetime and Thoreau was

not. [One *complex sentence,* containing a subordinate clause (introduced by *although*) and two independent clauses joined by a coordinating conjunction (*and*)]

You likely thought the *b* sentence in each pair was more readable, or perhaps you preferred some combination of *a* and *b* sentences. Most readers do not like to read all simple sentences, like the *a* examples. Variety among types of sentences makes writing more interesting and thus understandable.

Apply the Skill

Identify Sentence Varieties

Decide whether each of the following sentences is a simple sentence (*S*), a compound sentence (*CM*), or a complex sentence (*CP*).

1. Emerson attended Boston Latin School as a child, where he received a classical education.
2. He taught school for several years, and then he became an ordained minister.
3. After his wife's sudden death, he resigned his ministry.
4. He traveled to England in 1832.
5. When he returned to the United States, he was ready to begin a new career as a lecturer.

Improve Sentence Variety

Rewrite the following passage, varying sentence structure to make it more interesting.

Emerson published a short book in 1836. It was called *Nature*. It expressed the basic principles of Transcendentalism. Emerson wrote it to tell others what he had experienced in the world. He referred to his essays as "revelations." He wanted others to infer meaning from them. He believed people were too distanced from nature. He thought they should renew their ties with nature.

Concord Hymn

A Lyric Poem by Ralph Waldo Emerson

Build Background

Historical Context Ralph Waldo Emerson wrote **"Concord Hymn"** in 1837 for the dedication of the Obelisk, a monument honoring the soldiers who died while fighting the British during the Battle of Lexington and Concord. That battle, which occurred on April 19, 1775, was the first of the American Revolution and became known as "the shot heard 'round the world."

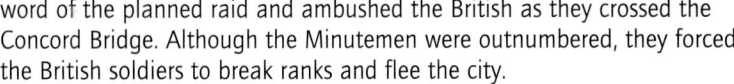

   The battle started when British Lieutenant Colonel Francis Smith planned to commandeer military supplies stored in Concord. The American Minutemen had received word of the planned raid and ambushed the British as they crossed the Concord Bridge. Although the Minutemen were outnumbered, they forced the British soldiers to break ranks and flee the city.

   Emerson's poem—written as a *hymn,* or song of praise or joy—actually was sung to the melody of a traditional Christian hymn during Concord's Fourth of July celebration in 1837.

Reader's Context The Vietnam War Memorial, in Washington, DC, consists of a black marble wall engraved with the names of the approximately 58,000 members of the U.S. military who died in that conflict. How might visitors to the site likely respond to the monument?

See the Author Focus on page 156 for biographical information about Ralph Waldo Emerson.

The Obelisk, erected in 1837 at the Old North Bridge, the site of the Battle of Lexington and Concord.

Analyze Literature

Consonance and Alliteration
Consonance is the repetition of consonant sounds at the ends of words, as in *world* and *flood.*

Alliteration is the repetition of consonant sounds at the beginnings of words, as in *them* and *thee.*

Set Purpose

Emerson's use of the word *hymn* in the title of this poem clearly reveals his attitude toward the historic battle that is its subject. Read "Concord Hymn" aloud several times, and identify its hymnlike qualities. Listen especially for examples of consonance and alliteration. Imagine the poem being set to music and sung.

Preview Vocabulary

foe, 166
redeem, 166
sire, 166

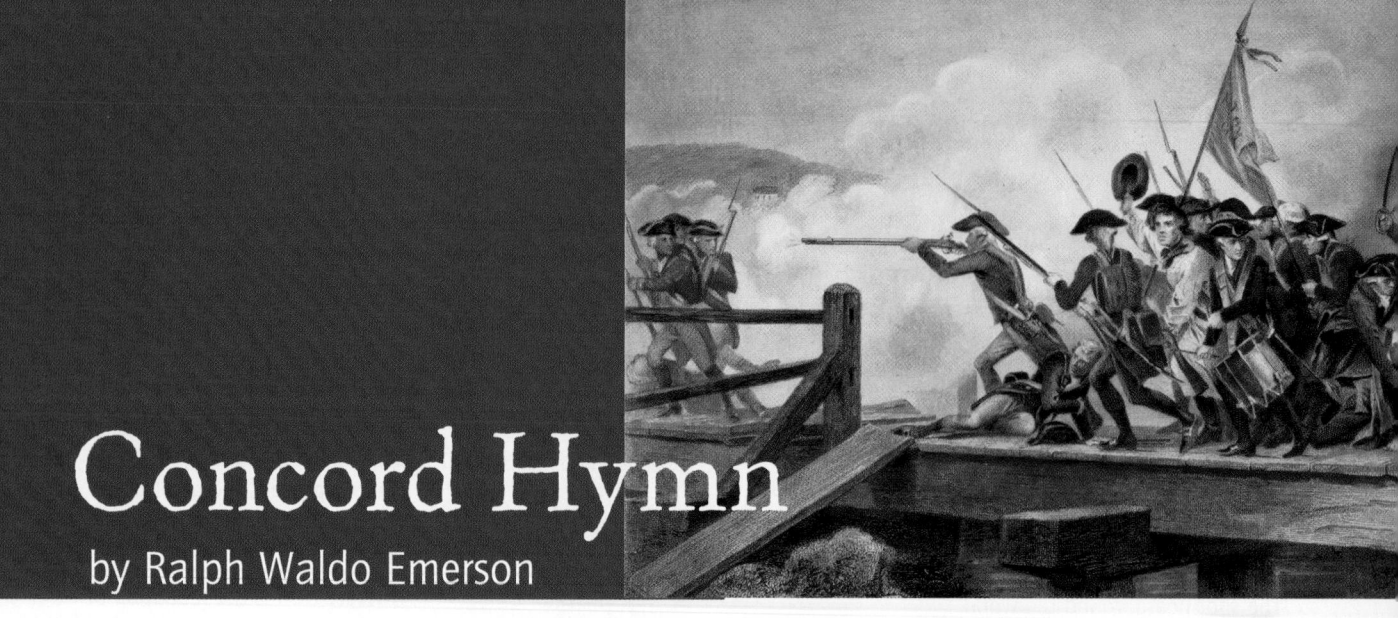

Concord Hymn

by Ralph Waldo Emerson

Sung at the Completion of the Battle Monument, April 19, 1836

By the rude[1] bridge that arched the flood,
   Their flag to April's breeze unfurled,
Here once the embattled farmers stood.
   And fired the shot heard round the world.

5   The <u>foe</u> long since in silence slept;
   Alike the conqueror silent sleeps;
And Time the ruined bridge has swept
   Down the dark stream which seaward creeps.

On this green bank, by this soft stream,
10   We set today a votive[2] stone;
That memory may their deed <u>redeem</u>,
   When, like our <u>sires</u>, our sons are gone.

Spirit, that made those heroes dare
   To die, and leave their children free,
15 Bid Time and Nature gently spare
   The shaft we raise to them and thee. ❖

---

1. **rude.** Roughly or hastily put together
2. **votive.** Offered as fulfillment of a promise or as an expression of gratitude

foe (fō) *n.*, enemy or opponent
re • deem (ri dēm´) *v.*, fulfill; restore
sire (sīr') *n.*, father or forefather

MIRRORS & WINDOWS

What purpose or purposes do war memorials serve? In what other ways might the war dead be remembered?

Refer to Text ▶ ▶ ▶ ▶ ▶	Reason with Text	
1a. Identify the comparison made in lines 5–6.	**1b.** What does the comparison suggest about war?	**Understand** Find meaning
2a. Name who fired the "shot heard round the world."	**2b.** "The shot heard round the world" is an *aphorism*, or a short saying that makes an often significant observation. The French Revolution occurred not long after the American Revolution. How does the aphorism reflect that fact?	**Apply** Use information
3a. Recall what the speaker asks the "Spirit" to do.	**3b.** What does the speaker suggest might happen if "Time and Nature" destroyed the "shaft"?	**Analyze** Take things apart
4a. Who are "our sires" and "our sons"?	**4b.** What will the monument continue to do after "our sons" are gone? Argue whether building such monuments is useful.	**Evaluate** Make judgments
5a. From the speaker's view, why did "those heroes dare" to die?	**5b.** Imagine that you have been asked to write a memorial to those who died in a fire, hurricane, war, or other disaster. How would you pay tribute to those who died?	**Create** Bring ideas together

Analyze Literature

Consonance and Alliteration

What examples did you find of words that demonstrate consonance and alliteration? How does repeating these sounds enrich the language of the poem? In particular, how does this make the poem musical and hymnlike?

Extend the Text

Writing Options

Creative Writing Suppose that you have been hired by your local chamber of commerce to write a description of an area monument or landmark for inclusion in a new brochure promoting tourism. Choose a monument or landmark, do brief research about it, and then write a description that will make people want to visit it.

Expository Writing What features of "Concord Hymn" make it a hymn as well as a poem? Provide a definition of *hymn*, and then in a one-paragraph literary analysis, explain why the work qualifies as a hymn.

Collaborative Learning

Produce a Pageant To celebrate the anniversary of the American Revolution, produce a *pageant*, in which group members role-play prominent historical figures, such as Paul Revere, Sam Adams, and Ralph Waldo Emerson. Do brief research on the events in Lexington and Concord that triggered the fighting there and on the individuals involved. Then present your pageant to the whole class.

Lifelong Learning

Research a Memorial Choose one of the memorials in Washington, DC. Research its planning and construction, including who initiated the project, how the artist/architect was chosen, and how long the project took. Write a report summarizing this information. In your conclusion, evaluate whether the memorial is a fitting tribute to the cause or individual it was intended to honor.

 Go to **www.mirrorsandwindows.com** for more.

Henry David Thoreau

> ## "Go confidently in the direction of your dreams. Live the life you have imagined."

Henry David Thoreau (1817–1862) was born in Concord, Massachusetts, and lived most of his life there, as well. Stories of his spending afternoons alone in the pasture, tending his mother's cows, suggest that he developed an appreciation for both nature and solitude early in life. Thoreau attended Concord Academy as a youth and then graduated from Harvard in 1837. In 1835, he contracted tuberculosis, a disease from which he would suffer his entire life.

Thoreau had read Ralph Waldo Emerson's *Nature* while in college, but actually meeting the man in Concord changed his life. Thoreau left his position as a teacher and became a member of Emerson's household, working for the family as a handyman and a gardener from 1841 to 1843. While there, he had access to Emerson's extensive library and met the leaders of the Transcendentalism movement, Emerson's inner circle. Thoreau participated in some of the group's activities, delivering lectures at the Concord Lyceum and publishing articles in *The Dial*.

In 1845, at the age of twenty-eight, Thoreau decided that he wanted to focus on his studies and writing in a solitary setting. He built a cabin on the shores of Walden Pond, just two miles from Concord, on land owned by Emerson. Over the next two years and two months, Thoreau recorded his observations and reflections, eventually publishing them in two books: *A Week on the Concord and Merrimack Rivers* (1849) and *Walden; or, Life in the Woods* (1854). These were the only book-length works that Thoreau published in his lifetime, and neither was a financial success. To support himself, Thoreau worked at various times as a pencil maker, surveyor, and lecturer. He continued writing, nonetheless, later publishing essays against the Mexican War and in favor of abolition. Some twenty volumes of journals were discovered after his death.

Thoreau won his place in American literature by, as he put it, traveling a good deal in Concord, the intellectual center of the Boston area. Still, he made numerous visits to Maine, Cape Cod, and New Hampshire, and he also traveled to Quebec, Canada, and Minnesota in unsuccessful attempts to strengthen his weakened lungs. Tuberculosis finally took Thoreau's life in 1862, when he was just forty-four years old.

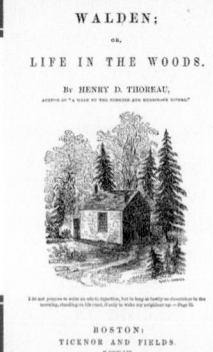

Noted Works

"Civil Disobedience" (1846)

A Week on the Concord and Merrimack Rivers (1849)

Walden; or, Life in the Woods (1854)

"Slavery in Massachusetts" (1854)

"A Plea for Capt. John Brown" (1859)

from **Walden**

An Essay by Henry David Thoreau

Build Background

Literary Context ***Walden; or, Life in the Woods***
is based on the journals Thoreau kept during his stay on
Emerson's property from July 4, 1845, to September 6,
1847. Thoreau reportedly built his cabin at Walden Pond
for twenty-eight dollars, using mostly secondhand materials, and while there, he lived off the land, raising some of
his own crops and eating wild berries and apples.

Thoreau was not shut off from civilization entirely,
however; he visited family and friends in nearby Concord
and performed various odd jobs to support himself. He
would later write in *Walden,* "For more than five years I maintained myself thus
solely by the labor of my hands, and I found, that by working about six weeks
in a year, I could meet all the expenses of living. The whole of my winters, as
well as most of my summers, I had free and clear for study."

Thoreau spent a good deal of this time revising and reworking the text of
Walden, ultimately writing seven full drafts over the nine years leading to its
publication. When it was published in 1854, *Walden* firmly established Thoreau's reputation not only as a writer but also as an outspoken individualist.

Reader's Context What might you consider doing if you felt it was time to
make significant changes in your life? Would you move or isolate yourself, as
Thoreau did? Why or why not?

A statue of Thoreau stands beside a re-creation of his cabin at Walden Pond.

Analyze Literature

Purpose and Tone
A writer's **purpose** is his or
her aim, or goal. Authors usually have one or more of the
following purposes: to inform
or explain, to describe, to persuade, or to tell a story.

Tone is the emotional attitude
toward the reader or the subject
suggested by a literary work—for
instance, serious or sarcastic,
playful or sincere.

Set Purpose

Walden has been described as
an essay, a narrative, a memoir,
and even a work of fiction by
a few scholars who question
whether life in the woods was
exactly as Thoreau described
it. In reading the excerpts that
follow, identify Thoreau's purpose or purposes for writing,
which may vary from one section to another. Also determine
the author's tone, as indicated
by his choices of words and
phrases.

Preview Vocabulary

resignation, 170
earnest, 171
saturate, 171
ethereal, 172
encumbrance, 173
posterity, 173
undulation, 174
superfluous, 175
fluctuate, 176
volatile, 178

from Walden

by Henry David Thoreau

Practically, the old have no very important advice to give the young.

From "Economy"

The mass of men lead lives of quiet desperation. What is called <u>resignation</u> is confirmed desperation. From the desperate city you go into the desperate country, and have to console yourself with the bravery of minks and muskrats. A stereotyped but unconscious despair is concealed even under what are called the games and amusements of mankind. There is no play in them, for this comes after work. But it is a characteristic of wisdom not to do desperate things. When we consider what, to use the words of the catechism, is the chief end of man,[1] and what are the true necessaries and means of life, it appears as if men had deliberately chosen the common mode of living because they preferred it to any other. Yet they honestly think there is no choice left. But alert and healthy natures remember that the sun rose clear. It is never too late to give up our prejudices. No way of thinking or doing, however

---

1. **When . . . man.** Refers to a line from the shorter Catechism in the *New England Primer:* "What is the chief end of man? Man's chief end is to glorify God and enjoy him forever."

---

re • sig • na • tion (re zig nā´ shən) *n.*, submissiveness; patient acceptance

ancient, can be trusted without proof. What every body echoes or in silence passes by as true today may turn out to be falsehood tomorrow, mere smoke of opinion, which some had trusted for a cloud that would sprinkle fertilizing rain on their fields. What old people say you cannot do you try and find that you can. Old deeds for old people, and new deeds for new. Old people did not know enough once, perchance, to fetch fresh fuel to keep the fire a-going; new people put a little dry wood under a pot, and are whirled round the globe with the speed of birds, in a way to kill old people, as the phrase is. Age is no better, hardly so well, qualified for an instructor as youth, for it has not profited so much as it has lost. One may almost doubt if the wisest man has learned any thing of absolute value by living. Practically, the old have no very important advice to give the young, their own experience has been so partial, and their lives have been such miserable failures, for private reasons, as they must believe; and it may be that they have some faith left which belies that experience, and they are only less young than they were. I have lived some thirty years on this planet and I have yet to hear the first syllable of valuable or even <u>earnest</u> advice from my seniors. They have told me nothing, and probably cannot tell me any thing, to the purpose. Here is life, an experiment to a great extent untried by me; but it does not avail me that they have tried it. If I have any experience which I think valuable, I am sure to reflect that this my Mentors[2] said nothing about. . . .

One may almost doubt if the wisest man has learned any thing of absolute value by living.

Near the end of March, 1845, I borrowed an axe and went down to the woods by Walden Pond, nearest to where I intended to build my house, and began to cut down some tall arrowy white pines, still in their youth, for timber. It is difficult to begin without borrowing, but perhaps it is the most generous course thus to permit your fellow-men to have an interest in your enterprise. The owner of the axe, as he released his hold on it, said that it was the apple of his eye; but I returned it sharper than I received it. It was a pleasant hillside where I worked, covered with pine woods, through which I looked out on the pond, and a small open field in the woods where pines and hickories were springing up. The ice in the pond was not yet dissolved, though there were some open spaces, and it was all dark colored and <u>saturated</u> with water. There were some slight flurries of snow during the days that I worked there, but for the most part when I came out on to the railroad, on my way home, its yellow sand heap stretched away gleaming in the hazy atmosphere, and the rails shone in the spring sun, and I heard the lark and pewee and other birds already come to commence another year with us.

They were pleasant spring days, in which the winter of man's discontent was thawing as well as the earth, and the life that had lain torpid began to stretch itself. One day, when my axe had come off and I had cut a green hickory for a wedge, driving it with a stone and had placed the whole to soak in a pond hole in order to swell the wood, I saw a striped snake run into the water, and he lay on the bottom, apparently without inconvenience, as long as I staid there, or more than a quarter of an hour; perhaps because he had not yet fairly come out of the torpid state. It appeared to me that for a like reason men remain in their present low and primitive condition; but if they should feel the influence of

---

2. **Mentors.** Wise advisers; from Mentor, the friend of Odysseus in Homer's *The Odyssey,* who educated the hero's son

ear • nest (ʉrʹ nəst) *adj.,* serious; sincere
sat • u • rate (saʹ chʉr āt) *v.,* thoroughly soak

the spring of springs arousing them, they would of necessity rise to a higher and more <u>ethereal</u> life. I had previously seen the snakes in frosty mornings in my path with portions of their bodies still numb and inflexible, waiting for the sun to thaw them. On the 1st of April it rained and melted the ice, and in the early part of the day, which was very foggy, I heard a stray goose groping about over the pond and cackling as if lost, or like the spirit of the fog.

They were pleasant spring days, in which the winter of man's discontent was thawing as well as the earth.

So I went on for some days cutting and hewing timber, and also studs and rafters, all with my narrow axe, not having many communicable or scholarlike thoughts, singing to myself,—

> Men say they know many things;
> But lo! they have taken wings,—
> The arts and sciences
> And a thousand appliances
> The wind that blows
> Is all that any body knows.

I hewed the main timbers six inches square, most of the studs on two sides only, and the rafters and floor timbers on one side, leaving the rest of the bark on, so that they were just as straight and much stronger than sawed ones. Each stick was carefully mortised or tenoned[3] by its stump, for I had borrowed other tools by this time. My days in the woods were not very long ones, yet I usually carried my dinner of bread and butter, and read the newspaper in which it was wrapped, at noon, sitting amid the green pine boughs which I had cut off, and to my bread was imparted some of their fragrance, for my hands were covered with a thick coat of pitch. Before I had done I was more the friend than the foe of the pine tree, though I had cut down some of them, having become better acquainted with it. Sometimes a rambler in the wood was attracted by the sound of my axe, and we chatted pleasantly over the chips which I had made.

By the middle of April, for I made no haste in my work, but rather made the most of it, my house was framed and ready for the raising. I had already bought the shanty of James Collins, an Irishman who worked on the Fitchburg Railroad, for boards. James Collins' shanty was considered an uncommonly fine one. When I called to see it he was not at home. I walked about the outside, at first unobserved from within, the window was so deep and high. It was of small dimensions, with a peaked cottage roof, and not much else to be seen, the dirt being raised five feet all around as if it were a compost heap. The roof was the soundest part, though a good deal warped and made brittle by the sun. Door-sill there was none, but a perennial passage for the hens under the door board. Mrs. C. came to the door and asked me to view it from the inside. The hens were driven in by my approach. It was dark, and had a dirt floor for the most part, dank, clammy, and aguish, only here a board and there a board which would not bear removal. She lighted a lamp to show me the inside of the roof and the walls, and also that the board floor extended under the bed, warning me not to step into the cellar, a sort of dust hole two feet deep. In her own words, they were "good boards overhead, good boards all around, and a good window,"—of two whole squares originally, only the cat had passed out that way lately. There was a stove, a bed, and a place to sit, an infant in the house where it was born, a silk parasol, gilt-framed looking-glass, and a patent new coffee mill nailed to an oak sapling, all told. The bargain was soon concluded, for James had in the mean while returned. I to pay four dollars and twenty-five cents tonight, he to vacate at five

---

3. **mortised or tenoned.** Joined or fastened

ethe • re • al (ē thē´ rē 'l) *adj.,* heavenly; delicate and refined

Irish Immigration

Thoreau mentions his Irish neighbors Collins, Seeley, and young Patrick, all of whom were likely recent additions to the area. From 1845 to 1847, a disastrous plant disease destroyed Ireland's potato crop, which half the nation's population depended on for food. About 750,000 people died of starvation and sickness, and hundreds of thousands more set sail for other lands.

A large number of these immigrants came to the United States, where many were employed by the railroad companies. Because of their willing-

ness to work for low wages at difficult jobs, Irish laborers were scorned by both the businesses who took advantage of them and the local workers who competed for the same jobs.

tomorrow morning, selling to nobody else meanwhile: I to take possession at six. It were well, he said, to be there early, and anticipate certain indistinct but wholly unjust claims on the score of ground rent and fuel. This he assured me was the only <u>encumbrance</u>. At six I passed him and his family on the road. One large bundle held their all,—bed, coffee-mill, looking-glass, hens, all but the cat, she took to the woods and became a wild cat, and, as I learned afterward, trod in a trap set for wood-chucks, and so became a dead cat at last.

I took down this dwelling the same morning, drawing the nails, and removed it to the pond side by small cartloads, spreading the boards on the grass there to bleach and warp back again in the sun. One early thrush gave me a note or two as I drove along the woodland path. I was informed treacherously by a young Patrick that neighbor Seeley, an Irishman, in the intervals of the carting, transferred the still tolerable, straight, and drivable nails, staples, and spikes to his pocket, and then stood when I came back to pass the time of day, and look freshly up, unconcerned, with spring thoughts, at the devastation; there being a dearth[4] of work, as he said. He was there to represent spectator-dom, and help make this seemingly insignificant event one with the removal of the gods of Troy.[5]

I dug my cellar in the side of a hill sloping to the south, where a woodchuck had formerly dug his burrow, down through sumach and blackberry roots, and the lowest stain of vegetation, six feet square by seven deep, to a fine sand where potatoes would not freeze in any winter. The sides were left shelving, and not stoned; but the sun having never shone on them, the sand still keeps its place. It was but two hours' work. I took particular pleasure in this breaking of ground, for in almost all latitudes men dig into the earth for an equable temperature. Under the most splendid house in the city is still to be found the cellar where they store their roots as of old, and long after the superstructure has disappeared <u>posterity</u> remark its dent in the earth. The house is still but a sort of porch at the entrance of a burrow.

At length, in the beginning of May, with the help of some of my acquaintances, rather to improve so good an occasion for neighborliness than from any necessity, I set up the frame of my house. No man was ever more honored in the character of his raisers than I. They are destined, I trust, to assist at the raising of loftier structures one day. I began to

---

4. **dearth.** Scarcity
5. **gods of Troy.** Reference to Virgil's *Aeneid,* in which Aeneas escapes with his household gods

---

en • cum • brance (ən kum´ brəns) *n.,* hindrance; burden
pos • ter • i • ty (pô stār´ ə tē) *n.,* succeeding generations

occupy my house on the 4th of July, as soon as it was boarded and roofed, for the boards were carefully feather-edged and lapped, so that it was perfectly impervious to rain;[6] but before boarding I laid the foundation of a chimney at one end, bringing two cartloads of stones up the hill from the pond in my arms. I built the chimney after my hoeing in the fall, before a fire became necessary for warmth, doing my cooking in the mean while out of doors on the ground, early in the morning: which mode I still think is in some respects more convenient and agreeable than the usual one. When it stormed before my bread was baked, I fixed a few boards over the fire, and sat under them to watch my loaf, and passed some pleasant hours in that way. In those days, when my hands were much employed, I read but little, but the least scraps of paper which lay on the ground, my holder, or table-cloth, afforded me as much entertainment, in fact answered the same purpose as the Iliad.[7]

♦ ♦ ♦

From "Where I Lived and What I Lived For"

Every morning was a cheerful invitation to make my life of equal simplicity, and I may say innocence, with Nature herself. I have been as sincere a worshipper of Aurora[8] as the Greeks. I got up early and bathed in the pond; that was a religious exercise, and one of the best things which I did. They say that characters were engraven on the bathing tub of king Tching-thang to this effect: "Renew thyself completely each day; do it again, and again, and forever again."[9] I can understand that. Morning brings back the heroic ages. I was as much affected by the faint hum of a mosquito making its invisible and unimaginable tour through my apartment at earliest dawn, when I was sitting with door and windows open, as I could be by any trumpet that ever sang of fame. It was Homer's requiem; itself an Iliad and Odyssey in the air, singing its own wrath and wanderings. There was something cosmical about it,

a standing advertisement, till forbidden,[10] of the everlasting vigor and fertility of the world. The morning, which is the most memorable season of the day, is the awakening hour. Then there is least somnolence in us; and for an hour, at least, some part of us awakes which slumbers all the rest of the day and night. Little is to be expected of that day, if it can be called a day, to which we are not awakened by our Genius, but by the mechanical nudgings of some servitor, are not awakened by our own newly-acquired force and aspirations from within, accompanied by the undulations of celestial music, instead of factory bells and a fragrance filling the air—to a higher life than we fell asleep from; and thus the darkness bear its fruit, and prove itself to be good, no less than the light. That man who does not believe that each day contains an earlier, more sacred, and auroral hour than he has yet profaned, has despaired of life, and is pursuing a descending and darkening way. After a partial cessation of his sensuous life, the soul of man, or its organs rather, are reinvigorated each day, and his Genius tries again what noble life it can make. All memorable events, I should say, transpire in morning time and in a morning atmosphere. The Vedas[11] say, "All intelligences awake with the morning." Poetry and art, and the fairest and most memorable of the actions of men, date from such an hour. All poets and heroes, like Memnon,[12] are the children of Aurora, and emit their music at sunrise. To him whose elastic and vigorous thought keeps pace with the

---

6. **feather-edged . . . rain.** The board's thin edges overlapped, making the roof watertight.
7. **Iliad.** Greek epic by Homer
8. **Aurora.** Goddess of dawn
9. **"Renew . . . again."** From Confucius, Chinese philosopher
10. **standing . . . forbidden.** Advertisement that was to be run "till forbidden," or withdrawn by the sponsor
11. **Vedas.** Hindu scriptures
12. **Memnon.** Killed by Achilles in the Trojan War

un • du • la • tion (un' jü lā´ shən) *n.*, act of moving in waves

sun, the day is a perpetual morning. It matters not what the clocks say or the attitudes and labors of men. Morning is when I am awake and there is a dawn in me. Moral reform is the effort to throw off sleep. Why is it that men give so poor an account of their day if they have not been slumbering? They are not such poor calculators. If they had not been overcome with drowsiness they would have performed something. The millions are awake enough for physical labor; but only one in a million is awake enough for effective intellectual exertion, only one in a hundred millions to a poetic or divine life. To be awake is to be alive. I have never yet met a man who was quite awake. How could I have looked him in the face?

To affect the quality of the day, that is the highest of arts.

We must learn to reawaken and keep ourselves awake, not by mechanical aids, but by an infinite expectation of the dawn, which does not forsake us in our soundest sleep. I know of no more encouraging fact than the unquestionable ability of man to elevate his life by a conscious endeavor. It is something to be able to paint a particular picture, or to carve a statue, and so to make a few objects beautiful; but it is far more glorious to carve and paint the very atmosphere and medium through which we look, which morally we can do. To affect the quality of the day, that is the highest of arts. Every man is tasked to make his life, even in its details, worthy of the contemplation of his most elevated and critical hour. If we refused, or rather used up, such paltry information as we get, the oracles[13] would distinctly inform us how this might be done.

I went to the woods because I wished to live deliberately, to front only the essential facts of life, and see if I could not learn what it had to teach, and not, when I came to die, discover that I had not lived. I did not wish to live what was not life, living is so dear; nor did I wish to practice resignation, unless it was quite necessary. I wanted to live deep and suck out all the marrow of life, to live so sturdily and Spartan-like[14] as to put to rout all that was not life, to cut a broad swath and shave close, to drive life into a corner, and reduce it to its lowest terms, and, if it proved to be mean, why then to get the whole and genuine meanness of it, and publish its meanness to the world; or if it were sublime, to know it by experience, and be able to give a true account of it in my next excursion. For most men, it appears to me, are in a strange uncertainty about it, whether it is of the devil or of God, and have somewhat hastily concluded that it is the chief end of man here to "glorify God and enjoy him forever."[15]

Still we live meanly, like ants; though the fable tells us that we were long ago changed into men;[16] like pygmies we fight with cranes; it is error upon error, and clout upon clout, and our best virtue has for its occasion a super-fluous and evitable wretchedness. Our life is frittered away by detail. An honest man has hardly need to count more than his ten fingers, or in extreme cases he may add his ten toes, and lump the rest. Simplicity, simplicity, simplicity! I say, let your affairs be as two or three, and not a hundred or a thousand; instead of a million count half a dozen, and keep your accounts on your thumb nail. In the midst of this chopping sea of civilized life, such are the clouds and storms and quicksands and thousand-and-one items to be allowed for,

---

13. **oracles.** People in communication with the gods
14. **Spartan-like.** Without excessive comforts
15. **"glorify . . . forever."** Reference to the *New England Primer*
16. **fable . . . men.** Refers to a Greek fable in which Zeus turns ants into men

su • per • flu • ous (sü pʉr´ flü əs) *adj.,* excessive; unnecessary

that a man has to live, if he would not founder and go to the bottom and not make his port at all, by dead reckoning, and he must be a great calculator indeed who succeeds. Simplify, simplify. Instead of three meals a day, if it be necessary eat but one, instead of a hundred dishes, five; and reduce other things in proportion. Our life is like a German Confederacy, made up of petty states, with its boundary forever <u>fluctuating</u>, so that even a German cannot tell you how it is bounded at any moment. The nation itself, with all its so called internal improvements, which, by the way, are all external and superficial, is just such an unwieldy and overgrown establishment, cluttered with furniture and tripped up by its own traps, ruined by luxury and heedless expense, by want of calculation and a worthy aim, as the million households in the land; and the only cure for it as for them is in a rigid economy, a stern and more than Spartan simplicity of life and elevation of purpose. It lives too fast. Men think that it is essential that the Nation have commerce, and export ice, and talk through a telegraph, and ride thirty miles an hour, without a doubt, whether they do or not; but whether we should live like baboons or like men, is a little uncertain. If we do not get out sleepers,[17] and forge rails, and devote days and nights to the work, but go to tinkering upon

our lives to improve them, who will build railroads? And if railroads are not built, how shall we get to heaven in season? But if we stay at home and mind our business, who will want railroads? We do not ride on the railroad; it rides upon us. Did you ever think what those sleepers are that underlie the railroad? Each one is a man, an Irish-man, or a Yankee man. The rails are laid on them, and they are covered with sand, and the cars run smoothly over them. They are sound sleepers, I assure you. And every few years a new lot is laid down and run over; so that, if some have the pleasure of riding on a rail, others have the misfortune to be ridden upon. And when they run over a man that is walking in his sleep, a supernumerary[18] sleeper in the wrong position, and wake him up, they suddenly stop the cars, and make a hue and cry about it, as if this were an exception. I am glad to know that it takes a gang of men for every five miles to keep the sleepers down and level in their beds as it is, for this is a sign that they may sometime get up again.

Why should we live with such hurry and waste of life? We are determined to be starved before we are hungry. Men say that a stitch in time saves nine, and so they take a thousand stitches today to save nine tomorrow. As for work, we haven't any of any consequence. We have the Saint Vitus' dance[19] and cannot possibly keep our heads still. If I should only give a few pulls at the parish bell-rope, as for a fire, that is, without setting the bell, there is hardly a man on his farm in the outskirts of Concord, notwithstanding that press of engagements which was his excuse so many times this morning, nor a boy, nor a woman, I might almost say, but would forsake all and follow

---

17. **sleepers.** Railroad ties
18. **supernumerary.** Extra
19. **Saint Vitus' dance.** Refers to a nervous disorder with symptoms of jerky motions

---

fluc • tu • ate (fluk´ chü āt) *v.*, change or vary continuously

that sound, not mainly to save property from the flames, but, if we will confess the truth, much more to see it burn, since burn it must, and we, be it known, did not set it on fire,—or to see it put out, and have a hand in it, if that is done as handsomely; yes, even if it were the parish church itself. Hardly a man takes a half hour's nap after dinner, but when he wakes he holds up his head and asks "What's the news?" as if the rest of mankind had stood his sentinels. Some give directions to be waked every half hour, doubtless for no other purpose; and then, to pay for it, they tell what they have dreamed. After a night's sleep the news is as indispensable as the breakfast. "Pray tell me any thing new that has happened to a man any where on this globe",—and he reads it over his coffee and rolls, that a man had had his eyes gouged out this morning on the Wachito River; never dreaming the while that he lives in the dark unfathomed mammoth cave of this world, and has but the rudiment of an eye himself.[20]

Why should we live with such hurry and waste of life? We are determined to be starved before we are hungry.

◆ ◆ ◆

I left the woods for as good a reason as I went there. Perhaps it seemed to me that I had several more lives to live, and could not spare any more time for that one. It is remarkable how easily and insensibly we fall into a particular route, and make a beaten track for ourselves. I had not lived there a week before my feet wore a path from my door to the pond-side; and though it is five or six years since I trod it, it is still quite distinct. It is true, I fear that others may have fallen into it, and so helped to keep it open. The surface of the earth is soft and impressible by the feet of men; and so with the paths which the mind travels. How worn and dusty, then, must be the highways of the world, how deep the ruts

of tradition and conformity! I did not wish to take a cabin passage, but rather to go before the mast and on the deck of the world, for there I could best see the moonlight amid the mountains. I do not wish to go below now.

I learned this, at least, by my experiment; that if one advances confidently in the direction of his dreams, and endeavors to live the life which he has imagined, he will meet with a success unexpected in common hours. He will put some things behind, will pass an invisible boundary; new, universal, and more liberal laws will begin to establish themselves around and within him; or old laws be expanded, and interpreted in his favor in a more liberal sense, and he will live with the license of a higher order of beings. In proportion as he simplifies his life, the laws of the universe will appear less complex, and solitude will not be solitude, nor poverty poverty, nor weakness weakness. If you have built castles in the air, your work need not be lost; that is where they should be. Now put the foundations under them.

It is a ridiculous demand which England and America make, that you shall speak so that they can understand you. Neither men nor toadstools grow so. As if that were important, and there were not enough to understand you without them. As if Nature could support but one order of understandings, could not sustain birds as well as quadrupeds, flying as well as creeping things, and *hush* and *who,* which Bright[21] can understand, were the best English. As if there were safety in stupidity alone. I fear chiefly lest my expression may not be *extra-vagant* enough, may not wander far enough beyond the narrow limits of my daily experience, so as to be adequate to the truth of which I have been convinced. *Extra vagance!* it depends on how you are yarded. The migrating buffalo, which seeks new pastures in another latitude, is not extravagant like the cow which kicks over the pail,

---

20. **dark . . . himself.** Reference to sightless fish found in Mammoth Cave
21. **Bright.** Name for an ox

leaps the cow-yard fence, and runs after her calf, in milking time. I desire to speak somewhere *without* bounds; like a man in a waking moment, to men in their waking moments; for I am convinced that I cannot exaggerate enough even to lay the foundation of a true expression. Who that has heard a strain of music feared then lest he should speak extravagantly any more forever? In view of the future or possible, we should live quite laxly and undefined in front, our outlines dim and misty on that side; as our shadows reveal an insensible perspiration toward the sun. The <u>volatile</u> truth of our words should continually betray the inadequacy of the residual statement. Their truth is instantly *translated*; its literal monument alone remains. The words which express our faith and piety are not definite; yet they are significant and fragrant like frankincense[22] to superior natures.

Why level downward to our dullest perception always, and praise that as common sense? The commonest sense is the sense of men asleep, which they express by snoring. Sometimes we are inclined to class those who are once-and-a-half witted with the half-witted, because we appreciate only a third part of their wit. Some would find fault with the morning-red, if they ever got up early enough. "They pretend," as I hear, "that the verses of Kabir have four different senses; illusion, spirit, intellect, and the exoteric doctrine of the Vedas;" but in this part of the world it is considered a ground for complaint if a man's writings admit of more than one interpretation. While England endeavors to cure the potato-rot, will not any endeavor to cure the brain-rot, which prevails so much more widely and fatally?

I do not suppose that I have attained to obscurity, but I should be proud if no more fatal fault were found with my pages on this score than was found with the Walden ice. Southern customers objected to its blue color, which is the evidence of its purity, as if it were muddy, and preferred the Cambridge ice, which is white, but tastes of weeds. The purity men love is like the mists which envelop the earth, and not like the azure ether beyond.

Some are dinning in our ears that we Americans, and moderns generally, are intellectual dwarfs compared with the ancients, or even the Elizabethan[23] men. But what is that to the purpose? A living dog is better than a dead lion.[24] Shall a man go and hang himself because he belongs to the race of pygmies, and not be the biggest pygmy that he can? Let every one mind his own business, and endeavor to be what he was made.

Why should we be in such desperate haste to succeed, and in such desperate enterprises? If a man does not keep pace with his companions, perhaps it is because he hears a different drummer. Let him step to the music which he hears, however measured or far away. It is not important that he should mature as soon as an apple-tree or an oak. Shall he turn his spring into summer? If the condition of things which we were made for is not yet, what were any reality which we can substitute? We will not be shipwrecked on a vain reality. Shall we with pains erect a heaven of blue glass over ourselves, though when it is done we shall be sure to gaze still at the true ethereal heaven far above, as if the former were not? ❖

---

22. **frankincense.** Type of incense
23. **Elizabethan.** From the time of Queen Elizabeth I (1533–1603)
24. **A living . . . lion.** From the Bible, Ecclesiastes 9:4

> **vol • a • tile** (väl´ ə tīl) *adj.*, unstable; likely to change without warning

MIRRORS & WINDOWS

Does Thoreau's plea to "Simplify, simplify" appeal to you? Why or why not?

Literature Connection

In 1974, **Annie Dillard** (b. 1945) won the Pulitzer Prize for general nonfiction for *Pilgrim at Tinker Creek,* the collection of essays from which **"The Present"** is taken. In this book, Dillard writes of her experiences and reflections over the course of a year, during which she took daily walks through the land around Tinker Creek, located in the Blue Ridge Mountains near Roanoke, Virginia. As you read this selection, notice Dillard's vivid descriptions and powers of observation. When it was published, Dillard's book was instantly recognized as reminiscent of Thoreau's *Walden.*

DILLARD

The Present
by Annie Dillard

Catch it if you can.

It is early March. I am dazed from a long day of interstate driving homeward; I pull in at a gas station in Nowhere, Virginia, north of Lexington. The young boy in charge ("Chick 'at oll?") is offering a free cup of coffee with every gas purchase. We talk in the glass-walled office while my coffee cools enough to drink. He tells me, among other things, that the rival gas station down the road, whose free coffee sign is visible from the interstate, charges you fifteen cents if you want your coffee in a Styrofoam cup, as opposed, I guess, to your bare hands.

All the time we talk, the boy's new beagle puppy is skidding around the office, sniffing impartially[1] at my shoes and at the wire rack of folded maps. The cheerful human conversation wakes me, recalls me, not to a normal consciousness, but to a kind of energetic readiness. I step outside, followed by the puppy.

I am absolutely alone. There are no other customers. The road is vacant, the interstate is out of sight and earshot. I have hazarded into a new corner of the world, an unknown spot, a Brigadoon.[2] Before me extends a low hill trembling in yellow brome,[3] and behind the hill, filling the sky, rises an enormous mountain ridge, forested, alive and awesome with brilliant blown lights. I have never seen anything so tremulous[4] and live. Overhead, great strips and chunks of cloud dash to the northwest in a gold rush. At my back the sun is setting—how can I not have noticed before that the sun is setting? My mind has been a blank slab of black asphalt for hours, but that doesn't stop the sun's wild wheel. I set my coffee beside me on the curb; I smell loam on the wind; I pat the puppy; I watch the mountain.

My hand works automatically over the puppy's fur, following the line of hair under his ears, down his neck, inside his forelegs, along his hot-skinned belly.

Shadows lope along the mountain's rumpled flanks; they elongate[5] like root tips, like lobes of spilling water, faster and faster. A warm purple pigment pools in each ruck and tuck of the rock; it deepens and spreads, boring crevasses, canyons. As the purple vaults and slides, it tricks out the unleafed forest and rumpled rock in gilt, in shape-shifting patches of glow. These gold lights veer and retract, shatter and glide in a series of dazzling splashes, shrinking, leaking, exploding. The

---

1. **impartially.** Without bias or favor
2. **Brigadoon.** A place that is unaffected by time or real-world events. The term comes from the title of a 1947 musical comedy by A. J. Lerner and F. Loewe.
3. **brome.** Tall grass; also called *bromegrass*
4. **tremulous.** Characterized by trembling or shaking
5. **elongate.** Extend or stretch out

ridge's bosses and hummocks[6] sprout bulging from its side; the whole mountain looms miles closer; the light warms and reddens; the bare forest folds and pleats itself like living protoplasm before my eyes, like a running chart, a wildly scrawling oscillograph[7] on the present moment. The air cools; the puppy's skin is hot. I am more alive than all the world.

This is it, I think, this is it, right now, the present, this empty gas station, here, this western wind, this tang of coffee on the tongue, and I am patting the puppy, I am watching the mountain. And the second I verbalize this awareness in my brain, I cease to see the mountain or feel the puppy. I am opaque, so much black asphalt. But at the same second, the second I know I've lost it, I also realize that the puppy is still squirming on his back under my hand. Nothing has changed for him. He draws his legs down to stretch the skin taut so he feels every fingertip's stroke along his furred and arching side, his flank, his flung-back throat.

I sip my coffee. I look at the mountain, which is still doing its tricks, as you look at a still-beautiful face belonging to a person who was once your lover in another country years ago: with fond nostalgia, and recognition, but no real feeling save a secret astonishment that you are now strangers. Thanks. For the memories. It is ironic that the one thing that all religions recognize as separating us from our creator—our very self-consciousness—is also the one thing that divides us from our fellow creatures. It was a bitter birthday present from evolution, cutting us off at both ends. I get in the car and drive home.

Catch it if you can. The present is an invisible electron; its lightning path traced faintly on a blackened screen is fleet, and fleeing, and gone.

That I ended this experience prematurely for myself—that I drew scales over my eyes between me and the mountain and gloved my hand between me and the puppy—is not the only point. After all, it would have ended anyway. I've never seen a sunset or felt a wind that didn't. The levitating[8] saints came down at last, and their two feet bore real weight. No, the point is that not only does time fly and do we die, but that in these reckless conditions we live at all, and are vouchsafed,[9] for the duration of certain inexplicable[10] moments, to know it. ❖

---

6. **bosses and hummocks.** *Bosses*—pieces that jut out; *hummocks*—small, rounded hill.
7. **oscillograph.** Device that records electrical variations
8. **levitating.** Rising or floating
9. **vouchsafed.** Given the privilege
10. **inexplicable.** Incapable of being explained or understood

---

Review Questions

1. What is "it" in "Catch it if you can"? At what point does Dillard lose "it"? How might she regain "it"?

2. Where is Dillard in this essay? What had she been doing before arriving there? Analyze how these circumstances might lead her to feel "more alive than all the world."

3. According to Dillard, what is "the point"? Does the fact that something cannot last make it seem more important or special? Why or why not?

TEXT ⇌ TEXT CONNECTION

If Thoreau and Dillard were to meet, what might each say about the other's work? How might Thoreau comment on Dillard's decision to return to the "black asphalt" and drive home? Would he agree with her assertion that the sense of the present is fleeting and infrequent? Explain.

Refer to Text ▶ ▶ ▶ ▶ ▶	**Reason with Text**	
1a. In Thoreau's view, what kind of lives do most people lead?	**1b.** The first sentence of this excerpt from *Walden* is a well-known *aphorism*, or statement commenting on life. Explain what Thoreau means by it.	**Understand** Find meaning
2a. Recall what Thoreau says will happen when individuals begin to simplify their lives (paragraph 14).	**2b.** Thoreau urges readers to simplify their lives. Is his advice easier or more difficult to follow today than it was in Thoreau's time? Explain.	**Apply** Use information
3a. Why did Thoreau go to the woods? Why did he leave the woods?	**3b.** Compare and contrast the two reasons.	**Analyze** Take things apart
4a. If a person "hears a different drummer," what does Thoreau say he or she should do?	**4b.** Do you agree with Thoreau's reasoning? Why or why not?	**Evaluate** Make judgments
5a. Identify the "highest of arts" (paragraph 9), according to Thoreau.	**5b.** Propose how American society would change if large groups of people followed Thoreau's advice to simplify their lives.	**Create** Bring ideas together

Analyze Literature

Purpose and Tone

What is Thoreau's primary purpose in *Walden?* What other secondary purposes does he have? How does recognizing a writer's purpose enrich your appreciation of the work?

What is the overall tone of the essay? Use examples of language from the selection to support your suggestion. Does the tone of this essay fit its content? Explain.

Extend the Text

Writing Options

Creative Writing Suppose you have some property you would like to sell or rent—for example, a city apartment, a house in the suburbs or a rural area, or a commercial building. Write a real estate advertisement for the property, listing its desirable features.

Persuasive Writing You are a local judge, and a citizen appears before your court to explain why he or she refuses to pay a parking ticket. The individual says the car was parked illegally but that he or she needed the spot to keep an appointment to donate blood. Issue a decision in this case, explaining in a paragraph whether the individual should have to pay the parking ticket.

Collaborative Learning

Design a Replica Working with a partner or in a small group, design a *replica*, or model, of the house that Thoreau built near Walden Pond. Start by doing research on the original house and the materials used. Look in a variety of sources, such as historical documents and newspaper articles from Thoreau's day. (Some may be available on the Internet.) Draw a sketch of the house and/or build a small model. Summarize your findings in a brief report.

Media Literacy

Hold a Forum With a group of classmates, organize a forum in which students compare and contrast Henry David Thoreau's and Annie Dillard's responses to nature. (See Dillard's essay on pages 179–180.) You can choose to read other short selections from *Walden* or other brief essays by Dillard and then discuss the similarities and differences between the two writers.

 Go to **www.mirrorsandwindows.com** for more.

1. Thoreau claims that what most people call *resignation* really is
   A. acceptance.
   B. disinterest.
   C. desperation.
   D. abandon.
   E. laziness.

2. What does Thoreau do with the shanty he purchases from James Collins?
   A. He dismantles it.
   B. He lives in it.
   C. He sells it.
   D. He uses it as an office.
   E. He uses it as a garden shed.

3. In the excerpts from *Walden,* what does the word *earnest* mean?
   A. accepting
   B. sensible
   C. questionable
   D. logical
   E. sincere

4. Which of the following best states the main idea of "The Present," the passage from *Pilgrim at Tinker Creek?*
   A. Being in the present is a temporary experience, and realizing that separates a person from the world.
   B. The knowledge of their mortality makes people hurry along in life.
   C. Connecting with nature only is possible if someone knows he or she is going to die someday.
   D. Verbalizing an experience can ruin it.
   E. People can commune with nature only in remote, isolated places.

5. In the excerpt from *Pilgrim at Tinker Creek,* what most likely is meant by the word *it* in the phrase "catch it if you can"?
   A. the light of the setting sun on a mountain
   B. the warmth of a puppy's belly
   C. a moment to rest
   D. the memory of things long forgotten
   E. the present moment

6. In the excerpts from *Walden,* the line "I have been as sincere a worshipper of Aurora as the Greeks" communicates Thoreau's love for which of the following?
   A. wine
   B. Greek mythology
   C. morning
   D. solitude
   E. the northern lights

7. In "The Present," the passage from *Pilgrim at Tinker Creek,* what does the word *vouchsafe* mean?
   A. hold in security
   B. swear to uphold
   C. give a privilege to
   D. redeem
   E. made mortal

8. Thoreau argues that striving for common sense and mutual understanding
   A. makes it easier for people to communicate with one another.
   B. keeps people awake.
   C. reduces originality and individuality.
   D. teaches people to live more simply.
   E. is pointless.

9. **Constructed Response:** Explain how the following statement from *Walden* illustrates Thoreau's view of conformity: "The surface of the earth is soft and impressible by the feet of men; and so with the paths which the mind travels."

10. **Constructed Response:** During Thoreau's lifetime, the "black asphalt" that Dillard mentions did not cover the land to the extent it does now. Given this and other changes in the modern world, argue whether Thoreau's ideas about leading a simple yet purposeful life are still relevant. Suggest how Dillard might reconcile the differences between the modern world and Thoreau's Walden.

TEST-TAKING TIP

If you take the SAT, don't answer a question if you have no idea of the correct response. You will not lose points for leaving a question unanswered, but you will lose one-quarter point for answering a question incorrectly. (You will score one point for answering a question correctly.) Only guess at the answer if you can eliminate one or more of the possible responses as being incorrect. Mathematically, that will give you the best chance of increasing your score.

Understand the Concept

The two types of word meanings are denotation and connotation. The **denotation** of a word is its dictionary definition; this meaning is objective and generally agreed upon. The **connotation** of a word is the emotional association or implication it makes; this meaning is subjective and often personal.

Connotations are often *positive* (favorable) or *negative* (unfavorable). For example, the adjectives *unique* and *freakish* both mean "different from what is typical." But *unique* suggests that something is original and distinctive, having a positive connotation. In contrast, *freakish* suggests that something is strange or abnormal and thus has a negative connotation. The word *different* is more neutral, having neither a positive nor a negative connotation.

Connotations also sometimes express degrees of *intensity*, or depth of feeling. Notice, for example, the increase in intensity among these words: *startled, surprised, shocked, outraged.*

When you are reading, try to determine the connotations of unfamiliar words from the context. Use clues from the surrounding text to help identify the emotional associations that words have. Consider, too, the overall tone of a passage to determine connotative word meanings. Compare the following sentences:

EXAMPLES

I hadn't realized how illness had ravaged Jorgé's body until I saw his *emaciated,* skeletal figure.

Vince was a *scrawny* kid who was always getting picked on.

You can tell from these sentences that the words *emaciated* and *scrawny* both mean "thin." In the first sentence, you can infer that Jorgé's thinness is the result of illness, and in the second sentence, you can infer that being thin is associated with being small and weak.

When you are writing and speaking, choose words that convey the specific meanings you intend. Although a dictionary won't include the connotative meanings of words, you can use the denotative definitions and examples of usage provided to distinguish between words. A *thesaurus,* which lists synonyms, near synonyms, and antonyms, also can be helpful in understanding the connotations of words.

Apply the Skill

Exercise A

Use your knowledge and a dictionary, if needed, to identify the denotation of each of these words from a selection in the unit. Then determine whether the word, as used in the selection, has a positive or a negative connotation. With a partner, use each word correctly in a sentence.

1. scourged ("Thanatopsis," line 79)
2. fetters ("Stanzas on Freedom," line 18)
3. redemption (*Nature,* paragraph 8)
4. refinement (Letter to Sophia Ripley, paragraph 1)
5. paltry (*Walden,* paragraph 9)

Exercise B

Use a dictionary and a thesaurus, as needed, to find three synonyms for each of the following words. Describe the connotation each synonym has and how this should affect your use of the word.

1. frugal (adjective)
2. house (noun)
3. question (verb)
4. stubborn (adjective)
5. throw (verb)

SPELLING PRACTICE

Words Ending with *-able/-ible*

Adding suffixes to words sometimes complicates their spelling, as is the case with *-able* and *-ible,* both of which mean "capable or worthy of." The general rule is to use *-able* with whole words and *-ible* with word parts—for instance, *prefer* + *-able* = *preferable* and *vis* + *-ible* = *visible.* However, there are many exceptions to this rule, such as *capable.* Familiarize yourself with the spellings and meanings of these words from "Walden."

agreeable	insensible	remarkable
drivable	invisible	tolerable
evitable	memorable	unimaginable
impressible	miserable	valuable
indispensable	possible	
inflexible	probable	

from **Civil Disobedience**
An Essay by Henry David Thoreau

from **Self-Reliance**
An Essay by Ralph Waldo Emerson

Build Background

Literary Context In 1846, during a day trip to town and away from Walden Pond, Thoreau was arrested for refusing to pay poll taxes (fees to vote) in protest against the Mexican-American War. He spent just one night in jail, but to Thoreau, his imprisonment was an act of conscience, not lawlessness. His description of being imprisoned underlies the central theme in what is perhaps his most famous essay, **"Civil Disobedience,"** published in 1849. The term refers to *nonviolent* protest against laws he considered unjust—*civil* as distinct from *military* protest.

Halfway around the world and more than half a century later, Mohandas Gandhi, the leader of India's struggle for independence from Great Britain, took up Thoreau's challenge. In 1916, Gandhi wrote the essay "On Civil Disobedience." Another fifty years later, in the 1960s, Martin Luther King Jr. led the Civil Rights movement by urging his followers to practice nonviolent resistance in their fight for freedom (see King's "Letter from Birmingham Jail" in Unit 8).

"Self-Reliance" is considered the finest expression of Ralph Waldo Emerson's beliefs on individualism. Over the years, the thoughts Emerson entered in his journal became the source of ideas for the many lectures he gave. After speaking, he would condense his ideas into essay form, as he does in "Self-Reliance," for a wider audience. "Self-Reliance" has remained an influential example of nineteenth-century Transcendentalism.

Reader's Context How can dissatisfaction with one's community or nation lead to efforts at improvement, both personal and public?

Meet the Authors

Ralph Waldo Emerson (1803–1882) and **Henry David Thoreau** (1817–1862) were not only contemporaries (living at the same time) but also neighbors in Concord, Massachusetts, a center of great cultural and intellectual achievement. Although the two had similar perspectives on important matters, Emerson was recognized during his time as a significant intellect and national leader, while Thoreau was seen as a local personality and something of an eccentric.

Today, Thoreau is highly regarded for his intelligence and insight. When he died at age forty-four, Emerson delivered his eulogy, writing of his friend, "He had in a short life exhausted the capabilities of this world; wherever there is knowledge, wherever there is virtue, wherever there is beauty, he will find a home."

See the Author Focuses on pages 156 (Emerson) and 168 (Thoreau) for biographical information about these authors.

Compare Literature

Thesis and Irony

The **thesis** is the main idea presented and supported in a work of nonfiction. It may be stated directly or implied.

Irony is a difference between appearance and reality. *Situational irony* occurs when an event violates the expectations of the reader or audience. *Verbal irony* occurs when a writer says one thing but means another.

Set Purpose

Emerson and Thoreau both advocated individualism over conformity and believed that citizens could help create a just society by acting on their deepest sense of what is right. As you read these authors' essays, identify the thesis in each one and where it is stated or implied. In addition, look for instances or irony and consider how each author uses this literary device to advance his main idea.

Preview Vocabulary

expedient, 185
unscrupulous, 187
endeavor, 187
predominate, 190
aversion, 190
arduous, 190

from Civil Disobedience

by Henry David Thoreau

Unjust laws exist: shall we be content to obey them, or shall we endeavor to amend them, and obey them until we have succeeded or shall we transgress them at once?

I heartily accept the motto, "That government is best which governs least;" and I should like to see it acted up to more rapidly and systematically. Carried out, it finally amounts to this, which also I believe,—"That government is best which governs not at all;" and when men are prepared for it, that will be the kind of government which they will have. Government is at best but an <u>expedient</u>; but most governments are usually, and all governments are sometimes, inexpedient. The objections which have been brought against a standing army, and they are many and weighty, and deserve to prevail, may also at last be brought against a standing government. The standing army is only an arm of the standing government. The government itself, which is only the mode which the people have chosen to execute their will, is equally liable to be abused and perverted before the people can act through it. Witness the present Mexican war, the work of comparatively a few individuals using the standing government as their tool; for, in the outset, the people would not have consented to this measure. . . .

But, to speak practically and as a citizen, unlike those who call themselves no-government men, I ask for, not at once no government, but *at once* a better government. Let every man make known what kind of government would command his respect, and that will be one step toward obtaining it.

After all, the practical reason why, when the power is once in the hands of the people, a majority are permitted, and for a long period continue, to rule is not because they are most likely to be in the right, nor because this seems fairest to the minority, but because they are physically the strongest. But a government in which the majority rule in all cases cannot be based on justice, even as far as men understand it. Can there not be a government in which the majorities do not virtually decide right and

ex • pe • di • ent (eks pē´ dē 'nt) *n.,* temporary means to an end

The Mexican-American War

The Mexican-American War (1846–1848) was fought primarily over land. By the middle of the 1800s, Americans had embraced the concept of *manifest destiny*, which encouraged expansion of the nation from coast to coast. However, doing so meant acquiring territory that belonged to Mexico.

Texas was annexed in 1845, and in 1846, the United States attempted to purchase the land that is now California and New Mexico. Mexico refused to sell, and after a series of military skirmishes between Mexican and American troops, the United States declared war on May 13, 1846. After nearly two years of fighting, Mexico agreed to sell the land and a treaty was signed.

Thoreau protested the Mexican-American War for several reasons. First, he and other Americans felt that President James K. Polk had entered into the conflict without an official declaration of war. (Some Americans even believed that U.S. troops had instigated the war by purposely engaging Mexican troops in battle.) Thoreau and others also opposed the war because the new American West was to be open to slavery. Both Thoreau and Emerson were involved in the abolitionist movement, which was centered in Boston.

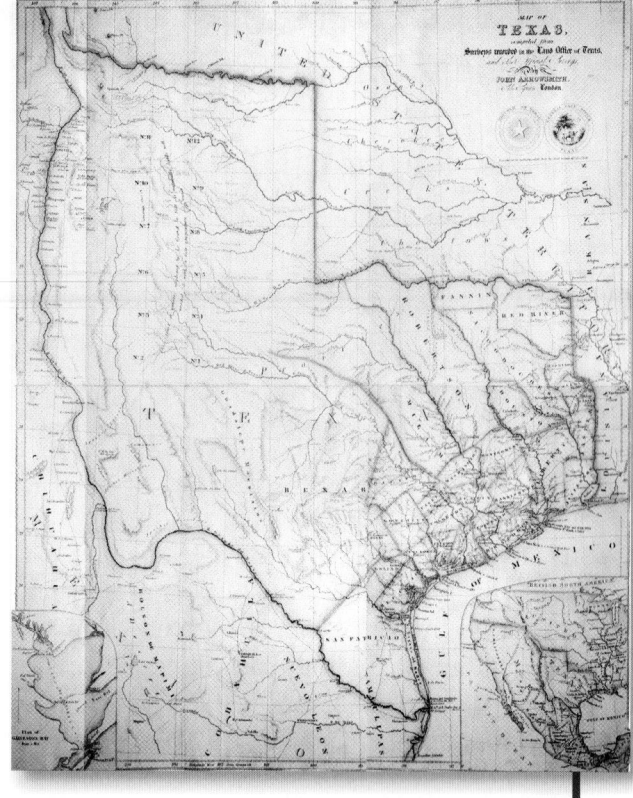

wrong, but conscience?—in which majorities decide only those questions to which the rule of expediency is applicable? Must the citizen ever for a moment, or in the least degree, resign his conscience to the legislator? Why has every man a conscience, then? I think that we should be men first, and subjects afterward. It is not desirable to cultivate a respect for the law, so much as for the right. The only obligation which I have a right to assume is to do at any time what I think right. It is truly enough said, that a corporation has no conscience; but a corporation of conscientious men is a corporation *with* a conscience. Law never made men a whit more just; and, by means of their respect for it, even the well-disposed are daily made

the agents of injustice. A common and natural result of an undue respect for law is, that you may see a file of soldiers, colonel, captain, corporal, privates, powder-monkeys,[1] and all, marching in admirable order over hill and dale to the wars, against their wills, ay, against their common sense and consciences, which makes it very steep marching indeed, and produces a palpitation of the heart. They have no doubt that it is a damnable business in which they are concerned; they are all peaceably inclined. Now, what are they? Men at all? or small movable forts and magazines, at the service of some

---

1. **powder-monkeys.** Boys who carried gunpowder to artillery units

unscrupulous man in power? Visit the Navy-Yard, and behold a marine, such a man as an American government can make, or such as it can make a man with its black arts—a mere shadow and reminiscence of humanity, a man laid out alive and standing, and already, as one may say, buried under arms with funeral accompaniments, though it may be,—

> "Not a drum was heard, not a funeral note,
>   As his corse to the rampart we hurried;
> Not a soldier discharged his farewell shot
>   O'er the grave where our hero was
>   buried."[2]

The mass of men serve the state thus, not as men mainly, but as machines, with their bodies. They are the standing army, and the militia, jailers, constables, *posse comitatus,*[3] etc. In most cases there is no free exercise whatever of the judgement or of the moral sense; but they put themselves on a level with wood and earth and stones; and wooden men can perhaps be manufactured that will serve the purpose as well. Such command no more respect than men of straw or a lump of dirt. They have the same sort of worth only as horses and dogs. Yet such as these even are commonly esteemed good citizens. Others—as most legislators, politicians, lawyers, ministers, and office-holders—serve the state chiefly with their heads; and, as they rarely make any moral distinctions, they are as likely to serve the Devil, without *intending* it, as God. A very few—as heroes, patriots, martyrs, reformers in the great sense, and *men*—serve the state with their consciences also, and so necessarily resist it for the most part; and they are commonly treated as enemies by it. . . .

U njust laws exist: shall we be content to obey them, or shall we endeavor to amend them, and obey them until we have succeeded or shall we transgress them at once? Men generally, under such a government as this, think that they ought to wait until they have persuaded the majority to alter them. They think that, if they should resist, the remedy would be worse than the evil. But it is the fault of the government itself that the remedy *is* worse than the evil. *It* makes it worse. Why is it not more apt to anticipate and provide for reform? Why does it not cherish its wise minority? Why does it cry and resist before it is hurt? Why does it not encourage its citizens to be on the alert to point out its faults, and *do* better than it would have them? Why does it always crucify Christ, and excommunicate Copernicus and Luther,[4] and pronounce Washington and Franklin rebels? . . .

If the injustice is part of the necessary friction of the machine of government, let it go, let it go: perchance it will wear smooth,—certainly the machine will wear out. If the injustice has a spring, or a pulley, or a rope, or a crank, exclusively for itself, then perhaps you may consider whether the remedy will not be worse than the evil; but if it is of such a nature that it requires you to be the agent of injustice to another, then, I say, break the law. Let your life be a counter-friction to stop the machine. What I have to do is to see, at any rate, that I do not lend myself to the wrong which I condemn. . . .

I meet this American government, or its representative, the state government, directly, and face to face, once a year—no more—in the person of its tax-gatherer; this is the only mode in which a man situated as I am necessarily

---

2. **"Not . . . buried."** First lines of a poem by Charles Wolfe, an Irish writer
3. ***posse comitatus.*** [Latin] Group assembled by a sheriff to help enforce the law
4. **Copernicus and Luther.** Nicolaus Copernicus (1473–1543)—Polish astronomer who first stated that the Earth revolves around the sun; Martin Luther (1483–1546)—German leader of the Protestant Reformation

un • scru • pu • lous (un skrü´ pyü ləs) *adj.,* lacking moral principles
en • deav • or (in de´ vər) *v.,* attempt

meets it; and it then says distinctly, Recognize me; and the simplest, most effectual, and, in the present posture of affairs, the indispensablest mode of treating with it on this head, of expressing your little satisfaction with and love for it, is to deny it then. My civil neighbor, the tax-gatherer, is the very man I have to deal with,—for it is, after all, with men and not with parchment that I quarrel,—and he has voluntarily chosen to be an agent of the government. How shall he ever know well what he is and does as an officer of the government, or as a man, until he is obliged to consider whether he shall treat me, his neighbor, for whom he has respect, as a neighbor and well-disposed man, or as a maniac and disturber of the peace, and see if he can get over this obstruction to his neighborliness without a ruder and more impetuous thought or speech corresponding with his action. I know this well, that if one thousand, if one hundred, if ten men whom I could name,—if ten *honest* men only,—ay, if *one* HONEST man, in this State of Massachusetts, *ceasing to hold slaves,* were actually to withdraw from this copartnership, and be locked up in the county jail therefor, it would be the abolition of slavery in America. For it matters not how small the beginning may seem to be: what is once well done is done forever. But we love better to talk about it: that we say is our mission. Reform keeps many scores of newspapers in its service, but not one man. . . .

U nder a government which imprisons any unjustly, the true place for a just man is also a prison. The proper place today, the only place which Massachusetts has provided for her freer and less desponding spirits, is in her prisons, to be put out and locked out of the State by her own act, as they have already put themselves out by their principles. It is there that the fugitive slave, and the Mexican prisoner on parole, and the Indian come to plead the wrongs of his race should find them; on that separate, but more free and honorable ground, where the State places those who are not *with* her, but *against* her,—the only house in a slave State in which a free man can abide with honor. If any think that their influence would be lost there, and their voices no longer afflict the ear of the State, that they would not be as an enemy within its walls, they do not know by how much truth is stronger than error, nor how much more eloquently and effectively he can combat injustice who has experienced a little in his own person. Cast your whole vote, not a strip of paper merely, but your whole influence. A minority is powerless while it conforms to the majority; it is not even a minority then; but it is irresistible when it clogs by its whole weight. If the alternative is to keep all just men in prison, or give up war and slavery, the State will not hesitate which to choose. If a thousand men were not to pay their tax bills this year, that would not be a violent and bloody measure, as it would be to pay them, and enable the State to commit violence and shed innocent blood. This is, in fact, the definition of a peaceable revolution, if any such is possible. If the tax-gatherer, or any other public officer, asks me, as one has done, "But what shall I do?" my answer is, "If you really wish to do anything, resign your office." When the subject has refused allegiance, and the officer has resigned from office, then the revolution is

If the alternative is to keep all just men in prison, or give up war and slavery, the State will not hesitate which to choose.

accomplished. But even suppose blood should flow. Is there not a sort of blood shed when the conscience is wounded? Through this wound a man's real manhood and immortality flow out, and he bleeds to an everlasting death. I see this blood flowing now. . . .

I have paid no poll tax for six years. I was put into a jail once on this account, for one night; and, as I stood considering the walls of solid stone, two or three feet thick, the door of wood and iron, a foot thick, and the iron grating which strained the light, I could not help being struck with the foolishness of that institution which treated me as if I were mere flesh and blood and bones, to be locked up. I wondered that it should have concluded at length that this was the best use it could put me to, and had never thought to avail itself of my services in some way. I saw that, if there was a wall of stone between me and my townsmen, there was a still more difficult one to climb or break through before they could get to be as free as I was. I did not for a moment feel confined, and the walls seemed a great waste of stone and mortar. I felt as if I alone of all my townsmen had paid my tax. They plainly did not know how to treat me, but behaved like persons who are underbred. In every threat and in every compliment there was a blunder; for they thought that my chief desire was to stand the other side of that stone wall. I could not but smile to see how industriously they locked the door on my meditations, which followed them out again without let or hindrance, and *they* were really all that was dangerous.

As they could not reach me, they had resolved to punish my body; just as boys, if they cannot come at some person against whom they have a spite, will abuse his dog. I saw that the State was half-witted, that it was timid as a lone woman with her silver spoons, and that it did not know its friends from its foes, and I lost all my remaining respect for it, and pitied it.

Thus the State never intentionally confronts a man's sense, intellectual or moral, but only his body, his senses. It is not armed with superior wit or honesty, but with superior physical strength. I was not born to be forced. I will breathe after my own fashion. Let us see who is the strongest. What force has a multitude? They only can force me who obey a higher law than I. They force me to become like themselves. I do not hear of *men* being *forced* to live this way or that by masses of men. What sort of life were that to live? When I meet a government which says to me, "Your money or your life," why should I be in haste to give it my money? It may be in a great strait, and not know what to do: I cannot help that. It must help itself; do as I do. It is not worth the while to snivel about it. I am not responsible for the successful working of the machinery of society. I am not the son of the engineer. I perceive that, when an acorn and a chestnut fall side by side, the one does not remain inert to make way for the other, but both obey their own laws, and spring and grow and flourish as best they can, till one, perchance, overshadows and destroys the other. If a plant cannot live according to nature, it dies; and so a man. ❖

MIRRORS & WINDOWS Why does society sometimes discourage individuals from acting according to their consciences?

from Self-Reliance

by Ralph Waldo Emerson

The Voyage of Life, 1842. Thomas Cole.

To be great is to be misunderstood.

There is a time in every man's education when he arrives at the conviction that envy is ignorance; that imitation is suicide; that he must take himself for better, for worse, as his portion; that though the wide universe is full of good, no kernel of nourishing corn can come to him but through his toil bestowed on that plot of ground which is given to him to till.

♦ ♦ ♦

Trust thyself: every heart vibrates to that iron string. Accept the place the divine Providence has found for you; the society of your contemporaries, the connexion of events. Great men have always done so and confided themselves childlike to the genius of their age, betraying their perception that the Eternal was stirring at their heart, working through their hands, pre-dominating in all their being.

♦ ♦ ♦

Society everywhere is in conspiracy against the manhood of every one of its members. Society is a joint-stock company[1] in which the members agree for the better securing of his bread to each shareholder, to surrender the liberty and culture of the eater. The virtue in most request is conformity. Self-reliance is its aversion. It loves not realities and creators, but names and customs.

♦ ♦ ♦

Whoso would be a man must be a nonconformist. He who would gather immortal palms must not be hindered by the name of goodness, but must explore if it be goodness. Nothing is at last sacred but the integrity of our own mind.

What I must do, is all that concerns me, not what the people think. This rule, equally arduous in actual and in intellectual life, may

---

1. **joint-stock company.** Business in which joint owners hold the capital, or money invested and earned

pre • dom • i • nate (prē dô´ mi nāt) *v.*, have authority or influence over
aver • sion (ä vʉr´ shən) *n.*, strong dislike
ar • du • ous (är´ jü əs) *adj.*, difficult

serve for the whole distinction between greatness and meanness. It is the harder, because you will always find those who think they know what is your duty better than you know it. It is easy in the world to live after the world's opinion; it is easy in solitude to live after our own; but the great man is he who in the midst of the crowd keeps with perfect sweetness the independence of solitude.

◆ ◆ ◆

A foolish consistency is the hobgoblin of little minds, adored by little statesmen and philosophers and divines.[2] With consistency a great soul has simply nothing to do. He may as well concern himself with his shadow on the wall. Out upon your guarded lips! Sew them up with packthread, do. Else, if you would be a man, speak what you think today in words as hard as cannon balls, and tomorrow speak what tomorrow thinks in hard words again, though it contradict everything you said today. Ah, then, exclaim the aged ladies, you shall be sure to be misunderstood. Misunderstood! It is a right fool's word. Is it so bad then to be misunderstood? Pythagoras was misunderstood, and Socrates, and Jesus, and Luther, and Copernicus, and Galileo, and Newton, and every pure and wise spirit that ever took flesh. To be great is to be misunderstood.

◆ ◆ ◆

I hope in these days we have heard the last of conformity and consistency. Let the words be gazetted and ridiculous henceforward.[3] Instead of the gong for dinner, let us hear a whistle from the Spartan fife.[4] Let us bow and apologize never more. A great man is coming to eat at my house. I do not wish to please him: I wish that he should wish to please me. I will stand here for humanity, and though I would make it kind, I would made it true. Let us affront and reprimand the smooth mediocrity and squalid[5] contentment of the times, and hurl in the face of custom, and trade, and office, the fact which is the upshot of all history, that there is a great responsible Thinker and Actor moving wherever moves a man; that a true man belongs to no other time or place, but is the center of things. Where he is, there is nature. . . . Every true man is a cause, a country, and an age; requires infinite spaces and numbers and time fully to accomplish his thought;—and posterity seem to follow his steps as a procession. A man Caesar is born, and for ages after, we have a Roman Empire. Christ is born, and millions of minds so grow and cleave to[6] his genius, that he is confounded with virtue and the possible of man. An institution is the lengthened shadow of one man; as, the Reformation, of Luther; Quakerism, of Fox; Methodism, of Wesley; Abolition, of Clarkson.[7] Scipio,[8] Milton called, "the height of Rome;" and all history resolves itself very easily into the biography of a few stout and earnest persons. ❖

---

2. **divines.** People who try to predict the future
3. **gazetted and ridiculous henceforward.** Labeled and not used from now on
4. **gong . . . fife.** The gong stands for leisurely life; the fife represents disciplined, alert living.
5. **squalid.** Wretched; miserable
6. **cleave to.** Cling to; follow
7. **Reformation . . . Clarkson.** Martin Luther (1483–1546), founder of the Reformation; George Fox (1624–1691), founder of Quakerism; John Wesley (1703–1791), founder of Methodism; and Thomas Clarkson (1760–1846), antislavery activist
8. **Scipio.** (237–183 BCE) Roman conqueror of Carthage, a city-state in ancient Africa

MIRRORS & WINDOWS

What is the difference between *self-reliance* and *conformity*? Do you tend to be more self-reliant or more conformist?

Refer to Text ▶ ▶ ▶ ▶ ▶ **Reason with Text**

1a. According to Emerson, what virtue does society ask of each person?	**1b.** What virtue does Emerson favor instead? Why?	**Understand** Find meaning
2a. According to Thoreau, what are people afraid will happen if they protest unfair laws?	**2b.** Under what conditions, in your view, might large numbers of people risk their safety or even their lives to protest injustice?	**Apply** Use information
3a. What kinds of people, in Emerson's opinion, value a "foolish consistency"?	**3b.** Identify the possible consequences of accepting a foolish consistency. Why might petty leaders encourage such consistency among their followers?	**Analyze** Take things apart
4a. According to Emerson, when is it difficult to be an independent thinker?	**4b.** Argue whether people should be encouraged to be self-reliant.	**Evaluate** Make judgments
5a. Recall the advice Emerson gives for acting as an individual. What advice does Thoreau give?	**5b.** Propose what social and political issues Emerson and Thoreau might be involved in if they were alive today. Explain why.	**Create** Bring ideas together

Compare Literature

Thesis and Irony

Write two sentences: one stating the thesis in "Civil Disobedience" and one stating the thesis in "Self-Reliance." Also note where in the essay you found the thesis and whether it was stated directly or implied. Finally, jot down examples of support the author provides to prove his thesis. Evaluate how effectively each author makes his point.

Discuss the irony in an innocent-sounding question such as "Is it so bad then to be misunderstood?" What might have been Emerson's reason for using irony? Identify examples of irony in Thoreau's essay, and explain their significance.

Extend the Text

Writing Options

Creative Writing Create a question-and-answer script in which audience members raise questions about "Self-Reliance" and "Civil Disobedience" and Emerson and Thoreau respond. Include some questions that both authors are expected to answer.

Persuasive Writing You would like to express an opinion about a school controversy but are not sure whether a gentle tone, like Emerson's, or an aggressive tone, like Thoreau's, will be more effective. Write two versions of a one-paragraph position statement: one using each tone. Then ask classmates which version seems more persuasive and why.

Collaborative Learning

Create a Mural With a group of students, create and display a mural showing scenes of civil disobedience during the Civil Rights movement of the 1950s and 1960s. Read accounts and look at photographs of sit-ins, boycotts, and other types of peaceful resistance.

Lifelong Learning

Compare Writers' Influence Thoreau's "Civil Disobedience" had a significant impact on Martin Luther King Jr. Was King also influenced by Emerson's "Self-Reliance"? Write a brief historical analysis to compare the influence the two essays have had on well-known individuals.

 Go to **www.mirrorsandwindows.com** for more.

1. Which of the following statements is *not* a reason for Thoreau's lack of support for the government?
   A. "The government itself . . . is equally liable to be abused and perverted before the people can act through it."
   B. "But a government in which the majority rule in all cases cannot be based on justice, even as far as men understand it."
   C. "I felt as if I alone of all my townsmen had paid my tax."
   D. "Under a government which imprisons any unjustly, the true place for a just man is also a prison."
   E. "Thus the state never intentionally confronts a man's sense, intellectual or moral, but only his body, his senses. It is not armed with superior wit or honesty, but with superior physical strength."

2. Which of the following ideas is expressed in both Thoreau's and Emerson's essays?
   A. People should do what they believe is right, not what others tell them is right.
   B. Individuals should put more value in what they think than what others think.
   C. A government in which the majority rules encourages people to conform.
   D. No one can lead an intellectual life without thinking primarily of himself or herself.
   E. Individuals should rely on themselves to meet their own needs.

3. In "Civil Disobedience," what does the word *inexpedient* mean?
   A. not having authority over
   B. fast
   C. lacking moral principles
   D. lacking necessary experience
   E. impeding progress

4. In Emerson's opinion, being able to follow one's own mind instead of public opinion may serve to
   A. distinguish between adults and children.
   B. distinguish between greatness and meanness.
   C. separate men from women.
   D. determine who should lead the country.
   E. achieve success and popularity.

5. Emerson argues that people should say what they think "in words as hard as cannon balls" even if
   A. they contradict what they said yesterday.
   B. no one wants to hear it.
   C. doing so goes against society.
   D. the message probably will be misunderstood.
   E. it hurts people they care about.

6. If you have an *aversion* to something, you will likely
   A. want to have or experience more of it.
   B. break out in hives or a rash when exposed to it.
   C. compare it something more familiar.
   D. try to avoid it.
   E. do it often.

7. Why does Thoreau compare soldiers and others who serve the government to "wood and earth and stones"?
   A. He thinks they are uneducated and slow witted.
   B. He believes they have lost their souls.
   C. He believes their bodies are acting against their consciences.
   D. He believes they are a natural part of the world.
   E. He believes they are the foundation on which society is built.

8. **Constructed Response:** Both Emerson and Thoreau refer to Jesus, Martin Luther, and Copernicus in their essays. Explain how each author uses these allusions to support his thesis, and evaluate the effectiveness of doing so.

9. **Constructed Response:** Explain this metaphor from Emerson: "Society is a joint-stock company in which the members agree for the better securing of his bread to each shareholder, to surrender the liberty and culture of the eater." What does it suggest about Emerson's views of society and human nature?

Understand the Concept

Many writers sometimes make the mistake of writing sentence fragments instead of complete sentences. A **sentence fragment** is a phrase or clause that does not express a complete thought but has been capitalized and punctuated as if it were a sentence.

EXAMPLES

Phrase fragment Thoreau's account of life at Walden Pond. [The verb, plus any modifiers, is missing.]

Sentence Thoreau's account of life at Walden Pond was revised over nine years.

Clause fragment When it was published in 1854. [This is a clause, not a sentence, because it begins with a subordinating conjunction, *when*. To become a sentence, the fragment needs to be linked to a main clause.]

Sentence When it was published in 1854, *Walden* established Thoreau's reputation as a writer.

Clause fragment Whom history would recognize as a visionary. [This is a clause, not a sentence, because it begins with a relative pronoun, *whom*. The fragment needs to be joined to a main clause to become a sentence.]

Sentence It was Thoreau whom history would recognize as a visionary.

To avoid writing fragments, make sure that every sentence has a subject and a verb. If you write a clause introduced by a subordinating conjunction or a relative pronoun, be sure to link the clause to a main clause to make a sentence. Another way to catch any fragments in your writing is to proofread your work carefully.

Apply the Skill

Identify Sentence Fragments

Indicate which of the following items are *sentences* (mark *S*) and which are *fragments* (mark *F*).

1. Henry David Thoreau a talented, skilled writer.
2. Enjoyed the solitude of being alone in nature.
3. He had read Emerson's *Nature* while in college.
4. Worked for Emerson as a gardener and handyman.
5. In 1845, when he was twenty-eight.
6. Thoreau's cabin was just two miles from Concord.
7. Over the next two years and two months.
8. Published essays against the Mexican War and in favor of abolition.
9. When he was just forty-four years old.
10. Twenty volumes of journals were discovered after his death.

Revise Sentence Fragments

The following items are all fragments. Rewrite each one to make it a sentence.

1. Based on the journals Thoreau kept.
2. Thoreau spent a good deal of time.
3. When it was published in 1854.
4. Writing seven full drafts over nine years.
5. To establish Thoreau's reputation as a writer.

Use Complete Sentences

Work with a partner to practice building sentences and avoiding fragments. Each of you should make a list of five phrases, including prepositional phrases (for example, *in the lunchroom*), participial phrases (*having waited long enough*), and infinitive phrases (*to arrive at the meeting on time*). Then exchange lists. From each phrase, build a sentence. (If necessary, make minor adjustments in the wording of the phrase.) Exchange papers again, and correct any fragments.

Evaluate the Use of Sentence Fragments

Using a sentence fragment is considered a grammatical mistake in academic writing and news reporting. However, professional writers such as novelists and columnists often use fragments for effect in their writing. A sentence fragment can be used to emphasize a certain point, to add a particular emotional tone, or to mimic the sound of everyday speech. Collect two or three examples of professional writing that include sentence fragments. Analyze each example to determine what effect the writer intended.

Letter to Sophia Ripley

by Margaret Fuller

August 27, 1839
On the nature of the proposed Conversations

(Sarah) Margaret Fuller
(1810–1850) was one of the primary women involved in the Transcendentalist movement. In the early 1840s, she was an editor, along with Ralph Waldo Emerson, of *The Dial*. She later turned one of her essays for the magazine into an influential book, *Woman in the Nineteenth Century* (1845).

On August 27, 1839, Fuller wrote a letter to Sophia Dana Ripley, suggesting that they and other "well-educated and thinking women" from the Boston area take part in weekly conversations on stimulating subjects. During the next five years, some two hundred women—including Emerson's wife, Lydia—attended the weekly meetings. Ironically, Emerson himself referred to the meetings as "Parlatorio" ("parlor oratory," or discussions in respectable homes). Nevertheless, the conversations sparked interest in the feminist movement.

The advantages of a weekly meeting, for conversation, might be great enough to repay the trouble of attendance, if they consisted only in supplying a point of union to well-educated and thinking women, in a city which, with great pretensions[1] to mental refinement, boasts, at present, nothing of the kind, and where I have heard many, of mature age, wish for some such means of stimulus and cheer, and those younger, for a place where they could state their doubts and difficulties, with a hope of gaining aid from the experience or aspirations[2] of others. And if my office were only to suggest topics, which would lead to conversation of a better order than is usual at social meetings, and to turn back the current when digressing into personalities or common-places, so that what is valuable in the experience of each might be brought to bear upon all, I should think the object not unworthy of the effort.

But my ambition goes much further. It is to pass in review the departments of thought and knowledge, and endeavor to place them in due relation to one another in our minds. To systematize thought, and give a precision and clearness in which our sex are so deficient, chiefly, I think, because they have so few inducements[3] to test and classify what they receive. To ascertain[4] what pursuits are best suited to us, in our time and state of society, and how we may make best use of our means for building up the life of thought upon the life of action.

---

1. **pretentions.** Claims or intentions
2. **aspirations.** Strong desires or ambitions
3. **inducements.** Motivations
4. **ascertain.** Make certain or exact

Could a circle be assembled in earnest, desirous to answer the questions,—What were we born to do? and how shall we do it?—which so few ever propose to themselves till their best years are gone by, I should think the undertaking a noble one, and, if my resources should prove sufficient to make me its moving spring, I should be willing to give to it a large portion of those coming years, which will, as I hope, be my best. I look upon it with no blind enthusiasm, nor unlimited faith, but with a confidence that I have attained a distinct perception of means, which, if there are persons competent to direct them, can supply a great want, and promote really high objects. So far as I have tried them yet, they have met with success so much beyond my hopes, that my faith will not easily be shaken, not my earnestness chilled. Should I, however, be disappointed in Boston, I could hardly hope that such a plan could be brought to bear on general society, in any other city of the United States. But I do not fear, if a good beginning can be made. I am confident that twenty persons cannot be brought together from better motives than vanity or pedantry,[5] to talk upon such subjects as we propose, without finding in themselves great deficiencies, which they will be very desirous to supply. ❖

---

5. **pedantry.** Here, eagerness to expand one's learning

MIRRORS & WINDOWS

What motivated the women who attended the conversations established by Fuller and Ripley? What would motivate women today to participate in discussions such as these?

Refer and Reason

1. According to Fuller, how might younger women benefit from the meetings? How might older women benefit? Explain how the two groups might benefit each other.

2. State what Fuller sees as the role of her office in organizing the groups. If you were working with Fuller, what ideas would you add to or remove from the letter? Be specific.

3. Identify Fuller's use of *parallelism* in paragraph 2, in which similar ideas are expressed in the same grammatical form. Using the same parallel structure, restate her ambition in your own words.

Writing Options

1. Travel back to 1839 and write a letter of acceptance to Fuller, explaining why you want to join the conversation group. You may use present-day wording or write in Fuller's more formal style.

2. Suppose that members of a men's club in Boston in the 1840s have asked you, a journalist, to write an editorial objecting to Fuller's conversation groups. Prepare a copy to show to the club members.

MW Go to **www.mirrorsandwindows.com** for more.

Not all of the literature of the New England Renaissance was sentimental and idealistic. Writers such as Washington Irving, Edgar Allan Poe, Nathaniel Hawthorne, and Herman Melville portrayed a decidedly darker view of the world.

Irving is representative of a group of New York writers who exposed the greed and pretentiousness of the newly formed American aristocracy, often through satire. Irving used folk tales and legends, both American and European, as the basis for some of his stories and to examine what he called "the unchanging principles of human nature."

The frailties of human nature were examined by Poe, Hawthorne, and Melville. Sin and guilt, madness and death, good and evil were explored in stories that often were *allegorical,* teaching lessons about the human condition. A related theme was the failure of traditional religion, especially Puritanism, to provide personal guidance and social control.

Among these authors, Poe stands out as the master of **Gothic fiction,** as characterized by medieval settings and grotesque, mysterious, and violent incidents. Poe said he purposefully chose subjects that would make people melancholy, such as death. A masterful storyteller, he generally is credited with having invented both the ghost story and the detective story.

Poe, along with Hawthorne and Irving, also is credited with establishing the short story as a literary form. In the 1800s, short stories often were published in periodicals, making them widely available to the American public.

Walk at Dusk, c. 1830–1835. David Casper Friedrich.
J. Paul Getty Museum, Los Angeles.

The Devil and Tom Walker

A Short Story by Washington Irving

Build Background

Literary Context **"The Devil and Tom Walker,"**
first published in 1824 as part of a collection of stories by
Washington Irving, is about a man who sells his soul to
the devil in exchange for wealth. There are several theories

about the origin of this story. Many literary scholars believe "The Devil and
Tom Walker" is an adaptation of *Faust,* the famous play by German writer
Johann Goethe, first published around 1806. Irving had traveled throughout
Germany by the time he wrote this story and likely was familiar with Goethe's
play. Other scholars contend that the story is rooted in a centuries-old New
England legend, one that Irving would have known.

Regardless, "The Devil and Tom Walker," as well as some of Irving's other
early short stories, was not well received upon publication. Some critics attribute
this response to the fact that the short story was a relatively new literary form
at the time. As noted earlier, writers such as Irving, Nathaniel Hawthorne, and
Edgar Allan Poe would establish this form in American literature by midcentury.

Reader's Context What makes people sacrifice their integrity for short-term
gain or success?

Meet the Author

Washington Irving (1783–1859) was born in New York City
into a large, prosperous family. He developed a love for books
early in life and would eventually learn to speak or write in
four languages. He trained privately to become a lawyer but
practiced only a short time before turning to writing.

Irving has the distinction of being the first American to
make a living full time as a writer and to have earned respect
among European literary circles. He is most famous for his
short stories, particularly "The Legend of Sleepy Hollow" and
"Rip Van Winkle," both published in 1819–1820. He began
his literary career, however, by writing satirical sketches for journals and newspapers, in which he poked fun at fashionable New York society.

Irving traveled extensively and spent nearly twenty years living in Europe
(1815–1832). He applied his skills as a lawyer, as well as a linguist, while
working for the American diplomatic corps in Great Britain and Spain. He
also wrote about many of the places he visited. His books on fifteenth-century
Spanish history, including several about Christopher Columbus, brought him
recognition in Europe. Irving traveled to the American West in the 1830s. In
writing about his experiences, he commented on the deplorable treatment of
the Native Americans by Europeans and Americans.

From 1846 until his death in 1859, Irving lived at Sunnyside, his home
along the Hudson River, in New York state. A century later, Sunnyside was
opened to the public; a tour of the estate offers a glimpse into Irving's life.

Analyze Literature

**Plot, Conflict, Exposition,
and Climax**
Plot refers to the series of
events related to a central
conflict, or struggle. Two key
elements of plot are the exposition and the climax.

In the **exposition,** the author
introduces the characters
and setting, sets the tone or
mood, and gives background
information.

The **climax** is the high point of
interest.

Set Purpose

As one of the pioneers of the
short story, Irving was a master
at weaving a cleverly crafted
tale. As you read "The Devil and
Tom Walker," analyze the plot.
Identify what parts of the story
comprise the exposition, the
conflict, and the climax. Trace
how Irving carefully develops
the plot to create a feeling of
suspense.

Preview Vocabulary

prevalent, 200
precarious, 200
propitiate, 203
surmise, 203
obliterate, 203
resolute, 203
speculate, 206
ostentation, 206
parsimony, 206

THE DEVIL
and Tom Walker

by Washington Irving

Man and Woman Contemplating the Moon, c. 1818. Caspar David Freidrich. Gemaeldegalerie, Staatliche Museen zu Berlin, Berlin, Germany. (See detail on page 198.)

Like most short-cuts, it was an ill-chosen route.

A few miles from Boston in Massachusetts, there is a deep inlet, winding several miles into the interior of the country from Charles Bay, and terminating in a thickly wooded swamp or morass. On one side of this inlet is a beautiful dark grove; on the opposite side the land rises abruptly from the water's edge into a high ridge, on which grow a few scattered oaks of great age and immense size. Under one of these gigantic trees, according to old stories, there was a great amount of treasure buried by Kidd the pirate. The inlet allowed a facility to bring the money in a boat secretly and at night to the very foot of the hill; the elevation of the place permitted a good look-out to be kept that no one was at hand; while the remarkable trees formed good landmarks by which the place might easily be found again. The old stories add, moreover, that the Devil presided at the hiding of the money, and took it under his guardianship; but this it is well known he always does with buried treasure, particularly when it has been ill-gotten.

Be that as it may, Kidd never returned to recover his wealth; being shortly after seized at Boston, sent out to England, and there hanged for a pirate.

About the year 1727, just at the time that earthquakes were <u>prevalent</u> in New England, and shook many tall sinners down upon their knees, there lived near this place a meager, miserly fellow, of the name of Tom Walker. He had a wife as miserly as himself: they were so miserly that they even conspired to cheat each other. Whatever the woman could lay hands on, she hid away; a hen could not cackle but she was on the alert to secure the new-laid egg. Her husband was continually prying about to detect her secret hoards, and many and fierce were the conflicts that took place about what ought to have been common property. They lived in a forlorn-looking house that stood alone, and had an air of starvation. A few straggling savin trees, emblems of sterility, grew near it; no smoke ever curled from its chimney; no traveller stopped at its door. A miserable horse, whose ribs were as articulate as the bars of a gridiron, stalked about a field, where a thin carpet of moss, scarcely covering the ragged beds of puddingstone,[1] tantalized and balked his hunger; and sometimes he would lean his head over the fence, look piteously at the passerby, and seem to petition deliverance from this land of famine.

The house and its inmates had altogether a bad name. Tom's wife was a tall termagant,[2] fierce of temper, loud of tongue, and strong of arm. Her voice was often heard in wordy warfare with her husband; and his face sometimes showed signs that their conflicts were not confined to words. No one ventured, however, to interfere between them. The lonely wayfarer shrunk within himself at the horrid clamor and clapperclawing;[3] eyed the den of discord

> **They were so miserly that they even conspired to cheat each other.**

askance; and hurried on his way, rejoicing, if a bachelor, in his celibacy.

One day that Tom Walker had been to a distant part of the neighborhood, he took what he considered a shortcut homeward, through the swamp. Like most shortcuts, it was an ill-chosen route. The swamp was thickly grown with great gloomy pines and hemlocks, some of them ninety feet high, which made it dark at noonday, and a retreat for all the owls of the neighborhood. It was full of pits and quagmires, partly covered with weeds and mosses, where the green surface often betrayed the traveler into a gulf of black, smothering mud; there were also dark and stagnant pools, the abodes of the tadpole, the bullfrog, and the watersnake; where the trunks of pines and hemlocks lay half-drowned, half-rotting, looking like alligators, sleeping in the mire.

Tom had long been picking his way cautiously through this treacherous forest; stepping from tuft to tuft of rushes and roots, which afforded <u>precarious</u> footholds among deep sloughs; or pacing carefully, like a cat, along the prostrate[4] trunks of trees; startled now and then by the sudden screaming of the bittern, or the quacking of a wild duck, rising on the wing from some solitary pool. At length he arrived at a piece of firm ground, which ran out like a peninsula into the deep bosom of the swamp. It had been one of the strongholds of the Indians during their wars with the first colonists. Here they had thrown up a kind of fort, which they had looked upon as almost impregnable, and had used as a place of refuge for their squaws

---

1. **puddingstone.** Rock made of pebbles and gravel in cement
2. **termagant.** Quarrelsome, scolding woman
3. **clapperclawing.** Scratching or clawing with the fingernails
4. **prostrate.** Flat on the ground

prev • a • lent (prĕ´ və lənt) *adj.,* widespread
pre • car • i • ous (prə kâr´ ē əs) *adj.,* dangerous

and children. Nothing remained of the old Indian fort but a few embankments, gradually sinking to the level of the surrounding earth, and already overgrown in part by oaks and other forest trees, the foliage of which formed a contrast to the dark pines and hemlocks of the swamp.

It was late in the dusk of evening when Tom Walker reached the old fort, and he paused there awhile to rest himself. Anyone but he would have felt unwilling to linger in this lonely, melancholy place, for the common people had a bad opinion of it, from the stories handed down from the time of the Indian wars; when it was asserted that the savages held incantations[5] here, and made sacrifices to the evil spirit.

Tom Walker, however, was not a man to be troubled with any fears of the kind. He reposed himself for some time on the trunk of a fallen hemlock, listening to the boding cry of the tree toad, and delving with his walking staff into a mound of black mold at his feet. As he turned up the soil unconsciously, his staff struck against something hard. He raked it out of the vegetable mold, and lo! a cloven skull, with an Indian tomahawk buried deep in it, lay before him. The rust on the weapon showed the time that had elapsed since this deathblow had been given. It was a dreary memento of the fierce struggle that had taken place in this last foothold of the Indian warriors.

"Humph!" said Tom Walker, as he gave it a kick to shake the dirt from it.

"Let that skull alone!" said a gruff voice. Tom lifted up his eyes, and beheld a great black man seated directly opposite him, on the stump of a tree. He was exceedingly surprised, having neither heard nor seen anyone approach; and he was still more perplexed on observing, as well as the gathering gloom would permit, that the stranger was neither Negro nor Indian. It is true he was dressed in a rude half-Indian garb, and had a red belt or sash swathed round his body; but his face was neither black nor copper color, but swarthy

and dingy, and begrimed with soot, as if he had been accustomed to toil among fires and forges. He had a shock of coarse black hair, that stood out from his head in all directions, and bore an ax on his shoulder.

He scowled for a moment at Tom with a pair of great red eyes.

"What are you doing in my grounds?" said the black man, with a hoarse growling voice.

"Your grounds?" said Tom with a sneer, "no more your grounds than mine; they belong to Deacon Peabody."

"Deacon Peabody be d—d," said the stranger, "as I flatter myself he will be, if he does not look more to his own sins and less to those of his neighbors. Look yonder, and see how Deacon Peabody is faring."

Tom looked in the direction that the stranger pointed, and beheld one of the great

---

5. **incantations.** Verbal charms or magic spells

The Salem Witch Trials

When Tom Walker meets the devil and asks who he is, the devil calls himself, among other things, "the grandmaster of the Salem witches." He is referring to the witch hunt that took place in 1692 in Salem, Massachusetts. The supposedly irrational behavior of a number of young women was, according to a local doctor, the work of the devil. Charged with witchcraft, nineteen of the women refused in court to admit to any wrongdoing and were hanged.

Some historians have explained the witch hunt by noting that Quakers and other religious groups, whose interpretation of Scripture differed from that of the Puritans, were gaining a following in colonies the Puritans had founded. Descendants of the earlier settlers may have felt threatened by the arrival of these newcomers and attacked individuals displaying unusual behavior.

A drama based on the events in Salem, *The Crucible* (1953), by prominent American playwright Arthur Miller (1915–2005), is an *allegory,* or symbolic re-enactment, of the anticommunist crusade conducted by Senator Joseph McCarthy (1908–1957). (See *The Crucible* and a transcript from the McCarthy hearings in Unit 7.)

---

trees, fair and flourishing without, but rotten at the core, and saw that it had been nearly hewn through, so that the first high wind was likely to blow it down. On the bark of the tree was scored the name of Deacon Peabody, an eminent man, who had waxed[6] wealthy by driving shrewd bargains with the Indians. He now looked round, and found most of the tall trees marked with the name of some great man of the colony, and all more or less scored by the ax. The one on which he had been seated, and which had evidently just been hewn down, bore the name of Crowninshield: and he recollected a mighty rich man of that name, who made a vulgar display of wealth, which it was whispered he had acquired by buccaneering.[7]

"He's just ready for burning!" said the black man, with a growl of triumph. "You see I am likely to have a good stock of firewood for winter."

"But what right have you," said Tom, "to cut down Deacon Peabody's timber?"

"The right of a prior claim," said the other. "This woodland belonged to me long before one of your white-faced race put foot upon the soil."

"And pray, who are you, if I may be so bold?" said Tom.

"Oh, I go by various names. I am the wild huntsman in some countries; the black miner in others. In this neighborhood I am known by the name of the black woodsman. I am he to whom the red men consecrated this spot, and in honor of whom they now and then roasted a white man, by way of sweet-smelling sacrifice. Since the red men have been exterminated by you white savages, I amuse myself by presiding at the persecutions of Quakers and Anabaptists;[8] I am the great patron and prompter of slave dealers, and the grandmaster of the Salem witches."

"The upshot of all which is, that, if I mistake not," said Tom, sturdily, "you are he commonly called Old Scratch."

"The same, at your service!" replied the black man, with a half-civil nod.

Such was the opening of this interview, according to the old story; though it has almost

---

6. **waxed.** Grew, became
7. **buccaneering.** Robbing ships at sea; piracy
8. **Quakers . . . Anabaptists.** Two religious groups whose beliefs were attacked by the Puritans

too familiar an air to be credited. One would think that to meet with such a singular personage, in this wild, lonely place, would have shaken any man's nerves; but Tom was a hard-minded fellow, not easily daunted, and he had lived so long with a termagant wife, that he did not even fear the Devil.

It is said that after this commencement, they had a long and earnest conversation together, as Tom returned homeward. The black man told him of great sums of money buried by Kidd the pirate, under the oak trees on the high ridge, not far from the morass. All these were under his command, and protected by his power, so that none could find them but such as <u>propitiated</u> his favor. These he offered to place within Tom Walker's reach, having conceived an especial kindness for him; but they were to be had only on certain conditions. What these conditions were may easily be <u>surmised</u>, though Tom never disclosed them publicly. They must have been very hard, for he required time to think of them, and he was not a man to stick at trifles where money was in view. When they had reached the edge of the swamp, the stranger paused—"What proof have I that all you have been telling me is true?" said Tom. "There is my signature," said the black man, pressing his finger on Tom's forehead. So saying, he turned off among the thickets of the swamp, and seemed, as Tom said, to go down, down, down, into the earth, until nothing but his head and shoulders could be seen, and so on, until he totally disappeared.

When Tom reached home, he found the black print of a finger, burnt, as it were, into his forehead, which nothing could <u>obliterate</u>.

The first news his wife had to tell him was the sudden death of Absalom Crowninshield, the rich buccaneer. It was announced in the papers with the usual flourish, that "A great man had fallen in Israel."[9]

When Tom reached home, he found the black print of a finger, burnt, as it were, into his forehead.

Tom recollected the tree which his black friend had just hewn down, and which was ready for burning. "Let the freebooter[10] roast," said Tom, "who cares!" He now felt convinced that all he had heard and seen was no illusion.

He was not prone to let his wife into his confidence; but as this was an uneasy secret, he willingly shared it with her. All her avarice was awakened at the mention of hidden gold, and she urged her husband to comply with the black man's terms and secure what would make them wealthy for life. However Tom might have felt disposed to sell himself to the Devil, he was determined not to do so to oblige his wife; so he flatly refused out of the mere spirit of contradiction. Many and bitter were the quarrels they had on the subject, but the more she talked, the more <u>resolute</u> was Tom not to be damned to please her.

At length she determined to drive the bargain on her own account, and if she succeeded, to keep all the gain to herself. Being of the same fearless temper as her husband, she set off for the old Indian fort towards the close of a summer's day. She was many hours absent. When she came back she was reserved and sullen in her replies. She spoke something of a black man, whom she had met about twilight, hewing at the root of a tall tree. He was sulky, however, and would not come to terms: she was to go again with a propitiatory offering, but what it was she forebore to say.

---

9. **great man . . . Israel.** Reference to the biblical passage "Know ye not that there is a prince and a great man fallen this day in Israel?" (2 Samuel 3:38). Irving is probably mocking the exaggerated importance of the newspaper's death announcement.
10. **freebooter.** Pirate

> **pro • pi • ti • ate** (prō pi´ shē āt) v., gain, as someone's goodwill, by treating agreeably
> **sur • mise** (sʉr mīz´) v., make a guess
> **ob • lit • er • ate** (ô bli´ tʉr āt) v., wipe away; erase
> **re • so • lute** (re zō lüt´) adj., strong in purpose; unyielding

The next evening she set off again for the swamp, with her apron heavily laden. Tom waited and waited for her, but in vain; midnight came, but she did not make her appearance: morning, noon, night returned, but still she did not come. Tom now grew uneasy for her safety, especially as he found she had carried off in her apron the silver teapot and spoons, and every portable article of value. Another night elapsed, another morning came; but no wife. In a word, she was never heard of more.

What was her real fate nobody knows, in consequence of so many pretending to know. It is one of those facts that have become confounded by a variety of historians. Some asserted that she lost her way among the tangled mazes of the swamp, and sank into some pit or slough; others, more uncharitable, hinted that she had eloped with the household booty, and made off to some other province; while others assert that the tempter had decoyed her into a dismal quagmire, on the top of which her hat was found lying. In confirmation of this, it was said a great black man, with an ax on his shoulder, was seen late that very evening coming out of the swamp, carrying a bundle tied in a check apron, with an air of surly triumph.

The most current and probable story, however, observes that Tom Walker grew so anxious about the fate of his wife and his property, that he set out at length to seek them both at the Indian fort. During a long summer's afternoon he searched about the gloomy place, but no wife was to be seen. He called her name repeatedly, but she was nowhere to be heard. The bittern alone responded to his voice, as he flew screaming by; or the bullfrog croaked dolefully from a neighboring pool. At length, it is said, just in the brown hour of twilight, when the owls began to hoot, and the bats to flit about, his attention was attracted by the clamor of carrion crows[11] hovering about a cypress tree. He looked up, and beheld a bundle tied in a checked apron, and hanging in the branches of the tree, with a great vulture perched hard by, as if keeping watch upon it. He leaped with joy; for he recognized his wife's apron, and supposed it to contain the household valuables.

"Let us get hold of the property," said he, consolingly to himself, "and we will endeavor to do without the woman."

As he scrambled up the tree, the vulture spread its wide wings, and sailed off screaming into the deep shadows of the forest. Tom seized the checked apron, but woeful sight! found nothing but a heart and liver tied up in it!

Such, according to the most authentic old story, was all that was to be found of Tom's wife. She had probably attempted to deal with the black man as she had been accustomed to deal with her husband; but though a female scold is generally considered a match for the Devil, yet in this instance she appears to have had the worst of it. She must have died game, however; for it is said Tom noticed many prints of cloven feet deeply stamped about the tree, and found handfuls of hair, that looked as if they had been plucked from the coarse black shock of the woodsman. Tom knew his wife's prowess by experience. He shrugged his shoulders, as he looked at the signs of a fierce clapperclawing. "Egad," said he to himself, "Old Scratch must have had a tough time of it!"

Tom consoled himself for the loss of his property, with the loss of his wife, for he was a man of fortitude. He even felt something like gratitude towards the black woodsman, who, he considered, had done him a kindness. He sought, therefore, to cultivate a further acquaintance with him, but for some time without success; the old blacklegs played shy, for whatever people may think, he is not always to be had for calling for: he knows how to play his cards when pretty sure of his game.

> **What was her real fate nobody knows.**

---

11. **carrion crows.** Crows that feed on dead or rotting flesh

The Story of "Rip Van Winkle"

Washington Irving is probably most famous for his story "Rip Van Winkle." Like Tom Walker, Rip is married to an unpleasant woman, although Rip himself, unlike Tom, is a gentle soul. On a

hillside along the Hudson River, a group of small-size men playing a kind of bowling game invite Rip to taste an unfamiliar drink. The potion puts Rip to sleep for twenty years. When he wakes up, he learns that his wife has died, and he makes the wonderful discovery that, during his extended nap, the American colonies have been victorious in their war for independence.

At length, it is said, when delay had whetted Tom's eagerness to the quick, and prepared him to agree to anything rather than not gain the promised treasure, he met the black man one evening in his usual woodman's dress, with his ax on his shoulder, sauntering along the swamp, and humming a tune. He affected to receive Tom's advance with great indifference, made brief replies, and went on humming his tune.

By degrees, however, Tom brought him to business, and they began to haggle about the terms on which the former was to have the pirate's treasure. There was one condition which need not be mentioned, being generally understood in all cases where the Devil grants favors; but there were others about which, though of less importance, he was inflexibly obstinate. He insisted that the money found through his means should be employed in his service. He proposed, therefore, that Tom should employ it in the black traffic; that is to say, that he should fit out a slave ship. This, however, Tom resolutely refused: he was bad enough in all conscience, but the Devil himself could not tempt him to turn slave-trader.

Finding Tom so squeamish on this point, he did not insist upon it, but proposed, instead, that he should turn usurer[12]; the Devil being extremely anxious for the increase of usurers, looking upon them as his peculiar[13] people.

To this no objections were made, for it was just to Tom's taste.

"You shall open a broker's shop in Boston next month," said the black man.

"I'll do it tomorrow, if you wish," said Tom Walker.

"You shall lend money at two per cent a month."

"Egad, I'll charge four!" replied Tom Walker.

"You shall extort bonds, foreclose mortgages, drive the merchant to bankruptcy—"

"I'll drive him to the D——l," cried Tom Walker.

"You are the usurer for my money!" said the blacklegs, with delight. "When will you want the rhino?"[14]

"This very night."

"Done!" said the Devil.

"Done!" said Tom Walker. So they shook hands and struck a bargain.

A few days' time saw Tom Walker seated behind his desk in a counting house in Boston.

His reputation for a ready-moneyed man, who would lend money out for a good consideration, soon spread abroad. Everybody remembers the time of Governor Belcher, when money was particularly scarce. It was a time of paper credit. The country had been deluged with government bills; the famous Land Bank[15] had been established; there had been a

---

12. **usurer.** Person who lends money, especially at an unusually or unlawfully high interest rate
13. **peculiar.** Here, belonging to an individual
14. **rhino.** Slang word for "money"
15. **Land Bank.** Institution, set up in Boston in 1739, that lent money to property owners. Many borrowers lost money when the bank was outlawed two years later.

rage for speculating; the people had run mad with schemes for new settlements, for building cities in the wilderness; land jobbers went about with maps of grants, and townships, and El Dorados,[16] lying nobody knew where, but which everybody was ready to purchase. In a word, the great speculating fever which breaks out every now and then in the country, had raged to an alarming degree, and everybody was dreaming of making sudden fortunes from nothing. As usual the fever had subsided; the dream had gone off, and the imaginary fortunes with it; the patients were left in doleful plight, and the whole country resounded with the consequent cry of "hard times."

At this propitious time of public distress did Tom Walker set up as usurer in Boston. His door was soon thronged by customers. The needy and adventurous, the gambling speculator, the dreaming land jobber, the thriftless tradesman, the merchant with cracked credit, in short, every-one driven to raise money by desperate means and desperate sacrifices, hurried to Tom Walker.

Thus Tom was the universal friend of the needy, and acted like a "friend in need"; that is to say, he always exacted good pay and good security. In proportion to the distress of the applicant was the hardness of his terms. He accumulated bonds and mortgages; gradually squeezed his customers closer and closer, and sent them at length, dry as a sponge, from his door.

In this way he made money hand over hand, became a rich and mighty man, and exalted his cocked hat upon 'Change.[17] He built himself, as usual, a vast house, out of ostentation; but left the greater part of it unfinished and unfurnished, out of parsimony. He even set up a carriage in the fullness of his vainglory,[18] though he nearly starved the horses which drew it; and as the ungreased wheels groaned and screeched on the

axletrees, you would have thought you heard the souls of the poor debtors he was squeezing.

As Tom waxed old, however, he grew thoughtful. Having secured the good things of this world, he began to feel anxious about those of the next. He thought with regret on the bargain he had made with his black friend, and set his wits to work to cheat him out of the conditions. He became, therefore, all of a sudden, a violent churchgoer. He prayed loudly and strenuously, as if heaven were to be taken by force of lungs. Indeed, one might always tell when he had sinned most during the week, by the clamor of his Sunday devotion. The quiet Christians who had been modestly and steadfastly travelling Zionward,[19] were struck with self-reproach at seeing themselves so suddenly outstripped in their career by this new-made convert. Tom was as rigid in religious as in money matters; he was a stern supervisor and censurer of his neighbors, and seemed to think

Having secured the good things of this world, he began to feel anxious about those of the next.

every sin entered up to their account became a credit on his own side of the page. He even talked of the expediency of reviving the persecution of Quakers and Anabaptists. In a word, Tom's zeal became as notorious as his riches.

Still, in spite of all this strenuous attention to forms, Tom had a lurking dread that the Devil, after all, would have his due. That he might not be taken unawares, therefore, it is said he always

---

16. **Eldorados.** Mocking reference to El Dorado, a mythical place in Latin America where Spanish explorers hoped to find gold
17. **'Change.** Short for "Exchange," or "Stock Exchange"
18. **vainglory.** Vanity; self-importance
19. **Zionward.** Toward heaven

---

spec • u • late (spek´ yü lāt) v., take a risk in business, with the hope of making a profit
os • ten • ta • tion (ô sten tā´ shən) n., showiness, often intended to attract attention
par • si • mo • ny (pär´ sə mō' nē) n., stinginess

carried a small Bible in his coat pocket. He had also a great folio Bible on his countinghouse desk, and would frequently be found reading it when people called on business; on such occasions he would lay his green spectacles in the book, to mark the place, while he turned round to drive some usurious bargain.

Some say that Tom grew a little crack-brained in his old days, and that fancying his end approaching, he had his horse newly shod, saddled and bridled, and buried with his feet uppermost; because he supposed that at the last day the world would be turned upside down, in which case he should find his horse standing ready for mounting, and he was determined at the worst to give his old friend a run for it. This, however, is probably a mere old wives' fable. If he really did take such a precaution, it was totally superfluous; at least so says the authentic old legend, which closes his story in the following manner.

One hot summer afternoon in the dog days, just as a terrible black thunder-gust was coming up, Tom sat in his countinghouse in his white linen cap and India silk morning gown. He was on the point of foreclosing a mortgage, by which he would complete the ruin of an unlucky land speculator for whom he had professed the greatest friendship. The poor land jobber begged him to grant a few months' indulgence. Tom had grown testy and irritated, and refused another day.

"My family will be ruined and brought upon the parish," said the land jobber.

"Charity begins at home," replied Tom; "I must take care of myself in these hard times."

Buffalo Trail: The Impending Storm, 1869. Albert Bierstadt. Corcoran Gallery of Art, Washington, DC.

"You have made so much money out of me," said the speculator.

Tom lost his patience and his piety—"The Devil take me," said he, "if I have made a farthing!"[20]

Just then there were three loud knocks at the street door. He stepped out to see who was there. A black man was holding a black horse, which neighed and stamped with impatience.

"Tom, you're come for," said the black fellow, gruffly. Tom shrunk back, but too late. He had left his little Bible at the bottom of his coat pocket, and his big Bible on the desk buried under the mortgage he was about to foreclose: never was sinner taken more unawares. The black man whisked him like a child into the saddle, gave the horse the lash, and away he galloped, with Tom on his back, in the midst of the thunderstorm. The clerks stuck their pens behind their ears, and stared after him from the windows. Away went Tom Walker, dashing down the streets, his white cap bobbing up and down, his morning gown fluttering in the wind, and his steed striking fire out of the pavement at every bound. When the clerks turned to look for the black man he had disappeared.

Tom Walker never returned to foreclose the mortgage. A countryman who lived on the border of the swamp, reported that in the height of the thunder-gust he had heard a great clattering of hoofs and a howling along the road, and running to the window caught sight of a figure, such as I have described, on a horse that galloped like mad across the fields, over the hills and down into the black hemlock swamp towards the old Indian fort; and that shortly after a thunderbolt falling in that direction seemed to set the whole forest in a blaze.

The good people of Boston shook their heads and shrugged their shoulders, but had been so much accustomed to witches and goblins and tricks of the Devil, in all kind of shapes from the first settlement of the colony, that they were not so much horror struck as might have been expected. Trustees were appointed to take charge of Tom's effects. There was nothing, however, to administer upon.

On searching his coffers[21] all his bonds and mortgages were found reduced to cinders. In place of gold and silver his iron chest was filled with chips and shavings; two skeletons lay in his stable instead of his half-starved horses, and the very next day his great house took fire and was burned to the ground.

Such was the end of Tom Walker and his ill-gotten wealth. Let all griping money brokers lay this story to heart. The truth of it is not to be doubted. The very hole under the oak trees, whence he dug Kidd's money, is to be seen to this day; and the neighboring swamp and old Indian fort are often haunted in stormy nights by a figure on horseback, in morning gown and white cap, which is doubtless the troubled spirit of the usurer. In fact, the story has resolved itself into a proverb, and is the origin of that popular saying, so prevalent throughout New England, of "The Devil and Tom Walker." ❖

> ## "The Devil take me," said he, "if I have made a farthing!"

---

20. **farthing.** British coin worth one-fourth of a penny
21. **coffers.** Secure boxes for holding money or other valuable items

MIRRORS & WINDOWS

What about your character or integrity would you be willing to sacrifice to receive a gift of, say, a million dollars? For instance, would you betray someone? Would you lie? Would you give up a personal goal or dream?

Refer to Text ▶ ▶ ▶ ▶ ▶   Reason with Text

1a. Identify the marks on the trees to which the devil points. What will happen to the trees?

1b. When the devil says he has a "prior claim" on the woodland, what does he mean?

Understand
Find meaning

2a. Trace the link between Captain Kidd and the devil.

2b. The devil is a character from legend, religious writings, and other literary works. What is the effect in Irving's story of using this stereotyped figure?

Apply
Use information

3a. When Tom and the devil meet sometime after Mrs. Walker's death, what do they discuss?

3b. Why does the narrator describe the outdoor setting (the swamp and the fort) in such detail? Infer why the last meeting between Tom and the devil takes place in the counting house.

Analyze
Take things apart

4a. Identify what Tom expects to find in his wife's bundled apron. What does he actually find?

4b. Irving calls Tom's wife a "female scold." Evaluate the role she plays in the story.

Evaluate
Make judgments

5a. At the end of the story, what does the narrator say about the swamp and the fort?

5b. Create a modern-day story, drama, painting, song, or other work that portrays people's excessive drive for wealth and status.

Create
Bring ideas together

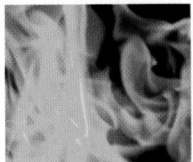

Analyze Literature

Plot, Conflict, Exposition, and Climax
Review your analysis of the plot. What characters, descriptions, and actions appear in the exposition? How do these details set the story in motion? What is the conflict? What event is the climax? How does the climax lead to the end of the story?

Extend the Text

Writing Options
Creative Writing Prepare a treasure hunt for a children's party. Write a series of notes for the hunt, each one giving directions for finding the next. The last note should tell where the treasure is hidden. You can write the directions in rhyme or in code ("under the table" might be "'neath the board on sticks"), or you can write step-by-step directions in ordinary language.

Expository Writing Briefly research the story of *Faust,* the play mentioned in the Build Background section. Then in a comparison-and-contrast essay, discuss how "The Devil and Tom Walker" is similar to and different from the play.

Collaborative Learning
Make a Map Have individual group members reread the selection and jot down notes on the *setting,* or the locations of various scenes. Come together and compare notes, and then create a map that shows all these locations. Use your imagination in drawing connecting roads and other places the story does not mention.

Media Literacy
Create a Flier Create a flier to inform unsuspecting investors about the dangers of, for example, buying shares of stock on the Internet or in an unknown company. Include a few real-life examples of people who have lost their money through legitimate or illegitimate investments.

 Go to **www.mirrorsandwindows.com** for more.

Edgar Allan Poe

> ## "Science has not yet taught us if madness is or is not the sublimity of the intelligence."

Edgar Allan Poe (1809–1849) led a short, tragic life filled with insecurity. By the time he was two years old, his father had deserted the family and his mother had died. He was raised in the household of John Allan, a prosperous merchant in Richmond, Virginia.

In 1826, Poe attended the University of Virginia, but he began to gamble and dropped out. He then joined the army and was appointed to West Point, but he was expelled in 1831 for not attending classes. His relationship with John Allan was strained during this time, resulting in what seems to have been a permanent break. At the age of twenty-seven, Poe married his first cousin, Virginia Clemm, who was not yet fourteen. Some scholars have interpreted the marriage as Poe's attempt to find a stable family life.

Poe went on to hold various editorial jobs, review literary works, and write a novel along with numerous short stories and poems. Publication of the poem "The Raven" in 1845 made him briefly famous, but he spent most of his adult life in poverty, losing one job after another. The death of his sickly young wife in 1847 left him with a deep sense of loss. Two years later, in 1849, Poe was found unconscious on a deserted street in Baltimore; he was taken to a hospital, where he died within hours. The specific cause of his death remains a topic of controversy; alcoholism, cholera, tuberculosis, and even murder all have been suggested as causes.

Despite his tragic life's circumstances, Poe made major contributions to literary form and criticism. Among the first writers of detective fiction, Poe also pioneered the psychological tale of horror. His contribution to this literary form was the use of *double meanings*, a technique for creating a tale that can be interpreted as being about the supernatural or about the highly charged imagination of a disturbed character. As a critic, Poe offered a superb definition of the *short story:* Its details, he said, were carefully chosen to create a single, vivid impression on the reader. Believing that a work of literature should be read in a single setting to have the desired effect, Poe was a champion of this genre.

Poe believed that peculiarity was an essential ingredient of beauty, and his writing often is exotic. His stories and poems are filled with doomed, introspective aristocrats. The twilight realm between life and death and the haunted settings of many of his stories reflect the morbid interiors of his characters' troubled minds. As symbolic expressions of the unconscious, these settings are central to Poe's art.

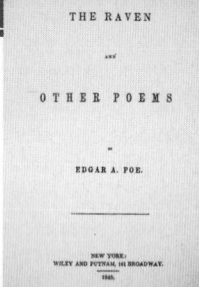

THE RAVEN

AND

OTHER POEMS

BY

EDGAR A. POE.

NEW YORK:
WILEY AND PUTNAM, 161 BROADWAY.
1845.

Noted Works

"The Fall of the House of Usher" (1839)

"The Pit and the Pendulum" (1840)

"The Raven" (poem, 1845)

"The Cask of Amontillado" (1846)

"The Tell-Tale Heart" (1848)

"Annabel Lee" (poem, 1849)

The Raven
A Narrative Poem by Edgar Allan Poe

Alone
A Lyric Poem by Edgar Allan Poe

Build Background

Literary Context When **"The Raven"** was published in the *New York Evening Mirror* (1845), the editor warned readers that "it would stick to the memory of everybody who reads it." That prophecy came true. The poem was an instant success worldwide among both readers and critics, and it is still one of the most famous poems in American literature.

Poe considered "The Raven" one of his best works and wrote an essay about composing it. In the essay, he described his writing process as calculated and formulaic. For instance, he determined that a poem should be about 100 lines to be read in one sitting; "The Raven" is 108. He also decided to write the tale backward, starting with the final stanza and working back from it. Knowing the effect he wanted to achieve helped him best develop the plot, he thought. Poe's choice of topic also was carefully chosen: He believed the death of a beautiful woman to be the most poetic of all topics.

Poe's choice of topic for **"Alone"** was similarly melancholy. In this poem, Poe describes his feelings of emotional isolation from other people and from the natural world. He wrote this poem, presumed to be about his own troubled childhood, in 1829, when he was just twenty years old. Literary scholars speculate that he provided several handwritten "facsimiles" of the poem to an editor at *Scribner's Magazine* over the years but asked that it not be published. *Scribner's* finally did publish the poem in 1875, well after Poe's death.

Reader's Context If you wanted to use an image from the natural world to create a mood of fear and loss in a poem, what image would you select? Explain.

Illustration to Edgar Allan Poe's *The Raven*, 1875. Edouard Manet. Museum of Fine Arts, Boston.

Analyze Literature

Mood and Alliteration
The **mood,** or atmosphere, is the emotion created in the reader by a literary work.

Alliteration is the repetition of initial consonant sounds, as in "weak and weary" ("The Raven," line 1). The term also can apply to the repetition of sounds within words, as in "silken sad uncertain rustling" (line 13).

Set Purpose

Many of the details of Poe's personal life suggest he was a desperate individual. Yet as a writer, he seemed very much in control, focused on the effect he wished to create. As you read "The Raven" and "Alone," write down the descriptive and narrative details he uses to evoke a mood of sadness and desolation. In reading "The Raven," also make note of Poe's use of alliteration. Read this poem aloud to hear Poe's powerful use of language.

Preview Vocabulary

surcease, 212
entreat, 212
obeisance, 213
craven, 213
beguiling, 213
ominous, 214
tempest, 214
undaunted, 214

The Raven

by Edgar Allan Poe

Once upon a midnight dreary, while I pondered, weak and weary,
Over many a quaint and curious volume of forgotten lore,
While I nodded, nearly napping, suddenly there came a tapping,
As of some one gently rapping, rapping at my chamber door.
5 "'Tis some visiter," I muttered, "tapping at my chamber door—
                   Only this, and nothing more."

Ah, distinctly I remember it was in the bleak December,
And each separate dying ember wrought its ghost upon the floor.
Eagerly I wished the morrow;—vainly I had tried to borrow
10 From my books <u>surcease</u> of sorrow—sorrow for the lost Lenore—
For the rare and radiant maiden whom the angels name Lenore—
                   Nameless here for evermore.

Thrilled me—filled me with fantastic terrors never felt before;
So that now, to still the beating of my heart, I stood repeating
15 "'Tis some visiter <u>entreating</u> entrance at my chamber door—
Some late visiter entreating entrance at my chamber door;—
                   This it is, and nothing more."

sur • cease (sʉr sēs´) *n.*, relief (from); end
en • treat (en trēt´) *v.*, beg; ask earnestly

And the silken sad uncertain rustling of each purple curtain
Presently my soul grew stronger; hesitating then no longer,
20   "Sir," said I, "or Madam, truly your forgiveness I implore;
But the fact is I was napping, and so gently you came rapping,
And so faintly you came tapping, tapping at my chamber door,
That I scarce was sure I heard you"—here I opened wide the door,—
                             Darkness there, and nothing more.

25   Deep into that darkness peering, long I stood there wondering, fearing,
Doubting dreaming dreams no mortal ever dared to dream before;
But the silence was unbroken, and the darkness gave no token,
And the only word there spoken was the whispered word, "Lenore!"
This I whispered, and an echo murmured back the word, "Lenore!"
30   Merely this, and nothing more.

Then into the chamber turning, all my soul within me burning,
Soon I heard again a tapping somewhat louder than before.
"Surely," said I, "surely that is something at my window lattice;[1]
Let me see, then, what thereat is, and this mystery explore—
35   Let my heart be still a moment and this mystery explore;—
                          'Tis the wind, and nothing more!"

Open here I flung the shutter, when, with many a flirt and flutter,
In there stepped a stately raven of the saintly days of yore;
Not the least <u>obeisance</u> made he; not an instant stopped or stayed he;
40   But, with mien[2] of lord or lady, perched above my chamber door—
Perched upon a bust of Pallas[3] just above my chamber door—
                        Perched, and sat, and nothing more.

Then this ebony bird <u>beguiling</u> my sad fancy into smiling,
By the grave and stern decorum of the countenance it wore,
45   "Though thy crest be shorn and shaven, thou," I said, "art sure no <u>craven</u>,
Ghastly grim and ancient raven wandering from the Nightly shore—
Tell me what thy lordly name is on the Night's Plutonian[4] shore!"
                        Quoth the raven, "Nevermore."

Much I marvelled this ungainly fowl to hear discourse so plainly,
50   Though its answer little meaning—little relevancy bore;
For we cannot help agreeing that no sublunary[5] being
Ever yet was blessed with seeing bird above his chamber door—
Bird or beast upon the sculptured bust above his chamber door,
                       With such name as "Nevermore."

---

1. **lattice.** Shutter; openwork structure used as a screen
2. **mien.** Manner; appearance
3. **Pallas.** Greek goddess of wisdom
4. **Plutonian.** Black; relating to the underworld
5. **sublunary.** Earthly (from Latin for "under the moon")

obei • sance (ō bā´ səns) *n.*, gesture of respect
cra • ven (krā´ vən) *n.*, coward
be • guil • ing (bə gī´ liŋ) *adj.*, charming; leading by deception

55 But the raven, sitting lonely on the placid bust, spoke only
That one word, as if his soul in that one word he did outpour.
Nothing farther then he uttered—not a feather then he fluttered—
Till I scarcely more than muttered, "Other friends have flown before—
On the morrow he will leave me, as my hopes have flown before."
60   Quoth the raven, "Nevermore."

Startled at the stillness broken by reply so aptly spoken,
"Doubtless," said I, "what it utters is its only stock and store
Caught from some unhappy master whom unmerciful Disaster
Followed fast and followed faster till his songs one burden bore—
65 Till the dirges of his Hope that melancholy bore
                          Of 'Never—nevermore.'"

But the raven still beguiling all my sad soul into smiling,
Straight I wheeled a cushioned seat in front of bird, and bust, and door;
Then upon the velvet sinking, I betook myself to linking
70 Fancy unto fancy thinking what this <u>ominous</u> bird of yore—
What this grim, ungainly, ghastly, gaunt, and ominous bird of yore
                           Meant in croaking "Nevermore."

This I sat engaged in guessing, but no syllable expressing
To the fowl whose fiery eyes now burned into my bosom's core;
75 This and more I sat divining, with my head at ease reclining
On the cushion's velvet lining that the lamplight gloated o'er,
But whose velvet violet lining with the lamplight gloating o'er,
                           She shall press, ah, nevermore!

Then, methought, the air grew denser, perfumed from an unseen censer[6]
80 Swung by angels whose faint foot-falls tinkled on the tufted floor.
"Wretch," I cried, "thy God hath lent thee—by these angels he hath sent thee
Respite—respite and Nepenthe[7] from thy memories of Lenore!
Let me quaff[8] this kind Nepenthe and forget this lost Lenore!"
                           Quoth the raven, "Nevermore."

85 "Prophet!" said I, "thing of evil!—prophet still, if bird or devil!—
Whether Tempter sent, or whether <u>tempest</u> tossed thee here ashore,
Desolate, yet all <u>undaunted</u>, on this desert land enchanted—
On this home by Horror haunted—tell me truly, I implore—
Is there—*is* there balm in Gilead?[9]—tell me—tell me, I implore!"
90   Quoth the raven, "Nevermore."

---

6. **censer.** Container for burning incense
7. **Nepenthe.** Potion to produce forgetfulness of pain or sorrow
8. **quaff.** Drink deeply
9. **balm in Gilead.** Gilead is a mountainous area in the Middle East where evergreens provide medicinal resins. The question echoes Jeremiah 8:22, "Is there no balm in Gilead?"

om • in • ous (ô´ min əs) *adj.*, forewarning evil
tem • pest (tem´ pəst) *n.*, violent storm
un • daunt • ed (un dän´ ted) *adj.*, firm in the face of danger; unafraid

"Prophet!" said I, "thing of evil!—prophet still, if bird or devil!
By that Heaven that bends above us—by that God we both adore—
Tell this soul with sorrow laden if, within the distant Aidenn,[10]
It shall clasp a sainted maiden whom the angels name Lenore—
95   Clasp a rare and radiant maiden whom the angels name Lenore."
                                    Quoth the raven, "Nevermore."

"Be that word our sign of parting, bird or fiend!" I shrieked, upstarting—
Get thee back into the tempest and the Night's Plutonian shore!
Leave no black plume[11] as a token of that lie thy soul hath spoken!
100   Leave my loneliness unbroken—quit the bust above my door!
Take thy beak from out my heart, and take thy form from off my door!"
                                    Quoth the raven, "Nevermore."

And the raven, never flitting, still is sitting, still is sitting
On the pallid bust of Pallas just above my chamber door;
105   And his eyes have all the seeming of a demon that is dreaming,
And the lamp-light o'er him streaming throws his shadow on the floor;
And my soul from out that shadow that lies floating on the floor
                                    Shall be lifted—nevermore! ❖

---

10. **Aidenn.** Name created by Poe to suggest Eden
11. **plume.** Feather

Poe believed the death of a beautiful woman to be the most poetic of subjects.
What subject or subjects do you believe to be poetic?

ART CONNECTION

Illustrations of Poe's Stories

Many famous European artists illustrated the works of Edgar Allan Poe. Alfred Kubin, a famous Austrian Expressionist who also drew accompaniments for the works of Fyodor Dostoevsky and E. T. A. Hoffmann, composed the sketch shown here. When Poe's work was anthologized in Great Britain, John Tenniel (who also illustrated *Alice in Wonderland*) drafted a series of drawings for the British edition. A renowned French woodcutter named Gustave Dore and the French Impressionist painter Edouard Manet (see page 211) both contributed art for French translations of Poe.

These were not typical projects for Impressionists and woodcutters, but Poe's artistic influence was so powerful that these artists could not refuse collaboration with the famous American writer.

Critical Viewing What do effective illustrations contribute to a story? In other words, what do they add to the reader's experience? How does not having illustrations affect the reader's experience?

Alone

by Edgar Allan Poe

The Reprimand, 1863. Edouard Frere.
Brooklyn Museum of Art, Brooklyn, New York.

From childhood's hour I have not been
As others were—I have not seen
As others saw—I could not bring
My passions from a common spring—
5 From the same source I have not taken
My sorrow—I could not awaken
My heart to joy at the same tone—
And all I lov'd—I lov'd alone—
Then—in my childhood—in the dawn
10 Of a most stormy life—was drawn
From ev'ry depth of good and ill
The mystery which binds me still—

From the torrent, or the fountain—
From the red cliff of the mountain—
15 From the sun that round me roll'd
In its autumn tint of gold—
From the lightning in the sky
As it pass'd me flying by—
From the thunder, and the storm—
20 And the cloud that took the form
(When the rest of Heaven was blue)
Of a demon in my view— ❖

MIRRORS & WINDOWS

What do the words *stormy, torrent,* and *thunder* suggest about the speaker's attitude toward his childhood? What words would you use to describe your own childhood?

Primary Source Connection

Both "The Raven" and "Alone" vividly portray Poe's emotional distress, especially his loneliness and sense of loss. In this **letter to John Allan,** the man who raised Poe after his parents' deaths, the writer expresses another source of despair: He tells Allan, who apparently does not respect Poe's lifestyle, that he is penniless. Various reasons have been offered to explain the estrangement (angry separation) between Allan and Poe, which seems to have occurred when Poe was about twenty years old. Allan never legally adopted Poe, but Poe took his surname as a middle name.

Letter to John Allan
by Edgar Allan Poe

Baltimore April 12th 1833

It has been more than two years since you have assisted me, and more than three since you have spoken to me. I feel little hope that you will pay any regard to this letter, but still I cannot refrain from making one more attempt to interest you in my behalf. If you will only consider in what a situation I am placed you will surely pity me. Without friends, without any means, consequently of obtaining employment, I am perishing— absolutely perishing for want of aid. And yet I am not idle, nor addicted to any vice—nor have I committed any offence against society which would render me deserving of so hard a fate. For God's sake pity me, and save me from destruction.

E. A. Poe

1. How long has it been since Poe has spoken to John Allan or received aid from him? Infer whether it was easy or hard for Poe to write this letter.

2. What does Poe claim will happen if he does not get assistance? List the words or phrases that indicate his desperation.

3. Poe does not believe he is "deserving of so hard a fate." What is his rationale? Evaluate whether his explanation is reasonable.

TEXT ^{TO} TEXT CONNECTION

In his letter, Poe does not mention his writing. Why not, do you think? How does the tone or style of this letter reflect the tone or style of Poe's poetry? If you were Poe's guardian, how might you respond to such a letter?

The letter in Poe's handwriting.

Refer to Text ▷ ▷ ▷ ▶ ▶	Reason with Text	
1a. Identify the cause of the speaker's sorrow in "The Raven" (line 10). According to the speaker, why has the raven come (lines 81–82)?	**1b.** Has the bird come for this reason? Explain.	**Understand** Find meaning
2a. In "Alone," what does the speaker say was "drawn" from his stormy life and experiences of nature?	**2b.** For many writers, nature is a source of inspiration and comfort. Examine how the speaker's attitude toward nature differs from that view.	**Apply** Use information
3a. In lines 43–45 of "The Raven," how does the speaker respond to the raven? How does the speaker respond to the raven beginning in lines 70–71?	**3b.** What causes the speaker to change his attitude toward the raven?	**Analyze** Take things apart
4a. How does the speaker describe the raven when it arrives (lines 37–40)?	**4b.** Assess whether the raven is an effective symbol of the speaker's mood.	**Evaluate** Make judgments
5a. Identify the unexpected word that appears in the last line of "Alone."	**5b.** Suggest why writers might share their demons—the thoughts and feelings that haunt them—with their readers.	**Create** Bring ideas together

Analyze Literature

Mood and Alliteration

How does Poe create the mood, or atmosphere, in "The Raven" and "Alone"? What descriptive and narrative details express this feeling of sadness and desolation?

What examples of alliteration did you identify in "The Raven"? How does repeating these sounds create a musical effect in the poem? How does the use of alliteration help create the tone?

Extend the Text

Writing Options

Creative Writing Write a diary entry about being visited by a bird or other animal. Use your imagination to describe the animal and why it visited you, how you fell about the visit, and how the visit ended. Make the story vivid so that you will enjoy rereading the diary entry when you are older.

Expository Writing Suppose you have been asked to give a reading of "The Raven" at a local book club and to provide a brief literary analysis of the poem. Choose a specific feature of the poem—for example, its emphatic rhyme or the significance of the raven as a symbol—and write an analytical essay about it.

Collaborative Learning

Draw a Comic Strip With a partner or in a small group, draw a comic strip of "The Raven" or "Alone." Include details about the appearance of the speaker and the setting.

Lifelong Learning

Create a Psychological Sketch What caused the break between Poe and John Allan, his guardian? (see the Primary Source Connection on pages 217–218). Look for information about the writer that gives details of his early years, especially his relationship with Allan. Create a chart that shows possible match-ups among events in Poe's life, in his poems, and in the letter.

 Go to **www.mirrorsandwindows.com** for more.

1. How has the speaker of "The Raven" been distracting himself from thoughts of Lenore?
   A. He has been sleeping.
   B. He has been walking.
   C. He has been reading.
   D. He has been writing poetry.
   E. He has been listening to music.

2. For what purpose does the speaker of "The Raven" believe the bird is there?
   A. It's there to help him forget Lenore.
   B. It was thrown off course by a storm.
   C. It's there to drive him insane with fear.
   D. It will help him remember Lenore.
   E. It's there to pluck out his heart with its beak.

3. What does the word *surcease* mean in the line "—vainly I had tried to borrow / From my books surcease of sorrow"?
   A. excess
   B. beginning
   C. small amount
   D. relief
   E. artistic expression

4. Which of the following statements best expresses the main idea of "Alone"?
   A. A devastating storm in the speaker's childhood made him afraid of nature.
   B. During an unhappy childhood, the speaker looked to nature to escape.
   C. The speaker was abandoned as a child and lived alone and terrified in the woods.
   D. From childhood, the speaker has had a unique perspective of the world that separates him from others.
   E. None of the above

5. Which of the following series of adjectives best expresses the character of the speakers in "The Raven" and "Alone" and Poe himself in the letter to his uncle? (The words should apply to all three selections.)
   A. desperate, angry, reckless
   B. fearful, lonely, dramatic
   C. pitiful, needy, self-centered
   D. crazed, defiant, morose
   E. hurt, weepy, lazy

6. The bust of Pallas on which the raven perches is an allusion to
   A. Lenore's last name.
   B. Greek mythology.
   C. a famous poet.
   D. a muse.
   E. a painting.

7. What literary technique is featured in the line "Doubting dreaming dreams no mortal ever dared to dream before;"?
   A. internal rhyme
   B. alliteration
   C. personification
   D. run-on line
   E. assonance

8. **Constructed Response:** The poem "The Raven" often is interpreted as containing many *symbols*, things that stand for or represent both themselves and other things. Think about the bird's behavior throughout the poem, about how the speaker and the raven interact, and about what the ending of the poem predicts will happen. Then write an analysis of the symbol of the raven in the poem.

9. **Constructed Response:** Describe how Poe uses natural elements in his writing, such as the wind and clouds. Based on "The Raven" and "Alone," analyze the significance of these natural elements in his poetry.

TEST-TAKING TIP

In a test with an analogy section, distinguish between answers that share a *literal* connection to the question but not an *analogous* connection. For example, the answer "monkey : banana" would be an incorrect response to "JUNGLE : BUGS," even though monkeys live in jungles. This is a literal connection. To establish an analogous connection, analyze the relationship between the terms. The nature of the relationship between a monkey and a banana is completely different from that between a jungle and bugs.

The Fall of the House of Usher

A Short Story by Edgar Allan Poe

Build Background

Literary Context **"The Fall of the House of Usher,"** one of Poe's early short stories, was first published in 1839 in the journal *Burton's Gentleman's Magazine,* of which Poe was coeditor for several years. The story later was revised and published in 1845 in a collection of stories entitled *Tales of the Grotesque and Arabesque.*

"The Fall of the House of Usher" is characteristically Poe in several respects. First, it portrays the themes of death in life—namely, being buried alive and returning from the grave—as well as themes of decay, illness, and insanity. In addition, the story contains double meanings, repeatedly pointing to the difference between appearance and reality. Poe's use of a narrator, an unnamed visiting friend, helps create this duality of meaning. For instance, through the observations of the narrator, readers see into the troubled mind of Usher, a man who is unaware that he is going insane. Finally, "The Fall of the House of Usher" is rich with symbolism, ranging from the house itself to the characters who occupy it.

Reader's Context Why do many people enjoy reading or hearing ghost stories or other scary tales? To what emotions do these works appeal?

See the Author Focus on page 210 for biographical information about Poe.

Wood engraving (1875) of Poe's monument in Baltimore, Maryland.

Analyze Literature

Gothic Fiction and Foreshadowing
Gothic fiction is a style characterized by the use of medieval settings, a murky atmosphere of horror and gloom, and grotesque, mysterious, or violent incidents.

Foreshadowing is the technique of hinting at events that will occur later in a story.

Set Purpose

In creating the title of this short story, Poe established the significance of the setting: the House of Usher. Providing a setting that evokes strong feelings of foreboding or anticipation is essential to Gothic fiction. Jot down descriptive details about the setting as you read this story. Also note what events Poe foreshadows in developing the plot of this suspenseful tale.

Preview Vocabulary

annihilate, 223
equivocal, 224
specious, 224
inordinate, 226
insipid, 226
palpable, 227
manifest, 229
impetuous, 232
obstinate, 233
prodigious, 234

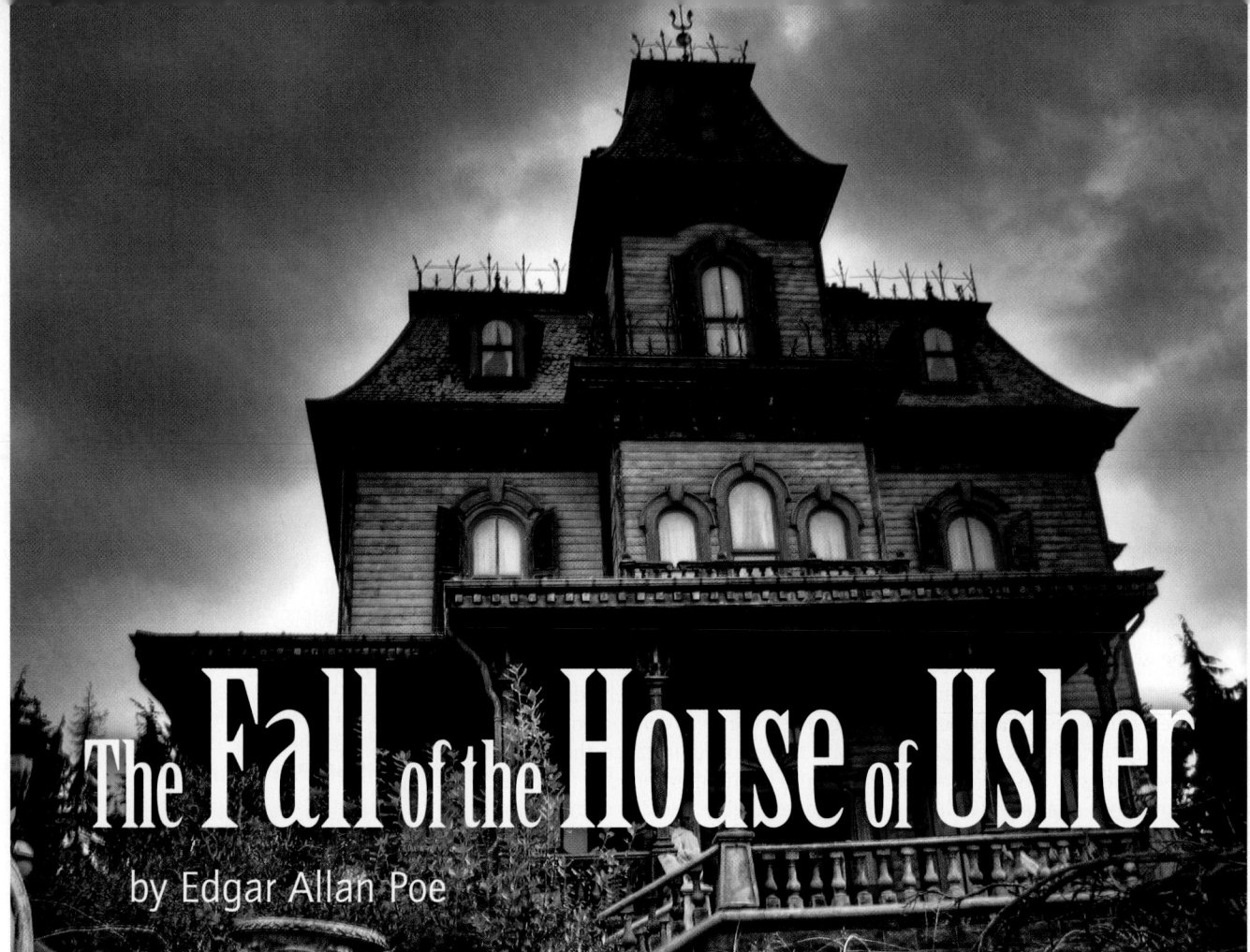

The Fall of the House of Usher

by Edgar Allan Poe

I felt that I breathed an atmosphere of sorrow.

Son cœur est un luth suspendu;
Sitôt qu'on le touche il résonne.[1]
—*de Béranger*

During the whole of a dull, dark, and soundless day in the autumn of the year, when the clouds hung oppressively low in the heavens, I had been passing alone, on horseback, through a singularly dreary tract of country; and at length found myself, as the shades of the evening drew on, within view of the melancholy House of Usher. I know not how it

was—but, with the first glimpse of the building, a sense of insufferable gloom pervaded my spirit. I say insufferable; for the feeling was unrelieved by any of that half-pleasurable, because poetic, sentiment, with which the mind usually receives even the sternest natural images of the desolate or terrible. I looked upon the scene before me—upon the mere[2] house, and

---

1. ***Son cœur . . . il résonne.*** "His heart is a suspended lute; / Whenever one touches it, it resounds." From *Le Refus* (*The Refusal*) by the French writer Pierre-Jean de Béranger (1780–1857)
2. **mere.** Lake

the simple landscape features of the domain—upon the bleak walls—upon the vacant eyelike windows—upon a few rank sedges[3]—and upon a few white trunks of decayed trees—with an utter depression of soul which I can compare to no earthly sensation more properly than to the afterdream of the reveler upon opium—the bitter lapse into everyday life—the hideous dropping off of the veil. There was an iciness, a sinking, a sickening of the heart—an unredeemed dreariness of thought which no goading of the imagination could torture into aught of the sublime. What was it—I paused to think—what was it that so unnerved me in the contemplation of the House of Usher? It was a mystery all insoluble; nor could I grapple with the shadowy fancies that crowded upon me as I pondered. I was forced to fall back upon the unsatisfactory conclusion, that while, beyond doubt, there *are* combinations of very simple natural objects which have the power of thus affecting us, still the analysis of this power lies among considerations beyond our depth. It was possible, I reflected, that a mere different arrangement of the particulars of the scene, of the details of the picture, would be sufficient to modify, or perhaps to <u>annihilate</u> its capacity for sorrowful impression; and, acting upon this idea, I reined my horse to the precipitous brink of a black and lurid tarn[4] that lay in unruffled luster by the dwelling, and gazed down—but with a shudder even more thrilling than before—upon the remodeled and inverted images of the gray sedge, and the ghastly tree stems, and the vacant and eyelike windows.

Nevertheless, in this mansion of gloom I now proposed to myself a sojourn of some weeks. Its proprietor, Roderick Usher, had been one of my boon companions in boyhood; but many years had elapsed since our last meeting. A letter, however, had lately reached me in a distant part of the country—a letter from him—which, in its wildly importunate nature, had admitted of no other than a personal reply. The MS.[5] gave evidence of nervous agitation. The writer spoke of acute bodily illness—of a mental disorder which oppressed him—and of an earnest desire to see me, as his best, and indeed his only personal friend, with a view of attempting, by the cheerfulness of my society, some alleviation of his malady. It was the manner in which all this, and much more, was said—it was the apparent *heart* that went with his request—which allowed me no room for hesitation; and I accordingly obeyed forthwith what I still considered a very singular summons.

> ## What was it—I paused to think— what was it that so unnerved me in the contemplation of the House of Usher?

Although, as boys, we had been even intimate associates, yet I really knew little of my friend. His reserve had been always excessive and habitual. I was aware, however, that his very ancient family had been noted, time out of mind, for a peculiar sensibility of temperament, displaying itself, through long ages, in many works of exalted art, and manifested, of late, in repeated deeds of munificent yet unobtrusive charity, as well as in a passionate devotion to the intricacies, perhaps even more than to the orthodox and easily recognizable beauties, of musical science. I had learned, too, the very remarkable fact, that the stem of the Usher race, all time-honored as it was, had put forth, at no period, any enduring branch; in other words, that the entire family lay in the direct

---

3. **rank sedges.** Rotting marsh plants
4. **tarn.** Mountain lake
5. **MS.** Manuscript

an • ni • hi • late (an nī′ il āt) *v.*, destroy

line of descent, and had always, with very tri-fling and very temporary variation, so lain. It was this deficiency, I considered, while running over in thought the perfect keeping of the character of the premises with the accredited character of the people, and while speculating upon the possible influence which the one, in the long lapse of centuries, might have exercised upon the other—it was this deficiency, perhaps, of collateral issue,[6] and the consequent undeviating transmission, from sire to son, of the patrimony with the name, which had, at length, so identified the two as to merge the original title of the estate in the quaint and equivocal appellation of the "House of Usher"—an appellation which seemed to include, in the minds of the peasantry who used it, both the family and the family mansion.

When I again uplifted my eyes to the house itself, from its image in the pool, there grew in my mind a strange fancy.

I have said that the sole effect of my somewhat childish experiment—that of looking down within the tarn—had been to deepen the first singular impression. There can be no doubt that the consciousness of the rapid increase of my superstition—for why should I not so term it?—served mainly to accelerate the increase itself. Such, I have long known, is the paradoxical law of all sentiments having terror as a basis. And it might have been for this reason only, that, when I again uplifted my eyes to the house itself, from its image in the pool, there grew in my mind a strange fancy—a fancy so ridiculous, indeed, that I but mention it to show the vivid force of the sensations which oppressed me. I had so worked upon my imagination as really to believe that about

the whole mansion and domain there hung an atmosphere peculiar to themselves and their immediate vicinity—an atmosphere which had no affinity with the air of heaven, but which had reeked up from the decayed trees, and the gray wall and the silent tarn—a pestilent and mystic vapor, dull, sluggish, faintly discernible,[7] and leaden-hued.

Shaking off from my spirit what *must* have been a dream, I scanned more narrowly the real aspect of the building. Its principal feature seemed to be that of an excessive antiquity. The discoloration of ages had been great. Minute fungi overspread the whole exterior, hanging in a fine tangled webwork from the eaves. Yet all this was apart from any extraordinary dilapidation. No portion of the masonry had fallen; and there appeared to be a wild inconsistency between its still perfect adaptation of parts, and the crumbling condition of the individual stones. In this there was much that reminded me of the specious totality of old woodwork which has rotted for long years in some neglected vault, with no disturbance from the breath of the external air. Beyond this indication of extensive decay, however, the fabric gave little token of instability. Perhaps the eye of a scrutinizing observer might have discovered a barely perceptible fissure, which, extending from the roof of the building in front, made its way down the wall in a zig-zag direction, until it became lost in the sullen waters of the tarn.

Noticing these things, I rode over a short cause-way to the house. A servant-in-waiting took my horse, and I entered the Gothic archway of the hall. A valet, of stealthy

---

6. **collateral issue.** Includes cousins, nieces and nephews, and other relatives except parents, grandparents, sisters and brothers, children, and grandchildren
7. **discernible.** Noticeable

> **equi • vo • cal** (e kwiv´ ə k'l) *adj.,* able to be understood in more than one way
> **spe • cious** (spē´ shəs) *adj.,* false; misleading

Fall of the House of Usher, 1938. Douglas Percy Bliss.

The valet now threw open a door and ushered me into the presence of his master.

The room in which I found myself was very large and lofty. The windows were long, narrow, and pointed, and at so vast a distance from the black oaken floor as to be altogether inaccessible from within. Feeble gleams of encrimsoned light made their way through the trellised panes, and served to render sufficiently distinct the more prominent objects around; the eye, however, struggled in vain to reach the remoter angles of the chamber, or the recesses of the vaulted and fretted ceiling. Dark draperies hung upon the walls. The general furniture was profuse, comfortless, antique, and tattered. Many books and musical instruments lay scattered about, but failed to give any vitality to the scene. I felt that I breathed an atmosphere of sorrow. An air of stern, deep, and irredeemable gloom hung over and pervaded all.

Upon my entrance, Usher arose from a sofa on which he had been lying at full length, and greeted me with a vivacious warmth which had much in it, I at first thought, of an overdone cordiality—of the constrained effort of the *ennuyé*[9] man of the world. A glance, however, at his countenance, convinced me of his perfect sincerity. We sat down; and for some moments, while he spoke not, I gazed upon him with a feeling half of pity, half of awe. Surely, man had never before so terribly altered, in so brief a period, as had Roderick Usher! It was with difficulty that I could bring myself to admit the identity of the wan being before me with the companion of my early boyhood. Yet the character of his face had been at all times remarkable. A cadaverousness of complexion; an eye large, liquid, and luminous beyond comparison; lips somewhat thin and very pallid, but of a surpassingly beautiful curve; a nose of a delicate Hebrew model, but with a breadth of nostril unusual in similar formations; a finely molded chin, speaking, in its

step, thence conducted me, in silence, through many dark and intricate passages in my progress to the *studio* of his master. Much that I encountered on the way contributed, I know not how, to heighten the vague sentiments of which I have already spoken. While the objects around me—while the carvings of the ceilings, the somber tapestries of the walls, the ebon blackness of the floors, and the phantasmagoric[8] armorial trophies which rattled as I strode, were but matters to which, or to such as which, I had been accustomed from my infancy—while I hesitated not to acknowledge how familiar was all this—I still wondered to find how unfamiliar were the fancies which ordinary images were stirring up. On one of the staircases, I met the physician of the family. His countenance, I thought, wore a mingled expression of low cunning and perplexity. He accosted me with trepidation and passed on.

8. **phantasmagoric.** Rapidly changing images, as in a dream
9. *ennuyé.* [French] Bored

want of prominence, of a want of moral energy; hair of a more than weblike softness and tenuity;[10] these features, with an <u>inordinate</u> expansion above the regions of the temple, made up altogether a countenance not easily to be forgotten. And now in the mere exaggeration of the prevailing character of these features, and of the expression they were wont to convey, lay so much of change that I doubted to whom I spoke. The now ghastly pallor of the skin, and the now miraculous luster of the eye, above all things startled and even awed me. The silken hair, too, had been suffered to grow all unheeded, and as, in its wild gossamer texture, it floated rather than fell about the face, I could not, even with effort, connect its arabesque[11] expression with any idea of simple humanity.

In the manner of my friend I was at once struck with an incoherence—an inconsistency; and I soon found this to arise from a series of feeble and futile struggles to overcome an habitual trepidancy—an excessive nervous agitation. For something of this nature I had indeed been prepared, no less by his letter, than by reminiscences of certain boyish traits, and by conclusions deduced from his peculiar physical conformation and temperament. His action was alternately vivacious and sullen. His voice varied rapidly from a tremulous indecision (when the animal spirits seemed utterly in abeyance) to that species of energetic concision—that abrupt, weighty, unhurried, and hollow-sounding enunciation—that leaden, self-balanced and perfectly modulated guttural utterance, which may be observed in the lost drunkard, or the irreclaimable eater of opium, during the periods of his most intense excitement.

It was thus that he spoke of the object of my visit, of his earnest desire to see me, and of the solace he expected me to afford him. He entered, at some length, into what he conceived to be the nature of his malady. It was, he said, a constitutional and a family evil, and one for which he despaired to find a remedy—a mere nervous affection,[12] he immediately added, which would undoubtedly soon pass. It displayed itself in a host of unnatural sensations. Some of these, as he detailed them, interested and bewildered me; although, perhaps, the terms, and the general manner of the narration had their weight. He suffered much from a morbid acuteness of the senses; the most <u>insipid</u> food was alone endurable; he could wear only garments of certain texture; the odors of all flowers were oppressive; his eyes were tortured by even a faint light; and there were but peculiar sounds, and these from stringed instruments, which did not inspire him with horror.

He entered, at some length, into what he conceived to be the nature of his malady.

To an anomalous[13] species of terror I found him a bounden slave. "I shall perish," said he, "I *must* perish in this deplorable folly. Thus, thus, and not otherwise, shall I be lost. I dread the events of the future, not in themselves, but in their results. I shudder at the thought of any, even the most trivial, incident, which may operate upon this intolerable agitation of soul. I have, indeed, no abhorrence of danger, except in its absolute effect—in terror. In this unnerved—in this pitiable condition—I feel that the period will sooner or later arrive when I must abandon life and reason together, in some struggle with the grim phantasm, FEAR."

I learned, moreover, at intervals, and through broken and equivocal hints, another singular feature of his mental condition. He

---

10. **tenuity.** Thinness
11. **arabesque.** Of an intricate design, often employing shapes of plants and animals
12. **affection.** Here, ailment or disorder
13. **anomalous.** Unusual

---

in • or • di • nate (in ōr´ di nət) *adj.,* excessive; beyond reasonable limits
in • sip • id (in sip´ əd) *adj.,* without flavor

was enchained by certain superstitious impressions in regard to the dwelling which he tenanted, and whence, for many years, he had never ventured forth—in regard to an influence whose supposititious[14] force was conveyed in terms too shadowy here to be restated—an influence which some peculiarities in the mere form and substance of his family mansion, had, by dint of long sufferance, he said, obtained over his spirit—an effect which the *physique* of the gray walls and turrets, and of the dim tarn into which they all looked down, had, at length, brought about upon the *morale* of his existence.

He admitted, however, although with hesitation, that much of the peculiar gloom which thus afflicted him could be traced to a more natural and far more <u>palpable</u> origin—to the severe and long-continued illness—indeed to the evidently approaching dissolution—of a tenderly beloved sister—his sole companion for long years—his last and only relative on earth. "Her decease," he said, with a bitterness which I can never forget, "would leave him (him the hopeless and the frail) the last of the ancient race of the Ushers." While he spoke, the lady Madeline (for so was she called) passed slowly through a remote portion of the apartment, and, without having noticed my presence, disappeared. I regarded her with an utter astonishment not unmingled with dread—and yet I found it impossible to account for such feelings. A sensation of stupor oppressed me, as my eyes followed her retreating steps. When a door, at length, closed upon her, my glance sought instinctively and eagerly the countenance of the brother—but he had buried his face in his hands, and I could only perceive that a far more than ordinary wanness had overspread the emaciated fingers through which trickled many passionate tears.

The disease of the lady Madeline had long baffled the skill of her physicians. A settled apathy, a gradual wasting away of the person, and frequent although transient affections of a partially cataleptical[15] character, were the

unusual diagnosis. Hitherto she had steadily borne up against the pressure of her malady, and had not betaken herself finally to bed; but, on the closing in of the evening of my arrival at the house, she succumbed (as her brother told me at night with inexpressible agitation) to the prostrating power of the destroyer; and I learned that the glimpse I had obtained of her person would thus probably be the last I should obtain—that the lady, at least while living, would be seen by me no more.

For several days ensuing, her name was unmentioned by either Usher or myself: And during this period I was busied in earnest endeavors to alleviate the melancholy of my friend. We painted and read together; or I

---

14. **supposititious.** Supposed; hypothetical
15. **cataleptical.** In a trancelike state, unable to move

> **pal • pa • ble** (pal´ pə b'l) *adj.*, able to be touched or felt; easily observed

THE FALL OF THE HOUSE OF USHER **227**

listened, as if in a dream, to the wild improvisations of his speaking guitar. And thus, as a closer and still closer intimacy admitted me more unreservedly into the recesses of his spirit, the more bitterly did I perceive the futility of all attempt at cheering a mind from which darkness, as if an inherent positive quality, poured forth upon all objects of the moral and physical universe, in one unceasing radiation of gloom.

I shall ever bear about me a memory of the many solemn hours I thus spent alone with the master of the House of Usher. Yet I should fail in any attempt to convey an idea of the exact character of the studies, or of the occupations, in which he involved me, or led me the way. An excited and highly distempered ideality[16] threw a sulfureous[17] luster over all. His long improvised dirges will ring forever in my ears. Among other things, I hold painfully in mind a certain singular perversion and amplification of the wild air of the last waltz of Von Weber.[18] From the paintings over which his elaborate fancy brooded, and which grew, touch by touch, into vaguenesses at which I shuddered the more thrillingly, because I shuddered knowing not why—from these paintings (vivid as their images now are before me) I would in vain endeavor to educe more than a small portion which should lie within the compass of merely written words. By the utter simplicity, by the nakedness of his designs, he arrested and overawed attention. If ever mortal painted an idea, that mortal was Roderick Usher. For me at least—in the circumstances then surrounding me—there arose out of the pure abstractions which the hypochondriac contrived to throw upon his canvas, an intensity of intolerable awe, no shadow of which felt I ever yet in the contemplation of the certainly glowing yet too concrete reveries of Fuseli.[19]

One of the phantasmagoric conceptions of my friend, partaking not so rigidly of the spirit of abstraction, may be shadowed forth, although feebly, in words. A small picture presented the interior of an immensely long and rectangular vault or tunnel, with low walls, smooth, white, and without interruption or device. Certain accessory points of the design served well to convey the idea that this excavation lay at an exceeding depth below the surface of the earth. No outlet was observed in any portion of its vast extent, and no torch, or other artificial source of light was discernible; yet a flood of intense rays rolled throughout, and bathed the whole in a ghastly and inappropriate splendor.

I have just spoken of that morbid condition of the auditory nerve which rendered all music intolerable to the sufferer with the exception of certain effects of stringed instruments. It was, perhaps, the narrow limits to which he thus

16. **distempered ideality.** Mental derangement
17. **sulfureous.** Hellish; a likely reference to the yellowish color of sulfur
18. **Von Weber.** Carl Maria von Weber (1786–1826), a German composer
19. **Fuseli.** Henry Fuseli (also known as Johann Heinrich Fuessli or Füssli; 1741–1825), an English-Swiss painter whose works had an otherworldly quality

confined himself upon the guitar, which gave birth, in great measure, to the fantastic character of his performances. But the fervid *facility* of his *impromptus*[20] could not be so accounted for. They must have been, and were, in the notes, as well as in the words of his wild fantasias (for he not unfrequently accompanied himself with rhymed verbal improvisations), the result of that intense mental collectedness and concentration to which I have previously alluded as observable only in the moments of the highest artificial excitement. The words of one of these rhapsodies I have easily remembered. I was, perhaps, the more forcibly impressed with it, as he gave it, because, in the under or mystic current of its meaning, I fancied that I perceived, and for the first time, a full consciousness on the part of Usher, of the tottering of his lofty reason upon her throne. The verses, which were entitled "The Haunted Palace," ran very nearly, if not accurately, thus:

I

In the greenest of our valleys,
    By good angels tenanted,
Once a fair and stately palace—
    Radiant palace—reared its head.
In the monarch Thought's dominion—
    It stood there!
Never seraph spread a pinion[21]
    Over fabric half so fair.

II

Banners yellow, glorious, golden,
    On its roof did float and flow;
(This—all this—was in the olden
    Time long ago)
And every gentle air that dallied,
    In that sweet day,
Along the ramparts plumed and pallid,
    A winged odor went away.

III

Wanderers in that happy valley
    Through two luminous windows saw
Spirits moving musically
    To a lute's well-tunéd law,

Round about a throne, where sitting
    (Porphyrogene!)[22]
In state his glory well befitting,
    The ruler of the realm was seen.

IV

And all with pearl and ruby glowing
    Was the fair palace door,
Through which came flowing, flowing,
      flowing,
    And sparkling evermore,
A troop of Echoes whose sweet duty
    Was but to sing,
In voices of surpassing beauty,
    The wit and wisdom of their king.

V

But evil things, in robes of sorrow,
    Assailed the monarch's high estate;
(Ah, let us mourn, for never morrow
    Shall dawn upon him, desolate!)
And, round about his home, the glory
    That blushed and bloomed
Is but a dim-remembered story
    Of the old time entombed.

VI

And travelers now within that valley,
    Through the red-litten windows, see
Vast forms that move fantastically
    To a discordant melody;
While, like a rapid ghastly river,
    Through the pale door,
A hideous throng rush out forever,
    And laugh—but smile no more.

I well remember that suggestions arising from this ballad led us into a train of thought wherein there became <u>manifest</u> an opinion of Usher's which I mention not so much on account of its novelty (for other men have

---

20. **impromptus.** Spontaneous performances
21. **seraph spread a pinion.** Angel spread a wing
22. **Porphyrogene.** Word invented by Poe to mean "royal offspring" from the Greek *porphyro,* meaning purple, the color of royalty

man • i • fest (man´ ə fest) *adj.,* noticeable

thought thus), as on account of the pertinacity with which he maintained it. This opinion, in its general form, was that of the sentience[23] of all vegetable things. But, in his disordered fancy, the idea had assumed a more daring character, and trespassed, under certain conditions, upon the kingdom of inorganization.[24] I lack words to express the full extent, or the earnest *abandon* of his persuasion. The belief, however, was connected (as I have previously hinted) with the gray stones of the home of his forefathers. The conditions of the sentience had been here, he imagined, fulfilled in the method of collocation of these stones—in the order of their arrangement, as well as in that of the many *fungi* which overspread them, and of the decayed trees which stood around—above all, in the long undisturbed endurance of this arrangement, and in its reduplication in the still waters of the tarn. Its evidence—the evidence of the sentience—was to be seen, he said (and I here started as he spoke), in the gradual yet certain condensation of an atmosphere of their own about the waters and the walls. The result was discoverable, he added, in that silent, yet importunate and terrible influence which for centuries had molded the destinies of his family, and which made *him* what I now saw him—what he was. Such opinions need no comment, and I will make none.

Our books—the books which, for years, had formed no small portion of the mental existence of the invalid—were, as might be supposed, in strict keeping with this character of phantasm. We pored together over such works as the *Ververt et Chartreuse* of Gresset; the *Belphegor* of Machiavelli; the *Heaven and Hell* of Swedenborg; *The Subterranean Voyage of Nicholas Klimm* by Holberg; the Chiromancy of Robert Flud, of Jean D'Indaginé, and of De la Chambre; the *Journey into the Blue Distance* of Tieck; and *The City of the Sun* of Campanella. One favorite volume was a small octavo edition of the *Directorium Inquisitorum,* by the Dominican Eymeric de Gironne; and there were passages in Pomponius Mela, about the old African Satyrs and Ægipans,[25] over which Usher would sit dreaming for hours. His chief delight, however, was found in the perusal of an exceedingly rare and curious book in quarto Gothic—the manual of a forgotten church—the *Vigiliae Mortuorum*[26] *secundum Chorum Ecclesiae Maguntinae.*

I could not help thinking of the wild ritual of this work, and of its probable influence upon the hypochondriac, when, one evening, having informed me abruptly that the lady Madeline was no more, he stated his intention of preserving her corpse for a fortnight (previously to its final interment), in one of the numerous vaults within the main walls of the building. The worldly reason, however, assigned for this singular proceeding, was one which I did not feel at liberty to dispute. The brother had been led to his resolution (so he told me) by consideration of the unusual character of the malady of the deceased, of certain obtrusive and eager inquiries on the part of her medical men, and of the remote and exposed situation of the burial ground of the family. I will not deny that when I called to mind the

---

23. **sentience.** Awareness; consciousness
24. **kingdom of inorganization.** Realm of inorganic things
25. **Ververt . . . Ægipans.** List of authors and books about magic and horror
26. **Vigiliae Mortuorum.** [Latin] "Vigil of the dead"

sinister countenance of the person whom I met upon the staircase, on the day of my arrival at the house, I had no desire to oppose what I regarded as at best but a harmless, and by no means an unnatural, precaution.

At the request of Usher, I personally aided him in the arrangements for the temporary entombment. The body having been encoffined, we two alone bore it to its rest. The vault in which we placed it (and which had been so long unopened that our torches, half smothered in its oppressive atmosphere, gave us little opportunity for investigation) was small, damp, and entirely without means of admission for light; lying, at great depth, immediately beneath that portion of the building in which was my own sleeping apartment. It had been used, apparently, in remote feudal times, for the worst purposes of a dungeon-keep, and, in later days, as a place of deposit for powder, or some other highly combustible substance, as a portion of its floor, and the whole interior of a long archway through which we reached it, were carefully sheathed with copper. The door, of massive iron, had been, also, similarly protected. Its immense weight caused an unusually sharp grating sound, as it moved upon its hinges.

Having deposited our mournful burden upon tressels within this region of horror, we partially turned aside the yet unscrewed lid of the coffin, and looked upon the face of the tenant. A striking similitude between the brother and sister now first arrested my attention; and Usher, divining, perhaps, my thoughts, murmured out some few words from which I learned that the deceased and himself had been twins, and that sympathies of a scarcely intelligible nature had always existed between them. Our glances, however, rested not long upon the dead—for we could not regard her unawed. The disease which had thus entombed the lady in the maturity of youth, had left, as usual in all maladies of a strictly cataleptical character, the mockery of a faint blush upon the bosom and the face, and that suspiciously lingering smile upon the lip which is so terrible in death. We replaced and screwed down the lid, and, having secured the door of iron, made our way, with toil, into the scarcely less gloomy apartments of the upper portion of the house.

An observable change came over the features of the mental disorder of my friend.

And now, some days of bitter grief having elapsed, an observable change came over the features of the mental disorder of my friend. His ordinary manner had vanished. His ordinary occupations were neglected or forgotten. He roamed from chamber to chamber with hurried, unequal, and objectless step. The pallor of his countenance had assumed, if possible, a more ghastly hue—but the luminousness of his eye had utterly gone out. The once occasional huskiness of his tone was heard no more; and a tremulous quaver, as if of extreme terror, habitually characterized his utterance. There were times, indeed, when I thought his unceasingly agitated mind was laboring with some oppressive secret, to divulge which he struggled for the necessary courage. At times, again, I was obliged to resolve all into the mere inexplicable vagaries[27] of madness, for I beheld him gazing upon vacancy for long hours, in an attitude of the profoundest attention, as if listening to some imaginary sound. It was no wonder that his condition terrified—that it infected me. I felt creeping upon me, by slow yet certain degrees, the wild influences of his own fantastic yet impressive superstitions.

It was, especially, upon retiring to bed late in the night of the seventh or eighth day after the placing of the lady Madeline within the dungeon, that I experienced the full power of such feelings. Sleep came not near my couch—while the hours waned and waned away. I struggled to reason off the nervousness which had dominion over me. I endeavored to believe that much, if not all of what I felt, was due to the bewildering influence of the gloomy furniture of the room—of the dark and tattered draperies, which, tortured into motion by the breath of a rising tempest, swayed fitfully to and fro upon the walls, and rustled uneasily about the decorations of the bed. But my efforts were fruitless. An irrepressible tremor gradually pervaded my frame; and, at length, there sat upon my very heart an incubus[28] of utterly causeless alarm. Shaking this off with a gasp and a struggle, I uplifted myself upon the pillows, and, peering earnestly within the intense darkness of the chamber, harkened—I know not why, except that an instinctive spirit prompted me—to certain low and indefinite sounds which came, through the pauses of the storm, at long intervals, I knew not whence. Overpowered by an intense sentiment of horror, unaccountable yet unendurable, I threw on my clothes with haste (for I felt that I should sleep no more during the night), and endeavored to arouse myself from the pitiable condition into which I had fallen, by pacing rapidly to and fro through the apartment.

I had taken but few turns in this manner, when a light step on an adjoining staircase arrested my attention. I presently recognized it as that of Usher. In an instant afterward he rapped, with a gentle touch, at my door, and entered, bearing a lamp. His countenance was, as usual, cadaverously wan—but, moreover, there was a species of mad hilarity in his eyes—an evidently restrained *hysteria* in his whole demeanor. His air appalled me—but anything was preferable to the solitude which I had so long endured, and I even welcomed his presence as a relief.

"And you have not seen it?" he said abruptly, after having stared about him for some moments in silence—"you have not then seen it?—but, stay! you shall." Thus speaking, and having carefully shaded his lamp, he hurried to one of the casements, and threw it freely open to the storm.

The <u>impetuous</u> fury of the entering gust nearly lifted us from our feet. It was, indeed, a tempestuous yet sternly beautiful night, and one wildly singular in its terror and its beauty. A whirlwind had apparently collected its force in our vicinity; for there were frequent and violent alterations in the direction of the wind; and the exceeding density of the clouds (which hung so low as to press upon the turrets of the house) did not prevent our perceiving the lifelike velocity with which they flew careering from all points against each other, without passing away into the distance. I say that even their

---

27. **vagaries.** Unpredictable ideas or actions
28. **incubus.** Nightmare

im • pet • u • ous (im pet´ chü əs) *adj.*, here, forceful; violent

exceeding density did not prevent our perceiving this—yet we had no glimpse of the moon or stars—nor was there any flashing forth of the lightning. But the under surfaces of the huge masses of agitated vapor, as well as all terrestrial objects immediately around us, were glowing in the unnatural light of a faintly luminous and distinctly visible gaseous exhalation which hung about and enshrouded the mansion.

The impetuous fury of the entering gust nearly lifted us from our feet.

"You must not—you shall not behold this!" said I, shudderingly, to Usher, as I led him, with a gentle violence, from the window to a seat. "These appearances, which bewilder you, are merely electrical phenomena not uncommon—or it may be that they have their ghastly origin in the rank miasma of the tarn. Let us close this casement—the air is chilling and dangerous to your frame. Here is one of your favorite romances. I will read, and you shall listen;—and so we will pass away this terrible night together."

The antique volume which I had taken up was the *Mad Trist* of Sir Launcelot Canning;[29] but I had called it a favorite of Usher's more in sad jest than in earnest; for, in truth, there is little in its uncouth and unimaginative prolixity[30] which could have had interest for the lofty and spiritual ideality of my friend. It was, however, the only book immediately at hand; and I indulged a vague hope that the excitement which now agitated the hypochondriac, might find relief (for the history of mental disorder is full of similar anomalies) even in the extremeness of the folly which I should read. Could I have judged, indeed, by the wild overstrained air of vivacity with which he harkened, or apparently harkened, to the words of the tale, I might well have congratulated myself upon the success of my design.

I had arrived at that well-known portion of the story where Ethelred, the hero of the *Trist,* having sought in vain for peaceable admission into the dwelling of the hermit, proceeds to make good an entrance by force. Here, it will be remembered, the words of the narrative run thus:

"And Ethelred, who was by nature of a doughty[31] heart, and who was now mighty withal, on account of the powerfulness of the wine which he had drunken, waited no longer to hold parley with the hermit, who, in sooth, was of an <u>obstinate</u> and maliceful turn, but, feeling the rain upon his shoulders, and fearing the rising of the tempest, uplifted his mace outright, and, with blows, made quickly room in the plankings of the door for his gauntleted hand; and now pulling therewith sturdily, he so cracked, and ripped, and tore all asunder, that the noise of the dry and hollow-sounding wood alarumed and reverberated throughout the forest."

It was, beyond doubt, the coincidence alone which had arrested my attention.

At the termination of this sentence I started, and for a moment, paused; for it appeared to me (although I at once concluded that my excited fancy had deceived me)—it appeared to me that, from some very remote portion of the mansion, there came, indistinctly, to my ears, what might have been, in its exact similarity of character, the echo (but a stifled and dull one certainly) of the very cracking and ripping sound which Sir Launcelot had so particularly

---

29. **Mad Trist of Sir Launcelot Canning.** Work made up by Poe
30. **prolixity.** Wordiness
31. **doughty.** Brave, valiant

ob • sti • nate (ôbʹ sti nət) *adj.,* stubborn

described. It was, beyond doubt, the coincidence alone which had arrested my attention; for, amid the rattling of the sashes of the casements, and the ordinary commingled noises of the still increasing storm, the sound, in itself, had nothing, surely, which should have interested or disturbed me. I continued the story:

"But the good champion Ethelred, now entering within the door, was sore enraged and amazed to perceive no signal of the maliceful hermit; but, in the stead thereof, a dragon of a scaly and <u>prodigious</u> demeanor, and of a fiery tongue, which sate in guard before a palace of gold, with a floor of silver; and upon the wall there hung a shield of shining brass with this legend enwritten—

Who entereth herein, a conqueror hath bin;
Who slayeth the dragon, the shield he shall win;

And Ethelred uplifted his mace, and struck upon the head of the dragon, which fell before him, and gave up his pesty breath, with a shriek so horrid and harsh, and withal so piercing, that Ethelred had fain to close his ears with his hands against the dreadful noise of it, the like whereof was never before heard."

Here again I paused abruptly, and now with a feeling of wild amazement—for there could be no doubt whatever that, in this instance, I did actually hear (although from what direction it proceeded I found it impossible to say) a low and apparently distant, but harsh, protracted, and most unusual screaming or grating sound—the exact counterpart of what my fancy had already conjured up for the dragon's unnatural shriek as described by the romancer.

Oppressed, as I certainly was, upon the occurrence of this second and most extraordinary coincidence, by a thousand conflicting sensations, in which wonder and extreme terror were predominant, I still retained sufficient presence of mind to avoid exciting, by any observation, the sensitive nervousness of my companion. I was by no means certain that he had noticed the sounds in question; although, assuredly, a strange alteration had, during the last few minutes, taken place in his demeanor. From a position fronting my own, he had gradually brought round his chair, so as to sit with his face to the door of the chamber; and thus I could but partially perceive his features, although I saw that his lips trembled as if he were murmuring inaudibly. His head had dropped upon his breast—yet I knew that he was not asleep, from the wide and rigid opening of the eye as I caught a glance of it in profile. The motion of his body, too, was at variance with this idea—for he rocked from side to side with a gentle yet constant and uniform sway. Having rapidly taken notice of all this, I resumed the narrative of Sir Launcelot, which thus proceeded:

A strange alteration had … taken place in his demeanor.

"And now, the champion, having escaped from the terrible fury of the dragon, bethinking himself of the brazen shield, and of the breaking up of the enchantment which was upon it, removed the carcass from out of the way before him, and approached valorously over the silver pavement of the castle to where the shield was upon the wall; which in sooth tarried not for his full coming, but fell down at his feet upon the silver floor, with a mighty great and terrible ringing sound."

No sooner had these syllables passed my lips, than—as if a shield of brass had indeed, at the moment, fallen heavily upon a floor of silver—I became aware of a distinct, hollow, metallic, and clangorous, yet apparently muffled reverberation. Completely unnerved, I leaped to my feet; but the measured rocking movement of Usher was undisturbed. I rushed to the chair in which he sat. His eyes were bent fixedly before him, and throughout his whole

---

pro • di • gious (prō di´ jəs) *adj.*, enormous

countenance there reigned a stony rigidity. But, as I placed my hand upon his shoulder, there came a strong shudder over his whole person; a sickly smile quivered about his lips; and I saw that he spoke in a low, hurried, and gibbering murmur, as if unconscious of my presence. Bending closely over him, I at length drank in the hideous import of his words.

"Not hear it?—yes, I hear it, and *have* heard it. Long—long—long—many minutes, many hours, many days, have I heard it—yet I dared not—oh, pity me, miserable wretch that I am!—I dared not—I *dared* not speak! *We have put her living in the tomb!* Said I not that my senses were acute? I *now* tell you that I heard her first feeble movements in the hollow coffin. I heard them—many, many days ago—yet I dared not—*I dared not speak!* And now—tonight—Ethelred—ha! ha!—the breaking of the hermit's door, and the death cry of the dragon, and the clangor of the shield!—say, rather, the rending of her coffin, and the grating of the iron hinges of her prison, and her struggles within the coppered archway of the vault! Oh whither shall I fly? Will she not be here anon? Is she not hurrying to upbraid me for my haste? Have I not heard her footstep on the stair? Do I not distinguish that heavy and horrible beating of her heart? *Madman!*"—here he sprang furiously to his feet, and shrieked out his syllables, as if in the effort he were giving up his soul—"*Madman! I tell you that she now stands without the door!*"

As if in the superhuman energy of his utterance there had been found the potency of a spell—the huge antique panels to which the speaker pointed, threw slowly back, upon the instant, their ponderous and ebony jaws. It was the work of the rushing gust—but then without those doors there *did* stand the lofty and enshrouded figure of the lady Madeline of Usher. There was blood upon her white robes, and the evidence of some bitter struggle upon every portion of her emaciated[32] frame. For a moment she remained trembling and reeling to and fro upon the threshold—then, with a low moaning cry, fell heavily inward upon the person of her brother, and in her violent and now final death agonies, bore him to the floor a corpse, and a victim to the terrors he had anticipated.

For a moment she remained trembling and reeling to and fro upon the threshold.

From that chamber, and from that mansion, I fled aghast. The storm was still abroad in all its wrath as I found myself crossing the old causeway. Suddenly there shot along the path a wild light, and I turned to see whence a gleam so unusual could have issued; for the vast house and its shadows were alone behind him. The radiance was that of the full, setting, and blood-red moon, which now shone vividly through that once barely discernible fissure, of which I have before spoken as extending from the roof of the building, in a zigzag direction, to the base. While I gazed, this fissure rapidly widened—there came a fierce breath of the whirlwind—the entire orb of the satellite burst at once upon my sight—my brain reeled as I saw the mighty walls rushing asunder—there was a long tumultuous shouting sound like the voice of a thousand waters—and the deep and dank tarn at my feet closed sullenly and silently over the fragments of the "*House of Usher.*" ❖

---

32. **emaciated frame.** Thin body

MIRRORS & WINDOWS

What harm comes from being isolated from others? Are people in the modern world more isolated than people from years past?

Refer to Text ▶ ▶ ▶ ▶ ▶	**Reason with Text**	
1a. Recall why Roderick says he has not left the house in many years.	**1b.** State another possible reason that Roderick never leaves the house.	**Understand** Find meaning
2a. When Roderick says he is suspicious of the doctor, what does the narrator remember?	**2b.** Stories that include unnatural events can sound unconvincing unless the reader is prepared for them. Examine how foreshadowing helps make this story believable.	**Apply** Use information
3a. Why does Roderick place Madeline's coffin in a temporary vault in the house rather than in the burial ground?	**3b.** Is Madeline buried alive on purpose or by accident? What clues in the story support your answer?	**Analyze** Take things apart
4a. Early in the story, what does the narrator say the phrase "House of Usher" refers to?	**4b.** Argue whether Poe has provided a fitting ending to the story.	**Evaluate** Make judgments
5a. What interrupts the narrator as he reads from "The Mad Trist"?	**5b.** Although "The Fall of the House of Usher" has no actual ghosts, do you consider it like a ghost story? Why or why not?	**Create** Bring ideas together

Analyze Literature

Gothic Fiction and Foreshadowing

How does Poe set the scene for his tale of Gothic fiction? How do the descriptions of the house and grounds, as well as the characters, contribute to the plot?

Authors use foreshadowing to develop suspense and sometimes to create irony; often, the incident that occurs later is the opposite of what readers have been led to expect. What instances of foreshadowing did you find in the story? What might the story have been like without them?

Extend the Text

Writing Options

Creative Writing Create a children's version of "The Fall of the House of Usher." Maintain the characters and events, but shorten some of the descriptions and use adjectives and adverbs that elementary or middle school students will know. Exchange papers with a partner, and read each other's retelling to be sure it is clear.

Narrative Writing Write a health column for a local newspaper in which you describe a visit to a family (real or imaginary) with one or more seriously ill members. Your column should discuss the problems that illness can cause within a family; you also may want to include some of your reactions, as a journalist, to the unfortunate situation.

Collaborative Learning

Develop a TV Show Playing the role of a TV producer, meet with your "staff" to discuss whether "The House of Usher" can be adapted as a weekly drama. With a group of classmates, write a one-page proposal describing what the sets would look like, what actors would play the main characters, and what would occur in the first two or three episodes.

Media Literacy

Prepare a Fund-Raising Letter Write a letter asking residents of your community to contribute money to repair a local mansion about to collapse. Suggest a plan for turning it into a history museum, music school, or other cultural institution. Also explain how the town could benefit from its restoration.

 Go to **www.mirrorsandwindows.com** for more.

1. Which of the following word pairs best describes the overall mood of "The Fall of the House of Usher"?
   A. awestruck and fearful
   B. contemptuous and pitying
   C. morbid and curious
   D. gloomy and freakish
   E. despairing and sarcastic

2. The mood of the story is conveyed primarily through
   A. descriptive details about the setting.
   B. the use of simple sentences.
   C. use of a third-person narrator.
   D. the limited use of dialogue.
   E. the use of alliteration.

3. If someone presents to you a *specious* argument, how would you best respond?
   A. Give in. You cannot argue against such a sound argument.
   B. Refute the argument. While it sounds good, it is full of false logic.
   C. Point out the "big picture," the main idea. The person arguing is focused on a detail.
   D. Ask for clarification. The person arguing is using specialized terms and jargon.
   E. Suggest an alternate viewpoint. The person is making a specific and unusual point.

4. Which of these is *not* a symptom of Roderick Usher's disorder?
   A. intolerance to spicy food
   B. hallucinations
   C. sensitivity to touch
   D. only tolerant to the sound of strings
   E. strong reaction to smells

5. Against what or whom does Roderick Usher struggle?
   A. his sister, Madeline
   B. the contempt of society
   C. the disrepair of the house
   D. the advice of the family physician
   E. his own feelings of fear

6. Which of the following lines foreshadows Madeline's return from the vault?
   A. "The disease which had thus entombed the lady in the maturity of youth, had left, as usual in all maladies of a strictly cataleptical character, the mockery of a faint blush upon the bosom and the face, and that suspiciously lingering smile upon the lip which is so terrible in death."

   B. "At times, again, I was obliged to resolve all into the mere inexplicable vagaries of madness, for I beheld him gazing upon vacancy for long hours, in an attitude of the profoundest attention, as if listening to some imaginary sound."
   C. "I was by no means certain that he had noticed the sounds in question; although, assuredly, a strange alteration had, during the last few minutes, taken place in his demeanor. From a position fronting my own, he had gradually brought round his chair, so as to sit with his face to the door of the chamber;"
   D. All of the above
   E. None of the above

7. Which of the following is most like the word *equivocal* in meaning?
   A. ambiguous
   B. of the same opinion
   C. even-tempered
   D. mistaken
   E. misleading

8. **Constructed Response:** Analyze the character of Roderick Usher as a symbol of the entire Usher family. Consider both his physical appearance and his state of mind. Which of Roderick's qualities seem contradictory or paradoxical?

9. **Constructed Response:** What is the significance of the two tales, "The Haunted Palace" and *Mad Trist,* mentioned within "The Fall of the House of Usher"? Discuss how they contribute to the mood, suspense, and theme of the story.

TEST-TAKING TIP

If you plan to take an Advanced Placement (AP) test, make certain you are familiar with the general terminology of the subject. For the AP English test, for example, you will need to know the meanings of literary terms such as *alliteration* and *protagonist*. Study the relevant terms diligently weeks before the test to ensure you won't have difficulty with the language.

Understanding Literary Criticism **Psychological Criticism**

A critic using the psychological lens is like a detective searching for clues to the workings of human nature. The literary text becomes a storehouse of symbols—some obvious, some hidden. The critic applies psychoanalytic concepts to the elements of setting, character, conflict, symbol, tone, and mood.

Overview of Psychological Criticism

The language of **psychological criticism** comes from the studies of Sigmund Freud and Carl Jung, two nineteenth-century Europeans who created the frame of reference for modern psychology. Freud and Jung studied the *unconscious,* the buried material in the human psyche. They explored the use of symbols in speech, in dreams, and in literature. Freud once said that it was the poets and philosophers, not he, who had discovered the unconscious. Both Freud and Jung believed that conflicts within a person were caused by deep fears and desires. When a person cannot act on these feelings, perhaps because they are inappropriate, he or she may develop an emotional disorder.

Perhaps the most popularized of Freudian theories is the *Oedipal complex.* Freud named his theory after Oedipus, a figure of classical Greek tragedy, who unwittingly killed his father and married his mother. Oedipus became Freud's vehicle for understanding the central conflict of childhood. The concept of the Oedipal complex, although modified by later interpreters, is still considered valid by many psychologists.

Jung developed the theory of *archetypes,* images and patterns with universal significance, such as the hero, the mother, and the fool. His theory of the masculine and feminine parts of the psyche also has influenced literary theory. He believed that a healthy person is in touch with both parts of the personality.

Application of Psychological Criticism

The usefulness of the psychological approach for understanding literature becomes clear when it is applied to a text such as Edgar Allan Poe's "The Fall of the House of Usher." In analyzing this work according to psychological theory, consider the following elements.

Setting and Mood

The fictional setting contains a wealth of symbolic detail that establishes the story's mood. Notice the narrator's first impressions of the ancient mansion:

> Minute fungi overspread the whole exterior, hanging in a fine, tangled web-work from the eaves. Yet all this was apart from any extraordinary dilapidation. No portion of the masonry had fallen; and there appeared to be a wild inconsistency between its still perfect adaptation of parts, and the crumbling condition of the individual stones. In this there was much that reminded me of the specious totality of old woodwork which has rotted for years in some neglected vault, with no disturbance from the breath of the external air. Beyond this indication of extensive decay, however, the fabric gave little token of instability. Perhaps the eye of a scrutinizing observer might have discovered a barely perceptible fissure, which, extending from the roof of the building in front, made its way down the wall in a zigzag direction, until it became lost in the sullen waters of the tarn.

❏ **Analyze** Note how Poe foreshadows the ultimate disintegration of the family manor, the narrator noticing "a barely perceptible fissure" running down the front of the building. What other details give the overall impression that the physical House of Usher is decaying? How does this description highlight the story's theme of disintegration and create a mood of fear?

Characterization

Next, consider Roderick Usher, the central character of Poe's Gothic tale of mental breakdown. Poe uses both direct and indirect characterization techniques. For instance, Usher's anxiety is revealed through descriptions of his odd, disheveled appearance and mannerisms and his rapid mood swings. The narrator describes his tone as sometimes marked by "overdone

FREUD

JUNG

POE

cordiality" and other times by a "sullen" quality. Here Usher is characterized directly:

> He suffered much from a morbid acuteness of the senses. The most insipid food was alone endurable; he could wear only garments of certain texture; the odors of all flowers were oppressive; his eyes were tortured by even a faint light; and there were but peculiar sounds, and these from stringed instruments, which did not inspire him with horror.

❏ **Analyze** Consider how Poe's direct and indirect characterization of Roderick Usher might lead readers to see him as a *hypochondriac*, a person who imagines he is sicker than he really is. Which details in the quotation above would lead you to make this diagnosis? Which other descriptions heighten this impression of instability?

Motivation and Conflict

In analyzing a character, consider the type of conflict that drives him or her. Is the conflict internal or external? Are the character's motivations conscious or unconscious? For instance, Roderick Usher inters his sister in a vault in the mansion, rather than arrange a proper burial. Notice the vagueness of his explanation for doing so:

> Having informed me abruptly that the lady Madeline was no more, he stated his intention of preserving her corpse for a fortnight (previously to its final interment) in one of the numerous vaults within the main walls of the building. The worldly reason, however, assigned for this singular proceeding, was one which I did not feel at liberty to dispute. The brother had been led to his resolution, so

he told me, by consideration of the unusual character of the malady of the deceased, of certain obtrusive and eager inquiries on the part of her medical men, and of the remote and exposed situation of the burial ground of the family.

❏ **Analyze** Does this reason seem valid? Which psychoanalytic theory could you use to explain Roderick Usher's extraordinary behavior upon the apparent death of his sister?

Metaphor and Symbol

"The Fall of the House of Usher" is full of metaphors and symbols. For example, the narrator perceives the mansion as human-like, with its "vacant and eye-like windows." This metaphor is extended throughout the story, becoming more sinister in its implications.

❏ **Analyze** Consider the relationship of this house to the generations that have inhabited it. Why do these forefathers oppress the mind of Roderick Usher, the last surviving male heir of the family? In what sense is the house a symbolic prison for Usher and his sister Madeline?

WRITING ABOUT

Psychological Criticism

Write an essay that answers this question: How does the physical disintegration of the House of Usher parallel the condition of its inhabitants? Use details from the story to illustrate the concept of disintegration.

Understand the Concept

Another common sentence error is a **run-on sentence,** which contains two or more sentences that have been strung together, as if a single sentence. Run-on sentences confuse readers, who cannot tell where one thought ends and another begins.

There are two types of run-on sentences. The first, called a **fused sentence,** has no punctuation mark or coordinating conjunction (*and, but, or, nor, yet,* or *for*) between the sentences. The two sentences run in, one after the other. To correct this error, identify the individual sentences and separate them using a semicolon:

EXAMPLES

Fused sentence The visitor to the House of Usher says that Roderick has invited him Roderick's letter reveals its writer's distress.

Corrected sentence The visitor to the House of Usher says that Roderick has invited him; Roderick's letter reveals its writer's distress. [Add a semicolon between the two sentences to create one correctly punctuated sentence.]

In the second type of run-on, called a **comma splice,** a comma separates two complete sentences. There are three options for fixing a comma splice:

EXAMPLES

Comma splice The visitor and Roderick have been friends since childhood, they have not seen each other for many years.

Corrected sentence 1 The visitor and Roderick have been friends since childhood, *but* they have not seen each other for many years. [Insert a coordinating conjunction after the comma to create a compound sentence.]

Corrected sentence 2 The visitor and Roderick have been friends since childhood; they have not seen each other for many years. [Add a semicolon between the two sentences to create one correctly punctuated sentence.]

Corrected sentence 3 The visitor and Roderick have been friends since childhood. They have not seen each other for many years. [Add a period at the end of the first sentence and a capital letter at the beginning of the second to create two correctly formed sentences.]

Examine your writing carefully for these two types of run-on sentences. Know how to correct the kinds of sentence errors you make.

Apply the Skill

Identify Run-On Sentences

Indicate which of the following items are *fused sentences* (mark *FS*) and which are *comma splices* (mark *CS*).

1. Roderick and his sister, Madeline, are the only remaining Ushers the family line will end at their deaths.
2. The narrator passes the family doctor, even he has an unpleasant, confused look.
3. Probably the narrator is most shocked on seeing Roderick his friend now has the look of the dying.
4. According to Roderick, he will die of fear, he is also afraid to leave the house.
5. Soon the visitor meets Madeline her brother expects her to die from a baffling illness.

Revise Run-On Sentences

Revise the following paragraph, correcting all the run-on sentences. Use your imagination to add details as you rewrite.

What happened to the mansion what happened to the people who lived there? In modern times Roderick might go to a psychiatrist, talking to someone about his distressing experience might help. The House of Usher couldn't be saved, the walls of the house were cracking, the exterior was falling down. The deteriorating condition of the mansion suggested the condition of the family the lightning-shape break symbolized the decline of the Ushers. Neither the mansion nor the family could be saved, both had deteriorated to the point of near death.

Death of Edgar Allan Poe

by H. A. Murena
Translated by Darwin J. Flakoll
and Claribel Alegría

H. A. Murena is the pen name of Héctor Alberto Alvarez (1923–1975), a distinguished Argentine writer of works of poetry, fiction, and drama. The poem "Muerte de Edgar Allan Poe," written in Spanish, was translated by Darwin J. Flakoll and Claribel Alegría.

In the poem **"Death of Edgar Allan Poe,"** the speaker is Poe himself, writing in first-person point of view. As he lies dying in the streets of Baltimore, Murena's speaker thinks of his life as an author: how he got his start as a poet, what he tried to say in his works, how his readers and critics responded, and what he did and did not achieve as an artist.

As you read the poem, consider how line 2, in which the speaker mentions "the horror" of his approaching death, echoes ideas in "The Fall of the House of Usher."

It is well, he said. I no longer complain.
I had already imagined this horror as well:
the hostile city of Baltimore;[1] the eternal,
frozen mist of autumn dawn
5 in the docks, all elfs missing;[2]
and becoming the refuse that brusque hands
could drag off in a cart to the hospital;
and seeing myself thus.
Because I was yet an adolescent I recall,
10 the night when I wrote my first verse,
when I heard the whisper, the diminutive[3] worm
of corruption initiating its march
in this Danish youth, the very minute
in which the valiant prince had already
15 been crowned for death, and then
I understood the deepest sense in which that prince was I.[4]

---

1. **Baltimore.** Poe was found unconscious on the streets of this Maryland city.
2. **all elfs missing.** Commonly spelled *elves*. The speaker may be saying that there was nothing cheerful or playful in the way he imagined his death.
3. **diminutive.** Small and familiar or lovable.
4. **diminutive worm of corruption . . . prince was I.** The "Danish youth" who was a "valiant prince" refers to Hamlet, in Shakespeare's famous tragedy. Most of Shakespeare's dramas are written as poetry rather than prose.

They did not forgive my conjuring,[5] my visions.
They would speak of gold and of cattle, of progress
and of sad machines, and I showed them
20   the vortex over which all trembles,
I wished to save them by one day bursting forth with
the poetry that through millenniums has slept
interred in the blood of men.
Unarmed gentleman of the real battle,
25   I went through cities with my staff; hated,
hearing the inextinguishable[6] race of earth
sharpening without pause in its caves
the dagger prepared for me.
And, although I could have been a Byron,[7]
30   although, perhaps for an instant could have spoken
to Shakespeare on equal terms, I reaped no more
than the hypnotic roses of crimes
and terror, and in this phantasmal[8] America,
bewitched from one end to the other,
35   I die obscurely, defeated and ignored.
Now I feel only a heaviness of countenance,[9]
the stupor[10] of one abruptly
wrenched from vast and profound dreams.
It is well. I no longer complain. ❖

---

5. **conjuring.** Bringing to mind
6. **inextinguishable.** Not able to be destroyed
7. **Byron.** George Gordon, Lord Byron (1788–1824), an English Romantic poet
   who achieved fame during his life for his poetry and daring adventures
8. **phantasmal.** Referring to an imaginary being or ghostly figure
9. **countenance.** Demeanor or composure
10. **stupor.** State of shock

Murena is one of many writers who have been influenced by Edgar Allan Poe.
Who has influenced you, for good or bad?

Refer and Reason

1. Poe, the speaker in the poem, sees a link between himself and Hamlet. (In Shakespeare's play, Prince Hamlet is distressed at the corruption in Denmark; his father, the recently murdered king, returns as a ghost to explain that Hamlet's uncle, now married to Hamlet's mother, murdered him. Uncertain about righting the situation, Hamlet hesitates and is murdered by a poisoned sword intended for his uncle.) Describe the link Poe sees. How is his death like Hamlet's?

2. Murena's poem and Poe's "Alone" are both written in the first-person point of view. Compare and contrast Murena's speaker with the speaker in "Alone."

3. Which phrase in line 38 in Murena's poem sums up his depiction of Poe's life? If you were to write a poem about the dying thoughts of a real or imaginary famous person, whom would you choose as the subject and what would your poem say about him or her?

Writing Options

1. Suppose that you are a TV correspondent investigating the circumstances surrounding Poe's death in 1849. Research the topic, and then present a news report for a network special called "How Did Poe Die? Looking Back a Century and a Half."

2. Write a short evaluative essay in which you consider Murena's ability to capture Poe's thoughts and feelings.

 Go to **www.mirrorsandwindows.com** for more.

LITERARY CONNECTION

The Influence of Poe

When Edgar Allan Poe died in 1849 at age forty, he was impoverished and largely unappreciated in American literary circles. Such a dishonorable ending is out of balance with the weight of Poe's influence on generations of writers since his time. Writers as diverse as Sir Arthur Conan Doyle, Walt Whitman, William Faulkner, and Jules Verne have been inspired by Poe's short fiction, poetry, literary criticism, and general themes and styles.

Initially, Poe's influence was felt most strongly overseas, particularly after poet Charles Baudelaire translated some of Poe's works into French. Marcel Proust (France), Vladimir Nabokov and Fyodor Dostoevsky (Russia), Franz Kafka (Czech Republic), and Jorge Luis Borges (Argentina) all cited Poe as an inspiration. Some even included references to him or his works in their own writing. Japanese writer Hirai Taro assumed the pen name *Edogawa Rampo,* a rendering of Poe's name in Japanese, for his series of detective fiction.

Poe's influence reached artistic circles beyond those in which he worked. H. P. Lovecraft and Ray Bradbury, prominent writers in the science fiction genre, both cited Poe as an influence, as did Friedrich Nietzsche, the famed German philosopher. At the other end of the literary spectrum, children's writer Lemony Snicket alluded to Poe in *A Series of Unfortunate Events,* in which a Mr. Poe and his sons Edgar and Albert take care of the Baudelaire children. Even though the stories often are humorous and are appropriate for children, they hint at macabre events.

In acknowledgment of Poe's mastery of the mysterious and macabre, the Mystery Writers of America bestow the Edgar Allan Poe Awards, or the Edgars for short. Awarded annually, the Edgars celebrate the best work in several categories, including both fiction and nonfiction writing and television, film, and theater productions. The award itself is a small bust of Edgar Allan Poe.

The Minister's Black Veil

by Nathaniel Hawthorne

Nathaniel Hawthorne (1804–1864) was born in Salem, Massachusetts, and descended from a prominent Puritan family. He struggled for years to become a successful writer, living in isolation and honing his craft. He finally published a collection of stories in 1837, *Twice-Told Tales,* which contained some of his finest stories, including "The Minister's Black Veil." In 1850, Hawthorne published his most famous work of fiction, the novel *The Scarlet Letter.*

A prominent theme in Hawthorne's work is that judging wrongdoers too harshly can be as destructive to individuals and to society as sinful behavior. This is the theme in *The Scarlet Letter,* in which Hester must wear a symbol on her clothing so that neither she nor the world will forget the sin for which society has condemned her. In "The Minister's Black Veil," Parson Hooper also seems to wear a symbol of shame or evil.

The sexton stood in the porch of Milford meetinghouse, pulling lustily at the bell-rope. The old people of the village came stooping along the street. Children, with bright faces, tripped merrily beside their parents, or mimicked a graver gait, in the conscious dignity of their Sunday clothes. Spruce bachelors looked sidelong at the pretty maidens, and fancied that the Sabbath sunshine made them prettier than on weekdays. When the throng had mostly streamed into the porch, the sexton began to toll the bell, keeping his eye on the Reverend Mr. Hooper's door. The first glimpse of the clergyman's figure was the signal for the bell to cease its summons.

"But what has good Parson Hooper got upon his face?" cried the sexton in astonishment.

All within hearing immediately turned about, and beheld the semblance of Mr. Hooper, pacing slowly his meditative way toward the meetinghouse. With one accord they started, expressing more wonder than if some strange minister were coming to dust the cushions of Mr. Hooper's pulpit.

"Are you sure it is our parson?" inquired Goodman[1] Gray of the sexton.

"Of a certainty it is good Mr. Hooper," replied the sexton. "He was to have exchanged pulpits with Parson Shute of Westbury; but Parson Shute sent to excuse himself yesterday, being to preach a funeral sermon."

The cause of so much amazement may appear sufficiently slight. Mr. Hooper, a gentlemanly person of about thirty, though still a bachelor, was dressed with due clerical neatness, as if a careful wife had starched his band, and brushed the weekly dust from his Sunday's garb. There was but one

---

1. **Goodman.** Polite address similar to *Mister*

Portrait of Franz Liszt, 1838. Henri Lehmann.
Musée Carnavalet, Paris, France.

thing remarkable in his appearance. Swathed about his forehead, and hanging down over his face, so low as to be shaken by his breath, Mr. Hooper had on a black veil. On a nearer view, it seemed to consist of two folds of crape,[2] which entirely concealed his features, except the mouth and chin, but probably did not intercept his sight, farther than to give a darkened aspect to all living and inanimate things. With this gloomy shade before him, good Mr. Hooper walked onward, at a slow and quiet pace, stooping somewhat and looking on the ground, as is customary with abstracted[3] men, yet nodding kindly to those of his parishioners who still waited on the meetinghouse steps. But so wonder-struck were they, that his greeting hardly met with a return.

"I can't really feel as if good Mr. Hooper's face was behind that piece of crape," said the sexton.

"I don't like it," muttered an old woman, as she hobbled into the meetinghouse. "He has changed himself into something awful, only by hiding his face."

"Our parson has gone mad!" cried Goodman Gray, following him across the threshold.

A rumor of some unaccountable phenomenon had preceded Mr. Hooper into the meetinghouse, and set all the congregation astir. Few could refrain from twisting their heads toward the door; many stood upright, and turned directly about; while several little boys clambered upon the seats, and came down again with a terrible racket. There was a general bustle, a rustling of the women's gowns and shuffling of the men's feet, greatly at variance with that hushed repose which should attend the entrance of the minister. But Mr. Hooper appeared not to notice the perturbation[4] of his people. He entered with an almost noiseless step, bent his head mildly to the pews on each side, and bowed as he passed his oldest parishioner, a white-haired great-grandsire, who occupied an armchair in the center of the aisle. It was strange to observe, how slowly this venerable man became conscious of something singular in the appearance of his pastor. He seemed not fully to partake of the prevailing wonder, till Mr. Hooper had ascended the stairs, and showed himself in the pulpit, face to face with his congregation, except for the black veil. That mysterious emblem was never once withdrawn. It shook with his measured breath as he gave out the psalm; it threw its obscurity[5] between him and the holy page, as he read the Scriptures; and while he prayed, the veil lay heavily on his uplifted countenance. Did he seek to hide it from the dread Being whom he was addressing?

Such was the effect of this simple piece of crape, that more than one woman of delicate nerves was forced to leave the meetinghouse. Yet perhaps the pale-faced congregation was

---

2. **crape.** Band of cloth worn during mourning
3. **abstracted.** Distracted; lost in thought
4. **perturbation.** Confusing; state of disorder
5. **obscurity.** Here, darkness

almost as fearful a sight to the minister, as his black veil to them.

Mr. Hooper had the reputation of a good preacher, but not an energetic one: He strove to win his people heavenward, by mild persuasive influences, rather than to drive them thither, by the thunders of the Word. The sermon which he now delivered, was marked by the same characteristics of style and manner, as the general series of his pulpit oratory. But there was something, either in the sentiment of the discourse itself, or in the imagination of the auditors, which made it greatly the most powerful effort that they had ever heard from their pastor's lips. It was tinged, rather more darkly than usual, with the gentle gloom of Mr. Hooper's temperament. The subject had reference to secret sin, and those sad mysteries which we hide from our nearest and dearest, and would fain conceal from our own consciousness, even forgetting that the Omniscient[6] can detect them. A subtle power was breathed into his words. Each member of the congregation, the most innocent girl, and the man of hardened breast, felt as if the preacher had crept upon them, behind his awful veil, and discovered their hoarded iniquity[7] of deed or thought. Many spread their clasped hands on their bosoms. There was nothing terrible in what Mr. Hooper said; at least, no violence; and yet, with every tremor of his melancholy voice, the hearers quaked. An unsought pathos[8] came hand in hand with awe. So sensible were the audience of some unwonted attribute in their minister, that they longed for a breath of wind to blow aside the veil, almost believing that a stranger's visage[9] would be discovered, though the form, gesture, and voice were those of Mr. Hooper.

At the close of the services, the people hurried out with indecorous[10] confusion, eager to communicate their pent-up amazement, and conscious of lighter spirits, the moment they lost sight of the black veil. Some gathered in little circles, huddled closely together, with their mouths all whispering in the center; some went homeward alone, wrapped in silent

meditation; some talked loudly, and profaned the Sabbath day with ostentatious[11] laughter. A few shook their sagacious[12] heads, intimating[13] that they could penetrate the mystery; while one or two affirmed that there was no mystery at all, but only that Mr. Hooper's eyes were so weakened by the midnight lamp, as to require a shade. After a brief interval, forth came good Mr. Hooper also, in the rear of his flock. Turning his veiled face from one group to another, he paid due reverence to the hoary heads,[14] saluted the middle-aged with kind dignity, as their friend and spiritual guide, greeted the young with mingled authority and love, and laid his hands on the little children's heads to bless them. Such was always his custom on the Sabbath day. Strange and bewildered looks repaid him for his courtesy. None,

---

6. **Omniscient.** All-knowing God
7. **iniquity.** Wickedness or injustice
8. **pathos.** Feelings of sympathy or sorrow
9. **visage.** Face or appearance
10. **indecorous.** Improper
11. **ostentatious.** Showy or excessive
12. **sagacious.** Wise
13. **intimating.** Suggesting; hinting
14. **hoary heads.** Reference to the white or gray hair of the elderly

as on former occasions, aspired to the honor of walking by their pastor's side. Old Squire Saunders, doubtless by an accidental lapse of memory, neglected to invite Mr. Hooper to his table, where the good clergyman had been wont[15] to bless the food, almost every Sunday since his settlement. He returned, therefore, to the parsonage, and, at the moment of closing the door, was observed to look back upon the people, all of whom had their eyes fixed upon the minister. A sad smile gleamed faintly from beneath the black veil, and flickered about his mouth, glimmering as he disappeared.

"How strange," said a lady, "that a simple black veil, such as any woman might wear on her bonnet, should become such a terrible thing on Mr. Hooper's face!"

"Something must surely be amiss with Mr. Hooper's intellects," observed her husband, the physician of the village. "But the strangest part of the affair is the effect of this vagary,[16] even on a sober-minded man like myself. The black veil, though it covers only our pastor's face, throws its influence over his whole person, and makes him ghostlike from head to foot. Do you not feel it so?"

"Truly do I," replied the lady; "and I would not be alone with him for the world. I wonder he is not afraid to be alone with himself!"

"Men sometimes are so," said her husband.

"I would not be alone with him for the world."

The afternoon service was attended with similar circumstances. At its conclusion, the bell tolled for the funeral of a young lady. The relatives and friends were assembled in the house, and the more distant acquaintances stood about the door, speaking of the good qualities of the deceased, when their talk was interrupted by the appearance of Mr. Hooper, still covered with his black veil. It was now an appropriate emblem. The clergyman stepped into the room where the corpse was laid, and bent over the coffin, to take a last farewell of his deceased parishioner. As he stooped, the veil hung straight down from his forehead, so that, if her eyelids had not been closed forever, the dead maiden might have seen his face. Could Mr. Hooper be fearful of her glance, that he so hastily caught back the black veil? A person, who watched the interview between the dead and living, scrupled[17] not to affirm, that, at the instant when the clergyman's features were disclosed, the corpse had slightly shuddered, rustling the shroud[18] and muslin cap, though the countenance retained the composure of death. A superstitious old woman was the only witness of this prodigy.[19] From the coffin, Mr. Hooper passed into the chamber of the mourners, and thence to the head of the staircase, to make the funeral prayer. It was a tender and heart-dissolving prayer, full of sorrow, yet so imbued with celestial[20] hopes, that the music of a heavenly harp, swept by the fingers of the dead, seemed faintly to be heard among the saddest accents of the minister. The people trembled, though they but darkly understood him, when he prayed that they, and himself, and all of mortal race, might be ready, as he trusted this young maiden had been, for the dreadful hour that should snatch the veil from their faces.[21] The bearers went heavily forth, and the mourners followed, saddening all the street, with the dead before them, and Mr. Hooper in his black veil behind.

"Why do you look back?" said one in the procession to his partner.

"I had a fancy," replied she, "that the minister and the maiden's spirit were walking hand in hand."

"And so had I, at the same moment," said the other.

---

15. **wont.** Accustomed
16. **vagary.** Unusual happening
17. **scrupled.** Hesitated; was reluctant
18. **shroud.** Cloth in which a body is wrapped for burial
19. **prodigy.** Startling event
20. **celestial.** Of the heavens
21. **snatch . . . faces.** The Puritans believed that at death, individuals would be stripped of their clothing and adornments.

That night, the handsomest couple in Milford village were to be joined in wedlock. Though reckoned a melancholy man, Mr. Hooper had a placid cheerfulness for such occasions, which often excited a sympathetic smile, where livelier merriment would have been thrown away. There was no quality of his disposition which made him more beloved than this. The company at the wedding awaited his arrival with impatience, trusting that the strange awe, which had gathered over him throughout the day, would now be dispelled.[22] But such was not the result. When Mr. Hooper came, the first thing that their eyes rested on was the same horrible black veil, which had added deeper gloom to the funeral, and could portend[23] nothing but evil to the wedding. Such was its immediate effect on the guests, that a cloud seemed to have rolled duskily from beneath the black crape, and dimmed the light of the candles. The bridal pair stood up before the minister. But the bride's cold fingers quivered in the tremulous[24] hand of the bridegroom, and her deathlike paleness caused a whisper, that the maiden who had been buried a few hours before, was come from her grave to be married. If ever another wedding were so dismal, it was that famous one, where they tolled the wedding knell.[25] After performing the ceremony, Mr. Hooper raised a glass of wine to his lips, wishing happiness to the new-married couple, in a strain of mild pleasantry that ought to have brightened the features of the guests, like a cheerful gleam from the hearth. At that instant, catching a glimpse of his figure in the looking glass, the black veil involved his own spirit in the horror with which it overwhelmed all others. His frame shuddered—his lips grew white—he spilt the untasted wine upon the carpet—and rushed forth into the darkness. For the Earth, too, had on her Black Veil.

The next day, the whole village of Milford talked of little else than Parson Hooper's black veil. That, and the mystery concealed behind it, supplied a topic for discussion between acquaintances meeting in the street, and good women gossiping at their open windows. It was the first item of news that the tavern keeper told to his guests. The children babbled of it on their way to school. One imitative little imp covered his face with an old black handkerchief, thereby so affrighting his playmates, that the panic seized himself, and he well nigh lost his wits by his own waggery.[26]

The next day, the whole village of Milford talked of little else than Parson Hooper's black veil.

It was remarkable, that all, of the busybodies and impertinent people in the parish, not one ventured to put the plain question to Mr. Hooper, wherefore he did this thing. Hitherto, whenever there appeared the slightest call for such interference, he had never lacked advisers, nor shown himself averse to be guided by their judgment. If he erred at all, it was by so painful a degree of self-distrust, that even the mildest censure[27] would lead him to consider an indifferent action as a crime. Yet, though so well acquainted with this amiable[28] weakness, no individual among his parishioners chose to make the black veil a subject of friendly remonstrance.[29] There was a feeling of dread, neither plainly confessed nor carefully concealed, which caused each to shift the responsibility upon another, till at length it was found expedient to send a deputation[30] of the church, in order to deal with Mr. Hooper about the mystery, before it should grow into a scandal. Never did an embassy so ill discharge its duties. The minister received them

---

22. **dispelled.** Broke up or scattered
23. **portend.** Indicate, especially about the future
24. **tremulous.** Trembling or shaking
25. **knell.** Ringing of a bell
26. **waggery.** Joke or prank
27. **censure.** Criticism or condemnation
28. **amiable.** Friendly; agreeable
29. **remonstrance.** Objection; complaint
30. **deputation.** Group of representatives

with friendly courtesy, but became silent, after they were seated, leaving to his visitors the whole burden of introducing their important business. The topic, it might be supposed, was obvious enough. There was the black veil, swathed round Mr. Hooper's forehead, and concealing every feature above his placid mouth, on which, at times, they could perceive the glimmering of a melancholy smile. But that piece of crape, to their imagination, seemed to hang down before his heart, the symbol of a fearful secret between him and them. Were the veil but cast aside, they might speak freely of it, but not till then. Thus they sat a considerable time, speechless, confused, and shrinking uneasily from Mr. Hooper's eye, which they felt to be fixed upon them with an invisible glance. Finally, the deputies returned abashed to their constituents, pronouncing the matter too weighty to be handled, except by a council of the churches, if, indeed, it might not require a general synod.[31]

But there was one person in the village, unappalled by the awe with which the black veil had impressed all beside herself. When the deputies returned without an explanation, or even venturing to demand one, she, with the calm energy of her character, determined to chase away the strange cloud that appeared to be settling round Mr. Hooper, every moment more darkly than before. As his plighted[32] wife, it should be her privilege to know what the black veil concealed. At the minister's first visit, therefore, she entered upon the subject, with a direct simplicity, which made the task easier both for him and her. After he had seated himself, she fixed her eyes steadfastly upon the veil, but could discern nothing of the dreadful gloom that had so overawed the multitude: It was but a double fold of crape, hanging down from his forehead to his mouth, and slightly stirring with his breath.

"No," said she aloud, and smiling, "there is nothing terrible in this piece of crape, except that it hides a face which I am always glad to look upon. Come, good sir, let the sun shine from behind the cloud. First lay aside your black veil: Then tell me why you put it on."

A Fair Puritain, 1897. E. Percy Moran. Library of Congress, Washington, DC.

Mr. Hooper's smile glimmered faintly.

"There is an hour to come," said he, "when all of us shall cast aside our veils. Take it not amiss, beloved friend, if I wear this piece of crape till then."

"Your words are a mystery too," returned the young lady. "Take away the veil from them, at least."

"Elizabeth, I will," said he, "so far as my vow may suffer[33] me. Know, then, this veil is a type and a symbol, and I am bound to wear it ever, both in light and darkness, in solitude and before the gaze of multitudes, and as with strangers, so with my familiar friends. No mortal eye will see it withdrawn. This dismal shade must separate me from the world: Even you, Elizabeth, can never come behind it!"

---

31. **synod.** Central agency of an association of churches
32. **plighted.** Engaged to be married
33. **suffer.** Allow or permit

"What grievous affliction hath befallen you," she earnestly inquired, "that you should thus darken your eyes forever?"

"If it be a sign of mourning," replied Mr. Hooper, "I, perhaps, like most other mortals, have sorrows dark enough to be typified by a black veil."

"But what if the world will not believe that it is the type of an innocent sorrow?" urged Elizabeth. "Beloved and respected as you are, there may be whispers, that you hide your face under the consciousness of secret sin. For the sake of your holy office, do away this scandal!"

The color rose into her cheeks, as she intimated the nature of the rumors that were already abroad in the village. But Mr. Hooper's mildness did not forsake him. He even smiled again—that same sad smile, which always appeared like a faint glimmering of light, proceeding from the obscurity beneath the veil.

The color rose into her cheeks, as she intimated the nature of the rumors that were already abroad in the village.

"If I hide my face for sorrow, there is cause enough," he merely replied; "and if I cover it for secret sin, what mortal might not do the same?"

And with this gentle, but unconquerable obstinacy[34] did he resist all her entreaties. At length Elizabeth sat silent. For a few moments she appeared lost in thought, considering, probably, what new methods might be tried, to withdraw her lover from so dark a fantasy, which, if it had no other meaning, was perhaps a symptom of mental disease. Though of a firmer character than his own, the tears rolled down her cheeks. But, in an instant, as it were, a new feeling took the place of sorrow: Her eyes were fixed insensibly on the black veil, when, like a sudden twilight in the air, its terrors fell around her. She arose, and stood trembling before him.

"And do you feel it then at last?" said he mournfully.

She made no reply, but covered her eyes with her hand, and turned to leave the room. He rushed forward and caught her arm.

"Have patience with me, Elizabeth!" cried he passionately. "Do not desert me, though this veil must be between us here on earth. Be mine, and hereafter there shall be no veil over my face, no darkness between our souls! It is but a mortal veil—it is not for eternity! Oh! you know not how lonely I am, and how frightened to be alone behind my black veil. Do not leave me in this miserable obscurity forever!"

"Lift the veil but once, and look me in the face," said she.

"Never! It cannot be!" replied Mr. Hooper.

"Then, farewell!" said Elizabeth.

She withdrew her arm from his grasp, and slowly departed, pausing at the door, to give one long, shuddering gaze, that seemed almost to penetrate the mystery of the black veil. But, even amid his grief, Mr. Hooper smiled to think that only a material emblem had separated him from happiness, though the horrors which it shadowed forth, must be drawn darkly between the fondest of lovers.

From that time no attempts were made to remove Mr. Hooper's black veil, or, by a direct appeal, to discover the secret which it was supposed to hide. By persons who claimed a superiority to popular prejudice, it was reckoned merely an eccentric whim, such as often mingles with the sober actions of men otherwise rational, and tinges them all with its own semblance of insanity. But with the multitude, good Mr. Hooper was irreparably a bugbear.[35] He could not walk the streets with any peace of mind, so conscious was he that the gentle and timid would turn aside to avoid him, and that others would make it a point of hardihood to throw themselves in his way. The impertinence

---

34. **obstinacy.** Stubbornness
35. **bugbear.** Source of irritation or dread

of the latter class compelled him to give up his customary walk, at sunset, to the burial ground; for when he leaned pensively[36] over the gate, there would always be faces behind the gravestones, peeping at his black veil. A fable went the rounds, that the stare of the dead people drove him thence. It grieved him, to the very depth of his kind heart, to observe how the children fled from his approach, breaking up their merriest sports, while his melancholy figure was yet afar off. Their instinctive dread caused him to feel, more strongly than aught else, that a preternatural[37] horror was interwoven with the threads of the black crape. In truth, his own antipathy[38] to the veil was known to be so great, that he never willingly passed before a mirror, nor stooped to drink at a still fountain, lest, in its peaceful bosom, he should be affrighted by himself. This was what gave plausibility[39] to the whispers, that Mr. Hooper's conscience tortured him for some great crime, too horrible to be entirely concealed, or otherwise than so obscurely intimated. Thus, from beneath the black veil, there rolled a cloud into the sunshine, an ambiguity of sin or sorrow, which enveloped the poor minister, so that love or sympathy could never reach him. It was said, that ghost and fiend consorted with him there. With self-shudderings and outward terrors, he walked continually in its shadow, groping darkly within his own soul, or gazing through a medium that saddened the whole world. Even the lawless wind, it was believed, respected his dreadful secret, and never blew aside the veil. But still good Mr. Hooper sadly smiled, at the pale visages of the worldly throng as he passed by.

Among all its bad influences, the black veil had the one desirable effect, of making its

wearer a very efficient clergyman. By the aid of his mysterious emblem—for there was no other apparent cause—he became a man of awful power, over souls that were in agony for sin. His converts always regarded him with a dread peculiar to themselves, affirming, though but figuratively, that, before he brought them to celestial light, they had been with him behind the black veil. Its gloom, indeed, enabled him to sympathize with all dark affections. Dying sinners cried aloud for Mr. Hooper, and would not yield their breath till he appeared; though ever, as he stooped to whisper consolation, they shuddered at the veiled face so near their own. Such were the terrors of the black veil, even when Death had bared his visage! Strangers came long distances to attend service at his church, with the mere idle purpose of gazing at his figure, because it was forbidden them to behold his face. But many were made to quake ere they departed! Once, during Governor Belcher's administration, Mr. Hooper was appointed to preach the election sermon. Covered with his black veil, he stood before the chief magistrate, the council, and the representatives, and wrought so deep an impression, that the legislative measures of that year, were characterized by all the gloom and piety of our earliest ancestral sway.

In this manner Mr. Hooper spent a long life, irreproachable[40] in outward act, yet shrouded in dismal suspicions; kind and loving, though unloved, and dimly feared; a man apart from men, shunned in their health and joy, but ever summoned to their aid in

---

36. **pensively.** Thoughtfully or seriously
37. **preternatural.** Supernatural; abnormal
38. **antipathy.** Strong dislike
39. **plausibility.** Believability
40. **irreproachable.** Blameless

mortal anguish. As years wore on, shedding their snows above his sable veil, he acquired a name throughout the New England churches, and they called him Father Hooper. Nearly all his parishioners, who were of mature age when he was settled, had been borne away by many a funeral: He had one congregation in the church, and a more crowded one in the churchyard; and having wrought so late into the evening, and done his work so well, it was now good Father Hooper's turn to rest.

Several persons were visible by the shaded candlelight, in the death chamber of the old clergyman. Natural connections he had none. But there was the decorously grave, though unmoved physician, seeking only to mitigate[41] the last pangs of the patient whom he could not save. There were the deacons, and other eminently pious members of his church. There, also, was the Reverend Mr. Clark, of Westbury, a young and zealous divine, who had ridden in haste to pray by the bedside of the expiring minister. There was the nurse, no hired hand-maiden of death, but one whose calm affection had endured thus long, in secrecy, in solitude, amid the chill of age, and would not perish, even at the dying hour. Who, but Elizabeth! And there lay the hoary head of good Father Hooper upon the death-pillow, with the black veil still swathed about his brow and reach-ing down over his face, so that each more dif-ficult gasp of his faint breath caused it to stir. All through life that piece of crape had hung between him and the world: It had separated him from cheerful brotherhood and woman's love, and kept him in that saddest of all prisons, his own heart; and still it lay upon his face, as if to deepen the gloom of his darksome chamber, and shade him from the sunshine of eternity.

For some time previous, his mind had been confused, wavering doubtfully between the past and the present, and hovering forward, as it were, at intervals, into the indistinctness of the world to come. There had been feverish turns, which tossed him from side to side, and wore away what little strength he had. But in his most convulsive struggles, and in the wildest vagaries of his intellect, when no other thought retained its sober influence, he still showed an awful solicitude lest the black veil should slip aside. Even if his bewildered soul could have forgotten, there was a faithful woman at his pillow, who, with averted eyes, would have covered that aged face, which she had last beheld in the comeli-ness of manhood. At length the death-stricken old man lay quietly in the torpor[42] of mental and bodily exhaustion, with an imperceptible pulse, and breath that grew fainter and fainter, except when a long, deep, and irregular inspiration[43] seemed to prelude the flight of his spirit.

The minister of Westbury approached the bedside.

"Venerable Father Hooper," said he, "the moment of your release is at hand. Are you ready for the lifting of the veil, that shuts in time from eternity?"

Father Hooper at first replied merely by a feeble motion of his head; then, apprehensive, perhaps, that his meaning might be doubtful, he exerted himself to speak.

"Yea," said he, in faint accents, "my soul hath a patient weariness until that veil be lifted."

"And is it fitting," resumed the Reverend Mr. Clark, "that a man so given to prayer, of such a blameless example, holy in deed and thought, so far as mortal judgment may pronounce; is it fitting that a father in the church should leave a shadow on his memory, that may seem to blacken a life so pure? I pray you, my venerable brother, let not this thing be! Suffer us to be gladdened by your trium-phant aspect, as you go to your reward. Before the veil of eternity be lifted, let me cast aside this black veil from your face!"

And thus speaking, the Reverend Mr. Clark bent forward to reveal the mystery of so many years. But, exerting a sudden energy, that made all the beholders stand aghast, Father Hooper snatched both his hands from beneath the

---

41. **mitigate.** Make less harsh
42. **torpor.** Mental or physical inactivity
43. **inspiration.** Breathing in

bedclothes, and pressed them strongly on the black veil, resolute[44] to struggle, if the minister of Westbury would contend with a dying man.

"Never!" cried the veiled clergyman. "On earth, never!"

"Dark old man!" exclaimed the affrighted minister, "with what horrible crime upon your soul are you now passing to the judgment?"

Father Hooper's breath heaved; it rattled in his throat; but, with a mighty effort, grasping forward with his hands, he caught hold of life, and held it back till he should speak. He even raised himself in bed; and there he sat, shivering with the arms of death around him, while the black veil hung down, awful, at that last moment, in the gathered terrors of a lifetime. And yet the faint, sad smile, so often there, now seemed to glimmer from its obscurity, and linger on Father Hooper's lips.

"Why do you tremble at me alone?" cried he, turning his veiled face round the circle of pale spectators. "Tremble also at each other! Have men avoided me, and women shown no pity, and children screamed and fled, only for my black veil? What, but the mystery which it obscurely typifies, has made this piece of crape so awful? When the friend shows his inmost heart to his friend; the lover to his best beloved; when man does not vainly shrink from the eye of his Creator, loathsomely treasuring up the secret of his sin; then deem me a monster, for the symbol beneath which I have lived, and die! I look around me, and, lo! on every visage a Black Veil!"

While his auditors shrank from one another, in mutual affright, Father Hooper fell back upon his pillow, a veiled corpse, with a faint smile lingering on the lips. Still veiled, they laid him in his coffin, and a veiled corpse they bore him to the grave. The grass of many years has sprung up and withered on that grave, the burial stone is moss-grown, and good Mr. Hooper's face is dust; but awful is still the thought, that it moldered beneath the Black Veil! ❖

---

44. **resolute.** Determined

Hawthorne's writing is sometimes criticized as being heavy handed in how it delivers a message. When you read, do you look for the so-called moral of the story?

Refer and Reason

1. What does Elizabeth ask Hooper to do for her? Why does she break their engagement after Hooper refuses her request?

2. Just before Hooper dies, what does he say he has lived beneath and is now dying beneath? Suggest what the veil symbolizes, and argue whether it is a convincing symbol.

3. On his deathbed, what does Hooper see as he looks around him? Relate his observation to the theme of the story.

Writing Options

1. Imagine you are a Puritan teenager. How do you feel about yourself and the world around you? Write a brief journal entry describing your thoughts, actions, feelings about your community or a similar topic.

2. Write an essay analyzing the character of Hooper, based on dialogue and events in the story. Try to bring the minister to life for someone who has not read the story.

 Go to **www.mirrorsandwindows.com** for more.

Loomings
from
Moby-Dick

by Herman Melville

Herman Melville
(1819–1891) was born into a relatively wealthy family whose fortune declined. Beginning at age twelve, he worked a variety of jobs to help support the family; then at twenty,

he sailed on a whaler to the South Seas in search of adventure. After jumping ship, he lived with a tribal group, was picked up by an Australian whaler, took part in a mutiny (an uprising against a ship's officers), and was imprisoned. When he returned home at age twenty-five, he wrote *Typee*, a story about his adventurous voyage. Published in 1846, the book was a huge success and soon was followed by other popular stories of seafaring life.

Melville's greatest work, *Moby-Dick*, published in 1851, was poorly received. In this narrative about a whaling expedition, Melville presents a metaphorical study of the nature of good, evil, and reality. Although it was little appreciated in its time, today *Moby-Dick* is regarded as a classic American novel.

Call me Ishmael. Some years ago—never mind how long precisely—having little or no money in my purse, and nothing particular to interest me on shore, I thought I would sail about a little and see the watery part of the world. It is a way I have of driving off the spleen, and regulating the circulation. Whenever I find myself growing grim about the mouth; whenever it is a damp, drizzly November in my soul; whenever I find myself involuntarily pausing before coffin warehouses, and bringing up the rear of every funeral I meet; and especially whenever my hypos[1] get such an upper hand of me, that it requires a strong moral principle to prevent me from deliberately stepping into the street, and methodically knocking people's hats off—then, I account it high time to get to sea as soon as I can. This is my substitute for pistol and ball. With a philosophical flourish Cato[2] throws himself upon his sword; I quietly take to the ship. There is nothing surprising in this. If they but knew it, almost all men in their degree, some time or other, cherish very nearly the same feelings towards the ocean with me.

There now is your insular city of the Manhattoes,[3] belted round by wharves as Indian isles by coral reefs—commerce surrounds it with her surf. Right and left, the streets take you waterward. Its extreme down-town is the battery, where that noble mole[4] is washed by waves, and cooled by breezes, which

---

1. **hypos.** Short for *hypochondria*, or excessive worry about illness
2. **Cato.** Cato the Younger (95 BCE–46 BCE) was a statesman in the last years of the Roman Republic. He killed himself with his own sword to avoid living under the rule of *Caesar*.
3. **Manhattoes.** Native American name for Manhattan (Island), one of the five boroughs of New York City
4. **mole.** Pier or breakwater

Book illustration from *Moby-Dick,* c. 1905.
Isaac Walton Taber.

a few hours previous were out of sight of land.
Look at the crowds of water-gazers there.

Circumambulate the city of a dreamy Sabbath afternoon. Go from Corlears Hook to Coenties Slip, and from thence, by Whitehall, northward.[5] What do you see?—Posted like silent sentinels all around the town, stand thousands upon thousands of mortal men fixed in ocean reveries.[6] Some leaning against the spiles; some seated upon the pier-heads; some looking over the bulwarks of ships from China; some high aloft in the rigging, as if striving to get a still better seaward peep. But these are all landsmen; of week days pent up in lath and plaster—tied to counters, nailed to benches, clinched to desks. How then is this? Are the green fields gone? What do they here?

But look! here come more crowds, pacing straight for the water, and seemingly bound for a dive. Strange! Nothing will content them but the extremest limit of the land; loitering under the shady lee of yonder warehouses will not suffice. No. They must get just as nigh the water as they possibly can without falling in. And there they stand—miles of them—leagues. Inlanders all, they come from lanes and alleys, streets and avenues—north, east, south, and west. Yet here they all unite. Tell me, does the magnetic virtue of the needles of the compasses of all those ships attract them thither?

Once more. Say, you are in the country; in some high land of lakes. Take almost any path you please, and ten to one it carries you down in a dale, and leaves you there by a pool in the stream. There is magic in it. Let the most absent-minded of men be plunged in his deepest reveries—stand that man on his legs, set his feet a-going, and he will infallibly[7] lead you to water, if water there be in all that region. Should you ever be athirst in the great American desert, try this experiment, if your caravan happen to be supplied with a metaphysical professor.[8] Yes, as every one knows, meditation and water are welded for ever.

But here is an artist. He desires to paint you the dreamiest, shadiest, quietest, most enchanting bit of romantic landscape in all the valley of the Saco.[9] What is the chief element he employs? There stand his trees, each with a hollow trunk, as if a hermit and a crucifix were within; and here sleeps his meadow, and there sleep his cattle; and up from yonder cottage goes a sleepy smoke. Deep into distant woodlands winds a mazy way, reaching to overlapping spurs of mountains bathed in their hill-side blue. But though the picture lies thus tranced, and though this pine-tree shakes down its sighs like leaves upon this shepherd's head, yet all were vain, unless the shepherd's

---

5. **Corlears Hook . . . Coenties Slip . . . Whitehall.** Areas at the southern tip of Manhattan
6. **reveries.** Daydreams
7. **infallibly.** Without error
8. **metaphysical professor.** *Metaphysics,* a branch of philosophy, deals with questions of reality. Melville is making a joke by saying that only someone who can think outside ordinary reality can produce water in the desert.
9. **Saco.** River that runs through New Hampshire and Maine

Whalers, 1845. Joseph Mallord William Turner.
Tate Gallery, London, England.

eye were fixed upon the magic stream before him. Go visit the Prairies in June, when for scores on scores of miles you wade knee-deep among Tiger-lilies—what is the one charm wanting?—Water—there is not a drop of water there! Were Niagara but a cataract[10] of sand, would you travel your thousand miles to see it? Why did the poor poet of Tennessee, upon suddenly receiving two handfuls of silver, deliberate[11] whether to buy him a coat, which he sadly needed, or invest his money in a pedestrian trip to Rockaway Beach? Why is almost every robust healthy boy with a robust healthy soul in him, at some time or other crazy to go to sea? Why upon your first voyage as a passenger, did you yourself feel such a mystical vibration, when first told that you and your ship were now out of sight of land? Why did the old Persians hold the sea holy? Why did the Greeks give it a separate deity, and own brother of Jove?[12] Surely all this is not without meaning. And still deeper the meaning of that story of Narcissus, who because he could not grasp the tormenting, mild image he saw in the fountain, plunged into it and was drowned. But that same image, we ourselves see in all rivers and oceans. It is the image of the ungraspable

phantom of life; and this is the key to it all.

Now, when I say that I am in the habit of going to sea whenever I begin to grow hazy about the eyes, and begin to be over conscious of my lungs, I do not mean to have it inferred that I ever go to sea as a passenger. For to go as a passenger you must needs have a purse, and a purse is but a rag unless you have something in it. Besides, passengers get sea-sick—grow quarrelsome—don't sleep at nights—do not enjoy themselves much, as a general thing;—no, I never go as a passenger; nor, though I am something of a salt, do I ever go to sea as a Commodore, or a Captain, or a Cook. I abandon the glory and distinction of such offices to those who like them. For my part, I abominate[13] all honorable respectable toils, trials, and tribulations of every kind whatsoever. It is quite as much as I can do to take care of myself, without taking care of ships, barques, brigs, schooners, and what not. And as for going as cook,—though I confess there is considerable glory in that, a cook being a sort of officer on ship-board—yet, somehow, I never fancied broiling fowls;—though once broiled, judiciously buttered, and judgmatically salted and peppered, there is no one who will speak more respectfully, not to say reverentially, of a broiled fowl than I will. It is out of the idolatrous[14] dotings of the old Egyptians upon broiled ibis and roasted river horse,[15] that you see the mummies of those creatures in their huge bake-houses the pyramids.

---

10. **cataract.** Waterfall
11. **deliberate.** Think about carefully
12. **Jove.** Chief Roman god, usually called Jupiter, and the equivalent of the Greek god Zeus. Neptune, a brother of Jupiter, was the Roman god of the sea; Poseidon, a brother of Zeus, was the Greek god of the oceans.
13. **abominate.** Hate
14. **idolatrous.** Worshiping physical objects as gods
15. **ibis . . . river horse.** Ibis is a wading bird; "river horse" is the literal meaning, from two Greek words, of *hippopotamus.*

No, when I go to sea, I go as a simple sailor, right before the mast, plumb down into the forecastle, aloft there to the royal mast-head. True, they rather order me about some, and make me jump from spar to spar, like a grasshopper in a May meadow. And at first, this sort of thing is unpleasant enough. It touches one's sense of honor, particularly if you come of an old established family in the land, the Van Rensselaers, or Randolphs, or Hardicanutes. And more than all, if just previous to putting your hand into the tar-pot, you have been lording it as a country schoolmaster, making the tallest boys stand in awe of you. The transition is a keen one, I assure you, from a schoolmaster to a sailor, and requires a strong decoction of Seneca and the Stoics[16] to enable you to grin and bear it. But even this wears off in time.

What of it, if some old hunks of a sea-captain orders me to get a broom and sweep down the decks? What does that indignity amount to, weighed, I mean, in the scales of the New Testament? Do you think the archangel Gabriel thinks anything the less of me, because I promptly and respectfully obey that old hunks in that particular instance? Who aint a slave? Tell me that. Well, then, however the old sea-captains may order me about—however they may thump and punch me about, I have the satisfaction of knowing that it is all right; that everybody else is one way or other served in much the same way—either in a physical or metaphysical point of view, that is; and so the universal thump is passed round, and all hands should rub each other's shoulder-blades, and be content.

Again, I always go to sea as a sailor, because they make a point of paying me for my trouble, whereas they never pay passengers a single penny that I ever heard of. On the contrary, passengers themselves must pay. And there is all the difference in the world between paying and being paid. The act of paying is perhaps the most uncomfortable infliction that the two orchard thieves[17] entailed upon us. But *being paid,*—what will compare with it? The urbane activity with which a man receives money is really marvellous, considering that we so earnestly believe money to be the root of all earthly ills, and that on no account can a monied man enter heaven. Ah! how cheerfully we consign ourselves to perdition![18]

There is all the difference in the world between paying and being paid.

Finally, I always go to sea as a sailor, because of the wholesome exercise and pure air of the forecastle deck. For as in this world, head winds are far more prevalent than winds from astern (that is, if you never violate the Pythagorean maxim),[19] so for the most part the Commodore on the quarterdeck gets his atmosphere at second hand from the sailors on the forecastle. He thinks he breathes it first; but not so. In much the same way do the commonalty lead their leaders in many other things, at the same time that the leaders little suspect it. But wherefore it was that after having repeatedly smelt the sea as a merchant sailor, I should now take it into my head to go on a whaling voyage; this the invisible police officer of the Fates, who has the constant surveillance of me, and secretly dogs me, and influences me in some unaccountable way—he can better answer than any one else. And, doubtless, my going on this whaling voyage, formed part of the grand programme of Providence that was drawn up a long time ago. It came in as a sort of brief interlude and solo between more extensive performances. I take it that this part of the bill must have run something like this:

"Grand Contested Election for the Presidency of the United States.
"WHALING VOYAGE BY ONE ISHMAEL.
"BLOODY BATTLE IN AFGHANISTAN."

16. **Seneca and the Stoics.** Seneca (c. 4 BCE–65 CE) was a Roman philosopher; the Stoics shunned the experience of personal feelings.
17. **two orchard thieves.** Probably a reference to Adam and Eve
18. **perdition.** Destruction; damnation
19. **Pythagorean maxim.** Theory that ships go faster when the wind comes from a particular direction

Though I cannot tell why it was exactly that those stage managers, the Fates, put me down for this shabby part of a whaling voyage, when others were set down for magnificent parts in high tragedies, and short and easy parts in genteel comedies, and jolly parts in farces—though I cannot tell why this was exactly; yet, now that I recall all the circumstances, I think I can see a little into the springs and motives which being cunningly presented to me under various disguises, induced me to set about performing the part I did, besides cajoling me into the delusion that it was a choice resulting from my own unbiased freewill and discriminating judgment.

Chief among these motives was the overwhelming idea of the great whale himself. Such a portentous and mysterious monster roused all my curiosity. Then the wild and distant seas where he rolled his island bulk; the undeliverable, nameless perils of the whale; these, with all the attending marvels of a thousand Patagonian[20] sights and sounds, helped to sway me to my wish. With other men, perhaps, such things would not have been inducements; but as for me, I am tormented with an everlasting itch for things remote. I love to sail forbidden seas, and land on barbarous coasts. Not ignoring what is good, I am quick to perceive a horror, and could still be social with it—would they let me—since it is but well to be on friendly terms with all the inmates of the place one lodges in.

By reason of these things, then, the whaling voyage was welcome; the great flood-gates of the wonder-world swung open, and in the wild conceits that swayed me to my purpose, two and two there floated into my inmost soul, endless processions of the whale, and, mid most of them all, one grand hooded phantom, like a snow hill in the air. ❖

---

20. **Patagonian.** Region in South America that includes parts of Argentina and Chile

Tales of adventure, both real and imagined, have always been popular among readers. Why do such stories appeal to people?

Refer and Reason

1. How does Ishmael describe himself when he goes to sea? Does this description seem believable? Why or why not?

2. According to Ishmael, who is responsible for his going on the whaling voyage? Explain what this notion indicates about *Moby-Dick* as a whole.

3. Identify the chief motive for joining the voyage, as stated by Ishmael. Evaluate why he says he can be on friendly terms with "inmates of the place [he] lodges in"—even "a horror."

Writing Options

1. You would like to sail across the ocean on a freighter as part of the crew. Write a letter of application to the captain, telling about yourself and explaining why you want to join the crew.

2. You are a modern-day member of the Aleut people, living near the North Pole, who are allowed to kill whales for food and supplies. Write a one-paragraph position statement, explaining how you feel about hunting these creatures.

 Go to **www.mirrorsandwindows.com** for more.

Understand the Concept

An **eponym** is a word derived from the name of a real or fictitious person. For instance, in the selection from *Moby-Dick,* Ishmael mentions the *Pythagorean* maxim. Pythagoras (c. 580–c. 500 BCE) was a Greek mathematician. According to his theorem, which relates to the measurement of right triangles, ships will go faster if they catch the wind from a certain direction.

One of the first uses of eponyms has been traced to the second century BCE, when the Assyrians named the years after high-ranking officials. The use of leaders' names to designate eras has continued to be one of the most common uses of eponyms. Both *Elizabethan England* and the *Victorian Era* refer to the reigns of noted British queens. Concepts and schools of thought also are often labeled with eponyms, as in *Jeffersonian democracy* and *Reaganomics.* Literary styles and themes, as well, frequently are identified with authors' names, such as *Dickensian* (Charles Dickens), *Faulknerian* (William Faulkner), and *Orwellian* (George Orwell).

There also are many less obvious eponyms in use in the English language:

- *Dahlia* from Swedish botanist Anders Dahl (1751–1789)
- *Sousaphone* from American bandmaster and composer John Philip Sousa (1854–1932)
- *America* from Italian explorer Amerigo Vespucci (1454–1512)
- *Doberman pinscher* from German dog breeder Ludwig Dobermann (nineteenth century)
- *Teddy bear* from President Theodore Roosevelt (1851–1919)

Many product names are eponyms that reflect names of inventors or heads of companies. For instance, *Dell, Hewlett-Packard, Bose, Dolby, Toyota,* and *Ford* are all eponyms. Some specific product names have, over time, become eponyms with generic meanings. The word *Kleenex,* for instance, is the name of a particular brand of facial tissue, but it is used as an eponym to mean any kind of facial tissue, as in "Please get me a Kleenex."

The use of eponyms reflects the changing nature of language, as words are added and dropped to accommodate developments in history, technology, literature, and culture. Given this, eponyms remain in the language only if they are useful.

Apply the Skill

Exercise A

Use the dictionary and other resources to determine what each of the following eponyms means and on whose name it is based.

1. Confucianism
2. Julian calendar
3. Cyrillic alphabet
4. Quixotic
5. Occam's razor
6. Hobson's choice
7. Mickey Mouse (*adj.*)
8. napoleon
9. melba toast
10. odyssey

Exercise B

Research the following people to determine what eponyms are based on their names. Write several sentences about each person and how the eponym was derived from his or her name.

1. General Ambrose Burnside
2. King Charles I of England
3. Edward A. Murphy Jr.
4. Axel Paulsen
5. Harold "Matt" Matson and Elliot Handler
6. Adi Dassler
7. Caesar Cardini
8. Ernesto Miranda

SPELLING PRACTICE

Words with *C* Sounds

The letter *c* can make different sounds, depending on what comes after it. Generally, when the letter *c* occurs before an *e* or *i*, it sounds like the letter *s*, as in the word *celery.* Yet at times, a *c* can sound like *sh*, as in *magician*, or *k*, as in *corn*. The digraph (two letters that make one sound) *ch* usually is pronounced as in *church*, but it also can be pronounced like *k*, as in *mechanic*. Sort these words from "Loomings" into groups representing the various *c* sounds.

archangel	conceits	methodically
because	conscious	oceans
cajoling	curiosity	perceive
chief	exercise	precisely
choice	inducements	schooners
circumstances	judiciously	social
commerce	magnificent	surveillance

Great Short Works of Herman Melville by Herman Melville

After finishing Moby-Dick, Herman Melville feared his writing career had peaked, but the quality of these later works demonstrates he was wrong. In them, Melville creates unforgettable characters (the noble Billy Budd) and situations (the shadowy, decaying slave ship in "Benito Cereno"), while questioning accepted moral standards.

The Scarlet Letter by Nathaniel Hawthorne

Hester Prynne is forced to wear the letter *A* (for *adulterer*) sewn on her dress. Her predicament worsens when her husband, who was thought dead, reappears and vows to hunt out her secret lover. Nathaniel Hawthorne's classic tale reveals enduring truths about the passions of the human heart and how an out cast ultimately can find peace. (EMC Access Edition)

American Women Poets of the Nineteenth Century: An Anthology (American Women Writers Series) edited by Cheryl Walker

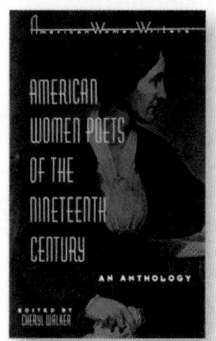

This anthology displays the diversity of women's creativity in an age known mostly for men writers, showcasing humorous parodies, rousing abolitionist poems, and reflections on issues such as the treatment of Native Americans and equal access to education. Although these women lived in an age that tried to confine them to the domestic sphere, they wrote their way into the larger world.

Undaunted Courage: Meriwether Lewis, Thomas Jefferson, and the Opening of the American West by Stephen E. Ambrose

Esteemed historian Stephen Ambrose retraces Lewis and Clark's famous voyage (1804–1806) into the uncharted American West. As the two men search for a waterway to the Pacific with Native American guides, they encounter both adventure and heartbreak. Ambrose treats his subjects as though they are close friends, making his prose lively and exciting.

The Last of the Mohicans by James Fenimore Cooper

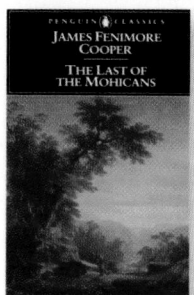

James Fenimore Cooper wrote the first American historical novel in 1826 about Native Americans during the French and Indian War. The book's popularity worldwide earned Cooper an international reputation. By today's standards, his depictions of Native Americans and women are unflattering, but the work remains a significant literary milestone worthy of critical study.

The Essential Writings of Ralph Waldo Emerson by Ralph Waldo Emerson

This anthology gathers Emerson's greatest writings into a single volume, including the complete versions of all his essays. In addition, the collection provides a comprehensive look at the Transcendentalist ethos and offers the famous thinker's ruminations on famous historical figures, politics, and contemporaries such as Henry David Thoreau and Abraham Lincoln.

What kind of speaker would you prefer to listen to: one who fumbles with pages of text while reading in a disinterested, droning voice or one who glances at a few note cards while speaking in a natural, conversational tone? What kind of speaker would you prefer to be? One of the keys to delivering an effective presentation is to prepare and use good notes.

1. Prepare Notes, Not the Full Text

Imagine that you are preparing a brief speech on a topic of interest to you and your audience—for instance, whether the school needs a new athletic field. First, research the subject by looking for information in the library or on the Internet, taking an opinion poll, and using other means. After you have gathered the information, organize the facts and ideas you plan to include in your presentation. Then, on index cards or sheets of paper, write down, in brief form, the information you will present. Consider these guidelines:

● Organize the information in condensed form as notes. Whatever the purpose or length of your presentation, your notes will serve as *prompts*, or *cues*, as you speak.

● Avoid writing out your speech, either on cards or sheets of paper. Writing out your speech will almost guarantee that you will *read* it, rather than deliver it in a natural, conversational style. Your audience will pay more attention if you speak naturally than if you read the text word by word. Also, when you read page after page of text, it's easy to stumble over a passage or lose your place altogether.

2. Make Sure Your Notes Are Useful

Preparing good notes, on cards or on paper, will help you deliver a good presentation. Your notes should be brief, so you do not have to read a lot of text, but the wording should be useful:

● Write down the main ideas you want to emphasize, along with briefly worded supporting details (for instance, *Athletic field is affected by weather; puddles, ice form*). Also jot down certain signal words and phrases, such as *for instance* or *in*

contrast, to ensure you explain how the details are related to the main ideas.

● Avoid having too much information on one card. Putting sections of your presentation on individual cards will make it easier to keep your place and control the pace of your delivery.

● For material that should be presented word for word, such as quotations and statistical data, write out the information in full.

● Consider how many notes you will need. If you prepare too few, you may forget important points. If you prepare too many, you might run over the time allotted for your presentation.

3. Practice Delivery with Your Notes

As you prepare, allow enough time to practice your delivery using the notes you have made. Ask a friend or family member to be your practice audience. Practicing should help you become more at ease in handling the cards or sheets of paper. Avoid shuffling a lot of papers or cards while you speak; doing so will distract your audience.

Be sure to time your presentation while you practice. If you realize you have too few or too many notes, make the needed adjustments.

SPEAKING & LISTENING RUBRIC

Your presentation and use of notes will be evaluated on these elements:

Content

❏ Your notes are well organized, clearly written, and easy to follow.

❏ Your notes emphasize main ideas and provide brief supporting details.

Delivery & Presentation

❏ You make good use of your notes during your delivery.

❏ Your use of notes is not distracting to your audience.

A well-written setting jumps off the page, taking on just as much life as any character. Try to imagine *Lord of the Rings* without the lushness of Middle-earth or Edgar Allan Poe's "The Fall of the House of Usher" without the looming, dilapidated house.

To describe a setting, a writer needs to engage all of the reader's senses. By doing this and by using specific language, the writer makes it easy for the reader to imagine this place.

Assignment Plan, write, and revise a description of a setting

Purpose To bring a scene to life for readers

Audience Someone who is unfamiliar with your setting and wants to learn more

❶ Prewrite

Select Your Topic
Any place, real or imaginary, can work as a setting for your description. Come up with a list of actual or invented places. Choose whatever place speaks to you most. Remember that a setting is made effective in the description, not in how unique the place is.

Gather Information
The best way to gather information on a place is to go there. If your location is local, visit it and observe your surroundings. Write down as many details as you can, remembering to include all five senses. If your location is far away, do research to find information. If your location is imaginary, make up the details, but keep in mind that they must fit together logically for readers.

WRITING RUBRIC

A successful description of a setting has these elements:
- ❏ an introduction that quickly puts the reader in the scene
- ❏ a body that includes specific details of sight, sound, smell, feel, and, if appropriate, taste
- ❏ a conclusion that gives the reader a sense of closure

Organize Your Ideas
Review your notes. Have you included as many sensory details as you can? Will someone who has never been to your location be able to imagine it fully?

Consider how to organize the information. Will you use a *spatial orientation,* moving your readers around the location? Will you use *general to specific* or *specific to general?* Number the details in the order they should appear in your description. Try not to describe the senses in different paragraphs, however. You experience senses all at once, not individually.

Write Your Organizing Statement
Your *organizing statement* will not appear in your description but will instead be used a device to help you maintain focus. What overall feeling do you want your setting to portray?

What Great Writers Do

A setting's success lies in the details. Neil Gaiman, creator of the *Sandman* comic series, notes, "You can take for granted that people know what a street, a shop, a beach, a sky, an oak tree look like. Tell them what makes this one different."

GAIMAN

❷ Draft

Write your essay by following this three-part framework: introduction, body, and conclusion.

Introduction Capture your readers' attention right away by dropping them into the scene.

Body Build interest by laying out compelling, specific details.

Conclusion Provide closure, perhaps by literally exiting the scene.

Draft Your Introduction
The introduction of a descriptive setting hooks readers. Consider beginning with a detail that will appeal to readers because it's unique or familiar.

Draft Your Body

In the body, continue to intrigue your reader by building your description, engaging senses and curiosity. This is information you already mapped out in the Prewrite stage.

Review your notes and the order in which you planned to present them. Develop each paragraph by presenting details together to engage the reader. Each detail you use should clearly relate to the feeling you are trying to create.

Draft Your Conclusion

Finally, write the conclusion for your descriptive setting. A good conclusion brings the description to a close, leaving the reader with the feeling you have been crafting through your paragraphs.

❸ Revise

Evaluate Your Draft

You can evaluate your own writing or exchange descriptions with a classmate and evaluate each other's work. Either way, think about whether you can easily picture the setting that's described.

Start by looking at the content and organization. Make sure the introduction, body, and conclusion work together to create the feeling you outlined in your organizing statement. Every paragraph should relate clearly to it, and each paragraph should flow into the next. Use the Revision Checklist that follows to help you evaluate.

Next, check the language for errors. Go back through your draft to make sure you have correctly applied the guidelines in the Grammar & Style workshops in this unit. Again, use the Revision Checklist to evaluate the writing.

The vividness of a description relies on well-worded modifiers. Make sure you have used appropriate adjectives that allow readers to imagine your setting and that convey your intended mood.

Revise for Content, Organization, and Style

Review the notes you or your partner made as you evaluated your draft. Then apply each comment in effectively revising your draft.

Proofread for Errors

In this stage, check for remaining errors. Use proofreader's symbols to mark any you find. To complete the assignment, print out a final draft and read it aloud before turning it in.

Writing Follow-Up

Publish and Present

- Have classmates share the settings they wrote. What are the similarities and differences between the descriptions?
- A descriptive setting is a beginning step to writing a short story. Try writing a story based on your setting or on one of your classmates' settings.

Reflect

Writing about something often gives you a fuller appreciation for the subject. Do you feel more of a connection to your setting having written about it? Explain your answer

---

REVISION CHECKLIST

Content & Organization

- ❏ Does the introduction start with a sentence that captures readers' interest?
- ❏ Does each paragraph in the body work to create the feeling you stated in your organizing statement?
- ❏ Does each body paragraph provide specific details that engage readers' senses, creating a full sense of the place?
- ❏ Does the conclusion leave readers with the feeling you aimed to create?

Grammar & Style

- ❏ Do you vary sentence structure? (page 164)
- ❏ Are all of your sentences complete? (page 194)
- ❏ Do you avoid writing run-on sentences? (page 240)

Reading Skills

Identify Mood and Tone

Mood is the atmosphere or emotion conveyed by a literary work. A writer creates mood by using concrete details to describe the setting, characters, and events. The writer can evoke in the reader a specific emotional response—such as fear, discomfort, longing, or anticipation—by working carefully with descriptive language and sensory details. The mood of a work might be dark, mysterious, gloomy, cheerful, inspiring, or peaceful.

Tone is the writer's attitude toward the subject or the reader of the work. When listening to someone talk, it usually is easy to recognize the speaker's tone from his or her voice. You can hear such emotions and attitudes as joy, sarcasm, and uncertainty in a speaker's voice. When reading, however, the only clues you have about the tone of the piece come from what is on the page. The writer establishes the tone by carefully choosing words and phrases.

To recognize the tone, ask yourself these questions: Who is the speaker? What is the situation or subject? Is it being described objectively, or does the writer make a judgment about it? Examples of different tones a work may have include familiar, ironic, playful, lighthearted, sarcastic, serious, academic, emphatic, proud, angry, melancholy, matter of fact, respectful, and sincere.

TEST-TAKING TIP

In answering a multiple-choice question, read the prompt and each possible response carefully. Pay special attention to any words that are bolded, italicized, written in all capital letters, or otherwise emphasized. Type treatments such as these often are used to focus readers on important terms and topics. Make sure you do not miss the word *not*.

Practice

Directions: Read the following story. The questions that come after it will ask you to identify the mood and tone.

FICTION: This passage is an excerpt from Edgar Allan Poe's short story "The Pit and the Pendulum."

1   I was sick—sick unto death with that long agony; and when they at length unbound me, and I was permitted to sit, I felt that my senses were leaving me. The
5 sentence—the dread sentence of death— was the last of distinct accentuation which reached my ears. After that, the sound of the inquisitorial voices seemed merged in one dreamy indeterminate hum. It conveyed
10 to my soul the idea of revolution—perhaps from its association in fancy with the burr of a mill wheel. This only for a brief period;

for presently I heard no more. Yet, for a while, I saw; but with how terrible an exag-
15 geration! I saw the lips of the black-robed judges. They appeared to me white—whiter than the sheet upon which I trace these words—and thin even to grotesqueness; thin with the intensity of their expression
20 of firmness—of immovable resolution—of stern contempt of human torture. I saw that the decrees of what to me was Fate were still issuing from those lips. I saw them writhe with a deadly locution. I saw them fashion
25 the syllables of my name; and I shuddered because no sound succeeded. I saw, too, for a few moments of delirious horror, the soft and nearly imperceptible waving of the sable draperies which enwrapped the walls
30 of the apartment. And then my vision fell upon the seven tall candles upon the table. At first they wore the aspect of charity, and seemed white slender angels who would

save me; but then, all at once, there came
35 a most deadly nausea over my spirit, and
I felt every fiber in my frame thrill as if I
had touched the wire of a galvanic battery,
while the angel forms became meaningless
specters, with heads of flame, and I saw that
40 from them there would be no help. And
then there stole into my fancy, like a rich
musical note, the thought of what sweet
rest there must be in the grave. The thought
came gently and stealthily, and it seemed

45 long before it attained full appreciation; but
just as my spirit came at length properly
to feel and entertain it, the figures of the
judges vanished, as if magically, from before
me; the tall candles sank into nothingness;
50 their flames went out utterly; the blackness of darkness supervened; all sensations
appeared swallowed up in a mad rushing
descent as of the soul into Hades. Then
silence, and stillness, and night were the
55 universe.

Multiple Choice

1. Which of the following phrases contributes
   the *least* to the prevailing mood near the
   beginning?
   A. "sick unto death with that long agony"
      (lines 1–2)
   B. "I felt that my senses were leaving me"
      (line 4)
   C. "merged in one dreamy indeterminate
      hum" (lines 8–9)
   D. "with how terrible an exaggeration"
      (lines 14–15)
   E. "I saw them fashion the syllables of my
      name" (lines 24–25)

2. What is the main mood of this excerpt?
   A. dark and dreamlike
   B. inspiring
   C. sad and lonely
   D. peaceful
   E. inquisitorial and grotesque

3. The tone of the author could best be
   described as
   A. angry.
   B. lighthearted.
   C. ironic.
   D. emphatic and apprehensive.
   E. academic and matter of fact.

4. What technique does Poe use here that
   contributes to creating *both* the mood
   and the tone?
   A. dramatic irony
   B. onomatopoeia
   C. repetition
   D. foreshadowing
   E. characterization

Constructed Response

5. Discuss how Poe's abundant use of sensory
   details contributes to the mood of the passage. What do the details have in common?

Writing Skills

Analyze the Prompt

Before you begin writing, be sure to analyze the prompt carefully. Exactly *what* is it asking? If you do not interpret the prompt correctly, you will not write on the correct topic and will not receive credit for your essay.

Evaluate the prompt for the clues it provides about what is expected of you. Some questions contain key words that identify exactly what is being asked. For example, are you being asked to *analyze* or *identify, describe* or *discuss, evaluate* or *argue for or against something,* or *justify* or *explain?* Underline any key words in the prompt.

It also may be helpful to make notes in the margin as you analyze the prompt. Perhaps reading the prompt will bring to mind a specific character in a story or other support details you can use in your essay. Jotting them down may help you formulate a plan for writing.

Finally, be sure to read *all* of the prompt. Some prompts have several parts and ask you to do several things. Evaluate the prompt carefully at the start of the timed writing session. Then reread the prompt again before you start writing to verify you have completely understood it. After drafting your essay, go back and reread the prompt once more. Make sure you have addressed everything it asks.

> ### TEST-TAKING TIP
>
> When writing an essay, do not be distracted by the thought that everything you put in writing needs to be perfect. Doing so can lead to *writer's block,* or the inability to put one's ideas on paper. If you find yourself immobilized when confronted by a blank page, do some forced writing. Make yourself write steadily for five minutes, not paying attention to the quality of what you produce for the time being. Once your ideas are flowing, then go back and respond to the prompt. Remember that you can always go back and revise what you have written.

Practice

Timed Writing: 25 minutes

Think carefully about the issue presented in the following excerpt and assignment below.

In today's world, various kinds of acts can be considered either inhumane or kind in the long term. An animal with a painful terminal illness or severe injury that has no hope of recovery might be given a lethal amount of a drug. Some people view euthanasia (or mercy killing) as wrong. Others consider it merciful and compassionate.

Assignment: What is your position on euthanasia of animals? Plan and write an essay in which you develop your point of view in response to this question. Support your viewpoint with reasoning and examples taken from your reading, studies, experience, or observations.

Revising and Editing Skills

As part of the Writing section, some standardized tests ask you to identify sentence errors. These errors deal with grammar, usage, word choice, idiom, and mechanics. Being able to identify and correct mistakes in what you have written is essential to writing well. Examples of common errors you should watch for include the following:

- incorrect spellings and capitalization
- dangling participles

- disagreement between subject and verb
- inconsistent verb tense
- incorrect forms of irregular verbs
- incorrect use of frequently confused words, such as *between* and *among*
- double negatives
- adjective/adverb confusion
- incorrect or missing punctuation

Practice

Directions: Each of the following sentences contains either a single error or no error. The error, if there is one, appears in one of the lettered and underlined series of words. Write down the letter that identifies the error in each sentence. If there is no error, write down "E" for "No error." Do not write down more than one letter, because no sentence contains more than one error.

Multiple Choice

1. One of the (A) reasons I favor euthanasia for animals (B) was based on a personal experience (C) with a dog I had (D) when I was little. (E) No error

2. (A) Scout, a (B) 12-year-old spaniel, was obviously in (C) pain but I selfishly (D) wanted him to remain in my life. (E) No error

3. (A) Although he wasn't able to play (B) with me or go on (C) walks, he was still around (D) for me to love. (E) No error

4. Then (A) my dad (B) had explained that it is (C) more kind and humane to stop (D) Scout's suffering. (E) No error

Rainy Day in Camp, 1871. Winslow Homer.
Metropolitan Museum of Art, New York.

Slavery and the Civil

Unit 3

War 1850–1865

Slavery and the Civil War 1850–1865

1850

1855

AMERICAN LITERATURE AMERICAN LITERATURE AMERICAN LITERATURE AME

1850
Nathaniel Hawthorne publishes *The Scarlet Letter*

1851
Sojourner Truth delivers her speech "Ain't I a Woman?"

1851
Herman Melville publishes *Moby-Dick*

1852
Harriet Beecher Stowe's *Uncle Tom's Cabin* becomes a best seller

1853
William Wells Brown publishes *Clotel,* becoming the first African-American novelist to be published

1853
Stephen C. Foster writes the song "My Old Kentucky Home"

1855
Walt Whitman publishes the first edition of *Leaves of Grass*

1855
Frederick Douglass publishes his second autobiography, *My Bondage and My Freedom*

1856
L. Frank Baum, author of *The Wizard of Oz,* is born on May 15

1859
The first novel by an African-American woman, *Our Nig* by Harriet E. Wilson, is published

AMERICAN HISTORY AMERICAN HISTORY AMERICAN HISTORY AMERICAN HIST

1850
Congress passes the Fugitive Slave Act

1850
Los Angeles is incorporated as a city

1853
The U.S. government buys Mexican land, which later becomes known as the Gadsden Purchase

1853
More than seven thousand people die in New Orleans from a yellow fever epidemic

1854
The Kansas-Nebraska Act is passed, escalating hostilities between abolitionists and proslavery Americans

1855
The first hospital for women is established in New York

1856
Open violence breaks out between abolitionists and proslavery Americans in the Kansas-Nebraska territory, dubbed "Bleeding Kansas" by the press

1857
The Supreme Court upholds slaveholders' rights in the Dred Scott case

1858
Abraham Lincoln loses the Illinois Senate race to Stephen A. Douglas, but debates held during the race make Lincoln famous

1859
John Brown raids Harpers Ferry, West Virginia; the raid fails and Brown is sentenced to death

BROWN

WORLD HISTORY WORLD HISTORY WORLD HISTORY WORLD HISTORY WORLD

1850
In China, the first clashes of the Taiping Rebellion occur between Imperialist militia and the Heavenly Army

1852
Napoleon III proclaims a new constitution for the French Second Republic and becomes Emperor of France

1852
Scottish missionary Dr. David Livingstone explores interior Africa

1853
Admiral Matthew Perry arrives in Japan

1854
The Crimean War begins, involving Russia against an alliance of France, the United Kingdom, and the Ottoman Empire

1856
France and England declare war on China in the Second Opium War

1858
The first trans-Atlantic cable is completed

1858
Charles Darwin introduces the theory of evolution to the London Linnaean Society

1858
Chinese ports are opened to British and French trade

1859
Work begins on the Suez Canal, linking the Mediterranean and the Red Sea

DARWIN

AURE AMERICAN LITERATURE AMERICAN LITERATURE AMERICAN LITERATURE AMERICAN

1860
Henry Wadsworth Longfellow writes "Paul Revere's Ride"

1861
Harriet Jacobs publishes *Incidents in the Life of a Slave Girl*

1862
Emily Dickinson writes several of her best-loved poems, including "This is my letter to the World"

1862
Julia Ward Howe writes "The Battle Hymn of the Republic"

1862
Ambrose Bierce joins the staff of Union General William Babcock Hazen

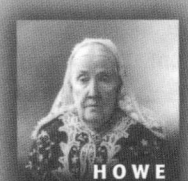
HOWE

1863
Henry Wadsworth Longfellow publishes *Tales of a Wayside Inn*

1863
John Greenleaf Whittier publishes *In War Time*

1863
Louisa May Alcott publishes *Hospital Sketches,* an account of her work as a nurse in a Union hospital

1864
Walt Whitman publishes *Drum-Taps,* a collection of Civil War poetry

1864
Nathaniel Hawthorne dies on May 19

1865
P. T. Barnum exposes psychics and other paranormal mediums as frauds in his book *The Humbugs of the World*

P. T. BARNUM'S
Greatest Show on Ea

CAN HISTORY AMERICAN HISTORY AMERICAN HISTORY AMERICAN HISTORY AMERICAN H

1860
Abraham Lincoln is elected president

1860
South Carolina secedes from the Union, followed later by ten other Southern states

1860
Elizabeth Cady Stanton argues for women's suffrage

1861
Seceded states form the Confederate States of America

1861
Confederate troops attack Fort Sumter, starting the Civil War

1862
Lincoln issues the Emancipation Proclamation

1863
The Battle of Gettysburg, the bloodiest of the Civil War, is fought July 1–3

1864
President Lincoln is re-elected

1865
The Civil War ends with the surrender of General Robert E. Lee at Appomattox, Virginia

1865
Congress ratifies the Thirteenth Amendment, which prohibits slavery

1865
President Lincoln is assassinated by John Wilkes Booth

BOOTH

ORLD HISTORY WORLD HISTORY WORLD HISTORY WORLD HISTORY WORLD HISTORY WO

1860
The Second Opium War ends in China

1860
The New Maori Revolt begins in New Zealand

1861
Umar Tall topples Mali's Bambara Empire in western Africa

1861
Italy unites as a country under Victor Emmanuel, its first king

1862
English and French troops arrive in Mexico, beginning the French intervention in Mexico

1862
Otto Von Bismarck becomes Prime Minister of Prussia

1863
The International Red Cross forms in Geneva, Switzerland

1864
In China, the Qing Empire defeats the Taiping Heavenly Army, ending the Taiping Rebellion

1865
The Salvation Army starts in Whitechapel, London

1865
Paul Bogle leads hundreds of Jamaicans in the Morant Bay Rebellion

1865
The first antiseptic surgery is performed

"A house divided against itself can not stand."

—ABRAHAM LINCOLN

North Versus South

In the early years of the nineteenth century, the North and South developed in two different directions. People in the North more frequently lived in cities and towns than those in the South, working in factories and mills or on small farms. Thus, the North became a center for industrial manufacturing and the export of finished goods. To protect its export business, the North favored high *tariffs,* or fees, on goods from other countries and saw the federal government as the preeminent authority. The South, in contrast, was almost entirely agricultural, producing rice, tobacco, cotton, and sugar and exporting many of these goods to Great Britain. Since it had little industry, the South needed to obtain finished products from elsewhere, and so it opposed high tariffs. Southerners most often worked the land and considered individual states as having their own authority.

With the invention of the cotton gin in 1793, it became economically feasible to grow the crop for export. As lands in Georgia, Alabama, and Mississippi came under cotton cultivation, more and more slaves were needed to work the plantations. Although slave importation had become illegal as early as 1808, smuggling thrived amid lax enforcement along the unprotected eastern coastline. As the number of slaves grew, so did the number of rebellions. The largest was in New Orleans in 1811, when more than 400 slaves revolted, and the most well known was that of Nat Turner in 1831.

The Issue of Slavery

Even as the United States was being created, differences arose between Northerners and Southerners over the issue of slavery. Thomas Jefferson had included a strong antislavery statement in his draft of the Declaration of Independence, but it was deleted because of Southern opposition. Proponents argued that slave owners treated their "valuable property" well, but the reality was unquestionably brutal. Slaves typically worked from sunup to sundown. They lived in squalid shacks and were fed meager portions. In addition, they were forbidden to learn to read and write, sold away from their families, and often whipped for minor offenses.

In the North, the abolitionist movement pushed for ending slavery by law. The abolitionists found a voice in the newspapers of the day, including William Lloyd Garrison's *The Liberator* and black-owned papers such as John Russwurm's and Samuel Cornish's *Freedom Journal* and Frederick Douglass's *The North Star.* Harriet Beecher Stowe's 1852 novel *Uncle Tom's Cabin* also influenced public opinion against slavery. Abolitionists organized the Underground Railroad, a system of safe houses and guides for slaves escaping to free states in the North. Its most famous "conductor" was Harriet Tubman, a runaway slave herself.

NOTABLE NUMBERS

2/3 Amount of the world's cotton produced by the South in 1850

250,000 Slaves imported illegally before the Civil War

200,000 Free blacks living in the North in 1850

300 Fugitive slaves led to freedom in the North by Harriet Tubman

9,000% Rise in the cost of consumer goods in the South during the course of the war

623,000 Troops who died during the Civil War, many more from disease than from battle wounds

$15 billion Estimated cost of the Civil War

A series of events intensified hostilities between North and South. The Fugitive Slave Act of 1850 was a concession to the South in exchange for its agreement to allow the Mexican war territories to enter the Union as nonslave states. It authorized the prosecution of anyone who assisted escaping slaves. The act made it easy for slave owners to recapture slaves who had fled to the North and to pick up any black whom they claimed was a runaway. It infuriated prominent Northerners who were active in the Underground Railroad.

The Kansas-Nebraska Act of 1854 allowed these new states to decide the issue of slavery for themselves. Both pro- and antislavery forces rushed to the two states to vote on the issue, which led to bloody fighting between armed bands in Kansas, known as

> *"What to the American slave is your Fourth of July? I answer, a day that reveals to him more than all other days of the year, the gross injustice and cruelty to which he is the constant victim."*
>
> —FREDERICK DOUGLASS

The Underground Railroad, 1893. Charles T. Webber. Cincinnati Art Museum, Cincinnati, Ohio.

"Bleeding Kansas." In the 1857 Dred Scott decision, the U.S. Supreme Court ruled that a slave who had fled to free territory could not sue for his freedom because he was property, not a person; this further fanned the flames of war. Abolitionist John Brown's raid on the arsenal at Harpers Ferry to capture weapons for slaves and his subsequent hanging gave the North a martyr.

Secession and the Outbreak of Civil War

When Abraham Lincoln became president in 1861, seven states had already voted to secede from the Union. At this point, the clash was not over slavery but economic interests. The Northern capitalists wanted free land, free labor, free markets, a high protective tariff for their manufactures, and a United States Bank—all of which the Southern slave interests opposed.

Early in 1861, delegates from throughout the South met in Montgomery, Alabama, to form the Confederate States of America, choosing Jefferson Davis as their president. When Lincoln attempted to retake federal Fort Sumter in the Charleston, South Carolina, harbor, four more Southern states seceded, beginning the most troubled period in American history.

At the start of the war, the main goal of the North was to restore the Southern states to the Union. The main goal of the South was to establish an independent nation that would allow preservation of its way of life. Each side had its strengths and weaknesses.

The North had a larger population, an industrial base, railroads, and control of the federal navy; however, having to fight in the unfamiliar South and poor military leadership were huge obstacles. The South had strong support from the white population, and its forces were led by skilled commanders, reflecting the Southern tradition of military service. The South had a smaller population, however, producing half as much food as the North; in addition, it had fewer factories to manufacture weapons and fewer lines of railroad tracks on which to move troops.

The North's military strategy was threefold: to blockade the Southern ports, to control the Mississippi

River, and to capture the Confederate capital of Richmond, Virginia. In contrast, the South planned to hold as much of its territory as possible until the North grew tired of fighting. Southern leaders hoped that Great Britain and France would pressure the North for peace in order to regain their cotton supply.

> *"My paramount object in this struggle is to save the Union, and is not either to save or destroy Slavery."*
>
> —ABRAHAM LINCOLN

People on both sides expected the war to be over in a short time, but it lasted five years. Many of the first major battles were losses for the Union forces, which were plagued by poor leadership. During the first three years of the war, President Abraham Lincoln went through three army commanders—McClellan, Burnside, and Hooker—while the Confederate forces were led by General Robert E. Lee throughout the war. On the seas, the Union blockade of Southern ports managed to reduce trade by two-thirds, and the battle of the two ironclad warships, the *Monitor* and the *Merrimac,* marked the beginning of a new type of naval warfare.

Emancipation and the War's End

Facing mounting criticism from the abolitionists, Lincoln finally issued the Emancipation Proclamation on January 1, 1863. It freed slaves in the Confederate states but not in the slave-holding states that had remained in the Union. The Proclamation galvanized the abolitionists, who pushed Congress to enact legislation ending slavery; their efforts ultimately resulted in passage of the Thirteenth Amendment in 1865. The Proclamation also opened the Union military forces to blacks, and by the war's end, 200,000 were enlisted in its army and navy.

Hoping that a Confederate victory in the North would persuade England and France to assist the South, General Lee marched into Pennsylvania on July 1, 1863, where his forces accidentally met those of General Meade outside the town of Gettysburg. The bloody three-day battle resulted in a Confederate loss. Coupled with General Ulysses S. Grant's victory at Vicksburg, which gave the Union complete control of the Mississippi, Gettysburg proved a turning point in the war.

Although Lincoln's hopes for re-election looked dim in early 1864, two more Union victories, in Mobile Bay and Atlanta, allowed him to win a second term. The war continued one more year, during which General Sherman cut a swath of destruction across

Georgia on his "march to the sea." Lee surrendered to Grant at Appomattox Court House on April 9, 1865, after losing the Confederate capital of Richmond.

The war's end found the South in ruins. Because most of the battles had been fought on Southern territory, farmland had been destroyed and rail lines torn up. Essential goods were scarce due to the Union blockade, and food shortages had caused riots in Atlanta and Richmond. In both the North and South, citizens of every city and town mourned their dead in the bloodiest war in American history, while their leaders struggled to find ways of bringing the war-torn nation back together.

Lincoln actually had begun planning for the Reconstruction period before the war had ended. A moderate politician, his goal was to reunite the nation quickly and without further acrimony; contrary to some in the North, he was not looking for revenge but rather healing. Tragically, Lincoln would not live to see the rebuilding of the nation. He was assassinated on April 14, 1865, just five days after Lee's surrender.

PART 1

A Nation Divided

Historians generally agree that the Civil War Era was the most tragic in U.S. history, in terms of both the crisis of ideals that divided Americans and the loss of life and destruction that ultimately resulted. Thus, it seems ironic that this tragic period produced no literary masterpiece about the war. Much of the recognized literature about the Civil War, such as Stephen Crane's *Red Badge of Courage* (1895), was written years later.

This isn't to say that Americans were not writing about the war. Both national leaders and everyday folks were recording and sharing their experiences in letters, diaries, and journals. A collection of letters by Confederate General Robert E. Lee, for instance, reveals his values about family and country and documents the details of his military campaigns. Countless letters were written by soldiers to loved ones at home, many of which were delivered upon the soldiers' deaths.

During the Civil War, newspapers and weekly magazines were important sources of information as well as entertainment. Poems and stories, often sentimental expressions of patriotism and valor, were printed in these publications, sometimes in serial installments.

Harriet Beecher Stowe's landmark novel about the depravity of slavery, *Uncle Tom's Cabin,* was first published in serial form in 1851 in the abolitionist newspaper *National Era.* It was published as a novel the next year, selling 300,000 copies, and it had been read by an estimated one million people by the time slavery was abolished in 1865. Although Stowe's novel has been criticized for its sentimental and perhaps stereotypical treatment of slaves, its historic impact cannot be overlooked.

The Second Minnesota Regiment at Missionary Ridge, 1906. Douglas Volk. Minnesota State Capitol, St. Paul.

from Narrative of the Life of Frederick Douglass, an American Slave, Written by Himself

An Autobiography by Frederick Douglass

Build Background

Historical Context In the excerpt from *Narrative of the Life of Frederick Douglass, an American Slave,* the author describes the organization and operation of the vast plantation where he was born. This selection is remarkable not only for its revelations about slavery but also for the fact that it was even written.

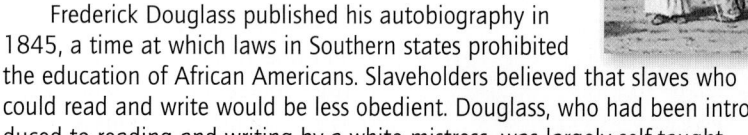

Frederick Douglass published his autobiography in 1845, a time at which laws in Southern states prohibited the education of African Americans. Slaveholders believed that slaves who could read and write would be less obedient. Douglass, who had been introduced to reading and writing by a white mistress, was largely self-taught.

Reader's Context When you are feeling sad or blue, how do you express your feelings? When someone hurts or disappoints you, how do you react?

Meet the Author

Born a slave in Maryland, **Frederick Douglass** (1818–1895) escaped to Massachusetts in 1838, where he associated with prominent abolitionists such as William Lloyd Garrison and became an influential force in the fight to end slavery. Douglass published *Narrative of the Life of Frederick Douglass, an American Slave,* the first of three autobiographies he would write, in 1845.

Knowing that publication of the book would reveal his identity and make him a target for slave catchers, Douglass went to England, where he lectured for the abolitionist cause. After friends helped him to buy his freedom, he moved to Rochester, New York, and began publishing an abolitionist newspaper.

Unjustly implicated in John Brown's attack on the arsenal at Harpers Ferry, West Virginia, which Brown had hoped would instigate a slave revolt, Douglass fled to Canada and England before the Civil War. Following enactment of the Emancipation Proclamation, he returned to the United States and helped to organize regiments of African-American soldiers to fight for the Northern cause. He also personally called on President Abraham Lincoln to secure fair compensation for these soldiers. In addition, Douglass worked as a "conductor" of the Underground Railroad, which helped smuggle slaves from slave states to freedom in the North.

After the war, Douglass held a number of political offices, including U.S. Marshall and Recorder of Deeds for the District of Columbia and Minister to Haiti. He also lobbied for legislation to prevent discrimination of all kinds.

Analyze Literature

Stereotype and Tone
A **stereotype** is an uncritically accepted fixed or conventional idea, particularly such an idea held about a whole group of people.

Tone is the emotional attitude toward the reader or toward the subject implied by a literary work. It may be expressed by word choice, imagery, and other techniques.

Set Purpose

Published sixteen years before the Civil War, Douglass's autobiography revealed to Americans the realities of slavery. Many Northerners, in particular, did not witness slavery firsthand and, as a result, formed false stereotypes about slaves and their conditions. Find the stereotype Douglass mentions in this excerpt, and note how he dispels it. In addition, trace how the tone of the narrative changes from beginning to end. Jot down words and images that express tone.

Preview Vocabulary

diligently, 279
rapturous, 279
incoherent, 280
obdurate, 280

Plantation Economy in the Old South, c. 1876. William Aiken Walker.
Warner Collection, Tuscaloosa, Alabama. (See detail on page 276.)

from Narrative of the Life of Frederick Douglass

an American Slave, Written by Himself

To those songs

I trace my first glimmering conception of the
dehumanizing character of slavery.

Colonel Lloyd[1] kept from three to four hundred slaves on his home plantation, and owned a large number more on the neighboring farms belonging to him. The names of the farms nearest to the home plantation were Wye Town and New Design. Wye Town was under the overseership of a man named Noah Willis. New Design was under the overseership of a Mr. Townsend. The overseers of these, and all the rest of the farms, numbering over twenty, received advice and direction from the managers of the home plantation. This was the great business place. It was the seat of government for

---

1. **Colonel Lloyd.** Owner of the large plantation in Maryland where Douglass was born

Spirituals

Kept from practicing their traditional religions, many African-American slaves adopted Christianity. Slave owners actively encouraged this Christianizing, some because of concern for their slaves' immortal souls but many more out of hope that people who looked for rewards in the next life might tolerate terrible circumstances in this one.

Combining elements of Christian hymns with traditional African and European music work songs, African Americans created a new kind of music known as the *spiritual.* This form of song was a

forerunner of many modern musical styles, including gospel and blues. Many of these songs followed a *call-and-response pattern,* which was typical of West African tribal music.

A lone singer sang a verse, and a group of people joined in on the refrain.

Spirituals often reflected the poetic text of hymns and incorporated Christian themes of salvation and the afterlife. They retold stories from the Bible, especially the story of the deliverance of the Israelites from slavery in Egypt, as in the spiritual "Go Down, Moses." The texts of spirituals were frequently ambiguous, or veiled in meaning. On one level, "Swing Low, Sweet Chariot" expresses slaves' longing to be taken to heaven. On another more hidden level, it expresses their hope of being rescued from slavery on Earth. Some spirituals even contained coded messages that helped runaway slaves find their way to freedom in the North. "Follow the Drinking Gourd," for instance, tells slaves to find the Big Dipper (the gourd) in the nighttime sky and use it as the compass point for north.

Deeply emotional and often melancholy, spirituals provided a way for slaves to share their hard lives and ease their suffering. Often sung by groups, with rhythmical accompaniments like those found in African music, spirituals were part of church services, revival meetings, and secret gatherings.

---

the whole twenty farms.[2] All disputes among the overseers were settled here. . . .

Here, too, the slaves of all the other farms received their monthly allowance of food, and their yearly clothing. The men and women slaves received, as their monthly allowance of food, eight pounds of pork, or its equivalent fish, and one bushel of corn meal. Their yearly clothing consisted of two coarse linen shirts, one jacket, one pair of trousers, for winter, made of coarse negro cloth, one pair of stockings, and one pair of shoes; the whole of which could not have cost more than seven dollars. The allowance of the slave children was given to their mothers, or the old women having the care of them. My mother and I were separated when I was but an infant—before I knew her as my mother. It is a common

custom, in the part of Maryland from which I ran away, to part children from their mothers at a very early age. Frequently, before the child has reached its twelfth month, its mother is taken from it, and hired out on some farm a considerable distance off, and the child is placed under the care of an old woman, too old for field labor. The children unable to work in the field had neither shoes, stockings, jackets, nor trousers, given to them; their clothing consisted of two coarse linen shirts per year. When these failed them, they went naked until the next allowance-day. Children from seven to ten years old, of both sexes, almost naked, might be seen at all seasons of the year.

---

2. **twenty farms.** Lloyd family papers indicate only thirteen farms.

My mother and I were separated
when I was but an infant—before I knew her as my mother.

The home plantation of Colonel Lloyd wore the appearance of a country village. All the mechanical operations for all the farms were performed here. The shoemaking and mending, the blacksmithing, cartwrighting, coopering,[3] weaving, and grain-grinding, were all performed by the slaves on the home plantation. The whole place wore a businesslike aspect very unlike the neighboring farms. The number of houses, too, conspired to give it advantage over the neighboring farms. It was called by the slaves the *Great House Farm.* Few privileges were esteemed higher, by the slaves of the out-farms, than that of being selected to do errands at the Great House Farm. It was associated in their minds with greatness. A representative could not be prouder of his election to a seat in the American Congress, than a slave on one of the out-farms would be of his election to do errands at the Great House Farm. They regarded it as evidence of great confidence reposed in them by their overseers; and it was on this account, as well as a constant desire to be out of the field from under the driver's lash, that they esteemed it a high privilege, one worth careful living for. He was called the smartest and most trusty fellow, who had this honor conferred upon him the most frequently. The competitors for this office sought as <u>diligently</u> to please their overseers, as the office-seekers in the political parties seek to please and deceive the people. The same traits of character might be seen in Colonel Lloyd's slaves, as are seen in the slaves of the political parties.

The slaves selected to go to the Great House Farm, for the monthly allowance for themselves and their fellow slaves, were peculiarly enthusiastic. While on their way, they would make the dense old woods, for miles around, reverberate with their wild songs, revealing at once the highest joy and the deepest sadness. They would compose and sing as they went along, consulting neither time nor tune. The thought that came up, came out—if not in the word, in the sound—and as frequently in the one as in the other. They would sometimes sing the most pathetic sentiment in the most <u>rapturous</u> tone, and the most rapturous sentiment in the most pathetic tone. Into all of their songs they would manage to weave something of the Great House Farm. Especially would they do this when leaving home. They would then sing most exultingly the following words:

> I am going away to the Great House Farm!
> O, yea! O, yea! O!

This they would sing, as a chorus, to words which to many would seem unmeaning jargon, but which, nevertheless, were full of meaning to themselves. I have sometimes thought that the mere hearing of those songs would do more to impress some minds with the horrible character of slavery, than the reading of whole volumes of philosophy on the subject could do.

---

3. **cartwrighting, coopering.** *Cartwrighting*—building carts; *coopering*—making barrels

---

dil • i • gent • ly (dil´ ə jənt lē) *adv.,* painstakingly; industriously
rap • tur • ous (rap´ chʊr əs) *adj.,* full of joy or pleasure

Every tone was a testimony
against slavery, and a prayer to God for deliverance from chains.

I did not, when a slave, understand the deep meaning of those rude and apparently <u>incoherent</u> songs. I was myself within the circle; so that I neither saw nor heard as those without might see and hear. They told a tale of woe which was then altogether beyond my feeble comprehension; they were tones loud, long, and deep; they breathed the prayer and complaint of souls boiling over with the bitterest anguish. Every tone was a testimony against slavery, and a prayer to God for deliverance from chains. The hearing of those wild notes always depressed my spirit, and filled me with ineffable sadness. I have frequently found myself in tears while hearing them. The mere recurrence to those songs, even now, afflicts me; and while I am writing these lines, an expression of feeling has already found its way down my cheek. To those songs I trace my first glimmering conception of the dehumanizing character of slavery. I can never get rid of that conception. Those songs still follow me, to deepen my hatred of slavery, and quicken my sympathies for my brethren in bonds. If any one wishes to be impressed with the soul-killing effects of slavery, let him go to Colonel Lloyd's plantation, and, on allowance-day, place himself in the deep pine woods; and there let him, in silence, analyze the sounds that shall pass through the chambers of his soul, and if he is not thus impressed, it will only be because "there is no flesh in his <u>obdurate</u> heart."

I have often been utterly astonished, since I came to the north, to find persons who could speak of the singing, among slaves, as evidence of their contentment and happiness. It is impossible to conceive of a greater mistake. Slaves sing most when they are most unhappy. The songs of the slave represent the sorrows of his heart; and he is relieved by them, only as an aching heart is relieved by its tears. At least, such is my experience. I have often sung to drown my sorrow, but seldom to express my happiness. Crying for joy, and singing for joy, were alike uncommon to me while in the jaws of slavery. The singing of a man cast away upon a desolate island might be as appropriately considered as evidence of contentment and happiness, as the singing of a slave; the songs of the one and of the other are prompted by the same emotion. ❖

---

in • co • her ent (in' kō hār´ ənt) *adj.,* unclear; not understandable
ob • dur • ate (ôb´ dʉr ət) *adj.,* unsympathetic; hardened

MIRRORS & WINDOWS

Douglass says hearing the songs sung by slaves deepens his hatred of slavery. What song or sound reminds you of a bad experience?

DOUGLASS

HAYDEN

Literature Connection

African-American poet and educator **Robert Hayden** (1913–1980) was raised by a foster family in Detroit, Michigan. Despite experiencing severe hardship as a youth, Hayden achieved great prominence during his literary career. He was elected to the American Academy of Poets in 1975 and served as the Library of Congress's Poet Laureate Consultant from 1975 to 1978.

Hayden wrote the poem **"Frederick Douglass"** in the mid-1940s, but it was not published until 1962, when it appeared in *A Ballad of Remembrance,* one of several collections of his poems. Inspired by African-American history, Hayden also wrote tributes to Nat Turner, Harriet Tubman, Bessie Smith, and Malcolm X. As you read "Frederick Douglass," determine why Hayden pays tribute to this nineteenth-century abolitionist.

Frederick Douglass
by Robert Hayden

When it is finally ours, this freedom, this liberty, this beautiful
and terrible thing, needful to man as air,
usable as earth; when it belongs at last to all,
when it is truly instinct, brain matter, diastole, systole,
5   reflex action; when it is finally won; when it is more
than the gaudy mumbo jumbo of politicians:
this man, this Douglass, this former slave, this Negro
beaten to his knees, exiled, visioning a world
where none is lonely, none hunted, alien,
10   this man, superb in love and logic, this man
shall be remembered. Oh, not with statues' rhetoric,
not with legends and poems and wreaths of bronze alone,
but with the lives grown out of his life, the lives
fleshing his dream of the beautiful, needful thing. ❖

Review Questions

1. To what is *freedom* compared? Explain why freedom is described as "beautiful," "terrible," and "needful."

2. Identify what Douglass envisions in the poem. Argue whether the shared vision of Douglass and Hayden has been realized in the contemporary United States.

3. According to the speaker, when will Douglass be remembered? Relate this poem to the autobiography of Frederick Douglass.

TEXT ^{TO} TEXT CONNECTION

Identify the lines in the poem that refer to the autobiography of Frederick Douglass. Explain what Douglass did to advance the cause of freedom for slaves. How does Hayden say he will be remembered for his efforts? Is that an appropriate tribute? Why or why not?

HISTORY CONNECTION

The Underground Railroad

The Underground Railroad was an expansive network of people, places, and routes that helped African-American slaves escape to freedom during the 1800s. Escaped slaves traveled along established routes primarily by foot and on horseback. They always traveled at night, covering between ten and twenty miles, and they stopped at designated stations to rest and eat during the day. So-called station masters maintained these safe houses and knew of others along the route in their immediate area. One station master would notify the next whenever an escapee was coming through the area. However, to keep the Underground Railroad secure, station masters typically did not have extensive knowledge of the route beyond their own area. In fact, the route from one station to another often was meandering and indirect to confuse potential pursuers.

Escaped slaves were shuttled between stations by individuals known as "conductors." There was no such thing as a typical conductor. Many were sympathetic whites, including some from religious groups such as the Quakers. Other conductors were Native Americans, and some were themselves escaped African-American slaves. Conductors of African descent sometimes infiltrated plantation homes disguised as slaves. Once inside, they encouraged actual slaves to escape and pointed them toward the nearest station.

The Underground Railroad became so successful that legislatures in Southern states began to enact fugitive slave laws, making it illegal to assist escaped slaves. Additionally, slave owners started posting bounties on runaway slaves, which encouraged legions of slave catchers to journey North in pursuit of escapees. Sometimes, slave catchers ensnared freed African Americans and returned them to slavery just to collect a bounty.

$100 REWARD!
RANAWAY
From the undersigned, living on Current River, about twelve miles above Doniphan, in Ripley County, Mo., on 3rd of March, 1860, A NEGRO MAN, about 30 years old, weighs about 160 pounds; high forehead, with a scar on it; had on brown pants and coat very much worn, and an old black wool hat; shoes size No. 11.
The above reward will be given to any person who may apprehend this
APOS TUCKER.

In the end, fugitive slave laws actually strengthened the abolitionist cause, since they encouraged the people operating the Underground Railroad to fortify their defenses and improve their security. Estimates vary, but from 1810 to 1850, up to 100,000 individuals were smuggled out of the slave-holding South to free states in the North, as well as to Canada and even Mexico.

Refer to Text ▶ ▶ ▶ ▶ ▶ Reason with Text

1a. What happened on allowance-day on the plantation where Douglass was born?	**1b.** Discuss how allowance-day also provided a means of controlling slave behavior.	**Understand** Find meaning
2a. Describe the songs that the slaves sang as they made their way through the woods.	**2b.** According to Douglass, why did the slaves sing on their way to the Great House Farm?	**Apply** Use information
3a. Identify the different aspects of the slave children's lives.	**3b.** How did the way in which children were treated benefit the slaveholder?	**Analyze** Take things apart
4a. To what does Douglass compare the slaves chosen to go to the Great House Farm? To what does he compare their singing?	**4b.** Argue whether Douglass is justified in making these comparisons.	**Evaluate** Make judgments
5a. Outline how the music we now call the blues is similar to the singing of the slaves sent for supplies on allowance-day.	**5b.** When have you chosen singing as a way of expressing sad feelings?	**Create** Bring ideas together

Analyze Literature

Stereotype and Tone

What stereotype about slaves does Douglass reject in his description of the slaves' singing? What is Douglass's nonstereotypical interpretation of the slaves' singing? Why might some Northerners have believed in the stereotype of the happy slave?

What tone does Douglass use at the beginning of the narrative to describe the organization and operation of the plantation? How does the tone change when he recalls the songs sung by the slaves? How does the changing tone of the narrative fit the change in topic?

Extend the Text

Writing Options

Creative Writing Write song lyrics about the slaves of Colonel Lloyd's farm, using Douglass's analogy of "a man cast away upon a desolate island" to describe a slave's feelings. Ask classmates to read your lyrics and identify the tone.

Expository Writing Obtain a newspaper listing of TV shows for the current week. Identify several TV series you watch that include teenage characters. Write the name of each teen character, and list the qualities he or she exhibits. Then write a two-page analysis for network executives of how teens are portrayed in these shows.

Collaborative Learning

Research an Abolitionist With a partner, research a person involved in abolitionism, such as Lyman Beecher, John Brown, Lydia Maria Child, William Lloyd Garrison, Angelina Grimké, Julia Ward Howe, or Harriet Beecher Stowe. With your partner, role-play an interview between one of these people and a modern-day interviewer. The interviewer should ask specific questions about the abolitionist's beliefs and involvement in abolitionist activities, based on his or her reading. The interviewee should give detailed answers based on the same research.

Lifelong Learning

Create a Dialogue Write a conversation between Frederick Douglass and Robert Hayden (see page 281), in which they discuss laws that have been passed to advance the legal rights of African Americans. Have Douglass explain the Thirteenth, Fourteenth, and Fifteenth Amendments to the U.S. Constitution. Have Hayden discuss the Civil Rights Act of 1964. Ask two classmates to read your dialogue to the class.

 Go to **www.mirrorsandwindows.com** for more.

1. Which of these statements best describes the lives of slave children?
   A. They stayed with their mothers until they were old enough to work in the fields.
   B. They were raised by elderly women who could no longer work in the fields.
   C. They were allowed to go to school only until they were ten years old.
   D. They were required to go to school until they were ten years old.
   E. They were well fed and well clothed.

2. The Great House Farm was all of the following *except*
   A. a prized assignment for slaves.
   B. the seat of government for the entire network of farms.
   C. the secret meeting place for slaves involved in the Underground Railroad.
   D. the site of all mechanical operations for the network of farms.
   E. the place slaves received their monthly allowance.

3. If you do something *diligently*, how are you doing it?
   A. with a light touch
   B. with joy
   C. with sadness
   D. without much thought
   E. with great care

4. Which of the following best states the main idea of the poem "Frederick Douglass"?
   A. The best way to honor Douglass would be to have all people live in freedom.
   B. A memorial should be built in Douglass's honor.
   C. Douglass didn't care whether he became famous.
   D. Being free is instinctive in humans and the most important condition of life.
   E. Freedom has its own problems and consequences, so it should be extended in small amounts and with restrictions.

5. Which of the following best describes the songs slaves sung on their way to and from Great House Farm?
   A. joyful, praising God
   B. sad and pathetic but also joyful
   C. describing the privilege of working at Great House Farm
   D. empty and meaningless
   E. bitter and angry

6. In the line "there is no flesh in his obdurate heart," what does the word *obdurate* mean?
   A. powerful
   B. hardened
   C. overly sensitive
   D. prone to excitement
   E. long lived

7. In the poem "Frederick Douglass," freedom "belongs at last to all" when what occurs?
   A. Frederick Douglass is honored with a bronze statue.
   B. Laws are passed ensuring equal rights for all Americans.
   C. Politicians talk about freedom and equal rights more than they do now.
   D. Freedom becomes an instinctual, natural part of living for everyone.
   E. None of the above

8. **Constructed Response:** Explain what it meant to a slave to be assigned to the Great House Farm. How did slaves make themselves available for this assignment, and how did they react when they were chosen? Why was getting this assignment important? Use evidence from the text to support your answer.

9. **Constructed Response:** Discuss what the treatment of the slaves suggests about the slave owners. What did the lives of the slaves mean to the owners? Review the lives slaves led, as described by Douglass: their allowances, the way infants and mothers were treated, the competition for assignment to the Great House Farm, and the songs the slaves sung.

> **TEST-TAKING TIP**
>
> If you are having trouble responding to a multiple-choice question, review the answer options to see whether two of them are opposites or nearly so. When there are opposite items, it's likely one of them is the correct answer.

Understand the Concept

A **paragraph** is a group of related sentences that develop one main idea. A paragraph can have any of several purposes: to narrate, to describe, to persuade, or to inform. In any case, an effective paragraph has two key characteristics: unity and a logical method of organization.

Most effective paragraphs have a **main idea,** a point that is developed with **supporting details,** such as examples, details, facts, and quotations. The main idea is often stated directly at the beginning of the paragraph in a **topic sentence,** which is followed by several supporting sentences.

Look at the following paragraph from *Narrative of the Life of Frederick Douglass, an American Slave, Written by Himself.* The main idea of the paragraph is stated in the first sentence:

> The slaves selected to go to the Great House Farm, for the monthly allowance for themselves and their fellow slaves, were peculiarly enthusiastic. While on their way, they would make the dense old woods, for miles around, reverberate with their wild songs, revealing at once the highest joy and the deepest sadness. They would compose and sing as they went along, consulting neither time nor tune. . . .

Note how the other sentences in the paragraph support the topic sentence, telling how the slaves showed their enthusiasm. All the sentences work together to create a unified paragraph.

The topic sentence does not always come first in a paragraph, however. Sometimes the supporting sentences come first and lead up to the topic sentence, which is stated at the end.

Apply the Skill

Identify the Main Idea and Topic Sentence

Read the following paragraph from *An Appeal in Favor of That Class of Americans Called Africans,* by Lydia Maria Child. Then identify the main idea and where it is stated in a topic sentence.

> We first debase the nature of man by making him a slave, and then very coolly tell him that he must always remain a slave because he does not know how to use freedom. We first crush people to the earth, and then claim the right of trampling on them forever, because they are prostrate. Truly, human selfishness never invented a rule which worked out so charmingly both ways!

Revise a Paragraph to Improve Unity

Revise the following paragraph, rearranging the numbered sentences to improve organization and unity. (The first sentence is the topic sentence and should remain in that position.) After you have decided the order of the sentences, edit the paragraph to eliminate repetition, replacing *Douglass* with pronouns such as *he* and *his.*

> Frederick Douglass was an influential force in the fight to end slavery. (1) Unjustly implicated in the attack on Harpers Ferry in 1859, Douglass left the country a second time. (2) Following enactment of the Emancipation Proclamation in 1863, Douglass returned to the United States and organized regiments of African-American soldiers to fight for the North. (3) Born a slave in Maryland, Douglass escaped to Massachusetts in 1838, where he associated with prominent abolitionists. (4) When publication of the book made Douglass a target for slave catchers, he fled to England, where he remained until friends helped him buy his freedom. (5) After the war, Douglass held a number of political offices and lobbied for legislation to prevent discrimination. (6) In 1845, Douglass published *Narrative of the Life of Frederick Douglass, an American Slave.*

Write a Unified Paragraph

For the following topic sentence, write four supporting sentences to create a short paragraph. Each supporting sentence should develop the main idea stated in the topic sentence, and all the sentences should be related.

> Snack foods and soft drinks should (should not) be sold in high school cafeterias.

An Occurrence at Owl Creek Bridge

A Short Story by Ambrose Bierce

Build Background

Literary Context **"An Occurrence at Owl Creek Bridge"** takes place during the Civil War. Ambrose Bierce skillfully uses details about military customs and regulations to lend authenticity to the story's setting and action.

In its use of factual, precisely observed details, this story is a fine early example of American *Realism*. It also is an early example of *Naturalism,* a type of writing that portrays humans' lives as being shaped not by free will but by powerful social, economic, and environmental forces beyond their control.

Originally published in the San Francisco *Examiner* in July 1890 and later included in the collection *Tales of Soldiers and Civilians* (1891), this story opens with a man about to be hanged. It then takes an unexpected twist when he drops from the platform.

Reader's Context If you knew you had only one day to live, how would you spend it? Whom would you see? What would you do?

Meet the Author

Ambrose Bierce (1842–c. 1914), known as "Bitter Bierce," was a cynical, unhappy man with a sharp, satirical wit. Born in Ohio, he grew up in a large, poor family. An unhappy childhood followed by exposure to unimaginable brutality during the Civil War combined to create in Bierce the pessimism that became the dominant trait of his character and his fiction.

After spending a year at a military academy, Bierce joined the Union army, rising to the rank of lieutenant. He was a distinguished soldier and participated in several major battles. His war experiences provided material for some of his best stories, including "An Occurrence at Owl Creek Bridge" and "Chickamauga."

After the Civil War, Bierce worked as a journalist in San Francisco, establishing himself by writing witty, satirical columns as a major literary figure in what was then a rough-and-tumble frontier city. There, he counted among his friends such major writers as Mark Twain and Bret Harte, both of whom traveled the American frontier and wrote similar journalistic accounts of their experiences.

Disaster plagued Bierce throughout his life: His marriage ended in divorce, one son was killed in a fight, and another son died of alcoholism. In 1913, Bierce traveled to Mexico, which was in civil war, and he disappeared without a trace.

Analyze Literature

Psychological Fiction and Flashback
Psychological fiction emphasizes the interior experiences, especially the emotionally painful experiences, of its characters.

A **flashback** interrupts the *chronological order,* or sequence of events, of a literary work and presents an event that occurred earlier.

Set Purpose

Bierce's literary legacy lies in stories such as "An Occurrence at Owl Creek Bridge," which are still acclaimed for their suspense and psychological realism. As you read, identify passages in the story that qualify it as psychological fiction. Determine, in particular, what Bierce is trying to suggest about the character Farquhar by examining his psyche. In addition, identify where Bierce uses flashback, interrupting the chronology of the story. Determine how he indicates these shifts for the reader.

Preview Vocabulary

acclivity, 288
embrasure, 288
imperious, 289
efface, 291
oscillation, 291
ludicrous, 291
undulation, 291
gesticulate, 292
malign, 294

An Occurrence
at Owl Creek Bridge

by Ambrose Bierce

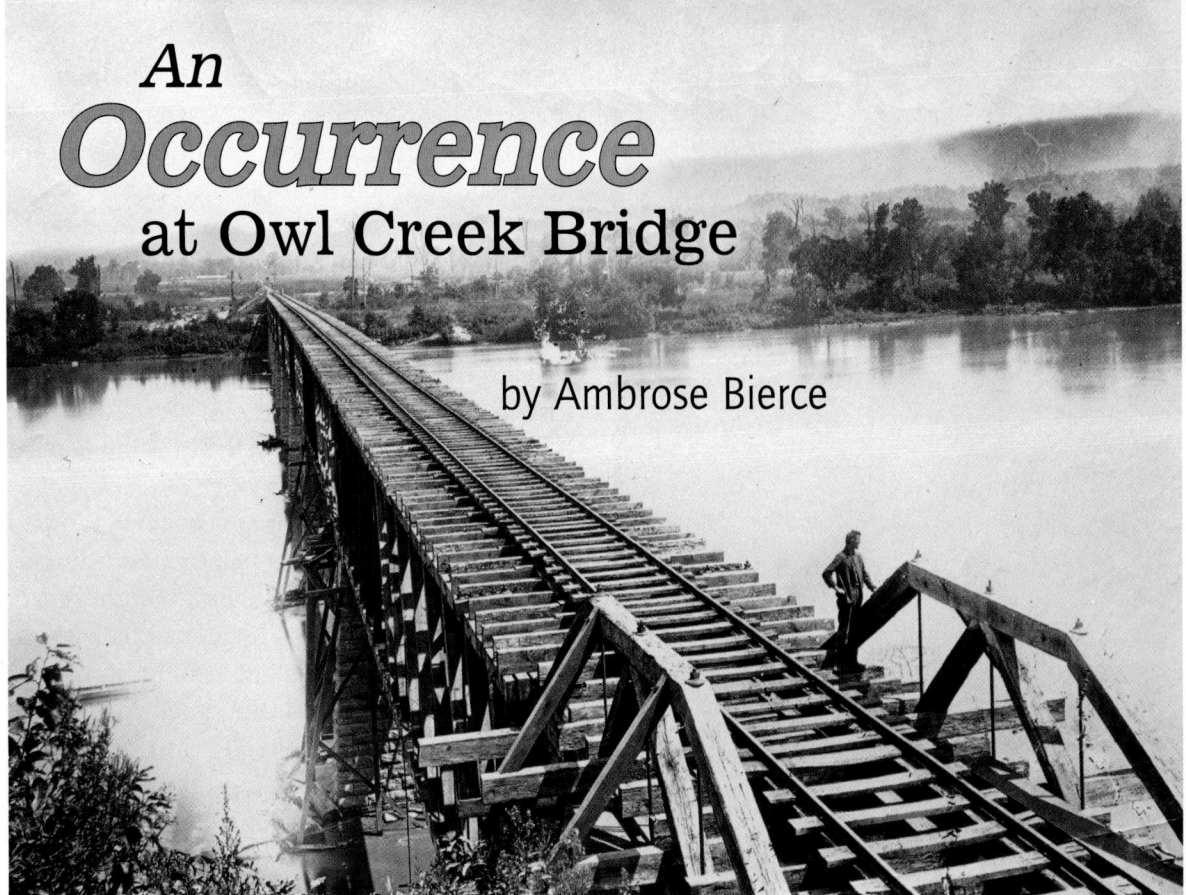

The Howe Bridge crossing the Tennessee River in Bridgeport, Alabama, (c. 1863).

To die of hanging at the bottom of a river!— the idea seemed to him ludicrous.

I

A man stood upon a railroad bridge in northern Alabama, looking down into the swift water twenty feet below. The man's hands were behind his back, the wrists bound with a cord. A rope closely encircled his neck. It was attached to a stout cross timber above his head and the slack fell to the level of his knees. Some loose boards laid upon the sleepers[1] supporting the metals of the railway supplied a footing for him and his executioners—two private soldiers of the Federal army, directed by a sergeant who in civil life may have been a deputy sheriff. At a short remove upon the same temporary platform was an officer in the uniform of his rank, armed. He was a captain. A sentinel[2] at each end of the bridge stood with his rifle in the position known as "support," that is to say, vertical in front of the left shoulder, the hammer resting on the forearm thrown straight across the chest—a formal and unnatural position, enforcing an erect carriage of the body. It did not appear to be the duty of these two men to know what was occurring at the center of the bridge; they merely blockaded the two ends of the foot planking that traversed it.

Beyond one of the sentinels nobody was in sight; the railroad ran straight away into a forest for a hundred yards, then, curving, was lost to view. Doubtless there was an outpost

---

1. **sleepers.** Ties that support railroad tracks
2. **sentinel.** Person acting as a guard

bridge, staring stonily, motionless. The sentinels, facing the banks of the stream, might have been statues to adorn the bridge. The captain stood with folded arms, silent, observing the work of his subordinates, but making no sign. Death is a dignitary who when he comes announced is to be received with formal manifestations of respect, even by those most familiar with him. In the code of military etiquette silence and fixity are forms of deference.

The man who was engaged in being hanged was apparently about thirty-five years of age. He was a civilian, if one might judge from his habit, which was that of a planter. His features were good—a straight nose, firm mouth, broad forehead, from which his long, dark hair was combed straight back, falling behind his ears to the collar of his well-fitting frock coat. He wore a mustache and pointed beard, but no whiskers; his eyes were large and dark gray, and had a kindly expression which one would hardly have expected in one whose neck was in the hemp.[3] Evidently this was no vulgar assassin. The liberal military code makes provision for hanging many kinds of persons, and gentlemen are not excluded.

The preparations being complete, the two private soldiers stepped aside and each drew away the plank upon which he had been standing. The sergeant turned to the captain, saluted and placed himself immediately behind that officer, who in turn moved apart one pace. These movements left the condemned man and the sergeant standing on the two ends of the same plank, which spanned three of the cross-ties of the bridge. The end upon which the civilian stood almost, but not quite, reached a fourth. This plank had been held in place by the weight of the captain; it was now held by that of the sergeant. At a signal from the former the latter

farther along. The other bank of the stream was open ground—a gentle <u>acclivity</u> topped with a stockade of vertical tree trunks, loop-holed for rifles with a single <u>embrasure</u> through which protruded the muzzle of a brass cannon commanding the bridge. Midway of the slope between bridge and fort were the spectators—a single company of infantry in line, at "parade rest," the butts of the rifles on the ground, the barrels inclining slightly backward against the right shoulder, the hands crossed upon the stock. A lieutenant stood at the right of the line, the point of his sword upon the ground, his left hand resting upon his right. Excepting the group of four at the center of the bridge, not a man moved. The company faced the

---

3. **hemp.** Rope made of hemp

> **ac • cliv • i • ty** (ə kliv´ ə tē) *n.,* upward slope
> **em • bra • sure** (em brā´ zhər) *n.,* slanted opening in a wall that increases the firing angle of a gun

would step aside, the plank would tilt and the condemned man go down between two ties. The arrangement commended itself to his judgment as simple and effective. His face had not been covered nor his eyes bandaged. He looked a moment at his "unsteadfast footing," then let his gaze wander to the swirling water of the stream racing madly beneath his feet. A piece of dancing driftwood caught his attention and his eyes followed it down the current. How slowly it appeared to move! What a sluggish stream!

> # He closed his eyes in order to fix his last thoughts upon his wife and children.

He closed his eyes in order to fix his last thoughts upon his wife and children. The water, touched to gold by the early sun, the brooding mists under the banks at some distance down the stream, the fort, the soldiers, the piece of drift—all had distracted him. And now he became conscious of a new disturbance. Striking through the thought of his dear ones was a sound which he could neither ignore nor understand, a sharp, distinct, metallic percussion like the stroke of a blacksmith's hammer upon the anvil; it had the same ringing quality. He wondered what it was, and whether immeasurably distant or near by—it seemed both. Its recurrence was regular, but as slow as the tolling of a death knell.[4] He awaited each stroke with impatience and—he knew not why—apprehension. The intervals of silence grew progressively longer; the delays became maddening. With their greater infrequency the sounds increased in strength and sharpness. They hurt his ear like the thrust of a knife; he feared he would shriek. What he heard was the ticking of his watch.

He unclosed his eyes and saw again the water below him. "If I could free my hands," he thought, "I might throw off the noose and spring into the stream. By diving I could evade the bullets and, swimming vigorously, reach the bank, take to the woods and get away home. My home, thank God, is as yet outside their lines; my wife and little ones are still beyond the invader's farthest advance."

As these thoughts, which have here to be set down in words, were flashed into the doomed man's brain rather than evolved from it the captain nodded to the sergeant. The sergeant stepped aside.

II

Peyton Farquhar was a well-to-do planter, of an old and highly respected Alabama family. Being a slave owner and like other slave owners a politician he was naturally an original secessionist[5] and ardently devoted to the Southern cause. Circumstances of an <u>imperious</u> nature, which it is unnecessary to relate here, had prevented him from taking service with the gallant army that had fought the disastrous campaigns ending with the fall of Corinth, and he chafed under the inglorious restraint, longing for the release of his energies, the larger life of the soldier, the opportunity for distinction. That opportunity, he felt, would come, as it comes to all in war time. Meanwhile he did what he could. No service was too humble for him to perform in aid of the South, no adventure too perilous for him to undertake if consistent with the character of a civilian who was at heart a soldier, and who in good faith and without too much qualification assented to at least a part of the frankly villainous dictum that all is fair in love and war.

---

4. **knell.** Sound of a bell rung slowly for a death, funeral, or disaster
5. **secessionist.** One who approved of Alabama's movement to withdraw from the United States. Before the Civil War began, seven states, including Alabama, voted to become the Confederate States of America.

> **im • pe • ri • ous** (im pir´ ē əs) *adj.,* intensely compelling

Union soldiers guarding a railroad bridge (1864).

One evening while Farquhar and his wife were sitting on a rustic bench near the entrance to his grounds, a gray-clad soldier rode up to the gate and asked for a drink of water. Mrs. Farquhar was only too happy to serve him with her own white hands. While she was fetching the water her husband approached the dusty horseman and inquired eagerly for news from the front.

"The Yanks are repairing the railroads," said the man, "and are getting ready for another advance. They have reached the Owl Creek bridge, put it in order and built a stockade on the north bank. The commandant has issued an order, which is posted everywhere, declaring that any civilian caught interfering with the railroad, its bridges, tunnels or trains will be summarily hanged. I saw the order."

"How far is it to the Owl Creek bridge?" Farquhar asked.

"About thirty miles."

"Is there no force on this side the creek?"

"Only a picket post[6] half a mile out, on the railroad, and a single sentinel at this end of the bridge."

"Suppose a man—a civilian and student of hanging—should elude the picket post and perhaps get the better of the sentinel," said Farquhar, smiling, "what could he accomplish?"

The soldier reflected. "I was there a month ago," he replied. "I observed that the flood of last winter had lodged a great quantity of driftwood against the wooden pier at this end of the bridge. It is now dry and would burn like tow."

The lady had now brought the water, which the soldier drank. He thanked her ceremoniously, bowed to her husband and rode away. An hour later, after nightfall, he repassed the plantation, going northward in the direction from which he had come. He was a Federal scout.

III

As Peyton Farquhar fell straight downward through the bridge he lost consciousness and was as one already dead. From this state he was awakened—ages later, it seemed to him—by the pain of a sharp pressure upon his throat, followed by a sense of suffocation. Keen, poignant agonies seemed to shoot from his neck downward through every fiber of his body and limbs. These pains appeared to flash

---

6. **picket post.** Troops that protect an army from a surprise attack

> # Keen, poignant agonies seemed to shoot from his neck downward through every fiber of his body and limbs.

along well defined lines of ramification and to beat with an inconceivably rapid periodicity. They seemed like streams of pulsating fire heating him to an intolerable temperature. As to his head, he was conscious of nothing but a feeling of fullness—of congestion. These sensations were unaccompanied by thought. The intellectual part of his nature was already effaced; he had power only to feel, and feeling was torment. He was conscious of motion. Encompassed in a luminous cloud, of which he was now merely the fiery heart, without material substance, he swung through unthinkable arcs of oscillation, like a vast pendulum. Then all at once, with terrible suddenness, the light about him shot upward with the noise of a loud splash; a frightful roaring was in his ears, and all was cold and dark. The power of thought was restored; he knew that the rope had broken and he had fallen into the stream. There was no additional strangulation; the noose about his neck was already suffocating him and kept the water from his lungs. To die of hanging at the bottom of a river!—the idea seemed to him ludicrous. He opened his eyes in the darkness and saw above him a gleam of light, but how distant, how inaccessible! He was still sinking, for the light became fainter and fainter until it was a mere glimmer. Then it began to grow and brighten, and he knew that he was rising toward the surface—knew it with reluctance, for he was now very comfortable. "To be hanged and drowned," he thought, "that

is not so bad; but I do not wish to be shot. No; I will not be shot; that is not fair."

He was not conscious of an effort, but a sharp pain in his wrist apprised him that he was trying to free his hands. He gave the struggle his attention, as an idler might observe the feat of a juggler, without interest in the outcome. What splendid effort!—what magnificent, what superhuman strength! Ah, that was a fine endeavor! Bravo! The cord fell away; his arms parted and floated upward, the hands dimly seen on each side in the growing light. He watched them with a new interest as first one and then the other pounced upon the noose at his neck. They tore it away and thrust it fiercely aside, its undulations resembling those of a watersnake. "Put it back, put it back!" He thought he shouted these words to his hands, for the undoing of the noose had been succeeded by the direst pang that he had yet experienced. His neck ached horribly; his brain was on fire; his heart, which had been fluttering faintly, gave a great leap, trying to force itself out at his mouth. His whole body was racked and wrenched with an insupportable anguish! But his disobedient hands gave no heed to the command. They beat the water vigorously with quick, downward strokes, forcing him to the surface. He felt his head emerge; his eyes were blinded by the sunlight; his chest expanded convulsively, and with a supreme and crowning agony his lungs engulfed a great draft of air, which instantly he expelled in a shriek!

He was now in full possession of his physical senses. They were, indeed, preternaturally[7] keen and alert. Something in the awful disturbance of his organic system had so exalted and

---

7. **preternaturally.** Inexplicably; without reason or explanation

---

ef • face (ə fās´) v., erase; wipe out
os • cil • la • tion (äs' ə lā´ shən) n., act of swinging back and forth
lu • di • crous (lü´ di krəs) adj., absurd; ridiculous
un • du • la • tion (un' jə lā´ shən) n., rising and falling in waves

Where Is Owl Creek?

Bierce's designation of Owl Creek as the setting for this story may have involved some *poetic license,* or alteration of the facts by the author. While there is an Owl Creek in northwestern Alabama, it is located within the Bankhead National Forest, a heavily wooded area. This seems unlikely terrain for a plantation. (In the story, Farquhar's plantation was an estimated thirty miles from Owl Creek Bridge.)

Bierce may have selected Owl Creek based on his familiarity with Civil War battles. Owl Creek runs through the area of southwestern Tennessee that was the site of the Battle of Shiloh, fought on April 6–7, 1862. Confederate forces, led by General Albert Sidney Johnston and P. G. T. Beauregard, launched a surprise attack against Union forces, led by Major General Ulysses S. Grant, and came close to defeating Grant's army and blocking his march into northern Mississippi. Fierce Union resistance, along with the arrival of reinforcements from Major General Don Carlos Buell, ultimately forced the Confederates to retreat. This two-day battle was the bloodiest in United States history up to that time, killing an estimated 3,500 soldiers and wounding more than 16,000.

Shiloh National Military Park was established by Congress in 1894 and became a national park in 1933.

and the veining of each leaf—saw the very insects upon them: the locusts, the brilliant-bodied flies, the gray spiders stretching their webs from twig to twig. He noted the prismatic colors in all the dewdrops upon a million blades of grass. The humming of the gnats that danced above the eddies of the stream, the insupportable beating of the dragonflies' wings, the strokes of the water spiders' legs, like oars which had lifted their boat—all these made audible music. A fish slid along beneath his eyes and he heard the rush of its body parting the water.

He had come to the surface facing down the stream; in a moment the visible world seemed to wheel slowly round, himself the pivotal point, and he saw the bridge, the fort, the soldiers upon the bridge, the captain, the sergeant, the two privates, his executioners. They were in silhouette against the blue sky. They shouted and <u>gesticulated</u>, pointing at him. The captain had drawn his pistol, but did not fire; the others were unarmed. Their movements were grotesque and horrible, their forms gigantic.

Suddenly he heard a sharp report and something struck the water smartly within a few inches of his head, spattering his face with spray. He heard a second report, and saw one of the sentinels with his rifle at his shoulder, a light cloud of blue smoke rising from the muzzle. The man in the water saw the eye of the man on the bridge gazing into his own through the sights of the rifle. He observed that it was a gray eye and remembered having read that gray eyes were keenest, and that all famous marksmen had them. Nevertheless, this one had missed.

A counterswirl had caught Farquhar and turned him half round; he was again looking into the forest on the bank opposite the fort. The sound of a clear, high voice in a monotonous singsong now rang out behind him and came across the water with a distinctness that

---

ges • tic • u • late (jes tik´ yü lāt´) *v.,* make gestures with hands or arms

refined them that they made record of things never before perceived. He felt the ripples upon his face and heard their separate sounds as they struck. He looked at the forest on the bank of the stream, saw the individual trees, the leaves

pierced and subdued all other sounds, even the beating of the ripples in his ears. Although no soldier, he had frequented camps enough to know the dread significance of that deliberate, drawling, aspirated chant; the lieutenant on shore was taking a part in the morning's work. How coldly and pitilessly—with what an even, calm intonation, presaging, and enforcing tranquillity in the men—with what accurately measured intervals fell those cruel words:

"Attention, company! . . . Shoulder arms! . . . Ready! . . . Aim! . . . fire!"

Farquhar dived—dived as deeply as he could. The water roared in his ears like the voice of Niagara, yet he heard the dulled thunder of the volley and, rising again toward the surface, met shining bits of metal, singularly flattened, oscillating slowly downward. Some of them touched him on the face and hands, then fell away, continuing their descent. One lodged between his collar and neck; it was uncomfortably warm and he snatched it out.

As he rose to the surface, gasping for breath, he saw that he had been a long time under water; he was perceptibly farther down stream—nearer to safety. The soldiers had almost finished reloading; the metal ramrods flashed all at once in the sunshine as they were drawn from the barrels, turned in the air, and thrust into their sockets. The two sentinels fired again, independently and ineffectually.

The hunted man saw all this over his shoulder; he was now swimming vigorously with the current. His brain was as energetic as his arms and legs; he thought with the rapidity of lightning.

"The officer," he reasoned, "will not make that martinet's[8] error a second time. It is as easy to dodge a volley as a single shot. He has probably already given the command to fire at will. God help me, I cannot dodge them all!"

An appalling splash within two yards of him was followed by a loud, rushing sound, *diminuendo,*[9] which seemed to travel back through the air to the fort and died in an explosion which stirred the very river to its

deeps! A rising sheet of water curved over him, fell down upon him, blinded him, strangled him! The cannon had taken a hand in the game. As he shook his head free from the commotion of the smitten water he heard the deflected shot humming through the air ahead, and in an instant it was cracking and smashing the branches in the forest beyond.

"They will not do that again," he thought; "the next time they will use a charge of grape.[10] I must keep my eye upon the gun; the smoke will apprise me—the report arrives too late; it lags behind the missile. That is a good gun."

Suddenly he felt himself whirled round and round— spinning like a top.

Suddenly he felt himself whirled round and round—spinning like a top. The water, the banks, the forests, the now distant bridge, fort and men—all were commingled and blurred. Objects were represented by their colors only; circular horizontal streaks of color—that was all he saw. He had been caught in a vortex and was being whirled on with a velocity of advance and gyration that made him giddy and sick. In a few moments he was flung upon the gravel at the foot of the left bank of the stream—the southern bank—and behind a projecting point which concealed him from his enemies. The sudden arrest of his motion, the abrasion of one of his hands on the gravel, restored him, and he wept with delight. He dug his fingers into the sand, threw it over himself in handfuls and audibly blessed it. It looked like diamonds, rubies, emeralds; he

---

8. **martinet.** Strict disciplinarian
9. **diminuendo.** Musical term meaning a reduction in volume
10. **grape.** Cluster of small iron balls fired from a cannon

could think of nothing beautiful which it did not resemble. The trees upon the bank were giant garden plants; he noted a definite order in their arrangement, inhaled the fragrance of their blooms. A strange, roseate light shone through the spaces among their trunks and the wind made in their branches the music of aeolian harps.[11] He had no wish to perfect his escape—was content to remain in that enchanting spot until retaken.

A whiz and rattle of grapeshot among the branches high above his head roused him from his dream. The baffled cannoneer had fired him a random farewell. He sprang to his feet, rushed up the sloping bank, and plunged into the forest.

All that day he traveled, laying his course by the rounding sun. The forest seemed interminable; nowhere did he discover a break in it, not even a woodman's road. He had not known that he lived in so wild a region. There was something uncanny in the revelation.

By night fall he was fatigued, footsore, famishing. The thought of his wife and children urged him on. At last he found a road which led him in what he knew to be the right direction. It was as wide and straight as a city street, yet it seemed untraveled. No fields bordered it, no dwelling anywhere. Not so much as the barking of a dog suggested human habitation. The black bodies of the trees formed a straight wall on both sides, terminating on the horizon in a point, like a diagram in a lesson in perspective. Overhead, as he looked up through this rift in the wood, shone great golden stars looking unfamiliar and grouped in strange constellations. He was sure they were arranged in some order which had a secret and <u>malign</u> significance. The wood on either side was full of singular noises, among which—once, twice, and again, he distinctly heard whispers in an unknown tongue.

His neck was in pain and lifting his hand to it he found it horribly swollen. He knew that it had a circle of black where the rope had bruised it. His eyes felt congested; he could no longer close them. His tongue was swollen with thirst; he relieved its fever by thrusting it forward from between his teeth into the cold air. How softly the turf had carpeted the untraveled avenue—he could no longer feel the roadway beneath his feet!

Doubtless, despite his suffering, he had fallen asleep while walking, for now he sees another scene—perhaps he has merely recovered from a delirium. He stands at the gate of his own home. All is as he left it, and all bright and beautiful in the morning sunshine. He must have traveled the entire night. As he pushes open the gate and passes up the wide white walk, he sees a flutter of female garments; his wife, looking fresh and cool and sweet, steps down from the veranda to meet him. At the bottom of the steps she stands waiting, with a smile of ineffable joy, an attitude of matchless grace and dignity. Ah, how beautiful she is! He springs forward with extended arms. As he is about to clasp her he feels a stunning blow upon the back of the neck; a blinding white light blazes all about him with a sound like the shock of a cannon—then all is darkness and silence!

Peyton Farquhar was dead; his body, with a broken neck, swung gently from side to side beneath the timbers of the Owl Creek bridge. ❖

---

11. **aeolian harps.** Harps that produce music when air blows over the strings

ma • lign (mə līn´) *adj.,* malicious; evil

Think of a time you made a decision and things turned out badly. Did you regret the decision?

Refer to Text ▶ ▶ ▶ ▶ ▶ **Reason with Text**

1a. Why is Farquhar hanged?	**1b.** Why does the gray-clad soldier visit the Farquhar home?	**Understand** Find meaning
2a. Recall how Peyton Farquhar is described.	**2b.** What was Farquhar trying to achieve for himself by getting involved unofficially?	**Apply** Use information
3a. State what happens to Farquhar at the end of the story.	**3b.** Consider the events that led to the story's conclusion. Which events did Farquhar put into action? Which events were beyond his control?	**Analyze** Take things apart
4a. What does Farquhar imagine happens to him?	**4b.** How effectively has the author depicted Farquhar's psychological trauma? Justify your response with evidence from the text.	**Evaluate** Make judgments
5a. Identify parts of the story that seem gruesome, frightening, or supernatural.	**5b.** Ambrose Bierce is known as a Realist, but this story is sometimes considered his "best ghost story." Do you agree that it's a type of ghost story? Why or why not?	**Create** Bring ideas together

Analyze Literature

Psychological Fiction and Flashback
Which parts of the story qualify it as psychological fiction? In other words, where does the writer effectively put the reader "inside the mind" of his main character?

Which part of the story makes up the flashback? In what ways does the flashback advance the plot? What necessary information does the flashback provide? How would the story be different if told in regular chronological order?

Extend the Text

Writing Options
Creative Writing Write the military order that the passing soldier describes to Peyton Farquhar and that was posted for Southern civilians to read. Think about the audience for this order, and pay attention to your tone and language.

Persuasive Writing Some literary critics suggest that knowing about an author's personal background can help readers understand his or her writing. Does knowing about Bierce's life and experiences affect your understanding of "An Occurrence at Owl Creek Bridge"? Do further research on Bierce. Then write an essay in which you agree or disagree with these critics' theory; use evidence from your research and the story to support your ideas.

Collaborative Learning
Reveal Narrator Attitude Ambrose Bierce was known for his cynical commentary on nineteenth-century life. Go back through the story with a partner and look for examples of the author's opinions, sarcasm, and dry humor. What do such comments reveal about the narrator? Do you like this person? Do you agree with his opinions? Write a summary of your impression of Bierce.

Media Literacy
Analyze a Film Adaptation Watch the 1962 film adaptation of "An Occurrence at Owl Creek Bridge," directed by Robert Enrico. How does the film compare with the way you envisioned the story and the character of Farquhar? For your school newspaper, write a review of the film. Consider what you like and dislike about the film and how faithfully it follows the story.

 Go to **www.mirrorsandwindows.com** for more.

1. Which of the following is *not* an oddity Farquhar notices as he walks through the woods toward his home?
   A. The forest seems to go on forever.
   B. There are no signs of life.
   C. The bullets buzz by him in what seems like slow motion.
   D. The stars are arranged in unfamiliar constellations.
   E. He hears whispers in an unknown language.

2. Which of the following is an example of irony from the selection?
   A. The story starts at the beginning of the hanging and then jumps back to the encounter with the Federal scout.
   B. The description of Farquhar's surroundings seems dreamlike.
   C. Farquhar fears he might be strangled by the rope underwater.
   D. Although Farquhar seems to escape, in fact, he is recaptured.
   E. The Federal soldiers act quite formally, even though they are killing an enemy.

3. Which of the following best defines the word *imperious,* as used in the story?
   A. intensely compelling
   B. arrogant and cold
   C. completely absurd
   D. secretly dangerous
   E. important only to a small group

4. Which obstacles must Farquhar overcome in order to make his escape?
   A. people shooting at him
   B. a whirlpool
   C. cannon fire
   D. strangulation from the rope
   E. All of the above

5. In the sentence "He was sure [the stars] were arranged in some order which had a secret and malign significance," what does the word *malign* mean?
   A. mysterious
   B. beneficial
   C. unknowable
   D. evil
   E. serious

6. From what you know about Ambrose Bierce, how does "An Occurrence at Owl Creek Bridge" demonstrate his worldview?
   A. Bierce thought emotional truth was more real than actual events, so Farquhar's dream is as valid as his death.
   B. The story shows that death and destruction are the results of war, which points to Bierce's bitter worldview.
   C. Bierce believed that hope exists in even the direst of circumstances; thus, Farquhar's dream of escape shows Bierce's hopeful worldview.
   D. Bierce upheld the dignity of warfare by showing a Confederate sympathizer perform brave deeds and face his death with honor.
   E. Bierce was fiercely pro-Union, so the story serves as a warning to those would sympathize with the Confederate cause.

7. **Constructed Response:** Write an analysis of this story as psychological fiction. Address elements of characterization and plot as well as Bierce's use of literary techniques such as flashback. Also address the theme of the story and what Bierce is suggesting about war.

8. **Constructed Response:** Examine what we learn about the Civil War and what we can infer about its effects on people from reading "An Occurrence at Owl Creek Bridge." For instance, how does Farquhar's attitude toward the war lead him to his death? How do the soldiers on the bridge treat him, and what is their attitude toward the hanging?

TEST-TAKING TIP

Although you cannot write on the test sheet, you can make notes in the accompanying booklet. When you come across a complicated question, write out the possible responses next to the question in the booklet. Putting your thoughts on paper will help clarify your thinking. Doing so also will help you retrace your thoughts when you check your work later.

The Gettysburg Address
The Second Inaugural Address
Speeches by Abraham Lincoln

Build Background

Historical Context Abraham Lincoln's **Gettysburg Address** and **Second Inaugural Address** are two of the most famous presidential speeches in American history. The words of both are etched into the walls of the Lincoln Memorial in Washington, DC.

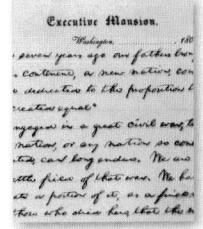

Lincoln delivered the Gettysburg Address at the dedication of the national cemetery at Gettysburg, Pennsylvania, on November 19, 1863. The previous July, Gettysburg had been the site of the bloodiest battle in the Civil War. Union and Confederate troops fought for three days on the farmlands of Pennsylvania. The Union army's ultimate victory at Gettysburg proved a turning point in the war, as it ended Confederate General Robert E. Lee's march into the North.

On March 4, 1865, Lincoln was inaugurated president for a second term. The gray skies that day matched the somber mood of the thousands of spectators who gathered to watch the swearing-in ceremony. The nation, weary of the war that was now drawing to a close, waited anxiously for the president's speech.

Reader's Context If you were the leader of a group of discouraged followers, what would you say to inspire them to continue their struggle?

Meet the Author

Abraham Lincoln (1809–1865) rose from obscurity to a place of reverence in American history. Born to frontier parents in a cabin in Kentucky, he schooled himself by reading. A strong, lanky youth, Lincoln worked on the family farm when they moved to Illinois and then held various jobs, such as flatboatman and storekeeper. After serving in the Blackhawk War, he prepared himself for a career in law and passed the bar exam in 1836. He then moved to Springfield, Illinois, and was elected to the state legislature, where he served four terms.

In 1858, Lincoln entered the U.S. senatorial race against Stephen A. Douglas. Lincoln lost that election, but the Lincoln-Douglas debates showed him to be a brilliant speaker, combining learned references with homespun wit and steel-trap logic. In 1860, running as the candidate of the newly formed Republican party, Lincoln was elected the sixteenth president of the United States and immediately became embroiled in the Civil War.

During the war, Lincoln issued the Emancipation Proclamation, freeing slaves in the states then in rebellion. After the war, he worked for passage of the Thirteenth Amendment, which ended slavery in the United States. In April 1865, shortly after being inaugurated to a second term, Lincoln was assassinated by John Wilkes Booth while watching a play at Ford's Theater in Washington.

Analyze Literature

Parallelism and Antithesis
Parallelism is a technique in which a writer emphasizes the equal value of two or more ideas by expressing them in the same grammatical form.

Antithesis is a technique in which words, phrases, or ideas are contrasted, often by repetition of a grammatical structure.

Set Purpose

Both the Gettysburg Address and Second Inaugural Address were delivered on somber, even sorrowful occasions. Think about how President Lincoln recognized Americans' solemn mood in preparing his remarks. Consider why he decided to use parallelism and antithesis to express his sentiments. As you read, note examples of each literary technique.

Preview Vocabulary

score, 298
consecrate, 298
insurgent, 301
rend, 301
scourge, 302
unrequited, 302
malice, 302

Four score and seven years ago our fathers brought forth on this continent, a new nation, conceived in Liberty, and dedicated to the proposition that all men are created equal.

Now we are engaged in a great civil war, testing whether that nation, or any nation so conceived and so dedicated, can long endure. We are met on a great battlefield of that war. We have come to dedicate a portion of that field, as a final resting place for those who here gave their lives that that nation might live. It is altogether fitting and proper that we should do this.

But, in a larger sense, we can not dedicate—we can not consecrate—we can not hallow—this ground. The brave men, living and dead, who struggled here, have consecrated it, far above our poor power to add or detract. The world will little note, nor long remember what we say here, but it can never forget what they did here. It is for us the living, rather, to be dedicated here to the unfinished work which they who fought here have thus far so nobly advanced. It is rather for us to be here dedicated to the great task remaining before us—that from these honored dead we take increased devotion to that cause for which they gave the last full measure of devotion—that we here highly resolve that these dead shall not have died in vain—that this nation, under God, shall have a new birth of freedom—and that government of the people, by the people, for the people, shall not perish from the earth. ❖

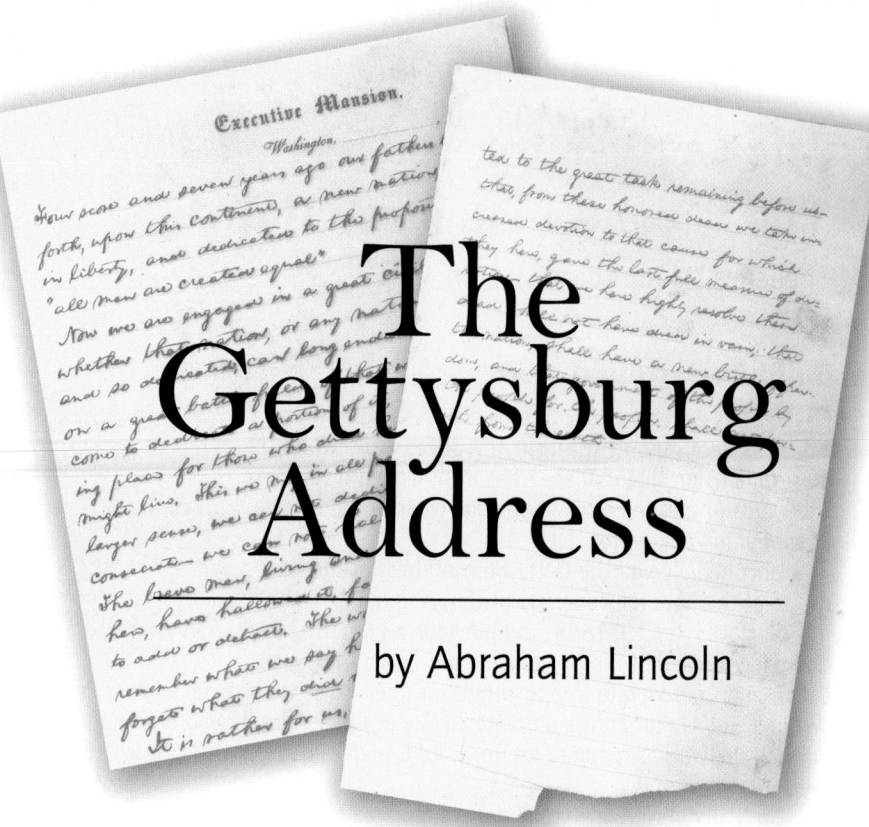

The Gettysburg Address

by Abraham Lincoln

Lincoln's original draft of the Gettysburg Address, which is on display at the Library of Congress.

score (skōr) *n.*, set of twenty
con • se • crate (kän´ sə krāt) *v.*, make or declare sacred

MIRRORS & WINDOWS

If you had been a relative of a soldier killed at Gettysburg, how would you have reacted to Lincoln's speech?

Primary Source Connection

President Lincoln wrote this **letter of condolence** to Mrs. Lydia Bixby, a Bostonian widow, in the fall of 1864 after hearing that she had lost five sons during the Civil War. (It later was learned that only two of her sons had been killed.) Lincoln's eloquent letter was reprinted in the *Boston Evening Transcript* and remains a tribute to all soldiers who have died in combat. Moviegoers became familiar with the letter in 1998, when it was read at the beginning of Steven Spielberg's *Saving Private Ryan* and set the stage for the movie's dramatic plot.

In fact, the authenticity of Lincoln's letter has been questioned by handwriting experts and historical scholars. Some believe the letter actually was written by John Hay, one of Lincoln's secretaries. Also, the original letter was believed to have been destroyed by Mrs. Bixby, suggesting that subsequent versions all have been forgeries. The validity of the Bixby letter remains a topic of scholarly debate.

Letter to Mrs. Bixby
by Abraham Lincoln

Executive Mansion, Washington,

November 21, 1864

Mrs. Bixby, Boston, Massachusetts:

Dear Madam:

I have been shown in the files of the War Department a statement of the Adjutant-General of Massachusetts that you are the mother of five sons who have died gloriously on the field of battle. I feel how weak and fruitless must be any words of mine which should attempt to beguile you from the grief of a loss so overwhelming. But I cannot refrain from tendering to you the consolation that may be found in the thanks of the Republic they

died to save. I pray that our Heavenly Father may assuage the anguish of your bereavement, and leave you only the cherished memory of the loved and lost, and the solemn pride that must be yours to have laid so costly a sacrifice upon the altar of freedom.

Yours very sincerely and respectfully,

Abraham Lincoln

Review Questions

1. Recall how Mrs. Bixby's sons died. Why does Lincoln thank her?

2. According to Lincoln, what is "weak and fruitless"? Infer how a parent might feel about the consolation expressed in this letter. How effectively does the letter express this sentiment?

3. At the end of the letter, what emotion does Lincoln assume Mrs. Bixby feels? What factors might influence how the family of someone who has died in battle feels about the war or the government?

TEXT $\xleftarrow{\text{TO}}$ TEXT CONNECTION

Many scholars rank Lincoln's letter to Mrs. Bixby among his top three writings, along with the Gettysburg Address and the Second Inaugural Address. How are these three similar in literary style? Which is most effective in achieving its purpose? Why?

The Second Inaugural Address

by Abraham Lincoln

Fellow-Countrymen:

At this second appearing to take the oath of the Presidential office there is less occasion for an extended address than there was at the first. Then a statement somewhat in detail of a course to be pursued seemed fitting and proper. Now, at the expiration of four years, during which public declarations have been constantly called forth on every point and phase of the great contest which still absorbs the attention and engrosses the energies of the nation, little that is new could be presented. The progress of our arms, upon which all else chiefly depends, is as well known to the public as to myself, and it is, I trust, reasonably satisfactory and encouraging to all. With high hope for the future, no prediction in regard to it is ventured.

On the occasion corresponding to this four years ago all thoughts were anxiously directed to an impending civil war. All dreaded it—all sought to avert it. While the inaugural address was being delivered from this place, devoted altogether to *saving* the Union without war, <u>insurgent</u> agents were in the city seeking to *destroy* it without war—seeking to dissol[v]e the Union, and divide effects, by negotiation. Both parties deprecated war; but one of them would *make* war rather than let the nation survive; and the other would *accept* war rather than let it perish. And the war came.

One eighth of the whole population were colored slaves, not distributed generally over the Union, but localized in the southern part of it. These slaves constituted a peculiar and powerful interest. All knew that this interest was, somehow, the cause of the war. To strengthen, perpetuate, and extend this interest was the object for which the insurgents would <u>rend</u> the Union, even by war; while the Government

---

in · sur · gent (in sur´ jənt) *adj.,* revolting against an established government
rend (rend) *v.,* tear apart

Lincoln taking the oath of office for his second term on March 4, 1865.

claimed no right to do more than to restrict the territorial enlargement of it. Neither party expected for the war, the magnitude, or the duration, which it has already attained. Neither anticipated that the *cause* of the conflict might cease with, or even before, the conflict itself should cease. Each looked for an easier triumph, and a result less fundamental and astounding. Both read the same Bible, and pray to the same God; and each invokes His aid against the other. It may seem strange that any men should dare to ask a just God's assistance in wringing their bread from the sweat of other men's faces; but let us judge not that we be not judged.[1] The prayers of both could not be answered; that of neither has been answered fully. The Almighty has His own purposes. "Woe unto the world because of offenses! for it must needs be that offenses come; but woe to that man by whom the offense cometh!"[2] If we shall suppose that American Slavery is

one of those offenses which, in the providence of God, must needs come, but which, having continued through His appointed time, He now wills to remove, and that He gives to both North and South, this terrible war, as the woe due to those by whom the offense came, shall we discern therein any departure from those divine attributes which the believers in a Living God always ascribe to Him? Fondly do we hope—fervently do we pray—that this mighty <u>scourge</u> of war may speedily pass away. Yet, if God wills that it continue, until all the wealth piled by the bond-man's two hundred and fifty years of <u>unrequited</u> toil[3] shall be sunk, and until every drop of blood drawn with the lash, shall be paid by another drawn with the sword, as was said three thousand years ago, so still it must be said "the judgments of the Lord, are true and righteous altogether."[4]

With <u>malice</u> toward none; with charity for all; with firmness in the right, as God gives us to see the right, let us strive on to finish the work we are in; to bind up the nation's wounds; to care for him who shall have borne the battle, and for his widow, and his orphan— to do all which may achieve and cherish a just and lasting peace, among ourselves, and with all nations. ❖

---

1. **let us . . . not judged.** Based on a verse from the Bible, Matthew 7:1
2. **"Woe unto the world . . . offense cometh!"** Quote from the Bible, Matthew 18:7
3. **bond-man's . . . toil.** Refers to the period of slavery in which the slaves were not requited or paid for their labor
4. **"the judgments . . . righteous altogether."** Quote from the Bible, Psalm 19:9

---

scourge (skʉrj) *n.,* cause of widespread suffering
un • re • quit • ed (un' rē kwīt´ əd) *adj.,* not rewarded or paid for
mal • ice (mal´ əs) *n.,* desire to cause pain or injury to another

When is it more important to be humble: in victory or in defeat?

Refer to Text ▶ ▶ ▶ ▶ ▶ Reason with Text

1a. Identify the event taking place when the Gettysburg Address is delivered. What is being tested by this event?	**1b.** According to Lincoln, under what circumstances would the dead have died in vain? What can the listeners do to ensure that the deaths were not futile?	**Understand** Find meaning
2a. As stated in the Second Inaugural Address, what was the position of the Union, or North, on the issue of slavery at the beginning of the Civil War?	**2b.** Why does Lincoln refrain from casting judgment on the South in the Second Inaugural Address?	**Apply** Use information
3a. Identify two quotations in the Second Inaugural Address. What is the source of each?	**3b.** Infer how Lincoln might have responded to Northerners who insisted that God was on their side.	**Analyze** Take things apart
4a. Recall the words Lincoln uses to evaluate the significance of the Gettysburg Address.	**4b.** The Gettysburg Address has been repeated for over one hundred years, and many students have memorized it. Consider why this speech has touched Americans so deeply.	**Evaluate** Make judgments
5a. In the Second Inaugural, what does Lincoln say should happen to Confederate soldiers?	**5b.** Summarize the most important point Lincoln is trying to make.	**Create** Bring ideas together

Analyze Literature

Parallelism and Antithesis

Lincoln uses parallelism extensively in the final sentence of the Gettysburg Address. Make a chart listing other examples of parallelism that begin with *that,* and paraphrase each one. Make a similar chart of examples for the Second Inaugural Address, and paraphrase each one.

Review the definition of antithesis provided earlier. What examples can you identify in the Gettysburg Address and the Second Inaugural Address?

Extend the Text

Writing Options

Creative Writing Write a *eulogy* for a young soldier killed in war, telling about his or her life, accomplishments, and personality. Consider that the audience will be mourners at the funeral or memorial service.

Persuasive Writing You are a speechwriter for the president of the United States. Write a persuasive speech in which the president asks for the support of the American public on a critical issue. The speech will be delivered on national television from the White House.

Collaborative Learning

Research the Battle of Gettysburg With three classmates, prepare a presentation about one aspect of

the Battle of Gettysburg, such as events leading up to the battle, events during the battle, or the significance of the battle. Everyone should do research and take notes. Then have group members carry out individual roles (secretary, writer, editor, presenter). Deliver your final presentation to the class.

Critical Literacy

Analyze Speeches Another famous speech in American history is Martin Luther King Jr.'s "I Have a Dream" speech. Locate a recording of the speech, and analyze it for rhetorical devices such as repetition, parallelism, and antithesis. Play the recording for the class, and explain what makes this speech memorable.

 Go to **www.mirrorsandwindows.com** for more.

Understand the Concept

A sentence has **parallel structure** or **parallelism** when it uses the same grammatical forms to express ideas of equal—or parallel—importance. Words, phrases, and clauses that have the same form and function in a sentence are called **parallel.**

One of the most famous examples of parallel structure appears in Abraham Lincoln's Gettysburg Address. Lincoln used a series of prepositional phrases—"of the people, by the people, for the people"—to emphasize his concept of American government.

Parallelism not only adds emphasis and rhythm to writing, but it also improves unity and balance. Faulty parallelism makes sentences sound awkward and can obscure their meaning.

EXAMPLES

Faulty The soldiers vowed *to fight,* even *dying,* to preserve the Union.

Parallel The soldiers vowed *to fight,* even *to die,* to preserve the Union. [*dying* was changed to *to die* to have the same structure as *to fight*]

Faulty At the end of the war, Southerners found *their farmlands destroyed, their railroads demolished,* and *they didn't have enough food.*

Parallel At the end of the war, Southerners found *their farmlands destroyed, their railroads demolished,* and *their food supply limited.* [*they didn't have enough food* was changed to *their food supply limited* to have the same structure as *farmlands destroyed* and *railroads demolished*]

To correct faulty parallelism, look for series of nouns and verbs and similarly constructed clauses and phrases. Match like elements and write them using the same grammatical structure.

Apply the Skill

Identify Parallel Structure

Find the uses of parallel structure in the following paragraphs from Lincoln's First Inaugural Address, delivered March 4, 1861:

In your hands, my dissatisfied fellow countrymen, and not in mine, is the momentous issue of civil war. The government will not assail you. You can have no conflict without being yourselves the aggressors. You have no oath registered in Heaven to destroy the government, while I shall have the most solemn one to preserve, protect, and defend it.

I am loath to close. We are not enemies, but friends. We must not be enemies. Though passion may have strained, it must not break our bonds of affection. The mystic chords of memory, stretching from every battlefield, and patriot grave, to every living heart and hearthstone, all over this broad land, will yet swell the chorus of the Union, when again touched, as surely they will be, by the better angels of our nature.

Improve Parallel Structure

Rewrite each of the following sentences using parallel structure.

1. Our ancestors brought forth a new nation conceived in liberty and it was also being dedicated to the principle of equality for all people.
2. It is fitting and proper to dedicate the cemetery and setting aside a portion of it to the fallen soldiers.
3. The brave men who were fighting and died here consecrated the ground better than we can.
4. The world does not note nor will it remember what we say here.
5. We must resolve that these dead shall not have died in vain and to dedicate ourselves to the preservation of the nation.

Use Parallel Structure in Your Own Writing

Imagine that you lived during Abraham Lincoln's time. Write a letter to the president in which you relate your feelings and observations about national events. Use five examples of parallelism in your letter. After completing your letter, read it aloud. Any errors in parallelism will sound awkward. Revise your writing to improve parallelism.

Farewell to His Army

A Letter by Robert E. Lee

Build Background

Historical Context Early in 1865, General Robert E. Lee, commander of all Confederate forces, recognized that the South could not win the war. After Union forces surrounded Lee's troops at Appomattox Court House, in Virginia, Lee surrendered to the Union commander, General Ulysses S. Grant, on April 9, 1865. The following letter, **Farewell to His Army,** was attached to Lee's surrender report to Confederate President Jefferson Davis. In the letter, Lee officially announces his action to his men, admiring their valor and thanking them for their devotion.

Reader's Context What are valid reasons for a country going to war?

Meet the Author

Robert E. Lee (1807–1870), the Confederacy's greatest soldier, was a colonel in the United States Army when his home state, Virginia, seceded with other Southern states from the Union in April 1861. At that time, President Lincoln offered him command of the Union forces. Although Lee did not favor secession and had shown his disapproval of slavery by freeing his own slaves years earlier, he declined Lincoln's offer and joined the Confederate Army instead.

As commander of the Army of Northern Virginia from 1862 to the end of the war, Lee made brilliant use of his limited manpower and supplies. Confederate forces defeated Union forces consistently in the major battles of the first years of the war. Nevertheless, Union forces were not seriously weakened by these losses, while Lee's forces dwindled.

Named general-in-chief of all Confederate forces early in 1865, Lee realized that the South could not win the war. Within months, he surrendered, bringing the Civil War to a close. After the war, Lee became president of Washington College in Lexington, Virginia. He took a strong stand against the bitterness that continued to divide the nation, working peaceably to restore the South.

The Surrender of General Lee to General Grant, 1867. Louis Guillaume.

Analyze Literature

Purpose and Tone
A writer's **purpose** is his or her aim, or goal, which may be one or more of the following: to inform or explain; to portray a person, place, object, or event; to convince people to accept a position; or to tell a story.

Tone is the emotional attitude toward the subject implied by a literary work, such as playful, sarcastic, or sincere. Tone may be revealed through word choice, imagery, and so on.

Set Purpose

General Lee was famous for treating his soldiers with respect, and that attitude is apparent in his final letter to his troops. As you read the letter, identify the purposes Lee has for writing on this occasion of surrender. Also analyze the tone of the letter and whether it suits the occasion and Lee's purposes. Write down the words and images that express tone.

Preview Vocabulary

arduous, 306
fortitude, 306
valor, 306

Farewell to His Army

by Robert E. Lee

Headquarters, Army Northern Virginia, April 10, 1865

After four years of <u>arduous</u> service, marked by unsurpassed courage and <u>fortitude</u>, the Army of Northern Virginia has been compelled to yield to overwhelming numbers and resources. I need not tell the survivors of so many hard-fought battles, who have remained steadfast to the last, that I have consented to this result from no distrust of them; but, feeling that <u>valor</u> and devotion could accomplish nothing that could compensate for the loss that would have attended the continuation of the contest, I have determined to avoid the useless sacrifice of those whose past services have endeared them to their countrymen. By the terms of the agreement, officers and men can return to their homes, and remain there until exchanged.[1]

You will take with you *the satisfaction that proceeds from the consciousness of duty faithfully performed*; and I earnestly pray that a merciful God will extend to you his blessing and protection. With an unceasing admiration of your constancy and devotion to your country, and a grateful remembrance of your kind and generous consideration of myself, I bid you an affectionate farewell. ❖

---

1. **exchanged.** Discharged from military service

> **ar • du • ous** (är´ jü əs) *adj.*, difficult; hard to accomplish or achieve
> **for • ti • tude** (fōr´ tə tüd) *n.*, strength of mind that enables a person to accomplish a goal
> **val • or** (val´ ər) *n.*, bravery

MIRRORS & WINDOWS How might Confederate soldiers have felt upon reading or listening to General Lee's letter?

Literature Connection

Some 130 years after the Civil War, **Jane Kenyon** wrote the poem **"At the Public Market Museum"** following a visit to the Charleston United Daughters of the Confederacy Museum. The museum contains one of the largest and most important collections of Confederate artifacts in the United States. In the poem, Kenyon describes a display of gray jackets, uniforms worn by Confederate soldiers. "At the Public Market Museum" was published in *Otherwise: New and Selected Poems* (1996).

At the Public Market Museum:
Charleston, South Carolina

by Jane Kenyon

A volunteer, a Daughter of the Confederacy,
receives my admission and points the way.
Here are gray jackets with holes in them,
red sashes with individual flourishes,[1]
5   things soft as flesh. Someone sewed
the gold silk cord onto that gray sleeve
as if embellishments[2]
could keep a man alive.

---

1. **flourishes.** Ornaments
2. **embellishments.** Decorations

I have been reading *War and Peace*,[3]

10 and so the particulars of combat
are on my mind—the shouts and groans
of men and boys, and the horses' cries
as they fall, astonished at what
has happened to them.

15   Blood on leaves,
blood on grass, on snow; extravagant
beauty of red. Smoke, dust of disturbed
earth; parch and burn.

Who would choose this for himself?
20 And yet the terrible machinery
waited in place. With psalters[4]
in their breast pockets, and gloves
knitted by their sisters and sweethearts,
the men in gray hurled themselves
25 out of the trenches, and rushed against
blue. It was what both sides agreed to do. ❖

---

3. **War and Peace.** Epic novel by Leo Tolstoy about Russian society
during the early 1800s
4. **psalters.** Books of psalms; prayer books

Review Questions

1. What, specifically, is the speaker in the poem looking at? What strikes the speaker as odd or touching about these items? Why?

2. What is on the speaker's mind? Why? Compare and contrast the images of the second stanza with those in the first and last stanzas. What view of the war do these images create?

3. According to the speaker, why did the Confederate and Union soldiers (the "men in gray" and "blue") fight one another? Suggest what the last line of the poem reveals about the speaker's feelings toward war. Do you agree or disagree? Explain.

TEXT ⇄ TO TEXT CONNECTION

Both Lee's Farewell to His Army and Kenyon's "At the Public Market Museum" acknowledge the sacrifices of soldiers in wartime. What does each say about the nature of war and the roles of those who serve in battle? How might the fact that the two were written more than one hundred years apart affect the perspectives taken on the Civil War?

Refer to Text ▶ ▶ ▶ ▶ ▶	Reason with Text	
1a. To what does Lee attribute the South's defeat?	**1b.** Explain what Lee wants his soldiers to understand.	**Understand** Find meaning
2a. Why has Lee decided to surrender? What terms has he negotiated for the surrender of his troops?	**2b.** Suggest how this letter might have influenced the feelings of Southerners toward Confederate troops.	**Apply** Use information
3a. Identify the words and phrases Lee uses to underscore his evaluation of his troops' performance.	**3b.** Compare Lee's reference to Confederate soldiers' sacrifice with Lincoln's reference to Union soldiers' sacrifice in his Letter to Mrs. Bixby. How are they alike and different?	**Analyze** Take things apart
4a. According to Lee, how have his soldiers treated him?	**4b.** Assess what the letter reveals about Lee personally.	**Evaluate** Make judgments
5a. How many years have Lee's soldiers been with him? What have they experienced together?	**5b.** Summarize Lee's purpose in writing this letter.	**Create** Bring ideas together

Analyze Literature

Purpose and Tone
What purposes does Lee have for writing? What does he want his soldiers to understand? Analyze how well he achieves these goals.

What is the overall tone of the letter? What words and images suggest this tone? Is this tone suitable for both the occasion and Lee's purposes in writing? Why or why not?

Extend the Text

Writing Options
Creative Writing Imagine that you are a Confederate soldier, fighting in General Lee's army. Write a personal letter from the battlefront to your family, sweetheart, or friend. What details and feelings will you include? What tone will you adopt?

Expository Writing Write two compare-and-contrast paragraphs. In the first paragraph, tell what a military recruiter in the midnineteenth century might have said to persuade a young person to volunteer for military service. In the second paragraph, tell what a military recruiter in the early twenty-first century might say to enlist new recruits.

Media Literacy
Make a Museum Catalog Museums often publish catalogs that provide information about the paintings, sculptures, and artifacts in an exhibit. Make a catalog for visitors to a Civil War museum. List items (such as uniforms) that visitors might see, along with a brief description of each item. If possible, include photos or sketches. Think about what view of war you want the exhibit to present. Display your catalog in the classroom.

Lifelong Learning
Interview a War Veteran Interview someone who fought in a war. (You can contact the American Legion or Veterans of Foreign Wars to locate interviewees.) To prepare for the interview, research the war to find out where it was fought and for what purpose. Prepare questions that ask about the veteran's role in the war and memories of serving. In conducting the interview, be sensitive to the veteran's feelings. There may be some things he or she does not want to discuss. After the interview, write a letter thanking the veteran for his or her service to the country.

 Go to **www.mirrorsandwindows.com** for more.

from
Incidents in the Life of a Slave Girl, Seven Years Concealed
by Harriet Jacobs (Linda Brent)

Harriet Jacobs (1813–1897) was born a slave in Edenton, North Carolina. Following the death of a kind mistress, Jacobs became the property of a young girl, whose father harassed her for seven years, beginning in her midteens. In 1835, at age twenty-two, Jacobs and her children escaped and lived for another seven years in a hidden crawl space, coming out only at night for exercise. In 1842, Jacobs fled to Philadelphia and then to New York, where she worked as a nurse maid and was reunited with several family members, also fugitive slaves.

Encouraged by abolitionist friends, Jacobs published her account of her experiences as a slave, writing under the pseudonym Linda Brent. *Incidents in the Life of a Slave Girl, Seven Years Concealed* was condemned by some abolitionists on moral grounds because it expressed a young woman's perspective on the mistreatment of slaves.

I. CHILDHOOD

I was born a slave; but I never knew it till six years of happy childhood had passed away. My father was a carpenter, and considered so intelligent and skillful in his trade, that, when buildings out of the common line were to be erected, he was sent for from long distances, to be head workman. On condition of paying his mistress two hundred dollars a year, and supporting himself, he was allowed to work at his trade, and manage his own affairs. His strongest wish was to purchase his children; but, though he several times offered his hard earnings for that purpose, he never succeeded. In complexion my parents were a light shade of brownish yellow, and were termed mulattoes.[1] They lived together in a comfortable home; and, though we were all slaves, I was so fondly shielded that I never dreamed I was a piece of merchandise, trusted to them for safe keeping, and liable to be demanded of them at any moment. I had one brother, William, who was two years younger than myself—a bright, affectionate child. I had also a great treasure in my maternal grandmother, who was a remarkable woman in many respects. She was the daughter of a planter in South Carolina, who, at his death, left her mother and his three children free, with money to go to St. Augustine, where they had relatives. It was during the Revolutionary War; and they were captured on their passage, carried back, and sold to different purchasers. Such was the story my grandmother used to tell me; but I do not remember all the particulars. She was a little girl when she was captured and sold to the keeper of a large hotel. I have often heard her tell how hard she fared during childhood. But as she grew older she evinced[2] so much intelligence, and was so faithful,

---

1. **mulattoes.** Persons of mixed white and African-American ancestry
2. **evinced.** Displayed clearly

A Visit from the Old Mistress, 1876. Winslow Homer.
Smithsonian American Art Museum, Washington, DC.

that her master and mistress could not help seeing it was for their interest to take care of such a valuable piece of property. She became an indispensable personage in the household, officiating in all capacities, from cook and wet nurse[3] to seamstress. She was much praised for her cooking; and her nice crackers became so famous in the neighborhood that many people were desirous of obtaining them. In consequence of numerous requests of this kind, she asked permission of her mistress to bake crackers at night, after all the household work was done; and she obtained leave to do it, provided she would clothe herself and her children from the profits. Upon these terms, after working hard all day for her mistress, she began her midnight baking, assisted by her two oldest children. The business proved profitable; and each year she laid by a little, which was saved for a fund to purchase her children. Her master died, and the property was divided among his heirs. The widow had her dower[4] in the hotel which she continued to keep open. My grandmother remained in her service as a slave; but her children were divided among her master's children. As she had five, Benjamin, the young-

est one, was sold, in order that each heir might have an equal portion of dollars and cents. There was so little difference in our ages that he seemed more like my brother than my uncle. He was a bright, handsome lad, nearly white; for he inherited the complexion my grandmother had derived from Anglo-Saxon ancestors. Though only ten years old, seven hundred and twenty dollars were paid for him. His sale was a terrible blow to my grandmother; but she was naturally hopeful, and she went to work with renewed energy, trusting in time to be able to purchase some of her children. She had laid up three hundred dollars, which her mistress one day begged as a loan, promising to pay her soon. The reader probably knows that no promise or writing given to a slave is legally binding; for, according to Southern laws, a slave, being property, can hold no property. When my grandmother lent her hard earnings to her mistress, she trusted solely to her honor. The honor of a slaveholder to a slave!

To this good grandmother I was indebted for many comforts. My brother Willie and I often received portions of the crackers, cakes, and preserves, she made to sell; and after we ceased to be children we were indebted to her for many more important services.

Such were the unusually fortunate circumstances of my early childhood. When I was six years old, my mother died; and then, for the first time, I learned, by the talk around me, that I was a slave. My mother's mistress was the daughter of my grandmother's mistress. She was the foster sister of my mother; they were both nourished at my grandmother's breast.

---

3. **wet nurse.** Woman who cares for and suckles infants not her own
4. **dower.** Part of or interest in the real estate of a deceased husband given by law to his widow

Winslow Homer

Winslow Homer (1836–1910), one of the most well-known American artists, began his career as an illustrator for the magazine *Harper's Weekly*. During the Civil War, he composed warfront illustrations for the magazine based on his experiences living among the soldiers. He also expressed many of the scenes he witnessed using watercolors and canvasses, rather than sketches and illustrations, including the painting of African-American slaves on page 311. This period marked Homer's transformation from a freelance illustrator to a serious painter.

In contrast to most American painters, Homer was entirely self-taught. Moreover, he developed a unique artistic style at a time when painting worldwide was dominated by Impressionism. Begun in Paris in the 1860s, Impressionism was a style in which artists used unmixed colors and rough brush strokes to capture a momentary image, creating an overall sensation rather than a detailed replica.

In sharp contrast to Impressionist paintings, Homer's work generally is objective and ultrarealistic, combining clean outlines with clear contrasts of color to create images that mirror the real world almost perfectly. Homer's subjects span from majestic landscapes to idyllic rural scenes, but all his paintings portray simple concepts in a straightforward manner.

Critical Viewing Homer belonged to a well-known artists' society called the Tile Club, which met every Wednesday to discuss their work. Many of the group's members appreciated Homer's ability to see beauty within simple subjects, but some were critical of his content, finding it too common and even boorish. Review several other paintings of Winslow Homer on pages 268, 379, and 463. What do you think of the subjects Homer chose to paint? Are his paintings interesting or dull?

In fact, my mother had been weaned[5] at three months old, that the babe of the mistress might obtain sufficient food. They played together as children; and, when they became women, my mother was a most faithful servant to her whiter foster sister. On her death-bed her mistress promised that her children should never suffer for any thing; and during her lifetime she kept her word. They all spoke kindly of my dead mother, who had been a slave merely in name, but in nature was noble and womanly. I grieved for her, and my young mind was troubled with the thought who would now take care of me and my little brother. I was told that my home was now to be with her mistress; and I found it a happy one. No toilsome or disagreeable duties were imposed on me. My mistress was so kind to me that I was always glad to do her bidding, and proud to labor for her as much as my young years would permit. I would sit by her side for hours, sewing diligently, with a heart as free from care as that of

any free-born white child. When she thought I was tired, she would send me out to run and jump; and away I bounded, to gather berries or flowers to decorate her room. Those were happy days—too happy to last. The slave child had no thought for the morrow; but there came that blight, which too surely waits on every human being born to be a chattel.[6]

When I was nearly twelve years old, my kind mistress sickened and died. As I saw the cheek grow paler, and the eye more glassy, how earnestly I prayed in my heart that she might live! I loved her; for she had been almost like a mother to me. My prayers were not answered. She died, and they buried her in the little churchyard, where, day after day, my tears fell upon her grave.

I was sent to spend a week with my grandmother. I was now old enough to begin to

---

5. **weaned.** Accustomed a child to take food other than by nursing
6. **chattel.** Movable property

think of the future; and again and again I asked myself what they would do with me. I felt sure I should never find another mistress so kind as the one who was gone. She had promised my dying mother that her children should never suffer for any thing; and when I remembered that, and recalled her many proofs of attachment to me, I could not help having some hopes that she had left me free. My friends were almost certain it would be so. They thought she would be sure to do it, on account of my mother's love and faithful service. But, alas! we all know that the memory of a faithful slave does not avail[7] much to save her children from the auction block.

After a brief period of suspense, the will of my mistress was read, and we learned that she had bequeathed[8] me to her sister's daughter, a child of five years old. So vanished our hopes. My mistress had taught me the precepts[9] of God's Word: "Thou shalt love thy neighbor as thyself." "Whatsoever ye would that men should do unto you, do ye even so unto them." But I was her slave, and I suppose she did not recognize me as her neighbor. I would give much to blot out from my memory that one great wrong. As a child, I loved my mistress; and, looking back on the happy days I spent with her, I try to think with less bitterness of this act of injustice. While I was with her, she taught me to read and spell; and for this privilege, which so rarely falls to the lot of a slave, I bless her memory.

She possessed but few slaves; and at her death those were all distributed among her relatives. Five of them were my grandmother's children, and had shared the same milk that nourished her mother's children. Notwithstanding my grandmother's long and faithful service to her owners, not one of her children escaped the auction block. These God-breathing machines are no more, in the sight of their masters, than the cotton they plant, or the horses they tend. ❖

---

7. **avail.** Be of advantage or result in
8. **bequeathed.** Gave or left by will, especially personal property
9. **precepts.** Principles

Unlike most slaves, Jacobs knew something about her roots. What do you know about your family's roots, and what does it mean to you?

Refer and Reason

1. At a young age, Harriet Jacobs learned that white people regarded her as chattel, or merchandise. Explain how this revelation might have affected her self-image.

2. What was remarkable about Jacobs's grandmother? Infer why Jacobs and her family might have enjoyed privileges that other slaves did not receive.

3. Why did Jacobs expect that her mistress would set her free? Why isn't she more critical of her mistress?

Writing Options

1. Based on the information given about Jacobs's grandmother, write a script for a scene based on when her mistress borrowed money from her and did not return it.

2. Write one paragraph explaining why Jacobs did not know she was a slave until she was six years old. How might that have shaped her personality and outlook on life? Use evidence from the text to support your answer.

 Go to **www.mirrorsandwindows.com** for more.

Understand the Concept

Transitions are words and phrases that provide logical connections in writing, usually between two clauses or two sentences. Using transitions improves the *coherence* of writing, linking ideas for readers and thus improving their understanding.

EXAMPLES

The North's military strategy was to block the Southern ports, to control the Mississippi River, and to capture the Confederate capital of Richmond. *In contrast,* the South planned to hold as much of its territory as possible until the North grew tired of fighting. [*In contrast,* followed by a comma, shows the shift in topic from North to South and points to the difference in strategies.]

Although people on both sides expected the war to be over in a short time, it lasted five long years. [*Although* shows that what people expected did not match the reality.]

To use transitions effectively, choose the words and phrases that provide the meanings you want. Here are some of the most commonly used transitions and their meanings:

To show contrast   However, Instead, In contrast, Although

To show comparison   Also, Likewise, Similarly, In comparison

To show time or sequence   Next, First, second, . . . , In addition, Finally

To introduce details and examples   For example, For instance, Specifically, Namely

To summarize or conclude   In conclusion, In summary, Therefore, Consequently

To show cause and effect   As a result, Since, Because, Accordingly

Apply the Skill

Identify Transitions

In the following paragraph, identify the transitional words and phrases and determine what meaning each one signals.

Most historians agree that the Civil War era was the most tragic in U.S. history. Specifically, the war caused a crisis of ideals that divided Americans and resulted in a tremendous loss of life and destruction of property. An estimated 623,000 troops died during the war, and another 300,000 Americans were wounded or killed. In the end, the Civil War cost an estimated $15 billion. It seems ironic, therefore, that this tragic period produced no literary masterpiece about the war.

Use Transitions Correctly

From the examples of commonly used transitions in column 1, choose the best word or phrase to link the two clauses or two sentences in each of the following numbered items. Be sure to use proper punctuation and capitalization.

1. Americans recorded their experiences by writing letters. Robert E. Lee wrote letters to document his military campaigns.
2. Soldiers wrote letters to their loved ones at home. Many of these letters were not delivered until after the soldiers had been killed.
3. Newspapers and magazines were important sources of information during the Civil War; they provided entertainment.
4. These publications often printed stories and novels in serial installments. Harriet Beecher Stowe's novel *Uncle Tom's Cabin* was first published as a serial in an abolitionist newspaper.
5. Stowe's novel has been criticized for its sentimental and perhaps stereotypical treatment of slaves; its historic impact cannot be overlooked.

PART 2

Lyric Poets

While the American poetic tradition was naturally influenced by its European ancestors, nineteenth-century poetry underwent a significant change as a result of industrialism and the Civil War. A modern consciousness was emerging, and it produced a new literature. Whereas earlier poets described the world in sentimental terms, a new generation addressed life's realities.

Walt Whitman and Emily Dickinson were key figures in this new generation of poets. Both observed and wrote about everyday life, producing primarily **lyric poetry,** which expresses the emotions of the speaker. Both also broke with traditional forms to lay the foundation for a truly American approach to poetry.

Although Whitman and Dickinson lived nearly identical life spans, they were opposites in terms of lifestyle and personality. Whitman was a public figure and something of a spokesperson for his time. Dickinson, on the other hand, lived a quiet life among a small circle of family and friends; few people even knew of her poetry during her lifetime.

Whitman's legacy as a poet lies in his use of **free verse:** poetry that does not use regular rhyme, meter, or stanza division. His work is characterized by long, rambling lines that imitate the natural patterns and rhythms of speech. In contrast, Emily Dickinson is known for an economy of expression; she created vivid, concrete images with carefully chosen, sometimes idiosyncratic words. She also experimented with language, defying conventions of punctuation, capitalization, and grammar.

Poppies on the Isles of Shoals, 1890. Childe Hassam. Brooklyn Museum of Art, Brooklyn, New York.

Poetry Defined

Poetry is a major genre of literature and includes narrative, dramatic, and lyric poems. It features imaginative language that is carefully chosen and arranged to communicate experiences, thoughts, and emotions. Poetry differs from **prose** in that it compresses meaning into fewer words and often uses meter, rhyme, and imagery. Although conventional poetry adheres strictly to meter and rhyme, much modern and contemporary poetry has an innovative, experimental quality.

A **lyric poem** is a highly musical type of poetry that expresses the emotions of a speaker. In form, the lyric usually relies on a regular metrical pattern or a combination of patterns. Lyric poems can be contrasted with **narrative poems,** which have storytelling as their main purpose. Lyric poems also can be contrasted with **dramatic poems,** which rely heavily on dramatic elements such as *monologue* (speech by a single character) and *dialogue* (conversation involving two or more characters).

The **themes** of lyric poetry are as varied as love and loss, war and peace, and religion and nature. Some lyric poems are **elegies,** mourning the dead in the manner of Walt Whitman's "O Captain! My Captain!" which was composed after the assassination of President Abraham Lincoln. Another lyric form is the **ode,** a poem on a serious theme, usually with varying line lengths and complex stanzas.

Lyric Poetry in American Literature

The lyric poems of Walt Whitman and Emily Dickinson were written in an era when Romanticism was slowly giving way to Realism in literature. As Chilean poet Pablo Neruda's "Ode to Walt Whitman" implies, Whitman tried to see what was extraordinary about humanity. He still nurtured the idealism of a Romantic, but he broke with poetic conventions, paying little attention to strict meter and form. Dickinson's strong connection to nature marks her as a fellow Romantic, but the sentiment in her work is undercut by a strong sense of Realism. This, along with her experimental use of form, demonstrates her modern consciousness.

Much of Whitman's poetry explores his individualism in relation to society; in his "Preface" to *Leaves of Grass,* he proclaims, "The United States themselves are essentially the greatest poem." To celebrate the nation, Whitman composed his *Leaves of Grass* as a "lyric-epic," an open form characterized by **free verse,** what he called his "language experiment." Dickinson, on the other hand, examines the self and its sensitive response to all it encounters. She writes, "I find ecstasy in living—the mere sense of living is joy enough."

> *"If I read a book [and] it makes my whole body so cold no fire can ever warm me I know that is poetry. If I feel physically as if the top of my head were taken off, I know that is poetry."*
>
> —EMILY DICKINSON

Elements of Poetry

Form and Structure

Form refers to the organization of the parts of a poem. You can look at poetic form broadly, asking yourself several questions: What type of poem is this? Is it a lyrical ode, an elegy, or perhaps an example of free verse? Next, you can analyze the poem's structure—how the author has arranged the lines on the page. Some poems have a continuous form; most, however, are divided into stanzas, which are similar to the paragraphs of prose. The **stanza,** a group of lines in a poem, varies in average length from two to eight lines.

Examining a stanza, you will notice the presence or absence of a **rhyme scheme.** The rhyme scheme is the pattern of **end rhymes,** or rhyming words at the ends of lines of verse. Even poems without exact end rhyme may include **slant rhyme,** in which the rhyming sounds are similar but not identical, or **internal rhyme,** the use of rhyming words within lines.

Digging deeper, you can analyze the grammar, syntax, and punctuation of the poem. Dickinson's poetry displays two idiosyncratic features: her use of dashes and her use of capital letters to stress certain

WHITMAN **DICKINSON**

words. Dickinson also frequently uses **enjambment,** continuing a statement beyond the end of a line, rather than the *end-stopped* line of verse, in which both the sense and the grammar are complete at the end of the line. She writes, "Because I could not stop for Death— / He kindly stopped for me—" rather than retaining the grammatical unit of the sentence.

In Whitman's poetry, you will find plenty of evidence of the experimental method through which he tried to express the dynamic character of a nation and an era. Literary critics have noted that his stanzas form a wavelike pattern, in which lines expand and contract. Whitman also incorporated into his poems **catalogs,** or lists of items, as you will see in the excerpt from "Song of Myself."

Meter and Rhythm

Meter is a regular rhythmic pattern in poetry. A poem's meter creates **rhythm,** the pattern of beats or stresses in a line of verse or prose. Rhythm can be regular or irregular. The metrical pattern is determined by the number of beats, or stresses, in each line. Stressed and unstressed syllables are divided into rhythmical units called **feet.**

Also look for the pattern of ideas and images that hold the poem together. Many poets use **figurative language**—writing or speech that is meant to be understood imaginatively instead of literally—to help readers to see things in new ways. Types of figurative language include **hyperbole, metaphor, personification, simile,** and **understatement.** Neruda uses personification when he says of Whitman, "He made me see how the high mountain tutors us." In "Because I could not stop for death—" Dickinson personifies death as a polite gentleman: "He knew no haste." The entire poem is an **extended metaphor,** in which Death is characterized as a carriage driver and the speaker of the poem as his passenger. Whitman uses hyperbole when he claims, "The narrowest hinge in my hand puts to scorn all machinery."

Sound Devices

Poets use a variety of sound devices to create and enhance meaning. **Repetition** is a writer's intentional reuse of a sound, word, phrase, or sentence. Writers often use repetition to emphasize ideas or, especially in poetry, to create musical effects; a *refrain* is found in many lyric poems. **Alliteration** is the repetition of an initial consonant sound, as in "the cow crunching" and "a mouse is a miracle." **Assonance** is the repetition of vowel sounds in stressed syllables that end with different consonant sounds. An example is the repetition in Dickinson's "Because I could not stop for Death—" of the long *a* sound: "We passed the fields of Gazing Grain—."

HOW TO READ

Poetry

Read the poem aloud. Many of the elements of poetry—including rhythm, meter, and sound devices—are best realized by reading a poem aloud. Doing so will let you hear and feel how the language is used, which is key both to understanding and appreciating poetry.

Visualize. Because poems often contain sensory details, they lend themselves well to visualization. Create images in your mind, using your senses to see, hear, smell, feel, and taste the poem.

Make inferences. Unlike other types of writing, poetry doesn't allow much room for explanation. To understand a poem, make inferences, or put together the clues given in the poem with your own prior knowledge.

Ask questions. As you read a poem, write down the words and phrases you don't understand. Also jot down questions you may have about imagery, form, rhyme, or other elements. Discuss your questions with your classmates and/or teacher.

Compare and contrast. The possibilities for comparing and contrasting poems are wide and varied. Doing so can help you better understand poetic forms, figurative language, themes, historical context, and authors. You can also identify what you like and dislike in poetry.

Walt Whitman

"I sound my barbaric yawp over the roofs of the world."

Walt Whitman (1819–1892) is considered by many to be the greatest of all American poets. The son of a Long Island farmer who turned carpenter and moved his family to Brooklyn in 1823, Whitman left school at age eleven to work as an office boy. By twelve, he was working in the printing office of a newspaper. By fifteen, he was on his own. In his mid-teens, he contributed pieces to a Manhattan newspaper and attended debating societies. After working as a journeyman printer, Whitman returned home, where he taught school and continued to work on newspapers.

Later in his life, Whitman held various newspaper positions, including reviewer of books, musicals, and theater events. As a newspaper man, he got to know people of all social classes. He purposefully placed himself at the center of political battles over slavery, territorial expansion, the Mexican War, sectionalism, free trade, states' rights, worker strife, and the new market economy. He believed in the idea of using poetry as a form of political action.

Always self-taught, Whitman began to write full time. His rise to fame was slow, and at times his poetry drew harsh criticism. Ralph Waldo Emerson was one of the few intellectuals to praise Whitman's work, writing him a famous congratu-latory letter. In an 1882 review in the *New York Examiner,* one critic said, "Walt Whitman is a great poet—in his own estimation, and in that of critics who make up in noise what they lack in numbers."

During the Civil War, Whitman worked as a volunteer hospital nurse in Washington, an experience that made him well loved by the American public. *Drum-Taps* and "When Lilacs Last in the Dooryard Bloom'd" are the two great products of Whitman's wartime years. Among his best work after the war are his prose collections *Specimen Days* and *Democratic Vistas,* in which he scorned an America "canker'd, crude, superstitious and rotten"—a nation he esteemed had failed all the common laborers and favored the wealthy.

Whitman worked in several government departments until he suffered a stroke in 1873. He spent the rest of his life in Camden, New Jersey, where he continued to write poems and articles. He was a major influence on later poets, inspiring them to experiment with metrical structure as well as subject matter.

Noted Works

Leaves of Grass (1855–1891, nine editions, poetry)

Drum Taps; Sequel to Drum Taps (1865, poetry)

Democratic Vistas (1871, prose)

Memoranda During the War (1875, prose)

Specimen Days (1882, prose)

November Boughs (1888, poetry)

from **Preface to Leaves of Grass**

A Preface by Walt Whitman

from **I Hear America Singing**

A Lyric Poem by Walt Whitman

Build Background

Literary Context Unconventional in both content and technique, **Leaves of Grass** is probably the most influential volume of poems in the history of American literature. It is the book of poetry for which Walt Whitman is best known.

Whitman spent his entire life revising and adding to *Leaves of Grass,* producing at least nine editions. He released the first edition, containing just twelve poems, on July 4, 1855, after having designed the cover and typesetting most of the book himself. He then released two larger editions in 1856 and 1860 and another edition containing Civil War poems in 1865. The final volume edited by Whitman, containing more than 300 poems, was published in 1892, the year of his death.

Although *Leaves of Grass* was a commercial failure, critics generally recognized Whitman as a bold new voice in poetry. Ralph Waldo Emerson called the book "the most extraordinary piece of wit and wisdom America has yet contributed." Some, however, did not like Whitman's use of free verse in long rhythmical lines with a natural, organic structure.

The 1855 edition of *Leaves of Grass* is the only one for which Whitman wrote a *preface,* or introduction. In it, he presented many of his opinions and beliefs, hoping to enlighten the American people and regenerate the ideals of the American republic. At that time, the United States was a young nation and just beginning to establish an identity separate from that of Europe. The following excerpt highlights Whitman's passion for American democracy and the common man and woman. Although written in prose format, the Preface is lyrical, or musical, in style and contains elements of free verse.

"I Hear America Singing" is one of the most famous poems from *Leaves of Grass.* It, too, celebrates the common man and woman. In this poem, Whitman salutes working-class people who take pride in their occupations. The poem is written in free verse and contains examples of Whitman's evocative word choice.

Reader's Context What do you like about living in the United States? What don't you like? Explain your answers.

Analyze Literature

Romanticism and Free Verse
Romanticism was a literary and artistic movement of the eighteenth and nineteenth centuries that placed value on emotion or imagination over reason, the individual over society, and freedom over authority.

Free verse is poetry that does not use regular rhyme, meter, or stanza division.

Set Purpose

In his day, Whitman sometimes was criticized for being unconventional. In reading Whitman's preface and poem, look for conventional Romantic elements, including his idealism and passion for America and Americans. Also look for ways Whitman broke from convention—for instance, his use of free verse.

Preview Vocabulary

stalwart, 320
teeming, 320
nonchalance, 320
disdain, 320
audacity, 320
prolific, 320
picturesque, 321
novelty, 321
susceptibility, 321
mason, 322
robust, 322

from Preface to *Leaves of Grass*

by Walt Whitman

The President's taking off his hat to them, not they to him.

America does not repel the past or what it has produced under its forms or amid other politics or the idea of castes or the old religions . . . accepts the lesson with calmness . . . is not so impatient as has been supposed that the slough still sticks to opinions and manners and literature while the life which served its requirements has passed into the new life of the new forms . . . perceives that the corpse is slowly borne from the eating and sleeping rooms of the house . . . perceives that it waits a little while in the door . . . that it was fittest for its days . . . that its action has descended to the <u>stalwart</u> and well shaped heir who

> **stal • wart** (stäl´ wʉrt) *adj.*, brave; hardy

approaches . . . and that he shall be fittest for his days.

The Americans of all nations at any time upon the earth, have probably the fullest poetical nature. The United States themselves are essentially the greatest poem. In the history of the earth hitherto the largest and most stirring appear tame and orderly to their ampler largeness and stir. Here at last is something in the doings of man that corresponds with the broadcast doings of the day and night. Here is not merely a nation but a <u>teeming</u> nation of nations. Here is action untied from strings necessarily blind to particulars and details magnificently moving in vast masses. Here is the hospitality which forever indicates heroes. . . . Here are the roughs[1] and beards and space and ruggedness and <u>nonchalance</u> that the soul loves. Here the performance <u>disdaining</u> the trivial unapproached in the tremendous <u>audacity</u> of its crowds and groupings and the push of its perspective spreads with crampless and flowing breadth and showers its <u>prolific</u> and splendid extravagance. One sees it must indeed own the riches of the summer and winter, and need never be bankrupt while corn grows from the ground or the orchards drop apples or the bays contain fish or men beget children upon women.

Other states indicate themselves in their deputies . . . but the genius of the United States is not best or most in its executives or legislatures, nor in its ambassadors or authors or colleges or churches or parlors, nor even in its newspapers or inventors . . . but always most in the common people. Their manners, speech, dress, friendship—the freshness and candor of their physiognomy[2]—the <u>picturesque</u> looseness of their carriage[3] . . . their deathless attachment to freedom—their aversion to anything indecorous[4] or soft or mean—the practical acknowledgment of the citizens of one state by the citizens of all other states—the fierceness of their roused resentment—their curiosity and welcome of <u>novelty</u>—their self-esteem and wonderful sympathy—their <u>susceptibility</u> to a slight[5]—the air they have of persons who never knew how it felt to stand in the presence of superiors—the fluency of their speech—their delight in music, the sure symptom of manly tenderness and native elegance of soul . . . their good temper and open handedness—the terrible significance of their elections—the President's taking off his hat to them, not they to him—these too are unrhymed poetry. It awaits the gigantic and generous treatment worthy of it. ❖

---

1. **roughs.** People accustomed to living in the wilds
2. **physiognomy.** Outward appearance or features that provide clues to a person's character
3. **carriage.** Posture; manner of carrying oneself
4. **indecorous.** Conflicting with standards of proper conduct or good taste
5. **slight.** Instance of being disregarded or insulted

teem • ing (tēm´ iŋ) *adj.*, overflowing; abounding
non • cha • lance (nôn shə läns´) *n.*, state of being seemingly unconcerned; coolness
dis • dain (dis dān´) *v.*, treat as unworthy
au • dac • i • ty (ô da´ sə tē) *n.*, boldness; daring
pro • lif • ic (prə li´ fik) *adj.*, creating abundant growth
pic • tur • esque (pik´ chər resk´) *adj.*, resembling a picture; charming or quaint
nov • el • ty (nä´ vəl tē) *n.*, something new or unusual
sus • cep • ti • bil • i • ty (sə sep tə bi´ lə tē) *n.*, sensitivity

MIRRORS & WINDOWS

In the 1855 preface, Whitman boasts that America is unique from other nations. Do you agree with his assessment?

from *I Hear America Singing*

by Walt Whitman

I hear America singing, the varied carols I hear;
Those of mechanics—each one singing his, as it
    should be, blithe[1] and strong;
The carpenter singing his, as he measures his
    plank or beam,
The <u>mason</u> singing his, as he makes ready for
    work, or leaves off work;
5 The boatman singing what belongs to him in
    his boat—the deckhand singing on the
    steamboat deck;
The shoemaker singing as he sits on his bench—
    the hatter singing as he stands;
The wood-cutter's song—the ploughboy's, on
    his way in the morning, or at the noon
    intermission, or at sundown;
The delicious singing of the mother—or of the
    young wife at work—or of the girl sewing
    or washing—Each singing what belongs to
    her, and to none else;
The day what belongs to the day—At night, the
    party of young fellows, <u>robust</u>, friendly,
10 Singing, with open mouths, their strong
    melodious songs. ❖

---

1. **blithe.** Happy; lighthearted

> **ma • son** (māˊ sən) *n.,* a skilled worker in brick and stone
> **ro • bust** (rō bustˊ) *adj.,* full of health and strength; vigorous

 **MIRRORS & WINDOWS** In his poem "I Hear America Singing," Whitman praises common laborers. Today, we might call them *blue-collar workers.* Do you value this type of work? Would you like to do this kind of work?

Refer to Text ▶ ▶ ▶ ▶ ▶ **Reason with Text**

1a. In the Preface to *Leaves of Grass*, to what does Whitman compare the United States?

1b. Discuss why Whitman believes that Americans have a poetical nature.

Understand
Find meaning

2a. What do the words *blithe* and *strong* in "I Hear America Singing" suggest about the feelings people have toward their work?

2b. Do most workers today feel happy about their jobs? Explain.

Apply
Use information

3a. List the different workers Whitman includes in his poem. How are the workers alike? How are they different?

3b. When Whitman celebrated the diversity of the American workforce, do you think he had workers of different races and ethnicities in mind as well? Why or why not?

Analyze
Take things apart

4a. What advantages does America have that other nations may not?

4b. Consider that in 1855, the United States was divided on the issue of slavery. Argue whether Whitman was justified in portraying the country in such positive tones.

Evaluate
Make judgments

5a. State the message Whitman conveys through his catalog of workers.

5b. Make a list of workers that Whitman might celebrate if he were writing his poem today.

Create
Bring ideas together

Analyze Literature

Romanticism and Free Verse
Which elements of Romanticism did you find in the preface to *Leaves of Grass* and "I Hear America Singing"? Do you think that laborers in the nineteenth century were as content as Whitman portrays them? Why or why not?

What elements of free verse are included in the Preface to *Leaves of Grass?* Why is "I Hear America Singing" an example of free verse?

Extend the Text

Writing Options
Creative Writing Your firm has been hired to create a campaign promoting American workers. Your duty is to write a jingle, a short, catchy poem or verse set to music. Write a simple jingle, and try it out on family and friends.

Descriptive Writing Write an essay describing how you feel about living in your country. Include what you like about living in this country and what you do not like. Use real-life experiences to support your opinions.

Lifelong Learning
Write a Job Description Since 1937, the United States has had official poet laureates. Imagine that you have been asked to help select the nation's next poet. Find out what a poet laureate does and how he or she

is chosen (see the Literary Connection in Unit 9, page 1285). Learn about the accomplishments of previous poet laureates. Then write a job description, including qualifications for the position and duties and responsibilities.

Collaborative Learning
Make a Time Line Whitman published the first edition of *Leaves of Grass* in 1855 and issued at least eight other editions over the next forty years. With a partner, make a time line showing the year of publication for each major edition. Next to each year, briefly note what was happening in the United States at the time. You might also include photos of Whitman and historical events (available on the Internet). Present your completed time line to the rest of the class.

 Go to **www.mirrorsandwindows.com** for more.

VOCABULARY & SPELLING
SUFFIXES

Understand the Concept

Recall from Unit 1 that a **suffix** is a group of letters that attaches to the end of a word (called a **root word**) and alters its meaning. Knowing how specific suffixes change word meanings will help you make sense of unfamiliar words in your reading and expand your own vocabulary.

Several suffixes are used to indicate people who perform certain jobs or are experts in certain areas. The most common are *-er* and *-or,* as in *teacher* and *inventor.* Others include *-ist* (*chemist*), *-ian* (*beautician*), and *-ant/-ent* (*attendant, superintendent*).

Suffixes for workers may be added to nouns or verbs and sometimes adjectives. Adding a suffix may mean a spelling change, such as doubling a final consonant, dropping a silent *e,* or changing *y* to *i.*

EXAMPLES

supervise (verb) + *-or* = *supervisor* (a person who supervises)

franchise (noun) + *-er* = *franchiser* (a person who owns or operates a franchise, such as a fast-food restaurant)

pharmacy (noun) + *-ist* = *pharmacist* (a person who works in a pharmacy)

technical (adjective) + *-ian* = *technician* (a specialist in the technical details of an occupation, such as a computer technician)

In some cases, the spelling of the root word may change, or the root word may be based on a foreign spelling. For example, a *vintner* is a person who makes or sells wine *(vino).*

Apply the Skill

Exercise A
Using your knowledge of root words and suffixes, identify the work done by each of the following people.

1. flutist
2. restaurateur
3. exterminator
4. cashier
5. lobbyist
6. assistant
7. mediator
8. lawyer
9. statistician
10. naturalist

Exercise B
Using a suffix, create the word that describes the person who does each of the following jobs. Check your spelling with a dictionary.

1. a person who plans weddings
2. an expert on healthy diets
3. a person who surveys land
4. a person who appraises the value of property
5. one who sells real estate
6. a person who gives physical therapy
7. a person who consults with businesses and organizations
8. a person who arranges and delivers flowers
9. an expert in physics
10. an expert on hair styles
11. a person who writes for newspapers or journals
12. a person who appears on TV game show contests

Exercise C
Write a paragraph about jobs you might like to have after you finish school. Use the correct suffixes for workers to name these jobs and give a brief description of each.

SPELLING PRACTICE

Consonant Blends and Digraphs

A *digraph* is a cluster of two or three consonants that together make a new sound, such as *sh* or *th.* A *consonant blend* is a cluster of consonants in which each letter maintains its original sound, such *br* or *cl.* When spelling words with consonant blends and digraphs, be sure to include each letter in the grouping. Identify the consonant blends and digraphs in these words from the Preface to *Leaves of Grass.*

acknowledgment	extravagance	presence
approaches	fluency	requirements
attachment	nonchalance	splendid
breadth	orchards	susceptibility
descended	picturesque	sympathy

from Song of Myself

A Lyric Poem by Walt Whitman

Build Background

Literary Context **"Song of Myself,"** one of Walt Whitman's most famous poems, is his effort to describe his personality, or as he put it: "one man's—the author's—identity, ardors, observations, faiths, and thoughts." This poem is the first work in *Leaves of Grass,* the collection of poetry that Whitman spent his life writing, and it well reflects the evolution of his work. In the first edition of *Leaves of Grass,* published in 1855, the poem appeared untitled. In the second edition, published just a year later, the poem was called "Poem of Walt Whitman, An American," and in the 1860 edition, it was titled simply "Walt Whitman." Whitman settled on the title "Song of Myself" in the 1881 edition of *Leaves of Grass.*

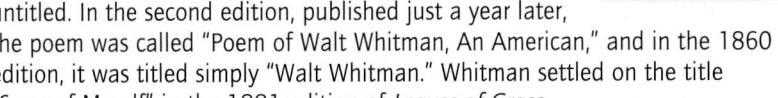

With each change to the title of the poem, Whitman also reworked and expanded its meaning, eventually writing fifty-two sections. The selected sections that follow exemplify all the themes for which Whitman is best known: his belief that insignificant, lowly subjects are in fact worthy of poetry; his democratic celebration of the common people; and his love of natural and animal pleasure. All of these themes are summed up in the *grass,* the symbol central to his life work.

Like all the poems in *Leaves of Grass,* "Song of Myself" is written in free verse: It does not fit into any planned form, and it has no regular pattern of rhyme, meter, or stanza length. To Whitman, the poet provides the energy necessary to the growth of a poem, but it develops spontaneously, in largely unpredictable ways.

WORDSWORTH

In writing "Song of Myself," Whitman was participating in the Romantic tradition of autobiographical verse that began in the late 1700s with English poet William Wordsworth's *The Prelude.* Similarly, Whitman's love of common speech and exaltation of lowly objects into poetic subjects was a doctrine first voiced in Wordsworth's Preface to *Lyrical Ballads.* Although Whitman followed in the tradition of English Romantic poets, his work has a distinctly American flavor.

Reader's Context When have you felt especially good about yourself? When have you felt connected to other people and to nature?

See the Author Focus on page 318 for biographical information about Walt Whitman.

Analyze Literature

Symbol and Elaboration
A **symbol** is something that stands for or represents both itself and something else.

Elaboration is a writing technique in which a subject is introduced and then expanded on by repetition with slight changes, the addition of details, or similar devices.

Set Purpose

As the first poem in Whitman's landmark collection *Leaves of Grass,* "Song of Myself" appropriately uses *grass* as a symbol to explore themes of nature, humanity, and society. As you read, jot down lines from the poem about grass, such as line 5, "I lean and loafe at my ease observing a spear of summer grass." Also note Whitman's use of elaboration to examine subjects from multiple angles, including grass.

Preview Vocabulary

suffice, 327
harbor, 327
indifference, 327
complacent, 327
impalpable, 327
linguist, 327
contender, 327
disposition, 328
infidel, 330
quadruped, 330
fissure, 331

Boy Sitting in the Grass, c. 1882. Georges Seurat.
Glasgow Art Gallery and Museum, Scotland. (See detail on page 325.)

from Song of Myself

by Walt Whitman

1

I celebrate myself, and sing myself,
And what I assume you shall assume,
For every atom belonging to me as good belongs to you.

I loafe and invite my soul,
5   I lean and loafe at my ease observing a spear of summer grass.

My tongue, every atom of my blood, form'd from this soil, this air,
Born here of parents born here from parents the same, and their
     parents the same,
I, now thirty-seven years old in perfect health begin,
Hoping to cease not till death.

10   Creeds and schools in abeyance,[1]
Retiring back a while <u>sufficed</u> at what they are, but never forgotten,
I <u>harbor</u> for good or bad, I permit to speak at every hazard,
Nature without check with original energy.

. . .

4

Trippers and askers surround me,
15   People I meet, the effect upon me of my early life or the ward and
     city I live in, or the nation,
The latest dates, discoveries, inventions, societies, authors old and new,
My dinner, dress, associates, looks, compliments, dues,
The real or fancied <u>indifference</u> of some man or woman I love,
The sickness of one of my folks or of myself, or ill-doing or loss or
     lack of money, or depressions or exaltations,
20   Battles, the horrors of fratricidal[2] war, the fever of doubtful news,
     the fitful events;
These come to me days and nights and go from me again,
But they are not the Me myself.

Apart from the pulling and hauling stands what I am,
Stands amused, <u>complacent</u>, compassionating, idle, unitary,
25   Looks down, is erect, or bends an arm on an <u>impalpable</u> certain rest,
Looking with side-curved head curious what will come next,
Both in and out of the game and watching and wondering at it.

Backward I see in my own days where I sweated through fog with
     <u>linguists</u> and <u>contenders</u>,
I have no mockings or arguments, I witness and wait.

. . .

---

1. **abeyance.** Temporary suspension, as of an activity or function
2. **fratricidal.** Characterized by the killing of a sibling or someone who is like a sibling

suf • fice (sə fīs´) *v.,* be enough; be sufficient or adequate
har • bor (här´ bər) *v.,* serve as, or provide, a place of protection
in • dif • fer • ence (in di´ frənts) *n.,* quality or state of being impartial or disinterested
com • pla • cent (kəm plā´ sənt) *adj.,* being unconcerned or self-satisfied
im • pal • pa • ble (im pal´ pə b'l) *adj.,* that which cannot be felt by touching
lin • guist (liŋ´ gwist) *n.,* specialist in the science of language
con • tend • er (kən ten´ dər) *n.,* one who strives or fights in competition

30 A child said *What is the grass?* fetching it to me with full hands;
How could I answer the child? I do not know what it is any more
　　than he.

I guess it must be the flag of my <u>disposition</u>, out of hopeful green
　　stuff woven.

Or I guess it is the handkerchief of the Lord,
A scented gift and remembrancer designedly dropt,
35 Bearing the owner's name someway in the corners, that we may
　　see and remark, and say *Whose?*

Or I guess the grass is itself a child, the produced babe of the
　　vegetation.

Or I guess it is a uniform hieroglyphic,[3]
And it means, Sprouting alike in broad zones and narrow zones,
Growing among black folks as among white,
40 Kanuck, Tuckahoe, Congressman, Cuff,[4] I give them the same,
　　I receive them the same.

And now it seems to me the beautiful uncut hair of graves.

Tenderly will I use you curling grass,
It may be you transpire from the breasts of young men,
It may be if I had known them I would have loved them,
45 It may be you are from old people, or from offspring taken soon
　　out of their mothers' laps,
And here you are the mothers' laps.

This grass is very dark to be from the white heads of old mothers,
Darker than the colorless beards of old men,
Dark to come from under the faint red roofs of mouths.

50 O I perceive after all so many uttering tongues,
And I perceive they do not come from the roofs of mouths for
　　nothing.

---

3. **hieroglyphic.** Picture or symbol representing a word, syllable, or sound, used by the
　ancient Egyptians and others in a system of writing
4. **Kanuck, Tuckahoe, Congressman, Cuff.** *Kanuck*—French Canadian; *Tuckahoe*—Virgin-
　ian; *Cuff*—from the African word *cuffee,* refers to African Americans

dis • po • si • tion (dis pə zi´ shən) *n.,* one's customary frame of mind

I wish I could translate the hints about the dead young men and
    women,
And the hints about old men and mothers, and the offspring taken
    soon out of their laps.

What do you think has become of the young and old men?
55 And what do you think has become of the women and children?

They are alive and well somewhere,
The smallest sprout shows there is really no death,
And if ever there was it led forward life, and does not wait at the
    end to arrest it,
And ceas'd the moment life appear'd.

60 All goes onward and outward, nothing collapses,
And to die is different from what any one supposed, and luckier.

7

Has any one supposed it lucky to be born?
I hasten to inform him or her it is just as lucky to die, and I
    know it.

I pass death with the dying and birth with the new-wash'd babe,
    and am not contain'd between my hat and boots,
65 And peruse manifold objects, no two alike and every one good,
The earth good and the stars good, and their adjuncts all good.

I am not an earth nor an adjunct of an earth,
I am the mate and companion of people, all just as immortal and
      fathomless as myself,
(They do not know how immortal, but I know.)

70   Every kind for itself and its own, for me mine male and female,
For me those that have been boys and that love women,
For me the man that is proud and feels how it stings to be
      slighted,
For me the sweet-heart and the old maid, for me mothers and the
      mothers of mothers,
For me lips that have smiled, eyes that have shed tears,
75   For me children and the begetters of children.

Undrape! you are not guilty to me, nor stale nor discarded,
I see through the broadcloth and gingham[5] whether or no,
And am around, tenacious, acquisitive, tireless, and cannot be
      shaken away.

. . .

31

I believe a leaf of grass is no less than the journey-work of the
      stars,
80   And the pismire[6] is equally perfect, and a grain of sand, and the
      egg of the wren,
And the tree-toad is a chef-d'oeuvre[7] for the highest,
And the running blackberry would adorn the parlors of heaven,
And the narrowest hinge in my hand puts to scorn all machinery,
And the cow crunching with depress'd head surpasses any statue,
85   And a mouse is miracle enough to stagger sextillions[8] of <u>infidels</u>.

I find I incorporate gneiss,[9] coal, long-threaded moss, fruits,
      grains, esculent[10] roots,
And am stucco'd with <u>quadrupeds</u> and birds all over,

---

5. **broadcloth and gingham.** *Broadcloth*—fine wool, cotton, or silk; *gingham*—cotton cloth
   woven in checks or plaids
6. **pismire.** Ant
7. **chef-d'oeuvre.** Master or culminating work
8. **sextillions.** Number represented by one followed by twenty-one zeros
9. **gneiss.** Metamorphic rock with minerals arranged in layers
10. **esculent.** Edible

in • fi • del (in´ fə del) *n.*, person who does not believe in a particular religion
quad • ru • ped (kwä´ drü ped) *n.*, animal, especially a mammal, with four feet

And have distanced what is behind me for good reasons,
But call any thing back again when I desire it.

90   In vain the speeding or shyness,
In vain the plutonic rocks[11] send their old heat against my
     approach,
In vain the mastodon retreats beneath its own powder'd bones,
In vain objects stand leagues off and assume manifold shapes,
In vain the ocean settling in hollows and the great monsters
     lying low,
95   In vain the buzzard houses herself with the sky,
In vain the snake slides through the creepers and logs,
In vain the elk takes to the inner passes of the woods,
In vain the razor-bill'd auk[12] sails far north to Labrador,[13]
I follow quickly, I ascend to the nest in the <u>fissure</u> of the cliff.

32

100   I think I could turn and live with animals, they are so placid and
     self-contain'd,
I stand and look at them long and long.

---

11. **plutonic rocks.** Rocks formed far below the surface of the earth
12. **auk.** Shore bird of northern seas with a heavy body, a short tail, and short wings used as
paddles
13. **Labrador.** Region along the Atlantic coast of northeastern Canada

fis • sure (fĭ′ zhər) *n.,* long, narrow, deep cleft or crack

They do not sweat and whine about their condition,
They do not lie awake in the dark and weep for their sins,
They do not make me sick discussing their duty to God,
105   Not one is dissatisfied, not one is demented with the mania of
      owning things,
Not one kneels to another, nor to his kind that lived thousands of
      years ago,
Not one is respectable or unhappy over the whole earth.

. . .

52

The spotted hawk swoops by and accuses me, he complains of my
      gab and my loitering.

I too am not a bit tamed, I too am untranslatable,
110   I sound my barbaric yawp[14] over the roofs of the world.

The last scud[15] of day holds back for me,
It flings my likeness after the rest and true as any on the shadow'd
      wilds,
It coaxes me to the vapor and the dusk.

I depart as air, I shake my white locks at the runaway sun,
115   I effuse[16] my flesh in eddies,[17] and drift it in lacy jags.[18]

I bequeath myself to the dirt to grow from the grass I love,
If you want me again look for me under your boot-soles.

You will hardly know who I am or what I mean,
But I shall be good health to you nevertheless,
120   And filter and fibre your blood.

Failing to fetch me at first keep encouraged,
Missing me one place search another,
I stop somewhere waiting for you. ❖

---

14. **yawp.** Loud, harsh cry or call
15. **scud.** Windblown mist or clouds
16. **effuse.** Spread out
17. **eddies.** Circular current of water or air
18. **jags.** Sharp projecting part; barb

MIRRORS & WINDOWS

"Song of Myself" might be considered Whitman's creed, or statement of beliefs about himself, about nature, and about dying. Do you share any of his beliefs?

Refer to Text ▷ ▷ ▶ ▶ ▶ **Reason with Text**

1a. How does Whitman respond to the question "What is the grass?" Why does he want to treat the grass tenderly?	**1b.** Interpret how the grass is a symbol of Whitman's democratic ideals.	**Understand** Find meaning
2a. What does Whitman say about dying in Sections 6 and 7?	**2b.** What are Whitman's hopes for his own death?	**Apply** Use information
3a. A *catalog* is a list of people or things. Identify four things Whitman catalogs in the poem.	**3b.** Why does Whitman catalog these things?	**Analyze** Take things apart
4a. In Section 32, Whitman says that he could "turn and live with animals." Why would he like to live with the animals? How are they different from humans?	**4b.** Determine the advantages and disadvantages of living with animals.	**Evaluate** Make judgments
5a. Identify what Whitman celebrates in Section 6.	**5b.** Propose what Whitman and today's environmentalists have in common.	**Create** Bring ideas together

Analyze Literature

Symbol and Elaboration

Review the lines you wrote down in which *grass* is used as a symbol. Next to or underneath each line, explain what the grass symbolizes. Look for recurring ideas in interpreting Whitman's use of symbolization.

Section 6 provides a good example of elaboration. What other examples did you find? How does Whitman elaborate? What is the purpose of doing so?

Extend the Text

Writing Options

Creative Writing Write a descriptive essay in which you celebrate yourself. Include things such as your talents and accomplishments, likes and dislikes, and personality and beliefs. Make your essay positive and energetic. Plan to read it at your high school graduation party or on your next birthday.

Expository Writing Imagine that a classmate is having difficulty understanding "Song of Myself." Write a one-paragraph paraphrase of one section of the poem for him or her. Explain difficult vocabulary; point out imagery, symbolism, and elaboration; and summarize main ideas.

Media Literary

Research Whitman on the Internet Walt Whitman's *contemporaries* (people who lived at the same time) were intensely divided about his work; a few praised him lavishly, but many were shocked and appalled by his poetry. Using the Internet, locate an article about Whitman's writing written during the nineteenth century. After reading the article, write a summary outlining its main points, and then share it with the class.

Lifelong Learning

Prepare Notes for Speaking You have been hired as a tour guide at the Walt Whitman House in Camden, New Jersey, and need to learn about Whitman's life so you can answer visitors' questions. Find out more about Whitman's life. Then prepare a set of notes you could use in speaking to tour groups about Whitman. Practice your presentation with a group of classmates, and let them ask you questions.

 Go to **www.mirrorsandwindows.com** for more.

1. To which of the following does the speaker *not* compare a spear of grass?
   A. the flag of his disposition
   B. a child
   C. the handkerchief of the Lord
   D. a hieroglyphic
   E. the spears of young men going off to war

2. The speaker says he "could turn and live with animals" for which of the following reasons?
   A. They are self-contained.
   B. They do not pity themselves.
   C. They are not concerned with religious matters.
   D. They are not dissatisfied or materialistic.
   E. All of the above

3. Which of the following is closest in meaning to the word *abeyance?*
   A. temporary suspension
   B. complete agreement
   C. simple purity
   D. bitter discord
   E. quiet resentment

4. Why does the speaker say he is like the spotted hawk?
   A. He is a hunter.
   B. He is loud and untamed.
   C. He is self-sufficient and unconcerned.
   D. He has extraordinarily keen senses.
   E. He is a rare species.

5. What is the speaker's attitude toward death in "Song of Myself"?
   A. He fears it like the mysterious "monsters" of the deep sea.
   B. He believes death either does not exist or is merely a prelude to another life.
   C. He rages against it as the end of life on earth.
   D. He is consoled by the idea of being reunited with long-departed loved ones.
   E. He yearns for the escape into oblivion.

6. Consider the meaning of the word *impalpable* in this line: "Nature without check with original energy / Looks down, is erect, or bends an arm on an impalpable certain rest." Which of the following means the opposite of *impalpable?*
   A. easily felt or noticed
   B. easily done or performed
   C. without substance
   D. likely to happen
   E. detrimental to one's health

7. In stanza 31, what do the rocks, mastodon, ocean, elk, and others in this catalog do in vain?
   A. They fight against him.
   B. They try to destroy the grass.
   C. They try to avoid the speaker.
   D. They try to give him a message about the meaning of life.
   E. They conceal the meaning of life.

8. What point does Whitman make by comparing grass with the work of the stars, a tree-toad to a master work, and a mouse with a religious miracle?
   A. His needs and desires in life are simple, so he is able to enjoy more of life.
   B. Humanmade objects and experiences are superficial and meaningless.
   C. He believes in one god who created all of life.
   D. It illustrates his democratic ideal that all things are magnificent.
   E. Things near us, in our environment, are just as capable of giving us pleasure as things far away.

9. **Constructed Response:** Explain Whitman's use of grass as a symbol "Song of Myself," providing examples from the poem to support your response. What do the images of grass suggest about Whitman's feelings about himself as well as nature, humanity, and society?

10. **Constructed Response:** Much of Whitman's poetry reflects the ideals of the American republic, such as the rights and responsibilities of common people and the superiority of democracy as a form of government. What American ideals are reflected in "Song of Myself"? Use examples from the poem to support your response.

By the Bivouac's Fitful Flame
Beat! Beat! Drums!

Lyric Poems by Walt Whitman

Build Background

Historical Context **"By the Bivouac's Fitful Flame"** and **"Beat! Beat! Drums!"** are two poems from Walt Whitman's volume of Civil War poetry, *Drum-Taps* (1865). These poems reflect his experiences as a volunteer nurse and companion to the wounded in the crowded military hospitals near Washington, DC. An estimated 623,000 troops died in the Civil War, more than in any war in which the United States has participated, and most of those deaths were caused by disease due to the poor conditions instead of by battle. Thus, the services of nurses were greatly needed to tend to the war wounded.

Whitman also spent time behind enemy lines in Virginia finding and caring for his brother George, a wounded Union soldier. He ended up staying in Washington, DC, for eleven years, during which time he worked as a clerk in the U.S. Department of the Interior. He was fired from that job when the Secretary of the Interior found out that Whitman was the author of the then-controversial *Leaves of Grass.*

Literary Context Rather than depict scenes of combat, Whitman's war poems deal with events and emotions that occur off the battlefield. "By the Bivouac's Fitful Flame" takes place in an army encampment as a lonely, homesick soldier sits by a campfire. "Beat! Beat! Drums!" shows the effects of an impending war on the civilian population.

Reader's Context If a family member or close friend were fighting in a war, how would your life be affected? What feelings would you have?

Hospital tents in the rear of Douglas Hospital, Washington, DC (1869).

Analyze Literature

Alliteration and Onomatopoeia
Alliteration is the repetition of initial consonant sounds in consecutive or slightly separated words.

Onomatopoeia (än' ō mat' ō pē´ ə) is the use of words or phrases that sound like the things to which they refer, such as *buzz, click,* and *pop.*

Set Purpose

Whitman enjoyed experimenting with language, as demonstrated by his use of *sound devices,* which create musical qualities in poetry. To hear these effects, read aloud the two poems in this grouping. In reading "By the Bivouac's Fitful Flame," listen for instances of alliteration, such as the repeated "f" sound in the phrase "fitful flame." In reading "Beat! Beat! Drums!" identify the use of onomatopoeia and consider how it creates rhythm and emphasis. For each poem, think about how the use of language fits the overall mood of the piece.

Preview Vocabulary

ruthless, 337
parley, 338
beseech, 338
entreaty, 338

By the Bivouac's Fitful Flame

by Walt Whitman

Tents at Lake O'Hara, 1916. John Singer Sargent.
Wadsworth Atheneum Museum of Art, Hartford, Connecticut.
(See detail on page 335.)

By the bivouac's[1] fitful flame,
A procession winding around me, solemn
    and sweet and slow—but first I note,
The tents of the sleeping army, the fields'
    and woods' dim outline,
The darkness lit by spots of kindled fire,
    the silence,
5 Like a phantom far or near an occasional
    figure moving,
The shrubs and trees, (as I lift my
    eyes they seem to be stealthily
    watching me,)
While wind in procession thoughts,
    O tender and wondrous thoughts,
Of life and death, of home and the past
    and loved, and of those that are far
    away;
A solemn and slow procession there as
    I sit on the ground,
10 By the bivouac's fitful flame. ❖

---

1. **bivouac.** Temporary camp or resting place for an army

MIRRORS & WINDOWS

If you were a soldier, what might you think about on the night before a battle?
What do you think about when you are alone and perhaps feeling lonely?

Samuel D. Badger (Drummer Boy), c. 1870.
Minnesota Historical Society, St. Paul, Minnesota.

Beat! Beat! Drums!

by Walt Whitman

Beat! beat! drums!—blow! bugles! blow!
Through the windows—through doors—burst like a <u>ruthless</u> force,
Into the solemn church, and scatter the congregation,
Into the school where the scholar is studying;
5   Leave not the bridegroom quiet—no happiness must he have now
     with his bride,
Nor the peaceful farmer any peace, ploughing his field or gathering
     his grain,
So fierce you whirr and pound you drums—so shrill you bugles blow.

ruth • less (rüth′ ləs) *adj.,* showing no mercy

Beat! beat! drums!—blow! bugles! blow!
Over the traffic of cities—over the rumble of wheels in the streets;
10 Are beds prepared for sleepers at night in the houses? no sleepers
        must sleep in those beds,
    No bargainers' bargains by day—no brokers or speculators[1]—
        would they continue?
    Would the talkers be talking? would the singer attempt to sing?
    Would the lawyer rise in the court to state his case before the judge?
    Then rattle quicker, heavier drums—you bugles wilder blow.

15 Beat! beat! drums!—blow! bugles! blow!
    Make no <u>parley</u>—stop for no expostulation,[2]
    Mind not the timid—mind not the weeper or prayer,
    Mind not the old man <u>beseeching</u> the young man,
    Let not the child's voice be heard, nor the mother's <u>entreaties</u>,
20 Make even the trestles[3] to shake the dead where they lie awaiting
        the hearses,
    So strong you thump O terrible drums—so loud you bugles blow. ❖

---

1. **brokers or speculators.** People buying and selling stocks, bonds, real estate, and other
   commodities
2. **expostulation.** Talk for the sake of reasoning with someone
3. **trestles.** Braced framework for support

> **par • ley** (pär′ lē) *n.,* conference with an enemy
> **be • seech** (bi sēch′) *v.,* beg; plead
> **en • treat • y** (en trēt′ ē) *n.,* plea; act of asking urgently

MIRRORS & WINDOWS "Beat! Beat! Drums!" describes people being swept up in an approaching war.
Why do people come together in times of crisis and tragedy?

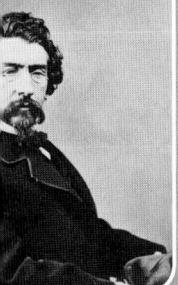

Informational Text Connection

Poet Walt Whitman and photographer Mathew Brady were contemporaries. They both started their careers in New York City in the mid-1840s, and they both lived in Washington, DC, during the Civil War. Whitman was among the many influential Americans whose portraits Brady photographed and then displayed in his gallery. Brady also photographed President Abraham Lincoln and most of the leading military figures of the Civil War, including Ulysses S. Grant and Robert E. Lee.

Whitman and Brady also had the common goal of using their art to record the horrors of the Civil War. In *Drum-Taps*, Whitman's collection of Civil War poetry, he wrote, "The real war will never get in the books. . . . Think how much, and of importance, will be—has already been—buried in the grave." As you read this **biographical article about Mathew Brady,** identify the artistic bond he shared with Whitman.

Mathew Brady: Civil War Photographer

Americans' understanding of the Civil War would be significantly diminished if photographic technology had not been developed in the years just before the conflict. Great American writers such as Stephen Crane and Walt Whitman were able to represent in their stories and poems some of the terror and tragedy that occurred during the war. However, they could not match the realism captured by a photograph in demonstrating fear in a young soldier's eyes or misery in a dead man's face.

Before photography, visual representations of war usually were illustrious paintings that glamorized battle as a heroic conflict. An artist could create a desired tone in his or her work, making battle seem less brutal and more gran-

diose than it likely was in reality. In contrast, the scorched earth and mounds of corpses shown in Civil War photographs contained no such illusions. In fact, these photographs dramatically shifted people's attitude toward war. Viewing the atrocities portrayed by wartime photography caused Americans to wonder whether war was a sensible solution to the nation's problems.

Mathew Brady (c. 1823–1896) is the most renowned photographer among the many who documented the Civil War. He was only a teenager when photographic technology emerged, but he quickly familiarized himself with the craft. In 1844, at age twenty-one, he opened a studio in New York City, and in

1856, he opened a second studio in Washington, DC.

Brady initially focused on photographing famous Americans, noting that "from the first, I regarded myself as under obligation to my country to preserve the faces of its historic men and mothers." Among the many people Brady met and photographed was Walt Whitman, who soon grew interested in Brady's work. Whitman saw an intimate connection between his poetry and Brady's photographs and became one of Brady's most frequent subjects over the next four decades.

Whitman saw an intimate connection between his poetry and Brady's photographs.

When the first shots of the Civil War were fired at Fort Sumter, South Carolina, on April 12, 1861, Brady saw an opportunity to secure his legacy in American history. He decided to photograph the Civil War, producing not just portraits of soldiers but also capturing the realities of war few people had ever seen: the wretched campsites in which the soldiers lived, the preparations they made for battle, the desolate landscapes they left in their wake, the wounded soldiers that lay dying in hospital camps, and, most famously, the dead bodies scattered across the battlefields. Brady's idea was risky, given the obvious dangers of putting oneself in the middle of a war.

In addition, he was abandoning a very successful portrait business at the height of his career. Friends and family attempted to dissuade him, but he remained committed to his plan. In his later years, Brady remarked, "I had to go. A spirit in my feet said 'Go,' and I went."

Brady initiated his project on July 21, 1861, with the First Battle of Bull Run—the first major land battle of the Civil War. During the fighting, he became so immersed in his work that the Confederates nearly captured him on their way to victory. Soon after, he recognized that he never would be able to complete his project working alone. To expand his effort, he commissioned twenty-three assistants, supplying each with photographic equipment that included a portable darkroom.

Brady's most famous Civil War exhibit came in 1862, shortly after the Battle of Antietam. This conflict, the most violent one-day battle in American history, involved 132,000 soldiers and resulted in over 23,000 casualties (soldiers killed and wounded). Brady's exhibition, simply titled "The Dead of Antietam," contained hideously detailed photographs of corpses lying strewn across the battlefield. In a review of the exhibit, the *New York Times* wrote, "Brady has brought home to us the terrible reality and earnestness of war."

Soldiers slain during the Battle of Antietam (September 1862).

A Union arsenal in Washington, DC (1862).

A group of Union lieutenants gathered in Antietam, Maryland (1862).

After the Civil War ended in 1865, Brady assumed the Library of Congress would purchase his entire collection of some seven hundred photographs. Because his project had been monumental in scope and employed the use of cutting-edge photographic technology, its costs had ballooned to over $100,000. Brady demanded $125,000 from the federal government, but his offer was refused.

When the interest on Brady's debt began to spiral out of control, he was forced to sell his New York studio and declare bankruptcy.

In 1875, Congress agreed to buy most of Brady's collection for $25,000, but the entire sum went directly to his collectors. Devastated by the failure of his life's greatest work, along with the death of his wife in 1887, Brady's health quickly deteriorated. He died in a charity hospital during the winter of 1896, alone and forgotten. Despite this sorrowful end to Brady's life, he is today recognized as one of the greatest contributors to the United States' historical narrative and as the founder of photojournalism. ❖

Review Questions

1. For what is Mathew Brady famous? Explain the difference between a *photographer* and a *photojournalist.* Why is Brady considered a photojournalist?

2. Beyond preserving history, what did Brady want to accomplish with his Civil War photos? Compare and contrast Brady's Civil War photos to current-day television news broadcasts from war zones. How might the effect on the American public be similar?

3. Give an example of a war scene Brady photographed. Look for an example of photojournalism in a current newspaper or magazine. In particular, look for a photo story related to war. What difference does it make to the audience to see pictures as well as read words?

TEXT ^{TO} TEXT CONNECTION

What belief did Whitman and Brady share regarding their art? How did they demonstrate this belief in chronicling the Civil War? Were they successful in documenting the war, not only during their time but for future generations? Explain your answer.

Refer to Text ► ► ► ► ►   **Reason with Text**

1a. Describe the scene in "By the Bivouac's Fitful Flame."	**1b.** How may the scene be different in the morning? What may happen to the soldier?	**Understand** Find meaning
2a. What is the "procession winding around me" in the first poem?	**2b.** Why is the soldier dwelling on these thoughts?	**Apply** Use information
3a. Describe Whitman's catalog technique in "Beat! Beat! Drums!"	**3b.** Explain the purpose of the catalog.	**Analyze** Take things apart
4a. In times of conflict between nations, some people might be accused of being "drum beaters"? What do you think this means?	**4b.** Assess how Whitman feels about the buildup for war.	**Evaluate** Make judgments
5a. Trace what happens to the sound of the drums and bugles from stanza 1 to stanza 3 in the second poem.	**5b.** How is the approaching war like a hurricane, flood, or other natural disaster?	**Create** Bring ideas together

Analyze Literature

Alliteration and Onomatopoeia

In "By the Bivouac's Fitful Flame," how many times do you hear the sound "f" in successive or slightly separated words? What other examples of alliteration do you hear? How does the use of this device fit the mood of the poem?

In "Beat! Beat! Drums!" where do you hear onomatopoeia? What effects does Whitman create with these words, particularly in repeating them throughout the poem? Again, how does the use of this device fit the poem's mood?

Extend the Text

Writing Options
Creative Writing Civil War photographer Mathew Brady (see the preceding Informational Text Connection) photographed many famous Americans from the 1840s through the 1860s, including Walt Whitman. Write a dialogue that might have occurred between the two men. What would they say about the war, photography and poetry, and the American people?

Expository Writing Write a one-page analysis of how the poem "Beat! Beat! Drums!" should be read aloud, whether by an individual or a group. Consider how to portray the tone and content of the poem. Should it be recited loudly or softly? What should be the *tempo,* or speed?

Media Literacy
Evaluate Websites Make a list of five websites that provide valuable information about the Civil War, and give it to your school's media center. To evaluate the websites, create a checklist of criteria. For instance, one way to evaluate whether a site is valuable is to determine who sponsors it. A site sponsored by a university, a government agency, or a well-known news organization is more credible, or believable, than a nonprofessional website or blog.

Collaborative Learning
Create a Photo Story Working with a partner, create a photo story. One person can take the photos, and the other can write words to go with the photos. Your story might be about a person or an event at your school or in your neighborhood. It might be a human interest story or a political or environmental statement. Ask the editor of your school newspaper to publish your story.

 Go to **www.mirrorsandwindows.com** for more.

1. Which of the following best describes the mood of "By the Bivouac's Fitful Flame"?
A. frightened and worried
B. content and peaceful
C. eager and ambitious
D. paranoid and suspicious
E. homesick and solemn

2. What is happening in "By the Bivouac's Fitful Flame"?
A. A spy is watching an enemy camp, waiting for the right moment to strike.
B. A procession of people dislocated by the war is passing by the soldiers' camp and looking for shelter.
C. A soldier in his camp at night remembers the life and people he has left behind.
D. Flames from a campfire have burnt the soldiers' camp to the ground.
E. None of the above

3. In "Beat! Beat! Drums!" what does the word *ruthless* mean?
A. without a cause
B. without mercy
C. without regret
D. without a plan
E. without risk or danger

4. Which of the following best describes the tone of "Beat! Beat! Drums!"?
A. urgent
B. proud
C. courageous
D. tormented
E. devotional

5. In the second stanza of "Beat! Beat! Drums!" why does the speaker call for the drums to be quicker and the bugles to be wilder?
A. The soldiers are marching on, so the drummer and bugler need to keep pace.
B. The drums and bugles need to be louder to help rally the soldiers and prepare them for battle.
C. They must disrupt those aspects of daily life that have not been affected by war.
D. Additional soldiers have died in battle, so the expression of grief must be more intense.
E. The marching soldiers have left the area of the church and school, so their procession can get louder.

6. In the selection about Mathew Brady, Walt Whitman is quoted as saying about the Civil War, "The real war will never get in the books." What did he mean by that?
A. The writers of history will focus only on a few significant battles.
B. The war will devastate society so much that many aspects of life, such as book publishing, will come to an end.
C. It will be impossible to calculate the actual monetary cost of the war.
D. The general public will never know about the real horrors of the war.
E. The Civil War effort would be considered minor compared to other wars.

7. If someone *beseeches* something of you, what is he or she doing?
A. borrowing something
B. stealing something
C. begging for something
D. insulting something
E. destroying something

8. Constructed Response: Based on your reading of "By the Bivouac's Fitful Flame," "Beat! Beat! Drums!" and the quotation from Whitman in the Brady selection, suggest what message Whitman was trying convey about the effects of war. Use evidence from the texts to support your answer.

> **TEST-TAKING TIP**
>
> Some test questions ask you to read two passages and consider what they have in common. Before choosing an answer, read through all the answers and eliminate those that pertain to only one of the selections. Doing so will help you narrow down the possibilities and increase your chances of choosing the right answer.

Ode to Walt Whitman

by Pablo Neruda

Chilean poet **Pablo Neruda** (1904–1973) has been called the "Walt Whitman of South America." Like Whitman, Neruda was a prolific writer,  publishing thirty-five volumes of poetry in his native Spanish that have since been translated into many languages. Whitman and Neruda both are considered "grass-roots poets," or poets who speak for the common people. Just as Whitman gave identity to North America, Neruda voiced the identity of South America. Both poets wrote on similar themes of nature, love, civil war, and religion.

Neruda, who was born twelve years after Whitman died, often spoke of Whitman's profound influence on his life. In a 1966 speech in New York City, Neruda said, "For my part, I, who am now nearing seventy, discovered Walt Whitman when I was just fifteen, and I hold him to be my greatest creditor. I stand before you feeling that I bear with me always this great and wonderful debt which has helped me to exist." The poem **"Ode to Walt Whitman,"** written in the mid-1950s, expresses Neruda's gratitude to his mentor and contains literary *allusions*, or references, to specific Whitman poems. Neruda received numerous awards in his lifetime, including the Nobel Prize for literature in 1971.

I can't recall my age, or if
I was in the vast streaming South,[1]
or on some forbidding coastline
where seagulls wheeled & cried . . .
5   But I touched a hand that day,
& it was Walt Whitman's hand.
And barefoot I walk the earth,
I wade through tenacious[2] dew
in the grasslands of Whitman.

10   Throughout my entire childhood,
my companion was that hand
with dew on it, the timber
of its patriarchal[3] pine,
the expanse of its prairie,
15   its mission of articulate[4] peace.

And Walt did not disdain[5]
all the gifts of the earth,
the capital's surfeit[6] of curves,
the purple initial of learning,

---

1. **South.** Temuco, a wilderness region in southern Chile where Neruda grew up
2. **tenacious.** Clinging not easily removed
3. **patriarchal.** Of or referring to a man who is a founder or father
4. **articulate.** Clear; well spoken
5. **disdain.** Scorn; have contempt for
6. **surfeit.** Abundance

Peasants, 1947. Diego Rivera. Museu de Arte, Sao Paulo, Brazil.

20   but taught me to be americano,
      & raised my eyes to books,
      toward the treasure that we find
      inside a kernel of wheat.

      Engirthed[7] by the clarity
25   of the plains, he made me see
      how the high mountain tutors us.
      From the subterranean echo
      he fetched it all in for me,
      whatever he could harvest
30   gallivanting[8] through the alfalfa,
      on the days he passed in the kitchen
      or at the bend of the river.

      But not just earth by itself
      was brought into the light
35   by the work of his shovel:
      he disinterred[9] humanity.
      And the slaves who were abased[10]
      along with him, balancing
      the black dignity of their stature,
40   went on to conquer happiness.

---

  7. **Engirthed.** Surrounded with; encompassed by
  8. **gallivanting.** Galloping; running lightheartedly
  9. **disinterred.** Dug up, especially a human body that had been buried
10. **abased.** Lowered in prestige or esteem

To the stoker,[11] down below
in the boiler room, Walt sent
a basket of strawberries,
& each corner of his city
45   was visited by his verse,
verse like a strip of clean flesh,
the beard of a true fisherman,
the solemn supple gait
of his acacian[12] legs.

50   Passing among the soldiers—
his bardic[13] silhouette.
Night nurse, camerado,
he knew painful, rasping breath,
& he waited with the dawn
55   for life's silent return.

Breadmaker supreme!
Prime old brother of my roots!
Cupola[14] of the conifers!
For the last hundred years
60   the wind has passed over
your germinating grassland
without consuming your vision.

But now your country is cruel—
full of persecution, tears,
65   prisons & lethal weapons,
uncivil wars that nonetheless
haven't crushed the grass of your book,
living source of originality.

And ay!, those who murdered Lincoln,
70   who now lie in that bed,
have dismantled the fragrant
lilac of his memorial[15]
& put a throne in its place,
splattered with blood & misfortune.

---

11. **stoker.** Person who shovels coal into a furnace
12. **acacian.** Of or pertaining to the acacia tree, a tree originally
    native to North America and known for its strength and
    durability
13. **bardic.** Of or relating to a poet; Shakespeare is known as
    "the Bard."
14. **Cupola.** Small structure built on top of a roof, as on a barn
15. **lilac of his memorial.** Whitman's poem "When Lilacs Last in
    the Dooryard Bloom'd," his tribute to the assassinated President
    Abraham Lincoln

75   Your voice, that's still singing
in the suburban stations, on
the unloading docks at night . . .
Your word, that's still splashing
like dark water . . .

80   And your people, black, white,
poor & simple, like all people
still not forgetting
the tolling of your bell . . .[16]

They congregate & sing
85   beneath the magnitude
of your spacious life.
They walk among the people
with your love. They caress
the pure development
90   of fraternity[17] on earth. ❖

---

16. **tolling of your bell.** Refers to the custom of ringing a church
bell upon the death of a person
17. **fraternity.** Brotherhood or sense of family

Think of someone from history you would like to meet, whether a famous individual or a family member. Why would you like to meet him or her?

Refer and Reason

1. According to Neruda, what did Whitman send to the stoker? Why would this gift be unusual? Infer what Neruda is conveying about Whitman.

2. Neruda begins his poem by speaking *about* Whitman. Look for the spot in the poem where Neruda begins speaking *to* Whitman. Suggest the reason for this shift in focus.

3. How does Neruda describe his first encounter with Whitman's poetry? Where did he often read the poet? Think of a favorite author from your childhood. Why did you like this author?

Writing Options

1. Write an essay in tribute to someone who has influenced your life or taught you something important. The person may be living or dead, famous or unknown. Tell how you became acquainted with the person and why he or she has been important in your life. Share your tribute with a close friend.

2. In 1952, Pablo Neruda stayed in a villa on the island of Capri off the coast of Italy. His visit was fictionalized in the 1994 Italian movie *Il Postino (The Postman)*. Nominated for an Academy Award, the movie shows Neruda befriending a postman and inspiring in him a love of poetry. Watch the movie, and then write a review about what you learned from it about Neruda's life and poetry.

 Go to **www.mirrorsandwindows.com** for more.

Emily Dickinson

"Saying nothing . . . sometimes says the most."

Emily Dickinson (1830–1886) was born in Amherst, Massachusetts, to a prominent family. She lived a private life, rarely venturing beyond her home and close circle of family and friends. Her primary relationships were with her sister, Lavinia; her brother, Austin; and Austin's wife, Susan Huntington Dickinson. Neither Emily nor Lavinia married. Although Emily seldom left Amherst, she spent one year at Mt. Holyoke Female Seminary, ten miles away, and visited Washington, DC, and Philadelphia with her father.

After Dickinson's year at Mt. Holyoke, she returned home, where she delighted in reading books that might "joggle the Mind." The volumes she appreciated the most included the Bible, Shakespeare's plays, and the works of such writers of her day as Ralph Waldo Emerson, the British writers John Keats and Alfred Tennyson, and George Eliot.

Early on, Dickinson befriended Benjamin Newton, a law student who encouraged her writing. His sudden death led to a spiritual crisis, during which Dickinson sought the advice of a well-known minister from Philadelphia, Charles Wadsworth, who became a close friend. In the late 1850s, Dickinson wrote drafts of love letters to an unknown person identified in the correspondence as "Master." Some of her poems of this time reflect the frustrations and tensions of unfulfilled longing.

Although Dickinson is considered by many literary scholars to be the United States' greatest lyric poet, she kept her writing to herself, sharing fragments of it only with the people closest to her. When she died at age fifty-five, her family discovered forty hand-bound volumes of poetry containing some one thousand poems. Yet during her lifetime, only seven of her poems were published, all anonymously and without her approval. In the first volumes of her poetry, the editors mangled the verse by "correcting" her unusual punctuation and her deliberate lapses in grammar. Only in 1955, with the publication of *The Poems of Emily Dickinson*, edited by T. H. Johnson, was the full extent of her achievement revealed.

Taken as a whole, Dickinson's verses, most of them brief, present a complex self-portrait, a sort of spiritual autobiography. Her voice alternately is humble and proud, personal and distant, joyful and sorrowful but always questioning, meditative, and intensely alive. She observed details keenly but created unexpected, surprising generalizations that synthesize the particulars into universal truths.

Noted Works

"Success is counted sweetest" (c. 1859)

"There is a certain slant of light" (c. 1861)

"I'm nobody! Who are you?" (c. 1861)

"I heard a Fly buzz—when I died—" (c. 1862)

"This is my letter to the World" (c. 1862)

"Because I could not stop for Death—" (c. 1863)

"A narrow Fellow in the Grass" (c. 1866)

Much Madness is divinest Sense—
I heard a Fly buzz—when I died—
Because I could not stop for Death—
This is my letter to the World

Lyric Poems by Emily Dickinson

Build Background

Literary Context Contemporary scholars have offered various explanations for Dickinson's withdrawal from society, including thwarted love and physical disabilities. Despite her isolation, she lived her life intensely, in vivid moments of observation and reflection captured in astonishingly original verse. Her poems themselves support the theory that her reclusiveness was the determined, willful act of someone who wished to encounter life on her own terms. This view is supported by Dickinson's tongue-in-cheek analysis in **"Much Madness is divinest Sense—"** of society's treatment of people who choose to think for themselves.

Dickinson analyzed the topic of death in several of her poems. In **"I heard a Fly buzz—when I died—,"** the speaker imagines her own death, expressing with brilliant irony her fears about the transition from this life to the next. In **"Because I could not stop for Death—,"** considered one of Dickinson's best poems, the speaker describes a journey through eternity and suggests accepting death with quiet civility.

"This is my letter to the World" provides insight into Dickinson's view of her poetry and her wish to someday connect with her readership. This wish seems to have gone unfulfilled, given that only seven of Dickinson's nearly eighteen hundred poems were published in her lifetime.

Reader's Context Think of someone you know who is quiet and withdrawn—someone who keeps to himself or herself. How is he or she generally treated by others? What might others discover if they got to know this person better?

Emily Dickinson's bedroom in the Dickinson home, Amherst, Massachusetts.

Analyze Literature

Personification and Slant Rhyme
Personification is a figure of speech in which an animal, object, force of nature, or idea is described as if it were human or given human characteristics.

In **slant rhyme,** the sounds are similar but not identical, as in *bear* and *bore.*

Set Purpose

The reason behind Emily Dickinson's reclusive lifestyle has been the subject of much speculation. Whatever the cause, it seems likely her isolation manifested itself in her poetry. For instance, Dickinson often personified forces she could not control, such as death. In reading her poems, look for examples of personification. Dickinson also experimented freely with poetic conventions, such as rhyme. Look for her use of slant rhyme in the following poems.

Preview Vocabulary

discerning, 350
assent, 350
demur, 350
civility, 353
surmise, 353

Portrait of Mrs. Jack Warner, 1945. Salvador Dali.
Gala-Salvador Dali Foundation, New York.

Much Madness is divinest Sense–

by Emily Dickinson

Much Madness is divinest Sense—
To a <u>discerning</u> Eye—
Much Sense—the starkest Madness—
'Tis the Majority
In this, as All, prevail—
<u>Assent</u>—and you are sane—
<u>Demur</u>—you're straightway dangerous—
And handled with a Chain— ❖

> **dis • cern • ing** (di sərn´ iŋ) *adj.,* critical
> **as • sent** (ə sent´) *v.,* agree
> **de • mur** (di mər´) *v.,* disagree

MIRRORS & WINDOWS

Some people believe there is a fine line between genius and insanity. What does this mean? Do you think that it is true?

I heard a Fly buzz— when I died—

by Emily Dickinson

I heard a Fly buzz—when I died—
The Stillness in the Room
Was like the Stillness in the Air—
Between the Heaves of Storm—

5   The Eyes around—had wrung them dry—
and Breaths were gathering firm
For that last Onset—when the King[1]
Be witnessed—in the Room

I willed my Keepsakes[2]—Signed away
10 What portion of me be
Assignable—and then it was
There interposed[3] a Fly—

With Blue—uncertain stumbling Buzz—
Between the light—and me—
15 And then the Windows failed—and then
I could not see to see— ❖

---

1. **King.** God or Jesus
2. **Keepsakes.** Personal items that are treasured
3. **interposed.** Appeared suddenly

MIRRORS & WINDOWS   Dickinson describes giving away her "Keepsakes," the things about her that were "assignable." What is your most treasured keepsake, or possession?

A Walk in the Snow, 1879. Lucien Frank. (See detail on page 349.)

Because I could not stop for Death—

by Emily Dickinson

Because I could not stop for Death—
He kindly stopped for me—
The Carriage held but just Ourselves—
And Immortality.

5 We slowly drove—He knew no haste
And I had put away
My labor and my leisure too,
For His <u>Civility</u>—

We passed the School, where Children strove
10 At recess—in the Ring—
We passed the Fields of Gazing Grain—
We passed the Setting Sun—

Or rather—He passed Us—
The Dews drew quivering and Chill—
15 For only Gossamer, my Gown—
My Tippet[1]—only Tulle[2]—

We paused before a House that seemed
A Swelling of the Ground—
The Roof was scarcely visible—
20 The Cornice[3]—in the Ground

Since then—'tis Centuries—and yet
Feels shorter than the Day
I first <u>surmised</u> the Horses Heads
Were toward Eternity— ❖

---

1. **Tippet.** Short cape worn over the shoulders
2. **Tulle.** Thin netting
3. **Cornice.** Molded projection at the top of a building

ci • vil • i • ty (sə vil´ ə tē) *n.*, gentleness; civilized manner
sur • mise (sər mīz´) *v.*, infer

Dickinson presents a peaceful, civil view of death in this poem. In what situations
might this be an accurate view of death? In what situations might it not be an
accurate view?

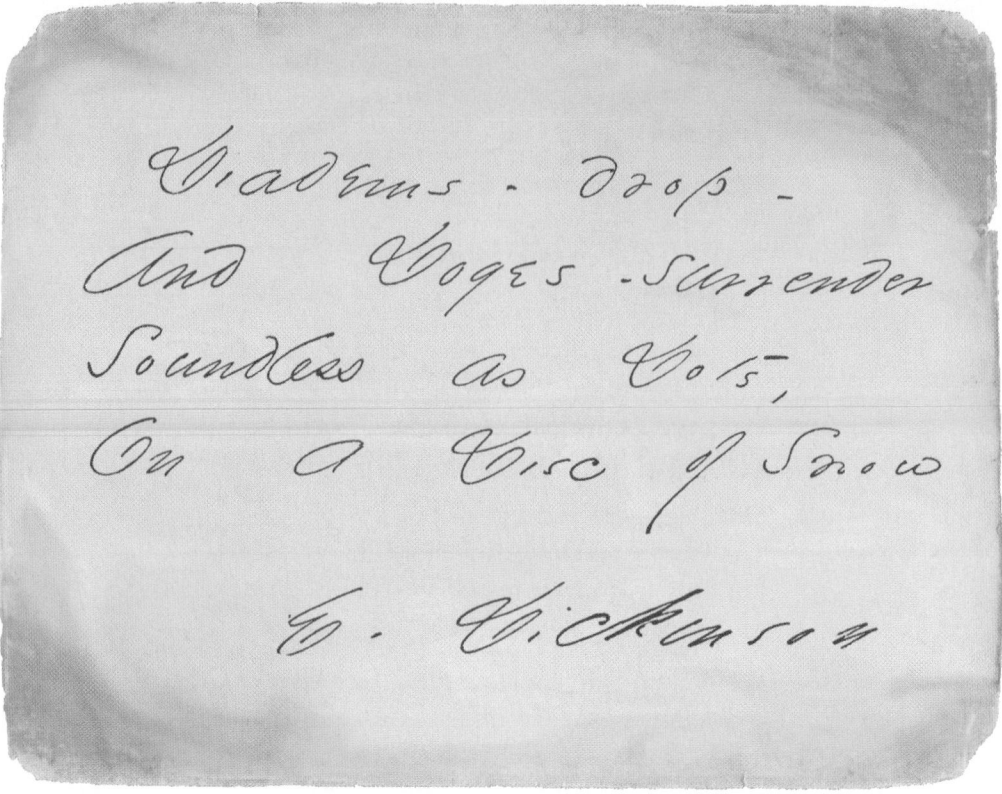

This is my letter to the World

by Emily Dickinson

This is my letter to the World
That never wrote to Me—
The simple News that Nature told—
With tender Majesty

Her Message is committed
To Hands I cannot see—
For love of Her—Sweet—countrymen—
Judge tenderly—of Me ❖

Putting down your thoughts in a letter you will never send is sometimes recommended as a way to vent frustration or anger. To whom would you write such a letter? What would you say?

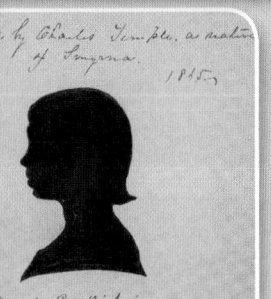

Informational Text Connection

Daniel Terdiman's online article **"Battle for the Belle of Amherst"** describes a mock-serious competition among computer experts to create a video game based on the life and work of Emily Dickinson. The "Belle of Amherst" is a label often applied to Dickinson, who was the daughter of a prominent Amherst, Massachusetts, family. As you read, look for references to Dickinson's life, personality, and poetry.

Battle for the Belle of Amherst
by Daniel Terdiman

SAN FRANCISCO—In this era of first-person shooters, successful video games seem to require lots of shooting, explosions and other assaults on the senses. But who says you can't write a game about the poetry of Emily Dickinson?

That was the question put to some of the biggest names in gaming during a special panel discussion Wednesday at the Game Developers Conference here.

The Sims creator Will Wright, *Black & White* designer Peter Molyneux and *Splinter Cell* lead designer Clint Hocking were set the task of developing a game concept based on the reclusive poet.

This was the second year of the challenge: Last year, several leading designers were asked to come up with games about love. Wright had the overflow crowd roaring with *Collateral Romance,* a love story set in the war game, *Battlefield 1942.*

"In a conference full of glitzy demos and very prepared and polished presentations, it's important that we look at games in a very raw way, and give all of you not just the sense of the finished product, but also the process that game designers go through," said the panel's chairman, Eric Zimmerman, founder of gameLab.

Splinter Cell's Hocking, the first to present, said his initial thoughts had been an Emily Dickinson

poetry slam.[1] That, he joked, would pit Dickinson against fellow writers "Mark Twain, aka Fathom," and "Robert 'Iceman' Frost."

Hocking finally decided on a game scenario in which players would mimic the physical act of writing. That led him to the Nintendo DS and its built-in stylus.

Players of Hocking's fantasy game *Muse* would collect symbols from an environment based on Dickinson's Massachusetts—things that might have influenced her writing, such as willow trees. Piecing the symbols together in a certain order, players would form the poems. Because Dickinson's poetry evolved conceptually over time, some symbols in the game would only unlock after players had already crafted some poems.

To make the game collaborative, Hocking suggested players could use the Nintendo DS' Wi-Fi feature to share symbols with each other, hastening the composition of the poems and the completion of the game.

Next up was Molyneux, but his presentation was less a concept for a game about Dickinson's poetry than a showcase for software he had designed. In the context of the challenge, the software presented

---

1. **poetry slam.** Poetry competition performed in front of judges

a house much like Dickinson's. Players would move around the house, unlocking Dickinson's experiences.

Unfortunately, it appeared that Molyneux and two assistants had put more time into their demo than in designing a game. Though graphically beautiful, the designers had no fleshed-out concept behind it.

Wright, the speaker most people in the room had come to see, riffed on Dickinson's reputation as a recluse.

"If she were alive today, she'd be an internet addict," Wright deadpanned, "and she'd probably have a really amazing blog."[2]

At first, he said, he'd thought he would mix Dickinson's poetry into a *Grand Theft Auto: San Andreas* environment. But in the end, he was inspired to create a kind of combination of Tamagotchi and Microsoft's universally hated paperclip helper, Clippy.[3]

Then came the idea to put the player in the role of Dickinson's therapist. The game, he said, would be stored on a USB flash drive.

"As you interact with her, you start with a cordial relationship," he said. "She (either) becomes romantically obsessed with you, or goes into a suicidal depression, and at the end, she can delete herself from the memory stick."

Along the way, Wright explained, Dickinson would reside in the player's computerized world, popping up from time to time with an e-mail, instant message, text message or desktop appearance. As an example, he showed the crowd a potential text message from Dickinson: "1t is b3tt3r t0 B th3 h4mm3r th4n th3 4nv1L" (geek writing for "it is better to be the hammer than the anvil").

With lines like that, Wright won the challenge, hands down. Many felt Hocking's design was technically a more complete game idea, but Wright won the room with his humor and by tying in the way people use technology on a daily basis with a morose character like Dickinson.

In the end, Wright, Molyneux and Hocking demonstrated that imagination is the key to game creation.

"You give (Wright) any off-the-wall topic, and he'll show you how his brain works," said Bruce Boston, who manages the in-world economy of the massively multiplayer online game, *There*. "He takes the core concept . . . and he'll turn it into a game you'll want to be playing in six months."

Raph Koster, chief creative officer at Sony Online Entertainment, said the presentations were "awesome," but summed up the lamentations of many in the room.

"It's a shame we won't actually make those games," he said. ❖

---

2. **blog.** Short for *Web log*: an online diary or journal
3. **Tamagotchi . . . Clippy.** Tamagotchi is a handheld digital "pet," created in Japan and popular in the late 1990s. Clippy is a cartoon figure that pops up onscreen to offer advice about the software program.

Review Questions

1. Identify each designer's concept for a video game based on Emily Dickinson. Why would major video game designers be interested in creating a game based on a very private poet like Dickinson?

2. What aspect of Dickinson's reputation did Wright discuss with the audience? Wright says that if Dickinson were alive today, she would be an Internet addict. Do you agree or disagree?

3. How was Wright able to win the competition? How would you develop Wright's concept for the game? Suggest two ideas for how the game could proceed.

TEXT ⇄ TEXT CONNECTION

Compare the lifestyle of nineteenth-century poet Emily Dickinson with that of a twenty-first-century video game designer. What do the two seem to have in common? Find a line in the article that supports your answer. Then find the Dickinson poem that most closely connects to "Battle for the Belle of Amherst." Explain each choice.

Refer to Text ▶ ▶ ▶ ▶ ▶	Reason with Text	
1a. In "This is my letter to the World," what does the speaker call her poem or her poetry in general?	**1b.** Explain what insight this poem provides on Dickinson's motives for keeping to herself.	**Understand** Find meaning
2a. In "Much Madness is divinest Sense—," what does the speaker say happens to people who do and do not go along with the majority?	**2b.** What aspects of Dickinson's life and work reveal a person who thinks for herself?	**Apply** Use information
3a. Identify the three visual images the speaker notes during the carriage ride in "Because I could not stop for Death—."	**3b.** Trace how the speaker changes by the end of the poem. What causes this change?	**Analyze** Take things apart
4a. In "I heard a Fly buzz—when I died—," what does the speaker notice about the fly? What does she notice about the rest of the room after the fly enters?	**4b.** Assess how realistic the moment of death is, as described by the speaker.	**Evaluate** Make judgments
5a. Although Dickinson wrote all these poems in the 1860s, each speaks to a concern that young people today might have. Identify the concern expressed in each poem.	**5b.** Choose one of these concerns. Acting as an advice columnist, write a response to a young person who has contacted you about this concern. Base your response on Dickinson's poems.	**Create** Bring ideas together

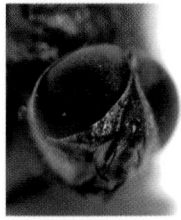

Analyze Literature

Personification and Slant Rhyme

How is personification used in "Because I could not stop for Death—"? How does it enrich Dickinson's portrayal of death?

Find two examples of slant rhyme in "Much Madness is divinest Sense—." Explain what ideas in the poem the rhymes reinforce.

Extend the Text

Writing Options
Creative Writing Reread "This is my letter to the World." Then write your own letter, explaining what you want the world to know about you and how you want it to regard or judge you.

Expository Writing Write an essay in which you compare and contrast the views of death presented in "Because I could not stop for Death—" and "I heard a Fly buzz—when I died—." Evaluate how well each view of death is portrayed and how realistic the portrayal is.

Media Literacy
Write a Movie Review Find and view the 1976 movie *The Belle of Amherst,* starring Julie Harris, to learn more about Emily Dickinson and her family relations. Considering what is known and not known about Dickinson, what did the creators of the movie have to speculate about? How did they portray Dickinson in her Amherst home? Write a movie review critiquing the portrayal of Dickinson.

Collaborative Learning
Hold a Panel Discussion Many writers do not earn enough money from the sales of their work, so they take jobs to support themselves. Hold a panel discussion on whether the government should support writers. Students on each side of the issue should prepare their arguments ahead of time. Students in the audience can ask questions and make comments on the topic.

 Go to **www.mirrorsandwindows.com** for more.

There's a certain Slant of light—
by Emily Dickinson

There's a certain Slant of light,
    Winter Afternoons—
That oppresses, like the Heft[1]
Of Cathedral Tunes—

Heavenly Hurt, it gives us—
5 We can find no scar,
But internal difference,
Where the Meanings, are—

None may teach it—Any—
'Tis the Seal Despair—
10 An imperial affliction
Sent us of the Air—

When it comes, the Landscape listens—
Shadows—hold their breath—
When it goes, 'tis like the Distance
15 On the look of Death— ❖

---

1. **Heft.** Weight

As a member of a solid New England family, **Emily Dickinson** was immersed in the Puritan tradition, and for many years, she attended church services twice each Sunday. Many of her poems deal with religious subjects, often with questions about the relationship of the individual soul to God and about immortality and the afterlife.

"There's a certain Slant of light—" is a poignant description of the feelings of loneliness and despair that come and go in people's lives.

"My life closed twice before its close—" compares death to separation from a loved one and wonders if immortality will be just as painful.

In **"The Soul selects her own Society—,"** Dickinson might be speaking about herself in terms of her decision to withdraw from society. The poem asserts an individual's freedom to choose associates.

My life closed twice before its close—
by Emily Dickinson

My life closed twice before its close—
It yet remains to see
If Immortality unveil
A third event to me

So huge, so hopeless to conceive
As these that twice befell.
Parting is all we know of heaven,
And all we need of hell. ❖

The Soul selects her own Society—
by Emily Dickinson

The Soul selects her own Society—
Then—shuts the Door—
To her divine Majority—
Present no more—

5 Unmoved—she notes the Chariots—pausing—
At her low Gate—
Unmoved—an Emperor be kneeling
Upon her Mat—

I've known her—from an ample nation—
10 Choose One—
Then—close the Valves of her attention—
Like Stone— ❖

What three words best describe Emily Dickinson, based on what you know about her?

Refer and Reason

1. Identify how the speaker uses word choice and punctuation to create a somber, lonely mood in "There's a certain Slant of light—." What might be the scene or situation in this poem?

2. The speaker in "My life closed twice before its close" states that "Parting is all we know of heaven / And all we need of hell." Analyze this idea in light of Dickinson's peculiar life.

3. Reread the final stanza of "The Soul selects her own Society—." How does the abruptness of the syllable pattern contribute to the meaning of the poem?

Writing Options

1. Although sparsely written, many of Dickinson's poems tell a story. Choose one of the poems in this section, and rewrite it as a short story. Read your story to the class.

2. Dickinson's poetry did not win acclaim until many years after her death. Even then, editors often tried to "correct" her punctuation and capitalization. Write a persuasive paragraph in which you defend Dickinson's poetry to an editor. Use examples from her poems to illustrate your argument.

 Go to **www.mirrorsandwindows.com** for more.

His Promised Land: The Autobiography of John P. Parker, Former Slave and Conductor on the Underground Railroad
by John P. Parker, edited by Stuart Seely Sprague

The story of John P. Parker, who was a slave and "conductor" on the Underground Railroad, is one of the few narratives told in a conductor's own words. In it, Parker recounts being sold at age eight, attempting many escapes, training as an iron worker, and purchasing his freedom.

The Belle of Amherst: A Play Based on the Life of Emily Dickinson
by William Luce

Although Emily Dickinson rarely left her father's house in fifty-six years, she was a keen, sensitive observer of the natural world. In Luce's one-woman drama, we look into Miss Emily's private world through her letters, diaries, and poetry and through dramatic flashback, discovering an enchanting spirit.

Bleeding Kansas by Nicole Etcheson

Etcheson employs a variety of primary sources to portray the violent yet fascinating conflict between abolitionists and pro-slavery forces in the Kansas Territory in the years leading up to the Civil War. Readers interested in learning more about John Brown and the abolitionist movement will enjoy this intriguing narrative.

The Civil War: An Illustrated History
by Geoffrey C. Ward and others

Based on Ken Burns's award-winning PBS television series *The Civil War,* this book includes accounts of the war by historical figures such as Abraham Lincoln, as well as the tragic stories of everyday men and women. Some five hundred photographs, paintings, lithographs, and maps accompany this fascinating text.

The Complete Poems
by Walt Whitman

Walt Whitman had a natural talent for expressing important social commentary in a lyrical language, and this anthology showcases his extraordinary range. Whitman's words help unlock the secret of what it means to be an American. This book includes original printings of Whitman's most famous poems, such as "Song of Myself."

The Killer Angels
by Michael Shaara

This fictionalized account of the Battle of Gettysburg, seen through the eyes of real-life Confederates such as Lee, Longstreet, Pickett, and Armistead, won the Pulitzer Prize for fiction in 1974. Shaara's book combines painstaking historical detail with lively narrative to provide a strikingly realistic account of the Civil War's most famous battle.

The best topics for an oral presentation are the ones you know about and find interesting. Given that, an experience you have had or an event you have attended might make an exciting topic for an oral presentation.

1. Choose a Suitable Experience or Event

When deciding on a topic, select one that you will be comfortable talking about and that your listeners will enjoy hearing about. Avoid picking a subject for which you do not have enough details to create a vivid narrative.

If you narrate a personal experience, do not include inappropriate details about you or anyone else who took part. If you narrate an event, it should be one you observed or participated in—for example, you watched the rescue of a person trapped in a smashed vehicle.

2. Use the Narrative Techniques Employed in Writing

Describing an experience you have had or an event you have lived through is similar to writing a story: You emphasize the *narrative,* or the storytelling. Here are some helpful suggestions:

- Decide on your purpose. Your goal might be to entertain your listeners with an amusing incident, to describe how you reacted in a frightening situation, or to describe an older person you cherished. As you prepare, keep your purpose in mind, because it will affect other aspects of your narrative, such as word choice, tone of voice, and mood.
- Determine the sequence of events. In a narrative, the details usually are presented in *chronological order,* the order in which they occurred. However, you can create suspense by withholding important information until the end (for example, stating that the elderly person you admired actually died before you were born). Another approach is to start at the end and then, using the *flashback* technique, present the incidents that led up to the finish.
- Use sensory details to make your narrative come alive, describing what you saw, heard, felt, and smelled. Be certain the images you describe fit your purpose and contribute to the narrative.

- Use transitions to connect parts of the narrative. Expressions such as *therefore, however, at the same time, later, next,* and *some years earlier* clarify the link between one incident or detail and another.
- Introduce other people and create dialogue, if doing so will contribute to the narrative. Try to describe characters in ways that will bring them to life for your listeners.
- To ensure you are well prepared and deliver an effective oral presentation, prepare note cards (see Speaking & Listening Workshop, Unit 2).

3. Practice Delivering Your Narrative

As with any oral presentation, practicing should strengthen your delivery and give you greater confidence when you speak. Practicing in front of an audience of family or friends can help you identify problems in the content or organization of your narrative. For instance, you may realize you left out an important part or have events out of order. Now is the time to correct these problems.

SPEAKING & LISTENING RUBRIC

Your narrative presentation will be evaluated on these elements:

Content

- ❏ Your topic is a personal experience or event and is of interest to your audience.
- ❏ The purpose and organization of your narrative are clear and consistent.
- ❏ Relevant sensory details contribute to the narrative; characters and dialogue, if used, are appropriate and believable.

Delivery & Presentation

- ❏ Your facial expressions, pace, word choice, and tone of voice suit your topic and purpose.
- ❏ You hold your audience's attention and achieve the purpose of your presentation.

In this unit, you read about the Civil War, a tragic era in which issues of slavery, economics, and states' rights divided the nation. Our understanding of these issues today is enhanced by reading the writing of the period. We can better understand slavery, for instance, by reading the autobiography of Frederick Douglass, who risked his life to publish this work and fight for abolition.

Think about the problems in your own life. While they may not be as large or serious as the issues dealt with in this unit, they matter to you. You can give them weight through writing about them and persuading others of the importance of solving them.

In this assignment, you will explain and then solve a problem you are dealing with in your own life, proposing one or more reasonable solutions.

Assignment Plan, write, and revise an essay that explains a problem and suggests one or more solutions

Purpose To persuade others of the importance of the problem and the feasibility of your solutions

Audience Someone who is aware of or affected by the problem and may be interested in helping to solve it

---

WRITING RUBRIC

A successful problem/solution essay has these elements:

- ❏ an introduction that identifies the problem, gives it context, and captures readers' interest
- ❏ a thesis statement that clearly expresses the argument the writer plans to make
- ❏ a body that demonstrates the scope of the problem and provides a feasible solution to it
- ❏ a conclusion that restates the thesis and brings closure to discussion

---

❶ Prewrite

Select Your Topic
Create a list of five to ten topics—problems you would like to solve. Then choose the one that you are most passionate about or that affects you most directly.

Next, brainstorm a list of possible solutions to that problem. Then focus on the ones that are feasible in terms of the time, cost, people, or effort needed to apply them. Choose one or two realistic solutions.

Gather Information
Think carefully about your problem. What do you need to demonstrate to others to convince them of the need to solve it?

Create a simple chart on which you record your feelings about the problem and why you have them (see page 363, columns 1 and 2). Provide four or five reasons that demonstrate why this issue is problematic. Next, consider how others might disagree with your views. By anticipating opposing viewpoints, you can strengthen your argument. Record these opposing viewpoints in column 3. Finally, think about how you will respond to these opposing viewpoints. Write your *rebuttal* to each point in column 4.

Analyze each solution the same way. Why is it feasible? Why might others disagree with it? How can you respond to people with opposing views?

Organize Your Ideas
Put Xs next to the three points that best demonstrate the problem. Number them in the order you want them to appear in the essay. You should begin with the strongest or most common argument.

If you have provided more than one solution, decide now which one is best. Circle the solution on the chart that you will propose in your essay.

Write Your Thesis Statement
Based on the points and solution you have identified, write a **thesis statement.** Using information from the Problem Chart, one student, Allison, wrote this thesis statement about controlling Internet access in schools:

> *Internet access in schools should be restricted by installing software to block out inappropriate websites.*

Problem Chart: Internet Use at Schools

My Feelings	Why I Feel This Way	Opposing Viewpoints	My Rebuttal
1 X Some websites contain offensive, even harmful content	Many sites contain materials that are pornographic, violent, racist, drug related, and so on	Students have seen it all	Not all students have seen it all; most don't want to see this content and shouldn't have to
3 X Viewing websites makes money for their owners	More inappropriate sites appear online every day; easy to access, even by accident	People can choose not to view these sites	Schools should not support these sites in any way
Viewing inappropriate websites corrupts people's morals	Students will be influenced by seeing and reading offensive materials	Students are old enough to decide for themselves	Students might have this option at home but should not at school
2 X Viewing inappropriate websites is a waste of time	This content is not school related, and viewing it takes away from schoolwork	Students should be able to look at whatever they want during their free time	Other students might be offended by or distracted by these sites
<u>Solution:</u> Install Internet-blocking software on school computers	Its the best way to ensure that only appropriate materials will be accessed	Doing so might restrict access to certain school-related topics	Such cases would be rare; the advantages of blocking would outweigh the drawbacks

❷ Draft

Write your essay by following this three-part framework: introduction, body, and conclusion.

Introduction Put the problem in a context that will interest readers, and state your thesis, proposing how to solve the problem.

Body First, define the problem and demonstrate why it is problematic, supporting each main point with evidence and addressing opposing views.

Conclusion Restate your thesis and bring the discussion to a close.

What Great Writers Do

According to Samuel Johnson, eighteenth-century British poet and essayist, "The two most engaging powers of an author are to make new things familiar, and familiar things new." Think about the writers whose work you read in this unit. How are they able to draw in readers by making a foreign topic accessible or by opening readers' eyes to see an old issue in a new way?

JOHNSON

Draft Your Introduction

In writing the introduction, focus on doing two things. First, put the problem in a context that will interest your readers. You can accomplish this by introducing the problem with a shocking fact or personalizing it with an anecdote. Think about what will get your audience's attention. Second, convince readers of the importance of your topic. Why should they care about this problem? Present a clear thesis statement that identifies how to solve the problem.

The introduction that Allison wrote during the Draft stage is shown in the first column on page 365. In the first sentence, Allison puts her problem in context, and in the second sentence, she states her thesis. Her introduction seems abrupt, however. How could she ease into her argument and make readers appreciate the seriousness of this issue?

Draft Your Body

Start by demonstrating the scope of the problem, and then offer a solution. Use the information from the Problem Chart you completed earlier.

Look at the draft of Allison's first body paragraph in the left-hand column of the chart on page 365. This paragraph presents what Allison believes is the most compelling reason for blocking Internet access to inappropriate websites: the content on these sites is offensive and even dangerous. Allison also wrote two more body paragraphs, presenting her other two reasons for controlling access, and another body paragraph presenting her solution.

Review the three statements you circled on your Problem Chart. Develop each into a paragraph by adding evidence based on personal knowledge or research. Ensure that the order in which you present the paragraphs will convince readers of the seriousness of the problem and lead them to your solution.

Draft Your Conclusion

Your conclusion should restate your thesis and close the discussion. In a problem/solution essay, the conclusion also often provides a warning or call to action.

Look at the draft of Allison's conclusion in the chart on page 366. Does she do these things?

❸ Revise

Evaluate Your Draft

Look at your own essay, or exchange essays with a classmate and evaluate each other's work. Think carefully about what parts of the essay are sound and what can be improved.

Start by looking at the content and organization. Make sure that the three parts of the essay—the introduction, body, and conclusion—function as a whole to prove the thesis. It should be obvious how each paragraph connects the next and relates to the thesis, or argument. Use the Revision Checklist on page 366 to help you evaluate.

Next, review your draft to ensure you have followed the guidelines in the Grammar & Style workshops in this unit. Again, use the Revision Checklist to assess the writing.

Another way to improve your writing is to replace vague words with more exact words. Notice some of the word changes Allison made in the Revise stage.

Revise for Content, Organization, and Style

Allison evaluated her essay and noted a number of things that could be improved. Look at the chart on pages 365–366 (this time, the right-hand column) to see how she revised the three paragraphs you read earlier:

- **Introduction:** Allison added an anecdote, providing a context that helped her student readers identify with the problem.
- **Body:** By adding details and improving word choices, Allison clarified the problem and led readers to her solution.
- **Conclusion:** By focusing on the idea of preventing harm, Allison further proved the importance of solving the problem.

Review the notes you or your partner made on your draft. Apply relevant comments as you revise your draft.

DRAFT STAGE		REVISE STAGE	
Introduction While it is true that the Internet offers the largest single source of information in schools, its use can have some negative consequences. Internet access at schools should be restricted by installing software to block out inappropriate websites.	Provides a context for the problem States the thesis	Four male students cluster around one of the Internet-ready computers against the wall. They snicker and gesture to one another. Their faces redden as their bodies shake with laughter. A nearby freshman abandons her work and leaves the library. Does this scene sound familiar to you? While ~~it is true that~~ the Internet offers the largest ~~single~~ source of information in schools, its unrestricted use can have ~~some~~ negative and unintended consequences for both students and schools. To avoid potential harm, Internet access at schools should be restricted by installing software to block out inappropriate websites.	Adds an anecdote to interest readers Eliminates unnecessary words Adds details for clarity Leads into thesis with transition
Body Paragraph Students can access a lot of offensive content on the Internet. In addition to websites that promote pornography, there are sites promoting racism, violence, hatred, and other views. Some websites glorify drug use and other dangerous behaviors. People against restricting Internet access argue that students today have seen it all, so that nothing shocks or entices them anymore. Many students have not been exposed to these kinds of materials and don't want to be.	Describes types of websites Identifies opposing view	Students can access a ~~lot~~ wide range of offensive content on the Internet. In addition to websites that promote pornography, there are sites ~~promoting~~ that promote racism, violence, hatred, and other views that may conflict with students' religious and ethical beliefs. Some websites glorify drug use and other dangerous behaviors, which may interest students in trying them. People against restricting Internet access argue that students today have seen it all, so that nothing shocks or entices them anymore. In fact, ~~M~~many students have not been exposed to these kinds of materials and don't want to be.	Makes description more specific Use parallel construction Explains potential harm from viewing these websites Adds transition

DRAFT STAGE		REVISE STAGE	
Conclusion			
The benefits of restricting students' Internet access far outweigh the potential drawbacks. Schools can prevent students from viewing inappropriate materials and make the time they spend in school more productive. In addition, schools can decide not to support individuals and companies who take advantage of children.	Restates thesis	The benefits of restricting students' Internet access far outweigh the potential drawbacks. Schools can ~~prevent~~ protect students from the potential harm of viewing inappropriate materials and make the time they spend in school more productive. In addition, schools can ~~decide not to support~~ take a stand against individuals and companies who take advantage of unsuspecting and immature consumers, such as children.	Restates goal of preventing harm

Uses more compelling language to issue a warning |

REVISION CHECKLIST

Content & Organization

❏ Does the introduction put the argument into a context that will interest readers?

❏ Does the introduction include a clear thesis statement?

❏ Does each paragraph in the body connect to the thesis, providing relevant evidence to back up its point? Are counterarguments successfully rebutted?

❏ Does the body offer a feasible solution to the problem?

❏ Does the conclusion restate the argument, or thesis? Does it bring the essay to a close and provide a warning or call for action?

Grammar & Style

❏ Have you written well-structured paragraphs? (page 285)

❏ Have you used parallel structures? (page 304)

❏ Have you used transitional words and phrases? (page 314)

Proofread for Errors

You can look for errors as you evaluate your essay, but focus now on any you might have missed or introduced in adding new material. Use proofreader's symbols to mark the errors you find. To complete the assignment, print out a final draft and read it aloud before turning it in.

Read Allison's final draft on the next page. Note how she worked through the three stages of the writing process: Prewrite, Draft, and Revise.

Writing Follow-Up

Publish and Present

● Set up a debate with any classmates who wrote about the same problem you did but made a different argument or provided a different solution.

● Submit your piece for publication as an editorial in the school newspaper or in a local publication.

Reflect

● Did developing and writing your argument change your feelings about this problem? Explain.

● What other solutions did you identify in brainstorming possible ways to solve this problem? Could you make a good argument for implementing any of them?

STUDENT MODEL

Consequences of Unrestricted Internet Access in Schools
by Allison Stewart

Four male students cluster around one of the computers against the wall. They snicker and gesture to one another. Then their faces redden as their bodies shake with laughter. A nearby freshman abandons her work and leaves the library. Does this scene sound familiar? While the Internet offers the largest source of information in schools, its unrestricted use can have negative and unintended consequences for both students and schools. To avoid potential harm, Internet access in schools should be restricted by installing software to block out inappropriate websites.

Students can access a wide range of offensive content on the Internet. In addition to websites that promote pornography, there are sites that promote racism, violence, hatred, and other views that may conflict with students' religious and ethical beliefs. Some websites glorify drug use and other dangerous behaviors, which may interest students in trying them. People against restricting Internet access argue that students today have seen it all, so that nothing shocks or entices them anymore. In fact, many students have not been exposed to these kinds of materials and don't want to be.

Another negative consequence of students being able to access inappropriate websites is that it wastes valuable time. The content of these sites clearly is not school related, and spending time viewing it takes away from learning. Students may have free time during the school day, but they should not waste it. Scenes like the one described earlier also distract other students, wasting their time, too.

Students' visiting inappropriate websites also has a disturbing consequence for schools: It puts them in the position of supporting these sites. Adult-themed websites, in particular, are a growing money-making industry, and their owners find ways to make them more and more accessible, even by accident. Although students can choose not to stay on these sites, schools should be able to prevent them from ever gaining access.

This problem of students' inappropriate access can be solved by installing Internet-blocking software on school computers. Doing so will ensure that students can visit only those websites with generally accepted subject matter. In some cases, students might be denied access to useful information. For instance, students doing online research for a paper about cocaine use might be barred from some websites. Such cases will be rare, however, and students will learn to use other sources of information.

The benefits of restricting students' Internet access far outweigh the potential drawbacks. Schools can protect students from the potential harm of viewing inappropriate materials and make the time they spend in school more productive. In addition, schools can take a stand against individuals and companies who take advantage of unsuspecting and immature consumers, such as children.

Margin notes:

What context does the writer provide for the argument?

What is the writer's thesis statement?

What is the potential harm of viewing inappropriate sites?

How does viewing inappropriate sites waste students' time?

What is the unintended consequence of this problem for students?

Name one drawback to installing Internet-blocking software.

What are the overall benefits of installing this software?

Reading Skills

Identify Author's Purpose

A writer's *purpose* is his or her aim or goal. Being able to determine an author's purpose or purposes is an important reading skill. To determine the writer's goal, ask yourself these questions: Why did the author write this piece? What is he or she trying to do? What response does he or she want to get from the reader?

An author may write with one or more of these purposes:

- to reflect
- to entertain, describe, enrich, or enlighten
- to tell a story or narrate a series of events
- to inform or explain
- to persuade

A writer's purpose corresponds to a specific *mode*, or type, of writing. The purpose of expressive writing—such as that found in a diary entry, personal letter, autobiography, or personal essay—tends to be to reflect on one's experiences or feelings. Character sketches, plays, and some poems are written to entertain readers or enrich their lives. Short stories, biogra-phies, myths, and historical accounts tell or narrate. The writers of news articles, research reports, expository essays, and book reviews want to inform readers about certain subjects. Editorials, petitions, political speeches, persuasive essays, and other forms of argu-mentative writing are intended to persuade.

Once you have identified what an author is trying to do, you can evaluate how well he or she achieved that purpose. For example, if you are convinced by the argument presented in a persuasive essay, then the author has been effective. If you view a play that does not hold your attention, then the author has failed to meet the goal of entertaining you.

> ### TEST-TAKING TIP
>
> When answering essay-type questions (often called *constructed responses*), remember that you are being evaluated on your understanding of the text. Although you can be somewhat creative in answering these questions, you still should include ideas, details, and examples from the passage you have read.

Practice

Directions: Read the following passage. The questions that come after it will concern identi-fying the author's purpose.

ORAL TRADITION / SPIRITUAL: The following is an anonymous African-American song called "Follow the Drinking Gourd."

When the sun comes back and the first quail calls,
Follow the drinking gourd,
For the old man is a-waiting for to carry you to freedom
If you follow the drinking gourd.

Chorus
5 Follow the drinking gourd,
Follow the drinking gourd,
For the old man is a-waiting for to carry you to freedom
If you follow the drinking gourd.

The river bank will make a very good road,
10   The dead trees show you the way,
The left foot, peg foot[1] traveling on
Follow the drinking gourd.

Repeat **Chorus**

The river ends between two hills,
Follow the drinking gourd.
15   There's another river on the other side,
Follow the drinking gourd.

Repeat **Chorus**

Where the little river meets the great big river,
Follow the drinking gourd.
The old man is a-waiting for to carry you to freedom
20   If you follow the drinking gourd.

---

1. **peg foot.** Wooden foot; orthopedic relpacement

Multiple Choice

1. What is the main purpose of the song's title?
   A. to create a strong visual image
   B. to entertain the listener
   C. to emphasize and summarize what the song is saying
   D. to provide something to which the listener could relate

2. Which of these best describes the purpose of the selection?
   F. to help slave owners find escaping slaves
   G. to state explicitly the route to freedom
   H. to remember the plight of slaves
   J. to help slaves escape to safety

3. How is the refrain connected to this purpose?
   A. It explains where to buy a ticket for the Underground Railroad.
   B. It tells listeners to follow the Big Dipper to get to freedom.
   C. It reminds listeners to bring water for the journey.
   D. It tells slave owners that the slaves are heading North.

4. The original main purpose of oral tradition in general is to
   F. pass on information to people who could not read.
   G. entertain people who like music.
   H. display the talents of the storyteller or singer.
   J. tell listeners what they need to do.

Constructed Response

5. Discuss the key details in this song and the specific purpose of each. Explain what these details have in common.

Writing Skills

Plan Your Response

After evaluating the essay prompt, your next step is to collect and organize your thoughts about it. First, determine the main point you want to make in your response. Jot it down on a piece of scratch paper. Next, think about the supporting ideas you will provide to prove your main point. These ideas should be broad enough that you can write a paragraph about each but not so broad as to be vague.

To organize your supporting ideas, number them to show the order in which they should be presented. If there is a natural order to your supporting ideas, such as *sequential* or *chronological,* you probably should use it in writing your response. When writing a persuasive response, using a *rhetorical* organization, in which you lead up to your strongest point, generally is most effective. Doing so allows you to build the case for your main idea and finish with your strongest point.

The result of planning your response should be an outline. Follow it when writing your essay to ensure it is focused and well organized.

TEST-TAKING TIP

Although you will be evaluated on the quality, not the quantity, of what you write, keep in mind that an essay generally has at least five paragraphs. The first paragraph should provide an introduction, the middle three paragraphs should discuss the topic, and the last paragraph should state a conclusion. Each paragraph should consist of three or more sentences in order to be fully developed.

Practice

Timed Writing: 30 minutes

The outcome of the Aesop's fable "The Tortoise and the Hare" suggests that "Slow and steady wins the race." Some people agree with this belief, suggesting that being thorough and working steadily toward a goal will ensure success. Others argue that in today's fast-changing world, doing things quickly and with flash or style is more important. In general, whom do you think will do better in high school: the student who is thorough and steady or the one who is fast and flashy?

In your essay, take a position on this question. You may write about either of the two perspectives given, or you may provide a different perspective on this question. Use specific reasons and examples to support your position.

Revising and Editing Skills

Some standardized tests ask you to read a draft of an essay and answer questions about how to improve it. As you read the draft, watch for errors such as these:

- incorrect spellings
- disagreement between subject and verb; inconsistent verb tense; incorrect forms for irregular verbs; sentence fragments and run-ons; double negatives; and incorrect use of frequently confused words, such as *affect* and *effect*

- missing end marks, incorrect comma use, and lowercased proper nouns and proper adjectives
- unclear purpose, unclear main ideas, and lack of supporting details
- confusing order of ideas and missing transitions
- language or mood that is inappropriate to the audience and purpose

After checking for errors, read each test question and decide which answer is best.

Practice

Directions: In the passage that follows, certain words and phrases are numbered and underlined. In the questions below the passage, alternatives are provided for each underlined word or phrase. In each case, choose the alternative that best expresses the idea, that is worded most consistently with the style and tone of the rest of the passage, or that makes the text correct according to the conventions of standard English. If you think the original version is best, choose the first alternative, "No change." To indicate your answer, circle the letter of the chosen alternative.

(1) We are surrounded by examples of people <u>today demanding speed: high-speed Internet,</u> overnight deliveries, faxes, instant messaging, 24-hour turnarounds. (2) In some <u>cases, speed is certainly desirable—like technology.</u> (3) <u>But somethings cannot be hurried; they</u> take planning, attention, and just plain time. (4) <u>The high school student whom is slow—within reason—and steady, like the hare,</u> will win the race.

Multiple Choice

1. A. No change.
   B. today, demanding speed: high-speed Internet
   C. today, demanding speed: high-speed internet
   D. today whom demand speed: high-speed Internet

2. F. No change.
   G. cases speed is certainly desirable—like technology
   H. cases, such as with technology, speed is certainly desirable
   J. cases, certainly, speed is desirable—like technology

3. A. No change.
   B. But some things cannot be hurried; they
   C. Somethings, however, cannot be hurried; they
   D. But some things cannot be hurried, they

4. F. No change.
   G. The high school student who is slow—within reason—and steady, like the hare,
   H. The high school student whom is slow—within reason—and steady like the hare,
   J. The high school student who is slow within reason and steady, like the hare,

Valley of the Yosemite, 1864. Albert Bierstadt.
Private collection.

Expanding Frontiers

Unit 4

1865–1910

Expanding Frontiers 1865–1910

1865

1875

AMERICAN LITERATURE AMERICAN LITERATURE AMERICAN LITERATURE AMI

1865
Mark Twain's short story "The Notorious Jumping Frog of Calaveras County" is published in the *New York Saturday Press*

1868
W. E. B. Du Bois is born on February 23

1868
Louisa May Alcott publishes *Little Women*

1873
Congress enacts the Comstock Law, making it illegal to send any "obscene, lewd, or lascivious" books through the mail

1876
Mark Twain publishes *The Adventures of Tom Sawyer*

1880
Henry James publishes *Portrait of a Lady* as a serialized novel in *Atlantic Monthly*

1881
Susan B. Anthony and Elizabeth Cady Stanton publish *History of Woman Suffrage*

1884
Mark Twain publishes *Adventures of Huckleberry Finn*

1884
Kate Chopin publishes *Bayou Folk*

1889
Theodore Roosevelt publishes the first volume of *The Winning of the West*

ROOSEVEL

AMERICAN HISTORY AMERICAN HISTORY AMERICAN HISTORY AMERICAN HIS

1865
Reconstruction begins under President Andrew Johnson

1867
Alaska is purchased from Russia for $7.2 million

1868
President Andrew Johnson is impeached; he avoids expulsion from office by one vote in the U.S. Senate

JOHNSON

1869
The transcontinental railroad is completed in Promontory, Utah

1870
Congress ratifies the Fifteenth Amendment, protecting African-American voting rights

1872
Yellowstone is established as the world's first national park

1876
Alexander Graham Bell invents the telephone

1876
Lakota Sioux and North Cheyenne forces defeat General George Armstrong Custer's cavalry at the Battle of Little Big Horn

1886
Samuel Gompers begins the American Federation of Labor (AFL) for skilled workers only

1886
A bomb is thrown during a labor union rally in Chicago, resulting in the Haymarket Riot

WORLD HISTORY WORLD HISTORY WORLD HISTORY WORLD HISTORY WORL

1866
Fyodor Dostoevsky publishes *Crime and Punishment*

1866
The Canadian parliament meets for the first time

1867
Karl Marx publishes the first volume of *Das Kapital*

1868
Emperor Meiji of Japan declares his own restoration to full power, ushering in a dramatic wave of Westernization

1870
The Franco-Prussian War begins in what is now Germany

1875
Egypt fails in an attempt to invade Ethiopia

1879
The Anglo-Zulu War begins in South Africa

1881
English troops attack Parihaka, a peaceful Maori community in New Zealand

1883
The volcanic island Krakatoa erupts, killing 36,000 people

1885
German inventor Karl Benz constructs the first gasoline-powered automobile

AMERICAN LITERATURE AMERICAN LITERATURE AMERICAN LITERATURE AMERICAN LITERATURE

1891
Herman Melville dies

1892
Walt Whitman dies

1892
Frances Ellen Watkins Harper publishes *Shadows Uplifted*, the second novel by an African-American woman released in the United States

1894
Robert Frost publishes his first poem

1895
Frederick Douglass dies

1897
Jack London sails to join the Klondike Gold Rush

WASHINGTON

1901
Booker T. Washington publishes *Up from Slavery*

1903
W. E. B. Du Bois publishes *The Souls of Black Folk*

1906
Jack London publishes *White Fang*

1906
Upton Sinclair publishes *The Jungle*, prompting Congress to pass the Pure Food and Drug Act

THE JUNGLE

UPTON SINCLAIR

AMERICAN HISTORY AMERICAN HISTORY AMERICAN HISTORY AMERICAN HISTORY AME

1890
The U.S. Seventh Cavalry kills 153 Lakota Sioux at Wounded Knee, including 63 women and children

1892
Preservationist John Muir founds the Sierra Club

1892
Ellis Island begins accepting immigrants into the United States

1894
The Pullman Strike occurs in Illinois

1898
The Spanish-American War begins with the sinking of the U.S.S. *Maine*

1901
Jazz trumpeter Louis Armstrong is born

1901
Theodore Roosevelt is elected president

1903
The Wright brothers make the first controlled airplane flight at Kitty Hawk, North Carolina

1909
W. E. B. Du Bois helps establish the National Association for the Advancement of Colored People (NAACP)

WORLD HISTORY WORLD HISTORY WORLD HISTORY WORLD HISTORY WORLD HISTORY WORLD HIS

1891
Lili'uokalani becomes Queen of Hawaii

1892
Lord Stanley of Preston donates the Stanley Cup as an annual award for Canada's top-ranking hockey team

1893
New Zealand becomes the first country to grant women voting rights

1895
The first Sino-Japanese War ends, making Korea a province of Japan

1899
The Boxer Rebellion breaks out in China

1901
The Commonwealth of Australia is formed

1902
The Second Boer War ends, resulting in two southern African republics being added to the British Empire

1904
Work begins on the Panama Canal

1904
The Russo-Japanese War begins

1905
Arthur Griffith establishes the Sinn Fèin party in Ireland

> # "What do I care about the law? Hain't I got the power?"
>
> —CORNELIUS VANDERBILT, AMERICAN ENTREPRENEUR

Reuniting the Nation

After the Civil War, U.S. leaders debated the political and economic rights of freed slaves and the role of federal power in the reunited states. Fearing the recently enacted Civil Rights Act of 1866 might be overturned by the courts, Congress passed the Fourteenth Amendment to the Constitution in 1868, granting full citizenship to all persons born in the United States. (However, a subsequent interpretation determined it did not apply to Native Americans.) The Fifteenth Amendment, which followed in 1870, granted male citizens the right to vote.

In the immediate years after the war, education in the South improved and African Americans played a significant role in politics, winning seats in the U.S. Congress. However, Southern white resistance to Reconstruction efforts (expressed in the rise of the Ku Klux Klan), growing Northern disinterest in Reconstruction, and court decisions limiting rights of new citizens led to passage of the Amnesty Act in 1872, pardoning most Confederates and allowing them to vote and hold office again. Predictably, the control of state governments returned to white elites. With the Compromise of 1877, which removed all federal troops from the South, Reconstruction was over. The way was open for Northern industrial capital to flow south and for state governments to legalize segregation through the adoption of "Jim Crow" laws.

> *"For there began to rise in America in 1876 a new capitalism and a new enslavement of labor."*
>
> —W. E. B. DU BOIS

Expanding Westward

Veterans of the Civil War, having traveled away from home for the first time in their lives, developed a taste for adventure. Some took advantage of the Homestead Act of 1862, which offered 160 acres for ten dollars to anyone who would live on the land for five years. The United States purchased Alaska from Russia, and the transcontinental railroad, completed in 1869, made travel far easier, although the graft ($86 million) associated with its construction was monumental.

Civil War veterans were joined in their westward trek by a flood of immigrants seeking a better life than they had found in the crowded cities of the East. The homesteaders turned the American plains into an agricultural region, surviving in sod houses, pumping water out of the ground with windmills, and fencing the land to protect their crops from wandering cattle herds.

Westward expansion was further fueled by dreams of discovering gold and silver, and the rough and tumble mining towns that sprung up gave rise to legends

of the "Wild West." Cattle raising, begun in Texas, became big business throughout the western plains, with herds of cattle driven to railroad stops that would take them to the Chicago stockyards.

Native American resentment grew as the new rail lines hastened the demise of the buffalo, the mainstay of many native cultures. Adding to the tension, the federal government broke treaty after treaty, moving native peoples to smaller and less desirable reservations of land so that settlers, railroads, and prospectors could take the better land. Thirty years of warfare ensued, ending tragically with the slaughter of mostly unarmed Lakota at Wounded Knee, South Dakota, in 1890.

The Native American quest for full citizenship was not successful until 1924, although the 1887 Dawes Act allowed those who took up a 160-acre allotment and lived separately from their tribes to become citizens. President Theodore Roosevelt described this provision as "a mighty pulverizing engine to break up the tribal mass." The hundreds of thousands of acres of land remaining after the individual allotments were then sold at bargain prices to land-hungry whites.

"I was born on the prairies where the wind blew free and there was nothing to break the light of the sun. I was born where there were no enclosures."

—GERONIMO, CHIRICAHUA APACHE LEADER

Population Growth and the Distribution of Wealth

A new wave of immigration starting in 1860 brought people from southern and eastern Europe (Italy, Poland, and Russia) and Asia to the United States, greatly diversifying the population. However, by the 1880s, anti-immigrant groups had formed, and they became successful in pushing through the legislature bills that required those seeking entry to have a minimum sum of money and that excluded the Chinese entirely.

Another trend during this period was the growth of cities, which attracted recent immigrants, freed African Americans from the South, and farmers seeking jobs in industry. Young women became increasingly important in the workforce, filling jobs in textile factories and so-called sweatshops. Cities began to build upward, and with the invention of the electric elevator, skyscrapers became possible.

After the Civil War, the use of kerosene lamps created a huge demand for oil, and steel replaced iron with the invention of the Bessemer process and open hearth. Benefiting from technological advances, a new class of millionaire industrialists emerged, controlling meatpacking, railroads, and oil and steel production. By 1877, the greatest economic expansion in history was underway.

Unfortunately, as the United States moved from a nation of farms to one of stores and factories, controls were not put in place to ensure a fair distribution of wealth. The government had no experience with large corporations, and consequently, shrewd businessmen were able to build empires by negotiating government subsidies, choking off competition, and keeping wages low and work hours long. Called "robber barons" by some and "captains of industry" by others, the trusts

NOTABLE NUMBERS

26 million Immigrants arriving in the United States between the end of the Civil War and 1900

40% Population living in cities by 1900; the urban population grew from 6 million to 44 million between 1860 and 1910

14,000 Children, many under age fourteen, working in the Pennsylvania coal mines in 1900

1,400 Strikes that occurred in 1886, involving 500,000 workers; up from about 500 a year, involving about 150,000 workers, over the previous four years

$50 Price paid for a buffalo hide in the late nineteenth century, at a time when an unskilled laborer made less than $1 per day

and monopolies formed by these giants destroyed small businesses.

When laborers began to form unions to improve their working conditions, creating the Knights of Labor and later the American Federation of Labor, company owners did all they could to break the unions. This sometimes resulted in loss of life, as in the 1892 strike at Carnegie Steel's Homestead Mine. Despite such determined opposition, the labor movement grew. Two landmark events in labor history were the 1886 Chicago Haymarket Square Affair, when a bomb exploded in the midst of a workers' rally, and the 1909 garment workers' strike in New York, when 20,000 workers, mostly women, walked off the job.

Populist Gains

Farming expanded after the Civil War, as the political situation stabilized and new lands were opened for settlement. The supply of farm products was larger than the demand for them, unfortunately, and so prices fell while costs for seed, storage, and transportation did not. Banding together in the Farmers' Alliance and its outgrowth, the Populist Party, farmers tried to create an independent culture for themselves in opposition to powerful industrial and political interests.

Child labor activists demonstrate for workers' rights.

In the cities, laborers also lived in poverty. Hostilities grew toward new immigrants, who often would work for lower wages than native workers. Overcrowded tenements proliferated, creating sanitation and health crises, while political bosses, such as New York's Tweed Ring, grew rich through graft.

Charitable enterprises attempted to help the poor by establishing settlement houses that offered services and education; among them was Chicago's Hull House, founded in 1889 by Jane Addams. Photographer Jacob Riis shot images of the New York slums, shocking citizens into calling for reform, and "muckraker" journalists exposed the unscrupulous practices of business owners and politicians.

Expanding Abroad

By 1890, the Bureau of the Census officially declared the United States' internal frontier closed. With the depression of 1893 and an enlarged industrial capacity, financial leaders began looking for overseas markets.

An opportunity arose in 1895 when Cuba rebelled against Spain. In 1898, the battleship *Maine*, anchored in the Havana harbor to convey U.S. interest in the situation, was mysteriously blown up, prompting President William McKinley to ask Congress for a declaration of war. When Spain was defeated three months later in "the splendid little war," the new Cuban government was forced to grant the United States the right to intervene in the country's affairs, and the United States acquired Puerto Rico, the Hawaiian Islands, and the Philippines. However, the Filipinos wanted independence and revolted against annexation. It took three years and thousands of Filipino deaths before the rebellion was crushed.

Acquiring these territories meant that huge new markets were opened for American enterprise. However, prominent voices were raised in moral outrage against these American forays, among them the members of the Anti-Imperialist League. Said Mark Twain, "We have pacified some thousands of the islanders and buried them, . . . and so by these Providences of God—and the phrase is the government's, not mine— we are a World Power."

Realism was the new and dominant mode in American fiction of the late nineteenth century. The early-nineteenth-century Romantics of New England had presented idealized writing designed to inspire lofty emotions. The Realists, in contrast, drew portraits from life, often shocking more sensitive readers with their grim depictions of realities, as the country itself had been shocked by the grim realities of the Civil War.

The use of local dialect and varied, unsavory characters were two expressions of Realism. In the short story "The Outcasts of Poker Flat," for instance, Bret Harte featured a gambler and prostitutes as main characters. Mark Twain, widely known for his satirical humor, often involving exaggerated, colorful characters, also showed elements of Realism. Because of its realistic use of a variety of dialects and its quintessentially American theme of the individual's quest for freedom, Twain's *Adventures of Huckleberry Finn* often is considered the greatest American novel.

At the turn of the century, **Naturalism,** an extension of Realism, became the dominant mode in American fiction. Inspired by nineteenth-century theorists such as Charles Darwin, Naturalism held that people's actions and beliefs resulted not from free will but from the arbitrary, outside forces of heredity and environment. In the United States, Naturalism found its champion in Stephen Crane in novels such as *The Red Badge of Courage* and stories such as "The Open Boat" and "A Mystery of Heroism." It was further realized in the works of such authors as Frank Norris, Jack London, and Theodore Dreiser.

Two Guides, c. 1875. Winslow Homer. Sterling and Francine Clark Art Institute, Williamstown, Massachusetts.

"A man cannot be comfortable without his own approval."

Mark Twain (1835–1910) was the pseudonym of Samuel Langhorne Clemens. He took the name from a term he encountered as a riverboat pilot that referred to water two fathoms deep, a safe depth for a riverboat. The leadsman on the boat would call out "Mark twain" when water of that depth had been reached.

Born in Florida, Missouri, Twain grew up in the nearby river town of Hannibal. His father died when he was just fourteen, forcing him to leave school and earn a living. He apprenticed himself to a printer, working for his older brother setting type. At twenty-one, he headed to New Orleans to depart for a trip to the Amazon River in South America. The plan fell apart, but Twain found a position as an apprentice riverboat pilot. When the Civil War interrupted trade on the Mississippi River, Twain was forced to find another job. He went west and found work as a reporter for several California newspapers.

Twain traveled to the Sandwich Islands (now Hawaii) as a correspondent for the *Sacramento Union*. On his return, he used the humorous articles he had written as the basis for a lecture series—the first in a long, successful career as a speaker. Twain won international attention in 1869 with his first book, *The Innocents Abroad*, which was a satire based on his travels in Europe and the Middle East. His next book, published in 1872, was *Roughing It*, a travel account in which he satirized life in the American West.

Twain eventually gave up newspaper reporting to concentrate full time on his books and public speaking. His most famous books—*The Adventures of Tom Sawyer* (1876), *Life on the Mississippi* (1883), and *Adventures of Huckleberry Finn* (1884)—all draw from his experiences on the Mississippi River. Twain's most famous novel, *Huckleberry Finn*, tells the story of a boy named Huck who, together with an escaped slave named Jim, travels down the Mississippi on a raft. Alternately funny and serious, the book is an indictment of racism, showing that beneath outward differences, people have similar feelings and dreams.

In the 1890s, Twain suffered a series of misfortunes, including the death of a daughter and monetary loss due to failed speculative investments. The writings of his last years are bitterly directed at the hypocrisies of his fellow human beings. Twain's most critical works were not published until long after his death.

Noted Works

The Innocents Abroad (1869)

Roughing It (1872)

The Adventures of Tom Sawyer (1876)

Life on the Mississippi (1883)

Adventures of Huckleberry Finn (1884)

The Notorious Jumping Frog of Calaveras County

A Short Story by Mark Twain

Build Background

Literary Context **"The Notorious Jumping Frog of Calaveras County"** is Mark Twain's retelling of a popular nineteenth-century **tall tale,** a lighthearted and humorous story that contains highly exaggerated, unrealistic events. Twain first became known nationally when the story was published in the *Saturday Press* in 1865. The story also is an outstanding example of Regionalist writing. It portrays the entertainments of simple, uneducated men living in a frontier mining camp in California.

Another of Twain's hallmarks—the pitting of East against West—also appears in this story. The narrator writes and speaks with a sophisticated vocabulary and shows mild disdain for the rustic and uneducated Westerners. Simon Wheeler, however, speaks in dialect and tells his stories like tall tales.

Historical Context Located about 130 miles east of San Francisco, at the foothills of the Sierra Nevada Mountains, Calaveras County was the site of the California Gold Rush, which drew thousands of prospectors from 1849 to 1859. The frog-jumping contest was started in 1928, when the town wanted to raise funds to pave roads in the growing mining town.

Reader's Context What story or fact have you exaggerated to impress a group of listeners?

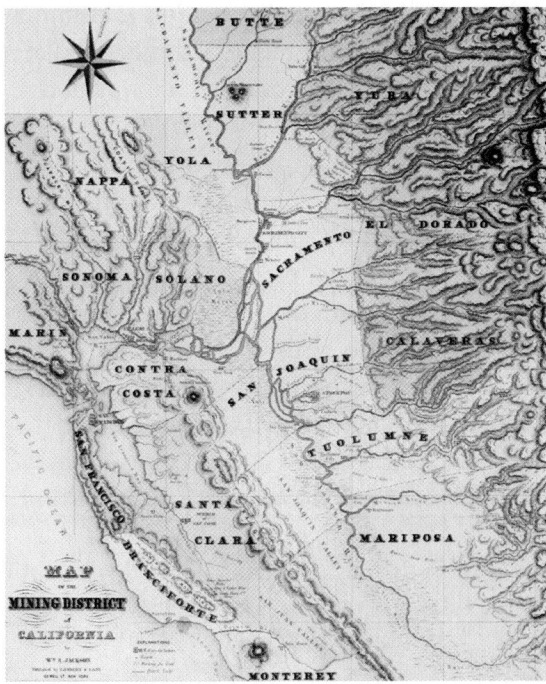

Map of California's mining district (c. 1850).

Analyze Literature

Dialect and Frame Tale
A **dialect** is a version of a language spoken by the people of a particular place, time, or social group.

A **frame tale** is a story that provides a vehicle for the telling of other stories.

Set Purpose

"The Notorious Jumping Frog" not only made Twain known to a national American audience, but it also demonstrated stylistic elements that would become trademarks of his storytelling. One of those elements was the use of dialect, which is found in the writing of many Realists. As you read, analyze Twain's use of western dialect and determine what it adds to the story. In addition, identify the story-within-a story, or frame tale, and evaluate whether this is an effective tool for telling a story.

Preview Vocabulary

garrulous, 382
append, 382
conjecture, 382
dilapidated, 382
interminable, 383
exhorter, 383
cavort, 384
ornery, 384
vagabond, 386
afflicted, 386

The Notorious Jumping Frog of Calaveras County

by Mark Twain

In compliance with the request of a friend of mine, who wrote me from the East, I called on good-natured, <u>garrulous</u> old Simon Wheeler, and inquired after my friend's friend, Leonidas W. Smiley, as requested to do, and I hereunto <u>append</u> the result. I have a lurking suspicion that *Leonidas W.* Smiley is a myth; that my friend never knew such a personage; and that he only <u>conjectured</u> that if I asked old Wheeler about him, it would remind him of his infamous *Jim* Smiley, and he would go to work and bore me to death with some exasperating reminiscence of him as long and as tedious as it should be useless to me. If that was the design, it succeeded.

I found Simon Wheeler dozing comfortably by the barroom stove of the <u>dilapidated</u> tavern in the decayed mining camp of Angel's, and I noticed that he was fat and bald-headed, and had an expression of winning gentleness and simplicity upon his tranquil countenance. He roused up, and gave me good-day. I told him a friend of mine had commissioned me to make some inquiries about a cherished companion of his boyhood named *Leonidas W.* Smiley— *Rev. Leonidas W.* Smiley, a young minister of the Gospel, who he had heard was at one time a resident of Angel's Camp. I added that if Mr. Wheeler could tell me anything about this Rev. Leonidas W. Smiley, I would feel under many obligations to him.

Simon Wheeler backed me into a corner and blockaded me there with his chair, and

gar • ru • lous (gär´ ə ləs) *adj.*, talking a lot or too much
ap • pend (ə pend´) *v.*, attach or affix
con • jec • ture (kən jek´ chər) *v.*, guess
di • lap • i • dat • ed (də lap´ ə dā təd) *adj.*, falling to pieces or into disrepair

then sat down and reeled off the monotonous narrative which follows this paragraph. He never smiled, he never frowned, he never changed his voice from the gentle-flowing key to which he tuned his initial sentence, he never betrayed the slightest suspicion of enthusiasm; but all through the <u>interminable</u> narrative there ran a vein of impressive earnestness and sincerity, which showed me plainly that, so far from his imagining that there was anything ridiculous or funny about his story, he regarded it as a really important matter, and admired its two heroes as men of transcendent genius in *finesse*.[1] I let him go on in his own way, and never interrupted him once.

Rev. Leonidas W. H'm, Reverend Le—well, there was a feller here once by the name of *Jim* Smiley, in the winter of '49—or maybe it was the spring of '50—I don't recollect exactly, somehow, though what makes me think it was one or the other is because I remember the big flume[2] warn't finished when he first come to the camp; but any way, he was the curiousest man about always betting on anything that turned up you ever see, if he could get anybody to bet on the other side; and if he couldn't he'd change sides. Any way that suited the other man would suit *him*—any way just so's he got a bet, *he* was satisfied. But still he was lucky, uncommon lucky; he most always come out winner. He was always ready and laying for a chance; there couldn't be no solit'ry thing mentioned but that feller'd offer to bet on it, and take any side you please, as I was just telling you. If there was a horserace, you'd find him flush[3] or you'd find him busted[4] at the end of it; if there was a dog-fight, he'd bet on it; if there was a cat-fight, he'd bet on it; if there was a chicken-fight, he'd bet on it; why, if there was two birds setting on a fence, he would bet you which one would fly first, or if there was a camp-meeting,[5] he would be there reg'lar to bet on Parson Walker, which he judged to be the best <u>exhorter</u> about here, and so he was too, and a good man. If he even see a straddle-bug[6] start to go anywheres, he would bet you how long it would take him to get to—to wherever he was going to, and if you took him up, he would foller that straddle-bug to Mexico but what he would find out where he was bound for and how long he was on the road. Lots of the boys here has seen that Smiley, and can tell you about him. Why, it never made no difference to *him*—he'd bet on *any* thing—the dangdest feller.

Parson Walker's wife laid very sick once, for a good while, and it seemed as if they warn't going to save her; but one morning he come in, and Smiley up and asked him how she was, and he said she was considable better—thank the Lord for his inf'nite mercy—and coming on so smart that with the blessing of Prov'dence she'd get well yet; and Smiley, before he thought says, "Well, I'll resk two-and-a-half she don't anyway."

> He was the curiousest man about always betting on anything that turned up you ever see.

---

1. **transcendent . . . finesse.** Extraordinary skill, cunning, or artfulness
2. **flume.** Artificial channel for carrying water to furnish power or transport objects
3. **flush.** Well supplied with money
4. **busted.** Penniless
5. **camp-meeting.** Religious gathering at a camp or mining community
6. **straddle-bug.** Long-legged insect

in • ter • mi • na • ble (in tʉr´ min ə bl´) *adj.*, without, or apparently without, end
ex • hor • ter (ig zôrt´ ər) *n.*, one who urges earnestly by advice or warning

Thish-yer Smiley had a mare—the boys called her the fifteen-minute nag, but that was only in fun, you know, because of course she was faster than that—and he used to win money on that horse, for all she was so slow and always had the asthma, or the distemper, or the consumption, or something of that kind. They used to give her two or three hundred yards start, and then pass her under way; but always at the fag end[7] of the race she'd get excited and desperate-like, and come <u>cavorting</u> and straddling up, and scattering her legs around limber, sometimes in the air, and sometimes out to one side among the fences, and kicking up m-o-r-e dust and raising m-o-r-e racket with her coughing and sneezing and blowing her nose—and *always* fetch up at the stand just about a neck ahead, as near as you could cipher it down.

And he had a little small bull-pup, that to look at him you'd think he warn't worth a cent but to set around and look <u>ornery</u> and lay for a chance to steal something. But as soon as money was up on him he was a different dog; his underjaw'd begin to stick out like the fo'castle[8] of a steamboat, and his teeth would uncover and shine like the furnaces. And a dog might tackle him and bully-rag him, and bite him, and throw him over his shoulder two or three times, and Andrew Jackson—which was the name of the pup—Andrew Jackson would never let on but what *he* was satisfied, and hadn't expected nothing else—and the

bets being doubled and doubled on the other side all the time, till the money was all up; and then all of a sudden he would grab that other dog jest by the j'int of his hind leg and freeze to it—not chaw, you understand, but only just grip and hang on till they throwed up the sponge, if it was a year. Smiley always come out winner on that pup, till he harnessed a dog once that didn't have no hind legs, because they'd been sawed off in a circular saw, and when the thing had gone along far enough, and the money was all up, and he come to make a snatch for his pet holt[9] he see in a minute how he's been imposed on, and how the other dog had him in the door, so to speak, and he 'peared surprised, and then he looked sorter discouraged-like, and didn't try no more to win the fight, and so he got shucked out bad. He give Smiley a look, as much as to say his heart was broke, and it was *his* fault, for putting up a dog that hadn't no hind legs for him to take holt of, which was his main dependence in a fight, and then he limped off a piece and laid down and died. It was a good pup, was that Andrew Jackson, and would have made a name for hisself if he'd lived, for the stuff was in him and he had genius—I know it, because he hadn't no opportunities to speak of, and it don't stand to reason that a dog could make such a fight as he could under them circumstances if he hadn't no talent. It always makes me feel sorry when I think of that last fight of his'n, and the way it turned out.

Well, thish-yer Smiley had rat-terriers[10] and chicken cocks,[11] and tomcats and all them kind of things, till you couldn't rest, and you couldn't fetch nothing for him to bet on but

---

7. **fag end.** Last part
8. **fo'castle.** Upper deck of a boat; part of a bow that protrudes
9. **pet holt.** Favorite hold
10. **rat-terriers.** Small, aggressive dogs
11. **chicken cocks.** Roosters trained to fight each other

---

ca • vort (kə vōrt´) *v.,* leap about; prance
or • nery (ōr´ nər ē) *adj.,* having an ugly or mean disposition

Mark Twain on Civilization

At the time Mark Twain wrote "The Notorious Jumping Frog of Calaveras County," the American West was relatively young and undeveloped. Easterners tended to feel superior to Westerners, whom they regarded as uneducated and uncivilized. (Europeans tended to feel superior to Americans for the same reasons.)

Twain satirized these arrogant, superficial individuals, making fun of their values and lifestyles and sometimes revealing their behavior to be self-serving and even cruel. He once remarked, "Good breeding consists of concealing how much we think of ourselves and how little we think of the other person." Avoiding the corrupting influence of civilization is another of the main themes in *The Adventures of Tom Sawyer* and *Adventures of Huckleberry Finn*.

he'd match you. He ketched a frog one day, and took him home, and said he cal'lated to educate him; and so he never done nothing for three months but set in his back yard and learn that frog to jump. And you bet you he *did* learn him, too. He'd give him a little punch behind, and the next minute you'd see that frog whirling in the air like a doughnut—see him turn one summerset, or maybe a couple, if he got a good start, and come down flat-footed and all right, like a cat. He got him up so in the matter of ketching flies, and kep' him in practice so constant, that he'd nail a fly every time as fur as he could see him. Smiley said all a frog wanted was education, and he could do 'most anything—and I believe him. Why, I've seen him set Dan'l Webster down here on this floor—Dan'l Webster was the name of the frog—and sing out, "Flies, Dan'l, flies!" and quicker'n you could wink he'd spring straight up and snake a fly off'n the counter there, and flop down on

the floor ag'in as solid as a gob of mud, and fall to scratching the side of his head with his hind foot as indifferent as if he hadn't no idea he'd been doin' any more'n any frog might do. You never see a frog so modest and straightfor'ard as he was, for all he was so gifted. And when it come to fair and square jumping on a dead level, he could get over more ground at one straddle than any animal of his breed you ever see. Jumping on a dead level was his strong suit, you understand; and when it come to that, Smiley would ante up money on him as long as he had a red.[12] Smiley was monstrous proud of his frog, and well he might be, for fellers that had traveled and been everywheres all said he laid over any frog that ever *they* see.

Well, Smiley kep' the beast in a little lattice box, and he used to fetch him down-town sometimes and lay for a bet. One day a feller—a stranger in the camp, he was—come acrost him with his box, and says:

"What might it be that you've got in the box?"

And Smiley says, sorter indifferent-like, "It might be a parrot, or it might be a canary, maybe, but it ain't—it's only just a frog."

And the feller took it, and looked at it careful, and turned it round this way and that, and says, "H'm—so 'tis. Well, what's *he* good for?"

"Well," Smiley says, easy and careless, "he's good enough for *one* thing, I should judge—he can outjump any frog in Calaveras county."

The feller took the box again, and took another long, particular look, and give it back to Smiley, and says, very deliberate, "Well," he says, "I don't see no p'ints about that frog that's any better'n any other frog."

"Maybe you don't," Smiley says. "Maybe you understand frogs and maybe you don't understand em; maybe you've had experience, and maybe you ain't only a amature, as it were. Anyways, I've got *my* opinion, and I'll resk forty dollars that he can outjump any frog in Calaveras county."

---

12. **red.** Red cent; very small amount of money

And the feller studied a minute, and then says, kinder sad like, "Well, I'm only a stranger here, and I ain't got no frog; but if I had a frog, I'd bet you."

And then Smiley says. "That's all right—that's all right—if you'll hold my box a minute, I'll go and get you a frog." And so the feller took the box and put up his forty dollars along with Smiley's, and set down to wait.

So he set there a good while thinking and thinking to hisself, and then he got the frog out and pried his mouth open and took a tea-spoon and filled him full of quailshot[13]—filled him pretty near up to his chin—and set him on the floor. Smiley he went to the swamp and slopped around in the mud for a long time, and finally he ketched a frog, and fetched him in, and give him to this feller, and says:

"Now, if you're ready, set him alongside of mDan'l, with his forepaws just even with Dan'l's, and I'll give the word." Then he says, "One—two—three—*git!*" and him and the feller touched up the frogs from behind, and the new frog hopped off lively, but Dan'l give a heave, and hysted up his shoulders—so—like a Frenchman, but it warn't no use—he couldn't budge; he was planted as solid as a church, and he couldn't no more stir than if he was anchored out. Smiley was a good deal sur-prised, and he was disgusted too, but he didn't have no idea what the matter was, of course.

The feller took the money and started away; and when he was going out at the door, he sorter jerked his thumb over his shoulder—so—at Dan'l, and says, again very deliberate, "Well," he says, "*I* don't see no p'ints about that frog that's any better'n any other frog."

Smiley he stood scratching his head and looking down at Dan'l a long time, and at last he says, "I do wonder what in the nation that frog throw'd off for—I wonder if there ain't something the matter with him—he 'pears to look mighty baggy, somehow." And he ketched Dan'l by the nap of the neck, and hefted him, and says, "Why blame my cats if he don't weigh five pound!" and turned him upside down and he belched out a double handful of shot. And then he see how it was, and he was the maddest man—he set the frog down and took out after that feller, but he never ketched him. And—

Here Simon Wheeler heard his name called from the front yard, and got up to see what was wanted. And turning to me as he moved away, he said: "Just set where you are, stranger, and rest easy—I ain't going to be gone a second."

But, by your leave, I did not think that a continuation of the history of the enterprising <u>vagabond</u> *Jim* Smiley would be likely to afford me much information concerning the *Rev. Leonidas W.* Smiley, and so I started away.

At the door I met the sociable Wheeler returning, and he button-holed[14] me and recommenced;

"Well, thish-yer Smiley had a yaller one-eyed cow that didn't have no tail, only jest a short stump like a bannanner, and—"

However, lacking both time and inclina-tion, I did not wait to hear about the <u>afflicted</u> cow, but took my leave. ❖

---

13. **quailshot.** Lead pellets used for hunting quail
14. **button-holed.** Made a person listen, as if by grabbing his or her coat by a buttonhole

---

vag • a • bond (văg´ ə bänd) *n.*, wandering, idle, disreputable, or shiftless person
af • flic • ted (ə flik´ təd) *adj.,* suffering from an illness or other painful physical condition

---

Would you have been interested in or bored by Wheeler's story of the cow? What makes someone a good storyteller?

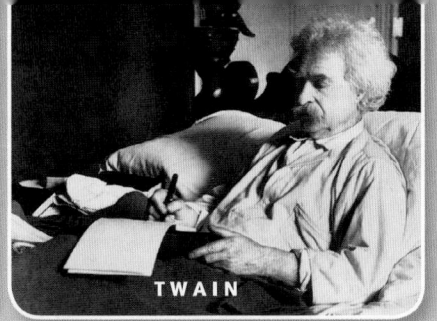

TWAIN

Primary Source Connection

Mark Twain is still considered one of America's greatest humorists and storytellers, as demonstrated by the continued popularity of stories such as "The Notorious Jumping Frog of Calaveras County" and novels such as *The Adventures of Tom Sawyer* and *Adventures of Huckleberry Finn*. To Twain, storytelling was an art.

Twain shared his secrets for successful storytelling in the essay **"How to Tell a Story."** Published in 1897, in the later years of Twain's career, the essay provides the author's insights on how to tell a humorous story, in particular. Twain forewarns his readers that doing so is difficult and later remarks, "This is art—and fine and beautiful, and only a master can compass it."

How to Tell a Story
by Mark Twain

The Humorous Story, an American Development.—Its Difference from Comic and Witty Stories.

I do not claim that I can tell a story as it ought to be told. I only claim to know how a story ought to be told, for I have been almost daily in the company of the most expert story-tellers for many years.

There are several kinds of stories, but only one difficult kind—the humorous. I will talk mainly about that one. The humorous story is American, the comic story is English, the witty story is French. The humorous story depends for its effect upon the *manner* of the telling; the comic story and the witty story upon the *matter*.

The humorous story may be spun out to great length, and may wander around as much as it pleases, and arrive nowhere in particular; but the comic and witty stories must be brief and end with a point. The humorous story bubbles gently along, the others burst.

The humorous story is strictly a work of art—high and delicate art—and only an artist can tell it; but no art is necessary in telling the comic and the witty story; anybody can do it. The art of telling a humorous story—understand, I mean by word of mouth, not print—was created in America, and has remained at home.

The humorous story is told gravely; the teller does his best to conceal the fact that he even dimly suspects that there is anything funny about it; but the teller of the comic story tells you beforehand that it is one of the funniest things he has ever heard, then tells it with eager delight, and is the first person to laugh when he gets through. And sometimes, if he has had good success, he is so glad and happy that he will repeat the "nub" of it and glance around from face to face, collecting applause, and then repeat it again. It is a pathetic thing to see.

Very often, of course, the rambling and disjointed humorous story finishes with a nub, point, snapper, or whatever you like to call it. Then the listener must be alert, for in many cases the teller will divert attention from that nub by dropping it in a carefully casual and indifferent way, with the pretence that he does not know it is a nub.

Artemus Ward[1] used that trick a good deal; then when the belated audience presently caught the joke he would look up with innocent surprise, as if wondering what they had found to laugh at. Dan Setchell[2] used it before him, Nye[3] and Riley[4] and others use it to-day.

But the teller of the comic story does not slur the nub; he shouts it at you—every time. And when he prints it, in England, France, Germany, and Italy, he italicizes it, puts some whooping exclamation-points after it, and sometimes explains it in a parenthesis. All of which is very depressing, and makes one want to renounce joking and lead a better life.

Let me set down an instance of the comic method, using an anecdote which has been popular all over the world for twelve or fifteen hundred years. The teller tells it in this way:

The Wounded Soldier

In the course of a certain battle a soldier whose leg had been shot off appealed to another soldier who was hurrying by to carry him to the rear, informing him at the same time of the loss which he had sustained; whereupon the generous son of Mars,[5] shouldering the unfortunate, proceeded to carry out his desire. The bullets and cannon-balls were flying in all directions, and presently one of the latter took the wounded man's head off—without, however, his deliverer being aware of it. In no long time he was hailed by an officer, who said:

"Where are you going with that carcass?"

"To the rear, sir—he's lost his leg!"

"His leg, forsooth?" responded the astonished officer; "you mean his head, you booby."

Whereupon the soldier dispossessed himself of his burden, and stood looking down upon it in great perplexity. At length he said:

"It is true, sir, just as you have said." Then after a pause he added, "*But he* TOLD *me* IT WAS HIS LEG!!!!!"

Here the narrator bursts into explosion after explosion of thunderous horse-laughter, repeating that nub from time to time through his gaspings and shriekings and suffocatings.

It takes only a minute and a half to tell that in its comic-story form; and isn't worth the telling, after all. Put into the humorous-story form it takes ten minutes, and is about the funniest thing I have ever listened to—as James Whitcomb Riley tells it.

He tells it in the character of a dull-witted old farmer who has just heard it for the first time, thinks it is unspeakably funny, and is trying to repeat it to a neighbor. But he can't remember it; so he gets all mixed up and wanders helplessly round and round, putting in tedious details that don't belong in the tale and only retard it; taking them out conscientiously and putting in others that are just as useless; making minor mistakes now and then and stopping to correct them and explain how he came to make them; remembering things which he forgot to put in their proper place and going back to put them in there; stopping his narrative a good while in order to try to recall the

---

1. **Artemus Ward.** Pen name of Charles Farrar Browne (1834–1867), popular American humorous writer and lecturer
2. **Dan Setchell.** American comic actor (1831–c. 1866)
3. **Nye.** Edgar Wilson Nye (1850–1896), also known as Bill Nye, well-known American humorist who spent much of his life out west
4. **Riley.** James Whitcomb Riley (1849–1916), known as the "Hoosier poet" and well liked for his humorous verse
5. **generous son of Mars.** Soldier; Mars was the Roman god of war

exhausted, and the tears are running down their faces.

The simplicity and innocence and sincerity and unconsciousness of the old farmer are perfectly simulated, and the result is a performance which is thoroughly charming and delicious. This is art—and fine and beautiful, and only a master can compass it; but a machine could tell the other story.

To string incongruities and absurdities together in a wandering and sometimes purposeless way, and seem innocently unaware that they are absurdities, is the basis of the American art, if my position is correct. Another feature is the slurring of the point. A third is the dropping of a studied remark apparently without knowing it, as if one were thinking aloud. The fourth and last is the pause. . . .

The pause is an exceedingly important feature in any kind of story, and a frequently recurring feature, too. It is a dainty thing, and delicate, and also uncertain and treacherous; for it must be exactly the right length—no more and no less—or it fails of its purpose and makes trouble. If the pause is too short the impressive point is passed, and the audience have had time to divine that a surprise is intended—and then you can't surprise them, of course. ❖

name of the soldier that was hurt, and finally remembering that the soldier's name was not mentioned, and remarking placidly that the name is of no real importance, anyway—better, of course, if one knew it, but not essential, after all—and so on, and so on, and so on.

The teller is innocent and happy and pleased with himself, and has to stop every little while to hold himself in and keep from laughing outright; and does hold in, but his body quakes in a jelly-like way with interior chuckles; and at the end of the ten minutes the audience have laughed until they are

Review Questions

1. List the three types of funny stories Twain describes. According to Twain, what makes the humorous story more difficult than the other two types?

2. What does it mean to "slur the nub"? Describe the manner a humorous storyteller must have to convey his or her tale successfully.

3. What is the basis of the American art, according to Twain? Would the story of the Wounded Soldier be better told in the way Twain suggests? Argue whether it is more difficult to have a humorous manner than tell a funny story.

TEXT $\overset{TO}{\underset{}{\rightleftarrows}}$ TEXT CONNECTION

Make two columns on a sheet of paper. In one column, list the characteristics of the humorous story. In the other column, list the characteristics of the comic story and witty story. What are the differences between the two? In "The Notorious Jumping Frog," how does Twain portray Simon Wheeler as the ideal humorous storyteller?

Refer to Text ▶ ▶ ▶ ▶ ▶ Reason with Text

1a. Why does the narrator go to see Simon Wheeler? About whom does Simon Wheeler tell a story?	**1b.** Describe the narrator's response to Wheeler's story. Why might the narrator have this response?	**Understand** Find meaning
2a. Describe how Smiley uses the horse and Andrew Jackson for gambling.	**2b.** How can you predict that Dan'l Webster will lose the contest?	**Apply** Use information
3a. Identify the elements that make this story humorous.	**3b.** What tale would Simon Wheeler have related about the cow if he had been given the chance?	**Analyze** Take things apart
4a. List all the different things on which Jim Smiley bets.	**4b.** Is Smiley a gifted gambler or an addicted gambler? Explain.	**Evaluate** Make judgments
5a. What is remarkable about Dan'l Webster? Why does he lose the contest?	**5b.** Read another tall tale, such as Paul Bunyan, Pecos Bill, John Henry, or Johnny Appleseed. Then compare and contrast it to "The Notorious Jumping Frog of Calaveras County."	**Create** Bring ideas together

Analyze Literature

Dialect and Frame Tale

Twain's use of a regional dialect adds color and interest to his story. How do Simon Wheeler and the narrator use English differently? How does Twain use language to characterize Wheeler and the narrator?

What is the frame tale in this story? What is Simon Wheeler's attitude toward his story about Jim Smiley? What is the frame narrator's attitude toward Wheeler's story? How does the attitude of the frame narrator toward Simon's story affect the story as a whole?

Extend the Text

Writing Options

Creative Writing Imagine that you are Jim Smiley writing a memoir for fellow gamblers about your experiences. Write the last chapter, in which you relate your worst gambling failure. Include the reason for your downfall.

Narrative Writing Write a one-paragraph summary of the tall tale about the cow that Wheeler mentions at the end of the story. Imagine you are Mark Twain submitting an idea for a follow-up story in the *Saturday Press;* your reader is the magazine's editor.

Collaborative Learning

Prepare an Oral Interpretation Working with a partner, select an excerpt from one of Mark Twain's pieces of fiction or some of his humorous quotations, and pre-

pare an oral interpretation based on the material. Decide how you will interpret the material. In other words, what tone, facial expressions, and gestures will you employ? Get tips from "How to Tell a Story" (see pages 387–389). Pretending to be Mark Twain, present your work to your partner.

Media Literacy

Write a Tall Tale Imagine that you want to join Tall-Tale Tellers of America, an organization of people who enjoy stretching the truth. To become a member, you must prove that you can spin a humorous yarn. Write a tall tale to submit with your application. You might base it on a funny personal experience or a lesson you have learned. Develop a humorous sequence of events. You may want to use nonstandard language for humorous effect.

 Go to **www.mirrorsandwindows.com** for more.

1. The narrator of "The Notorious Jumping Frog of Cala-veras County" believes that his friend wanted him to ask about Leonidas W. Smiley because
   A. the friend wanted to learn about him.
   B. the friend needed to contact him.
   C. the friend wanted the narrator to have to listen to Wheeler's story about Jim Smiley.
   D. the friend was afraid Leonidas W. Smiley had been harmed at the mining camp.
   E. the friend thought Leonidas W. Smiley would prove helpful to the narrator.

2. Andrew Jackson won fights by doing what?
   A. pinning the other dog by the neck
   B. biting the other dog's ear
   C. holding onto the other dog's hind leg
   D. severely injuring the other dog
   E. playing dead until the other dog turned away

3. Simon Wheeler is described as *garrulous*. What does this word mean?
   A. argumentative
   B. risk taking
   C. sophisticated
   D. wrinkled
   E. talkative

4. Why does the narrator leave before Wheeler can tell the story about the cow?
   A. He has an appointment and does not want to be late.
   B. Someone from the front yard calls him.
   C. He does not have the time or the interest to hear the story.
   D. He wants to save that story for later.
   E. He already has heard that story.

5. What does the stranger do to make Dan'l Webster lose the jumping contest?
   A. He holds down one of his hind legs.
   B. He poisons him to make him feel sick.
   C. He overfeeds the frog so he is too fat to move quickly.
   D. He feeds the frog quailshot.
   E. He drugs the frog to make him sleepy.

6. What are you doing if you *conjecture?*
   A. You are performing a magic trick.
   B. You are making a guess.
   C. You are leading a meeting.
   D. You are agreeing with a common idea.
   E. You are predicting the future.

7. Which of the following is *not* characteristic of a humorous story, according to Twain in "How to Tell a Story"?
   A. It can be told at length.
   B. It should be told in a serious manner.
   C. The subject of the story is more important than the manner in which it is told.
   D. It is an artistic work.
   E. It is American in origin.

8. **Constructed Response:** What makes "The Notori-ous Jumping Frog of Calaveras County" and "How to Tell a Story" humorous? What literary devices add to the humor of the selections? Identify these devices, and explain how Twain uses them to create humor. Support your opinions with quotations from the selections.

> ### TEST-TAKING TIP
>
> During the writing portion of a test, focus on the provided topic and avoid responding in unconventional formats or structures. For instance, don't respond to a question about poetry by writing in verse—unless doing so is requested. Also avoid using overly complicated vocabulary and mak-ing obscure references.
>
> In addition to evaluating the quality of your response, test graders will assess your ability to follow directions and work within a given format. Provide them with an essay that makes its point clearly and directly with sound gram-mar and syntax.

Understand the Concept

Using verbs correctly is one of the greatest challenges in writing and speaking the English language. The primary reason for this difficulty is that many verbs in English are **irregular.** That is, they do not follow the standard rules for creating past and past-participle forms.

Consider, for example, the verb *talk,* which is a **regular verb.** To create its past-tense form, we add *-ed* to make *talked.* To form its past-participle form, we again add *-ed* plus the helping verb *have: have talked.* These are the rules for forming the past and past-participle forms of regular verbs. For irregular verbs, the past and part-participle forms often are created by changing interior vowel sounds.

Here are some examples:

Present Tense	Past Tense	Part Participle
eat	ate	(have) eaten
drink	drank	(has) drunk
grow	grew	(has) grown
write	wrote	(has) written

By knowing irregular verb forms, you will be able to tell the difference between past and present or past-perfect forms:

> **EXAMPLES**
>
> **Past** I *went* to the store yesterday.
>
> **Present perfect** I *have gone* to the store many times this week.
>
> **Past perfect** I *had gone* to the store twice before buying the turkey.
>
> **Incorrect** I *had went* to the store. (Simple past-tense verb used with helping verb)
>
> **Incorrect** I *gone* to the store many times. (Past participle used without helping verb)

If you are unsure how to create the various forms of a verb, look it up in the dictionary. If the verb is a regular verb, the dictionary will list only the present-tense form. If the verb is irregular, the other forms will be listed, as well.

Apply the Skill

Identify Correct and Incorrect Verb Forms
For each of the following sentences, replace the irregular verb in parentheses with the correct form of verb.

1. The dog Andrew Jackson (bite) the hind legs of the other dog last week.
2. The quailshot has (sink) into the stomach of the frog.
3. Jim Smiley (teach) his frog about jumping.
4. He (lend) a hand to the stranger to help him find a frog.
5. Has Simon (bring) up the story about the yellow cow yet?

Fix Incorrect Verb Forms
On your paper, rewrite each of these sentences with the correct form of irregular verb. Use the past tense or a perfect tense, which uses the past participle.

1. Simon Wheeler seen Jim Smiley's frog turn somersaults in the air.
2. Jim had gave the stranger his frog box to hold.
3. Dan'l Webster couldn't jump because he had ate quailshot.
4. The stranger had took Jim's money and left town.
5. The narrator grown tired of hearing Simon's stories.

Use Correct Verb Forms in Your Writing
Write a tall tale about a pet you have had or an animal about which you have heard stories. Tell the tale in a humorous way, and exaggerate the animal's abilities. For example, you could tell about a squirrel that could outwit any protective birdfeeder device.

When you finish your tale, check your verbs to make sure you have used the correct past forms of irregular verbs. Share your story with your class.

from **Life on the Mississippi**

A Memoir by Mark Twain

Build Background

Literary Context Published in 1883, just one year before *Adventures of Huckleberry Finn*, **Life on the Mississippi** is Mark Twain's memoir of the steamboat era on the Mississippi River before the American Civil War. The book begins with a brief history of the river, starting with its discovery by Spanish explorer Hernando de Soto in the sixteenth century. The next section describes Twain's career as a Mississippi steamboat pilot, a prestigious job that fulfilled his childhood dream. The final section tells of Twain's return, many years later, to travel the river from St. Louis to New Orleans, when competition from railroads had made steamboats passé. Twain records his observations on greed, gullibility, tragedy, and bad architecture.

Mark Twain often claimed that if the Civil War had not disrupted riverboat traffic on the Mississippi, he would have spent his entire life as a steamboat pilot. The following excerpt from *Life on the Mississippi* describes how steamboat traffic affected small river towns prior to the war and how every boy's dream was to become a steamboatman.

In 1902, Twain returned to the river to receive an honorary degree from the University of Missouri in Columbia. There, he also dedicated a steamboat that was named after him. Later that year, he recounted in an interview with the *New York World* how his first trip on a steamboat had been as a stowaway who said, considering the rainstorm that pelted him and the hot cinders from the smokestack that fell on him, "If it hadn't been a steamboat that I was on I would have wanted be safe at home in time for supper." In 2003, Hannibal, Missouri, erected a new statue to commemorate Mark Twain's brief career as a steamboat pilot and his love for the river.

Reader's Context Who was your childhood hero? What did you want to be when you grew up?

Statue of Mark Twain in Hannibal, Missouri.

Analyze Literature

Memoir

A **memoir** is a type of autobiography that focuses on one incident or period in a person's life. Memoirs are often based on a person's memories of and reactions to historical events.

Set Purpose

The Mississippi River featured prominently in Twain's youth and was a focal point in much of his writing, as well. *Life on the Mississippi* is thus a fitting title for his memoir. As you read the following excerpt, determine what makes it a memoir. Consider the differences between a *memoir* and an *autobiography*. Also compare and contrast Twain's style of writing in his memoir with that in his other works.

Preview Vocabulary

transient, 394
prodigious, 395
conspicuous, 397
tarry, 397
tranquil, 397
renowned, 397
disconsolate, 398

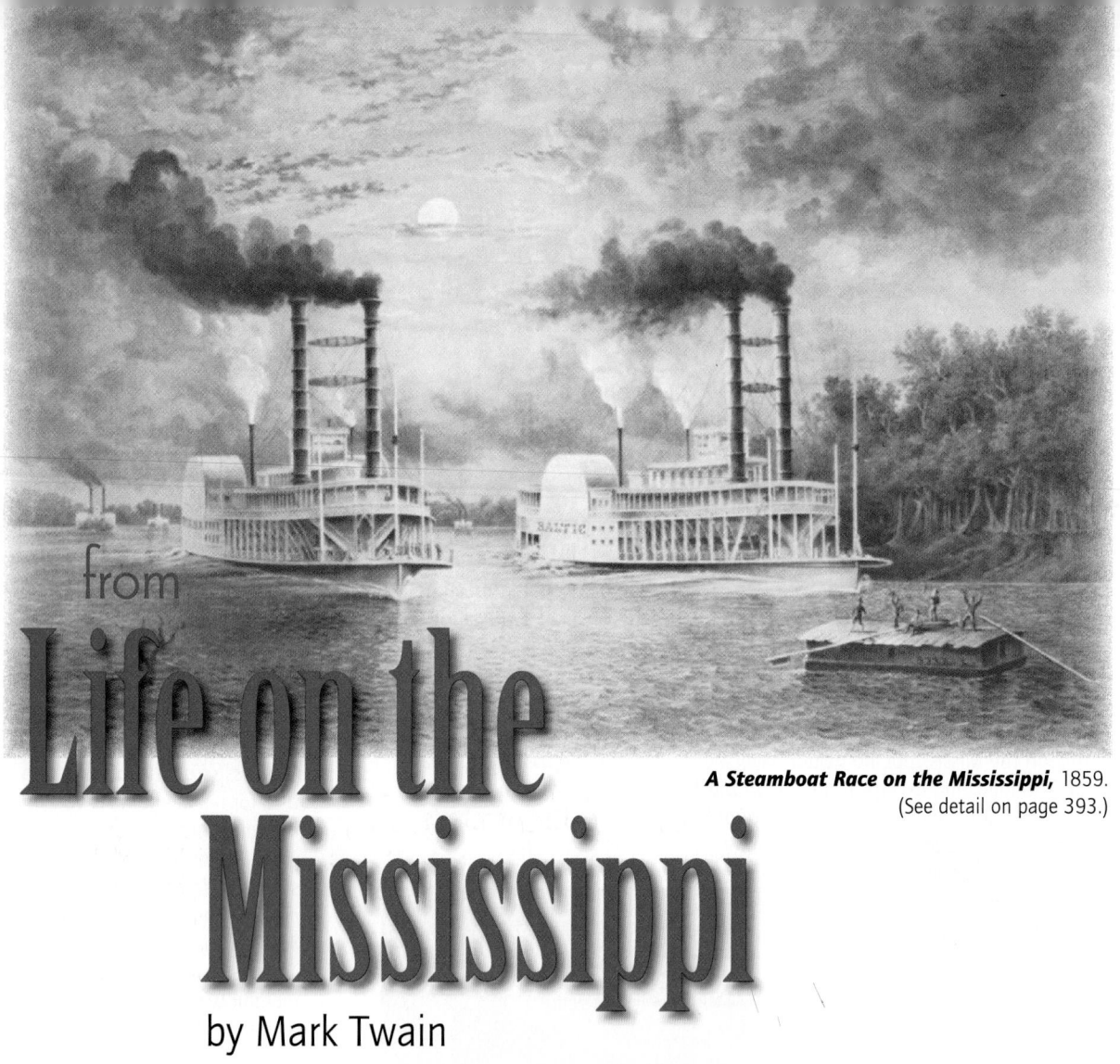

A Steamboat Race on the Mississippi, 1859.
(See detail on page 393.)

from
Life on the
Mississippi

by Mark Twain

After all these years I can picture that old time to myself now, just as it was then.

When I was a boy, there was but one permanent ambition among my comrades in our village[1] on the west bank of the Mississippi River. That was, to be a steamboatman. We had <u>transient</u> ambitions of other sorts, but they were only transient.

When a circus came and went, it left us all burning to become clowns; the first Negro minstrel show that came to our section left us all suffering to try that kind of life; now and then we had a hope that if we lived and were good, God would permit us to be pirates.

---

1. **our village.** Hannibal, Missouri

tran • sient (tranʹ zē ənt) *adj.,* fleeting; passing quickly

These ambitions faded out, each in its turn; but the ambition to be a steamboatman always remained.

Once a day a cheap, gaudy packet[2] arrived upward from St. Louis, and another downward from Keokuk.[3] Before these events, the day was glorious with expectancy; after them, the day was a dead and empty thing. Not only the boys, but the whole village, felt this. After all these years I can picture that old time to myself now, just as it was then: the white town drowsing in the sunshine of a summer's morning; the streets empty, or pretty nearly so; one or two clerks sitting in front of the Water Street stores, with their splint-bottomed chairs tilted back against the wall, chins on breasts, hats slouched over their faces, asleep—with shingle shavings enough around to show what broke them down; a sow and a litter of pigs loafing along the sidewalk, doing a good business in watermelon rinds and seeds; two or three lonely little freight piles scattered about the levee; a pile of skids[4] on the slope of the stone-paved wharf, and the fragrant town drunkard asleep in the shadow of them; two or three wood flats[5] at the head of the wharf, but nobody to listen to the peaceful lapping of the wavelets against them; the great Mississippi, the majestic, the magnificent Mississippi, rolling its mile-wide tide along, shining in the sun; the dense forest away on the other side; the point above the town, and the point below, bounding the river-glimpse and turning it into a sort of sea, and withal a very still and brilliant and lonely one. Presently a film of dark smoke appears above one of those remote points; instantly a Negro drayman,[6] famous for his quick eye and prodigious voice, lifts up the cry, "S-t-e-a-m-boat a-comin'!" and the scene changes! The town drunkard stirs, the clerks wake up, a furious clatter of drays follows, every house and store pours out a human contribution, and all in a twinkling the dead town is alive and moving. Drays, carts, men, boys, all go hurrying from many quarters to a common center, the wharf. Assembled there, the people fasten their eyes upon the coming boat as upon a wonder they are seeing for the first time. And the boat *is* rather a handsome sight, too. She is long and sharp and trim and pretty; she has two tall, fancy-topped chimneys, with a gilded device of some kind swung between them; a fanciful pilothouse, all glass and gingerbread, perched on top of the texas deck[7] behind them; the paddle-boxes are gorgeous with a picture or with gilded rays above the boat's name; the boiler, the hurricane deck, and the texas deck are fenced and ornamented with clean white railings; there is a flag gallantly flying from the jackstaff;[8] the furnace doors are open and the fires glaring bravely; the upper decks are black with passengers; the captain stands by the big bell, calm, imposing, the envy of all; great volumes of the blackest smoke are rolling and tumbling out of the chimneys—a husbanded grandeur created with a bit of pitch pine just before arriving at a town; the crew are grouped on the forecastle;[9] the broad stage is run far out over the port

The great Mississippi, the majestic, the magnificent Mississippi, rolling its mile-wide tide along, shining in the sun.

---

2. **packet.** Boat on a regular route
3. **Keokuk.** Town in southeastern Iowa
4. **skids.** Wooden platforms
5. **flats.** Flat-bottomed boats
6. **drayman.** Driver of a low cart called a dray
7. **texas deck.** Deck next to the officers' cabins
8. **jackstaff.** Rope running up and down a mast
9. **forecastle.** Front of the upper deck

pro • di •gious (prô di´ jəs) *adj.,* enormous; monstrous

The Mississippi River

The subject of Twain's famous memoir also is an integral feature of the United States' geography and a vital element in the nation's history. The Mississippi River derives its name from the Anishinabe, an Ojibwe band who lived at the river's origin in northwestern Minnesota. They called it *Misi-ziibi*, meaning "great river." The first European to view the Mississippi River is believed to have been Hernando de Soto in 1541; the river was explored in 1673 by Jacques Marquette and Louis Jolliet. La Salle claimed the entire region for France after traveling down to the mouth of the river in 1682.

When measured from its mouth to its most distant tributary, the Mississippi is the third-longest river in the world and the largest river system in North America. Flowing out of Lake Itasca in northwestern Minnesota, the river runs 2,350 miles and then empties into the Gulf of Mexico in southeastern Louisiana. It takes approximately ninety days for the water to travel this distance. The Mississippi River drains forty-one percent of the mainland United States, and its basin stretches over one million square miles.

Contributing to the massive water flow of the Mississippi River are its hundreds of tributaries. (A *tributary* is a stream or river that has an independent source but flows into another river at its mouth instead of a larger body of water, such as a sea or ocean.) The largest tributaries to the Mississippi are the Missouri River (which is roughly the same length as the Mississippi), the Arkansas River, and the Ohio River.

The Mississippi River has been at the center of some key events in American history. The western basin of the river comprised the land the United States purchased from France in 1803, known as the Louisiana Purchase, which doubled the size of the nation. In years following, the U.S. government used the river to establish borders for several states in the nation's midsection, including Iowa, Missouri, Illinois, Arkansas, and the state of Mississippi. During the Civil War, the Union realized the importance of establishing control over the river's trade pathways in order to block the Confederate Army's supply lines. General Ulysses S. Grant's victorious Vicksburg Campaign accomplished this on July 4, 1863, ultimately leading to the defeat of the Confederates.

bow, and an envied deckhand stands picturesquely on the end of it with a coil of rope in his hand; the pent steam is screaming through the gauge cocks; the captain lifts his hand, a bell rings, the wheels stop; then they turn back, churning the water to foam, and the steamer is at rest. Then such a scramble as there is to get aboard, and to get ashore, and to take in freight and to discharge freight, all at one and the same time; and such a yelling and cursing as the mates facilitate it all with! Ten minutes later the steamer is under way again, with no flag on the jackstaff and no black smoke issuing from the chimneys. After ten more minutes the town is dead again, and the town drunkard asleep by the skids once more.

My father was a justice of the peace, and I supposed he possessed the power of life and death over all men and could hang anybody that offended him. This was distinction enough for me as a general thing; but the desire to be a steamboatman kept intruding, nevertheless.

I first wanted to be a cabin boy, so that I could come out with a white apron on and shake a tablecloth over the side, where all my old comrades could see me; later I thought I would rather be the deckhand who stood on the end of the stage plank with the coil of rope in his hand, because he was particularly <u>conspicuous</u>. But these were only daydreams—they were too heavenly to be contemplated as real possibilities. By and by one of our boys went away. He was not heard of for a long time. At last he turned up as apprentice engineer or striker on a steamboat. This thing shook the bottom out of all my Sunday-school teachings. That boy had been notoriously worldly, and I just the reverse; yet he was exalted to this eminence, and I left in obscurity and misery. There was nothing generous about this fellow in his greatness. He would always manage to have a rusty bolt to scrub while his boat <u>tarried</u> at our town, and he would sit on the inside guard and scrub it, where we could all see him and envy him and loathe him. And whenever his boat was laid up he would come home and swell around the town in his blackest and greasiest clothes, so that nobody could help remembering that he was a steamboatman; and he used all sorts of steamboat technicalities in his talk, as if he were so used to them that he forgot common people could not understand them. He would speak of the labboard[10] side of a horse in an easy, natural way that would make one wish he was dead. And he was always talking about "St. Looey" like an old citizen; he would refer casually to occasions when he "was coming down Fourth Street," or when he was "passing by the Planter's House," or when there was a fire and he took a turn on the brakes of "the old Big Missouri"; and then he would go on and lie about how many towns the size of ours were burned down there that day. Two or three of

This thing shook the bottom out of all my Sunday-school teachings.

the boys had long been persons of consideration among us because they had been to St. Louis once and had a vague general knowledge of its wonders, but the day of their glory was over now. They lapsed into a humble silence, and learned to disappear when the ruthless cub engineer approached. This fellow had money, too, and hair oil. Also an ignorant silver watch and a showy brass watch chain. He wore a leather belt and used no suspenders. If ever a youth was cordially admired and hated by his comrades, this one was. No girl could withstand his charms. He cut out every boy in the village. When his boat blew up at last, it diffused a <u>tranquil</u> contentment among us such as we had not known for months. But when he came home the next week, alive, <u>renowned</u>, and appeared in church all battered up and bandaged, a shining hero, stared at and wondered over by everybody, it seemed to us that the partiality of Providence for an undeserving reptile had reached a point where it was open to criticism.

This creature's career could produce but one result, and it speedily followed. Boy after boy managed to get on the river. The minister's son became an engineer. The doctor's and the postmaster's sons became mud clerks; the wholesale liquor dealer's son became a barkeeper on a boat; four sons of the chief merchant, and two sons of the county judge, became pilots. Pilot was the grandest position of all. The pilot, even in those days of trivial wages, had a princely salary—from a hundred and fifty to two hundred and fifty dollars a

---

10. **labboard.** Left side of a ship

con • spic • u • ous (kən spik´ yü əs) *adj.,* easily seen
tar • ry (tär´ ē) *v.,* stay longer; linger
tran • quil (tranˊ kwil) *adj.,* peaceful
re • nowned (rə nound´) *adj.,* famous

month, and no board to pay. Two months of his wages would pay a preacher's salary for a year. Now some of us were left <u>disconsolate</u>. We could not get on the river—at least our parents would not let us.

So by and by I ran away. I said I never would come home again till I was a pilot and could come in glory. But somehow I could not manage it. I went meekly aboard a few of the boats that lay packed together like sardines at the long St. Louis wharf, and very humbly inquired for the pilots, but got only a cold shoulder and short words from mates and clerks. I had to make the best of this sort of treatment for the time being, but I had comforting daydreams of a future when I should be a great and honored pilot, with plenty of money, and could kill some of these mates and clerks and pay for them. ❖

dis • con • so • late (dis kôn′ sə lət) *adj.,* saddened; not capable of being consoled

MIRRORS & WINDOWS

Twain writes that every boy in his village had the same "permanent ambition" to be a steamboatman. What is every boy's "permanent ambition" today? What is every girl's?

Refer to Text ▶ ▶ ▶ ▶ ▶ Reason with Text

1a. Why did Sam (Mark Twain) and his pals despise the cub engineer so much?	**1b.** Explain why the job of cub engineer might not have been as glorious as the boys imagined.

Understand
Find meaning

2a. Describe Hannibal, Missouri, in the riverboat days.	**2b.** *Life on the Mississippi* was written after the Civil War, in a time of great expansion and industrial change. Why might Twain's description of Hannibal have appealed to readers?

Apply
Use information

3a. State the tasks involved in the job *steamboatman*. Which task was the most desirable? Why?	**3b.** What seems to be the main reason the boys wanted to work on a steamboat?

Analyze
Take things apart

4a. What parts of the story are exaggerations?	**4b.** Which lines or parts from Twain's memoir do you find humorous?

Evaluate
Make judgments

5a. Trace how Twain's experience as a riverboat pilot is evident in this selection.	**5b.** If you were to write your memoirs, what special knowledge could you share with your readers?

Create
Bring ideas together

Analyze Literature

Memoir
How is *Life on the Mississippi,* Twain's memoir, different from an autobiography he might have written? Is it acceptable for an author to embellish the facts of his or her life in a memoir? Explain. How does Twain's written style in this memoir compare to that in his fiction and essay?

Extend the Text

Writing Options

Creative Writing Look at a map and identify towns along the Mississippi River that Mark Twain might have visited in his days as a riverboat pilot. Write a postcard that Twain might have sent to his brother, Orion, from a town along the river.

Applied Writing Write a job description for a riverboat pilot prior to the Civil War. Describe the nature of the job and the knowledge and skills required. Imagine that you will post the job description for the boys in Hannibal to read.

Lifelong Learning

Make a Scrapbook Mark Twain was fond of keeping scrapbooks. In fact, he invented a process to make "scrapbooking" neat and easy. Make a list of items Twain might have included in a scrapbook about his days as a river-

boat pilot, and write a brief description of each item. For example, a photo of famed riverboat pilot Horace Bixby might include the description "Twain served under him as an apprentice." Get ideas for what to include in the scrapbook from *Life on the Mississippi* and by doing research on Twain's riverboat days.

Media Literacy

Take a Virtual Tour Twain and his family lived in Hartford, Connecticut, from 1874 to 1891, and he wrote his most memorable books while living there. In lieu of traveling to Hartford, take a virtual tour of the Mark Twain House and Museum (which are open for visitors year round) by going to the website for the Mark Twain House. After your tour, send an e-mail to the museum, commenting on what you liked about the tour and/or requesting more information.

 Go to **www.mirrorsandwindows.com** for more.

No work of art is completely independent of the historical period and culture in which it is created, and every work is, in some respects, shaped by the artist's personal experiences. In examining a literary text from the **biographical-historical perspective,** the critic draws on the fabric of a time and place to discover the greater context of the work. The basic premise of this theory is refreshingly clear: We examine the writer's life and influences and look for ways in which his or her experience is tied to the historical moment.

Overview of Biographical-Historical Criticism

The River
In *Life on the Mississippi,* the author describes the background and motivation for his boyhood desire to be a steamboat pilot. Samuel Langhorne Clemens, who wrote under the pseudonym *Mark Twain,* grew up in the town of Hannibal, Missouri. He watched the steamboats move up and down the Mississippi River, wishing he were onboard.

The steamboat was an important form of transportation in the nineteenth century; it carried passengers and freight between Minnesota and the Gulf of Mexico. Settlers heading west traveled on the Mississippi, along with gamblers and rogues. This was America's Big River: It both divided East from West and united the country by making possible a lively commercial trade.

The Writer
Working for his brother in the newspaper business gave Twain the chance to publish some of his own work. He eventually found his way to the world of the riverfront, where he realized his boyhood dream. Although he piloted the Mississippi only from 1857 to 1861, Twain's experiences on the great river gave him a wealth of material for his writings.

At this point, history intervened in both the life of the nation and the young steamboat pilot. As mentioned earlier, the Civil War temporarily halted river traffic, and by the time it resumed, Mark Twain was busy establishing himself as a reporter, novelist, and lecturer. Twain never forgot his colorful years on the Big River. This period of his life features prominently in many of his articles and books, notably his 1876 series "High Times on the Mississippi" and his 1883 memoir *Life on the Mississippi.*

"I have been through some terrible things in my life, some of which actually happened."

—MARK TWAIN

Application of Biographical-Historical Criticism

Although readers must be careful not to take a writer's remarks about himself at face value (and Twain was notorious for exaggeration), the excerpt from *Life on the Mississippi* provides a revealing commentary on Twain's childhood and nineteenth-century America. Yet there is much that Twain does not tell us here. In analyzing the excerpt in this unit, consider not only Twain's humorous account but also the turbulent times he describes, which held very real dangers.

Setting and Mood
Twain's description of the town of Hannibal is rich in realistic detail, even as seen through the humorous gaze of the narrator. The sleepy town, a place where pigs scavenge on the sidewalk and clerks doze in the sunlight, seems unaware of its proximity to "the majestic, the magnificent Mississippi." Hannibal comes alive only when the steamboats arrive:

Presently a film of dark smoke appears. . . . Instantly a Negro drayman, famous for his quick eye and prodigious voice, lifts up the cry "S-t-e-a-m-boat a-comin'!" and the scene changes! The town drunkard stirs, the clerks wake up, a furious clatter of drays follows, every house and store pours out a human

TWAIN

contribution, and all in a twinkling the dead town is alive and moving. Drays, carts, men, boys, all go hurrying from many quarters to a common center, the wharf. Assembled there, the people fasten their eyes upon the coming boat as upon a wonder they are seeing for the first time.

❏ **Analyze** Note how Twain skillfully portrays the abrupt change in the town's mood from a state of slumbering quiet to one of hectic activity. Which other details give the impression that only the whistle of the steamboat can wake up this dull place? How does this description fix the historical moment for the reader and re-create the spirit of Hannibal as it was in Twain's boyhood?

Symbol and Irony

Twain provides a neat rationale for his desire to pilot a steamboat. A "notoriously worldly," self-assured boy manages to get a job on a steamboat and later returns to town to "swell around." He uses the lingo of the steamboatman, oils his hair, sports new clothing, and impresses all the local girls. In short, he becomes the symbol of every boy's dreams, just as the steamboat is the symbol of freedom and manhood.

When the obnoxious youth's boat blows up, he survives with minor injuries and becomes a hero. His success, Twain tells us, "shook the bottom out of all my Sunday-school teachings." This comment is ironic in that the mature author knows something of which his younger self was ignorant.

To understand the darker side of the Mississippi years, the reader would have to know that the Clemens family lost a son, Henry, when the steamboat *Pennsylvania* blew up in 1858. But for a twist of fate, young Sam would have been on that boat.

❏ **Analyze** Consider the point at which biography and history converge. The death toll from explosions of steamboat boilers numbered in the thousands, even after 1852, when the government imposed stricter

regulations on boat building and maintenance. Twain wrote his account of his years on the Mississippi thirty years after the death of his brother. How did the author's *nostalgia,* or longing for a time of lost innocence, color his ironic account of the boy who stirred up envy among the town's youth? How are personal experience and historical truth symbolized in Twain's narrative?

Motivation and Conflict

Finally, we learn in *Life on the Mississippi* that the sons of the civilized men of the town—the minister, judge, and postmaster—all want to be steamboat pilots. In his longing to escape the confines of civilization for the rough-and-ready life of the steamboatman, Twain was a youth of the times. His personal frontier paralleled the expansion of the American West, where individuals pursued their destinies far from the genteel Northeast and the class-stratified South.

❏ **Analyze** The values of orderly civilization and personal independence clashed during Twain's boyhood. He was not alone in his frustration: "We could not get on the river—at least our parents would not let us." Which details from the passage suggest what the steamboat represented to the boys growing up in this region?

WRITING ABOUT

Biographical-Historical Criticism

Write an essay that answers this question: In what sense were young Twain's motivation and conflict a natural outgrowth of the historical era and the spirit of a particular region? Use details from the excerpt to illustrate how personal history and social history inform one another.

The Outcasts of Poker Flat

A Short Story by Bret Harte

Build Background

Literary Context Bret Harte's **"The Outcasts of Poker Flat,"** published in 1869, is an example of nineteenth-century **Regionalism.** Regional writers portray a particular place, writing about its landscape, people, values, and lifestyle. Regionalists explore issues that are common to all people, but they do so by writing about a certain time and place.

In this story, Harte treats the conflict between a society and its "outcasts," those people whose behavior is unacceptable to the moral values that the majority at least pretend to uphold. Harte explores this timeless conflict by describing the fate of some stereotypical characters from the American frontier. Today, these characters are familiar to anyone who has watched a Western movie, but in the nineteenth century, they were new, and Harte was one of the first to describe them.

Reader's Context Who are the outcasts in American society today?

Meet the Author

Bret Harte (1836–1902) was the pen name of Francis Brett Harte, who gave many Easterners their first glimpse of the Old West in his amusing stories, characterized by local color, juxtapositions of characters, and surprise endings.

Although associated with the West, Harte was born in Albany, New York. He moved to California in 1854, after his father died. There, he gathered the material he would later use in his stories, riding shotgun on Wells Fargo stagecoaches and prospecting during the Gold Rush. In San Francisco, he worked as a typesetter and then a writer for the *Californian.* In 1861, he took a job as editor of the *Overland Monthly,* in which he published the work that would make him famous, including the stories "The Luck of Roaring Camp" and "The Outcasts of Poker Flat" and the poem "Plain Language from Truthful James."

Harte's Regionalism met with an eager audience back East, so eager that the *Atlantic Monthly* in Boston offered him the then-astronomical sum of ten thousand dollars to write twelve pieces for the magazine. Harte left for Boston, but the pieces he produced were mediocre and his fame subsided. After that, Harte produced several collections of stories, two novels, and two plays, none of which equaled the success of his earlier work. He served as a United States diplomat in Prussia and in Scotland and then settled in London, England, where he lived for the rest of his life.

Analyze Literature

Character and Motivation A **character** is an individual who takes part in the action of a literary work.

A **motivation** is a force that moves a character to think, feel, or behave in a certain way. Characters might be motivated by their values, goals, or past experiences.

Set Purpose

People from every kind of background were drawn to the American West in search of adventure and opportunity. Harte drew on this diversity, populating his stories with a colorful mix of characters. Many of his characters are *stock characters,* who represent stereotypes such as the lawman, the gunslinger, and so on. As you read, make a simple two-column chart, jotting down the characters and their primary qualities. Also try to determine what motivates each character, particularly Oakhurst, the main character.

Preview Vocabulary

predisposing, 403
conjecture, 403
precipitous, 405
bellicose, 405
equanimity, 406
guileless, 406
felonious, 408
extemporize, 408
ostentatiously, 408
querulous, 410

The OUTCASTS of POKER FLAT

by Bret Harte

The Fall of the Cowboy, 1895. Frederic Remington. Amon Carter Museum, Fort Worth, Texas. (See detail on page 402.)

The spot was singularly wild and impressive.

As Mr. John Oakhurst, gambler, stepped into the main street of Poker Flat on the morning of the twenty-third of November, 1850, he was conscious of a change in its moral atmosphere from the preceding night. Two or three men, conversing earnestly together, ceased as he approached, and exchanged significant glances. There was a Sabbath lull in the air, which, in a settlement unused to Sabbath influences, looked ominous.

Mr. Oakhurst's calm, handsome face betrayed small concern of these indications. Whether he was conscious of any <u>predisposing</u> cause, was another question. "I reckon they're after somebody," he reflected; "likely it's me."

He returned to his pocket the handkerchief with which he had been whipping away the red dust of Poker Flat from his neat boots, and quietly discharged his mind of any further <u>conjecture</u>.

In point of fact, Poker Flat was "after somebody." It had lately suffered the loss of several thousand dollars, two valuable horses,

---

pre • dis • pos • ing (prē dəs pōz´ iŋ) *adj.,* making likely to happen
con • jec • ture (kən jek´ chər) *n.,* prediction based on guesswork

and a prominent citizen. It was experiencing a spasm of virtuous reaction, quite as lawless and ungovernable as any of the acts that had provoked it. A secret committee[1] had determined to rid the town of all improper persons. This was done permanently in regard of two men who were then hanging from the boughs of a sycamore in the gulch, and temporarily in the banishment of certain other objectionable characters. I regret to say that some of these were ladies. It is but due to the sex, however, to state that their impropriety was professional, and it was only in such easily established standards of evil that Poker Flat ventured to sit in judgment.

Mr. Oakhurst was right in supposing that he was included in this category. A few of the committee had urged hanging him as a possible example, and a sure method of reimbursing themselves from his pockets of the sums he had won from them. "It's agin justice," said Jim Wheeler, "to let this yer young man from Roaring Camp—an entire stranger—carry away our money." But a crude sentiment of equity residing in the breasts of those who had been fortunate enough to win from Mr. Oakhurst, overruled this narrower local prejudice.

With him life was at best an uncertain game, and he recognized the usual percentage in favor of the dealer.

Mr. Oakhurst received his sentence with philosophic calmness, none the less coolly, that he was aware of the hesitation of his judges. He was too much of a gambler not to accept Fate. With him life was at best an uncertain game, and he recognized the usual percentage in favor of the dealer.

A body of armed men accompanied the deported wickedness of Poker Flat to the outskirts of the settlement. Besides Mr. Oakhurst, who was known to be a coolly desperate man, and for whose intimidation the armed escort was intended, the expatriated[2] party consisted of a young woman familiarly known as the "Duchess"; another, who had gained the infelicitous[3] title of "Mother Shipton,"[4] and "Uncle Billy," a suspected sluice[5] robber and confirmed drunkard. The cavalcade[6] provoked no comments from the spectators, nor was any word uttered by the escort. Only when the gulch which marked the uttermost limit of Poker Flat was reached, the leader spoke briefly and to the point. The exiles were forbidden to return at the peril of their lives.

As the escort disappeared, their pent-up feelings found vent in a few hysterical tears from the Duchess, some bad language from Mother Shipton, and a Partheian[7] volley of expletives from Uncle Billy. The philosophic Oakhurst alone remained silent. He listened calmly to Mother Shipton's desire to cut somebody's heart out, to the repeated statements of the Duchess that she would die in the road, and to the alarming oaths that seemed to be bumped out of Uncle Billy as he rode forward. With the easy good-humor characteristic of his class, he insisted upon exchanging his own ridinghorse, "Five Spot," for the sorry mule which the Duchess rode. But even this act did not draw the party into any closer sympathy. The young woman readjusted her somewhat draggled plumes with a feeble, faded

---

1. **secret committee.** Vigilance committee; group that helps maintain order and punish crime when processes of law are not effective
2. **expatriated.** Driven from one's land
3. **infelicitous.** Unfortunate; unsuitable
4. **Mother Shipton.** Lived from 1488 to 1560; known as a witch and believed to have been taken by the devil and to have borne him an imp
5. **sluice.** Trough used to separate gold from other materials
6. **cavalcade.** Procession (of horses)
7. **Partheian.** Like the Partheians, an ancient people from Asia known for firing shots while in retreat

The Deputy Sheriff, 1929. Frank Tenney Johnson. Private collection.

coquetry;[8] Mother Shipton eyed the possessor of "Five Spot" with malevolence, and Uncle Billy included the whole party in one sweeping anathema.[9]

The road to Sandy Bar—a camp that not having as yet experienced the regenerating influences of Poker Flat, consequently seemed to offer some invitation to the emigrants—lay over a steep mountain range. It was distant, a day's severe journey. In that advanced season, the party soon passed out of the moist, temperate regions of the foot-hills, into the dry, cold, bracing air of the Sierras.[10] The trail was narrow and difficult. At noon the Duchess, rolling out of her saddle upon the ground, declared her intention of going no further, and the party halted.

The spot was singularly wild and impressive. A wooded amphitheater, surrounded on three sides by <u>precipitous</u> cliffs of naked granite, sloped gently toward the crest of another precipice that overlooked the valley. It was undoubtedly the most suitable spot for a camp, had camping been advisable. But Mr. Oakhurst knew that scarcely half the journey to Sandy Bar was accomplished, and the party were not equipped or provisioned for delay. This fact he pointed out to his companions curtly, with a philosophic commentary on the folly of "throwing up their hand before the game was played out." But they were furnished with liquor, which in this emergency stood them in place of food, fuel, rest and prescience. In spite of his remonstrances,[11] it was not long before they were more or less under its influence. Uncle Billy passed rapidly from a <u>bellicose</u> state into one of stupor, the Duchess became maudlin, and Mother Shipton snored. Mr. Oakhurst alone remained erect, leaning against a rock, calmly surveying them.

Mr. Oakhurst did not drink. It interfered with a profession which required coolness, impassiveness and presence of mind, and, in his own language, he "couldn't afford it." As he gazed at his recumbent fellow-exiles, the loneliness begotten of his pariah-trade,[12] his habits of life, his very vices, for the first time seriously oppressed him. He bestirred himself in dusting his black clothes, washing his hands and face, and other acts characteristic of his studiously neat habits, and for a moment forgot his annoyance. The thought of deserting his

---

8. **coquetry.** Flirting
9. **anathema.** Curse
10. **Sierras.** Mountains in California
11. **remonstrances.** Protests; objections
12. **pariah-trade.** Profession scorned by others

---

pre • cip • i • tous (prē sip′ ə təs) *adj.,* steep
bel • li • cose (bel′ ə kōs) *adj.,* hostile; eager to fight

weaker and more pitiable companions never perhaps occurred to him. Yet he could not help feeling the want of that excitement, which singularly enough was most conducive to that calm <u>equanimity</u> for which he was notorious. He looked at the gloomy walls that rose a thousand feet sheer above the circling pines around him; at the sky, ominously clouded; at the valley below, already deepening into shadow. And doing so, suddenly he heard his own name called.

A horseman slowly ascended the trail. In the fresh, open face of the newcomer, Mr. Oakhurst recognized Tom Simson, otherwise known as the "Innocent" of Sandy Bar. He had met him some months before over a "little game," and had, with perfect equanimity, won the entire fortune—amounting to some forty dollars—of that <u>guileless</u> youth. After the game was finished, Mr. Oakhurst drew the youthful speculator behind the door and thus addressed him: "Tommy, you're a good little man, but you can't gamble worth a cent. Don't try it over again." He then handed him his money back, pushed him gently from the room, and so made a devoted slave of Tom Simson.

There was a remembrance of this in his boyish and enthusiastic greeting of Mr. Oakhurst. He had started, he said, to go to Poker Flat to seek his fortune. "Alone?" No, not exactly alone; in fact—a giggle—he had run away with Piney Woods. Didn't Mr. Oakhurst remember Piney? She that used to wait on the table at the Temperance House? They had been engaged a long time, but old Jake Woods had objected, and so they had run away, and were going to Poker Flat to be married, and here they were. And they were tired out, and how lucky it was they had found a place to camp and company. All this the Innocent delivered rapidly, while Piney—a stout, comely damsel of fifteen—emerged from behind the pine tree, where she had been blushing unseen, and rode to the side of her lover.

Mr. Oakhurst seldom troubled himself with sentiment. Still less with propriety. But he had

HISTORY CONNECTION

The Story of Nat Love

More than one-third of the cowboys who participated in the massive cattle drives of the late 1800s were of African, Mexican, or Native American heritage. The most prominent among them was Nat Love, a former slave from Tennessee who assumed the name Deadwood Dick. Love earned this nickname at a Deadwood, South Dakota, rodeo in 1876, where he greatly outperformed his competition in sharp shooting and cattle wrestling.

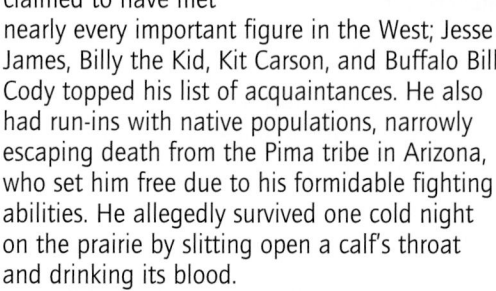

Love's life story is so saturated with wild adventure and improbable feats that it is hard to determine the facts. For instance, he claimed to have met nearly every important figure in the West; Jesse James, Billy the Kid, Kit Carson, and Buffalo Bill Cody topped his list of acquaintances. He also had run-ins with native populations, narrowly escaping death from the Pima tribe in Arizona, who set him free due to his formidable fighting abilities. He allegedly survived one cold night on the prairie by slitting open a calf's throat and drinking its blood.

These escapades made Deadwood Dick the subject of many popular Western-themed dime novels, although their protagonists were always white. Love spent the end of his life working as a Pullman porter on a train and writing his autobiography, *The Life and Adventures of Nat Love.*

equa • nim • i • ty (e kwä nim′ ə tē) *n.,* evenness of temper; quality of remaining calm
guile • less (gīl′ ləs) *adj.,* without deceit

a vague idea that the situation was not felicitous.[13] He retained, however, his presence of mind sufficiently to kick Uncle Billy, who was about to say something, and Uncle Billy was sober enough to recognize in Mr. Oakhurst's kick a superior power that would not bear trifling. He then endeavored to dissuade Tom Simson from delaying further, but in vain. He even pointed out the fact that there was no provision, nor means of making a camp. But, unluckily, the Innocent met this objection by assuring the party that he was provided with an extra mule loaded with provisions, and by the discovery of a rude attempt at a loghouse near the trail. "Piney can stay with Mrs. Oakhurst," said the Innocent, pointing to the Duchess, "and I can shift for myself."

Mr. Oakhurst seldom troubled himself with sentiment.

Nothing but Mr. Oakhurst's admonishing foot saved Uncle Billy from bursting into a roar of laughter. As it was, he felt compelled to retire up the canyon until he could recover his gravity. There he confided the joke to the tall pine trees, with many slaps of his leg, contortions of his face, and the usual profanity. But when he returned to the party, he found them seated by a fire—for the air had grown strangely chill and the sky overcast—in apparently amicable conversation. Piney was actually talking in an impulsive, girlish fashion to the Duchess, who was listening with an interest and animation she had not shown for many days. The Innocent was holding forth, apparently with equal effect, to Mr. Oakhurst and Mother Shipton, who was actually relaxing into amiability. "Is this yer a d——d picnic?" said Uncle Billy, with inward scorn, as he surveyed the sylvan group, the glancing fire-light and the tethered animals in the foreground. Suddenly an idea mingled with the alcoholic fumes that disturbed his brain. It was apparently of a jocular nature, for he felt impelled to slap his leg again and cram his fist into his mouth.

As the shadows crept slowly up the mountain, a slight breeze rocked the tops of the pine trees, and moaned through their long and gloomy aisles. The ruined cabin, patched and covered with pine boughs, was set apart for the ladies. As the lovers parted, they unaffectedly exchanged a parting kiss, so honest and sincere that it might have been heard above the swaying pines. The frail Duchess and the malevolent Mother Shipton were probably too stunned to remark upon this last evidence of simplicity, and so turned without a word to the hut. The fire was replenished, the men lay down before the door, and in a few minutes were asleep.

Mr. Oakhurst was a light sleeper. Toward morning he awoke benumbed and cold. As he stirred the dying fire, the wind, which was now blowing strongly, brought to his cheek that which caused the blood to leave it—snow!

He started to his feet with the intention of awakening the sleepers, for there was no time to lose. But turning to where Uncle Billy had been lying he found him gone. A suspicion leaped to his brain and a curse to his lips. He ran to the spot where the mules had been tethered; they were no longer there. The tracks were already rapidly disappearing in the snow.

The momentary excitement brought Mr. Oakhurst back to the fire with his usual calm. He did not waken the sleepers. The Innocent slumbered peacefully, with a smile on his good humored, freckled face; the virgin Piney slept beside her frailer sisters as sweetly as though attended by celestial guardians, and Mr. Oakhurst, drawing his blanket over his shoulders, stroked his mustachios and waited for the dawn. It came slowly in a whirling mist of snowflakes, that dazzled and confused the eye. What could be seen of the landscape appeared magically changed. He looked over

---

13. **felicitous.** Pleasant; acceptable

the valley, and summed up the present and future in two words—"Snowed in!"

A careful inventory of the provisions, which, fortunately for the party, had been stored within the hut, and so escaped the <u>felonious</u> fingers of Uncle Billy, disclosed the fact that with care and prudence they might last ten days longer. "That is," said Mr. Oakhurst, *sotto voce*[14] to the Innocent, "if you're willing to board us. If you ain't—and perhaps you'd better not—you can wait till Uncle Billy gets back with provisions." For some occult reason, Mr. Oakhurst could not bring himself to disclose Uncle Billy's rascality, and so offered the hypothesis that he had wandered from the camp and had accidentally stampeded the animals. He dropped a warning to the Duchess and Mother Shipton, who of course knew the facts of their associate's defection. "They'll find out the truth about us all, when they find out anything," he added, significantly, "and there's no good frightening them now."

They'll find out the truth about us all, when they find out anything.

Tom Simson not only put all his worldly store at the disposal of Mr. Oakhurst, but seemed to enjoy the prospect of their enforced seclusion. "We'll have a good camp for a week, and then the snow'll melt, and we'll all go back together." The cheerful gayety of the young man and Mr. Oakhurst's calm infected the others. The Innocent, with the aid of pine boughs, <u>extemporized</u> a thatch for the roofless cabin, and the Duchess directed Piney in the rearrangement of the interior with a taste and tact that opened the blue eyes of that provincial maiden to their fullest extent. "I reckon now you're used to fine things at Poker Flat," said

Piney. The Duchess turned away sharply to conceal something that reddened her cheeks through its professional tint, and Mother Shipton requested Piney not to "chatter." But when Mr. Oakhurst returned from a weary search for the trail, he heard the sound of happy laughter echoed from the rocks. He stopped in some alarm, and his thoughts first naturally reverted to the whiskey—which he had prudently *cachéd*.[15] "And yet it don't somehow sound like whiskey," said the gambler. It was not until he caught sight of the blazing fire through the still blinding storm, and the group around it, that he settled to the conviction that it was "square fun."

Whether Mr. Oakhurst had *cachéd* his cards with the whiskey as something debarred the free access of the community, I cannot say. It was certain that, in Mother Shipton's words, he "didn't say cards once" during that evening. Haply the time was beguiled by an accordion, produced somewhat <u>ostentatiously</u> by Tom Simson, from his pack. Notwithstanding some difficulties attending the manipulation of this instrument, Piney Woods managed to pluck several reluctant melodies from its keys, to an accompaniment by the Innocent on a pair of bone castanets. But the crowning festivity of the evening was reached in a rude camp-meeting hymn, which the lovers, joining hands, sang with great earnestness and vociferation.[16] I fear that a certain defiant tone and Covenanter's swing[17] to its chorus, rather

---

14. *sotto voce* (sō tō vō´ chā). In an undertone, so as not to be overheard
15. *cachéd* (ka shād´). Hidden
16. **vociferation.** Shouting
17. **Covenanter's swing.** Sung with a vigorous rhythm with a martial beat, as done by the covenanters, a group of Scottish Presbyterians who wished to separate from the Church of England

---

fe • lo • ni • ous (fə lōn´ ē əs) *adj.*, of a criminal
ex • tem • po • rize (eks tem p´ ə rīz) *v.*, contrive in a makeshift way to meet a pressing need
os • ten • ta • tious • ly (ôs ten tā´ shəs lē) *adv.*, so as to attract attention

than any devotional quality, caused it to speedily infect the others, who at last joined in the refrain:

> *"I'm proud to live in the service of the Lord*
> *And I'm bound to die in His army."*[18]

The pines rocked, the storm eddied and whirled above the miserable group, and the flames of their altar leaped heavenward, as if in token of the vow.

At midnight the storm abated, the rolling clouds parted, and the stars glittered keenly above the sleeping camp. Mr. Oakhurst, whose professional habits had enabled him to live on the smallest possible amount of sleep, in dividing the watch with Tom Simson, somehow managed to take upon himself the greater part of that duty. He excused himself to the Innocent, by saying that he had "often been a week without sleep." "Doing what?" asked Tom. "Poker!" replied Oakhurst, sententiously; "when a man gets a streak of luck—he don't get tired. The luck gives in first. Luck," continued the gambler, reflectively, "is a mighty queer thing. All you know about it for certain is that it's bound to change. And it's finding out when it's going to change that makes you. We've had a streak of bad luck since we left Poker Flat—

you come along and slap you get into it, too. If you can hold your cards right along you're all right. For," added the gambler, with cheerful irrelevance,

> *"I'm proud to live in the service of the Lord,*
> *And I'm bound to die in His army."*

The third day came, and the sun, looking through the white-curtained valley, saw the outcasts divide their slowly decreasing store of provisions for the morning meal. It was one of the peculiarities of that mountain climate that its rays diffused a kindly warmth over the wintry landscape, as if in regretful commiseration of the past. But it revealed drift on drift of snow piled high around the hut; a hopeless, uncharted, trackless sea of white lying below the rocky shores to which the castaways still clung. Through the marvelously clear air, the smoke of the pastoral village of Poker Flat rose miles away. Mother Shipton saw it, and from a remote pinnacle of her rocky fastness, hurled in that direction a final malediction. It was her last vituperative[19] attempt, and perhaps for that reason was invested with a certain degree

---

18. **"I'm proud . . . His army."** Refrain of the early American spiritual "Service of the Lord"

19. **vituperative.** Abusive; viciously fault finding

of sublimity. It did her good, she privately informed the Duchess. "Just you go out there and cuss, and see." She then set herself to the task of amusing "the child," as she and the Duchess were pleased to call Piney. Piney was no chicken, but it was a soothing and ingenious theory of the pair to thus account for the fact that she didn't swear and wasn't improper.

Music failed to fill entirely the aching void left by insufficient food.

When night crept up again through the gorges, the reedy notes of the accordion rose and fell in fitful spasms and longdrawn gasps by the flickering campfire. But music failed to fill entirely the aching void left by insufficient food, and a new diversion was proposed by Piney—story-telling. Neither Mr. Oakhurst nor his female companions caring to relate their personal experiences, this plan would have failed, too, but for the Innocent. Some months before he had chanced upon a stray copy of Mr. Pope's[20] ingenious translation of the Iliad. He now proposed to narrate the principal incidents of that poem—having thoroughly mastered the argument and fairly forgotten the words—in the current vernacular of Sandy Bar. And so for the rest of that night the Homeric demi-gods again walked the earth. Trojan bully and wily Greek wrestled in the winds, and the great pines in the canyon seemed to bow to the wrath of the son of Peleus.[21] Mr. Oakhurst listened with quiet satisfaction. Most especially was he interested in the fate of "Ash-heels,"[22] as the Innocent persisted in denominating the "swift-footed Achilles."

So with small food and much of Homer and the accordion, a week passed over the heads of the outcasts. The sun again forsook them, and again from leaden skies the snow-flakes were sifted over the land. Day by day closer around them drew the snowy circle, until at last they looked from their prison over drifted walls of dazzling white, that towered twenty feet above their heads. It became more and more difficult to replenish their fires, even from the fallen trees beside them, now half-hidden in the drifts. And yet no one complained. The lovers turned from the dreary prospect and looked into each other's eyes, and were happy. Mr. Oakhurst settled himself coolly to the losing game before him. The Duchess, more cheerful than she had been, assumed the care of Piney. Only Mother Shipton—once the strongest of the party—seemed to sicken and fade. At midnight on the tenth day she called Oakhurst to her side. "I'm going," she said, in a voice of querulous weakness, "but don't say anything about it. Don't waken the kids. Take the bundle from under my head and open it." Mr. Oakhurst did so. It contained Mother Shipton's rations for the last week, Homeric untouched. "Give 'em to the child," she said, pointing to the sleeping Piney. "You've starved yourself," said the gambler. "That's what they call it," said the woman querulously, as she lay down again, and turning her face to the wall, passed quietly away.

The accordion and the bones were put aside that day, and Homer was forgotten. When the body of Mother Shipton had been committed to the snow, Mr. Oakhurst took the Innocent aside, and showed him a pair of snow-shoes, which he had fashioned from the old pack-saddle. "There's one chance in a hundred to save her yet," he said, pointing to Piney; "but

---

20. **Mr. Pope's.** English poet Alexander Pope (1688–1744), whose translation of Homer's *Iliad* was written in heroic couplets
21. **son of Peleus.** Achilles (ä kil´ ēz), chief hero on the Greek side of the Trojan War
22. **Ash-heels.** The speaker means Achilles, whose only vulnerable spot was his heel, a fact emphasized by the mispronunciation

---

quer • u • lous (kwār´ yə ləs) *adj.,* full of complaint

it's there," he added pointing toward Poker Flat. "If you can reach there in two days she's safe." "And you?" asked Tom Simson. "I'll stay here," was the curt reply.

The lovers parted with a long embrace. "You are not going, too," said the Duchess, as she saw Mr. Oakhurst apparently waiting to accompany him. "As far as the canyon," he replied. He turned suddenly, and kissed the Duchess, leaving her pallid face aflame, and her trembling limbs rigid with amazement.

Night came, but not Mr. Oakhurst. It brought the storm again and the whirling snow. Then the Duchess, feeding the fire, found that some one had quietly piled beside the hut enough fuel to last a few days longer. The tears rose to her eyes, but she hid them from Piney.

The women slept but little. In the morning, looking into each other's faces, they read their fate. Neither spoke; but Piney, accepting the position of the stronger, drew near and placed her arm around the Duchess's waist. They kept this attitude for the rest of the day. That night the storm reached its greatest fury, and rending asunder the protecting pines, invaded the very hut.

Toward morning they found themselves unable to feed the fire, which gradually died away. As the embers slowly blackened, the Duchess crept closer to Piney, and broke the silence of many hours: "Piney, can you pray?" "No, dear," said Piney, simply. The Duchess, without knowing exactly why, felt relieved, and putting her head upon Piney's shoulder, spoke no more. And so reclining, the younger and purer pillowing the head of her soiled sister upon her virgin breast, they fell asleep.

The wind lulled as if it feared to waken them. Feathery drifts of snow, shaken from the long pine boughs, flew like white-winged birds, and settled about them as they slept. The moon through the rifted clouds looked down upon what had been the camp. But all human stain, all trace of earthy travail, was hidden beneath the spotless mantle mercifully flung from above.

They slept all that day and the next, nor did they waken when voices and footsteps broke the silence of the camp. And when pitying fingers brushed the snow from their wan faces, you could scarcely have told from the equal peace that dwelt upon them, which was she that had sinned. Even the Law of Poker Flat recognized this, and turned away, leaving them still locked in each other's arms.

But at the head of the gulch, on one of the largest pine trees, they found the deuce of clubs pinned to the bark with a bowie knife. It bore the following, written in pencil, in a firm hand:

†

BENEATH THIS TREE
LIES THE BODY
OF
JOHN OAKHURST,
WHO STRUCK A STREAK OF BAD LUCK
ON THE 23RD OF NOVEMBER, 1850,
AND
HANDED IN HIS CHECKS
ON THE 7TH DECEMBER, 1850

†

And pulseless and cold, with a Derringer[23] by his side and a bullet in his heart, though still calm as in life, beneath the snow, lay he who was at once the strongest and yet the weakest of the outcasts of Poker Flat. ❖

---

23. **Derringer.** Short-barreled pocket pistol; invented by Henry Derringer

An old adage says that "People make their own luck." What does it mean? Do you agree or disagree?

Refer to Text ▶ ▶ ▶ ▶ ▶	Reason with Text	
1a. What happens to Oakhurst at the end of the story?	**1b.** Explain why Oakhurst is "at once the strongest and yet the weakest of the outcasts of Poker Flat."	**Understand** Find meaning
2a. Outline what parts of the story a modern-day audience might find overly emotional, or *sentimental*.	**2b.** What is the purpose of sentimentality in fiction?	**Apply** Use information
3a. Identify the three main groups of people in the story.	**3b.** Contrast Harte's portrayal of the townspeople with that of the outcasts.	**Analyze** Take things apart
4a. Why are the outcasts thrown out of Poker Flat?	**4b.** Are the townspeople of Poker Flat justified in taking this action? Why or why not?	**Evaluate** Make judgments
5a. How is the outcasts' time together in the snowbound cabin different from what might be expected? Would they have changed if Tom and Piney had not joined them?	**5b.** Propose what would have happened to the outcasts if they had made it to Sandy Bar. Would they have continued their old lives or refashioned themselves? Explain.	**Create** Bring ideas together

Analyze Literature

Character and Motivation

Review your chart of characters and their qualities. Which characters seem to be stock characters, or stereotypes of Western figures? What qualities distinguish them as such?

Oakhurst could have ridden off and left his cranky, quarrelsome companions to fend for themselves. What was Oakhurst's motivation to stay and help them?

Extend the Text

Writing Options

Creative Writing Actors often create a *back story* (personal history) for the characters they portray to help them understand their characters' motivation. Choose one of the outcasts, and write a one-paragraph back story for that character. What brought the person to Poker Flat? Does he or she have a family or home? What experiences have shaped the person's life? Compare back stories with your classmates.

Expository Writing Write a critical essay that describes how "The Outcasts of Poker Flat" is an example of Regional literature. In portraying the American West, how does Harte characterize its landscape, people, values, and lifestyle? What impression does he create of this time and place?

Collaborative Learning

Write a Parody A *parody* is a literary work that imitates another work for humorous, often satirical purposes.

Work with other students to plan short story that parodies a piece of Western fiction. Begin by creating a list of stock characters from Westerns, such as the fearless sheriff, the silent gunslinger, and the sophisticated Eastern lady. Create a setting, naming the town in which these characters live. Next, create a plot by thinking of a conflict that might arise. Finally, create a humorous, surprise ending for your story.

Lifelong Learning

Make a Map of the Gold Rush The discovery of gold in 1849 drew thousands of fortune seekers to California. Draw a map to show the routes people took to get to the gold fields. Include the Sierra Mountains, and indicate where Poker Flat and Sandy Bar may have been. Display your map in the classroom.

 Go to **www.mirrorsandwindows.com** for more.

Understand the Concept

Adjectives and adverbs are **modifiers,** words that change or explain the meanings of other words. Modifiers not only add detail to writing, but they also make it more interesting. In fact, colorful modifiers can turn a dull text into a dynamic one.

Adjectives modify nouns, which are persons, places, things, and ideas. Adjectives can indicate color, number, quality, and material, among other things. **Adverbs** modify verbs, adjectives, and other adverbs, explaining how something is done or to what intensity. Many adverbs end in -ly.

Look at the following examples, in which the original vague, nondescript sentence is revised twice by adding modifiers:

EXAMPLES

Vague and nondescript The wind blew.

More detailed but dull The *cold* wind blew *hard.*

More detailed and colorful The *frigid* wind blew *furiously.*

In the second sentence, inserting the adjective *cold* and the adverb *hard* added detail to the original, but these modifiers are so common that the writing seems dull. In the third sentence, using the more colorful modifiers *frigid* (adjective) and *furiously* (adverb) make the sentence much more vivid and engaging.

Apply the Skill

Identify Adjectives and Adverbs

Copy on your own paper these sentences from "The Outcasts of Poker Flat." For each sentence, underline the adjectives once and the adverbs twice.

1. Two or three men, conversing earnestly together, ceased as he approached, and exchanged significant glances.

2. He returned to his pocket the handkerchief with which he had been whipping away the red dust of Poker Flat from his neat boots, and quietly discharged his mind of any further conjecture.

3. This was done permanently in regard of two men who were then hanging from the boughs of a sycamore in the gulch, and temporarily in the banishment of certain other objectionable characters.

4. The young woman readjusted her somewhat draggled plumes with a feeble, faded coquetry.

5. But when he returned to the party, he found them seated by a fire—for the air had grown strangely chill and the sky overcast—in apparently amicable conversation.

Improve the Use of Adjectives and Adverbs

Improve the interest level of this paragraph about "The Outcasts of Poker Flat" by adding colorful adjectives and adverbs where appropriate.

The townspeople form a committee to throw Mr. Oakhurst and the other people out of Poker Flat. On the way to Sandy Bar, they encounter a couple headed to Poker Flat to get married. Then the snow starts falling hard and they get snowed in. The group from Poker Flat tries to protect the couple from their bad histories and vices. They realize that they will die without more provisions, so Mr. Oakhurst and the Innocent set out. By the end of the story, some die but one survives.

Use Adjectives and Adverbs in Your Writing

Write a paragraph in which you describe a time you got caught in bad weather. Explain where you were and what you were doing. Use adjectives and adverbs to clarify the scene for the reader and to make your writing more interesting. Share your story with a classmate.

Richard Cory
Miniver Cheevy

Lyric Poems by Edwin Arlington Robinson

Build Background

Literary Context The poems **"Richard Cory"** and **"Miniver Cheevy"** are part of a *trilogy,* or group of three literary works on the same topic or theme. The third poem in the series is "Luke Havergal." Each poem portrays a character in Edwin Arlington Robinson's fictional Tilbury Town, and each parallels someone in Robinson's life. For instance, Richard Cory may be based on Robinson's brother, Herman, who became an alcoholic after some failed business endeavors, and Miniver Cheevy is similar to Robinson himself, who felt misunderstood and unappreciated as a writer.

The themes that run through these poems are personal failure and unfulfilled desire. In writing about the disappointments of everyday life, Robinson broke with the idealistic themes of earlier poets and established himself as a Realist.

Reader's Context Think of someone you have envied, only to find out that his or her life was not as wonderful as it seemed. What insight did that discovery give you into your own life?

Meet the Author

Edwin Arlington Robinson (1869–1935) was born in Head Tide, Maine, and grew up in Gardiner, Maine. He loved words from the time he learned to read, and he began writing poetry at age twelve.

Robinson attended Harvard, where he published the poem "Ballade of a Ship" in one of the university's literary journals. He was forced to leave after two years, however, due to his family's bankruptcy and his mother's ill health. He returned to Gardiner, which became the setting for many of his poems.

Robinson published several volumes of poetry early in his career, but he was unable to make a living at writing and worked for the New York City subway system for several years. He once wrote to a friend, "Writing has been my dream ever since I was old enough to lay a plan for an air castle." Although his career had several false starts, he continued to write until finally achieving success with *The Man Against the Sky* (1916). During the 1920s, he won three Pulitzer Prizes. Robinson spent the last twenty-five summers of his life at the Macdowell Colony of artists and musicians in New Hampshire.

Sometimes described as a "bridge" poet, Robinson's work reflects much of the traditional form of the nineteenth century yet dwells on the problems of the inner self, which is more characteristic of twentieth-century literature.

Analyze Literature

Irony and Allusion

Irony is a difference between appearance and reality. One type of irony is *irony of situation,* in which an event occurs that violates the expectations of the characters, the reader, or the audience.

An **allusion** is a reference to a well-known person, event, object, or work from history or literature.

Set Purpose

Although Robinson ultimately experienced great success in his career, he never felt appreciated as a writer. A similar sense of disappointment, even bitterness, runs throughout his writing and is one of the qualities that characterizes him as a Realist. In reading "Richard Cory," examine how Robinson uses irony to portray the sad reality of one man's life. In reading "Miniver Cheevy," identify the allusions Robinson makes and evaluate the effectiveness of doing so.

Preview Vocabulary

imperially, 415
array, 415
assail, 416
albeit, 416
incessantly, 416

Caballero con Lentes de la Familia Canals (Gentleman with Glasses from the Canals Family), c. 1840–1855. Artist unknown. Teodoro Vidal Collection, Smithsonian American Art Museum, Washington, DC.

Richard Cory

by Edwin Arlington Robinson

Whenever Richard Cory went down town,
We people on the pavement looked at him:
He was a gentleman from sole to crown,
Clean favored, and <u>imperially</u> slim.

5　And he was always quietly <u>arrayed</u>,
And he was always human when he talked;
But still he fluttered pulses when he said,
"Good-morning," and he glittered when he walked.

And he was rich—yes, richer than a king—
And admirably schooled in every grace:
10　In fine, we thought that he was everything
To make us wish that we were in his place.

So on we worked, and waited for the light,
And went without the meat, and cursed the bread;
And Richard Cory, one calm summer night,
15　Went home and put a bullet through his head. ❖

im • pe • ri • al • ly (im pēr´ ē əl ē) *adv.,* grandly or majestically
ar • ray (ə rā´) *v.,* dress somebody in particular clothes; arrange something for display

MIRRORS & WINDOWS

Everyone in town envied and admired Richard Cory, but did they really know him? How much can we know about the day-to-day realities of other people's lives?

Miniver Cheevy

by Edwin Arlington Robinson

Representation of Parsifal, c. 1800s. Hermann Hendrich. Richard Wagner Museum, Bayreuth, Germany. (See detail on page 414.)

Miniver Cheevy, child of scorn,
    Grew lean while he <u>assailed</u> the seasons;
He wept that he was ever born,
    And he had reasons.

5 Miniver loved the days of old
    When swords were bright and steeds
    were prancing;
The vision of a warrior bold
    Would set him dancing.

Miniver sighed for what was not,
10   And dreamed, and rested from his labors;
He dreamed of Thebes[1] and Camelot,[2]
    And Priam's[3] neighbors.

Miniver mourned the ripe renown
    That made so many a name so fragrant;
15 He mourned Romance, now on the town,[4]
    And Art, a vagrant.

Miniver loved the Medici,[5]
    <u>Albeit</u> he had never seen one;
He would have sinned <u>incessantly</u>
20   Could he have been one.

Miniver cursed the commonplace
    And eyed a khaki suit with loathing;
He missed the mediæval grace
    Of iron clothing.

25 Miniver scorned the gold he sought,
    But sore annoyed was he without it;
Miniver thought, and thought, and thought,
    And thought about it.

Miniver Cheevy, born too late,
30   Scratched his head and kept on thinking;
Miniver coughed, and called it fate,
    And kept on drinking. ❖

---

1. **Thebes.** City-state in ancient Greece
2. **Camelot.** Legendary site of King Arthur's court
3. **Priam.** In Homer's *Iliad*, King of Troy
4. **on the town.** On welfare
5. **Medici.** Noble, rich, powerful family in Florence, Italy (1300–1500)

as • sail (ə sāl´) *v.*, attack vigorously with words or actions
al • be • it (əl bē´ it) *conj.*, even though
in • ces • sant • ly (in ses´ ənt lē) *adv.*, continuing for a long time without stopping

If you could choose to live in another time, what would it be? How would you expect your life to be different?

Refer to Text ▶ ▶ ▶ ▶ ▶	Reason with Text	
1a. Describe Richard Cory's appearance, demeanor, and background. Describe Miniver Cheevy's appearance and outlook on life.	**1b.** How do the townspeople feel about Cory? Do they like or dislike him? How does society regard Miniver Cheevy? Explain.	**Understand** Find meaning
2a. What does Cory do "one calm summer night"?	**2b.** Why is this a stunning turn of events?	**Apply** Use information
3a. Make a list of the verbs Robinson uses, such as *assailed* and *wept,* in regard to Miniver Cheevy. How many times does he use the verb *thought?*	**3b.** Analyze what these verbs suggest about Cheevy.	**Analyze** Take things apart
4a. Identify the speaker in "Richard Cory."	**4b.** Suggest why Robinson does not tell the reader what was troubling Cory.	**Evaluate** Make judgments
5a. What does the line "He missed the mediae-val grace / Of iron clothing" suggest about the days of old in "Miniver Cheevy"?	**5b.** Would you like to have lived in another time and place? Explain.	**Create** Bring ideas together

Analyze Literature

Irony and Allusion

"Richard Cory" is considered by literary scholars one of the best examples of *situational irony* in American literature. Explain why.

What allusions did you find in "Miniver Cheevy"? Which of them did you recognize from other reading or studies? Why is the use of allusions effective in this poem?

Extend the Text

Writing Options

Creative Writing Write a newspaper article reporting the death of Richard Cory. Explain the circumstances surrounding his death, as well as basic facts about his life. Feel free to make up any missing details, including quotes from Cory's family members. Look in your local newspaper's obituary section for sample articles.

Expository Writing Write a comparison-and-contrast essay in which you explain the differences and similarities of the characters in "Richard Cory" and "Miniver Cheevy." Use specific examples from the poems to support your analyses of these characters.

Critical Literacy

Conduct a Role-Play Imagine that Richard Cory and Miniver Cheevy have been asked to appear together on a local radio talk show to discuss the meaning of life. With two partners, play the roles of the talk-show host, Richard Cory, and Miniver Cheevy. The talk-show host should ask questions about each guest's perspective on life. Other class members could be part of the listening audience and call in with questions and comments.

Media Literacy

Prepare a Travel Brochure Use the Internet to research the town of Gardiner, Maine—Robinson's hometown and the setting for many of his poems. Prepare a brochure designed to attract tourists to Gardiner. Indicate where Robinson's characters might have been seen in the town. You also may want to address the fact that Robinson did not always portray Gardiner in a positive light.

 Go to **www.mirrorsandwindows.com** for more.

To Build a Fire
A Short Story by Jack London

Build Background

Historical Context Published in 1908, **"To Build a Fire"** is a survival tale set in the Yukon, a region of northwest Canada adjacent to Alaska's eastern border. The Canadian government acquired this region in 1870 from the Hudson's Bay Company, a British trading firm, and established it as a territory in 1898.

Literary Context As one of the hundreds of thousands of people who joined the Klondike Gold Rush, which also started in 1898, Jack London had firsthand experience surviving a winter in the Yukon. London portrayed that experience in realistic detail in "To Build a Fire," one of the finest examples of **Naturalism,** a literary movement of the late nineteenth and early twentieth centuries that saw actions and events as resulting inevitably from biological or environmental forces.

Reader's Context Think of a time when someone wisely advised you not to do something but you did it anyway. What was the result?

Meet the Author

Jack London (1876–1916), born in San Francisco, helped support his family from the time he was fourteen. By eighteen, he had worked in a cannery and as an oyster pirate, seaman, jute-mill worker, and coal shoveler.

While still a teenager, London traveled halfway across the country with a group protesting the high level of national unemployment. After spending thirty days in jail for vagrancy, he returned to California in 1896, intent on attending the state university at Berkeley. He was admitted but left after just one year due to financial problems and frustration with higher education. Seeking a new adventure, London traveled to the Yukon in search of gold. Like most prospectors, he failed to strike it rich, and the year he spent in the extreme Yukon conditions left him with lifelong health problems.

London returned to California again, this time determined to make a living as a writer. He won a local writing contest, which was followed by numerous rejections and then a string of small successes. His break came when the *Atlantic Monthly* paid $120 for his story "The Odyssey of the North."

Although London often said he disliked his profession and wrote to make money, he nevertheless was a master storyteller who published prodigiously during his career. His two most famous novels, *The Call of the Wild* (1903) and *The Sea-Wolf* (1904), were written before he was thirty.

Analyze Literature

Setting, Plot, and Conflict
The **setting** of a literary work is the time and place in which it occurs, together with all the details used to create it.

A **plot** is a series of events related to a central **conflict,** or struggle between two forces in a literary work. That struggle may be between the main character and a person, society, fate, or nature, or it may be an internal struggle within the character.

Set Purpose

London chose the Yukon as the setting for nearly every short story and novel he wrote. As you read "To Build a Fire," write down the details he provides to create this setting, and decide which details are particularly effective in portraying the harshness of the Yukon. Also consider how London uses this setting to set up the central conflict of the plot. Identify the primary struggle in this story.

Preview Vocabulary

pall, 419
undulation, 420
apprehension, 421
reiterate, 422
imperative, 424
agitation, 426
nucleus, 427
apathetically, 428
peremptorily, 428
poignant, 428

To Build a Fire

by Jack London

The trouble with him was that he was without imagination.

Day had broken cold and gray, exceedingly cold and gray, when the man turned aside from the main Yukon[1] trail and climbed the high earth-bank, where a dim and little-traveled trail led eastward through the fat spruce timberland. It was a steep bank, and he paused for breath at the top, excusing the act to himself by looking at his watch. It was nine o'clock. There was no sun nor hint of sun, though there was not a cloud in the sky. It was a clear day, and yet there seemed an intangible <u>pall</u> over the face of things, a subtle gloom that made the day dark, and that was due to the absence of sun. This fact did not worry the man. He was used

to the lack of sun. It had been days since he had seen the sun, and he knew that a few more days must pass before that cheerful orb, due south, would just peep above the skyline and dip immediately from view.

The man flung a look back along the way he had come. The Yukon lay a mile wide and hidden under three feet of ice. On top of this ice were as many feet of snow. It was all pure

---

1. **Yukon.** Territory and river in northwest Canada

pall (pôl) *n.,* covering that obscures or cloaks gloomily

Miners cross Chilkoot Pass in Alaska on their way to the Yukon (1898).

as a creature of temperature, and upon man's frailty in general, able only to live within certain narrow limits of heat and cold; and from there on it did not lead him to the conjectural field of immortality and man's place in the universe. Fifty degrees below zero stood for a bite of frost that hurt and that must be guarded against by the use of mittens, earflaps, warm moccasins, and thick socks. Fifty degrees below zero was to him just precisely fifty degrees below zero. That there should be anything more to it than that was a thought that never entered his head.

As he turned to go on, he spat speculatively. There was a sharp, explosive crackle that startled him. He spat again. And again, in the air, before it could fall to the snow, the spittle crackled. He knew that at fifty below spittle crackled on the snow, but this spittle had crackled in the air. Undoubtedly it was colder than fifty below—how much colder he did not know. But the temperature did not matter. He was bound for the old claim on the left fork of Henderson Creek, where the boys were already. They had come over across the divide from the Indian Creek country, while he had come the roundabout way to take a look at the possibilities of getting out logs in the spring from the islands in the Yukon. He would be in to camp by six o'clock: a bit after dark, it was true, but the boys would be there, a fire would be going, and a hot supper would be ready. As for lunch, he pressed his hand against the protruding bundle under his jacket. It was also under his shirt, wrapped up in a handkerchief and lying against the naked skin. It was the only way to keep the biscuits from freezing. He smiled agreeably to himself as he thought

white, rolling in gentle <u>undulations</u> where the ice jams of the freeze-up had formed. North and south, as far as his eye could see, it was unbroken white, save for a dark hairline that curved and twisted from around the spruce covered island to the south, and that curved and twisted away into the north, where it disappeared behind another spruce-covered island. This dark hairline was the trail—the main trail—that led south five hundred miles to the Chilcoot Pass, Dyea,[2] and salt water; and that led north seventy miles to Dawson, and still on to the north a thousand miles to Nulato,[3] and finally to St. Michael on Bering Sea, a thousand miles and half a thousand more.

But all this—the mysterious, far-reaching hairline trail, the absence of sun from the sky, the tremendous cold, and the strangeness and weirdness of it all—made no impression on the man. It was not because he was long used to it. He was a newcomer in the land, a *chechaquo*,[4] and this was his first winter. The trouble with him was that he was without imagination. He was quick and alert in the things of life, but only in the things, and not in the significances. Fifty degrees below zero meant eighty-odd degrees of frost. Such fact impressed him as being cold and uncomfortable, and that was all. It did not lead him to meditate upon his frailty

---

2. **Chilcoot Pass, Dyea.** *Chilcoot Pass*—mountain pass leading to the Klondike; *Dyea*—once a town in Alaska that marked the beginning of the Yukon Trail
3. **Dawson . . . Nulato.** Gold-mining towns in the Yukon
4. *chechaquo.* Newcomer

---

un • du • la • tion (un jü lā′ shən) *n.,* wave; curve

of those biscuits, each cut open and sopped in bacon grease, and each enclosing a generous slice of fried bacon.

He plunged in among the big spruce trees. The trail was faint. A foot of snow had fallen since the last sled had passed over, and he was glad he was without a sled, traveling light. In fact, he carried nothing but the lunch wrapped in the handkerchief. He was surprised, however, at the cold. It certainly was cold, he concluded, as he rubbed his numb nose and cheekbones with his mittened hand. He was a warm-whiskered man, but the hair on his face did not protect the high cheekbones and the eager nose that thrust itself aggressively into the frosty air.

At the man's heels trotted a dog, a big native husky, the proper wolf dog, gray-coated and without any visible or temperamental difference from its brother, the wild wolf. The animal was depressed by the tremendous cold. It knew that it was no time for traveling. Its instinct told it a truer tale than was told to the man by the man's judgment. In reality, it was not merely colder than fifty below zero: it was colder than sixty below, than seventy below. It was seventy-five below zero. Since the freezing point is thirty-two above zero, it meant that one hundred and seven degrees of frost obtained. The dog did not know anything about thermometers. Possibly in its brain there was no sharp consciousness of a condition of very cold such as was in the man's brain. But the brute had its instinct. It experienced a vague but menacing <u>apprehension</u> that subdued it and made it slink along at the man's heels, and that made it question eagerly every unwonted movement of the man as if expecting him to go into camp or to seek shelter somewhere and build a fire. The dog had learned fire, and it wanted fire, or else to burrow under the snow and cuddle its warmth away from the air.

> The animal was depressed by the tremendous cold. It knew that it was no time for traveling.

The frozen moisture of its breathing had settled on its fur in a fine powder of frost, and especially were its jowls, muzzle, and eyelashes whitened by its crystalled breath. The man's red beard and mustache were likewise frosted, but more solidly, the deposit taking the form of ice and increasing with every warm, moist breath he exhaled. Also, the man was chewing tobacco, and the muzzle of ice held his lips so rigidly that he was unable to clear his chin when he expelled the juice. The result was that a crystal beard of the color and solidity of amber was increasing its length on his chin. If he fell down it would shatter itself, like glass, into brittle fragments. But he did not mind the appendage. It was the penalty all tobacco chewers paid in that country, and he had been out before in two cold snaps. They had not been so cold as this, he knew, but by the spirit thermometer[5] at Sixty Mile he knew they had been registered at fifty below and at fifty-five.

He held on through the level stretch of woods for several miles, crossed a wide flat, and dropped down a bank to the frozen bed of a small stream. This was Henderson Creek, and he knew he was ten miles from the forks. He looked at his watch. It was ten o'clock. He was making four miles an hour, and he calculated that he would arrive at the forks at half past twelve. He decided to celebrate that event by eating his lunch there.

The dog dropped in again at his heels, with a tail drooping discouragement, as the man swung along the creek bed. The furrow of the old sled trail was plainly visible, but a dozen inches of snow covered the marks of the last runners. In a month no man had come up or

---

5. **spirit thermometer.** Thermometer that uses alcohol instead of mercury because of the lower freezing point of alcohol

ap • pre • hen • sion (a' prē hen´ shən) n., anxiety; dread

down that silent creek. The man held steadily on. He was not much given to thinking, and just then particularly he had nothing to think about save that he would eat lunch at the forks and that at six o'clock he would be in camp with the boys. There was nobody to talk to; and, had there been, speech would have been impossible because of the ice-muzzle on his mouth. So he continued monotonously to chew tobacco and to increase the length of his amber beard.

Once in a while the thought <u>reiterated</u> itself that it was very cold and that he had never experienced such cold. As he walked along he rubbed his cheekbones and nose with the back of his mittened hand. He did this automatically, now and again changing hands. But rub as he would, the instant he stopped his cheekbones went numb, and the following instant the end of his nose went numb. He was sure to frost his cheeks; he knew that, and experienced a pang of regret that he had not devised a nose strap of the sort Bud wore in cold snaps. Such a strap passed across the cheeks, as well, and saved them. But it didn't matter much, after all. What were frosted cheeks? A bit painful, that was all: they were never serious.

Empty as the man's mind was of thoughts, he was keenly observant, and he noticed the changes in the creek, the curves and bends and timber jams, and always he sharply noted where he placed his feet. Once, coming around a bend, he shied abruptly, like a startled horse, curved away from the place where he had been walking, and retreated several paces back along the trail. The creek he knew was frozen clear to the bottom—no creek could contain water in that arctic winter—but he knew also that there were springs that bubbled out from the hillsides and ran along under the snow and on top the ice of the creek. He knew that the coldest snaps never froze these springs, and he knew likewise their danger. They were traps. They hid pools of water under the snow that might be three inches deep, or three feet. Sometimes a skin of ice half an inch thick covered them, and in turn was covered by the snow. Sometimes there were alternate layers of water and ice skin, so that when one broke through he kept on breaking through for a while, sometimes wetting himself to the waist.

That was why he had shied in such panic. He had felt the give under his feet and heard the crackle of a snow-hidden ice skin. And to get his feet wet in such a temperature meant trouble and danger. At the very least it meant delay, for he would be forced to stop and build a fire, and under its protection to bare his feet while he dried his socks and moccasins. He stood and studied the creek bed and its banks, and decided that the flow of water came from the right. He reflected awhile, rubbing his nose and cheeks, then skirted to the left, stepping gingerly and testing the footing for each step. Once clear of the danger, he took a fresh chew of tobacco and swung along at his four-mile gait.

In the course of the next two hours he came upon several similar traps. Usually the snow above the hidden pools had a sunken, candied appearance that advertised the danger. Once again, however, he had a close call; and once, suspecting danger, he compelled the dog to go on in front. The dog did not want to go. It hung back until the man shoved it forward, and then it went quickly across the white, unbroken surface. Suddenly it broke through, floundered to one side, and got away to firmer footing. It had wet its forefeet and legs, and

> Once in a while the thought reiterated itself that it was very cold and that he had never experienced such cold.

---

re • it • er • ate (rē i′ tər āt) *v.*, repeat

almost immediately the water that clung to it turned to ice. It made quick efforts to lick the ice off its legs, then dropped down in the snow and began to bite out the ice that had formed between the toes. This was a matter of instinct. To permit the ice to remain would mean sore feet. It did not know this. It merely obeyed the mysterious prompting that arose from the deep crypts of its being. But the man knew, having achieved a judgment on the subject, and he removed the mitten from his right hand and helped tear out the ice particles. He did not expose his fingers more than a minute, and was astonished at the swift numbness that smote them. It certainly was cold. He pulled on the mitten hastily, and beat the hand savagely across his chest.

At twelve o'clock the day was at its brightest. Yet the sun was too far south on its winter journey to clear the horizon. The bulge of the earth intervened between it and Henderson Creek, where the man walked under a clear sky at noon and cast no shadow. At half-past twelve, to the minute, he arrived at the forks of the creek. He was pleased at the speed he had made. If he kept it up, he would certainly be with the boys by six. He unbuttoned his jacket and shirt and drew forth his lunch. The action consumed no more than a quarter of a minute, yet in that brief moment the numbness laid hold of the exposed fingers. He did not put the mitten on, but, instead, struck the fingers a dozen sharp smashes against his leg. Then he sat down on a snow-covered log to eat. The sting that followed upon the striking of his fingers against his leg ceased so quickly that he was startled. He had had no chance to take a bite of biscuit. He struck the fingers repeatedly and returned them to the mitten, baring the other hand for the purpose of eating. He tried to take a mouthful, but the ice muzzle prevented. He had forgotten to build a fire and thaw out. He chuckled at his foolishness, and as he chuckled he noted the numbness creeping into the exposed fingers. Also, he noted that the stinging which had first come to

A Klondike miner in the White Pass between Canada and Alaska (1897).

his toes when he sat down was already passing away. He wondered whether the toes were warm or numb. He moved them inside the moccasins and decided that they were numb.

He pulled the mitten on hurriedly and stood up. He was a bit frightened. He stamped up and down until the stinging returned into the feet. It certainly was cold, was his thought. That man from Sulphur Creek had spoken the truth when telling how cold it sometimes got in the country. And he had laughed at him at the time! That showed one must not be too sure of things. There was no mistake about it, it was cold. He strode up and down, stamping his feet and threshing his arms, until reassured by the returning warmth. Then he got out matches and proceeded to make a fire. From the undergrowth, where high water of the previous spring had lodged a supply of seasoned twigs, he got his firewood. Working carefully from a small beginning, he soon had a roaring fire, over which he thawed the ice from his face and in the protection of which he ate his biscuits. For the moment the cold of space was outwitted. The dog took satisfaction in the fire, stretching out close enough for warmth and far enough away to escape being singed.

When the man had finished, he filled his pipe and took his comfortable time over a smoke. Then he pulled on his mittens, settled the earflaps of his cap firmly about his ears, and took the creek trail up the left fork. The dog was disappointed and yearned back toward the fire. This man did not know cold. Possibly all the generations of his ancestry had been ignorant of cold, of real cold, of cold one hundred and seven degrees below freezing point. But the dog knew; all its ancestry knew, and it had inherited the knowledge. And it knew that it was not good to walk abroad in such fearful cold. It was the time to lie snug in a hole in the snow and wait for a curtain of cloud to be drawn across the face of outer space whence this cold came. On the other hand, there was no keen intimacy between the dog and the man. The one was the toil slave of the other, and the only caresses it had ever received were the caresses of the whiplash and of harsh and menacing throat sounds that threatened the whiplash. So the dog made no effort to communicate its apprehension to the man. It was not concerned in the welfare of the man; it was for its own sake that it yearned back toward the fire. But the man whistled, and spoke to it with the sound of whiplashes, and the dog swung in at the man's heels and followed after.

The man took a chew of tobacco and proceeded to start a new amber beard. Also, his moist breath quickly powdered with white his mustache, eyebrows, and lashes. There did not seem to be so many springs on the left fork of the Henderson, and for half an hour the man saw no signs of any. And then it happened. At a place where there were no signs, where the soft, unbroken snow seemed to advertise solidity beneath, the man broke through. It was not deep. He wet himself halfway to the knees before he floundered out to the firm crust.

He was angry, and cursed his luck aloud. He had hoped to get into camp with the boys at six o'clock, and this would delay him an hour, for he would have to build a fire and dry

out his footgear. This was <u>imperative</u> at that low temperature—he knew that much; and he turned aside to the bank, which he climbed. On top, tangled in the underbrush about the trunks of several small spruce trees, was a high-water deposit of dry firewood—sticks and twigs, principally, but also larger portions of seasoned branches and fine, dry, last year's grasses. He threw down several large pieces on top of the snow. This served for a foundation and prevented the young flame from drowning itself in the snow it otherwise would melt. The flame he got by touching a match to a small shred of birch bark that he took from his pocket. This burned even more readily than paper. Placing it on the foundation, he fed the young flame with wisps of dry grass and with the tiniest dry twigs.

He worked slowly and carefully, keenly aware of his danger. Gradually, as the flame grew stronger, he increased the size of the twigs with which he fed it. He squatted in the snow, pulling the twigs out from their entanglement in the brush and feeding directly to the flame. He knew there must be no failure. When it is seventy-five below zero, a man must

im • per • a • tive (im pār´ ə tiv) *adj.,* absolutely necessary not fail in his first attempt to build a fire—that is, if his feet are wet. If his feet are dry, and he fails, he can run along the trail for half a mile and restore his circulation. But the circulation of wet and freezing feet cannot be restored by running when it is seventy-five below. No matter how fast one runs, the wet feet will freeze the harder.

All this the man knew. The old-timer on Sulphur Creek had told him about it the previous fall, and now he was appreciating the advice. Already all sensation had gone out of his feet. To build the fire he had been forced to remove his mittens, and the fingers had quickly gone numb. His pace of four miles an hour had kept his heart pumping blood to the surface of his body and to all the extremities. But the instant he stopped, the action of the pump eased down. The cold of space smote the unprotected tip of the planet, and he, being on that unprotected tip, received the full force of the blow.

The blood of his body recoiled before it. The blood was alive, like the dog, and like the dog it wanted to hide away and cover itself up from the fearful cold. So long as he walked four miles an hour, he pumped that blood, willy-nilly, to the surface; but now it ebbed away and sank down into the recesses of his body. The extremities were the first to feel its absence. His wet feet froze the faster, and his exposed fingers numbed the faster, though they had not yet begun to freeze. Nose and cheeks were already freezing, while the skin of all his body chilled as it lost its blood.

But he was safe. Toes and nose and cheeks would be only touched by the frost, for the fire was beginning to burn with strength. He was feeding it with twigs the size of his finger. In another minute he would be able to feed it with branches the size of his wrist, and then he could remove his wet foot-gear, and, while it dried, he could keep his naked feet warm by the fire, rubbing them at first, of course, with snow. The fire was a success. He was safe. He remembered the advice of the old-timer on Sulphur Creek, and smiled. The old-timer had been very serious in laying down the law that no man must travel alone in the Klondike after fifty below. Well, here he was; he had had the accident; he was alone; and he had saved himself. Those old-timers were rather womanish, some of them, he thought. All a man had to do was to keep his head, and he was all right. Any man who was a man could travel alone. But it was surprising, the rapidity with which his cheeks and nose were freezing. And he had not thought his fingers could go lifeless in so short a time. Lifeless they were, for he could scarcely make them move together to grip a twig, and they seemed remote from his body and from him. When he touched a twig, he had to look and see whether or not he had hold of it. The wires were pretty well down between him and his finger ends.

All of which counted for little. There was the fire, snapping and crackling and promising life with every dancing flame. He started to untie his moccasins. They were coated with ice; the thick German socks were like sheaths of iron halfway to the knees; and the moccasin strings were like rods of steel all twisted and knotted as by some conflagration. For a moment he tugged with his numb fingers, then, realizing the folly of it, he drew his sheath-knife.

But before he could cut the strings, it happened. It was his own fault or, rather, his mistake. He should not have built the fire under the spruce tree. He should have built it in the open. But it had been easier to pull the twigs from the brush and drop them directly on the fire. Now the tree under which he had done this carried a weight of snow on its boughs. No wind had blown for weeks, and each bough was fully freighted. Each time he had pulled a twig he had

All a man had to do was to keep his head, and he was all right.

communicated a slight <u>agitation</u> to the tree—an imperceptible agitation, so far as he was concerned, but an agitation sufficient to bring about the disaster. High up in the tree one bough capsized its load of snow. This fell on the boughs beneath, capsizing them. This process continued, spreading out and involving the whole tree. It grew like an avalanche, and it descended without warning upon the man and the fire, and the fire was blotted out! Where it had burned was a mantle of fresh and disordered snow.

The man was shocked. It was as though he had just heard his own sentence of death. For a moment he sat and stared at the spot where the fire had been. Then he grew very calm. Perhaps the old-timer on Sulphur Creek was right. If he had only had a trail mate he would have been in no danger now. The trail mate could have built the fire. Well, it was up to him to build the fire over again, and this second time there must be no failure. Even if he succeeded, he would most likely lose some toes. His feet must be badly frozen by now, and there would be some time before the second fire was ready.

Such were his thoughts, but he did not sit and think them. He was busy all the time they were passing through his mind. He made a new foundation for a fire, this time in the open, where no treacherous tree could blot it out. Next, he gathered dry grasses and tiny twigs from the high-water flotsam.[6] He could not bring his fingers together to pull them out, but he was able to gather them by the handful. In this way he got many rotten twigs and bits of green moss that were undesirable, but it was the best he could do. He worked methodically, even collecting an armful of the larger branches to be used later when the fire gathered strength. And all the while the dog sat and watched him, a certain yearning wistfulness in its eyes, for it looked upon him as the fire provider, and the fire was slow in coming.

When all was ready, the man reached in his pocket for a second piece of birch bark. He knew the bark was there, and, though he could not feel it with his fingers, he could hear its crisp rustling as he fumbled for it. Try as he would, he could not clutch hold of it. And all the time, in his consciousness, was the knowledge that each instant his feet were freezing. This thought tended to put him in a panic, but he fought against it and kept calm. He pulled on his mittens with his teeth, and threshed his arms back and forth, beating his hands with all his might against his sides. He did this sitting down, and he stood up to do it; and all the while the dog sat in the snow, its wolf brush of a tail curled around warmly over its forefeet, its sharp wolf ears pricked forward intently as it watched the man. And the man, as he beat and threshed with his arms and hands, felt a great surge of envy as he regarded the creature that was warm and secure in its natural covering.

After a time he was aware of the first faraway signals of sensation in his beaten fingers. The faint tingling grew stronger till it evolved into a stinging ache that was excruciating, but which the man hailed with satisfaction. He stripped the mitten from his right hand and fetched forth the birch bark. The exposed fingers were quickly going numb again. Next he brought out his bunch of sulphur matches. But the tremendous cold had already driven the life out of his fingers. In his effort to separate one match from the others, the whole bunch

6. **flotsam.** Odds and ends washed up by the water

ag • i • ta • tion (aˈ jə tāˈ shən) *n.*, appreciable motion or disturbance

fell in the snow. He tried to pick it out of the snow, but failed. The dead fingers could neither touch nor clutch. He was very careful. He drove the thought of his freezing feet, and nose, and cheeks, out of his mind, devoting his whole soul to the matches. He watched, using the sense of vision in place of that of touch, and when he saw his fingers on each side the bunch, he closed them—that is, he willed to close them, for the wires were down, and the fingers did not obey. He pulled the mitten on the right hand, and beat it fiercely against his knee. Then, with both mittened hands, he scooped the bunch of matches, along with much snow, into his lap. Yet he was no better off.

After some manipulation he managed to get the bunch between the heels of his mittened hands. In this fashion he carried it to his mouth. The ice crackled and snapped when by a violent effort he opened his mouth. He drew the lower jaw in, curled the upper lip out of the way, and scraped the bunch

He beat his hands, but failed in exciting any sensation.

with his upper teeth in order to separate a match. He succeeded in getting one, which he dropped on his lap. He was no better off. He could not pick it up. Then he devised a way. He picked it up in his teeth and scratched it on his leg. Twenty times he scratched before he succeeded in lighting it. As it flamed he held it with his teeth to the birch bark. But the burning brimstone went up his nostrils and into his lungs, causing him to cough spasmodically. The match fell into the snow and went out.

The old-timer on Sulphur Creek was right, he thought in the moment of controlled despair that ensued: after fifty below, a man should travel with a partner. He beat his hands, but failed in exciting any sensation. Suddenly he bared both hands, removing the mittens with his teeth. He caught the whole bunch between the heels of his hands. His arm muscles not being frozen enabled him to press the hand heels tightly against the matches. Then he

scratched the bunch along his leg. It flared into flame, seventy sulphur matches at once! There was no wind to blow them out. He kept his head to one side to escape the strangling fumes, and held the blazing bunch to the birch bark. As he so held it, he became aware of sensation in his hand. His flesh was burning. He could smell it. Deep down below the surface he could feel it. The sensation developed into pain that grew acute. And still he endured it, holding the flame of the matches clumsily to the bark that would not light readily because his own burning hands were in the way, absorbing most of the flame.

At last, when he could endure no more, he jerked his hands apart. The blazing matches fell sizzling into the snow, but the birch bark was alight. He began laying dry grasses and the tiniest twigs on the flame. He could not pick and choose, for he had to lift the fuel between the heels of his hands. Small pieces of rotten wood and green moss clung to the twigs, and he bit them off as well as he could with his teeth. He cherished the flame carefully and awkwardly. It meant life, and it must not perish. The withdrawal of blood from the surface of his body now made him begin to shiver, and he grew more awkward. A large piece of green moss fell squarely on the little fire. He tried to poke it out with his fingers, but his shivering frame made him poke too far, and he disrupted the <u>nucleus</u> of the little fire, the burning grasses and tiny twigs separating and scattering. He tried to poke them together again, but in spite of the tenseness of the effort, his shivering got away with him, and the twigs were hopelessly scattered. Each twig gushed a puff of smoke and went out. The fire provider had failed. As

nu • cle • us (nü′ klē əs) n., core; central part

he looked <u>apathetically</u> about him, his eyes chanced on the dog, sitting across the ruins of the fire from him, in the snow, making restless, hunching movements, slightly lifting one forefoot and then the other, shifting its weight back and forth on them with wistful eagerness.

The sight of the dog put a wild idea into his head. He remembered the tale of the man, caught in a blizzard, who killed a steer and crawled inside the carcass, and so was saved. He would kill the dog and bury his hands in the warm body until the numbness went out of them. Then he could build another fire. He spoke to the dog, calling it to him; but in his voice was a strange note of fear that frightened the animal, who had never known the man to speak in such way before. Something was the matter, and its suspicious nature sensed danger—it knew not what danger, but somewhere, somehow, in its brain arose an apprehension of the man. It flattened its ears down at the sound of the man's voice, and its restless, hunching movements and the liftings and shiftings of its forefeet became more pronounced; but it would not come to the man. He got on his hand and knees and crawled toward the dog. This unusual posture again excited suspicion, and the animal sidled mincingly away.

The man sat up in the snow for a moment and struggled for calmness. Then he pulled on his mittens, by means of his teeth, and got upon his feet. He glanced down at first in order to assure himself that he was really standing up, for the absence of sensation in his feet left him unrelated to the earth. His erect position in itself started to drive the webs of suspicion from the dog's mind; and when he spoke <u>peremptorily</u>, with the sound of whiplashes in his voice, the dog rendered its customary allegiance and came to him. As it came within reaching distance, the man lost his control. His arms flashed out to the dog, and he experienced genuine surprise when he discovered that his hands could not clutch, that there was neither bend nor feeling in the fingers. He had

forgotten for the moment that they were frozen and that they were freezing more and more. All this happened quickly, and before the animal could get away, he encircled its body with his arms. He sat down in the snow, and in this fashion held the dog, while it snarled and whined and struggled.

But it was all he could do, hold its body encircled in his arms and sit there. He realized that he could not kill the dog. There was no way to do it. With his helpless hands he could neither draw nor hold his sheath-knife nor throttle the animal. He released it, and it plunged wildly away, with tail between its legs, and still snarling. It halted forty feet away and surveyed him curiously, with ears sharply pricked forward. The man looked down at his hands in order to locate them, and found them hanging on the ends of his arms. It struck him as curious that one should have to use his eyes in order to find out where his hands were. He began threshing his arms back and forth, beating the mittened hands against his sides. He did this for five minutes, violently, and his heart pumped enough blood up to the surface to put a stop to his shivering. But no sensation was aroused in the hands. He had an impression that they hung like weights on the ends of his arms, but when he tried to run the impression down, he could not find it.

A certain fear of death, dull and oppressive, came to him. This fear quickly became <u>poignant</u> as he realized that it was no longer a mere matter of freezing his fingers and toes, or of losing his hands and feet, but that it was a matter of life and death with the chances against him. This threw him into a panic, and he turned and ran up the creekbed along the

---

ap • a • thet • i • cal • ly (a′ pə the′ tik lē) *adv.,* without emotion
per • emp • to • ri • ly (pʉr emp′ tər ə lē) *adv.,* in a commanding manner
poi • gnant (poi′ nyənt) *adj.,* sharp; painful

Transportation in the Klondike

With the Klondike Gold Rush came immediate and enormous growth in Canadian and American transportation systems, as both trains and ships were needed to move large amounts of people and supplies in and out of the region. There also was great demand for animals such as horses, mules, oxen, and dogs, which were

needed to move prospectors to and from the mountainous gold fields.

Dogs soon became the most popular of these animals because of their low cost, relatively simple care, and hardiness. A single dog could pull a sled carrying two hundred pounds of cargo.

The Canadian husky was the favorite among Klondike miners. As a northern dog, the husky probably had been bred for work and companionship—both important qualities to a miner. The dog's double coat suited it for the extreme cold: a soft, downy coat next to the skin and a longer, stiffer, external guard coat. The soft coat trapped the animal's body heat, and the guard coat kept the heat from escaping and water from penetrating to the skin. In addition, the husky's magnificent brush tail curled over its back, protecting its nose and forefeet. Jack London provides a masterful description of a husky in "To Build a Fire."

old, dim trail. The dog joined in behind and kept up with him. He ran blindly, without intention, in fear such as he had never known in his life. Slowly, as he plowed and floundered through the snow, he began to see things again—the banks of the creek, the old timber jams, the leafless aspens, and the sky. The running made him feel better. He did not shiver. Maybe, if he ran on, his feet would thaw out: and, anyway, if he ran far enough, he would

reach camp and the boys. Without doubt he would lose some fingers and toes and some of his face; but the boys would take care of him, and save the rest of him when he got there. And at the same time there was another thought in his mind that said he would never get to the camp and the boys; that it was too many miles away, that the freezing had too great a start on him, and that he would soon be stiff and dead. This thought he kept in the background and refused to consider. Sometimes it pushed itself forward and demanded to be heard, but he thrust it back and strove to think of other things.

It struck him as curious that he could run at all on feet so frozen that he could not feel them when they struck the earth and took the weight of his body. He seemed to himself to skim along above the surface, and to have no connection with the earth. Somewhere he had once seen a winged Mercury,[7] and he wondered if Mercury felt as he felt when skimming over the earth.

His theory of running until he reached camp and the boys had one flaw in it: he lacked the endurance. Several times he stumbled, and finally he tottered, crumpled up, and fell. When he tried to rise, he failed. He must sit and rest, he decided, and next time he would merely walk and keep on going. As he sat and regained his breath, he noted that he was feeling quite warm and comfortable. He was not shivering, and it even seemed that a warm glow had come to his chest and trunk. And yet, when he touched his nose or cheeks, there was no sensation. Running would not thaw them out. Nor would it thaw out his hands and feet. Then the thought came to him that the frozen portions of his body must be extending. He tried to keep this thought down, to forget it, to think of something else; he was aware of the panicky feeling that it caused, and

---

7. **Mercury.** In Roman mythology, Mercury, the messenger of the gods, is depicted with winged feet.

he was afraid of the panic. But the thought asserted itself, and persisted, until it produced a vision of his body totally frozen. This was too much, and he made another wild run along the trail. Once he slowed down to a walk, but the thought of the freezing extending itself made him run again.

And all the time the dog ran with him, at his heels. When he fell down a second time, it curled its tail over its forefeet and sat in front of him, facing him, curiously eager and intent. The warmth and security of the animal angered him, and he cursed it till it flattened down its ears appeasingly. This time the shivering came more quickly upon the man. He was losing in his battle with the frost. It was creeping into his body from all sides. The thought of it drove him on, but he ran no more than a hundred feet, when he staggered and pitched headlong. It was his last panic. When he had recovered his breath and control, he sat up and entertained in his mind the conception of meeting death with dignity. However, the conception did not come to him in such terms. His idea of it was that he had been making a fool of himself, running around like a chicken with its head cut off—such was the simile that occurred to him. Well, he was bound to freeze anyway, and he might as well take it decently. With this new-found peace of mind came the first glimmerings of drowsiness. A good idea, he thought, to sleep off to death. It was like taking an anaesthetic. Freezing was not so bad as people thought. There were lots worse ways to die.

He pictured the boys finding his body next day. Suddenly he found himself with them, coming along the trail and looking for himself. And, still with them, he came around a turn in the trail and found himself lying in the snow. He did not belong with himself any more, for even then he was out of himself; standing with the boys and looking at himself in the snow. It certainly was cold, was his thought. When he got back to the States he could tell the folks what real cold was. He drifted on from this to a vision of the old-timer on Sulphur Creek. He could see him quite clearly, warm and comfortable, and smoking a pipe.

"You were right, old hoss; you were right," the man mumbled to the old-timer of Sulphur Creek.

Then the man drowsed off into what seemed to him the most comfortable and satisfying sleep he had ever known. The dog sat facing him and waiting. The brief day drew to a close in a long, slow twilight. There were no signs of a fire to be made, and, besides, never in the dog's experience had it known a man to sit like that in the snow and make no fire. As the twilight drew on, its eager yearning for the fire mastered it, and with a great lifting and shifting of forefeet, it whined softly, then flattened its ears down in anticipation of being chidden[8] by the man. But the man remained silent. Later, the dog whined loudly. And still later it crept close to the man and caught the scent of death. This made the animal bristle and back away. A little longer it delayed, howling under the stars that leaped and danced and shone brightly in the cold sky. Then it turned and trotted up the trail in the direction of the camp it knew, where were the other food providers and fire providers. ❖

---

8. **chidden.** Scolded

Think of a situation in which you did not want to accept the obvious outcome or decision. What made you face reality?

Informational Text Connection

The Forest Service, established in 1905 as part of the United States Department of Agriculture (USDA), manages more than 193 million acres of forests and grasslands. Every year, many hundreds, if not thousands, of acres of woods and grasslands burn, some due to natural causes, such as lightning, and some due to accidents and human carelessness.

To prevent such devastation and avoid the risk to people's lives, every camper and hiker should know how to care properly for a campfire. **How to Build a Campfire,** a how-to document, was created by the **USDA Forest Service** and is available online, as is a variety of other information for enjoying the outdoors.

How to Build a Campfire
by USDA Forest Service

1. Dig a small pit away from overhanging branches. (Most parks have campfire pits ready and waiting for you.) Circle the pit with rocks, or be sure it already has a metal fire ring.
2. Clear a five-foot area around the pit down to the soil. Stack extra wood upwind and away from the fire.
3. Start with a handful of dry twigs and small sticks, and add larger sticks as the fire builds up. Put the largest pieces of wood on last. Be careful not to make a sudden shower of sparks.
4. In lighting the fire, conserve your matches. Carry a candle as a fire starter.
5. To keep a good fire going, place large pieces of wood outside and gradually push them into the flames.
6. Keep a bucket of water and a shovel nearby. To extinguish the fire, cover with dirt or pour water over it.
7. Never leave a campfire unattended.

How to Be Sure Your Campfire Is Out

1. Drown it with water. Make sure all embers, coals, and sticks are wet. Move rocks to see whether there are burning embers underneath.

2. Stir. Add more water and stir again. Be sure all burning material has been extinguished and cooled.

3. Feel all sticks and charred material. Feel the coals and ashes. Make sure no roots are burning.

4. No water? Use dirt. Mix enough soil or sand with the embers, and the fire will go out. Continue adding and stirring until all material is cold enough to feel with your bare hand. Don't just bury the fire; it may smolder and break out again.

Review Questions

1. How should the fire pit be prepared? Explain why the fire pit should be away from overhanging branches.

2. Explain how to conserve using matches. Which instructions are essentially for safety and which are more for preventing wildfires? Which are for both?

3. Describe how to put out a fire if you do not have any water. If you were going camping, what equipment would you bring to ensure being able to follow these instructions for building and putting out a campfire?

TEXT ^{TO} TEXT CONNECTION

How do the Forest Service guidelines for building and maintaining a campfire overlap with the description given in "How to Build a Fire"? What additional information from the story could you add to the Forest Service recommendations for building a campfire in the winter? In what way did the man in the story not heed the Forest Service advice about building a fire?

Refer to Text ▶ ▶ ▶ ▶ ▶ **Reason with Text**

1a. What signals the man that it is much colder than he had estimated?

1b. Determine why the man fails to take these signals more seriously.

Understand
Find meaning

2a. Make a list of the main events in the man's trek to the mining camp.

2b. On your list, circle the events that make his situation increasingly desperate.

Apply
Use information

3a. Identify the mistakes the man makes.

3b. Why does the author state that the man's limitation is that he is "without imagination"?

Analyze
Take things apart

4a. What are positive qualities of the man's character? What are the negative qualities?

4b. Argue whether the man would have survived if he had formed a better relationship with the dog.

Evaluate
Make judgments

5a. Identify elements of Naturalism in the story.

5b. How is the viewpoint of Naturalism reflected in this story? Why is the man not given a name?

Create
Bring ideas together

Analyze Literature

Setting, Plot, and Conflict
Review your list of details about setting. Which details are effective in creating the harsh Yukon setting? How important is the setting to the story? In what ways does London's setting reflect his interest in Naturalism?

In examining the plot, what is the external conflict, or outside force, against which the main character struggles? How does he fare against that force? How does the dog, a creature of nature, fare? Does the main character face any internal conflicts?

Extend the Text

Writing Options
Creative Writing Imagine that you are an old-timer at Sulphur Creek. Write a pamphlet to serve as a brief survival guide for newcomers who want to travel in the Yukon. Include what to wear, what supplies to bring, and what to do in an emergency. Also provide advice on when to travel and what trail to follow.

Expository Writing Write the directions for how to build a fire in the snow. Use information from the story. Give your directions to the old-timer to include in his or her survival guide (see Creative Writing above).

Lifelong Learning
Write Directions In this short story, Jack London describes the process of building a fire in the wilderness. Think of a procedure with which you are familiar, such as operating a DVD player or making a favorite food.

Write a set of how-to guidelines, documenting the procedure that someone else could follow. To get started, think through all the steps in the procedure. Then break each step into a series of simple chronological tasks. Use simple and precise language, and write the directions in the imperative voice (for example, *First, gather all the supplies*).

Critical Literacy
Read Jack London's Letters Much of what we know about famous people and the times in which they lived comes from their letters, which are *primary sources* of information. Go online to find letters written by Jack London. Read these original letters and take notes on the biographical data you collect. Then write a paragraph explaining what you learned about London. Share your paragraph with classmates.

 Go to **www.mirrorsandwindows.com** for more.

1. The speaker in "To Build a Fire" says that the trouble with the main character is that
A. he is hearing impaired.
B. he is homesick.
C. he has no imagination.
D. he is heartbroken.
E. he is uneducated and foolish.

2. How can the main character tell when it is fifty degrees below zero?
A. His spit cracks when it hits the snow.
B. His spit cracks in the air, before hitting the snow.
C. His dog fights to stay inside his cage.
D. Ice starts to form on his beard and eyelashes.
E. He can no longer feel his feet.

3. If you do something *apathetically,* how are you doing it?
A. with great feeling
B. according to routine
C. carefully, with attention to detail
D. without emotion
E. desperately

4. What two forces are struggling against each other in "To Build a Fire"?
A. cold and warmth
B. dog and man
C. life and death
D. opportunity and safety
E. human and nature

5. In "To Build a Fire," the old-timer from Sulphur Creek advises the main character by suggesting that
A. any conflict should be resolved before the sun goes down.
B. no one should travel alone in the Klondike when it is fifty degrees below zero or colder.
C. family and then work should be the priorities of a working man.
D. no one should travel in the Klondike without a dog.
E. one should never try to start a fire too close to tree branches.

6. What does the word *poignant* mean in the following sentence? "This fear quickly became poignant as he realized that it was no longer a mere matter of freezing his fingers and toes, . . . but that it was a matter of life and death with the chances against him."
A. sharp
B. motivating
C. overwhelming
D. spread out
E. irrelevant

7. According to the information from the USDA Forest Service, how can you make sure a campfire has been put out?
A. Cover and stir the embers with dirt or sand.
B. Drown the burning material with water.
C. Stir the burning material to check for embers.
D. Feel the extinguished burning material with your hands.
E. All of the above

8. Constructed Response: Explain how "To Build a Fire" is an example of Naturalism. Support your answer using specific evidence from the text.

9. Constructed Response: Explain how the central conflict in "To Build a Fire" is resolved and what this resolution might indicate about Jack London's view of the world.

> **TEST-TAKING TIP**
>
> Keep track of time while taking a timed test. Pay attention when each section of the test is introduced to learn how many questions there are and how long you have to complete them. To prepare, complete practice tests. Determine how long it takes you to answer half the test questions. If you tend to use more than half the time to complete half the questions, revisit your test-taking strategy.

Understand the Concept

When you come across an unfamiliar word in your reading, you often can figure out what it means by using **context clues,** words and phrases in the surrounding text that suggest the word's meaning. While you may use these clues unconsciously, learning several strategies will help you be a more effective reader.

There are two basic strategies for using context clues. The first is to compare the unknown word to words you already know, looking for similarities. The three main types of **comparison context clues** are restatement, apposition, and examples.

Using **restatement,** the author may tell you the meaning of the word by using different words to express the same idea in the same or another sentence.

> EXAMPLE
>
> There seemed a <u>pall</u> over the face of things. That is, *a gloom covered the scene.*

An **apposition** renames something in different words. Look for a word or phrase that has been placed in the sentence to clarify the word you do not know.

> EXAMPLE
>
> The <u>undulations</u> in the snow, *the small hill-like waves,* spread as far as the man could see.

The **examples** used in a sentence can help illustrate a term you do not know.

> EXAMPLE
>
> <u>Conifers</u>, *such as pine, spruce, and fir trees,* are the most common type of tree in the Yukon.

The second strategy involves contrasting the unknown word to words you already know. **Contrast context clues** help you find differences between words, which are often signaled by transitions such as *but, however, although,* and *yet.*

> EXAMPLE
>
> The dog was apprehensive about trekking, <u>but</u> the man fearlessly continued on his way.

Apply the Skill

Exercise A

Use context clues to help you determine the vocabulary word from "To Build a Fire" that fits each of the following sentences. See page 418 for a list of words.

1. The funeral director placed a _____, or heavy cloth, over the casket. (*Comparison: Apposition*)
2. Susy suffers from test-taking anxiety, so she has decided to seek help to overcome her _____. (*Comparison: Restatement*)
3. Recalling lost opportunities and missed chances can be especially _____. (*Comparison: Examples*)
4. Frank reacted _____, while Carol reacted enthusiastically. (*Contrast*)
5. Replacing a leaking water heater or fixing a broken furnace is _____. (*Comparison: Examples*)
6. The police restored calm to the streets following the _____ of the previous evening. (*Contrast*)

Exercise B

Find five words that you don't know from "To Build a Fire" or another selection in this unit. Look up the definition of each word in a dictionary. Then write a sentence using the word that provides context clues to its meaning. Exchange papers with a classmate, and try to determine the meanings of each other's words.

SPELLING PRACTICE

Words with *ei* or *ie*

To decide whether to use the vowel combination *ei* or *ie,* many people repeat the saying they learned in grade school: "*I* before *e,* except after *c,* or when sounded long *a* as in *neighbor* or *weigh.*" That saying does not cover every possible *ei* or *ie* question, however. Another rule states that if the vowel combination is pronounced with a long *e,* it should be spelled *ie,* as in the word *thief.* But if the syllable starts with the sound "see," it should be spelled *ei,* as in *receipt* and *seize.* If the syllable contains the "shuh" sound, the correct spelling is *ie,* as in *ancient.* Examine these words from "To Build a Fire," and determine which rule each word follows.

achieved	freighted	sufficient
brief	handkerchief	their
eighty	neither	view
experience	pieces	weights
field	received	weirdness
fiercely		

Stephen Crane (1871–1900) lived to be only twenty-eight, but in that time, he established himself as a great American writer of fiction and poetry. He was born in Newark, New Jersey, the youngest of fourteen children. His first novel, *Maggie: A Girl of the Street,* was rejected by publishers in 1893 because of its grim realism, and so Crane paid for its publication himself. His masterful novel about the Civil War, *The Red Badge of Courage,* was published in 1894 to great acclaim, establishing Crane's literary reputation.

A literary pioneer, Crane was a *Naturalist,* expressing the notion that human beings are pawns, moved by forces beyond their control. That perspective underlies both of the poems that follow. In addition, **"Do not weep, maiden, for war is kind"** illustrates typical characteristics of Crane's poetry: irony, realistic details, and a conversational tone, all expressed in *free verse,* without traditional patterns of rhyme, rhythm, and stanza form. Although Crane's poems were, in his day, considered experimental in form and structure, he did adopt poetic conventions such as repetition, metaphor, alliteration, and personification. In **"A Man Said to the Universe,"** Crane presents an imaginary dialogue between man and the universe.

Do not weep, maiden, for war is kind

by Stephen Crane

Do not weep, maiden, for war is kind.
Because your lover threw wild hands toward the sky
And the affrighted[1] steed ran on alone,
Do not weep.
5   War is kind.

    Hoarse, booming drums of the regiment,
    Little souls who thirst for fight,
    These men were born to drill and die.
    The unexplained glory flies above them,
10   Great is the Battle-God, great, and his Kingdom—
    A field where a thousand corpses lie.

Do not weep, babe, for war is kind.
Because your father tumbled in the yellow trenches,
Raged at his breast, gulped and died,
15   Do not weep.
War is kind.

    Swift blazing flag of the regiment,
    Eagle with crest of red and gold,
    These men were born to drill and die.
20   Point for them the virtue[2] of slaughter,
    Make plain to them the excellence of killing
    And a field where a thousand corpses lie.

Mother whose heart hung humble as a button
On the bright splendid shroud[3] of your son,
25   Do not weep.
War is kind. ❖

---

1. **affrighted.** Frightened
2. **virtue.** Moral excellence
3. **shroud.** Cloth used to wrap a corpse

Aurora Borealis, 1865. Frederic Church.
Smithsonian American Art Museum, Washington, DC.

A Man Said to the Universe

by Stephen Crane

A man said to the universe,
"Sir, I exist!"
"However," replied the universe,
"The fact has not created in me
A sense of obligation." ❖

MIRRORS & WINDOWS

According to the Naturalist philosophy, human beings are pawns, moved by forces beyond their control. Is this idea pessimistic or realistic?

ART CONNECTION

Frederic Church

Frederic Church (1826–1900) was a famous American landscape artist affiliated with the Hudson River School of the mid-1800s (see Unit 2, page 131). He was born in Hartford, Connecticut, to wealthy parents who encouraged him to pursue his art. He studied under esteemed painter Thomas Cole, generally considered the founder of the Hudson River School, and enjoyed immediate critical and financial success.

Like many painters of the era, Church often portrayed scenes from the Catskill Mountains and other New England settings. However, his interest in Naturalism and the complexities of nature motivated him to travel. In 1853 and again in 1857, he journeyed to South America and studied the diverse landscape.

Church's most famous painting, *Heart of the Andes,* was produced during the 1857 trip. This colossal canvas, measuring five feet by ten feet, showed a river lined by lush tropical vegetation, along with the upland plains and snow-capped Andes Mountains—elements too diverse to occur in one natural setting. Nonetheless, Church's painting drew wide acclaim for its quality of detail and use of color.

Church continued to travel widely, creating sketches and paintings based on his travels. He painted *Aurora Borealis,* shown on page 437, in 1865 from sketches he made of the so-called northern lights during a trip to the Arctic six years earlier. He reportedly was inspired by an odd occurrence of the lights in 1864, witnessed by millions of Americans as far south as Virginia, that followed two Union victories late in the Civil War.

Critical Viewing When *Aurora Borealis* was displayed in 1865, many Americans viewed it as symbolic of the Union cause and believed it foreshadowed victory. What about the painting might have given people such hope during a dark time in the nation's history? Consider both the content and artistic qualities of the painting.

Refer and Reason

1. In "Do not weep, maiden, for war is kind," identify the feelings evoked in the reader by the phrases "Little souls who thirst for fight," "the virtue of slaughter," "a field where a thousand corpses lie," and "the excellence of killing." Does the speaker believe in the "virtue of slaughter" and "the excellence of killing"? What in the poem suggests this?

2. In "A Man Said to the Universe," what is implied about the relationship between the universe and human beings? Is the universe indifferent to people? Explain.

3. Restate the main message Crane relates about war in "Do not weep, maiden, for war is kind." If you were the relative or friend of someone killed in battle, how would you respond to this message?

Writing Options

1. Write a poem that expresses your views of war. In choosing words and creating images, think of the *tone,* or emotional attitude, you want to portray. Write your poem in the unstructured style of free verse, as Crane did, or using traditional meter and rhyme.

2. Several online newspapers and bookstores allow readers to post reviews of literature they have read. Write your own review of a work by Stephen Crane, such as one of these poems or *The Red Badge of Courage,* and post it on the Internet.

 Go to **www.mirrorsandwindows.com** for more.

Oratory, or public speaking, was an important part of the oral tradition of Native Americans. In fact, many native peoples viewed oratorical skill as a requirement for leadership. Oratory was used in ceremonial events to address supernatural powers and at council meetings to decide legal and political issues. It was used to inspire warriors and celebrate victories, as well as to settle disputes and foster cooperation between tribes.

Another need for oratory developed when Native Americans began to negotiate with nonnative governments. A very early example was a speech by Wahunsonacock, or King Powhatan, to the colonists at Jamestown in 1609, in which he pleaded for peaceful relations. This type of oratory culminated in the late 1800s, when leaders such as Chief Joseph of the Nez Percé and Cochise of the Chiricahua Apache petitioned the U.S. government for compassionate and fair treatment of native peoples. These leaders' speeches were memorable not only for their eloquence but also for the glimpses they provided into Native American history and tradition.

Native American oratory became written literature when it was recorded by nonnative interpreters, who may have been witnesses to treaty negotiations or travelers, missionaries, captives, or soldiers. Many printed versions of Native American speeches became well known to the American public.

During the late 1800s and early 1900s, stories of Native American life, written by interviewers or natives themselves, also became popular. Like slave narratives, these accounts were of particular interest to people who were critical of U.S. government policy toward native peoples. Like the speeches, these stories provided an invaluable source of information about Native American cultures.

Buffalo Hunt on the Plains, 1872. William Jacob Hays. Buffalo Bill Historical Center, Cody, Wyoming.

I Will Fight No More Forever
A Speech by Chief Joseph of the Nez Percé

I Am the Last of My Family
A Speech by Cochise of the Chiricahua Apache

Build Background

Historical Context **"I Will Fight No More Forever"** is the surrender speech of In-mut-too-yah-lat-lat, known as Chief Joseph, leader of the Wal-lam-wat-kin band of the Chute-pa-lu. The French who first encountered the Chute-pa-lu referred to them as the *Nez Percé,* a name that refers to the custom of piercing the nose for personal adornment. This speech was delivered on October 5, 1877, when Chief Joseph surrendered to the U.S. Army. Joseph was told that after the surrender, his people would be returned to their homeland, but that promise was not kept.

Cochise, leader of the Chiricahua Apache, delivered his **"I Am the Last of My Family"** speech in 1872 during the negotiations with the U.S. government that followed his surrender. There are several accounts of this speech, all recorded years after it was delivered. The account presented here is from Henry Stuart Turrill, who witnessed the negotiations as a young soldier. In recounting the speech many years later, Turrill noted that Cochise started speaking in Apache but shifted to Spanish, in which he was fluent.

Reader's Context What would you find hardest to give up if you were forced to leave your home? Why?

Meet the Authors

Chief Joseph (c. 1840–1904) was a valiant leader who attempted to preserve his people's way of life in the face of overwhelming odds. In 1877, Chief Joseph was preparing to move with his people to a reservation in Idaho when he learned of an attack against white settlers by three Native Americans. Fearing reprisal, Joseph decided to flee with his people to Canada. Pursued by the U.S. Army, Joseph and his band traveled over one thousand miles, often meeting and defeating their pursuers. Surrounded by troops, Chief Joseph surrendered in October, only forty miles from the Canadian border.

Cochise (1812–1874) and the Chiricahua, one of the four main Apache tribes, entered into conflict with white settlers and soldiers around 1860, resulting in a series of wars that would last until 1886 with the capture of Geronimo, the last of the Apache leaders. Cochise was pursued by the U.S. Army for ten years and surrendered only when the government promised to negotiate with him over the relocation of his people. Those negotiations resulted in establishment of an Apache reservation in southwestern Arizona. Following Cochise's death two years later, the government reneged and relocated the Chiricahua.

Compare Literature

Oral Tradition and Purpose
An **oral tradition** is a work, a motif, an idea, or a custom that is passed by word of mouth from generation to generation.

A writer's **purpose** is his or her aim or goal, which may be one or more of the following: to inform or explain; to portray a person, place, object, or event; to convince people to accept a position; and to express thoughts and ideas or to tell a story.

Set Purpose

Chief Joseph and Cochise both were respected leaders who guided their people through difficult times. Although their words eventually were written down, their speeches remain part of the oral tradition of the Native American people. As you read each speech, note the phrases that likely helped people remember and retell it. Also determine each leader's purpose or purposes in speaking.

Preview Vocabulary

feeble, 443
perish, 444
remnant, 444

Guardian of the Trail, c. 1900. Carl Oscar Borg. Bowers Museum of Cultural Art, Santa Ana, California. (See detail on page 440).

I Will Fight No More FOREVER

by Chief Joseph

Tell General Howard[1] I know his heart. What he told me before, I have in my heart. I am tired of fighting. Our chiefs are killed. Looking Glass is dead. Toohoolhoolzote[2] is dead. The old men are all dead. It is the young men who say yes and no. He who led on the young men is dead. It is cold and we have no blankets. The little children are freezing to death. My people, some of them, have run away to the hills and have no blankets, no food; no one knows where they are—perhaps freezing to death. I want to have time to look for my children and see how many I can find. Maybe I shall find them among the dead. Hear me, my chiefs. I am tired; my heart is sick and sad. From where the sun now stands I will fight no more forever. Here me, my chiefs! I am tired; my heart is sick and sad. ❖

---

1. **General Howard.** Oliver Howard (1830–1909), who conducted the 1877 operation against Chief Joseph and the Nez Percé
2. **Looking Glass . . . Toohoolhoolzote.** Two Nez Percé leaders

---

MIRRORS & WINDOWS — At what point should a leader abandon a goal or plan for the sake of the people he or she represents?

HISTORY CONNECTION

Broken Promises

JOSEPH

In April 1879, Chief Joseph provided this account of his attempt to achieve justice for his people by political means:

At last I was granted permission to come to Washington. . . . I am glad we came. I have shaken hands with a great many friends, but there are some things I want to know which no one seems able to explain. . . . I cannot understand why so many chiefs are allowed to talk in so many different ways, and promise so many different things. I have seen the Great Father Chief, the next Great Chief, the Commissioner Chief, the Law Chief, and many other law chiefs,[1] and they all say they are my friends and that I shall have justice; but while their mouths all talk right, I do not understand why nothing is done for my people. I have heard talk and talk, but nothing is done. Good words do not last long unless they amount to something. Words do not pay for my dead people. They do not pay for my country, now overrun by white men. They do not protect my father's grave. They do not pay for all my horses and cattle. Good words will not give me back my children. . . . It makes my heart sick when I remember all the good words and all the broken promises. . . . All men were made by the same Great Spirit Chief. They are all brothers. The earth is the mother of all people, and all people should have equal rights upon it.

Another well-known address from Cochise is believed to have been presented in a resettlement negotiation meeting with the U.S. Army in 1866, six years before the leader's surrender. It was during this earlier round of negotiations that Cochise first realized the army planned to relocate the

Chiricahua Apache to the Tularosa Reservation in New Mexico. In expressing his sorrow over the loss of his people's lands, Cochise remarked,

When I was young I walked all over this country, east and west, and saw no other people than the Apaches. After many summers I walked again and found another race of people had come to take it. How is that? . . .

I have no father or mother; I am alone in the world. No one cares for Cochise; that is why I do not care to live, and wish the rocks to fall on me and cover me up. . . .

I want to live in these mountains; I do not want to go to Tularosa. That is a long ways off. The flies on those mountains eat out the eyes of horses. The bad spirits live there. I have drunk of these waters and they have cooled me; I do not want to leave here.

---

1. **Great Father Chief . . . other law chiefs.** President Theodore Roosevelt, various members of his administration, and various members of Congress

Indian with Drum, 1859. Joseph Henry Sharp.

I Am the Last
of My Family
by Cochise

This for a very long time has been the home of my people; they came from the darkness, few in numbers and <u>feeble</u>. The country was held by a much stronger and more numerous people, and from their stone houses we were quickly driven. We were a hunting people, living on the animals that we could kill. We came to these mountains about us; no one lived here, and so we took them for our home and country. Here we grew from the first feeble band to be a great people, and covered the whole country as the clouds cover the mountains. Many people came to our country. First the Spanish, with their horses and their iron shirts, their long knives[1] and guns,

---

1. **horses . . . knives.** Spaniards introduced horses to the Americas. Metal armor and swords are referred to here.

fee • ble (fē´ bl) *adj.,* weak

great wonders to my simple people. We fought some, but they never tried to drive us from our homes in these mountains. After many years the Spanish soldiers were driven away and the Mexican ruled the land. With these little wars came, but we were now a strong people and we did not fear them. At last in my youth came the white man, your people. Under the counsels of my grandfather, who had for a very long time been the head of the Apaches, they were received with friendship. Soon their numbers increased and many passed through my country to the great waters of the setting sun.[2] Your soldiers came and their strong houses[3] were all through my country. I received favors from your people and did all that I could in return and we lived at peace. At last your soldiers did me a very great wrong,[4] and I and my whole people went to war with them. At first we were successful and your soldiers were driven away and your people killed and we again possessed our land. Soon many soldiers came from the north and from the west, and my people were driven to the mountain hiding places; but these did not protect us, and soon my people were flying from one mountain to another, driven by the soldiers, even as the wind is now driving the clouds. I have fought long and as best I could against you. I have destroyed many of your people, but where I have destroyed one white man many have come in his place; but where an Indian has been killed, there has been none to come in his place, so that the great people that welcomed you with acts of kindness to this land are now but a feeble band that fly before your soldiers as the deer before the hunter, and must all perish if this war continues. I have come to you, not from any love for you or for your great father in Washington,[5] or from any regard for his or your wishes, but as a conquered chief, to try to save alive the few people that still remain to me. I am the last of my family, a family that for very many years have been the leaders of this people, and on me depends their future, whether they shall utterly vanish from the land or that a small remnant remain for a few years to see the sun rise over these mountains, their home. I here pledge my word, a word that has never been broken, that if your great father will set aside a part of my own country, where I and my little band can live, we will remain at peace with your people forever. If from his abundance he will give food for my women and children, whose protectors his soldiers have killed, with blankets to cover their nakedness, I will receive them with gratitude. If not, I will do my best to feed and clothe them, in peace with the white man. I have spoken. ❖

> I have fought long and as best I could against you.

---

2. **great . . . sun.** Pacific Ocean
3. **strong houses.** Military forts
4. **a very great wrong.** Likely refers to Cochise's falsely being accused of stealing farm animals in 1861
5. **great father in Washington.** President

per • ish (pār´ ish) *v.,* die
rem • nant (rem´ nənt) *n.,* remainder

MIRRORS & WINDOWS
Cochise describes himself as a "conquered chief." Does he maintain his dignity and honor in surrendering? Is there ever honor in surrendering?

Refer to Text ▶ ▶ ▶ ▶ ▶   Reason with Text

1a. In Cochise's speech, whom does he describe as visitors to the Apaches' land?	**1b.** Explain how the Apache react to each group of newcomers.	**Understand** Find meaning
2a. According to Chief Joseph, what has happened to the people's leaders, the chiefs, and the old men?	**2b.** What is dangerous about having the young men in charge?	**Apply** Use information
3a. Identify what motivates Cochise to come to the white conquerors to surrender.	**3b.** How does Cochise regard the "great father in Washington" (the president)?	**Analyze** Take things apart
4a. What does Chief Joseph need time to do?	**4b.** Judge what makes Chief Joseph's speech touching and memorable.	**Evaluate** Make judgments
5a. Recall the images Cochise uses to describe his people running and scattering as the soldiers approach.	**5b.** Why does Chief Joseph mention the sun?	**Create** Bring ideas together

Compare Literature

Oral Tradition and Purpose

Works in the oral tradition often contain memorable language—words and phrases people will remember and repeat in passing down these works to future generations. Make a list of memorable lines from Chief Joseph's speech. Then next to each line, explain why it is memorable. Do the same for Cochise's speech.

What purpose or purposes did Chief Joseph have in speaking? What purpose or purposes did Cochise have? Compare and contrast the speakers' purposes and how well they achieved them.

Extend the Text

Writing Options

Creative Writing Imagine that you are one of Chief Joseph's fellow chiefs, the group to whom he directed his speech, and prepare a response to deliver to him in the oral tradition. State whether you understand his sentiments and support his decision not to fight. Decide what tone you will take in addressing this revered leader.

Narrative Writing Write a paragraph explaining what happened to the Nez Percé after Chief Joseph's surrender in October 1877. Imagine that it will be used in a book such as this to provide a follow-up to Chief Joseph's speech. Search the Internet for photographs, Native American art, and historical documents to accompany your paragraph.

Lifelong Learning

Research a Native American Treaty Do research to identify a treaty that the U.S. government made with a Native American tribe in your region. Find out about the

events leading up to the treaty, the terms of the agreement, and whether both groups fulfilled the terms. Also determine the current status of the tribe and identify problems or disputes faced by modern-day members. Prepare a written report that students might read during Native American history month at their school.

Critical Literacy

Address a Jury Imagine that you are an attorney representing the Nez Percé in a lawsuit against the U.S. government. Prepare an address to a civil jury, stating what Chief Joseph's people have lost and how they should be compensated. Ask six of your classmates (the number of people on a civil jury) to be jurors and listen to your presentation. After the address, ask jurors whether they were persuaded by your speech. Have them comment on your delivery (tone, eye contact, body language) and the content of your argument.

Go to **www.mirrorsandwindows.com** for more.

from Black Elk Speaks

An Oral History by Nicholas Black Elk and John G. Neihardt

Build Background

Historical Context The pace of westward expansion in the late 1800s meant that Native Americans and whites engaged in increasing competition and conflict. Settlers encroached on the land designated in 1834 as the *Indian Territory* (modern-day Oklahoma) as they extended the Overland Trail to Utah, California, and Oregon. Then, in 1854, the U.S. government abolished the northern half of the Indian Territory so the transcontinental railroad could be built. The Native American tribes in the area (some of whom already had been relocated there) signed treaties, accepting reduced reservations or small individual pieces of land. Many ended up selling their lands to whites (usually under pressure), losing both their identities and control over their lives.

Literary Context In this excerpt from **Black Elk Speaks,** a warrior and *shaman* (medicine man) of the Oglala Lakota tells of his youth. He describes his first spiritual vision of the role of shaman, which would establish him as a spiritual leader to his people. The excerpt also focuses on the difficulties faced by the Lakota, one of the tribes of the Great Sioux Nation, as white settlers moved in and claimed ownership of the Great Plains.

Reader's Context Are people more likely to remember life's sorrows and disappointments or its triumphs and joys? Why?

Meet the Authors

Nicholas Black Elk (1863–1950) was almost seventy years old when John Neihardt interviewed him and several other Lakota elders in 1930–1931. Black Elk dictated his autobiography to Neihardt and recounted his people's history and traditions in an effort to preserve them. Because Neihardt's account was filtered through translators, experts have questioned the real authorship of the book. Still, it remains an important chronicle of Native American life and spirituality.

John G. Neihardt (1881–1973) was born in Illinois and grew up in Kansas and Nebraska. The close connections he formed with Native Americans in Nebraska strongly influenced his poems, short stories, and novels. *Black Elk Speaks,* his most popular work, evolved from interviews with the shaman during Neihardt's research for a long poetic work, *A Cycle of the West.* Black Elk said of the author, "He is a word sender. This world is like a garden and over it go his words like rain, and where they go they leave everything greener. After his words have passed, the memory of them shall stand long in the West like a flaming rainbow."

Analyze Literature

Narrative and Magical Realism
A **narrative** is a story told in fiction, nonfiction, poetry, or drama. The events of a narrative are usually told in *chronological order,* or the order in which they occurred.

Magical Realism is a form of fiction in which elements of fantasy appear within a primarily realistic narrative.

Set Purpose

In recording this oral history, Neihardt included not only Black Elk's account of the past but also the perspectives of several others. Note when other voices contribute to the narrative and how including them affects the telling of the story. Also identify which passages are realistic and which ones represent Black Elk's visions. Consider what the use of Magical Realism adds to the narrative.

Preview Vocabulary

bison, 448
gully, 449
sorrel, 450
treaty, 453

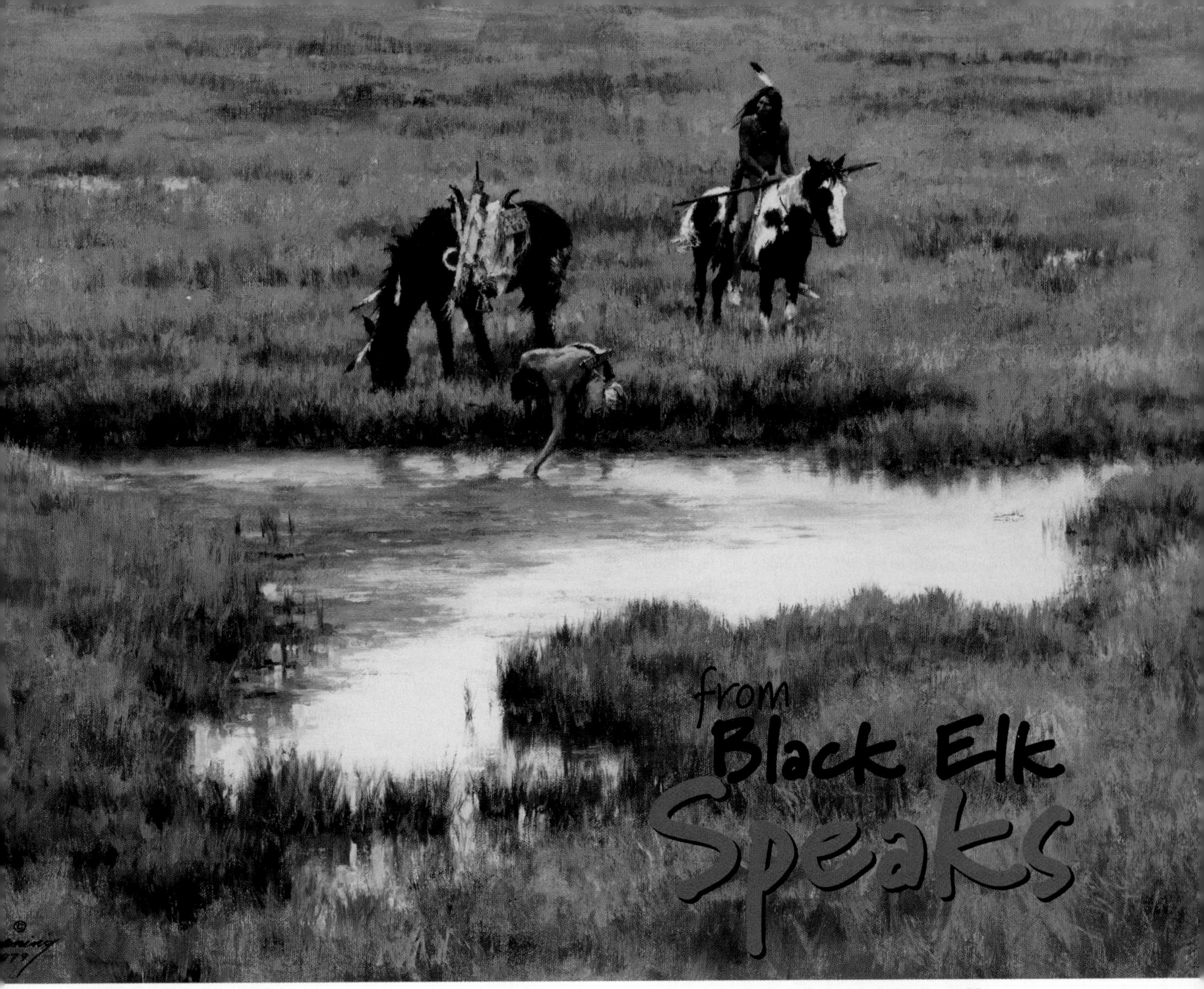

Good Medicine, 1979. Howard Terpning.
(See detail on page 446.)

by Nicholas Black Elk
and John G. Neihardt

It is like some fearful thing in a fog, for it was a time when everything seemed troubled and afraid.

I am a Lakota of the Ogalala[1] band. My father's name was Black Elk, and his father before him bore the name, and the father of his father, so that I am the fourth to bear it. He was a medicine man and so were several of his brothers. Also, he and the great Crazy Horse's father were cousins, having the same grandfather. My mother's name was White Cow Sees; her father was called Refuse-to-go, and her mother, Plenty Eagle Feathers. I can remember my mother's mother and her father. My father's

---

1. **Ogalala.** Although this spelling is used throughout Neihardt's narrative, *Oglala* is now the preferred spelling.

father was killed by the Pawnees when I was too little to know, and his mother, Red Eagle Woman, died soon after.

I was born in the Moon of the Popping Trees (December) on the Little Powder River in the Winter When the Four Crows Were Killed (1863), and I was three years old when my father's right leg was broken in the Battle of the Hundred Slain.[2] From that wound he limped until the day he died, which was about the time when Big Foot's band was butchered on Wounded Knee[3] (1890). He is buried here in these hills.

I can remember that Winter of the Hundred Slain as a man may remember some bad dream he dreamed when he was little, but I can not tell just how much I heard when I was bigger and how much I understood when I was little. It is like some fearful thing in a fog, for it was a time when everything seemed troubled and afraid. I had never seen a Wasichu[4] then, and did not know what one looked like; but every one was saying that the Wasichus were coming and that they were going to take our country and rub us all out and that we should all have to die fighting. It was the Wasichus who got rubbed out in that battle, and all the people were talking about it for a long while; but a hundred Wasichus was not much if there were others and others without number where those came from.

I remember once that I asked my grandfather about this. I said: "When the scouts come back from seeing the prairie full of <u>bison</u> somewhere, the people say the Wasichus are coming; and when strange men are coming to kill us all, they say the Wasichus are coming. What does it mean?" And he said, "That they are many."

When I was older, I learned what the fighting was about that winter and the next summer. Up on the Madison Fork the Wasichus

Every one was saying that the Wasichus were coming and that they were going to take our country.

had found much of the yellow metal that they worship and that makes them crazy, and they wanted to have a road up through our country to the place where the yellow metal was; but my people did not want the road. It would scare the bison and make them go away, and also it would let the other Wasichus come in like a river. They told us that they wanted only to use a little land, as much as a wagon would take between the wheels; but our people knew better. And when you look about you now, you can see what it was they wanted.

Once we were happy in our own country and we were seldom hungry, for then the two-leggeds and the four-leggeds lived together like relatives, and there was plenty for them and for us. But the Wasichus came, and they have made little islands for us and other little islands for the four-leggeds, and always these islands are becoming smaller, for around them surges the gnawing flood of the Wasichu; and it is dirty with lies and greed.

A long time ago my father told me what his father told him, that there was once a Lakota[5] holy man, called Drinks Water, who dreamed what was to be; and this was long before the coming of the Wasichus. He dreamed that the four-leggeds were going back into the earth and that a strange race had woven a spider's web all around the Lakotas. And he said: "When this happens, you shall live in square

---

2. **Battle of the Hundred Slain.** Also called the Fetterman Fight, a Lakota victory in which Captain Fetterman and eighty-one men were slain near Peno Creek in December 1866.

3. **Wounded Knee.** Creek in South Dakota, site of a terrible massacre of Native Americans in 1890. This massacre symbolized the defeat of the Great Sioux Nation and the end of the Indian wars.

4. **Wasichu.** Term used to describe a white settler

5. **Lakota.** Division of the Great Sioux Nation

---

bi • son (bī´ s'n) *n.,* type of mammal having a shaggy mane, short, curved horns, and humped back; commonly referred to as the American buffalo

Red Cloud of the Oglala Sioux.

gray houses, in a barren land, and beside those square gray houses you shall starve." They say he went back to Mother Earth soon after he saw this vision, and it was sorrow that killed him. You can look about you now and see that he meant these dirt-roofed houses we are living in, and that all the rest was true. Sometimes dreams are wiser than waking.

And so when the soldiers came and built themselves a town of logs there on the Piney Fork of the Powder, my people knew they meant to have their road and take our country and maybe kill us all when they were strong enough. Crazy Horse was only about 19 years old then, and Red Cloud was still our great chief. In the Moon of the Changing Season (October) he called together all the scattered bands of the Lakota for a big council on the Powder River, and when we went on the warpath against the soldiers, a horseback could

ride through our villages from sunrise until the day was above his head, so far did our camp stretch along the valley of the river; for many of our friends, the Shyela and the Blue Clouds,[6] had come to help us fight.

And it was about when the bitten moon was delayed (last quarter) in the Time of the Popping Trees when the hundred were rubbed out. My friend, Fire Thunder here, who is older than I, was in that fight and he can tell you how it was.

Fire Thunder Speaks:
I was 16 years old when this happened, and after the big council on the Powder we had moved over to the Tongue River where we were camping at the mouth of Peno Creek. There were many of us there. Red Cloud was over all of us, but the chief of our band was Big Road. We started out on horseback just about sunrise, riding up the creek toward the soldiers' town on the Piney, for we were going to attack it. The sun was about half way up when we stopped at the place where the Wasichus' road came down a steep, narrow ridge and crossed the creek. It was a good place to fight, so we sent some men ahead to coax the soldiers out. While they were gone, we divided into two parts and hid in the gullies on both sides of the ridge and waited. After a long while we heard a shot up over the hill, and we knew the soldiers were coming. So we held the noses of our ponies that they might not whinny at the soldiers' horses. Soon we saw our men coming back, and some of them were walking and leading their horses, so that the soldiers would think they were worn out. Then the men we had sent ahead came running down the road between us, and the soldiers on horseback followed, shooting. When they came

---

6. **Shyela and the Blue Clouds.** Cheyenne and Arapaho; two Native American groups from the Great Plains region

gul • ly (gŭl´ lē) *n.,* channel or hollow worn by running water

Battle of Little Big Horn, c. 1890–1900. Kicking Bear.
Southwest Museum, Los Angeles.

to the flat at the bottom of the hill, the fighting began all at once. I had a <u>sorrel</u> horse, and just as I was going to get on him, the soldiers turned around and began to fight their way back up the hill. I had a six-shooter that I had traded for, and also a bow and arrows. When the soldiers started back, I held my sorrel with one hand and began killing them with the six-shooter, for they came close to me. There were many bullets, but there were more arrows—so many that it was like a cloud of grasshoppers all above and around the soldiers; and our people, shooting across, hit each other. The soldiers were falling all the while they were fighting back up the hill, and their horses got loose. Many of our people chased the horses, but I was not after horses; I was after Wasichus. When the soldiers got on top, there were not many of them left and they had no place to hide. They were fighting hard. We were told to crawl up on them, and we did. When we were close, someone yelled: "Let us go! This is a good day to die. Think of the helpless ones at home!" Then we all cried, "Hoka hey!" and

ART CONNECTION

Kicking Bear

Kicking Bear (1848–?), a religious leader and warrior of the Lakota, fought at the Battle of Little Big Horn, also called *Custer's Last Stand.* Using a traditional style of Plains Indian painting, Kicking Bear recorded the eyewitness account of the Lakota's last great victory in defense of their homeland. Rather than portray one scene from a single perspective, Kicking Bear created a *pictograph,* which tells a narrative with pictures.

Critical Viewing Write several sentences that tell the story portrayed in Kicking Bear's pictograph, which is a visual narrative. Consider the setting, the people involved, and the events of the narrative.

sor • rel (sôr´ əl) *adj.,* light reddish-brown

rushed at them. I was young then and quick on my feet, and I was one of the first to get in among the soldiers. They got up and fought very hard until not one of them was alive. They had a dog with them, and he started back up the road for the soldiers' town, howling as he ran. He was the only one left. I did not shoot at him because he looked too sweet, but many did shoot, and he died full of arrows. So there was nobody left of the soldiers. Dead men and horses and wounded Indians were scattered all the way up the hill, and their blood was frozen, for a storm had come up and it was very cold and getting colder all the time. We left all the dead lying there, for the ground was solid, and we picked up our wounded and started back; but we lost most of them before we reached our camp at the mouth of the Peno. There was a big blizzard that night; and some of the wounded who did not die on the way, died after we got home. This was the time when Black Elk's father had his leg broken.

Black Elk Continues:
I am quite sure that I remember the time when my father came home with a broken leg that he got from killing so many Wasichus, and it seems that I can remember all about the battle too, but I think I could not. It must be the fear that I remember most. All this time I was not allowed to play very far away from our tepee, and my mother would say, "If you are not good the Wasichus will get you."

We must have broken camp at the mouth of the Peno soon after the battle, for I can remember my father lying on a pony drag with bison robes all around him, like a baby, and my mother riding the pony. The snow was deep and it was very cold, and I remember sitting in another pony drag beside my father and mother, all wrapped up in fur. We were

going away from where the soldiers were, and I do not know where we went, but it was west.

It was a hungry winter, for the deep snow made it hard to find the elk; and also many of the people went snowblind.[7] We wandered a long time, and some of the bands got lost from each other. Then at last we were camping in the woods beside a creek somewhere, and the hunters came back with meat.

I think it was this same winter when a medicine man, by the name of Creeping, went around among the people curing snowblinds. He would put snow upon their eyes, and after he had sung a certain sacred song that he had heard in a dream, he would blow on the backs of their heads and they would see again, so I have heard. It was about the dragonfly that he sang, for that was where he got his power, they say.

When it was summer again we were camping on the Rosebud, and I did not feel so much afraid, because the Wasichus seemed farther away and there was peace there in the valley and there was plenty of meat. But all the boys from five or six years up were playing war. The little boys would gather together from the different bands of the tribe and fight each other with mud balls that they threw with willow sticks. And the big boys played the game called Throwing-Them-Off-Their-Horses, which is a battle all but the killing; and sometimes they got hurt. The horsebacks from the different bands would line up and charge upon each other, yelling; and when the ponies came together on the run, they would rear and flounder and scream in a big dust, and the riders would seize each other, wrestling until one side had lost all its men, for those who fell upon the ground were counted dead.

> It was a hungry winter, for the deep snow made it hard to find the elk.

---

7. **went snowblind.** Were blinded temporarily by ultraviolet rays reflected from the snow

When I was older, I, too, often played this game. We were always naked when we played it, just as warriors are when they go into battle if it is not too cold, because they are swifter without clothes. Once I fell off on my back right in the middle of a bed of prickly pears,[8] and it took my mother a long while to pick all the stickers out of me. I was still too little to play war that summer, but I can remember watching the other boys, and I thought that when we all grew up and were big together, maybe we could kill all the Wasichus or drive them far away from our country.

It was in the Moon When the Cherries Turn Black (August) that all the people were talking again about a battle, and our warriors came back with many wounded. It was The Attacking of the Wagons, and it made me afraid again, for we did not win that battle as we did the other one, and there was much mourning for the dead. Fire Thunder was in that fight too, and he can tell you how it was that day.

Fire Thunder Speaks:
It was very bad. There is a wide flat prairie with hills around it, and in the middle of this the Wasichus had put the boxes of their wagons in a circle, so that they could keep their mules there at night. There were not many Wasichus, but they were lying behind the boxes and they shot faster than they ever shot at us before. We thought it was some new medicine of great power that they had, for they shot so fast that it was like tearing a blanket. Afterwards I learned that it was because they had new guns that they loaded from behind, and this was the first time they used these guns. We came on after sunrise. There were many, many of us, and we meant to ride right

over them and rub them out. But our ponies were afraid of the ring of fire the guns of the Wasichus made, and would not go over. Our women were watching us from the hills and we could hear them singing and mourning whenever the shooting stopped. We tried hard, but we could not do it, and there were dead warriors and horses piled all around the boxes and scattered over the plain. Then we left our horses in a gulch and charged on foot, but it was like green grass withering in a fire. So we picked up our wounded and went away. I do not know how many of our people were killed, but there were very many. It was bad.

Black Elk Continues:
I do not remember where we camped that winter but it must have been a time of peace and of plenty to eat.

I do not know how many of our people were killed, but there were very many. It was bad.

Standing Bear Speaks:
I am four years older than Black Elk, and he and I have been good friends since boyhood. I know it was on the Powder that we camped where there were many cottonwood trees. Ponies like to eat the bark of these trees and it is good for them. That was the winter when High Shirt's mother was killed by a big tree that fell on her tepee. It was a very windy night and there were noises that 'woke me, and then I heard that an old woman had been killed, and it was High Shirt's mother.

Black Elk Continues:
I was four years old then, and I think it must have been the next summer that I first heard the voices. It was a happy summer and nothing was afraid, because in the Moon When the

---

8. **prickly pears.** Plants belonging to a variety of cactus

Moon Names

Native Americans commonly identified different times of the year with moon names, as illustrated by Black Elk's reference to August as the *Moon When the Cherries Turn Black.* Although there are some similarities between the names created by different groups, most are different because they are based on the geographic regions in which the various groups lived and reflect what the groups hunted and harvested. For example, in contrast to the Oglala Lakota name for August, the Algonquin tribe called it the *Moon When Indian Corn Is Edible.*

Ponies Shed (May) word came from the Wasichus that there would be peace and that they would not use the road any more and that all the soldiers would go away. The soldiers did go away and their towns were torn down; and in the Moon of Falling Leaves (November), they made a <u>treaty</u> with Red Cloud that said our country would be ours as long as grass should grow and water flow. You can see that it is not the grass and the water that have forgotten.

Maybe it was not this summer when I first heard the voices, but I think it was, because I know it was before I played with bows and arrows or rode a horse, and I was out playing alone when I heard them. It was like somebody calling me, and I thought it was my mother, but there was nobody there. This happened more than once, and always made me afraid, so that I ran home.

trea • ty (trē′ tē) *n.,* formal agreement between two or more nations

Winter Count Calendar [detail], 1907. Battiste Good. Library of Congress, Washington, DC.

It was when I was five years old that my Grandfather made me a bow and some arrows. The grass was young and I was horseback. A thunderstorm was coming from where the sun goes down, and just as I was riding into the woods along a creek, there was a kingbird sitting on a limb. This was not a dream, it happened. And I was going to shoot at the kingbird with the bow my Grandfather made, when the bird spoke and said: "The clouds all over are one-sided." Perhaps it meant that all the clouds were looking at me. And then it said: "Listen! A voice is calling you!" Then I looked up at the clouds, and two men were coming there, headfirst like arrows slanting down; and as they came, they sang a sacred song and the thunder was like drumming. I will sing it for you. The song and the drumming were like this:

> "Behold, a sacred voice is calling you;
> All over the sky a sacred voice is calling."

I sat there gazing at them, and they were coming from the place where the giant lives (north). But when they were very close to me, they wheeled about toward where the sun goes down, and suddenly they were geese. Then they were gone, and the rain came with a big wind and a roaring.

I did not tell this vision to any one. I liked to think about it, but was afraid to tell it. ❖

MIRRORS & WINDOWS

Based on the events described in the selection, what future do you think Black Elk saw for his people?

Refer to Text ▶ ▶ ▶ ▶ ▶ **Reason with Text**

1a. What did the Oglala believe the Wasichus planned to do? What did the Wasichus wish to build? Why did the Oglala oppose their wishes?

1b. How did the Wasichus change the lives of the Oglala? How did the Oglala in the selection feel about the Wasichus and the things they seemed to value?

Understand
Find meaning

2a. How successful were the Oglala in the first battle described by Black Elk and Fire Thunder?

2b. Examine how real-life events affected the play of Oglala children.

Apply
Use information

3a. Recall how the medicine man named Creeping cured people of snow blindness.

3b. Identify specific references that demonstrate the Oglala Lakota's respect for the natural world.

Analyze
Take things apart

4a. What did Black Elk see in his vision?

4b. Interpret why Black Elk's vision had such an effect on him.

Evaluate
Make judgments

5a. What was the dream of the holy man Drinks Water?

5b. Using the information in this piece, summarize the main religious beliefs of the Oglala Sioux.

Create
Bring ideas together

Analyze Literature

Narrative and Magical Realism

How do the recollections and views Black Elk presents in his narrative differ from those of Fire Thunder and Standing Bear? Does having three people describe the same events give you get a better understanding of them? Why or why not?

Which passages in the narrative are realistic, and which ones qualify as Magical Realism, representing Black Elk's visions? Why might Neihardt have included these elements of fantasy within a nonfiction narrative? What do these passages contribute to the narrative?

Extend the Text

Writing Options
Creative Writing Imagine that you are negotiating a treaty between the Wasichus and the Oglala Lakota. Write a compromise document that will enable the two groups to live in peace. To make it a fair compromise, address the needs, desires, and hardships of both groups.

Expository Writing During the 1960s and 1970s, *Black Elk Speaks* became important to activists pursuing Native American civil rights. Historian Vine Deloria referred to the autobiography as the "Indian Bible." Write an essay suggesting why the autobiography became so significant. Support your opinion with details from the selection.

Media Literacy
Research Native American Groups Select a Native American tribe that interests you, whether one from the region in which you live or one about which you have heard or read. Then research one aspect of that tribe's culture, such as religion, art, architecture, ceremonies, child rearing, or food gathering. Prepare and deliver an oral report to the class. Use visual aids such as maps and photographs to make your report vivid and interesting.

Lifelong Learning
Tell a Story Many Native American groups traditionally have used storytelling to preserve and pass on their history and legends. Think about an event important to your family's history, and create a story about it to share with classmates. Make some notes to ensure you will present the events of the story in chronological order. Also provide the background information necessary for your audience to understand the story.

 Go to **www.mirrorsandwindows.com** for more.

1. What did the Wasichus want that caused a conflict with the Lakota, according to Black Elk?
   A. a road up the hills to the gold deposits
   B. control of the river for trade
   C. herds of bison
   D. for the Lakota to live in small gray houses
   E. for animals and humans to live on separate islands

2. Which of the following was *not* part of Drink Water's vision?
   A. animals returning to the earth
   B. a spider web around the Lakota
   C. yellow metal that drives people crazy
   D. his people living in square gray houses
   E. the starvation of his people

3. Which of the following is the best definition of the word *sorrel?*
   A. a type of horse
   B. a medicinal plant with gray-green leaves
   C. a light reddish-brown color
   D. short but sturdy
   E. young and strong

4. What is Black Elk referring to when he says, "You can see that it is not the grass and the water that have forgotten"?
   A. Black Elk cannot remember specifics because events occurred so long ago, but nature remembers.
   B. Nature continues through its cycles, but the Lakota have started to forget their traditions.
   C. The Lakota had promised not to attack the soldiers, but they did anyway and the many who are buried remember that.
   D. The Lakota vowed to remain on the land as long as grass would grow and water would flow, but many have since left to seek opportunities elsewhere.
   E. The treaty with Red Cloud was violated by the white people.

5. Why did Black Elk not tell anyone about his vision?
   A. The voices told him not to.
   B. Because he was young, no one would have believed him.
   C. He wanted to forget the frightening vision.
   D. He was afraid to tell it.
   E. He wanted to be the only one to know about it.

6. How does Black Elk describe the Winter of the Hundred Slain?
   A. as a time of victory
   B. as a hungry winter when many went snowblind
   C. like a fearful thing in a fog
   D. as a time of peace and plenty of meat
   E. as a bad time when his father was killed in battle

7. What do the games Black Elk played as a child indicate about the time in which he grew up?
   A. There was a growing peace between the Lakota and the Wasichus.
   B. The Lakota were preparing their children for harvesting and home building.
   C. The Lakota had surrendered to the Wasichus.
   D. Black Elk and the other children had an easier childhood than the generation before them.
   E. The Oglala anticipated further conflicts with the Wasichus.

8. **Constructed Response:** Describe Black Elk's point of view, and explain how the points of view of his friends Standing Bear and Fire Thunder support or detract from his viewpoint. What is the effect of having several people tell the story? Use examples from the text to support your ideas.

9. **Constructed Response:** Discuss the use of tone in this excerpt from *Black Elk Speaks,* first describing the tone and then analyzing how it affects readers' understanding of the content. Remember that Black Elk originally told this story in his own language. It later was translated by a relative, and then John Neihardt transcribed the story and published it as a book. What in the narrative suggests that the words were first spoken, rather than written?

> **TEST-TAKING TIP**
>
> Struggling with the meanings of unfamiliar words slows down many test takers. To help you decipher the meaning of an unknown word, use *context clues:* words and phrases in the surrounding text that suggest the word's meaning. If using context clues is not one of your strongest reading skills, work on learning specific strategies. See the Vocabulary & Spelling workshop on page 435 for explanations and examples of different strategies for using context clues.

I Tried to Be Like My Mother

by Pretty Shield

Rock medicine bundle with buckskin wrapper and beads. Buffalo Bill Historical Center, Cody, Wyoming. This bundle was opened by the Crow during the first sound of thunder in spring and at the onset of winter.

Pretty Shield (1856–1944) was a Crow medicine woman who recounted the story of life among the Crow people of Plum Creek before their life-changing contact with white settlers and soldiers. Her story, told using sign language to Frank B. Linder-man, shows how children's play prepared the youngsters for life as Crow adults. Her memoirs can be read in Linderman's book, *Pretty Shield: Medicine Woman of the Crows.*

The Crow historically have lived in the Yellowstone River Valley in Montana.

I tried to be like my mother, and like another woman, besides . . . I carried my doll on my back just as mothers carry their babies; and besides this I had a little teepee [lodge] that I pitched whenever my aunt pitched hers. It was made exactly like my aunt's, had the same number of poles, only of course my teepee was very small. My horse dragged the poles and packed the lodge-skin, so that I often beat my aunt in setting up my lodge, which she pretended made her jealous. And how I used to hurry in setting up my lodge, so that I might have a fire going inside it before my aunt could kindle one in hers! I did not know it then, but now I feel sure that she often let me beat her just to encourage me. Each year, as was our custom, I made myself a new lodge and set it up, as the grownups did, when we went into our winter camps. Each time I made a new one I cut my lodge-skin larger than the old one, took more and more pains to have it pretty. I played with these little lodges, often lived in them, until I was a married woman, and even after. I have never lost my love for play.

Once several of us girls made ourselves a play village with our tiny teepees. Of course our children were dolls, and our horses dogs, and yet we managed to make our village look very real, so real that we thought we ought to have some meat to cook. We decided to kill it ourselves. A girl named Beaver-that-passes borrowed her father's lance that was very sharp, and longer than both our bodies put together. We caught and saddled two gentle packhorses; and both the old fools went crazy before we managed to kill a calf. I helped all I could, but it was Beaver-that-passes who wounded a big calf that gave us both a lot of trouble before we finally got it down, and dead. I hurt my leg, and Beaver-that-passes cut her hand with the lance. The calf itself looked pretty bad by the time we got it to our play-village. But we had a big feast, and forgot our hurts. . . .

And sometimes . . . we made ourselves into mud-clowns and entertained the village, riding double on old horses that we made to look as funny as ourselves. There was one old man who would always drum for us, because drumming is not for women; and we would sing and dance through the village, stopping to show off before the lodges of our particular friends. Often women would come out and as though to pay us for our performances, give us meat and berries to eat. [The Crows are fond of clowning. With mud alone they are able to transform themselves, and even their horses, into grotesque figures] . . . one day several girls and a boy were going to have a play sun-dance. . . . Our lodges were pitched on Spotted-fish creek [Judith country], a nice place for us children to play. The day was warm. Flowers were everywhere, and birds were singing in the bushes and trees. There is a cliff not far from where the Crow lodges were pitched that day, and we children pitched our brush-lodge for our play sun-dance[1] at the foot of this cliff. We believed that our dance was real. We felt very serious. I said that there was but one boy with us. There were two, one to beat the drum, and one who danced. The dancer wore only his moccasins and breech-clout, as men do, and of course, he was painted. We girls wore our usual clothes, as dancing women do, painting our faces to please ourselves.

The dance made us forget everything else . . . The beating drum, our whistles, made from the big bone of an eagle's wing, our dancing, made us grownups whose hearts were in the sun-dance. ❖

---

1. **sun-dance.** Four- to eight-day ceremony performed by many Native American Plains tribes that includes singing, dancing, drumming, fasting, and having visions. The U.S. government outlawed sun-dances in 1904.

MIRRORS & WINDOWS

Participating in the dance made Shield and the other children feel as though they were grown-ups. What customs in your family or culture indicate that children are becoming adults?

Refer and Reason

1. What activities engaged the young girls? What would they not do, even in play? Infer how gender roles are reinforced by the children's games.

2. How did the adults participate in the children's play? How much did the adult guide the children to play in certain ways? Explain.

3. Identify the children's activities that would be considered dangerous for children now. Interpret what this suggests about Crow culture at that time.

Writing Options

1. Create a one-page description of an activities program for a child care center that includes a playtime aimed at preparing and educating young children about adult activities, such as shopping, cooking, and driving. Explain how this play might develop positive behaviors in the children.

2. Research the types of play enjoyed by children of white settlers during this time period (approximately 1860–1880). Describe what types of materials the toys were made of and how they were used. Write a paragraph in which you compare and contrast this information with that from Pretty Shield's narrative.

 Go to **www.mirrorsandwindows.com** for more.

Although the end of the Civil War brought with it an end to slavery, achieving equality would prove difficult for African Americans. Many people in the Reconstruction South were opposed to African Americans taking their place as citizens and tried to prevent them from exercising their rights, using both legal and illegal means. Moreover, not all African Americans agreed on the role they should play in American society. The writings of Booker T. Washington and W. E. B. Du Bois reveal two opposing views.

Having achieved the abolition of slavery, social reformers turned to women's rights after the war. Women worked for reform through the primary avenues open to them: ladies' groups, schools, and churches. They wrote articles, gave speeches, and held meetings, usually on a small, local level, but their efforts grew into a national crusade for women's suffrage. Sojourner Truth, Susan B. Anthony, and Elizabeth Cady Stanton rallied supporters to their cause and demonstrated women's strength as well as eloquence. Those qualities also characterized the fiction of writers such as Kate Chopin, Sarah Orne Jewett, Charlotte Perkins Gilman, and Louisa May Alcott, whose stories of domestic life challenged traditional gender roles, thus initiating American feminist literature.

Immigrants also struggled to find a place in American society, often facing discrimination in the land that had promised freedom and equality. In letters, journals, poems, and stories, immigrants wrote of anger, sorrow, disappointment, and alienation—themes that pervade the writing of modern-day immigrant Americans, as well.

The Blessing, 1905. Harry Herman Roseland. Brooklyn Museum of Art, Brooklyn, New York.

The Speech Defined

A **speech** is a public communication or expression of thought in spoken words. The **purpose** of a speech often is to inform an audience about a given subject or to persuade them to a particular point of view.

The ancient Greeks probably were the first to analyze **oratory** (public speaking) and to categorize the elements of public speaking. Because spoken language was still the primary means of communication in ancient times, public speaking was elevated to the status of art. It provided a way to inspire, to educate, and to entertain. In the fourth century BCE, Greek philosopher Aristotle wrote down a theory of **rhetoric,** or effective language use, that is still referred to today. He assumed that his listeners were average people who had no particular expertise in a subject but were capable of reason and common sense.

The objective, rational approach of Aristotle stands in sharp contrast to the subjective, highly charged oratory often heard today. Politicians, in particular, tend to speak to people's prejudices and fears and to employ unfair tactics to win support, even distorting the truth in many cases. Whereas classical rhetoric was judged according to a set of formal principles, the oratory of the political world often is a free-for-all, in which speakers are less concerned with means than with ends.

The speeches you will read in this unit are different in tone and diction yet share a viewpoint: that women deserve the right to vote, along with all the privileges and responsibilities of citizenship. Each of the four women speakers approaches the issue of voting from a particular cultural vantage point, yet all are united in their goal of achieving equal rights.

Elements of the Speech

Argument

An **argument** is a form of persuasion that makes a case to the audience for accepting or rejecting a proposition or course of action. In a persuasive speech, the argument is the **thesis,** or the main idea the speaker wants to share with the audience.

A speaker may approach the argument directly, as Maria Eugenia Echenique does in the opening of her speech: "To try to oppose women's emancipation is to oppose something that is almost a fact, it is to attack our laws and destroy the Republic." Echenique's introduction is forceful and undoubtedly challenged those listeners who believed that women's natural role was limited to keeping house and raising children. Susan B. Anthony makes a constitutional argument when she proclaims that it is "a downright mockery to talk to women of their enjoyment of liberty while they are denied the use of the only means of securing them provided by this democratic–republican government—the ballot."

"Nothing is so unbelievable that oratory cannot make it acceptable."

—MARCUS TULLIUS CICERO, ROMAN STATESMAN

Style

Style is the manner in which something is said or written, as characterized by qualities like word choice (*diction*), sentence structure and length, and other regular features of a writer's or speaker's work. Sojourner Truth's style is characterized by *dialect,* or the language spoken by the people of a particular place, time, or social group. She uses the word *chil'n* for *children,* the word *ain't* for *isn't,* and the word *racket* to describe the uproar over the issue of women's rights. There is sly humor in her observation about "that man over there" who insists that women should be "lifted over ditches" and otherwise spared life's inconveniences and hardships. To a woman such as Truth, who was born into slavery, this sort of gallantry must have seemed highly ironic.

Rhetoric

A **rhetorical device** is a technique used by a speaker or writer to achieve a particular effect, especially to persuade or influence. One such technique is *emotive language,* which stirs listeners' feelings. Elizabeth Cady Stanton does this when she exclaims, "See what a record of blood and cruelty the pages of history

reveal!" Truth's emotional pain becomes clear when she laments, "I have borne thirteen children, and seen most all sold off to slavery, and when I cried out with my mother's grief, none but Jesus heard me!"

A second rhetorical device, **repetition,** reinforces a message and creates a rhythmic effect. In her speech by the same title, Truth asks four times, "Ain't I a woman?" Elsewhere, she uses the device effectively when she declares, "I have been forty years a slave and forty years free, and would be here forty years more to have equal rights for all." The positioning of words and phrases in a sentence also creates meaning. Notice how Stanton builds meaning by using three-word phrases: "intrigue, bribery, and corruption," "falsehood, selfishness, and violence," and "oppression, violence, and war."

Many effective speakers use **rhetorical questions,** which are asked for effect but not meant to be answered because the answers are clear from the context. For example, in commenting on women's lack of legal protection, Echenique asks her audience, "Is it so easy for all women to look for a stranger to defend their offended dignity, their belittled honor, their stolen interests?" In responding to the notion that only educated, intelligent people should be allowed to vote, Truth asks, in her signature colloquial style, "If my cup won't hold but a pint, and yours holds a quart, wouldn't you be mean not to let me have my little half measure full?"

Figurative Language

Language that is meant to be understood imaginatively instead of literally is called **figurative language.** Writers and speakers may use figurative language to help readers to see things in new ways.

An **analogy** is a comparison of two things that are alike in some ways but otherwise quite different. Often, an analogy explains or describes something unfamiliar by comparing it to something more familiar. Notice how Stanton uses the device to effect: "Nature, like a loving mother, is ever trying to keep land and sea, mountain and valley, each in its place. . . . The present disorganization of society warns us that in the dethronement of woman we have let loose the elements of violence and ruin that she only has the power to curb." Thus, Stanton compares woman's primal position in civilization to Mother Nature, an entity that has boundless power to do harm or good.

Echenique uses a **metaphor** to suggest how woman's emancipation would ensure a more just world: "Generous and abnegated by nature, women would teach men humanitarian principles and would condemn the frenzy and insults that make a battlefield out of the courtroom."

A Speech

Understand the author's purpose. The most common purposes for giving a speech are to inform and to persuade. Historical speeches also are often connected to a specific time, place, or occasion. As you read or listen to a speech, try to determine the speaker's purpose.

Make inferences. Make inferences by connecting what you hear or read with what you already know. When reading a significant speech in American literature, use knowledge of its historical context when making inferences.

Analyze the argument. To analyze the argument in a persuasive speech, consider whether it has been supported using reasonable and credible evidence. Also consider what may have been left out, such as contrary opinions or unanswered questions.

Distinguish fact from opinion. Determine whether the details that support a writer's thesis are facts or opinions. A *fact* is a statement that can be proven true or false. An *opinion* expresses an attitude or desire. You can agree or disagree with an opinion but not prove it true or false.

Keeping the Thing Going While Things Are Stirring

A Speech by Sojourner Truth

Build Background

Literary Context Influenced by Elizabeth Cady Stanton, a leader in the struggle for women's suffrage, Sojourner Truth lent her unique oratory skills to the women's suffrage movement. In fact, Stanton recorded and printed transcripts of some of Truth's speeches in the landmark work she edited with Susan B. Anthony and Matilda Gage, *History of Woman Suffrage* (1881).

The powerful nature of Truth's oratorical style was born in a combination of elements: personal magnetism, a strong voice, and the courage to speak directly. Speaking English with a Dutch accent, Truth was legendary for her direct platform style. On one particular occasion, she challenged Frederick Douglass's stand on the issue of using violence against slavery, exclaiming, "Frederick! Is God dead?" Truth delivered her speech **"Keeping the Thing Going While Things Are Stirring"** on May 9, 1867, at the first annual meeting of the American Equal Rights Association.

Reader's Context For what issues have you spoken up or would you like to speak up? Why?

Meet the Author

Sojourner Truth (c. 1797–1883) was born to slave parents in Ulster County, New York, the second youngest of ten or twelve children. Originally named Isabella Baumfree, Truth served as a slave for twenty-one years, beginning at the age of nine when she was put up for auction.

Truth escaped to freedom in 1827, initially adopting the name of the Van Wagener family, who protected her. One year later, when emancipation became mandatory in New York state, she successfully fought to have one of her sons, who had been sold illegally, returned to her. In doing so, she became the first African-American woman to take a white man to court and win.

Truth moved to New York City and became involved in social and moral reform. A street-corner preacher, she had a wide knowledge of the Bible. In 1843, Isabella claimed that God told her to change her name to Sojourner Truth. She became a wandering orator, launching the speaking tours that made her famous. Unable to read or write, Truth dictated her life story, barely supporting herself by selling to audiences her published autobiographical account, *Narrative of Sojourner Truth,* as well as photographs of herself.

Truth settled in Battle Creek, Michigan, in the mid-1850s and worked from there until she died at age eighty-six. She met many important figures of her day, including Abraham Lincoln, Frederick Douglass, and Harriet Beecher Stowe.

Analyze Literature

Style and Dialect

Style is the manner in which something is said or written, as characterized by word choice (diction), sentence structure and length, and other recurring features.

Dialect is a version of a language spoken by the people of a particular place, time, or social group.

Set Purpose

The speeches of Sojourner Truth reflect several remarkable facts about her. First, she endured oppression both as a woman and as a slave, making her experience and thus perspective unique among leaders of the women's suffrage movement. In addition, while Truth could neither read nor write, she was a dynamic speaker. She incorporated her personality, vocal qualities, and other traits into a unique oratorical style. As you read Truth's speech, make a list of the qualities that indicate her style. In particular, analyze how her use of dialect influences her spoken style.

Keeping the Thing Going While Things Are Stirring

by Sojourner Truth

We do as much, we eat as much, we want as much.

Near Andersonville, c. 1865–1866. Winslow Homer. Newark Museum, Newark, New Jersey.

Address to the first annual meeting of the American Equal Rights Association delivered by Sojourner Truth on May 9, 1867

My friends, I am rejoiced that you are glad, but I don't know how you will feel when I get through. I come from another field—the country of the slave. They have got their liberty—so much good luck to have slavery partly destroyed; not entirely. I want it root and branch destroyed. Then we will all be free indeed. I feel that if I have to answer for the deeds done in my body just as much as a man, I have a right to have just as much as a man. There is a great stir about colored men getting their rights, but not a word about the colored women; and if colored men get their rights, and not colored women theirs, you see the

I am for keeping the thing going while things are stirring; because if we wait till it is still, it will take a great while to get it going again.

colored men will be masters over the women, and it will be just as bad as it was before. So I am for keeping the thing going while things are stirring; because if we wait till it is still, it will take a great while to get it going again. White women are a great deal smarter, and know more than colored women, while colored women do not know scarcely anything. They go out washing, which is about as high as a colored woman gets, and their men go about idle, strutting up and down; and when the women come home, they ask for their money and take it all, and then scold because there is no food. I want you to consider on that, chil'n. I call you chil'n; you are somebody's chil'n, and I am old enough to be mother of all that is here. I want women to have their rights. In the courts women have no right, no voice; nobody speaks for them. I wish woman to have her voice there among the pettifoggers.[1] If it is not a fit place for women, it is unfit for men to be there.

I am above eighty years old; it is about time for me to be going. I have been forty years a slave and forty years free, and would be here forty years more to have equal rights for all. I suppose I am kept here because something remains for me to do; I suppose I am yet to help to break the chain. I have done a great deal of work; as much as a man, but did not get so much pay. I used to work in the field and bind grain, keeping up with the cradler; but men doing no more, got twice as much pay; so with the German women. They work in the field and do as much work, but do not get the pay. We do as much, we eat as much, we want as much. I suppose I am about the only colored woman that goes about to speak for the rights of the colored women. I want to keep the thing stirring, now that the ice is cracked. What we want is a little money. You men know that you get as much again as women when you write, or for what you do. When we get our rights we shall not have to come to you for money, for then we shall have money enough in our own pockets; and maybe you will ask us for money. But help us now until we get it. It is a good consolation to know that when we have got this battle once fought we shall not be coming to you any more. You have been having our rights so long, that you think, like a slaveholder, that you own us. I know that it is hard for one who has held the reins for so long to give up; it cuts like a knife. It will feel all the better when it closes up again. I have been in Washington about three years, seeing about these colored people. Now colored men have the right to vote.[2] There ought to be equal rights now more than ever, since colored people have got their freedom. I am going to talk several times while I am here; so now I will do a little singing. I have not heard any singing since I came here. ❖

---

1. **pettifoggers.** People who argue over trifling, insignificant matters
2. **Now colored . . . to vote.** African-American men did not receive the right to vote under the U.S. Constitution until 1870 with passage of the Fifteenth Amendment. However, at the time of Truth's speech (May 1867), several states had ratified the Fourteenth Amendment, which provided the rights of citizenship. Some states interpreted this amendment as allowing African-American men to vote, and many did vote in the 1868 presidential election.

MIRRORS & WINDOWS

Truth states, "I want to keep the thing stirring, now that the ice is cracked." How has having momentum, or forward movement, kept you going on a project or goal?

Literature Connection

Sojourner Truth (c. 1797–1883) gave her famous **"Ain't I a Woman?"** speech at the 1851 Women's Rights Convention in Akron, Ohio. In this speech, Truth answers opponents to women's rights with forceful arguments, including personal testimony. A review of her speech at the time noted "her powerful form [Truth was six feet tall], her whole-souled, earnest gesture, and . . . her strong and truthful tones." Compare Truth's language in this speech with that in "Keeping the Thing Going While Things Are Stirring," which she delivered sixteen years later.

AIN'T I A WOMAN?

by Sojourner Truth

Well, children, where there is so much racket there must be something out of kilter.[1] I think that 'twixt[2] the negroes of the South and the women at the North, all talking about rights, the white men will be in a fix[3] pretty soon. But what's all this here talking about?

That man over there says that women need to be helped into carriages, and lifted over ditches, and to have the best place everywhere. Nobody ever helps me into carriages, or over mud-puddles, or gives me any best place! And ain't I a woman? Look at me! Look at my arm! I have ploughed and planted, and gathered into barns, and no man could head[4] me! And ain't I a woman? I could work as much and eat as much as a man—when I could get it—and bear the lash as well! And ain't I a woman? I have borne thirteen children, and seen most all sold off to slavery, and when I cried out with my mother's grief, none but Jesus heard me! And ain't I a woman?

Then they talk about this thing in the head; what's this they call it? [a member of the audience whispers "intellect"] That's it, honey. What's that got to do with women's rights or negroes' rights? If my cup won't hold but a pint, and yours holds a quart,[5] wouldn't you be mean not to let me have my little half measure full?

Then that little man in black there, he says women can't have as much rights as men, 'cause Christ wasn't a woman! Where did your Christ come from? Where did your Christ come from? From God and a woman! Man had nothing to do with Him.

If the first woman[6] God ever made was strong enough to turn the world upside down all alone, these women together ought to be able to turn it back, and get it right side up again! And now they is asking to do it, the men better let them.

Obliged to you for hearing me, and now old Sojourner ain't got nothing more to say. ❖

---

1. **out of kilter.** Out of order
2. **'twixt.** Between
3. **fix.** Position of difficulty or embarrassment
4. **head.** Take a lead over; surpass
5. **pint . . . quart.** A pint is half a quart.
6. **first woman.** In the book of Genesis in the Bible, the first woman God created was Eve. She, along with the first man, Adam, was expelled from the Garden of Eden for eating the fruit of the tree of knowledge of good and evil.

HISTORY CONNECTION

Ida B. Wells

Although Ida B. Wells (1862–1931) is not widely known of today, she was one of the most dynamic women of her time. Born a slave in Holly Springs, Mississippi, Wells was heavily influenced by her father's engagement in local politics after emancipation. Her parents stressed education for their children, which Wells took seriously, especially after both parents died in a yellow fever epidemic when she was fourteen. Young and poor, Wells insisted on keeping the family together and so took a teaching job at Rust College to support her six younger siblings.

Wells's first public act of defiance against racism was in 1884, when she refused to leave the first-class ladies' carriage of the train on which she was riding. The conductor attempted to remove her physically, and she bit him on the hand. It took three men to get her off the train. Wells sued the railroad for violating the "separate but equal" law—the first such case ever in the South. The district court decided in favor of Wells, granting her $500, but the Tennessee Supreme Court overturned the verdict three years later.

In 1892, three of Wells's African-American friends were lynched (hanged), which sent her on a crusade. In her role as editor of the Memphis newspaper, Wells published reports about the frequency of lynchings in the South. Moreover, she spoke around the country and met with President William McKinley to discuss the violence. On a speaking tour of Great Britain, Wells also became interested in the women's rights movement and befriended Susan B. Anthony and Jane Addams.

In 1909, Wells joined with W. E. B. Du Bois and several others to found the National Association for the Advancement of Colored People (NAACP). Today, the NAACP is the oldest and most influential civil rights organization in the United States. In 1930, nearly seventy years old, Wells ran for the Illinois state senate, one of the first African-American women to run for public office. She lost to the incumbent and died a year later, leaving behind a legacy of commitment to equal rights.

Refer to Text ▶ ▶ ▶ ▶ ▶ **Reason with Text**

1a. Who recently has been granted the rights of citizenship?	**1b.** Restate Truth's basic argument about why women deserve equal rights.	**Understand** Find meaning
2a. List the types of work Truth says she has done.	**2b.** How did Truth's experiences allow her to see the inequality between men and women?	**Apply** Use information
3a. What does Truth say it will be like for men to give up their rights over women?	**3b.** Analyze her argument that compares women's lack of rights to slavery.	**Analyze** Take things apart
4a. How long has Truth been traveling around and speaking out in Washington, DC?	**4b.** Do you agree with Truth that when fighting for a cause, you should keep fighting even if you have already made progress? Explain.	**Evaluate** Make judgments
5a. According to Truth, what are the money issues between black men and women?	**5b.** Suggest why Truth ends her speech with singing.	**Create** Bring ideas together

Analyze Literature

Style and Dialect

Review your list of stylistic qualities. What about her style made Sojourner Truth such an effective speaker? Also review Truth's speech "Ain't I a Woman?" (see pages 465–466) for more examples of her style.

How does Truth's use of dialect affect her style? Look for instances in which the syntax (word order) and grammar are unconventional, indicating use of a dialect. Does Truth's use of dialect strengthen or weaken the presentation of her message?

Extend the Text

Writing Options

Creative Writing Write lyrics for a song that Sojourner Truth might have sung at this meeting. For inspiration, read the lyrics of spirituals from the 1800s. You might try substituting the words in a spiritual to fit the theme of Truth's speech, or you can write entirely new lyrics.

Expository Writing Rewrite Truth's speech in a more formal, academic style without changing the message. Read your speech aloud to a classmate. Then compare your rewritten speech with Truth's original version, evaluating the impact of style on the message.

Media Literacy

Do a Multimedia Presentation Sojourner Truth was involved in both the abolitionist and women's suffrage movements. Research the historical relationship between the two, including conflicts over differing goals and discriminatory practices. Deliver your findings in an oral report accompanied by a PowerPoint, video, or other presentation using visual and auditory materials.

Lifelong Learning

Research Equality Issues Much progress has been made for equality between the sexes since the late 1800s, but there are still areas of inequality in modern life. With a partner, research an area of gender inequality, such as differences in pay, women's sports, or career advancement. Look for objective sources that present facts and statistics. Use this information to write a letter to your local newspaper that suggests how to make progress toward gender equality.

 Go to **www.mirrorsandwindows.com** for more.

1. What does Truth mean when she says "I want to keep the thing stirring, now that the ice is cracked"?
- **A.** Now that it's spring, it's a good time to start campaigning for women's rights.
- **B.** Women cannot continue in their roles as wives and mothers and achieve equality.
- **C.** African-American men should exercise their new rights and help women get equality.
- **D.** Some progress has been made in achieving equality for women, so the effort must continue.
- **E.** None of the above

2. According to Truth, how will it affect African-American couples' marriages if the women do not get the same rights as the men?
- **A.** Only one member of the household will be able to vote in elections.
- **B.** The men will have to work even harder to make up for the women's lack of opportunity.
- **C.** The men will think less of the women for not having rights.
- **D.** The men will expect twice the pay of the women for the same amount of work.
- **E.** The men will have power over the women, and the women will not have any legal recourse.

3. In her speech "Ain't I a Woman?" what does Truth point out to "that little man in black" about Jesus Christ?
- **A.** that he was not a woman
- **B.** that he was born of a woman
- **C.** that he considered women equal to men
- **D.** that he never married
- **E.** that he had one female disciple

4. Which of the following is *not* something Truth states she can do or endure as well as a man?
- **A.** read
- **B.** plow
- **C.** eat
- **D.** bear the lash
- **E.** plant

5. Why doesn't Truth boast about her intellect in "Ain't I a Woman?"
- **A.** She doesn't think she is very intelligent.
- **B.** The other members of the audience are smarter than she is.
- **C.** She thinks intellect is the one area in which men have an advantage over women.
- **D.** She believes that equal rights should not be granted according to people's intelligence.
- **E.** Her other accomplishments are more noteworthy than her intellectual feats.

6. Truth offers an allusion to the biblical story of the Garden of Eden to illustrate
- **A.** how deceitful women are.
- **B.** how strong women are.
- **C.** what happens when women are oppressed.
- **D.** that women are capable of influencing men.
- **E.** why the Bible is not a good source of arguments in support of equal rights.

7. The tone of "Ain't I a Woman?" may best be described as
- **A.** challenging.
- **B.** intellectual.
- **C.** tragic.
- **D.** celebratory.
- **E.** condescending.

8. Constructed Response: Explain how Truth used the circumstances of her life to shape the content and style of her speeches. What hardships did she endure, and what triumphs did she enjoy? How did these events affect her?

9. Constructed Response: Analyze the argument Truth presents in one of her speeches. What is her claim, or main point, and how does she support it? How does she anticipate and address counterarguments? How do her diction, style, and tone support her argument?

The Destructive Male
A Speech by Elizabeth Cady Stanton

Woman's Right to Suffrage
A Speech by Susan B. Anthony

Build Background

Historical Context Elizabeth Cady Stanton's speech **"The Destructive Male"** was given at the Women's Suffrage Convention in 1868 in Washington, DC. Stanton was one of the founders of the women's rights movement, which started in 1848 at a convention in Seneca Falls, New York. There, Stanton presented her Declaration of Sentiments, stating that men and women were created equal and calling for women's right to vote.

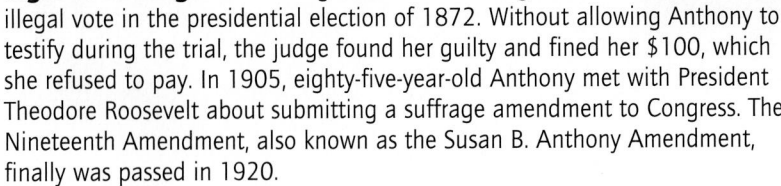

Susan B. Anthony, another founder of the women's rights movement, gave her well-known speech **"Woman's Right to Suffrage"** after being arrested for casting an illegal vote in the presidential election of 1872. Without allowing Anthony to testify during the trial, the judge found her guilty and fined her $100, which she refused to pay. In 1905, eighty-five-year-old Anthony met with President Theodore Roosevelt about submitting a suffrage amendment to Congress. The Nineteenth Amendment, also known as the Susan B. Anthony Amendment, finally was passed in 1920.

Reader's Context Think of a time you felt discriminated against or otherwise treated unfairly. How did you react?

Meet the Authors

Elizabeth Cady Stanton (1815–1902) was born in Johnstown, New York. An active abolitionist, she befriended Frederick Douglass and met her husband, Henry Stanton, at an abolition meeting. The Stantons had seven children, which required Stanton to stay home. She supported the suffragist cause by writing articles and speeches; many of her speeches were delivered by her close friend Susan B. Anthony. As Anthony stated in Stanton's obituary, Stanton "forged the thunderbolts" that Anthony "fired." Stanton's concern for women's rights went beyond voting to include family planning, custody and property rights, and income and divorce laws.

Susan B. Anthony (1820–1906) was born on February 15, 1820, in Adams, Massachusetts, into a Quaker family with a history of activism. She met Stanton in 1851, and from that time until Stanton's death in 1902, they were considered the leaders of the women's movement. From 1868 to 1870, Anthony and Stanton published a liberal New York newspaper, *The Revolution,* which called for equal pay and rights for women, and in 1881, with Matilda Gage, they compiled a collection of women's writings and speeches, *History of Woman Suffrage.*

Compare Literature

Argument and Rhetoric
An **argument** is the case for accepting or rejecting a proposition or course of action. It is a form of rhetorical expression that is intended to convince or persuade.

Rhetoric is the art of speaking or writing effectively, and it involves studying how language affects an audience.

Set Purpose

Stanton and Anthony spent most of their lives trying to convince Americans that women deserved the right to vote, but they often used different rhetorical approaches in doing so. After you read each woman's speech, summarize her main argument and analyze how she supports it. Predict how an audience of the day (around 1870) might have responded to each woman's rhetoric.

Preview Vocabulary

aggrandize, 471
disfranchised, 471
arrant, 471
expend, 472
subjugate, 472
indictment, 473
alleged, 473
posterity, 473
odious, 474
oligarchy, 474

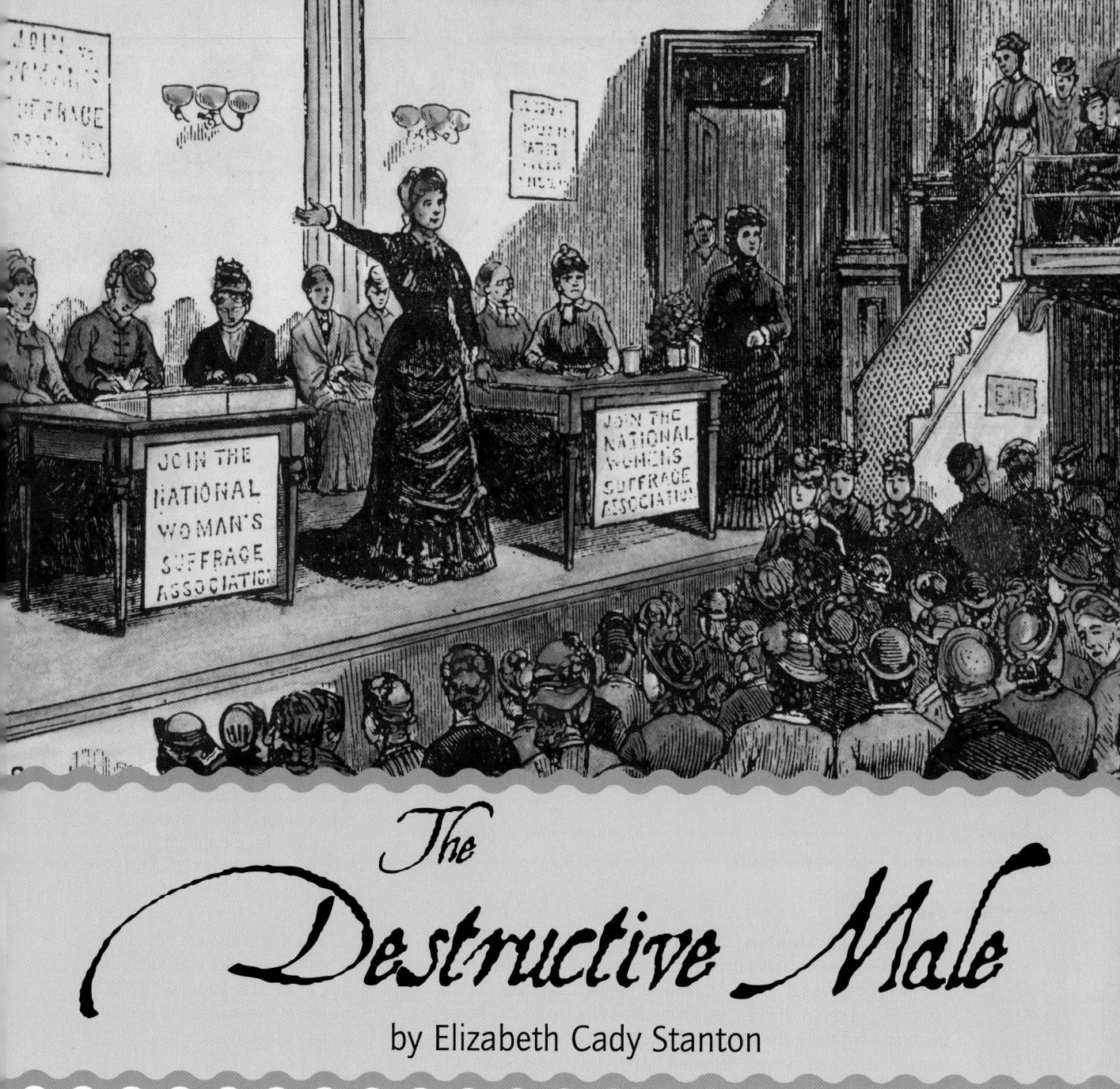

The Destructive Male

by Elizabeth Cady Stanton

**Whatever is done to lift woman to her true
position will help to usher in a new day of peace
and perfection for the race.**

I urge a sixteenth amendment,[1] because "manhood suffrage," or a man's government, is civil, religious, and social disorganization. The male element is a destructive force, stern, selfish, <u>aggrandizing</u>, loving war, violence, conquest, acquisition, breeding in the material and moral world alike discord, disorder, disease, and death. See what a record of blood and cruelty the pages of history reveal! Through what slavery, slaughter, and sacrifice, through what inquisitions and imprisonments, pains and persecutions, black codes and gloomy creeds, the soul of humanity has struggled for the centuries, while mercy has veiled her face and all hearts have been dead alike to love and hope!

The male element has held high carnival[2] thus far; it has fairly run riot from the beginning, overpowering the feminine element everywhere, crushing out all the diviner qualities in human nature, until we know but little of true manhood and womanhood, of the latter comparatively nothing, for it has scarce been recognized as a power until within the last century. Society is but the reflection of man himself, untempered by woman's thought; the hard iron rule we feel alike in the church, the state, and the home. No one need wonder at the disorganization, at the fragmentary condition of everything, when we remember that man, who represents but half a complete being, with but half an idea on every subject, has undertaken the absolute control of all sublunary[3] matters.

People object to the demands of those whom they choose to call the strong-minded, because they say "the right of suffrage will make the women masculine." That is just the difficulty in which we are involved today. Though <u>disfranchised</u>, we have few women in the best sense; we have simply so many reflections, varieties, and dilutions of the masculine

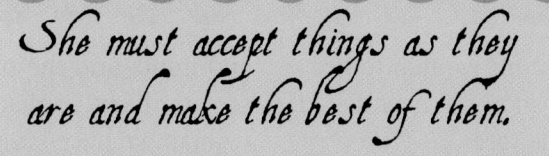

She must accept things as they are and make the best of them.

gender. The strong, natural characteristics of womanhood are repressed and ignored in dependence, for so long as man feeds woman she will try to please the giver and adapt herself to his condition. To keep a foothold in society, woman must be as near like man as possible, reflect his ideas, opinions, virtues, motives, prejudices, and vices. She must respect his statutes, though they strip her of every inalienable right, and conflict with that higher law written by the finger of God on her own soul.

She must look at everything from its dollar-and-cent point of view, or she is a mere romancer.[4] She must accept things as they are and make the best of them. To mourn over the miseries of others, the poverty of the poor, their hardships in jails, prisons, asylums, the horrors of war, cruelty, and brutality in every form, all this would be mere sentimentalizing. To protest against the intrigue, bribery, and corruption of public life, to desire that her sons might follow some business that did not involve lying, cheating, and a hard, grinding selfishness, would be <u>arrant</u> nonsense.

In this way man has been molding woman to his ideas by direct and positive influences, while she, if not a negation, has used indirect

---

1. **sixteenth amendment.** At the time of the speech, there were only fifteen amendments to the Constitution. The Fifteenth Amendment gave the right to vote to African-American men.
2. **held high carnival.** Nineteenth-century expression meaning "to have one's way"; to act without regard for others
3. **sublunary.** Relating to the terrestrial world; Earth
4. **romancer.** Someone who thinks mainly about things that have no basis in fact

---

ag • grand • ize (ə grand´ īz) *v.,* increase one's power and wealth
dis • fran • chised (dis fran´ chīzd) *adj.,* deprived of legal rights, particularly voting
ar • rant (ār´ ənt) *adj.,* extreme

means to control him, and in most cases developed the very characteristics both in him and herself that needed repression. And now man himself stands appalled at the results of his own excesses, and mourns in bitterness that falsehood, selfishness, and violence are the law of life. The need of this hour is not territory, gold mines, railroads, or specie payments[5] but a new evangel[6] of womanhood, to exalt purity, virtue, morality, true religion, to lift man up into the higher realms of thought and action.

We ask woman's enfranchisement, as the first step toward the recognition of that essential element in government that can only secure the health, strength, and prosperity of the nation. Whatever is done to lift woman to her true position will help to usher in a new day of peace and perfection for the race.

> *Woman knows the cost of life better than man does*

In speaking of the masculine element, I do not wish to be understood to say that all men are hard, selfish, and brutal, for many of the most beautiful spirits the world has known have been clothed with manhood; but I refer to those characteristics, though often marked in woman, that distinguish what is called the stronger sex. For example, the love of acquisition and conquest, the very pioneers of civilization, when <u>expended</u> on the earth, the sea, the elements, the riches and forces of nature, are powers of destruction when used to <u>subjugate</u> one man to another or to sacrifice nations to ambition.

Here that great conservator of woman's love, if permitted to assert itself, as it naturally would in freedom against oppression, violence, and war, would hold all these destructive forces in check, for woman knows the cost of life better than man does, and not with her consent would one drop of blood ever be shed, one life sacrificed in vain.

With violence and disturbance in the natural world, we see a constant effort to maintain an equilibrium of forces. Nature, like a loving mother, is ever trying to keep land and sea, mountain and valley, each in its place, to hush the angry winds and waves, balance the extremes of heat and cold, of rain and drought, that peace, harmony, and beauty may reign supreme. There is a striking analogy between matter and mind, and the present disorganization of society warns us that in the dethronement of woman we have let loose the elements of violence and ruin that she only has the power to curb. If the civilization of the age calls for an extension of the suffrage, surely a government of the most virtuous educated men and women would better represent the whole and protect the interests of all than could the representation of either sex alone. ❖

---

5. **specie payments.** Payments of a similar kind
6. **evangel.** Gospel

---

ex • pend (ik spend´) *v.,* use for a specific purpose
sub • ju • gate (sub´ jə gāt) *v.,* conquer or subdue

Stanton says that women traditionally have had to "accept things as they are and make the best of them." When is making the best of things a sensible idea? When might it be considered settling or giving up?

Woman's Right to Suffrage

by Susan B. Anthony

It is a downright mockery to talk to women of their enjoyment of the blessings of liberty while they are denied the use of the only means of securing them.

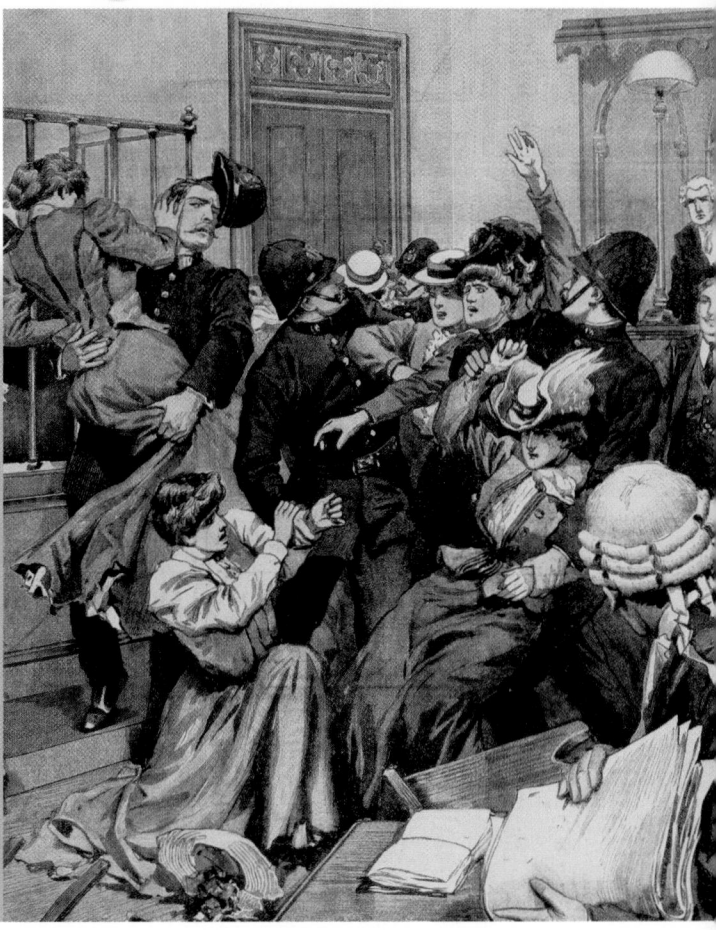

Friends and fellow citizens: I stand before you tonight under <u>indictment</u> for the <u>alleged</u> crime of having voted at the last presidential election, without having a lawful right to vote. It shall be my work this evening to prove to you that in thus voting, I not only committed no crime, but, instead, simply exercised my citizen's rights, guaranteed to me and all United States citizens by the National Constitution, beyond the power of any state to deny.

The preamble of the Federal Constitution says: "We, the people of the United States, in order to form a more perfect union, establish justice, insure domestic tranquillity, provide for the common defense, promote the general welfare, and secure the blessings of liberty to ourselves and our <u>posterity</u>, do ordain and establish this Constitution for the United States of America."

> **in • dict • ment** (in dīt´ mənt) *n.*, state of being charged with a crime or offense
> **al • leged** (ə lejd´) *adj.*, accused but not proven or convinced
> **pos • ter • i • ty** (pô tār´ ə tē) *n.*, all future generations

The only question left to be settled is:
Are women persons?

It was we, the people; not we, the white male citizens; nor yet we, the male citizens; but we, the whole people, who formed the Union. And we formed it, not to give the blessings of liberty, but to secure them; not to the half of ourselves and the half of our posterity, but to the whole people—women as well as men. And it is a downright mockery to talk to women of their enjoyment of the blessings of liberty while they are denied the use of the only means of securing them provided by this democratic-republican government—the ballot.

For any state to make sex a qualification that must ever result in the disfranchisement of one entire half of the people, is to pass a bill of attainder,[1] or, an ex post facto law,[2] and is therefore a violation of the supreme law of the land. By it the blessings of liberty are forever withheld from women and their female posterity. To them this government has no just powers derived from the consent of the governed. To them this government is not a democracy. It is not a republic. It is an <u>odious</u> aristocracy; a hateful <u>oligarchy</u> of sex; the most hateful aristocracy ever established on the face of the globe; an oligarchy of wealth, where the rich govern the poor. An oligarchy of learning, where the educated govern the ignorant, or even an oligarchy of race, where the Saxon rules the African, might be endured; but this oligarchy of sex, which makes father, brothers, husband, sons, the oligarchs over the mother and sisters, the wife and daughters, of every household—which ordains all men sovereigns, all women subjects, carries dissension, discord, and rebellion into every home of the nation.

Webster, Worcester, and Bouvier[3] all define a citizen to be a person in the United States, entitled to vote and hold office.

The only question left to be settled now is: Are women persons? And I hardly believe any of our opponents will have the hardihood[4] to say they are not. Being persons, then, women are citizens; and no state has a right to make any law, or to enforce any old law, that shall abridge their privileges or immunities. Hence, every discrimination against women in the constitutions and laws of the several states is today null and void, precisely as is every one against Negroes. ❖

---

1. **bill of attainder.** Act of legislature finding a person guilty of treason or felony without trial
2. **ex post facto law.** Law passed from or by subsequent action
3. **Webster, Worcester, and Bouvier.** Daniel Webster (1782–1852), American statesman, lawyer, and orator; Noah Worcester (1758–1837), American Congregational clergy; John Bouvier (1787–1851), American writer on law
4. **hardihood.** Boldness or daring

> **odi • ous** (ō´ dē əs) *adj.,* arousing or deserving hatred
> **ol • i • gar • chy** (ä´ lə gär' kē) *n.,* government in which a small group exercises control, especially for corrupt and selfish purposes

Women and African Americans are among several groups of U.S. citizens that struggled to win the right to vote. Do people today take for granted the right to vote? Why do so many people choose not to vote?

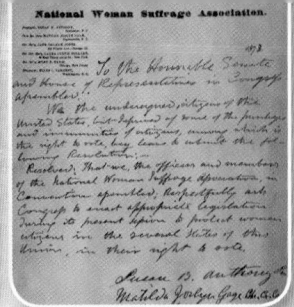

Primary Source Connection

In this **letter to Elizabeth Cady Stanton,** written in October 1902, **Susan B. Anthony** agrees to spend Stanton's eighty-seventh birthday with her. Anthony expresses her disappointment at their not yet having won the right to vote, despite having worked toward that goal for half a century. However, she also remarks that the younger generation of women has benefited from their efforts and will complete their work. Interestingly, Anthony closes the letter by mentioning that the two old friends will "move on to the next sphere of existence." Stanton died just a few days after receiving this letter.

Letter to Elizabeth Cady Stanton
by Susan B. Anthony

My dear Mrs. Stanton

I shall indeed be happy to spend with you November 12, the day on which you round out your four-score and seven,[1] over four years ahead of me, but in age as in all else I follow you closely. It is fifty-one years since first we met and we have been busy through every one of them, stirring up the world to recognize the rights of women. The older we grow, the more keenly we feel the humiliation of disfranchisement and the more vividly we realize its disadvantages in every department of life and most of all in the labor market.

We little dreamed when we began this contest, optimistic with the hope and buoyancy of youth, that half a century later we would be compelled to leave the finish of the battle to another generation of women. But our hearts are filled with joy to know that they enter upon this task equipped with a college education, with business experience, with the fully admitted right to speak in public—all of which were denied to women fifty years ago. They have practically but one point to gain—the suffrage; we had all. These strong, courageous, capable young women will take our place and complete our

---

1. **four-score and seven.** Eighty-seven (a score is twenty)

work. There is an army of them where we were but a handful. Ancient prejudice has become so softened, public sentiment so liberalized and women have so thoroughly demonstrated their ability as to leave not a shadow of doubt that they will carry our cause to victory.

And we, dear old friend, shall move on to the next sphere of existence—higher and larger, we cannot fail to believe, and one where women will not be placed in an inferior position but will be welcomed on a plane of perfect intellectual and spiritual equality.

Ever lovingly yours,

Susan B. Anthony

Review Questions

1. How old is Stanton at the time of this letter? How long have Anthony and Stanton been working together toward women's rights? Trace what has changed in the struggle for women's rights in that time.

2. Describe how new generations of women compare to Anthony and her contemporaries. How does Anthony feel about the future of women's suffrage and rights in general? Why does she feel this way?

3. What battles does Anthony state are left for future generations of women to fight? Determine what modern-day issues likely will not be resolved in your lifetime but rather passed to future generations.

TEXT $\xrightarrow{\text{TO}}$ TEXT CONNECTION

Susan B. Anthony was single minded in her pursuit of getting women the right to vote, but she died fourteen years before that goal was achieved. How does she determine success or failure in this cause? What gives her satisfaction and hope?

Suffragettes march in New York City (c. 1910).

Refer to Text ▷ ▷ ▷ ▷ ▷   **Reason with Text**

1a. Recall how Stanton describes the "male element."	**1b.** What aspects of the "female element," then, does Stanton say society is lacking?	**Understand** Find meaning
2a. What part of the U.S. Constitution does Anthony quote?	**2b.** What point is Anthony trying to make by quoting the Constitution?	**Apply** Use information
3a. Identify the types of *oligarchies* Anthony mentions in the fourth paragraph of her speech. What type of oligarchy does she believe to be the most unacceptable?	**3b.** In the closing of her speech, Anthony compares the discrimination against women to the discrimination against African Americans at that time. Is this comparison valid?	**Analyze** Take things apart
4a. According to Stanton, why do some people think suffrage would be bad for women?	**4b.** Critique Stanton's description of the male and female characters. How would a modern audience feel about her descriptions?	**Evaluate** Make judgments
5a. In Anthony's view, does the government's refusal to let women vote come from "the consent of the governed"? In other words, is that what most people want?	**5b.** Which speech is focused on the general condition of women, and which is more specific in its aim? What is the aim of the more general speech? Explain your answers.	**Create** Bring ideas together

Compare Literature

Argument and Rhetoric
What argument is each speaker making? How does each speaker support her argument? Whose approach is more effective in achieving its aim? Explain your answer.

If you had been in the audience when Anthony or Stanton gave her speech, would you have been persuaded by her rhetoric? Would you have agreed or disagreed with each woman's argument? Support your answer.

Extend the Text

Writing Options
Creative Writing Imagine that Stanton and Anthony are appearing together on a radio talk show. Write a dialogue between the two women, in which they discuss women's rights. Try to portray each woman's speaking style.

Descriptive Writing Write a paragraph for your school newspaper in which you introduce Stanton and Anthony and summarize their arguments for women's rights. Research each woman further to identify what she contributed to the movement.

Critical Literacy
Practice Deductive Reasoning Anthony proves her argument using *deductive reasoning,* a form of inference in

which specific conclusions are reached by reasoning from general principles assumed to be true. For example, she deduces that if a *citizen* is a person entitled to vote and women are persons, then women are entitled to vote. Write down five other examples of deductive reasoning, and share them with the class.

Lifelong Learning
Create a Time Line Anthony and Stanton were early leaders of the women's rights movement in the United States, but many others aided the condition of women around the world. Create a time line of the women's rights movement, identifying significant people and events and including photographs for illustration.

 Go to **www.mirrorsandwindows.com** for more.

The Emancipation of Women

by Maria Eugenia Echenique

Translated by Francisco Manzo Robledo

The struggle for women's rights, such as access to education and suffrage, started later in Argentina than in the United States and faced more obstacles. For example, the Argentine Constitution of 1853 defined a *citizen* as someone who could bear arms for the military. Women were prohibited from joining the military and thus were denied the full rights of citizenship.

Another difficulty was that the women's rights movement was, for many years, restricted to upper-class women, whose concerns did not coincide with those of women of lesser means. In fact, many of the advocates of women's education were not feminists; rather, some advocates supported these issues because they were perceived to result in the general betterment of society, not women in particular.

This 1876 speech by **Maria Eugenia Echenique** reveals the concerns of the time. Argentine women did not receive the right to vote until 1947.

When emancipation was given to men, it was also given to women in recognition of the equality of rights, consistent with the principles of nature on which they are founded, that proclaim the identity of soul between men and women. Thus, Argentine women have been emancipated by law for a long time. The code of law that governs us authorizes a widow to defend her rights in court, just as an educated woman can in North America, and like her, we can manage the interests of our children, these rights being the basis for emancipation. What we lack is sufficient education and instruction to make use of them, instruction that North American women have; it is not just recently that we have proclaimed our freedom. To try to question or to oppose women's emancipation is to oppose something that is almost a fact, it is to attack our laws and destroy the Republic.

So let the debate be there, on the true point where it should be: whether or not it is proper for women to make use of those granted rights, asking as a consequence the authorization to go to the university so as to practice those rights or make them effective. And this constitutes another right and duty in woman: a duty to accept the role that our own laws bestow on her when extending the circle of her jurisdiction and which makes her responsible before the members of her family.

This, assuming that the woman is a mother. But, are all women going to marry? Are all going to be relegated to a life of inaction during their youth or while they remain single? Is it so easy for all women to look for a stranger to defend their offended dignity, their belittled honor, their stolen interests? Don't we see every day how the laws are trodden underfoot, and the victim, being a woman, is forced to bow her head because she does not know how to defend herself, exposed to lies and tricks because she does not know the way to clarify the truth?

Far from causing the breakdown of the social classes, the emancipation of women would establish morality and justice in them; men would have a brake that would halt the "imperious need" that they have made of the "lies and tricks" of litigations, and the science of jurisprudence,[1] so sacred and magnificent in itself but degenerated today because of abuses, would return to its splendor and true objective once women take part in the forum. Generous and abnegated[2] by nature, women would teach men humanitarian principles and would condemn the frenzy and insults that make a battlefield out of the courtroom.

"Women either resolve to drown the voice of their hearts, or they listen to that voice and renounce emancipation." If emancipation is opposed to the tender sentiments, to the voice of the heart, then men who are completely emancipated and study science are not capable of love. The beautiful and tender girl who gives her heart to a doctor or to a scientist, gives it, then, to a stony man, incapable of appreciating it or responding to her; women could not love emancipated men, because where women find love, men find it too; in both burns the same heart's flame. I have seen that those who do not practice science, who do not know their duties or the rights of women, who are ignorant, are the ones who abandon their wives, not the ones who, concentrated on their studies and duties, barely have time to give them a caress.

Men as much as women are victims of the indifference that ignorance, not science, produces. Men are more slaves of women who abuse the prestige of their weakness and

The Boston Rocker, c. 1800s. Eastman Johnson. Private collection.

become tyrants in their home, than of the schooled and scientific women who understand their duties and are capable of something. With the former the husband has to play the role of man and woman, because she ignores everything: she is not capable of consoling nor helping her husband, she is not capable of giving tenderness, because, preoccupied with herself, she becomes demanding, despotic, and vain, and she does not know how to make a happy home. For her there are no responsibilities to carry out, only whims to satisfy. This is typical, we see it happening every day.

The ignorant woman, the one who voluntarily closes her heart to the sublime principles that provoke sweet emotions in it and elevate the mind, revealing to men the deep secrets of the All-Powerful; the woman incapable of helping her husband in great enterprises for fear of losing the prestige of her weakness and ignorance; the woman who only aspires to get mar-

---

1. **jurisprudence.** Law
2. **abnegated.** Prone to surrendering or giving up goods

ried and reproduce, and understands maternity as the only mission of women on earth—she can be the wife of a savage, because in him she can satisfy all her aspirations and hopes, following that law of nature that operates even on beasts and inanimate beings.

I would renounce and disown my sex if the mission of women were reduced only to procreation, yes, I would renounce it; but the mission of women in the world is much more grandiose and sublime, it is more than the beasts', it is the one of teaching humankind, and in order to teach it is necessary to know. A mother should know science in order to inspire in her children great deeds and noble sentiments, making them feel superior to the other objects in the universe, teaching them from the cradle to become familiar with great scenes of nature where they should go to look for God and love Him. And nothing more sublime and ideal than the scientific mother who, while her husband goes to cafes or to the political club

to talk about state interests, she goes to spend some of the evening at the astronomical observatory, with her children by the hand to show them Jupiter, Venus, preparing in that way their tender hearts for the most legitimate and sublime aspirations that could occupy men's minds. This sacred mission in the scientific mother who understands emancipation—the fulfillment of which, far from causing the abandonment of the home, causes it to unite more closely—instead of causing displeasure to her husband, she will cause his happiness.

The abilities of men are not so miserable that the carrying out of one responsibility would make it impossible to carry out others. There is enough time and competence for cooking and mending, and a great soul such as that of women, equal to that of their mates, born to embrace all the beauty that exists in Creation of divine origin and end, should not be wasted all on seeing if the plates are clean and rocking the cradle. ❖

 Echenique's speech reveals what Argentineans of the late 1800s believed to be a woman's role and characteristics. Do people today have any of these beliefs? What has and has not changed?

Refer and Reason

1. According to Echenique's critics, to what is women's emancipation opposed? How does Echenique refute this argument?

2. Identify Echenique's main arguments for the education of women. How might her vision of a "scientific mother" seem outdated and still unequal to modern thinking?

3. Based on the arguments presented in this speech, what does Echenique mean when she states that women's souls are "equal to that of their mates." Describe her vision of equality.

Writing Options

1. Write a one-paragraph response to Echenique's speech from the perspective of a poor or middle-class Argentine. How might her arguments not address the needs of these women?

2. Write a comparison-and-contrast essay of the views of Maria Eugenia Echenique, Sojourner Truth, Elizabeth Cady Stanton, and Susan B. Anthony regarding the nature of women, based on the evidence in their speeches.

 Go to **www.mirrorsandwindows.com** for more.

The Story of an Hour

A Short Story by Kate Chopin

Build Background

Cultural Context Kate Chopin began her career as a Regionalist writer, carefully portraying the landscape of the Gulf Islands and the people of Louisiana: the French Creoles of New Orleans and the rural Cajuns of Natchitoches. Many of the stories Chopin wrote were about the everyday lives of the Creoles and Cajuns she came to know during the ten years she lived there as a young woman. In this respect, her writing demonstrates elements of Realism and Naturalism.

Literary Context Chopin also was a pioneering feminist writer. When she first tried to publish **"The Story of an Hour"** in 1894, several magazine editors rejected the work, finding its portrayal of women radical and even immoral. Chopin's second novel, *The Awakening* (1899), met with much censorship in its time but is today considered a masterpiece. Chopin was rediscovered by literary critics in the 1950s and is revered by modern readers for her strong feminist message.

Reader's Context When have you experienced an emotion that was considered inappropriate by your friends, family, or co-workers?

Meet the Author

Kate Chopin (1851–1904), born Kate O'Flaherty, was raised in St. Louis, Missouri. After her father died in a train wreck when she was four years old, she was brought up by her French-speaking Creole mother, her grandmother, and her great-grandmother, who was a fine storyteller. Until age seventeen, Chopin attended a Catholic school called the St. Louis Academy of the Sacred Heart.

At eighteen, the author met a twenty-five-year-old banker named Oscar Chopin, whom she married. The Chopins moved to New Orleans, her husband's hometown, and before she was thirty years old, Kate Chopin had given birth to six children. When her husband's cotton business failed, the couple moved to Cloutierville in Natchitoches Parish, Louisiana.

Chopin was encouraged to write by her family physician in St. Louis, who recognized the quality of the prose in her letters home and felt writing would provide an outlet for her emotions. When Chopin's husband suddenly died of swamp fever, she moved back to St. Louis and began her literary career. She wrote two novels, more than one hundred short stories, and a variety of poetry, book reviews, and literary criticism—all while raising her six children as a single mother.

Analyze Literature

Reversal and Irony

A **reversal** is a dramatic change in the direction of events in a drama or narrative, especially a change in the fortunes of the *protagonist,* or main character.

Irony is a difference between appearance and reality. *Dramatic irony* occurs when a situation appears one way to the reader of the story and another way to the characters.

Set Purpose

The title "The Story of an Hour" suggests that this story will unfold quickly and perhaps bring about a dramatic change or surprise. As you read it, trace the feelings of the protagonist, Mrs. Mallard, by creating a sequence chart, noting especially how her feelings change after she learns of her husband's death. Look for two instances of reversal. Also look for an instance of dramatic irony, and analyze its effect on the ending of the story.

Preview Vocabulary

tumultuously, 483
importunity, 484

The Story of an Hour

by Kate Chopin

Madame Paul Escuider, 1882. John Singer Sargent.
Private collection. (See detail on page 481.)

There was something coming to her
and she was waiting for it, fearfully.

Knowing that Mrs. Mallard was afflicted with a heart trouble, great care was taken to break to her as gently as possible the news of her husband's death.

It was her sister Josephine who told her, in broken sentences; veiled hints that revealed in half concealing. Her husband's friend Richards was there, too, near her. It was he who had been in the newspaper office when intelligence of the railroad disaster was received, with Brently Mallard's name leading the list of "killed." He had only taken the time to assure himself of its truth by a second telegram, and had hastened to forestall any less careful, less tender friend in bearing the sad message.

She did not hear the story as many women have heard the same, with a paralyzed inability to accept its significance. She wept at once, with sudden, wild abandonment, in her sister's arms. When the storm of grief had spent itself she went away to her room alone. She would have no one follow her.

There stood, facing the open window, a comfortable, roomy armchair. Into this she sank, pressed down by a physical exhaustion that haunted her body and seemed to reach into her soul.

She could see in the open square before her house the tops of trees that were all aquiver with the new spring life. The delicious breath

John Singer Sargent

John Singer Sargent (1856–1925) was an American but lived nearly his entire life in Europe. He studied art in Italy during his teens, and in 1874, he was accepted at the Paris studio of Emile Auguste Carolus-Duran, a famous portrait artist. Carolus-Duran taught Sargent a painting technique called *alla prima,* in which the artist painted directly on the canvas, rather than sketching out forms and designs in advance.

Sargent was a prolific artist, producing almost three thousand paintings and countless sketches during his career. Although he painted many landscapes, his earliest and most enduring success came from painting portraits. In the late 1870s and early 1880s, Sargent was in great demand among the Paris elite. Then in 1884, his painting *Madame X,* which portrayed a twenty-three-old, bare-shouldered American woman, was criticized as being overly revealing. Fearing the ensuing scandal had ruined his career, Sargent moved to England. His reputation soon was restored, however, and by the turn of the twentieth century, Sargent was recognized as the most famous portrait artist in the United States and Europe.

In his early fifties, Sargent grew tired of portrait work and accepted few commissions. He resumed his travels and painted primarily landscapes, many of them watercolors. He also created murals for public buildings, including the Boston Public Library and the Museum of Fine Arts (also in Boston). Not only did he find painting murals challenging, but he also felt he was contributing to American cultural development.

Because much of Sargent's success came from painting portraits, his talent sometimes was overlooked and even criticized by those in the art community. In recent years, however, his work has been re-evaluated, and most contemporary art historians consider him among the greatest American artists.

Critical Viewing Based on your viewing of Sargent's *Madame Paul Escuider* (see facing page), what do you imagine this young woman is like? List details from the painting, and infer what they might reveal about the subject. Does the woman in the painting fit your impression of Mrs. Mallard, the protagonist of the story? Explain.

---

of rain was in the air. In the street below a peddler was crying his wares. The notes of a distant song which someone was singing reached her faintly, and countless sparrows were twittering in the eaves.

There were patches of blue sky showing here and there through the clouds that had met and piled one above the other in the west facing her window.

She sat with her head thrown back upon the cushion of the chair, quite motionless except when a sob came up into her throat and shook her, as a child who has cried itself to sleep continues to sob in its dreams.

She was young, with a fair, calm face, whose lines bespoke repression and even a certain strength. But now there was a dull stare in her eyes, whose gaze was fixed away off yonder on one of those patches of blue sky. It was not

a glance of reflection but rather indicated a suspension of intelligent thought.

There was something coming to her and she was waiting for it, fearfully. What was it? She did not know: it was too subtle and elusive to name. But she felt it, creeping out of the sky, reaching toward her through the sounds, the scents, the color that filled the air.

Now her bosom rose and fell <u>tumultuously</u>. She was beginning to recognize this thing that was approaching to possess her, and she was striving to beat it back with her will—as powerless as her two white slender hands would have been.

When she abandoned herself, a little whispered word escaped her slightly parted lips. She said it over and over under her breath:

---

tu • mul • tu • ous • ly (tü môl´ chü əs lē) *adv.,* wildly "free, free, free!" The vacant stare and the look of terror that had followed it went from her eyes. They stayed keen and bright. Her pulses beat fast, and the coursing blood warmed and relaxed every inch of her body.

She said it over and over under her breath:
"free, free, free!"

She did not stop to ask if it were or were not a monstrous joy that held her. A clear and exalted perception enabled her to dismiss the suggestion as trivial.

She knew that she would weep again when she saw the kind, tender hands folded in death; the face that had never looked save with love upon her, fixed and gray and dead. But she saw beyond that bitter moment a long procession of years to come that would belong to her absolutely. And she opened and spread her arms out to them in welcome.

There would be no one to live for her during those coming years; she would live for herself. There would be no powerful will bending hers in that blind persistence with which men and women believe they have a right to impose a private will upon a fellow creature. A kind intention or a cruel intention made the act seem no less a crime as she looked upon it in that brief moment of illumination.

And yet she had loved him—sometimes. Often she had not. What did it matter! What could love, the unsolved mystery, count for in face of this possession of self-assertion which she suddenly recognized as the strongest impulse of her being!

"Free! Body and soul free!" she kept whispering.

Josephine was kneeling before the closed door with her lips to the keyhole, imploring for admission. "Louise, open the door! I beg; open the door—you will make yourself ill. What are you doing, Louise? For heaven's sake open the door."

"Go away. I am not making myself ill." No; she was drinking in a very elixir of life[1] through that open window.

Her fancy was running riot along those days ahead of her. Spring days, and summer days, and all sorts of days that would be her own. She breathed a quick prayer that life might be long. It was only yesterday she had thought with a shudder that life might be long.

She arose at length and opened the door to her sister's <u>importunities</u>. There was a feverish triumph in her eyes, and she carried herself unwittingly like a goddess of Victory. She clasped her sister's waist, and together they descended the stairs. Richards stood waiting for them at the bottom.

Someone was opening the front door with a latchkey. It was Brently Mallard who entered, a little travel-stained, composedly carrying his gripsack[2] and umbrella. He had been far from the scene of accident, and did not know there had been one. He stood amazed at Josephine's piercing cry; at Richards's quick motion to screen him from the view of his wife.

But Richards was too late. When the doctors came they said she had died of heart disease—of joy that kills. ❖

---

1. **elixir of life.** Substance sought by medieval alchemists to prolong life indefinitely
2. **gripsack.** Small bag for traveling clothes

> im • por • tu • ni • ty (im' pōr tü´ nə tē) *n.*, persistent demand

MIRRORS & WINDOWS
Just after hearing the news about her husband, Mrs. Mallard says "over and over under her breath: 'free, free, free!'" Suggest what she now feels she can do. What might be her first act of freedom?

Refer to Text ▶ ▶ ▶ ▶ ▶ Reason with Text

1a. What does Mrs. Mallard learn from her sister, Josephine, at the beginning of the story?	**1b.** Why does Josephine have to break this news gently to her sister?	**Understand** Find meaning
2a. List the sights and smells Mrs. Mallard experiences at the open window in her room.	**2b.** Infer what these sights and smells represent to her and make her recognize.	**Apply** Use information
3a. What is Mrs. Mallard's immediate reaction to the news of her husband's death?	**3b.** How does Mrs. Mallard experience grief, happiness, and shocked disappointment? Chronicle her progression through these emotions as the story reveals them.	**Analyze** Take things apart
4a. Identify who enters the house just as Josephine and Mrs. Mallard are descending the stairs. What happens to Mrs. Mallard?	**4b.** In the context of nineteenth-century marriage, is Mrs. Mallard's joy at her husband's death understandable? Is it understandable in a modern context? Explain.	**Evaluate** Make judgments
5a. How does Mrs. Mallard appear when she opens the door to her sister?	**5b.** Propose why the story is called "The Story of an Hour." How does Mrs. Mallard come to a new realization during this time period?	**Create** Bring ideas together

Analyze Literature

Reversal and Irony

What are the two reversals in the story? What does the first reversal reveal about Mrs. Mallard? Why does the second reversal have such an impact?

At the end of the story, the doctors say Mrs. Mallard died of "joy that kills." How is this an example of dramatic irony? What actually caused her death?

Extend the Text

Writing Options

Creative Writing Write a *eulogy* for Mrs. Mallard, a speech honoring her life that would be read at her funeral. You may write from the perspective of her husband, sister, or friend. Describe what her life was like, and also mention how she died.

Expository Writing Write a paragraph explaining the love/hate relationship Mrs. Mallard has with her husband. Support your explanation using details from the story. What does Mrs. Mallard think of her husband? How does she react to him?

Critical Literacy

Write Biographical-Historical Criticism The theory of *biographical-historical criticism* analyzes a literary work in the context of the life and times of the author.

Research the life of Kate Chopin and the era in which she lived. Then write a short paper discussing the ways in which her life experience influenced her fiction. For example, her father died in a train wreck, just as Mr. Mallard is reported to have died in a "railroad disaster."

Lifelong Learning

Write a Personals Ad Research gender roles at the turn of the twentieth century. Then, pretending it is 1900, write an ad for the "personals" section of the local newspaper, seeking a conventional spouse. Describe all your requirements, including perhaps physical characteristics, dress, manners, educational background, financial status, and hobbies and interests.

 Go to **www.mirrorsandwindows.com** for more.

1. Who informed Mrs. Mallard of her husband's death?
   A. Richards, her husband's friend
   B. a railroad representative
   C. a telegraph
   D. her sister, Josephine
   E. a minister

2. How was Mrs. Mallard's reaction to the news of her husband's death different from what might be expected of most women?
   A. She started crying immediately, showing tremendous grief.
   B. She seemed paralyzed by her inability to accept the significance of the news.
   C. She turned and looked out the window, showing no sign of grief.
   D. She fainted.
   E. She did not believe the news.

3. In the sentence "Now her bosom rose and fell tumultuously," what does the word *tumultuously* mean?
   A. steadily
   B. irregularly
   C. unnoticeably
   D. heavily
   E. wildly

4. Why does Mrs. Mallard experience joy while sitting in her room, looking out the window?
   A. Her husband was brutal to her, so she is glad to be free of his tyranny.
   B. She realizes that her husband has not really died after all.
   C. She realizes that she will be free to live the rest of her life as she chooses.
   D. The hysteria of her emotion makes her confuse extreme grief with joy.
   E. Despite her husband's tragic death, she still can experience the joy of a sunny day.

5. Which of the following best defines the word *importunities?*
   A. questions
   B. demands
   C. awkward advances
   D. reasonable chances
   E. oddities

6. Why does the shock of seeing her husband alive kill Mrs. Mallard?
   A. She has a weak heart and is overjoyed to find out he is alive.
   B. She has a weak heart and is surprised at this turn of events.
   C. She has a weak heart and thinks he's a ghost.
   D. She has a weak heart and has lost her newfound freedom.
   E. She has a weak heart and is afraid he will beat her.

7. Which of the following literary elements is most important in the ending of this story?
   A. dramatic irony
   B. mood
   C. characterization
   D. setting
   E. foreshadowing

8. **Constructed Response:** Evaluate how "The Story of an Hour" is a commentary on women's lives in the late 1800s. Based on the story, what sort of life did a traditional woman lead? What might be symbolized by Mrs. Mallard's discovery of her feelings? Does Chopin seem optimistic about the possibility of change?. Include quotations and examples from the story to support your evaluation.

9. **Constructed Response:** Analyze the discovery Mrs. Mallard makes about herself as she ponders her husband's death. Compare her self-discovery to that of a character from another story. Evaluate each author's technique for presenting the self-discovery of the character. How does he or she bring about the discovery? Support your analysis with quotations and examples from the text.

TEST-TAKING TIP

In responding to a sentence-completion question, try to think of a word that makes sense in the sentence before looking at the available answers. Use the other words in the sentence to discover the purpose or general meaning of the missing word. Following this approach also will help you avoid cluttering your mind with unfavorable options.

Understand the Concept

Verbals are verb forms that act as namers (*nouns*) or modifiers (*adjectives* or *adverbs*). There are three kinds of verbals: participials, gerunds, and infinitives.

Participles, verb forms ending in *-ing, -d,* or *-ed,* are used as adjectives. A **participial phrase,** which can precede or follow the word it modifies, is made up of a participle and all the words related to it.

EXAMPLES

Singing loudly every song in her repertoire, Lucia tried to conquer her fears.

Worried about the coming thunderstorm, Mom shut all the windows in the house.

Be sure to place the participial phrase close to the word it modifies. Otherwise, you may imply something you do not mean.

Incorrect *Chugging along the tracks, we heard the train.*

Correct We heard the train *chugging along the tracks.*

Gerunds are verb forms ending in *-ing* that are used as nouns. In a sentence, a **gerund phrase** may be used as a subject, object, or object of a preposition.

EXAMPLES

Running was one of the events.

Before each basketball game, Colin practices *breathing deeply.*

I need help with *writing* my paper.

Infinitives are base verb forms preceded by the word *to.* An **infinitive phrase** can function as a noun, adjective, or adverb.

EXAMPLES

To tap dance in a Broadway musical is Marla's fondest dream. [Noun]

Right now Marla is practicing *to get into the school talent show.* [Adverb]

Sometimes, the *to* of an infinitive phrase is left out because it is understood. This happens frequently with the verbs *see, hear, feel, help, know, need, make,* and *let.*

EXAMPLE

Omar helps [to] *plaster the ceiling.*

Apply the Skill

Identify Verbal Phrases

For each of these sentences from "The Story of an Hour," identify what type of verbal phrase is used.

1. Knowing that Mrs. Mallard was afflicted with a heart trouble, great care was taken to break to her as gently as possible the news of her husband's death.
2. It was her sister Josephine who told her, in broken sentences; veiled hints that revealed in half concealing.
3. There stood, facing the open window, a comfortable, roomy armchair.
4. She was beginning to recognize this thing that was approaching to possess her, and she was striving to beat it back with her will.
5. She knew that she would weep again when she saw the kind, tender hands folded in death.

Fix Problems with Verbal Phrases

Rewrite each sentence, placing the verbal phrase in a better position and adding words as needed.

1. Paddling down the river, bears eyed our canoe but quickly lost interest.
2. Walking out to the piano onstage, the audience applauded loudly.
3. To provide contact information to her students, her office phone number was displayed on the overhead.
4. The front yard of our house was like a war zone pulling into the driveway.
5. After waking up in the morning, a strange creaking sound distracted him for a few minutes.

Use Verbal Phrases in Your Own Writing

Write a paragraph about a surprise you have received, good or bad. Use verbal phrases to add interest and variety to your sentences.

from Songs of Gold Mountain

Lyric Poems by Anonymous

Build Background

Historical Context In the mid-1800s, thousands of Chinese, usually young men, immigrated to California, intending to get rich in the "Gold Mountain," as the United States was called. At first, these laborers were welcomed, but eventually, efforts were made to limit their numbers. Many of these young men had five-year labor contracts and planned to return to China once they had made their fortunes. Nearly half of them never did, however, including many who were married and had families in China.

In 1882, the U.S. government passed the Chinese Exclusion Act, making it difficult for Chinese to immigrate. This law, the first in the United States targeted at a specific ethnic group, remained in effect until 1943. Because of the difficulties imposed by the act, those who did try to immigrate usually had the longest waiting times in the immigration detention center on Angel Island, off the coast of San Francisco. Known as the "Ellis Island of the West," Angel Island served as the first stop for immigrants who crossed the Pacific from Asia, Australia, and South America from 1910 to 1940.

During this time, immigration was restricted for citizens of certain countries, so Angel Island became the place where immigrants would wait for weeks, months, or even years while the Bureau of Immigration processed their applications. The processes often were humiliating and laborious: checking for parasites and a variety of diseases and verifying that the immigrant's story exactly matched that of his or her relatives or sponsors already in the United States. Failing an exam meant deportation. For those detained at Angel Island, the conditions were harsh. The food was bad, and the overcrowded buildings were considered firetraps.

Chinese immigrants wait outside the hospital at Angel Island (c. 1910).

Literary Context Several anonymous Chinese immigrants carved poems into the walls of their detention cells during their seemingly interminable waits. ***Songs of Gold Mountain*** is a collection of these Chinese poems.

Reader's Context How patient are you? What do you do to pass the time while waiting for something?

Analyze Literature

Speaker and Allusion

The **speaker** is the character who speaks in, or narrates, a poem—the voice assumed by the writer. The speaker and the writer of a poem are not necessarily the same person.

An **allusion** is a reference to a well-known person, event, object, or work from history or literature.

Set Purpose

The poems from *Songs of Gold Mountain* offer intimate details about the experiences and expectations of detained Chinese immigrants. For each of the four poems, infer what you can about the speaker, recording details from the poem to support your inferences. In the first poem, also identify the allusion the speaker makes and what it might indicate about his life before coming to the United States.

Preview Vocabulary

barrack, 489
scarcity, 490
deplorable, 490
encompass, 490

from Songs of *Gold Mountain*

1

As soon as it is announced
    the ship has reached America:
I burst out cheering,
    I have found precious pearls.
How can I bear the detention upon arrival,
Doctors and immigration officials refusing
    to let me go?
All the abuse—
I can't describe it with a pen.
I'm held captive in a wooden <u>barrack</u>, like King Wen[1]
    in Youli:[2]
No end to the misery and sadness in my heart.

---

1. **King Wen.** Wise Chinese ruler who became popular after his death
2. **Youli.** Place where King Wen was imprisoned by the Shang Dynasty king. Wen's sons defeated the Shang and started the Zhou Dynasty around 1122 BCE.

> **bar • rack** (bār´ ək) *n.,* shed for temporary dwelling

2

The moment I hear we've entered the port,
I am all ready:
    my belongings wrapped in a bundle.
Who would have expected joy to become sorrow:
Detained in a dark, crude, filthy room?
What can I do?
Cruel treatment, not one restful breath of air.
Scarcity of food, severe restrictions—all unbearable.
Here even a proud man bows his head low.

3

Fellow countrymen, four hundred million strong;
Many are great, with exceptional talents.
We want to come to the Flowery Flag Nation[3]
    but are barred;
The Golden Gate[4] firmly locked, without even
    a crack to crawl through.
This moment—
Truly deplorable is the imprisonment.
Our hearts ache in pain and shame;
Though talented, how can we put on wings and
    fly past the barbarians?

4

I am a man of heroic deeds;
I am a man with pride and dignity.
My bosom encompasses the height of Heaven
    and the brilliance of Earth;
Everywhere they know me as a truly noble man.
In search of wealth—
Greed led me on the road to Golden Mountain.
Denied landing upon reaching the shore, I am filled with rage.
With no means to pass the border, what can a person do? ❖

---

3. **Flowery Flag Nation.** Nickname for the United States
4. **Golden Gate.** Narrow body of water connecting San Francisco Bay and the Pacific Ocean

> **scar • ci • ty** (sker′ sə tē) *n.*, insufficient amount
> **de • plor • a • ble** (di plôr′ ə bəl) *adj.*, wretched; awful
> **en • com • pass** (in kəm′ pəs) *v.*, include; enclose

MIRRORS & WINDOWS The emotions expressed by the poets include sorrow, despair, shame, and rage. How would you respond to being denied something you feel you deserve?

Refer to Text ▷ ▷ ▷ ▷ ▷ **Reason with Text**

1a. Recall what the first two speakers do as soon as they arrive in the United States.	**1b.** How do they feel about what happens to them shortly after they arrive?	**Understand** Find meaning
2a. What do the speakers in the third and fourth poems call the United States?	**2b.** Infer what their nicknames for the United States suggest about how they felt about the country before arriving here.	**Apply** Use information
3a. According to the second speaker, how do proud men react to being detained?	**3b.** How do the speakers feel about their fellow countrymen? How can you tell?	**Analyze** Take things apart
4a. How does the third speaker refer to his captors?	**4b.** Judge what effect these poems had on the other detainees who read them.	**Evaluate** Make judgments
5a. Identify the conditions the speakers describe in their poems.	**5b.** Do the detainees regret their decision to come? If they had known about the detention before immigrating, would they have immigrated anyway? Explain.	**Create** Bring ideas together

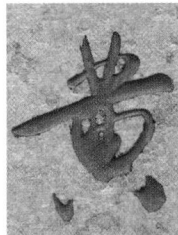

Analyze Literature

Speaker and Allusion

What did you infer about each speaker? For which one do you feel the most sympathy? Which do you feel has the most powerful way of expressing his situation? How is that achieved?

The first speaker makes an allusion to a king from Chinese history. For those who know the story of King Wen, how would this allusion shed light on the speaker's situation? How do allusions provide shortcuts to understanding for those who understand them?

Extend the Text

Writing Options

Creative Writing Write a poem about waiting for something and being disappointed by the results you anticipated. For example, you could write about being excited to go to an event, such as a concert or movie, that turned out to be boring or otherwise not enjoyable.

Expository Writing Write an essay analyzing the language of these poems. Examine the use of imagery, and decide whether it is concrete (realistic, direct language) or abstract (possibly fanciful or metaphorical). Explain what effect the different types of language might have on a reader.

Collaborative Learning

Investigate Immigration in the West With a group, research the different waves of immigrants that entered the western United States at facilities such as Angel Island. Look for information on what countries the immigrants came from, why they left their homelands, how many people immigrated in what time periods, and how they were treated on arrival in the United States. Present your information to the class as either a time line or a PowerPoint or other audiovisual presentation.

Critical Literacy

Research Literature Written by Prisoners The writing of people who have been incarcerated, whether for political or criminal reasons, not only describes their feelings and experiences but also provides insights into American history and culture. Using Internet and library sources, research literature written by people in prison to learn about its history and identify noted authors and works. Choose one author and research the circumstances that landed him or her in prison and the topics and themes he or she wrote about. Present your findings to the class in a brief oral presentation.

 Go to **www.mirrorsandwindows.com** for more.

We Wear the Mask

A Lyric Poem by Paul Laurence Dunbar

Build Background

Literary Context Paul Dunbar was one of the first African-American poets to gain national eminence, and he is considered a precursor to the Harlem Renaissance of the early 1900s (see Unit 5). Dunbar's reputation rests on his poems and short stories written in African-American dialect; however, the author considered his nondialectical work his best. During the late 1800s and early 1900s, the use of dialect among African-American poets was quite popular. Consequently and regrettably, many of Dunbar's poems not written in dialect were neglected.

In its formal language and use of rhyme, **"We Wear the Mask"** shows the influence of Scottish poet Robert Burns and American poet James Whitcomb Riley, both of whom Dunbar admired.

Reader's Context When do you hide your feelings from others? Why?

Meet the Author

Paul Laurence Dunbar (1872–1906) was born in Dayton, Ohio, the son of former slaves. Although his mother had no formal education, she taught her son to read when he was just four. Both his parents were "fond of books," according to Dunbar, and read aloud to the family in the evenings as they sat around the fire. Dunbar made his first attempt at rhyming when he was about six and read a poem by British Romantic William Wordsworth.

Dunbar was a good student but could not afford to go to college. He took a job as an elevator operator and wrote in his free time, submitting poems to local newspapers. In 1892, a former teacher invited him to read his work at a meeting of the Western Association of Writers. Their enthusiastic response encouraged the young writer to self-publish a collection of poems called *Oak and Ivy* (1893). To pay for the project, Dunbar sold the books for one dollar apiece to the people who rode in his elevator.

By 1895, Dunbar's poetry was being published in major newspapers and magazines. He published a second collection of poems, *Majors and Minors,* in 1895 with the financial support of friends. Dunbar gained national recognition in 1896 with the publication of *Lyrics of Lowly Life,* the collection in which "We Wear the Mask" appears. That launched him onto the lecture circuit in the United States and in Europe and eventually landed him a series of jobs at the Library of Congress, where he worked until sickness forced him to leave. Dunbar also published a novel, a short story collection, and some song lyrics in his later years.

A U.S. postage stamp was issued in honor of Dunbar in 1975.

Analyze Literature

Speaker and Metaphor
The **speaker** is the character who speaks in or narrates a poem—the voice assumed by the writer.

A **metaphor** is a figure of speech in which one thing is spoken or written about as if it were another. This figure of speech makes a comparison between the writer's actual subject (the *tenor* of the metaphor) and another thing to which the subject is likened (the *vehicle* of the metaphor).

Set Purpose

As indicated in the title, the speaker in this poem uses the plural *We.* As you read, determine who the speaker is speaking for and who is meant by the reference to *them* in line 8. In addition, analyze the metaphor of the mask, also introduced in the title. What is the tenor for the vehicle of the mask?

Preview Vocabulary

guile, 493
myriad, 493
vile, 493

We Wear the Mask

by Paul Laurence Dunbar

Les Fetiches, 1938. Lois Mailou Jones.
Smithsonian American Art Museum, Washington, DC.

We wear the mask that grins and lies,
It hides our cheeks and shades our eyes—
This debt we pay to human <u>guile</u>;
With torn and bleeding hearts we smile,
5   And mouth with <u>myriad</u> subtleties.

Why should the world be otherwise,
In counting all our tears and sighs?
Nay, let them only see us, while
    We wear the mask.

10   We smile, but, O great Christ, our cries
To thee from tortured souls arise.
We sing, but oh the clay is <u>vile</u>
Beneath our feet, and long the mile;
But let the world dream otherwise,
15   We wear the mask! ❖

guile (gīl) *n.,* secretiveness; sneakiness
my • ri • ad (mīr´ ē əd) *adj.,* of a varied nature
vile (vīl) *adj.,* offensive

MIRRORS & WINDOWS

When or with whom do you wear a mask, hiding your emotions?

Refer to Text ▶ ▶ ▶ ▶ ▶	Reason with Text	
1a. What is paid to "human guile"?	**1b.** Determine whether the speaker expresses a positive or negative attitude toward human duplicity.	**Understand** Find meaning
2a. What does the speaker suggest is not counted by the world?	**2b.** Why does the speaker suggest "Nay, let them only see us, while / We wear the mask"?	**Apply** Use information
3a. State what the mask hides.	**3b.** Identify the *we* mentioned in the poem. Who is the *them?*	**Analyze** Take things apart
4a. From what kinds of souls do the cries mentioned in the poem arise?	**4b.** Does the speaker justify use of the mask? Why or why not?	**Evaluate** Make judgments
5a. Under what conditions do the mask wearers sing?	**5b.** Deduce why people wear the mask.	**Create** Bring ideas together

Analyze Literature

Speaker and Metaphor

For whom is the speaker in this poem speaking? Why did Dunbar make the speaker plural (*we*) instead of singular (*I*)? Who is the *them* mentioned in line 8? What is the speaker's attitude toward *them?* Explain using details from the poem.

For what is the mask a metaphor in this poem? How appropriate a choice is the mask as a vehicle? What else could Dunbar have used as a vehicle?

Extend the Text

Writing Options

Creative Writing The speaker says the wearer of the mask speaks with "myriad subtleties." Imagine wearing the mask at work. Write a letter to your boss, listing your common utterances and explaining what they really mean. Also explain why you feel the need to "wear a mask" at work.

Expository Writing Review the information in the Meet the Author feature about Paul Laurence Dunbar. Using that as a starting point, conduct research to learn more about his background. Then write a paragraph analyzing "We Wear the Mask" in the context of Dunbar's life. Try to determine what inspired Dunbar to write the poem and whether he felt that he wore a mask.

Media Literacy

Compare Dunbar's Language Use the Internet to locate a poem by Dunbar that uses dialect. Then rewrite the poem in standard English. Read both versions of the poem aloud to your classmates. Discuss which version of the poem is more powerful and why.

Collaborative Learning

Enact a Role-Play With a partner, identify a character from film, literature, or television who "wears a mask." Discuss these questions: From whom is the character trying to hide his or her feelings? How successful is he or she? What would happen if the character revealed his or her true feelings? Then have a dialogue with your partner. One of you should take on the persona of a character wearing a mask, and the other should try to get the character to disclose his or her true feelings and explain the reason for wearing a mask.

 Go to **www.mirrorsandwindows.com** for more.

from

Up from Slavery

by Booker T. Washington

Booker T. Washington
(1856–1915) was born to a
mother who was
a slave in Hale's
Ford, Virginia. Like
most slaves, Booker
had only a first
name; he adopted
his stepfather's first
name as his last
name.

While attending makeshift
schools, Washington worked as
a salt packer, coal miner, and
houseboy. Filled with the desire
to learn to read and write, he
earned his way through Hampton Normal and Agricultural
Institute in Virginia by working
as a janitor. He graduated with
honors and, in 1881, became
the first principal of what is
now Tuskegee Institute. He
became a national figure as a
result of a short address, Chapter 14 of **Up from Slavery,** at
the Atlanta Exposition of 1895.

Known as the "Moses of
his Race," Washington received
an honorary degree from Harvard University, dined with
President Theodore Roosevelt,
and advised politicians and
business leaders.

In those days, and later as a young man, I used to try to picture
in my imagination the feelings and ambitions of a white boy
with absolutely no limit placed upon his aspirations and activities. I used to envy the white boy who had no obstacles placed
in the way of his becoming a Congressman, Governor, Bishop, or
President by reason of the accident of his birth or race. I used to
picture the way that I would act under such circumstances; how
I would begin at the bottom and keep rising until I reached the
highest round of success.

In later years, I confess that I do not envy the white boy as
I once did. I have learned that success is to be measured not so
much by the position that one has reached in life as by the obstacles which he has overcome while trying to succeed. Looked at
from this standpoint, I almost reach the conclusion that often the
Negro boy's birth and connection with an unpopular race is an
advantage, so far as real life is concerned. With few exceptions,
the Negro youth must work harder and must perform his task
even better than a white youth in order to secure recognition.
But out of the hard and unusual struggle which he is compelled
to pass, he gets a strength, a confidence, that one misses whose
pathway is comparatively smooth by reason of birth and race.

From any point of view, I had rather be what I am, a member of the Negro race, than be able to claim membership with
the most favored of any other race. I have always been made
sad when I have heard members of any race claiming rights

and privileges, or certain badges of distinction, on the ground simply that they were members of this or that race, regardless of their own individual worth or attainments. I have been made to feel sad for such persons because I am conscious of the fact that mere connection with what is known as a superior race will not permanently carry an individual forward unless he has individual worth, and mere connection with what is regarded as an inferior race will not finally hold an individual back if he possesses intrinsic, individual merit. Every persecuted individual and race should get much consolation out of the great human law, which is universal and eternal, that merit, no matter under what skin found, is in the long run, recognized and rewarded. This I have said here, not to call attention to myself as an individual, but to the race to which I am proud to belong. ❖

Booker T. Washington Legend, c. 1944–1945.
William H. Johnson. Smithsonian American Art Museum, Washington, DC.

Washington believes that "Merit . . . is in the long run, recognized and rewarded." Do you agree that people ultimately are recognized for their hard work and achievement? Has this been your experience?

Refer and Reason

1. Why did Washington initially envy white boys? Why does he no longer envy them? Restate his definition of *success.*

2. Who saddens Washington? What assumptions do they make? When is pride in one's race or ethnicity a good thing, and when is it not?

3. According to Washington, what must an African-American youth do to succeed? Find examples of people who have overcome significant obstacles to achieve success. Suggest what lessons can be learned from such people.

Writing Options

1. Write the text for a series of three motivational posters about overcoming obstacles and earning success. Include quotations from famous people to support the themes of the posters.

2. Write a two-paragraph narrative about a time you strove for success. Explain what it meant to be successful in that situation and what difficulties you faced.

 Go to **www.mirrorsandwindows.com** for more.

from *The Souls of Black Folk*

by W. E. B. Du Bois

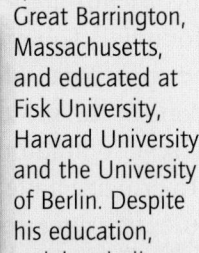

W. E. B. Du Bois (1868–1963), whose full name was William Edward Burghardt Du Bois (dü boiz´), was born in Great Barrington, Massachusetts, and educated at Fisk University, Harvard University, and the University of Berlin. Despite his education, racial prejudice prevented him from getting a faculty appointment at a major university, so he taught at various other colleges before going to Atlanta University in 1897.

Du Bois's essay "Of Mr. Booker T. Washington and Others" was first printed in the *Guardian* on July 27, 1902, and later published in Du Bois's collection of essays, *The Souls of Black Folk.* The essay was considered extremely controversial. At the time it was written, Booker T. Washington was the leading spokesperson for African Americans, and he believed that they should accept the discriminatory conditions imposed on them. In this essay, Du Bois calmly but completely rejects Washington's opinions.

Easily the most striking thing in the history of the American Negro since 1876[1] is the ascendancy of Mr. Booker T. Washington. It began at the time when war memories and ideals were rapidly passing; a day of astonishing commercial development was dawning; a sense of doubt and hesitation overtook the freedmen's sons,—then it was that his leading began. Mr. Washington came, with a simple definite program, at the psychological moment when the nation was a little ashamed of having bestowed so much sentiment on Negroes, and was concentrating its energies on Dollars. His program of industrial education, conciliation of the South, and submission and silence as to civil and political rights, was not wholly original; the Free Negroes from 1830 up to war-time had striven to build industrial schools, and the American Missionary Association had from the first taught various trades; and Price[2] and others had sought a way of honorable alliance with the best of the Southerners. But Mr. Washington first indissolubly linked these things; he put enthusiasm, unlimited energy, and perfect faith into this program, and changed it from a bypath into a veritable Way of Life. And the tale of the methods by which he did this is a fascinating study of human life.

It startled the nation to hear a Negro advocating such a program after many decades of bitter complaint; it startled and won the applause of the South, it interested and won the admiration of the North; and after a confused murmur of protest, it silenced if it did not convert the Negroes themselves.

---

1. **1876.** In 1876, Reconstruction following the Civil War ended, federal troops withdrew from the South, and African Americans lost political power.
2. **Price.** Thomas Frederick Price (1860–1919), editor, Roman Catholic priest, and founder of the American Missionary Association

Tuskegee Normal and Industrial Institute (c. 1900).

To gain the sympathy and cooperation of the various elements comprising the white South was Mr. Washington's first task; and this, at the time Tuskegee[3] was founded, seemed, for a black man, well-nigh impossible. And yet ten years later it was done in the word spoken at Atlanta: "In all things purely social we can be as separate as the five fingers, and yet one as the hand in all things essential to mutual progress." This "Atlanta Compromise"[4] is by all odds the most notable thing in Mr. Washington's career. The South interpreted it in different ways: the radicals received it as a complete surrender of the demand for civil and political equality; the conservatives, as a generously conceived working basis for mutual understanding. So both approved it, and today its author is certainly the most distinguished Southerner since Jefferson Davis, and the one with the largest personal following.

Next to this achievement comes Mr. Washington's work in gaining place and consideration in the North. Others less shrewd and tactful had formerly essayed to sit on these two stools and had fallen between them, but as Mr. Washington knew the heart of the South from birth and training, so by singular insight he intuitively grasped the spirit of the age which was dominating the North. And so thoroughly did he learn the speech and thought of triumphant commercialism, and the ideals of material prosperity, that the picture of a lone black boy poring over a French grammar amid the weeds and dirt of a neglected home soon seemed to him the acme of absurdities.[5]

One wonders what Socrates and St. Francis of Assisi[6] would say to this.

And yet this very singleness of vision and thorough oneness with his age is a mark of the successful man. It is as though Nature must needs make men narrow in order to give them force. So Mr. Washington's cult has gained unquestioning followers, his work has wonderfully prospered, his friends are legion, and his enemies are confounded. Today he stands as the one recognized spokesman of his ten million fellows, and one of the most notable figures in a nation of seventy millions. One hesitates, therefore, to criticize a life which, beginning with so little, has done so much. And yet the time is come when one may speak in all sincerity and utter courtesy of the mistakes and shortcomings of Mr. Washington's career, as well as of his triumphs, without being thought captious or envious, and without forgetting that it is easier to do ill than well in the world.

The criticism that has hitherto met Mr. Washington has not always been of this broad character. In the South especially has he had to

3. **Tuskegee.** Tuskegee Institute, a vocational school for African Americans founded in 1881 by Booker T. Washington
4. **Atlanta Compromise.** Washington's speech at the Atlanta Exposition of 1895 essentially traded the political, civil, and social rights of African Americans for the promise of jobs and vocational schools.
5. **acme of absurdities.** Refers to a passage in *Up From Slavery,* in which Washington describes nonpractical knowledge as absurd
6. **Socrates and St. Francis of Assisi.** *Socrates*—(c. 470–399 BCE), Greek philosopher; *St. Francis of Assisi*—(c. 1182–1226), founder of the Franciscan orders and leader of movements to reform the Catholic Church

walk warily to avoid the harshest judgments,—and naturally so, for he is dealing with the one subject of deepest sensitiveness to that section. Twice—once when at the Chicago celebration of the Spanish-American War he alluded to the color-prejudice that is "eating away the vitals of the South," and once when he dined with President Roosevelt[7]—has the resulting Southern criticism been violent enough to threaten seriously his popularity. In the North the feeling has several times forced itself into words, that Mr. Washington's counsels of submission overlooked certain elements of true manhood, and that his educational program was unnecessarily narrow. Usually, however, such criticism has not found open expression, although, too, the spiritual sons of the Abolitionists have not been prepared to acknowledge that the schools founded before Tuskegee, by men of broad ideals and self-sacrificing spirit, were wholly failures or worthy of ridicule. While, then, criticism has not failed to follow Mr. Washington, yet the prevailing public opinion of the land has been but too willing to deliver the solution of a wearisome problem into his hands, and say, "If that is all you and your race ask, take it."

Among his own people, however, Mr. Washington has encountered the strongest and most lasting opposition, amounting at times to bitterness, and even today continuing strong and insistent even though largely silenced in outward expression by the public opinion of the nation. Some of this opposition is, of course, mere envy; the disappointment of displaced demagogues and the spite of narrow minds. But aside from this, there is among educated and thoughtful colored men in all parts of the land a feeling of deep regret, sorrow, and apprehension at the wide currency and ascendancy which some of Mr. Washington's theories have gained. These same men admire his sincerity of purpose, and are willing to forgive much to honest endeavor which is doing something worth doing. They cooperate with Mr. Washington as far as they conscientiously can; and, indeed, it is no ordinary tribute to this man's tact and power that, steering as he must between so many diverse interests and opinions, he so largely retains the respect of all.

But the hushing of the criticism of honest opponents is a dangerous thing.

But the hushing of the criticism of honest opponents is a dangerous thing. It leads some of the best of the critics to unfortunate silence and paralysis of effort, and others to burst into speech so passionately and intemperately as to lose listeners. Honest and earnest criticism from those whose interests are most nearly touched,—criticism of writers by readers, of government by those governed, of leaders by those led,—this is the soul of democracy and the safeguard of modern society. If the best of the American Negroes receive by outer pressure a leader whom they had not recognized before, manifestly there is here a certain palpable gain. Yet there is also irreparable loss,—a loss of that peculiarly valuable education which a group receives when by search and criticism it finds and commissions its own leaders. The way in which this is done is at once the most elementary and the nicest problem of social growth. History is but the record of such group leadership, and yet how infinitely changeful is its type and character! And of all types and kinds, what can be more instructive than the leadership of a group within a group?—that curious double movement where real progress may be negative and actual advance be relative retrogression. All this is the social student's inspiration and despair.

---

7. **he dined with President Roosevelt.** Theodore Roosevelt (1858–1919) asked Washington to dine with him in 1901, stirring up controversy and criticism around the country.

Jim Crow Laws

In 1868 and 1870, respectively, Congress passed the Fourteenth and Fifteenth Amendments to the U.S. Constitution, guaranteeing civil liberties and voting rights to African-American men. Since African Americans could now vote and ex-Confederates could not, the political landscape of the South underwent a dramatic change.

Many white Southerners reacted to this change with fierce opposition, forming organizations such as the Ku Klux Klan and the Redeemers. Through their use of violence and unethical political dealings, these groups had successfully thwarted the goals of Reconstruction by 1876.

Three members of the Ku Klux Klan arrested in Mississippi for attempting to murder an entire family (1871).

When Southern whites regained political control over the region in the 1880s, they enacted what came to be known as Jim Crow laws. The name *Jim Crow* originated from a minstrel song called "Jump Jim Crow" that was popular in the Deep South. Jim Crow laws legalized segregation, which meant that white and black people could not attend the same schools, drink from the same water fountains, or even be buried in the same graveyards. If blacks tried to use white facilities, they were immediately arrested.

Although the African-American community fought Jim Crow laws, the U.S. Supreme Court upheld the states' rights to enact them in 1896. That landmark case, *Plessy v. Ferguson,* set the legal precedent for "separate but equal," which would not change until 1954, when the Court decided in *Brown v. Board of Education* that segregation was unconstitutional (see Unit 7).

Now in the past the American Negro has had instructive experience in the choosing of group leaders, founding thus a peculiar dynasty which in the light of present conditions is worthwhile studying. When sticks and stones and beasts form the sole environment of a people, their attitude is largely one of determined opposition to and conquest of natural forces. But when to earth and brute is added an environment of men and ideas, then the attitude of the imprisoned group may take three main forms,—a feeling of revolt and revenge; an attempt to adjust all thought and action to the will of the greater group; or, finally, a determined effort at self-realization and self-development despite environing opinion. The influence of all of these attitudes at various times can be traced in the history of the American Negro, and in the evolution of his successive leaders.

Before 1750, which the fire of African freedom still burned in the veins of the slaves,

there was in all leadership or attempted leadership but the one motive of revolt and revenge,—typified in the terrible Maroons, the Danish black, and Cato of Stono,[8] and veiling all the Americas in fear of insurrection. The liberalizing tendencies of the latter half of the eighteenth century brought, along with kindlier relations between black and white, thoughts of ultimate adjustment and assimilation. Such aspiration was especially voiced in the earnest songs of Phyllis, in the martydom of Attacks, the fighting of Salem and Poor, the intellectual accomplishments of Banneker and Derham, and the political demands of the Cuffes.[9]

---

8. **Maroons . . . Stono.** *Maroons*—fugitive slaves or their descendants; *Danish blacks*—slaves in the Danish West Indies who revolted in 1733; *Cato of Stono*—leader of a slave revolt in South Carolina
9. **Phyllis . . . the Cuffes.** *Phillis Wheatley*—(c. 1753–1784) African-American poet; *Crispus Attucks*—(c. 1723–1770) slain

Stern financial and social stress after the war cooled much of the previous humanitarian ardor. The disappointment and impatience of the Negroes at the persistence of slavery and serfdom voiced itself in two movements. The slaves in the South, aroused undoubtedly by vague rumors of the Haytian revolt, made three fierce attempts at insurrection,—in 1800 under Gabriel in Virginia, in 1822 under Vesey in Carolina, and in 1831 again in Virginia under the terrible Nat Turner.[10] In the Free States, on the other hand, a new and curious attempt at self-development was made. In Philadelphia and New York color prescription led to a withdrawal of Negro communicants from white churches and the formation of a peculiar socio-religious institution among the Negroes known as the African Church,—an organization still living and controlling in its various branches over a million of men.

Walker's[11] wild appeal against the trend of the times showed how the world was changing after the coming of the cotton-gin. By 1830, slavery seemed hopelessly fastened on the South, and the slaves thoroughly cowed into

Stern financial and social stress after the war cooled much of the previous humanitarian ardor.

submission. The free Negroes of the North, inspired by the mulatto immigrants from the West Indies, began to change the basis of their demands; they recognized the slavery of slaves, but insisted that they themselves were freemen, and sought assimilation and amalgamation with the nation on the same terms with other men. Thus, Forten and Purvis of Philadelphia, Shad of Wilmington, Du Bois of New Haven, Barbadoes[12] of Boston, and others, strove singly and together as men, they said, not as slaves; as

"people of color," not as "Negroes." The trend of the times, however, refused them recognition save in individual and exceptional cases, considered them as one with all the despised blacks, and they soon found themselves striving to keep even the rights they formerly had of voting and working and moving as freemen. Schemes of migration and colonization arose among them; but these they refused to entertain, and they eventually turned to the Abolition movement as a final refuge.

Here, led by Remond, Nell, Wells-Brown, and Douglass,[13] a new period of self-assertion and self-development dawned. To be sure, ultimate freedom and assimilation was the ideal before the leaders, but the assertion of the manhood rights of the Negro by himself was the main reliance, and John Brown's raid was the extreme of its logic. After the war and emancipation, the great form of Frederick Douglass, the greatest of American Negro leaders, still led the host. Self-assertion, especially in political lines, was the main program, and

leader of the Boston Massacre; *Peter Salem*—(d. 1816) African-American patriot killed in the battle of Bunker Hill; *Benjamin Banneker*—(1731–1800) African-American mathematician; *James Derham*—(1762–?) first recognized African-American physician; *Paul Cuffe*—(1759–1817) organizer of a movement to resettle African Americans in African colonies

10. **Gabriel . . . Turner.** *Gabriel*—(c. 1775–1800) conspired to attack Richmond, Virginia; *Denmark Vesey*—(c. 1767–1822) led an unsuccessful uprising in 1822; *Nat Turner*—(1800–1831) led the Southampton insurrection in 1831, in which one hundred slaves and sixty-one whites were killed

11. **Walker's.** *David Walker*—(1785–1830) author of an inflammatory antislavery pamphlet

12. **Forten . . . Barbadoes.** *James Forten*—(1766–1842) African-American philanthropist and civic leader; *Robert Purvis*—(1810–1898) founder of the American Anti-Slavery Society and president of the Underground Railroad; *Abraham Shadd*—African-American abolitionist and activist; *Alexander Du Bois*—(1803–1887) W. E. B. Du Bois's grandfather, cofounder of the Negro Episcopal Parish of St. Luke; *James G. Barbadoes*—(c. 1796–1841) delegate to the first National Negro Convention

13. **Remond . . . Douglass.** *Charles Lenox Remond*—(1810–1873) African-American leader; *William Cooper Nell*—(1816–1874) first African American to acquire a government position (clerk in the post office), abolitionist, writer, and advocate for equal education; *William Wells Brown*—(c. 1816–1884) publisher of *Clotel*, the first novel and play by an African American; *Fredrick Douglass*—(1817–1895) African-American abolitionist and diplomat

Four generations of slaves in Beaufort, South Carolina (c. 1862).

behind Douglass came Elliot, Bruce, and Langston, and the Reconstruction politicians, and, less conspicuous but of greater social significance Alexander Crummell and Bishop Daniel Payne.[14]

Then came the Revolution of 1876, the suppression of the Negro votes, the changing and shifting of ideals, and the seeking of new lights in the great night. Douglass, in his old age, still bravely stood for the ideals of his early manhood,—ultimate assimilation *through* self-assertion, and on no other terms. For a time Price arose as a new leader, destined, it seemed, not to give up, but to restate the old ideals in a form less repugnant to the white South. But he passed away in his prime. Then came the new leader. Nearly all the former ones had become leaders by the silent suffrage of their fellows, had sought to lead their own people alone, and were usually, save Douglass, little known outside their race. But Booker T. Washington arose as essentially the leader not of one race but of two,—a compromiser between the South, the

North, and the Negro. Naturally the Negroes resented, at first bitterly, signs of compromise which surrendered their civil and political rights, even though this was to be exchanged for larger chances of economic development. The rich and dominating North, however, was not only weary of the race problem, but was investing largely in Southern enterprises, and welcomed any method of peaceful cooperation. Thus, by national opinion, the Negroes began to recognize Mr. Washington's leadership; and the voice of criticism was hushed.

Mr. Washington represents in Negro thought the old attitude of adjustment and submission; but adjustment at such a peculiar time as to make his program unique. This is an age of unusual economic development, and Mr. Washington's program naturally takes an economic cast, becoming a gospel of Work and Money to such an extent as apparently almost completely to overshadow the higher aims of life. Moreover, this is an age when the more advanced races are coming in closer contact with the less developed races, and the race-feeling is therefore intensified; and Mr. Washington's program practically accepts the alleged inferiority of the Negro races. Again, in our own land, the reaction from the sentiment of wartime has given impetus to race-prejudice against Negroes, and Mr. Washington withdraws many of the high demands of Negroes as men and American citizens. In other periods of intensified prejudice all the Negro's tendency to self-assertion has been called forth; at this period a policy of submission is advocated. In the history of nearly all

---

14. **Elliot . . . Payne.** *Robert Brown Elliot*—(1842–1884) African-American congressman from South Carolina who served in the U.S. House of Representatives; *Blanche K. Bruce*—(1841–1898) first African-American man to serve a full term in the U.S. Senate (1875–1881); *John Mercer Langston*—(1829–1897) African-American congressman, lawyer, diplomat, educator; *Alexander Crummell*—(1819–1898) clergy of the Episcopal Church, missionary in Liberia for twenty years and then in Washington, DC; *Daniel Alexander Payne*—(1811–1893) bishop of the African Methodist Episcopal Church and president of Wilberforce University (1863–1876)

other races and peoples the doctrine preached at such crises has been that manly self-respect is worth more than lands and houses, and that a people who voluntarily surrender such respect, or cease striving for it, are not worth civilizing.

Mr. Washington represents in Negro thought the old attitude of adjustment and submission.

In answer to this, it has been claimed that the Negro can survive only through submission. Mr. Washington distinctly asks that black people give up, at least for the present, three things,—

First, political power,

Second, insistence on civil rights,

Third, higher education of Negro youth,—and concentrate all their energies on industrial education, the accumulation of wealth, and the conciliation of the South. This policy has been courageously and insistently advocated for over fifteen years, and has been triumphant for perhaps ten years. As a result of this tender of the palm-branch, what has been the return? In these years there have occurred:

1. The disfranchisement of the Negro.

2. The legal creation of a distinct status of civil inferiority for the Negro.

3. The steady withdrawal of aid from institutions for the higher training of the Negro.

These movements are not, to be sure, direct results of Mr. Washington's teachings; but his propaganda has, without a shadow of doubt, helped their speedier accomplishment. The question then comes: Is it possible, and probable, that nine millions of men can make effective progress in economic lines if they are deprived of political rights, made a servile caste, and allowed only the most meager chance for

developing their exceptional men? If history and reason give any distinct answer to these questions, it is an emphatic *No.* And Mr. Washington thus faces the triple paradox of his career:

1. He is striving nobly to make Negro artisans businessmen and property-owners; but it is utterly impossible, under modern competitive methods, for workingmen and property-owners to defend their rights and exist without the right of suffrage.

2. He insists on thrift and self-respect, but at the same time counsels a silent submission to civic inferiority such as is bound to sap the manhood of any race in the long run.

3. He advocates common-school and industrial training, and depreciates institutions of higher learning; but neither the Negro common schools, nor Tuskegee itself, could remain open a day were it not for teachers trained in Negro colleges, or trained by their graduates.

This triple paradox in Mr. Washington's position is the object of criticism by two classes of colored Americans. One class is spiritually descended from Toussaint the Savior,[15] through Gabriel, Vesey, and Turner, and they represent the attitude of revolt and revenge, they hate the white South blindly and distrust the white race generally, and so far as they agree on definite action, think that the Negro's only hope lies in emigration beyond the borders of the United States. And yet, by the irony of fate, nothing has more effectually made this program seem hopeless than the recent course of the United States toward weaker and darker peoples in the West Indies, Hawaii, and the Philippines,—for where in the world may we go and be safe from lying and brute force?

The other class of Negroes who cannot agree with Mr. Washington has hitherto said little aloud. They deprecate the sight of scattered counsels, of internal disagreement; and especially they dislike making their just criticism

---

15. **Toussaint the Savior.** *Pierre-Dominique Toussaint—* (c. 1743–1803) Haitian general and liberator

of a useful and earnest man an excuse of a general discharge of venom from small-minded opponents. Nevertheless, the questions involved are so fundamental and serious that it is difficult to see how men like the Grimkes, Kelly Miller, J. W. E. Bowen,[16] and other representatives of this group, can much longer be silent. Such men feel in conscience bound to ask of this nation three things:

1. The right to vote.
2. Civic equality.
3. The education of youth according to ability.

They acknowledge Mr. Washington's invaluable service in counselling patience and courtesy in such demands; they do not ask that ignorant black men vote when ignorant whites are debarred, or that any reasonable restrictions in the suffrage should not be applied; they know that the low social level of the mass of the race is responsible for much discrimination against it, but they also know, and the nation knows, that relentless color-prejudice is more often a cause than a result of the Negro's degradation; they seek the abatement of this relic of barbarism, and not its systematic encouragement and pampering by all agencies of social power from the Associated Press to the Church of Christ. They advocate, with Mr. Washington, a broad system of Negro common schools supplemented by thorough industrial training; but they are surprised that a man of Mr. Washington's insight cannot see that no such education system ever has rested or can rest on any other basis than that of the well-equipped college and university, and they insist that there is a demand for a few such institutions throughout the South to train the best of the Negro youth as teachers, professional men, and leaders.

This group of men honor Mr. Washington for his attitude of conciliation toward the white South; they accept the "Atlanta Compromise" in its broadest interpretation; they recognize, with him, many signs of promise, many men

of high purpose and fair judgment, in this section; they know that no easy task has been laid upon a region already tottering under heavy burdens. But, nevertheless, they insist that the way to truth and right lies in straightforward honesty, not in indiscriminate flattery; in praising those of the South who do well and criticizing uncompromisingly those who do ill; in taking advantage of the opportunities at hand and urging their fellows to do the same, but at the same time in remembering that only a firm adherence to their higher ideals and aspirations will ever keep those ideals within the realm of possibility. They do not expect that the free right to vote, to enjoy civic rights, and to be educated will come in a moment; they do not expect to see the bias and prejudices of years disappear at the blast of a trumpet; but they are absolutely certain that the way for a people to gain their reasonable rights is not by voluntarily throwing them away and insisting that they do not want them; that the way for a people to gain respect is not by continually belittling and ridiculing themselves that, on the contrary, Negroes must insist continually, in season and out of season, that voting is necessary to modern manhood, that color discrimination is barbarism, and that black boys need education as well as white boys.

> *The way to truth and right lies in straightforward honesty, not in indiscriminate flattery;*

In failing thus to state plainly and unequivocally the legitimate demands of their people, even at the cost of opposing an honored leader,

---

16. **Grimkes . . . Bowen.** *Archibald Grimke* (1849–1930) and *Francis Grimke* (1850–1937)—civic leaders concerned with African-American issues; *Kelly Miller*—(1863–1939) dean of Howard University, lecturer on African-American issues; *John Wesley Edward Bowen*—(1855–?) clergyman and educator

Elizabeth Freeman

W. E. B. Du Bois was not the first person from his family to fight for equality. More than a century before he was born, Du Bois's great-grandmother, a freedwoman named Elizabeth Freeman, played an important part in abolishing slavery in Massachusetts.

Freeman was born in 1742 to slave parents and christened Mum Bett. She was sold immediately to John Ashley of Sheffield, Massachusetts, whom she served for nearly forty years. In 1780, at age thirty-eight, Bett discovered her mistress attempting to strike her sister, Lizzy, with a heated shovel. When Bett intervened, Mrs. Ashley struck her with the shovel instead. Infuriated by her treatment, Bett immediately left the Ashley house and vowed never to return.

The same year, Massachusetts passed a revised Bill of Rights that ensured the equality of all people. Bett thought this might provide legal justification for her freedom as well as that of her sister. She secured the aid of Theodore Segwick, an early abolitionist lawyer, who agreed to argue the women's case before a court. The jury found in favor of Bett and her sister, granting them their freedom and thirty shillings in damages.

Although Ashley begged Bett to return to his estate and work for wages, she ignored him. Instead, she changed her name to Elizabeth Freeman and went to work for the attorney who had won her freedom. She later became a nurse and midwife and owned her own home. Her case set an important legal precedent in Massachusetts, the first state in the nation to ban slavery outright.

---

the thinking classes of American Negroes would shirk a heavy responsibility,—a responsibility to themselves, a responsibility to the struggling masses, a responsibility to the darker races of men whose future depends so largely on this American experiment, but especially a responsibility to this nation,—this common Fatherland. It is wrong to encourage a man or a people in evil-doing, it is wrong to aid and abet a national crime simply because it is unpopular not to do so. The growing spirit of kindliness and reconciliation between the North and South after the frightful differences of a generation ago ought to be a source of deep congratulation to all, and especially to those whose mistreatment caused the war; but if that reconciliation is to be marked by the industrial slavery and civic death of those same black men, with permanent legislation into a position of inferiority, then those black men, if they are really men, are called upon by every consider-ation of patriotism and loyalty to oppose such a course by all civilized methods, even though such opposition involves disagreement with Mr. Booker T. Washington. We have no right to sit silently by while the inevitable seeds are sown for a harvest of disaster to our children black and white.

First, it is the duty of black men to judge the South discriminatingly. The present generation of Southerners are not responsible for the past, and they should not be blindly hated or blamed for it. Furthermore, to no class is the indiscriminate endorsement of the recent course of the South toward Negroes more nauseating than to the best thought of the South. The South is not "solid"; it is a land in the ferment of social change, wherein forces of all kinds are fighting for supremacy; and to praise the ill the South is today perpetrating is just as wrong as to condemn the good. Discriminating and broad-minded criticism is

Photograph displayed by W. E. B. Du Bois in the Paris Exposition of 1900 as part of an exhibit on African-American culture and history.

Senator Ben Tillman,[17] is not only sane, but the imperative duty of thinking black men.

It would be unjust to Mr. Washington not to acknowledge that in several instances he has opposed movements in the South which were unjust to the Negro; he sent memorials to the Louisiana and Alabama constitutional conventions, he has spoken against lynching, and in other ways has openly or silently set his influence against sinister schemes and unfortunate happenings. Notwithstanding this, it is equally true to assert that on the whole the distinct impression left by Mr. Washington's propaganda is, first, that the South is justified in its present attitude toward the Negro because of the Negro's degradation; secondly, that the prime cause of the Negro's failure to rise more quickly is his wrong education in the past; and, thirdly, that his future rise depends primarily on his own efforts. Each of these propositions is a dangerous half-truth. The supplementary truths must never be lost sight of: first, slavery and race-prejudice are potent if not sufficient causes of the Negro's position; second, industrial and common-school training were necessarily slow in planting because they had to await the black teachers trained by higher institutions,—it being extremely doubtful if any essentially different development was possible, and certainly a Tuskegee was unthinkable before 1880; and, third, while it is a great truth to say that the Negro must strive and strive mightily to help himself, it is equally true that unless his striving be not simply seconded, but rather aroused and encouraged, by the initiative of the richer and wiser environing group, he cannot hope for great success.

what the South needs,—needs it for the sake of her own white sons and daughters, and for the insurance of robust, healthy mental and moral development.

Today even the attitude of the Southern whites toward the blacks is not, as so many assume, in all cases the same; the ignorant Southerner hates the Negro, the workingmen fear his competition, the money-makers wish to use him as a laborer, some of the educated see a menace in his upward development, while others—usually the sons of the masters— wish to help him to rise. National opinion has enabled this last class to maintain the Negro common schools, and to protect the Negro partially in property, life, and limb. Through the pressure of the money-makers, the Negro is in danger of being reduced to semi-slavery, especially in the country districts; the workingmen, and those of the educated who fear the Negro, have united to disfranchise him, and some have urged his deportation; while the passions of the ignorant are easily aroused to lynch and abuse any black man. To praise this intricate whirl of thought and prejudice is nonsense; to inveigh indiscriminately against "the South" is unjust; but to use the same breath in praising Governor Aycock, exposing Senator Morgan, arguing with Mr. Thomas Nelson Page, and denouncing

17. **Governor Aycock . . . Ben Tillman.** *Charles Brantley Aycock*— (1859–1905) governor of North Carolina; *Edwin Denison Morgan*— governor of New York (1859–1863) and U.S. senator; *Thomas Nelson Page*—(1853–1922) novelist who glamorized the Southern plantation; *Benjamin Ryan Tillman*—(1847–1918) U.S. senator who presented the views of Southern extremists

In his failure to realize and impress this last point, Mr. Washington is especially to be criticized. His doctrine has tended to make the whites, North and South, shift the burden of the Negro problem to the Negro's shoulders and stand aside as critical and rather pessimistic spectators; when in fact the burden belongs to the nation, and the hands of none of us are clean if we bend not our energies to righting these great wrongs.

The South ought to be led, by candid and honest criticism, to assert her better self and do her full duty to the race she has cruelly wronged and is still wronging. The North—her co-partner in guilt—cannot salve her conscience by plastering it with gold. We cannot settle this problem by diplomacy and suaveness, by "policy" alone. If worse come to worst, can the moral fiber of this country survive the slow throttling and murder of nine millions of men?

The black men of America have a duty to perform, a duty stern and delicate,—a forward movement to oppose a part of the work of their greatest leader. So far as Mr. Washington preaches Thrift, Patience, and Industrial Training for the masses, we must hold up his hands and strive with him, rejoicing in his honors and glorifying in the strength of this Joshua called of God and of man to lead the headless host. But so far as Mr. Washington apologizes for injustice, North or South, does not rightly value the privilege and duty of voting, belittles the emasculating effects of caste distinctions, and opposes the higher training and ambition of our brighter minds,—so far as he, the South or the Nation, does this,—we must unceasingly and firmly oppose them. By every civilized and peaceful method we must strive for the rights which the world accords to men, clinging unwaveringly to those great words which the sons of the Fathers would fain forget: "We hold these truths to be self-evident: That all men are created equal; that they are endowed by their Creator with certain inalienable rights; that among these are life, liberty, and the pursuit of happiness." ❖

MIRRORS & WINDOWS

Du Bois writes that "the hushing of the criticism of honest opponents is a dangerous thing." When have you spoken out against a popular opinion? How were your ideas received?

Refer and Reason

1. What does Du Bois claim is the "soul of democracy"? Describe how he uses this definition of democracy to support his criticism of Booker T. Washington.

2. According to Du Bois, what three things is Washington asking African Americans to give up? Does his criticism of Washington seem well founded? Explain.

3. What has Washington contributed to U.S. society? Why were his teachings considered by many to be advantageous to African Americans? Explain how, in this case, something positive can become negative if not correctly used.

Writing Options

1. Choose a topic of public concern, large or small, and write a brief article in opposition of popular opinion. Try to emulate Du Bois's polite, rational rhetoric.

2. Du Bois invokes the words of the Declaration of Independence at the end of this essay. Write a paragraph about the relevance and appropriateness of this reference.

 Go to **www.mirrorsandwindows.com** for more.

Booker T. *and* W. E. B.

Dudley Randall (1914–2000) had his first poem published at the age of thirteen in the *Detroit Free Press*. After serving in the military during World War II, Randall earned degrees in both English and library science, which led to his becoming a librarian and poet-in-residence at the University of Detroit. In 1965, Randall established Broadside Press, an independent publisher that helped launch the careers of many African-American writers. Randall's poem **"Booker T. and W. E. B."** is his summary, in dialogue form, of the philosophical and political differences between Booker T. Washington and W. E. B. Du Bois, two prominent African-American leaders of the late nineteenth and early twentieth centuries. The poem appeared in the first collection printed by Broadside, *Poem Counterpoem* (1966). In 1981, the mayor of Detroit named Randall poet laureate of the city.

by Dudley Randall

"It seems to me," said Booker T.,
"It shows a mighty lot of cheek
To study chemistry and Greek
When Mister Charlie needs a hand
5   To hoe the cotton on his land,
And when Miss Ann looks for a cook,
Why stick our nose inside a book?"

"I don't agree," said W. E. B.
"If I should have the drive to seek
10   Knowledge of chemistry or Greek,
I'll do it. Charles and Miss can look
Another place for hand or cook.
Some men rejoice in skill of hand,
And some in cultivating land,
15   But there are others who maintain
The right to cultivate the brain."

"It seems to me," said Booker T.,
"That all you folks have missed the boat
Who shout about the right to vote,
20   And spend vain days and sleepless nights
In uproar over civil rights.
Just keep your mouths shut, do not grouse,
But work, and save, and buy a house."

"I don't agree," said W. E. B.,
25 "For what can property avail
If dignity and justice fail?
Unless you help to make the laws,
They'll steal your house with trumped-up clause,
A rope's as tight, a fire as hot,
30 No matter how much cash you've got.
Speak soft, and try your little plan,
But as for me, I'll be a man."

"It seems to me," said Booker T.—

"I don't agree,"
35 Said W. E. B. ❖

Bronze plaque of Du Bois and Washington.
Hampton Memorial Chapel, Hampton University, Virginia.

Do you agree with the position of Booker T. Washington or W. E. B. DuBois?
Do you tend to be complacent and accept what you get in life, or do you
always want more?

Refer and Reason

1. Which activities does Booker T. encourage in this poem? Which does he criticize? According to the poem, why would an African-American leader hold such opinions?

2. Why does W. E. B. say property is not enough? Why does he think it is more manly to "cultivate the brain" than merely do physical tasks? Do you agree or disagree? Why?

3. Analyze the last two short stanzas. Identify what they suggest about the argument between the two men.

Writing Options

1. Write a brief, humorous summary of a disagreement between two people, either people you know personally or people in the news.

2. Write a one-paragraph paraphrase of the argument between Booker T. Washington and W. E. B. Du Bois, based on the content of this poem. Try to present each side of the argument equally.

 Go to **www.mirrorsandwindows.com** for more.

Adventures of Huckleberry Finn
by Mark Twain

Adventures of Huckleberry Finn, considered by some literary scholars to be the greatest American novel, chronicles the journey of a young boy, Huck, and a runaway slave, Jim, as they travel down the Mississippi River. Along the way, Huck learns important lessons about race, friendship, betrayal, and honesty. (EMC Access Edition)

Touch the Earth: A Self-Portrait of Indian Existence **compiled by T. C. McLuhan**

In this compilation of excerpts from speeches and writings spanning five centuries, Native Americans speak in their own voices, offering their ideas to white society with courtesy, mystification, anger, and finally desperation. Accompanied by archival photos, the selections include the words of familiar leaders such as Seattle, Tecumseh, and Joseph as well as lesser-known chiefs.

The Jungle **by Upton Sinclair**

Crime, corruption, poverty, and danger characterize the lives of Lithuanian immigrants working in Chicago's meat-packing industry at the turn of the twentieth century. Sinclair's graphic description of this industry launched a government investigation of the meat-packing industry and led to passage of legislation to ensure the quality of U.S. food products.

Sister Carrie **by Theodore Dreiser**

Caroline Meeber is a pretty country girl who moves to the big city and becomes involves first with a traveling salesman and then a saloon manager. She is used by men and uses them in return, ending up a glamorous Broadway actress. Dreiser's unsentimental account is considered a masterpiece of Naturalism. (EMC Access Edition)

Failure Is Impossible: Susan B. Anthony in Her Own Words
by Lynn Sherr

Although Anthony is best known for her fifty-year campaign for women's suffrage, she also fought for abolition, temperance, and an end to domestic violence. Journalist Sherr has paired selections from Anthony's speeches, letters, interviews, and writings with contemporary news reports and biographical essays to present an engaging portrait of one of America's earliest civil rights activists.

Reconstruction: America's Unfinished Revolution, 1863–1877
by Eric Foner

In this treatise on the period following the Civil War, Foner provides a detailed perspective on a nation's desperate but failed attempt to mend itself after its most violent conflict. Foner's revisionist approach dissolves old myths about Reconstruction using the testimony of ordinary people.

Speaking and listening is a two-way activity. When the audience pays attention, the speaker gains confidence, knowing that his or her message is being received and appreciated. At the same time, alert listeners obtain information, hear an amusing or interesting story, or otherwise benefit from the speaker's presentation.

1. Become an Active Listener

Active listeners pay attention to the speaker and to what is being said. They are respectful of the speaker and eager to be informed or entertained. In contrast, *passive listeners* "tune out" the presentation and may even display rudeness by not paying attention to the speaker.

Here are ways in which you can become an active listener:

- Listen with a purpose—for instance, to gain useful information or to hear a suspenseful story narrated well. Stay focused on what the speaker is saying, and avoid letting your attention wander.
- Be courteous. Keep in mind that the speaker probably spent time preparing for the presentation and thus deserves your respect. Also consider that when it's your turn to speak, you will expect your listeners to be polite.
- If the speaker is providing information, take brief notes on the main ideas. Doing so will help you understand and remember what is being said. If you have questions or would like to hear more about a particular point, ask the speaker for clarification in the question-and-answer session after the presentation.

2. Practice Active-Listening Skills in Conversation

Most people have had the experience of being in a one-way conversation, in which one person does all the talking and the others just listen. In fact, this is not a conversation, which is by definition an exchange of information and ideas. In a true conversation, everyone has the chance to be heard.

Here are some things you can do to sharpen your active-listening skills in conversation:

- Do not monopolize the conversation. Give the other person (or persons) an opportunity to talk.

- Pay attention when others are speaking. Show your interest in what is being said by making eye contact and asking questions.
- Avoid interrupting. When you interrupt someone, you not only show your disinterest in what he or she is saying, but you also suggest that what you have to say is more important.

3. Use Role-Playing to Develop Active-Listening Skills

Sharpen your active-listening skills by taking part in a role-playing activity with classmates:

- *Speaker presentations:* One student can role-play a person giving a speech, reciting a literary work, or making a presentation. The rest of the group can be audience members, either active or passive listeners. After the role-playing, group members can discuss what they learned from the activity.
- *Conversations:* Group members can conduct conversations between two or more people. Students can take turns role-playing polite, respectful speakers and rude, conversation-hogging talkers. After the activity, group members can discuss what the activity taught them.

SPEAKING & LISTENING RUBRIC

Your active-listening skills will be evaluated on these elements:

Preparation

- ❏ You can explain the differences between active listening and passive listening.
- ❏ You can explain how both the speaker and audience benefit when listeners are respectful and attentive.

Participation

- ❏ While listening to a presentation, you focus on what the speaker has to say.
- ❏ While taking part in a conversation, you show interest in what the other person says, avoid interrupting, and ask questions as appropriate.

While most of us will never face the hardships experienced by the authors in this unit—recovering from slavery like Booker T. Washington or fighting to keep a country together like Abraham Lincoln—even the most seemingly ordinary person has a story to tell. Often, we assume we know someone, but we really have no idea how fascinating his or her life is until we stop to ask.

For this assignment, you will create a profile using a combination of narration, biography, and oral history. A *profile* is not meant to tell someone's life story but rather to focus on one aspect of it. How do you want this person to come across to readers?

> **Assignment** Plan, write, and revise a profile
>
> **Purpose** To introduce one aspect of a person
>
> **Audience** An acquaintance of the subject

❶ Prewrite

Select Your Topic
Since everyone has a story, anyone can be the subject of a profile. Create a list of people you would like to know better. Choose whomever you think will be most willing to answer your questions.

Gather Information
To write a profile, you will need to interview your subject. Produce a list of questions you would like him or her to answer, but also be attuned to opportunities during the interview to ask more questions about topics you had not thought of earlier. Take good notes. You may need to quote your subject in the profile.

Organize Your Ideas
Review your notes. Have you taken down all of the essential details? Do you have enough information to produce an accurate, absorbing account?

> **WRITING RUBRIC**
>
> A successful profile has these elements:
> - ❑ an introduction that presents the person in an intriguing way
> - ❑ a body that develops a detailed account of one aspect of the person's life
> - ❑ a conclusion that gives the account closure

Since this piece is about someone's life, organizing the information using either a **narrative structure** (organized like a story, with an introduction, building action, climax, and resolution) or a **chronological structure** (sequenced according to time) will probably work best. However, you should reveal the details in whatever way will maintain readers' interest.

Write Your Organizing Statement
This sentence will not appear in your profile but will instead help you focus your piece. What is the overall message you want to portray about your subject?

> *What Great Writers Do*
>
> For readers to become invested in your piece, you need to make your person's story appealing. As H. L. Mencken, an early-twentieth-century journalist, remarked, "There are no dull subjects, . . . only dull writers."
>
>
> MENCKEN

❷ Draft

Write your essay by following this three-part framework: introduction, body, and conclusion.

> **Introduction** Invoke readers' curiosity from the very first sentence.
>
> **Body** Continue creating interest by using concrete details and effective storytelling.
>
> **Conclusion** Leave readers satisfied by offering closure.

Draft Your Introduction
The introduction of a profile presents your subject in a compelling way, perhaps by starting in the middle of your subject's story at a tense moment. Doing so will grab readers' attention from the start.

Draft Your Body
In the body, keep drawing in your readers by slowly revealing your subject's story. This is the information you mapped out in the Prewrite stage.

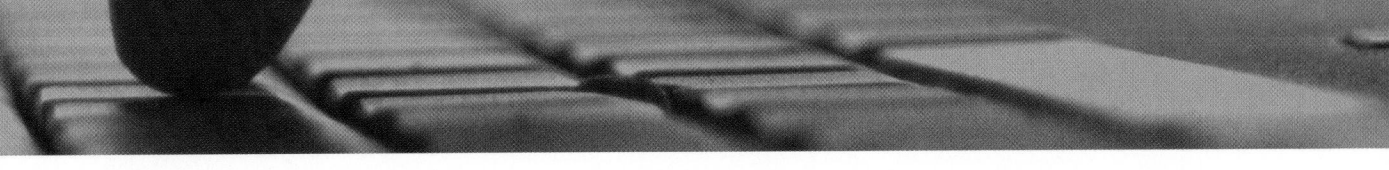

Review your notes and the order in which you planned to present the information. Develop each paragraph by sequencing details in a storylike fashion. Each detail should tie into the overall message you are trying to depict, as proposed in your organizing statement.

Draft Your Conclusion

Finally, write the conclusion for your profile. The conclusion should gratify readers with a sense of completion and a fuller understanding of the person you profiled.

❸ Revise

Evaluate Your Draft

You can evaluate your own profile or exchange drafts with a classmate and evaluate each other's work. In either case, decide how successfully the profile presents the person to you. What works well, and what can be improved?

Start by looking at the content and organization. Make sure the introduction, body, and conclusion work together to present the message about your subject from your organizing statement. Every paragraph should relate clearly to it, and every paragraph should flow into the next. Use the Revision Checklist below to help you evaluate. Make notes directly on the essay about what changes need to be made.

Also consider the pace at which you present details about your subject. Pacing is especially important when writing a narrative-type piece. Follow the advice of post-Romantic composer Gustav Mahler, who said, "If you think you're boring your audience, go slower not faster."

Next, check each sentence for mistakes. Make sure you have correctly used the concepts outlined in the Grammar & Style workshops in this unit. Again, use the Revision Checklist to assess the writing. Fine-tune the language, checking for clarity and specificity.

Revise for Content, Organization, and Style

Read the comments you and your partner made on your draft, and make the changes needed to improve your writing.

Proofread for Errors

Now look for remaining mistakes, using proofreader's symbols to mark any you find. To complete the assignment, print out a final draft and read it aloud before turning it in. This will help you slow down to catch things you might not normally see.

Writing Follow-Up

Publish and Present

- Readers often interpret pieces differently. Read your profile to your classmates, and see if they can infer your organizing statement. What might have caused their differing views?
- Submit your profile for publication in a "community interest" section of a newspaper or journal.

Reflect

- How would the subject of your profile likely feel about how you described him or her? Explain. Think about reversing roles. Would you rather be the observer or the observed? Why?

REVISION CHECKLIST

Content & Organization

- ❏ Is the introduction engaging, making readers want to read on?
- ❏ Does the body effectively imply the message stated in your organizing statement, each paragraph working with the next to create a full story?
- ❏ Does the conclusion leave readers feeling as though they know your subject?

Grammar & Style

- ❏ Are all irregular verbs formed correctly? (page 392)
- ❏ Do you properly use modifiers (adjectives and adverbs)? (page 413)
- ❏ Do your phrases (gerund, infinitive, and participial) receive proper verb treatment? (page 487)

Reading Skills

Identify Motifs

A **motif** is a recurring element that has symbolic significance in one or more works of literature. A motif can be an object, location, formula, situation, statement, structure, or literary device. It also can be two contrasting items or concepts, such as good and evil.

The term *motif* often is confused with *theme* and *symbol*. A *theme* is an abstract idea or paraphrase of the main idea or concept of a work, whereas a *motif* is a representation of that idea or concept. Motifs help the author to develop the theme and the reader to recognize it. A *symbol* is a person, place, thing, pattern, or event that represents something else.

In the fiction of Mark Twain, for example, one of the primary themes is the corrupting influence of civilization on human beings. In his "boys books" *Tom Sawyer* and *Huck Finn,* Twain develops that theme, in part, by using the motif of childhood. Childhood represents a pure, natural state—one characterized by innocence, honesty, and freedom. That state can be maintained only by rejecting the institutions of the civilized world, such as school, church, family, and government. The boyhood pranks and adventures of Tom and Huck represent attempts to remain free from the trappings of civilization.

In reading a literary work, it is important to be able to identify motifs because they help reveal the work's main points and themes. Understanding these elements will better equip you to interpret the work correctly.

> **TEST-TAKING TIP**
>
> When taking a multiple-choice test, beware of *distractors:* answer options that are partially correct and thus seem reasonable. For instance, a distractor might present a commonly misunderstood idea or apply the right information in the wrong way. Read each answer option carefully before making your choice. Don't be in such a hurry that you will be fooled by distractors.

Practice

Directions: Read the following passage. The questions that come after it will ask you to identify the motif.

PROSE FICTION: This passage is an excerpt from Sarah Orne Jewett's short story "A White Heron."

1   All night the door of the little house
stood open and the whippoorwills came
and sang upon the very step. The young
sportsman and his old hostess were sound
5   asleep, but Sylvia's great design kept her
broad awake and watching. She forgot
to think of sleep. The short summer
night seemed as long as the winter darkness, and at last when the whippoorwills
10   ceased, and she was afraid the morning
would after all come too soon, she stole
out of the house and followed the pasture
path through the woods, hastening toward
the open ground beyond, listening with
15   a sense of comfort and companionship to
the drowsy twitter of a half-awakened bird,
whose perch she had jarred in passing. Alas,
if the great wave of human interest which
flooded for the first time this dull little life
20   should sweep away the satisfactions of an
existence heart to heart with nature and the
dumb life of the forest! . . .

She crept out along the swaying oak
limb at last, and took the daring step across
25   into the old pine tree. The way was harder
than she thought; she must reach far and
hold fast, the sharp dry twigs caught and
held her and scratched her like angry talons,
the pitch made her thin little fingers clumsy
30   and stiff as she went round and round the

tree's great stem, higher and higher upward. The sparrows and robins in the woods below were beginning to wake and twitter to the dawn, yet it seemed much lighter there 35 aloft in the pine tree, and the child knew that she must hurry if her project were to be of any use. . . .

Sylvia's face was like a pale star, if one had seen it from the ground, when the last 40 thorny bough was past, and she stood trembling and tired but wholly triumphant, high in the treetop. Yes, there was the sea with the dawning sun making a golden dazzle over it, and toward that glorious east flew 45 two hawks with slow-moving pinions. How low they looked in the air from that height when one had only seen them before far up, and dark against the blue sky. Their gray

feathers were as soft as moths; they seemed 50 only a little way from the tree, and Sylvia felt as if she too could go flying away among the clouds. Westward, the woodlands and farms reached miles and miles into the distance; here and there were church steeples, 55 and white villages; truly it was a vast and awesome world!

The birds sang louder and louder. At last the sun came up bewilderingly bright. Sylvia could see the white sails of ships out 60 at sea, and the clouds that were purple and rose-colored and yellow at first began to fade away. Where was the white heron's nest in the sea of green branches, and was this wonderful sight and pageant of the world 65 the only reward for having climbed to such a giddy height?

Multiple Choice

1. What motif is repeated through this story?
   A. the white heron
   B. trees
   C. birds
   D. the innocence of children
   E. the cruelty of adults

2. The central motif of this story suggests
   A. that people and nature are connected.
   B. that Sylvia is good and innocent.
   C. that nature is cruel.
   D. that money can't buy happiness.
   E. that it pays to have big dreams.

3. The archetypal pine (see line 25) is an image of
   A. loneliness, just like the white heron and Sylvia.
   B. lofty dreams.
   C. the universal pillar, which connects heaven and earth.
   D. fauna and how it is different from flora.
   E. the vastness of night.

4. The importance of the character Sylvia to the motif is most apparent in which of the following?
   A. Sylvia's great design kept her broad awake. (lines 5–6)
   B. She crept out along the swaying oak limb at last. (lines 23–24)
   C. She must hurry if her project were to be of any use. (lines 36–37)
   D. Sylvia's face was like a pale star. (line 38)
   E. Sylvia felt as if she too could go flying away. (lines 50–51)

Constructed Response

5. Describe how seeing things through Sylvia's eyes contributes to the effectiveness of the motif.

Writing Skills

Write a Good Introduction

Once you have outlined your essay, you will be ready to begin writing. Provide an effective opening to your essay by writing a good introduction. The purposes of the introduction are to introduce your subject in an engaging way and to establish your thesis.

An effective introduction hooks the reader and makes him or her want to keep reading. When writing an essay for a standardized test, you won't have the opportunity to look for a quotation or interesting fact to use in your opener, like you would in writing a conventional essay. Instead, try to introduce your subject in an engaging way that is appropriate for your audience. You might ask a question or relate the subject to the reader in some relevant way.

The second purpose of an introduction is to state your thesis. In a persuasive essay, providing a clear thesis statement is even more important than getting your reader's attention. Your thesis statement should comprise a single sentence that summarizes your answer to the essay prompt. It should be specific, clear, and matter of fact yet strong. Your thesis statement should make a claim or assertion about the topic, which you will prove with supportive evidence in the rest of the essay.

In most cases, the introductory paragraph of an essay also should indicate the general organization of the essay, or the order in which you will present the evidence. A statement that identifies the three or so supporting points often follows the thesis. In a short essay, however, this preview sometimes can be eliminated.

TEST-TAKING TIP

When writing an essay in a testing situation, you will have to streamline some of your normal writing practices. Focus on these basic guidelines:

- Connect with the audience.
- Use language precisely.
- Develop ideas sufficiently.
- Provide appropriate evidence.
- Organize information effectively.

Use these points as a mental checklist when reviewing and revising your essay.

Practice

Timed Writing: 25 minutes

Think carefully about the issue presented in the following excerpt and assignment below. Allow twenty-five minutes to write your response to the prompt.

You probably have heard the saying "Honesty is the best policy." Is that true? Some people believe that lying always is wrong, no matter what the situation. Others believe that, in some circumstances, it's acceptable and even appropriate not to tell the entire truth.

Assignment: Is honesty always the best policy? Plan and write an essay in which you develop your perspective on this issue. Support your position with reasoning and examples from your reading, studies, experience, or observations.

Revising and Editing Skills

As part of the writing section, some standardized tests ask you to identify sentence errors. These errors deal with grammar, usage, word choice, idiom, and mechanics. Being able to identify and correct mistakes in what you have written is essential to writing well. Examples of common errors you should watch for include the following:

- incorrect spellings and capitalization
- dangling participles

- disagreement between subject and verb
- inconsistent verb tense
- incorrect forms of irregular verbs
- incorrect use of frequently confused words, such as *between* and *among*
- double negatives
- adjective/adverb confusion
- incorrect or missing punctuation

Practice

Directions: Each of the following numbered items consists of a sentence, part or all of which is underlined. Beneath each sentence are five restatements of the underlined material. Choice A repeats the underlined portion of the original sentence. Choices B through E are different ways to reword the underlined text. If the original phrasing is better than any of the alternatives, then select A. If not, circle the choice that provides the best alternative.

Multiple Choice

1. Having finished dessert, Tyler's dog coaxed him for a doggy treat.
   A. Having finished dessert, Tyler's
   B. Having had finished dessert, Tyler's
   C. After finishing dessert, Tyler's
   D. After Tyler had finished dessert, his
   E. Being finished with his dessert, Tyler's

2. Bicycling is preferable to driving because it's good exercise, doesn't contribute to air pollution, and it uses no gas.
   A. doesn't contribute to air pollution, and it uses no gas.
   B. contributes nothing to air pollution, and it uses no gas.
   C. does not contribute to air pollution, and uses no gas.
   D. does not contribute to air pollution, and using no gas.
   E. does not contribute to air pollution, and no gas is used.

3. The large number of items available at convenience stores have resulted in their increased popularity.
   A. have resulted in their
   B. having resulted in their
   C. have resulted in its
   D. has resulted in their
   E. have resulted in it's

4. *The Catcher in the Rye,* which is my favorite book, having been written by J. D. Salinger.
   A. book, having been written
   B. book, was written
   C. book, it was written
   D. book, being written
   E. book, it having been written

I Shall Be Expelled from School, c. 1916–1935. Charles Demuth.
Barnes Foundation, Merion Station, Pennsylvania.

Early Twentieth Century

Unit 5

1910–1929

1910

1915

AMERICAN LITERATURE AMERICAN LITERATURE AMERICAN LITERATURE AME

1911
Tennessee Williams is born

1911
Joseph Pulitzer dies, leaving funds to endow awards for journalistic and literary excellence

1911
Edith Wharton publishes *Ethan Frome*

1912
Western novelist Zane Grey publishes *Riders of the Purple Sage*

1913
Robert Frost publishes *A Boy's Will*

1914
The first issue of *The New Republic* is released

1915
Booker T. Washington dies

1916
Carter Godwin Woodson founds *The Journal of Negro History*

1916
Carl Sandburg publishes *Chicago Poems*

1917
The first Pulitzer Prizes are awarded

1917
T. S. Eliot publishes *Prufrock and Other Observations*

1918
Willa Cather publishes *My Antonia*

1919
Sherwood Anderson publishes *Winesburg, Ohio*

WHARTON

AMERICAN HISTORY AMERICAN HISTORY AMERICAN HISTORY AMERICAN HIST

1911
The U.S. Supreme Court declares Standard Oil a monopoly and orders John Rockefeller to dissolve the corporation

1912
The *Titanic* strikes an iceberg and sinks, killing 1,500

1914
Ford's Model T dominates the automobile market, selling more than all other models combined

1916
Jeannette Rankin becomes the first woman elected to Congress

1916
The Punitive Expedition sends 12,000 American troops into Mexico to find Pancho Villa

1917
The first Red Scare begins, creating hysteria over the potential spread of communism

1917
The United States enters World War I

1918
The Sedition Act is passed, making it illegal to speak against the government

1919
The Chicago White Sox intentionally lose the World Series, resulting in the "Black Sox" scandal

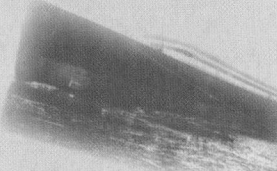

WORLD HISTORY WORLD HISTORY WORLD HISTORY WORLD HISTORY WORLD

1910
The Union of South Africa is formed

1911
The Xinhai Revolution establishes the Republic of China

1913
Mohandas Gandhi is arrested for leading a march of Indian miners in South Africa

1914
Archduke Ferdinand of Austria is assassinated, leading to World War I

1917
Vladimir Lenin leads the Bolsheviks in the Russian revolution

1915
Albert Einstein presents his general theory of relativity

1918
A ceasefire is reached on the Western Front, ending World War I

1918
A worldwide flu epidemic strikes; 20 million die in two years

1919
Mahatma Gandhi initiates his campaign of nonviolent resistance against British rule in India

LENIN

1920   # 1925

LEWIS

1920
Sinclair Lewis publishes
Main Street

1920
Frederick Jackson Turner
completes his *Frontier Thesis*

1921
Edith Wharton wins the
Pulitzer Prize for *The Age
of Innocence*

1923
Edna St. Vincent Millay wins
the Pulitzer Prize in poetry,
the first woman recipient

1924
Mark Twain publishes his
autobiography

1924
Jean Toomer publishes *Cane*

1925
Countee Cullen publishes his
first volume of poetry, *Colors*

1925
F. Scott Fitzgerald publishes
The Great Gatsby

1926
Ernest Hemingway writes
The Sun Also Rises

1927
Random House publishing is
founded in New York City

1928
Claude McKay publishes
Home to Harlem

1929
Thomas Wolfe publishes
Look Homeward, Angel

WOLFE

1920
The Eighteenth Amendment
prohibits the sale and
manufacturing of alcoholic
beverages

1920
Congress ratifies the
Nineteenth Amendment,
granting women the right
to vote

1921
The Tomb of the Unknown
Soldier is built in Arlington
National Cemetery

1923
President Warren G. Harding
dies while in office; Calvin
Coolidge takes office

1924
J. Edgar Hoover is appointed
head of the Federal Bureau
of Investigation (FBI)

1925
The Scopes Monkey Trial
takes place after a teacher
is arrested for teaching
evolution in a Tennessee
school

1927
Charles Lindbergh completes
the first trans-Atlantic flight

1928
Amelia Earhart becomes the
first woman to complete a
trans-Atlantic flight

1929
The stock market
plunges, leading
to the Great
Depression

1921
Adolf Hitler becomes
chairman of the Nazi Party

1922
Howard Carter discovers the
tomb of Tutankhamun
in Egypt

1922
Benito Mussolini becomes
prime minister of Italy

1923
Pancho Villa is assassinated
in Parral, Chihuahua

1923
A massive earthquake
destroys one-third of Tokyo,
Japan, killing an estimated
140,000

1924
Vladimir Lenin dies

1925
George Bernard Shaw wins
the Nobel Prize for literature

1926
Hirohito becomes emperor
of Japan

1927
Werner Heisenberg
formulates his uncertainty
principle

1928
Alexander Fleming discovers
penicillin

1928
Josef Stalin assumes
complete control over
the Soviet government

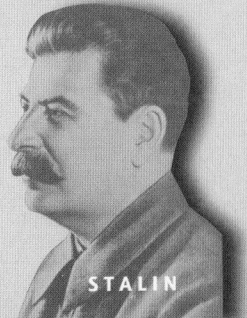

STALIN

"You are all a lost generation."

—GERTRUDE STEIN

The Progressive Era

After the abuses of the Gilded Age were exposed at the end of the nineteenth century, reformers sought new controls. The work of journalist Lincoln Steffens and photographer Jacob Riis led to urban reforms, such as turning over control of local governments to boards of commissioners. Congress passed meat, food, and drug inspection acts in response to articles written by muckraking journalist Upton Sinclair. An exposé of oil industry practices by Ida Tarbell led to stiffer controls over big business.

To give citizens more control over government, many states passed primary election, initiative, referendum, and recall statutes. Some states went further, passing laws regulating wages, hours, and factory safety. Congress established the Federal Trade Commission to investigate unfair trade practices, the Interstate Commerce Commission to regulate the telephone and telegraph system, and the Federal Reserve System to oversee the nation's money and banking system. Also ratified were the Sixteenth Amendment, creating a graduated income tax, and the Seventeenth Amendment, providing for direct election of senators, rather than selection by state legislatures.

> "The cost of liberty is less than the price of repression."
>
> —W. E. B. DU BOIS

To create an organized voice for African-American civil rights, constricted since the end of Reconstruction through Jim Crow segregation laws, W. E. B. Du Bois and other leaders founded the National Association for the Advancement of Colored People (NAACP) in 1909. Although women had begun calling for the right to vote since the Seneca Falls Convention in 1848, it wasn't until 1910 that suffragists saw their first victory, when Wyoming gave women the vote. The Nineteenth Amendment was ratified in 1920, giving voting rights to all women.

Industrial Ferment

After the financial collapse of 1907, profits were not as high as business leaders had hoped, so new cost-cutting measures were implemented. Among them was *Taylorism,* wherein each job in a mill was closely analyzed and then a system put in place that increased mechanization and the division of labor and based wages on piecework completed.

The system operated well in the auto and steel industries but not in the textile mills, where strikes resulted. Then came the infamous Triangle Shirtwaist Company fire in New York in 1911, in which 146 women were burned or crushed to death as they jumped out windows, unable to exit from the locked doors in the factory's upper floors.

Although the reforms of the Progressive Era benefited many ordinary citizens, conditions did not improve much for factory workers, tenant farmers, and miners—thus, the continued labor agitation. Especially threatening to business was the rise of the International Workers of the World, nicknamed *Wobblies,* which attempted to build a working-class movement,

NOTABLE NUMBERS

- **44** Families making $1 million or more in 1914
- **19 million** Combatants that died on World War I battlefields, 117,000 of them Americans; another 20 million died from hunger and disease related to the war
- **$10 billion** Amount owed by the Allies to the United States in 1920, after the war
- **4 million** Employees who took part in 4,000 strikes in 1919
- **4.5 million** Members of the Ku Klux Klan in 1924
- **3 million** Americans with money in the stock market when it crashed in 1929

and the organizing of such leaders as Mother Mary Jones of the United Mine Workers and Eugene Debs of the Socialist Party.

The First World War

The causes of World War I can be summarized in a series of *-isms: imperialism, nationalism,* and *militarism.* Defense agreements, negotiated by European powers to protect their interests, were triggered by the assassination of the heir to the throne of the Austrian-Hungarian Empire in 1914. Since no international organization was in place to mediate, war erupted. The United States was neutral, mired in the depression of 1914. Soon, however, British orders for war equipment, totaling $2 billion by 1917, and loans stimulated the economy and tied the United States to an Allied victory.

When the war became a stalemate, with neither side making progress on the battlefield, the Germans began using deadly mustard gas and the British established a naval blockade of German trade with neutral countries. The Germans responded by ordering their submarines to target American ships carrying materials to the Allies, prompting the U.S. Congress to declare war. To provide troops for the conflict, Congress passed the Selective Service Act, which proved very unpopular. Also widely criticized was the Espionage Act, which forbade speaking and writing against the war.

The United States' entry to the war came just as Russia was withdrawing after the Bolshevik Revolution and gave the Allies the reinforcements needed for victory. Major battles involving American troops were Chateau Thierry, Belleau Wood, and the Meuse-Argonne campaign.

By the war's end, the carnage of trench warfare, mustard gas, and modern armaments had shocked the world, and many leaders called for an organization that would mediate future international disputes. Consequently, the Versailles Peace Treaty created the League of Nations but also imposed severe economic hardships on Germany that would eventually lead to World War II. Meanwhile, President Woodrow Wilson was unable to persuade Congress to join the League, crippling its effectiveness.

The Twenties

After the horrors of World War I, Americans became increasingly isolationist. Although labor unions went on strike in a number of industries, they won few concessions. With the rise of Bolshevism in Russia, Americans grew worried about internal communist

Triangle Shirtwaist Company fire (1911).

"It was borrowed time anyway—the whole upper tenth of a nation living with the insouciance of a grand duc and the casualness of chorus girls."

—F. SCOTT FITZGERALD

people from western Europe. As the so-called Red Scare spread, anyone with radical ideas became suspect. In this environment, four thousand aliens were deported in 1920 and two radical Italian workers, Sacco and Vanzetti, were executed after a notorious trial deemed unfair fifty years later.

During the decade, many of the hard-won Progressive Era reforms were weakened, as government increasingly sided with industry. President Warren G. Harding's administration was plagued with graft and bribery. During President Calvin Coolidge's two terms, business boomed, as the wages of skilled workers rose and they purchased cars and appliances. For farmers and miners, however, economic conditions worsened. Race riots became increasingly common in northern cities, and thousands joined the Ku Klux Klan.

The passage of the Eighteenth Amendment initiated the Prohibition Era, in which the production and sale of liquor was illegal. The alcohol was kept flowing in establishments known as "speakeasies" and "blind pigs." Soon, criminals took over the liquor business, among them Al Capone. (Prohibition was revoked in 1933 with passage of the Twenty-First Amendment.)

Women had stepped in to do so-called men's work during the war and were not about to go back to their previous roles when the war ended. These modern young women were called "flappers" and did much to change gender roles. They cut their hair, wore short dresses, frequented speakeasies, and danced the Charleston and Black Bottom. Meanwhile, in Harlem, a vibrant African-American culture was developing under the leadership of political activists, writers, and musicians. It became known as the *Harlem Renaissance,* and jazz was its unique contribution to American culture.

People thought the Roaring Twenties would go on and on. However, the good times were fueled by the purchase of material goods, many of which were bought on time, rather than purchased outright. It

seemed everyone was also buying stock, often "on the margin" by paying only ten percent of the stock's face value and planning to pay the rest later.

Values climbed higher and higher—until September 3, 1929. Prices slipped and then slipped again and again, until what would become known as Black Thursday, October 24, 1929. Payments for stocks purchased on the margin became due. To get money, the margin purchasers had to sell their stock, no matter how little it was worth. Many Americans were wiped out completely. And so began the Great Depression.

1920s Era flappers.

odernism was an international literary and artistic movement that emerged in the early 1900s and flourished for about twenty years. **Modernists** rejected artistic conventions, preferring the *avant-garde:* experimental art forms that consciously broke with tradition. As such, Modernism was a response to the perceived breakdown of modern culture that followed World War I.

Disillusioned with the culture and values of the United States that emerged after the war, many American writers went to Europe, settling in the cosmopolitan cities of Paris and London. Chief among these *expatriates* were novelists F. Scott Fitzgerald, Ernest Hemingway, Sherwood Anderson, and John Dos Passos and poets Ezra Pound, T. S. Eliot, Gertrude Stein, Amy Lowell, and Hilda Doolittle. Stein labeled this group of writers "the Lost Generation" because of their sense of dislocation and alienation from American culture.

Lost Generation novelists made significant contributions to the Modern Era of American literature. They deviated from styles of the past, which they considered rigid and unrealistic, and experimented with stream-of-consciousness prose and different narrative points of view. Their writing often was spare and impersonal, and it questioned traditional American values, such as achieving success through hard work and self-reliance.

Modernist poets reacted against the wordiness, sentimentality, and predictable rhythms of previous generations. They experimented with nontraditional forms, including free verse and Japanese haiku. They attempted to present concise images, or word pictures, and thus also referred to themselves as **Imagists.** Rather than moralize or express their own emotions and opinions, Modernist poets let readers derive their own interpretations.

Still Life with Radishes, 1944. Pablo Picasso.

The Novel Defined

A **novel** may be defined most simply as a long work of fiction with an involved plot, many characters, and numerous settings. Although the novel shares many features with the short story and the novella, it is a more extended form of narrative.

One of the first European novels was *Don Quijote de la Mancha,* published by Miguel de Cervantes between 1605 and 1615. However, the novel as an acknowledged literary form did not really flourish until the eighteenth century, when it became the focus of literary discussion and formal analysis. Novels of various kinds began to appear—some intended to teach a moral, others to shock and scandalize. By the nineteenth century, there was an established canon of fine European and American fiction.

The modern novel resembles its forebears in structure and scope but departs in significant ways. To begin, its author seldom intends to teach a moral or exalt sentiment over intellect. An experimentalist, the modern novelist manipulates form, point of view, and narrative technique, sometimes emulating the modern filmmaker.

> *"There is no rule on how to write. Sometimes it comes easily and perfectly; sometimes it's like drilling rock and then blasting it out with charges."*
>
> —ERNEST HEMINGWAY, AMERICAN NOVELIST

Elements of the Novel

A long prose work usually is divided into chapters and sometimes into parts. Notice how the structure of the novel supports the development of plot, characterization, and other elements of fiction.

Plot

A **plot** is a series of events related to a central **conflict,** or struggle. A plot typically introduces a conflict, develops it, and eventually resolves it. The **exposition,** or introduction, sets the tone or mood, introduces the characters and setting, and provides necessary background information. In the **rising action,** the conflict is developed and intensified. The **climax** is the high point of interest or suspense. The **falling action** consists of all the events that follow the climax. The **resolution,** or *denouement* (dā′ nü män′), is the point at which the central conflict is ended, or resolved.

Elements of Plot

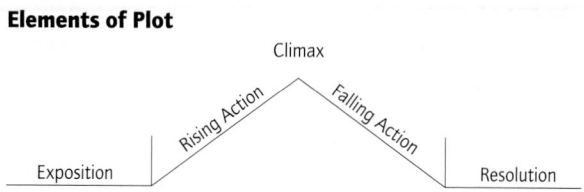

Setting and Mood

The **setting** is the time and place of the unfolding action together with all the details used to create a sense of a particular time and place. F. Scott Fitzgerald sets much of *The Great Gatsby* on the Long Island estate of the millionaire Jay Gatsby. The historical period is also significant. *Gatsby* takes place over the summer of 1922, in the era known as the Jazz Age.

The details that create the setting also establish a **mood,** or atmosphere, the emotion created in the reader by part or all of a literary work. In *Gatsby,* the details of the catered foods at the party—the two hundred oranges and masses of hams and turkeys—suggest a mood of opulence and extravagance.

Characterization

A **character** is an individual who takes part in the action of a literary work. The main character, or **protagonist,** is the most important character in the work and is in conflict with the **antagonist.**

Characterization is the act of creating or describing a character. In *direct characterization,* the writer *tells* what a character is like. In *Gatsby,* Jordan Baker's admirer is "a persistent undergraduate given to violent innuendo." *Indirect characterization* involves showing what characters say, do, or think; showing what other characters say or think about them; and describing what physical features, dress, and personality characters display.

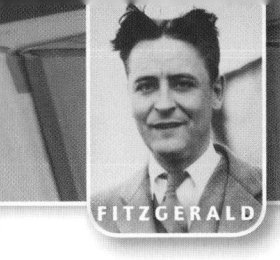

Ernest Hemingway frequently constructed fictional characters from people he knew, a habit that understandably caused ill feeling. Fitzgerald and Hemingway disagreed over the use of the *composite character,* one based on aspects of several real people.

Point of View

A **narrator** is a character or speaker who tells a story. **Point of view** is the vantage point, or perspective, from which the story is told—in other words, who is telling the story.

In *first-person point of view,* the story is told by someone who participates in or witnesses the action. A first-person narrator tends to be limited by what he or she can directly observe about other characters and situations. For example, Nick Carraway, who tells the story in *Gatsby,* does not really know his new friends or understand their past relationships with one other.

In *third-person point of view,* the narrator usually stands outside the action and observes. The perspective may be *limited,* revealing the thoughts of only the narrator or a single character, or *omniscient,* revealing the thoughts of all the characters. In the excerpt from Hemingway's *For Whom the Bell Tolls,* the voice of Robert Jordan takes over the narrative.

Tone

Tone is the emotional attitude toward the reader or toward the subject implied by a literary work. Consider the tone of this passage, which sums up the letter from home that Robert Jordan is reading in *For Whom the Bell Tolls:*

> There was quite a lot of religion in the letter and she prayed to Saint Anthony, to the Blessed Virgin of Pilar, and to other Virgins to protect him and she wanted him never to forget that he was also protected by the Sacred Heart of Jesus that he wore still, she trusted, at all times over his own heart where it had proven innumerable—this was underlined—times to have the power of stopping bullets.

The tone of mockery underscores the irony of the soldier's position: No one at home comprehends either the casual, inevitable brutality of war or the pervasive sense of death the soldier feels at all times.

Theme

A **theme** is a central message or perception about life revealed through a literary work. A *stated theme* is presented directly, whereas an *implied theme* must be inferred.

It usually is possible to find several major themes in a work of literature. Robert Jordan touches on a central theme of *For Whom the Bell Tolls* when he tells himself, "But you musn't believe in killing. . . . You must do it as a necessity but you must not believe in it. If you believe in it the whole thing is wrong."

HOW TO READ

The Novel

Identify the point of view. The author's choice of narrator, or point of view, determines how much and what kind of information readers will be given about the events and characters. Identify who is telling the story, and determine how his or her perspective may be limited or even biased.

Trace the sequence of events. As you read, trace the sequence of events, including the main plot and any subplots. In particular, identify the central conflict and trace its development to the climax. Predict how the conflict might be resolved to bring the story to a satisfying end.

Identify the theme. Without reducing the novel to a single moral or lesson, look for its central message. Think about what is suggested by how the conflict is resolved at the end of the story. Also consider the outcome of the story for the various characters, especially the protagonist.

from **The Great Gatsby**

A Novel by F. Scott Fitzgerald

Build Background

Literary Context When **The Great Gatsby** was published in 1925, author F. Scott Fitzgerald worried that the book's price of twenty-five cents would prevent people from buying it. In fact, the book was not a popular success in its day or for the remainder of Fitzgerald's life, selling fewer than 25,000 copies over the next fifteen years. It generally was praised by literary critics, however, and is today considered one of the greatest American novels.

The story is set in the 1920s, the Jazz Age, a phrase coined by Fitzgerald to capture the excitement and glamour of the time. Corruption and greed also marked the era, due largely to the illegal sale of liquor that thrived during Prohibition. Jay Gatsby, the novel's central character, seems to embody the American dream of the self-made man, but there are questions about his past. In this excerpt, the novel's narrator, Gatsby's neighbor on Long Island, describes attending one of Gatsby's lavish parties and meeting the host.

Reader's Context Think of a time you have gone to a party or other event where you didn't know the host or many of the guests. What was it like? Would you do it again? Why or why not?

Meet the Author

F. Scott Fitzgerald (1896–1940) was born in St. Paul, Minnesota, to an upper-middle-class family. After graduating from prep school in 1913, he attended Princeton, where he mingled with America's wealthy elite.

An average student, Fitzgerald left college after three years to join the army, hoping to see action in World War I. The war was soon over and Fitzgerald never went abroad; instead, he spent the next few years writing his first novel, *This Side of Paradise*. While stationed in Alabama, Fitzgerald also met the woman he would marry, Zelda Sayre.

After being discharged from the army, Fitzgerald went to New York to make his fortune. Publication of *This Side of Paradise* in 1920 brought him instant success. He married Zelda, and the two became known as madcap socialites. In 1921, the Fitzgeralds moved to France, where they joined a celebrated circle of American writers and artists. Over the next fifteen years, Fitzgerald published four short story collections and several more novels, including *The Great Gatsby* (1925) and *Tender Is the Night* (1934).

After 1930, Zelda was frequently hospitalized for schizophrenia. Fitzgerald moved to Hollywood in 1934 and turned to screenwriting. He died of a heart attack in 1940 at age forty-four.

Analyze Literature

Setting and Narrator

The **setting** of a literary work is the time and place in which it occurs, together with all the details used to create a sense of a particular time and place.

A **narrator** is a character or speaker who tells a story. It may be a major or a minor character or simply someone who has witnessed or heard about the events being related.

Set Purpose

As the man who coined the expression "the Jazz Age," Fitzgerald was especially qualified to write about 1920s American society. As you read this excerpt, record the details he provides to give readers a sense of the time and place. Also identify the narrator and determine his relationship to Gatsby. Consider why Fitzgerald chose this character to tell the story.

Preview Vocabulary

ravages, 529
innuendo, 530
prodigality, 530
erroneous, 530
contemptuous, 531
homogeneity, 532
cynical, 532
ascertain, 533
vacuous, 534
corpulent, 535

from

The Great Gatsby

by F. Scott Fitzgerald

People were not invited—they went there.

Chapter III

There was music from my neighbor's house through the summer nights. In his blue gardens men and girls came and went like moths among the whisperings and the champagne and the stars. At high tide in the afternoon I watched his guests diving from the tower of his raft or taking the sun on the hot sand of his beach while his two motor boats slit the waters of the Sound,[1] drawing aquaplanes over cataracts[2] of foam. On week-ends his Rolls-Royce became an omnibus,[3] bearing parties to and from the city, between nine in the morning and long past midnight, while his station wagon scampered like a brisk yellow bug to meet all trains. And on Mondays eight ser-vants including an extra gardener toiled all day with mops and scrubbing-brushes and ham-mers and garden shears, repairing the <u>ravages</u> of the night before.

Every Friday five crates of oranges and lem-ons arrived from a fruiterer in New York—every Monday these same oranges and lemons left his back door in a pyramid of pulpless halves. There was a machine in the kitchen which

---

1. **Sound.** Long Island Sound, off the coast of New York
2. **cataracts.** Cascades
3. **omnibus.** Archaic word for *bus*

rav • ag •es (ra´ və jəz) *n.*, damaging effects of something

could extract the juice of two hundred oranges in half an hour, if a little button was pressed two hundred times by a butler's thumb.

At least once a fortnight[4] a corps[5] of caterers came down with several hundred feet of canvas and enough colored lights to make a Christmas tree of Gatsby's enormous garden. On buffet tables, garnished with glistening hors d'œuvre, spiced baked hams crowded against salads of harlequin[6] designs and pastry pigs and turkeys bewitched to a dark gold. In the main hall a bar with a real brass rail was set up, and stocked with gins and liquors and with cordials so long forgotten that most of his female guests were too young to know one from another.

By seven o'clock the orchestra has arrived—no thin five piece affair but a whole pit full of oboes and trombones and saxophones and viols and cornets and piccolos and low and high drums. The last swimmers have come in from the beach now and are dressing upstairs; the cars from New York are parked five deep in the drive, and already the halls and salons and verandas are gaudy with primary colors and hair shorn in strange new ways and shawls beyond the dreams of Castile.[7] The bar is in full swing and floating rounds of cocktails permeate the garden outside until the air is alive with chatter and laughter and casual <u>innuendo</u> and introductions forgotten on the spot and enthusiastic meetings between women who never knew each other's names.

The lights grow brighter as the earth lurches away from the sun and now the orchestra is playing yellow cocktail music and the opera of

voices pitches a key higher. Laughter is easier, minute by minute, spilled with <u>prodigality</u>, tipped out at a cheerful word. The groups change more swiftly, swell with new arrivals, dissolve and form in the same breath—already there are wanderers, confident girls who weave here and there among the stouter and more stable, become for a sharp, joyous moment the center of a group and then excited with triumph glide on through the sea-change of faces and voices and color under the constantly changing light.

Suddenly one of these gypsies in trembling opal seizes a cocktail out of the air, dumps it down for courage and moving her hands like Frisco dances out alone on the canvas platform. A momentary hush; the orchestra leader varies his rhythm obligingly for her and there is a burst of chatter as the <u>erroneous</u> news goes around that she is Gilda Gray's[8] understudy from the "Follies."[9] The party has begun.

I believe that on the first night I went to Gatsby's house I was one of the few guests who had actually been invited. People were not invited—they went there. They got into automobiles which bore them out to Long Island and somehow they ended up at Gatsby's door. Once there they were introduced by somebody who knew Gatsby and after that they conducted themselves according to the rules of behavior associated with amusement parks. Sometimes they came and went without having met Gatsby at all, came for the party with a simplicity of heart that was its own ticket of admission.

---

4. **fortnight.** Period of two weeks
5. **corps.** Group of people who work together as a team
6. **harlequin.** Varied in color with an irregular geometric pattern
7. **Castile.** Region in Spain where ornate shawls are traditionally worn
8. **Gilda Gray.** Theater and film star from the 1920s
9. **the "Follies."** Ziegfeld Follies, a series of elaborate Broadway productions in the early 1900s

> **in • nu • en • do** (in´ yü en´ dō) *n.,* indirect remark or gesture with a suggestion of impropriety
> **prod • i • gal • i • ty** (prô´ də gal´ ə tē) *n.,* excess; waste
> **er • ro • ne • ous** (i rōn´ ē əs) *adj.,* incorrect or based on an incorrect assumption

I had been actually invited. A chauffeur in a uniform of robin's egg blue crossed my lawn early that Saturday morning with a surprisingly formal note from his employer—the honor would be entirely Gatsby's, it said, if I would attend his "little party" that night. He had seen me several times and had intended to call on me long before but a peculiar combination of circumstances had prevented it—signed Jay Gatsby in a majestic hand.

Dressed up in white flannels I went over to his lawn a little after seven and wandered around rather ill-at-ease among swirls and eddies of people I didn't know—though here and there was a face I had noticed on the commuting train. I was immediately struck by the number of young Englishmen dotted about; all well dressed, all looking a little hungry and all talking in low earnest voices to solid and prosperous Americans. I was sure that they were all selling something: bonds or insurance or automobiles. They were, at least, agonizingly aware of the easy money in the vicinity and convinced that it was theirs for a few words in the right key.

> ## I was sure that they were all selling something: bonds or insurance or automobiles.

As soon as I arrived I made an attempt to find my host but the two or three people of whom I asked his whereabouts stared at me in such an amazed way and denied so vehemently any knowledge of his movements that I slunk off in the direction of the cocktail table—the only place in the garden where a single man could linger without looking purposeless and alone.

I was on my way to get roaring drunk from sheer embarrassment when Jordan Baker came out of the house and stood at the head of the marble steps, leaning a little backward and looking with <u>contemptuous</u> interest down into the garden.

Welcome or not, I found it necessary to attach myself to someone before I should begin to address cordial remarks to the passers-by.

"Hello!" I roared, advancing toward her. My voice seemed unnaturally loud across the garden.

"I thought you might be here," she responded absently as I came up. "I remembered you lived next door to—"

She held my hand impersonally, as a promise that she'd take care of me in a minute, and gave ear to two girls in twin yellow dresses who stopped at the foot of the steps.

"Hello!" they cried together. "Sorry you didn't win."

That was for the golf tournament. She had lost in the finals the week before.

"You don't know who we are," said one of the girls in yellow, "but we met you here about a month ago."

"You've dyed your hair since then," remarked Jordan and I started but the girls had moved casually on and her remark was addressed to the premature moon, produced like the supper, no doubt, out of a caterer's basket. With Jordan's slender golden arm resting in mine we descended the steps and sauntered about the garden. A tray of cocktails floated at us through the twilight and we sat down at a table with the two girls in yellow and three men, each one introduced to us as Mr. Mumble.

"Do you come to these parties often?" inquired Jordan of the girl beside her.

"The last one was the one I met you at," answered the girl in an alert, confident voice. She turned to her companion: "Wasn't it for you, Lucille?"

It was for Lucille too.

"I like to come," Lucille said. "I never care what I do, so I always have a good time. When I was here last I tore my gown on a chair, and

---

con • temp • tu • ous (kən temp′ chü əs) *adj.,* demonstrating a strong dislike or lack of respeact

he asked me my name and address—inside of a week I got a package from Croirier's with a new evening gown in it."

"Did you keep it?" asked Jordan.

"Sure I did. I was going to wear it tonight, but it was too big in the bust and had to be altered. It was gas blue with lavender beads. Two hundred and sixty-five dollars."

"There's something funny about a fellow that'll do a thing like that," said the other girl eagerly. "He doesn't want any trouble with *anybody*."

"Who doesn't?" I inquired.

"Gatsby. Somebody told me——"

The two girls and Jordan leaned together confidentially.

"Somebody told me they thought he killed a man once."

A thrill passed over all of us. The three Mr. Mumbles bent forward and listened eagerly.

"I don't think it's so much *that*," argued Lucille skeptically; "it's more that he was a German spy during the war."

One of the men nodded in confirmation.

"I heard that from a man who knew all about him, grew up with him in Germany," he assured us positively.

"Oh no," said the first girl, "it couldn't be that, because he was in the American army during the war." As our credulity switched back to her she leaned forward with enthusiasm. "You look at him sometime when he thinks nobody's looking at him. I'll bet he killed a man."

"Somebody told me they thought he killed a man once."

She narrowed her eyes and shivered. Lucille shivered. We all turned and looked around for Gatsby. It was testimony to the romantic speculation he inspired that there were whispers about him from those who had found little that it was necessary to whisper about in this world.

The first supper—there would be another one after midnight—was now being served and Jordan invited me to join her own party who were spread around a table on the other side of the garden. There were three married couples and Jordan's escort, a persistent undergraduate given to violent innuendo and obviously under the impression that sooner or later Jordan was going to yield him up her person to a greater or lesser degree. Instead of rambling this party had preserved a dignified <u>homogeneity</u>, and assumed to itself the function of representing the staid nobility of the countryside—East Egg condescending to West Egg, and carefully on guard against its spectroscopic gayety.

"Let's get out," whispered Jordan, after a somehow wasteful and inappropriate half hour. "This is much too polite for me."

We got up and she explained that we were going to find the host—I had never met him, she said, and it was making me uneasy. The undergraduate nodded in a <u>cynical</u>, melancholy way.

The bar, where we glanced first, was crowded but Gatsby was not there. She couldn't find him from the top of the steps, and he wasn't on the veranda. On a chance we tried an important-looking door, and walked into a high Gothic library, panelled with carved English oak, and probably transported complete from some ruin overseas.

A stout, middle-aged man with enormous owl-eyed spectacles was sitting somewhat drunk on the edge of a great table, staring with unsteady concentration at the shelves of books. As we entered he wheeled excitedly around and examined Jordan from head to foot.

"What do you think?" he demanded impetuously.

---

ho • mo • ge • ne • i • ty (hō′ mō jə nā′ ə tē) *n.,* quality of being the same or similar in nature

cyn • ic • al (sin′ ə k'l) *adj.,* mocking or scornful

The Prohibition Era

The Great Gatsby was published in the middle of the Prohibition Era, when the manufacture, consumption, and transportation of alcohol were against the law in the United States. Passage of the Eighteenth Amendment to the U.S. Constitution in 1917 made these acts illegal, but in fact, the movement to ban alcohol started shortly after the Revolutionary War.

In 1784, a Pennsylvanian physician named Benjamin Rush claimed that excessive alcohol consumption threatened people's health. Five years later, a group of Connecticut farmers formed the United States' first *Temperance* group, which advocated abstinence. The Temperance movement gained momentum in the mid-1800s when leaders of the Methodist Church incorporated the philosophy of abstinence into their religion. Although the movement was sidetracked during the Civil War, the issue of abstinence remained the focus of social activists throughout the nineteenth century.

By 1917, the Temperance movement had gained enough support for the U.S. Congress to pass

a constitutional amendment banning alcohol. By January 1919, thirty-six states had ratified (approved) the Eighteenth Amendment, and it became law in January 1920.

Ironically, issuing a total ban on alcohol proved an unwise solution to the problem of consumption. Doing so put the power of manufacturing and distributing liquor directly in the hands of organized crime, which flourished during the 1920s. Mobsters such as Al Capone made millions of dollars from the illegal sale of alcohol. As illustrated in *The Great Gatsby,* alcohol was readily available throughout the United States during Prohibition, particularly for people of wealth.

The Prohibition Era ended in 1933, when Congress repealed the Eighteenth Amendment by passing the Twenty-First Amendment. This remains the only time in U.S. history that an amendment has been entirely overturned.

"About what?"

He waved his hand toward the book-shelves.

"About that. As a matter of fact you needn't bother to ascertain. I <u>ascertained</u>. They're real."

"The books?"

He nodded.

"Absolutely real—have pages and everything. I thought they'd be a nice durable cardboard. Matter of fact they're absolutely real. Pages and—— Here! Lemme show you."

Taking our skepticism for granted he rushed to the book-cases and returned with Volume One of the "Stoddard Lectures."

"See!" he cried triumphantly. "It's a bona fide piece of printed matter. It fooled me. This fella's a regular Belasco.[10] It's a triumph. What thoroughness! What realism! Knew when to stop too—didn't cut the pages. But what do you want? What do you expect?"

He snatched the book from me and replaced it hastily on its shelf muttering that if one brick was removed the whole library was liable to collapse.

"Who brought you?" he demanded. "Or did you just come? I was brought. Most people were brought."

Jordan looked at him alertly, cheerfully without answering.

"I was brought by a woman named Roosevelt," he continued. "Mrs. Claud Roosevelt. Do you know her? I met her somewhere last night. I've been drunk for about a week now, and I thought it might sober me up to sit in a library."

---

10. **Belasco.** David Belasco, a popular playwright and Broadway theater producer in the early 1900s

as · cer · tain (a sʉr tān´) *v.,* determine

"Has it?"

"A little bit, I think. I can't tell yet. I've only been here an hour. Did I tell you about the books? They're real. They're——"

"You told us."

We shook hands with him gravely and went back outdoors.

There was dancing now on the canvas in the garden, old men pushing young girls backward in eternal graceless circles, superior couples holding each other tortuously, fashionably and keeping in the corners—and a great number of single girls dancing individualistically or relieving the orchestra for a moment of the burden of the banjo or the traps. By midnight the hilarity had increased. A celebrated tenor had sung in Italian and a notorious contralto had sung in jazz and between the numbers people were doing "stunts" all over the garden while happy <u>vacuous</u> bursts of laughter rose toward the summer sky. A pair of stage "twins"—who turned out to be the girls in yellow—did a baby act in costume and champagne was served in glasses bigger than finger bowls. The moon had risen higher, and floating in the Sound was a triangle of silver scales, trembling a little to the stiff, tinny drip of the banjoes on the lawn.

I was still with Jordan Baker. We were sitting at a table with a man of about my age and a rowdy little girl who gave way upon the slightest provocation to uncontrollable laughter. I was enjoying myself now. I had taken two finger bowls of champagne and the scene had changed before my eyes into something significant, elemental and profound.

At a lull in the entertainment the man looked at me and smiled.

"Your face is familiar," he said politely. "Weren't you in the Third Division during the war?"

"Why, yes. I was in the Ninth Machine-Gun Battalion."

"I was in the Seventh Infantry until June nineteen-eighteen. I knew I'd seen you somewhere before."

The front cover of the first edition of *The Great Gatsby* is one of the most famous book covers ever produced. The novel was so highly anticipated that its publisher, Charles Scribner, hired artist Francis Cugat to design the cover before Fitzgerald had even finished writing the manuscript. This cover still appears on the Scribner edition of the book.

We talked for a moment about some wet, grey little villages in France. Evidently he lived in this vicinity for he told me that he had just bought a hydroplane and was going to try it out in the morning.

"Want to go with me, old sport? Just near the shore along the Sound."

"What time?"

"Any time that suits you best."

It was on the tip of my tongue to ask his name when Jordan looked around and smiled.

vac • u • ous (vak´ yü əs) *adj.*, lacking intelligence

"Having a gay time now?" she inquired.

"Much better." I turned again to my new acquaintance. "This is an unusual party for me. I haven't even seen the host. I live over there—" I waved my hand at the invisible hedge in the distance, "and this man Gatsby sent over his chauffeur with an invitation."

For a moment he looked at me as if he failed to understand.

"I'm Gatsby," he said suddenly.

"What!" I exclaimed. "Oh, I beg your pardon."

"I thought you knew, old sport. I'm afraid I'm not a very good host."

He smiled understandingly—much more than understandingly. It was one of those rare smiles with a quality of eternal reassurance in it, that you may come across four or five times in life. It faced—or seemed to face—the whole external world for an instant, and then concentrated on *you* with an irresistible prejudice in your favor. It understood you just so far as you wanted to be understood, believed in you as you would like to believe in yourself and assured you that it had precisely the impression of you that, at your best, you hoped to convey. Precisely at that point it vanished—and I was looking at an elegant young rough-neck, a year or two over thirty, whose elaborate formality of speech just missed being absurd. Some time before he introduced himself I'd got a strong impression that he was picking his words with care.

Almost at the moment when Mr. Gatsby identified himself a butler hurried toward him with the information that Chicago was calling him on the wire. He excused himself with a small bow that included each of us in turn.

"If you want anything just ask for it, old sport," he urged me. "Excuse me. I will rejoin you later."

When he was gone I turned immediately to Jordan—constrained to assure her of my surprise. I had expected that Mr. Gatsby would be a florid and <u>corpulent</u> person in his middle years.

"Who is he?" I demanded. "Do you know?"

"He's just a man named Gatsby."

"Where is he from, I mean? And what does he do?"

"Now *you're* started on the subject," she answered with a wan smile. "Well,—he told me once he was an Oxford[11] man."

A dim background started to take shape behind him but at her next remark it faded away.

"However, I don't believe it."

"Why not?"

"I don't know," she insisted. "I just don't think he went there."

Something in her tone reminded me of the other girl's "I think he killed a man," and had the effect of stimulating my curiosity. I would have accepted without question the information that Gatsby sprang from the swamps of Louisiana or from the lower East Side of New York. That was comprehensible. But young men didn't—at least in my provincial[12] inexperience I believed they didn't—drift coolly out of nowhere and buy a palace on Long Island Sound.

"Anyhow he gives large parties," said Jordan, changing the subject with an urban distaste for the concrete. "And I like large parties. They're so intimate. At small parties there isn't any privacy." ❖

---

11. **Oxford.** Oxford University in England
12. **provincial.** Unsophisticated

cor • pu • lent (kôr´ pyü lənt) *adj.,* obese

The narrator says that Gatsby looked at people in a way that "understood you just so far as you wanted to be understood." Do you feel that the people around you know you well? Do you want people to know you well?

Refer to Text ▶ ▶ ▶ ▶ ▶	Reason with Text	
1a. What surprises the man that the narrator and Jordan meet in the library?	**1b.** Explain why the man in the library was surprised by this.	**Understand** Find meaning
2a. How do people react when the narrator asks where the host of the party is?	**2b.** What is the narrator's overall impression of Gatsby by the end of the party?	**Apply** Use information
3a. What happened the last time Lucille was at Gatsby's house?	**3b.** Identify elements of Gatsby's character that are revealed in this excerpt.	**Analyze** Take things apart
4a. What happens at Gatsby's house on weekends?	**4b.** Describe how Fitzgerald viewed the lifestyle described in this selection. Did he admire it or disapprove of it? Explain.	**Evaluate** Make judgments
5a. What do the narrator and Gatsby have in common?	**5b.** Predict how the narrator's relationship with Gatsby will develop.	**Create** Bring ideas together

Analyze Literature

Setting and Narrator

Identify the time and place in which the novel is set. What details convey the setting? Why is the setting important to the story?

Who is the narrator? What is his relationship to Gatsby? Why did Fitzgerald choose this person to narrate the story? Would Gatsby or another character have been a more effective narrator? Explain.

Extend the Text

Writing Options

Creative Writing Choose one of the scenes from the party, and rewrite it to be set in the current time. In a one-paragraph description, include details that indicate the scene's new setting. Compare your description with that of a classmate.

Expository Writing Imagine that it's 1924, and F. Scott Fitzgerald has sent you a copy of the manuscript for *The Great Gatsby* before its publication, asking what you think of his choice of narrator. Write Fitzgerald a letter in which you analyze the narrator. Is he a credible and reliable person to tell Gatsby's story? Why or why not?

Collaborative Learning

Evaluate Literature With a small group, discuss the value of *The Great Gatsby* as a literary work. Explore the following questions: What gives a piece of writing literary value? Is this judgment purely subjective, or do universal traits characterize good literature? Why might *The Great Gatsby* have been unpopular with readers of the 1920s and 1930s?

Media Literacy

Research the 1920s With two or three classmates, research an aspect of the 1920s, also called the Roaring Twenties and the Jazz Age. You might choose from these topics: Prohibition, music and entertainment, historical events, and the economy. Create a multimedia presentation on your topic, combining photographs, video, illustrations, and text.

 Go to **www.mirrorsandwindows.com** for more.

Understand the Concept

To *subordinate* something means to make it secondary or less important. In writing, **subordination** is a strategy for combining ideas when one idea is more important than another.

To use subordination effectively, you need to understand how the parts of a sentence function together. A **clause** has a subject and a verb. An **independent clause** expresses a complex thought and can stand alone. By definition, a sentence is an independent clause. A **subordinate clause** does not express a complete thought and cannot stand alone. It must be joined to an independent clause.

A **complex sentence** contains one independent clause (stating the most important idea) and one or more subordinate clauses (stating less important ideas). These two clauses are joined by either a **subordinating conjunction** (such as *although* or *if*) or a **relative pronoun** (such as *who, whom, whose,* or *which*). The conjunction or pronoun usually expresses the relationship between the two clauses.

There are three types of subordinate clauses: adjective, adverb, and noun clauses. In each of the following examples, the subordinate clause is italicized and the conjunction or relative pronoun is in bold italic type.

An **adjective clause** modifies a noun or pronoun:

EXAMPLE

Nick, ***who*** *was Gatsby's neighbor,* had not met the host.

An **adverb clause** modifies a verb, an adjective, or another adverb:

EXAMPLES

Because *he heard so many rumors,* Nick became curious about his host. [modifies verb *became*]

The narrator became even more curious ***after*** *he met Gatsby.* [modifies adjective *more curious*]

The guests behaved more oddly ***than*** *they had at last week's party.* [modifies adverb *more oddly*]

A **noun clause** functions the same way as a one-word noun in a sentence:

EXAMPLES

Subject ***That*** *the party was expensive* did not trouble Gatsby.

Direct object The man explained ***why*** *he had come to the party.*

Predicate nominative The information ***that*** *Chicago was calling him on the wire* interrupted our conversation.

These clauses also can function as an indirect object, the object of a preposition, or an appositive.

Apply the Skill

Identify Subordinate Clauses

The following complex sentences are from *The Great Gatsby.* Write each sentence on a piece of paper. Then underline the subordinate clause or clauses, circle the subordinating conjunctions or relative pronouns, and indicate the type of clause.

1. Welcome or not, I found it necessary to attach myself to someone before I should begin to address cordial remarks to the passers-by.
2. She held my hand impersonally, as a promise that she'd take care of me in a minute, and gave ear to two girls in twin yellow dresses who stopped at the foot of the stairs.
3. As our credulity switched back to her she leaned forward with enthusiasm.
4. For a moment he looked at me as if he failed to understand.
5. I had expected that Mr. Gatsby would be a florid and corpulent person in his middle years.
6. Some time before he introduced himself I'd got a strong impression that he was picking his words with care.

Use Subordinate Clauses in Your Writing

Write a short story or essay about a time when you felt awkward or out of place in a social situation. In your writing, include at least five sentences with subordinate clauses. After drafting your story or essay, go through it and underline all the subordinate clauses you used. Also check your punctuation.

"Writing at its best is a lonely life."

Ernest Hemingway (1899–1961) was born and raised in Oak Park, Illinois. He began his writing career after high school, working as a reporter for the *Kansas City Star*.

When World War I broke out and an eye problem prevented him from joining the U.S. Army, Hemingway worked for the American Red Cross in Italy as an ambulance driver. Just before his nineteenth birthday, he was hit by artillery, and his knee and foot were severely injured. He spent several months recovering in a hospital in Milan. There, he met an American nurse with whom he had a romance that was fleeting but nonetheless left an impression on the young writer. Their relationship became the basis of a later novel, *A Farewell to Arms* (1929).

After the war, Hemingway continued to work as a journalist, moving to Paris in 1921. He became part of the large community of expatriate artists and writers, who encouraged his literary talent. After publishing a series of stories and a novel, his first success came in 1926 with publication of *The Sun Also Rises*. Hemingway had written and rewritten the novel while touring various parts of Spain and France, where the novel is set, between 1924 and 1926.

Many of Hemingway's works can be linked with his life's experiences. *Death in the Afternoon*, published in 1932, is a nonfiction work about Spanish bullfighting, a subject that fascinated the author. *The Green Hills of Africa*, published in 1935, is the story of a safari in East Africa, where Hemingway hunted throughout his life. *For Whom the Bell Tolls*, published in 1940, is set during the Spanish Civil War, which Hemingway had experienced firsthand.

The Old Man and the Sea, the story of an old Cuban fisherman, seems to have been inspired while the author was living in Cuba, where he bought a farm in 1940. This story took him more than ten years to write, but after it was finally published in 1952, it earned Hemingway the Pulitzer Prize for fiction. In 1954, he was awarded the Nobel Prize for literature.

In 1953, Hemingway was seriously injured in a plane crash in Africa, from which he never fully recovered. He left Cuba in 1959, after Fidel Castro came to power, and moved to Ketchum, Idaho. He died there in 1961.

Noted Works

The Sun Also Rises (1926)
A Farewell to Arms (1929)
Death in the Afternoon (1932)
For Whom the Bell Tolls (1940)
The Old Man and the Sea (1952)

from **The Sun Also Rises**
from **For Whom the Bell Tolls**

Novels by Ernest Hemingway

Build Background

Literary Context As noted earlier, ***The Sun Also Rises*** was Hemingway's first novel, published in 1926. Set in post–World War I Europe, the novel includes a cast of wealthy American and British expatriates living in Paris. At the center of this group is the novel's narrator, Jake Barnes, an American journalist and war veteran who is in love with Brett, a beautiful and flirtatious English socialite. Jake, Brett, and their expatriate group travel to Pamplona, Spain, for a weeklong fiesta, where Brett falls in love with a young bullfighter, Romero. This excerpt describes a bullfight that Jake attends with Brett in Pamplona.

   For Whom the Bell Tolls is set during the Spanish Civil War, a 1937 conflict between a fascist group of rebels and the liberal government of Spain. The novel's hero, Robert Jordan, is a demolitions expert working with a local antifascist guerilla leader, Pablo. Jordan's strong sense of duty conflicts with Pablo's weariness of war, but this excerpt also reveals Jordan's inner conflict in this highly regarded war novel.

   Both Jake Barnes and Robert Jordan exemplify a character prototype that appears in many of Hemingway's stories and novels. Called the *Hemingway hero,* this character is a man who struggles to find meaning and dignity in a world characterized by cynicism and desperation. Many of these characters have suffered wounds, physical or emotional. In Hemingway's words, "[They] hurt very badly; in the body, mind, and spirit, and also morally." Enduring his pain, the Hemingway hero is stoic, brave, and honorable. He lives by a code of "grace under pressure," which Hemingway said was the definition of *courage.* Attempting to find meaning in life, this character engages in rituals and traditions such as bullfighting, big-game hunting, and trout fishing—all passions of the author.

   While some literary critics have dismissed the Hemingway hero as a masculine stereotype, others have recognized in him the image of Hemingway and many men of his generation. Regardless, this character prototype is one of the most analyzed elements of Hemingway's work.

Reader's Context Think of a time when you were in a difficult situation and could do nothing to improve or otherwise change things. Did you complain? Did you perhaps criticize or blame others? What is most difficult about maintaining "grace under pressure"?

Analyze Literature
Plot and Motivation

The **plot** is the series of events related to a central conflict, or struggle. It typically introduces a conflict, develops it, and eventually resolves it.

Motivation is a force that moves a character to think, feel, or behave in a certain way.

Set Purpose

Both of these novels are set in Spain, and their events take place only fifteen or so years apart. Even so, the two books tell very different stories. As you read each excerpt, trace the series of events that comprise the plot. In particular, identify the central conflict. Consider, too, the roles of the characters in the novels. In *The Sun Also Rises,* what motivates Romero, the bullfighter? In *For Whom the Bell Tolls,* what motivates Robert Jordan, the demolitions expert? Jot down details about each character's thoughts and actions that suggest his motivation.

Preview Vocabulary

terrain, 541
defraud, 542
aesthetics, 543
mystification, 546
brusqueness, 546
desultory, 547
innumerable, 548
fascist, 549
pompous, 550
abeyance, 550

The Bull-Fighter's Salute, 1869. Mariano Fortuny y Marsal.
National Gallery, London, England.

from

The Sun Also Rises

by Ernest Hemingway

Neither he nor Romero seemed to have anything in common with the others. They were all alone.

I looked through the glasses and saw the three matadors.[1] Romero was in the centre, Belmonte on his left, Marcial on his right. Back of them were their people, and behind the banderilleros,[2] back in the passageway and in the open space of the corral, I saw the picadors.[3] Romero was wearing a black suit. His tricornered hat was low down over his eyes. I could not see his face clearly under the hat, but it looked badly marked. He was looking straight ahead. Marcial was smoking a cigarette guardedly, holding it in his hand. Belmonte looked ahead, his face wan and yellow, his long wolf jaw out. He was looking at nothing. Neither he nor Romero seemed to have anything in common with the others. They were all alone. The President came in; there was handclapping above us in the grand stand, and I handed the glasses to Brett. There was applause. The music started. Brett looked through the glasses.

"Here, take them," she said.

Through the glasses I saw Belmonte speak to Romero. Marcial straightened up and dropped his cigarette, and, looking straight ahead, their heads back, their free arms swinging, the three matadors walked out. Behind them came all the procession, opening out, all striding in step, all the capes furled, everybody with free arms swinging, and behind rode the picadors, their pics rising like lances. Behind all came the two trains of mules and the bull-ring servants. The matadors bowed, holding their hats on, before the President's box, and then came over to the barrera[4] below us. Pedro Romero took off his heavy gold-brocaded cape and handed it over the fence to his sword-handler. He said something to the sword-handler. Close below us we saw Romero's lips were puffed, both eyes were discolored. His face was discolored and swollen. The sword-handler took the cape, looked up at Brett, and came over to us and handed up the cape.

"Spread it out in front of you," I said.

Brett leaned forward. The cape was heavy and smoothly stiff with gold. The sword-handler looked back, shook his head, and said something. A man beside me leaned over toward Brett.

"He doesn't want you to spread it," he said. "You should fold it and keep it in your lap."

Brett folded the heavy cape.

Romero did not look up at us. He was speaking to Belmonte. Belmonte had sent his formal cape over to some friends. He looked across at them and smiled, his wolf smile that was only with the mouth. Romero leaned over the barrera and asked for the water-jug. The sword-handler brought it and Romero poured water over the percale of his fighting-cape, and then scuffed the lower folds in the sand with his slippered foot.

"What's that for?" Brett asked.

"To give it weight in the wind."

"His face looks bad," Bill said.

"He feels very badly," Brett said. "He should be in bed."

The first bull was Belmonte's. Belmonte was very good. But because he got thirty thousand pesetas[5] and people had stayed in line all night to buy tickets to see him, the crowd demanded that he should be more than very good. Belmonte's great attraction is working close to the bull. In bull-fighting they speak of the <u>terrain</u> of the bull and the terrain of the bull-fighter. As long as a bull-fighter stays in

---

1. **matadors.** [Spanish] Bullfighters
2. **banderilleros.** [Spanish] Assistants on foot who do the initial capework and place barbed darts in the bull
3. **picadors.** [Spanish] Assistants mounted on horseback who lance the bull in the first stage of the fight
4. **barrera.** [Spanish] Wall encircling the ring
5. **pesetas.** [Spanish] Spanish currency

> **ter • rain** (tə rān´) *n.*, ground seen in terms of its features or physical nature; territory in this context

Bullfight, 1934. Pablo Picasso. Collection of Victor Ganz, New York.

nor too dangerously armed with horns, and so the element that was necessary to give the sensation of tragedy was not there, and the public, who wanted three times as much from Belmonte, who was sick with a fistula, as Belmonte had ever been able to give, felt <u>defrauded</u> and cheated, and Belmonte's jaw came further out in contempt, and his face turned yellower, and he moved with greater difficulty as his pain increased, and finally the crowd were actively against him, and he was utterly contemptuous and indifferent. He had meant to have a great afternoon, and instead it was an afternoon of sneers, shouted insults, and finally a volley of cushions and pieces of bread and vegetables, thrown down at him in the plaza where he had had his greatest triumphs. His jaw only went further out. Sometimes he turned to smile that toothed, long-jawed, lipless smile when he was called something particularly insulting, and always the pain that any movement produced grew stronger and stronger, until finally his yellow face was parchment color, and after his second bull was dead and the throwing of bread and cushions was over, after he had saluted the President with the same wolf-jawed smile and contemptuous eyes, and handed his sword over the barrera to be wiped, and put back in its case, he passed through into the callejon[7] and leaned

his own terrain he is comparatively safe. Each time he enters into the terrain of the bull he is in great danger. Belmonte, in his best days, worked always in the terrain of the bull. This way he gave the sensation of coming tragedy. People went to the corrida[6] to see Belmonte, to be given tragic sensations, and perhaps to see the death of Belmonte. Fifteen years ago they said if you wanted to see Belmonte you should go quickly, while he was still alive. Since then

Fifteen years ago they said if you wanted to see Belmonte you should go quickly, while he was still alive.

he has killed more than a thousand bulls. When he retired the legend grew up about how his bull-fighting had been, and when he came out of retirement the public were disappointed because no real man could work as close to the bulls as Belmonte was supposed to have done, not, of course, even Belmonte.

Also Belmonte imposed conditions and insisted that his bulls should not be too large,

---

6. **corrida.** [Spanish] Bullfight
7. **callejon.** [Spanish] Passageway

> **de • fraud** (də fräd´) *v.*, take someone's money or property dishonestly; to cheat

Bullfighting

Ernest Hemingway was fascinated with bull-fighting, a traditional Spanish spectacle in which a *matador,* or bullfighter, fights and usually kills a bull. In 1925, Hemingway attended

the fiesta in Pamplona, a city in northern Spain, on which this excerpt from *The Sun Also Rises* is based.

In a traditional bullfight, three matadors work together in a circular dirt ring to kill six bulls. Each matador has a team of assistants who help condition the bull, provoking the animal while they observe its personality and test its bravery. The matador then toys with the bull for a time and finally slays it with his sword. The matador's success relies on his skill and performance during this final stage of the bullfight. Demonstrating courage is one of the foundations of bullfighting, and any cowardly behavior on the part of the matador or the bull is condemned.

In recent years, bullfighting has become extremely controversial. Many people believe that animals should not be slaughtered for entertainment. Some Spaniards also oppose bullfighting due to its association with Francisco Franco, who was dictator of Spain from 1939 to 1975. In response, the Spanish government has eliminated some of the crueler aspects of bullfighting but continues to treat it as a distinguished cultural tradition.

on the barrera below us, his head on his arms, not seeing, not hearing anything, only going through his pain. When he looked up, finally, he asked for a drink of water. He swallowed a little, rinsed his mouth, spat the water, took his cape, and went back into the ring.

Because they were against Belmonte the public were for Romero. From the moment he left the barrera and went toward the bull they

applauded him. Belmonte watched Romero, too, watched him always without seeming to. He paid no attention to Marcial. Marcial was the sort of thing he knew all about. He had come out of retirement to compete with Marcial, knowing it was a competition gained in advance. He had expected to compete with Marcial and the other stars of the decadence of bull-fighting, and he knew that the sincerity of his own bull-fighting would be so set off by the false <u>aesthetics</u> of the bull-fighters of the decadent period that he would only have to be in the ring. His return from retirement had been spoiled by Romero. Romero did always, smoothly, calmly, and beautifully, what he, Belmonte, could only bring himself to do now sometimes. The crowd felt it, even the people from Biarritz,[8] even the American ambassador saw it, finally. It was a competition that Belmonte would not enter because it would lead only to a bad horn wound or death. Belmonte was no longer well enough. He no longer had his greatest moments in the bull-ring. He was not sure that there were any great moments. Things were not the same and now life only came in flashes. He had flashes of the old greatness with his bulls, but they were not of value because he had discounted them in advance when he had picked the bulls out for their safety, getting out of a motor and leaning on a fence, looking over at the herd on the ranch of his friend the bull-breeder. So he had two small, manageable bulls without much horns, and when he felt the greatness again coming, just a little of it through the pain that was always with him, it had been discounted and sold in advance, and it did not give him a good feeling. It was the greatness, but it did not make bull-fighting wonderful to him any more.

---

8. **Biarritz.** Town in southwestern France

aes · thet · ics (as thet´ iks) *n.,* set of principles, often related to appearance

Hemingway's Titles

In choosing titles for the novels *The Sun Also Rises* and *For Whom the Bell Tolls,* Hemingway looked to several literary sources. The title *The Sun Also Rises* is based on a passage from the Bible, Ecclesiastes 1, which describes the cycle of life:

> One generation goeth, and another generation cometh; but the earth abideth for ever.
>
> The sun also ariseth, and the sun goeth down, and hasteth to its place where it ariseth.
>
> The wind goeth toward the south, and turneth about unto the north; it turneth about continually in its course, and the wind returneth again to its circuits.

Ecclesiastes is part of the Old Testament and was written around 250 BCE. Its thematic focus is *mortality,* or the idea that human life is temporary and fleeting. Throughout Ecclesiastes, readers are instructed to enjoy life in the present, rather than live for the hereafter.

For the title of *For Whom the Bell Tolls,* Hemingway drew from a well-known passage by John Donne (1573–1631), a seventeenth-century British poet whose work often contained morbid themes. That passage was from Donne's Meditation 17, a reflective essay from *Devotions Upon Emergent Occasions* (1624):

DONNE

> No man is an island, entire of itself; every man is a piece of the continent, a part of the main. If a clod be washed away by the sea, Europe is the less, as well as if a promontory were, as well as if a manor of they friend's or of thine own were. Any man's death diminishes me, because I am involved in mankind; and therefore never send to know for whom the bell tolls; it tolls for thee.

Pedro Romero had the greatness. He loved bull-fighting, and I think he loved the bulls, and I think he loved Brett. Everything of which he could control the locality he did in front of her all that afternoon. Never once did he look up. He made it stronger that way, and did it for himself, too, as well as for her. Because he did not look up to ask if it pleased he did it all for himself inside, and it strengthened him, and yet he did it for her, too. But he did not do it for her at any loss to himself. He gained by it all through the afternoon.

His first "quite" was directly below us. The three matadors take the bull in turn after each charge he makes at a picador. Belmonte was the first. Marcial was the second. Then came Romero. The three of them were standing at the left of the horse. The picador, his hat down over his eyes, the shaft of his pic angling sharply toward the bull, kicked in the spurs and held them and with the reins in his left hand walked the horse forward toward the bull. The bull was watching. Seemingly he watched the white horse, but really he watched the triangular steel point of the pic. Romero, watching, saw the bull start to turn his head. He did not want to charge. Romero flicked his cape so the color caught the bull's eye. The bull charged with the reflex, charged, and found not the flash of color but a white horse, and a man leaned far over the horse, shot the steel point of the long hickory shaft into the hump of muscle on the bull's shoulder, and pulled his horse sideways as he pivoted on the pic, making a wound, enforcing the iron into the bull's shoulder, making him bleed for Belmonte.

The bull did not insist under the iron. He did not really want to get at the horse. He turned and the group broke apart and Romero was taking him out with his cape. He took him out softly and smoothly, and then stopped and, standing squarely in front of the bull, offered him the cape. The bull's tail went up and he charged, and Romero moved his arms ahead of the bull, wheeling, his feet firmed. The dampened, mud-weighted cape swung open and full as a sail fills, and Romero pivoted with it just ahead of the bull. At the end of the pass they were racing each other again. Romero smiled. The bull wanted it again, and Romero's cape filled again, this time on the other side. Each time he let the bull pass so close that the man and the bull and the cape that filled and pivoted ahead of the bull were all one sharply etched mass. It was all so slow and so controlled. It was as though he were rocking the bull to sleep. He made four veronicas[9] like that, and finished with a half-veronica that turned his back on the bull and came away toward the applause, his hand on his hip, his cape on his arm, and the bull watching his back going away.

In his own bulls he was perfect. His first bull did not see well. After the first two passes with the cape Romero knew exactly how bad the vision was impaired. He worked accordingly. It was not brilliant bull-fighting. It was only perfect bull-fighting. The crowd wanted the bull changed. They made a great row. Nothing very fine could happen with a bull that could not see the lures, but the President would not order him replaced.

"Why don't they change him?" Brett asked.

"They've paid for him. They don't want to lose their money."

"It's hardly fair to Romero."

"Watch how he handles a bull that can't see the color."

"It's the sort of thing I don't like to see."

It was not nice to watch if you cared anything about the person who was doing it. With the bull who could not see the colors of the capes, or the scarlet flannel of the muleta,[10] Romero had to make the bull consent with his body. He had to get so close that the bull saw his body, and would start for it, and then shift the bull's charge to the flannel and finish out the pass in the classic manner. The Biarritz crowd did not like it. They thought Romero was afraid, and that was why he gave that little sidestep each time as he transferred the bull's charge from his own body to the flannel. They preferred Belmonte's imitation of himself or Marcial's imitation of Belmonte. There were three of them in the row behind us.

"What's he afraid of the bull for? The bull's so dumb he only goes after the cloth."

"He's just a young bull-fighter. He hasn't learned it yet."

It was not nice to watch if you cared anything about the person who was doing it.

"But I thought he was fine with the cape before."

"Probably he's nervous now."

Out in the centre of the ring, all alone, Romero was going on with the same thing, getting so close that the bull could see him plainly, offering the body, offering it again a little closer, the bull watching dully, then so close that the bull thought he had him, offering again and finally drawing the charge and then, just before the horns came, giving the bull the red cloth to follow with that little, almost imperceptible, jerk that so offended the critical judgment of the Biarritz bull-fight experts.

"He's going to kill now," I said to Brett. "The bull's still strong. He wouldn't wear himself out."

---

9. **veronica.** Basic pass technique used by bullfighters at the beginning of a fight
10. **muleta.** [Spanish] Small red cape used by a bullfighter at the end of the fight

Out in the centre of the ring Romero profiled in front of the bull, drew the sword out from the folds of the muleta, rose on his toes, and sighted along the blade. The bull charged as Romero charged. Romero's left hand dropped the muleta over the bull's muzzle to blind him, his left shoulder went forward between the horns as the sword went in, and for just an instant he and the bull were one, Romero way out over the bull, the right arm extended high up to where the hilt of the sword had gone in between the bull's shoulders. Then the figure was broken. There was a little jolt as Romero came clear, and then he was standing, one hand up, facing the bull, his shirt ripped out from under his sleeve, the white blowing in the wind, and the bull, the red sword hilt tight between his shoulders, his head going down and his legs settling.

"There he goes," Bill said.

Romero was close enough so the bull could see him. His hand still up, he spoke to the bull. The bull gathered himself, then his head went forward and he went over slowly, then all over, suddenly, four feet in the air.

Romero
was close enough
so the bull could see him.

They handed the sword to Romero, and carrying it blade down, the muleta in his other hand, he walked over to in front of the President's box, bowed, straightened, and came over to the barrera and handed over the sword and muleta.

"Bad one," said the sword-handler.

"He made me sweat," said Romero. He wiped off his face. The sword-handler handed him the water-jug. Romero wiped his lips. It hurt him to drink out of the jug. He did not look up at us.

Marcial had a big day. They were still applauding him when Romero's last bull came in. It was the bull that had sprinted out and killed the man in the morning running.

During Romero's first bull his hurt face had been very noticeable. Everything he did showed it. All the concentration of the awkwardly delicate working with the bull that could not see well brought it out. The fight with Cohn had not touched his spirit but his face had been smashed and his body hurt. He was wiping all that out now. Each thing that he did with this bull wiped that out a little cleaner. It was a good bull, a big bull, and with horns, and it turned and recharged easily and surely. He was what Romero wanted in bulls.

When he had finished his work with the muleta and was ready to kill, the crowd made him go on. They did not want the bull killed yet, they did not want it to be over. Romero went on. It was like a course in bull-fighting. All the passes he linked up, all completed, all slow, templed and smooth. There were no tricks and no <u>mystifications</u>. There was no <u>brusqueness</u>. And each pass as it reached the summit gave you a sudden ache inside. The crowd did not want it ever to be finished. ❖

---

mys • ti • fic • a • tion (mis tə fi kā´ shən) *n.,* act of making something mysterious or hard to explain
brusque • ness (brusk´ nes) *n.,* abrupt or blunt manner

The narrator says, "It was not nice to watch if you cared anything about the person who was doing it." Would you want to watch a bullfight? Why do some people enjoy watching violent events or movies?

Guernica, 1937. Pablo Picasso. Museo Nacional Centro de Arte Reina Sofia, Madrid, Spain.

from
FOR WHOM THE BELL TOLLS
by Ernest Hemingway

You never kill any one that you want to kill in a war.

Chapter Twenty-Six

It was three o'clock in the afternoon before the planes came. The snow had all been gone by noon and the rocks were hot now in the sun. There were no clouds in the sky and Robert Jordan sat in the rocks with his shirt off browning his back in the sun and reading the letters that had been in the pockets of the dead cavalryman. From time to time he would stop reading to look across the open slope to the line of the timber, look over the high country above and then return to the letters. No more cavalry had appeared. At intervals there would be the sound of a shot from the direction of El Sordo's camp. But the firing was <u>desultory</u>.

From examining his military papers he knew the boy was from Tafalla in Navarra,[1] twenty-one years old, unmarried, and the son of a blacksmith. His regiment was the Nth cavalry, which surprised Robert Jordan, for he had believed that regiment to be in the North. He was a Carlist,[2] and he had been wounded at the fighting for Irun[3] at the start of the war.

---

1. **Tafalla in Navarra.** Tafalla is a city in the province of Navarra in northern Spain, near the border with France.
2. **Carlist.** Conservative Spanish political group
3. **Irun.** City in northern Spain on the Bay of Biscay

des • ul • to • ry (de səl′ tōr ē) *adj.,* irregular; uneven

Pablo Picasso

Pablo Picasso (1881–1973), one of the most celebrated artists of the twentieth century, was born in Málaga, Spain. As a child, he was recognized as a prodigy and received formal instruction from his father, himself a painter. The young Picasso also attended several distinguished art academies, including those in Barcelona and Madrid.

Like many artists and writers of the Modern Era, Picasso went to Paris to develop his talent. He lived off and on in the French capital beginning in 1900. As a struggling artist in his twenties, Picasso lived in extreme poverty. He burned many of his early paintings to keep warm in the winter.

Picasso was remarkably versatile and prolific. He created an estimated 22,000 artworks in his lifetime, ranging from drawings and paintings to prints, ceramics, and sculptures. He is best known, however, for developing a new artistic style called *Cubism.* Cubism was rooted in the idea of taking objects apart, reducing them to geometric shapes, and presenting the shapes in reorganized fashion.

Many Cubist works of art also have qualities of *Surrealism,* depicting fantastic, dream-like images and employing extensive symbolism.

Guernica, which appears on page 547, displays both Cubist and Surrealist elements and is perhaps Picasso's most famous artwork. It depicts the horrific bombing of Guernica, an unprotected village in northeastern Spain, during the Spanish Civil War in 1937. An outspoken pacifist, Picasso dedicated the work, which is a large mural, to the bombing's estimated 1,600 victims.

Critical Viewing When asked to explain the symbolism in his paintings, Picasso remarked, "It isn't up to the painter to define the symbols. . . . The public who look at the picture must interpret the symbols as they understand them." What images in this painting seem symbolic? What might they suggest about the horrors of war? Compare and contrast Picasso's depiction of war with Hemingway's in *For Whom the Bell Tolls.*

I've probably seen him run through the streets ahead of the bulls at the Feria in Pamplona,[4] Robert Jordan thought. You never kill any one that you want to kill in a war, he said to himself. Well, hardly ever, he amended and went on reading the letters.

The first letters he read were very formal, very carefully written and dealt almost entirely with local happenings. They were from his sister and Robert Jordan learned that everything was all right in Tafalla, that father was well, that mother was the same as always but with certain complaints about her back, that she hoped he was well and not in too great danger and she was happy he was doing away with the Reds[5] to liberate Spain from the domination of the Marxist[6] hordes. Then there was a list of those boys from Tafalla who had been killed or badly wounded since she wrote last. She mentioned ten who were killed. That is a great many for a town the size of Tafalla, Robert Jordan thought.

There was quite a lot of religion in the letter and she prayed to Saint Anthony, to the Blessed Virgin of Pilar, and to other Virgins to protect him and she wanted him never to forget that he was also protected by the Sacred Heart of Jesus that he wore still, she trusted, at all times over his own heart where it had been proven <u>innumerable</u>—this was underlined—times to have the power of stopping bullets. She was as always his loving sister Concha.

This letter was a little stained around the edges and Robert Jordan put it carefully back with the military papers and opened a letter with a less severe handwriting. It was from the

---

4. **Feria in Pamplona.** Festival of the bulls in Pamplona, also in Navarra, Spain
5. **Reds.** Derogatory term referring to communists
6. **Marxist.** Political philosophy of communism developed by Karl Marx

in • nu • mer • a • ble (i nü´ mʉr ə b'l) *adj.,* too many to count

Do you think you have a right to kill any one? No. But I have to.

boy's *novia*, his fiancée, and it was quietly, formally, and completely hysterical with concern for his safety. Robert Jordan read it through and then put all the letters together with the papers into his hip pocket. He did not want to read the other letters.

I guess I've done my good deed for today, he said to himself. I guess you have all right, he repeated.

"What are those you were reading?" Primitivo asked him.

"The documentation and the letters of that *requeté*[7] we shot this morning. Do you want to see it?"

"I can't read," Primitivo said. "Was there anything interesting?"

"No," Robert Jordan told him. "They are personal letters."

"How are things going where he came from? Can you tell from the letters?"

"They seem to be going all right," Robert Jordan said. "There are many losses in his town." He looked down to where the blind for the automatic rifle had been changed a little and improved after the snow melted. It looked convincing enough. He looked off across the country.

"From what town is he?" Primitivo asked.

"Tafalla," Robert Jordan told him.

All right, he said to himself. I'm sorry, if that does any good.

It doesn't, he said to himself.

All right then, drop it, he said to himself.

All right, it's dropped.

But it would not drop that easily. How many is that you have killed? he asked himself. I don't know. Do you think you have a right to kill any one? No. But I have to. How many of those you have killed have been real <u>fascists</u>? Very few. But they are all the enemy to whose force we are opposing force. But you like the people of Navarra better than those of any other part of Spain. Yes. And you kill them. Yes. If you don't believe it go down there to the camp. Don't you know it is wrong to kill? Yes. But you do it? Yes. And you still believe absolutely that your cause is right? Yes.

It is right, he told himself, not reassuringly, but proudly. I believe in the people and their right to govern themselves as they wish. But you mustn't believe in killing, he told himself. You must do it as a necessity but you must not believe in it. If you believe in it the whole thing is wrong.

But how many do you suppose you have killed? I don't know because I won't keep track. But do you know? Yes. How many? You can't be sure how many. Blowing the trains you kill many. Very many. But you can't be sure. But of those you are sure of? More than twenty. And of those how many were real fascists? Two that I am sure of. Because I had to shoot them when we took them prisoners at Usera.[8] And you did not mind that? No. Nor did you like it? No. I decided never to do it again. I have avoided it. I have avoided killing those who are unarmed.

Listen, he told himself. You better cut this out. This is very bad for you and for your work. Then himself said back to him, You listen, see? Because you are doing something very serious and I have to see you understand it all the time. I have to keep you straight in your head. Because if you are not absolutely straight in your head you have no right to do the things you do for all of them are crimes and no man has a right to take another man's life unless it is to prevent something worse happening to other people. So get it straight and do not lie to yourself.

But I won't keep a count of people I have killed as though it were a trophy record or a disgusting business like notches in a gun, he told himself. I have a right to not keep count and I have a right to forget them.

---

7. *requeté*. [Spanish] Prisoner
8. **Usera.** District of Madrid, the capital of Spain

fas • cist (fa´ shist) *n.,* member of an oppressive political movement

No, himself said. You have no right to forget anything. You have no right to shut your eyes to any of it nor any right to forget any of it nor to soften it nor to change it.

Shut up, he told himself. You're getting awfully <u>pompous</u>.

Nor ever to deceive yourself about it, himself went on.

All right, he told himself. Thanks for all the good advice and is it all right for me to love Maria?

Yes, himself said.

Even if there isn't supposed to be any such thing as love in a purely materialistic conception of society?

Since when did you ever have any such conception? himself asked. Never. And you never could have. You're not a real Marxist and you know it. You believe in Liberty, Equality and Fraternity.[9] You believe in Life, Liberty and the Pursuit of Happiness.[10] Don't ever kid yourself with too much dialectics.[11] They are for some but not for you. You have to know them in order not to be a sucker. You have put many things in <u>abeyance</u> to win a war. If this war is lost all of those things are lost.

But afterwards you can discard what you do not believe in. There is plenty you do not believe in and plenty that you do believe in.

And another thing. Don't ever kid yourself about loving some one. It is just that most people are not lucky enough ever to have it. You never had it before and now you have it. What you have with Maria, whether it lasts just through today and a part of tomorrow, or whether it lasts for a long life is the most important thing that can happen to a human being. There will always be people who say it does not exist because they cannot have it. But I tell you it is true and that you have it and that you are lucky even if you die tomorrow.

Cut out the dying stuff, he said to himself. That's not the way we talk. That's the way our friends the anarchists[12] talk. Whenever things get really bad they want to set fire to something and to die. It's a very odd kind of mind they have. Very odd. Well, we're getting through today, old timer, he told himself. It's nearly three o'clock now and there is going to be some food sooner or later. They are still shooting up at Sordo's, which means that they have him surrounded and are waiting to bring up more people, probably. Though they have to make it before dark.

I wonder what it is like up at Sordo's. That's what we all have to expect, given enough time. I imagine it is not too jovial up at Sordo's. We certainly got Sordo into a fine jam with that horse business. How does it go in Spanish? *Un callejón sin salida.* A passageway with no exit. I suppose I could go through with it all right. You only have to do it once and it is soon over with. But wouldn't it be luxury to fight in a war some time where, when you were surrounded, you could surrender? *Estamos copados.* We are surrounded. That was the great panic cry of this war. Then the next thing was that you were shot; with nothing bad before if you were lucky. Sordo wouldn't be lucky that way. Neither would they when the time ever came.

It was three o'clock. Then he heard the far-off, distant throbbing and, looking up, he saw the planes. ❖

---

9. **Liberty, Equality, and Fraternity.** Slogan of the French Revolution, which became France's national motto
10. **Life, Liberty, and the Pursuit of Happiness.** "Inalienable rights" listed in the Declaration of Independence
11. **dialectics.** Dialogue for the purpose of reasoning or argument
12. **anarchist.** Someone who rebels against order or authority

> **pomp • ous** (päm´ pəs) *adj.,* showing great self-importance; arrogant
> **abey • ance** (ä bā´ yents) *n.,* temporary inactivity

When you do something that is controversial or wrong, how do you justify your actions? How do you convince yourself you are doing the right thing?

PARKER

Literature Connection

Dorothy Parker (1893–1967) was a humorist who lived in New York from the 1920s to the 1940s. Despite ending her formal education at age thirteen, Parker managed to become an editor of the magazine *Vanity Fair* and a contributor to the *New Yorker*.

The title of the following essay, **"The Artist's Reward,"** came from a letter from Ernest Hemingway to F. Scott Fitzgerald, in which he described the challenges of being a writer. He said, "I am now in the state of depression where you've gone over and over until you can't tell whether anything you've written is any good or not; this is called the Artist's Reward."

The Artist's Reward
by Dorothy Parker

There is a thing about him that I have not yet mentioned, for I am a slow worker. He has the most profound bravery that it has ever been my privilege to see; and I am not the one who over-readily discerns examples of courage among my opposite sex. He has had pain, ill-health, and the kind of poverty that you don't believe—the kind of which actual hunger is the attendant; he has had about eight times the normal allotment of responsibilities. And he has never once compromised. He has never turned off on an easier path than the one he staked himself. It takes courage.

That brings me to the point which I have been trying to reach all this time: Ernest Hemingway's definition of courage—his phrase that, it seems to me, makes Barrie's[1] "Courage is immortality" sound like one of the more treble trillings of Tinker Bell. Mr. Hemingway did not use the term "courage." Ever the euphemist, he referred to the quality as "guts," and he was attributing its possession to an absent friend.

"Now just a minute," somebody said, for it was one of those argumentative evenings. "Listen. Look here a minute. Exactly what do you mean by 'guts'?"

"I mean," Ernest Hemingway said, "grace under pressure."

That grace is his. The pressure, I suppose, comes in, *gratis,* under the heading of the Artist's Reward. ❖

---

1. **Barrie's.** Refers to J. M. Barrie, author of *Peter Pan*

LITERARY CONNECTION

The Fitzgerald/Hemingway Relationship

F. Scott Fitzgerald and Ernest Hemingway met in Paris in 1925. Both were members of a group of talented American writers who had gone to Europe after the war. Hemingway was working as a journalist, although he had published a few literary pieces in small magazines. Fitzgerald, on the other hand, was a recognized author, having gained success with the publication of *This Side of Paradise* in 1920 and enjoying the recent release of his second novel, *The Great Gatsby.*

Hemingway and Fitzgerald became close but cautious friends. Hemingway felt that success came too easily to Fitzgerald, whom he thought was naturally talented but lazy about his art. He described Fitzgerald as having "jumped straight from youth to senility." Fitzgerald viewed Hemingway as the definition of masculinity and courage but believed both his writing and his character were too raw.

While Hemingway was writing his first novel, *The Sun Also Rises,* he sought Fitzgerald's critical opinion. Fitzgerald reviewed the manuscript and returned a ten-page handwritten letter, expressing criticism and praise for the budding writer's efforts. Hemingway acted on Fitzgerald's suggestion that the novel was wordy and cut the first sixteen pages, along with making other changes.

Fitzgerald further assisted his friend by mentioning him to Max Perkins, his own editor at Scribner's, an established literary press. Fitzgerald wrote to Perkins, "This is to tell you about a young writer named Ernest Hemingway. . . . I'd look him up right away. He's the real thing." When Perkins learned that several other publishers were interested in Hemingway's forthcoming novel, he pursued the writer and persuaded him to sign with Scribner's. Scribner's published *The Sun Also Rises* in 1926.

Despite enjoying tremendous success, Hemingway became increasingly resentful of those who had mentored him, including Fitzgerald. An incredibly competitive man, Hemingway alienated many people in his personal and professional lives. Regardless, Fitzgerald continued to refer to him as "the greatest living writer of our time."

THE SUN ALSO RISES

ERNEST HEMINGWAY
Author of
"IN OUR TIMES" and "THE TORRENTS OF SPRING"

Refer to Text ▶ ▶ ▶ ▶ ▶ Reason with Text

1a. In *For Whom the Bell Tolls*, whose letters does Robert Jordan read?	**1b.** Explain how reading the letters affects Jordan.	**Understand** Find meaning
2a. In *The Sun Also Rises*, what does Romero give Brett before the fight?	**2b.** How does the narrator in *The Sun Also Rises* feel about Romero's interest in Brett?	**Apply** Use information
3a. In *The Sun Also Rises*, identify which bullfighter is the crowd's favorite.	**3b.** Compare and contrast Romero and Belmonte.	**Analyze** Take things apart
4a. Describe what Robert Jordan is doing in the excerpt from *For Whom the Bell Tolls*.	**4b.** What kind of person is Jordan? Do you sympathize with him? Why or why not?	**Evaluate** Make judgments
5a. In the excerpt from *For Whom the Bell Tolls*, what is Robert Jordan waiting for?	**5b.** Based on the background information provided, predict what will happen next in each novel. Will Brett and Jake Barnes fall in love? Which side of Robert Jordan's inner conflict will win out? Explain your answers.	**Create** Bring ideas together

Analyze Literature

Plot and Motivation

What is the central conflict in each novel excerpt? How is it developed? Is it resolved by the end of the excerpt? If not, predict how the conflict might be resolved in the rest of the novel.

What is the motivation for Romero in *The Sun Also Rises*? What is the motivation for Robert Jordan in *For Whom the Bell Tolls*? How is each character's motivation reflected in his thoughts and actions? Support your opinion with details from the text.

Extend the Text

Writing Options

Creative Writing Based on your predictions from question 5b above, write the next paragraph of either *The Sun Also Rises* or *For Whom the Bell Tolls*. Try to imitate Hemingway's writing style as much as possible, and stay true to the plot.

Descriptive Writing Imagine that you met Jake Barnes or Robert Jordan and are writing a letter to a friend telling about the meeting. Based on the background information provided for the selections and what you have gleaned from reading them, write a one-paragraph character sketch of either Barnes or Jordan.

Collaborative Learning

Analyze Author Style With a partner, compare the writing styles of Ernest Hemingway and F. Scott Fitzgerald. Refer to the selections and identify distinctive features of each writer's style, such as sentence structure and length, word choice, use of figurative language, and use of dialogue. Make a comparison chart of your observations.

Lifelong Learning

Research on the Internet Imagine that you are writing a biography of Ernest Hemingway. Using the Internet, identify places to which you should travel to conduct research. Write an itinerary listing each location, what you should research there, and how long you should spend there.

 Go to **www.mirrorsandwindows.com** for more.

1. In the excerpt from *The Sun Also Rises,* what is meant by the sentence "[Belmonte's greatness] had been discounted and sold in advance"?
   A. Spectators have placed bets against him, reducing his confidence.
   B. Tickets for his bullfights are being sold more cheaply than tickets for others.
   C. He can no longer live up to his past accomplishments.
   D. He fights less-challenging bulls, which cheapens his victories.
   E. Tickets for his bullfights sell out quickly, because everyone expects to see him get killed.

2. From Belmonte's perspective, how has Romero spoiled his return from retirement?
   A. Romero's style of bullfighting is now in fashion, so Belmonte's style looks odd.
   B. Romero and others have copied Belmonte's style, so Belmonte no longer stands out.
   C. Romero skillfully performs the dangerous moves for which Belmonte used to be known.
   D. Romero selects safe bulls to ensure he will appear skillful and emerge victorious.
   E. The gossip about Romero's affair with Brett has drawn attention away from the bullfight.

3. What is the main reason Hemingway repeatedly compares Belmonte to a wolf—for example, "his long wolf jaw out," "his wolf smile that was only with the mouth," "the same wolf-jawed smile"?
   A. Wolves are the worst enemy of bulls.
   B. The story's main idea is that everyone is a beast.
   C. These vivid descriptions help the reader visualize Belmonte.
   D. Hemingway is characterizing Belmonte as a wolf not only in appearance but also in behavior and personality.
   E. The comparison itself isn't important, but the use of repetition emphasizes Belmonte's importance.

4. In *For Whom the Bell Tolls,* what is character Robert Jordan's motivation for fighting?
   A. He thinks it makes men out of boys.
   B. He believes in his side's cause or purpose.
   C. He wants adventure and excitement.
   D. He is a patriotic and political person.
   E. He was drafted and has no choice in the matter.

5. In *For Whom the Bell Tolls,* the sound of gunshots from the direction of El Sordo's camp is described as *desultory.* What does that mean?
   A. irregular
   B. aggressive
   C. rapid
   D. sending up an alarm
   E. for show

6. Which of the following quotations from *For Whom the Bell Tolls* best describes the Hemingway hero?
   A. "The boy was from Tafalla in Navarra, twenty-one years old, unmarried, and the son of a blacksmith."
   B. "He was also protected by the Sacred Heart of Jesus that he wore still, she trusted, at all times over his own heart where it had been proven innumerable—this was underlined—times to have the power of stopping bullets."
   C. "It is right, he told himself, not reassuringly but proudly. I believe in the people and their right to govern themselves as they wish. But you mustn't believe in killing, he told himself. You must do it as a necessity but you must not believe in it."
   D. "He was well and not in too great danger and she was happy he was doing away with the Reds to liberate Spain from the domination of the Marxist hordes."
   E. "You're not a real Marxist and you know it."

7. According to Dorothy Parker in "The Artist's Reward," what was a sign of the depth of Hemingway's poverty?
   A. He needed to write in order to live.
   B. He was unable to pay his bills.
   C. He occasionally went hungry.
   D. He was unable to join other writers in Europe.
   E. He argued with people who had easier lives.

8. **Constructed Response:** Characterize Hemingway's writing style by describing its most striking and consistent qualities. Consider qualities such as word choice, sentence and paragraph length, level of detail, use of dialogue, and so on. Use details from the novel excerpts to support your characterization of style.

9. **Constructed Response:** Compare and contrast Jake Barnes from *The Sun Also Rises* and Robert Jordan from *For Whom the Bell Tolls.* How does each demonstrate the qualities of the Hemingway hero—for instance, stoicism, bravery, and honor? How does each live by the code of "grace under pressure"? Use examples from the texts to support your analysis.

Understand the Concept

To *coordinate* things means to join them in an equal or balanced way. In writing, **coordination** is a strategy for combining related ideas of the same importance.

Ideas are combined using **coordinating conjunctions.** The most common coordinating conjunctions are *and, or, nor, for, but, yet,* and *so.* Each conjunction indicates a different relationship between the words that it connects. For instance, *or* indicates an option or choice. The words *but* and *yet* indicate a contrast or variation.

Coordinating conjunctions can be used to connect several words, such as nouns, verbs, adjectives, and adverbs. They also can be used to connect groups of words, such as phrases, clauses, and sentences.

> **EXAMPLES**
>
> The spectators in the arena were excited but respectful. [The coordinating conjunction *but* joins two adjectives, showing the contrast between *excited* and *respectful*.]
>
> The matadors entered the ring, greeted the crowd, and prepared for the bullfight. [The coordinating conjunction *and* joins a series of three verb phrases. Note the use of commas to separate the phrases.]

When a coordinating conjunction joins two or more independent clauses (which are sentences), a **compound sentence** is formed. A comma is placed before the coordinating conjunction joining the two clauses.

> **EXAMPLE**
>
> He felt guilty about what he had done, so he spent a lot of time trying to justify it. [The coordinating conjunction *so* joins two complete sentences.]

Apply the Skill

Identify Coordinating Conjunctions

Identify the coordinating conjunction in each of the following sentences.

1. Hemingway was born and raised in Illinois.
2. He had an eye problem that prevented him from joining the army, so he served for the American Red Cross instead.
3. After the war, he returned to Europe and began his writing career.
4. Hemingway had written and rewritten the novel while touring various parts of Spain and France.
5. Hemingway was seriously injured in a 1953 plane crash in Africa and never fully recovered.

Correct Coordinating Conjunctions

Each of the following sentences contains an incorrectly used coordinating conjunction. Correct the sentence by rewriting it with the appropriate subordinating conjunction.

1. In Europe, Hemingway was part of a community of expatriate artists or writers.
2. In *The Sun Also Rises,* the narrator is interested in Brett, so she is interested in Romero.
3. Neither the narrator or Brett wanted to leave the bullfight.
4. Hemingway was passionate about bullfighting and many people find it cruel.
5. The hero prototype appears in many of Hemingway's stories or novels.

Use Coordination in Your Writing

Write a paragraph summarizing one of the Hemingway selections you have read. Then review your writing. Identify the coordinating clauses you have used, and confirm that you used them correctly. Revise the paragraph needed to use coordinating clauses more effectively.

In a Station of the Metro
The River-Merchant's Wife: A Letter

Lyric Poems by Ezra Pound

Build Background

Literary Context One day, as Ezra Pound emerged from the Paris subway (called the *Metro*), he suddenly saw "a beautiful face, and then another and another." He captured that experience in the poem **"In a Station of the Metro."** The original version was thirty lines long, but the final version was distilled into just two lines. As such, it exemplifies the characteristic for which Pound's poetry is most noted: imagery.

    "The River-Merchant's Wife: A Letter" is a tribute to Chinese poet Li Po (701–762), whose work Pound translated in a collection called *Cathay* (1915). Literary scholars have catalogued more than one thousand of Li Po's poems and identified natural imagery, imagination, Taoist sentiments, and keen observations about life as hallmarks of Li Po's writing.

Reader's Context What do you see when you look into a crowd of people?

Meet the Author

Ezra Pound (1885–1972) was born in Idaho but grew up in Pennsylvania. He attended the University of Pennsylvania for two years and graduated from Hamilton College in 1905. Strongly interested in Classical and Romance literature, he earned a master's degree in the Romance languages.
    In 1908, after teaching college for two years, Pound left the United States for Europe, where he would live most of his life. He traveled widely, working as a journalist and self-publishing several small volumes of poetry between 1908 and 1911. Through his acquaintance with William Butler Yeats and other British writers, Pound explored a wide range of poetry, much of it Japanese and Chinese.
    Around 1912, Pound formulated the concept of **Imagism,** poetry that presents concise images that readers are to interpret for themselves. His motto "Make it new" expressed the philosophy of this new movement. In 1914, Pound edited the first anthology of Imagist poetry, *Des Imagistes,* which included works by then-novice poets Hilda Doolittle and William Carlos Williams. Pound supported the careers of many young poets, including Robert Frost, Marianne Moore, James Joyce, and T. S. Eliot.
    Pound moved to Paris in 1920, where he was part of the expatriate group that included Hemingway and Fitzgerald. Four years later, he settled in Italy, where he lived for more than twenty years. He published some seventy books of poetry, plays, and essays during his lifetime.

Analyze Literature

Imagism and Imagery
Imagism was a literary movement of the early twentieth century in which poets sought to present single moments of sensory perception without reference to the emotions or opinions of the author, narrator, or speaker.

Imagery is the figurative or descriptive language used to create word pictures, or images. This language can describe real objects or places, or it can create a feeling, mood, or idea.

Set Purpose

Ezra Pound often is called the "poet's poet" because of his profound influence on twentieth-century poetry. As the founder of Imagism, he set a new course for Modernist poets. Look for elements of Imagism as you read "In a Station of the Metro" and "The River-Merchant's Wife." Evaluate each poem according to the goals stated in Pound's essay "A Few Don'ts by an Imagiste," which appears on pages 560–561. In addition, evaluate Pound's use of imagery in each poem. Identify the moods, feelings, or ideas he creates.

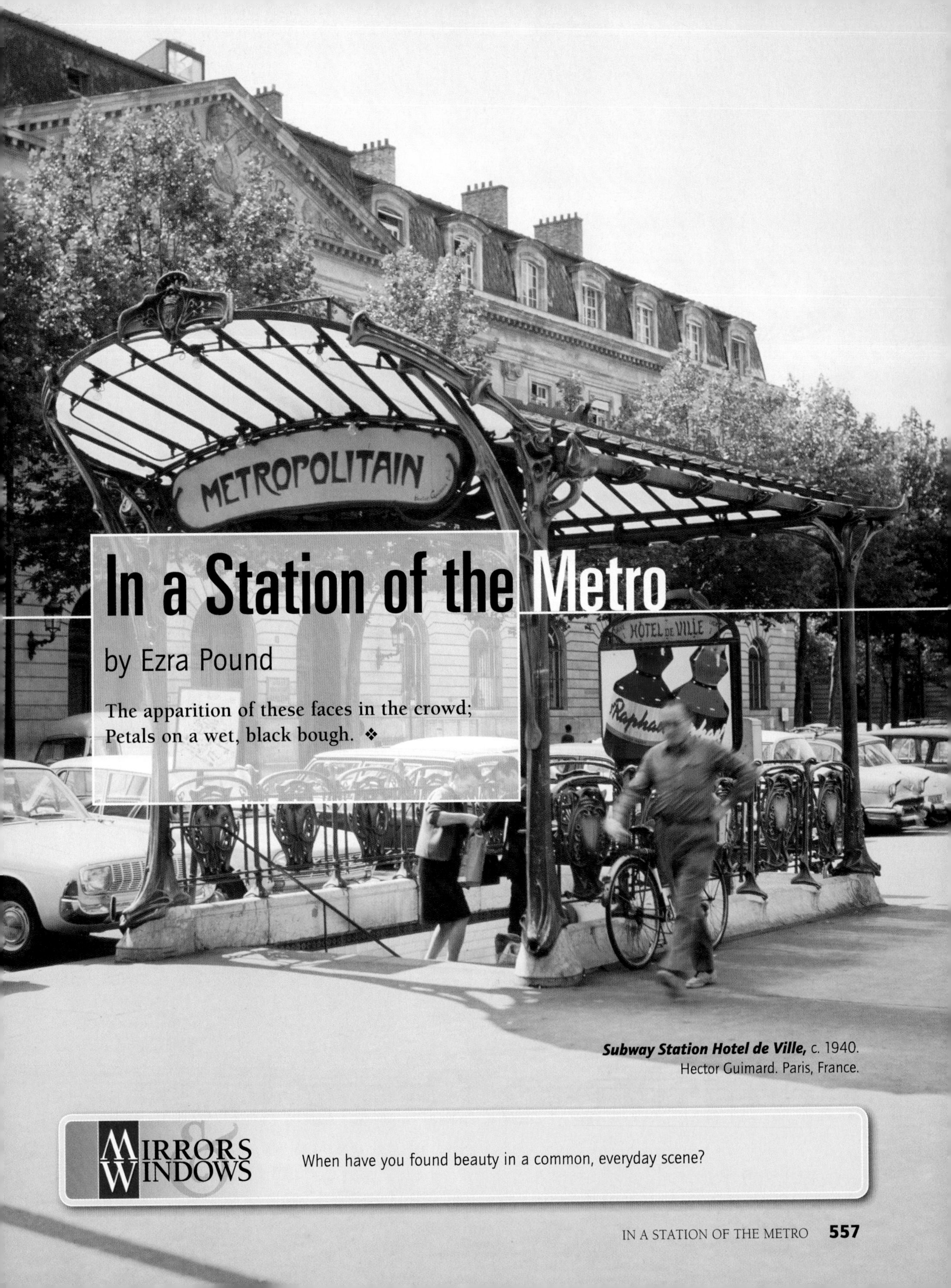

In a Station of the Metro

by Ezra Pound

The apparition of these faces in the crowd;
Petals on a wet, black bough. ❖

Subway Station Hotel de Ville, c. 1940.
Hector Guimard. Paris, France.

MIRRORS & **W**INDOWS

When have you found beauty in a common, everyday scene?

The River-Merchant's Wife
A Letter

by Ezra Pound

While my hair was still cut straight across my forehead
I played about the front gate, pulling flowers.
You came by on bamboo stilts, playing horse,
You walked about my seat, playing with blue plums.
5 And we went on living in the village of Chokan:[1]
Two small people, without dislike or suspicion.

At fourteen I married My Lord you.
I never laughed, being bashful.
Lowering my head, I looked at the wall.
10 Called to, a thousand times, I never looked back.

At fifteen I stopped scowling,
I desired my dust to be mingled with yours
Forever and forever and forever.
Why should I climb the lookout?

15 At sixteen you departed,
You went into far Ku-to-yen,[2] by the river of swirling eddies,
And you have been gone five months.
The monkeys make sorrowful noise overhead.

You dragged your feet when you went out.
20 By the gate now, the moss is grown, the different mosses,
Too deep to clear them away!
The leaves fall early this autumn, in wind.
The paired butterflies are already yellow with August
Over the grass in the West garden;
25 They hurt me. I grow older.
If you are coming down through the narrows of the river Kiang,
Please let me know beforehand,
And I will come out to meet you, As far as Cho-fu-Sa.[3] ❖

---

1. **Chokan.** Suburb of Nanking, a Chinese city
2. **Ku-to-yen.** Island in the Yangtze River
3. **Cho-fu-Sa.** Beach along the Yangtze River, hundreds of miles from Nanking

 **MIRRORS & WINDOWS** Recall a time you missed someone. What memories of that person come to mind when you think of him or her?

Literature Connection

"A Few Don'ts by an Imagiste," a work of literary criticism by **Ezra Pound,** was originally published in *Poetry* magazine in 1913. In this essay, Pound outlines some "rules" for poets and writers. In fact, he compares the writing of poetry not just to other types of writing but to music and science, as well.

As an Imagist, Pound believed that the only true poetic expression was conveyed by concrete (real and tangible) images, as opposed to abstract ideas such as love and happiness. Note Pound's frank, conversational tone in this essay.

A Few Don'ts by an Imagiste

by Ezra Pound

It is better to present one Image in a lifetime than to produce voluminous works.

All this, however, some may consider open to debate. The immediate necessity is to tabulate A LIST OF DON'TS for those beginning to write verses. I can not put all of them into Mosaic negative.[1]

To begin with, consider the three propositions (demanding direct treatment, economy of words, and the sequence of the musical phrase), not as dogma[2]—never consider anything as dogma—but as the result of long contemplation, which, even if it is some one else's contemplation, may be worth consideration.

Pay no attention to the criticism of men who have never themselves written a notable work. Consider the discrepancies[3] between the actual writing of the Greek poets and dramatists, and the theories of the Graeco-Roman grammarians, concocted to explain their metres.

Language

Use no superfluous[4] word, no adjective which does not reveal something.

Don't use such an expression as "dim lands *of peace.*" It dulls the image. It mixes an abstraction with the concrete. It comes from the writer's not realizing that the natural object is always the *adequate* symbol.

Go in fear of abstractions. Do not retell in mediocre verse what has already been done in good prose. Don't think any intelligent person is going to be deceived when you try to shirk all the difficulties of the unspeakably difficult art of good prose by chopping your composition into line lengths. . . .

Don't imagine that the art of poetry is any simpler than the art of music, or that you can please the expert before you have spent at least as much effort on the art of verse as an average piano teacher spends on the art of music.

Be influenced by as many great artists as you can, but have the decency either to acknowledge the debt outright, or to try to conceal it.

Don't allow "influence" to mean merely that you mop up the particular decorative vocabulary of some one or two poets whom you happen to admire. . . .

Use either no ornament or good ornament.

Rhythm and Rhyme

. . . Let the neophyte know assonance and alliteration,[5] rhyme immediate and delayed, simple and polyphonic, as a musician would expect

---

1. **Mosaic negative.** Refers to Mosaic law, or the law of Moses, which begins with the Ten Commandments; many of the commandments begin with "Thou shall not . . ." Pound means that he cannot list every possible thing a poet should not do.
2. **dogma.** Authoritative statement of belief
3. **discrepancies.** Differences
4. **superfluous.** Unnecessary; extra
5. **neophyte . . . alliteration.** *Neophyte*—beginner, new person; *assonance*—repetition of vowel sounds in different words; *alliteration*—repetition of the initial sound of words

to know harmony and counterpoint and all the minutiae of his craft. No time is too great to give to these matters or to any one of them, even if the artist seldom have need of them.

Don't imagine that a thing will "go" in verse just because it's too dull to go in prose.

Don't be "viewy"—leave that to the writers of pretty little philosophic essays. Don't be descriptive; remember that the painter can describe a landscape much better than you can, and that he has to know a deal more about it.

When Shakespeare talks of the "Dawn in russet mantle clad" he presents something which the painter does not present. There is in this line of his nothing that one can call description; he presents.

Consider the way of the scientists rather than the way of an advertising agent for a new soap.

The scientist does not expect to be acclaimed as a great scientist until he has *discovered* something. He begins by learning what has been discovered already. He goes from that point onward. He does not bank on being a charming fellow personally. He does not expect his friends to applaud the results of his freshman class work. Freshmen in poetry are unfortunately not confined to a definite and recognizable class room. They are "all over the shop." Is it any wonder "the public is indifferent to poetry?"

Don't chop your stuff into separate *iambs*.[6] Don't make each line stop dead at the end and then begin every next line with a heave.

Let the beginning of the next line catch the rise of the rhythm wave, unless you want a definite longish pause.

In short, behave as a musician, a good musician, when dealing with that phase of your art which has exact parallels in music. The same laws govern, and you are bound by no others. . . .

A rhyme must have in it some slight element of surprise if it is to give pleasure, it need not be bizarre or curious, but it must be well used if used at all. . . .

Don't mess up the perception of one sense by trying to define it in terms of another. This is usually only the result of being too lazy to find the exact word. To this clause there are possibly exceptions.

The first three simple prescriptions will throw out nine-tenths of all the bad poetry now accepted as standard and classic; and will prevent you from many a crime of production. ❖

---

6. *iambs.* Metrical feet in poetry with one unstressed syllable followed by a stressed syllable

Review Questions

1. According to Pound, what do abstractions do to images? Explain why a natural symbol is preferable to an abstraction.

2. Compare and contrast the writing of poetry to the making of music or the painting of landscapes. How does the phrase from Shakespeare meet Pound's rules?

3. How is a scientist a good model for a poet, according to Pound? Evaluate Pound's rules. Do they strike you as workable and insightful or as limiting and discouraging? Why?

TEXT $\xrightarrow[\longleftarrow]{\text{TO}}$ TEXT CONNECTION

Using the criteria in this essay, how would Pound evaluate his poems "In a Station of the Metro" and "The River-Merchant's Wife: A Letter"? Which criteria do the poems meet? Which do they not meet? What other poems have you read that follow Pound's suggestions?

Refer to Text ▶ ▶ ▶ ▶ ▶ Reason with Text

1a. In "In a Station of the Metro," what does the speaker see in the crowd?

1b. Explain why the speaker describes the faces as an "apparition."

Understand
Find meaning

2a. To what does the speaker liken the faces he sees?

2b. Based on the background information given about this poem, suggest why Pound reduced it to two lines.

Apply
Use information

3a. In "The River-Merchant's Wife," what happened when the speaker was fourteen?

3b. How do the speaker's feelings toward her husband evolve over time?

Analyze
Take things apart

4a. What hurts the speaker in "The River-Merchant's Wife"?

4b. Describe the poem's feeling or mood. Assess how well Pound conveys it.

Evaluate
Make judgments

5a. Name the images in "The River-Merchant's Wife" that suggest time has passed.

5b. Why did Pound use natural imagery to express his ideas, instead of stating them more directly?

Create
Bring ideas together

Analyze Literature

Imagism and Imagery

Evaluate "In a Station of the Metro" according to the goals of Imagism, as outlined in the Literature Connection selection on pages 560–561. For instance, does the poem capture a "single moment of perception"? Does it refer to an author, speaker, or narrator?

What mood is created by the single image in "In a Station of the Metro"? What feelings are conveyed by the imagery in "The River-Merchant's Wife"?

Extend the Text

Writing Options

Creative Writing Write a poem in which you describe a scene that made an impression on you. Try to recreate Ezra Pound's style by describing the scene using an image or images from nature, instead of directly stating how the scene affected you.

Persuasive Writing Write a letter to the editor of *Poetry* magazine in which you express your opinion about the advice Pound offers in "A Few Don'ts by an Imagiste" on pages 560–561. Does he offer sound advice that all writers can use to improve their writing? Explain.

Collaborative Learning

Create Poetry Rules Pound was the founder of Imagism, a movement in early-twentieth-century poetry. In groups, choose another poetic movement and conduct research to learn more about it. As a group, create a set of guidelines for writing that type of poetry. Then have each group member write a poem following those guidelines. Exchange and evaluate one another's poems.

Critical Literacy

Learn More About Imagism In groups of four, identify other Imagist poets and research their lives and works. Choose three of these poets, and assign three group members to role-play them in a panel discussion about Imagism. Have a fourth student mediate the discussion. The panel should discuss what Imagism is, why it is important, what it contributed to modern poetry, and any other topic your group finds relevant.

 Go to **www.mirrorsandwindows.com** for more.

Petals
A Lyric Poem by Amy Lowell

Mid-Day
A Lyric Poem by Hilda Doolittle

Build Background

Literary Context Amy Lowell and Hilda Doolittle (known as H. D.) were the primary women writers of the Imagist movement. Lowell embraced the principles of the movement after meeting Ezra Pound. She then served as a mentor to H. D., promoting her work and that of other Imagist poets in the United States. Women writers of the day had difficulty being recognized and were often spoken for by men. In fact, Pound submitted the first of H. D.'s poems for publication.

Amy Lowell's poem **"Petals"** compares life to a stream into which flower petals are dropped and carried away. In Hilda Doolittle's poem **"Mid-Day,"** the speaker compares her thoughts to a tree dropping seedpods. Both of these melancholy poems use figurative language to compare human experience to nature.

Reader's Context Think of something in nature that reminds you of your life or your mood. What is it? Why do you make this association?

Meet the Authors

Amy Lowell (1874–1925) was born in Brookline, Massachusetts, into one of Boston's wealthiest families. As a woman from a prominent family, she was not allowed to attend college, so she educated herself by reading extensively. She managed to have an independent life, rare for a woman of her day, because she had the resources to support herself. Lowell's desire to contribute to public life found its outlet when, at age thirty-eight, she published her poetry in *A Dome of Many Coloured Glass.*
She soon adopted the Imagist style for which she is best known. Lowell won the Pulitzer Prize for poetry in 1926, one year after her death.

Hilda Doolittle, or **H. D.** (1896–1961), was born in Bethlehem, Pennsylvania. She attended Bryn Mawr College, where she befriended Ezra Pound and Marianne Moore, both American poets. Upon moving to England in 1911, she met Pound again, and he introduced her to the members of London's literary circle, including Amy Lowell. H. D.'s first poems were published in *Poetry* magazine in 1913. After World War II, she experienced chronic health problems but remained a prolific writer until she died in 1961. While best known as an Imagist poet, H. D. also wrote fiction and nonfiction.

Compare Literature

Speaker and Mood
The **speaker** is the character who speaks in, or narrates, a poem—the voice assumed by the writer. The speaker and the writer are not always the same person, however.

Mood, or atmosphere, is the emotion created in the reader by a literary work.

Set Purpose

Women's unique perspectives are represented in the works of both Lowell and Doolittle. In reading each woman's poem, identify and describe the speaker. Record specific words and phrases from the poem to support your opinion. Also think about the mood of the poem, or the emotional response it evokes. Write down one word that captures the feeling you are left with at the end of the poem.

Preview Vocabulary

freighted, 564
crimsoned, 564
employ, 564
anguished, 565
perish, 565

Petals

by Amy Lowell

Life is a stream
On which we strew
Petal by petal the flower of our heart;
The end lost in dream,
5 They float past our view,
We only watch their glad, early start.

<u>Freighted</u> with hope,
<u>Crimsoned</u> with joy,
We scatter the leaves of our opening rose;
10 Their widening scope,
Their distant <u>employ</u>,
We never shall know. And the stream as it flows
Sweeps them away,
Each one is gone
15 Ever beyond into infinite ways.
We alone stay
While years hurry on,
The flower fared forth, though its fragrance still stays. ❖

---

freight • ed (frā′ təd) *adj.,* loaded
crim • soned (krim′ sənd) *adj.,* reddened
em • ploy (em ploi′) *n.,* use

If you could see into the future, what would you want to know? What wouldn't you want to know?

Mid-Day

by Hilda Doolittle

The light beats upon me.
I am startled—
a split leaf crackles on the paved floor—
I am <u>anguished</u>—defeated.

5 A slight wind shakes the seed-pods—
my thoughts are spent
as the black seeds.
My thoughts tear me,
I dread their fever.
10 I am scattered in its whirl.
I am scattered like
the hot shrivelled seeds.

The shriveled seeds
are split on the path—
15 the grass bends with dust,
the grape slips
under its cracked leaf:
yet far beyond the spent seed-pods,
and the blackened stalks of mint,
20 the poplar is bright on the hill,
the poplar spreads out,
deep-rooted among trees.

O poplar, you are great

among the hill-stones,
25 while I <u>perish</u> on the path
among the crevices of the rocks. ❖

Meadowlawn Road: Afternoon, 1991.
Gerrit Greve. Private collection.

> **an • guished** (āŋ´ gwisht) *adj.,* extremely anxious;
> tormented
> **per • ish** (pār´ ish) *v.,* die

MIRRORS & WINDOWS   What images from nature best describe how you feel about life right now?

Refer to Text ▶ ▶ ▶ ▶ ▶   Reason with Text

1a. In "Petals," to what does the speaker compare life?	**1b.** What do the flower petals represent?	**Understand** Find meaning
2a. In the second stanza of "Mid-Day," to what does the speaker compare herself?	**2b.** Suggest another possible metaphor for the speaker's state of mind.	**Apply** Use information
3a. In "Petals," how do the flower petals start their journey?	**3b.** Infer what happens to the flower petals on their journey.	**Analyze** Take things apart
4a. In "Mid-Day," what does the speaker dread?	**4b.** Is the poet's use of imagery effective in illustrating the speaker's feelings? Why or why not?	**Evaluate** Make judgments
5a. What happens to the speaker in the last stanza of "Mid-Day"?	**5b.** Compare and contrast the speaker's state of mind in "Mid-Day" with that of the speaker in "Petals."	**Create** Bring ideas together

Compare Literature

Speaker and Mood

What can you infer about the speaker in each poem? How are the two speakers similar and different? With which speaker do you most identify? Explain.

What feeling are you left with at the end of each poem? What word best describes the mood? How is that mood created using imagery from nature? Support your answer using examples from the selection.

Extend the Text

Writing Options

Creative Writing Write a poem in which you use an image from nature to express your mood today. In your poem, try to use vivid images without expressly referencing yourself or your emotions, following the principles of Imagism.

Expository Writing Write a short comparison-and-contrast essay in which you discuss how nature imagery is used to create mood in "Petals" and "Mid-Day." Compare the imagery, mood, and ideas each author wants to convey in her poem.

Collaborative Learning

Conduct an Author Dialogue When Hilda Doolittle lived in Europe, she met and became friends with Amy Lowell. What was their first meeting like? What did they talk about? Conduct research to learn more about these two poets. Then write and perform a skit in which you and a classmate depict these poets' first meeting.

Media Literacy

Collect Song Lyrics Make a collection of song lyrics that use images of nature to convey a message or mood. Select three of these songs, and write a brief analysis of how imagery is used to create the meaning of each song. You may also compare how similar images are used differently in the songs.

 Go to **www.mirrorsandwindows.com** for more.

1. In the poem "Petals," what do the flower petals leave behind?
   A. stems
   B. pollen
   C. fragrance
   D. memory
   E. color

2. Which of the following best expresses the main idea of "Petals"?
   A. What we value in life gets scattered and swept away like the petals of a flower.
   B. Our hopes and dreams spread out from us and into the world, leaving behind happy memories.
   C. Hopes and dreams are easily discarded.
   D. When we are old and alone, we will have only our memories for comfort.
   E. We never know how what we do in the world ultimately will affect us.

3. Which of the following could be described as *crimson* in color?
   A. a golden necklace
   B. a mossy stone
   C. a moonless night sky
   D. a ripe apple
   E. a cloudless sky

4. Which of the following images does *not* represent the mood of "Mid-Day"?
   A. blackened stalks of mint
   B. shriveled seeds
   C. a cracked leaf
   D. dusty grass
   E. a deep-rooted poplar

5. Which of the following best expresses the main idea of "Mid-Day"?
   A. The speaker feels withered, weak, and scattered, unlike the poplar tree, which is rooted, secure, and majestic.
   B. Everything eventually perishes and turns to stone and dust, even the poplar on the hill.
   C. The dying of plant life in the autumn saddens many people.
   D. Nature can be kind and healing if we open ourselves up to it.
   E. Our thoughts can overcome the mood of the environment that surrounds us.

6. Which of the following lines sharply contrasts the overall mood of "Mid-Day"?
   A. "The light beats upon me."
   B. "I am anguished—defeated."
   C. "I dread their fever."
   D. "the poplar is bright on the hill"
   E. "while I perish on the path"

7. Which of the following statements best summarizes the meaning or meanings of "Mid-Day" and "Petals"?
   A. Some people view nature's inevitable cycle of life and death as signaling rebirth and continuation, while others view it as indicating dying and fading away.
   B. Poets who write about pretty scenes in nature produce upbeat poems, whereas those who write about harsh scenes produce solemn poems.
   C. In literature, trees usually symbolize strength and stability.
   D. People can't see beyond their own environment and place in life.
   E. All of the above

8. **Constructed Response:** Describe a dialogue between the speakers of "Petals" and "Mid-Day." What views might they exchange? What advice might they give one another? Cite evidence from the poems to support your description of what the speakers might say.

9. **Constructed Response:** Identify the strongest and most effective images in "Petals" or "Mid-Day." Describe how the images create the mood of the poem and contribute to its main idea, or theme. Discuss at least three images.

> **TEST-TAKING TIP**
>
> In many tests, the questions are easier at the beginning and get progressively more difficult. Make sure to answer all the easy questions. When you come to a difficult question, don't spend a lot of time on it. Rather, answer it the best you can but flag it somehow. Keep going and complete the rest of the test, and then return to the problematic items you flagged.

William Carlos Williams

> *"If they give you lined paper,
> write the other way."*

William Carlos Williams (1883–1963) was born in Rutherford, New Jersey. He began writing poetry while in high school but also was interested in medicine. His goal upon starting college was to become a dentist, but he soon switched to medicine.

While in medical school at the University of Pennsylvania, William met and became friends with Ezra Pound and Hilda Doolittle (H. D.), both of whom would become influential American figures in the Imagist movement. These relationships fed Williams's interest in literature and poetry, even as he was completing his medical internship in New York City and doing postgraduate study in Germany.

Williams became active in New York City's avant-garde poetry movement and kept in touch with Pound and his literary circle in Europe. Even though Pound served as a mentor to Williams and helped publish his early work, Williams felt that Pound was too tied to European values, culture, and literature. Williams desired instead to create a more American style of poetry, one based on the ideas, experiences, and language of everyday people. Along with poets Marianne Moore and Wallace Stevens, he was one of the leaders of the Modernist movement in the United States. Also, like Pound, Williams mentored a new generation of poets, including several of those who would become known as the Beats (see Unit 7, Part 3).

In 1910, Williams returned to Rutherford and began his medical practice. Specializing in pediatrics, he gained a reputation as a dedicated, old-fashioned doctor. He lived and practiced medicine in Rutherford for the rest of his life, with few of his patients ever knowing he was an accomplished writer.

Regardless, Williams had a full, active literary career, writing short stories, plays, novels, and literary criticism in addition to poetry. His first major collection of poems, *The Tempers*, was published in 1913; he would publish fifty more collections of poetry and prose over the next fifty years. Key works include a five-volume epic poem, *Paterson* (1946–1958), which was based on Patterson, New Jersey (near Rutherford), and an autobiography (1951), which explains the close relationship between his medical and writing careers.

Williams was awarded the National Book Award in 1950, the Bollingen Prize in 1953, and the Pulitzer Prize in 1963. A heart attack in 1948 and a series of strokes beginning in 1951 eventually forced him to end his medical practice. By 1961, he also had stopped writing because of his health.

The Collected Poems of William Carlos Williams
Volume II · 1939-1962
Edited by Christopher MacGowan

Noted Works

The Tempers (1913)

Spring and All (1923)

The Edge of the Knife (1932)

Paterson (1946–1958)

Pictures from Brueghel (1962)

The Red Wheelbarrow
This Is Just to Say
The Dance

Lyric Poems by William Carlos Williams

Build Background

Literary Context William Carlos Williams's lifelong desire to create a modern American poetry can be traced in the three poems that follow, which represent works from the beginning, middle, and end of his prolific fifty-year career.

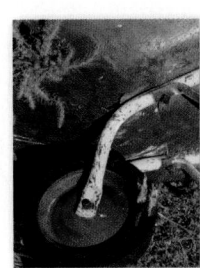

"The Red Wheelbarrow," one of Williams's early poems (published in 1923), reflects the impact of Imagism, the movement that championed the use of free verse and concise images, or word pictures. In just one sentence, sixteen words, Williams creates a series of vivid images. This poem often is compared to Ezra Pound's "In a Station of the Metro."

In 1924, Williams rejected the poetic form of free verse and began experimenting with controlled measure, eventually developing his signature *variable feet,* or, as Williams called them, "loose verses." Commenting on the *iamb,* a common metric foot, Williams remarked, "The iamb is not the normal measure of American speech. The foot has to be expanded or contracted in terms of actual speech. The key to modern poetry is measure, which must reflect the flux of modern life."

"This Is Just to Say" was published in 1934, while Williams still was refining and experimenting with verse. It sometimes is classified as a *found poem,* one in which an existing text has been refashioned and presented as a poem. In terms of structure, a found poem is comparable to a verbal collage: words and phrases that have been collected and rearranged to create new meaning. As with a collage, the meaning of a found poem is left to the interpretation of the audience, which is one of the principles of Imagism.

"The Dance" was published in 1962, at the end of Williams's career. In it, Williams describes the dance in the painting *The Wedding Dance in the Open Air,* which he refers to as *The Kermess.* The painting was the work of Pieter Brueghel, a Flemish artist from the 1500s best known for his scenes of daily life, as portrayed in the living world of field and forest and of sturdy peasants at work and play. As noted elsewhere, Williams aimed to represent scenes of daily life in his own work.

Reader's Context Focus on an everyday object or event, and think about what it means. How would you explain the meaning of this event or object? What details would you include in your explanation?

Analyze Literature

Imagery, Rhythm, and Meter
Imagery is the figurative or descriptive language used to create word pictures, or images.

Rhythm is the pattern of beats, or stresses, in a line of verse or prose, which can be regular or irregular.

Meter is a regular rhythmic pattern in poetry. This pattern is determined by the number of beats, or stresses, in each line.

Set Purpose

Like the other Imagists, Williams developed vivid imagery to create word pictures. As you read each poem, record the specific images in a simple two-column chart. Jot down the image in one column and the sense it appeals to in the second column. Also consider Williams's use of rhythm and meter—qualities he experimented with throughout his career. Read each poem aloud to determine the rhythm, whether regular or irregular. Then decide whether each poem has meter.

Wheelbarrow, 1934. Morris Graves.
Smithsonian American Art Museum, Washington, DC.

The Red Wheelbarrow

by William Carlos Williams

so much depends
upon

a red wheel
barrow

glazed with rain
water

beside the white
chickens ❖

The speaker starts out by saying "so much depends on a red wheel barrow."
What might depend on it? Who might depend on it?

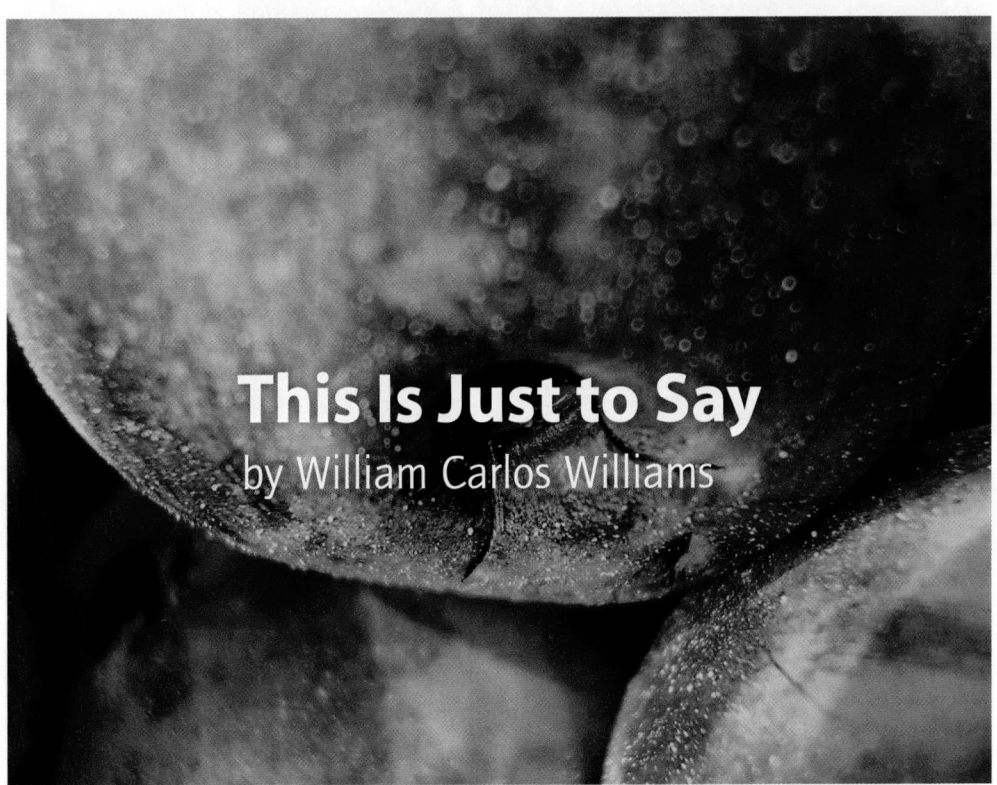

This Is Just to Say
by William Carlos Williams

I have eaten
the plums
that were in
the icebox[1]

5   and which
you were probably
saving
for breakfast

Forgive me
10 they were delicious
so sweet
and so cold ❖

---

1. **icebox.** Refrigerator

 MIRRORS & WINDOWS

When have you done something that you knew you were not supposed to do? How did things turn out?

The Wedding Dance in the Open Air, 1566. Pieter Brueghel the Elder. Detroit Institute of Arts, Detroit, Michigan.

The Dance

by William Carlos Williams

In Brueghel's great picture, The Kermess,[1]
the dancers go round, they go round and
around, the squeal and the blare and the
tweedle of bagpipes, a bugle and fiddles
5   tipping their bellies (round as the thick-
sided glasses whose wash they impound)[2]
their hips and their bellies off balance
to turn them. Kicking and rolling about
the Fair Grounds, swinging their butts, those
10   shanks[3] must be sound to bear up under such
rollicking measures, prance as they dance
in Brueghel's great picture, The Kermess. ❖

---

1. **The Kermess.** Referring to *The Wedding Dance in Open Air*, by
   Pieter Brueghel the Elder, a Flemish painter
2. **whose wash they impound.** Whose beverage they drink
3. **shanks.** Thighs

MIRRORS & WINDOWS

Both Brueghel, the painter, and Williams, the poet, tried to capture everyday life in their works. Is this what most people expect from art and literature? What do you expect?

Refer to Text ▶ ▶ ▶ ▶ ▶ Reason with Text

1a. In "This Is Just to Say," how does the speaker say the plums tasted?	**1b.** Explain why the speaker asks for forgiveness. Does he or she regret eating the plums?	**Understand** Find meaning
2a. In "The Dance," what is off balance? Why?	**2b.** If you were one of the dancers depicted by Williams in this poem, would you be pleased by his description of you? Explain.	**Apply** Use information
3a. List the details provided about the wheelbarrow in "The Red Wheelbarrow."	**3b.** Why are these details significant?	**Analyze** Take things apart
4a. What kind of dance is described in "The Dance"?	**4b.** Judge how Williams feels about the painting he describes. Explain.	**Evaluate** Make judgments
5a. What is on the red wheelbarrow?	**5b.** Suggest how this emphasizes the temporary nature of the image in this poem. What moment is captured?	**Create** Bring ideas together

Analyze Literature

Imagery, Rhythm, and Meter

Review the chart of images you created for each poem. To which senses do the images appeal? What object or experience is created in each poem using this imagery?

What rhythm, or pattern of beats, did you find in each poem? Is the pattern regular or irregular? Does the poem have meter, or a regular rhythmic pattern? How does the use of rhythm and meter affect your reading and understanding of the poem?

Extend the Text

Writing Options

Creative Writing Imagine that you are the owner of the plums in "This Is Just to Say." Write a note to the speaker, explaining why you were saving the plums and why you do or do not forgive him or her.

Expository Writing Each poem represents a different stage in Williams's career. Write an essay of literary criticism in which you explore the differences and similarities in the style and subject matter of these three poems.

Collaborative Learning

Visualize Images Look online and in books and magazines for drawings and photographs that match or are similar to the image that formed in your mind while reading each poem. Compare the photos and drawings you find with those of a classmate, and discuss the process of visualization. How do your mental images differ from the actual images? How are they similar?

Lifelong Learning

Annotate a Bibliography Locate one of each of the following four types of resources by or about William Carlos Williams: (1) a book with one author; (2) a poem, short story, essay, or chapter in a collection of works by one author; (3) an introduction, preface, foreword, or afterword written by someone other than the author(s) of a work; and (4) an article in an encyclopedia or other reference work. For each resource, write an annotated bibliography entry, in which you provide a brief summary of the work along with the publication information.

 Go to **www.mirrorsandwindows.com** for more.

Understand the Concept

What specific color do you think of when you hear the word *red?* Do you think of the color of a rose? A ripe strawberry? A cherry? A stop sign?

There are many shades of red: *carmine, scarlet, cerise, ruby, auburn, burgundy,* and *cardinal.* There are *brick red, fire engine red, candy apple red,* and *blood red.* Each shade is different. Some reds have a purplish tint; others are more orange. Some are darker, and some are lighter and brighter.

You probably could make similar lists of words and phrases for other colors. In doing so, you would be identifying members of a semantic family of words—color words, to be specific.

The word *semantics* refers to the study of meanings of words. **Semantic families** are groups of words that have related meanings because they name or describe related ideas or items. There are semantic families of words for families, school, sports, medicine, work, and just about any other topic or field you can name. Semantic families include everyday words, more complex words, and even slang and personal terms.

Consider the **connotations** of words from these various levels of vocabulary—that is, what the words suggest. For instance, in the group of *family words,* someone who is a *grandmother* could be named in several ways: She could be called *my grammy, my grandmother,* or *the matriarch of our family.* Each of these labels has a slightly different meaning and suggests something different about the relationship with this person.

Think about the connotations of the color words you choose. Select words that suggest the meanings you intend. In addition, choose words that produce vivid images of what you are naming or describing.

Understanding the links among words in a semantic family can help you determine the meanings of unfamiliar words. Recognizing semantic families also can extend your vocabulary, both in speaking and writing.

Apply the Skill

Exercise A

For each color listed below, brainstorm a list of words or phrases for shades of that color. Then choose three words or phrases and explain how they differ. For example, if you chose *brick red, burgundy,* and *ruby,* you might say that *brick red* has brown tones, *burgundy* has purplish tones, and *ruby* is the truest red and the brightest of the three. Use each color word or phrase in a sentence that illustrates the meaning of that specific shade.

1. blue
2. green
3. brown
4. purple
5. black

Exercise B

Choose one of the color words or phrases you identified in Exercise A. Think of an object that can be described as that color. Write an Imagistic poem about the object in the style of "The Red Wheelbarrow."

SPELLING PRACTICE

Homophones

Many people make mistakes using *homophones:* words that sound alike but are spelled differently and have different meanings, such as *to, too,* and *two.* Be sure you know the proper uses of the homophones listed below from "The Red Wheelbarrow," "This Is Just to Say," and "The Dance." Note that a computer spell-check program will not flag an incorrectly used homophone as a misspelled word.

be (bee)	rain (reign, rein)
bear (bare)	red (read)
for (fore, four)	so (sew)
great (grate)	their (there, they're)
in (inn)	which (witch)
picture (pitcher)	you (ewe)

The Love Song of J. Alfred Prufrock

A Dramatic Monologue by T. S. Eliot

Build Background

Literary Context T. S. Eliot's **"The Love Song of J. Alfred Prufrock"** has been described as "the conversation with himself" of the speaker, Prufrock, a timid, indecisive, middle-aged man. In this dramatic monologue, Eliot uses the Modernist **stream-of-consciousness** technique to capture the conversation inside the speaker's mind. "Prufrock" is characteristic of Eliot's work in its lack of nonessential detail and use of allusions and vague images.

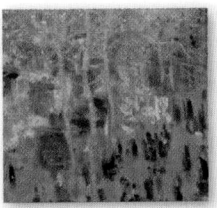

Reader's Context When have you hesitated to say or do something? Explain why you hesitated.

Meet the Author

T(homas) S(tearns) Eliot (1888–1965) was born in St. Louis, Missouri, to a prominent family. His father was a successful businessman, and his mother was a social worker and amateur poet.

After graduating from prep school, Eliot attended Harvard University, where he earned both bachelor's and master's degrees in literature in four years. In 1910, the year he completed his master's, he wrote one of his most famous poems, "The Love Song of J. Alfred Prufrock," which was radically experimental for its day.

Over the next few years, Eliot attended the Sorbonne in France and then Oxford University in England, studying philosophy and religion and supporting himself as a teacher, editor, and bank teller. In 1914, he met Ezra Pound, the unofficial leader of the American expatriate writers living in London, and became part of the city's intellectual and artistic set. At Pound's recommendation, "Prufrock" was published in *Poetry* magazine in 1915, bringing Eliot the attention of the literary world. Publication in 1917 of *Prufrock and Other Observations,* Eliot's first book, further established the young writer. Additional collections of poetry and literary criticism followed in 1920.

After a series of family difficulties, Eliot experienced a brief period of writer's block. Then in 1922, again aided by Pound, Eliot published an even more challenging poem, *The Waste Land,* a view of the moral bankruptcy of the interwar period posed against what Eliot saw as the superior values of the past. Publication of *The Waste Land* established Eliot as one of the most significant poets of the twentieth century.

In 1927, Eliot became a member of the Church of England and a British citizen. He continued to write not only poetry but also several plays and volumes of literary criticism. In 1948, he was awarded the Nobel Prize for literature.

Analyze Literature

Dramatic Monologue and Allusion
A **dramatic monologue** is a poem that presents the speech of a single character in a dramatic situation.

An **allusion** is a figure of speech in which a reference is made to a person, event, object, or work from history or literature.

Set Purpose

T. S. Eliot is best known as a poet, but he also was an accomplished playwright and literary critic. His interest in drama is apparent in this poem, which takes the form of a dramatic monologue. Determine the dramatic situation of J. Alfred Prufrock: What does he want to do? Eliot's vast knowledge of literary and historic topics is apparent in this poem, as well. Jot down three allusions as you read "The Love Song of J. Alfred Prufrock."

Preview Vocabulary

tedious, 577
insidious, 577
linger, 577
assert, 578
presume, 578
formulated, 578
digress, 578
malinger, 579
deferential, 580
obtuse, 580

The Boulevard des Capucines, Paris, 1873. Claude Monet.
La Seine a Vetheuil, Giverny, Paris. (See detail on page 575.)

The Love Song of J. Alfred Prufrock

by T. S. Eliot

S'io credessi che mia risposta fosse
a persona che mai tornasse al mondo,
questa fiamma staria senza più scosse.
Ma per ciò che giammai di questo fondo
non tornò vivo alcun, s'i'odo il vero,
senza tema d'infamia ti rispondo.[1]

---

1. **S'io . . . rispondo.** [Italian] Epigraph from Dante's *Inferno*, Canto 27, lines 61–66.
The speaker is one of the damned telling of his torment: "If I believed that my
response would be / to somebody who would ever return to the world, / this flame
would be without more movement. / But since nobody has returned from this depth
alive, / if I hear the truth, / without fear of infamy, I answer you."

Let us go then, you and I,
When the evening is spread out against the sky
Like a patient etherised[2] upon a table;
Let us go, through certain half-deserted streets,
5   The muttering retreats
Of restless nights in one-night cheap hotels
And sawdust restaurants with oyster-shells:
Streets that follow like a <u>tedious</u> argument
Of <u>insidious</u> intent
10   To lead you to an overwhelming question . . .
Oh, do not ask, "What is it?"
Let us go and make our visit.

In the room the women come and go
Talking of Michelangelo.[3]

15   The yellow fog that rubs its back upon the window-panes,
The yellow smoke that rubs its muzzle on the window-panes,
Licked its tongue into the corners of the evening,
<u>Lingered</u> upon the pools that stand in drains,
Let fall upon its back the soot that falls from chimneys,
20   Slipped by the terrace, made a sudden leap,
And seeing that it was a soft October night,
Curled once about the house, and fell asleep.

And indeed there will be time
For the yellow smoke that slides along the street
25   Rubbing its back upon the window-panes;
There will be time, there will be time
To prepare a face to meet the faces that you meet;
There will be time to murder and create,
And time for all the works and days of hands
30   That lift and drop a question on your plate;
Time for you and time for me,
And time yet for a hundred indecisions,
And for a hundred visions and revisions,
Before the taking of a toast and tea.

---

2. **etherised.** Rendered groggy or numb
3. **Michelangelo.** (1475–1564) Italian sculptor, painter, architect, and poet

---

te • di • ous (tē´ dē əs) *adj.*, long and tiresome
in • sid • i • ous (in sid´ ē əs) *adj.*, deceitful
lin • ger (liŋ´ gər) *v.*, remain or stay longer than usual

35 In the room the women come and go
Talking of Michelangelo.

And indeed there will be time
To wonder, "Do I dare?" and, "Do I dare?"
Time to turn back and descend the stair,
40 With a bald spot in the middle of my hair—
(They will say: "How his hair is growing thin!")
My morning coat, my collar mounting firmly to the chin,
My necktie rich and modest, but <u>asserted</u> by a simple pin—
(They will say: "But how his arms and legs are thin!")
45 Do I dare
Disturb the universe?
In a minute there is time
For decisions and revisions which a minute will reverse.

For I have known them all already, known them all—
50 Have known the evenings, mornings, afternoons,
I have measured out my life with coffee spoons;
I know the voices dying with a dying fall
Beneath the music from a farther room.
          So how should I <u>presume</u>?

55 And I have known the eyes already, known them all—
The eyes that fix you in a <u>formulated</u> phrase,
And when I am formulated, sprawling on a pin,
When I am pinned and wriggling on the wall,
Then how should I begin
60 To spit out all the butt-ends of my days and ways?
          And how should I presume?

And I have known the arms already, known them all—
Arms that are braceleted and white and bare
(But in the lamplight, downed with light brown hair!)
65 Is it perfume from a dress
That makes me so <u>digress</u>?
Arms that lie along a table, or wrap about a shawl.
          And should I then presume?
          And how should I begin?

                                        · · · · ·

70 Shall I say, I have gone at dusk through narrow streets
And watched the smoke that rises from the pipes
Of lonely men in shirt-sleeves, leaning out of windows? . . .

---

as • sert (ä surt´) *v.,* declare; affirm
pre • sume (prē züm´) *v.,* dare; venture; take upon oneself
for • mu • lat • ed (fôr´ myü lā təd) *adj.,* systematical; precise
di • gress (dī gres´) *v.,* deviate from the main topic in speaking or writing

I should have been a pair of ragged claws
Scuttling across the floors of silent seas.
. . . . .

75 And the afternoon, the evening, sleeps
      so peacefully!
Smoothed by long fingers,
Asleep . . . tired . . . or it <u>malingers</u>,
Stretched on the floor, here beside you
      and me.
80 Should I, after tea and cakes and ices,
Have the strength to force the moment to
      its crisis?

A View of the Seine, Paris, 1917. Paul Mathieu.

But though I have wept and fasted,
      wept and prayed,
Though I have seen my head (grown slightly bald) brought in
      upon a platter,
I am no prophet[4]—and here's no great matter;
I have seen the moment of my greatness flicker,
85 And I have seen the eternal Footman hold my coat, and snicker,
And in short, I was afraid.

And would it have been worth it, after all,
After the cups, the marmalade, the tea,
Among the porcelain, among some talk of you and me,
90 Would it have been worth while,
To have bitten off the matter with a smile,
To have squeezed the universe into a ball
To roll it towards some overwhelming question,
To say: "I am Lazarus,[5] come from the dead,
95 Come back to tell you all, I shall tell you all"—
If one, settling a pillow by her head,
      Should say: "That is not what I meant at all.
      That is not it, at all."

And would it have been worth it, after all,
100 Would it have been worth while,
After the sunsets and the dooryards and the sprinkled streets,
After the novels, after the teacups, after the skirts that trail along
      the floor—
And this, and so much more?—
It is impossible to say just what I mean!

---

4. **I am no prophet.** The head of the prophet John the Baptist was brought to Princess
   Salome on a platter.
5. **Lazarus.** In the Bible, John 11:1–44, Lazarus is resurrected.

ma • lin • ger (mə liŋ′ gər) *v.,* pretend illness

105　But as if a magic lantern threw the nerves in patterns on a screen:
　　　Would it have been worth while
　　　If one, settling a pillow or throwing off a shawl,
　　　And turning toward the window, should say:
　　　　　"That is not it at all,
110　　　That is not what I meant, at all."
　　　　　　　　　. . . . .

　　　No! I am not Prince Hamlet, nor was meant to be;
　　　Am an attendant lord, one that will do
　　　To swell a progress,⁶ start a scene or two,
　　　Advise the prince; no doubt, an easy tool,
115　Deferential, glad to be of use,
　　　Politic, cautious, and meticulous;
　　　Full of high sentence,⁷ but a bit obtuse;
　　　At times, indeed, almost ridiculous—
　　　Almost, at times, the Fool.

120　I grow old . . . I grow old . . .
　　　I shall wear the bottoms of my trousers rolled.

　　　Shall I part my hair behind? Do I dare to eat a peach?
　　　I shall wear white flannel trousers, and walk upon the beach.
　　　I have heard the mermaids singing, each to each.

125　I do not think that they will sing to me.

　　　I have seen them riding seaward on the waves
　　　Combing the white hair of the waves blown back
　　　When the wind blows the water white and black.

　　　We have lingered in the chambers of the sea
130　By sea-girls wreathed with seaweed red and brown
　　　Till human voices wake us, and we drown. ❖

---

6. **progress.** Procession
7. **sentence.** Opinions

> **def • er • en • tial** (def′ ər en′ ch'l) *adj.,* respectful
> **ob • tuse** (ôb tüs′) *adj.,* slow to understand or perceive; insensitive

MIRRORS & WINDOWS　Prufrock says, "In a minute there is time for decisions and revisions which a minute will reverse." Are you a decisive person? Do you tend to make decisions and follow through on them, or do you usually change your mind at some point?

Refer to Text ▶ ▶ ▶ ▶ ▶ **Reason with Text**

1a. What curls around the house and falls asleep?	**1b.** What does the color suggest?	**Understand** Find meaning
2a. Identify the "crisis" to which the speaker refers in the second section of the poem. Of what is he afraid?	**2b.** When you experience a moment of self-doubt, what strategies help you build a more confident picture of yourself?	**Apply** Use information
3a. List the sea imagery used in the poem.	**3b.** Analyze what this imagery reveals about the speaker's psychological state.	**Analyze** Take things apart
4a. Does the speaker believe his life has been bold or fast paced?	**4b.** Argue whether "The Love Song of J. Alfred Prufrock" is an accurate portrayal of a modern person. Explain.	**Evaluate** Make judgments
5a. Does the speaker believe he is a modern-day hero? Explain.	**5b.** What qualities should a modern-day hero have? Explain.	**Create** Bring ideas together

Analyze Literature

Dramatic Monologue and Allusion

What is the dramatic situation of J. Alfred Prufrock? What does Prufrock reveal about himself in the dramatic monologue that makes him sympathetic or unsympathetic?

What allusions did you find in this poem? Research each allusion, and write a sentence or two explaining its meaning. Evaluate what each allusion contributes to the meaning of the poem.

Extend the Text

Writing Options

Creative Writing A *parody* is a literary work that imitates another work for a humorous, often satirical purpose. Write a parody in free verse on the topic of *indecision.* Exchange poems with a classmate, and discuss one another's work.

Expository Writing Suppose a friend tells you he or she doesn't understand the title of this poem. Write a brief essay analyzing the poem's title. How is the poem a love song? Does it fit the traditional concept of a love song?

Collaborative Learning

Write a Situation Comedy Work with a small group to write an episode of a situation comedy about a man like J. Alfred Prufrock. Change the tragic elements of his psychological profile into humorous traits. Perform the episode for your class.

Critical Literacy

Research Allusions T. S. Eliot often uses allusions in his poems to evoke in his readers echoes of others works and other ideas, thus enriching the context of the poem. With a partner, research the following original texts (all alluded to in "Prufrock"), noting where you located each source. Then write a footnote for each allusion, explaining how Eliot changed the reference for his own purpose and what point the allusion makes in the stated lines of the poem. *Original Texts:* (1) Hesiod's "Works and Days" (referenced in line 29 of "Prufrock"); (2) William Shakespeare's *Twelfth Night,* Act I, scene i, line 4 (referenced in line 52 of "Prufrock"), (3) Emily Dickinson's "I cannot live with you" (referenced in line 89 of "Prufrock"); and (4) Andrew Marvell's "To His Coy Mistress" (referenced in line 92 of "Prufrock").

 Go to **www.mirrorsandwindows.com** for more.

If you and a friend ever have read the same story or poem and disagreed about what it means, you already know that a work of literature can have multiple interpretations. In fact, the theory of **reader-response criticism** suggests that the reader creates the meaning of a text by reading and responding to it.

As you delve into a literary work, you are engaged in a creative process that takes in the text and extends its significance in countless directions. According to this theory, the reading process is as much about you as it is about the words printed on the page.

"A poem is what the reader lives through under the guidance of the text and experiences as relevant to the text."

—LOUISE ROSENBLATT, LITERARY CRITIC

Overview of Reader-Response Criticism

Literary critic Louise Rosenblatt, an early advocate of reader-response theory, introduced the notion that a poem is "produced" by the interaction between the work and the reader. Rosenblatt and fellow critic Stanley Fish have argued that a literary work should not be viewed as a self-enclosed object, containing a fixed meaning or set of associations. Rather, many different interpretations of a work can be justified, as long as the reading respects the text.

Reader-response theory also recognizes that how a work is read will vary from culture to culture and perhaps even from gender to gender. Similarly, people of different ages will respond differently to the same work. The high school student reading T. S. Eliot's poem "The Love Song of J. Alfred Prufrock" will react to Prufrock's dilemma with a particular set of expectations and emotions, while a middle-aged reader most likely will take another view of the hesitant narrator and his conflict. According to reader-response theory, both will be correct.

What is it about a poem, for instance, that allows so many possible analyses? The reader-response lens focuses on the gaps created by the poem, spaces for which the reader is free to supply the meaning. When you use this critical lens, you become conscious of your-self as an active participant in the construction of meaning. You do not attempt to fit a single key to the work but allow yourself a full range of associations and ideas as you read. If you pay attention to your own mental processes as a reader, you may find that you are skilled at constructing a unique meaning from a literary work.

Application of Reader-Response Criticism

The richness of the reader-response approach to literature is apparent when we apply it to a complex and subtle poem such as "The Love Song of J. Alfred Prufrock." As you read the poem using the reader-response lens, consider the role *you* play in analyzing the following elements.

Literary Devices: Dramatic Monologue and Tone

As noted earlier, Eliot's narrative poem takes the form of a dramatic monologue. The speaker invites you, the reader, to accompany him through the London streets on a visit of great significance to him. Consider how the speaker's tone prepares you for the experience to come:

> Let us go, then, you and I,
> When the evening is spread out against the sky
> Like a patient etherised upon a table;
> Let us go, through certain half-deserted streets,
> The muttering retreats
> Of restless nights in one-night cheap hotels
> And sawdust restaurants with oyster shells;
> Streets that follow like a tedious argument
> Of insidious intent
> To lead you to an overwhelming question . . .

❏ **Analyze** Notice the images that Prufrock, the narrator, selects as representative of his journey through the city. What tone is set in this first stanza? How do you respond to the similes in lines 2–3 and 8–9? Why might Prufrock want to avoid discussing the "overwhelming question" on his mind? Do you find any irony at this point in the poem? Jot down some notes about your response to the opening stanza.

ELIOT

Setting and Mood

The shifting setting of the poem reflects not only Prufrock's physical progress from the streets to the room where a party is taking place; it also reveals his inner consciousness. Notice all the details that your companion points out, like the yellow fog that takes on a life of its own and the women who talk of the artist Michelangelo. These images absorb and perhaps oppress the lonely middle-aged man and create a particular mood.

Consider the speaker's hesitation at ending his walk at the very place where he must ask his pressing question:

> And indeed there will be time
> For the yellow smoke that slides along the street
> Rubbing its back upon the window-panes;
> There will be time, there will be time
> To prepare a face to meet the faces that you meet.

❑ **Analyze** What is Prufrock feeling as he nears his destination? What aspects of your own social experiences can you draw on to understand this man? Use your memories and observations as you construct meaning from these lines.

Desire and Conflict

Recall that the critic using the reader-response lens examines the gaps in the text, the places where the reader must supply the meaning. "The Love Song of J. Alfred Prufrock," with its numerous ellipses (. . .) and overall stylistic fragmentation, provides you with many opportunities to participate imaginatively in the poem.

This fragmentation deepens our understanding of Prufrock as a man in conflict with his own desires. For example, he sees himself not as a hero but as "an attendant lord. . . . Almost, at times, the Fool." He wonders, "Do I dare to eat a peach?" And he fears that the mermaids, those fabulous sirens of desire, will not sing their song to him.

❑ **Analyze** As you examine the structure of the poem, you will see that Eliot uses ellipses to indicate each significant break and leap in the consciousness of Prufrock. What seems to be happening to this character between lines 69 and 70, between lines 74 and 75, and between lines 111 and 112? How do the speaker's emotions shift at each break in the text and serve to highlight his emotional conflict?

Metaphor and Symbol

In analyzing the metaphors and symbols in this poem, leave your mind free to form associations and ideas. You are not looking for the one right interpretation but for the interpretation that fits your overall response to the poem. For instance, what emotions are stirred in you by these lines?

> I should have been a pair of ragged claws
> Scuttling across the floors of silent seas.

❑ **Analyze** Find three uses of figurative language that speak to you or move you. How does each example strengthen your unique interpretation of the poem? Why do these examples seem to sum up the experience of reading "The Love Song of J. Alfred Prufrock"?

> **WRITING ABOUT**
>
> ## Reader-Response Criticism
>
> Write an essay that answer this question: How does the speaker's thought process make his ultimate refusal to act seem inevitable or unavoidable? Use details from the poem to illustrate the concept of a mind defeating its own desires and needs.

Poetry

A Lyric Poem by Marianne Moore

Ars Poetica

A Lyric Poem by Archibald MacLeish

Build Background

Literary Context Many poets have attempted to describe their theory of their art. The first was Roman poet Horace (c. 65–8 BCE), who wrote an essay called "Ars Poetica," or "The Art of Poetry." In it, he addresses concepts such as the relationship between style and subject and the need for poems to be brief in length but lasting in meaning.

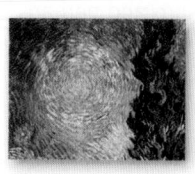

In **"Poetry,"** published in 1924, Marianne Moore suggests that poetry must be accessible to engage readers, writing "We do not admire what we cannot understand." In this poem, Moore uses a *catalog* of particulars to define a general term, which is characteristic of her work.

Archibald MacLeish presents his perspective in a poem entitled **"Ars Poetica,"** published in 1926. MacLeish's theory of poetry is stated simply in lines such as "A poem should not mean but be." Although MacLeish wrote this poem after the Imagist movement had ended, his presentation of a sequence of distinct images is clearly Imagist in style.

Reader's Context How would you define *poetry?* What makes a poem good?

Meet the Authors

Marianne Moore (1887–1972) was born in Kirkwood, Missouri. She attended Bryn Mawr College, where she published poetry in the college literary magazine and studied history, law, and politics. In 1918, she and her mother moved to New York City, where Moore became an assistant at the New York Public Library. Meanwhile, she wrote poetry. Friend and fellow poet Hilda Doolittle (H. D.) recognized Moore's genius and arranged to publish a book of her poetry without telling her. That first book, entitled simply *Poems,* came out in 1921. Throughout her life, Moore was widely recognized for her writing and won numerous awards and honors.

Archibald MacLeish (1906–2001), born in Glencoe, Illinois, graduated from Yale in 1915 and earned a law degree from Harvard in 1919. He left for France in 1917 to serve in a medical unit during World War I. *Tower of Ivory,* his first book of poetry, was published the same year. MacLeish's experiences during the war and the Great Depression shaped his intellectual interests and work. His growing social awareness was reflected in this writing. A prolific writer, he was awarded three Pulitzer Prizes: two for poetry (*Conquistador* in 1933 and *Collected Poems* in 1953) and one for drama (*J. B.* in 1958).

Compare Literature

Theme and Stanza

A **theme** is a central message or perception about life that is revealed through a literary work. It may be stated or implied.

A **stanza** is a group of lines in a poem. Types of stanzas include the *couplet* (two lines), *triplet* (three), *quatrain* (four), and *octave* (eight).

Set Purpose

Like the Roman poet Homer, Modernist poets Moore and MacLeish wrote about their art—in effect, stating their own theories of poetry. Write a sentence summarizing each poet's theory, which is presented as the theme of his or her poem. Decide whether the theme is stated or implied. Also evaluate the poet's use of stanzas, an important element of form. What type or types of stanzas are used in each poem?

Preview Vocabulary

dilate, 585
derivative, 586
valid, 586
prominence, 586
insolence, 586
triviality, 586
palpable, 587

Poetry

by Marianne Moore

Nude Descending a Staircase #2, 1912.
Marcel Duchamp. Philadelphia Museum of Art,
Philadelphia, Pennsylvania.

I, too, dislike it: there are things that are important beyond all this fiddle.[1]
    Reading it, however, with a perfect contempt for it, one discovers in
    it after all, a place for the genuine.
        Hands that can grasp, eyes
5   that can <u>dilate</u>, hair that can rise
            if it must, these things are important not because a

---

1. **fiddle.** Nonsense

di • late (dī´ lāt) *v.*, become larger or wider

high-sounding interpretation can be put upon them but because they are
    useful. When they become so <u>derivative</u> as to become unintelligible,
      the same thing may be said for all of us, that we
10   do not admire what
          we cannot understand: the bat
            holding on upside down or in quest of something to

    eat, elephants pushing, a wild horse taking a roll, a tireless wolf under
      a tree, the immovable[2] critic twitching his skin like a horse that feels a flea, the base-
15   ball fan, the statistician[3]—
          nor is it <u>valid</u>
            to discriminate against "business documents and

    school-books"; all these phenomena are important. One must make a distinction
      however: when dragged into <u>prominence</u> by half poets, the result is not poetry,
20   nor till the poets among us can be
          "literalists of
          the imagination"[4]—above
            <u>insolence</u> and <u>triviality</u> and can present

    for inspection, "imaginary gardens with real toads in them," shall we have
25   it. In the meantime, if you demand on the one hand,
      the raw material[5] of poetry in
        all its rawness and
        that which is on the other hand
          genuine, then you are interested in poetry. ❖

---

2. **immovable.** Stubborn
3. **statistician.** Expert in statistics
4. **"literalists of the imagination."** Term from W. B. Yeats's *Ideas of Good and Evil*, describing people who take words at their precise meaning
5. **raw material.** Basic ingredients

> de • riv • a • tive (də riv´ ə tiv) *adj.,* based on something else; imitative
> val • id (va´ ləd) *adj.,* sound; just
> prom • i • nence (prôm´ ə nents) *n.,* conspicuousness
> in • so • lence (in´ sə lənts) *n.,* disrespectfulness
> triv • i • al • i • ty (triv' ē al´ ə tē) *n.,* something insignificant

 **MIRRORS & WINDOWS** — The speaker states that "we do not admire what we cannot understand." Do you agree with this idea?

Ars Poetica

by Archibald MacLeish

Road with Cypress and Star, 1890. Vincent van Gogh. Kroller-Muller Museum, Otterlo, The Netherlands.

A poem should be <u>palpable</u> and mute.
As a globed fruit,

Dumb
As old medallions[1] to the thumb,

5 Silent as the sleeve-worn stone
Of casement ledges where the moss has
     grown—

A poem should be wordless
As the flight of birds.

A poem should be motionless in time
10 As the moon climbs,

Leaving, as the moon releases
Twig by twig the night-entangled trees,

Leaving, as the moon behind the winter leaves,
Memory by memory the mind—

15 A poem should be motionless in time
As the moon climbs.

A poem should be equal to:
Not true.

For all the history of grief
20 An empty doorway and a maple leaf.

For love
The leaning grasses and two lights above
     the sea—

A poem should not mean
But be. ❖

---

1. **medallions.** Medals

pal • pa • ble (pal´ pə b'l) *adj.,* easily perceived; obvious; clear

MIRRORS & WINDOWS

Do MacLeish and Moore agree on what poetry should be? Which poem best expresses what you think of poetry?

Refer to Text ▶ ▶ ▶ ▶ ▶ **Reason with Text**

1a. In "Poetry," about what must we "make a distinction"?	**1b.** Describe the speaker's attitude toward what the "half poets" create.	**Understand** Find meaning
2a. According to Moore, what does one discover in poetry?	**2b.** Examine one of the poems in this unit in terms of Moore's definition of poetry.	**Apply** Use information
3a. According to the speaker in "Ars Poetica," what should be "palpable and mute"?	**3b.** Consider the following phrases: "all the history of grief" and "An empty doorway and a maple leaf." Which of these lines "means" in the speaker's sense, and which line simply "is"?	**Analyze** Take things apart
4a. In what sense should a poem be "as the moon climbs," according to the speaker in "Ars Poetica"?	**4b.** Judge whether the speaker in "Ars Poetica" would approve of Marianne Moore's poem "Poetry."	**Evaluate** Make judgments
5a. Describe what makes someone interested in poetry.	**5b.** Summarize what demands the reader or listener should make on poetry.	**Create** Bring ideas together

Compare Literature

Theme and Stanza

What is the central theme of "Ars Poetica"? How is it similar to that of Moore's "Poetry"? What are these poets saying about the nature and purpose of poetry? Is the theme in each poem stated or implied?

What two types of stanzas does Moore use in "Poetry"? How does using stanzas of different lengths affect the way you read the poem? What type of stanza does MacLeish use in "Ars Poetica?" How does this stanza type affect the way you read the poem?

Extend the Text

Writing Options

Creative Writing Write a dialogue between Marianne Moore and Archibald MacLeish. What might they say to each other? What attitude might each have toward the other and about his or her own ideas? Share your dialogue with the class.

Persuasive Writing You and a friend are debating the ideas expressed in these two poems. As a way of continuing the conversation, write your friend a paragraph explaining which view of poetry—Moore's or MacLeish's—most corresponds with your own and why.

Collaborative Learning

Define Poetry With two or three classmates, discuss the ideas presented in "Poetry" and "Ars Poetica." Do you agree or disagree with the ideas about poetry expressed in these poems? What does poetry mean to you? Together, write your own definition of poetry. Use both abstract and concrete language.

Lifelong Learning

Use Searching Tools Identify a source of information about each of the following topics: Archibald MacLeish, "Ars Poetica," *Conquistador* (the title of MacLeish's poetry collection), Marianne Moore, *Poems* (the title of Moore's poetry collection). What information do you see in the catalog entry for each source? How does this information help determine whether the sources may be useful to someone writing about these poems or poets?

 Go to **www.mirrorsandwindows.com** for more.

ARS POETICA

by Vicente Huidobro

Vicente Huidobro (1893–1948) was born in Chile to a wealthy family. He founded his own magazine in 1913, *Azul,* and published his first work in it. In 1916, he went to Europe, where he met artists such as painter Pablo Picasso and poet Pierre Reverdy. Upon returning to Chile in 1925, he became a newspaper editor and launched an unsuccessful campaign for the presidency. He returned to Europe again, where he completed a series of poems that became his master work, *Altazor.*

Huidobro's poem **"Ars Poetica"** is a manifesto of the *Creacionismo* (Creationism) artistic movement, which emerged out of the avant-garde movement in the early 1900s. Followers of this movement believed that poetry should do more than describe its subjects; it also should give them life. In "Ars Poetica," Huidobro creates a powerful image of what he believes poetry can do. This idea is encapsulated in the famous line "The poet is a little God."

Let poetry be like a key
That opens a thousand doors.
A leaf falls; something flies overhead;
Let as much as the eyes see be created,
5   And the soul of the listener tremble.

Invent new worlds and watch your word;
The adjective, when it does not create life, kills.

We are in the age of nerves.
Muscles hang,
10   Like a memory, in museums,
But we are not the weaker for it:
True vigor
Lives in the head.

Do not sing the rose, O poets!
15   Make it bloom in the poem.

For us alone
All things live under the sun.

The poet is a little God. ❖

MIRRORS & WINDOWS

This poem ends with the line "The poet is a little God." Do you agree with the speaker's view of the power of poetry?

A New Planet, 1921. K. F. Yuon.
Tretiakov Gallery, Moscow, Russia.

Refer and Reason

1. Where does "true vigor" live? Identify the ways that poetry has power, according to the speaker.

2. What does the speaker want poets to do with the rose? Determine whether this poem meets the speaker's own criteria for true poetry.

3. To what does the speaker compare the poet? Summarize the speaker's view of poetry, as described in this poem.

Writing Options

1. Write your own "Ars Poetica" poem, expressing your view of what poetry should be. Write your poem in the style that best reflects your view of poetry.

2. Write a letter to Vicente Huidobro, agreeing or disagreeing with his view of poetry. In your letter, explain your view of poetry and compare it with the view he expressed in "Ars Poetica."

Go to **www.mirrorsandwindows.com** for more.

somewhere
i have never travelled,gladly
beyond

by e. e. cummings

somewhere i have never travelled,gladly beyond
any experience,your eyes have their silence:
in your most frail gesture are things which enclose me,
or which i cannot touch because they are too near

5   your slightest look easily will unclose me
though i have closed myself as fingers,
you open always petal by petal myself as Spring opens
(touching skilfully,mysteriously)her first rose

or if your wish be to close me, i and
10   my life will shut very beautifully,suddenly,
as when the heart of this flower imagines
the snow carefully everywhere descending;

nothing which we are to perceive in this world equals
the power of your intense fragility:whose texture
15   compels me with the colour of its countries,
rendering death and forever with each breathing

(i do not know what it is about you that closes
and opens; only something in me understands
the voice of your eyes is deeper than all roses)
20   nobody,not even the rain,has such small hands ❖

The speaker tells the subject of the poem, "i do not know what it is about you that closes and opens; only something in me understands." Who has the power to "open" or "close" you?

Self Portrait, c. 1940. E. E. Cummings.

Refer and Reason

1. What does the speaker say happens when the person being addressed looks at him? Identify the various things to which the speaker compares the person addressed. How are the descriptions contradictory?

2. What does the speaker understand about the subject of this poem? Evaluate the effect the subject has on the speaker of that poem.

3. Identify the line that indicates whether the speaker is happy or unhappy about his relationship with the subject. Considering the perspective of the speaker, how do you think the person addressed feels about him? What effect does the person being addressed have on the speaker? Give evidence to support your response.

Writing Options

1. Write a greeting card message for the person who is addressed in "somewhere I have never travelled,gladly beyond." Expand on the metaphor of *spring* expressed in the second stanza.

2. Imagine that a classmate tells you he or she thinks that Cummings's unconventional style makes his poetry less valuable as art. Do you agree or disagree? In response to your classmate's statement, write a brief paragraph in which you explore Cummings's unconventional style.

 Go to **www.mirrorsandwindows.com** for more.

Wallace Stevens (1879–1955) was born and raised in Reading, Pennsylvania. After spending three years at Harvard, he went to work for a newspaper; disliking journalism, he left and went to law school. He was admitted to the bar in 1904 and maintained a private practice until 1908, when he joined the legal staff of an insurance company. In 1916, Stevens joined the Hartford Accident and Indemnity Company, eventually becoming its vice president. Although he held this position until his death, few of his colleagues knew that he wrote poetry. He once told a reporter, "It gives a man character as a poet to have this daily contact with a job." His *Collected Poems* (1954) won a Pulitzer Prize and the National Book Award.

"Anecdote of the Jar" was published in 1923. In this short poem, Stevens juxtaposes a human-made object against the Tennessee wilderness to show the relationship between humans and nature. As you read, note Stevens's straightforward, almost conversational style.

Anecdote of the Jar

by Wallace Stevens

I placed a jar in Tennessee,
And round it was, upon a hill.
It made the slovenly[1] wilderness
Surround that hill.

The wilderness rose up to it,
And sprawled around, no longer wild.
The jar was round upon the ground
And tall and of a port in air.

It took dominion[2] everywhere.
The jar was gray and bare.
It did not give of bird or bush,
Like nothing else in Tennessee. ❖

---

1. **slovenly.** Untidy in appearance
2. **dominion.** Power; control

The jar is out of place in the wilderness but takes control over it. Is it possible to achieve progress or growth without damaging the environment?

Refer and Reason

1. How does the speaker describe the jar? Compare and contrast the jar and the wilderness, as described by the speaker in this poem.

2. How did the wilderness change after the jar was placed on the hill? Evaluate the speaker's view of nature and human-made objects. Does the speaker have more respect for nature or for the jar? Explain your answer.

3. Why was the jar "like nothing else in Tennessee"? What has more power: the jar or the wilderness? Why?

Writing Options

1. Imagine that you are the wilderness in "Anecdote of the Jar." Write a letter to the editor, in which you respond to the ideas Stevens expresses about humans and nature in the poem.

2. Write a critical essay in which you examine the ideas Wallace Stevens expresses in the poem "Anecdote of the Jar" and compare them to your own.

Go to **www.mirrorsandwindows.com** for more.

As described in Part 1, many early-twentieth-century authors felt alienated from American culture and went to Europe to seek inspiration and fellowship. However, another group rooted themselves deeply in their homeland and examined the common values and experiences of everyday Americans. Some of these authors have been called **Regionalists**—writers whose work is characterized by a particular geographical setting—but that label is too confining. In their poems, short stories, and novels, these authors explored universal topics and themes that reached beyond any given locale.

Willa Cather's best-known novels and short stories depicted life in the small towns and homesteads of rural Nebraska. Through her strong, spirited female characters, Cather portrayed both the stability and integrity that came from living a traditional life and the desire to defy traditional roles and experience new interests and lifestyles.

In detailed descriptions of life in rural New England, poet Robert Frost explored people's everyday worries, disappointments, and tragedies and their ability to endure them. Although a traditionalist in his commitment to regular rhyme and meter, Frost broke with convention in using everyday language. Given these qualities, his poems were accessible to an audience of general readers yet sophisticated enough to draw critical interest and appreciation.

Like Frost, poets Carl Sandburg and Edgar Lee Masters wrote in simple, straightforward language about common topics and themes, including disappointment and death. However, like many Modernist poets, Sandburg and Masters abandoned poetic conventions such as form, meter, and verse. Both acknowledged being influenced by nineteenth-century poet Walt Whitman.

Hills, South Truro, 1930. Edward Hopper.
Cleveland Museum of Art, Cleveland, Ohio.

A Wagner Matinee

A Short Story by Willa Cather

Build Background

Literary Context Published in 1904, **"A Wagner Matinee"** is one of Willa Cather's earliest stories. In it, she juxtaposes pioneer life in Red Willow, Nebraska, with city life in Boston, Massachusetts.

When Aunt Georgiana visits her nephew, Clark, it stirs in him appreciation for the care she provided him as a child but also sadness at the realization of what her life in Nebraska has lacked. Clark's conflicting feelings emerge when he takes Georgiana to an afternoon performance of the operatic music of Richard Wagner (Väg´nər), a nineteenth-century German composer. Music was one of Cather's passionate interests.

Reader's Context Imagine that you are listening to favorite piece of music. What emotions do you feel?

Meet the Author

Willa Cather (1873–1947) was born in Virginia, but when she was ten, her family moved to frontier Nebraska to homestead a tract of land. The family later moved to the town of Red Cloud, where Cather's father operated a loan and insurance business. He was a successful businessman but never wealthy or influential, which Cather attributed to his pursuit of intellectual and spiritual interests over financial ones.

The family borrowed money to send Cather to the University of Nebraska, where she wrote reviews of books, plays, and music for the *Nebraska Journal*. After graduating in 1895, she moved to Pittsburgh, Pennsylvania, and worked as a newspaper and magazine writer and editor. She also published collections of poetry and short stories. In 1906, she moved to New York City and joined *McClure's* magazine, first as a contributing editor and then as managing editor. Her first novel, *Alexander's Bridge,* was serialized in that publication in 1912. It told the story of a restless middle-aged engineer looking for diversion in life and ultimately sacrificing his integrity to acquire it.

At the suggestion of fellow author Sarah Orne Jewett, Cather turned to the subject she knew best: the Nebraska prairie and its people. Over the next five years, she wrote two of her most famous novels, *O Pioneers!* (1913) and *My Antonia* (1918). She was awarded the Pulitzer Prize for her novel *One of Ours* in 1923 and the Howells Medal from the American Academy and Institute of Arts and Letters in 1930 for *Death Comes for the Archbishop*.

Cather continued to write novels and short stories until her death in 1947. Her work is known for its strong, unconventional female characters and its well-defined sense of time and place.

Analyze Literature

Narrator, Point of View, and Characterization
A **narrator** is a character or speaker who tells a story.

Point of view is the vantage point from which a story is told.

Characterization is the act of creating or describing a character.

Set Purpose

Given Cather's reputation for creating strong woman characters, her decision to have a man narrate "A Wagner Matinee" is an interesting one. A writer's decisions about narrator and point of view determine how much and what kinds of information readers are given. As you read, consider what information is provided by Clark, the narrator, and whether it is reliable. On what does he base his opinion of his aunt? Consider, too, the other ways Cather creates the character of Aunt Georgiana.

Preview Vocabulary

callow, 598
revert, 598
reverential, 598
tremulously, 599
respective, 600
overture, 601
prelude, 601
interminably, 602
jocularity, 603
reproach, 603

First Row Orchestra, 1951. Edward Hopper.
Hirshhorn Museum, Washington, DC.

A Wagner Matinee

by Willa Cather

**The name of my Aunt Georgiana opened before me
a gulf of recollection so wide and deep.**

I received one morning a letter, written in pale ink on glassy, blue-lined note-paper, and bearing the postmark of a little Nebraska village. This communication, worn and rubbed, looking as if it had been carried for some days in a coat pocket that was none too clean, was from my Uncle Howard, and informed me that his wife had been left a small legacy[1] by a bach-elor relative, and that it would be necessary for her to go to Boston to attend to the settling of the estate. He requested me to meet her at the station and render her whatever services might be necessary. On examining the date indicated as that of her arrival, I found it to be no

---

1. **legacy.** Inheritance

later than tomorrow. He had characteristically delayed writing until, had I been away from home for a day, I must have missed my aunt altogether.

The name of my Aunt Georgiana opened before me a gulf of recollection so wide and deep that, as the letter dropped from my hand, I felt suddenly a stranger to all the present conditions of my existence, wholly ill at ease and out of place amid the familiar surroundings of my study. I became, in short, the gangling farmer-boy my aunt had known, scourged with chilblains[2] and bashfulness, my hands cracked and sore from the corn husking. I sat again before her parlor organ, fumbling the scale with my stiff, red fingers, while she, beside me, made canvas mittens for the huskers.

The next morning, after preparing my landlady for a visitor, I set out for the station. When the train arrived I had some difficulty in finding my aunt. She was the last of the passengers to alight, and it was not until I got her into the carriage that she seemed really to recognize me. She had come all the way in a day coach; her linen duster[3] had become black with soot and her black bonnet grey with dust during the journey. When we arrived at my boarding-house the landlady put her to bed at once, and I did not see her again until the next morning.

Whatever shock Mrs. Springer experienced at my aunt's appearance, she considerately concealed. As for myself, I saw my aunt's battered figure with that feeling of awe and respect with which we behold explorers who have left their ears and fingers north of Franz-Joseph-Land, or their health somewhere along the Upper Congo.[4] My Aunt Georgiana had been a music teacher at the Boston Conservatory, somewhere back in the latter sixties.[5] One summer, while visiting in the little village among the Green Mountains where her ancestors had dwelt for generations, she had kindled the <u>callow</u> fancy of my uncle, Howard Carpenter, then an idle, shiftless boy of twenty-one. When she returned to her duties in Boston, Howard followed her, and the upshot of this infatuation was that she eloped with him, eluding the reproaches of her family and the criticism of her friends by going with him to the Nebraska frontier.[6] Carpenter, who, of course, had no money, took up a homestead in Red Willow County, fifty miles from the railroad. There they had measured off their land themselves, driving across the prairie in a wagon, to the wheel of which they had tied a red cotton handkerchief, and counting its revolutions. They built a dug-out in the red hillside, one of those cave dwellings whose inmates so often <u>reverted</u> to primitive conditions. Their water they got from the lagoons where the buffalo drank, and their slender stock of provisions[7] was always at the mercy of bands of roving Indians. For thirty years my aunt had not been farther than fifty miles from the homestead.

> **Whatever shock Mrs. Springer experienced at my aunt's appearance, she considerately concealed.**

I owed to this woman most of the good that ever came my way in my boyhood, and had a <u>reverential</u> affection for her. During the years when I was riding herd for my uncle,

---

2. **scourged with chilblains.** Tormented by blisters on hands and feet
3. **duster.** Lightweight coat
4. **north of Franz-Joseph-Land . . . Congo.** *Franz-Joseph-Land*—group of tiny islands in the Arctic Ocean; *Congo*—river in central Africa
5. **sixties.** 1860s
6. **Nebraska frontier.** Western border of Nebraska; uncharted territory
7. **provisions.** Supplies

---

cal • low (ka´ lō) *adj.,* lacking adult sophistication
re • vert (rə vʉrt´) *v.,* return to a former practice or state
rev • er • en • tial (rev´ ər en´ ch'l) *adj.,* showing a feeling of deep respect, love, and awe

The Homestead Act

When Aunt Georgiana married Howard Carpenter, they went to Nebraska and "took up a homestead," most likely under the Homestead Act of 1862, which made public lands in the western United States available at no cost to settlers. Ten percent of the land area of the United States was claimed and settled through this act.

A homesteader had to be at least twenty-one years old and the head of a household. After paying eighteen dollars for the filing fee, the homesteader would be given 160 acres of land. In order to prove the right to maintain the land he or she was given, the homesteader had to build a home, farm the land, and live there for at least five years. After that, he or she was rewarded with a patent on the land, signed with the name of the president.

The Homestead Act was repealed in 1976, although allowances were made for Alaska, the last state in the nation where homesteading was still a workable option for land distribution. The Homestead Act helped create more than 372,000 farms.

my aunt, after cooking the three meals—the first of which was ready at six o'clock in the morning—and putting the six children to bed, would often stand until midnight at her ironing board, with me at the kitchen table beside her, hearing me recite Latin declensions and conjugations, gently shaking me when my drowsy head sank down over a page of irregular verbs. It was to her, at her ironing or mending, that I read my first Shakespeare, and her old textbook on mythology was the first that ever came into my empty hands. She taught me my scales and exercises[8] on the little parlor organ which her husband had bought her after fifteen years during which she had not so much as seen a musical instrument. She would sit beside me by the hour, darning and counting, while I struggled with the "Joyous Farmer." She seldom talked to me about music, and I understood why. Once when I had been doggedly beating out some easy passages from an old score of *Euryanthe* I had found among her music books, she came up to me and, putting her hands over my eyes, gently drew my head back upon her shoulder, saying <u>tremulously</u>, "Don't love it so well, Clark, or it may be taken from you."

When my aunt appeared on the morning after her arrival in Boston, she was still in a semisomnambulant[9] state. She seemed not to realize that she was in the city where she had spent her youth, the place longed for hungrily half a lifetime. She had been so wretchedly train-sick throughout the journey that she had no recollection of anything but her discomfort, and, to all intents and purposes, there were but a few hours of nightmare between the farm in Red Willow County and my study on Newbury Street. I had planned a little pleasure for her that afternoon, to repay her for some of the glorious moments she had given me when we used to milk together in the straw-thatched cowshed and she, because I was more than usually tired, or because her husband had spoken sharply to me, would tell me of the splendid performance of the *Huguenots* she had seen in Paris, in her youth.

---

8. **scales and exercises.** Musical scales and practice pieces
9. **semisomnambulant.** Like one who is sleepwalking

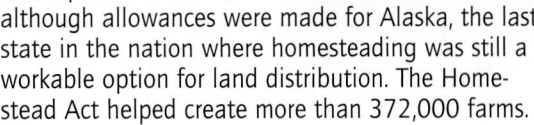

trem • u • lous • ly (trem´ yə ləs lē) *adv.,* in a trembling or quivering manner

At two o'clock the Symphony Orchestra was to give a Wagner[10] program, and I intended to take my aunt; though, as I conversed with her, I grew doubtful about her enjoyment of it. I suggested our visiting the Conservatory and the Common[11] before lunch, but she seemed altogether too timid to wish to venture out. She questioned me absently about various changes in the city, but she was chiefly concerned that she had forgotten to leave instructions about feeding half-skimmed milk to a certain weakling calf, "old Maggie's calf, you know, Clark," she explained, evidently having forgotten how long I had been away. She was further troubled because she had neglected to tell her daughter about the freshly-opened kit of mackerel[12] in the cellar, which would spoil if it were not used directly.

I asked her whether she had ever heard any of the Wagnerian operas, and found that she had not, though she was perfectly familiar with their <u>respective</u> situations, and had once possessed the piano score of *The Flying Dutchman.* I began to think it would be best to get her back to Red Willow County without waking her, and regretted having suggested the concert.

From the time we entered the concert hall, however, she was a trifle less passive and inert, and for the first time seemed to perceive her surroundings. I had felt some trepidation lest she might become aware of her queer, country clothes, or might experience some painful embarrassment at stepping suddenly into the world to which she had been dead for a quarter of a century. But, again, I found how superficially I had judged her. She sat looking about her with eyes as impersonal, almost as stony, as those with which the granite Rameses[13] in a museum watches the froth and fret that ebbs and flows about his pedestal. I have seen this same aloofness in old miners who drift into the Brown hotel at Denver, their pockets full of bullion, their linen soiled, their haggard faces unshaven; standing in the thronged corridors

as solitary as though they were still in a frozen camp on the Yukon.

The matinee audience was made up chiefly of women. One lost the contour of faces and figures, indeed any effect of line whatever, and there was only the color of bodices past counting, the shimmer of fabrics soft and firm, silky and sheer; red, mauve, pink, blue, lilac, purple, ecru, rose, yellow, cream, and white, all the colors that an impressionist[14] finds in a sunlit landscape, with here and there the dead shadow of a frock coat. My Aunt Georgiana regarded them as though they had been so many daubs of tube-paint on a palette.

When the musicians came out and took their places, she gave a little stir of anticipation, and looked with quickening interest down over the rail at that invariable grouping, perhaps the first wholly familiar thing that had greeted her eye since she had left old Maggie and her

---

10. **Wagner.** Richard Wagner (1813–1883), German composer
11. **the Common.** Boston Common; park in a historic section of Boston
12. **kit of mackerel.** Container of pickled fish
13. **Rameses.** Name of a number of Egyptian kings who ruled from circa 1315 BCE to circa 1090 BCE
14. **impressionist.** Painter, writer, or composer who seeks to render impressions and moods in which the chief aim is to capture a momentary glimpse of a subject

---

re • spec • tive (rə spekʹ tiv) *adj.,* as relates individually to each of two or more persons or things

weakling calf. I could feel how all those details sank into her soul, for I had not forgotten how they had sunk into mine when I came fresh from ploughing forever and forever between green aisles of corn, where, as in a treadmill, one might walk from daybreak to dusk without perceiving a shadow of change. The clean profiles of the musicians, the gloss of their linen, the dull black of their coats, the beloved shapes of the instruments, the patches of yellow light on the smooth, varnished bellies of the cellos and the bass viols in the rear, the restless, wind-tossed forest of fiddle necks and bows— I recalled how, in the first orchestra I ever heard, those long bow-strokes seemed to draw the heart out of me, as a conjurer's stick[15] reels out yards of paper ribbon from a hat.

The first number was the *Tannhauser* <u>overture</u>. When the horns drew out the first strain of the Pilgrim's chorus, Aunt Georgiana clutched my coat sleeve. Then it was I first realized that for her this broke a silence of thirty years. With the battle between the two motives, with the frenzy of the Venusberg theme and its ripping of strings, there came to me an overwhelming sense of the waste and wear we are so powerless to combat; and I saw again the tall, naked house on the prairie, black and grim as a wooden fortress; the black pond where I had learned to swim, its margin pitted with sun-dried cattle tracks; the rain gullied clay banks about the naked house, the four dwarf ash seedlings where the dishcloths were always hung to dry before the kitchen door. The world there was the flat world of the ancients; to the east, a cornfield that stretched to daybreak; to the west, a corral that reached to sunset; between, the conquests of peace, dearer-bought than those of war.

The overture closed, my aunt released my coat sleeve, but she said nothing. She sat staring dully at the orchestra. What, I wondered, did she get from it? She had been a good pianist in her day, I knew, and her musical education had been broader than that of most music teachers of a quarter of a century ago. She had often told me of Mozart's operas and Meyerbeer's and I could remember hearing her sing, years ago, certain melodies of Verdi. When I had fallen ill with a fever in her house, she used to sit by my cot in the evening—when the cool, night wind blew in through the faded mosquito netting tacked over the window and I lay watching a certain bright star that burned red above the cornfield—and sing "Home to our mountains, O, let us return!" in a way fit to break the heart of a Vermont boy near dead of homesickness already.

She sat staring dully at the orchestra. What, I wondered, did she get from it?

I watched her closely through the <u>prelude</u> to *Tristan and Isolde,* trying vainly to conjecture what that seething turmoil of strings and winds might mean to her, but she sat mutely staring at the violin bows that drove obliquely downward, like the pelting streaks of rain in a summer shower. Had this music any message for her? Had she enough left to at all comprehend this power which had kindled the world since she had left it? I was in a fever of curiosity, but Aunt Georgiana sat silent upon her peak in Darien.[16] She preserved this utter immobility throughout the number from *The Flying Dutchman,* though her fingers worked mechanically upon her black dress, as if, of themselves, they were recalling the piano score they had once

---

15. **conjurer's stick.** Magician's wand
16. **peak in Darien.** Mountain in Panama (formerly called the Isthmus of Darien) where Cortés was said to have looked westward at the Pacific Ocean, a new discovery for Europeans

---

over • ture (ōv´ rə chur) *n.*, musical introduction to an opera or other large musical work
pre • lude (prā´ lüd) *n.*, first movement of an opera; introduction

Old Barn in Field of Asters, c. 1940. Henry Varnum Poor.

played. Poor hands! They had been stretched and twisted into mere tentacles to hold and lift and knead with—on one of them a thin, worn band that had once been a wedding ring. As I pressed and gently quieted one of those groping hands, I remembered with quivering eyelids their services for me in other days.

Soon after the tenor began the "Prize Song," I heard a quick drawn breath and turned to my aunt. Her eyes were closed, but the tears were glistening on her cheeks, and I think, in a moment more, they were in my eyes as well. It never really died, then—the soul which can suffer so excruciatingly and so <u>interminably</u>; it withers to the outward eye only; like that strange moss which can lie on a dusty shelf half a century and yet, if placed in water, grows green again. She wept so throughout the development and elaboration of the melody.

During the intermission before the second half, I questioned my aunt and found that the "Prize Song" was not new to her. Some years before there had drifted to the farm in Red Willow County a young German, a tramp cow-puncher, who had sung in the chorus at Bayreuth[17] when he was a boy, along with the other peasant boys and girls. Of a Sunday

---

17. **Bayreuth.** Site of international music festivals in Germany

in • ter • mi • na • bly (in tʉr´ min ə blē) *adv.*, endlessly

morning he used to sit on his gingham-sheeted bed in the hands' bedroom which opened off the kitchen, cleaning the leather of his boots and saddle, singing the "Prize Song," while my aunt went about her work in the kitchen. She had hovered over him until she had prevailed upon him to join the country church, though his sole fitness for this step, in so far as I could gather, lay in his boyish face and his possession of this divine melody. Shortly afterward, he had gone to town on the Fourth of July, been drunk for several days, lost his money at a faro[18] table, ridden a saddled Texas steer on a bet, and disappeared with a fractured collar-bone. All this my aunt told me huskily, wanderingly, as though she were talking in the weak lapses of illness.

"Well, we have come to better things than the old *Trovatore* at any rate, Aunt Georgie?" I queried, with a well meant effort at <u>jocularity</u>.

Her lip quivered and she hastily put her handkerchief up to her mouth. From behind it she murmured, "And you have been hearing this ever since you left me, Clark?" Her question was the gentlest and saddest of <u>reproaches</u>.

The second half of the program consisted of four numbers from the *Ring,* and closed with Siegfried's funeral march. My aunt wept quietly, but almost continuously, as a shallow vessel overflows in a rain-storm. From time to time her dim eyes looked up at the lights, burning softly under their dull glass globes.

The deluge of sound poured on and on; I never knew what she found in the shining current of it; I never knew how far it bore her, or past what happy islands. From the trembling of her face I could well believe that before the last number she had been carried out where the myriad[19] graves are, into the grey, nameless burying grounds of the sea; or into some world of death vaster yet, where, from the beginning of the world, hope has lain down with hope and dream with dream and, renouncing, slept.

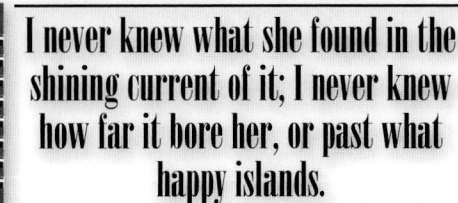

I never knew what she found in the shining current of it; I never knew how far it bore her, or past what happy islands.

The concert was over; the people filed out of the hall chattering and laughing, glad to relax and find the living level again, but my kinswoman made no effort to rise. The harpist slipped the green felt cover over his instrument; the flute-players shook the water from their mouthpieces; the men of the orchestra went out one by one, leaving the stage to the chairs and music stands, empty as a winter cornfield.

I spoke to my aunt. She burst into tears and sobbed pleadingly. "I don't want to go, Clark, I don't want to go!"

I understood. For her, just outside the concert hall, lay the black pond with the cattle-tracked bluffs; the tall, unpainted house, with weather-curled boards, naked as a tower; the crook-backed ash seedlings where the dish-cloths hung to dry; the gaunt, moulting[20] turkeys picking up refuse about the kitchen door. ❖

---

18. **faro.** Gambling game
19. **myriad.** Numerous
20. **moulting.** Shedding feathers

joc • u • lar • i • ty (jŏk' yü lär´ ə tē) *n.*, humor; joking
re • proach (rə prōch´) *n.*, blaming or reproving; rebuke

During her trip to Boston, Aunt Georgiana is sadly reminded of what she has given up in life. Do most people regret what they have or have not done? What do you regret?

Refer to Text ▶ ▶ ▶ ▶ ▶ Reason with Text

1a. State why Aunt Georgiana visits Boston.

1b. List the details from the story that portray the hardship of Aunt Georgiana's life on the Nebraska frontier.

Understand
Find meaning

2a. Why did Aunt Georgiana give up music?

2b. Describe a time you had to give up something you loved, and examine what that loss meant to you.

Apply
Use information

3a. Describe Aunt Georgiana's life experiences with music.

3b. Compare and contrast the role music had in Aunt Georgiana's life before and after she homesteaded in Nebraska.

Analyze
Take things apart

4a. In what kind of home did Aunt Georgiana and Howard live?

4b. Decide which setting, rural Nebraska or cosmopolitan Boston, is described most effectively. Give details to support your answer.

Evaluate
Make judgments

5a. What advice did Aunt Georgiana give Clark about music when he lived with her in Nebraska?

5b. Summarize the relationship between music and the human soul that Cather suggests in this story.

Create
Bring ideas together

Analyze Literature

Narrator, Point of View, and Characterization
In what ways does Clark, the narrator, misjudge or underestimate his aunt? How does this affect the first-person point of view of the narrator? Evaluate whether Clark is a reliable narrator.

What techniques does the author use to reveal Aunt Georgiana's character to readers? Summarize what kind of person you think she is after reading this story.

Extend the Text

Writing Options
Creative Writing Aunt Georgiana warned her nephew when he was a boy, "Don't love it so well, Clark, or it may be taken from you." Write a monologue in which Aunt Georgiana finishes her thought by sharing her own experience. Base your monologue on evidence from the story about what she might say.

Expository Writing For a literary journal focusing on the works of Willa Cather, write an essay in which you explore how her own life may be reflected in this story. Use the biographical information about Cather on page 596 as well as information you find through research. Use examples from the selection to support your ideas.

Collaborative Learning
Role-Play the Character With a classmate, conduct a role-play in which one of you plays Aunt Georgiana as a young woman and the other plays her at the age she is in the story. Discuss how the young and old Georgianas feel about how her life turned out.

Lifelong Learning
Research Music in Willa Cather's Work Research the role of music in Willa Cather's work. Based on examples of her other short stories and novels, develop a thesis statement that summarizes how she uses music in her writing. Use your thesis statement to prepare an expository speech on the subject. Present your speech to the class.

 Go to **www.mirrorsandwindows.com** for more.

1. Clark, the narrator, states that he owes to Aunt Georgiana "most of the good" from his childhood. Which of the following actions by Georgiana does *not* support this statement?
   A. She kept him awake to study.
   B. She taught him to play scales on the organ.
   C. She took care of him when he had a fever.
   D. She convinced him to join the church choir.
   E. She entertained him with stories of performances she had seen.

2. The narrator compares Aunt Georgiana's regard for the crowd around her and her experience at the music hall to all of the following *except* what?
   A. an Egyptian statue in a museum
   B. a weakling calf
   C. miners in the Brown Hotel in Denver
   D. the paints on a palette
   E. old moss placed in water

3. Reread this sentence from the first paragraph of "A Wagner Matinee": "He requested me to meet her at the station and render her whatever services might be necessary." What does the word *render* mean here?
   A. exchange with
   B. provide or deliver to
   C. assign to
   D. change or convert for
   E. evaluate for

4. The narrator states, "I began to think it would be best to get [Aunt Georgiana] back to Red Willow Country without waking her, and regretted having suggested the concert." What best explains this statement?
   A. Georgiana had a rough journey and needs to sleep.
   B. Georgiana is not interested in music.
   C. Georgiana's country clothes and mannerisms will stand out in urban Boston society.
   D. Rekindling Georgiana's former life in music does not seem like a good idea.
   E. Georgiana is too preoccupied with events on her Nebraska homestead to care about an orchestra concert.

5. What might you expect to hear if a situation involves a lot of *jocularity?*
   A. laughter
   B. crying
   C. angry voices
   D. music
   E. sarcastic remarks

6. What does the narrator understand about Aunt Georgiana at the end of the story?
   A. She is frightened by how much Boston society has changed.
   B. She cannot stop worrying about conditions on the homestead.
   C. She has changed so much that she does not fully recognize the elements of her former life.
   D. She was planning on leaving her family at the homestead when she received the legacy.
   E. She made a great sacrifice for the life she now lives and has had to numb herself to her former life to endure.

7. Which of the following is *not* an example of *callousness?*
   A. "wholly ill at ease and out of place"
   B. "the gangling farmer-boy my aunt had known, scourged with chilblains and bashfulness"
   C. "fumbling the scale with my stiff, red fingers"
   D. "I did not see her again until the next morning"
   E. "an idle, shiftless boy of twenty-one"

8. **Constructed Response:** Analyze the narrator's use of imagery from nature to describe the orchestra and music. How is this imagery used to show that Aunt Georgiana's life of music has been replaced with life on the homestead? Support your analysis using specific images from the story.

9. **Constructed Response:** Discuss Cather's choice of Clark as narrator in "A Wagner Matinee." What unique perspective does he bring to the story? How might the story be different if told by Aunt Georgiana or from an omniscient third-person point of view? Support your ideas with evidence from the text.

Understand the Concept

An **appositive** is a noun that is placed next to or near another noun to identify it or add information about it. If the information in an appositive specifically identifies the noun that precedes it, then the appositive is **essential** (or *restrictive*) and is not set off with commas. In the example below, the noun *Willa Cather* specifically identifies the noun *Pulitzer Prize winner*.

> **EXAMPLE**
>
> This selection was written by Pulitzer Prize winner Willa Cather.

If the information in the appositive does not specifically identify the noun that precedes it, then the appositive is **nonessential** (or *nonrestrictive*) and is set off with commas. In the following example, *a Pulitzer Prize winner* could describe any number of writers, not just *Willa Cather*.

> **EXAMPLE**
>
> This selection was written by Willa Cather, a Pulitzer Prize winner.

An **appositive phrase** is a group of words that includes an appositive and the words that modify it, such as adjectives and prepositional phrases. The group of words adds information about the noun it modifies. In the next example, the appositive phrase *who was born in Virginia and raised in Nebraska* gives further information about the noun *Cather*.

> **EXAMPLE**
>
> Cather, who was born in Virginia and raised in Nebraska, started writing when she was in college.

Apply the Skill

Identify Appositives

Identify the appositives and appositive phrases in the sentences below. Then on a separate sheet of paper, write the noun or pronoun the appositive identifies or renames.

1. In *A Wagner Matinee,* the narrator's aunt, a former musician, visits him in Boston.
2. Cather's first novel, *Alexander's Bridge,* was published when she was thirty-nine.
3. Aunt Georgiana had left the musical world to marry Howard Carpenter, a country boy from the Green Mountains.
4. Aunt Georgiana had once owned the piano score to the Wagnerian opera *The Flying Dutchman.*
5. In 1922, Cather was awarded the Pulitzer Prize for the novel *One of Ours.*

Correct the Punctuation with Appositives

Copy the following paragraph onto a separate sheet of paper. Underline all the appositives and appositive phrases. Then insert commas where they are needed to set off nonessential information.

> In the short story "A Wagner Matinee" the narrator takes his aunt to a concert. His aunt a homesteader from Nebraska has come to Boston to attend to the affairs of a relative. Before getting married she was a music teacher at the Boston Conservatory a music school in Boston, Massachusetts. She left Boston to take up a homestead on the Nebraska frontier with her husband Howard.

Use Appositives in Your Writing

Write a short story about a person who regrets some choice he or she made in life, or write an essay about you or someone you know who regrets the path his or her life took. After drafting your story or essay, look for appositives in your writing. Which type of appositive did you use more often: essential (restrictive) or nonessential (nonrestrictive)? Check to make sure you used commas to set off nonrestrictive appositives but not restrictive appositives.

Lucinda Matlock
Petit, the Poet

Dramatic Poems by Edgar Lee Masters

Build Background

Literary Context **"Lucinda Matlock"** and **"Petit, the Poet"** are from Edgar Lee Masters's *Spoon River Anthology,* a collection of *epitaphs,* or verses written to be inscribed on tombs or read in commemoration of people who have died. Masters's complete collection includes 212 characters who address readers from beyond the

grave, telling about such topics as how they lived their lives, how they died, and even how they are faring in death. The topic of an afterlife, however, rarely is mentioned.

First serialized in the *St. Louis Mirror* in 1914–1915 under Masters's pseudonym, Webster Ford, the epitaphs in *Spoon River Anthology* tell stories reminiscent of the life stories of people whom Masters knew or heard about in Petersburg and Lewiston, Illinois, near the Spoon River. Many of the names that Masters used in his anthology can be found on tombstones in the Lewiston cemetery.

Reader's Context Think about an elderly person you know. What is his or her attitude toward life? How does it differ from your own?

Meet the Author

Edgar Lee Masters (1868–1950) was born in Garnett, Kansas, but grew up in two small Illinois towns, Petersburg and Lewiston, which would inspire his best-known work, *Spoon River Anthology* (1915).

Masters briefly attended Knox College in Galesburg, Illinois, before studying law in his father's office and passing the bar. In 1891, he moved to Chicago, where he worked as a bill collector for the Edison Company until he was able to build a successful law practice. He later formed a law firm in which Clarence Darrow, the great criminal defense lawyer, was a partner. All the while, Masters was writing poems, having some published but many rejected.

When an editor sent him a copy of *Select Epigrams from the Greek Anthology,* a collection of classical *epigrams* (short, often witty sayings, many of which were originally used on gravestones), Masters began using the concise style of the epigram in his own work. Harriet Monroe, editor of *Poetry; A Magazine of Verse,* discovered Masters's work in this style and helped him get it published.

Spoon River Anthology was an instant and unanticipated success. Masters gave up law and moved to New York City in the 1920s. During his career, he wrote novels, plays, and biographies, but none of his other work achieved the recognition of *Spoon River Anthology.*

Analyze Literature

Free Verse and Tone
Free verse is poetry that avoids use of regular rhyme, meter, or division into stanzas.

Tone is the emotional attitude toward the reader or toward the subject implied by a literary work.

Set Purpose

The popularity of *Spoon River Anthology* can be attributed, in large part, to Masters's ability to capture the lives and voices of everyday people. As you read, analyze his use of free verse, including irregular line breaks, sentence fragments, and other qualities that mimic ordinary speech. Write down examples from each poem. Also analyze how Masters uses language to create tone. Identify the attitude or mood conveyed by each poem.

Preview Vocabulary

repose, 609
degenerate, 609
valor, 610

Stone City, Iowa, c. 1930. Grant Wood. Joslyn Museum, Omaha, Nebraska.
Art © Estate of Grant Wood/Licensed by VAGA, New York, NY.

Lucinda Matlock
by Edgar Lee Masters

I went to the dances at Chandlerville,
And played snap-out[1] at Winchester.
One time we changed partners,
Driving home in the moonlight of middle June,
5   And then I found Davis.
We were married and lived together for seventy years,
Enjoying, working, raising the twelve children,
Eight of whom we lost
Ere[2] I had reached the age of sixty.
10 I spun, I wove, I kept the house, I nursed the sick,
I made the garden, and for holiday
Rambled over the fields where sang the larks,
And by Spoon River gathering many a shell,
And many a flower and medicinal weed—
15 Shouting to the wooded hills, singing to the green valleys.
At ninety-six I had lived enough, that is all,

---

1. **snap-out.** Parlor game
2. **Ere.** Before

And passed to a sweet <u>repose</u>.
What is this I hear of sorrow and weariness,
Anger, discontent and drooping hopes?
20 <u>Degenerate</u> sons and daughters,
Life is too strong for you—
It takes life to love Life. ❖

re • pose (rə pōz´) *n.,* rest
de • gen • er • ate (dē jen´ ʉr ət) *adj.,* having sunk to a lower level of
    quality or being

MIRRORS & WINDOWS

Imagine that you are ninety-six years old, like Lucinda Matlock. What have you done and how have you lived to be able to say you have "lived enough"?

ART CONNECTION

Grant Wood

Like Regionalist literature, Regionalist art focused on the artist's home region and celebrated rural life through a simple, realistic style. *American Gothic,* by Grant Wood (1891–1942), is one of the most recognizable pieces of twentieth-century art and an outstanding example of Regionalism.

Wood was born on a farm in Anamosa, Iowa, and spent his youth working with blacksmiths. He briefly attended the Art Institute of Chicago, where he learned how to paint in the ultrarealistic style pioneered by fifteenth-century Flemish painter Jan van Eyck.

In 1932, early in the Great Depression, Wood established an artistic community in his hometown. The Stone City Art Colony was a place artists could live and continue to create without having to worry about economic survival. President Franklin D. Roosevelt eventually commissioned many of these artists to paint murals on government buildings, a number of which still exist throughout the Midwest.

Critical Viewing Examine the paintings *American Gothic* and *Stone City, Iowa* (see page 608). What techniques does Wood use to make the scenes seem realistic? What qualities of his work seem especially middle American?

American Gothic, 1930. Grant Wood.
Art Institute of Chicago, Chicago, Illinois.
Art © Estate of Grant Wood/
Licensed by VAGA, New York, NY.

Petit, the Poet

by Edgar Lee Masters

Seeds in a dry pod, tick, tick, tick,
Tick, tick, tick, like mites[1] in a quarrel—
Faint iambics that the full breeze wakens—
But the pine tree makes a symphony thereof.
5   Triolets, villanelles, rondels, rondeaus,[2]
Ballades by the score with the same old thought:
The snows and the roses of yesterday are vanished,
And what is love but a rose that fades?
Life all around me here in the village:
10   Tragedy, comedy, valor and truth,
Courage, constancy, heroism, failure—
All in the loom, and oh what patterns!
Woodlands, meadows, streams and rivers—
Blind to all of it all my life long.
15   Triolets, villanelles, rondels, rondeaus,
Seeds in a dry pod, tick, tick, tick,
Tick, tick, tick, what little iambics,
While Homer and Whitman[3] roared in the pines? ❖

---

1. **mites.** Small insects
2. **Triolets . . . rondeaus.** Types of poems
3. **Homer and Whitman.** *Homer*—ancient Greek poet; *Whitman*—Walt
   Whitman (1819–1892), American poet, one of the first to write in
   free verse

va • lor (va´ lər) *n.,* bravery

Why do people sometimes fail to see the important things in life? What do they focus on instead?

Refer to Text ▶ ▶ ▶ ▶ ▶	**Reason with Text**	
1a. Whom did Lucinda marry?	**1b.** Summarize the kind of life Lucinda had with her husband.	**Understand** Find meaning
2a. To what was Petit blind all his life?	**2b.** What was Lucinda Matlock's philosophy of life?	**Apply** Use information
3a. Identify what Lucinda Matlock did to relax.	**3b.** Outline the qualities that may have enabled Lucinda to live to be ninety-six.	**Analyze** Take things apart
4a. To what sound does Petit compare his triolets, villanelles, and other poems?	**4b.** Look at the last line of "Petit, the Poet." Interpret what it indicates about Petit's feelings about how he lived his life.	**Evaluate** Make judgments
5a. What is Lucinda Matlock's message to the younger generation?	**5b.** Some people argue that each successive generation is weaker than the last. Write a response to this statement. How would Petit respond to this statement? How might Lucinda respond to Petit?	**Create** Bring ideas together

Analyze Literature

Free Verse and Tone

What examples of language did you find that mimic ordinary speech? Explain how this conversational quality of free verse fits Masters's purpose in writing about everyday people. What other qualities of free verse did you identify, such as lack of rhyme, meter, stanzas, and so on?

Describe the tone of each poem using one or two words. How does Masters create tone? Again, how is his use of language well suited to his purpose?

Extend the Text

Writing Options

Creative Writing Write brief (one or two lines) tombstone inscriptions for Lucinda Matlock and Petit the Poet. Be sure the inscription expresses each character's attitude toward life.

Expository Writing Write a one-paragraph critical analysis of Lucinda Matlock's or Petit's attitude toward life and death. Explain how that attitude may have enhanced or detracted from the quality of the character's life. Exchange paragraphs with a classmate, and discuss how your analyses are similar and/or different.

Collaborative Learning

Interpret a Poem Select a poem from *Spoon River Anthology* for each person in your small group. Then sit in a circle and take turns reading aloud the poems. As you listen to the speaker before you, take notes on the character he or she presents. Then write a transition to present a logical bridge to your selection. The first presenter should write a general introduction to the selections.

Media Literacy

Design an Internet Site Research Edgar Lee Masters and the Spoon River using library and Internet sources. Then design an Internet site about Masters that includes a biographical time line and virtual tour of the Spoon River. Write the text for the virtual tour and, if possible, select and provide copies of the photos you would include on the site. Display the time line, photos, and text on poster board, and explain your planned Internet site to the class.

 Go to **www.mirrorsandwindows.com** for more.

Robert Frost

> ## *"Take what is given, and make it over in your own way."*

Robert Frost (1874–1963) was born in San Francisco but moved to New England with his mother at age eleven, after his father died. He graduated at the top of his high school class, sharing the position of valedictorian with Elinor White, whom he married in 1895.

The couple taught for a short time at Dartmouth, but the demands of teaching left Frost little time to write, so he quit. After performing a series of odd jobs, he entered Harvard in 1897; ill health forced him to leave after two years without completing his degree. For the next nine years, he and his wife lived in Derry, New Hampshire, on a farm Frost's grandfather purchased for them. Although Frost was not a successful farmer, the agrarian lifestyle allowed him time to write.

In 1912, Frost took his family to England, and it was there that his poetry first found a major audience with the publication of *A Boy's Will* (1913) and *North of Boston* (1914). After England entered World War I, the Frosts returned to the United States and settled on another farm in New Hampshire. During this time, Frost began to enjoy financial stability from the sale of his books. He also taught and lectured at various colleges, including Dartmouth, Amherst, Harvard, and the University of Michigan.

Frost was awarded the Pulitzer Prize for poetry in 1924, 1931, 1937, and 1943 and received honorary degrees from many universities—so many, in fact, that he had the honorary hoods made into a quilt. In 1961, he recited his poem "The Gift Outright" at the inauguration of John F. Kennedy, thirty-fifth president of the United States.

Robert Frost was unquestionably the most popular American poet of the twentieth century. He had a rare talent that allowed him to produce poetry simple and clear enough to appeal to a mainstream audience yet intellectually rich enough to appeal to sophisticated literary critics. While Frost's poems were well received by the critics, many misunderstood his use of simple, direct language—what Frost called "the sound of sense." According to Frost, the best poems conveyed the sense of ordinary people talking.

Noted Works

"After Apple-Picking" (1915)

"The Death of the Hired Man" (1915)

"Mending Wall" (1915)

"The Road Not Taken" (1915)

"Nothing Gold Can Stay" (1923)

"Stopping by Woods on a Snowy Evening" (1923)

Birches
Mending Wall
The Death of the Hired Man

Poems by Robert Frost

Build Background

Literary Context Robert Frost's many popular works often deal with the character, people, and landscape of New England. However, his work goes beyond the scope of **Regionalism,** or writing in which a particular geographical setting plays an important role. The careful local observations and homely details of Frost's poems often have deeper symbolic meanings. Frost delved into people's tragedies and fears, their reactions to the complexities of life, and their ultimate acceptance of life's burdens.

All three of the poems that follow are from early in Frost's career, between 1915 and 1920, the time when his work became popular among both readers and critics. Moreover, all three describe experiences common to anyone who has spent time outdoors in the country or on a farm.

The poem **"Birches,"** for example, recalls the boyhood experience of swinging on the branches of trees. The speaker in the poem is an elderly man, and his sense of longing for the simple, carefree attitude of youth is felt throughout the poem. The speaker also reflects on how his boyhood experiences prepared him for the challenges of adulthood.

"Mending Wall," one of Frost's best-known poems, is about two neighbors walking along the stone wall that divides their property, repairing the wall by putting back in place the stones that have fallen to the ground. One of the neighbors, the speaker in the poem, ponders the purpose of having a wall, but the other neighbor, a conventional fellow, believes that "Good fences make good neighbors." In fact, this commonly quoted line often is viewed as the primary theme of the poem, but that is a limited interpretation. In presenting both neighbors' viewpoints, Frost explores not only the value of setting arbitrary boundaries but also the wisdom of maintaining convention for convention's sake.

"The Death of the Hired Man" is a narrative poem that presents a dialogue between a farm husband and wife. In this realistic-sounding conversation, the couple discuss how to treat their elderly hired man, whose health is failing. In doing so, they explore themes of home and belonging as well as death.

Reader's Context What items, events, and experiences do you associate with the region in which you live? How has your perception of these things changed as you have grown older?

Analyze Literature

Meter and Symbol

Meter is a regular rhythmic pattern in poetry, which is determined by the number of beats, or stresses, in each line.

A **symbol** is anything that stands for or represents both itself and something else.

Set Purpose

Like Edgar Lee Masters, Robert Frost wrote using the language of everyday conversation. Unlike Masters, however, Frost adhered to poetic conventions such as meter. Read aloud each of the following poems to hear the meter. Determine the general pattern of stressed and unstressed syllables. (Keep in mind that not every line has to have exactly the same pattern of beats for a poem to have meter.) Also review each poem for the use of symbols. In particular, review the use of nature symbols in "Birches."

Preview Vocabulary

bracken, 614
subdue, 615
poise, 615
lash, 615
grudge, 621
assurance, 622
pique, 622
abide, 624

Birches

by Robert Frost

Fishing from a Punt, c. 1866–1901.
Arthur W. Redgate. Private collection.
(See detail on page 613.)

When I see birches bend to the left and right
Across the lines of straighter darker trees,
I like to think some boy's been swinging them.
But swinging doesn't bend them down to stay.
5   As ice storms do. Often you must have seen them
Loaded with ice a sunny winter morning
After a rain. They click upon themselves
As the breeze rises, and turn many-colored
As the stir cracks and crazes their enamel.[1]
10   Soon the sun's warmth makes them shed crystal shells
Shattering and avalanching on the snow crust—
Such heaps of broken glass to sweep away
You'd think the inner dome of heaven had fallen.
They are dragged to the withered <u>bracken</u> by the load,
15   And they seem not to break; though once they are bowed
So low for long, they never right themselves:
You may see their trunks arching in the woods
Years afterwards, trailing their leaves on the ground
Like girls on hands and knees that throw their hair
20   Before them over their heads to dry in the sun.
But I was going to say when Truth broke in
With all her matter of fact about the ice storm,
I should prefer to have some boy bend them

---

1. **crazes their enamel.** Scratches the shiny white surfaces of the birch trunks

brack • en (brak´ ən) *n.,* large, coarse, weedy ferns occurring in meadows and woods

As he went out and in to fetch the cows—
25 Some boy too far from town to learn baseball,
Whose only play was what he found himself,
Summer or winter, and could play alone.
One by one he <u>subdued</u> his father's trees
By riding them down over and over again
30 Until he took the stiffness out of them,
And not one but hung limp, not one was left
For him to conquer. He learned all there was
To learn about not launching out too soon
And so not carrying the tree away
35 Clear to the ground. He always kept his <u>poise</u>
To the top branches, climbing carefully
With the same pains you use to fill a cup
Up to the brim, and even above the brim.
Then he flung outward, feet first, with a swish,
40 Kicking his way down through the air to the ground.
So was I once myself a swinger of birches.
And so I dream of going back to be.
It's when I'm weary of considerations,
And life is too much like a pathless wood
45 Where your face burns and tickles with the cobwebs[2]
Broken across it, and one eye is weeping
From a twig's having <u>lashed</u> across it open.
I'd like to get away from earth awhile
And then come back to it and begin over.
50 May no fate willfully misunderstand me
And half grant what I wish and snatch me away
Not to return. Earth's the right place for love:
I don't know where it's likely to go better.
I'd like to go by climbing a birch tree,
55 And climb black branches up a snow-white trunk
Toward heaven, till the tree could bear no more,
But dipped its top and set me down again.
That would be good both going and coming back.
One could do worse than be a swinger of birches. ❖

---

2. **cobwebs.** The speaker refers to the weblike pattern of lines across the face,
perhaps brought on by his grief as well as his age.

---

sub • due (sub dü´) *v.,* overcome; control; reduce
poise (poiz) *n.,* balance; self-control
lash (lash) *v.,* strike hard with great force

MIRRORS & WINDOWS

What activities from your childhood made you feel free and happy? Do you do
any of those things now? What made you stop?

FROST

FROST

Primary Source Connection

Published in 2000, **Jay Parini's** biography ***Robert Frost: A Life*** explores the life and work of this popular American poet. In this excerpt, Parini recounts the origins of the poem "Birches," which was inspired by a poem by Lucy Larcom, another American poet. Other biographical accounts of Frost's boyhood report his own experiences with swinging birches.

Frost wrote "Birches" and many of his other famous poems during the time he and his family lived in Beaconsfield, England, in a cottage called the Bungalow. It was in England that Frost's writing career was launched in earnest with the help of American poet Ezra Pound and British poet Frank S. Flint and critic T. E. Hulme.

from **Robert Frost: A Life**
by Jay Parini

Having settled into Beaconsfield once again, with the older children in school and Elinor teaching the younger ones, Frost found himself on fire with the urge to write. The homesickness that had begun in late spring was now yielding marvelous fruit in poems such as "After Apple-Picking," "Mending Wall," and "Birches"—all written in Beaconsfield. The last one, inspired by a poem on the same subject by the American poet Lucy Larcom, began from a fragment about icicles dating back to 1906. It opens fetchingly:[1]

> *When I see birches bend to left and right*
> *Across the lines of straighter darker trees,*
> *I like to think some boy's been swinging them.*

Lesley, in the journal she kept when she was six, wrote alluringly[2] about the New England game of swinging birches: "On the way home," she said, "I climbed up a hi birch and came down with it and I stopt in the air about three feet and pap cout me." Her father had

been taught how to do this in the summer of 1886 by Charlie Peabody, a neighbor from Lawrence. The practice of climbing birches until your weight brought the trunk plunging to earth had caught his imagination, as it now caught Lesley's:

> i like to climb trees very much but mam doesnt like me to becose i tare my stockings so i have to stop i do not like to but i have to at frst i was scared to swing with birchis but now i am not so much scared becose it wont hurt me. an i am not scared if it swings down with me if it does klere down with me i don't like it if it dosnt i climb uther threes but they downt swing as the birchis do so i downt like them aswell i climb oak and mapel but with me they swing with me. i like that to but not as well but papa likes to

---

1. **fetchingly.** In a pleasant or appealing manner
2. **alluringly.** In a charming or luring manner

swing beter. i climb apale trees but those dont swing a tall do they.

Frost's later accounts of the writing of "Birches" were often misleading. He would tell admiring audiences that he wrote it one morning in Beaconsfield "with one stroke of the pen." But he explained to Robert Penn Warren many years later that the poem was "two fragments soldered together so long ago I have forgotten where the joint is." The poem,

which was originally called "Swinging Birches," catches perfectly the "sound of sense" in poetry; while it is written in classic blank verse, one cannot help but hear Frost's grainy, idiosyncratic[3] voice ushering the syllables into his own strong vernacular.[4] ❖

---

3. **idiosyncratic.** Characteristic of an individual's oddness or peculiarity
4. **vernacular.** Native language or expression of a group or class of people

Review Questions

1. Where did Frost write some of his best poems? What emotion seemed to prompt this outpouring of poetry? Explain how that emotion prompted Frost to write about swinging birches.

2. Who taught Frost to swing birches? How has Frost's daughter taken to the sport? Infer what her journal reveals about her father.

3. How does Frost's explanation to audiences of how he wrote "Birches" differ from what he told Robert Penn Warren? Suggest why Frost might give two accounts of writing this poem. Does it affect your appreciation or understanding of the poem to know how he wrote it? Explain.

TEXT ⇄ TEXT CONNECTION

Identify the similarities between Frost's daughter's journal entry and Frost's poem. What did his daughter Lesley likely think about the poem "Birches"? Do you think she liked it? Why or why not?

LITERARY CONNECTION

The Pulitzer Prize

PULITZER

Robert Frost was rare among writers in enjoying both popular and critical praise during his lifetime. The critical acclaim of his work was evidenced by his winning four Pulitzer Prizes for poetry, the most of any writer.

The Pulitzer Prize is named after Joseph Pulitzer, an American journalist of the late 1800s who owned several widely read newspapers, including the *St. Louis Post–Dispatch* and the *New York World.* His vicious circulation battle with William Randolph Hearst, owner of the *New York Journal,* largely contributed to the practice of *yellow jour-*

nalism, in which journalists exaggerate facts and distort news to bolster readership.

Before Pulitzer died in 1911, he donated two million dollars to Columbia University to create a school of journalism and establish a national prize for writers of various materials, ranging from news stories to literature. Columbia awarded the first Pulitzer Prizes in 1917, and today, the university recognizes writers in twenty-one categories each year. Each recipient is awarded ten thousand dollars and a certificate. Because of its prestige and career-enhancing tendency, the Pulitzer has become a highly coveted award for many American writers.

MENDING WALL

by Robert Frost

Something there is that doesn't love a wall,
That sends the frozen-ground-swell[1] under it,
And spills the upper boulders in the sun,
And makes gaps even two can pass abreast.
5   The work of hunters is another thing:
I have come after them and made repair
Where they have left not one stone on a stone,

---

1. **frozen-ground-swell.** Heaving of the ground caused by its freezing during
winter

But they would have the rabbit out of hiding,
To please the yelping dogs. The gaps I mean,
10 No one has seen them made or heard them made,
But spring mending-time we find them there.
I let my neighbor know beyond the hill;
And on a day we meet to walk the line
And set the wall between us once again.
15 We keep the wall between us as we go.
To each the boulders that have fallen to each.
And some are loaves and some so nearly balls
We have to use a spell to make them balance:
"Stay where you are until our backs are turned!"
20 We wear our fingers rough with handling them.
Oh, just another kind of outdoor game.
One on a side. It comes to little more;
There where it is we do not need the wall:
He is all pine and I am apple orchard.
25 My apple trees will never get across
And eat the cones under his pines, I tell him.
He only says, "Good fences make good neighbors."
Spring is the mischief in me, and I wonder
If I could put a notion in his head:
30 "*Why* do they make good neighbors? Isn't it
Where there are cows? But here there are no cows.
Before I built a wall I'd ask to know
What I was walling in or walling out,
And to whom I was like to give offense.
35 Something there is that doesn't love a wall,
That wants it down." I could say "Elves" to him,
But it's not elves exactly, and I'd rather
He said it for himself. I see him there
Bringing a stone grasped firmly by the top
40 In each hand, like an old-stone savage armed.
He moves in darkness as it seems to me,
Not of woods only and the shade of trees.
He will not go behind his father's saying,
And he likes having thought of it so well
45 He says again, "Good fences make good neighbors." ❖

Do you agree with the statement "Good fences make good neighbors"?

The Death of the Hired Man
by Robert Frost

Old Man and Tree, 1947. Karl Zerbe.

Mary sat musing on the lamp-flame at the table,
Waiting for Warren. When she heard his step,
She ran on tiptoe down the darkened passage
To meet him in the doorway with the news
5   And put him on his guard. "Silas is back."
She pushed him outward with her through
    the door
And shut it after her. "Be kind," she said.
She took the market things from Warren's arms
And set them on the porch, then drew him down
10   To sit beside her on the wooden steps.

"When was I ever anything but kind to him?
But I'll not have the fellow back," he said.
"I told him so last haying,[1] didn't I?
If he left then, I said, that ended it.
15   What good is he? Who else will harbor him
At his age for the little he can do?
What help he is there's no depending on.
Off he goes always when I need him most.
He thinks he ought to earn a little pay,
20   Enough at least to buy tobacco with,
So he won't have to beg and be beholden.[2]
'All right,' I say, 'I can't afford to pay
Any fixed wages, though I wish I could.'
'Someone else can.' 'Then someone else will have to.'
25   I shouldn't mind his bettering himself
If that was what it was. You can be certain,
When he begins like that, there's someone at him
Trying to coax him off with pocket money—

---

1. **haying.** Harvest; gathering of hay
2. **beholden.** Indebted to anyone

In haying time, when any help is scarce.
30 In winter he comes back to us. I'm done."

"Sh! not so loud: he'll hear you," Mary said.

"I want him to: he'll have to soon or late."

"He's worn out. He's asleep beside the stove.
When I came up from Rowe's I found him here,
35 Huddled against the barn-door fast asleep,
A miserable sight, and frightening, too—
You needn't smile—I didn't recognize him—
I wasn't looking for him—and he's changed.
Wait till you see."

40   "Where did you say he'd been?"

"He didn't say. I dragged him to the house,
And gave him tea and tried to make him smoke.
I tried to make him talk about his travels.
Nothing would do: he just kept nodding off."

45 "What did he say? Did he say anything?"

"But little."

                 "Anything? Mary, confess
He said he'd come to ditch the meadow for me."

"Warren!"

50   "But did he? I just want to know."

"Of course he did. What would you have him say?
Surely you wouldn't <u>grudge</u> the poor old man
Some humble way to save his self-respect.
He added, if you really care to know,
55 He meant to clear the upper pasture, too.
That sounds like something you have heard before?
Warren, I wish you could have heard the way
He jumbled everything. I stopped to look
Two or three times—he made me feel so queer—
60 To see if he was talking in his sleep.
He ran on Harold Wilson—you remember—
The boy you had in haying four years since.
He's finished school, and teaching in his college.
Silas declares you'll have to get him back.

grudge (grŭj) *v.,* allow or give something reluctantly; be envious or resentful

Curving Road, View of the Seine River, 1875.
Alfred Sisley. Private collection.

He says they two will make a team for work:
Between them they will lay this farm as
  smooth!
The way he mixed that in with other things.
He thinks young Wilson a likely lad, though
  daft
On education—you know how they fought
All through July under the blazing sun,
Silas up on the cart to build the load,
Harold along beside to pitch it on."

"Yes, I took care to keep well out of earshot."

"Well, those days trouble Silas like a dream.
75 You wouldn't think they would. How some things linger!
Harold's young college-boy's <u>assurance</u> <u>piqued</u> him.
After so many years he still keeps finding
Good arguments he sees he might have used.
I sympathize. I know just how it feels
80 To think of the right thing to say too late.
Harold's associated in his mind with Latin.
He asked me what I thought of Harold's saying
He studied Latin, like the violin,
Because he liked it—that an argument!
85 He said he couldn't make the boy believe
He could find water with a hazel prong—
Which showed how much good school had ever done him.
He wanted to go over that. But most of all
He thinks if he could have another chance
90 To teach him how to build a load of hay—"

"I know, that's Silas' one accomplishment.
He bundles every forkful in its place,
And tags and numbers it for future reference,
So he can find and easily dislodge it
95 In the unloading. Silas does that well.
He takes it out in bunches like big birds' nests.
You never see him standing on the hay
He's trying to lift, straining to lift himself."

"He thinks if he could teach him that he'd be
100 Some good perhaps to someone in the world.
He hates to see a boy the fool of books.

as • sur • ance (ä shʉr´ ənts) *n.,* confidence in ability or status
pique (pēk) *v.,* irritate; provoke

Poor Silas, so concerned for other folk,
And nothing to look backward to with pride,
And nothing to look forward to with hope,
105 So now and never any different."
Part of a moon was falling down the west,
Dragging the whole sky with it to the hills.
Its light poured softly in her lap. She saw it
And spread her apron to it. She put out her hand
110 Among the harplike morning-glory strings,
Taut with the dew from garden bed to eaves,
As if she played unheard some tenderness
That wrought on him beside her in the night.
"Warren," she said, "he has come home to die:
115 You needn't be afraid he'll leave you this time."

"Home," he mocked gently.

       "Yes, what else but home?
It all depends on what you mean by home.
Of course he's nothing to us, any more
120 Than was the hound that came a stranger to us
Out of the woods, worn out upon the trail."
"Home is the place where, when you have to go there,
They have to take you in."

       "I should have called it
125 Something you somehow haven't to deserve."

Warren leaned out and took a step or two,
Picked up a little stick, and brought it back
And broke it in his hand and tossed it by.
"Silas has better claim on us you think
130 Than on his brother? Thirteen little miles
As the road winds would bring him to his door.
Silas has walked that far no doubt today.
Why doesn't he go there? His brother's rich,
A somebody—director in the bank."

135 "He never told us that."

       "We know it though."

"I think his brother ought to help, of course.
I'll see to that if there is need. He ought of right
To take him in, and might be willing to—
140 He may be better than appearances.
But have some pity on Silas. Do you think
If he had any pride in claiming kin

Or anything he looked for from his brother,
He'd keep so still about him all this time?"

145   "I wonder what's between them."

                    "I can tell you.
Silas is what he is—we wouldn't mind him—
But just the kind that kinsfolk can't <u>abide</u>.
He never did a thing so very bad.
150   He don't know why he isn't quite as good
As anybody. Worthless though he is,
He won't be made ashamed to please his brother."

"*I* can't think Si ever hurt anyone."

"No, but he hurt my heart the way he lay
155   And rolled his old head on that sharp-edged chair-back.
He wouldn't let me put him on the lounge.
You must go in and see what you can do.
I made the bed up for him there tonight.
You'll be surprised at him—how much he's broken.
160   His working days are done; I'm sure of it."

"I'd not be in a hurry to say that."

"I haven't been. Go, look, see for yourself.
But, Warren, please remember how it is:
He's come to help you ditch the meadow
165   He has a plan. You mustn't laugh at him.
He may not speak of it, and then he may.
I'll sit and see if that small sailing cloud
Will hit or miss the moon."

                    It hit the moon.
170   Then there were three there, making a dim row,
The moon, the little silver cloud, and she.
Warren returned—too soon, it seemed to her,
Slipped to her side, caught up her hand and waited.

"Warren?" she questioned.

175   "Dead," was all he answered. ❖

---

abide (ə bīd´) *v.,* accept; tolerate

The speakers in the poem define *home* as a place "where, when you have to
go there, They have to take you in" and "something you somehow haven't to
deserve." What is your definition of *home*?

Refer to Text ▸ ▸ ▸ ▸ ▸ **Reason with Text**

1a. In "Birches," how does the narrator describe the birch trees when they lose their ice? Why does the narrator talk about the ice storms and their effect on birches?

1b. Explain what it says about human frailty and the power of nature if an ice storm, not some boy, bent the trees.

Understand
Find meaning

2a. What does the speaker in "Mending Wall" tell his neighbor as they repair the fence?

2b. Why might the neighbor want to have a wall where one is not necessary? What does this tell you about him?

Apply
Use information

3a. In "The Death of the Hired Man," what did Warren tell Silas at the last haying?

3b. Point out the reasons Warren gives for not accepting back Silas.

Analyze
Take things apart

4a. Where does Warren think Silas should have gone instead of to his farm?

4b. Assess what kind of person Warren seems to be. Was his reaction to Silas too coldhearted or justified? Explain your answer.

Evaluate
Make judgments

5a. In "Mending Wall," what would the speaker ask before building a wall?

5b. Beyond walls and fences, what other things keep people apart?

Create
Bring ideas together

Analyze Literature

Meter and Symbol

What general pattern of stressed and unstressed syllables did you find? How many stressed beats do most lines have? Focus on the use of meter in "Mending Wall." Copy the poem in your notebook, and mark the stressed and unstressed syllables.

Discuss the symbols you identified in each poem. For instance, what do the birch trees represent in "Birches"? What other nature symbols does Frost use in this poem? How does the use of symbols contribute to the meaning of the poem?

Extend the Text

Writing Options

Creative Writing Imagine you are a young person swinging from birches. Write step-by-step directions for a friend, telling him or her how to swing from birches.

Expository Writing Suppose a classmate tells you she does not understand why these three poems were grouped in this textbook. Write a comparison-and-contrast essay, in which you compare the themes explored in "Birches," "Mending Wall," and "The Death of the Hired Man." Provide a plausible explanation for grouping these selections.

Collaborative Learning

Conduct a Poetry Reading With your classmates, plan a poetry reading of five works of Robert Frost. To prepare, discuss the meaning of each poem in a small group. What is its central idea or theme? For the reading, have one person give a brief introduction to each poem, including when it was written, where it was first published, and what theme it presents.

Lifelong Learning

Create a Time Line With a partner, use the Internet to research Frost's life. Perhaps start with the site of the Academy of American Poets, which provides biographical information. Use the information you find to make a time line of key personal and literary events in the poet's life.

 Go to **www.mirrorsandwindows.com** for more.

1. In "Mending Wall," which of the following lines does *not* express the mystery or magic behind why the boulders fall down?
   A. "'Good fences make good neighbors.'"
   B. "Something there is that doesn't love a wall"
   C. "No one has seen them made or heard them made"
   D. "We have to use a spell to make them balance"
   E. "But it's not elves exactly"

2. In line 13, "walk the line" means both to walk along the edge of the property and
   A. to stay out of trouble.
   B. to follow directions.
   C. to follow tradition.
   D. to measure the distance.
   E. None of the above

3. In lines 41–42 of "Mending Wall," what does the speaker mean when he says the neighbor "moves in darkness as it seems to me, / Not of woods only and the shade of trees"?
   A. They have been working so long that it's getting dark outside.
   B. The neighbor has a dark purpose in wanting to maintain the wall.
   C. The neighbor has been knocking down parts of the wall at night.
   D. The neighbor has had a sad, lonely life.
   E. The neighbor is narrow minded and stuck in his ways.

4. What would the speaker ask before building a wall?
   A. What is the wall keeping in or out?
   B. Does the wall accurately divide the property?
   C. Who might be offended by the wall?
   D. A and B
   E. A and C

5. Reread line 1 of "The Death of the Hired Man": "Mary sat musing *on* the lamp-flame at the table." Why does Frost use the word *on* instead of *by*?
   A. *On* fits with the meter of the poem.
   B. Mary is thinking about why Warren is not home yet.
   C. It alerts the reader to the importance of light in the poem.
   D. *On* meant *by* at the time Frost wrote the poem.
   E. Mary is trying to figure out whether she needs the lamp on.

6. In line 76 of "The Death of the Hired Man," young Harold is described as having *assurance*. What synonym could be substituted here?
   A. regret
   B. education
   C. employment
   D. confidence
   E. difficulty

7. What is Silas's argument with Harold Wilson?
   A. Harold does not hay very well, which interrupts Silas's system.
   B. Harold got a job from Warren that Silas felt should be his.
   C. Silas resents Harold's education and thinks it has no practical use.
   D. Silas is upset that Harold left for college instead of help him clear Warren's fields.
   E. Harold does not believe in Silas's folk wisdom.

8. In "The Death of the Hired Man," what reason does Mary give for why Silas does not stay with his wealthier brother?
   A. His brother will have nothing to do with him.
   B. The two brothers have had a serious argument.
   C. Silas does not want to be made to feel ashamed.
   D. Silas invented the story about his brother; he's not real.
   E. His brother lives too far away away.

9. **Constructed Response:** Analyze "Mending Wall" and "The Death of the Hired Man" as narrative poems, or poems that tell a story. Discuss literary elements such as plot, setting, characterization, and theme. Identify the central conflict in each story.

10. **Constructed Response:** Compare and contrast two characters from these Frost poems: either the neighbor in "Mending Wall" and Silas in "The Death of the Hired Man" or the speaker in "Mending Wall" and Mary in "The Death of the Hired Man." Describe the characters' similarities and differences and what motivates them to act as they do. Cite examples from the poems to support your ideas.

Chicago
Grass

Lyric Poems by Carl Sandburg

Build Background

Literary Context Like Robert Frost, Carl Sandburg often is considered a poet of the common people, writing about American experiences, lifestyles, and values.

His poem **"Chicago"** was published in 1914 in his first book of verse, *Chicago Poems.* The previous year, Sandburg had moved to Chicago from Galesburg, a small town in rural Illinois, and likely was struck by the contrast between the two. In this poem, he uses bold language to  describe both the positive and negative qualities of Chicago, which had grown dramatically in the late nineteenth and early twentieth centuries. The city Sandburg writes about had become a national transportation hub, particularly for railroads, but also a center for organized crime.

"Grass" is one of the most eloquent antiwar poems ever written, largely because of its simplicity. Although Sandburg was a veteran of the Spanish-American War, he hated warfare. In this poem, he alludes to several battle-fields: Austerlitz and Waterloo from the Napoleonic wars, Gettysburg from the American Civil War, and Ypres and Verdun from World War I. "Grass" was published in 1918, the same year World War I ended.

Reader's Context Think of a place that evokes strong emotions in you. What does it represent to you? Why?

Meet the Author

Carl Sandburg (1878–1967) was born in Galesburg, Illinois, the son of immigrant Swedish parents. He left school after the eighth grade and held a variety of jobs until he was twenty, when he enlisted as a volunteer to fight in the Spanish-American War. After returning home, he attended Lombard College in Illinois but left in 1902 without graduating.

Sandburg's first poems were published in 1904, the year he began his journalism career at the Galesburg newspaper. In 1914, several of his poems were published in the magazine *Poetry,* and two years later, his first book of verse, *Chicago Poems,* was published. During these years, Sandburg held a variety of political jobs and wrote editorials for the *Milwaukee Leader* and other newspapers. He wrote for the *Chicago Daily News* from 1922 to 1930.

In his later years, Sandburg enjoyed extraordinary acclaim. He won two Pulitzer Prizes, one for poetry and one for a biography of Abraham Lincoln, and a Grammy for his recording of composer Aaron Copland's "Lincoln Portrait." In 1964, Sandburg was awarded the Presidential Medal of Freedom, one of the nation's highest civilian honors.

Analyze Literature

Sensory Details and Parallelism
Sensory details are words and phrases that describe how things look, sound, smell, taste, or feel.

Parallelism is a rhetorical technique in which a writer emphasizes the equal value or weight of two or more ideas by expressing them in the same grammatical form.

Set Purpose

Much of Sandburg's poetry is based on his personal experiences and observations. "Chicago" and "Grass" present his impressions of city life and war. As you read each poem, make a chart of the sensory details it contains, recording words and phrases that appeal to sight, sound, touch, smell, and taste. Think about what mood or idea Sandburg is trying to convey using these details. Also note Sandburg's use of parallelism in these poems. What ideas does he express in parallel fashion?

Preview Vocabulary

husky, 628
wanton, 628
ignorant, 629

CHICAGO

by Carl Sandburg

Hog Butcher for the World,
Tool Maker, Stacker of Wheat,
Player with Railroads and the Nation's Freight Handler;
Stormy, <u>husky</u>, brawling,
5   City of the Big Shoulders:

They tell me you are wicked and I believe them, for I have seen your
    painted women under the gas lamps luring the farm boys.
And they tell me you are crooked and I answer: Yes, it is true I have
    seen the gunman kill and go free to kill again.
And they tell me you are brutal and my reply is: On the faces of women
    and children I have seen the marks of <u>wanton</u> hunger.

---

husk • y (hus´ kē) *adj.*, solid; burly; strong
wan • ton (wän´ tən) *adj.*, unrestrained; merciless

And having answered so I turn once more to those who sneer at this
    my city, and I give them back the sneer and say to them:

10 Come and show me another city with lifted head singing so proud to
    be alive and coarse and strong and cunning.
Flinging magnetic curses amid the toil of piling job on job, here is a
    tall bold slugger set vivid against the little soft cities;
Fierce as a dog with tongue lapping for action, cunning as a savage
    pitted against the wilderness,
Bareheaded,
Shoveling,
15 Wrecking,
Planning,
Building, breaking, rebuilding,
Under the smoke, dust all over his mouth, laughing with white teeth,
Under the terrible burden of destiny laughing as a young man laughs,
20 Laughing even as an <u>ignorant</u> fighter laughs who has never lost a battle,
Bragging and laughing that under his wrist is the pulse. and under
    his ribs the heart of the people,
                        Laughing!
Laughing the stormy, husky, brawling laughter of Youth, half-naked,
    sweating, proud to be Hog Butcher, Tool Maker, Stacker of
    Wheat, Player with Railroads and Freight Handler to the Nation. ❖

ig • no • rant (ig′ nɵr ənt) *adj.,* unaware

Sandburg embraces both the positive and negative qualities of Chicago. What do
you like about the city or town in which you live? What don't you like about it?

BURNHAM

Informational Text Connection

This **architectural map of Chicago** reflects the primary events that have marked the city's growth and development and established it as a noted architectural center. In 1871, most of the downtown was destroyed by a tremendous fire, and an era of rapid rebuilding followed. Many of the city's oldest structures date back to the 1880s and 1890s and were designed by a group of architects known as the Chicago School. They created some of the world's first skyscrapers using steel-frame construction and large sheets of plate glass. In 1893, Chicago hosted the World's Fair, called the Columbian Exposition. Designed by noted Chicago architect Daniel Burnham, the exposition presented an architectural model of the ideal city. In 1909, Burnham unveiled his Plan of Chicago, one of the earliest and most well-known documents of urban planning. It set down principles not only for controlling the pace and aesthetics of urban development but also for improving the quality of urban living.

The Architecture of Chicago

1 Adler Planetarium

1300 South Lake Shore Drive

Philanthropist Max Adler commissioned architect Ernest Grunsfeld Jr. to build the Adler Planetarium in 1930. Despite its name, the Adler is more than just a planetarium. It also is a museum that houses over 35,000 square feet of astronomical exhibits and two full-sized planetarium theaters.

2 Aon Center

200 East Randolph Street

The Aon Center was designed in 1972 by architect Edward Durell Stone. At 1,136 feet, it is the third-tallest building in the United States, behind the Sears Tower and Empire State Building. The Aon Center is famous for its striking resemblance to the former World Trade Center.

3 Art Institute of Chicago

111 South Michigan Avenue

The Art Institute of Chicago, originally built as part of the 1893 Chicago World's Fair, houses one of the most prestigious art collections in the United States. Several of the paintings in this book, including Edward Hopper's *Nighthawks* and Grant Wood's *American Gothic,* are on permanent display there.

4 Board of Trade Building

141 West Jackson Boulevard

The Chicago Board of Trade Building, built in 1930 by the architectural firm Holabird & Root, is home to the world's largest futures and options exchange. The main commodity exchanged is grain, which is reflected in the building's Art Deco design. Egyptian, Greek, and Native American representations of grain are featured, as well.

5 Buckingham Fountain

500 South Lake Shore Drive

Buckingham Fountain, located in Grant Park, is one of the largest fountains in the world, spouting over 14,000 gallons per minute at heights that reach 150 feet. Edward H. Bennett designed the fountain in 1924 to look like the famous Latona Fountain in Versailles, France.

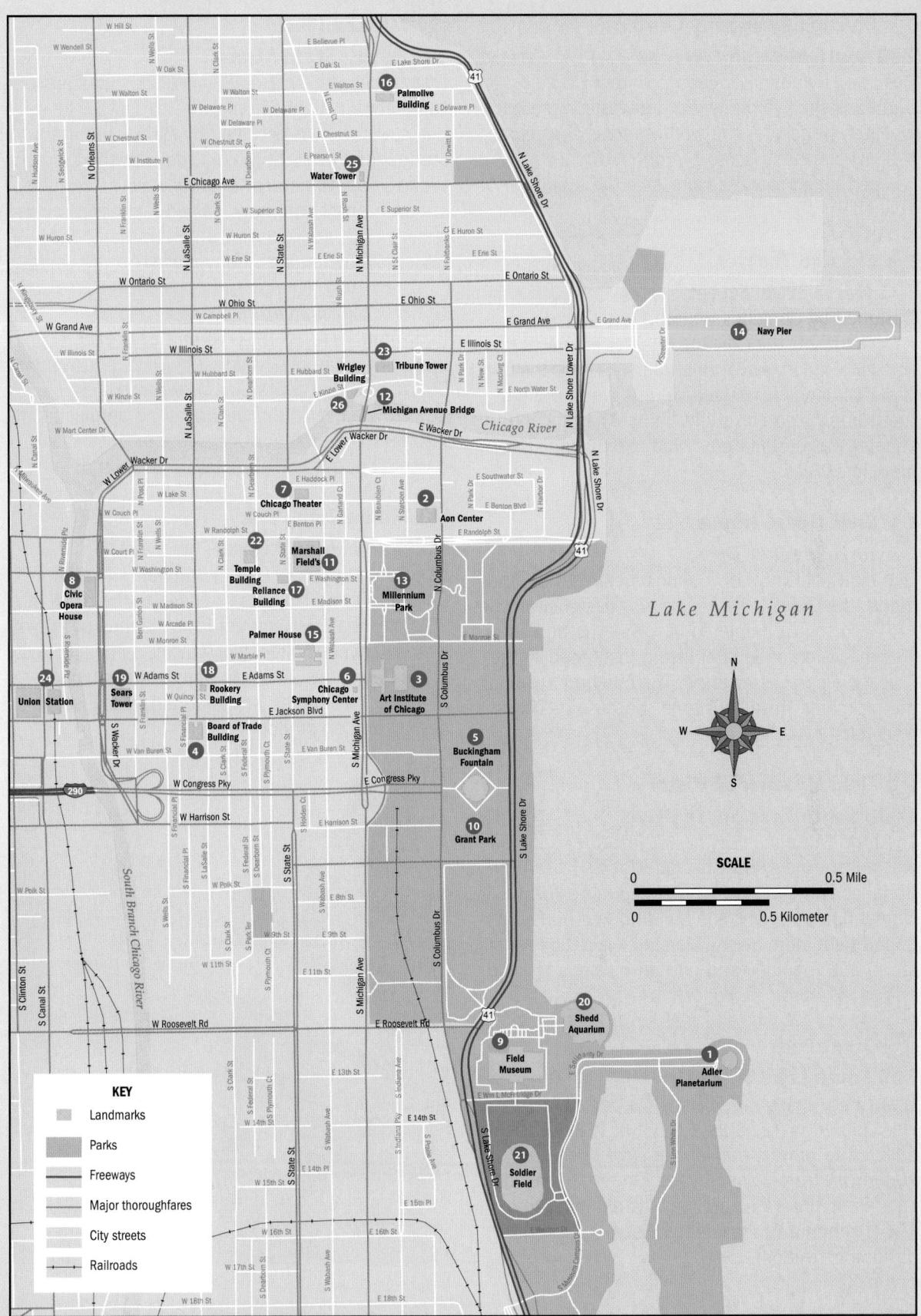

KEY

- Landmarks
- Parks
- Freeways
- Major thoroughfares
- City streets
- Railroads

16 Palmolive Building

25 Water Tower

14 Navy Pier

23 Wrigley Building

Tribune Tower

12 Michigan Avenue Bridge

26

7 Chicago Theater

2

Aon Center

22

11 Marshall Field's

Temple Building

17 Reliance Building

13 Millennium Park

8 Civic Opera House

15 Palmer House

19 Sears Tower

18

6 Chicago Symphony Center

3 Art Institute of Chicago

Rookery Building

24 Union Station

4 Board of Trade Building

5 Buckingham Fountain

10 Grant Park

Lake Michigan

Chicago River

South Branch Chicago River

20 Shedd Aquarium

9 Field Museum

1 Adler Planetarium

21 Soldier Field

SCALE

0   0.5 Mile

0   0.5 Kilometer

6 Chicago Symphony Center
220 South Michigan Avenue
Designed by noted Chicago architect Daniel Burnham, the Symphony Center was completed in 1904. It includes the world-famous Orchestra Hall, where the Chicago Symphony Orchestra has performed every season since the building opened.

7 Chicago Theater
175 North State Street
Designed by Cornelius W. Rapp and George L. Rapp in 1921, the Chicago Theater emulates the classical French-revival Baroque style. The theater is most famous for its vertical red sign featuring the word *Chicago* in bright lights. The Chicago Theater was designated a National Historic Landmark in 1983.

8 Civic Opera House
20 North Wacker Drive
Like many of Chicago's famous architectural landmarks, the Civic Opera House was designed in the Art Deco style. Completed in 1929, the building was the vision of Samuel Insull, then head of the Chicago Opera Association. The building acquired the nickname "Insull's Throne" because its shape resembles a massive chair.

9 Field Museum of History
1400 South Lake Shore Drive
The Field Museum, like the Art Institute, originally was part of the 1893 Chicago World's Fair. Additional construction was completed in 1906 by Daniel Burnham, and the building was named for department store owner Marshall Field. Specializing in anthropology and natural history, the Field has an extraordinary collection.

10 Grant Park
500 South Lake Shore Drive
Grant Park, known as "Chicago's front yard," was created in 1835 as a result of legislation enacted to protect part of the Lake Michigan waterfront from development. Originally called Lake Park, the 319-acre site was renamed in 1901 in honor of President Ulysses S. Grant, an Illinois resident.

11 Marshall Field's
111 North State Street
Construction on Marshall Field's flagship store was completed in stages from 1892 to 1915. The original structure was designed by Daniel Burnham and opened in 1893 to coincide with the Chicago World's Fair. It featured hydraulic elevators, modern bathrooms, and hand-carved mahogany counters. In 1906, a Neoclassical atrium was added, featuring the largest Tiffany mosaic in the world.

12 Michigan Avenue Bridge
Built from 1917 to 1920 as part of Daniel Burnham's Plan of Chicago, the Michigan Avenue Bridge provided a vital link between the city's downtown and north side. Spanning approximately 220 feet, the bridge is one of the most famous bascule bridges (drawbridges) in the world.

13 Millennium Park
North Michigan Avenue
As a continuation of Daniel Burnham's Plan of Chicago, Grant Park was extended to the north in 2004 to create Millennium Park. Planned by mayor Richard Daley and renowned avant-garde architect Frank Gehry, this 24.5-acre park features unique Modernist sculptures, an extraordinary landscape design, and an outdoor concert hall.

Millennium Park.

14 Navy Pier
600 East Grand Avenue
Intended as a place for cargo ships to unload freight, Navy Pier was completed in 1916 as part a two-pier plan by Daniel Burnham. The second pier was never built, and by 1965, the original pier had been abandoned. After a major renovation in 1989, Navy Pier reopened as a public center featuring a ferris wheel, children's museum, Shakespearean theater, and many public sculptures.

15 Palmer House
17 East Monroe Street
After opening on September 26, 1871, the Palmer House burned down just thirteen days later during the Great Chicago Fire. Owner Potter Palmer immediately set about building a new hotel that would surpass the old one in grandeur. When completed in 1875, the opulent structure was promoted as "the world's only fireproof hotel."

16 Palmolive Building
919 North Michigan Avenue
Designed by architectural firm Holabird & Root, the Palmolive Building was completed in 1929 and remains famous for its spirited Art Deco design. From 1930 to 1981, the building featured an operating beacon light atop its summit

17 Reliance Building
20 North State Street
Built in 1895, the Reliance Building was the first skyscraper to have most of its surface area covered with plate-glass panels. Built by John Root and Charles Atwood, the Reliance is home to the famous Hotel Burnham, named for fellow architect and city planner Daniel Burnham. The Reliance was designated a National Historic Landmark in 1976.

18 Rookery Building
209 South LaSalle Street
Considered the oldest standing high-rise in Chicago, the Rookery was built in 1888 by the architectural firm Burnham & Root. The building's large skylit lobby was remodeled in 1905 by noted Chicago architect Frank Lloyd Wright, who introduced elements of his Prairie School style. The Rookery was designated a National Historic Landmark in 1975.

The Sears Tower.

19 Sears Tower
233 South Wacker Drive
When built in 1973, the Sears Tower was the tallest building in the world at 1,451 feet. Today, it is the tallest building in North America and the fourth tallest in the world, by most accounts. The Sears Tower could be extended, as architect Bruce Graham built steel tubes within its framework to allow for future growth.

20 Shedd Aquarium
1200 Lake Shore Drive
The Shedd Aquarium is the world's second-largest indoor aquarium; its 5 million gallons of water hold 1,500 different species of fish, numbering 22,000 in all. Built as part of the 1893 Chicago World's Fair, the aquarium's first exhibits were shown in 1930 as a gift from John G. Shedd, then president of Marshall Field's.

21 Soldier Field
1410 South Museum Campus Drive
Built in 1924, Soldier Field is the home of the Chicago Bears, a franchise of the National Football League. Located on the shore of Lake Michigan, Soldier Field is an open-air stadium, with no retractable roof or other protection from harsh weather. This makes it a notoriously difficult environment for visiting teams, especially during the winter months.

22 Temple Building
77 West Washington Street
Built in 1924 by architects Holabird & Roche, the Temple Building was the tallest in Chicago for six years before being surpassed by the Board of Trade Building. Originally built as a church for Chicago's First United Methodist congregation, three sanctuaries still operate regularly within the building; the rest is rented out to businesses.

23 Tribune Tower
435 North Michigan Avenue
The Tribune Tower was built in 1925 by architects Howells & Hood, who were awarded the project after winning a competition that called for creating "the most beautiful and eye-catching building in the world." Reminiscent of the Woolworth Building in New York, the Tribune Tower is Neogothic in design, standing in sharp contrast to the more modern style preferred at the time by Chicago architects.

24 Union Station
225 South Canal Street
Construction on Union Station began in 1913, one year after the death of its designer, architect Daniel Burnham. His Neoclassical design was completed in 1925 by Graham, Anderson, Probst & White. When Union Station opened, its Great Hall was heralded as one of the United States' great indoor public places, with its vaulted skylight, towering columns, marble floors, and connecting balconies, staircases, and lobbies.

25 Water Tower
800 North Michigan Avenue
Constructed in 1869 of limestone blocks, the 150-foot, Gothic-style Water Tower resembles a small castle and stands in stark contrast to the modern high-rise buildings that surround it. As one of the few structures to survive the Great Chicago Fire in 1871, the Water Tower is a symbol of the city's strength and continuity.

26 Wrigley Building
410 North Michigan Avenue
Chewing gum mogul William Wrigley Jr. hired architects Graham, Anderson, Probst & White to build his corporate headquarters in 1920. Designed in the French Renaissance style, the gleaming-white building consists of two towers of different heights, which are joined by two suspended enclosed walkways and an open walkway at street level.

Review Questions

1. How many square miles is the downtown area? How much of this area comprises park space? What does this suggest about the philosophy underlying Chicago's development?

2. During what ten-year period were the most structures erected? Explain how this boom corresponds with the release of the Plan of Chicago in 1909.

3. Identify the buildings constructed as part of the 1893 Chicago World's Fair. Describe the legacy of the fair for Chicago's citizens.

TEXT $\xleftrightarrow{\text{TO}}$ TEXT CONNECTION

In his poem "Chicago," Sandburg describes the city as "Planning / Building, breaking, rebuilding." How does this description correspond to actual events in the city's growth and development? How did Chicago's city planners address some of the negative qualities Sandburg describes?

Grass by Carl Sandburg

Pile the bodies high at Austerlitz and Waterloo.[1]
Shovel them under and let me work—
    I am the grass; I cover all.

And pile them high at Gettysburg[2]
And pile them high at Ypres and Verdun.[3]
Shovel them under and let me work.
Two years, ten years; and passengers ask the conductor:
    What place is this?
    Where are we now?

    I am the grass.
    Let me work. ❖

---

1. **Austerlitz and Waterloo.** Northern European battle sites in the Napoleonic wars
2. **Gettysburg.** Civil War battlefield in southern Pennsylvania, which was the site of the most deadly battle of the war
3. **Ypres and Verdun.** World War I battle sites in Belgium and France, respectively, where heavy casualties resulted

MIRRORS & WINDOWS What is the best way to reclaim or reuse a former battle site? Should it be preserved, perhaps as a monument or park dedicated to those who died there? Or should it be built on for the sake of progress and moving on with life?

Refer to Text ▶ ▶ ▶ ▶ ▶ Reason with Text

Refer to Text	Reason with Text	
1a. State what the passengers ask the conductor in "Grass."	**1b.** Describe the change that occurs on the battlefields over time because of the work of the grass.	**Understand** Find meaning
2a. What does the speaker in "Chicago" give back to those who "sneer" at his city?	**2b.** Relate the attitude of the speaker in "Grass" to that of the speaker in "Chicago." What do these two poems tell you about Sandburg's view of the world?	**Apply** Use information
3a. In "Chicago," what is the speaker's answer to those who say the city is "brutal"?	**3b.** Identify the negative and positive aspects of Chicago the speaker describes in this poem.	**Analyze** Take things apart
4a. In "Grass," does the speaker think the soldiers and battles will be remembered?	**4b.** Do you agree with the speaker's attitude toward the soldiers and battles? Explain.	**Evaluate** Make judgments
5a. In "Chicago," what details does Sandburg give to describe the city?	**5b.** Summarize the impression you have of Chicago based on reading Sandburg's poem.	**Create** Bring ideas together

Analyze Literature

Sensory Details and Parallelism

Review the chart of sensory details you made for each poem. To what senses does Sandburg appeal? What mood or idea is he trying to convey? How does the use of sensory details help accomplish that purpose? How would the poem be different if Sandburg expressed the same mood or idea using abstract language?

Give an example of parallelism in each poem. Explain what ideas Sandburg is giving equal value or weight. Why is parallelism an effective rhetorical technique?

Extend the Text

Writing Options

Creative Writing Imagine that you are the grass at Gettysburg, which is maintained as a national military park and visited by two million people a year. Write an inscription for a monument there that captures what you saw at the Battle of Gettysburg.

Expository Writing Suppose you work as a writer in the city of Chicago's tourism bureau. Your supervisor has asked you to consider whether including Carl Sandburg's poem "Chicago" on the bureau's website would help bring visitors to the city. Write a brief analysis in which you evaluate whether Sandburg's portrayal of Chicago in the poem is consistent with the goal of attracting visitors to the city.

Collaborative Learning

Analyze Free Verse Sandburg's "Chicago" is written in free verse, using conversational language and having no regular rhyme, meter, or stanza divisions. With several classmates, analyze three or four other free-verse poems. Prepare a chart showing which qualities of free verse are found in which poems.

Lifelong Learning

Write a Tour Guide Script Imagine that you are a tour guide at Verdun, located in northeastern France, which was the site of one of the longest and deadliest battles in World War I. After researching the battle and the area, write a script that you would deliver as a tour guide to visitors to the area.

 Go to **www.mirrorsandwindows.com** for more.

Sonnet XXX

by Edna St. Vincent Millay

Edna St. Vincent Millay
(1892–1950) wrote, "I am glad that I paid so little attention to good advice. Had I abided by it I might have been saved from some of my most valuable mistakes."

Following her heart proved successful for the Maine-born Millay, who began to write poetry at an early age. She became a master of the *sonnet,* one of the most difficult of English poetic forms, and her poetry reached a large and enthusiastic audience. In 1923, she became the first woman to win the Pulitzer Prize, receiving the poetry award for *The Ballad of the Harp-Weaver.*

That same year, Millay married and bought a farm in upstate New York, where she continued her writing, including a *sonnet cycle,* or group of related sonnets, called *Fatal Interview.* Millay's **"Sonnet XXX,"** which tells of her own great love, continues the long tradition of love poetry.

Love is not all: it is not meat nor drink
Nor slumber nor a roof against the rain;
Nor yet a floating spar[1] to men that sink
And rise and sink and rise and sink again;
5   Love can not fill the thickened lung with breath,
Nor clean the blood, nor set the fractured bone;
Yet many a man is making friends with death
Even as I speak, for lack of love alone.
It well may be that in a difficult hour,
10   Pinned down by pain and moaning for release,
Or nagged by want[2] past resolution's power,
I might be driven to sell your love for peace,
Or trade the memory of this night for food.
It well may be. I do not think I would. ❖

---

1. **spar.** Pole supporting or extending the sail of a ship; here, the parts of a ship that can be used to keep sailors afloat after the ship has wrecked
2. **want.** Physical need

The speaker talks about love in terms of hunger and pain and death. Is love a physical need? Is it the most important thing in life?

1. According to lines 7 and 8, what might drive a person to make friends with death? Does the speaker believe love is a fundamental need? Support your answer with evidence from the poem.

2. What might move the speaker to sell his or her love for peace? To trade the memory of that love for food? Do you agree with the speaker's conclusions? Does the speaker seem convinced that he or she would not trade love for food or release from pain? Explain.

3. List the basic needs the speaker in the poem says cannot be fulfilled by love. Then make your own list of people's most basic needs. Compare and contrast the two lists, identifying how they are alike and different.

Writing Options

1. Write a thank-you letter to one of your parents or to someone who loved and supported you while you were growing up. In your letter, tell the person how his or her love affected your life.

2. Suppose you have been asked to contribute to an issue of a popular psychology magazine dedicated to the subject of *love*. Write a paragraph stating whether you agree or disagree with Millay's perspective of love, as stated in "Sonnet XXX."

 Go to **www.mirrorsandwindows.com** for more.

from

A Few Figs from Thistles

by Edna St. Vincent Millay

First Fig

My candle burns at both ends;
　　It will not last the night;
But ah, my foes, and oh, my friends—
　　It gives a lovely light!

Second Fig

Safe upon the solid rock the ugly houses stand:
Come and see my shining palace built upon the sand!

During the high-spirited 1920s, Harlem, the African-American community in uptown New York City, was the site of great passion and creativity. Writers, poets, philosophers, musicians, artists, and filmmakers all gathered to form a diverse talent base. Never before had so much African-American artistry bloomed in so short a time. This flowering of African-American culture came to be known as the **Harlem Renaissance.**

Although comprehensive in its scope of creative forms, the Harlem Renaissance was foremost a period of literature. The best-known poets of the era included James Weldon Johnson, Langston Hughes, and Countee Cullen, and the outstanding prose writers included Jean Toomer and Zora Neale Hurston. The work of these writers often reflected the experiences of blacks in northern cities and the rural South.

Beyond entertaining readers, the literature of the Harlem Renaissance also had a social purpose. Poets and novelists used their writing to protest racial prejudice and express pride in African-American cultural traditions. Their works were directed both to highly educated African Americans and also less well-educated members of the black community. Many writers chose techniques and styles that would appeal to white audiences, as well.

The economic opportunities that had sparked the so-called Great Migration of southern blacks to northern cities after World War I ended with the Great Depression. Harlem's concentration of talent was scattered away from the city, and writers and artists were forced to take other jobs to support themselves. The rich heritage of the Harlem Renaissance lived on, however, in the entirety of American art and literature.

Harlem, 1942. Jacob Lawrence. Private collection.

Langston Hughes

"There are ways of getting almost anywhere you want to go, if you really want to go."

Langston Hughes (1902–1967) was born in Joplin, Missouri, but spent most of his childhood in Lawrence, Kansas, living with his maternal grandmother. Among his ancestors were several famous individuals, including the first African American to be elected to public office and one of the men killed in John Brown's raid on Harpers Ferry in 1859.

Hughes's grandmother died when he was thirteen, at which time he went to live with his mother. After graduating from high school in Cleveland, Ohio, where he was named class poet, he spent more than a year with his father in Mexico. There, he wrote the poem "The Negro Speaks of Rivers," which would later gain him recognition. He claimed as his inspiration poets Walt Whitman, Carl Sandburg, Paul Laurence Dunbar, and Claude McKay.

Hughes's father wanted him to pursue a more practical career than writing and paid for him to study engineering at Columbia University. Hughes dropped out after a year, preferring instead to write poetry. He also was drawn to Harlem. "More than Paris, or the Shakespeare country, or Berlin, or the Alps," he wrote, "I wanted to see Harlem, the greatest Negro city in the world."

Hughes left New York after a year, and for the next several years, he traveled to various parts of Africa and Europe, taking whatever jobs he found. During this period, he continued to write and experienced some success, seeing his work published in important African-American periodicals such as *Opportunity* and the *Crisis*.

Hughes accepted a scholarship from Lincoln University in Pennsylvania and graduated in 1929. While there, he wrote his first novel, *Not Without Laughter* (1930). Political activism in the 1930s resulted in his being called to testify in 1953 before the House Un-American Activities Committee (see Unit 7) and being listed as a security risk by the Federal Bureau of Investigation (FBI) until 1959.

A prolific, versatile writer, Hughes published in his forty-year career sixteen collections of poetry, two novels, three collections of short stories, twenty plays, four musicals and operas, three autobiographies, twelve radio and television scripts, many children's poems, and dozens of magazine articles. His interest in jazz runs through much of his writing.

Among the many awards and honors recognizing Hughes's work were Rosenwald and Guggenheim Fellowships and a grant from the American Academy of Arts and Letters. Hughes's rich literary legacy was acknowledged in 2002, the centennial of his birth, with a commemorative stamp bearing his image.

Noted Works

The Weary Blues (poetry, 1926)

"The Negro Artist and the Racial Mountain" (essay, 1926)

The Ways of White Folks (stories, 1934)

The Big Sea (autobiography, 1940)

Montage of a Dream Deferred (poetry, 1951)

Black Nativity (Christmas pageant, 1961)

The Negro Speaks of Rivers
I, Too, Sing America

Lyric Poems by Langston Hughes

Build Background

Literary Context Langston Hughes published his first collection of verse, *The Weary Blues,* in 1926 at age twenty-four. Included in it were the two poems that follow, "The Negro Speaks of Rivers" and "I, Too, Sing America."

"The Negro Speaks of Rivers" actually was first published in 1921 in the *Crisis,* a magazine of the National Association for Colored People (NAACP), and Hughes dedicated the work to W. E. B. Du Bois. This poem traces the historic journey of African Americans through the world's rivers, starting in the Middle East, the birthplace of civilization, and ending in the American South.

Although written in the first person, the speaker in the poem is not presumed to be Hughes but rather an *omniscient* (all-knowing) observer who describes the proud heritage and enduring strength of the African-American people. By one account, the poem was inspired by Hughes's crossing the Mississippi River during a train trip just after high school, during which he observed the light reflecting off the water, creating a golden aura.

Hughes's admiration for Walt Whitman is reflected by the poem **"I, Too, Sing America,"** written in imitation of or perhaps response to Whitman's "I Hear America Singing" (see Unit 3, page 322). In Whitman's poem, the speaker praises the various voices of the ordinary people he encounters, but in Hughes's poem, the speaker decries the discriminatory treatment of African Americans and looks to the future, to a time when all Americans will be treated equally.

WHITMAN

Hughes reportedly wrote "I, Too, Sing America" after being denied passage on a ship because of his color. Jim Crow laws, which legalized many forms of segregation, still were in force in the South during the 1920s. Such segregation would not be outlawed until passage of the Civil Rights Act of 1964 and the Voting Rights Act of 1965.

While writing these poems during the 1920s, Hughes worked to unite the elements of blues and jazz with formal poetry. He stated, "Jazz to me is one of the inherent expressions of Negro life in America; the eternal tom-tom beating in the Negro soul—the tom-tom of revolt against weariness in a white world, a world of subway trains, and work, work, work; the tom-tom of joy and laughter, and pain swallowed in a smile."

Reader's Context When have you been excluded from a group? How did it make you feel? What, if anything, did you do about it? Why?

Analyze Literature

Speaker and Tone

The **speaker** is the character who speaks in, or narrates, a poem—the voice assumed by the writer. The speaker and the writer of the poem are not necessarily the same person, however.

Tone is the emotional attitude toward the reader or toward the subject implied by a literary work.

Set Purpose

As one of the key writers of the Harlem Renaissance, Langston Hughes lent a voice to African Americans that still resonates today. In the poems that follow, he uses unnamed speakers to express both pride in African Americans' heritage and frustration over their history of discrimination. As you read, characterize the speaker in each poem. Think about how the speaker's perspective is different from or similar to that of the author. Also compare and contrast the tones of the two poems. Again, think about how the attitude conveyed by the poem relates to Hughes's experience and perspective.

Blue Lagoon, c. 1940. John Wesley Hardrick.
Indiana State Museum, Indianapolis, Indiana.

The Negro Speaks of Rivers

by Langston Hughes

I've known rivers:
I've known rivers ancient as the world and older than the flow of
     human blood in human veins.

My soul has grown deep like the rivers.

    I bathed in the Euphrates when dawns were young.
5   I built my hut near the Congo and it lulled me to sleep.
    I looked upon the Nile[1] and raised the pyramids above it.
    I heard the singing of the Mississippi when Abe Lincoln went
     down to New Orleans,[2] and I've seen its muddy bosom turn
     all golden in the sunset.

    I've known rivers:
    Ancient, dusky rivers.

10   My soul has grown deep like the rivers. ❖

---

1. **Euphrates . . . Nile.** *Euphrates*—river that flows through Turkey, Syria, and Iraq; *Congo*—
river in central Africa; *Nile*—river in northeastern Africa
2. **when Abe Lincoln went down to New Orleans.** President Abraham Lincoln is reported
to have first stated his goal to abolish slavery after seeing the brutal treatment of slaves in
New Orleans.

What is your attitude toward your heritage? How much do you know about your
family's history?

I, Too, Sing America

by Langston Hughes

I, too, sing America.

I am the darker brother.
They send me to eat in the kitchen
When company comes,
5   But I laugh,
And eat well,
And grow strong.

Tomorrow,
I'll be at the table
10 When company comes.
Nobody'll dare
Say to me,
"Eat in the kitchen,"
Then.

15 Besides,
They'll see how beautiful I am
And be ashamed—

I, too, am America. ❖

Langston Hughes, 1925. Winold Reiss.
National Portrait Gallery, Washington, DC.

Imagine that the speaker of the poem is alive today. Would he be satisfied with the level of social progress that has been made since the 1920s, when the poem was written?

Primary Source Connection

In **Langston Hughes's** autobiography ***The Big Sea,*** published in 1940, he writes about his life to the age of twenty-eight. In this excerpt, he describes Harlem's popularity as an entertainment venue among whites in the 1920s. One of the most famous landmarks in Harlem was the Cotton Club, a nightclub featuring the so-called big bands of Duke Ellington and Cab Calloway and African-American performers such as Louis Armstrong.

Unfortunately, the Cotton Club had a strict whites-only policy for its customers until 1930, thus creating a color division in the heart of Harlem. An increase in the level of poverty in Harlem caused the Cotton Club to move to a midtown location; it closed in 1940.

from **The Big Sea**
by Langston Hughes

White people began to come to Harlem in droves. For several years they packed the expensive Cotton Club on Lenox Avenue. But I was never there, because the Cotton Club was a Jim Crow club for gangsters and monied whites. They were not cordial to Negro patronage, unless you were a celebrity like Bojangles.[1] So Harlem Negroes did not like the Cotton Club and never appreciated its Jim Crow policy in the very heart of their dark community. Nor did ordinary Negroes like the growing influx of whites toward Harlem after sundown, flooding the little cabarets and bars where formerly only colored people laughed and sang.

The Negroes said: "We can't go downtown and sit and stare at you in your clubs. You won't even let us in your clubs." But they didn't say it out loud—for Negroes are practically never rude to white people. So thousands of whites came to Harlem night after night, thinking the Negroes loved to have them there, and firmly believing that all Harlemites left their houses at sundown to sing and dance in cabarets, because most of the whites saw nothing but the cabarets, not the house.

It was a period when every season there was at least one hit play on Broadway acted by a Negro cast. And when books by Negro authors were being published with much greater frequency and much more publicity than ever before or since in history. It was a

---

1. **Bojangles.** Bill "Bojangles" Robinson (1878–1949)—famous African-American tap dancer

period when white writers wrote about Negroes more successfully (commercially speaking) than Negroes did about themselves. It was the period (God help us!) when Ethel Barrymore[2] appeared in blackface in *Scarlet Sister Mary!* It was the period when the Negro was in vogue.

I was there. I had a swell time while it lasted. But I thought it wouldn't last long. (I remember the vogue for things Russian, the season the Chauve-Souris[3] first came to town.) For how could a large and enthusiastic number of people be crazy about Negroes forever? But some Harlemites thought the millennium had come. They thought the race problem had at last been solved through Art plus Gladys Bentley.[4] They were sure the New Negro would lead a new life from then on in green pastures of tolerance created by Countee Cullen, Ethel Waters, Claude McKay, Duke Ellington, Bojangles, and Alain Locke.[5]

I don't know what made any Negroes think that—except that they were mostly intellectuals doing the thinking. The ordinary Negroes hadn't heard of the Negro Renaissance. And if they had, it hadn't raised their wages any. As for all those white folks in the speakeasies and night clubs of Harlem—well, maybe a colored man could find *some* place to have a drink that the tourists hadn't yet discovered. ❖

---

2. **Ethel Barrymore.** (1879–1959) Famous white stage and film actress who won an Academy Award in 1944
3. **Chauve-Souris.** Opera by Johann Strauss featuring a Russian prince; "the bat" in French
4. **Gladys Bentley.** (1907–1960) African-American blues singer known for dressing like a man
5. **Countee Cullen . . . Alain Locke.** *Countee Cullen* (1903–1946)—African-American poet; *Ethel Waters* (1896–1977)—blues vocalist and actress, second African American to be nominated for an Academy Award; *Claude McKay* (1889–1948)—African-American poet and novelist; *Duke Ellington* (1899–1974)—jazz composer, pianist, and band leader; *Alain Locke* (1886–1954)—writer, educator, philosopher, and the first African American to receive a Ph.D. from Harvard

Review Questions

1. Who were the primary patrons of the Cotton Club? Who were the performers? Discuss why the African-American residents of Harlem did not like the Cotton Club or the influx of white people to the area's nightclubs.

2. What evidence does Hughes give for his statement that, in the 1920s, "the Negro was in vogue"? Why did Hughes know that this period of vogue would not last?

3. According to Hughes, who in the African-American community was not aware of this period of vogue? Why were they not aware? Summarize how the arts can bring about understanding and peaceful co-existence between people of different races, ethnicities, cultures, and religions.

TEXT ⟷ TO ⟷ TEXT CONNECTION

Explain the parallels in content between "I, Too, Sing America" and this excerpt from *The Big Sea.* How was it possible that the "Negro was in vogue" yet still faced discrimination and abuse for being African American?

Refer to Text ▶ ▶ ▶ ▶ ▶   **Reason with Text**

1a. Name the specific rivers the speaker mentions in "The Negro Speaks of Rivers."	**1b.** Describe the accomplishments and experiences associated with each river.	**Understand** Find meaning
2a. In "I, Too, Sing America," where will the speaker eat tomorrow?	**2b.** What does eating at the table symbolize? Do African Americans "eat at the table" today? Explain.	**Apply** Use information
3a. In "I, Too, Sing America," how does the speaker view himself in relation to "them"?	**3b.** Identify the details in "I, Too, Sing America" that suggest that Americans are one family.	**Analyze** Take things apart
4a. In "The Negro Speaks of Rivers," how does the speaker feel about the rivers he has known?	**4b.** Assess the differences in tone between "The Negro Speaks of Rivers" and "I, Too, Sing America."	**Evaluate** Make judgments
5a. In "The Negro Speaks of Rivers," what did the speaker hear the Mississippi do when Abe Lincoln went to New Orleans?	**5b.** Compare and contrast how the African-American experience is depicted in the two poems.	**Create** Bring ideas together

Analyze Literature

Speaker and Tone

What qualities do you infer about the speaker in each poem? How are the speakers in the two poems alike and different? How is each speaker's perspective different from or similar to that of the author? Use details from the poems to support your analysis.

What attitude is implied in each poem? How does the tone of each poem compare to that of Hughes's autobiography, "When the Negro Was in Vogue"? How does Hughes's own experience and perspective seem to be reflected in his writing?

Extend the Text

Writing Options

Creative Writing Blues music is a central feature of Hughes's poetry. Write your own blues poem, setting it to music if you would like. Then read it to or perform it for the class.

Expository Writing Write a two-paragraph analysis of the significance of "The Negro Speaks of Rivers" and "I, Too, Sing America" to the Harlem Renaissance Era. How do these poems reflect key issues among African-American artists of the time? Use specific examples from the selections to support your analysis.

Collaborative Learning

Compare Literary Movements With a small group, read additional poetry by Langston Hughes. In addition, read poems representative of these literary movements:

Realism, Naturalism, Transcendentalism, and Imagism. As a group, compare and contrast Hughes's writing from the Harlem Renaissance with the work of writers from these other movements. Prepare a chart showing the similarities and differences across movements.

Lifelong Learning

Use Reference Works Most libraries have an assortment of reference works, and many can be found online as well. For each of the following items, identify the type of reference that would provide the information: (1) the location of the Congo River, (2) the history of the Nile River, (3) a news story about the most recent flood of the Mississippi River, (4) a quotation about rivers, and (5) the name of the river with which the Euphrates unites.

 Go to **www.mirrorsandwindows.com** for more.

America

A Sonnet by Claude McKay

A Black Man Talks of Reaping

A Lyric Poem by Arna Bontemps

Build Background

Literary Context Claude McKay is best known for his works about social injustice. His poem "If We Must Die," written in response to the Harlem race riots of 1919, expresses the frustration and anger of African Americans living in an age of blatant discrimination and violence. In **"America,"** published three years later, McKay describes his love/hate relationship with the country that held enormous promise but continually dashed his hopes and dreams.

Like McKay, Arna Bontemps also portrays the struggles of African Americans, a theme that can be seen in **"A Black Man Talks of Reaping."** In this allegorical poem, Bontemps uses the metaphor of farming to express the bitterness felt by African Americans in a racist United States.

Reader's Context What do you like about your country? What do you dislike about it? Why?

Meet the Authors

Claude McKay (1889–1948) was born in Jamaica to poor farm workers. His first two collections of poems, written in native dialect, were published in 1912 and earned him the prize money that helped him emigrate to the United States. After studying agriculture for several years, McKay moved to Harlem in 1914, where he became a prominent figure in the Harlem Renaissance. During the 1920s, McKay spent much of his time in Europe, largely due to his frustration with the discriminatory climate of the United States. While living abroad, he wrote most of the poetry that would appear in *Harlem Shadows* (1922) along with his award-winning novel *Home to Harlem* (1928), one of the first best sellers by an African-American writer.

Arna (Wendell) Bontemps (1902–1973) was born in Alexandria, Louisiana. His mother was a teacher and his father, a mason. In his work as a teacher, librarian, poet, novelist, playwright, and children's author, Bontemps dealt almost exclusively with African-American life and culture. He worked as a high school teacher and principal, as well as a freelance writer, before serving as Librarian of Fisk University from 1943 to 1965. He also taught at the University of Chicago and Yale University. Much of Bontemps's writing, in all genres, reflects his attempts to reconcile his respect for the richness of African-American folk culture with his rejection of negative ethnic stereotypes.

Compare Literature

Sonnet and Allegory

A **sonnet** is a fourteen-line poem, usually written in iambic pentameter. An English sonnet has three quatrains and a final couplet, with an *abab cdcd efef gg* rhyme scheme. An Italian sonnet has an octave and a sestet. The rhyme scheme of the octave is *abbaabba*, and that of the sestet can be *cdecde*, *cdcdcd*, or *cdedce*.

An **allegory** is a work in which characters, events, or settings symbolize, or represent, something else.

Set Purpose

Both McKay and Bontemps chose traditional poetic forms to express their anger and frustration over discrimination. McKay chose the sonnet form in writing "America." Review the structure and rhyme scheme of this poem, and determine whether it is an English or Italian sonnet. Bontemps's poem is an allegory. In reading "A Black Man Talks of Reaping," identify what the characters, events, and setting symbolize.

Preview Vocabulary

vigor, 649
malice, 649
unerring, 649

Study of a Tiger, c. 1900. Rudolph Ernst.

Although she feeds me bread of bitterness.[1]
And sinks into my throat her tiger's tooth,
Stealing my breath of life, I will confess
I love this cultured hell that tests my youth!
5   Her <u>vigor</u> flows like tides into my blood,
Giving me strength erect against her hate.
Her bigness sweeps my being like a flood.
Yet as a rebel fronts[2] a king in state,
I stand within her walls with not a shred
10 Of terror, <u>malice</u>, not a word of jeer.
Darkly I gaze into the days ahead,
And see her might and granite wonders there,
Beneath the touch of Time's <u>unerring</u> hand,
Like priceless treasures sinking in the sand. ❖

---

1. **bread of bitterness.** Reference to Psalm 80:5 in the Bible:
   "Thou feedest them with the bread of tears; and givest them tears
   to drink in great measure."
2. **fronts.** Confronts

vig • or (vig´ ər) *n.,* active physical or mental force or strength;
   intensity
ma • lice (ma´ lis) *n.,* active ill will; evil intent
un • err • ing (un ār´ iŋ) *adj.,* free from error; certain

MIRRORS & WINDOWS   What kind of future do you see for yourself in America? What kind of future
do you see for the country itself?

A Black Man Talks of Reaping[1]

by Arna Bontemps

Sowing, c. 1940. William H. Johnson.
Smithsonian American Art Museum, Washington, DC.

I have sown[2] beside all waters in my day.
I planted deep, within my heart the fear
that wind or fowl would take the grain away.
I planted safe against this stark, lean year.

5   I scattered seed enough to plant the land
in rows from Canada to Mexico
but for my reaping only what the hand
can hold at once is all that I can show.

Yet what I sowed and what the orchard yields
10 my brother's sons are gathering stalk and root:
small wonder then my children glean[3] in fields
they have not sown, and feed on bitter fruit. ❖

---

1. **Reaping.** Harvesting
2. **sown.** Planted
3. **glean.** Pick up bits of grain or produce left behind after a harvest

Imagine that you are the speaker in the poem. How would you feel after watching
your children eat what others have left behind in the fields?

William H. Johnson

William H. Johnson (1901–1970) was born in Florence, South Carolina, and aspired to become an artist from an early age. He moved to New York when he was seventeen to attend the National Academy of Design. A few years later, he went to Europe, where he studied art for most of the 1920s.

Johnson was strongly influenced by European Expressionist painting, which featured flurried brushstrokes and vibrant colors. His own paintings *Midnight Sun, Lofoten* (at right) and *Mountain Blossoms, Volda* (see page 667) reflect the Expressionist style.

Johnson returned to Harlem in 1930, near the end of the Harlem Renaissance, and embraced the topics and themes of the movement. In paintings such as *Sowing* (see the previous

Midnight Sun, Lofoten, 1937. William H. Johnson. Smithsonian American Art Museum, Washington, DC.

page), he focused on African-American subjects such as jazz musicians and sharecroppers. Johnson also painted a series of portraits of famous African Americans such as Booker T. Washington (see page 496), and he created a number of self-portraits, as well, including the one shown at left.

Johnson's mental health began to deteriorate in the early 1940s, and he spent most of his remaining years institutionalized. Before his death in 1970, he donated most of his artwork to the Smithsonian American Art Museum, where many of his paintings are on permanent display.

Critical Viewing Compare and contrast the paintings mentioned, looking for similarities and differences in style. Also consider the year each was painted and what was happening in Johnson's life at the time, based on this short biography. Can you trace the development or loss of certain qualities across his work?

Self-Portrait, c. 1934–1935. William H. Johnson. Smithsonian American Art Museum, Washington, DC.

Refer to Text ▶ ▶ ▶ ▶ ▶ **Reason with Text**

1a. In McKay's poem, what does America sink into the speaker's throat?	**1b.** Determine whether the speaker accepts the "bread of bitterness" America feeds him.	**Understand** Find meaning
2a. Identify what America steals from the speaker in McKay's poem.	**2b.** Based on what you know about the treatment of African Americans in the 1920s, suggest why the speaker in his poem expresses such bitterness.	**Apply** Use information
3a. What does America's "vigor" give the speaker?	**3b.** Point out the things the speaker likes and dislikes about America.	**Analyze** Take things apart
4a. What do the children "feed on" at the end of the second poem, "A Black Man Talks of Reaping"?	**4b.** Summarize the theme of Bontemps's poem.	**Evaluate** Make judgments
5a. Is the speaker in "A Black Man Talks of Reaping" surprised that his children are gleaning in "fields they have not sown"? Explain.	**5b.** Compare and contrast the tone of "A Black Man Talks of Reaping" with that of "America." How do Bontemps and McKay differ in their views of the African-American experience?	**Create** Bring ideas together

Compare Literature

Sonnet and Allegory

What type of sonnet is "America"? Discuss how you reached this conclusion. Why might McKay have used this traditional form?

For what is "A Black Man Talks of Reaping" an allegory? What does the planter's plight symbolize? What message is Bontemps trying to convey? Identify each symbol in the poem, and analyze what it means.

Extend the Text

Writing Options

Creative Writing Imagine that you are Arna Bontemps and have just read Claude McKay's "America." Write a letter to McKay, telling him what you think about the ideas expressed in "America."

Expository Writing Write a brief analysis of McKay's use of the sonnet to express the ideas related to the Harlem Renaissance. In what ways did he break from the traditional sonnet form? Is the sonnet an effective vehicle for expressing the ideas in this poem? Why or why not?

Collaborative Learning

Role-Play a Dialogue With a classmate, role-play a dialogue between Claude McKay and Arna Bontemps that occurs in the present day. Discuss the following questions: How do you feel about the United States? How have things changed for African Americans since the 1920s? What challenges still face African Americans? What does the future hold?

Media Literacy

Research Tenant Farming Research the history of tenant farming in the South, and then create a website on this subject. Your website should be appropriate for elementary school students and have the purpose of educating them and sparking their interest in this part of American history. Include quotations from Bontemps's poem "A Black Man Talks of Reaping" in appropriate locations in your website.

 Go to **www.mirrorsandwindows.com** for more.

Understand the Concept

Synonyms are words that have the same or similar meanings. **Antonyms** are words that have opposite meanings. Knowing both the synonyms and antonyms of a word can help you expand your vocabulary and thus add variety, accuracy, and interest to your writing.

Consider these synonyms and antonyms for the word *happy:*

| **Synonyms** | glad, joyful, pleased |
| **Antonyms** | sad, displeased, distraught |

Note that the words in each group have slightly different meanings. For instance, the synonym *joyful* indicates a more enthusiastic level of happiness than either *glad* or *pleased.* Similarly, the antonym *distraught* suggests a deeper level of emotion than *sad* or *displeased.*

To choose the appropriate synonym or antonym, you need to know the exact meaning or context of the original word. For instance, the word *light,* used as an adjective, has different meanings. It can refer to either the level of brightness or the weight of something. The antonym for *light,* therefore, could be *dark* or *heavy,* depending on the context. Likewise, you would need to know in what context *light* is used to choose from among the synonyms *pale, bright,* and *insubstantial.*

A useful source of information about synonyms and antonyms is a *thesaurus,* a reference book organized much like a dictionary that lists words with alternative and opposite meanings. Keep a thesaurus nearby as you write, and use it to find more specific and interesting words.

Apply the Skill

Exercise A

Brainstorm synonyms and antonyms for these words from Claude McKay's poem "America": *vigor, bigness, terror, malice, priceless, treasures.* Record your ideas in a three-column chart, writing the word in the first column, its synonyms in the second column, and its antonyms in the third column.

Exercise B

Use some of the synonyms you identified in Exercise A by substituting them for the words in McKay's poem. Discuss with a partner how each different word choice affects the meaning of the poem. Next, write a poem about your city, state, or country using several of the antonyms you identified.

Exercise C

Write a short comparison-and-contrast essay about the tones and themes of "America" and "A Black Man Talks of Reaping." Use a thesaurus to find appropriate and accurate words to describe the tone and theme of each poem. Make sure the words you choose express exactly what you mean; cross-checking a new word with its dictionary definition will help you.

SPELLING PRACTICE

Sounds of the Letter *g*

The letter *g* can be pronounced in several ways, depending on what letters are around it and what position it has in a word. For instance, at the beginning of a word, the letter *g* can have a hard or soft sound, as in *gossip* or *gentle,* respectively. Look for pronunciation patterns in these words from "America" and "A Black Man Talks of Reaping."

against	glean	strength
although	grain	tiger
enough	granite	unerring
gathering	might	vigor
gaze	reaping	
giving	stealing	

James Weldon Johnson

"We must begin to tell our young, There's a world waiting for you, Yours is the quest that's just begun."

James Weldon Johnson (1871–1938) was born in Jacksonville, Florida, in the early years of the Reconstruction Era. Because Jacksonville did not have a high school for African Americans, Johnson moved to Atlanta, where he attended preparatory school and later graduated from college. In 1896, Johnson returned to Jacksonville and became principal of his former grammar school.

While a principal, Johnson studied and then practiced law, becoming the first African American to be admitted to the Florida bar. He soon grew tired of being a lawyer, however, and collaborated with his brother writing songs. In 1900, to commemorate Abraham Lincoln's birthday, the brothers wrote an anthem called "Lift Every Voice and Sing," which became popular throughout the country. In later years, it would become the anthem for the Civil Rights movement. In 1901, the brothers went to New York, where they worked on Broadway musicals.

Johnson became active in politics, and from 1906 to 1914, he was U.S. Consul to Venezuela and Nicaragua. During this time, he also published poetry in several magazines. Literary success came with publication of *The Autobiography of an Ex-Colored Man,* the fictional story of a light-skinned black man living in the twentieth-century United States. When originally published in 1912, Johnson did not claim authorship of the book; he republished it in 1927 under his own name.

Upon returning to the United States, Johnson became active in African-American affairs. From 1920 to 1931, he worked for the National Association for the Advancement of Colored People (NAACP), eventually becoming its secretary. In 1922, he edited *The Book of American Negro Poetry,* a landmark in African-American literature, and in 1927, he published *God's Trombones: Seven Negro Sermons in Verse,* a celebration of folk preachers.

By this time, Johnson had become a key figure in the Harlem Renaissance. He urged African-American writers and other artists to draw on everyday life for their creative inspiration, believing that African Americans could best gain respect by producing great art.

Noted Works

The Autobiography of an Ex-Colored Man (novel, 1912)

The Book of American Negro Poetry (1922)

God's Trombones: Seven Negro Sermons in Verse (1927)

Black Manhattan (1930)

Along This Way (autobiography, 1934)

My City
Go Down, Death

Poems by James Weldon Johnson

Build Background

Literary Context James Weldon Johnson spent much of his life in New York City, ultimately settling there. His poem **"My City,"** published in 1935, is an ode to Manhattan, one of the five boroughs of New York (see below). Similarly to Carl Sandburg's "Chicago," Johnson's "My City" uses strong language to give readers a vivid portrait of the city. "My City" also examines the theme of death. Using the form of a Petrarchan sonnet, Johnson asks in the first stanza what will be his greatest loss upon dying; he answers that question in the second stanza.

    "Go Down, Death," published in 1927, is written in free verse and was inspired by the artistry of the classic African-American sermon. In this poem, the preacher asks mourners not to weep at the loss of Sister Caroline, because dying has ended her suffering. Death is personified in this poem as a merciful agent of God who has relieved Sister Caroline of her pain and brought her "home."

    Johnson had a deep respect for African-American folk traditions. However, he did not feel that using misspellings to capture the sound of the spoken language helped promote African-American culture. On this point, writers Zora Neale Hurston, Langston Hughes, and others disagreed with Johnson. In *The Book of American Negro Poetry,* which Johnson edited, he wrote, "What the colored poet in the United States needs to do is . . . find a form that will express the racial spirit by symbols from within rather than symbols from without, such as the mere mutilation of English spelling and pronunciation."

Reader's Context If you moved to a new city or country, what would you miss most about where you live now? Why?

Manhattan (labeled 1) is an island that lies between the Hudson and East Rivers. It is one of the five *boroughs,* or regions, of New York City; the others are Brooklyn (2), Queens (3), the Bronx (4), and Staten Island (5).

Analyze Literature

Alliteration and Repetition
Alliteration is the repetition of consonant sounds. Although alliteration usually refers to sounds at the beginning of words, it also can be used to refer to sounds within words.

Repetition is the writer's intentional reuse of a sound, word, phrase, or sentence. Writers often use repetition to emphasize ideas or to create a musical effect.

Set Purpose

The poems "My City" and "Go Down, Death" demonstrate Johnson's range as a writer. "My City" follows the traditional form of a Petrarchan sonnet, and "Go Down, Death" is written in free verse to emulate an African-American sermon. Despite these differences in form, both poems contain alliteration. Write down examples of repeated consonant sounds as you read. In reading "Go Down, Death," also look for examples of repetition. Read the poem aloud to consider how repeating certain words and phrases might affect listeners.

Preview Vocabulary

subtle, 656
unutterable, 656
furrow, 658

My City

by James Weldon Johnson

When I come down to sleep death's endless night,
The threshold of the unknown dark to cross,
What to me then will be the keenest loss,
When this bright world blurs on my fading sight?
5   Will it be that no more I shall see the trees
Or smell the flowers or hear the singing birds
Or watch the flashing streams or patient herds?
No, I am sure it will be none of these.

But, ah! Manhattan's sights and sounds, her smells,
10   Her crowds, her throbbing force, the thrill that comes
From being of her a part, her <u>subtle</u> spells,
Her shining towers, her avenues, her slums—
O God! the stark, <u>unutterable</u> pity,
To be dead, and never again behold my city! ❖

---

sub • tle (sut´ l) *adj.,* slight and not obvious
un • ut • ter • a • ble (ən ə´ tə rə bəl) *adj.,* beyond description or
   expression

Does the speaker in this poem make Manhattan sound attractive to you?
Would you want to live there?

Go Down, Death

by James Weldon Johnson

Weep not, weep not,
She is not dead;
She's resting in the bosom of Jesus.
Heart-broken husband—weep no more;
5   Grief-stricken son—weep no more;
Left-lonesome daughter—weep no more;
She only just gone home.

Day before yesterday morning,
God was looking down from his great, high heaven,
10 Looking down on all his children,
And his eye fell on Sister Caroline,
Tossing on her bed of pain.
And God's big heart was touched with pity,
With the everlasting pity.

15 And God sat back on his throne,
And he commanded that tall, bright angel standing at his right hand:
Call me Death!
And that tall, bright angel cried in a voice
That broke like a clap of thunder:
20 Call Death!—Call Death!
And the echo sounded down the streets of heaven
Till it reached away back to that shadowy place,
Where Death waits with his pale, white horses.[1]

And Death heard the summons,
25 And he leaped on his fastest horse,
Pale as a sheet in the moonlight.
Up the golden street Death galloped,
And the hooves of his horses struck fire from the gold,
But they didn't make no sound.
30 Up Death rode to the Great White Throne,
And waited for God's command.

And God said: Go down, Death, go down,
Go down to Savannah, Georgia,
Down in Yamacraw,
35 And find Sister Caroline.
She's borne the burden and heat of the day,
She's labored long in my vineyard,[2]
And she's tired—

---

1. **pale, white horses.** In the Bible (Revelations 6:8), Death sits on a pale horse.
2. **vineyard.** Land where grapes are cultivated; in the Bible, a symbol of spiritual labor

She's weary—
40   Go down, Death, and bring her to me.

And Death didn't say a word,
But he loosed the reins on his pale, white horse,
And he clamped the spurs to his bloodless sides,
And out and down he rode,
45   Through heaven's pearly gates,
Past suns and moons and stars;
on Death rode,
Leaving the lightning's flash behind;
Straight down he came.

50   While we were watching round her bed,
She turned her eyes and looked away,
She saw what we couldn't see;
She saw Old Death. She saw Old Death
Coming like a falling star.
55   But Death didn't frighten Sister Caroline;
He looked to her like a welcome friend.
And she whispered to us: I'm going home,
And she smiled and closed her eyes.

And Death took her up like a baby,
60   And she lay in his icy arms,
But she didn't feel no chill.
And death began to ride again—
Up beyond the evening star,
Into the glittering light of glory,
65   On to the Great White Throne.
And there he laid Sister Caroline
On the loving breast of Jesus.

And Jesus took his own hand and wiped away her tears,
And he smoothed the <u>furrows</u> from her face,
70   And the angels sang a little song,
And Jesus rocked her in his arms,
And kept a-saying: Take your rest,
Take your rest.

Weep not—weep not,
75   She is not dead;
She's resting in the bosom of Jesus. ❖

fur • row (fʉrʹ ō) *n.,* narrow rut or groove

How does the image of Death in this poem compare to your image of death?
Has reading this poem changed the way you think about death?

Primary Source Connection

James Weldon Johnson's *Black Manhattan* is a history of African Americans in New York City, beginning in the seventeenth century when the Dutch founded New Amsterdam (the original name for New York). At that time, according to Johnson, only eleven African Americans (all men) lived there. In describing slavery, abolition, and lynchings, Johnson points to the collective will of the African-American community to resist oppression and develop a culture that would help shape the wider American culture. When *Black Manhattan* was published in 1930, reviews from such diverse publications as the *Journal of Negro History* and the *New York Times* were full of praise.

from **Black Manhattan**

by James Weldon Johnson

Within the past ten years Harlem has acquired a world-wide reputation. It has gained a place in the list of famous sections of great cities. It is known in Europe and the Orient, and it is talked about by natives in the interior of Africa. It is farthest known as being exotic, colourful, and sensuous; a place of laughing, singing, and dancing; a place where life wakes up at night. This phase of Harlem's fame is most widely known because, in addition to being spread by ordinary agencies, it has been proclaimed in story and song. And certainly this is Harlem's most striking and fascinating aspect. New Yorkers and people visiting New York from the world over go to the night-clubs of Harlem and dance to such jazz music as can be heard nowhere else; and they get an exhilaration[1] impossible to duplicate. Some of these seekers after new sensations go beyond the gay night-clubs; they peep in under the more seamy side of things; they nose down into lower strata[2] of life. A visit to Harlem at night—the principal streets never deserted, gay crowds skipping from one place of amusement to another, lines of taxicabs and limousines standing under the sparkling lights of the entrances to the famous night-clubs, the subway kiosks swallowing and disgorging crowds all night long—gives the impression that Harlem never sleeps and that the inhabitants thereof jazz through existence. But, of course, no one can seriously think that the two hundred thousand and more Negroes in Harlem spend their nights on any such pleasance. Of a necessity the vast majority of them are ordinary, hard-working people, who spend their time in just about the same way that other

---

1. **exhilaration.** Thrill
2. **strata.** Layer; level

ordinary, hard-working people do. Most of them have never seen the inside of a night-club. The great bulk of them are confronted with the stern necessity of making a living, of making both ends meet, of finding money to pay the rent and keep the children fed and clothed nearly enough to attend school; their waking hours are almost entirely consumed in this unromantic task. And it is a task in which they cannot escape running up against a barrier erected especially for them, a barrier which pens them off on the morass[3]— no, the quicksands—of economic insecurity. Fewer jobs are open to them than to any other group; and in such jobs as they get, they are subject to the old rule, which still obtains "the last to be hired and the first to be fired."

Notwithstanding all that, gaiety is peculiarly characteristic of Harlem. The people who live there are by nature a pleasure-loving people; and though most of them must take their pleasures in a less expensive manner than in nightly visits to clubs, they nevertheless, as far as they can afford—and often much

---

3. **morass.** Swamp
4. **Mrs. C. J. Walker.** Born Sarah Breedlove (1867–1919); creator of a line of women's hair care products and the first self-made African-American woman to become a millionaire

---

Music, Theater, and Art of the Harlem Renaissance

In the 1920s, African Americans contributed to several musical styles that are still popular today. The sounds of African-American jazz invigorated and popularized mainstream American music, and jazz musicians and composers such as Duke Ellington and Cab Calloway became beloved stars at home and abroad. Bessie Smith and other blues singers presented bold, witty, emotionally raw lyrics, and songs such as Eubie Blake's catchy "I'm Just Wild about Harry" had a lively ragtime style. African-American spirituals became widely appreciated as uniquely beautiful religious music.

ELLINGTON

The Harlem Renaissance also was an era of innovative theater. Many young African-American actors performed in the Lafayette and Lincoln Theaters, including Ethel Waters and Noble Sissle. Harlem's first theater group was founded at the Lafayette in 1916. Other theater groups that

ROBESON

emerged during the Harlem Renaissance included the Harlem Experimental Theater, the Krigwa Players, the Negro Art Theater, the Utopia Players, and the Harlem Community Players. The play *The Emperor Jones,* by white playwright Eugene O'Neill (1920), focused on the black experience and brought fame to two black actors, Charles Gilpin and Paul Robeson.

Many African-American visual artists across the United States also gained prominence at this time. Aaron Douglas's illustrations for magazines such as *Crisis* and *Opportunity* and his book covers for the leading Harlem writers made his style the "look" of the Harlem Renaissance. James Van Der Zee photographed many of the defining images of Harlem's middle class.

African-American painters and sculptors developed a wide range of styles, based on the art of Africa and ancient Egypt, American folk art, and representational and abstract European art. African tribal art, in particular, previously dismissed as "primitive," began to be appreciated for its intelligence and beauty. Even among white artists, attention shifted to African art, and Cubists and Expressionists began to base their radical new forms on traditional African sculpture.

farther—do satisfy their hunger for enjoyment. And since they are constituted as they are, enjoyment being almost as essential to them as food, perhaps really a compensation which enables them to persist, it is well that they are able to extract pleasure easily and cheaply. An average group of Negroes can in dancing to a good jazz band achieve a delightful state of intoxication that for others would require nothing short of a certain per capita imbibition of synthetic gin. The masses of Harlem get a good deal of pleasure out of things far too simple for most other folks. In the evenings of summer and on Sundays they get lots of enjoyment out of strolling. Strolling is almost a lost art in New York; at least, in the manner in which it is so generally practised in Harlem. Strolling in Harlem does not mean merely walking along Lenox or upper Seventh Avenue or One Hundred and Thirty-fifth Street; it means that those streets are places for socializing. One puts on one's best clothes and fares forth to pass the time pleasantly with the friends and acquaintances and, most important of all, the strangers he is sure of meeting. One saunters along, he hails this one, exchanges a word or two with that one, stops for a short chat with the other one. He comes up to a laughing, chattering group, in which he may have only one friend or acquaintance, but that gives him the privilege of joining in. He does join in and takes part in the joking, the small talk and gossip, and makes new acquaintances. He passes on and arrives in front of one of the theatres, studies the bill for a while, undecided about going in. He finally moves on a few steps farther and joins another group and is introduced to two or three pretty girls who have just come to Harlem, perhaps only for a visit; and finds a reason to be glad that he postponed going into the theatre. The hours of a summer evening run by rapidly. This is not simply going out for a walk; it is more like going out for adventure. ❖

Review Questions

1. How does Johnson describe nighttime Harlem in the selection? What atmosphere does his description suggest?

2. State one of the ways Johnson says African Americans enjoy themselves. In Johnson's view, does pleasure depend on economic security? Why or why not?

3. How does Johnson contrast the experiences of whites and blacks in Harlem? Johnson describes the difference between the outside world's perception of Harlem and its reality. Think of another example of this kind of inaccurate perception of a place. Explain whom it hurts and whom it benefits.

TEXT ^{TO} TEXT CONNECTION

What does Johnson say is characteristic of Harlem? Compare and contrast the *tone* (the author's emotional attitude) of this selection with the tones of "My City" and "Go Down, Death." What does Johnson predict for African Americans in New York?

Refer to Text ▷ ▷ ▶ ▶ ▶ Reason with Text

1a. In "My City," what does the speaker think will be the greatest loss when he dies?	**1b.** Describe how the speaker feels about Manhattan. Give examples to support your answer.	**Understand** Find meaning
2a. In "Go Down, Death," what does God tell Death to do?	**2b.** Examine the primary message intended for the sermon's audience.	**Apply** Use information
3a. How is Death described in "Go Down, Death"?	**3b.** Compare and contrast the views of death expressed in "My City" and "Go Down, Death."	**Analyze** Take things apart
4a. Identify the speaker in "Go Down, Death." Also identify the setting of this poem.	**4b.** Would "Go Down, Death" be as effective if it were written in more formal language? Support your answer by contrasting the poem with "My City" or another poem.	**Evaluate** Make judgments
5a. What does the speaker in "My City" say happens after death?	**5b.** Suggest how the speaker in "My City" likely would feel about the funeral sermon "Go Down, Death"? What can you infer about Johnson's perspective on death?	**Create** Bring ideas together

Analyze Literature

Alliteration and Repetition

What instances of alliteration did you find in each poem? How does the use of alliteration help create the tone of each poem?

List the words and phrases that are repeated in "Go Down, Death." Why does Johnson repeat these particular words and phrases? If this poem were read at a funeral, how might the repetition affect the listeners?

Extend the Text

Writing Options

Creative Writing Imagine that the speaker in "My City" has met the sermon leader in "Go Down, Death." Write a dialogue in which they discuss their opinions on death and the afterlife.

Expository Writing Write a character analysis of the speaker in "My City." What does he believe? What are his values? What does he like to do? Use details from the poem to support your analysis.

Collaborative Learning

Perform a Dramatic Reading With a partner, rehearse and perform a dramatic reading of one or more of James Weldon Johnson's poems. Take turns reading separate poems, or have several people read parts of the same poem. As you read, experiment with pace and volume, and use gestures where appropriate.

Media Literacy

Create a Multimedia Presentation Using the information in the Cultural Connection on page 660 as a starting point, research the music, theater, and art produced during the Harlem Renaissance. Choose one individual and conduct further research about his or her life and work. Prepare and deliver a multimedia presentation about this individual's contribution to the Harlem Renaissance.

 Go to **www.mirrorsandwindows.com** for more.

1. Why is it appropriate that "My City" is a sonnet?
   A. It is essentially a love poem to Manhattan.
   B. Johnson invented the sonnet form.
   C. The poem asks and then answers a question.
   D. Johnson wants to shock readers.
   E. The loose structure goes well with the subject matter.

2. Which of the following lines from "My City" has alliteration?
   A. "When I come down to sleep death's endless night"
   B. "When this bright world blurs on my fading sight"
   C. "But, ah! Manhattan's sights and sounds, her smells"
   D. "O God! The stark, unutterable pity"
   E. "To be dead, and never again behold my city!"

3. Johnson describes Manhattan as having "subtle spells." Which of the following words means the opposite of *subtle?*
   A. soft
   B. silent
   C. obvious
   D. unknown
   E. vulgar

4. In "Go Down, Death," which of these images is *not* associated with Death?
   A. "took her up like a baby"
   B. "on his pale, white horse"
   C. "coming like a falling star"
   D. "lay in his icy arms"
   E. "a voice that broke like a clap of thunder"

5. In "Go Down, Death," Sister Caroline most likely has *furrows* on her face because of
   A. worry.
   B. surprise.
   C. happiness.
   D. sleeping.
   E. illness.

6. In "Go Down, Death," repeated phrases such as "Weep not, weep not" and "Take your rest, / Take your rest" create what quality or emotion?
   A. sadness
   B. anxiety
   C. monotony
   D. curiosity
   E. comfort

7. According to Johnson in the excerpt from *Black Manhattan,* how do the residents of Harlem usually find entertainment?
   A. They go to nightclubs.
   B. They stroll along the avenues.
   C. They dance.
   D. A and C
   E. B and C

8. Johnson writes in *Black Manhattan* that observers have the impression that "Harlem never sleeps and that the inhabitants thereof jazz through existence." What does this mistakenly suggest about the residents of Harlem?
   A. that they listen only to jazz music
   B. that they depend on the jazz clubs for work
   C. that they walk with a swing in their step
   D. that they lead easy-going, colorful lives
   E. that they are unaware of the poor conditions around them

9. **Constructed Response:** Compare and contrast the views of death presented in "My City" and "Go Down, Death." Explain which view is most similar to your own. Use details from the poems to support your analysis.

10. **Constructed Response:** Analyze Johnson's use of the Petrarchan sonnet form in "My City." Identify what question is asked and answered in the two stanzas of the poem. Discuss how the form supports the theme of the poem. Suggest why Johnson might have decided to use this traditional form.

TEST-TAKING TIP

Start preparing for a major test weeks in advance, not days. If you cram the night before the test, you will not remember most of what you studied on the next day. In fact, it's a good idea to take a break from studying and practicing twenty-four hours before the test. Doing so will help you clear your mind and approach the test in a calm manner.

Any Human to Another

by Countee Cullen

Countee Cullen (1903–1946) was born Countee Leroy Porter in New York City. Like many African-American writers of his time, Cullen's writing was, in large part, a reaction to the racism he encountered. Recalling an incident in 1930 when he was barred from eating in a restaurant, he later said, "There may have been many things in my life that have hurt me, and I find that the surest relief from these hurts is in writing. Most things I write, I do for the sheer love of the music in them. Somehow or other, however, I find my poetry of itself treating of the Negro, of his joys and his sorrows, mostly of the latter, and of the heights and the depths of emotion which I feel as a Negro."

The poem **"Any Human to Another,"** published in 1935, is a lyric addressing the sorrow that afflicts all humans and the need to share one another's pain.

The ills I sorrow at
Not me alone
Like an arrow
Pierce to the marrow,
5 Through the fat
And past the bone.

Your grief and mine
Must intertwine
Like sea and river,
10 Be fused and mingle,
Diverse yet single,
Forever and forever.

Let no man be so proud
And confident,
15 To think he is allowed
A little tent
Pitched in a meadow
Of sun and shadow
All his little own.

20 Joy may be shy, unique,
Friendly to a few,
Sorrow never scorned[1] to speak
To any who
Were false or true.

25 Your every grief
Like a blade
Shining and unsheathed
Must strike me down.
Of bitter aloes[2] wreathed,
30 My sorrow must be laid
On your head like a crown. ❖

---

1. **scorned.** Rejected or dismissed as contemptible or unworthy
2. **aloe.** Succulent plant known for its medicinal quality

The speaker says only some people experience joy in life, but everyone experiences sorrow. Do you agree? What would you rather share with others: your sorrow or your joy?

Can Fire in the Park, 1946. Beauford Delaney.
Smithsonian American Art Museum, Washington, DC.

Refer and Reason

1. Identify what all people share, according to the speaker. The British poet John Donne said, "No man is an island, entire of itself." What stanza in "Any Human to Another" does this statement echo?

2. In the final stanza, what expectation does the speaker have of others' pain? Assess whether the speaker offers a healthy psychological perspective.

3. Where must the speaker lay his sorrow? Relate this poem to the racial issues that were important to many Harlem Renaissance writers.

Writing Options

1. Imagine that you are Countee Cullen. Write a letter to your readers explaining why you entitled your poem "Any Human to Another."

2. Write a journal entry describing a sorrow or joy you have recently experienced. Explain whether you kept it to yourself or shared it with other people.

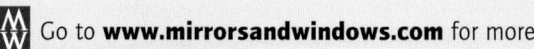 Go to **www.mirrorsandwindows.com** for more.

Jean Toomer (1896–1967), writer, poet, and playwright, was born in Washington, DC, the son of a Georgia farmer. As a light-skinned African-American man, he "passed" for white during certain periods of his life, but he was raised in a predominantly African-American community and attended African-American high schools. Describing his college education, which ended in 1917, Toomer said, "Neither the universities of Wisconsin or New York gave me what I wanted, so I quit them."

Working in Georgia as a teacher inspired Toomer to write *Cane* (1923), a book of prose poetry in which an African American struggles to discover his selfhood in various African-American communities. Toomer was praised for uniting "folk culture and the elite culture of the white avant-garde."

In **"Storm Ending,"** Toomer describes a storm using such figures of speech as metaphor, simile, and personification. Typical of his verse, "Storm Ending" follows established poetic traditions, not new African-American forms.

STORM ENDING

by Jean Toomer

Thunder blossoms gorgeously above our heads,
Great, hollow, bell-like flowers,
Rumbling in the wind,
Stretching clappers to strike our ears . . .
Full-lipped flowers
Bitten by the sun
Bleeding rain
Dripping rain like golden honey—
And the sweet earth flying from the thunder. ❖

How are you affected by thunderstorms and other kinds of severe weather? Are you frightened or invigorated?

Mountain Blossoms, Volda, c. 1936. William H. Johnson.
Smithsonian American Art Museum, Washington, DC.

Refer and Reason

1. As described in the poem, what do the clouds look like? Identify the senses to which the speaker refers.

2. What blossoms "gorgeously above our heads"? Determine which aspect of the storm has the most impact on the speaker.

3. What do the clouds stretch out to the speaker? Evaluate why the speaker pays more attention to how the storm looks than how it sounds.

Writing Options

1. Images in the poem evoke the senses of sight and sound. Write two new lines to the poem that add another sense, whether touch, taste, or smell.

2. Write a dialogue in which two people discuss the weather on the day of the storm.

MW Go to **www.mirrorsandwindows.com** for more.

from
Dust Tracks on a Road

by Zora Neale Hurston

Zora Neale Hurston (c. 1901–1960), writer and folklorist, was born and raised in Eatonville, Florida. As a novelist, Hurston is noted for her storytelling abilities, use of metaphoric language, and celebration of southern African-American culture. Her writing influenced the Harlem Renaissance writers of the 1930s, as well as later African-American writers. *Their Eyes Were Watching God* (1937), her most famous novel, is widely read in college classes.

Hurston's memoir, ***Dust Tracks on a Road,*** describes her childhood in the first all-black incorporated town of Eatonville, Florida, and her rise to prominence as a Harlem Renaissance writer. In this excerpt, she describes a childhood episode that inspired her enthusiasm for books and reading.

Although Hurston's memoir was a commercial success when published in 1942, it has been harshly criticized. Even her admirers condemned the book as being unreliable and promoting the assimilation of African Americans into mainstream American culture.

I used to take a seat on top of the gate-post and watch the world go by. One way to Orlando ran past my house, so the carriages and cars would pass before me. The movement made me glad to see it. Often the white travelers would hail me, but more often I hailed them, and asked, "Don't you want me to go a piece of the way with you?" They always did. I know now that I must have caused a great deal of amusement among them, but my self-assurance must have carried the point, for I was always invited to come along. I'd ride up the road for perhaps a half-mile, then walk back. I did not do this with the permission of my parents, nor with their foreknowledge. When they found out about it later, I usually got a whipping. My grandmother worried about my forward ways a great deal. She had known Slavery and to her my brazenness[1] was unthinkable.

"Git down offa dat gate-post! You li'l sow, you! Cit down! Setting up dere looking dem white folks right in de face! They's gowine[2] to lynch you, yet. And don't stand in dat doorway lacing out at 'em neither. Youse too brazen to live long."

Nevertheless, I kept right on gazing at them, and "going a piece of the way" whenever I could make it. The village seemed dull to me most of the time. If the village was singing a chorus, I must have missed the tune.

---

1. **brazenness.** Boldness; defiance
2. **gowine.** Dialect for "going"

A Back Road, c. 1880. Childe Hassam.
Brooklyn Museum of Art, New York.

the visitors and beam as much as to say it was a great privilege and pleasure to teach lovely children like us. They couldn't see that palmetto hickory in her hand behind all those benches, but we knew where our angelic behavior was coming from.

Usually, the visitors gave warning a day ahead and we would be cautioned to put on shoes, comb our heads, and see to ears and fingernails. There was a close inspection of every one of us before we marched in that morning. Knotty heads, dirty ears and fingernails got hauled out of line, strapped and sent home to lick the calf over[7] again.

> ## We were all little angels for the duration, because we'd better be.

This particular afternoon, the two young ladies just popped in. Mr. Calhoun was flustered, but he put on the best show he could. He dismissed the class that he was teaching up at the front of the room, then called the fifth grade in reading. That was my class.

So we took our readers and went up front. We stood up m the usual line, and opened to the lesson. It was the story of Pluto and Persephone.[8] It was new and hard to the class in general, and Mr. Calhoun was very uncomfortable as the readers stumbled along, spelling out words with their lips, and in mumbling undertones before they exposed them experimentally to the teacher's ears.

Perhaps a year before the old man[3] died, I came to know two other white people for myself. They were women.

It came about this way. The whites who came down from the North were often brought by their friends to visit the village school. A Negro school was something strange to them, and while they were always sympathetic and kind, curiosity must have been present, also. They came and went, came and went. Always, the room was hurriedly put in order, and we were threatened with a prompt and bloody death if we cut one caper[4] while the visitors were present. We always sang a spiritual, led by Mr. Calhoun himself. Mrs. Calhoun always stood in the back, with a palmetto switch[5] in her hand as a squelcher. We were all little angels for the duration, because we'd better be. She would cut her eyes[6] and give us a glare that meant trouble, then turn her face towards

---

3. **the old man.** White farmer who was a friend of Zora Neale and her family
4. **cut one caper.** Slang for "play a trick or prank" or "behave extravagantly or noisily"
5. **palmetto switch.** Whip made from the stem of a leaf from a palmetto palm
6. **cut her eyes.** Slang for "look at with contempt or scorn"
7. **lick the calf.** Slang for "get cleaned up"
8. **Pluto and Persephone.** Roman myth that explains the origin of the seasons. Pluto, a god, rules the underworld with his wife, Persephone.

Then it came to me. I was fifth or sixth down the line. The story was not new to me, because I had read my reader through from lid to lid, the first week that Papa had bought it for me.

That is how it was that my eyes were not in the book, working out the paragraph which I knew would be mine by counting the children ahead of me. I was observing our visitors who held a book between them, following the lesson. They had shiny hair, mostly brownish. One had a looping gold chain around her neck. The other one was dressed all over in black and white with a pretty finger ring on her left hand. But the thing that held my eyes were their fingers. They were long and and thin, and very white, except up near the tips. There they were baby pink. I had never seen such hands. It was a fascinating discovery for me. I wondered how they felt. I would have given those hands more attention, but the child before me was almost through. My turn next, so I got on my mark, bringing my eyes back to the book and made sure of my place. Some of the stories I had re-read several times and this Greco-Roman myth was one of my favorites. I was exalted[9] by it, and that is the way I read my paragraph.

"Yes, Jupiter[10] had seen her (Persephone). He had seen the maiden picking flowers in the field. He had seen the chariot of the dark monarch pause by the maiden's side. He had seen him when he seized Persephone. He had seen the black horses leap down Mount Aetna's[11] fiery throat. Persephone was now in Pluto's dark realm and he had made her his wife."

The two women looked at each other and then back to me. Mr. Calhoun broke out with a proud smile beneath his bristly moustache and instead of the next child taking up where I had ended, he nodded to me to go on. So I read the story to the end, where flying Mercury, the messenger of the Gods, brought Persephone back to the sunlit earth and restored her to the arms of Dame Ceres, her mother, that the world might have springtime and summer flowers, autumn and harvest. But because she

had bitten the pomegranate while in Pluto's kingdom, she must return to him for three months of each year, and be his queen. Then the world had winter, until she returned to earth.

The class was dismissed and the visitors smiled us away and went into a low-voiced conversation with Mr. Calhoun for a few minutes. They glanced my way once or twice and I began to worry. Not only was I barefooted, but my feet and legs were dusty. My hair was more uncombed than usual, and my nails were not shiny clean. Oh. I'm going to catch it now. Those ladies saw me, too. Mr. Calhoun is promising to 'tend to me. So I thought.

Then Mr. Calhoun called me. I went up thinking how awful it was to get a whipping before company. Furthermore, I heard a snicker run over the room. Hennie Clark and Stell Brazzlee did it out loud, so I would be sure to hear them. The smart-aleck was going to get it. I slipped one hand behind me and switched my dress tail at them, indicating scorn.

> **I went up thinking how awful it was to get a whipping before company.**

"Come here, Zora Neale," Mr. Calhoun cooed as I reached the desk. He put his hand at my shoulder and gave me little pats. The ladies smiled and held out those flower-looking fingers towards me. I seized the opportunity for a good look.

"Shake hands with the ladies, Zora Neale," Mr. Calhoun prompted and they took my hand one after the other and smiled. They asked me if I loved school, and I lied that I did. There was *some* truth in it, because I liked geography and reading, and I liked to play at recess time. Whoever it was invented writing and arithmetic got no thanks from me. Neither did I like

---

9. **exalted.** In high spirits; uplifted
10. **Jupiter.** King of the gods and Pluto's brother
11. **Mount Aetna.** Volcano in eastern Sicily, Italy; also known as Etna

the arrangement where the teacher could sit up there with a palmetto stem and lick me whenever he saw fit. I hated things I couldn't do anything about But I knew better than to bring that up right there, so l said yes, I *loved* school.

"I can tell you do," Brown Taffeta gleamed. She patted my head, and was lucky enough not to get sandspurs[12] in her hand. Children who roll and tumble in the grass in Florida are apt to get sandspurs in their hair. They shook hands with me again and I went back to my seat.

When school let out at three o'clock, Mr. Calhoun told me to wait. When everybody had gone, he told me I was to go to the Park House, that was the hotel in Maitland, the next afternoon to call upon Mrs. Johnstone and Miss Hurd. I must tell Mama to see that I was clean and brushed from head to feet, and I must wear shoes and stockings. The ladies liked me, he said, and I must be on my best behavior.

The next day I was let out of school an hour early, and went home to be stood up in a tub of suds and be scrubbed and have my ears dug into. My sandy hair sported a red ribbon to match my red and white checked gingham dress, starched until it could stand alone. Mama saw to it that my shoes were on the right feet, since I was careless about left and right. List thing, I was given a handkerchief to carry, warned again about my behavior, and sent off, with my big brother John to go as far as the hotel gate with me.

First thing, the ladies gave me strange things, like stuffed dates and preserved ginger, and encouraged me to eat all that I wanted. Then they showed me their Japanese dolls and just talked. I was then handed a copy of *Scribner's Magazine,* and asked to read a place that was pointed out to me. After a paragraph or two, I was told with smiles, that that would do.

I was led out on the grounds and they took my picture under a palm tree. They handed me what was to me then a heavy cylinder done up in fancy paper, tied with a ribbon, and they told me goodbye, asking me not to open it until I got home.

My brother was waiting for me down by the lake, and we hurried home, eager to see what was in the thing. It was too heavy to be candy or anything like that. John insisted on toting it for me.

My mother made John give it back to me and let me open it. Perhaps, I shall never experience such joy again. The nearest thing to that moment was the telegram accepting my first book. One hundred goldy-new pennies rolled out of the cylinder. Their gleam lit up the world. It was not avarice[13] that moved me. It was the beauty of the thing. I stood on the mountain. Mama let me play with my pennies for a while, then put them away for me to keep.

That was only the beginning. The next day I received an Episcopal hymn-book bound in white leather with a golden cross stamped into the front cover, a copy of The Swiss Family Robinson, and a book of fairy tales.

I set about to commit the song words to memory. There was no music written there, just the words. But there was to my consciousness music in between them just the same. "When I survey the Wondrous Cross" seemed the most beautiful to me, so I committed that to memory first of all. Some of them seemed dull and without life, and I pretended they were not there. If white people liked trashy singing like that, there must be something funny about them that I had not noticed

---

12. **sandspurs.** Prickly burs that grow on a grass of the same name; also called sandburs
13. **avarice.** Greed

before. I stuck to the pretty ones where the words marched to a throb I could feel.

A month or so after the two young ladies returned to Minnesota, they sent me a huge box packed with clothes and books. The red coat with a wide circular collar and the red tam pleased me more than any of the other things. My chums pretended not to like anything that I had, but even then I knew that they were jealous. Old Smarty had gotten by them again. The clothes were not new, but they were very good. I shone like the morning sun.

But the books gave me more pleasure than the clothes. I had never been too keen on dressing up. It called for hard scrubbings with Octagon soap suds getting in my eyes, and none too gentle fingers scrubbing my neck and gouging in my ears.

I had never been too keen on dressing up.

In that box were Gulliver's Travels, Grimm's Fairy Tales, Dick Whittington, Greek and Roman Myths, and best of all, Norse Tales. Why did the Norse tales strike so deeply into my soul? I do not know, but they did. I seemed to remember seeing Thor[14] swing his mighty short-handled hammer as he sped across the sky in rumbling thunder, lightning flashing from the tread of his steeds and the wheels of his chariot. The great and good Odin,[15] who went down to the well of knowledge to drink, and was told that the price of a drink from that fountain was an eye. Odin drank deeply, then plucked out one eye without a murmur and handed it to the grizzly keeper, and walked away. That held majesty for me.

Of the Greeks, Hercules moved me most. I followed him eagerly on his tasks. The story of the choice of Hercules as a boy when he met Pleasure and Duty, and put his hand in that of Duty and followed her steep way to the blue hills of fame and glory, which she pointed out at the end, moved me profoundly. I resolved[16] to be like him. The tricks and turns of the

Thor, the Norse god of thunder.

other Gods and Goddesses left me cold. There were other thin books about this and that sweet and gentle little girl who gave up her heart to Christ and good works. Almost always they died from it, preaching as they passed. I was utterly indifferent[17] to their deaths. In the first place I could not conceive of death, and in the next place they never had any funerals that amounted to a hill of beans, so I didn't care how soon they rolled up their big, soulful, blue eyes and kicked the bucket. They had no meat on their bones.

But I also met Hans Andersen and Robert Louis Stevenson. They seemed to know what I wanted to hear and said it in a way that tingled me. Just a little below these friends was

---

14. **Thor.** Norse god of thunder
15. **Odin.** Father of Thor in Norse mythology; considered the supreme god
16. **resolved.** Decided
17. **indifferent.** Without concern

Rudyard Kipling in his Jungle Books. I loved his talking snakes as much as I did the hero.

I came to start reading the Bible through my mother. She gave me a licking one afternoon for repeating something I had overheard a neighbor telling her. She locked me in her room after the whipping, and the Bible was the only thing in there for me to read. I happened to open to the place where David[18] was doing some mighty smiting,[19] and I got interested. David went here and he went there, and no matter where he went, he smote 'em hip and thigh. Then he sung songs to his harp awhile, and went out and smote some more. Not one time did David stop and preach about sins and things. All David wanted to know from God was who to kill and when. He took care of the other details himself. Never a quiet moment. I liked him a lot. So I read a great deal more in the Bible, hunting for some more active people like David. Except for the beautiful language of Luke and Paul,[20] the New Testament still plays a poor second to the Old Testament for me. The Jews had a God who laid about[21] Him when they needed Him. I could see no use waiting till Judgment Day to see a man who was just crying for a good killing, to be told to go and roast. My idea was to give him a good killing first, and then if he got roasted later on, so much the better. ❖

---

18. **David.** Second king of Israel who killed the giant Goliath
19. **smiting.** Striking with a weapon, such as a sword
20. **Luke and Paul.** Apostles of Jesus who wrote much of the New Testament of the Bible
21. **laid about.** Slang for "hit out in all directions"

 **MIRRORS & WINDOWS** Receiving the box of books helped instill in Huston a love for reading. What were your favorite books or stories when you were a young child?

Refer and Reason

1. Why does Hurston think Mr. Calhoun wants her to approach his desk after she reads to the visitors at the school? Compare and contrast the description of Hurston's appearance with that of the visitors. What conclusions can you draw about these individuals?

2. Explain what happens when Hurston calls on the ladies at the hotel. Do the ladies respect Hurston? Why or why not?

3. Of the books the ladies mailed to Hurston after their meeting, which was her favorite? Which were her least favorites? Assess how the ladies influenced Zora Neale Hurston's life.

Writing Options

1. Write a brief memoir about an experience with someone giving you a special gift, either tangible or intangible. Focus on a single experience that stands out in your memory.

2. Should talented people reap most of life's rewards? Or should everyone be rewarded for doing his or her best, even if it is not as good as the "best" of more talented people? Write a one-page essay explaining your opinion.

 Go to **www.mirrorsandwindows.com** for more.

The St. Paul Stories of F. Scott Fitzgerald by F. Scott Fitzgerald, with an Introduction by Patricia Hampl and Dave Page

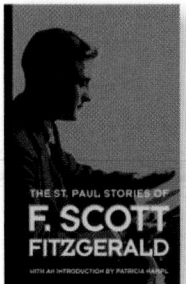

This collection contains Fitzgerald's early short stories—some classic, some almost unknown. Among the classics are the delightful "Bernice Bobs Her Hair" and the wistful "Winter Dreams." The stories are about boyhood pranks, lakeside parties, an ice palace, and young love. Lyrical and nostalgic, the stories demonstrate the importance of place in fiction.

In Our Time by Ernest Hemingway

In this, his first commercially published work, Hemingway introduces young Nick Adams and inaugurates his lean, tough writing style. Included are some of his early classic stories, such as "Indian Camp," telling of the emergency delivery of a baby in the wilderness, and "Soldier's Home," describing a veteran's return to his hometown after the "greeting of war heroes was over." The fourteen-story collection ends with "Big Two-Hearted River," detailing Nick's trout-fishing trip and one of Hemingway's best-loved stories.

My Antonia by Willa Cather

Fourteen-year-old Antonia Shimerda is strong, spirited, and intelligent. Her story, told by neighbor boy Jim Burden, reveals not only 1880s immigrant life on the unbroken plains, small-town classism, and the restraints placed on women but also the beauty of the rolling grasslands, where Jim discovers "The best days are the first to flee." (EMC Access Edition)

Classic Fiction of the Harlem Renaissance by William L. Andrews

This fine collection brings together many of the classic fictional works of the Harlem Renaissance, highlighting the political issues, race consciousness, and artistic innovations of both well-known and lesser-known writers of the era. Included are two complete novels, Claude McKay's *Home to Harlem* and Nella Larsen's *Quicksand,* as well as a major excerpt from Jean Toomer's *Cane* and pieces by Zora Neale Hurston, Langston Hughes, Rudolph Fisher, and Wallace Thurman.

Autobiography of Mother Jones by Mary Harris Jones

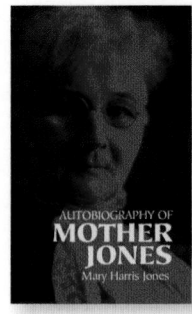

The labor activist whom Teddy Roosevelt once labeled "the most dangerous woman in America" writes about her career as a champion of the working class. Jones's exciting narrative takes the reader on a journey from the Appalachian Mountains to the Salinas Valley, providing plenty of adventure in between.

Main Street by Sinclair Lewis

This classic novel satirizes life in small-town America, taking aim at institutions such as religion, medicine, politics, and the arts. City girl Carol Milford marries a successful doctor and moves to his hometown in rural Minnesota, only to discover that she cannot fit into small-town society. Tensions mount as the townspeople reject Carol's attempts to enrich their lives.

Many oral presentations can be enhanced with the use of visual aids: illustrations, diagrams, models, and other materials listeners can see. Selecting appropriate visual aids and handling them purposefully are the keys to their effective use.

1. Use Visual Aids to Enhance Your Presentation

Using visuals is a good idea if doing so will help support the audience's understanding of your message. Here are some tips on deciding whether and how to include visual aids:

- For some subjects, such as art and travel, the value of using visual aids is obvious. Using visuals also makes sense in a how-to speech, in which you demonstrate a process. Visuals are useful, as well, for topics that involve statistics and other numbers, which lend themselves to charts and graphs. In any case, avoid using visual aids as filler for your presentation.
- Choose a reasonable number and variety of visual aids. What matters is the appropriateness, not the quantity, of items. In fact, having too many visuals may interfere with your delivery and make your presentation run over the allotted time.

2. Locate Visual Aids

There are many sources of visual aids. Photographs, reproductions of artworks, and charts and diagrams are available in magazines, newspapers, and books and on the Internet. Some libraries have folders containing pamphlets, illustrations, and similar materials. If you photocopy printed materials or download items from the Internet, be sure you follow copyright law. For assistance, check with your teacher or librarian.

Another option is to create visual aids, such as charts of statistics. Prepare each chart on a large piece of cardboard or tagboard using felt-tip pens. Ensure that all type and graphics are legible. At the bottom of the chart, in smaller type, provide the source of the information.

3. Practice Your Presentation with Visual Aids

If you plan to use an overhead or PowerPoint projector, make sure the display can be viewed clearly from all areas of the room. Likewise, ensure everyone will be able to see any photograph, chart, or diagram you show. Audience members will lose interest and become distracted if you use visuals they cannot see.

Passing materials among audience members may distract their attention from your presentation. If you need to distribute materials, place them on audience members' seats before they arrive.

To ensure your presentation will go smoothly, practice with your visual aids:

- If possible, practice in the room where you will speak with the equipment you will use. Perhaps ask a classmate to operate the projector while you concentrate on delivery.
- Coordinate using your notes with your visual aids. Your notes should indicate when each particular visual should be displayed.

SPEAKING & LISTENING RUBRIC

Your presentation will be evaluated on these elements:

Content

- ❏ Your visual aids are suitable to your topic, help convey the content, and capture listeners' attention.
- ❏ The visual aids you have created are legible and easy to understand.

Delivery & Presentation

- ❏ The visual aids can be seen by all audience members.
- ❏ The equipment used is in good condition, and you handle it skillfully.
- ❏ Your visual aids do not overwhelm your delivery.

Each year, colleges receive thousands of applications from prospective students. As part of the application process, most schools ask applicants to write an essay. To distinguish yourself within this sea of applicants, you need to write a strong application essay. Although your essay will not by itself determine whether you are admitted, it is an extremely important part of the application materials. So plan to put substantial time and thought into writing your college essay.

Colleges differ in the directives they give for the essay. Some ask for an essay that explains why the student would be a good fit for the college. Others seek something creative, such as a poem or an opinion on a national issue. Some ask students to write about a person, book, or movie that influenced them. Still others may ask students to tell about an experience that led to the student's personal growth or self-discovery.

Your assignment for this lesson is to write a college application essay of five hundred words that tells how an experience you had led to your personal growth or some discovery about yourself.

Assignment Plan, write, and revise an application essay telling of an experience that led to personal growth or self-discovery

Purpose To distinguish yourself from other applicants and gain admittance

Audience An admissions review committee who reads volumes of these essays

WRITING RUBRIC

A successful application essay has these qualities:

❏ an introduction that identifies a specific topic pertaining to the assignment and generates interest

❏ a body that provides details clarifying the topic

❏ a conclusion that brings closure and reinforces the thesis

❶ Prewrite

Select Your Topic

List four or five experiences that have led to your personal growth or through which you discovered something about yourself. Consider experiences from your distant or recent past, in which you were a main figure or a witness. For each experience, jot down how it affected you or taught you something about yourself—for example, "Whaling trip: Gave me a greater appreciation of the natural world."

Choose the experience you think will best represent your individual character in an application essay.

Gather Information

Think about the various parts of the experience—actions that took place, as well as things that were said or thought. Include details of sight, sound, touch, taste, and smell that were a part of the experience. Including these different kinds of details will help re-create the experience for the reader.

Put these details in a list or some graphic organizer, such as the web cluster shown on the next page. Jot down the particulars in whatever order they come to you. You will organize them later.

Organize Your Ideas

Review the information in your graphic organizer. Move items from one cluster to another if they are out of place. Then number the items in the order that will best re-create the experience for your reader. When narrating an experience, the best order usually is chronological—the order in which things happened.

In the model, for instance, the feelings of anger and boredom come before the sighting of the whale, which comes before the student's noticing the mountains.

Write Your Thesis Statement

Your thesis statement should summarize the main point of your essay. Here is the thesis statement of Jacob, a student writer:

Although I arrived in Alaska feeling resentful and angry, I left with a new appreciation for the natural world.

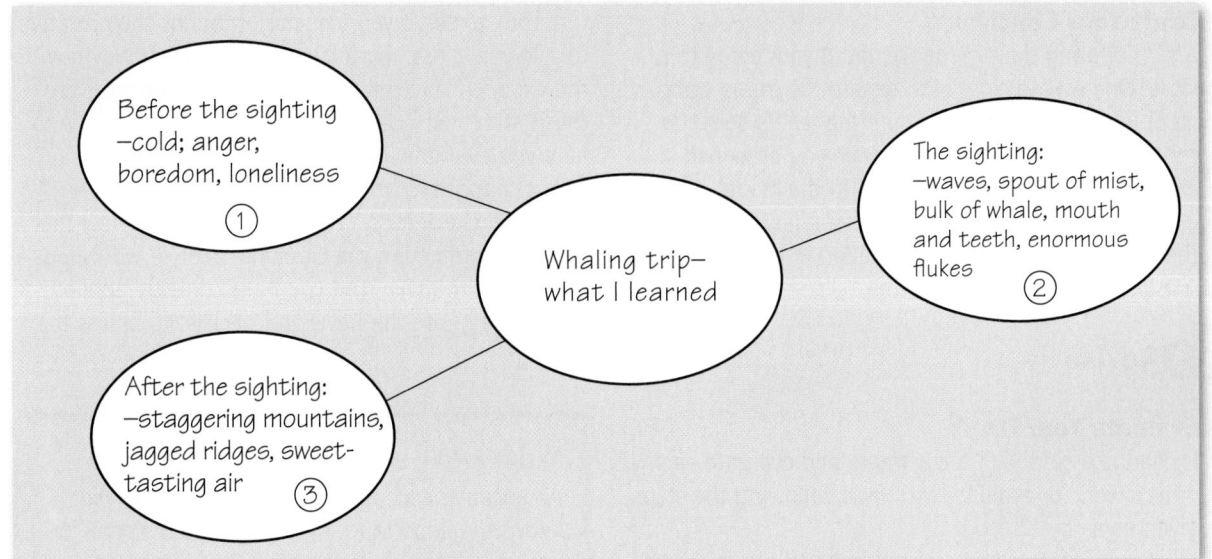

What Great Writers Do

MORRISON

If you write about an event in your life, dramatize your retelling to make it interesting to readers. Contemporary novelist Toni Morrison once said, "The vitality of language lies in its ability to [describe in detail] the actual, imagined and possible lives of its speakers, readers, writers."

➋ Draft

Write your essay by following this three-part framework: Introduction, Body, and Conclusion.

Introduction Present your experience and your topic in a way that will interest someone unfamiliar with both

Body Re-create the experience, conveying not only what happened but also its effect on you

Conclusion Close in a way that seems logical and reinforces the main idea

Draft Your Introduction

Your introduction should do two things: (1) pique the reader's interest and (2) identify the topic of the essay.

The introduction to a narrative about a personal experience might begin with some action to arouse readers' interest, such as "The tumultuous waves threw me clear across the deck of the ship." Follow that with a few more action details, and then identify your topic.

Another way to begin your essay might be to make a provocative comment, such as "One might not think the wet, cold deck of a whaling ship would be a place to learn life's lessons, but it was for me." Try a few different introductions until you find the one you like.

Draft the Body

Next, put into paragraph form the details of the experience you gathered earlier and recorded in your graphic organizer. Your focus in the body is to relate the important actions, words, and details so readers can visualize the experience and feel as you did while living it.

Build paragraphs with related pieces of information. For example, in the model, the details surrounding the actions of the whale logically go together. What Jacob, the student, notices after the whale sighting is in a separate paragraph.

Draft Your Conclusion

After narrating the experience, bring your essay to a close. One way to close is to restate the thesis statement in different words. Be sure the reader sees the connection between the experience you described and the point you want to make. In the model, Jacob expresses in the conclusion the lesson learned from the experience, namely, "I had fallen in love with Alaska—and the world of nature."

❸ Revise

Evaluate Your Draft

Exchange essays with a classmate and evaluate each other's work, or evaluate your own, following the steps given here.

Begin by reviewing the content and organization. Make sure the introduction identifies your topic and includes an interesting action, detail, or comment that will generate reader interest.

Examine the body paragraphs to see if they all help to clarify and flesh out the topic presented in the introduction. Be sure the order of events is logical—perhaps in chronological order. Unify each paragraph around a particular aspect. Insert transitions to move the reader from one paragraph to the next.

REVISION CHECKLIST

Content & Organization

❑ Does the introduction present you and your experience in an interesting way?

❑ Is the body organized in a logical way? In what order would you tell the essay's events if you were relaying it to a friend in conversation?

❑ Does the conclusion effectively draw closure to your essay without repeating anything?

Grammar & Style

❑ Have you used subordination, coordination, and appositives correctly and effectively? (pages 537, 555, 606)

Look to see if your conclusion brings the narrative to a logical close, reinforcing in some clear way how the experience re-created in the essay illustrates the thesis statement. Use the Revision Checklist below to help you evaluate. Make notes directly on the essay about changes to be made.

Next, check for sentence-level errors. Review the concepts outlined in the Grammar & Style workshops in this unit to make sure you have correctly applied them. Again, use the Revision Checklist to assess the writing.

What Great Writers Do

American science fiction author Stanley Schmidt knows the importance of letting content speak for itself. He offers this suggestion to writers: "Resist the temptation to try to use dazzling style to conceal weakness of substance."

With an essay like this, honesty is key. Using a simple, down-to-earth style will give your essay authenticity, improving your chances for acceptance.

Revise for Content, Organization, and Style

Read the notes you or your partner made on your draft, and make the appropriate changes.

Proofread for Errors

Now look for remaining sentence-level mistakes, using proofreader's symbols to mark any you find. To complete the assignment, print out a final draft and read it aloud before turning it in. This will allow you to check for flow as well as help you catch remaining errors.

DRAFT STAGE		REVISE STAGE	
Introduction When I first got to Alaska, I was really angry. I asked myself, "Why am I here? I don't even like whales, and I *hate* the cold." None of my friends were with me. I was alone with my father and a few stupid seamen. This was my birthday present, and all I could think about was how you're supposed to get something you *want* for your birthday. Although I arrived in Alaska feeling resentful and angry, I departed with a new appreciation for the natural world.	Explains the central conflict States thesis at the end of the introductory paragraph	The tumultuous waves threw me clear across the ferry's deck. I was tossed forward and aft like a forgotten scarecrow in the midst of a tornado. As I picked myself up off the deck, wincing from the fall, ~~When I first got to Alaska, I was really angry.~~ I asked myself, "Why am I here? I don't even like whales, and I *hate* the cold." None of my friends were with me; I was alone with my father and a few ~~stupid~~ smudgy, salt-stained old seamen. This was my birthday present, and all I could think about was how you're supposed to get something you *want* for your birthday. Although I arrived in Alaska feeling resentful and angry, I departed with a new appreciation for the natural world.	Adds details to entice the reader Eliminates "telling" Adds semicolon for smoother transition Adds descriptive language
Body Paragraph After what seemed like centuries, the captain pointed to a small spout of mist that appeared on the horizon. The whale's body was like that of a wondrous dazzling alien, with a rubbery ridged skin that encased its frame like some kind of amazing spectacular jumpsuit. It opened its strange gargantuan maw to reveal a set of bizarre plastic-like combs. Before I could get my fill the beast re-submerged beneath the Arctic waters flapping its enormous flukes as if it were waving goodbye to us.		After what seemed like centuries, the captain pointed to a small spout of mist that appeared on the horizon. "That's it?" I asked incredulously. But before I could continue, the whale leaped out of the water and into the air, blotting out the horizon with its massive bulk. ~~The whale's body~~ The whale was ~~like that of~~ a wondrous ~~dazzling~~ alien, with a rubbery, ridged skin that encased its frame like some kind of amazing ~~spectacular~~ jumpsuit. It opened its strange, gargantuan maw to reveal a set of bizarre, plastic-like combs. Before I could get my fill, the beast re-submerged beneath the Arctic waters, flapping its enormous flukes as if it were waving goodbye to us.	Elaborates on whale's entrance Breaks long paragraph into shorter ones Eliminates unnecessary modifiers Adds commas to separate adjectives

DRAFT STAGE	REVISE STAGE	
Conclusion I noticed for the first time that staggering mountains loomed over the shoreline like giant guardsmen watching our boat. I wanted to climb and explore all of the jagged ridges and minute details, which could be seen from the boat. I realized that the air, though brisk, carried a fresh sweet taste that I had never felt growing up in Los Angeles. The pure ocean beneath us carried waves of colorful fish that probed around the boat like the tendrils of a curious monster. I could not wait to return to land, for I wanted to trek across the broad green forestlands and see the unending stretches of icy tundra.	As we sailed back, I noticed for the first time that staggering mountains loomed over the shoreline like giant guardsmen watching our boat. ~~I wanted to climb and explore all of the jagged ridges and minute details, which could be seen from the boat.~~ I could identify minute details within their jagged ridges and found myself desperately wanting to climb all of them. I realized that the air, though brisk, carried a fresh, sweet taste that I had never felt growing up in Los Angeles. The pure ocean beneath us carried waves of colorful fish that probed around the boat like the tendrils of a curious monster. I could not wait to return to land, for I wanted to trek across the broad green forestlands and see the unending stretches of icy tundra. I had fallen in love with Alaska—and the world of nature.	Adds transitional phrase Changes sentence from passive to active voice Breaks long paragraph into two shorter ones Reinforces thesis statement

Writing Follow-Up

Publish and Present
- Use this essay in applying to colleges when the application requires an essay about personal growth or self-discovery.
- Submit your essay to college-prep resources. They may publish it as an example for future applicants.

Reflect
- How has this exercise boosted your confidence in terms of writing a college application essay?
- How might you use this writing technique in other types of writing?

STUDENT MODEL

A Whale of a Trip
by Jacob Johnson

The tumultuous waves threw me clear across the ferry's deck. I was tossed forward and aft like a forgotten scarecrow in the midst of a tornado. As I picked myself up off the deck, wincing from the fall, I asked myself, "Why am I here? I don't even like whales, and I *hate* the cold." None of my friends were with me; I was alone with my father and a few smudgy, salt-stained old seamen. This was my birthday present, and all I could think about was how you're supposed to get something you *want* for your birthday. Although I arrived in Alaska feeling resentful and angry, I departed with a new appreciation for the natural world.

After we stepped off the ferry and secured a hotel room, my father announced that we would be embarking yet again on a different boat. When I started to complain, he interrupted me and said, "You'll have fun." We met up with a tour boat full of old people and sailed out against the bitter wind. Just when I thought it couldn't get any worse, the captain set his anchor and announced, "We'll wait here until a whale arrives." When I asked what we were supposed to do until then, he replied, "Be patient."

After what seemed like centuries, the captain pointed to a small spout of mist that appeared on the horizon. "That's it?" I asked incredulously. But before I could continue, the whale leaped out of the water and into the air, blotting out the horizon with its massive bulk.

The whale was a wondrous alien, with a rubbery, ridged skin that encased its frame like some kind of amazing jumpsuit. It opened its strange, gargantuan maw to reveal a set of bizarre, plastic-like combs. Before I could get my fill, the beast re-submerged beneath the Arctic waters, flapping its enormous flukes as if it were waving goodbye to us.

As we sailed back, I noticed for the first time that staggering mountains loomed over the shoreline like giant guardsmen watching our boat. I could identify minute details within their jagged ridges and found myself desperately wanting to climb all of them. I realized that the air, though brisk, carried a fresh, sweet taste that I had never felt growing up in Los Angeles. The pure ocean beneath us carried waves of colorful fish that probed around the boat like the tendrils of a curious monster.

I could not wait to return to land, for I wanted to trek across the broad green forestlands and see the unending stretches of icy tundra. I had fallen in love with Alaska—and the world of nature.

How does the writer draw the reader into the essay?

What do you expect to learn about the writer?

How does the writer organize the events of the narrative?

How does the use of descriptive details enhance the narrative?

How does the writer reinforce his thesis without merely restating it?

Reading Skills

Evaluate Cause and Effect

Cause and effect is the relationship between two actions or events when one makes the other happen. For example, if you eat too much food and do not exercise enough, you gain weight. Eating too much combined with failing to exercise is the *cause;* gaining weight is the *effect.* Being able to recognize cause-and-effect relationships is key to understanding how many things works.

In written texts, sometimes the cause-and-effect relationship is stated directly. Transitional words and phrases that signal cause and effect include *as a result, for this reason, because, since, so, if/then, thus, consequently, accordingly,* and *therefore.* Other times, the cause-and-effect relationship is not directly stated, which means readers must infer it from what has been said. For example, a character might be described early on in a novel, but the reason for his or her nature or behavior might not be revealed until the last chapter.

In writing about cause and effect, many writers present the cause or causes first and then identify the effect or effects. Doing so is logical and will make sense to readers. For some topics, however, it may be more effective to present the effect(s) first and then identify the cause(s). In writing about the pollution of a local beach, for instance, starting with a list of health hazards (effects of the pollution) would demonstrate the need for action (the solution). In a more complicated structure, one effect may be the cause of another effect, establishing a chain reaction of connected causes and effects.

When you evaluate cause and effect, look for a logical relationship between one or more causes and one or more effects. Your purpose as a reader is to determine whether the connection between the two is reasonable.

> **TEST-TAKING TIP**
>
> In responding to a multiple-choice question, first eliminate the answer options that you immediately know are wrong. Once you have narrowed down the possible answers, the odds are better you will choose the correct one.

Practice

Directions: Read the following poem. The questions that come after it will ask you to evaluate cause and effect.

POEM: This poem is "The Tropics in New York," by Claude McKay.

> Bananas ripe and green, and ginger-root,
> Cocoa in pods and alligator pears,
> And tangerines and mangoes and grapefruit,
> Fit for the highest prize at parish fairs,

5   Set in the window, bringing memories
Of fruit-trees laden by low-singing rills,
And dewy dawns, and mystical blue skies
In benediction over nun-like hills.

My eyes grew dim, and I could no more gaze;
10   A wave of longing through my body swept,
And, hungry for the old, familiar ways,
I turned aside and bowed my head and wept.

Multiple Choice

1. Which word from the poem signals that an effect will follow?
   A. fit (line 4)
   B. bringing (line 5)
   C. laden (line 6)
   D. over (line 8)

2. What is the cause of the memories (line 5)?
   F. fruit-laden trees
   G. seeing produce in the window
   H. green bananas
   J. winning a prize at a parish fair

3. In line 9, the speaker's eyes grew dim because of
   A. unshed tears.
   B. old age.
   C. physical hunger.
   D. dizziness from bowing of the head.

4. Which of the following is an effect described in this poem?
   F. low-singing rills (line 6)
   G. benediction over nun-like hills (line 8)
   H. homesickness
   J. a New York market

Constructed Response

5. Describe the significance of the poem's title in the cause-and-effect relationship the poem presents. Evaluate whether this relationship is reasonable. Use details from the poem to support your analysis.

Writing Skills

Provide Support for Your Point of View

The readers who score the essays written in testing situations do not evaluate the point of view a writer takes but rather how well a writer supports his or her point of view. A strong essay states a clear thesis and then supports it using a variety of specific information.

Before you begin writing your essay, create a rough outline of the points you want to cover. Write down several main ideas that support or prove your thesis statement. Then under each main idea, list supporting details: statements, facts, examples, quotes, and illustrations that explain or demonstrate the idea.

When writing the essay, refer to your outline. Write one paragraph about each main idea. State the main idea in the first sentence of the paragraph, the *topic sentence*. Then incorporate the supporting details you listed in several more sentences. Write quickly and steadily, without spending too much time on any one paragraph. At the same time, cover each main point in adequate detail.

In writing a persuasive essay, your goal is to be convincing but not conniving or arrogant. To achieve that, be knowledgeable and fair in your presentation of evidence. Use a balance of reason and emotion. While you can use personal experience as support, you also should include some objective evidence.

Allow a few minutes to review and edit your essay after you have written it. A good way to proofread your own work is to read it aloud. Since you cannot do that in a testing situation, focus on hearing the text in your head as read it silently.

TEST-TAKING TIP

As you review and edit your essay, add transitional words and phrases to connect your ideas, especially from one paragraph to the next. Transitions in a persuasive essay may be as simple as *my first point, next, another reason,* and *most importantly.*

Practice

Timed Writing: 30 minutes

The high school years tend to be turbulent in terms of relationships. Teenagers tend to fall in and out of love and frequently break up with boyfriends and girlfriends. They also sometimes lose individuals and things they love in other ways—for example, a grandparent or pet that dies. Some people believe as Alfred Lord Tennyson wrote: "'Tis better to have loved and lost than never to have loved at all." Others think that the sadness and pain that come with losing love negate the original positive feelings. In your opinion, is it wise to experience love and risk feeling sadness and pain?

In your essay, take a position on this question. You may write about either of the two perspectives given, or you may provide a different perspective on this question. Use specific reasons and examples to support your position.

Revising and Editing Skills

Some standardized tests ask you to read a draft of an essay and answer questions about how to improve it. As you read the draft, watch for errors such as these:

- incorrect spellings
- disagreement between subject and verb; inconsistent verb tense; incorrect forms for irregular verbs; sentence fragments and run-ons; double negatives; and incorrect use of frequently confused words, such as *affect* and *effect*
- missing end marks, incorrect comma use, and lowercased proper nouns and proper adjectives

- unclear purpose, unclear main ideas, and lack of supporting details
- confusing order of ideas and missing transitions
- language that is inappropriate to the audience and purpose, and mood that is inappropriate for the purpose

After checking for errors, read each test question and decide which answer is best.

Practice

Directions: In the passage that follows, certain words and phrases are numbered and underlined. In the questions below the passage, alternatives are provided for each underlined word or phrase. In each case, choose the alternative that best expresses the idea, that is worded most consistently with the style and tone of the rest of the passage, or that makes the text correct according to the conventions of standard English. If you think the original version is best, choose the first alternative, MAKE NO CHANGE. To indicate your answer, circle the letter of the chosen alternative.

(1) At first, right after <u>loosing somebody, I wish that I had never loved that person at all</u>. (2) My feelings <u>change later however,</u> I realize what I gained from the experience. (3) Life is empty without <u>love, which is why it's loss</u> hurts so much. (4) <u>Therefore, I agree with Tennyson's statement:</u> "'Tis better to have loved and lost than never to have loved at all."

Multiple Choice

1. A. MAKE NO CHANGE.
   B. loosing somebody, I wish I'd never loved that person at all.
   C. losing somebody, I wish that I had never loved that person.
   D. losing somebody I wish that I had never loved that person at all.

2. F. MAKE NO CHANGE.
   G. change later however, and
   H. change later, however; and
   J. change later, however, and

3. A. MAKE NO CHANGE.
   B. love which is why it's loss
   C. love, which is why its loss
   D. love, which is the reason why it's loss

4. F. MAKE NO CHANGE.
   G. So I agree with Tennyson's statement, "'Tis
   H. Therefore, I agree with Tennyson stating, "'Tis
   J. Therefore, I agree with Tennyson's statement "'Tis

Nighthawks, 1942. Edward Hopper.
Art Institute of Chicago, Chicago, Illinois.

Depression and World

Unit 6

War II 1929–1945

Depression and World War II 1929–1945

1929   1935

AMERICAN LITERATURE AMERICAN LITERATURE AMERICAN LITERATURE AME

1929
William Faulkner publishes
The Sound and the Fury

1930
Sinclair Lewis becomes the
first American to win the
Nobel Prize for literature

1932
Pearl S. Buck wins the Pulitzer
Prize for her novel *The Good
Earth*

1933
Newsweek magazine is
published for the first time

1933
Jack Conroy publishes
The Disinherited

1934
Henry Miller publishes
Tropic of Cancer

MILLER

1935
The Federal Writers' Project
(FWP) is established

1936
Margaret Mitchell publishes
Gone with the Wind

1936
Eugene O'Neill wins the Nobel
Prize for literature

1937
Zora Neale Hurston publishes
Their Eyes Were Watching God

1939
John Steinbeck publishes
The Grapes of Wrath

AMERICAN HISTORY AMERICAN HISTORY AMERICAN HISTORY AMERICAN HIS

1929
The stock market plunges
dramatically, leading to the
Great Depression

1931
Congress designates "The
Star-Spangled Banner" as
the national anthem

1932
Hattie W. Caraway becomes
the first woman elected to
the U.S. Senate

1932
A series of dust storms begins
in the Great Plains states,
creating the Dust Bowl

1933
President Franklin D. Roosevelt
introduces the New Deal

1933
Prohibition ends with
passage of the Twenty-First
Amendment

1935
The Social Security Act
provides benefits for retired
workers, the unemployed,
people with disabilities, and
others in need

1935
Parker Brothers introduces
the game Monopoly

1936
African-American track star
Jesse Owens wins four gold
medals in the Olympics, held
in Berlin

1936
The Hoover Dam is completed

1938
A statutory minimum wage is
enforced for the first time

1939
The Baseball Hall of Fame is
established in Cooperstown,
New York

WORLD HISTORY WORLD HISTORY WORLD HISTORY WORLD HISTORY WORLD

1929
Vatican City is established as
an independent state within
Rome

1932
British physicist James
Chadwick proves the
existence of the neutron,
which led to creation of the
atomic bomb

1932
The Nazi Party gains a majority
in Germany's national election

1932
The first concentration camps
are established in Germany

1933
Adolf Hitler is appointed
Chancellor of Germany

1933
Japan withdraws from the
League of Nations

1933
The Soviet Party begins the
Great Purge, executing and
expelling members

1936
The Spanish Civil War begins;
Francisco Franco is named
head of state

1937
The *Hindenburg*, a German
zeppelin, explodes

1938
The Munich Agreement cedes
Austria and Czechoslovakia
to Adolf Hitler

1939
England and France declare
war on Germany following
Germany's invasion of Poland

1939
Adolf Hitler and Josef Stalin
agree to a nonaggression
pact between Germany
and Russia

AMERICAN LITERATURE AMERICAN LITERATURE AMERICAN LITERATURE AMER

1940
Richard Wright publishes
Native Son

1940
Carson McCullers publishes
The Heart Is a Lonely Hunter

1940
Ernest Hemingway publishes
For Whom the Bell Tolls

1941
Edmund Wilson edits and
publishes F. Scott Fitzgerald's
unfinished manuscript *The
Last Tycoon*

1942
The *New York Times* releases
its best-seller list

1944
Tennessee Williams's play
The Glass Menagerie is first
performed

WILLIAMS

1945
Ebony magazine debuts

1945
Richard Wright publishes
Black Boy

1945
Randall Jarrell publishes
Little Friend, Little Friend, a
wartime poetry collection

1945
Gwendolyn Brooks publishes
A Street in Bronzeville

STEINBECK

1945
John Steinbeck publishes
Cannery Row

1945
Annie Dillard is born

AN HISTORY AMERICAN HISTORY AMERICAN HISTORY AMERICAN HISTORY AMERIC

1940
The first modern-day freeway
opens in Pasadena, California

1941
Orson Welles's film
Citizen Kane premieres

1941
The Japanese attack Pearl
Harbor; the United States
enters World War II

1942
Under the Manhattan Project,
American scientists start
developing nuclear weapons

1943
Duke Ellington
performs
for the first
time at
Carnegie
Hall

ELLINGTON

1944
The United Negro College
Fund is established

1945
The first atomic bomb
is detonated in a test
in New Mexico

1945
On August 6 and 9,
the United States drops
atomic bombs on Japan

1945
President Roosevelt dies
suddenly; Harry Truman
assumes the presidency

ORLD HISTORY WORLD HISTORY WORLD HISTORY WORLD HISTORY WORLD HISTORY WORLD HISTOR

1940
Winston Churchill becomes
Prime Minister of Great
Britain

1940
Hitler invades France;
France surrenders

1940
Auschwitz, the largest Nazi
concentration camp, is
established in Poland

1941
Hitler invades Russia, nullifying
the nonaggression pact

1943
Italy surrenders to the
Allies

1944
Allied forces
invade German-
occupied France on
D-Day, June 6;
Paris is liberated
in late August

1945
Benito Mussolini is killed
by Italian partisans

1945
Hitler commits suicide
on April 30; Germany
surrenders on May 7

1945
Allied leaders
discuss postwar
occupation of
Germany at the
Yalta Conference

HITLER

1945
Allied leaders make plans
for postwar Europe at the
Potsdam Conference

1945
Japan agrees to an
unconditional surrender on
August 15, ending World
War II

1945
Representatives of fifty
nations meet to form the
United Nations

Depression and World War II 1929–1945

"Let me assert my firm belief that the only thing we have to fear is fear itself."

—PRESIDENT FRANKLIN D. ROOSEVELT

The Great Depression and 1930s Radicalism

The financial collapse of 1929 initiated the period known as the Great Depression. Although the easy credit that fueled soaring stock values during the 1920s was one cause of the Depression, other factors cited by economists were the global economic downturn after World War I, overproduction, and unequal distribution of income in the United States. Had workers received better wages for their labor and farmers better prices for their crops, they would have been able to make purchases that boosted the economy and lessened the effects of the Depression.

Millions were out of work, families waited in breadlines for a crust of bread and watery soup, tenants were turned out of their homes, and factory workers went on strike. Farmers in debt lost their land, while others burned their crops to increase prices. As drought hit the Great Plains, thousands in Dust Bowl states such as Kansas, Oklahoma, and Texas packed up and headed to California, only to find no work there either.

President Herbert Hoover opposed giving direct relief to jobless factory workers and farmers, believing voluntary efforts would relieve the crisis. Consequently, the miles of shacks that were thrown up outside cities for the new homeless became known as *Hoovervilles*. The president did persuade Congress to fund several public works projects to fuel the economy, among them the giant Hoover Dam in Nevada. However, when 10,000 World War I veterans marched to Washington, DC, in 1932 to demand payment of their pension bonuses, Hoover called out the army to disburse those who refused to return home, further alienating the citizenry.

The number of unemployed seemed proof that policies allowing the unbridled capitalism of the great industrialists, such as Andrew Carnegie, J. P. Morgan, and John D. Rockefeller, had not benefited most Americans. Hunger, labor unrest, and anarchist bombings seemed to indicate that the United States was headed toward a revolution.

"We shall soon . . . be in sight of the day when poverty shall be banished from this nation."

—PRESIDENT HERBERT HOOVER

A New Deal

Angry with Hoover, voters overwhelmingly elected Franklin Delano Roosevelt to the presidency in 1932. Roosevelt had pledged a "new deal for the American people," including direct relief for the needy, a massive public works program, and regulation of the stock market.

NOTABLE NUMBERS

300 million Tons of soil that often blew away in one day during the 1932 Dust Bowl

1 in 3 Americans who were either unemployed or the family member of someone unemployed in 1932

6.5 million Women who joined the workforce between 1941 and 1945; by the end of the war, one in three workers was a woman

$320 billion Amount spent by the United States to fight World War II

409,000 Americans killed fighting World War II

100,000 Deaths resulting from the 1945 Allied bombing of Dresden, Germany; almost all were civilians

After taking office, Roosevelt closed all the banks so that their records could be examined and then allowed only strong banks to reopen. Major new agencies were created, among them the Agriculture Adjustment Act (AAA), the Civilian Conservation Corps (CCC), the Works Progress Administration (WPA), and later Social Security (SS). Although these government programs provided some relief, unemployment continued to be high and wages remained low. Unions grew stronger, and in 1936, a strike shut down West Coast shipping for three months.

A poster advertising an exhibition sponsored by the Works Progress Administration (WPA). Established in 1935, the WPA put millions of Americans to work, including many artists, writers, and actors, in programs intended to foster culture across the nation.

European nations also suffered economic and political instability after World War I. Deeply in debt to the United States, the victor nations insisted that Germany pay them steep monetary reparations. In Latin America, totalitarian military leaders came to power as prices for coffee, bananas, and other crops dropped and unrest among the poor grew. When civil war broke out in Nicaragua, U.S. Marines were sent to protect American business interests and remained for nine years.

In several European nations, communists and conservatives clashed over strategies to reduce inflation and unemployment. Reacting to economic hardship and fighting between political parties, citizens welcomed ultranationalist leaders. In Spain, it was Francisco Franco and the Fascists; in Italy, Benito Mussolini and the Blackshirts; and in Germany, Adolf Hitler and the Nazis. Expounding mystical, pseudoscientific theories of racial purity and a belief that the so-called Aryan race was destined to rule the world, Hitler initiated a campaign to conquer new territories.

Moving Toward War

World War I was called "the war to end all wars," but events soon showed that title unrealistic. In 1936, Germany and Italy formed the Axis military alliance, which later would include Japan. Germany began taking territories to its east, Italy moved into Africa, and Japan invaded Asia (first Manchuria and then China).

At first, other nations followed a policy of appeasement, trying to get along with the Axis nations but hoping each act of aggression would be the last. However, with Hitler's invasion of Poland in 1939, England and France recognized the futility of this policy and declared war on Germany. In the next six months, Hitler's *blitzkrieg* crashed through defenses in France, Luxembourg, the Netherlands, Belgium, Denmark, and Norway; the Soviet Union occupied the Baltic countries; and Italy joined the war.

Meanwhile, in response to the national desire to stay out of European affairs, the U.S. Congress passed a series of neutrality laws. The conflict was a major

issue in the 1940 election, and both candidates promised to keep the United States out of the war.

However, after winning an unprecedented third term, Roosevelt became increasingly worried about Axis aggression and pushed for the Lend-Lease Act to provide needed materials to England, which was standing alone against Germany. Following the Japanese invasion of French Indochina in 1941, Roosevelt halted all U.S. shipments of oil and scrap metal to Japan, depriving it of resources critical to its economy. After Japan's December 7, 1941, surprise attack on Pearl Harbor, Hawaii, crippled the U.S. Navy, the United States entered the conflict.

World War II

By the time the United States entered the war, the Allied and Axis powers had been fighting for two years. It would be almost another year, November 1942, before American forces joined British troops to drive the Germans out of North Africa. Next, the joint forces invaded Sicily. To the northeast, Germany invaded the Soviet Union, violating their earlier non-aggression pact. Unprepared for winter on the steppes, German forces had to retreat before reaching Moscow and later were defeated at Stalingrad. As Allied forces advanced up the Italian peninsula in 1943, Mussolini was overthrown and the new government surrendered. However, German forces in Italy continued to fight.

The Manzanar Relocation Center in central California, established in 1941 to intern Japanese Americans during World War II.

On the home front, wartime industrial mobilization lifted the U.S. economy out of the last years of the Great Depression. Women entered the armed forces in larger numbers than ever, and many others took over jobs formerly held almost exclusively by men.

When the U.S. government declared people of Japanese ancestry a security threat, those living on the West Coast were forced from their homes and into internment camps for three years. Approximately three-fourths of the 120,000 people in these internment camps in 1942 were American born.

In the Pacific theater of the war, Japanese troops landed in the Philippines, forcing American and Filipino forces to surrender. However, naval victories at the Battles of Coral Sea and Midway allowed the United States to begin a strategy of island hopping. In Europe, 1944 saw the D-Day invasion to retake France from the Germans, the final Battle of the Bulge in the West, and the Soviet drive to Berlin in the East.

Germany surrendered on May 7, 1945, a week after Hitler's suicide. After retaking Guadalcanal and Guam in the western Pacific, American forces destroyed most of the Japanese fleet in the Leyte Gulf in the Philippines. Japan surrendered August 15, 1945, just days after the United States dropped atomic bombs on the cities of Hiroshima and Nagasaki.

"The unleashed power of the atom has changed everything save our modes of thinking and we thus drift toward unparalleled catastrophe."

—ALBERT EINSTEIN

After the war, the full extent of the atrocities committed by Hitler's Nazis become known when it was revealed that Germany had conducted a systematic campaign to exterminate millions of Jews, Gypsies, and others in death camps such as Auschwitz, Treblinka, and Buchenwald. Other combatants, too, had moral issues to ponder after the war, including Japan's destruction of Nanking, the Allied firebombing of civilian Dresden, and the United States' dropping of a second atomic bomb.

As the Depression worsened, Americans looked for distraction from their destitution. Popular culture flourished, particularly movies and radio. President Franklin D. Roosevelt recognized Americans' affection for radio and began broadcasting short speeches, dubbed "fireside chats," in 1933, bringing comfort to a troubled nation.

However, many American authors refused to divert their attention from the nation's woes. Jack Conroy portrayed the grim realities of urban, industrial life in *The Disinherited* (1933), and John Steinbeck delivered a harshly realistic account of life in rural America in *The Grapes of Wrath* (1939).

The horrors of World War II were captured in first-hand accounts published just after the war, including works by poet Randall Jarrell and novelist/playwright Norman Mailer. In *Hiroshima,* journalist John Hersey told the stories of six Japanese survivors of the atomic bombing. Americans were both fascinated with and horrified by the realities of what had occurred.

Mabel and the Goat, 1961. Thomas Hart Benton. Burstein Collection. Art © Thomas Hart Benton and Rita P. Benton Testamentary Trusts/UMB Bank Trustee/Licensed by VAGA, New York, NY.

Novelists John Heller and Kurt Vonnegut would publish their accounts of the war in the 1960s.

During the 1950s, several other writers shared experiences from the Holocaust, the greatest atrocity of the twentieth century. In 1952, *The Diary of Anne Frank* was translated into English, compiling the writings of a young Jewish girl who had died in a concentration camp. Six years later, Holocaust survivor Elie Wiesel published *Night,* a memoir that detailed the tragedy from a teen's perspective. Coming from children, these primary accounts made a profound impression on the American public.

from Let Us Now Praise Famous Men

Literary Nonfiction by James Agee, with Photography by Walker Evans

Build Background

Historical Context During the Depression, photographers, journalists, and fiction writers used their talents to convey the devastating effects of poverty and joblessness on the lives of ordinary people. In 1936, *Fortune* magazine hired writer James Agee and photographer Walker Evans to produce a series of articles on the condition of white sharecroppers in the rural South. (*Sharecroppers* are farmers who pay to use others' land by giving them part of the crop.) Agee and Evans spent about six weeks in Alabama, mostly with three families. Evans took photographs, and Agee took notes.

Although their work was rejected by *Fortune,* it eventually was published in 1941 in the book ***Let Us Now Praise Famous Men.*** Breaking with the tradition of using photographs to illustrate text, the two men chose to display fifty of Evans's starkly realistic photographs at the beginning of the book. Agee and Evans's work is considered one of the earliest examples of **literary nonfiction,** a modern genre in which literary techniques are combined with factual, journalistic reporting to describe a real event (see Unit 9, Understanding Literary Forms, pages 1238–1239).

Literary Context The title *Let Us Now Praise Famous Men* is from a biblical passage, Ecclesiasticus 44:1–15, which appears as an epigraph in the book and is reprinted in this book on page 699. The passage describes the legacies left not only by famous people but also common individuals, those who "have no memorial."

Reader's Context Has viewing a photograph ever helped you better understand the people or events of another time and place? Explain.

Meet the Authors

James Agee (1909–1955) is known for his delicate, moving, and lyrical prose. He worked as a reporter, film critic, and scriptwriter for television and movies after his collaboration with Evans. His novel *A Death in the Family,* published posthumously and considered his masterpiece, won the Pulitzer Prize for fiction in 1958. Agee's other books include a volume of poems, *Permit Me Voyage* (1934); another novel, *The Morning Watch* (1951); and several collections of correspondence, reviews, and film scripts.

Walker Evans (1903–1975) made a significant contribution to the development of American documentary photography. Although primarily a photographer of environments, not people, Evans's social concerns led him to photograph victims of the Depression, whose quiet courage in the face of adversity he tried to convey. He was an editor for both *Fortune* and *Time* magazines and became a professor of graphic arts at Yale. His other books include *American Photographs* and *Message from the Interior.*

Analyze Literature

Description and Mood
A **description** is a picture in words. Descriptive writing uses *sensory details:* words and phrases that describe how things look, sound, smell, taste, or feel.

Mood, or atmosphere, is the emotion created in the reader by part or all of a literary work.

Set Purpose

According to author John Hersey, whose work appears later in this unit, Agee "strove through the sounds and meaning of words to . . . achieve photography" that equaled Evans's images. As you read, try to envision the building Agee describes. Identify the senses he concentrates on in describing the scene. Also identify the mood that Agee and Evans create with their words and photographs. What is your emotional response toward the people and place they describe?

Preview Vocabulary

infinitesimal, 696
symmetry, 697
effigy, 697
profligate, 697
apathy, 697
intrinsic, 698
dishevelment, 698
rectilinear, 698
embellishment, 698
esthetic, 698

from Let Us Now Praise Famous Men

by James Agee

But these were merciful men, whose righteousness hath not been forgotten.

The Gudger House

The house is left alone

Slowly they diminished along the hill path, she, and her daughter, and her three sons, in leisured enfilade[1] beneath the light. The mother first, her daughter next behind, her eldest son, her straggler, whimpering; their bare feet pressed out of the hot earth gentle explosions of gold. She carried her youngest child, his knees locked simian[2] across her, his light hands at her neck, and his erected head, hooded with night, next hers, swiveled mildly upon the world's globe, a periscope.[3] The dog, a convoy, plaited his wanderings round them through the briars. She wore the flower-like beauty of the sunbonnet in which she is ashamed to appear before us. At length, well up the hill, their talking shrank and became inaudible, and at that point will give safe warning on the hill of their return. Their slanted bodies slowly straightened, one by one, along the brim, and turned into the east, a slow frieze,[4] and sank beneath the brim in order of their height, masts foundered in a horizon; the

---

1. **enfilade.** Interconnected group
2. **simian.** Resembling monkeys or apes
3. **periscope.** Tubular optical instrument containing lenses and mirrors by which an observer obtains an otherwise obstructed field of view
4. **frieze.** Sculptured or richly ornamental band as on a building

and a segment of the barn: and all of this framed image a little unnaturally brilliant and vital, as all strongly lighted things appear through corridors of darkness:

And this hall between, as the open valve of a sea creature, steadfastly flushing the free width of ocean through its <u>infinitesimal</u> existence: and on its either side, the square boxes, the square front walls, raised vertical to the earth, and facing us as two squared prows of barge or wooden wings, shadow beneath their lower edge and at their eaves; and the roof:

And these walls:

Nailed together of boards on beams, the boards facing the weather, into broad cards of wood inlet with windows stopped with shutters: walls, horizontals, of somewhat narrow weatherboarding; the windows bounded by boards of that same width in a square: the shutters, of wide vertical boards laid edge to edge, not overlapped: each of these boards was once of the living flesh of a pine tree; it was cut next the earth, and was taken between the shrieking of saws into strict ribbons; and now, which was vertical, is horizontal to the earth, and another is clamped against the length of its outward edge and its downward clamps another, and these boards, nailed tightly together upon pine beams, make of their horizontalities a wall: and the sun makes close horizontal parallels along the edges of these weatherboards, of sharp light and shade, the parallels strengthened here in slight straight-line lapse from level, in the subtle knife-edged curve of warping loose in another place: another irregular 'pattern' is made in the endings and piecings-out of boards:

dog, each of the walking children, at length; at last, the guileless cobra gloatings of the baby, the mother's tall, flared head.

They are gone.

No one is at home, in all this house, in all this land. It is a long while before their return. I shall move as they would trust me not to, and as I could not, were they here. I shall touch nothing but as I would touch the most delicate wounds, the most dedicated objects.

The silence of the brightness of this middle morning is increased upon me moment by moment and upon this house, and upon this house the whole of heaven is drawn into one lens; and this house itself, in each of its objects, it, too, is one lens.

> ## No one is at home, in all this house, in all this land.

In front of the house: The façade

The porch: stands in its short square shade: The hall: it is in shadow also, save where one wall, fifteen feet back, is slantingly slashed with light:

At the far end of this well of hall, the open earth, lifted a little, bald hard dirt; the faced frontages of the smokehouse and the henhouse,

in · fin · i · tes · i · mal (in' fin ə tes´ ə mäl) *adj.*, immeasurably or incalculably small

And the roof:

It is of short hand-hewn boards so thick and broad, they are shingles only of a most antique sort: crosswise upon rigid beams, laths[5] have been nailed, not far apart, and upon these laths, in successive rows of dozens and of hundreds, and here again, though regularly, with a certain shuffling of erratism[6] against pure symmetry, these broad thick shingles are laid down overlapping from the peak to the overhung edge like the plumage of a bird who must meet weather: and not unlike some square and formalized plumage, as of a holy effigy, they seem, and made in profligate plates of a valuable metal; for they have never been stained, nor otherwise touched or colored save only by all habits of the sky: nor has any other wood of this house been otherwise ever touched: so that, wherever the weathers of the year have handled it, the wood of the whole of this house shines with the noble gentleness of cherished silver, much as where (yet differently), along the floors, in the pathings of the millions of soft wavelike movements of naked feet, it can be still more melodiously charmed upon its knots, and is as wood long fondled in a tender sea:

Upon these structures, light:

It stands just sufficiently short of vertical that every leaf of shingle, at its edges, and every edge of horizontal plank (blocked, at each center, with squared verticals) is a most black and cutting ink: and every surface struck by light is thus: such an intensity and splendor of silver in the silver light, it seems to burn, and burns and blinds into the eyes almost as snow; yet in none of that burnishment or blazing whereby detail is lost: each texture in the wood, like those of bone, is distinct in the eye as a razor: each nail-head is distinct: each seam and split; and each slight warping; each random knot and knothole: and in each board, as lovely a music as a contour map and unique as a thumbprint, its grain, which was its living strength, and these wild creeks cut stiff across by saws; and moving nearer, the close-laid arcs and shadows even of those tearing wheels: and

this, more poor and plain than bone, more naked and noble than sternest Doric,[7] more rich and more variant than watered silk, is the fabric and the stature of a house.

> **It is put together out of the cheapest available pine lumber.**

It is put together out of the cheapest available pine lumber, and the least of this is used which shall stretch a skin of one thickness alone against the earth and air; and this is all done according to one of the three or four simplest, stingiest, and thus most classical plans contrivable, which are all traditional to that country: and the work is done by half-skilled, half-paid men under no need to do well, who therefore take such vengeance on the world as they may in a cynical and part willful apathy; and this is what comes of it: Most naïve, most massive symmetry and simpleness. Enough lines, enough off-true, that this symmetry is strongly yet most subtly sprained against its centers, into something more powerful than either full symmetry or deliberate breaking and balancing of 'monotonies' can hope to be. A look of being most earnestly hand-made, as a child's drawing, a thing created out of need, love, patience, and strained skill in the innocence of a race. Nowhere one ounce or inch spent with ornament, not one trace of

---

5. **laths.** Thin strips of wood nailed to rafters or studding as a groundwork for slates, tiles, or plaster
6. **erratism.** Variant of *erraticism*; characterized by lack of consistency, regularity, or uniformity
7. **Doric.** Belonging to the simplest Greek architectural style

sym • me • try (sim′ ə trē) *n.,* beauty of form arising from balanced proportion
ef • fi • gy (ef′ ə gē) *n.,* image or representation of a person
prof • li • gate (prôf′ li gət) *adj.,* wildly extravagant
ap • a • thy (a′ pə thē) *n.,* lack of interest or concern; indifference

relief or of disguise: a matchless monotony, and in it a matchless variety and this again throughout restrained, held rigid: and of all this, nothing which is not <u>intrinsic</u> between the materials of structure, the earth, and the open heaven. The major lines of structure, each horizontal of each board, and edge of shingle, the strictness yet subtle <u>dishevelment</u> of the shingles, the nailheads, which are driven according to geometric need, yet are not in perfect order, the grain, differing in each foot of each board and in each board from any other, the many knots in this cheap lumber: all these fluencies and irregularities, all these shadows of pattern upon each piece of wood, all these in <u>rectilinear</u> ribbons caught into one squared, angled, and curled music, compounding a chord of four chambers upon a soul and center of clean air: and upon all these masses and edges and chances and flowerings of grain, the changes of colorings of all weathers, and the slow complexions and marchings of pure light.

Or by another saying:

'In all this house:

'In all of this house not any one inch of lumber being wasted on <u>embellishment</u>, or on trim, or on any form of relief, or even on any doubling of walls: it is, rather, as if a hard thin hide of wood has been stretched to its utmost to cover exactly once, or a little less than once, in all six planes the skeletal beams which, with the inside surface of the weatherboarding, are the inside walls; and no touch, as I have said, of any wash or paint, nor, on the floors, any kind of covering, nor, to three of the rooms, any kind of ceiling, but in all places left bare the plain essences of structure; in result all these almost perfect symmetries have their full strength, and every inch of the structure, and every aspect and placement of the building materials, comes inevitably and purely through into full <u>esthetic</u> existence, the one further conditioner, and discriminator between the functions and properties of indoors and out, being the lights and operations of the sky.' ❖

> A look of being most earnestly hand-made, as a child's drawing, a thing created out of need, love, patience, and strained skill in the innocence of a race.

in • trin • sic (in trinz´ ək) *adj.*, belonging to the essential nature or constitution of a thing
di • shev • el • ment (di shev´ 'l mənt) *n.*, disorderliness
rec • ti • lin • e • ar (rek' tə lin´ ē ər) *adj.*, moving or forming a straight line
em • bel • lish • ment (em bel´ ish mənt) *n.*, act or process of making beautiful with ornamentation
es • the • tic (es the´ tik) *adj.*, pleasing in appearance

Agee and Evans used pseudonyms to conceal the identities of the tenant farmers portrayed in their book. This photo is of George Gudger Jr., a member of the family whose house is described in the excerpt.

Let Us Now Praise Famous Men includes the following biblical passage as an epigraph. The passage is from Ecclesiasticus (44:1–15), one of the books of the Apocrypha, which comprises biblical texts of unknown origin.

Let us now praise famous men, and our fathers that begat us.

The Lord hath wrought great glory by them through his great power from the beginning.

Such as did bear rule in their kingdoms, men renowned for their power, giving counsel by their understanding, and declaring prophecies:

Leaders of the people by their counsels, and by their knowledge of learning meet for the people, wise and eloquent in their instructions:

Such as found out musical tunes, and recited verses in writing:

Rich men furnished with ability, living peaceably in their habitations:

All these were honoured in their generations, and were the glory of their times.

There be of them, that have left a name behind them, that their praises might be reported.

And some there be which have no memorial; who perished, as though they had never been; and are become as though they had never been born; and their children after them.

But these were merciful men, whose righteousness hath not been forgotten.

With their seed shall continually remain a good inheritance, and their children are within the covenant.

Their seed standeth fast, and their children for their sakes. Their seed shall remain for ever, and their glory shall not be blotted out.

Their bodies are buried in peace; but their name liveth for evermore.

MIRRORS & **W**INDOWS

What advantages and disadvantages do photos have compared with words in portraying a person or place?

Refer to Text ▶ ▶ ▶ ▶ ▶ Reason with Text

1a. Who are the inhabitants of the Gudger house, and where are they going?	**1b.** Explain what Agee means when he writes that "this house itself, in each of its objects, it, too, is one lens."	**Understand** Find meaning
2a. What is the result of using "half-skilled, half-paid men under no need to do well" to build this house?	**2b.** What might Agee be trying to say about the people who live in this house when he states that it has a "look of being most earnestly hand-made, as a child's drawing"?	**Apply** Use information
3a. To what living things does the author compare the materials used in the building?	**3b.** Analyze how Agee uses words to mimic the effects achieved by Evans's photography. Find examples and describe the effect.	**Analyze** Take things apart
4a. What does the passage from Ecclesiasticus (page 699) say will happen to those who "have no memorial; who perished, as though they had never been"?	**4b.** How does reading this passage affect your understanding of Agee's attitude toward his subject?	**Evaluate** Make judgments
5a. What details in the limited descriptions of the landscape confirm that the location is rural?	**5b.** How might Agee's descriptions have changed if he and Evans had been sent to cover poverty in a city, rather than the rural South.	**Create** Bring ideas together

Analyze Literature

Description and Mood

In describing the Gudger house, which of the five senses does Agee evoke the most? Provide examples to support your choice.

What mood does Agee create in this excerpt? Cite the descriptive language and sensory details that led you to your conclusion.

Extend the Text

Writing Options

Creative Writing Imagine that you, like Agee, are one of the journalists who tried to make the nation aware of the effects of the Depression. Write a short magazine article about George Gudger Jr., the man whose photo appears on page 699. Describe how his life has changed during the Depression.

Expository Writing Go through the selection paragraph by paragraph, evaluating the order in which Agee describes specific aspects of the Gudger house and the people who live in it. What does he describe first, next, and so on? Write a paragraph evaluating the organization of this excerpt. Is it effective in creating vivid images of the people and house?

Lifelong Learning

Research the Great Depression Research the effects of the Great Depression on a family you know. Construct a family tree from the present to the early twentieth century. Interview older family members, if possible, and check historical records. Try to determine what their lives were like. Write an essay on your findings to share with the class.

Media Literacy

Make a Photo Catalog Using the Internet, research the subjects Walker Evans photographed in different periods of his life and select ten to twelve representative photos. Prepare a catalog for an exhibit, listing the title and year and briefly describing each photograph.

 Go to **www.mirrorsandwindows.com** for more.

Understand the Concept

One of James Agee's goals in writing *Let Us Now Praise Famous Men* was to achieve the effect of photography through the sounds and meanings of words. One of the ways in which he achieved this goal was by using **precise language.**

For example, rather than simply writing "As the mother carried the child, the child looked about at his surroundings," Agee used vivid language to make this scene come to life:

> "She carried her youngest child, his knees locked simian across her, his light hands at her neck, and his erected head, hooded with night, next to hers, swiveled mildly upon the world's globe, a periscope."

Your writing will be more effective and interesting if you use words that show your readers exactly what you mean. Precise nouns give readers a clear picture of who or what is involved in a sentence:

EXAMPLES

Original sentence The *people* made *noise.*

Revised sentence The *crowd* made an *uproar.*

Colorful verbs indicate the specific action in a sentence:

EXAMPLES

Original sentence He *took* the pitcher and *drank* the cool water.

Revised sentence He *grabbed* the pitcher and *gulped* the cool water.

Modifiers—adjectives and adverbs—change or describe the meanings of other words. Colorful or surprising modifiers can turn dull writing into dynamic writing:

EXAMPLES

Original sentence The *cold* wind blew *hard.*

Revised sentence The *frigid* wind blew *furiously.*

Apply the Skill

Identify Dull Nouns, Verbs, and Modifiers

Copy the following sentences on your paper. Then evaluate each one and underline the dull, vague nouns, verbs, and modifiers it contains.

1. The Dust Bowl was caused by a big drought that dried up the dirt of the Great Plains.
2. Strong winds then blew all the dried dust into big, dark clouds.
3. The clouds dimmed the skies above Chicago, and dirt fell from the sky, piling up in city streets.
4. Because the Great Plains farmland was no longer productive, farm families lost their money and homes and went west to find work.
5. The Dust Bowl was one of the causes of the Great Depression, a time of economic hardship that hurt many Americans' dreams of economic success.

Replace Dull Nouns, Verbs, and Modifiers

For each sentence in the previous exercise, replace the dull and vague nouns, verbs, and modifiers you underlined with more precise words and phrases.

Use Precise Language in Your Writing

Write a paragraph that describes a building or other structure, using as many sensory details as possible to create a vivid description. Then review the paragraph, considering your use of nouns, verbs, and modifiers. Replace any that are dull or imprecise with more interesting and specific words and phrases.

John Steinbeck

> *"No man really knows about other human beings. The best he can do is to suppose that they are like himself."*

John Steinbeck (1902–1968) was born in Salinas, California, in the heart of northern California's agricultural region. While he revered the fertile valleys and rolling hills of his native country, he deplored the conditions imposed on the workers who grew and harvested the crops and managed the herds. Both the region and themes of dispossession and oppression would authentically be portrayed in his short stories and novels.

From 1919 until 1925, Steinbeck took marine biology classes sporadically at Stanford University but never earned a degree. He went to New York City, intent on becoming a freelance writer, but he failed and returned to California. After publishing several short stories and a novel, he enjoyed his first critical success in 1935 with *Tortilla Flat,* the story of two young men during the Depression. This novel, along with seventeen of Steinbeck's other novels, later was made into a movie. Further literary success came with *Of Mice and Men* (1937), the tragic tale of the complex relationship between two migrant farm workers who help each other fight loneliness and despair. In 1938, Steinbeck published *The Long Valley,* a collection of some of his most enduring short stories, including "The Red Pony" and "Leader of the People."

Increasing fame brought offers from newspapers and magazines to cover stories related to the social crisis of the Depression. The material Steinbeck gathered while writing articles for a San Francisco newspaper formed the basis for the novel *The Grapes of Wrath* (1939); the work generally is considered his finest. A year later, the novel earned the Pulitzer Prize for fiction.

Steinbeck returned to his interest in marine biology in 1940 when he accompanied a friend, Ed Ricketts, on a voyage to collect biological specimens in the Gulf of California. Ricketts was the model for the protagonist in Steinbeck's next novel, *Cannery Row* (1945), and Steinbeck later published a nonfiction account of their journey, *The Log from the Sea of Cortez* (1951). Many of the author's later novels were examples of philosophical and moral fiction, including *The Pearl* (1947), *East of Eden* (1952), and *The Winter of Our Discontent* (1961).

In 1962, John Steinbeck was awarded the Nobel Prize for literature for his "realistic and imaginative writing, combining as it does sympathetic humor and keen social perception." In his acceptance speech, he remarked, "I hold that a writer who does not believe in the perfectibility of man has no dedication nor any membership in literature."

Noted Works
Tortilla Flat (1935)
Of Mice and Men (1937)
The Grapes of Wrath (1939)
The Pearl (1947)
East of Eden (1952)

from **The Grapes of Wrath**

A Novel by John Steinbeck

The Chrysanthemums

A Short Story by John Steinbeck

Build Background

Literary Context Published in 1939, **The Grapes of Wrath** is a novel about the Joad family's migration from Oklahoma to California in search of a better life. Steinbeck created a unique structure for the novel, using alternating chapters to tell the story of the Joads and to describe the plight of the so-called Okies, the poor migrant farmers who fled the Dust Bowl in the 1930s.

Steinbeck's written style alternates by chapter, as well. In the short chapters about the Okies and the social and economic conditions that led to their migration, Steinbeck's writing is descriptive and lyrical, almost poetic. In contrast, the chapters about the Joad family are long narratives that portray the hardship of their lives and capture their colorful native language and mannerisms. These two types of chapters and styles of writing are demonstrated in the excerpt that follows.

Throughout *The Grapes of Wrath*, Steinbeck explores themes of **Naturalism,** a literary movement that suggests actions and events inevitably result from biological, natural, or environmental forces. In depicting the banks and landowners as uncaring and unyielding, Steinbeck suggests that social and economic forces also control people's lives. His harsh portrayal of capitalism drew a sharp response when the novel was published, with some critics condemning the work as radical and even un-American. Regardless, *The Grapes of Wrath* was the best-selling novel of 1939; an estimated half million copies were sold during the first nine months after publication.

The second selection, **"The Chrysanthemums,"** often is described as one of Steinbeck's best short stories. It is from his collection *The Long Valley*, which is named for his native Salinas Valley. "The Chrysanthemums" is set in the Salinas Valley and contains vivid descriptions of its landscape, seasons, and weather. The story's main character, Elisa Allen, is a farm woman who seems trapped in a narrow existence and dreams of a more fulfilling life.

Steinbeck wrote "The Chrysanthemums" in 1934, during the decade sometimes called "the hungry thirties." This was the middle of the Depression and thus a time when many people dreamed of having more, in terms of both material and emotional satisfaction. Many of Steinbeck's characters pursue dreams with little or no chance of success, again demonstrating the author's Naturalistic perspective.

Reader's Context If you had to leave home with only one or two possessions, what would you take with you. Why?

Analyze Literature

Setting and Dialogue
The **setting** of a literary work is the time and place in which it occurs, together with all the details and dialogue.

Dialogue is conversation between two or more characters.

Set Purpose

Like many of Steinbeck's novels and stories, "The Chrysanthemums" is set in the Salinas Valley. As you read this short story, pay attention to Steinbeck's description of the setting, including the landscape and other details of time and place. Similarly, as you read the excerpt from *The Grapes of Wrath,* consider how Steinbeck creates a picture of the Joad family farm. In reading each selection, also make note of what is revealed about the characters exclusively through their dialogue.

Preview Vocabulary

ruthless, 704
implement, 705
moon, 705
refuse, 705
pilgrimage, 705
sedately, 712
fawning, 715

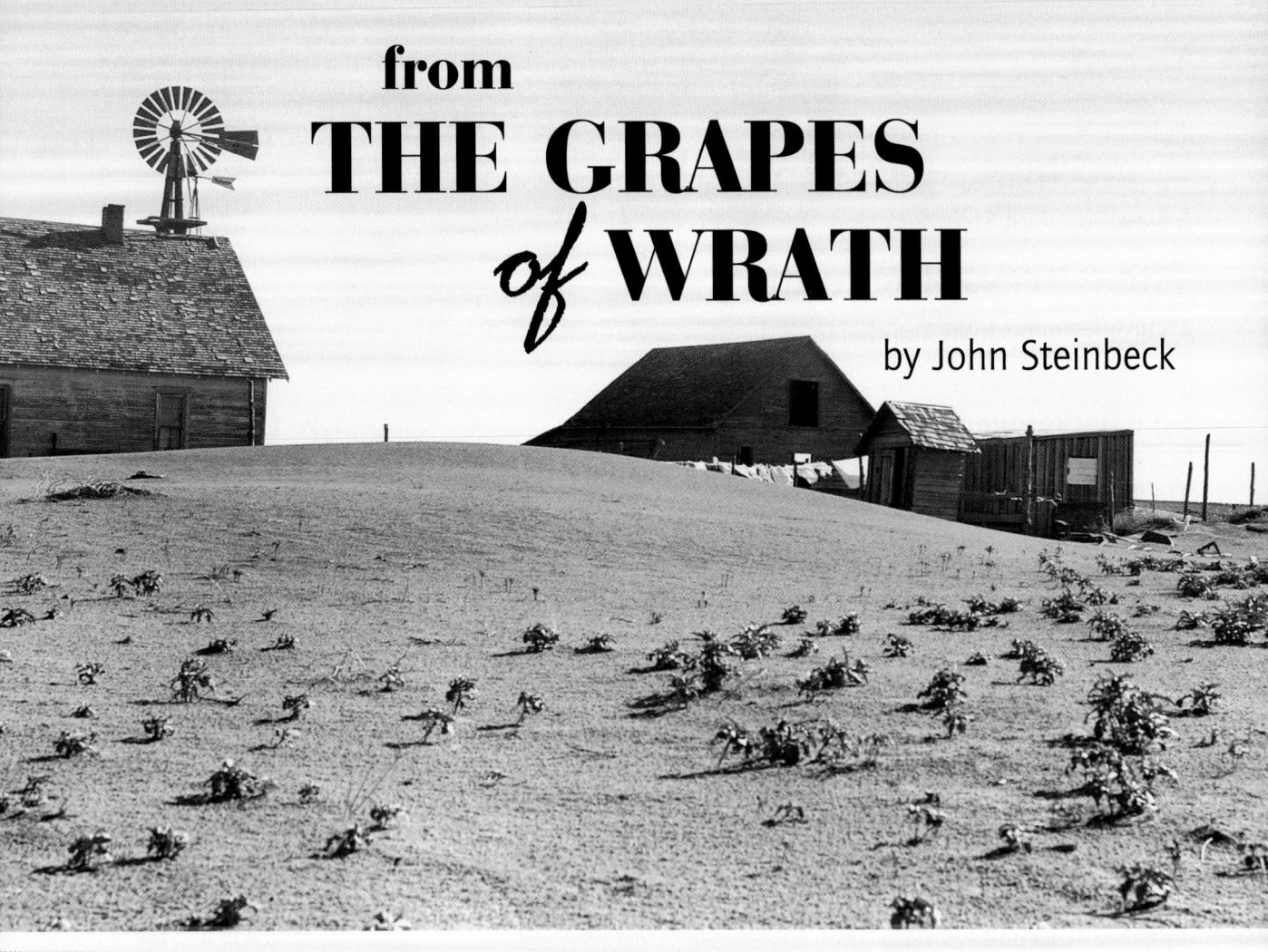

from
THE GRAPES
of WRATH

by John Steinbeck

YOU'RE NOT BUYING ONLY JUNK,
YOU'RE BUYING JUNKED LIVES.

Chapter Nine

In the little houses the tenant people sifted their belongings and the belongings of their fathers and of their grandfathers. Picked over their possessions for the journey to the west. The men were <u>ruthless</u> because the past had been spoiled, but the women knew how the past would cry to them in the coming days. The men went into the barns and the sheds.

That plow, that harrow,[1] remember in the war we planted mustard? Remember a fella wanted us to put in that rubber bush they call guayule? Get rich, he said. Bring out those tools—get a few dollars for them. Eighteen dollars for that plow, plus freight—Sears Roebuck.

Harness, carts, seeders, little bundles of hoes. Bring 'em out. Pile 'em up. Load 'em in the wagon. Take 'em to town. Sell 'em for what you can get. Sell the team and the wagon, too. No more use for anything.

---

1. **harrow.** Tool for breaking up and smoothing the soil

ruth • less (rüth´ ləs) *adj.,* cruel; without mercy

Fifty cents isn't enough to get for a good plow. That seeder cost thirty-eight dollars. Two dollars isn't enough. Can't haul it all back— Well, take it, and a bitterness with it. Take the well pump and the harness. Take halters, collars, hames, and tugs.[2] Take the little glass brow-band jewels, roses red under glass. Got those for the bay gelding.[3] 'Member how he lifted his feet when he trotted?

Junk piled up in a yard.

Can't sell a hand plow any more. Fifty cents for the weight of the metal. Disks and tractors, that's the stuff now.

BUT I WARN YOU, YOU'RE BUYING WHAT WILL PLOW YOUR OWN CHILDREN UNDER.

Well, take it—all junk—and give me five dollars. You're not buying only junk, you're buying junked lives. And more—you'll see— you're buying bitterness. Buying a plow to plow your own children under, buying the arms and spirits that might have saved you. Five dollars, not four. I can't haul 'em back— Well, take 'em for four. But I warn you, you're buying what will plow your own children under. And you won't see. You can't see. Take 'em for four. Now, what'll you give for the team and wagon? Those fine bays, matched they are, matched in color, matched the way they walk, stride to stride. In the stiff pull—straining hams and buttocks, split-second timed together. And in the morning, the light on them, bay light. They look over the fence sniffing for us, and the stiff ears swivel to hear us, and the black forelocks![4] I've got a girl. She likes to braid the manes and forelocks, puts little red bows on them. Likes to do it. Not any more. I could tell you a funny story about that girl and that off bay. Would make you laugh. Off horse is eight, near is ten, but might of been twin colts the way they work together. See? The teeth. Sound all over. Deep lungs. Feet fair and clean. How much? Ten dollars? For both? . . .

Chapter Ten

When the truck had gone, loaded with implements, with heavy tools, with beds and springs, with every movable thing that might be sold, Tom hung around the place. He mooned into the barn shed, into the empty stalls, and he walked into the implement lean-to and kicked the refuse that was left, turned a broken mower tooth with his foot. He visited places he remembered—the red bank where the swallows nested, the willow tree over the pig pen. Two shoats[5] grunted and squirmed at him through the fence, black pigs, sunning and comfortable. And then his pilgrimage was over, and he went to sit on the doorstep where the shade was lately fallen. Behind him Ma moved about in the kitchen, washing children's clothes in a bucket; and her strong freckled arms dripped soapsuds from the elbows. She stopped her rubbing when he sat down. She looked at him a long time, and at the back of his head when he turned and stared out at the hot sunlight. And then she went back to her rubbing.

She said, "Tom, I hope things is all right in California."

He turned and looked at her. "What makes you think they ain't?" he asked.

"Well—nothing. Seems too nice, kinda. I seen the han'bills fellas pass out,[6] an' how much work they is, an' high wages an' all; an' I seen in the paper how they want folks to come

---

2. **halters, collars, hames, and tugs.** Equipment for harnessing a workhorse
3. **bay gelding.** Reddish-brown male horse
4. **forelocks.** Hair growing from the front of a horse's head
5. **shoat.** Young pig
6. **han'bills fellas pass out.** Flyers distributed among poor people in the Dust Bowl states by representatives of large West Coast landowners

---

im • ple • ment (im´ plə mənt) n., tool; utensil
moon (mün) v., behave in a dreamy abstracted manner
ref • use (re´ fyüs) n., worthless materials; garbage
pil • grim • age (pil´ grə mij) n., journey to a sacred place

Dramatizations of *The Grapes of Wrath*

FONDA

DARWELL

The Grapes of Wrath has been dramatized several times since its publication in 1939. Just one year later, the best-selling novel was adapted into a screenplay and released as a movie. Directed by legendary filmmaker John Ford and starring Henry Fonda and Jane Darwell in the roles of Tom and Ma Joad, the movie was both a popular and critical success. Ford and Darwell won Oscars for their work on the film, and Steinbeck is said to have found the movie superior to the book.

In 1988, a stage version of *The Grapes of Wrath,* written and directed by Frank Galati, debuted in Chicago.

After productions in San Diego and London, the play arrived in New York in 1990, where it ran for nearly two hundred performances. The Broadway production earned seven Tony nominations in 1990 and won the awards for best play and best direction.

In 2007, the Minnesota Opera premiered an operatic adaptation of *The Grapes of Wrath,* the culmination of twelve years' effort. Composer Ricky Ian Gordon and librettist Michael Korie described Steinbeck's writing as having a rhythm that lends itself to musical expression. Given the significance of the novel in the body of American literature, the opera company acknowledged its sense of responsibility in bringing the work to the stage. Critics remarked on the timelessness of the story and its themes of perseverance and oppression.

---

an' pick grapes an' oranges an' peaches. That'd be nice work, Tom, pickin' peaches. Even if they wouldn't let you eat none, you could maybe snitch a little ratty one sometimes. An' it'd be nice under the trees, workin' in the shade. I'm scared of stuff so nice. I ain't got faith. I'm scared somepin ain't so nice about it."

Tom said, "Don't roust your faith bird-high an' you won't do no crawlin' with the worms."

"I know that's right. That's Scripture, ain't it?"

"I guess so," said Tom. "I never could keep Scripture straight sence I read a book name' *The Winning of Barbara Worth.*[7]

Ma chuckled lightly and scrounged the clothes in and out of the bucket. And she wrung out overalls and shirts, and the muscles of her forearms corded out. "Your Pa's pa, he quoted Scripture all the time. He got it all roiled up, too. It was the *Dr. Miles' Almanac* he got mixed up. Used to read ever' word in that almanac out loud—letters from folks that couldn't sleep or had lame backs. An' later he'd give them people for a lesson, an' he'd

say, 'That's a par'ble from Scripture.' Your Pa an' Uncle John troubled 'im some about it when they'd laugh." She piled wrung clothes like cord wood on the table. "They say it's two thousan' miles where we're goin'. How far ya think that is, Tom? I seen it on a map, big mountains like on a post card, an' we're goin' right through 'em. How long ya s'pose it'll take to go that far, Tommy?"

"I dunno," he said. "Two weeks, maybe ten days if we got luck. Look, Ma, stop your worryin'. I'm a-gonna tell you somepin about bein' in the pen.[8] You can't go thinkin' when you're gonna be out. You'd go nuts. You got to think about that day, an' then the nex' day, about the ball game Sat'dy. That's what you got to do. Ol' timers does that. A new young fella gets buttin'

---

7. ***The Winning of Barbara Worth.*** Historical 1926 novel by Harold Wright Bell about the reclamation of the lower California desert near San Diego
8. **bein' in the pen.** *Pen* is slang for *penitentiary,* or prison. Tom Joad has just been released from prison for having committed manslaughter

get jobs an' all work—maybe we can get one of them little white houses. An' the little fellas go out an' pick oranges right off the tree. They ain't gonna be able to stand it, they'll get to yellin' so."

Tom watched her working, and his eyes smiled. "It done you good jus' thinkin' about it. I knowed a fella from California. He didn't talk like us. You'd of knowed he come from some far-off place jus' the way he talked. But he says they's too many folks lookin' for work right there now. An' he says the folks that pick the fruit live in dirty ol' camps an' don't hardly get enough to eat. He says wages is low an' hard to get any."

A shadow crossed her face. "Oh, that ain't so," she said. "Your father got a

his head on the cell door. He's thinkin' how long it's gonna be. Whyn't you do that? Jus' take ever' day."

"That's a good way," she said, and she filled up her bucket with hot water from the stove, and she put in dirty clothes and began punching them down into the soapy water. "Yes, that's a good way. But I like to think how nice it's gonna be, maybe, in California. Never cold. An' fruit ever'place, an' people just bein' in the nicest places, little white houses in among the orange trees. I wonder—that is, if we all

han'bill on yella paper, tellin' how they need folks to work. They wouldn' go to that trouble if they wasn't plenty work. Costs 'em good money to get them han'bills out. What'd they want ta lie for, an' costin' 'em money to lie?"

Tom shook his head. "I don' know, Ma. It's kinda hard to think why they done it. Maybe—" He looked out at the hot sun, shining on the red earth.

"Maybe what?"

"Maybe it's nice, like you says." ❖

Describe a time when you were suspicious of something that sounded unbelievably good. How did it turn out?

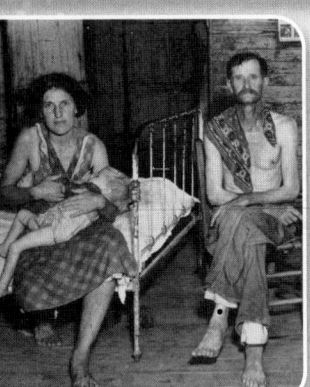

Primary Source Connection

As **John Steinbeck's** literary agent, Elizabeth Otis was to find writing assignments for the author and publishers for his work. In this 1938 **letter to Otis,** he explains to her his rejection of some assignments for "slicks," or magazines, and he describes his increasing emotional involvement in the plight of migrant workers on California farms during the Dust Bowl. Steinbeck ultimately did some field assignments, writing about the Dust Bowl for various publications. His experiences during this time inspired his 1939 novel, *The Grapes of Wrath.*

Letter to Elizabeth Otis
by John Steinbeck

Los Gatos
March 7, 1938

Dear Elizabeth:

I shouldn't have repeated that for the sake of the letter but it was true enough in intention and quite unconscious. I guess unconscious is very correct as an evaluation of my condition. Just got back from another week in the field. The floods have aggravated the starvation and sickness. I went down for Life[1] this time. Fortune[2] wanted me to do an article for them but I won't. I don't like the audience. Then Life sent me down with a photographer from its staff and we took a lot of pictures of the people. They guarantee not to use it if they change it and will send me the proofs.[3] They paid my expenses and will put up money for the help of some of these people.

I'm sorry but I simply can't make money on these people. That applies to your query about an article for a national magazine. The suffering is too great for me to cash in on it. I hope this doesn't sound either quixotic[4] or martyrish to you. A short trip into the fields where the water is a foot deep in the tents

---

1. **Life.** Popular photojournalist magazine, published weekly from 1936 to 1972
2. **Fortune.** Popular business magazine, published monthly since 1930
3. **proofs.** Preliminary copies of magazine or book pages, submitted for approval
4. **quixotic.** Striving for or characterized by lofty, unrealistic ideals; derived from the character Don Quixote, from a seventeenth-century novel of the same name by Miguel de Cervantes Saavedra

and the children are up on the beds and there is no food and no fire, and the county has taken off all the nurses because "the problem is so great that we can't do anything about it." So they do nothing. And we found a boy in jail for a felony because he stole two old radiators because his mother was starving to death and in stealing them he broke a little padlock on a shed. We'll either spring him or the district attorney will do the rest of his life explaining.

But you see what I mean. It is the most heartbreaking thing in the world. If Life does use the stuff there will be lots of pictures and swell ones. It will give you an idea of the kind of people they are and the kind of faces. I break myself every time I go out because the argument that one person's effort can't really do anything doesn't seem to apply when you come on a bunch of starving children and you have a little money. I can't rationalize it for myself anyway. So don't get me a job for a slick.[5] I want to put a tag of shame on the greedy [people] who are responsible for this but I can best do it through newspapers.

I'm going to see the Secretary of Agriculture in a little while and try to find out for my own satisfaction anyway just how much of the government's attitude is political and how much humanitarian. Then I'll know what course to take.

I'm in a mess trying to catch up with things that have piled up in the week I was gone. And of course I was in the mud for three days and nights and I have a nice cold to beat, but I haven't time right now for a cold so I won't get a very bad one.

Sorry for the hectic quality of this letter. I am hectic and angry.

Thank you for everything.

Bye,
John

---

5. **slick.** Magazine printed on glossy paper

Review Questions

1. Where has Steinbeck been for the past week? What was he doing there? Why does Steinbeck refuse to "make money on these people"?

2. Describe the conditions Steinbeck has encountered. Why does he refute the idea that one person cannot make a difference? What example does he give of being able to make a clear difference?

3. Identify the emotions Steinbeck feels at the end of the letter, and suggest why he may feel this way. What can one person do to bring about change in the face of overwhelming circumstances? Give examples from current events of people who have made a difference.

TEXT ^{TO} TEXT CONNECTION

John Steinbeck once said, "If you're in trouble, or hurt or need—go to the poor people. They're the only ones that'll help—the only ones." How does this statement relate both to the letter and the excerpt from *The Grapes of Wrath?* How does reading Steinbeck's letter help you better understand the novel?

The Angelus, 1857. Jean Francois Millet. Musée d'Orsay, Paris, France.

THE CHRYSANTHEMUMS

by John Steinbeck

"I'm strong," she boasted. "I never knew before how strong."

The high grey-flannel fog of winter closed off the Salinas Valley[1] from the sky and from all the rest of the world. On every side it sat like a lid on the mountains and made of the great valley a closed pot. On the broad, level land floor the gang plows bit deep and left the black earth shining like metal where the shares had cut. On the foothill ranches across the Salinas River, the yellow stubble fields seemed to

---

1. **Salinas Valley.** Coast Ranges region of California, south of San Francisco

be bathed in pale cold sunshine, but there was no sunshine in the valley now in December. The thick willow scrub along the river flamed with sharp and positive yellow leaves.

It was a time of quiet and of waiting. The air was cold and tender. A light wind blew up from the southwest so that the farmers were mildly hopeful of a good rain before long; but fog and rain do not go together.

Across the river, on Henry Allen's foothill ranch there was little work to be done, for the hay was cut and stored and the orchards were plowed up to receive the rain deeply when it should come. The cattle on the higher slopes were becoming shaggy and rough-coated.

Elisa Allen, working in her flower garden, looked down across the yard and saw Henry, her husband, talking to two men in business suits. The three of them stood by the tractor shed, each man with one foot on the side of the little Fordson. They smoked cigarettes and studied the machine as they talked.

Elisa watched them for a moment and then went back to her work. She was thirty-five. Her face was lean and strong and her eyes were as clear as water. Her figure looked blocked and heavy in her gardening costume, a man's black hat pulled low down over her eyes, clodhopper shoes, a figured print dress almost completely covered by a big corduroy apron with four big pockets to hold the snips, the trowel and scratcher,[2] the seeds and the knife she worked with. She wore heavy leather gloves to protect her hands while she worked.

She was cutting down the old year's chrysanthemum stalks with a pair of short and powerful scissors. She looked down toward the men by the tractor shed now and then. Her face was eager and mature and handsome; even her work with the scissors was over-eager, over-powerful. The chrysanthemum stems seemed too small and easy for her energy.

She brushed a cloud of hair out of her eyes with the back of her glove, and left a smudge of earth on her cheek in doing it. Behind her stood the neat white farm house with red geraniums close-banked around it as high as the windows. It was a hard-swept looking little house with hard-polished windows, and a clean mud-mat on the front steps.

Elisa cast another glance toward the tractor shed. The strangers were getting into their Ford coupe. She took off a glove and put her strong fingers down into the forest of new green chrysanthemum sprouts that were growing around the old roots. She spread the leaves and looked down among the close-growing stems. No aphids were there, no sowbugs or snails or cutworms. Her terrier fingers destroyed such pests before they could get started.

Elisa started at the sound of her husband's voice. He had come near quietly, and he leaned over the wire fence that protected her flower garden from cattle and dogs and chickens.

"At it again," he said. "You've got a strong new crop coming."

Elisa straightened her back and pulled on the gardening glove again. "Yes. They'll be strong this coming year." In her tone and on her face there was a little smugness.

"You've got a gift with things," Henry observed. "Some of those yellow chrysanthemums you had this year were ten inches across. I wish you'd work out in the orchard and raise some apples that big."

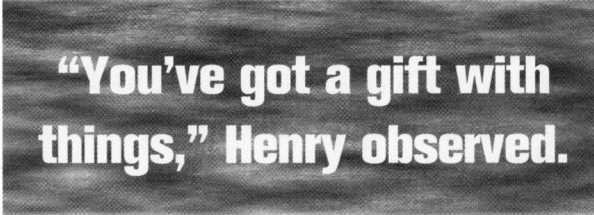

"You've got a gift with things," Henry observed.

Her eyes sharpened. "Maybe I could do it, too. I've a gift with things, all right. My mother had it. She could stick anything in the ground and make it grow. She said it was having planters' hands that knew how to do it."

---

2. **the snips, the trowel and scratcher.** Gardening tools

"Well, it sure works with flowers," he said.

"Henry, who were those men you were talking to?"

"Why, sure, that's what I came to tell you. They were from the Western Meat Company. I sold those thirty head of three-year-old steers. Got nearly my own price, too."

"Good," she said. "Good for you."

"And I thought," he continued, "I thought how it's Saturday afternoon, and we might go into Salinas for dinner at a restaurant, and then to a picture show—to celebrate, you see."

"Good," she repeated. "Oh, yes. That will be good."

Henry put on his joking tone. "There's fights tonight. How'd you like to go to the fights?"

"Oh, no," she said breathlessly. "No, I wouldn't like fights."

"Just fooling, Elisa. We'll go to a movie. Let's see. It's two now. I'm going to take Scotty and bring down those steers from the hill. It'll take us maybe two hours. We'll go in town about five and have dinner at the Cominos Hotel. Like that?"

"Of course I'll like it. It's good to eat away from home."

"All right, then. I'll go get up a couple of horses."

She said, "I'll have plenty of time to transplant some of these sets, I guess."

She heard her husband calling Scotty down by the barn. And a little later she saw the two men ride up the pale yellow hillside in search of the steers.

There was a little square sandy bed kept for rooting the chrysanthemums. With her trowel she turned the soil over and over, and smoothed it and patted it firm. Then she dug ten parallel trenches to receive the sets. Back at the chrysanthemum bed she pulled out the little crisp shoots, trimmed off the leaves of each one with her scissors and laid it on a small orderly pile.

A squeak of wheels and plod of hoofs came from the road. Elisa looked up. The country road ran along the dense bank of willows and cottonwoods that bordered the river, and up this road came a curious vehicle, curiously drawn. It was an old spring-wagon, with a round canvas top on it like the cover of a prairie schooner. It was drawn by an old bay horse and a little grey-and-white burro. A big stubble-bearded man sat between the cover flaps and drove the crawling team. Underneath the wagon, between the hind wheels, a lean and rangy mongrel dog walked <u>sedately</u>. Words were painted on the canvas, in clumsy, crooked letters. "Pots, pans, knives, sisors, lawn mores, Fixed." Two rows of articles, and the triumphantly definitive "Fixed" below. The black paint had run down in little sharp points beneath each letter.

Elisa, squatting on the ground, watched to see the crazy, loose-jointed wagon pass by. But it didn't pass. It turned into the farm road in front of her house, crooked old wheels skirling and squeaking. The rangy dog darted from between the wheels and ran ahead. Instantly the two ranch shepherds flew out at him. Then

se • date • ly (sə dāt′ lē) *adv.,* with a quiet, steady pace

all three stopped, and with stiff and quivering tails, with taut straight legs, with ambassadorial dignity, they slowly circled, sniffing daintily. The caravan pulled up to Elisa's wire fence and stopped. Now the newcomer dog, feeling outnumbered, lowered his tail and retired under the wagon with raised hackles and bared teeth.

The man on the wagon seat called out, "That's a bad dog in a fight when he gets started."

Elisa laughed. "I see he is. How soon does he generally get started?"

The man caught up her laughter and echoed it heartily. "Sometimes not for weeks and weeks," he said. He climbed stiffly down, over the wheel. The horse and the donkey drooped like unwatered flowers.

Elisa saw that he was a very big man. Although his hair and beard were greying, he did not look old. His worn black suit was wrinkled and spotted with grease. The laughter had disappeared from his face and eyes the moment his laughing voice ceased. His eyes were dark, and they were full of the brooding that gets in the eyes of teamsters and of sailors. The calloused hands he rested on the wire fence were cracked, and every crack was a black line. He took off his battered hat.

> **The laughter had disappeared from his face and eyes the moment his laughing voice ceased.**

"I'm off my general road, ma'am," he said. "Does this dirt road cut over across the river to the Los Angeles highway?"

Elisa stood up and shoved the thick scissors in her apron pocket. "Well, yes, it does, but it winds around and then fords the river. I don't think your team could pull through the sand."

He replied with some asperity.[3] "It might surprise you what them beasts can pull through."

"When they get started?" she asked.

He smiled for a second. "Yes. When they get started."

"Well," said Elisa, "I think you'll save time if you go back to the Salinas road and pick up the highway there."

He drew a big finger down the chicken wire and made it sing. "I ain't in any hurry, ma'am. I go from Seattle to San Diego and back every year. Takes all my time. About six months each way. I aim to follow nice weather."

Elisa took off her gloves and stuffed them in the apron pocket with the scissors. She touched the under edge of her man's hat, searching for fugitive hairs. "That sounds like a nice kind of a way to live," she said.

He leaned confidentially over the fence. "Maybe you noticed the writing on my wagon. I mend pots and sharpen knives and scissors. You got any of them things to do?"

"Oh, no," she said quickly. "Nothing like that." Her eyes hardened with resistance.

"Scissors is the worst thing," he explained. "Most people just ruin scissors trying to sharpen 'em, but I know how. I got a special tool. It's a little bobbit kind of thing, and patented. But it sure does the trick."

"No. My scissors are all sharp."

"All right, then. Take a pot," he continued earnestly, "a bent pot, or a pot with a hole. I can make it like new so you don't have to buy no new ones. That's a saving for you."

"No," she said shortly. "I tell you I have nothing like that for you to do."

His face fell to an exaggerated sadness. His voice took on a whining undertone. "I ain't had a thing to do today. Maybe I won't have no supper tonight. You see I'm off my regular road. I know folks on the highway clear from Seattle to San Diego. They save their things for me to sharpen up because they know I do it so good and save them money."

---

3. **asperity.** Sharpness

"I'm sorry," Elisa said irritably. "I haven't anything for you to do."

His eyes left her face and fell to searching the ground. They roamed about until they came to the chrysanthemum bed where she had been working. "What's them plants, ma'am?"

The irritation and resistance melted from Elisa's face. "Oh, those are chrysanthemums, giant whites and yellows. I raise them every year, bigger than anybody around here."

"Kind of a long-stemmed flower? Looks like a quick puff of colored smoke?" he asked.

"That's it. What a nice way to describe them."

"They smell kind of nasty till you get used to them," he said.

"It's a good bitter smell," she retorted, "not nasty at all."

He changed his tone quickly. "I like the smell myself."

"I had ten-inch blooms this year," she said.

The man leaned farther over the fence. "Look. I know a lady down the road a piece, has got the nicest garden you ever seen. Got nearly every kind of flower but no chrysanthemums. Last time I was mending a copper-bottom washtub for her (that's a hard job but I do it good), she said to me, 'If you ever run acrost some nice chrysanthemums I wish you'd try to get me a few seeds.' That's what she told me."

Elisa's eyes grew alert and eager. "She couldn't have known much about chrysanthemums. You *can* raise them from seed, but it's much easier to root the little sprouts you see there."

"Oh," he said. "I s'pose I can't take none to her, then."

"Why yes you can," Elisa cried. "I can put some in damp sand, and you can carry them right along with you. They'll take root in the pot if you keep them damp. And then she can transplant them."

"She'd sure like to have some, ma'am. You say they're nice ones?"

"Beautiful," she said. "Oh, beautiful." Her eyes shone. She tore off the battered hat and

shook out her dark pretty hair. "I'll put them in a flower pot, and you can take them right with you. Come into the yard."

While the man came through the picket gate Elisa ran excitedly along the geranium-bordered path to the back of the house. And she returned carrying a big red flower pot. The gloves were forgotten now. She kneeled on the ground by the starting bed and dug up the sandy soil with her fingers and scooped it into the bright new flower pot. Then she picked up the little pile of shoots she had prepared. With her strong fingers she pressed them in the sand and tamped around them with her knuckles. The man stood over her. "I'll tell you what to do," she said. "You remember so you can tell the lady."

This photograph of Florence Owens Thompson, a poverty-stricken migrant mother of seven young children, came to symbolize the Depression for many Americans. The photo was taken in February 1936 by Dorothea Lange, one of the first women photojournalists.

"Yes, I'll try to remember."

"Well, look. These will take root in about a month. Then she must set them out, about a foot apart in good rich earth like this, see?" She lifted a handful of dark soil for him to look at. "They'll grow fast and tall. Now remember this: In July tell her to cut them down, about eight inches from the ground."

"Before they bloom?" he asked.

"Yes, before they bloom." Her face was tight with eagerness. "They'll grow right up again. About the last of September the buds will start."

She stopped and seemed perplexed. "It's the budding that takes the most care," she said hesitantly. "I don't know how to tell you." She looked deep into his eyes, searchingly. Her mouth opened a little, and she seemed to be listening. "I'll try to tell you," she said. "Did you ever hear of planting hands?"

"Can't say I have, ma'am."

"Well, I can only tell you what it feels like. It's when you're picking off the buds you don't want. Everything goes right down into your fingertips. You watch your fingers work. They do it themselves. You can feel how it is. They pick and pick the buds. They never make a mistake. They're with the plant. Do you see? Your fingers and the plant. You can feel that, right up your arm. They know. They never make a mistake. You can feel it. When you're like that you can't do anything wrong. Do you see that? Can you understand that?"

She was kneeling on the ground looking up at him. Her breast swelled passionately.

The man's eyes narrowed. He looked away self-consciously. "Maybe I know," he said. "Sometimes in the night in the wagon there—"

Elisa's voice grew husky. She broke in on him, "I've never lived as you do but I know what you mean. When the night is dark—why, the stars are sharp pointed, and there's quiet. Why, you rise up and up! Every pointed star get driven into your body. It's like that. Hot and sharp and—lovely."

Kneeling there, her hand went out toward his legs in the greasy black trousers. Her hesitant fingers almost touched the cloth. Then her hand dropped to the ground. She crouched low like a <u>fawning</u> dog.

He said, "It's nice, just like you say. Only when you don't have no dinner, it ain't."

She stood up then, very straight, and her face was ashamed. She held the flower pot out to him and placed it gently in his arms. "Here. Put it in your wagon on the seat, where you can watch it. Maybe I can find something for you to do."

At the back of the house she dug in the can pile and found two old and battered aluminum saucepans. She carried them back and gave them to him. "Here, maybe you can fix these."

fawn • ing (fän´ iŋ) *adj.*, showing affection with flattery or in a cringing manner

His manner changed. He became professional. "Good as new I can fix them." At the back of his wagon he set a little anvil, and out of an oily tool box dug a small machine hammer. Elisa came through the gate to watch him while he pounded out the dents in the kettles. His mouth grew sure and knowing. At a difficult part of the work he sucked his under-lip.

"You sleep right in the wagon?" Elisa asked.

"Right in the wagon, ma'am. Rain or shine I'm dry as a cow in there."

"It must be nice," she said. "It must be very nice. I wish women could do such things."

"It ain't the right kind of a life for a woman."

> **"It must be nice," she said. "It must be very nice. I wish women could do such things."**

Her upper lip raised a little, showing her teeth. "How do you know? How can you tell?" she said.

"I don't know, ma'am," he protested. "Of course I don't know. Now here your kettles, done. You don't have to buy no new ones."

"How much?"

"Oh, fifty cents'll do. I keep my prices down and my work good. That's why I have all them satisfied customers up and down the highway."

Elisa brought him a fifty-cent piece from the house and dropped it in his hand. "You might be surprised to have a rival some time.

I can sharpen scissors, too. And I can beat the dents out of little pots. I could show you what a woman might do."

He put his hammer back in the oily box and shoved the little anvil out of sight. "It would be a lonely life for a woman, ma'am, and a scarey life, too, with animals creeping under the wagon all night." He climbed over the single-tree steadying himself with a hand on the burro's white rump. He settled himself in the seat, picked up the lines. "Thank you kindly, ma'am," he said. "I'll do like you told me; I'll go back and catch the Salinas road."

"Mind," she called, "if you're long in getting there, keep the sand damp."

"Sand, ma'am? . . . Sand? Oh, sure. You mean around the chrysanthemums. Sure I will." He clucked his tongue. The beasts leaned luxuriously into their collars. The mongrel dog took his place between the back wheels. The wagon turned and crawled out the entrance road and back the way it had come, along the river.

Elisa stood in front of her wire fence watching the slow progress of the caravan. Her shoulders were straight, her head thrown back, her eyes half-closed, so that the scene came vaguely into them. Her lips moved silently, forming the words "Good-bye—good-bye." Then she whispered, "That's a bright direction. There's a glowing there." The sound of her whisper startled her. She shook herself free and looked about to see whether anyone had been listening. Only the dogs had heard. They lifted their heads toward her from their sleeping in the dust, and then stretched out their chins and settled asleep again. Elisa turned and ran hurriedly into the house.

In the kitchen she reached behind the stove and felt the water tank. It was full of hot water from the noonday cooking. In the bathroom she tore off her soiled clothes and flung them into the corner. And then she scrubbed herself with a little block of pumice, legs and thighs, loins and chest and arms, until her skin was scratched and red. When she had dried herself she stood in front of a mirror in her bedroom and looked at her body. She tightened her stomach and threw out her chest. She turned and looked over her shoulder at her back.

After a while she began to dress, slowly. She put on her newest under-clothing and her nicest stockings and the dress which was the symbol of her prettiness. She worked carefully on her hair, penciled her eyebrows and rouged her lips.

Before she was finished she heard the little thunder of hoofs and the shouts of Henry and his helper as they drove the red steers into the corral. She heard the gate bang shut and set herself for Henry's arrival.

His step sounded on the porch. He entered the house calling, "Elisa, where are you?"

"In my room, dressing. I'm not ready. There's hot water for your bath. Hurry up. It's getting late."

When she heard him splashing in the tub, Elisa laid his dark suit on the bed, and shirt and socks and tie beside it. She stood his polished shoes on the floor beside the bed. Then she went to the porch and sat primly and stiffly

down. She looked toward the river road where the willow-line was still yellow with frosted leaves so that under the high grey fog they seemed a thin band of sunshine. This was the only color in the grey afternoon. She sat unmoving for a long time. Her eyes blinked rarely.

Henry came banging out of the door, shoving his tie inside his vest as he came. Elisa stiffened and her face grew tight. Henry stopped short and looked at her. "Why—why, Elisa. You look so nice!"

> "Nice? You think I look nice? What do you mean by 'nice'?"

"Nice? You think I look nice? What do you mean by 'nice'?"

Henry blundered on. "I don't know. I mean you look different, strong and happy."

"I am strong? Yes, strong. What do you mean 'strong'?"

He looked bewildered. "You're playing some kind of a game," he said helplessly. "It's a kind of a play. You look strong enough to break a calf over your knee, happy enough to eat it like a watermelon."

For a second she lost her rigidity. "Henry! Don't talk like that. You didn't know what you said." She grew complete again. "I'm strong," she boasted. "I never knew before how strong."

Henry looked down toward the tractor shed, and when he brought his eyes back to her, they were his own again. "I'll get out the car. You can put on your coat while I'm starting."

Elisa went into the house. She heard him drive to the gate and idle down his motor, and then she took a long time to put on her hat. She pulled it here and pressed it there. When Henry turned the motor off she slipped into her coat and went out.

The little roadster bounced along on the dirt road by the river, raising the birds and

GOODMAN

The Swing Era

Jazz musicians had been playing Swing since the 1920s. Band leaders such as Count Basie, Duke Ellington, Fletcher Henderson, and Chick Webb played integral roles in developing jazz from its Dixieland roots into the Swing form popularized by jazz clarinetist Benny Goodman, who would become known as "the King of Swing." However, all these early band leaders were African American. Given the social boundaries of the time, Swing did not become popular among mainstream Americans until white musicians such as Goodman started performing it.

Swing jazz is characterized by a strong rhythm section (drums and bass) that anchors a series of accompanying woodwind and brass instruments (generally, clarinets, saxophones, trumpets, and trombones). Swing bands typically were large (about twenty players), which meant a band leader would invest significant time into composing songs the entire group could perform. Improvisation by individual players also was an important part of Swing, but it was more controlled than it had been in earlier jazz forms.

Swing music had a powerful cultural impact that extended beyond the scope of popular music. Its energetic, carefree tone gave listeners a reprieve from the harshness of life during the Depression. In addition, the extravagant dance form that grew out of Swing allowed people to vent their frustrations constructively during tough times and provided young people with a much-needed means of expression.

---

driving the rabbits into the brush. Two cranes flapped heavily over the willow-line and dropped into the river-bed.

Far ahead on the road Elisa saw a dark speck. She knew.

She tried not to look as they passed it, but her eyes would not obey. She whispered to herself sadly, "He might have thrown them off the road. That wouldn't have been much trouble, not very much. But he kept the pot," she explained. "He had to keep the pot. That's why he couldn't get them off the road."

The roadster turned a bend and she saw the caravan ahead. She swung full around toward her husband so she could not see the little covered wagon and the mismatched team as the car passed them.

In a moment it was over. The thing was done. She did not look back.

She said loudly, to be heard above the motor, "It will be good, tonight, a good dinner."

"Now you're changed again," Henry complained. He took one hand from the wheel and patted her knee. "I ought to take you in to dinner oftener. It would be good for both of us. We get so heavy out on the ranch."

"Henry," she asked, "could we have wine at dinner?"

"Sure we could. Say! That will be fine."

She was silent for a while; then she said, "Henry, at those prize fights, do the men hurt each other very much?"

"Sometimes a little, not often. Why?"

"Well, I've read how they break noses, and blood runs down their chests. I've read how the fighting gloves get heavy and soggy with blood."

> "I ought to take you in to dinner oftener. It would be good for both of us.

Kallmunz, Stormy Atmosphere, 1904. Wassily Kandinsky.

He looked around at her. "What's the matter, Elisa? I didn't know you read things like that." He brought the car to a stop, then turned to the right over the Salinas River bridge.

"Do any women ever go to the fights?" she asked.

"Oh, sure, some. What's the matter, Elisa? Do you want to go? I don't think you'd like it, but I'll take you if you really want to go."

She relaxed limply in the seat. "Oh, no. No. I don't want to go. I'm sure I don't." Her face was turned away from him. "It will be enough if we can have wine. It will be plenty." She turned up her coat collar so he could not see that she was crying weakly—like an old woman. ❖

MIRRORS & WINDOWS

When someone does something nice for you, do you tend to be appreciative and grateful or suspicious of his or her motive?

Refer to Text ▶ ▶ ▶ ▶ ▶   Reason with Text

1a. At the start of the excerpt from *The Grapes of Wrath,* why are the people selling their belongings?	**1b.** Explain how men and women view this experience differently. What different emotions do they feel?	**Understand** Find meaning
2a. Why doesn't Tom Joad believe the handbill that advertises jobs in California? Why does Ma Joad continue to believe it?	**2b.** What does Ma's trust in the handbill reveal about her? What does Tom's skepticism reveal about him?	**Apply** Use information
3a. Review the description of Elisa Allen from the beginning of "The Chrysanthemums." Which details suggest her strength?	**3b.** Trace how the changes in Elisa's appearance and manner are tied to her feelings of self-confidence.	**Analyze** Take things apart
4a. In *The Grapes of Wrath,* how does Tom answer Ma's question about how long it will take to get to California? What advice does he give her?	**4b.** Evaluate how well Tom and Ma understand one another's expectations about life in California.	**Evaluate** Make judgments
5a. In "The Chrysanthemums," how does the traveling fix-it man's visit affect Elisa, both immediately and in the long term?	**5b.** Summarize Steinbeck's views on human nature, based on his portrayal of the fix-it man.	**Create** Bring ideas together

Analyze Literature

Setting and Dialogue

Review the first several paragraphs of "The Chrysanthemums," which describe the Salinas Valley on a December day. How is this setting appropriate for a story about Elisa Allen? What is significant about the line "It was a time of quiet and of waiting"?

How effectively does Steinbeck use dialogue to develop the characters of Ma and Tom Joad in *The Grapes of Wrath?* What pieces of dialogue give the most insight into Ma? Into Tom?

Extend the Text

Writing Options

Creative Writing Write a journal entry for either Ma Joad or Elisa Allen. Have the character describe her day, confide her feelings about the day's events, and express her hopes and fears about the future.

Expository Writing Write an essay analyzing the importance of setting in both *The Grapes of Wrath* and "The Chrysanthemums." Is setting more important in one story than the other, or are different aspects of setting more important in each story? Use examples from the novel and the story to support your opinion.

Lifelong Learning

Compare Historical Accounts Using both print and online sources, find historical accounts of people's lives during the Depression. Consider these questions: What hardships did many people experience in the Depression? Did the Depression affect people differently in urban and rural areas? What lasting effects did the Depression have on people's lives? Using this information, prepare and present a speech in which you analyze the differences and similarities of historical accounts. Include excerpts from the accounts to support your analysis.

Media Literacy

Analyze Movie Reviews Work in small groups to research the films made from Steinbeck novels. Which films attained the most popular and critical success? Present your findings in an oral presentation that will help your classmates decide which movies to view.

 Go to **www.mirrorsandwindows.com** for more.

1. Which of the following seem(s) to explain Steinbeck's decision in writing *The Grapes of Wrath* to use alternating chapters to tell the story of the Joads and to describe the plight of the Okies?
   A. The chapters about the Okies allow describing the Depression, which is the larger social and historical story.
   B. The chapters about the Joads portray the personalities and experiences of the real people who lived during the Depression.
   C. Using alternating chapters allowed Steinbeck to demonstrate his wide-ranging ability as a writer.
   D. Both A and B
   E. Both B and C

2. In the Chapter Ten excerpt from *The Grapes of Wrath*, about what does Ma Joad fantasize concerning the move to California?
   A. the nice weather
   B. picking peaches
   C. the little white houses
   D. Both A and B
   E. A, B, and C

3. In the Chapter Ten excerpt, Tom says, "Don't roust your faith bird-high an' you won't do no crawlin' with the worms." What does this colloquial expression mean?
   A. To understand people, you must get down to their level.
   B. You will get a lot done if you start working early in the day.
   C. You will fail if you do not believe in what you are doing.
   D. Having low expectations will prevent you from being disappointed if things turn out poorly.
   E. You should not let doubt ruin your dreams.

4. Which idea from Steinbeck's letter to Elizabeth Otis resonates with the themes in the excerpt from *The Grapes of Wrath* and the short story "The Chrysanthemums"?
   A. People are generally willing to help others.
   B. People's dreams often are shattered by the harsh realities of life.
   C. People tend to help others only when it is in their own best interest.
   D. A lot of people are taken advantage of or not treated with respect.
   E. The nation's problems are too big for one person to solve.

5. Which of the following best summarizes what happens in the story "The Chrysanthemums"?
   A. Elisa feels she makes a personal connection with the fix-it man, but he only plays on her pride so she will give him work.
   B. The fix-it man feels Elisa was condescending to him, so he throws away the flowers she gave him.
   C. Elisa is insecure and suspicious about how other people value her and her abilities. She just imagines seeing her prized flowers on the road.
   D. Elisa imagines running off and living like the fix-it man, but she sees that what she values most in her life would not be compatible with that lifestyle.
   E. Elisa's strength of character and natural abilities blind her to the fact that other people's lives are more difficult than her own.

6. Why does Elisa show interest in going to the fights at the end of the story?
   A. She wants to prove to herself and her husband that she is strong.
   B. She wants to be around a crowd of people.
   C. Her interest in the fights is an expression of her anger at the fix-it man.
   D. She wants to show her husband that she knows a little about boxing.
   E. She is curious about what the sport involves.

7. If you respond with *asperity*, you are being
   A. enthusiastic.
   B. pleasant.
   C. intellectual.
   D. harsh.
   E. patient.

8. **Constructed Response:** Compare and contrast the characters of Ma and Tom Joad in the excerpt from *The Grapes of Wrath*. How does each feel about the move to California? What from each character's past seems to underlie his or her expectations? Use evidence from the text to support your ideas.

9. **Constructed Response:** Analyze how Steinbeck depicts men's and women's different approaches to life and its challenges in the excerpt from *The Grapes of Wrath* and the short story "The Chrysanthemums." Note both how men and women are described and what they say and do. Cite examples from both texts to support your argument.

A Date Which Will Live in Infamy
A Speech by Franklin Delano Roosevelt

Build Background

Historical Context Early on the morning of Sunday, December 7, 1941, Japanese planes suddenly filled the sky above the U.S. naval base at Pearl Harbor, Hawaii, attacking naval vessels at anchor in the harbor and taking their unsuspecting crews by surprise. An estimated 2,500 U.S. military personnel and civilians were killed, and more than 1,100 were injured. In addition to the human casualties, the U.S. Navy suffered a crippling blow: Nineteen ships had been sunk or damaged, and more than 300 planes had been damaged or destroyed.

After learning of the attack late that afternoon, President Franklin Delano Roosevelt dictated to his secretary, Grace Tully, a speech he planned to deliver the next day, asking Congress to declare war on Japan. Roosevelt reportedly composed the speech in his head, preferring to make a short, direct appeal rather than a lengthy recitation of Japan's offenses, as some of his advisers had recommended. Congress responded to **"A Date Which Will Live in Infamy"** by approving a declaration of war.

Reader's Context When have you had to deliver bad news to someone? What concerns did you have? How did you prepare yourself for this task?

Meet the Author

Franklin Delano Roosevelt (1882–1945) was born in Hyde Park, New York, to parents from wealthy, prestigious families. An only child, he was well traveled and well educated. He attended Harvard University and Columbia Law School.

Roosevelt entered politics in 1910 as a New York state senator. In 1921, he contracted polio and became almost completely paralyzed. He later regained much of his mobility and resumed his political career, becoming governor of New York in 1928. However, he would never walk again without the use of leg braces, and he used a wheelchair when out of the public eye.

Roosevelt was elected president in 1932, beating incumbent Herbert Hoover. Assuming office in the early years of the Depression, Roosevelt worked to turn around the country's economy. Through his New Deal, he initiated innovative economic reforms and reassured a weary and frightened nation that "the only thing we have to fear is fear itself." Roosevelt was re-elected in 1936, 1940, and 1944 and is the only president to serve more than two terms.

In 1939, Roosevelt's attention turned to world events when World War II broke out in Europe. Under Roosevelt's leadership, the United States and its allies ultimately won the war. Unfortunately, Roosevelt never was able to see his country's efforts result in victory. He died in office on April 12, 1945, less than one month before the Allied victory in Europe.

Analyze Literature

Purpose and Repetition
A writer's or speaker's **purpose** is his or her aim, or goal. That purpose might be to inform or explain (expository); to portray a person, place, object, or event (descriptive); to convince people to respond in some way (persuasive); or to tell a story (narrative).

Repetition is a writer's intentional reuse of a sound, word, phrase, or sentence.

Set Purpose

President Roosevelt's speech about the bombing of Pearl Harbor is one of the most famous examples of oratory (public speaking) in U.S. history. As you read, think about the purpose or purposes Roosevelt had in delivering this speech. Also look for examples of repeated words and phrases. Orators often use repetition to emphasize ideas and stir emotions.

Preview Vocabulary

infamy, 723
solicitation, 723
offensive, 724
onslaught, 724
premeditated, 724
treachery, 724
unbounding, 724
inevitable, 724

The U.S.S. *Arizona* ablaze in Pearl Harbor (December 7, 1941).

A Date Which Will Live in Infamy

by Franklin Delano Roosevelt

The facts of yesterday and today speak for themselves.

To the Congress of the United States:

Yesterday, December 7, 1941—a date which will live in infamy—the United States of America was suddenly and deliberately attacked by naval and air forces of the Empire of Japan.

The United States was at peace with that nation, and, at the solicitation of Japan, was still in conversation with its government and its emperor looking toward the maintenance of peace in the Pacific.

Indeed, one hour after Japanese air squadrons[1] had commenced bombing in the American

---

1. **air squadrons.** Military flight formations; groups of aircraft

> **in • fa • my** (in′ fə mē) *n.*, evil reputation brought about by something grossly criminal, shocking, or brutal
> **so • lic • i • ta • tion** (sô li′ si tā′ shən) *n.*, entreaty; petition; request

island of Oahu, the Japanese ambassador to the United States and his colleagues delivered to the Secretary of State a formal reply to a recent American message. While this reply stated that it seemed useless to continue the existing diplomatic negotiations, it contained no threat or hint of war or armed attack.

It will be recorded that the distance of Hawaii from Japan makes it obvious that the attack was deliberately planned many days or even weeks ago. During the intervening time, the Japanese government has deliberately sought to deceive the United States by false statements and expressions of hope for continued peace.

The attack yesterday on the Hawaiian islands has caused severe damage to American naval and military forces. Very many American lives have been lost. In addition, American ships have been reported torpedoed on the high seas between San Francisco and Honolulu.

Yesterday, the Japanese government also launched an attack against Malaya.[2]

Last night, Japanese forces attacked Hong Kong.

Last night, Japanese forces attacked Guam.

Last night, Japanese forces attacked the Philippine Islands.

Last night, Japanese forces attacked Wake Island.

This morning, the Japanese attacked Midway Island.

Japan has, therefore, undertaken a surprise offensive extending throughout the Pacific area. The facts of yesterday and today speak for themselves. The people of the United States have already formed their opinions and well understand the implications to the very life and safety of our nation.

As commander in chief of the Army and Navy, I have directed that all measures be taken for our defense.

Always will we remember the character of the onslaught against us.

No matter how long it may take us to overcome this premeditated invasion, the American people in their righteous might will win through to absolute victory.

I believe I interpret the will of the Congress and of the people when I assert that we will not only defend ourselves to the uttermost, but will make very certain that this form of treachery shall never endanger us again.

Hostilities exist. There is no blinking at the fact that that our people, our territory and our interests are in grave danger.

With confidence in our armed forces— with the unbounding determination of our people—we will gain the inevitable triumph— so help us God.

I ask that the Congress declare that since the unprovoked and dastardly attack by Japan on Sunday, December 7, a state of war has existed between the United States and the Japanese Empire. ❖

---

2. **Malaya.** Now Malaysia

of • fen • sive (ō fenʹ siv) *n.,* attack
on • slaught (änʹ slôt) *n.,* especially fierce attack
pre • med • i • tat • ed (prē meʹ də tā təd) *adj.,* characterized by willful intent and a degree of forethought and planning
treach • er • y (treʹ chə rē) *n.,* violation of allegiance or trust
un • bound • ing (un baůndʹ iŋ) *adj.,* without limit or restraint
in • ev • i • ta • ble (i neʹ və tə bəl) *adj.,* incapable of being avoided or evaded

Roosevelt tells the American people, "We will not only defend ourselves to the uttermost, but will make very certain that this form of treachery shall never endanger us again." When, if ever, is a nation justified in going to war?

GOODWIN

Literature Connection

Doris Kearns Goodwin (b. 1943) is a noted historian, biographer, and teacher. Her 1995 biography *No Ordinary Time: Franklin and Eleanor Roosevelt: The Home Front in World War II* was awarded the Pulitzer Prize in history. Goodwin also has received acclaim for her books about Lyndon B. Johnson, Abraham Lincoln, and the Kennedy family.

Consider what this excerpt from the biography reveals about how President Roosevelt and others in the White House reacted to learning of the attack on Pearl Harbor and how the president set about writing his momentous speech requesting a declaration of war against Japan.

from *No Ordinary Time*
by Doris Kearns Goodwin

Shortly after 7:30 A.M., local time, while sailors were sleeping, eating breakfast, and reading the Sunday papers, the first wave of 189 Japanese planes descended upon Pearl Harbor, dropping clusters of torpedo bombs on the unsuspecting fleet. Half the fleet, by fortunate coincidence, was elsewhere, including all three aircraft carriers, but the ships that remained were tied up to the docks so "snugly side by side," Harold Ickes[1] later observed, "that they presented a target that none could miss. A bomber could be pretty sure that he would hit a ship even if not the one he aimed at." Within minutes—before any anti-aircraft fire could be activated, and before a single fighter plane could get up into the air—all eight of the American battleships in Pearl Harbor, including the *West Virginia,* the *Arizona,* and the *California,* had been hit, along with three destroyers and three light cruisers.

Bodies were everywhere—trapped in the holds of sinking ships, strewn in the burn-ing waters, scattered on the smoke-covered ground. Before the third wave of Japanese planes completed its final run, thirty-five hundred sailors, soldiers, and civilians had lost their lives. It was the worst naval disaster in American history.

Knox[2] relayed the horrifying news to the president shortly after 1:30 P.M. Roosevelt was sitting in his study with Harry Hopkins[3] when the call came. "Mr. President," Knox said, "it looks like the Japanese have attacked Pearl Harbor." Hopkins said there must be some mistake; the Japanese would never attack Pearl Harbor. But the president reckoned it was

---

1. **Harold Ickes.** Harold LeClaire Ickes (1874–1952), Roosevelt's Secretary of the Interior and director of the Public Works Administration (PWA)
2. **Knox.** Colonel Frank Knox (1874–1944), Secretary of the Navy from 1940 until his death in 1944
3. **Harry Hopkins.** Harry Lloyd Hopkins (1890–1946) was one of President Roosevelt's closest advisers. He supervised various New Deal programs and was sent on the president's behalf to London and Moscow to meet with Winston Churchill and Joseph Stalin.

probably true—it was just the kind of thing the Japanese would do at the very moment they were discussing peace in the Pacific. All doubt was settled a few minutes later, when Admiral Stark[4] called to confirm the attack. With bloody certainty, the United States had finally discovered the whereabouts of the Japanese fleet.

> *The president reckoned it was probably true—it was just the kind of thing the Japanese would do at the very moment they were discussing peace in the Pacific.*

While the president was on the phone with Stark, Eleanor[5] was bidding luncheon guests goodbye. Heading back toward her sitting room on the second floor, she knew by one glance in her husband's study that something had happened. "All the secretaries were there, two telephones were in use, the senior military aides were on their way with messages. I said nothing because the words I heard over the telephone were quite sufficient to tell me that finally the blow had fallen and we had been attacked." Realizing at once that this was no time to disturb her husband with questions, Eleanor returned to work in her room. Earlier that morning, she had begun a chatty letter to Anna[6] which spoke of her plans to come to California for a visit in early January. When she resumed writing after lunch, she told Anna, "the news of the war has just come and I've put in a call for you and Johnny as you may want to send the children East." In the confusion of the first news of Pearl Harbor, it was thought that Japan might attack the West Coast as well. Finally, she drew the letter to a close. "I must go dear and talk to Father."

The first thing Eleanor noticed when she went into her husband's study was his "deadly calm" composure. While his aides and Cabinet members were running in and out in a state of excitement, panic, and irritation, he was sitting quietly at his desk, absorbing the news from Hawaii as it continued to flow in—"each report more terrible than the last." Though he looked strained and tired, Eleanor observed, "he was completely calm. His reaction to any event was always to be calm. If it was something that was bad, he just became almost like an iceberg, and there was never the slightest emotion that was allowed to show." Sumner Welles[7] agreed with Eleanor's assessment. In all the situations over the years in which he had seen the president, he "had never had such reason to admire him."

Beneath the president's imperturbable demeanor, however, Eleanor detected great bitterness and anger toward Japan for the treachery involved in carrying out the surprise attack while the envoys of the two countries were still talking. "I never wanted to have to fight this war on two fronts," Franklin told Eleanor. "We haven't got the Navy to fight in both the Atlantic and the Pacific . . . so we will have to build up the Navy and the Air Force and that will mean that we will have to take a good many defeats before we can have a victory." . . .

Meanwhile, a little bit at a time, the public at large was learning the news. "No American who lived through that Sunday will ever forget it," reporter Marquis Childs later wrote. "It seared deeply into the national consciousness," creating in all a permanent memory of where they were when they first heard the news.

◆ ◆ ◆

---

4. **Admiral Stark.** Harold Rainsford Stark (1880–1972), the U.S. Navy's Chief of Naval Operations from 1939 to 1942
5. **Eleanor.** Eleanor Roosevelt, the president's wife
6. **Anna.** Anna Eleanor Roosevelt (1906–1975), the Roosevelts' oldest child
7. **Sumner Welles.** Sumner Welles (1892–1961), an American diplomat who served as Undersecretary of State from 1937 to 1942

Churchill[8] was sitting at Chequers with envoy Averell Harriman[9] and Ambassador John Winant[10] when news of the Japanese attack came over the wireless. Unable to contain his excitement, he bounded to his feet and placed a call to the White House. "Mr. President, what's this about Japan?" "It's quite true," Roosevelt replied. "They have attacked us at Pearl Harbor. We are all in the same boat now."

"To have the United States at our side," Churchill later wrote, "was to me the greatest joy." After seventeen months of lonely fighting, he now believed the war would be won. "England would live; Britain would live; the Commonwealth of Nations and the Empire would live." The history of England would not come to an end. "Silly people—and there were many . . . ," Churchill mused, "—might discount the force of the United States," believing the Americans were soft, divided, paralyzed, averse to bloodshed. He knew better: he had studied the Civil War, the bloodiest war in history fought to the last inch. Saturated with emotion, Churchill thought of a remark British politician Sir Edward Grey had made to him more than 30 years before. The U.S. was like "a gigantic boiler. Once the fire is lighted under it there is no limit to the power it can generate."

Shortly before 5 P.M., the president called Grace Tully[11] to his study. "He was alone," Tully recalled, with two or three neat piles of notes stacked on his desk containing all the information he had been receiving during the afternoon. "Sit down, Grace. I'm going before Congress tomorrow. I'd like to dictate my message. It will be short." ❖

---

8. **Churchill.** Winston Churchill (1874–1965), Prime Minister of Great Britain during World War II (1940–1945)
9. **Averell Harriman.** William Averell Harriman (1871–1986), a special envoy to Great Britain early in the war
10. **John Winant.** John Gilbert Winant (1889–1947), U.S. Ambassador to Great Britain from 1941 to 1946
11. **Grace Tully.** Grace Tully (1900–1984), President Roosevelt's personal secretary

Review Questions

1. How did Prime Minister Winston Churchill react to the news that Pearl Harbor had been attacked? Summarize what the attack on the United States meant for Great Britain and the Allies in World War II.

2. How did President Roosevelt react to the news? Why was the Japanese attack a surprise, according to this excerpt? Why did Sumner Welles consider Roosevelt's reaction to the news admirable?

3. President Roosevelt was enormously popular in his time and is consistently rated as one of the best U.S. presidents. Identify the traits he showed in this time of crisis. Argue whether Americans still value these traits in a leader.

TEXT $\xleftrightarrow{\text{TO}}$ TEXT CONNECTION

Identify the details in this excerpt that suggest the relationship between the United States and Japan was strained before the attack on Pearl Harbor. Given that background, explain why President Roosevelt still might have felt "great bitterness and anger" toward Japan for the attack, leading him to call December 7, 1941, "a date which will live in infamy."

Refer to Text ▷ ▷ ▶ ▶ ▶ **Reason with Text**

1a. In his speech, how does President Roosevelt assess the attack in terms of human casualties and military losses?

1b. Infer why the president does not dwell on the American lives lost.

Understand
Find meaning

2a. In the last message received from the Japanese ambassador, what was and was not stated?

2b. Suggest why the president's speech persuaded Americans to become involved in World War II.

Apply
Use information

3a. Identify the main idea of each paragraph of the speech.

3b. Why might a short speech, like this one, have been more effective than a longer, more detailed speech?

Analyze
Take things apart

4a. Does the president use more nouns and verbs or more adjectives and adverbs in describing the attack? What words and phrases reveal the president's emotion?

4b. Judge whether this speech would have been more effective if it had contained more emotional language.

Evaluate
Make judgments

5a. What does the president say the people of the United States understand? What actions has the president taken?

5b. Imagine hearing this speech at the time it was delivered. Would it have been possible for the United States to resolve its difficulties peaceably with Japan? Why or why not?

Create
Bring ideas together

Analyze Literature

Purpose and Repetition
What is the primary purpose of Roosevelt's speech: to inform? to describe? to persuade? to narrate? What other purpose or purposes might he have had?

How does Roosevelt's use of repetition affect his speech? In particular, what main idea does his use of repetition help emphasize? What emotions does it stir?

Extend the Text

Writing Options
Creative Writing Imagine that you are a newspaper editor on December 8, 1941. Write an editorial about the president's speech from the perspective of an isolationist who believes the United States should stay out of the war or someone who feels the country must join in the war.

Narrative Writing Write one page about a specific aspect of President Roosevelt's life, such as his childhood; his wife, Eleanor; his battle with polio; or the New Deal. Research this aspect of the president's life using primary sources such as speeches and the work of biographers.

Critical Literacy
Compare Wartime Speeches Find a famous World War II speech in the library or on the Internet. Then write two paragraphs comparing and contrasting the themes and rhetorical techniques of that speech to Roosevelt's speech. (Possible speeches include "Appeal of June 18," by French General Charles de Gaulle, and "Never Was So Much Owed by So Many to So Few," by British Prime Minister Winston Churchill.)

Media Literacy
Analyze Media Coverage In small groups, research media coverage of the attack on Pearl Harbor. How was it covered in the newspaper, on the radio, and on film newsreels? Compile copies of articles, photos, and audio and video clips. Discuss with classmates each example of media coverage and whether it is objective or inflammatory.

 Go to **www.mirrorsandwindows.com** for more.

The Death of the Ball Turret Gunner

A Lyric Poem by Randall Jarrell

Build Background

Historical Context **"The Death of the Ball Turret Gunner,"** by Randall Jarrell, is perhaps the best-known American poem about World War II. Published in 1945, at the end of the war, this poem is from one of Jarrell's wartime collections called *Little Friend, Little Friend.*

In a footnote that accompanied the poem, Jarrell explained to readers the job of the ball turret gunner:

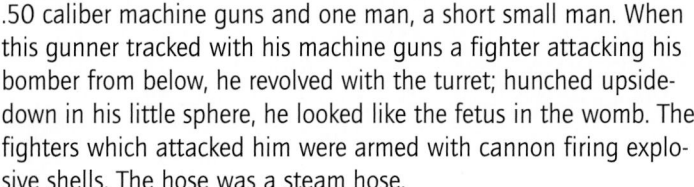

A ball turret was a plexiglass sphere set into the belly of a B-17 or B-24, and inhabited by two .50 caliber machine guns and one man, a short small man. When this gunner tracked with his machine guns a fighter attacking his bomber from below, he revolved with the turret; hunched upside-down in his little sphere, he looked like the fetus in the womb. The fighters which attacked him were armed with cannon firing explosive shells. The hose was a steam hose.

Reader's Context What sacrifices are people asked to make for their country? What sacrifices would you make for your country? Why?

Meet the Author

Randall Jarrell (1914–1965) was born in Nashville, Tennessee. After earning bachelor's and master's degrees from Vanderbilt University, he taught writing at Kenyon College and published his first volume of poetry, *Blood for a Stranger,* in 1942.

That same year, Jarrell left his teaching and writing career to enlist in the U.S. Army Air Force and serve in World War II. His poor vision prevented him from being a pilot, so he worked as a flight control tower operator.

Jarrell never saw combat, but he trained many pilots who did and knew well the harsh realities of war. These experiences provided inspiration for two volumes of poetry, *Little Friend, Little Friend* (1945) and *Losses* (1948). In these collections, Jarrell emphasized the evils of war and examined the lives of individual fighting men in compassionate detail. According to many critics, these collections remain unsurpassed in the body of poetry about World War II.

In subsequent poems, Jarrell turned his attention to the "dailiness of life" in civilian America. He was particularly interested in the role of women in society. His collection *The Woman at the Washington Zoo* received the National Book Award for Poetry in 1961. Childhood was the subject of his last book of poems, *The Lost World* (1965). His only novel, *Pictures from an Institution* (1954), is an affectionate satire of academic life.

Analyze Literature

Extended Metaphor and Imagery
An **extended metaphor** is a point-by-point presentation of one thing as though it were another. The description is intended to imply a comparison, inviting the reader to associate the thing being described with something quite different.

Imagery is the figurative or descriptive language used to create word pictures, or images.

Set Purpose

Reread Jarrell's explanation of a ball turret gunner in the Build Background section, and notice the simile he makes in describing the gunner: "he looked like the fetus in the womb." With that description in mind, analyze the poem as an extended metaphor. What two things are being compared, point by point? Also record the images Jarrell uses to portray the gunner, identifying the senses to which they relate.

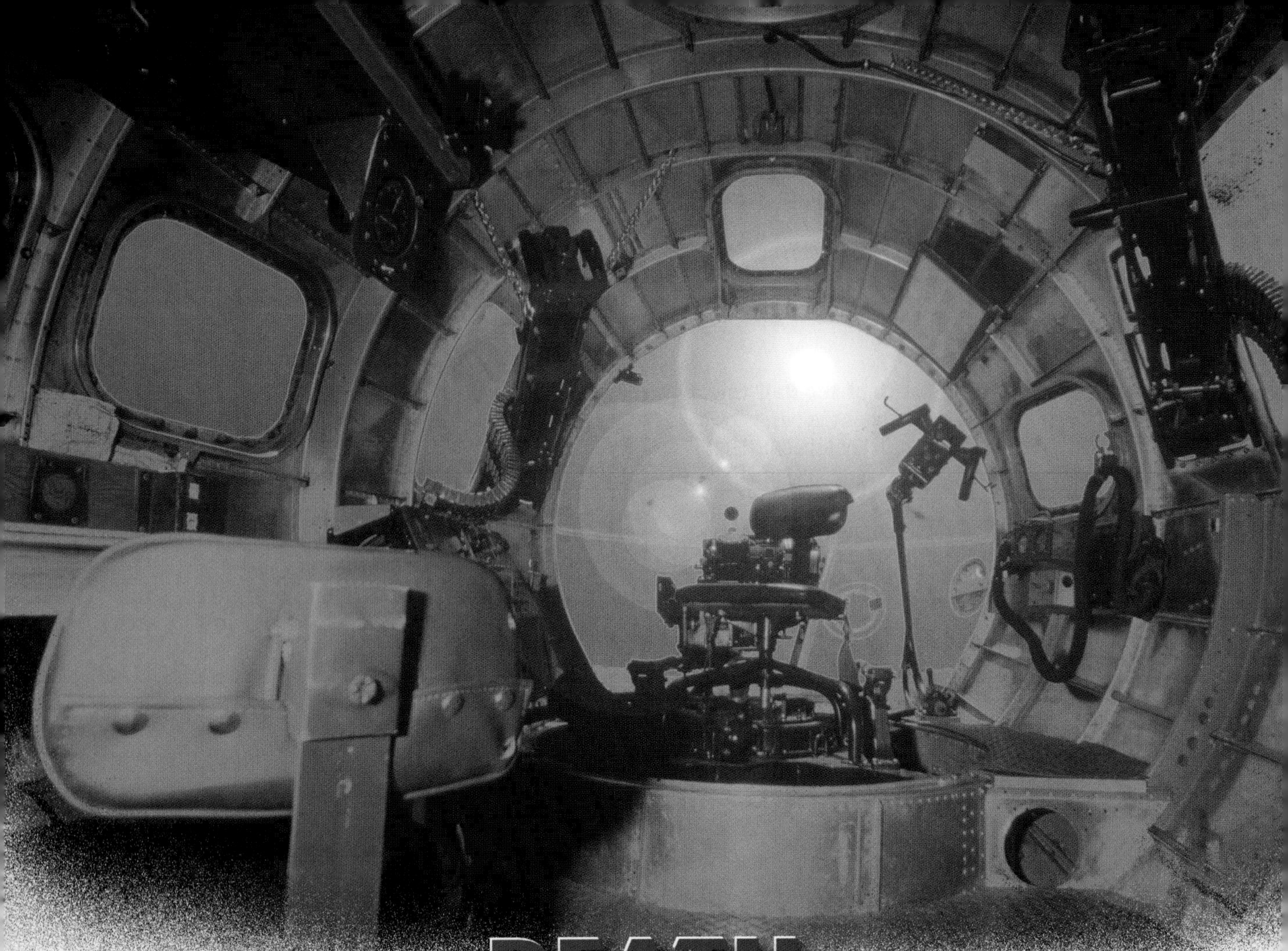

THE DEATH OF THE BALL TURRET GUNNER

by Randall Jarrell

From my mother's sleep I fell into the State,
And I hunched in its belly till my wet fur froze.
Six miles from earth, loosed from its dream of life,
I woke to black flak[1] and the nightmare fighters.
When I died they washed me out of the turret with a hose. ❖

---

1. **black flak.** Antiaircraft bullet shells

MIRRORS & WINDOWS Does the speaker consider his death heroic? What makes for a heroic death in wartime?

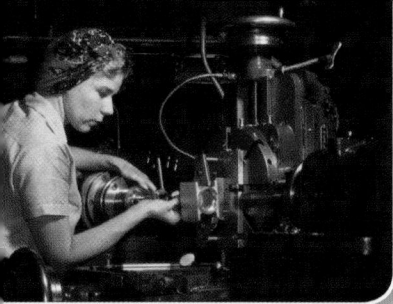

Informational Text Connection

Like Randall Jarrell, many Americans volunteered to support their country when the United States entered World War II. Among those volunteers were six million American women who fueled the war effort both at home and abroad. Many enlisted in all-female divisions of the military, such as the Navy's Women Accepted for Volunteer Emergency Service (WAVES) and the Army's Women's Army Corps (WACS). Others joined the Red Cross, serving in support roles to care for wounded troops overseas. At home, women responded to the wartime call to produce military supplies and equipment, filling jobs previously performed by men in shipyards, munitions plants, foundries, and steel mills. The proud image of Rosie the Riveter is an ongoing symbol of women's productivity and contribution to winning the war.

The **World War II posters** shown here were designed to recruit women into these roles. As you view them, consider what emotions they were designed to evoke to achieve that goal.

World War II Recruitment Posters

Released in late 1943, midway during the war, this poster of the fictional Rosie the Riveter was used to recruit women to work in manufacturing plants that produced equipment and materiel for the war. The poster was the central piece in a concentrated advertising campaign by the War Advertising Council that encouraged women to do their patriotic duty and take jobs outside the home. More than two million Americans responded, making this recruitment campaign the most successful in U.S. history.

Women in the war

WE CAN'T WIN WITHOUT THEM

Are you a girl with a Star-Spangled heart?

JOIN THE WAC NOW!

THOUSANDS OF ARMY JOBS NEED FILLING!

Women's Army Corps United States Army

(Left) Getting women to join the workforce meant changing long-held attitudes about their being employed outside the home and doing jobs typically performed by men. By the end of the war, an estimated six million women held war-related manufacturing and service positions. Although many would leave their jobs and return home after the war, their employment marked a permanent change in the American workforce. Having a job not only became socially acceptable but even desirable for many women.

IT'S A WOMAN'S WAR TOO!

JOIN THE WAVES

YOUR COUNTRY NEEDS YOU NOW

JOHN FALTER USNR

Apply to your nearest
NAVY RECRUITING STATION OR OFFICE OF NAVAL OFFICER PROCUREMENT

(Above) After serving in the U.S. Navy during World War I, performing mostly clerical work, all women were released from duty except those who were nurses. Then in 1942, after lengthy political discussion, legislation was passed to allow women to serve as officers as well as volunteers. By the next year, 27,000 women were serving as WAVES (Women Accepted for Volunteer Emergency Service), doing not only clerical work but also medical, technological, and intelligence jobs. By the end of World War II, more than 75,000 women had enlisted as WAVES.

(Left) More than 150,000 women served in the Women's Army Corps (WAC) during World War II. These WACs, as they were known, were the first women other than nurses to serve as full-fledged members of the U.S. Army. At the time of the war, most Americans were uncomfortable with the idea of women serving in the military. The WACs were the first of the women's service groups to be allowed to serve overseas in combat areas.

YOUR RED CROSS NEEDS YOU!

During World War II, the American Red Cross recruited an estimated 7.5 million volunteers, including 104,000 nurses for military service. At home, Red Cross workers held blood drives, helped staff medical centers and hospitals, prepared packages for American and Allied prisoners of war, and supported families of military personnel. Overseas, Red Cross personnel worked in military hospitals and on hospital ships and trains, caring for some one million wounded during the course of the war.

Review Questions

1. For what organization or industry is each poster designed? Analyze the image and text in each poster. Explain what each poster is designed to make women think, feel, and do.

2. In what activities are the women engaged? Critique how these posters maintain or contradict stereotypes about women and their traditional roles.

3. How realistic are these posters in their portrayal of war? Summarize why these posters might have been effective in encouraging women to volunteer. Would they be effective today? Why or why not?

TEXT $\xleftrightarrow{\text{TO}}$ TEXT CONNECTION

Compare and contrast the impression of war created by these posters with that created by Randall Jarrell's poem "The Death of the Ball Turret Gunner." In particular, consider the visual images used in the posters against the word images Jarrell created in his poem. Which seems to provide the most realistic view of war?

Refer to Text ▷ ▷ ▶ ▶ ▶ Reason with Text

1a. In the first line of the poem, what does the speaker say he "fell into"? From where or what did he fall?

1b. Identify what event in his life the speaker is describing in line 1. Was this event voluntary? Identify the event the speaker is describing in line 2.

Understand
Find meaning

2a. In line 3, from what is the speaker "loosed"? To what does the speaker wake in line 4?

2b. In lines 3–4, what does the language about dreams and sleep suggest about the speaker's feelings about war and his role in it?

Apply
Use information

3a. What happens to the speaker in the poem's last line?

3b. Compare and contrast the last line of the poem with the first four lines. What did Jarrell want to achieve in the last line?

Analyze
Take things apart

4a. Identify the language in the poem that refers to motherhood, unborn babies, and birth.

4b. Evaluate the relationship between the mother figure and the gunner. Why might the author have chosen such language in a poem about war and death?

Evaluate
Make judgments

5a. What words does the speaker use to describe aerial combat?

5b. If the speaker had survived the war, what attitude might he have had toward his country and the war itself? Why?

Create
Bring ideas together

Analyze Literature

Extended Metaphor and Imagery
What two things are being compared in this extended metaphor? Identify the points of comparison that help you make the association between these two things. Is Jarrell's use of this metaphor effective in portraying death and war?

Review the list of images you identified in this poem. In particular, to what sense do the images relate?

Extend the Text

Writing Options
Creative Writing In the role of the ball turret gunner, write a letter to a family member or friend back home that describes what you do. Include your feelings about your job, the war, and so on.

Expository Writing Write a paragraph to introduce "The Death of the Ball Turret Gunner" in a collection of poems written during wartime. Explain to readers what you perceive Jarrell says about war in this poem.

Collaborative Learning
Research Wartime Propaganda With a small group, research World War II *propaganda,* or materials intended to spread ideas and facts to promote or damage a cause.

In particular, look for advertisements and posters that use exaggerated or unfounded claims to manipulate people's thoughts and actions. Choose two examples of propaganda, and analyze the purpose and effectiveness of each. Present your analyses in an oral presentation for your class.

Media Literacy
Compare a Film and Poem Numerous films have been made about World War II, from *Sands of Iwo Jima* in 1949 to *Tora! Tora! Tora!* in 1970 to *Pearl Harbor* in 2001. Choose and watch a film. Then write a paragraph comparing and contrasting the portrayal of World War II in the film with that in Jarrell's poem.

 Go to **www.mirrorsandwindows.com** for more.

A Noiseless Flash, from Hiroshima

Literary Nonfiction by John Hersey

Build Background

Historical Context On August 6, 1945, in an effort to force an end to World War II, the United States dropped an atomic bomb on Hiroshima, Japan. A second bomb was dropped on Nagasaki three days later. On August 15, Japanese Emperor Hirohito announced his nation's surrender, telling his people, "The enemy now possesses a new and terrible weapon with the power to destroy many innocent lives and do incalculable damage."

The bombing of Hiroshima destroyed two-thirds of the city's buildings. Between 70,000 and 130,000 people were killed instantly. Thousands more survived the initial blast but later died of radiation sickness, and countless other survivors suffered lifelong injuries and illnesses, such as cancer.

Journalist John Hersey tells the story of six survivors in his book *Hiroshima*, from which **"A Noiseless Flash"** is excerpted. First published in 1946 in the *New Yorker* magazine, *Hiroshima* is based on Hersey's interviews with atomic bomb survivors and recounts events of the morning of the blast and over the next few days and weeks.

Reader's Context News reports often tell stories of people who escape tragedy because of some last-minute change in plans, such as missing an airplane flight. When have you or someone close to you had such an experience, even on a less dramatic scale? What sorts of emotions or thoughts follow this kind of experience?

Meet the Author

John Hersey (1914–1993) was born in China to missionary parents. He graduated from Yale and the University of Cambridge in England, where he studied English literature.

After serving as a private secretary for American novelist Sinclair Lewis, Hersey became a journalist for *Time* and *Life* magazines and traveled to Asia and Europe to cover World War II. His first two books, *Men on Bataan* (1942) and *Into the Valley* (1943), are examples of his skillful war reporting. His novel *A Bell for Adano* (1944), set in Italy in World War II, won the Pulitzer Prize for fiction.

In *Hiroshima* (1946), Hersey combined factual reporting with literary techniques to describe a real event. In doing so, he created one of the earliest landmark works of *literary nonfiction* (see Unit 9, Understanding Literary Forms, pages 1238–1239). According to Hersey, "Fiction is a clarifying agent. It makes truth plausible. . . . Among all the means of communication now available, imaginative literature comes closer than any other to being able to give an impression of the truth."

Analyze Literature

Point of View and Irony
Point of view is the vantage point, or perspective, from which the story is told. In *first-person point of view*, the story is told by someone who participates in or witnesses the action. In *third-person point of view*, the narrator usually stands outside the action and observes.

Irony is a difference between appearance and reality. One type of irony is *irony of situation*, in which an event occurs that violates the expectations of the characters or reader.

Set Purpose

John Hersey's *Hiroshima* is considered one of the most significant works of modern American journalism. As you read this excerpt, determine the point of view Hersey uses to recount survivors' stories of the bombing and consider why he decided on this perspective. Also look for examples of irony of situation in this retelling of actual events.

Preview Vocabulary

volition, 737
philanthropy, 738
intermittent, 740
incendiary, 740
hedonistic, 741
incessant, 742
convivial, 742
xenophobic, 743
theological, 743
repugnant, 743

A NOISELESS FLASH

FROM HIROSHIMA

by John Hersey

THEN, FOR A FEW SECONDS OR MINUTES, HE WENT OUT OF HIS MIND.

At exactly fifteen minutes past eight in the morning, on August 6, 1945, Japanese time, at the moment when the atomic bomb flashed above Hiroshima, Miss Toshiko Sasaki, a clerk in the personnel department of the East Asia Tin Works, had just sat down at her place in the plant office and was turning her head to speak to the girl at the next desk. At that same moment, Dr. Masakazu Fujii was settling down cross-legged to read the Osaka *Asahi* on the porch of his private hospital, overhanging one of the seven deltaic[1] rivers which divide Hiroshima; Mrs. Hatsuyo Nakamura, a tailor's widow, stood by the window of her kitchen, watching a neighbor tearing down his house because it lay in the path of an air-raid-defense fire lane; Father Wilhelm Kleinsorge, a German

priest of the Society of Jesus, reclined in his underwear on a cot on the top floor of his order's three-story mission house, reading a Jesuit magazine, *Stimmen der Zeit;*[2] Dr. Terufumi Sasaki, a young member of the surgical staff of the city's large, modern Red Cross Hospital, walked along one of the hospital corridors with a blood specimen for a Wassermann test[3] in his hand; and the Reverend Mr. Kiyoshi Tanimoto, pastor of the Hiroshima Methodist Church, paused at the door of a rich man's house in Koi, the city's western suburb, and prepared to unload a handcart full of things he had evacu-

---

1. **deltaic.** Related to the triangular deposits at the mouth of a river
2. *Stimmen der Zeit.* [German] "Voices of the time"
3. **Wassermann test.** Blood test used to diagnose syphilis

ated from town in fear of the massive B-29 raid which everyone expected Hiroshima to suffer. A hundred thousand people were killed by the atomic bomb, and these six were among the survivors. They still wonder why they lived when so many others died. Each of them counts many small items of chance or <u>volition</u>—a step taken in time, a decision to go indoors, catching one streetcar instead of the next—that spared him. And now each knows that in the act of survival he lived a dozen lives and saw more death than he ever thought he would see. At the time, none of them knew anything.

The Reverend Mr. Tanimoto got up at five o'clock that morning. He was alone in the parsonage,[4] because for some time his wife had been commuting with their year-old baby to spend nights with a friend in Ushida, a suburb to the north. Of all the important cities of Japan, only two, Kyoto and Hiroshima, had been visited in strength by *B-san,* or Mr. B, as the Japanese, with a mixture of respect and unhappy familiarity, called the B-29; and Mr. Tanimoto, like all his neighbors and friends, was almost sick with anxiety. He had heard uncomfortably detailed accounts of mass raids on Kure, Iwakuni, Tokuyama, and other nearby towns; he was sure Hiroshima's turn would come soon. He had slept badly the night before, because there had been several air raid warnings. Hiroshima had been getting such warnings almost every night for weeks, for at that time the B-29s were using Lake Biwa, northeast of Hiroshima, as a rendezvous point, and no matter what city the Americans planned to hit, the Superfortresses streamed in over the coast near Hiroshima. The frequency of the warnings and the continued abstinence of Mr. B with respect to Hiroshima had made its citizens jittery; a rumor was going around that the Americans were saving something special for the city.

Mr. Tanimoto is a small man, quick to talk, laugh, and cry. He wears his black hair parted in the middle and rather long; the prominence of the frontal bones just above his eyebrows

> A RUMOR WAS GOING AROUND THAT THE AMERICANS WERE SAVING SOMETHING SPECIAL FOR THE CITY.

and the smallness of his mustache, mouth, and chin give him a strange, old-young look, boyish and yet wise, weak and yet fiery. He moves nervously and fast, but with a restraint which suggests that he is a cautious, thoughtful man. He showed, indeed, just those qualities in the uneasy days before the bomb fell. Besides having his wife spend the nights in Ushida, Mr. Tanimoto had been carrying all the portable things from his church, in the close-packed residential district called Nagaragawa, to a house that belonged to a rayon manufacturer in Koi, two miles from the center of town. The rayon man, a Mr. Matsui, had opened his then unoccupied estate to a large number of his friends and acquaintances, so that they might evacuate whatever they wished to a safe distance from the probable target area. Mr. Tanimoto had had no difficulty in moving chairs, hymnals, Bibles, altar gear, and church records by pushcart himself, but the organ console and an upright piano required some aid. A friend of his named Matsuo had, the day before, helped him get the piano out to Koi; in return, he had promised this day to assist Mr. Matsuo in hauling out a daughter's belongings. That is why he had risen so early.

Mr. Tanimoto cooked his own breakfast. He felt awfully tired. The effort of moving the piano the day before, a sleepless night, weeks of worry and unbalanced diet, the cares of his parish—all combined to make him feel hardly adequate to the new day's work. There was another thing, too: Mr. Tanimoto had studied theology at Emory College, in Atlanta, Georgia;

---

4. **parsonage.** Home that a church provides for its pastor

vo • li • tion (vō li′ shən) *n.,* choice or decision made

he had graduated in 1940; he spoke excellent English; he dressed in American clothes; he had corresponded with many American friends right up to the time the war began; and among a people obsessed with a fear of being spied upon—perhaps almost obsessed himself—he found himself growing increasingly uneasy. The police had questioned him several times, and just a few days before, he had heard that an influential acquaintance, a Mr. Tanaka, a retired officer of the Toyo Kisen Kaisha steamship line, an anti-Christian, a man famous in Hiroshima for his showy <u>philanthropies</u> and notorious for his personal tyrannies, had been telling people that Tanimoto should not be trusted. In compensation, to show himself publicly a good Japanese, Mr. Tanimoto had taken on the chairmanship of his local *tonarigumi,* or Neighborhood Association, and to his other duties and concerns this position had added the business of organizing air raid defense for about twenty families.

Before six o'clock that morning, Mr. Tanimoto started for Mr. Matsuo's house. There he found that their burden was to be a *tansu,* a large Japanese cabinet, full of clothing and household goods. The two men set out. The morning was perfectly clear and so warm that the day promised to be uncomfortable. A few minutes after they started, the air raid siren went off—a minute-long blast that warned of approaching planes but indicated to the people of Hiroshima only a slight degree of danger, since it sounded every morning at this time, when an American weather plane came over. The two men pulled and pushed the handcart through the city streets. Hiroshima was a fanshaped city, lying mostly on the six islands formed by the seven estuarial rivers[5] that branch out from the Ota River; its main commercial and residential districts, covering about four square miles in the center of the city, contained three-quarters of its population, which had been reduced by several evacuation programs from a wartime peak of 380,000 to about 245,000. Factories and other residential

districts, or suburbs, lay compactly around the edges of the city. To the south were the docks, an airport, and the island-studded Inland Sea. A rim of mountains runs around the other three sides of the delta. Mr. Tanimoto and Mr. Matsuo took their way through the shopping center, already full of people, and across two of the rivers to the sloping streets of Koi, and up them to the outskirts and foothills. As they started up a valley away from the tight-ranked houses, the all-clear sounded. (The Japanese radar operators, detecting only three planes,

---

5. **estuarial rivers.** Rivers that meet the sea

phi • lan • thro • py (fə lanʹ thrō pē) *n.,* act or gift of dispensing aid or funds set aside for humanitarian purposes

This torii (gate) is part of the Itsukushima Shrine, which is located on the island of Miyajima ("shrine island") near Hiroshima. The Shinto shrine was established in 1168, although shrines have existed on this site since the sixth century. Visitors to the shrine pass under the torii by boat to purify themselves before entering.

supposed that they comprised a reconnaissance.[6]) Pushing the handcart up to the rayon man's house was tiring, and the men, after they had maneuvered their load into the driveway and to the front steps, paused to rest awhile. They stood with a wing of the house between them and the city. Like most homes in this part of Japan, the house consisted of a wooden frame and wooden walls supporting a heavy tile roof. Its front hall, packed with rolls of bedding and clothing, looked like a cool cave full of fat cushions. Opposite the house, to the right of the front door, there was a large, finicky rock garden. There was no sound of planes. The morning was still; the place was cool and pleasant.

Then a tremendous flash of light cut across the sky. Mr. Tanimoto has a distinct recollection that it traveled from east to west, from the city toward the hills. It seemed a sheet of sun. Both he and Mr. Matsuo reacted in terror—and both had time to react (for they were 3,500 yards, or two miles, from the center of the explosion). Mr. Matsuo dashed up the front steps into the house and dived among the bedrolls and buried himself there. Mr. Tanimoto took four or five steps and threw himself between two big rocks in the garden. He bellied up very hard against one of them. As his face was against the stone, he did not see what happened. He felt a sudden pressure, and then splinters and pieces of board and fragments of tile fell on him. He heard no roar. (Almost no one in Hiroshima recalls hearing any noise of the bomb. But a fisherman in his sampan[7] on the Inland Sea near Tsuzu, the man with whom Mr. Tanimoto's mother-in-law and sister-in-law were living, saw the flash and heard a tremendous explosion; he was nearly twenty miles from Hiroshima, but the thunder was greater than when the B-29s hit Iwakuni, only five miles away.)

> THEN A TREMENDOUS FLASH OF LIGHT CUT ACROSS THE SKY.

When he dared, Mr. Tanimoto raised his head and saw that the rayon man's house had collapsed. He thought a bomb had fallen directly on it. Such clouds of dust had risen that there was a sort of twilight around. In panic, not thinking for the moment of Mr. Matsuo under the ruins, he dashed out into the street. He noticed as he ran that the concrete wall of the estate had fallen over—toward the house rather than away from it. In the street, the first thing he saw was a squad of soldiers who had been burrowing into the hillside opposite, making one of the thousands of dugouts in which the Japanese

6. **reconnaissance.** Exploratory military survey of enemy territory
7. **sampan.** Small, flat-bottomed Asian boat

apparently intended to resist invasion, hill by hill, life for life; the soldiers were coming out of the hole, where they should have been safe, and blood was running from their heads, chests, and backs. They were silent and dazed.

Under what seemed to be a local dust cloud, the day grew darker and darker.

At nearly midnight, the night before the bomb was dropped, an announcer on the city's radio station said that about two hundred B-29s were approaching southern Honshu[8] and advised the population of Hiroshima to evacuate to their designated "safe areas." Mrs. Hatsuyo Nakamura, the tailor's widow, who lived in the section called Noboricho and who had long had a habit of doing as she was told, got her three children—a ten-year-old boy, Toshio, an eight-year-old girl, Yaeko, and a five-year-old girl, Myeko—out of bed and dressed them and walked with them to the military area known as the East Parade Ground, on the northeast edge of the city. There she unrolled some mats and the children lay down on them. They slept until about two, when they were awakened by the roar of the planes going over Hiroshima.

> THEY SLEPT UNTIL ABOUT TWO, WHEN THEY WERE AWAKENED BY THE ROAR OF THE PLANES GOING OVER HIROSHIMA.

As soon as the planes had passed, Mrs. Nakamura started back with her children. They reached home a little after two-thirty and she immediately turned on the radio, which, to her distress, was just then broadcasting a fresh warning. When she looked at the children and saw how tired they were, and when she thought of the number of trips they had made in past weeks, all to no purpose, to the East Parade Ground, she decided that in spite of the instructions on the radio, she simply could

not face starting out all over again. She put the children in their bedrolls on the floor, lay down herself at three o'clock, and fell asleep at once, so soundly that when the planes passed over later, she did not waken to their sound.

The siren jarred her awake at about seven. She arose, dressed quickly, and hurried to the house of Mr. Nakamoto, the head of her Neighborhood Association, and asked him what she should do. He said that she should remain at home unless an urgent warning—a series of intermittent blasts of the siren—was sounded. She returned home, lit the stove in the kitchen, set some rice to cook, and sat down to read that morning's Hiroshima *Chugoku*. To her relief, the all-clear sounded at eight o'clock. She heard the children stirring, so she went and gave each of them a handful of peanuts and told them to stay on their bedrolls, because they were tired from the night's walk. She had hoped that they would go back to sleep, but the man in the house directly to the south began to make a terrible hullabaloo[9] of hammering, wedging, ripping, and splitting. The prefectural[10] government, convinced, as everyone in Hiroshima was, that the city would be attacked soon, had begun to press with threats and warnings for the completion of wide fire lanes, which, it was hoped, might act in conjunction with the rivers to localize any fires started by an incendiary

---

8. **Honshu.** Largest island of Japan
9. **hullabaloo.** Loud, confused noise
10. **prefectural.** Relating to a district governed by a chief officer

---

in • ter • mit • tent (in tʉr mit′ ənt) *adj.*, coming and going at intervals; not continuous

in • cen • di • ary (in sen′ dē ār ē) *adj.*, relating to or involving deliberate burning of property

raid; and the neighbor was reluctantly sacrificing his home to the city's safety. Just the day before, the prefecture had ordered all able-bodied girls from the secondary schools to spend a few days helping to clear these lanes, and they started work soon after the all-clear sounded.

Mrs. Nakamura went back to the kitchen, looked at the rice, and began watching the man next door. At first, she was annoyed with him for making so much noise, but then she was moved almost to tears by pity. Her emotion was specifically directed toward her neighbor, tearing down his home, board by board, at a time when there was so much unavoidable destruction, but undoubtedly she also felt a generalized, community pity, to say nothing of self-pity. She had not had an easy time. Her husband, Isawa, had gone into the Army just after Myeko was born, and she had heard nothing from or of him for a long time, until, on March 5, 1942, she received a seven-word telegram: "Isawa died an honorable death at Singapore." She learned later that he had died on February 15th, the day Singapore fell, and that he had been a corporal. Isawa had been a not particularly prosperous tailor, and his only capital was a Sankoku sewing machine. After his death, his allotments[11] stopped coming, Mrs. Nakamura got out the machine and began to take in piecework herself, and since then had supported the children, but poorly, by sewing.

As Mrs. Nakamura stood watching her neighbor, everything flashed whiter than any white she had ever seen. She did not notice what happened to the man next door; the reflex of a mother set her in motion toward her children. She had taken a single step (the house was 1,350 yards, or three-quarters of a mile, from the center of the explosion) when something picked her up and she seemed to fly into the next room over the raised sleeping platform, pursued by parts of her house.

Timbers fell around her as she landed, and a shower of tiles pommelled her; everything became dark, for she was buried. The debris

AS MRS. NAKAMURA STOOD WATCHING HER NEIGHBOR, EVERYTHING FLASHED WHITER THAN ANY WHITE SHE HAD EVER SEEN.

did not cover her deeply. She rose up and freed herself. She heard a child cry, "Mother, help me!," and saw her youngest—Myeko, the five-year-old—buried up to her breast and unable to move. As Mrs. Nakamura started frantically to claw her way toward the baby, she could see or hear nothing of her other children.

In the days right before the bombing, Dr. Masakazu Fujii, being prosperous, hedonistic, and at the time not too busy, had been allowing himself the luxury of sleeping until nine or nine-thirty, but fortunately he had to get up early the morning the bomb was dropped to see a house guest off on a train. He rose at six, and half an hour later walked with his friend to the station, not far away, across two of the rivers. He was back home by seven, just as the siren sounded its sustained warning. He ate breakfast and then, because the morning was already hot, undressed down to his underwear and went out on the porch to read the paper. This porch—in fact, the whole building—was curiously constructed. Dr. Fujii was the proprietor of a peculiarly Japanese institution: a private, single-doctor hospital. This building, perched beside and over the water of the Kyo River, and next to the bridge of the same name, contained thirty rooms for thirty patients and their kinfolk—for, according to Japanese custom, when a person falls sick and goes to a hospital, one or more members of his family go and live there with him, to cook for him, bathe, massage, and read to

---

11. **allotments.** Monetary payments provided by the government

he • do • nis • tic (hē də nis´ tik) *adj.*, relating to or characterized by pleasure

An aerial view of Hiroshima one day after the bombing (August 7, 1945).

him, and to offer <u>incessant</u> familial sympathy, without which a Japanese patient would be miserable indeed. Dr. Fujii had no beds—only straw mats—for his patients. He did, however, have all sorts of modern equipment: an x-ray machine, diathermy apparatus,[12] and a fine tiled laboratory. The structure rested two-thirds on the land, one-third on piles over the tidal waters of the Kyo. This overhang, the part of the building where Dr. Fujii lived, was queer-looking, but it was cool in summer and from the porch, which faced away from the center of the city, the prospect of the river, with pleasure boats drifting up and down it, was always refreshing. Dr. Fujii had occasionally had anxious moments when the Ota and its mouth branches rose to flood, but the piling was apparently firm enough and the house had always held.

Dr. Fujii had been relatively idle for about a month because in July, as the number of untouched cities in Japan dwindled and as Hiroshima seemed more and more inevitably a target, he began turning patients away, on the ground that in case of a fire raid he would not be able to evacuate them. Now he had only two patients left—a woman from Yano, injured in the shoulder, and a young man of twenty-five recovering from burns he had suffered when the steel factory near Hiroshima in which he worked had been hit. Dr. Fujii had six nurses to tend his patients. His wife and children were safe; his wife and one son were living outside Osaka, and another son and two daughters were in the country on Kyushu.[13] A niece was living with him, and a maid and a manservant. He had little to do and did not mind, for he had saved some money. At fifty, he was healthy, <u>convivial</u>, and calm, and he was pleased to pass the evenings drinking whiskey with friends, always sensibly and for the sake of conversation. Before the war, he had *affected* brands imported from Scotland and America; now he was perfectly satisfied with the best Japanese brand, Suntory.

Dr. Fujii sat down cross-legged in his underwear on the spotless matting of the porch, put on his glasses, and started reading the Osaka *Asahi*. He liked to read the Osaka news because his wife was there. He saw the flash. To him—faced away from the center and looking at his paper—it seemed a brilliant yellow. Startled, he began to rise to his feet. In that moment (he was 1,550 yards from the center), the hospital leaned behind his rising and, with a terrible ripping noise, toppled into the river. The Doctor, still in the act of getting to his feet, was thrown forward and around

---

12. **diathermy apparatus.** Equipment for heat treatments
13. **Kyushu.** Southernmost of the main islands of Japan

in • ces • sant (in ses´ ənt) *adj.,* continuing or following without interruption
con • viv • i • al (kən vi´ vē əl) *adj.,* relating to feasting, drinking, and good company

and over; he was buffeted and gripped; he lost track of everything, because things were so speeded up; he felt the water.

Dr. Fujii hardly had time to think that he was dying before he realized that he was alive, squeezed tightly by two long timbers in a V across his chest, like a morsel suspended between two huge chopsticks—held upright, so that he could not move, with his head miraculously above water and his torso and legs in it. The remains of his hospital were all around him in a mad assortment of splintered lumber and materials for the relief of pain. His left shoulder hurt terribly. His glasses were gone.

> DR. FUJII HARDLY HAD TIME TO THINK THAT HE WAS DYING BEFORE HE REALIZED THAT HE WAS ALIVE.

Father Wilhelm Kleinsorge, of the Society of Jesus, was, on the morning of the explosion, in rather frail condition. The Japanese wartime diet had not sustained him, and he felt the strain of being a foreigner in an increasingly xenophobic Japan; even a German, since the defeat of the Fatherland,[14] was unpopular. Father Kleinsorge had, at thirty-eight, the look of a boy growing too fast—thin in the face, with a prominent Adam's apple, a hollow chest, dangling hands, big feet. He walked clumsily, leaning forward a little. He was tired all the time. To make matters worse, he had suffered for two days, along with Father Cieslik, a fellow-priest, from a rather painful and urgent diarrhea, which they blamed on the beans and black ration bread they were obliged to eat. Two other priests then living in the mission compound, which was in the Noboricho section—Father Superior LaSalle and Father Schiffer—had happily escaped this affliction.

Father Kleinsorge woke up about six the morning the bomb was dropped, and half an hour later—he was a bit tardy because of his sickness—he began to read Mass in the mission chapel, a small Japanese-style wooden building which was without pews, since its worshipers knelt on the usual Japanese matted floor, facing an altar graced with splendid silks, brass, silver, and heavy embroideries. This morning, a Monday, the only worshipers were Mr. Takemoto, a theological student living in the mission house; Mr. Fukai, the secretary of the diocese;[15] Mrs. Murata, the mission's devoutly Christian housekeeper; and his fellow-priests. After Mass, while Father Kleinsorge was reading the Prayers of Thanksgiving, the siren sounded. He stopped the service and the missionaries retired across the compound to the bigger building. There, in his room on the ground floor, to the right of the front door, Father Kleinsorge changed into a military uniform which he had acquired when he was teaching at the Rokko Middle School in Kobe and which he wore during air raid alerts.

After an alarm, Father Kleinsorge always went out and scanned the sky, and in this instance, when he stepped outside, he was glad to see only the single weather plane that flew over Hiroshima each day about this time. Satisfied that nothing would happen, he went in and breakfasted with the other Fathers on substitute coffee and ration bread, which, under the circumstances, was especially repugnant to him. The Fathers sat and talked a while, until, at eight, they heard the all-clear. They went then to various parts of the building. Father Schiffer retired to his room to do some writing. Father Cieslik sat in his room in a straight chair with a pillow over his stomach to ease his pain, and read. Father Superior LaSalle stood at the window of his room, thinking. Father Kleinsorge went up to a room on the third

---

14. **defeat of the Fatherland.** Germany surrendered in May 1945.
15. **diocese.** Territorial jurisdiction of a bishop

> **xe • no • pho • bic** (zē' nō fō´ bik) *adj.*, fearful of or showing hatred toward foreigners
> **theo • log • i • cal** (thē ō lä´ jik 'l) *adj.*, of, or relating to theology, or the study of religious faith, practice, and experience
> **re • pug • nant** (rē pug´ nənt) *adj.*, causing distaste or aversion

An American soldier views the rubble of a formerly luxurious mansion in Hiroshima.

floor, took off all his clothes except his under-wear, and stretched out on his right side on a cot and began reading his *Stimmen der Zeit.*

FATHER KLEINSORGE NEVER KNEW HOW HE GOT OUT OF THE HOUSE.

After the terrible flash—which, Father Kleinsorge later realized, reminded him of something he had read as a boy about a large meteor colliding with the earth—he had time (since he was 1,400 yards from the center) for one thought: A bomb has fallen directly on us. Then, for a few seconds or minutes, he went out of his mind.

Father Kleinsorge never knew how he got out of the house. The next things he was con-scious of were that he was wandering around in the mission's vegetable garden in his under-wear, bleeding slightly from small cuts along his left flank; that all the buildings round about had fallen down except the Jesuits' mission

house, which had long before been braced and double-braced by a priest named Groppe, who was terrified of earthquakes; that the day had turned dark; and that Murata-*san,* the house-keeper, was nearby, crying over and over, "*Shu Jesusu, awaremi tamia!* Our Lord Jesus, have pity on us!"

On the train on the way into Hiroshima from the country, where he lived with his mother, Dr. Terufumi Sasaki, the Red Cross Hospital surgeon, thought over an unpleasant nightmare he had had the night before. His mother's home was in Mukaihara, thirty miles from the city, and it took him two hours by train and tram[16] to reach the hospital. He had slept uneasily all night and had wakened an hour earlier than usual, and, feeling sluggish and slightly feverish, had debated whether to go to the hospital at all; his sense of duty finally forced him to go, and he had started out on an earlier train than he took most mornings. The

---

16. **tram.** Streetcar

After the bombing, Japanese children used face masks and umbrellas to protect themselves from fumes and falling ashes.

dream had particularly frightened him because it was so closely associated, on the surface at least, with a disturbing actuality. He was only twenty-five years old and had just completed his training at the Eastern Medical University, in Tsingtao,[17] China. He was something of an idealist and was much distressed by the inadequacy of medical facilities in the country town where his mother lived. Quite on his own, and without a permit, he had begun visiting a few sick people out there in the evenings, after his eight hours at the hospital and four hours' commuting. He had recently learned that the penalty for practicing without a permit was severe; a fellow-doctor whom he had asked about it had given him a serious scolding. Nevertheless, he had continued to practice. In his dream, he had been at the bedside of a country patient when the police and the doctor he had consulted burst into the room, seized him, dragged

him outside, and beat him up cruelly. On the train, he just about decided to give up the work in Mukaihara, since he felt it would be impossible to get a permit, because the authorities would hold that it would conflict with his duties at the Red Cross Hospital.

At the terminus,[18] he caught a streetcar at once. (He later calculated that if he had taken his customary train that morning, and if he had had to wait a few minutes for the streetcar, as often happened, he would have been close to the center at the time of the explosion and would surely have perished.) He arrived at the hospital at seven-forty and reported to the chief surgeon. A few minutes later, he went to a room on the first floor and drew blood from the arm of a man in order to perform a

---

17. **Tsingtao.** Large Chinese city on the Yellow River, which was occupied by Japan during World War II
18. **terminus.** Station at the end of a transportation line

The ruined framework of the Museum of Science and Industry was left in place after the Hiroshima bombing as a memorial to the tragedy.

Wassermann test. The laboratory containing the incubators for the test was on the third floor. With the blood specimen in his left hand, walking in a kind if distraction he had felt all morning, probably because of the dream and his restless night, he started along the main corridor on his way toward the stairs. He was one step beyond an open window when the light of the bomb was reflected, like a gigantic photograph flash, in the corridor. He ducked down on one knee and said to himself, as only a Japanese would, "Sasaki, *gambare!* Be brave!" Just then (the building was 1,650 yards from the center), the blast ripped through the hospital. The glasses he was wearing flew off his face; the bottle of blood crashed against one wall, his Japanese slippers zipped out from under his feet—but otherwise, thanks to where he stood, he was untouched.

Dr. Sasaki shouted the name of the chief surgeon and rushed around to the man's office and found him terribly cut by glass. The hospi-

HE WAS ONE STEP BEYOND AN OPEN WINDOW WHEN THE LIGHT OF THE BOMB WAS REFLECTED, LIKE A GIGANTIC PHOTOGRAPH FLASH, IN THE CORRIDOR.

tal was in horrible confusion: heavy partitions and ceilings had fallen on patients, beds had overturned, windows had blown in and cut people, blood was spattered on the walls and floors, instruments were everywhere, many of the patients were running about screaming, many more lay dead. (A colleague working in the laboratory to which Dr. Sasaki had been walking was dead; Dr. Sasaki's patient, whom he had just left and who a few moments before had been dreadfully afraid of syphilis, was also dead.) Dr. Sasaki found himself the only doctor in the hospital who was unhurt.

Dr. Sasaki, who believed that the enemy had hit only the building he was in, got bandages and began to bind the wounds of those inside the hospital; while outside, all over Hiroshima, maimed and dying citizens turned their unsteady steps toward the Red Cross Hospital to begin an invasion that was to make Dr. Sasaki forget his private nightmare for a long, long time.

Miss Toshiko Sasaki, the East Asia Tin Works clerk, who is not related to Dr. Sasaki, got up at three o'clock in the morning on the day the bomb fell. There was extra housework to do. Her eleven-month-old brother, Akio, had come down the day before with a serious stomach upset; her mother had taken him to the Tamura Pediatric Hospital and was staying there with him. Miss Sasaki, who was about twenty, had to cook breakfast for her father, a brother, a sister, and herself, and—since the hospital, because of the war, was unable to provide food—to prepare a whole day's meals for her mother and the baby, in time for her Father, who worked in a factory making rubber earplugs for artillery crews, to take the food by on his way to the plant. When she had finished and had cleaned and put away the cooking things, it was nearly seven. The family lived in Koii, and she had a forty-five minute trip to the Kannonmachi. She was in charge of personnel records in the factory. She left Koi at seven, and as soon as she reached the plant, she went with some of the other girls from the personnel department to the factory auditorium. A prominent local Navy man, a former employee, had commit-

ted suicide the day before by throwing himself under a train—a death considered honorable enough to warrant a memorial service, which was to be held at the tin works at ten o'clock that morning. In the large hall, Miss Sasaki and the others made suitable preparations for the meeting. This work took about twenty minutes.

Miss Sasaki went back to her office and sat down at her desk. She was quite far from the windows, which were off to her left, and behind her were a couple of tall bookcases containing all the books of the factory library, which the personnel department had organized. She settled herself at her desk, put some things in a drawer, and shifted papers. She thought that before she began to make entries in her lists of new employees, discharges, and departures for the Army, she would chat for a moment with the girl at her right. Just as she turned her head away from the windows, the room was filled with a blinding light. She was paralyzed by fear, fixed still in her chair for a long moment (the plant was 1,600 yards from the center).

Everything fell, and Miss Sasaki lost consciousness. The ceiling dropped suddenly and the wooden floor above collapsed in splinters and the people up there came down and the roof above them gave way; but principally and first of all, the bookcases right behind her swooped forward and the contents threw her down, with her left leg horribly twisted and breaking underneath her. There, in the tin factory, in the first moment of the atomic age, a human being was crushed by books. ❖

 **MIRRORS & WINDOWS**

Hersey wrote, "And now each [of the survivors] knows that in the act of survival he lived a dozen lives and saw more death than he ever thought he would see." What emotions might be evoked in someone who survives a tragedy of this magnitude?

The U.S.S. *Indianapolis*

On July 26, 1945, the U.S.S. *Indianapolis,* a state-of-the-art navy cruiser, delivered an atomic bomb to a U.S. airbase on Tinian, one of the Marianas Islands. Eleven days later, that bomb, code named "Little Boy," was dropped on Hiroshima, Japan. After returning to Guam to restock and receive new orders, the ship sailed again on July 28 to the Philippines.

Just after midnight on July 29–30, the *Indianapolis* was hit by two torpedoes from a Japanese submarine. The ship capsized and sank within twelve minutes. Approximately 300 men died in the attack. The remainder of the crew, almost 900 sailors and marines, spent the next four or five days in the water with only life jackets to keep them afloat.

When the survivors finally were rescued on August 2, just 321 were still alive. The rest had died of lack of food and water, exposure to the elements, and attacks by sharks. With nearly 900 dead, the sinking of the *Indianapolis* remains the worst at-sea loss of life in the history of the U.S. Navy.

Captain Charles McVay was court-martialed for hazarding his ship by not following a zig-zagging course (a maneuver intended to avert submarine attacks). In McVay's trial, Mochitsura Hashimoto, commander of the Japanese submarine that sank the *Indianapolis,* testified that even if the captain had performed this maneuver, the Japanese still would have torpedoed her. Most of McVay's crew also stood in support of him. Nonetheless, McVay was convicted, the only captain to be court martialed of the hundreds who lost ships during World War II.

The stain on McVay's record remained in place until 1996, when a curious schoolboy got involved. Hunter Scott, an eleven-year-old from Pensacola, Florida, decided to do a report on the sinking of the *Indianapolis.* He had learned about the tragedy from a scene in the movie *Jaws,* in which a character recounts surviving the shark attacks after the cruiser sank. Scott sent out questionnaires to the ship's remaining survivors, asking for their opinions about McVay's conviction. After receiving responses strongly in defense of the captain, Scott set out to clear McVay's name.

In 1999, Scott and the survivors testified at a hearing before the Senate Armed Services Committee. The strongest piece of the testimony in defense of McVay was, once again, from Mochitsura Hashimoto, the Japanese submarine commander. In a letter to the chairman of the committee, he wrote:

> I have met many of your brave men who survived the sinking of the *Indianapolis.* I would like to join them in urging that your national legislature clear their captain's name. Our peoples have forgiven each other for that terrible war and its consequences. Perhaps it is time your peoples forgave Captain McVay for the humiliation of his unjust conviction.

In October 2000, the U.S. Congress passed a resolution exonerating Captain Charles McVay in the loss of the U.S.S. *Indianapolis.* President Bill Clinton also signed the resolution, finally ending the proud ship's tragic story.

Refer to Text ▶ ▶ ▶ ▶ ▶ Reason with Text

1a. Name the people Hersey identifies in the opening paragraph, and describe what each was doing at the time of the bombing.	**1b.** Summarize Hersey's purpose for focusing on six individuals.	**Understand** Find meaning
2a. What "strain" does Father Kleinsorge feel that the other survivors do not? What did he do whenever the air raid sirens sounded?	**2b.** Relate Father Kleinsorge's actions to the strain he feels.	**Apply** Use information
3a. Identify the images Hersey uses to describe the explosion of the bomb, as seen by each survivor. Which survivors are hurt?	**3b.** Compare and contrast the survivors' experiences of the blast and its immediate physical effects on them.	**Analyze** Take things apart
4a. How is *Hiroshima* more like a fictional work of literature, such as a novel or short story, than a work of journalism, such as a newspaper story?	**4b.** According to Hersey, "[Journalism] allows the reader to witness history; fiction gives its readers an opportunity to live it." Assess this statement in relation to the selection.	**Evaluate** Make judgments
5a. List the details Hersey provides about the Japanese medical system of the time.	**5b.** How were sick people cared for in Japan during World War II? How does that standard of care compare to that of today?	**Create** Bring ideas together

Analyze Literature

Point of View and Irony

From what point of view is *Hiroshima* told? What makes this point of view effective for this particular genre and subject matter?

Identify several examples of situational irony in this excerpt. Which example is the most powerful? Why?

Extend the Text

Writing Options

Creative Writing Write a journal entry from one of the people in Hersey's account dated August 5, 1945—the day before the bombing. Try to portray a normal day in this person's life by describing everyday activities, conversations, and so on.

Persuasive Writing Write one page in which you argue which would be more effective: a novel about the bombing of Hiroshima, told by a fictional character in the story, or a nonfiction account about the survivors, written from a journalist's perspective. Address the benefits and drawbacks of each type of work.

Lifelong Learning

Create a Bibliography Working in a small group, create a bibliography of five works of literary nonfiction.

For each work, provide the author, title, and publication information and offer a brief description. Then have each group member write a few sentences explaining which works he or she would most like to read and why.

Media Literacy

Analyze a Documentary Many documentaries have been made about the Hiroshima bombing. Choose one, such as ABC's *Hiroshima: Why the Bomb Was Dropped* (1995), to view as a class. Then discuss these questions: Does the documentary seem fair and accurate? What position, if any, do the filmmakers seem to promote? Have Americans' views of the bombing changed over time?

 Go to **www.mirrorsandwindows.com** for more.

1. Which of the following most likely explains why Hersey decided to present the specific accounts of individual survivors, rather than describe the effects of the bombing in more general terms?
   A. Telling individuals' stories makes the piece seem more real and personal.
   B. Presenting the survivors as characters makes the piece seem more literary.
   C. Describing specific individuals' experiences shows what a narrow range of people were directly affected by the bombing.
   D. Describing others' experiences helps create distance from the tragedy, ensuring that those who read the piece will know this could never happen to them.
   E. Recounting a few people's stories makes the tragedy seem less immense and thus less grim.

2. Why did Mr. Tanimoto take on chairmanship of his local Neighborhood Association?
   A. to prove that he was not a spy
   B. because he was a spy
   C. to meet new people
   D. to help the people in his neighborhood
   E. to pass time while his family was hiding safely away from the city

3. To what do the six people Hersey interviewed credit their miraculous survival?
   A. having a strong will to live
   B. heeding warnings of attack and being prepared for the disaster
   C. having important work yet to do in their lives
   D. being far away from the center of the blast
   E. making seemingly unimportant decisions that affected where they were and what they were doing

4. Which of the following does *not* illustrate some aspect of Japanese culture?
   A. Dr. Sasaki first reacts to the blast by telling himself to be brave.
   B. Dr. Fujii's hospital has rooms for the patients' family members to stay and take care of them.
   C. Mrs. Nakamura has her children sleep on bedrolls on the floor.
   D. Dr. Sasaki wears slippers in the hospital.
   E. Everyone wakes up very early in the morning.

5. Father Kleinsorge is described as "breakfast[ing] with the other Fathers on substitute coffee and ration bread, which, under the circumstances, was especially repugnant to him." What word could be substituted for *repugnant* in this description?
   A. filling
   B. disgusting
   C. pleasing
   D. tiresome
   E. unsatisfying

6. What does *buffeted* mean, as used in the following sentence? "The Doctor, still in the act of getting to his feet, was thrown forward and around and over; he was *buffeted* and gripped; he lost track of everything, because things were so speeded up; he felt the water."
   A. seized or restrained
   B. battered or beaten
   C. forced or attacked
   D. cushioned or protected
   E. made unconscious

7. **Constructed Response:** Describe how Hersey uses irony in his retelling of the survivors' accounts in "A Noiseless Flash." How does the use of irony enhance your understanding of what happened? Use examples from the text to support your answer.

8. **Constructed Response:** Explain how Hersey develops the people in "A Noiseless Flash" as characters in a story. What information does he provide about them? How does knowing this information affect your understanding of the account? Focus on two characters, and support your explanation using details from the text.

Understand the Concept

A verb is in the **active voice** when the subject of the verb *performs* the action. A verb is in the **passive voice** when the subject of the verb *receives* the action.

> **EXAMPLES**
>
> **Active** The United States *dropped* an atomic bomb on Hiroshima.
>
> **Passive** An atomic bomb *was dropped* on Hiroshima by the United States.

Although most writers use a combination of active and passive verbs, skillful writers tend to use more active verbs. Active verbs make writing sound more natural, alive, and interesting. In *Hiroshima,* for example, John Hersey uses active voice sentences to describe the effects of dropping the atomic bomb on Hiroshima. Consider this active voice sentence from the selection:

> **EXAMPLE**
>
> The two men pulled and pushed the handcart through the city streets.

If Hersey had written this sentence using passive voice, it would have been much less vivid:

> **EXAMPLE**
>
> The handcart was pulled and pushed through the city streets.

To eliminate passive voice from your own writing, construct sentences in which the subject is the *actor.* Notice how each passive voice sentence is rewritten in the following examples:

> **EXAMPLES**
>
> **Passive** The school *was flooded* with requests from students for a longer vacation.
> **Active** Students *flooded* the school with requests for a longer vacation.
> **Passive** The decision to extend spring break an extra week *was accepted* by everyone.
> **Active** Everyone *accepted* the decision to extend spring break an extra week.

Apply the Skill

Identify Passive and Active Voice Sentences
Copy the following sentences on a separate sheet of paper. Then label each as being written in active (A) or passive (P) voice.

1. Asia, Italy, and the Soviet Union were visited by John Hersey, a foreign correspondent.
2. Novelist Sinclair Lewis hired Hersey as his private secretary.
3. In writing *Hiroshima,* Hersey helped develop a new genre, a combination of journalism and literature.
4. In 1945, the Pulitzer Prize in fiction was received by Hersey for *A Bell for Adano.*
5. For this novel, Hersey's experiences as a war correspondent were recalled by him.

Revise Passive Voice Sentences
Rewrite each sentence that you labeled "P" using the active voice. Then compare the original and revised versions. Do you prefer the passive voice for any of the sentences? If so, why?

Evaluate Use of Passive Voice
Working in small groups, identify sentences from *Hiroshima* that are written in passive voice. Then rewrite each using active voice. As a class, discuss which sentences you prefer: the passive voice sentences Hersey wrote or your own active voice revisions. Why might Hersey have used passive voice in these instances?

Use Active and Passive Voice
Write six sentences about the bombing of Hiroshima: three in active voice and three in passive voice.

The Watch

by Elie Wiesel

Elie Wiesel (b. 1928) is a survivor of the Holocaust, Nazi Germany's program for systematically killing Jews and other minorities during World War II. Born in Sighet, Romania, Wiesel was deported to the concentration camp at Auschwitz in 1944 and later moved to Buchenwald, another camp. His parents and younger sister also were sent to camps, but they did not survive.

After the war, Wiesel moved to France, and in 1956, he settled in the United States. In 1958, he published his first book, *Night,* a memoir of his experiences in concentration camps. Since then, he has written thirty-some other works on religion, hatred, and genocide. In addition, Wiesel operates a foundation whose mission is "to combat indifference, intolerance, and injustice." Wiesel was awarded the Nobel Peace Prize in 1986.

In the memoir **"The Watch,"** Wiesel brings readers to Sighet in late April 1944 to show how the Jewish people of that town were treated by their fellow townspeople after the German occupation. To explain why he dedicated himself to writing about the Holocaust, Wiesel once said, "I felt that having survived I owe something to the dead, . . . and anyone who does not remember betrays them again."

For my bar mitzvah,[1] I remember, I had received a magnificent gold watch. It was the customary gift for the occasion, and was meant to remind each boy that henceforth he would be held responsible for his acts before the Torah[2] and its timeless laws.

But I could not keep my gift. I had to part with it the very day my native town became the pride of the Hungarian nation by chasing from its confines every single one of its Jews. The glorious masters of our municipality[3] were jubilant: they were rid of us, there would be no more kaftans[4] on the streets. The local newspaper was brief and to the point: from now on, it would be possible to state one's place of residence without feeling shame.

The time was late April, 1944.

In the early morning hours of that particular day, after a sleepless night, the ghetto was changed into a cemetery and its residents into gravediggers. We were digging feverishly in the courtyard, the garden, the cellar, consigning to the earth, temporarily we thought, whatever remained of the belongings accumulated by several generations, the sorrow and reward of long years of toil.

My father took charge of the jewelry and valuable papers. His head bowed, he was silently digging near the barn. Not far away, my mother, crouched on the damp ground, was burying the silver candelabra she used only on Shabbat[5] eve; she was moaning softly, and I avoided her eyes. My sisters burrowed near the cellar. The youngest, Tziporah, had chosen the garden, like myself. Solemnly shoveling, she declined my help. What did she have to hide? Her toys? Her school notebooks? As

---

1. **bar mitzvah.** Initiation ceremony held to celebrate the thirteenth birthday of a Jewish boy and his beginning of religious responsibility
2. **Torah.** First five books of the Hebrew scriptures
3. **municipality.** Urban political unit having certain powers of self-government
4. **kaftans.** Ankle-length garments with elbow-length or longer sleeves
5. **Shabbat.** Jewish Sabbath, or day of rest and worship

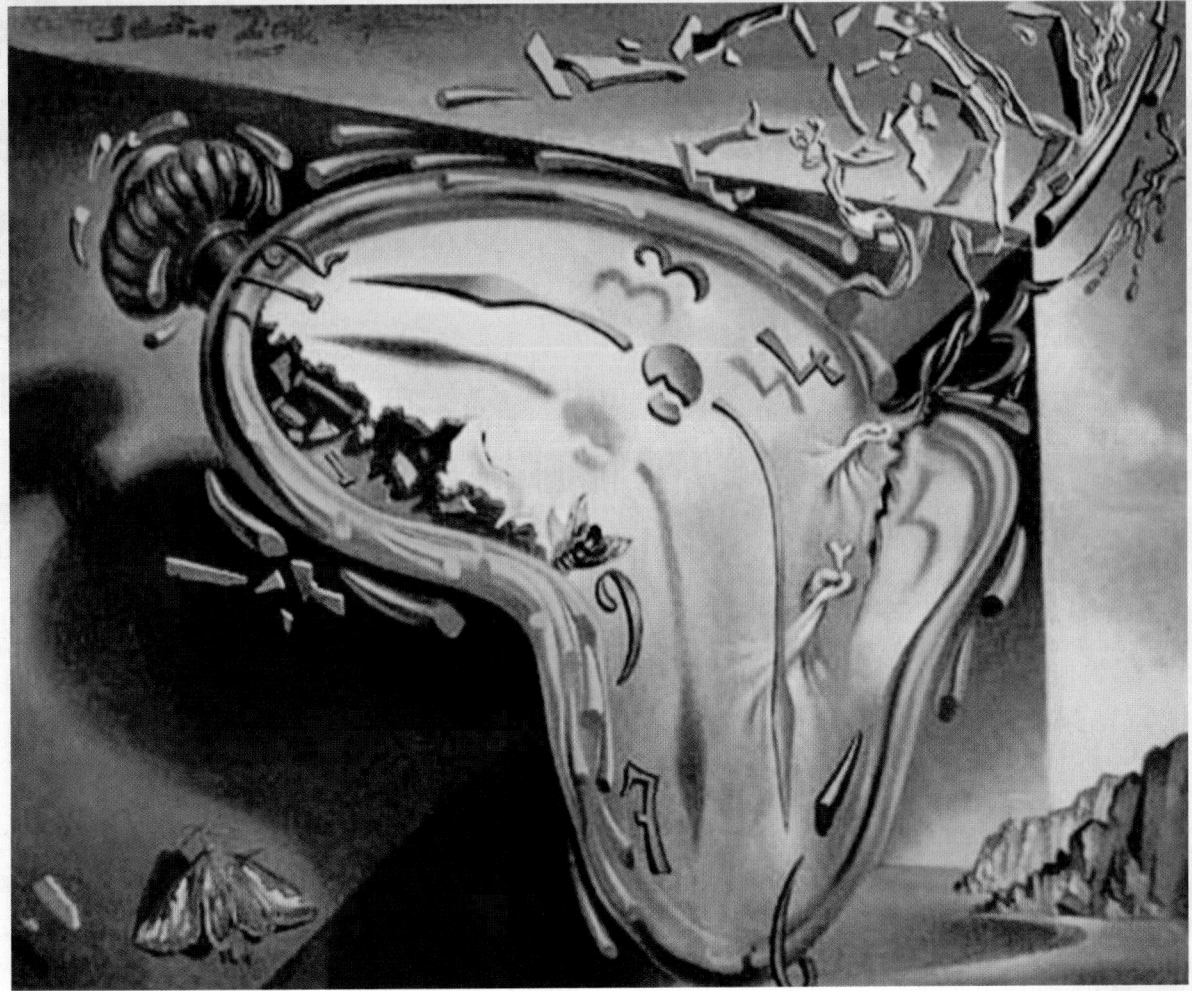

Soft Watch, 1954. Salvador Dali.

for me, my only possession was my watch. It meant a lot to me. And so I decided to bury it in a dark, deep hole, three paces away from the fence, under a poplar tree whose thick, strong foliage seemed to provide a reasonably secure shelter.

All of us expected to recover our treasures. On our return, the earth would give them back to us. Until then, until the end of the storm, they would be safe.

Yes, we were naïve. We could not foresee that the very same evening, before the last train had time to leave the station, an excited mob of well-informed friendly neighbors would be rushing through the ghetto's wide-open houses and courtyards, leaving not a stone or beam unturned, throwing themselves upon the loot.

> All of us expected to recover our treasures. On our return, the earth would give them back to us.

Twenty years later, standing in our garden, in the middle of the night, I remember the first gift, also the last, I ever received from my parents. I am seized by an irrational, irresistible desire to see it, to see if it is still there in the same spot, and if defying all laws of probabil-

After enduring two months of unceasing German artillery, residents of Warsaw, Poland, were moved to a concentration camp just outside the city (October 24, 1944).

my memory recalls. I fall on my knees. What can I use to dig? There is a shovel in the barn; its door is never locked. But by groping around in the dark I risk stumbling and waking the people sleeping in the house. They would take me for a marauder, a thief, and hand me over to the police. They might even kill me. Never mind, I'll have to manage without a shovel. Or any other tool. I'll use my hands, my nails. But it is difficult; the soil is hard, frozen, it resists as if determined to keep its secret. Too bad, I'll punish it by being the stronger.

ity, it has survived—like me—by accident, not knowing how or why. My curiosity becomes obsession. I think neither of my father's money nor of my mother's candlesticks. All that matters in this town is my gold watch and the sound of its ticking.

Despite the darkness, I easily find my way in the garden. Once more I am the bar mitzvah child; here is the barn, the fence, the tree. Nothing has changed. To my left, the path leading to the Slotvino Rebbe's[6] house. The Rebbe, though, had changed: the burning bush[7] burned itself out and there is nothing left, not even smoke. What could he possibly have hidden the day we went away? His phylacteries?[8] His prayer shawl? The holy scrolls inherited from his famous ancestor Rebbe Meirl of Premishlan? No, probably not even that kind of treasure. He had taken everything along, convinced that he was thus protecting not only himself but his disciples as well. He was proved wrong, the wonder rabbi.

But I mustn't think of him, not now. The watch, I must think of the watch. Maybe it was spared. Let's see, three steps to the right. Stop. Two forward. I recognize the place. Instinctively, I get ready to re-enact the scene

Feverishly, furiously, my hands claw the earth, impervious to cold, fatigue and pain. One scratch, then another. No matter. Continue. My nails inch ahead, my fingers dig in, I bear down, my every fiber participates in the task. Little by little the hole deepens. I must hurry. My forehead touches the ground. Almost. I break out in a cold sweat, I am drenched, delirious. Faster, faster. I shall rip the earth from end to end, but I must know. Nothing can stop or frighten me. I'll go to the bottom of my fear, to the bottom of night, but I will know.

What time is it? How long have I been here? Five minutes, five hours? Twenty years. This night was defying time. I was laboring to exhume not an object but time itself, the soul and memory of that time. Nothing could be more urgent, more vital.

Suddenly a shiver goes through me. A sharp sensation, like a bite. My fingers touch some-

---

6. **Slotvino Rebbe's.** Rabbi or spiritual leader of the community
7. **burning bush.** In the Hebrew scriptures, the burning bush burned without being consumed by fire, and God's voice spoke to Moses from the bush.
8. **phylacteries.** Small leather cases that contain texts from the Hebrew Scriptures and that are traditionally worn by Jewish men during their prayers

thing hard, metallic, rectangular. So I have not been digging in vain. The garden is spinning around me, over me. I stand up to catch my breath. A moment later, I'm on my knees again. Cautiously, gently I take the box from its tomb. Here it is, in the palm of my hand: the last relic, the only remaining symbol of everything I had loved, of everything I had been. A voice inside me warns: Don't open it, it contains nothing but emptiness, throw it away and run. I cannot heed the warning; it is too late to turn back. I need to know, either way. A slight pressure of my thumb and the box opens. I stifle the cry rising in my throat: the watch is there. Quick, a match. And another. Fleetingly, I catch a glimpse of it. The pain is blinding: could this thing, this object, be my gift, my pride? My past? Covered with dirt and rust, crawling with worms, it is unrecognizable, revolting. Unable to move, wondering what to do, I remain staring at it with the disgust one feels for love betrayed or a body debased. I am angry with myself for having yielded to curiosity. But disappointment gives way to profound pity: the watch too lived through war and holocaust, the kind reserved for watches perhaps. In its way, it too is a survivor, a ghost infested with humiliating sores and obsolete memories. Suddenly I feel the urge to carry it to my lips, dirty as it is, to kiss and console it with my tears, as one might console a living being, a sick friend returning from far away and requiring much kindness and rest, especially rest.

I touch it, I caress it. What I feel, besides compassion, is a strange kind of gratitude. You see, the men I had believed to be immortal had vanished into fiery clouds. My teachers, my friends, my guides had all deserted me. While this thing, this nameless, lifeless thing had survived for the sole purpose of welcoming me on my return and providing an epilogue[9] to my childhood. And there awakens in me a desire to confide in it, to tell it my adventures, and in exchange, listen to its own. What had happened in my absence: who had first taken possession of my house, my bed? Or rather, no;

our confidences could wait for another time, another place: Paris, New York, Jerusalem. But first I would entrust it to the best jeweler in the world, so that the watch might recover its luster, its memory of the past.

> The pain is blinding: could this thing, this object, be my gift, my pride? My past?

It is growing late. The horizon is turning a deep red. I must go. The tenants will soon be waking, they will come down to the well for water. No time to lose. I stuff the watch into my pocket and cross the garden. I enter the courtyard. From under the porch a dog barks. And stops at once: he knows I am not a thief, anything but a thief. I open the gate. Halfway down the street I am overcome by violent remorse: I have just committed my first theft.

I turn around, retrace my steps through courtyard and garden. Again I find myself kneeling, as at Yom Kippur[10] services, beneath the poplar. Holding my breath, my eyes refusing to cry, I place the watch back into its box, close the cover, and my first gift once more takes refuge deep inside the hole. Using both hands, I smoothly fill in the earth to remove all traces.

Breathless and with pounding heart, I reach the still deserted street. I stop and question the meaning of what I have just done. And find it inexplicable.

In retrospect, I tell myself that probably I simply wanted to leave behind me, underneath the silent soil, a reflection of my presence. Or that somehow I wanted to transform my watch into an instrument of delayed vengeance: one day, a child would play in the garden, dig near

---

9. **epilogue.** Closing section added to a novel, play, or other work to provide further comment, interpretation, or explanation
10. **Yom Kippur.** Day of atonement that Jews observe with fasting and prayer

The sun was rising and I was still walking through the empty streets and alleys. For a moment I thought I heard the chanting of schoolboys studying Talmud; I also thought I heard the invocations of Hasidim[12] reciting morning prayers in thirty-three places at once. Yet above all these incantations, I heard distinctly, but as though coming from far away, the tick-tock of the watch I had just buried in accordance with Jewish custom. It was, after all, the very first gift that a Jewish child had once been given for his very first celebration.

Jewish men, as denoted by the Star of David patches on their jackets, who were liberated from a Polish concentration camp (November 1944).

the tree and stumble upon a metal box. He would thus learn that his parents were usurpers,[11] and that among the inhabitants of his town, once upon a time, there had been Jews and Jewish children, children robbed of their future.

Since that day, the town of my childhood has ceased being just another town. It has become the face of a watch. ❖

---

11. **usurpers.** Those who hold something in possession by force or without right
12. **Hasidim.** Group of Orthodox Jews who follow Jewish laws strictly

The watch is often interpreted as a symbol of Wiesel's childhood. What possession do you consider a symbol of your childhood?

Refer and Reason

1. List the details in this memoir excerpt that imply what happened to Wiesel's family and the other Jews of Sighet. Analyze Wiesel's motivation for not directly stating these people's fate.

2. What emotions does Wiesel feel while digging to find his watch? How does he feel after he finds it? Consider Wiesel's decision to return to his former hometown. What did this visit likely mean to him?

3. What do the people of Sighet feel about the fate of the Jews who once lived there? What events in the world today might Wiesel attribute to indifference? Explain how indifference harms people in daily life, in families, and in interactions with classmates.

Writing Options

1. Write a descriptive paragraph about an object that either is significant to you now or was special in your past. Use your writing style to convey your feelings about this object.

2. Write a review of "The Watch," focusing on Wiesel's writing style. Explain what qualities underlie his style. Also evaluate whether Wiesel's writing style is effective for a work such as "The Watch."

Go to **www.mirrorsandwindows.com** for more.

PART 2

Southern Renaissance

The **Southern Renaissance** movement marked a deliberate break from the region's traditional literary aesthetic. The majority of Southern literature, such as Margaret Mitchell's *Gone with the Wind* (1939), tended to employ stock characters—for example, the submissive slave and the charming Southern belle—to idealize the antebellum (pre–Civil War) South. This literature also tended to minimize the poor treatment of African Americans in order to celebrate traditional Southern values and lifestyles.

Southern Renaissance writers were borne of a different generation and consequently had a much different view of their region's heritage and legacy. Authors such as William Faulkner, Katherine Anne Porter, and Tennessee Williams treated slavery as a horrible affliction that lingered long after the Civil War, like an impervious stain. These writers attempted to reveal the beauty and grace of Southern culture without condoning the racism and cruelty it had endorsed. In their short stories, novels, and plays, Southern Renaissance writers often crafted tragic narratives that characterized the South as still recovering from the shame of military defeat, resembling epic Greek drama in this respect.

Faulkner, and later Flannery O'Connor (see Unit 7), pioneered the *Southern Gothic* literary tradition, which used established Gothic elements in a contemporary Southern setting. Grotesque and sometimes violent characters often were used to portray the dark underside of Southern society. These innovative writers renewed the South's artistic sensibility and influenced generations of writers throughout the twentieth century.

The Whittling Boy, 1873. Winslow Homer.
Malden Public Library, Malden, Massachusetts.

The Short Story Defined

The **short story** is a condensed form of fictional narrative. Like a novel, a short story must contain a well-developed plot, authentic characters, and a theme. In contrast to a novel, a story has a narrow focus. It can introduce only a few important characters, and the conflict it presents must be resolved in relatively few pages. Moreover, since short story authors work on a smaller scale, they must quickly establish the setting and develop a particular mood.

Elements of the Short Story

As you read a short story, notice how the author provides a setting and mood, establishes a point of view, breathes life into characters, develops and advances the plot, and suggests one or more major themes.

Setting and Mood

The **setting** is the time and place of the unfolding action, together with all the details used to create a sense of a particular time and place. This might be a dank Mississippi swamp at dawn or a busy main street at noon. The historical period of the story also is significant.

The details that create the setting also create the **mood,** or atmosphere. The mood is the emotion created in the reader by part or all of a literary work.

The relationship between setting and mood is highlighted in this passage from William Faulkner's "A Rose for Emily." In it, the narrator describes the scene that greets the alderman who enters the home of the town's aging, eccentric spinster, Miss Emily Grierson:

> It smelled of dust and disuse—a close, dank smell. The Negro led them into the parlor. It was furnished in heavy, leather-covered furniture. When the Negro opened the blinds of one window, they could see that the leather was cracked; and when they sat down, a faint dust rose sluggishly about their thighs, spinning with slow motes in the single sun-ray. On a tarnished gilt easel before the fireplace stood a crayon portrait of Miss Emily's father.

The details in the passage tell us a great deal about Miss Emily's life. The furniture is leather and thus expensive, but it is cracked, which suggests that these are old possessions that Miss Emily has been unable or unwilling to replace. The furniture also is dusty, suggesting neglect. A tarnished easel, which clearly has not been polished for some time, holds a picture of the long-dead father. Through these details, the author establishes a mood of melancholy and nostalgia for a happier time in Miss Emily's life.

"In a short story, . . . almost every word has to be almost exactly right. In the novel you can be careless but in the short story you can't."

—WILLIAM FAULKNER

Narrative Voice and Point of View

The **narrator** is the character or speaker who tells a story. **Point of view** is the vantage point, or perspective, from which the story is told—in other words, who is telling the story.

First-person narrators, who are characters in the story, tend to be limited by what they can observe directly about other characters and situations. The narrator of "A Rose for Emily" is one of the townspeople. He quickly identifies himself in the story's opening sentence: "When Miss Emily Grierson died, our whole town went to her funeral." His views of people and events are necessarily limited by his role as an onlooker.

Third-person narrators, who are observers outside the story, fall into two distinct categories: those with a *limited* point of view and those who are *omniscient,* or all knowing. A narrator with a limited point of view does not possess all the information needed to understand a situation. Sometimes, the narrator knows the thoughts and feelings of only one character, as in the case of Katherine Anne Porter's "The Jilting of Granny Weatherall." Granny, whose **stream-of-consciousness narrative** gives us the significant facts of her adulthood, is not, in fact, the narrator. She has limited consciousness and is referred to in the third person. While she clearly and painfully remembers the great

PORTER   WELTY   FAULKNER

and small disappointments in her life, she is unaware through much of the story that she is dying.

An omniscient third-person narrator knows everything about the characters and the plot. The narrator of Eudora Welty's "A Worn Path" describes the actions and thoughts of Phoenix Jackson as she makes her way to the small town where she must do a vital errand. Although her perspective dominates the story, the narrator's consciousness is not limited to her but extends to other characters and to the larger world.

Characterization

Characterization is the act of creating or describing a character. Using *direct characterization,* the writer *tells* what a character is like. *Indirect characterization* involves showing what characters say, do, or think; showing what other characters say or think about them; and describing what physical features, dress, and personality characters display.

For example, Granny Weatherall believes she is as sharp as ever, but the people gathered around her bed whisper, "She was never like this, *never* like this!" "Well, what can we expect?" "Yes, eighty years old." The reader understands that Granny is struggling to remain in control, while those around her know she is quickly slipping away.

Plot

A **plot** is a series of events related to a central **conflict,** or struggle. In sum, a plot typically introduces

a conflict, develops it, and eventually resolves it (see plot diagram in Unit 5, page 526).

The first element of plot, the **exposition,** provides background information about the characters, setting, and conflict and usually occurs at the beginning of a story. The exposition helps readers understand what is to follow. The **rising action** sets up the conflict or problem that the protagonist (main character) must resolve. The **climax** of a story is the high point of interest or suspense. It is the turning point of the action, during which the character takes a critical step or reaches an understanding of the problem. The **falling action** consists of all the events that follow the climax. The **resolution** is the point in the story when the central conflict is ended.

Theme

A **theme** is a central message or perception about life revealed through a literary work. A *stated theme* is presented directly, whereas an *implied theme* must be inferred.

One theme of "A Rose for Emily" is spelled out by the narrator, who comments, "People in our town, remembering how old lady Wyatt, her great-aunt, had gone completely crazy at last, believed that the Griersons held themselves a little too high for what they really were." Other themes emerge for the reader who reflects thoughtfully on the author's purpose and attitude toward the material.

HOW TO READ

A Short Story

Identify the point of view. In deciding who will tell the story, the author determines how much and what kind of information to give readers about events and characters. Identify the point of view, and determine how the narrator's perspective may be limited or biased.

Trace the sequence of events. In a short story, the plot must be established and developed quickly. Pay attention to the exposition at the start of the story to ensure you understand

crucial background information. Then identify the conflict and trace its development to the climax. Predict how the conflict might be resolved at the end of the story.

Identify the theme. One or more themes might run through a short story. To identify the theme, consider what is suggested by how the conflict is resolved. Also consider the outcome of the story for the various characters, especially the protagonist.

The Jilting of Granny Weatherall

A Short Story by Katherine Anne Porter

Build Background

Literary Context Katherine Anne Porter's **"The Jilting of Granny Weatherall"** is the story of a dying woman's memory of being left at the altar on her wedding day. The title character presumably is based on Porter's own grandmother, with whom she lived as a young child. The story also is set in Texas, where Porter grew up.

A third parallel between the story and the author's life is that Porter herself nearly died from influenza at age twenty-eight. In fact, her funeral arrangements had been made and her obituary had been written. Porter later claimed that this experience caused her to contemplate the realities of death and the possibility of an afterlife. Religious themes run through much of her writing, as do themes of lost Southern values and lifestyles.

Like all the short stories published in Porter's 1930 collection *Flowering Judas,* "The Jilting of Granny Weatherall" first was published in a literary magazine, *transitions.* Porter's early audience comprised mostly writers who read these types of magazines. Although small, that audience nonetheless was enthusiastic about her perfection of style and the short story form.

Reader's Context Imagine what you will be like when you are old. What memories likely will stay with you? Why?

Meet the Author

Katherine Anne Porter (1890–1980) was born Callie Porter in Indian Creek, Texas. Her mother died when she was about two, and her father moved the family to live with his mother. That grandmother had a house "full of books," Porter recalled, but also was extremely poor. Porter's grandmother died when she was eleven. Just five years later, at age sixteen, Porter got married so she could leave home, but it was a short union.

Porter was an independent, self-supporting woman, and her life was filled with travel and activity. By 1916, she had begun her writing career as a reporter, working for newspapers in Texas and Colorado. She moved to New York City in 1918 and then spent from 1918 to 1924 living mainly in Mexico, doing freelance writing. She wrote her first short story, "Maria Conception" (1922), while living in Mexico, and it drew critical acclaim. In 1931, Porter used a Guggenheim Fellowship to return to Mexico for several years.

Among Porter's most noted works are several short story collections: *Flowering Judas* (1929), *Noon Wine* (1937), *Pale Horse, Pale Rider* (1939), and *The Leaning Tower* (1944). Her only novel, *Ship of Fools,* which she wrote over a thirty-year period, was published in 1962. In 1965, her *Collected Stories* received a National Book Award, the Pulitzer Prize for fiction, and the Gold Medal for fiction from the National Institute of Arts and Letters.

Analyze Literature

Point of View and Stream-of-Consciousness Writing The **point of view** is the vantage point, or perspective, from which a story is told. In *first-person point of view,* the story is told by someone who participates in or witnesses the action. In *third-person point of view,* the narrator usually stands outside the action and observes. In a *limited point of view,* the thoughts of only the narrator or a single character are revealed. In an *omniscient point of view,* the thoughts of all the characters are revealed.

Stream-of-consciousness writing attempts to present the flow of feelings, thoughts, and impressions within the minds of characters.

Set Purpose

Porter is one of several Southern Renaissance writers who experimented with point of view. As you read "The Jilting of Granny Weatherall," determine who is telling the story. Specifically, when does a narrator tell the story and when does Granny's consciousness take over the narration? Consider why knowing Granny's thoughts and feelings is key to understanding the story.

Preview Vocabulary

rummage, 762
jilt, 765
dwindle, 768

The Jilting
of
Granny Weatherall

by Katherine Anne Porter

New England Woman (Mrs. Jedediah H. Richards),
1895. Cecilia Beaux. Pennsylvania Academy of the Fine Arts,
Philadelphia, Pennsylvania.

Tomorrow was far away and there was nothing to trouble about.

She flicked her wrist neatly out of Doctor Harry's pudgy careful fingers and pulled the sheet up to her chin. The brat ought to be in knee breeches. Doctoring around the country with spectacles on his nose! "Get along now, take your schoolbooks and go. There's nothing wrong with me."

Doctor Harry spread a warm paw like a cushion on her forehead where the forked green vein danced and made her eyelids twitch. "Now, now, be a good girl, and we'll have you up in no time."

"That's no way to speak to a woman nearly eighty years old just because she's down. I'd have you respect your elders, young man."

"Well, Missy, excuse me," Doctor Harry patted her cheek. "But I've got to warn you, haven't I? You're a marvel, but you must be careful or you're going to be good and sorry."

"Don't tell me what I'm going to be. I'm on my feet now, morally speaking. It's Cornelia. I had to go to bed to get rid of her."

Her bones felt loose, and floated around in her skin, and Doctor Harry floated like a balloon around the foot of the bed. He floated and pulled down his waistcoat and swung his glasses on a cord. "Well, stay where you are, it certainly can't hurt you."

"Get along and doctor your sick," said Granny Weatherall. "Leave a well woman alone. I'll call for you when I want you. . . . Where were you forty years ago when I pulled through milk leg[1] and double pneumonia? You weren't even born. Don't let Cornelia lead you on," she shouted, because Doctor Harry appeared to float up to the ceiling and out. "I pay my own bills, and I don't throw my money away on nonsense!"

She meant to wave good-bye, but it was too much trouble. Her eyes closed of themselves, it was like a dark curtain drawn around the bed. The pillow rose and floated under her, pleasant as a hammock in a light wind. She listened to the leaves rustling outside the window. No, somebody was swishing newspapers: no, Cornelia and Doctor Harry were whispering together. She leaped broad awake, thinking they whispered in her ear.

> Her eyes closed of themselves, it was like a dark curtain drawn around the bed.

"She was never like this, *never* like this!" "Well, what can we expect?" "Yes, eighty years old. . . ."

Well, and what if she was? She still had ears. It was like Cornelia to whisper around doors. She always kept things secret in such a public way. She was always being tactful and kind. Cornelia was dutiful: that was the trouble with her. Dutiful and good: "So good and dutiful," said Granny, "that I'd like to spank her." She saw herself spanking Cornelia and making a fine job of it.

"What'd you say, Mother?" Granny felt her face tying up in hard knots.

"Can't a body think, I'd like to know?"

"I thought you might want something."

"I do. I want a lot of things. First off, go away and don't whisper."

She lay and drowsed, hoping in her sleep that the children would keep out and let her rest a minute. It had been a long day. Not that she was tired. It was always pleasant to snatch a minute now and then. There was always so much to be done, let me see: tomorrow.

Tomorrow was far away and there was nothing to trouble about. Things were finished somehow when the time came: thank God there was always a little margin over for peace: then a person could spread out the plan of life and tuck in the edges orderly. It was good to have everything clean and folded away, with the hair brushes and tonic bottles sitting straight on the white embroidered linen: the day started without fuss and the pantry shelves laid out with rows of jelly glasses and brown jugs and white stonechina jars with blue whirligigs and words painted on them: coffee, tea, sugar, ginger, cinnamon, allspice: and the bronze clock with the lion on top nicely dusted off. The dust that lion could collect in twenty-four hours! The box in the attic with all those letters tied up, well, she'd have to go through that tomorrow. All those letters—George's letters and John's letters and her letters to them both—lying around for the children to find afterwards made her uneasy. Yes, that would be tomorrow's business. No use to let them know how silly she had been once.

While she was <u>rummaging</u> around she found death in her mind and it felt clammy and unfamiliar. She had spent so much time preparing for death there was no need for bringing it up again. Let it take care of itself now. When she was sixty she had felt very old, finished, and went around making farewell trips to see her children and grandchildren,

---

1. **milk leg.** Painful swelling of the leg

rum • mage (rum´ əj) *v.*, search through thoroughly; ransack

with a secret in her mind: This is the very last of your mother, children! Then she made her will and came down with a long fever. That was all just a notion like a lot of other things, but it was lucky too, for she had once for all got over the idea of dying for a long time. Now she couldn't be worried. She hoped she had better sense now. Her father had lived to be one hundred and two years old and had drunk a noggin of strong hot toddy on his last birthday. He told the reporters it was his daily habit, and he owed his long life to that. He had made quite a scandal and was very pleased about it. She believed she'd just plague Cornelia a little.

"Cornelia! Cornelia!" No footsteps, but a sudden hand on her cheek. "Bless you, where have you been?"

"Here, mother."

"Well, Cornelia, I want a noggin of hot toddy."

"Are you cold, darling?"

"I'm chilly, Cornelia. Lying in bed stops the circulation. I must have told you that a thousand times."

Well, she could just hear Cornelia telling her husband that Mother was getting a little childish and they'd have to humor her. The thing that most annoyed her was that Cornelia thought she was deaf, dumb, and blind. Little hasty glances and tiny gestures tossed around

> ## She found death in her mind and it felt clammy and unfamiliar.

her and over her head saying, "Don't cross her, let her have her way, she's eighty years old," and she sitting there as if she lived in a thin glass cage. Sometimes Granny almost made up her mind to pack up and move back to her own house where nobody could remind her every minute that she was old. Wait, wait, Cornelia, till your own children whisper behind your back!

In her day she had kept a better house and had got more work done. She wasn't too old yet for Lydia to be driving eighty miles for advice when one of the children jumped the track, and Jimmy still dropped in and talked things over: "Now, Mammy, you've a good business head, I want to know what you think of this? . . ." Old. Cornelia couldn't change the furniture around without asking. Little things, little things! They had been so sweet when they were little. Granny wished the old days were back again with the children young and everything to be done over. It had been a hard pull, but not too much for her. When she thought of all the food she had cooked, and all the clothes she had cut and sewed, and all the gardens she had made—well, the children showed it. There they were, made out of her, and they couldn't get away from that. Sometimes she wanted to see John again and point to them and say, Well, I didn't do so badly, did I? But that would have to wait. That was for tomorrow. She used to think of him as a man, but now all the children were older than their father, and he would be a child beside her if she saw him now. It seemed strange and there was something wrong in the idea. Why, he couldn't possibly recognize her. She had fenced in a hundred acres once, digging the post holes herself and clamping the wires with just a negro boy to help. That changed a woman. John would be looking for a young woman with the peaked Spanish comb in her hair and the painted fan. Digging post holes changed a woman. Riding country roads in the winter when women had their babies was another thing: sitting up nights with sick horses and sick children and hardly ever losing one. John, I hardly ever lost one of them! John would see that in a minute, that would be something he could understand, she wouldn't have to explain anything!

It made her feel like rolling up her sleeves and putting the whole place to rights again. No matter if Cornelia was determined to be everywhere at once, there were a great many things left undone on this place. She would start tomorrow and do them. It was good to be strong enough for everything, even if all you made melted and changed and slipped under your hands, so that by the time you finished you almost forgot what you were working for. What was it I set out to do? she asked herself intently, but she could not remember. A fog rose over the valley, she saw it marching across the creek swallowing the trees and moving up the hill like an army of ghosts. Soon it would be at the near edge of the orchard, and then it was time to go in and light the lamps. Come in, children, don't stay out in the night air.

Lighting the lamps had been beautiful. The children huddled up to her and breathed like little calves waiting at the bars in the twilight. Their eyes followed the match and watched the flame rise and settle in a blue curve, then they moved away from her. The lamp was lit, they didn't have to be scared and hang on to mother any more. Never, never, never more. God, for all my life I thank Thee. Without Thee, my God, I could never have done it. Hail Mary, full of grace.

I want you to pick all the fruit this year and see that nothing is wasted. There's always someone who can use it. Don't let good things rot for want of using. You waste life when you waste good food. Don't let things get lost. It's bitter to lose things. Now, don't let me get to thinking, not when I am tired and taking a little nap before supper. . . .

The pillow rose about her shoulders and pressed against her heart and the memory was being squeezed out of it: oh, push down the pillow, somebody: it would smother her if she tried to hold it. Such a fresh breeze blowing and such a green day with no threats in it. But he had not come, just the same. What does a woman do when she has put on the white veil and set out the white cake for a man and he doesn't come? She tried to remember. No, I swear he never harmed me but in that. He never harmed me but in that . . . and what if he did? There was the day, the day, but a whirl of dark smoke rose and covered it, crept up and over into the bright field where everything was planted so carefully in orderly rows. That was hell, she knew hell when she saw it. For sixty years she had prayed against remembering him and against losing her soul in the deep pit of hell, and now the two things were mingled in one and the thought of him was a smoky cloud from hell that moved and crept in her head when she had just got rid of Doctor Harry and was trying to rest a minute. Wounded vanity, Ellen, said a sharp voice in the top of her mind. Don't let your wounded vanity get the upper hand of you. Plenty of girls get jilted. You were jilted, weren't you? Then stand up to it. Her eyelids wavered and let in streamers of blue-gray light like tissue paper over her eyes. She must get up and pull the shades down or she'd never sleep. She was in bed again and the shades were not down. How could that happen? Better turn over, hide from the light, sleeping in the light gave you nightmares. "Mother, how do you feel now?" and a stinging wetness on her forehead. But I don't like having my face washed in cold water!

Hapsy? George? Lydia? Jimmy? No, Cornelia, and her features were swollen and full of little puddles. "They're coming, darling, they'll all be here soon." Go wash your face, child, you look funny.

> What does a woman do when she has put on the white veil and set out the white cake for a man and he doesn't come?

Instead of obeying, Cornelia knelt down and put her head on the pillow. She seemed to be talking but there was no sound. "Well, are you tongue-tied? Whose birthday is it? Are you going to give a party?"

Cornelia's mouth moved urgently in strange shapes. "Don't do that, you bother me, daughter."

"Oh, no, Mother. Oh, no. . . ."

Nonsense. It was strange about children. They disputed your every word. "No what, Cornelia?"

"Here's Doctor Harry."

"I won't see that boy again. He just left five minutes ago."

"That was this morning, Mother. It's night now. Here's the nurse."

"This is Doctor Harry, Mrs. Weatherall. I never saw you look so young and happy!"

"Ah, I'll never be young again—but I'd be happy if they'd let me lie in peace and get rested."

She thought she spoke up loudly, but no one answered. A warm weight on her forehead, a warm bracelet on her wrist, and a breeze went on whispering, trying to tell her something. A shuffle of leaves in the everlasting hand of God, He blew on them and they danced and rattled. "Mother, don't mind, we're

---

jilt (jilt) v., reject; cast off

going to give you a little hypodermic."[2] "Look here, daughter, how do ants get in this bed? I saw sugar ants yesterday." Did you send for Hapsy too?

It was Hapsy she really wanted. She had to go a long way back through a great many rooms to find Hapsy standing with a baby on her arm. She seemed to herself to be Hapsy also, and the baby on Hapsy's arm was Hapsy and himself and herself, all at once, and there was no surprise in the meeting. Then Hapsy melted from within and turned flimsy as gray gauze and the baby was a gauzy shadow, and Hapsy came up close and said. "I thought you'd never come," and looked at her very searchingly and said, "You haven't changed a bit!" They leaned forward to kiss, when Cornelia began whispering from a long way off. "Oh, is there anything you want to tell me? Is there anything I can do for you?"

> I want you to find George.
> Find him and be sure to
> tell him I forgot him.

Yes, she had changed her mind after sixty years and she would like to see George. I want you to find George. Find him and be sure to tell him I forgot him. I want him to know I had my husband just the same and my children and my house like any other woman. A good house too and a good husband that I loved and fine children out of him. Better than I hoped for even. Tell him I was given back everything he took away and more. Oh, no, oh, God, no, there was something else besides the house and the man and the children. Oh, surely they were not all? What was it? Something not given back. . . . Her breath crowded down under her ribs and grew into a monstrous frightening shape with cutting edges; it bored up into her head, and the agony was unbelievable: Yes, John, get the Doctor now, no more talk, my time has come.

When this one was born it should be the last. The last. It should have been born first, for it was the one she had truly wanted. Everything came in good time. Nothing left out, left over. She was strong, in three days she would be as well as ever. Better. A woman needed milk in her to have her full health.

"Mother, do you hear me?"

"I've been telling you—"

"Mother, Father Connolly's here."

"I went to Holy Communion only last week. Tell him I'm not so sinful as all that."

"Father just wants to speak to you."

He could speak as much as he pleased. It was like him to drop in and inquire about her soul as if it were a teething baby, and then stay on for a cup of tea and a round of cards and gossip. He always had a funny story of some sort, usually about an Irishman who made his little mistakes and confessed them, and the point lay in some absurd thing he would blurt out in the confessional showing his struggles between native piety and original sin. Granny felt easy about her soul. Cornelia, where are your manners? Give Father Connolly a chair. She had her secret comfortable understanding with a few favorite saints who cleared a straight road to God for her. All as surely signed and sealed as the papers for the new Forty Acres. Forever . . . heirs and assigns[3] forever. Since the day the wedding cake was not cut, but thrown out and wasted. The whole bottom dropped out of the world, and there she was blind and sweating with nothing under her feet and the walls falling away. His hand had caught her under the breast, she had not fallen, there was the freshly polished floor with the green rug on it, just as before. He had cursed like a sailor's parrot and said, "I'll kill him for you." Don't lay a hand on him, for my sake leave something to God. "Now, Ellen, you must believe what I tell you. . . ."

So there was nothing, nothing to worry about any more, except sometimes in the night

---

2. **hypodermic.** Injection

3. **assigns.** People to whom property is transferred

one of the children screamed in a nightmare, and they both hustled out shaking and hunting for the matches and calling, "There, wait a minute, here we are!" John, get the doctor now. Hapsy's time has come. But there was Hapsy standing by the bed in a white cap. "Cornelia, tell Hapsy to take off her cap. I can't see her plain."

Her eyes opened very wide and the room stood out like a picture she had seen somewhere. Dark colors with the shadows rising towards the ceiling in long angles. The tall black dresser gleamed with nothing on it but John's picture, enlarged from a little one, with John's eyes very black when they should have been blue. You never saw him, so how do you know how he looked? But the man insisted the copy was perfect, it was very rich and handsome. For a picture, yes, but it's not my husband. The table by the bed had a linen cover and a candle and a crucifix. The light was blue from Cornelia's silk lampshades. No sort of light at all, just frippery. You had to live forty years with kerosene lamps to appreciate honest electricity. She felt very strong and she saw Doctor Harry with a rosy nimbus[4] around him.

"You look like a saint, Doctor Harry, and I vow that's as near as you'll ever come to it."

"She's saying something."

"I heard you, Cornelia. What's all this carrying on?"

"Father Connolly's saying—"

> ## Her eyes opened very wide and the room stood out like a picture she had seen somewhere.

Cornelia's voice staggered and bumped like a cart in a bad road. It rounded corners and turned back again and arrived nowhere. Granny stepped up in the cart very lightly and reached for the reins, but a man sat beside her and she knew him by his hands, driving the cart. She did not look in his face, for she knew without seeing, but looked instead down the

Neighborhood Physician, 1939. Jack Levine. Burstein Collection. Art © Jack Levine/Licensed by VAGA, New York, NY.

road where the trees leaned over and bowed to each other and a thousand birds were singing a Mass. She felt like singing too, but she put her hand in the bosom of her dress and pulled out a rosary, and Father Connolly murmured Latin in a very solemn voice and tickled her feet.[5] My God, will you stop that nonsense? I'm a married woman. What if he did run away and leave me to face the priest by myself? I found another a whole world better. I wouldn't have exchanged my husband for anybody except St. Michael himself, and you may tell him that for me with a thank you in the bargain.

---

4. **nimbus.** Halo; circle of light around the head of a saint or divinity
5. **murmured . . . feet.** Administered last rites, a sacrament in the Catholic Church for a person who is dying

Light flashed on her closed eyelids, and a deep roaring shook her. Cornelia, is that lightning? I hear thunder. There's going to be a storm. Close all the windows. Call the children

in. "Mother, here we are, all of us." "Is that you, Hapsy?" "Oh, no, I'm Lydia. We drove as fast as we could." Their faces drifted above her, drifted away. The rosary fell out of her hands and Lydia put it back. Jimmy tried to help, their hands fumbled together, and Granny closed two fingers around Jimmy's thumb. Beads wouldn't do, it must be something alive. She was so amazed her thoughts ran round and round. So, my dear Lord, this is my death and I wasn't even thinking about it. My children have come to see me die. But I can't, it's not time. Oh, I always hated surprises. I wanted to give Cornelia the amethyst set—Cornelia, you're to have the amethyst set, but Hapsy's to wear it when she wants, and, Doctor Harry, do shut up. Nobody sent for you. Oh, my dear Lord, do wait a minute. I meant to do something about the Forty Acres, Jimmy doesn't need it and Lydia will later on, with that worthless husband of hers. I meant to

finish the altar cloth and send six bottles of wine to Sister Borgia for her dyspepsia.[6] I want to send six bottles of wine to Sister Borgia, Father Connolly, now don't let me forget.

Cornelia's voice made short turns and tilted over and crashed. "Oh, Mother, oh, Mother, oh Mother. . . ."

"I'm not going, Cornelia. I'm taken by surprise. I can't go."

You'll see Hapsy again. What about her? "I thought you'd never come." Granny made a long journey outward, looking for Hapsy. What if I don't find her? What then? Her heart sank down and down, there was no bottom to death, she couldn't come to the end of it. The blue light from Cornelia's lampshade drew into a tiny point in the center of her brain, it flickered and winked like an eye, quietly it fluttered and <u>dwindled</u>. Granny lay curled down within herself, amazed and watchful, staring at the point of light that was herself: her body was now only a deeper mass of shadow in an endless darkness and this darkness would curl around the light and swallow it up. God, give a sign!

For the second time there was no sign. Again no bridegroom and the priest in the house. She could not remember any other sorrow because this grief wiped them all away. Oh, no, there's nothing more cruel than this— I'll never forgive it. She stretched herself with a deep breath and blew out the light. ❖

---

6. **dyspepsia.** Indigestion

dwin • dle (dwin′ d'l) v., languish; fade

MIRRORS & WINDOWS

As she nears the end of her life, Granny Weatherall focuses on a negative, painful experience. Do you tend to focus on the positive or the negative in life?

Refer to Text ▷ ▶ ▶ ▶ ▶	**Reason with Text**	
1a. What does Granny Weatherall remember most about her first wedding day?	**1b.** Interpret why Granny Weatherall mingles the thought of her bridegroom with the thought of losing her soul in hell.	**Understand** Find meaning
2a. Who is *John?* Identify what Granny Weatherall wants him to know.	**2b.** Granny Weatherall recalls some of the sayings she used to repeat to her children, such as "Don't let good things rot for want of using." What place do these sayings have in her life, and why is she remembering them now?	**Apply** Use information
3a. State two times when Granny Weatherall was jilted.	**3b.** What do these two experiences have in common? Which seems most difficult for her?	**Analyze** Take things apart
4a. How did Granny Weatherall prepare herself for death when she was sixty years old?	**4b.** Assess how much the past and the future influence Granny Weatherall's thinking.	**Evaluate** Make judgments
5a. List the traits that characterized Granny Weatherall before she became ill.	**5b.** Explain why *Granny Weatherall* is an appropriate name for the character in this story.	**Create** Bring ideas together

Analyze Literature

Point of View and Stream-of-Consciousness Writing

In the opening sentence, who is telling the story? Where does the narration shift to reveal Granny's consciousness? Where else does the point of view shift in this way? Explain how moving from one perspective to another affects the telling of the story.

What do you learn about Granny Weatherall from the stream-of-consciousness flow of her thoughts and feelings? Pick out specific details from the story. How is Porter's use of stream-of-consciousness writing effective in telling this story?

Extend the Text

Writing Options

Creative Writing Imagine that you are Granny Weatherall's daughter, Cornelia. Write a retelling of the story from your point of view, covering the same events. Decide whether to use stream-of-consciousness techniques in writing your account.

Descriptive Writing Suppose a classmate is having trouble following the stream-of-consciousness writing in "The Jilting of Granny Weatherall." Write a descriptive essay that explains the basic storyline to him or her. Address what is happening in the present as well as in Granny Weatherall's memories.

Media Literacy

Write an Obituary Review several obituaries in local newspapers to familiarize yourself with this form of writ-ing and the types of details typically included. Then write an obituary for Granny Weatherall, including details that will communicate to readers not only the facts of her life but also what was unique about her.

Lifelong Learning

Library Research Visit the reference section of your school or local library to find critical analyses of Katherine Anne Porter's work, specifically the story "The Jilting of Granny Weatherall." Ask your librarian for guidance. Select one critical analysis, and write a one-paragraph summary of it. Then write a second paragraph explaining whether you agree or disagree with the critical analysis.

 Go to **www.mirrorsandwindows.com** for more.

William Faulkner

> ## "I believe that man will not merely endure: he will prevail."

William Faulkner (1897–1962) was born in New Albany, Mississippi, to a prominent Southern family and spent most of his life in Oxford, home to the University of Mississippi. Despite his proximity to the academic world, Faulkner had little formal education; he dropped out of high school and spent only one year as a student at the university.

Faulkner's first novel, *Soldier's Pay*, was published in 1926 with the help of acclaimed fiction writer Sherwood Anderson and earned him an advance of two hundred dollars each on his next two novels. Recalling these events, Faulkner is reported to have said "I liked the money" and to have noted that Anderson "worked only in the morning," which seemed to him "a mighty easy way to earn money."

Most of Faulkner's novels are set in the mythical Yoknapatawpha (yäk´ nə pə tô fə) County, Mississippi, and tell stories about the decline of traditional Southern ways of life. Literary scholars have speculated that Yoknapatawpha County is based on the real Lafayette County, where Oxford is located. At least seventeen of Faulkner's stories are set in Yoknapatawpha, including *The Sound and the Fury, As I Lay Dying,* and *Absalom, Absalom!* Many of the characters that populate Yoknapatawpha County appear in more than one story, such as Colonel Sartoris, the main character in *Sartoris* (1929), who also is mentioned in the short stories "The Bear" and "A Rose for Emily."

The use of long, resonant sentences with abundant details is one of the hallmarks of Faulkner's writing style. He also experimented considerably with point of view. The stories in some of his novels are told by several different characters, including a mentally challenged man in *The Sound and the Fury* (1929) and the members of a poor, mentally deficient farm family in *As I Lay Dying* (1930). Much of Faulkner's fiction employed a stream-of-consciousness mode, presenting characters' random thoughts, feelings, and impressions in interior monologues.

In addition to novels, Faulkner wrote screenplays, the most notable of which were his adaptations of Ernest Hemingway's *To Have and Have Not* and Raymond Chandler's *The Big Sleep.* Faulkner's work was recognized in 1950 with a Nobel Prize for literature and in 1954 and 1962 with Pulitzer Prizes for fiction. His Nobel Prize acceptance speech often is referenced as one of the most eloquent descriptions of the purpose of literature (see pages 780–781).

Noted Works

The Sound and the Fury (1929)

As I Lay Dying (1930)

Light in August (1932)

Absalom, Absalom! (1936)

Go Down, Moses (1942)

A Rose for Emily
A Short Story by William Faulkner

Darl, from As I Lay Dying
A Novel by William Faulkner

Build Background

Literary Context In the tradition of the Southern Renaissance movement, William Faulkner chronicled the social and economic rise and fall of the American South during the period from the end of the Civil War through the Depression. As described in the Author Focus, his stories and novels are characterized by recurring fictional places and characters and experimentation with literary elements such as point of view.

"A Rose for Emily" first was published in 1930, early in Faulkner's career, and it became one of his most famous short stories. The setting is the home of an aging spinster, Miss Emily Grierson. Like Miss Emily, her home is decaying but refuses to fall. It protects her until the end from the prying eyes of Jefferson, Mississippi, the small-town Southern community in which she has lived her entire life.

The large and ornate but disintegrating mansion is a typical setting for **Gothic fiction,** a type of writing that Faulkner helped develop into a uniquely Southern Gothic tradition. It is characterized by a murky atmosphere of horror and gloom and grotesque, mysterious, and violent incidents. In "A Rose for Emily," Faulkner also uses a series of flashbacks to develop the plot, revealing the personal details of Miss Emily's life and relating her ongoing conflict with the external world.

Faulkner's novel **As I Lay Dying,** also published in 1930, is an excellent example of his use of distinctive narrative structures—specifically, multiple points of view and the inner psychological voices of the characters. Faulkner tells the darkly comic tale of the death of Addie Bundren, the matriarch of the Bundren family, through the eyes of each family member, including Addie herself. As the novel begins, Addie, a Mississippi farm woman, is dying. During the course of the book, her husband, Anse; her four sons, Cash, Darl, Jewel, and Vardaman; her daughter, Dewey Dell; and various neighbors reveal through words and actions their relationship with Addie, who has made Anse promise to take her to Jefferson to be buried. The excerpt that follows is from the perspective of her son Darl.

Be aware that Faulkner's writing sometimes contains racial slurs. He considered it important to portray the South as realistically as possible, including the prevalence and effects of racial segregation and discrimination.

Reader's Context If you were to create a mythical setting based on where you live, what would it be like? Describe what the houses would look like, how the people would look and act, and so on. Explain your choices.

Analyze Literature

Setting and Conflict
The **setting** of a literary work is the time and place in which it occurs.

A **conflict** is a struggle between two forces. In an *external conflict,* the main character struggles against another character, forces of nature, society, or fate. In an *internal conflict,* the main character struggles against some element within himself or herself.

Set Purpose

By setting many of his novels and stories in the mythical Yoknapatawpha County, Faulkner was able to create a rich fabric of community and culture. As you read "A Rose for Emily" and "Darl," record the details provided about the setting and consider what they reveal about the characters. In addition, identify the types of conflict in each selection and trace how they are resolved.

Preview Vocabulary

august, 772
perpetuity, 773
temerity, 774
vindicate, 775
circumvent, 778
virulent, 778
doddering, 779
gaunt, 783
juxtaposition, 783
ubiquity, 785

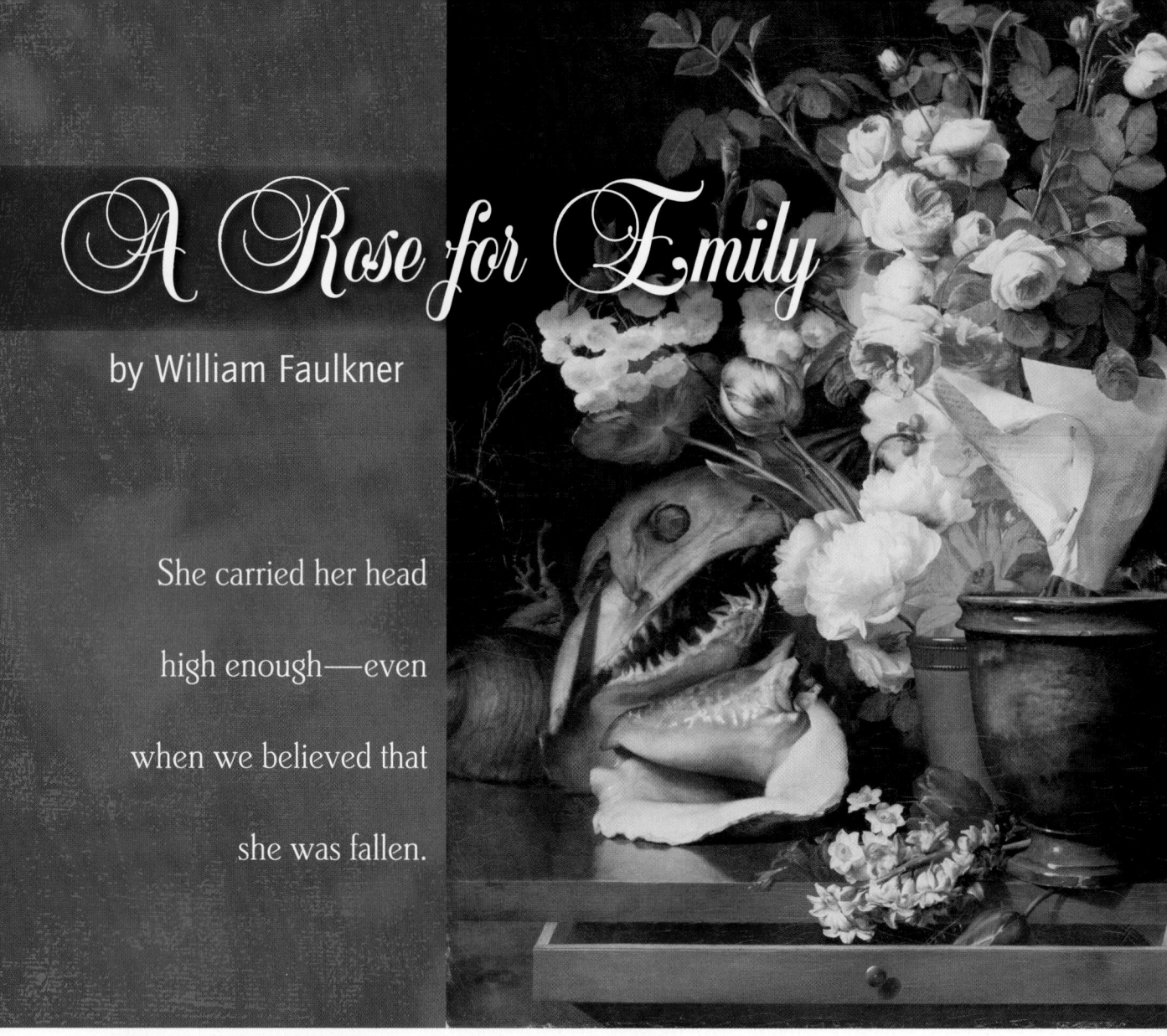

A Rose for Emily

by William Faulkner

She carried her head

high enough—even

when we believed that

she was fallen.

Roses with Other Flowers, Shells, a Shark's Head, and Petrifications, 1819. Antoine Berjon.
Philadelphia Museum of Art, Philadelphia, Pennsylvania. (See detail on page 771.)

I

When Miss Emily Grierson died, our whole town went to her funeral: the men through a sort of respectful affection for a fallen monument, the women mostly out of curiosity to see the inside of her house, which no one save an old manservant—a combined gardener and cook—had seen in at least ten years.

It was a big, squarish frame house that had once been white, decorated with cupolas[1] and spires and scrolled balconies in the heav-ily lightsome style of the seventies,[2] set on what had once been our most select street. But garages and cotton gins had encroached and obliterated even the <u>august</u> names of that

---

1. **cupolas.** Small dome-shaped superstructures on roofs, often holding weathervanes
2. **the seventies.** 1870s

---

au • gust (ä´ gəst) *adj.,* majestic, noble, and impressive

neighborhood; only Miss Emily's house was left, lifting its stubborn and coquettish decay above the cotton wagons and the gasoline pumps—an eyesore among eyesores. And now Miss Emily had gone to join the representatives of those august names where they lay in the cedar-bemused cemetery among the ranked and anonymous graves of Union and Confederate soldiers who fell at the battle of Jefferson.

Alive, Miss Emily had been a tradition, a duty, and a care; a sort of hereditary obligation upon the town, dating from that day in 1894 when Colonel Sartoris, the mayor—he who fathered the edict that no Negro woman should appear on the streets without an apron—remitted her taxes,[3] the dispensation dating from the death of her father on into perpetuity. Not that Miss Emily would have accepted charity. Colonel Sartoris invented an involved tale to the effect that Miss Emily's father had loaned money to the town, which the town, as a matter of business preferred this way of repaying. Only a man of Colonel Sartoris' generation and thought could have invented it, and only a woman could have believed it.

When the next generation, with its more modern ideas, became mayors and aldermen, this arrangement created some little dissatisfaction. On the first of the year they mailed her a tax notice. February came, and there was no reply. They wrote her a formal letter, asking her to call at the sheriff's office at her convenience. A week later the mayor wrote her himself, offering to call or to send his car for her and received in reply a note on paper of an archaic shape in a thin, flowing calligraphy in faded ink, to the effect that she no longer went out at all. The tax notice was also enclosed, without comment.

They called a special meeting of the Board of Aldermen. A deputation waited upon her, knocked at the door through which no visitor had passed since she ceased giving china-painting lessons eight or ten years earlier. They were admitted by the old Negro into a dim hall from which a stairway mounted into still more

shadow. It smelled of dust and disuse—a close, dank smell. The Negro led them into the parlor. It was furnished in heavy, leather-covered furniture. When the Negro opened the blinds of one window they could see that the leather was cracked; and when they sat down, a faint dust rose sluggishly about their thighs spinning with slow motes in the single sun-ray. On a tarnished gilt easel before the fireplace stood a crayon portrait of Miss Emily's father.

They rose when she entered—a small, fat woman in black, with a thin gold chain descending to her waist and vanishing into her belt, leaning on an ebony cane with a tarnished gold head. Her skeleton was small and spare; perhaps that was why what would have been merely plumpness in another was obesity in her. She looked bloated, like a body long submerged in motionless water, and of that pallid hue. Her eyes, lost in the fatty ridges of her face, looked like two small pieces of coal pressed into a lump of dough as they moved from one face to another while the visitors stated their errand.

She looked bloated, like a body long submerged in motionless water, and of that pallid hue.

She did not ask them to sit. She just stood in the door and listened quietly until the spokesman came to a stumbling halt. Then they could hear the invisible watch ticking at the end of the gold chain.

Her voice was dry and cold. "I have no taxes in Jefferson. Colonel Sartoris explained it to me. Perhaps one of you can gain access to the city records and satisfy yourselves."

---

3. **remitted her taxes.** Excused her from paying taxes

per • pe • tu • i • ty (pʉr′ pə tü′ ə tē) *n.*, eternity

"But we have. We are the city authorities, Miss Emily. Didn't you get a notice from the sheriff, signed by him?"

"I received a paper, yes," Miss Emily said. "Perhaps he considers himself the sheriff . . . I have no taxes in Jefferson."

"But there is nothing on the books to show that, you see. We must go by the—"

"See Colonel Sartoris. I have no taxes in Jefferson."

"But, Miss Emily—"

"See Colonel Sartoris." (Colonel Sartoris had been dead almost ten years.) "I have no taxes in Jefferson. Tobe!" The Negro appeared. "Show these gentlemen out."

II

So she vanquished them, horse and foot, just as she had vanquished their fathers thirty years before about the smell. That was two years after her father's death and a short time after her sweetheart—the one we believed would marry her—had deserted her. After her father's death she went out very little; after her sweetheart went away, people hardly saw her at all. A few of the ladies had the <u>temerity</u> to call, but were not received, and the only sign of life about the place was the Negro man—a young man then— going in and out with a market basket.

"Just as if a man—any man—could keep a kitchen properly," the ladies said; so they were not surprised when the smell developed. It was another link between the gross, teeming world and the high and mighty Griersons.

A neighbor, a woman, complained to the mayor, Judge Stevens, eighty years old.

"But what will you have me do about it, madam?" he said.

"Why, send her word to stop it," the woman said. "Isn't there a law?"

"I'm sure that won't be necessary," Judge Stevens said. "It's probably just a snake or a rat that nigger of hers killed in the yard. I'll speak to him about it."

The next day he received two more complaints, one from a man who came in diffident deprecation.[4] "We really must do something about it, Judge. I'd be the last one in the world to bother Miss Emily, but we've got to do something." That night the Board of Aldermen met—three graybeards and one younger man, a member of the rising generation.

"It's simple enough," he said. "Send her word to have her place cleaned up. Give her a certain time to do it in, and if she don't . . ."

"Dammit, sir," Judge Stevens said, "will you accuse a lady to her face of smelling bad?"

So the next night, after midnight, four men crossed Miss Emily's lawn and slunk about the house like burglars, sniffing along the base of the brickwork and at the cellar openings

---

4. **diffident deprecation.** Timid criticism or disapproval

te • mer • i • ty (tə mār´ ə tē) *n.,* recklessness

while one of them performed a regular sowing motion with his hand out of a sack slung from his shoulder. They broke open the cellar door and sprinkled lime there, and in all the outbuildings. As they recrossed the lawn, a window that had been dark was lighted and Miss Emily sat in it, the light behind her, and her upright torso motionless as that of an idol. They crept quietly across the lawn and into the shadow of the locusts that lined the street. After a week or two the smell went away.

That was when people had begun to feel really sorry for her. People in our town, remembering how old lady Wyatt, her great-aunt, had gone completely crazy at last, believed that the Griersons held themselves a little too high for what they really were. None of the young men were quite good enough for Miss Emily and such. We had long thought of them as a tableau,[5] Miss Emily a slender figure in white in the background, her father a spraddled silhouette in the foreground, his back to her and clutching a horsewhip, the two of them framed by the back-flung front door. So when she got to be thirty and was still single, we were not pleased exactly, but <u>vindicated</u>; even with insanity in the family she wouldn't have turned down all of her chances if they had really materialized.

That was when people had begun to feel really sorry for her.

When her father died, it got about that the house was all that was left to her; and in a way, people were glad. At last they could pity Miss Emily. Being left alone, and a pauper, she had become humanized. Now she too would know the old thrill and the old despair of a penny more or less.

The day after his death all the ladies prepared to call at the house and offer condolence and aid, as is our custom. Miss Emily met them at the door, dressed as usual and with no trace of grief on her face. She told them that her father was not dead. She did that for three days, with the ministers calling on her, and the doctors, trying to persuade her to let them dispose of the body. Just as they were about to resort to law and force, she broke down, and they buried her father quickly.

We did not say she was crazy then. We believed she had to do that. We remembered all the young men her father had driven away, and we knew that with nothing left, she would have to cling to that which had robbed her, as people will.

III

She was sick for a long time. When we saw her again, her hair was cut short, making her look like a girl, with a vague resemblance to those angels in colored church windows— sort of tragic and serene.

The town had just let the contracts for paving the sidewalks, and in the summer after her father's death they began the work. The construction company came with niggers and mules and machinery, and a foreman named Homer Barron, a Yankee—a big, dark, ready man, with a big voice and eyes lighter than his face. The little boys would follow in groups to hear him cuss the niggers, and the niggers singing in time to the rise and fall of picks. Pretty soon he knew everybody in town. Whenever you heard a lot of laughing anywhere about the square, Homer Barron would be in the center of the group. Presently we began to see him and Miss Emily on Sunday afternoons driving in the yellow-wheeled buggy and the matched team of bays from the livery stable.

At first we were glad that Miss Emily would have an interest, because the ladies all said, "Of course a Grierson would not think seriously of a

---

5. **tableau.** Theatrical scene

vin • di • cate (vin´ də kāt) v., prove correct

Northerner, a day laborer." But there were still others, older people, who said that even grief could not cause a real lady to forget *noblesse oblige*[6]—without calling it *noblesse oblige*. They just said, "Poor Emily. Her kinsfolk should come to her." She had some kin in Alabama; but years ago her father had fallen out with them over the estate of old lady Wyatt, the crazy woman, and there was no communication between the two families. They had not even been represented at the funeral.

And as soon as the old people said, "Poor Emily," the whispering began. "Do you suppose it's really so?" they said to one another. "Of course it is. What else could . . ." This behind their hands; rustling of craned[7] silk and satin behind jalousies[8] closed upon the sun of Sun-day afternoon as the thin, swift, clop-clop-clop of the matched teams passed: "Poor Emily."

She carried her head high enough—even when we believed that she was fallen. It was as if she demanded more than ever the recognition of her dignity as the last Grierson; as if it had wanted that touch of earthiness to reaffirm her imperiousness. Like when she bought the rat poison, the arsenic. That was over a year after they had begun to say "Poor Emily," and while the two female cousins were visiting her.

"I want some poison," she said to the druggist. She was over thirty then, still a slight woman though thinner than usual, with cold, haughty black eyes in a face the flesh of which was strained across the temples and about the eye-sockets as you imagine a lighthouse-keeper's face ought to look. "I want some poison," she said.

"Yes, Miss Emily. What kind? For rats and such I'd recom—"

"I want the best you have. I don't care what kind."

The druggist named several. "They'll kill anything up to an elephant. But what you want is—"

"Arsenic," Miss Emily said. "Is that a good one?"

"Is . . . arsenic? Yes, ma'am. But what you want—"

"I want arsenic."

The druggist looked down at her. She looked back at him, erect, her face like a strained flag. "Why, of course," the druggist said. "If that's what you want. But the law requires you to tell what you are going to use it for."

Miss Emily just stared at him, her head tilted back in order to look him eye for eye, until he looked away and went and got the arsenic and wrapped it up. The Negro delivery boy brought her the package; the druggist didn't come back. When she opened the package at home there was written on the box, under the skull and bones: "For rats."

---

6. ***noblesse oblige.*** [French] Idea from the French code of chivalry that people from the upper classes (the nobles) are obligated to be kind to people from the lower classes
7. **craned.** Stretched
8. **jalousies.** Slatted windows or shades

Abstraction White Rose, 1927. Georgia O'Keeffe. Georgia O'Keeffe Museum, Santa Fe, New Mexico.

IV

So the next day we all said, "She will kill herself"; and we said it would be the best thing. When she had first begun to be seen with Homer Barron, we had said, "She will marry him." Then we said, "She will persuade him yet," because Homer himself had remarked—he liked men, and it was known that he drank with the younger men in the Elks' Club—that he was not a marrying man. Later we said, "Poor Emily," behind the jalousies as they passed on Sunday afternoon in the glittering buggy, Miss Emily with her head high and Homer Barron with his hat cocked and a cigar in his teeth, reins and whip in a yellow glove.

Then some of the ladies began to say that it was a disgrace to the town and a bad example to the young people. The men did not want to interfere, but at last the ladies forced the Baptist minister—Miss Emily's people were Episcopal—to call upon her. He would never divulge what happened during that interview, but he refused to go back again. The next Sunday they again drove about the streets, and the following day the minister's wife wrote to Miss Emily's relations in Alabama.

So she had blood-kin under her roof again and we sat back to watch developments. At first nothing happened. Then we were sure that they were to be married. We learned that Miss Emily had been to the jeweler's and ordered a man's toilet set[9] in silver, with the letters H. B.

---

9. **man's toilet set.** Set of grooming aids, such as a brush and comb

---

ART CONNECTION

Georgia O'Keeffe

American artist Georgia O'Keeffe (1887–1986) was born on a Wisconsin dairy farm in 1887. After showing great artistic promise at an early age, she was admitted to the Art Institute of Chicago when she was eighteen. She quickly grew dissatisfied with the school's stifling creative climate, however.

O'Keeffe stopped painting for the next decade but resumed her work in 1915, working with an art instructor named Arthur Dow. His expertise in Asian art forms helped O'Keeffe break free of the creative shackles she had encountered as a student in Chicago. She began to paint in a style uniquely her own.

In 1916, a friend showed O'Keeffe's work to Alfred Stieglitz, one of the most prominent members of the New York art community. After several years' correspondence, Stieglitz convinced O'Keeffe to come to New York and began exhibiting her work; the two were married in 1924. Around this time, O'Keeffe also began to paint the large-scale floral images for which she would become famous. Paintings such as *Abstraction White Rose*, shown at left, brought her both popular and critical recognition.

In 1929, O'Keeffe and Stieglitz vacationed in New Mexico, and O'Keeffe became fascinated with its vibrant desert landscapes. She celebrated that natural beauty in many of her later paintings, incorporating in them the bones of steers and unending southwestern horizons. O'Keeffe moved to New Mexico in 1949, several years after her husband's death.

O'Keeffe's eyesight deteriorated in the 1970s, and her output diminished greatly after that. In 1985, she received a Medal of Arts from President Ronald Reagan, securing her legacy as one of the most important American artists of the twentieth century.

Critical Viewing O'Keeffe was an individualist who forged her own style and painted her own subjects, defying what was popular in the European art community. How is *Abstraction White Rose* different from other paintings of flowers you have seen? Consider such qualities as the scope of the image, level of detail, use of color, and so on.

on each piece. Two days later we learned that she had bought a complete outfit of men's clothing, including a nightshirt, and we said, "They are married." We were really glad. We were glad because the two female cousins were even more Grierson than Miss Emily had ever been.

So we were not surprised when Homer Barron—the streets had been finished some time since—was gone. We were a little disappointed that there was not a public blowing-off, but we believed that he had gone on to prepare for Miss Emily's coming, or to give her a chance to get rid of the cousins. (By that time it was a cabal,[10] and we were all Miss Emily's allies to help <u>circumvent</u> the cousins.) Sure enough, after another week they departed. And, as we had expected all along, within three days Homer Barron was back in town. A neighbor saw the Negro man admit him at the kitchen door at dusk one evening.

And that was the last we saw of Homer Barron. And of Miss Emily for some time. The Negro man went in and out with the market basket, but the front door remained closed. Now and then we would see her at a window for a moment, as the men did that night when they sprinkled the lime, but for almost six months she did not appear on the streets. Then we knew that this was to be expected too; as if that quality of her father which had thwarted her woman's life so many times had been too <u>virulent</u> and too furious to die.

When we next saw Miss Emily, she had grown fat and her hair was turning gray. During the next few years it grew grayer and grayer until it attained an even pepper-and-salt iron-gray, when it ceased turning. Up to the day of her death at seventy-four it was still that vigorous iron-gray, like the hair of an active man.

From that time on her front door remained closed, save for a period of six or seven years,

when she was about forty, during which she gave lessons in china-painting. She fitted up a studio in one of the downstairs rooms, where the daughters and granddaughters of Colonel Sartoris' contemporaries were sent to her with the same regularity and in the same spirit that they were sent to church on Sundays with a twenty-five-cent piece for the collection plate. Meanwhile her taxes had been remitted.

Then the newer generation became the backbone and the spirit of the town, and the painting pupils grew up and fell away and did not send their children to her with boxes of color and tedious brushes and pictures cut from the ladies' magazines. The front door closed upon the last one and remained closed for good. When the town got free postal delivery, Miss Emily alone refused to let them fasten the metal numbers above her door and attach a mailbox to it. She would not listen to them.

Daily, monthly, yearly we watched the Negro grow grayer and more stooped, going in and out with the market basket. Each December we sent her a tax notice, which would be returned by the post office a week later, unclaimed. Now and then we would see her in one of the downstairs windows—she had evidently shut up the top floor of the house—like the carven torso of an idol in a niche, looking or not looking at us, we could never tell which. Thus she passed from generation to generation—dear, inescapable, impervious, tranquil, and perverse.

---

10. **cabal.** Group of persons involved in secret activity or plotting

cir • cum • vent (sʉr kum vent´) *v.*, outwit; get around
vir • u • lent (vēr´ ə lənt) *adj.*, malignant; bitterly hostile

And so she died. Fell ill in the house filled with dust and shadows, with only a <u>doddering</u> Negro man to wait on her. We did not even know she was sick; we had long since given up trying to get any information from the Negro. He talked to no one, probably not even to her, for his voice had grown harsh and rusty, as if from disuse.

She died in one of the downstairs rooms, in a heavy walnut bed with a curtain, her gray head propped on a pillow yellow and moldy with age and lack of sunlight.

V

The Negro met the first of the ladies at the front door and let them in, with their hushed, sibilant[11] voices and their quick, curious glances, and then he disappeared. He walked right through the house and out the back and was not seen again.

The two female cousins came at once. They held the funeral on the second day, with the town coming to look at Miss Emily beneath a mass of bought flowers, with the crayon face of her father musing profoundly above the bier[12] and the ladies sibilant and macabre;[13] and the very old men—some in their brushed Confederate uniforms—on the porch and the lawn, talking of Miss Emily as if she had been a contemporary of theirs, believing that they had danced with her and courted her perhaps, confusing time with its mathematical progression, as the old do, to whom all the past is not a diminishing road but, instead, a huge meadow which no winter ever quite touches, divided from them now by the narrow bottle-neck of the most recent decade of years.

Already we knew that there was one room in that region above stairs which no one had seen in forty years, and which would have to be forced. They waited until Miss Emily was decently in the ground before they opened it.

The violence of breaking down the door seemed to fill this room with pervading dust. A thin, acrid[14] pall as of the tomb seemed to lie everywhere upon this room decked and furnished as for a bridal: upon the valance curtains of faded rose color, upon the rose-shaded lights, upon the dressing table, upon the delicate array of crystal and the man's toilet things backed with tarnished silver, silver so tarnished that the monogram was obscured. Among them lay a collar and tie, as if they had just been removed, which, lifted, left upon the surface a pale crescent in the dust. Upon a chair hung the suit, carefully folded; beneath it the two mute shoes and the discarded socks.

The man himself lay in the bed.

For a long while we just stood there looking down at the profound and fleshless grin. The body had apparently once lain in the attitude of an embrace, but now the long sleep that outlasts love, that conquers even the grimace of love, had cuckolded[15] him. What was left of him, rotted beneath what was left of the nightshirt, had become inextricable from the bed in which he lay; and upon him and upon the pillow beside him lay that even coating of the patient and biding dust.

Then we noticed that in the second pillow was the indentation of a head. One of us lifted something from it, and leaning forward, that faint and invisible dust dry and acrid in the nostrils, we saw a long strand of iron-gray hair. ❖

---

11. **sibilant.** Hissing
12. **bier.** Coffin on a supporting platform
13. **macabre.** Gruesome; suggestive of death
14. **acrid.** Bitter; irritating
15. **cuckolded.** Betrayed, especially by an unfaithful wife

dod • der • ing (dä´ də riŋ) *adj.*, senile; feeble

MIRRORS & WINDOWS

What in your life have you found difficult to give up, even after it has no longer been useful, appropriate, or appealing?

NOBEL PRIZE MEDAL

Literature Connection

William Faulkner received the Nobel Prize for literature in 1950 for his powerful and artistically unique contribution to the modern American novel. Although he admired other contemporary writers, especially Ernest Hemingway, he felt that the role of the writer was to "try for the impossible" by experimenting with style, narration, and other literary elements. His brief **Nobel Prize acceptance speech,** one of the shortest yet most memorable acceptance speeches on record, presents a noble view of the purpose of literature in the modern age.

Nobel Prize Acceptance Speech
by William Faulkner

I feel that this award was not made to me as a man, but to my work—a life's work in the agony and sweat of the human spirit, not for glory and least of all for profit, but to create out of the materials of the human spirit something which did not exist before. So this award is only mine in trust.[1] It will not be difficult to find a dedication for the money part of it commensurate[2] with the purpose and significance of its origin. But I would like to do the same with the acclaim too, by using this moment as a pinnacle from which I might be listened to by the young men and women already dedicated to the same anguish and travail,[3] among whom is already that one who will some day stand here where I am standing.

Our tragedy today is a general and universal physical fear so long sustained by now that we can even bear it. There are no longer problems of the spirit. There is only the question: When will I be blown up?[4] Because of this, the young man or woman writing today has forgotten the problems of the human heart in conflict with itself which alone can make good writing because only that is worth writing about, worth the agony and the sweat.

He must learn them again. He must teach himself that the basest of all things is to be afraid; and, teaching himself that, forget it forever, leaving no room in his workshop for anything but the old verities[5] and truths of the heart, the old universal truths lacking which any story is ephemeral[6] and doomed—love and honor and pity and pride and compassion and sacrifice. Until he does so, he labors under a curse. He writes not of love but of lust, of defeats in which nobody loses anything of value, of victories without hope and, worst of all, without pity or compassion. His griefs grieve on no universal bones, leaving no scars. He writes not of the heart but of the glands.

Until he relearns these things, he will write as though he stood among and watched the end of man. I decline to accept the end of man. It is easy enough to say that man is immortal simply because he will endure: that when the last ding-dong of doom has clanged and faded

---

1. **in trust.** In another's care
2. **commensurate.** Equal in measure or size; proportionate
3. **travail.** Hard work
4. **When will I be blown up?** Reference to people's general fear of being annihilated following the use of atomic weapons in World War II
5. **verities.** Fundamental principles or beliefs that are believed to be true
6. **ephemeral.** Temporary; short lived

from the last worthless rock hanging tideless in the last red and dying evening, that even then there will still be one more sound: that of his puny inexhaustible voice, still talking. I refuse to accept this. I believe that man will not merely endure: he will prevail. He is immortal, not because he alone among creatures has an inexhaustible voice, but because he has a soul, a spirit capable of compassion and sacrifice and endurance. The poet's, the writer's, duty is to write about these things. It is his privilege to help man endure by lifting his heart, by reminding him of the courage and honor and hope and pride and compassion and pity and sacrifice which have been the glory of his past. The poet's voice need not merely be the record of man, it can be one of the props, the pillars to help him endure and prevail. ❖

Review Questions

1. Reread the first sentence of Faulkner's speech. What does he say is his purpose in writing? Reread the first paragraph of the speech. What does he say is his purpose in speaking?

2. According to Faulkner, what is the only subject worth writing about? Why might young writers not understand this? Outline what they need to learn or relearn to be effective storytellers.

3. Why will people not only endure but prevail, according to Faulkner? Summarize the writer's role in helping people prevail.

TEXT ⟷ᵀᴼ TEXT CONNECTION

In his speech, Faulkner reminds writers of their responsibility to explore universal issues of human desire and conflict, rather than superficial topics. Does Faulkner achieve that in his own writing? Is "A Rose for Emily" just a Gothic horror story? Is the excerpt from *As I Lay Dying*, which follows, only about a death in the family?

LITERARY CONNECTION

The Nobel Prize

Alfred Nobel (1833–1896) was born into a wealthy Swedish family that encouraged its children to study science, particularly chemistry and physics. Nobel traveled extensively around Europe and the United States, working with scientists. He developed and patented dynamite (one of his 355 patents) and helped develop the oil industry in Russia, making him one of the wealthiest men of his time.

Nobel also was interested in the worldwide peace movement. Before he died in 1896, he stipulated that his fortune was to be used to create the Nobel Foundation, which would award prizes yearly to accomplished individuals in chemistry, physics, medicine, literature, peace, and economics.

The Nobel Prize for literature is considered the most prestigious literary award in the world. In contrast to most literary prizes, which honor particular works, the Nobel Prize honors a writer's body of work. The winner of the Nobel Prize for literature receives a monetary award and a medal inscribed with these words: "And they who bettered life on earth by new found mastery." American winners of the literature prize have included Sinclair Lewis (1930), Eugene O'Neill (1936), Pearl Buck (1938), William Faulkner (1949), Ernest Hemingway (1954), John Steinbeck (1962), and Toni Morrison (1993).

Young Woman on Her Deathbed, 1621. Anonymous.
Musée des Beaux-Arts, Rouen, France.

Darl,
from As I Lay Dying

by William Faulkner

Pa stands beside the bed. From behind his leg Vardaman peers, with his round head and his eyes round and his mouth beginning to open. She looks at pa; all her failing life appears to drain into her eyes, urgent, irremediable.[1] "It's Jewel she wants," Dewey Dell says.

"Why, Addie," pa says, "him and Darl went to make one more load. They thought there was time. That you would wait for them, and

that three dollars and all . . ." He stoops laying his hand on hers. For a while yet she looks at him, without reproach, without anything at all, as if her eyes alone are listening to the irrevocable[2] cessation[3] of his voice. Then she raises

---

1. **irremediable.** Unable to be remedied or cured
2. **irrevocable.** Impossible to change
3. **cessation.** Stopping

"She taken and left us," pa says.

herself, who has not moved in ten days. Dewey Dell leans down, trying to press her back.

"Ma," she says; "ma."

She is looking out the window, at Cash stooping steadily at the board in the failing light, laboring on toward darkness and into it as though the stroking of the saw illumined[4] its own motion, board and saw engendered.[5]

"You, Cash," she shouts, her voice harsh, strong, and unimpaired. "You, Cash!"

He looks up at the <u>gaunt</u> face framed by the window in the twilight. It is a composite picture of all time since he was a child. He drops the saw and lifts the board for her to see, watching the window in which the face has not moved. He drags a second plank into position and slants the two of them into their final <u>juxtaposition</u>, gesturing toward the ones yet on the ground, shaping with his empty hand in pantomime[6] the finished box. For a while still she looks down at him from the composite picture, neither with censure nor approbation.[7] Then the face disappears.

She lies back and turns her head without so much as glancing at pa. She looks at Vardaman; her eyes, the life in them, rushing suddenly upon them; the two flames glare up for a steady instant. Then they go out as though someone had leaned down and blown upon them.

"Ma," Dewey Dell says; "ma!" Leaning above the bed, her hands lifted a little, the fan still moving like it has for ten days, she begins to keen.[8] Her voice is strong, young, tremulous and clear, rapt with its own timbre and volume, the fan still moving steadily up and down, whispering the useless air. Then she flings herself across Addie Bundren's knees, clutching her, shaking her with the furious strength of the young before sprawling suddenly across the handful of rotten bones that Addie Bundren left, jarring the whole bed into a chattering sibilance[9] of mattress shucks, her arms outflung and the fan in one hand still beating with expiring breath into the quilt.

From behind pa's leg Vardaman peers, his mouth full open and all color draining from his face into his mouth, as though he has by some means fleshed his own teeth in himself, sucking. He begins to move slowly backward from the bed, his eyes round, his pale face fading into the dusk like a piece of paper pasted on a failing wall, and so out of the door.

Pa leans above the bed in the twilight, his humped silhouette partaking of that owl-like quality of awry-feathered, disgruntled outrage within which lurks a wisdom too profound or too inert[10] for even thought.

"Durn them boys," he says.

Jewel, I say. Overhead the day drives level and gray, hiding the sun by a flight of gray spears. In the rain the mules smoke a little, splashed yellow with mud, the off one clinging in sliding lunges to the side of the road above the ditch. The tilted lumber gleams dull yellow, water-soaked and heavy as lead, tilted at a steep angle into the ditch above the broken wheel; about the shattered spokes and about Jewel's ankles a runnel of yellow neither water nor earth swirls, curving with the yellow road neither of earth nor water, down the hill dissolving into a streaming mass of dark green neither of earth nor sky. Jewel, I say.

Cash comes to the door, carrying the saw. Pa stands beside the bed, humped, his arms dangling. He turns his head, his shabby profile,

---

4. **illumined.** Illuminated
5. **engendered.** Joined in form
6. **pantomime.** Communication conveyed only by body movements
7. **neither with censure nor approbation.** Without criticism or approval
8. **keen.** Mourn or lament loudly
9. **sibilance.** Hissing
10. **inert.** Sluggish; inactive

---

gaunt (gônt) *adj.,* excessively thin and angular
jux · ta · po · si · tion (juks′ tə pō zi′ shən) *n.,* state of being side by side

his chin collapsing slowly as he works the snuff against his gums.

"She's gone," Cash says.

"She taken and left us," pa says. Cash does not look at him.

"How nigh are you done?" pa says. Cash does not answer. He enters, carrying the saw. "I reckon you better get at it," pa says. "You'll have to do the best you can, with them boys gone off that-away." Cash looks down at her. He is not listening to pa at all. He does not approach the bed. He stops in the middle of the floor, the saw against his leg, his sweating arms powdered lightly with sawdust, his face composed. "If you get in a tight, maybe some of them'll get here tomorrow and help you," pa says. "Vernon could." Cash is not listening. He is looking down at her peaceful, rigid face fading into the dusk as though darkness were a precursor[11] of the ultimate earth, until at last the face seems to float detached upon it, lightly as the reflection of a dead leaf. "There is Christians enough to help you," pa says. Cash is not listening. After a while he turns without looking at pa and leaves the room. Then the saw begins to snore again. "They will help us in our sorrow," pa says.

The sound of the saw is steady, competent, unhurried, stirring the dying light so that at each stroke her face seems to wake a little into an expression of listening and of waiting, as though she were counting the strokes. Pa looks down at the face, at the black sprawl of Dewey Dell's hair, the outflung arms, the clutched fan now motionless on the fading quilt. "I reckon you better get supper on," he says.

Dewey Dell does not move.

"Git up, now, and put supper on," pa says. "We got to keep our strength up. I reckon

> *Cash is not listening. He is looking down at her peaceful, rigid face fading into the dusk.*

---

11. **precursor.** Something that comes before; forerunner

Doctor Peabody's right hungry, coming all this way. And Cash'll need to eat quick and get back to work so he can finish it in time."

Dewey Dell rises, heaving to her feet. She looks down at the face. It is like a casting of fading bronze upon the pillow, the hands alone still with any semblance[12] of life: a curled, gnarled inertness; a spent yet alert quality from which weariness, exhaustion, travail has not yet departed, as though they doubted even yet the actuality of rest, guarding with horned and penurious[13] alertness the cessation which they know cannot last.

Dewey Dell stoops and slides the quilt from beneath them and draws it up over them to the chin, smoothing it down, drawing it smooth. Then without looking at pa she goes around the bed and leaves the room.

She will go out where Peabody is, where she can stand in the twilight and look at his back with such an expression that, feeling her eyes and turning, he will say: I would not let it grieve me, now. She was old, and sick too. Suffering more than we knew. She couldn't have got well. Vardaman's getting big now, and with you to take good care of them all. I would try not to let it grieve me. I expect you'd better go and get some supper ready. It don't have to be much. But they'll need to eat, and she looking at him, saying You could do so much for me if you just would. If you just knew. I am I and you are you and I know it and you don't know it and you could do so much for me if you just would and if you would then I could tell you and then nobody would have to know it except you and me and Darl.

> *I would not let it grieve me, now.*
> *She was old, and sick too.*
> *Suffering more than we knew.*

Pa stands over the bed, dangle-armed, humped, motionless. He raises his hand to his head, scouring his hair, listening to the saw. He comes nearer and rubs his hand, palm and back, on his thigh and lays it on her face and then on the hump of quilt where her hands are. He touches the quilt as he saw Dewey Dell do, trying to smoothe it up to the chin, but disarranging it instead. He tries to smoothe it again, clumsily, his hand awkward as a claw, smoothing at the wrinkles which he made and which continue to emerge beneath his hand with perverse <u>ubiquity</u>, so that at last he desists, his hand falling to his side and stroking itself again, palm and back, on his thigh. The sound of the saw snores steadily into the room. Pa breathes with a quiet, rasping sound, mouthing the snuff against his gums. "God's will be done," he says. "Now I can get them teeth."

Jewel's hat droops limp about his neck, channelling water onto the soaked towsack tied about his shoulders as, ankle-deep in the running ditch, he pries with a slipping two-by-four, with a piece of rotting log for fulcrum, at the axle. Jewel, I say, she is dead, Jewel. Addie Bundren is dead. ❖

---

12. **semblance.** Likeness
13. **penurious.** Extremely frugal; stingy

> **ubiq • ui • ty** (yü bi´ kwə tē) *n.*, state of seeming to be everywhere

---

MIRRORS & WINDOWS

Much of what the Bundren family thinks and feels is left unsaid. When is it best for people to talk about their emotions, and when is it best for people to let their actions demonstrate how they feel?

Refer to Text ▷ ▷ ▷ ▶ ▶ **Reason with Text**

1a. List five situations from "A Rose for Emily" in which Miss Emily breaks the law and is not punished. Which situation occurs first chronologically?	**1b.** Explain how Miss Emily is able to avoid the consequences of her illegal activities.	**Understand** Find meaning
2a. What excuse did the townspeople offer to explain Miss Emily's refusal to give up her father's body for burial?	**2b.** Relate Miss Emily's appearance and behavior after her father's death to events later in the story.	**Apply** Use information
3a. As described in "Darl," what does Addie Bundren look like at this stage in life? List details about her physical appearance.	**3b.** Analyze what the physical description of Addie suggests about the life she led or the kind of person she was.	**Analyze** Take things apart
4a. How does Pa react to his wife's death in "Darl"? What does he do when Dewey Dell leaves the room?	**4b.** Based on what Pa says and does, judge whether he is grieving. Support your answer using details from the excerpt.	**Evaluate** Make judgments
5a. In "A Rose for Emily," why were young women sent to take china-painting lessons from Miss Emily? Why did the lessons stop?	**5b.** Explain how Miss Emily is "a fallen monument." Summarize what she represents to the town of Jefferson.	**Create** Bring ideas together

Analyze Literature

Setting and Conflict
In "A Rose for Emily," review the setting in the scene when the door to the locked bedroom is broken down. What probably occurred on that night forty years before, and what might have occurred since? In "Darl," how does the setting indicate the family's situation? Use details from the selections to support your answers.

Describe the external and internal conflicts in "A Rose for Emily" and "Darl." Which type of conflict seems more difficult to overcome: external or internal? Explain.

Extend the Text

Writing Options
Creative Writing Write a dialogue of the conversation that Miss Emily and Homer Barron might have had the night he died. Try to use Southern dialect and colloquial (informal, everyday) language, as Faulkner does, to make the conversation realistic.

Expository Writing Think about the mood created by Faulkner's style of writing, which includes the use of long, often complex sentences. What emotions does it evoke in readers? Select one sentence from "A Rose for Emily" and one sentence from "Darl." Write a paragraph analyzing what each sentence accomplishes in creating mood.

Critical Literacy
Interview the Author Suppose you have an opportunity to interview William Faulkner about the influence of Gothic fiction on "A Rose for Emily." What would you ask him about creating a setting, developing characters, and formulating a plot? Write a summary of Faulkner's answers to your questions, and share it with your class.

Collaborative Learning
Create a Dramatic Script With a partner, create a dramatic script of the events in "Darl." Decide whether dialogue will be sufficient to tell the story or if props and scenery are needed. Act out your script for your class. Then discuss the benefits and drawbacks of reading the story versus seeing it acted out.

 Go to **www.mirrorsandwindows.com** for more.

1. In "A Rose for Emily," why does Colonel Sartoris make up an explanation for why Miss Emily does not have to pay taxes?
A. He knows Miss Emily cannot understand the complicated tax laws.
B. He owes Miss Emily's family money, and this is a sneaky way to repay it.
C. He knows Miss Emily's father gave the town money years ago so his daughter would not have to deal with the townsfolk.
D. He does not feel the founding families of the town should have to bother themselves with taxes.
E. He knows Miss Emily does not have much money, and he does not want to insult her by asking for payment.

2. Many of the conflicts between Miss Emily and the townspeople are, in fact,
A. racial conflicts.
B. conflicts between the older and younger generations.
C. economic conflicts.
D. conflicts between Northerners and Southerners.
E. conflicts between the wealthy and the poor or middle class.

3. Which of the following descriptions of setting in "A Rose for Emily" is most Gothic?
A. "It was a big, squarish frame house that had once been white, decorated with cupolas and spires and scrolled balconies in the heavily lightsome style of the seventies, set on what had once been our most select street."
B. "They were admitted . . . into a dim hall from which a stairway mounted into still more shadow. It smelled of dust and disuse—a close, dank smell."
C. "[The parlor] was furnished in heavy, leather-covered furniture. . . . [T]he leather was cracked; and when they sat down, a faint dust rose sluggishly about their thighs."
D. "The violence of breaking down the door seemed to fill this room with pervading dust."
E. "They crept quietly across the law and into the shadow of the locusts that lined the street."

4. In Faulkner's Nobel Prize acceptance speech, he tells young writers that "the basest of all things" is
A. to write for profit.
B. to be afraid.
C. to search for universal truths.
D. to lose honor.
E. to make sacrifices.

5. "Darl," the excerpt from *As I Lay Dying,* is written in which point or points of view?
A. first-person
B. second-person
C. third-person
D. first- and third-person
E. first- and second-person

6. In "Darl," what is Cash doing while his mother lies in bed inside the house?
A. chopping wood
B. building a wagon
C. standing by her bed
D. working on the house
E. making her coffin

7. At the end of the "Darl" excerpt when pa is left alone with his dead wife, what do his actions reveal about his feelings?
A. He is at a loss for how to show how he feels.
B. He is overwhelmed with grief.
C. He is ready to move on to with his life.
D. A and B
E. A and C

8. Constructed Response: In Faulkner's Nobel Prize acceptance speech, he says that "man will not merely endure; he will prevail." How can this idea be considered a theme in "A Rose for Emily" and the excerpt from *As I Lay Dying?* Analyze how each selection addresses the idea of overcoming one's challenges in life. Use details from the selections for support.

9. Constructed Response: Analyze Faulkner's use of sensory details in the two selections. Include the descriptions of the Grierson house in "A Rose for Emily" and the metaphorical imagery used to describe the faces of the Bundren family in "Darl." How do those details convey meaning about the people and circumstances in each story?

> ### TEST-TAKING TIP
>
> Although practice tests do not contain the same questions as the actual test, their format is identical. In preparing for a test, take the time to learn the rules and expectations of each of its sections. Becoming familiar with a test's format will help you be more comfortable when you actually take the test.

Understand the Concept

Possessive nouns are nouns that modify other words. Generally, to form a possessive noun, an apostrophe plus an *s* is added to a singular noun. If the noun is plural, only an apostrophe is added. Consider this example from "A Rose for Emily":

EXAMPLE

On a tarnished gilt easel before the fireplace stood a crayon portrait of *Miss Emily's* father.

In this sentence, *Miss Emily's* might seem to be a noun. However, it functions as an adjective because it modifies the word *father.*

Possessive pronouns act much the same way as possessive nouns. Many possessive pronoun forms are the same as other pronouns, but a few pronoun forms are uniquely possessive. Some of the unique forms are *mine, your, yours, hers, its, our, their,* and *theirs.* Two other possessive forms, *her* and *his,* are not always possessive.

My and *mine* look like pronouns, but in these sentences, they function as modifiers (adjectives):

EXAMPLES

My favorite short story is "A Rose for Emily."

The best essay in the class written about "A Rose for Emily" was *mine.*

Keep in mind that the possessive form of the pronoun *it* is *its,* not *it's.* Adding an apostrophe and *s* to *it* creates the contraction *it's,* meaning "it is."

Apply the Skill

Identify Possessive Nouns and Pronouns
Review the following sentences. For each one, write down the possessive nouns and pronouns that function as modifiers. After each possessive noun or pronoun, write in parentheses the word or words it modifies.

1. Many of Faulkner's novels are set in Mississippi, where the author spent most of his life.
2. "A Rose for Emily" is set in the author's famous fictional locale, Yoknapatawpha County.
3. One of the short story's unusual features is its use of the first-person plural point of view.
4. For example, the story begins, "When Miss Emily Grierson died, our whole town went to her funeral."
5. The Board of Aldermen's efforts to collect taxes from Miss Emily fails.
6. The townspeople gossip about Miss Emily's relationship with her father and her suitor, Homer Barron.
7. The townspeople's disapproval of Homer Barron as a suitor is the subject of much of their gossip.
8. Although the townspeople know of Miss Emily's visit to the town druggist to purchase arsenic, they do not learn of her horrible secret until after her death.
9. One of the story's main themes is women's role in traditional Southern society.
10. A film adaptation of Faulkner's "A Rose for Emily" was released in 1982, with Anjelica Huston serving in the film's starring role.

Improve the Use of Possessive Nouns and Pronouns
Correct the mistaken uses of possessive nouns and pronouns in this paragraph about "A Rose for Emily":

Emily Grierson is the towns' symbol of it's past grandeur. Just as its obvious that she is crumbling, along with hers large home, so, too, are the values and behavior's of the past's crumbling. When the horror of the dead mans body is revealed, the town's people know exactly who's hair it is that is found next to him on the bed.

Use Possessive Nouns and Pronouns
Practice using possessive nouns and possessive pronouns by writing a paragraph describing your favorite hobbies and those of your family and friends.

The Son

by Horacio Quiroga

Danger always exists for man at any age.

Horacio Quiroga (1878–1937), one of Latin America's finest short story writers, knew firsthand of the death and madness about which he wrote. Born in Uruguay, Quiroga was just an infant when his father was killed accidentally. Later tragedies include the unexpected deaths of his stepfather, his wife, and a friend.

A comparison of Quiroga's stories with those of William Faulkner reveals several similarities. Both authors' short stories often are set in the wild and contain elements of Gothic fiction, such as madness, hallucinations, death, and the supernatural. Quiroga's short story **"The Son,"** which is from his collection *The Decapitated Chicken and Other Stories* (1925), uses a literary technique that Faulkner also employs in his writing: telling the story from an unusual point of view.

It is a powerful summer day in Misiones,[1] with all the sun, heat, and calm the season can offer. Nature, at its fullest and most open, seems satisfied with itself.

Like the sun, the heat, and the calm surroundings, the father, too, opens his heart to nature.

"Be careful, little one," he says to his son, summing up all his warnings for the occasion in the one phrase, which his son fully understands.

"Yes, *papá*," responds the child as he picks up the shotgun, fills his shirt pockets with shells, and then carefully buttons the pockets.

"Come back by noon," his father says.

"Yes, *papá*," the young boy repeats.

Balancing the shotgun in his hand, he smiles at his father, kisses him, and leaves.

The father follows him for a moment with his eyes and then returns to his day's tasks, made happy by his young one's joy.

He knows that his son, raised from tender infancy to be cautious in the presence of danger, can handle a firearm and hunt anything that presents itself. Although very tall for his age, he is only thirteen. And he might seem even younger if one were to judge by the purity of his blue eyes, still fresh with childish surprise.

---

1. **Misiones.** Province in northeastern Argentina

Rio Juchitan [detail], c. 1900s. Diego Rivera.
Museo del Palacio de Bellas Artes, Mexico.

The father doesn't have to raise his eyes from his task to follow in his mind the son's progress. Now, he has crossed the red path and is heading straight for the woods through the opening in the esparto grass.[2]

He knows that hunting in the woods—hunting game—requires more patience than his son can muster. After cutting through the woods his cub will skirt the line of cactus and go to the marsh in search of doves, toucans, or perhaps a pair of herons like the one his friend Juan sighted several days ago.

Only now, a ghost of a smile touches the father's lips as he recalls the two young boys' love of hunting. Sometimes they get only a *yacútoro*, even less frequently a *surucuá*,[3] and, even so, return in triumph, Juan to his own ranch with the nine-gauge shotgun that he himself has given him, and his son to their mesa with the huge sixteen-gauge Saint-Etienne—a white powder, four-lock shotgun.

The father had been exactly the same. At thirteen he would have given his life for a shotgun. Now at that age his son has one—and the father smiles.

It isn't easy, nevertheless, for a widowed father, whose only hope and faith lies in the life of his son, to raise the boy as he has, free within his limited range of action, sure of hand and foot since he was four years old, conscious of the immensity of certain dangers and the limitations of his own strength.

The father has had to battle fiercely against what he considers his own selfishness. So easy for a child to miscalculate, to place a foot in empty space, and . . . one loses a son! Danger always exists for man at any age, but its threat is lessened if, from the time one is a child, he is accustomed to rely on nothing but his own strength.

2. **esparto grass.** Type of grass used for making paper and baskets
3. ***yacútoro . . . surucuá.*** [Spanish] Both terms refer to types of birds

This is the way the father has raised his son. And to achieve it he has had to resist his heart as well as his moral torments, because this father, a man with a weak stomach and poor sight, has suffered for some time from hallucinations.

He has seen visions of a former happiness—embodied in most painful illusions—that should have remained forever buried in the oblivion in which he has shut himself. He has not escaped the torment of visions concerning his own son. He has *seen* him hammering a *parabellum*[4] bullet on the shop forge, *seen* him fall to the ground covered in blood—when what the boy was really doing was polishing the buckle of his hunting belt.

Horrible things. . . . But today, this burning, vital summer day, the love of which the son seems to have inherited, the father feels happy, tranquil, and sure of the future.

In that instant, not far away, a sharp crack sounds.

"The Saint-Etienne," the father thinks, recognizing the detonation. "Two fewer doves in the woods. . . ." Paying no further attention to the insignificant event, the man once again loses himself in his task.

The sun, already very high, continues to rise. Everywhere one looks—rocks, land, trees—the air, as rarefied[5] as if in an oven, vibrates with heat. A deep humming sound fills the soul and saturates the surrounding countryside as far as the eye can see—at this hour the essence of all tropical life.

The father glances at his wrist: twelve o'clock. And he raises his eyes to the woods.

His son should be on his way back now. They never betray the confidence each has in the other—the silver-haired father and the thirteen-year-old boy. When his son responds, "Yes, *papá*," he will do what he says. He had

said he would be back before twelve, and the father had smiled as he watched him set off.

But the son has not returned.

The man returns to his chores, forcing himself to concentrate on his task. It is easy, so easy, to lose track of time in the woods, to sit on the ground for a while, resting, not moving. . . .

Suddenly the noonday light, the tropical hum, and the father's heart skip a beat at the thought he has just had: his son resting, not moving. . . .

Time has gone by: it is 12:30. The father steps out of his workshop, and, as he rests his hand on the mechanic's bench, the explosion of a *parabellum* bullet surges from the depths of his memory; and instantly, for the first time in three hours, he realizes he has heard nothing since the blast from the Saint-Etienne. He has not heard stones turning under a familiar step. His son has not returned, and all nature stands arrested at the edge of the woods, awaiting him. . . .

Ah! A temperate character and blind confidence in the upbringing of a son are not sufficient to frighten away the specter of calamity that a weak-sighted father sees rising from the edge of the woods. Distraction, forgetfulness, an unexpected delay: his heart cannot accept any of these reasons; none would delay his son's return.

One shot, one single shot, has sounded, and that a long time ago. The father has heard no sound since, has seen no bird; not one single person has come out of the opening in the esparto grass to tell him that at a wire fence . . . a great disaster. . . .

Without his machete,[6] distracted, the father sets out. He cuts through the opening in the grass, enters the woods, skirts the line of

> **He has seen visions of a former happiness—embodied in most painful illusions—that should have remained forever buried.**

---

4. **parabellum.** Type of semiautomatic pistol or machine gun
5. **rarefied.** Thin or less dense
6. **machete.** Large, heavy-bladed knife used to cut through underbrush

cactus—without finding the least trace of his son.

All nature seems to stand still. And after the father has traveled the well-known hunting paths and explored the marsh in vain, he knows surely that each step forward carries him, fatally and inexorably,[7] toward the body of his son.

Nothing even to reproach himself for, poor creature. Only the cold, terrible, and final realization: his son has killed himself going over a . . .

But where . . . where! There are so many wire fences and the woods are so foul. Oh, so very foul . . . ! If one is not careful crossing a fence with a shotgun in his hand . . .

The father stifles a shout. He has seen something rising. . . . No, it isn't his son, no . . . ! And he turns in a different direction, and then another and another. . . .

Nothing would be gained here by showing the pallor of the man's skin or the anguish in

> **He is sure that the mere act of pronouncing his son's name, of calling him aloud, will be the confession of his death.**

his eyes. The man still has not called his son. Although his heart clamors for him, his mouth remains mute. He is sure that the mere act of pronouncing his son's name, of calling him aloud, will be the confession of his death.

"Boy!" escapes from him abruptly. . . . No one, nothing, responds. The father, who has aged ten years, walks down the sun-reddened paths searching for the son who has just died.

"Sonny! My little boy!" The diminutive rises from the depths of his soul.

Once before, in the midst of happiness and peace, this father had suffered the hallucination of seeing his son rolling on the ground, his forehead pierced by a bullet. Now, in every dark corner of the woods he sees sparkling wire; and at the foot of a fence post, his discharged shotgun at his side, he sees . . .

"Son! My little boy!"

---

7. **inexorably.** Relentlessly; unalterably

Even the forces that submit a poor hallucinated father to the most atrocious nightmares have their limits. And our father feels his reason slipping away—when suddenly he sees his son step out of a cross path.

The look on the face of a father in the woods without his machete is enough to cause a thirteen-year-old boy to hasten his step, his eyes moist.

"My little boy," the man murmurs and drops exhausted to the white sand, clasping his arms about his son's legs.

The child stands, his legs encircled, and, as he understands his father's pain, slowly caresses his head, "Poor *papá*. . . ."

Time begins again. Soon it will be three o'clock. Together now, father and son undertake the return home; and if one can admit to tears in the voice of a strong man, let us mercifully close our ears to the anguish crying in that voice.

"Why didn't you watch the sun to keep track of the time?" the father murmurs.

"I looked, *papá*. . . . But as I started back I saw Juan's herons and I followed them. . . ."

"What you have put me through, my son . . . !"

"Pah-pah . . . ," the boy murmurs, too.

After a long silence: "And the herons, did you kill them?" the father asks.

"No. . . ."

An unimportant detail, after all. Under the blazing sky, in the open, cutting through the esparto, the man returns home with his son, his arm resting happily on the boy's shoulders, almost as high as his own. He returns bathed in sweat, and, though broken in body and soul, he smiles with happiness. . . .

He smiles with hallucinated happiness. . . . Because this father walks alone. He has found no one, and his arm is resting upon empty air. Because behind him, at the foot of a fence post, with his legs higher than his body, caught in a wire fence, his beloved son, dead since ten o'clock in the morning, lies in the sun. ❖

Do you believe in the saying "Prepare for the worst and hope for the best"? When is worrying about potential danger productive, and when is doing so pointless?

Refer and Reason

1. What does the father imagine he sees in the woods? What does he really see? Compare and contrast the father's final vision of his son to his previous visions.

2. What passages make you question the accuracy of the father's perceptions and even his mental stability? Characterize his mental state both before and after he finds his son.

3. Infer whether this story reflects Quiroga's own fears and feelings about his family. If you could ask the author to reveal the theme of the story, what do you think he would say?

Writing Options

1. Imagine that you are the dead son in Quiroga's story and have the opportunity to communicate with your father one last time. Write a personal letter to your father, explaining what happened on your hunting trip. Consider your purpose: Do you want to blame him? Comfort him? Thank him for allowing you to be independent?

2. Write a few paragraphs about the similarities and differences in Quiroga's and Faulkner's writing. Compare and contrast "The Son" with "A Rose for Emily" or "Darl."

 Go to **www.mirrorsandwindows.com** for more.

A Worn Path

A Short Story by Eudora Welty

Build Background

Literary Context In her autobiography, Eudora Welty wrote, "A sheltered life can be a daring life as well. For all serious daring starts from within." Like many of Welty's stories, **"A Worn Path"** explores the intricacies of the inner life and small heroisms of an ordinary person. In the story, Phoenix Jackson makes an archetypal journey in which she demonstrates determination, generosity, and resourcefulness. Welty also explores the complexities of relationships in many of her stories, examining the intimate but often strange bonds within families and communities.

Reader's Context Do you prefer to live a sheltered life or a daring life? What are the benefits and drawbacks of each?

Meet the Author

Eudora Welty (1909–2001) was born in Jackson, Mississippi, and lived much of her life there. She left to attend Mississippi State College for Women, the University of Wisconsin, and Columbia's Graduate School of Business. She returned to Jackson in 1931 after her father's unexpected death and worked at a local newspaper and radio station.

From 1933 to 1936, Welty traveled Mississippi working as a publicist and photographer for the Works Progress Administration (WPA), a Depression Era program that gave unemployed people work building roads, libraries, and other public facilities. She proved herself an adept photographer, and many of the photos she took during this time later were exhibited and published.

Welty was foremost a writer, however, stating that "there's so much more of life that only words can convey." In 1936, she published her first short story, "Death of a Traveling Salesman," in the literary magazine *Manuscript.* It attracted the attention of writer Katherine Anne Porter, who became Welty's mentor and wrote the foreword to her first collection of stories, *A Curtain of Green.* Published in 1941, that collection was inspired by the images of rural Mississippi that Welty gleaned while working for the WPA. It contained many of Welty's best-known works, including "A Worn Path," and established her as a major fiction writer.

Welty enjoyed success throughout her career, producing four collections of short stories, five novels, two collections of photographs, and three works of nonfiction. She also was in demand as a speaker and served residencies at a number of universities, including both Oxford and Cambridge in England. In 1972, she won the Pulitzer Prize for her novel *The Optimist's Daughter.* In 1984, she published an autobiography, *One Writer's Beginnings,* detailing her life and its relationship to her writing. She cautioned people not to make too strong a connection between the two, stating that "the writer's mind and heart . . . can't be mapped and plotted."

Analyze Literature

Character and Archetype

A **character** is an individual who takes part in the action of a literary work. A *flat character* shows only one character trait. A *round character* shows the multiple traits of a real person.

An **archetype** is a character, theme, symbol, plot, or other literary element that has appeared in the literature of the world throughout time. For example, the story of a *journey* in which someone faces danger and becomes wiser is considered archetypal.

Set Purpose

How an individual faces life's obstacles reveals a great deal about him or her. As you read "A Worn Path," list the obstacles Phoenix Jackson faces along her journey and note how she overcomes each one. Also write down details about the character's appearance, actions, mannerisms, and so on. Finally, consider how Phoenix's journey is archetypal. Think about what emotion enables her to overcome the obstacles she faces.

Preview Vocabulary

pendulum, 795
quivering, 796
limber, 796
rouse, 796
ravine, 798
obstinate, 801

Georgia Landscape, 1934. Hale Woodruff. Smithsonian American Art Museum, Washington, DC.

A Worn Path
by Eudora Welty

"Tell us quickly about your grandson, and get it over. He isn't dead, is he?"

It was December—a bright frozen day in the early morning. Far out in the country there was an old Negro woman with her head tied in a red rag, coming along a path through the pinewoods. Her name was Phoenix Jackson. She was very old and small and she walked slowly in the dark pine shadows, moving a little from side to side in her steps, with the bal-anced heaviness and lightness of a <u>pendulum</u> in a grandfather clock. She carried a thin, small cane made from an umbrella, and with this she

> **pen • du • lum** (pen´ jə lum) *n.*, object suspended from a fixed point that swings freely back and forth; commonly used to regulate movement, as in a clock

kept tapping the frozen earth in front of her. This made a grave and persistent noise in the still air, that seemed meditative like the chirping of a solitary little bird.

She wore a dark striped dress reaching down to her shoe tops, and an equally long apron of bleached sugar sacks, with a full pocket: all neat and tidy, but every time she took a step she might have fallen over her shoelaces, which dragged from her unlaced shoes. She looked straight ahead. Her eyes were blue with age. Her skin had a pattern all its own of numberless branching wrinkles and as though a whole little tree stood in the middle of her forehead, but a golden color ran underneath, and the two knobs of her cheeks were illumined by a yellow burning under the dark. Under the red rag her hair came down on her neck in the frailest of ringlets, still black, and with an odor like copper.

"Something always take a hold of me on this hill—pleads I should stay."

Now and then there was a quivering in the thicket. Old Phoenix said, "Out of my way, all you foxes, owls, beetles, jack rabbits, coons and wild animals! . . . Keep out from under these feet, little bob-whites. . . . Keep the big wild hogs out of my path. Don't let none of those come running my direction. I got a long way." Under her small black-freckled hand her cane, limber as a buggy whip, would switch at the brush as if to rouse up any hiding things.

On she went. The woods were deep and still. The sun made the pine needles almost too bright to look at, up where the wind rocked. The cones dropped as light as feathers. Down in the hollow was the morning dove—it was not too late for him.

The path ran up a hill. "Seem like there is chains about my feet, time I get this far," she said, in the voice of argument old people keep to use with themselves. "Something always take a hold of me on this hill—pleads I should stay."

After she got to the top she turned and gave a full, severe look behind her where she had come. "Up through pines," she said at length. "Now down through oaks."

Her eyes opened their widest, and she started down gently. But before she got to the bottom of the hill a bush caught her dress.

Her fingers were busy and intent, but her skirts were full and long, so that before she could pull them free in one place they were caught in another. It was not possible to allow the dress to tear. "I in the thorny bush," she said. "Thorns, you doing your appointed work. Never want to let folks pass, no sir. Old eyes thought you was a pretty little *green* bush."

Finally, trembling all over, she stood free, and after a moment dared to stoop for her cane.

"Sun so high!" she cried, leaning back and looking, while the thick tears went over her eyes. "The time getting all gone here."

At the foot of this hill was a place where a log was laid across the creek.

"Now comes the trial," said Phoenix.

Putting her right foot out, she mounted the log and shut her eyes. Lifting her skirt, leveling her cane fiercely before her, like a festival figure in some parade, she began to march across. Then she opened her eyes and she was safe on the other side.

"I wasn't as old as I thought," she said.

But she sat down to rest. She spread her skirts on the bank around her and folded her

---

quiv • er • ing (kwiv′ ər iŋ) *n.*, shaking or moving characterized by a slight trembling motion
lim • ber (lim′ bər) *adj.*, having a supple and resilient quality
rouse (rowz) *v.*, become stirred

hands over her knees. Up above her was a tree in a pearly cloud of mistletoe. She did not dare to close her eyes, and when a little boy brought her a plate with a slice of marble-cake on it she spoke to him. "That would be acceptable," she said. But when she went to take it there was just her own hand in the air.

So she left that tree, and had to go through a barbed-wire fence. There she had to creep and crawl, spreading her knees and stretching her fingers like a baby trying to climb the steps. But she talked loudly to herself: she could not let her dress be torn now, so late in the day, and she could not pay for having her arm or her leg sawed off if she got caught fast where she was.

At last she was safe through the fence and risen up out in the clearing. Big dead trees, like black men with one arm, were standing in the purple stalks of the withered cotton field. There sat a buzzard.

"Who you watching?"

In the furrow she made her way along.

"Glad this not the season for bulls," she said, looking sideways, "and the good Lord made his snakes to curl up and sleep in the winter. A pleasure I don't see no two-headed snake coming around that tree, where it come once. It took a while to get by him, back in the summer."

She passed through the old cotton and went into a field of dead corn. It whispered and shook and was taller than her head. "Through the maze now," she said, for there was no path.

Then there was something tall, black, and skinny there, moving before her.

At first she took it for a man. It could have been a man dancing in the field. But she stood still and listened, and it did not make a sound. It was as silent as a ghost.

"Ghost," she said sharply, "who be you the ghost of? For I have heard of nary death close by."

But there was no answer—only the ragged dancing in the wind.

She shut her eyes, reached out her hand, and touched a sleeve. She found a coat and inside that an emptiness, cold as ice.

"You scarecrow," she said. Her face lighted. "I ought to be shut up for good," she said with laughter. "My senses is gone. I too old. I the oldest people I ever know. Dance, old scarecrow," she said, "while I dancing with you."

She kicked her foot over the furrow, and with mouth drawn down, shook her head once or twice in a little strutting way. Some husks blew down and whirled in streamers about her skirts.

Then she went on, parting her way from side to side with the cane, through the whispering field. At last she came to the end, to a wagon track where the silver grass blew between the red ruts. The quail were walking around like pullets,[1] seeming all dainty and unseen.

---

1. **pullets.** Young hens

Deep, deep the road went down between the high green-colored banks. Overhead the live-oaks met, and it was as dark as a cave.

A black dog with a lolling tongue came up out of the weeds by the ditch. She was meditating, and not ready, and when he came at her she only hit him a little with her cane. Over she went in the ditch, like a little puff of milkweed.

Down there, her senses drifted away. A dream visited her, and she reached her hand up, but nothing reached down and gave her a pull. So she lay there and presently went to talking. "Old woman," she said to herself, "that black dog come up out of the weeds to stall you off, and now there he sitting on his fine tail, smiling at you."

A white man finally came along and found her—a hunter, a young man, with his dog on a chain.

"Well, Granny!" he laughed. "What are you doing there?"

"Lying on my back like a June-bug waiting to be turned over, mister," she said, reaching up her hand.

He lifted her up, gave her a swing in the air, and set her down. "Anything broken, Granny?"

"No sir, them old dead weeds is springy enough," said Phoenix, when she had got her breath. "I thank you for your trouble."

"Where do you live, Granny?" he asked, while the two dogs were growling at each other.

"Away back yonder, sir, behind the ridge. You can't even see it from here."

"Walk pretty," she said. "This the easy place. This the easy going."

She followed the track, swaying through the quiet bare fields, through the little strings of trees silver in their dead leaves, past cabins silver from weather, with the doors and windows boarded shut, all like old women under a spell sitting there. "I walking in their sleep," she said, nodding her head vigorously.

In a <u>ravine</u> she went where a spring was silently flowing through a hollow log. Old Phoenix bent and drank. "Sweet-gum makes the water sweet," she said, and drank more. "Nobody know who made this well, for it was here when I was born."

The track crossed a swampy part where the moss hung as white as lace from every limb. "Sleep on, alligators, and blow your bubbles." Then the track went into the road.

---

ra • vine (rä vēn´) *n.,* small, narrow, steep-sided valley larger than a gully and smaller than a canyon

"On your way home?"

"No sir, I going to town."

"Why, that's too far! That's as far as I walk when I come out myself, and I get something for my trouble." He patted the stuffed bag he carried, and there hung down a little closed claw. It was one of the bob-whites, with its beak hooked bitterly to show it was dead. "Now you go on home, Granny!"

"I bound to go to town, mister," said Phoenix. "The time come around."

He gave another laugh, filling the whole landscape. "I know you old colored people! Wouldn't miss going to town to see Santa Claus!"

But something held old Phoenix very still. The deep lines in her face went into a fierce and different radiation. Without warning, she had seen with her own eyes a flashing nickel fall out of the man's pocket onto the ground.

"How old are you, Granny?" he was saying.

"There is no telling, mister," she said, "no telling."

Then she gave a little cry and clapped her hands and said, "Git on away from here, dog! Look! Look at that dog!" She laughed as if in admiration. "He ain't scared of nobody. He a big black dog." She whispered, "Sic him!"

"Watch me get rid of that cur," said the man. "Sic him, Pete! Sic him!"

Phoenix heard the dogs fighting, and heard the man running and throwing sticks. She even heard a gunshot. But she was slowly bending forward by that time, further and further forward, the lids stretched down over her eyes, as if she were doing this in her sleep. Her chin was lowered almost to her knees. The yellow palm of her hand came out from the fold of her apron. Her fingers slid down and along the ground under the piece of money with the grace and care they would have in lifting an egg from under a setting hen. Then she slowly straightened up, she stood erect, and the nickel was in her apron pocket. A bird flew by. Her lips moved: "God watching me the whole time. I come to stealing."

The man came back, and his own dog panted about them. "Well, I scared him off that time," he said, and then he laughed and lifted his gun and pointed it at Phoenix.

She stood straight and faced him.

"Doesn't the gun scare you?" he said, still pointing it.

"No, sir, I seen plenty go off closer by, in my day, and for less than what I done," she said, holding utterly still.

He smiled, and shouldered the gun. "Well, Granny," he said, "you must be a hundred years old, and scared of nothing. I'd give you a dime if I had any money with me. But you take my advice and stay home, and nothing will happen to you."

"God watching me the whole time. I come to stealing."

"I bound to go on my way, mister," said Phoenix. She inclined her head in the red rag. Then they went in different directions, but she could hear the gun shooting again and again over the hill.

She walked on. The shadows hung from the oak trees to the road like curtains. Then she smelled wood-smoke, and smelled the river, and she saw a steeple and the cabins on their steep steps. Dozens of little black children whirled around her. There ahead was Natchez shining. Bells were ringing. She walked on.

In the paved city it was Christmas time. There were red and green electric lights strung and criss-crossed everywhere, and all turned on in the daytime. Old Phoenix would have been lost if she had not distrusted her eyesight and depended on her feet to know where to take her.

She paused quietly on the sidewalk where people were passing by. A lady came along in the crowd, carrying an armful of red-, green- and silver-wrapped presents; she gave off perfume like the red roses in hot summer, and Phoenix stopped her.

"Please, missy, will you lace up my shoe?" She held up her foot.

"What do you want, Grandma?"

"See my shoe," said Phoenix. "Do all right for out in the country, but wouldn't look right to go in a big building."

"Stand still then, Grandma," said the lady. She put her packages down on the sidewalk beside her and laced and tied both shoes tightly.

"Can't lace 'em with a cane," said Phoenix. "Thank you, missy. I doesn't mind asking a nice lady to tie up my shoe, when I gets out on the street."

Moving slowly and from side to side, she went into the big building, and into a tower of steps, where she walked up and around and around until her feet knew to stop.

She entered a door, and there she saw nailed up on the wall the document that had been stamped with the gold seal and framed in the gold frame, which matched the dream that was hung up in her head.

"Here I be," she said. There was a fixed and ceremonial stiffness over her body.

"A charity case, I suppose," said an attendant who sat at the desk before her.

But Phoenix only looked above her head. There was sweat on her face, the wrinkles in her skin shone like a bright net.

"Speak up, Grandma," the woman said. "What's your name? We must have your history, you know. Have you been here before? What seems to be the trouble with you?"

Old Phoenix only gave a twitch to her face as if a fly were bothering her.

"Are you deaf?" cried the attendant.

But then the nurse came in.

"Oh, that's just old Aunt Phoenix," she said. "She doesn't come for herself—she has a little grandson. She makes these trips just as regular as clockwork. She lives away back off the Old Natchez Trace." She bent down. "Well, Aunt Phoenix, why don't you just take a seat? We won't keep you standing after your long trip." She pointed.

The old woman sat down, bolt upright in the chair.

"Now, how is the boy?" asked the nurse.

Old Phoenix did not speak.

"I said, how is the boy?"

But Phoenix only waited and stared straight ahead, her face very solemn and withdrawn into rigidity.

"Is his throat any better?" asked the nurse. "Aunt Phoenix, don't you hear me? Is your grandson's throat any better since the last time you came for the medicine?"

With her hands on her knees, the old woman waited, silent, erect and motionless, just as if she were in armor.

"You mustn't take up our time this way, Aunt Phoenix," the nurse said. "Tell us quickly about your grandson, and get it over. He isn't dead, is he?"

At last there came a flicker and then a flame of comprehension across her face, and she spoke.

"My grandson. It was my memory had left me. There I sat and forgot why I made my long trip."

"Forgot?" The nurse frowned. "After you came so far?"

Then Phoenix was like an old woman begging a dignified forgiveness for waking up frightened in the night. "I never did go to school, I was too old at the Surrender,"[2] she said in a soft voice. "I'm an old woman without an education. It was my memory fail me. My little grandson, he is just the same, and I forgot it in the coming."

"Throat never heals, does it?" said the nurse, speaking in a loud, sure voice to old Phoenix. By now she had a card with something written on it, a little list. "Yes. Swallowed lye. When was it?—January—two-three years ago—"

Phoenix spoke unasked now. "No, missy, he not dead, he just the same. Every little while his throat begin to close up again, and he not able to swallow. He not get his breath. He not able to help himself. So the time come around, and I go on another trip for the soothing medicine."

"All right. The doctor said as long as you came to get it, you could have it," said the nurse. "But it's an <u>obstinate</u> case."

"My little grandson, he sit up there in the house all wrapped up, waiting by himself," Phoenix went on. "We is the only two left in the world. He suffer and it don't seem to put him back at all. He got a sweet look. He going to last. He wear a little patch quilt and peep out holding his mouth open like a little bird. I remembers so plain now. I not going to forget him again, no, the whole enduring time. I could tell him from all the others in creation."

"All right." The nurse was trying to hush her now. She brought her a bottle of medicine. "Charity," she said, making a check mark in a book.

Old Phoenix held the bottle close to her eyes, and then carefully put it into her pocket.

"I thank you," she said.

"It's Christmas time, Grandma," said the attendant. "Could I give you a few pennies out of my purse?"

"Five pennies is a nickel," said Phoenix stiffly.

"Here's a nickel," said the attendant.

Phoenix rose carefully and held out her hand. She received the nickel and then fished the other nickel out of her pocket and laid it beside the new one. She stared at her palm closely, with her head on one side.

Then she gave a tap with her cane on the floor.

"This is what come to me to do," she said. "I going to the store and buy my child a little windmill they sells, made out of paper. He going to find it hard to believe there such a thing in the world. I'll march myself back where he waiting, holding it straight up in this hand."

She lifted her free hand, gave a little nod, turned around, and walked out of the doctor's office. Then her slow step began on the stairs, going down. ❖

---

2. **Surrender.** Surrender of the South to the North at the end of the Civil War in 1865

ob • sti • nate (äb´ stə nət), *adj.*, stubborn; not easily changed

MIRRORS **&** **W**INDOWS

If Phoenix Jackson had taken a new path to Natchez, rather than the "worn" path, would the meaning of the story change? When have you chosen a familiar path over a new path in your own life?

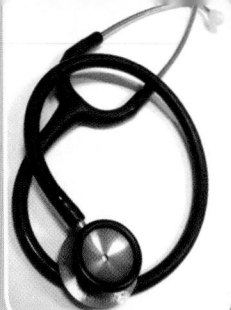
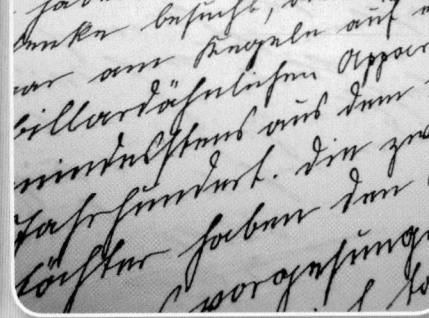
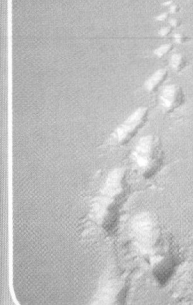

Primary Source Connection

In the essay **"Is Phoenix Jackson's Grandson Really Dead?" Eudora Welty** responds to readers of "A Worn Path" who have written her asking this question. Welty argues that the question is irrelevant: Phoenix makes the journey out of love for her grandson, and whether he is actually dead or still alive will not change the outcome or the central idea of the story. "A Worn Path" works on the theme of love. Other stories and novels by Welty deal with the many dimensions and stages of women's lives, including their roles as daughters, wives, mothers, and grandmothers.

Is Phoenix Jackson's Grandson Really Dead?

by Eudora Welty

A story writer is more than happy to be read by students; the fact that these serious readers think and feel something in response to his work he finds life-giving. At the same time he may not always be able to reply to their specific questions in kind. I wondered if it might clarify something, for both the questioners and myself, if I set down a general reply to the question that comes to me most often in the mail, from both students and their teachers, after some classroom discussion. The unrivaled favorite is this: "Is Phoenix Jackson's grandson really dead?"

It refers to a short story I wrote years ago called "A Worn Path," which tells of a day's journey an old woman makes on foot from deep in the country into town and into a doctor's office on behalf of her little grandson; he is at home, periodically ill, and periodically she comes for his medicine; they give it to her as usual, she receives it and starts the journey back.

I had not meant to mystify readers by withholding any fact; it is not a writer's business to tease. The story is told through Phoenix's mind as she undertakes her errand. As the author at one with the character as I tell it, I must assume that the boy is alive. As the reader, you are free to think as you like, of course: the story invites you to believe that no matter what happens, Phoenix for as long as she is able to walk and can hold to her purpose will make her journey. The *possibility* that she would keep on even if he were dead is there in her devotion and its single-minded, single-track errand. Certainly the *artistic* truth, which should be good enough for the fact, lies in Phoenix's own answer to

Cemetery Monument, 1937. Eudora Welty. Private collection.

tions, too, become facts, in the larger, fictional sense. But it is not all right, not in good faith, for things not to mean what they say.

The grandson's plight was real and it made the truth of the story, which is the story of an errand of love carried out. If the child no longer lived, the truth would persist in the "wornness" of the path. But his being dead can't increase the truth of the story, can't affect it one way or the other. I think I signal this, because the end of the story has been reached before old Phoenix gets home again: she simply starts back. To the question "Is the grandson really dead?" I could reply that it doesn't make any difference. I could also say that I did not make him up in order to let him play a trick on Phoenix. But my best answer would be: "*Phoenix* is alive."

The origin of a story is sometimes a trustworthy clue to the author—or can provide him with the clue—to its key image; maybe in this case it will do the same for the reader. One day I saw a solitary old woman like Phoenix. She was walking; I saw her, at middle distance, in a winter country landscape, and watched her slowly make her way across my line of vision. That sight of her made me write the story. I invented an errand for her, but that only seemed a living part of the figure she was herself: what errand other than for someone else could be making her go? And her going was the first thing, her persisting in her landscape was the real thing, and the first and the real were what I wanted and worked to keep. I brought her up close enough, by imagination, to describe her face, make her present to the eyes, but the full-length figure moving across the winter fields was the indelible one and the image to keep, and the perspective extending into the vanishing distance the true one to hold in mind.

that question. When the nurse asks, "He isn't dead, is he?" she speaks for herself: "He still the same. He going to last."

The grandchild is the incentive. But it is the journey, the going of the errand, that is the story, and the question is not whether the grandchild is in reality alive or dead. It doesn't affect the outcome of the story or its meaning from start to finish. But it is not the question itself that has struck me as much as the idea, almost without exception implied in the asking, that for Phoenix's grandson to be dead would somehow make the story "better."

It's *all right*, I want to say to the students who write to me, for things to be what they appear to be, and for words to mean what they say. It's all right, too, for words and appearances to mean more than one thing—ambiguity is a fact of life. A fiction writer's responsibility covers not only what he presents as the facts of a given story but what he chooses to stir up as their implications; in the end, these implica-

I invented for my character, as I wrote, some passing adventures—some dreams and harassments and a small triumph or two, some jolts to her pride, some flights of fancy to console her, one or two encounters to scare her, and a moment that gave her cause to feel ashamed, a moment to dance and preen— for it had to be a *journey,* and all these things belonged to that, parts of life's uncertainty.

A narrative line is in its deeper sense, of course, the tracing out of a meaning and the real continuity of a story lies in this probing forward. The real dramatic force of a story depends on the strength of the emotion that has set it going. The emotional value is the measure of the reach of the story. What gives any such content to "A Worn Path" is not its circumstances but its *subject:* the deep-grained habit of love.

What I hoped would come clear was that in the whole surround of this story, the world it threads through, the only certain thing at all is the worn path. The habit of love cuts through confusion and stumbles or contrives its way out of difficulty, it remembers the way even when it forgets, for a dumbfounded moment, its reason for being. The path is the thing that matters.

Her victory—old Phoenix's—is when she sees the diploma in the doctor's office, when she finds "nailed up on the wall the document that had been stamped with the gold seal and framed in the gold frame, which matched the dream that was hung up in her head." The return with the medicine is just a matter of retracing her own footsteps. It is the part of the journey, and of the story, that can now go without saying.

In the matter of function, old Phoenix's way might even do as a sort of parallel to your way of work if you are a writer of stories. The way to get there is the all-important, all-absorbing problem, and this problem is your reason for undertaking the story. Your only guide, too, is your sureness about your subject, about what this subject is. Like Phoenix, you work all your life to find your way, through all the obstructions and the false appearances and the upsets you may have brought on yourself, to reach a meaning—using inventions of your imagination, perhaps helped out by your dreams and bits of good luck. And finally too, like Phoenix, you have to assume that what you are working in aid of is life, not death.

But you would make the trip anyway— wouldn't you?—just on hope. ❖

Review Questions

1. According to Welty, what truly matters in this story—the "only certain thing"? Explain why it does not matter whether Phoenix Jackson's grandson is dead.

2. What inspired Welty to write "A Worn Path"? Analyze why Welty focuses on the incidents that happen to Phoenix Jackson along the way, not the results of her actions.

3. According to Welty, what is "all right" and "not all right" in fiction writing? Does the meaning of the story change if Phoenix Jackson's grandson is dead or alive? Why or why not? Judge whether Welty's explanation is acceptable.

TEXT $\xleftrightarrow{\text{TO}}$ TEXT CONNECTION

Eudora Welty believes that a story should be able to stand alone so the reader can find its truth. Do you agree or disagree? What does Welty identify as the responsibilities of a writer? Evaluate whether she fulfills these responsibilities in "A Worn Path."

Refer to Text ▶ ▶ ▶ ▶ ▶ **Reason with Text**

1a. Identify the areas through which Phoenix walks.	**1b.** Which obstacle in Phoenix's journey poses the greatest threat to her? Why?	**Understand** Find meaning
2a. Why is the woman who ties Phoenix's shoes carrying presents?	**2b.** Relate the Christmas story to Phoenix's journey. What associations can you make?	**Apply** Use information
3a. List the obstacles Phoenix encounters during her journey, and describe how she overcomes each one.	**3b.** Analyze the methods Phoenix uses to overcome each obstacle. What do they reveal about her character?	**Analyze** Take things apart
4a. Is Phoenix Jackson's grandson alive or dead? Find examples from the story to support each answer.	**4b.** Argue whether "The Worn Path" would be a better story if readers knew for certain whether the grandson were alive or dead.	**Evaluate** Make judgments
5a. How old is Phoenix? Identify places in the story that Phoenix and her behavior are compared to a clock.	**5b.** Explain why Welty waits until the end of the story to reveal why Phoenix made the journey. Address the use of clock imagery in your explanation.	**Create** Bring ideas together

Analyze Literature

Character and Archetype

Review the list of obstacles you made. What do you learn about Phoenix from these encounters? What else do you learn about Phoenix's appearance, actions, and so on? Based on these details, is Phoenix a flat or round character?

What emotion makes it possible for Phoenix to overcome the obstacles of her journey? Explain how her journey is an archetype.

Extend the Text

Writing Options

Creative Writing Write a personal narrative to share with classmates about a journey you have taken to help someone important to you. The journey need not be long, but it should contain obstacles you can describe vividly. For example, have you ever approached your parents to speak on behalf of a brother or sister?

Descriptive Writing Imagine you are nominating Phoenix Jackson for a special award honoring African-American women of character. Write an essay to submit to the awards committee in which you describe her character. Include what you learn about Phoenix's character from the obstacles she faces.

Collaborative Learning

Create a Board Game With a small group of students, develop a board game based on Phoenix Jackson's journey. Determine how players will advance around the board, what penalties will impede their progress, and how the winner be determined. Divide tasks among members for writing directions and making the board and accessories. Have classmates play your game.

Media Literacy

Research the Author Use the Internet to locate news items about Eudora Welty, such as information about adaptations of her work, interviews with her, reviews of her work, and winners of the Eudora Welty Writing Contest for high school students. Then lay out a page of a newsletter dedicated to Welty, including articles on the topics you find most interesting. Share your newsletter with the class.

 Go to **www.mirrorsandwindows.com** for more.

1. Which of the following obstacles does Phoenix Jackson *not* meet along her journey?
   A. a log across the creek
   B. a barbed-wire fence
   C. a bull in a cotton field
   D. a large black dog
   E. a bush of thorns

2. How does the man who helps Phoenix out of the ditch show disrespect for her?
   A. He points his gun at her.
   B. He calls her "Granny."
   C. He assumes she is going to town to see Santa Claus.
   D. He tells her she should go home.
   E. All of the above

3. Phoenix's cane is described as "limber as a buggy whip." Which of the following is an antonym for the word *limber*?
   A. stiff
   B. supple
   C. thick
   D. sharp
   E. lightweight

4. In the sentence "Big dead trees, like black men with one arm, were standing in the purple stalks of the withered cotton field," the trees are described using which type or types of figurative language?
   A. a metaphor
   B. a simile
   C. personification
   D. A and C
   E. B and C

5. Which of the following best states the theme of "A Worn Path"?
   A. The personal sacrifices we make for the people we love become habitual.
   B. Love overcomes all of life's obstacles, even death.
   C. Making sacrifices for the people we love eventually wears us down.
   D. Every loving relationship is tested by countless obstacles.
   E. Elderly family members have a lifelong responsibility to care for the young.

6. Which of the following is *not* a sign that Phoenix Jackson may be losing touch with reality?
   A. When she arrives at the doctor's office, she forgets for a moment why she has come there.
   B. Rather than tie her own shoes, she asks a woman she meets on the sidewalk to do it.
   C. While sitting on the bank of the creek, she sees a boy offer her a slice of cake.
   D. She talks to the animals she sees and hears as she walks down the road.
   E. She thinks she sees a ghost in a cornfield.

7. According to Welty in her essay, why doesn't it matter whether Phoenix Jackson's grandson is dead or alive?
   A. He is not a real person; Phoenix has imagined him.
   B. He is only a minor character and thus not important to the outcome of the story.
   C. Phoenix makes the journey out of love for her grandson; whether he is dead or alive is irrelevant.
   D. Phoenix does not think about or mention her grandson until she gets to the doctor's office; he is not important to the story.
   E. Welty never answers this question in her essay; she wants the answer to be a mystery.

8. **Constructed Response:** Explain how Phoenix Jackson's journey in "A Worn Path" can be considered archetypal. Identify the elements of an archetype, and use details from the story to support your explanation. Consider what Phoenix's determination to complete her journey suggests about human nature.

9. **Constructed Response:** Explain whether your understanding of "A Worn Path" differs depending on whether Phoenix's grandson is dead or alive. Use examples from the story and Welty's essay to support your answer.

TEST-TAKING TIP

When you take the analogy portion of a test, consider how the first two words in each analogy relate to one another before reviewing the answer options. Test makers often include a choice that is synonymous with one word in the first part of the analogy but not both words.

VOCABULARY & SPELLING
CONTRACTIONS

Understand the Concept

In "Is Phoenix Jackson's Grandson Really Dead?" Eudora Welty writes, "But his being dead can't increase the truth of the story, can't affect it one way or the other." In this sentence, the word *can't* is a **contraction,** which is formed by combining a pronoun and a verb or the words in a verb phrase. One or more letters are omitted and replaced with an apostrophe.

Commonly used contractions formed from the pronouns *I, you, we,* and *they* include the following:

I'm (I am)	we're (we are)
I've (I have)	we've (we have)
I'll (I will)	we'll (we will)
you're (you are)	they're (they are)
you've (you have)	they've (they have)
you'll (you will)	they'll (they will)

Commonly used contractions formed from verb phrases with *not* include these:

isn't (is not)	don't (do not)
wasn't (was not)	didn't (did not)
won't (will not)	doesn't (does not)

Several other commonly used contractions are sometimes mistakenly used as possessives to show ownership. The word *it's* is a contraction that means "it is"; the possessive *its* is written without an apostrophe. Similarly, the word *who's* is a contraction meaning "who is"; the possessive of *who* is *whose.*

> **EXAMPLES**
> **Contraction** *It's* almost time to leave for the movie.
> **Possessive** The car was due for *its* annual inspection.
> **Contraction** We need to decide *who's* attending.
> **Possessive** *Whose* turn is next?

Welty's use of contractions in her essay is well suited to its informal, conversational tone. Note how much more formal the same sentence sounds when the word *cannot* is used instead of *can't:*

> But his being dead cannot increase the truth of the story, cannot affect it one way or the other.

The informal nature of contractions makes their use inappropriate for most academic writing. In developing your writing skills, learn how to match your tone and thus your word choices to the occasion, whether formal or informal.

Apply the Skill

Exercise A
Write the following sentences on a sheet of paper. Then review each one, underlining the contractions and circling the possessives.

1. In her essay, Welty argues that it's irrelevant whether Phoenix Jackson's grandson is dead or alive.
2. That fact won't change the story's outcome or central idea.
3. Welty wasn't afraid to write about the intimate but often strange bonds within families and communities.
4. However, she didn't want her readers or critics to make too strong a connection between her life and her writing.
5. In her autobiography, *One Writer's Beginnings,* she stated, "The writer's mind and heart . . . can't be mapped and plotted."

Exercise B
Revise the sentences in Exercise A, writing out each contraction above the line. Note the difference in formality between the original and revised sentences.

> **SPELLING PRACTICE**
>
> **Plurals**
> In most cases, making a word plural is the simple matter of adding an *-s* to the end. However, in some cases, you need to add *-es,* as in *dresses,* or change a *y* to an *i* before adding *-es,* as in *stories.* Words that have irregular plural forms, such as *goose/geese* and *ox/oxen,* also can be confusing. Review the following words from "A Worn Path," and note how each plural has been formed.
>
> | | | |
> |---|---|---|
> | bubbles | feathers | pennies |
> | cabins | foxes | pines |
> | doors | ladies | roses |
> | echoes | needles | senses |
> | eyes | packages | tears |

Portrait of a Girl in Glass

by Tennessee Williams

Thomas Lanier "Tennessee" Williams (1911–1983), one of the United States' finest playwrights, grew up in Mississippi and St. Louis. He was nicknamed "Tennessee" by college friends because of his pronounced Southern accent and his father's Tennessee roots.

Williams's first real success came in 1944 with production of *The Glass Menagerie,* a play based on one of his short stories, **"Portrait of a Girl in Glass"** (1941). The central character of that work—a socially isolated young woman whose fragility is symbolized by her collection of glass figurines—is believed to be modeled on Williams's sister, Rose, who spent much of her life institutionalized.

A prolific writer, Williams wrote twenty-five full-length plays, dozens of short plays and screenplays, two novels, sixty short stories, over one hundred poems, and an autobiography. His most noted plays, *A Streetcar Named Desire* (1947) and *Cat on a Hot Tin Roof* (1955), both won Pulitzer Prizes and were made into award-winning films. Much of Williams's writing is set in the South and features individuals struggling with the loss of traditional values and lifestyles.

We lived in a third floor apartment on Maple Street in Saint Louis, on a block which also contained the Everready Garage, a Chinese laundry, and a bookie shop[1] disguised as a cigar store.

Mine was an anomalous[2] character, one that appeared to be slated for radical change or disaster, for I was a poet who had a job in a warehouse. As for my sister Laura, she could be classified even less readily than I. She made no positive motion toward the world but stood at the edge of the water, so to speak, with feet that anticipated too much cold to move. She'd never have budged an inch, I'm pretty sure, if my mother who was a relatively aggressive sort of woman had not shoved her roughly forward, when Laura was twenty years old, by enrolling her as a student in a nearby business college. Out of her "magazine money" (she sold subscriptions to women's magazines), Mother had paid my sister's tuition for a term of six months. It did not work out. Laura tried to memorize the typewriter keyboard, she had a chart at home, she used to sit silently in front of it for hours, staring at it while she cleaned and polished her infinite number of little glass ornaments. She did this every evening after dinner. Mother would caution me to be very quiet. "Sister is looking at her typewriter chart!" I felt somehow that it would do her no good, and I was right. She would seem to know the positions of the keys until the weekly speed-drill[3] got under way, and then they would fly from her mind like a bunch of startled birds.

At last she couldn't bring herself to enter the school any more. She kept this failure a secret for a while. She left the house each morning as before and spent six hours walking around the park. This was in February, and all the walking out-doors regardless of weather brought on influenza. She

---

1. **bookie shop.** Place where bets are illegally made for events such as horse races
2. **anomalous.** Being or seeming inconsistent, contradictory, or abnormal
3. **speed-drill.** Method of teaching involving timed repetition of an exercise; here refers to a timed typing test

Portrait of a Woman, 1909. Alexej von Jawlensky.
Uzbekistan Art Museum, Tashkent, Uzbekistan.

was in bed for a couple of weeks with a curiously happy little smile on her face. Of course Mother phoned the business college to let them know she was ill. Whoever was talking on the other end of the line had some trouble, it seems, in remembering who Laura was, which annoyed my mother and she spoke up pretty sharply. "Laura has been attending that school of yours for two months, you certainly ought to recognize her name!" Then came the stunning disclosure. The person sharply retorted, after a moment or two, that now she *did* remember the Wingfield girl, and that she had not been at the business college *once* in about a month.

Whoever was talking on the other end of the line had some trouble, it seems, in remembering who Laura was, which annoyed my mother.

Mother's voice became strident.[4] Another person was brought to the phone to verify the statement of the first. Mother hung up and went to Laura's bedroom where she lay with a tense and frightened look in place of the faint little smile. Yes, admitted my sister, what they said was true. "I couldn't go any longer, it scared me too much, it made me sick at the stomach!"

After this fiasco,[5] my sister stayed at home and kept in her bedroom mostly. This was a narrow room that had two windows on a dusky areaway between two wings of the building. We called this areaway Death Valley for a reason that seems worth telling. There were a great many alley-cats in the neighborhood and one particularly vicious dirty white Chow[6] who stalked them continually. In the open or on the fire-escapes they could usually elude him but now and again he cleverly contrived[7] to run some youngster among them into the cul-de-sac of this narrow areaway at the far end of which, directly beneath my sister's bedroom windows, they made the blinding discovery that what had appeared to be an avenue of escape was really a locked arena, a gloomy vault of concrete and brick with walls too high for any cat to spring, in which they must suddenly turn to spit at their death until it was hurled upon them. Hardly a week went by without a repetition of this violent drama. The areaway had grown to be hateful to Laura because she could not look out on it without recalling the screams and the snarls of killing. She kept the shades drawn down, and as Mother would not permit the use of electric

4. **strident.** Harsh and insistent
5. **fiasco.** Complete failure
6. **Chow.** Breed of dog
7. **contrived.** Planned in a clever manner

current except when needed, her days were spent almost in perpetual[8] twilight. There were three pieces of dingy ivory furniture in the room, a bed, a bureau, a chair. Over the bed was a remarkably bad religious painting, a very effeminate head of Christ with teardrops visible just below the eyes. The charm of the room was produced by my sister's collection of glass. She loved colored glass and had covered the walls with shelves of little glass articles, all of them light and delicate in color. These she washed and polished with endless care. When you entered the room there was always this soft, transparent radiance in it which came from the glass absorbing whatever faint light came through the shades on Death Valley. I have no idea how many articles there were of this delicate glass. There must have been hundreds of them. But Laura could tell you exactly. She loved each one.

She lived in a world of glass and also a world of music. The music came from a 1920 victrola[9] and a bunch of records that dated from about the same period, pieces such as *Whispering* or *The Love Nest* or *Dardanella*.[10] These records were souvenirs of our father, a man whom we barely remembered, whose name was spoken rarely. Before his sudden and unexplained disappearance from our lives he had made this gift to the household, the phonograph and the records, whose music remained as a sort of apology for him. Once in a while, on pay-day at the warehouse, I would bring home a new record. But Laura seldom cared for these new records, maybe because they reminded her too much of the noisy tragedies in Death Valley or the speed-drills at the business college. The tunes she loved were the ones she had always heard. Often she sang to herself at night in her bedroom. Her voice was thin, it usually wandered off-key. Yet it had a curious childlike sweetness. At eight o'clock in the evening I sat down to write in my own mouse-trap of a room. Through the closed doors, through the walls, I would hear my sister singing to herself, a piece like *Whispering* or *I Love You* or *Sleepy Time Gal,* losing the tune now and then but always preserving the minor atmosphere of the music. I think that was why I always wrote such strange and sorrowful poems in those days. Because I had in my ears the wispy sound of my sister serenading her pieces of colored glass, washing them while she sang or merely looking down at them with her vague blue eyes until the points of gem-like radiance in them gently drew the aching particles of reality from her mind and finally produced a state of hypnotic calm in which she even stopped singing or washing the glass and merely sat without motion until my mother knocked at the door and warned her against the waste of electric current.

I don't believe that my sister was actually foolish. I think the petals of her mind had simply closed through fear, and it's no telling how much they had closed upon in the way

---

8. **perpetual.** Continuing forever
9. **victrola.** Type of home music player that played music recorded on a circular record
10. ***Dardanella.*** Wildly popular dance songs from the 1920s

of secret wisdom. She never talked very much, not even to me, but once in a while she did pop out with something that took you by surprise.

After work at the warehouse or after I'd finished my writing in the evening, I'd drop in her room for a little visit because she had a restful and soothing effect on nerves that were worn rather thin from trying to ride two horses simultaneously in two opposite directions.

I usually found her seated in the straight-back ivory chair with a piece of glass cupped tenderly in her palm.

"What are you doing? Talking to it?" I asked.

"No," she answered gravely, "I was just looking at it."

On the bureau were two pieces of fiction which she had received as Christmas or birthday presents. One was a novel called the *Rose-Garden Husband*[11] by someone whose name escapes me. The other was *Freckles* by Gene Stratton Porter.[12] I never saw her reading the *Rose-Garden Husband,* but the other book was one that she actually lived with. It had probably never occurred to Laura that a book was something you read straight through and then laid aside as finished. The character Freckles, a one-armed orphan youth who worked in a lumber-camp, was someone that she invited into her bedroom now and then for a friendly visit just as she did me. When I came in and found this novel open upon her lap, she would gravely remark that Freckles was having some trouble with the foreman of the lumber-camp or that he had just received an injury to his spine when a tree fell on him. She frowned with genuine sorrow when she reported these misadventures of her story-book hero, possibly not recalling how successfully he came through them all, that the injury to the spine fortuitously[13] resulted in the discovery of rich parents and that the bad-tempered foreman had a heart of gold at the end of the book. Freckles became involved in romance with a girl he called The Angel, but my sister usually stopped reading when this girl became too prominent in the story. She closed the book or turned back to the lonelier periods in the orphan's story. I only remember her making one reference to this heroine of the novel. "The Angel is nice," she said, "but seems to be kind of conceited about her looks."

Then one time at Christmas, while she was trimming the artificial tree, she picked up the Star of Bethlehem that went on the topmost branch and held it gravely toward the chandelier.

"Do stars have five points really?" she enquired.

This was the sort of thing that you didn't believe and that made you stare at Laura with sorrow and confusion.

"No," I told her, seeing she really meant it, "they're round like the earth and most of them much bigger."

She was gently surprised by this new information. She went to the window to look up at the sky which was, as usual during Saint Louis winters, completely shrouded by smoke.

"It's hard to tell," she said, and returned to the tree.

This was the sort of thing that you didn't believe and that made you stare at Laura with sorrow and confusion.

So time passed on till my sister was twenty-three. Old enough to be married, but the fact of the matter was she had never even had a date with a boy. I don't believe this seemed as awful to her as it did to Mother.

---

11. **Rose-Garden Husband.** Novel by Margaret Widdemer (1884–1978), award-winning American poet and novelist
12. **Freckles by Gene Stratton Porter.** Porter (1863–1924) was an American naturalist and novelist who wrote romantic stories; *Freckles* was a novel published in 1904.
13. **fortuitously.** Fortunately; luckily

At breakfast one morning Mother said to me, "Why don't you cultivate some nice young friends? How about down at the warehouse? Aren't there some young men down there you could ask to dinner?"

This suggestion surprised me because there was seldom quite enough food on her table to satisfy three people. My mother was a terribly stringent[14] housekeeper, God knows we were poor enough in actuality, but my mother had an almost obsessive dread of becoming even poorer. A not unreasonable fear since the man of the house was a poet who worked in a warehouse, but one which I thought played too important a part in all her calculations.

Almost immediately Mother explained herself.

"I think it might be nice," she said, "for your sister."

I brought Jim home to dinner a few nights later. Jim was a big red-haired Irishman who had the scrubbed and polished look of well-kept chinaware. His big square hands seemed to have a direct and very innocent hunger for touching his friends. He was always clapping them on your arms or shoulders and they burned through the cloth of your shirt like plates taken out of an oven. He was the best-liked man in the warehouse and oddly enough he was the only one that I was on good terms with. He found me agreeably ridiculous I think. He knew of my secret practice of retiring to a cabinet in the lavatory and working on rhyme schemes when work was slack in the warehouse, and of sneaking up on the roof now and then to smoke my cigarette with a view across the river at the undulant[15] open country of Illinois.

No doubt I was classified as screwy in Jim's mind as much as in the others', but while their attitude was suspicious and hostile when they first knew me, Jim's was warmly tolerant from

Scene from the original 1945 production of *The Glass Menagerie,* the play based on "Portrait of a Girl in Glass."

the beginning. He called me Slim, and gradually his cordial acceptance drew the others around, and while he remained the only one who actually had anything to do with me, the others had now begun to smile when they saw me as people smile at an oddly fashioned dog who crosses their path at some distance.

The others had now begun to smile when they saw me as people smile at an oddly fashioned dog who crosses their path at some distance.

Nevertheless it took some courage for me to invite Jim to dinner. I thought about it all week and delayed the action till Friday noon, the last possible moment, as the dinner was set for that evening.

"What are you doing tonight?" I finally asked him.

"Not a [darn] thing," said Jim. "I had a date but her Aunt took sick and she's hauled her freight[16] to Centralia!"

14. **stringent.** Strict with money
15. **undulant.** Rising and falling in waves
16. **hauled her freight.** Colloquialism for "gone" or "left for"

"Well," I said, "why don't you come over for dinner?"

"Sure!" said Jim. He grinned with astonishing brightness.

I went outside to phone the news to Mother.

Her voice that was never tired responded with an energy that made the wires crackle.

"I suppose he's Catholic?" she said.

"Yes," I told her, remembering the tiny silver cross on his freckled chest.

"Good!" she said. "I'll bake a salmon loaf!"

And so we rode home together in his jalopy.[17]

I had a curious feeling of guilt and apprehension as I led the lamb-like Irishman up three flights of cracked marble steps to the door of Apartment F, which was not thick enough to hold inside it the odor of baking salmon.

Never having a key, I pressed the bell.

"Laura!" came Mother's voice. "That's Tom and Mr. Delaney! Let them in!"

There was a long, long pause.

"Laura?" she called again. "I'm busy in the kitchen, you answer the door!"

Then at last I heard my sister's footsteps. They went right past the door at which we were standing and into the parlor. I heard the creaking noise of the phonograph crank. Music commenced. One of the oldest records, a march of Sousa's,[18] put on to give her the courage to let in a stranger.

The door came timidly open and there she stood in a dress from Mother's wardrobe, a black chiffon ankle-length and high-heeled slippers on which she balanced uncertainly like a tipsy crane[19] of melancholy plumage.[20] Her eyes stared back at us with a glass brightness and her delicate wing-like shoulders were hunched with nervousness.

"Hello!" said Jim, before I could introduce him.

He stretched out his hand. My sister touched it only for a second.

"Excuse me!" she whispered, and turned with a breathless rustle back to her bedroom door, the sanctuary[21] beyond it briefly revealing itself with the tinkling, muted radiance of glass before the door closed rapidly but gently on her wraithlike figure.

Jim seemed to be incapable of surprise.

"Your sister?" he asked.

"Yes, that was her," I admitted. "She's terribly shy with strangers."

"She looks like you," said Jim, "except she's pretty."

Laura did not reappear till called to dinner. Her place was next to Jim at the drop-leaf table and all through the meal her figure was slightly tilted away from his. Her face was feverishly bright and one eyelid, the one on the side toward Jim, had developed a nervous wink. Three times in the course of the dinner she dropped her fork on her plate with a terrible clatter and she was continually raising the water-glass to her lips for hasty little gulps. She went on doing this even after the water was gone from the glass. And her handling of the silver became more awkward and hurried all the time.

Her face was feverishly bright and one eyelid, the one on the side toward Jim, had developed a nervous wink.

I thought of nothing to say.

To Mother belonged the conversational honors, such as they were. She asked the caller about his home and family. She was delighted to learn that his father had a business of his own, a retail shoe store somewhere in Wyoming. The news that he went to night-school to study accounting was still more edifying.[22] What was his heart set on beside the

---

17. **jalopy.** Automobile that is old and falling apart
18. **Sousa.** John Philip Sousa (1854–1932), an American bandmaster and composer
19. **crane.** Bird with very long legs, a long neck, and a long, straight bill
20. **plumage.** Feathers of a bird
21. **sanctuary.** Place of protection and refuge
22. **edifying.** Enlightening or informative

warehouse? Radio-engineering? My, my, my! It was easy to see that here was a very up-and-coming young man who was certainly going to make his place in the world!

Then she started to talk about her children. Laura, she said, was not cut out for business. She was domestic, however, and making a home was really a girl's best bet.

Jim agreed with all this and seemed not to sense the ghost of an implication.[23] I suffered through it dumbly, trying not to see Laura trembling more and more beneath the incredible unawareness of Mother.

And bad as it was, excruciating[24] in fact, I thought with dread of the moment when dinner was going to be over, for then the diversion of food would be taken away, we would have to go into the little steam-heated parlor. I fancied the four of us having run out of talk, even Mother's seemingly endless store of questions about Jim's home and his job all used up finally—the four of us, then, just sitting there in the parlor, listening to the hiss of the radiator and nervously clearing our throats in the kind of self-consciousness that gets to be suffocating.

But when the blanc-mange[25] was finished, a miracle happened.

Mother got up to clear the dishes away. Jim gave me a clap on the shoulders and said, "Hey, Slim, let's go have a look at those old records in there!"

He sauntered carelessly into the front room and flopped down on the floor beside the victrola. He began sorting through the collection of worn-out records and reading their titles aloud in a voice so hearty that it shot like beams of sunlight through the vapors of self-consciousness engulfing my sister and me.

He was sitting directly under the floor-lamp and all at once my sister jumped up and said to him, "Oh—you have freckles!"

Jim grinned. "Sure that's what my folks call me—Freckles!"

Head of a Young Woman in Profile, c. 1895. Odilon Redon.

"Freckles?" Laura repeated. She looked toward me as if for the confirmation of some too wonderful hope. I looked away quickly, not knowing whether to feel relieved or alarmed at the turn that things were taking.

Jim had wound the victrola and put on *Dardanella.*

He grinned at Laura.

"How about you an' me cutting the rug[26] a little?"

23. **implication.** Suggestion
24. **excruciating.** Causing great pain or disress
25. **blanc-mange.** Sweet, molded jellylike dessert made with milk
26. **cutting the rug.** Colloquialism for "dancing"

"What?" said Laura breathlessly, smiling and smiling.

"Dance!" he said, drawing her into his arms.

As far as I knew she had never danced in her life. But to my everlasting wonder she slipped quite naturally into those huge arms of Jim's, and they danced round and around the small steam-heated parlor, bumping against the sofa and chairs and laughing loudly and happily together. Something opened up in my sister's face. To say it was love is not too hasty a judgment, for after all he had freckles and that was what his folks called him. Yes, he had undoubtedly assumed the identity—for all practical purposes—of the one-armed orphan youth who lived in the Limberlost, that tall and misty region to which she retreated whenever the walls of Apartment F became too close to endure.

Something opened up in my sister's face. To say it was love is not too hasty a judgment.

Mother came back in with some lemonade. She stopped short as she entered the portieres.[27]

"Good heavens! Laura? Dancing?"

Her look was absurdly grateful as well as startled.

"But isn't she stepping all over you, Mr. Delaney?"

"What if she does?" said Jim, with bearish gallantry. "I'm not made of eggs!"

"Well, well, well!" said Mother, senselessly beaming.

"She's light as a feather!" said Jim. "With a little more practice she'd dance as good as Betty!"

There was a little pause of silence.

"Betty?" said Mother.

"The girl I go out with!" said Jim.

"Oh!" said Mother.

She set the pitcher of lemonade carefully down and with her back to the caller and her eyes on me, she asked him just how often he and the lucky young lady went out together.

"Steady!" said Jim.

Mother's look, remaining on my face, turned into a glare of fury.

"Tom didn't mention that you went out with a girl!"

"Nope," said Jim. "I didn't mean to let the cat out of the bag. The boys at the warehouse'll kid me to death when Slim gives the news away."

He laughed heartily but his laughter dropped heavily and awkwardly away as even his dull senses were gradually penetrated by the unpleasant sensation the news of Betty had made.

"Are you thinking of getting married?" said Mother.

"First of next month!" he told her.

It took her several moments to pull herself together. Then she said in a dismal tone, "How nice! If Tom had only told us we could have asked you *both!*"

Jim had picked up his coat.

"Must you be going?" said Mother.

"I hope it don't seem like I'm rushing off," said Jim, "but Betty's gonna get back on the eight o'clock train an' by the time I get my jalopy down to the Wabash depot—"

"Oh, then, we mustn't keep you."

Soon as he'd left, we all sat down, looking dazed.

Laura was the first to speak.

"Wasn't he nice?" she said. "And all those freckles!"

"Yes," said Mother. Then she turned on me.

"You didn't mention that he was engaged to be married!"

"Well, how did I know that he was engaged to be married?"

"I thought you called him your best friend down at the warehouse?"

---

27. **portieres.** Curtains hanging across a doorway

"Yes, but I didn't know he was going to be married!"

"How peculiar!" said Mother. "How very peculiar!"

"No," said Laura gently, getting up from the sofa. "There's nothing peculiar about it."

She picked up one of the records and blew on its surface a little as if it were dusty, then set it softly back down.

"People in love," she said, "take everything for granted."

What did she mean by that? I never knew.

She slipped quietly back to her room and closed the door.

Not very long after that I lost my job at the warehouse. I was fired for writing a poem on the lid of a shoe-box. I left Saint Louis and took to moving around. The cities swept about me like dead leaves, leaves that were brightly colored but torn away from the branches. My nature changed. I grew to be firm and sufficient.

In five years' time I had nearly forgotten home. I had to forget it, I couldn't carry it with me. But once in a while, usually in a strange town before I have found companions, the shell of deliberate hardness is broken through. A door comes softly and irresistibly open. I hear the tired old music my unknown father left in the place he abandoned as faithlessly as I. I see the faint and sorrowful radiance of the glass, hundreds of little transparent pieces of it in very delicate colors. I hold my breath, for if my sister's face appears among them—the night is hers! ❖

In "Portrait of a Girl in Glass," Tom describes Laura as someone who "made no positive motion toward the world but stood at the edge of the water." What fears do you have about going into the world beyond high school?

Refer and Reason

1. List some of the story's many references to animals. Analyze the use of animal imagery by explaining what the animals reveal about individual characters and their situations.

2. What does Laura say about people in love that Tom cannot understand? Explain what Laura seems to mean.

3. How are Tom and his father alike? Explain whether Tom feels he has made the right choice at the end of the story. Could he have realized his own dreams and continued his relationship with his family? Why or why not?

Writing Options

1. Rewrite the scene when Jim Delaney comes to dinner from Laura's point of view. Make your version consistent with both the events that occurred and Laura's character, but reveal more of Laura's thoughts, feelings, and perceptions.

2. Imagine that a literary critic has reviewed "Portrait of a Girl in Glass" and written, "The narrator doesn't really care about his sister." Write a paragraph in which you either support or refute this statement. Use evidence from the short story to support your position.

 Go to **www.mirrorsandwindows.com** for more.

Understand the Concept

Tennessee Williams's stories and plays are known for their realistic dialogue, reflecting both Southern dialect and natural patterns of conversation. Williams achieved that realism, in part, by using **colloquial language,** the informal language of everyday speech. Consider this example from "Portrait of a Girl in Glass," in which Jim, the dinner guest, explains why he has to leave:

> "I hope it don't seem like I'm rushing off, but Betty's gonna get back on the eight o'clock train an' by the time I get my jalopy down to the Wabash depot—"

This example is colloquial in several ways. For instance, the informal word *jalopy* is used to mean "an old, broken-down car." In addition, four contractions are used: *don't* (do not), *I'm* (I am), *Betty's* (Betty is), and *an'* (and). The use of *don't* is grammatically incorrect (the correct contraction here would be *doesn't*), and *gonna* is used for *going to* but actually is not a word. Phrases such as *rushing off, get back,* and *get . . . down to* all are conversational, as well.

Using formal language, Jim's explanation might be stated as follows:

> "I do not want you to think I am leaving hurriedly, but Betty is returning home on the train due in at eight o'clock, and given the amount of time required to drive my old, broken-down automobile to the Wabash depot—"

Note the dramatic change in tone along with the addition of nine words.

Contemporary examples of colloquial language include these words and expressions:

cool (excellent, popular)	funny (odd, different)
flunked (failed)	wired (high strung)
get across (communicate)	check out (investigate)

Clearly, all these words and expressions have other more standard (*denotative*) meanings. For instance, the dictionary defines the word *cool* as meaning "lacking in warmth." Yet in most instances of everyday conversation, the meanings of these words would be clear. They have generally accepted informal meanings. These meanings may not be clear, however, among people of another generation or those from another culture.

As a speaker and writer, you should know when the use of colloquial language is appropriate. Consider the occasion and audience. In an informal situation that involves communicating with friends, family, and other familiar people, colloquial language is appropriate. However, in any situation—even an informal one—that includes people who speak English as a second language, the use of colloquial language likely would cause confusion and so should be avoided. In academic settings, colloquial language generally is not appropriate.

Apply the Skill

Rewrite each of the following sentences to eliminate the use of colloquial language.

1. Tom knows his job at the warehouse isn't a good fit for him.
2. Typing school is too much for Laura, so she starts skipping class.
3. Tom knows Laura is a funny girl and has a hard time fitting in.
4. Tom's mom bugs him about getting Laura a date with one of his buddies from work.
5. Laura had a huge crush on Jim in high school.
6. After Tom gets fired, he takes off.

SPELLING PRACTICE

Verbs That End with *y*

Forming the past tense of a verb that ends with *y* can result in a spelling error if you do not know whether to change the *y* to an *i* before adding -*ed*. For instance, the past tense of *cry* is *cried*, not *cryed*. Determine how to spell the past-tense form of each these verbs from "Portrait of a Girl in Glass."

classify	marry	study
delay	pay	try
fly	satisfy	verify
lay	stay	

Three Famous Short Novels: Spotted Horses, Old Man, The Bear
by William Faulkner

This collection shows Faulkner in three very different modes. *The Bear* relates young Ike McCaslin's hunt for an aged bear, in which he learns about blood connection with the land and respect for the old ways. *Spotted Horses* is a tall tale of the Southwest featuring three con men, the disreputable Snopes family, and a suspicious wild horse auction. *Old Man* requires some digging to figure out how a gentle convict ends up back in prison, serving an additional ten years.

All the King's Men by Robert Penn Warren

In this classic novel, Robert Penn Warren chronicles the rise and fall of a Southern politican through the eyes of his closest associate. Based loosely on the exploits of Louisiana governor and senator Huey P. Long, this popular political thriller has been adapted into two films, a play, and an opera.

The Good War: An Oral History of World War II by Studs Terkel

Studs Terkel collected the testimonies of more than 120 Americans who lived through World War II and anthologized them, producing one continuous narrative. His unique approach to history provides firsthand accounts of the experiences of a wide range of Americans during this turbulent era of history.

Hiroshima by John Hersey

John Hersey went to Hiroshima, Japan, a month after the atomic bomb was dropped to write a magazine article on the survivors. In a factual, journalistic style, he follows the survivors from just before the blast through the next several days as they cope with radiation sickness and injury. An immediate sensation, Hersey's work put a human face on devastation that was impossible to comprehend.

Native Son by Richard Wright

From the beginning of Wright's controversial novel, it is clear that his protagonist, Bigger Thomas, is headed for trouble. What follows is a gripping murder mystery that boldly confronts America's difficult and inescapable race conflict. Wright's painfully honest discussion will chill most readers to the bone.

Impounded: Dorothea Lange and the Censored Images of Japanese American Internment by Dorothea Lange, Linda Gordon, and Gary Okihiro

Dorothea Lange was commissioned by the U.S. government to photograph the Japanese internment camps erected during World War II, but when government officials saw the sorrowful content of her work, they confiscated her entire portfolio. Published for the first time in 2006, Lange's historic pictures capture the humiliation and anguish forced on Japanese-American communities during this period.

Knowing how to give a *how-to,* or *process,* presentation is one of the most useful things you can learn about speaking. Giving clear directions is important not only in the classroom but also in the world of work. Many people's jobs involve giving this type of presentation—for example, to train new employees or to demonstrate a product to potential buyers.

When you create a set of directions for others to follow, think through the process carefully. Make certain the steps you provide are complete, accurate, and in the proper sequence.

1. Choose a Suitable Topic

The topic you choose for your how-to presentation should be one you are familiar with or can learn about easily. Also keep in mind your listeners' interests. Try to select a process that will appeal to the audience. Processes you might explain include the following:

- Getting a driver's license
- Cooking a favorite food
- Working as a volunteer
- Finding a summer job
- Applying to colleges

It's best not to demonstrate a process that includes complicated steps or requires difficult-to-obtain or possibly dangerous equipment. In other words, keep your presentation simple. If you are not sure whether a topic is suitable, check with your teacher.

2. Develop Well-Organized Directions

Begin by arranging the major steps of the process in logical order. Then give the details needed to complete each step. Be sure to specify the materials needed and carefully explain the tasks involved.

Also follow these guidelines:

- Use transitional words such as *first, second,* and *next* to help readers keep track of the steps of the process. Using transitional words also will help you keep your place in the presentation.
- Before you move from one step to step the next, be sure your listeners have understood what you have described. If they look confused, review what you have said or ask if they need clarification.

- Use visual aids so you can demonstrate the process while you describe it (see Speaking & Listening Workshop, Unit 5). Doing so will make your presentation more interesting to listeners and also may help calm your nerves. To ensure audience members will be able to see what you are doing, use large photographs and diagrams or an oversized model.

3. Practice Your Delivery

Assemble all the materials, including your visual aids. Plan how to arrange and use them in the location where you will be speaking. For instance, will you need a table? An electrical outlet? A whiteboard? Also consider how to arrange the setting so your listeners can see and hear your presentation.

Practice your presentation in front of one or two friends or family members, and ask them to provide feedback on both your content and delivery. In particular, verify whether they can follow the steps you present in explaining your process.

SPEAKING & LISTENING RUBRIC

Your presentation will be evaluated on these elements:

Content

- ❑ The topic is of interest to your listeners and avoids complicated steps and equipment.
- ❑ The steps proceed in logical order.
- ❑ The visual aids are appropriate for the content.

Delivery & Presentation

- ❑ You use transitional words to track the steps in the process.
- ❑ You handle your visual aids effectively.
- ❑ You arrange the setting appropriately.
- ❑ You take note of the audience's response to monitor whether your explanation is clear.

As American society grows more reliant on technology, mediums such as video, PowerPoint, and Flash are becoming increasingly prevalent. Learning how to use these and other multimedia tools will help expand your communication skills and better equip you for today's technology-reliant world.

For this assignment, you will create a multimedia presentation that discusses an aspect of World War II or the Depression.

Assignment Plan, create, and edit a multimedia presentation

Purpose To explore a topic related to World War II or the Depression

Audience Students in an American or world history class

❶ Prewrite

Select Your Topic

Both World War II and the Depression offer a wide variety of topics, including people, places, and events in the United States and overseas. Since your presentation will rely heavily on visuals, choose a topic that will translate well to the screen. Many of the most dramatic events and people of the 1930s and 1940s were captured in photographs and documentaries.

Gather Information

Research your topic using both Internet and library sources. Take detailed notes that document facts about your topic, and collect corresponding images.

WRITING RUBRIC

A successful multimedia presentation has these elements:

- ❏ an intriguing introduction that presents the topic
- ❏ a body that provides information and builds interest
- ❏ a conclusion that brings the presentation to a satisfying close

Write Your Controlling Idea

What overall message do you want to convey to your audience? Write a one-sentence statement in response to that question. You may not include this *controlling idea* in your presentation, but you should use it to help focus your thoughts.

Organize Your Ideas

For a historical topic, it is logical to organize the information in **chronological order,** in which details are presented in order of occurrence. Create an informal outline, listing the details you want to present. Then review your notes. Do you have enough content to present a complete, accurate discussion of your topic? Have you located images that match your content and will enhance your discussion of it?

Also keep in mind your audience's interest level and attention span. How can you make your topic appealing to students? Finally, consider the length requirement and other details of the assignment. Be sure you can cover your topic in the appropriate time frame and level of detail.

❷ Draft

Although this assignment is a multimedia presentation, it should follow the traditional structure of a written assignment, such as an essay. Write a draft or script to use in delivering or recording your presentation. Follow this three-part framework: Introduction, Body, and Conclusion.

Introduction Command audience attention by suggesting your topic's importance.

Body Maintain interest through compelling imagery and narration.

Conclusion Close the discussion and reinforce the importance of your topic.

Draft Your Introduction

In creating the introduction, make good use of images as well as words. What is the most dramatic or shocking aspect of your topic? Consider starting with this point to seize your audience's attention.

Draft Your Body

In the body, continue to build on the interest you created in your introduction. Use chronological order to create a sense of drama, presenting each detail in order, as it happened.

Review your outline and notes. Think about which details you want to narrate with words versus visuals. Also verify that each detail relates to your controlling idea.

> ### What Great Writers Do
> British writer and critic V. S. Pritchett notes, "Stories can be rather stark and bare unless you put in the right details. Details make stories human, and the more human a story can be, the better."

Draft Your Conclusion

Next, compose the conclusion. Again, use a mixture of imagery and narration. Your goal is to leave readers with a feeling of closure but also an understanding of why this historical topic still is important.

❸ Revise

Evaluate Your Draft

Exchange drafts with a classmate, or evaluate your own work. First, review the content and organization.

REVISION CHECKLIST

Content & Organization

- ❏ Does the introduction create interest and identify the topic?
- ❏ Does the body discuss the topic in a logical yet interesting way?
- ❏ Does the conclusion wrap up the discussion and reinforce the importance of the topic?

Grammar & Style

- ❏ Have you used precise language to portray history accurately? (page 701)
- ❏ Do you use active and passive voice effectively to highlight meaning? (page 751)
- ❏ Have you used possessive nouns and pronouns correctly? (page 788)

Is the information organized in a logical way that will make sense to listeners? Does all the information relate clearly to the controlling idea? Are visuals used effectively?

Next, check the flow of the narration, the spoken part of your presentation. Pay particular attention to *coherence,* or how well ideas are connected. Add transitions such as *first, next,* and *in addition* to link ideas. In a historical discussion, citing the years in which events occurred also provides coherence.

Finally, make sure you have correctly applied the concepts presented in the Grammar & Style workshops in this unit. Use the Revision Checklist to evaluate the language for clarity and specificity.

Revise for Content, Organization, and Style

Review the notes you or your partner made on your draft. Consider each point as you edit and revise your presentation.

❹ Deliver or Record

Whether you will deliver your multimedia presentation live to an audience or record and show it later, practice well in advance. Your narration and presentation of images must be well timed and polished, as delays and other slip-ups will distract listeners.

The primary advantage of recording a presentation is that you have the opportunity to review and revise it. The corresponding disadvantage is that audience members will have greater expectations of a recorded presentation than a live one.

Writing Follow-Up

Publish and Present

- ● Contact ninth-grade history or social studies teachers to see if they will show your presentation to their students, your intended audience. If you can, observe students' responses and decide whether you successfully reached your target audience.

Reflect

- ● A famous saying suggests that "Those who forget history are destined to repeat it." What lessons were learned or should have been learned from the Depression and World War II?

Reading Skills

Compare and Contrast Characters

Comparing and contrasting are closely related processes. When you **compare** one item with another, you describe how the two are alike, noting the similarities between them. When you **contrast** two items, you describe their differences.

To compare and contrast characters from a literary selection, begin by listing the traits of each character. To identify these traits, review the selection for direct descriptions of the character, the character's behavior, the character's thoughts and emotions, and the character's interaction with other characters—that is, how he or she treats and behaves with others and what others say or think about him or her. Record the characters' traits in a simple two-column chart, using one column for each character.

After you have listed the characters' traits, compare lists to see which traits they have in common. As you identify matching or similar characteristics, draw a line from one column of your chart to the other. These paired traits are the characters' similarities; those traits that are left unpaired are the characters' differences.

Not all character traits are equally important. In comparing and contrasting characters, focus on the most important traits. To judge whether a trait is important, think about how often it is mentioned or how much it affects the character's thoughts and actions. Also consider the result of the character being this way. Would the story change much if the character did not have this trait?

TEST-TAKING TIP

In responding to a multiple-choice question, think of the correct response on your own before reading the options provided. Then read the options and identify the one that most closely matches your initial response.

Practice

Directions: Read the following passage from *The Glass Menagerie*, a play by Tennessee Williams. Answer the questions after it based on what is stated or implied in the passage.

1   **TOM.** In high school, Jim was a hero. He had tremendous Irish good nature and vitality with the scrubbed and polished look of white chinaware. He seemed to move in a
5   continual spotlight. He was a star in basketball, captain of the debating club, president of the senior class and the glee club, and he sang the male lead in the annual light opera. He was forever running or bounding,
10   never just walking. He seemed always just at the point of defeating the law of gravity. He was shooting with such velocity through his adolescence that you would just logically expect him to arrive at nothing short of
15   the White House by the time he was thirty. But Jim apparently ran into more interference after his graduation from high school because his speed had definitely slowed. And so, at this particular time in our lives
20   he was holding a job that wasn't much better than mine. . . . I knew that Jim and Laura had known each other in high school because I had heard my sister Laura speak admiringly of Jim's voice. I didn't know if
25   Jim would remember her or not. Because in high school Laura had been as unobtrusive as Jim had been astonishing. . . .
  LAURA. There was a Jim O'Connor we both knew in high school. If that is the one
30   that Tom is bringing home to dinner—Oh, Mother, you'd have to excuse me, I wouldn't come to the table!
  AMANDA. What's this now? What sort of silly talk is this?

35 **LAURA.** You asked me once if I'd ever liked a boy. Don't you remember I showed you this boy's picture? . . .

AMANDA. (*Stopping* LAURA.) I've got to put courage in you, honey, for living. (*Exits*
40 *through living-room curtains, and exits R. into kitchen.* LAURA *opens door.* TOM *and* JIM *enter.* LAURA *remains hidden in hall behind door.*)

TOM. Laura—(LAURA *crosses C.*) this is
45 Jim. Jim, this is my sister Laura.

JIM. I didn't know that Shakespeare had a sister! How are you, Laura?

LAURA. (*Retreating stiff and trembling. Shakes hands.*) How—how do you do?

50 **JIM.** Well, I'm okay! Your hand's *cold*, Laura! (TOM *puts hats on phone table.*)

LAURA. Yes, well—I've been playing the victrola. . . .

JIM. Must have been playing classical music
55 on it. You ought to play a little hot swing music to warm you up. (LAURA *crosses to phonograph.* TOM *crosses up to* LAURA. LAURA *starts phonograph—looks at* JIM. *Exits through living-room curtains.*)

60 **JIM.** What's the matter?

TOM. Oh—Laura? Laura is—is terribly shy. (*Crosses and sits on day-bed.*)

JIM. (*Crosses down C.*) Shy, huh? Do you know it's unusual to meet a shy girl nowa-
65 days? I don't believe you ever mentioned you had a sister.

Multiple Choice

1. We learn about Jim in all of the following ways *except* by
   A. direct description.
   B. his behavior.
   C. his interaction with Laura.
   D. his interaction with Tom.
   E. what other characters say about him.

2. Which line(s) tells of a difference between Jim and Laura?
   A. And so, at this particular time in our lives he was holding a job that wasn't much better than mine. (lines 19–21)
   B. I had heard my sister Laura speak admiringly of Jim's voice. (lines 23–24)
   C. Because in high school Laura had been as unobtrusive as Jim had been astonish-ing. (lines 25–27)
   D. Well, I'm okay! Your hand's *cold*, Laura! (line 50)
   E. Oh—Laura? Laura is—is terribly shy. (line 61)

3. What difference between characters is revealed in Jim's last lines in this passage?
   A. How unusual Laura is
   B. How Laura is shy whereas most girls of the time are not
   C. How well Jim and Laura remember each other
   D. How admiring Jim is of Laura
   E. How inattentive Jim is, because Tom has mentioned his sister before

4. Laura's assertion that she will not come to the table if Jim is there (lines 30–32) reveals that she
   A. never liked Jim.
   B. once liked Jim but feels he has changed.
   C. is bitter because Jim never paid attention to her.
   D. likes Jim but is shy and uncomfortable.
   E. does not like having company for dinner.

Constructed Response

5. Compare and contrast the characters of Jim and Laura, discussing three of their most important characteristics.

Writing Skills

Address Alternate Viewpoints

In writing an essay, it is important to acknowledge different viewpoints. Doing so shows that you have thought carefully about the subject and that your response is not uninformed or strictly emotional. To demonstrate this, you can use either of two approaches.

One approach is to mention the alternative viewpoints in the opening sentence or sentences of your introduction. Then dismiss them in your thesis statement and state your viewpoint, which you will prove in the essay.

Another way to address other viewpoints is within the body paragraphs of the essay. In each paragraph, provide a reason in support of your viewpoint. Then compare and contrast your supporting evidence with the other viewpoints. Note what the various viewpoints have in common as well as the fallacies (errors in judgment) you see in the other points of view.

Also try to anticipate your reader's viewpoint and what evidence he or she would offer as support. Then address each of these ideas. Otherwise, the reader will be thinking "But what about . . . ?"

Be careful not to spend all your time criticizing other viewpoints. Although you want to provide reasons for dismissing other perspectives, your focus should be on providing support for your point of view. You may lose the reader's interest and support if you are too negative in discussing alternate viewpoints.

TEST-TAKING TIP

Even in a timed testing situation, be sure to take time to read over what you have written and make revisions. You will be amazed at the improvements you can make in just a few minutes. When looking over your response, read slowly and carefully. In addition to checking grammar, spelling, and punctuation, look for missing words and places where you may have written the wrong word accidentally. Catching such obvious mistakes takes very little time and makes a big difference in the presentation of your ideas.

Practice

Timed Writing: 25 minutes

Think carefully about the issue presented in the following excerpt and the assignment below. On occasions such as birthdays, graduations, and New Year's, people commonly look back on their lives. Most people agree that the fewer regrets, the better. But if we have to have regrets, which is preferable: regrets over things we have done or have not done?

Assignment: Is it better to have regrets over something you did or something that you did not do? Plan and write an essay in which you develop your point of view on this issue. Support your position with reasoning and examples taken from your reading, studies, experience, or observations.

Revising and Editing Skills

As part of the Writing section, some standardized tests ask you to improve paragraphs. You are presented with the draft of a short essay. Then you are asked questions about how the sentences and paragraphs fit together. To answer, you make revisions by combining sentences and changing structures within sentences.

Practice

Directions: The following passage is an early draft of an essay. Some parts need to be rewritten. Read the passage. Then select the best answer for each question that follows. Some questions address particular sentences or parts of sentences; they ask you to revise the sentence structure or word choice. Other questions ask you about the organization and development of the paragraph.

(1) I think the worst regrets are over things that you didn't do in your life. (2) It's been said that "what might have been" are the very saddest words. (3) This is true. (4) Because although it's painful to think of the bad things we have done in the past, it's even more painful to think of how different our lives might have been if only we had dared to do some things. (5) I mean to go after a goal that we really wanted.

Multiple Choice

1. In this paragraph, which change in organization is most needed?
   A. Move sentence 1 to the end.
   B. Move sentence 4 to the beginning.
   C. Move sentence 2 to the end.
   D. Move sentences 2 and 3 to the end.
   E. Move sentences 4 and 5 to the beginning.

2. In context, which is the best way to revise and combine the following underlined portions of sentences 3 and 4?

   <u>This is true. Because</u> although it's painful to think of the bad things we have done in the past, it's even more painful to think of how different our lives might have been if only we had dared to do some things.
   A. (As it is now)
   B. This is true; because
   C. This is true, because
   D. This is true because
   E. This is true—because

3. Which sentence should be deleted?
   A. 1   D. 4
   B. 2   E. 5
   C. 3

4. In context, which is the best way to revise and combine the following underlined portions of sentences 4 and 5?

   Because although it's painful to think of the bad things we have done in the past, it's even more painful to think of how different our lives might have <u>been if only we had dared to do some things. I mean to go after a goal</u> that we really wanted.
   A. (As it is now)
   B. been if only we had dared to do some things and go after a goal
   C. been if we had dared to do some things and, thus, pursue a goal
   D. been if only we had dared to do some things (that is, to go after a goal)
   E. been had we dared to do some things— namely, to go after a goal

Convergence, 1952. Jackson Pollock.
Albright-Knox Art Gallery, Buffalo, New York.

Postwar Era

Unit 7

1945–1960

Postwar Era 1945–1960

1945

1950

AMERICAN LITERATURE AMERICAN LITERATURE AMERICAN LITERATURE AM

1946
Robert Penn Warren publishes *All the King's Men*

1947
Novelist and screenwriter Dalton Trumbo is sentenced to prison for refusing to testify before the House Un-American Activities Committee

1947
The Diary of Anne Frank is published for the first time

1948
Norman Mailer publishes *The Naked and the Dead*

MAILER

1949
Arthur Miller wins the Pulitzer Prize for *Death of a Salesman*

1950
Poets Edna St. Vincent Millay and Edgar Lee Masters die

1951
J. D. Salinger publishes *Catcher in the Rye*

1952
Flannery O'Connor publishes her first novel, *Wise Blood*

1952
Ralph Ellison publishes *Invisible Man*

1953
Arthur Miller's *The Crucible* opens on Broadway

1953
James Baldwin publishes *Go Tell It on the Mountain*

ELLISON

AMERICAN HISTORY AMERICAN HISTORY AMERICAN HISTORY AMERICAN HIS

1945
On August 6 and 9, the United States drops two nuclear weapons on Japan; Japan surrenders on August 15, ending World War II

1946
The House Un-American Activities Committee begins questioning citizens suspected of being communist sympathizers

FOR EUROPEAN RECOVERY
SUPPLIED BY THE
UNITED STATES OF AMERICA

1947
Jackie Robinson becomes the first African American to play major league baseball in the twentieth century

1947
The Marshall Plan provides aid to countries devastated by World War II

1948
Alger Hiss, a former member of the U.S. Department of State, is accused of being a Soviet spy

1950
Harry Truman sends troops to Vietnam to assist the French in fighting communism

1950
Joseph McCarthy claims to have evidence of communist sympathizers in the federal government

1952
The United States successfully detonates the first hydrogen bomb on the island of Enewetak

1952
Jonas Salk first tests his polio vaccine

1953
Julius and Ethel Rosenberg are executed for selling nuclear arms secrets to the Soviet Union

WORLD HISTORY WORLD HISTORY WORLD HISTORY WORLD HISTORY WORL

1945
Nazi officers accused of war crimes go on trial in Nuremberg, Germany

1948
Israel becomes the world's only Jewish state

1949
The Soviet Union explodes its first nuclear bomb in a trial

1949
North American and European countries form the North Atlantic Treaty Organization (NATO) with the goal of preserving peace

1949
The Communist People's Republic of China assumes control of China

1950
Communist forces invade South Korea, prompting a military response by United Nations forces and initiating the Korean War

1952
In Kenya, the Mau Mau revolt against British rule

1952
The Central Intelligence Agency (CIA) overthrows the Guatemalan government and installs a U.S.-supported government

1953
Long-time Soviet leader Joseph Stalin dies

1954   1957

1954
Dr. Seuss writes *Horton Hears a Who*

1954
E. B. White publishes the children's novel *Charlotte's Web*

1955
Allen Ginsberg performs his poem *Howl* for the first time

1956
Elizabeth Bishop wins the Pulitzer Prize for her collection *Poems: North and South—A Cold Spring*

1957
Jack Kerouac publishes *On the Road*

1958
Vladimir Nabokov's *Lolita* is published in the United States

1958
Truman Capote publishes *Breakfast at Tiffany's*

1959
William S. Burroughs publishes *Naked Lunch*

1960
Richard Wright and Zora Neale Hurston die

1960
Harper Lee publishes *To Kill a Mockingbird*, which wins the Pulitzer Prize for fiction in 1961

1954
The U.S. Supreme Court rules in *Brown v. Board of Education* that school segregation is illegal

1954
Joseph Welch humiliates Joseph McCarthy during televised hearings, leading to a decline in McCarthyism

1955
Dr. Martin Luther King Jr. helps coordinate the Montgomery, Alabama, bus boycott

1955
Jonas Salk's polio vaccine is introduced to the American public

1956
The U.S. national motto, *E Pluribus Unum* ("Out of Many, One"), is changed to *In God We Trust*

1957
President Eisenhower sends troops to desegregate public schools in Little Rock, Arkansas

1957
Elvis Presley becomes the best-selling musical artist in the United States

1958
Congress establishes the National Aeronautics and Space Administration (NASA)

1959
Alaska and Hawaii are admitted as states

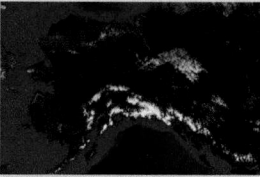

1960
Americans view the first televised presidential debate between John F. Kennedy and Richard Nixon

1954
Roger Bannister of Great Britain breaks the four-minute mile in running

1954
At the Geneva Conference, Vietnam is divided along the seventeenth parallel, forming communist and noncommunist regions

1955
The Soviet Union organizes the Warsaw Pact in response to NATO

1956
The Suez Crisis is fought between Egypt and the United Kingdom

1956
Sudan, Tunisia, and Morocco become independent African nations

1957
The Soviet Union launches *Sputnik 1*, an unmanned satellite, initiating the space race

1958
World War II hero General Charles de Gaulle becomes president of France

1959
The fourteenth and current Dalai Lama escapes from Tibet to India after the Chinese Army crushes a Tibetan resistance movement

CASTRO

1959
Fidel Castro leads the Cuban revolution and assumes leadership of the nation

1960
The Democratic Republic of the Congo gains independence from Belgium

"For it isn't enough to talk about peace. One must believe in it. And it isn't enough to believe in it. One must work at it."

—ELEANOR ROOSEVELT

Postwar Challenges

At the close of World War II, the Allies faced the challenge of keeping the peace in the nuclear age. To ensure Germany and Japan did not rearm, both were occupied by Allied forces after the war: Germany by England, France, the Soviet Union, and the United States and Japan by the United States. War criminals were put on trial in Nuremburg, Germany, and Tokyo, Japan, establishing the principle of individual responsibility for wartime acts. To institutionalize a means of working together to promote peace, the United Nations was created, and Eleanor Roosevelt helped draft its 1948 Universal Declaration of Human Rights.

Demobilization created problems, as troops returned home hoping to find jobs, many of which had been taken by women, African Americans, and Mexican Americans. To help veterans make the transition, the G.I. Bill of Rights was passed, providing pensions, government loans, and education benefits. Prices skyrocketed with the lifting of wartime price controls, and millions of workers went on strike for higher wages. The political climate became increasingly conservative, with Congress passing antilabor legislation and defeating a civil rights bill.

The Cold War

The postwar ideological, political, and economic tensions between the Soviet Union and satellite nations in eastern Europe, on the one hand, and the United States and western Europe, on the other, created what became known as the *Cold War,* which lasted from 1945 to 1989. The United States followed a policy of containment, aimed at restricting Soviet expansion. The ten-month Berlin Airlift, during which supplies were flown into the city during the Soviet blockade, was an early face-off between the world powers. Two other initiatives based on the containment policy were rebuilding free institutions in Europe through a massive economic aid program known as the Marshall Plan and creation of the North Atlantic Treaty Organization (NATO). The Soviet Union countered with the Warsaw Pact alliance.

The most chilling aspect of the Cold War was the nuclear arms race, with U.S. scientists developing the hydrogen bomb and the Soviets testing their own atomic weapons—both spewing radioactive fallout into

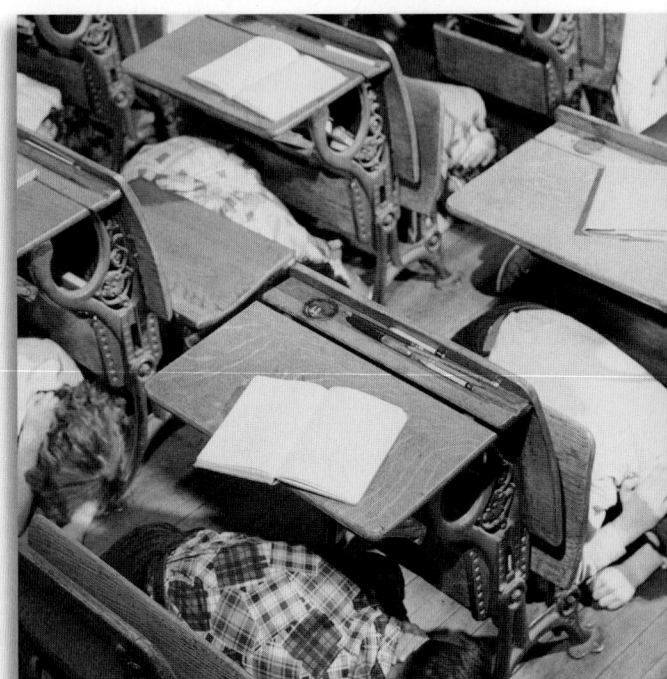

Schoolchildren practice a "duck-and-cover" drill to learn how to protect themselves in case of a nuclear attack (1951).

the atmosphere. As concern grew about the outbreak of nuclear war, schools held routine "duck-and-cover" practices, during which children crawled under their desks for protection. In addition, more than one million American families dug fallout shelters in their backyards and studied manuals on how to survive a nuclear attack.

Tensions escalated throughout the 1940s and 1950s, particularly with the outbreak of the Korean War in 1950. Involvement of U.S. troops to support South Korea against Communist North Korea and later its ally Communist China ended in a stalemate. Troops from both sides faced each other across the thirty-eighth parallel, where they had been stationed at the onset of the war.

The Korean War stimulated a spectacular rise in U.S. defense spending and growth in what war hero President Dwight D. Eisenhower named the *military-industrial complex.* In the late 1950s, Eisenhower used covert tactics to put in place leaders favorable to U.S. business interests in Iran and Guatemala, stirring up bitter and enduring resentment.

> *"History does not long entrust the care of freedom to the weak or the timid."*
>
> —PRESIDENT DWIGHT D. EISENHOWER

The Red Scare at Home

Given the conservative political climate of the United States and Americans' revulsion against communism, the country was more than ready to listen in 1950 when Senator Joseph McCarthy of Wisconsin accused the Truman administration of harboring communists. McCarthy's comments instigated a wave of investigations by congressional bodies such as the House Un-American Activities Committee, which interrogated thousands of persons suspected of being Communist party members, among them peace activists, labor leaders, and prominent writers and entertainers. Televised hearings exposed McCarthy's bullying, and finally in 1954, the Senate condemned his tactics.

When the Soviet Union launched *Sputnik,* the first orbital satellite, in 1957, the United States feared it was falling behind technologically. Schools were encouraged to strengthen their math and science offerings with funding from the National Defense Education Act. The National Aeronautics and Space Administration (NASA) also was created, and the first American satellite, *Explorer I,* was launched.

NOTABLE NUMBERS

54,000 U.S. troops killed in the Korean War, along with 1.5 million Chinese and Korean troops

2.5 million New York schoolchildren issued dog tags in 1952 so they could be identified in event of a nuclear attack

45 Pounds of unnecessary chrome fixtures on a midline car of the late 1950s

1 in 3 Proportion of Americans who lived in suburbs by 1960

50 Percentage of a white worker's earnings paid on average to an African American in the booming 1950s

The Soviet satellite Sputnik resting on a stand prior to launch. The four protruding rods are antennae (1957).

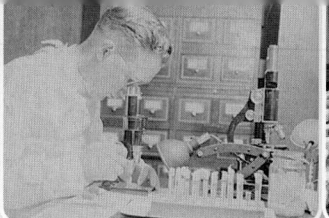

The Domestic Scene

By the time Dwight D. Eisenhower was elected president in 1952, the country's economy was strong and employment was high. With the troops returning, many women left wartime work in factories and public services and became homemakers and mothers. During the 1950s, couples married at younger ages and had more children than in previous decades.

In 1956, Congress authorized an interstate highway system that crossed the United States from east to west and north to south. This new mobility spawned motels and drive-in restaurants and movies. Colorful fin-tailed cars moved Americans to and from sprawling new suburbs, where young families were buying new homes with the low-interest loans available to veterans.

Automation dramatically changed the American workplace, increasing efficiency but reducing the number of workers needed both in factories and on farms. The farming population shrank by almost one-third. At the same time, there was an increase in the number of professional and service jobs. Service positions often were filled by women, and by 1960, women represented one-third of the American workforce.

"Music should be something that makes you gotta move, inside or outside."

—ELVIS PRESLEY

The new middle-class affluence sent Americans on a buying spree, purchasing new automobiles and appliances. Consumerism bred conformity, as families tried to "keep up with the Joneses." Television, the new communication and entertainment medium, promoted consumerism and the myth of the good life, often reinforcing racial and ethnic stereotypes. Teens expressed their discontent by turning to rock 'n' roll, an adaptation of black rhythm-and-blues music, and attending integrated performances by black and white artists such as Elvis Presley, Little Richard, Jerry Lee Lewis, Buddy Holly, and Fats Domino.

The Civil Rights Movement

Despite the United States' postwar affluence, the nation's inner cities grew increasingly poor and ethnically diverse. African Americans continued the rural-to-urban movement, known as the *Great Migration,* that had begun during World War I. Widespread unemployment forced Puerto Ricans to migrate to the mainland, most settling in New York City. Native Americans were pressured by the Relocation Act of 1956 to leave their tribal lands and move to urban areas. Urban renewal programs bulldozed older city neighborhoods to make way for low-income public housing, which destroyed communities and often became plagued by crime. Within twenty years, these vertical ghettos were themselves being bulldozed.

"Separate but equal" was the policy that had allowed maintaining separate educational facilities for white and black students since the 1896 *Plessy v. Ferguson* decision by the U.S. Supreme Court. With the landmark *Brown v. Board of Education* decision in 1954, the Court declared, "Separate educational facilities are inherently unequal." In 1955, the Court ordered schools to be desegregated "with all deliberate speed," launching the Civil Rights movement.

Another significant event in the early days of the movement occurred on December 1, 1955, when Rosa Parks, a forty-two-year-old African American, refused to give up her seat on a Montgomery, Alabama, bus. Her arrest prompted African Americans to begin a bus boycott under the leadership of Dr. Martin Luther King Jr. A year later, the U.S. Supreme Court ruled Montgomery's bus segregation laws unconstitutional.

In 1957, Little Rock, Arkansas, was ready to desegregate the schools until the governor ordered the state's national guard to prevent nine African-American students from enrolling. Only when President Eisenhower ordered in one thousand federal troops were the students able to enter the school. Meanwhile, the Civil Rights Act of 1957 was passed, making it a federal crime to prevent eligible persons from voting. Even so, the future would hold many more engagements in the struggle for equal civil rights.

At the end of World War II and the Great Depression, Americans were eager to get on with their lives. Men who had spent years away in combat eagerly returned home to their families, and women gave up wartime jobs to resume their traditional roles as wives and mothers. The year 1946 signaled the start of the baby boom, which would peak in 1957 and trail off in the early 1960s. For many Americans, the 1950s was an era of opportunity: They were going to college, getting jobs, buying houses and cars, and raising families—in short, living the American dream.

Many writers of this period examined the nuances of ordinary life, creating detailed, personal portraits of everyday folks—some sublime, others grotesque. Flannery O'Connor's short stories and novels, set in the American South, portrayed ordinary people in situations that often were marked by immorality, cruelty, and violence. Similarly, fiction writer Bernard Malamud depicted people's search for hope and meaning within the grim entrapment of poor urban America.

The realities of life in the modern postwar world were explored in literature about change and loss. Poets Theodore Roethke, Elizabeth Bishop, and Gabriela Mistral all shared intimate reflections on loss, including the pain of losing a loved one. Essayist E. B. White commented on many aspects of modern American life, including the inevitability of change and the need to live each day to its fullest.

Untitled, c. 1944. Willem de Kooning.

The Life You Save May Be Your Own

A Short Story by Flannery O'Connor

Build Background

Literary Context Flannery O'Connor's short story **"The Life You Save May Be Your Own"** is a prime example of Southern Gothic literature, an extension of the Southern Renaissance movement. Set in rural Georgia, the story features characters that include a man with an amputated arm and a young woman who is deaf and mentally challenged. The story's central concern is the abstract idea of good and evil, a theme common to O'Connor's fictional works. A devout Roman Catholic throughout her life, the author believed in a spiritual center and an acceptance of divine grace in people's lives.

"The Life You Save" received critical acclaim when it was first published in 1953 in the *Kenyon Review,* a literary journal. The next year, it earned the O. Henry Award for Short Fiction.

Reader's Context What qualities do you need to see in someone before you will trust him or her?

Meet the Author

(Mary) Flannery O'Connor (1925–1964), a short story writer and novelist, knew her calling from an early age. Born in Savannah, Georgia, she and her family later returned to their roots in the town of Milledgeville.

After graduating from the Georgia State College for Women, O'Connor left her home state to study writing at the University of Iowa. Her first story, "The Geranium," was published while she was there. She later moved to a writer's colony in Saratoga Springs, New York, and then to New York City and Connecticut.

While still in her twenties, O'Connor contracted disseminated lupus, from which her father had also suffered, and returned to Milledgeville to live with her mother. She wrote her darkest fiction after the onset of her illness, although she had never shied away from such themes as human limitations and mortality. "The truth does not change," she once wrote, "according to our ability to stomach it." Although increasingly confined, O'Connor did not allow her illness to destroy her enjoyment of life, her sense of humor, or her ability to work until her death at age thirty-nine.

O'Connor's first novel, *Wise Blood,* was published in 1952. This was followed by a collection of short stories, *A Good Man Is Hard to Find* (1953); a second novel, *The Violent Bear It Away* (1960); and a second short story collection, *Everything That Rises Must Converge* (1965).

Analyze Literature

Characterization and Dialect
Characterization is the act of creating or describing a character. *Indirect techniques* include showing what characters say, do, or think and showing what other characters say or think about them. The *direct technique* involves describing a character's physical features and personality.

A **dialect** is a version of a language spoken by the people of a particular place, time, or social group. A *regional dialect* is one spoken in a particular place. A *social dialect* is one spoken by a particular social group or class.

Set Purpose

O'Connor is famous for populating her stories with bizarre characters. As you read, analyze the characterization techniques she uses to develop the characters in this story. Also analyze her use of dialect in creating characters. Write down specific examples of dialect in the story.

Preview Vocabulary

list, 836
ominous, 837
sullen, 838
ravenous, 839
tinker, 840
morose, 841
placid, 842
sultry, 842
guffawing, 843

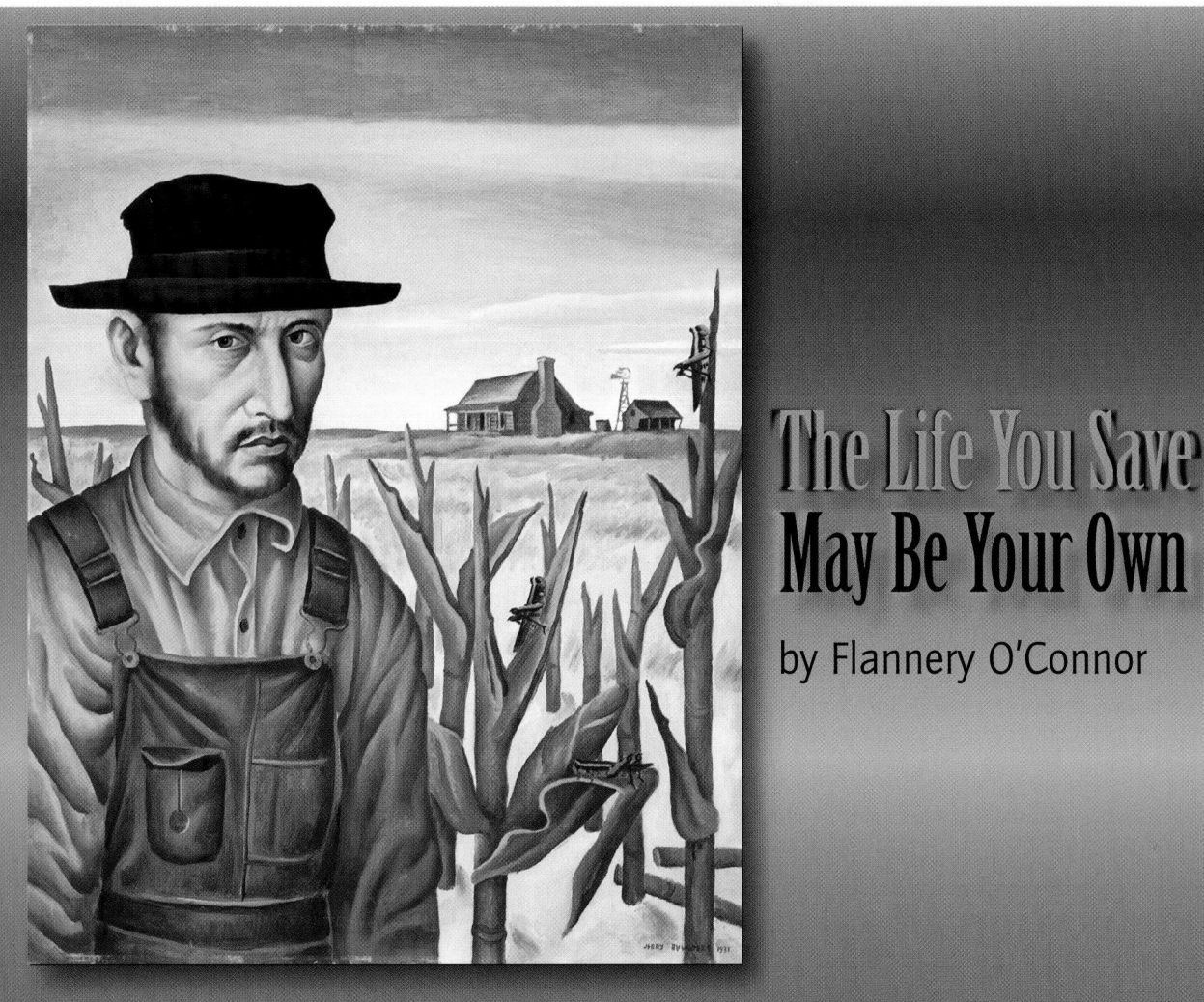

Sharecropper, 1937. Jerry Bywaters.
Dallas Museum of Art, Dallas, Texas.

The Life You Save May Be Your Own

by Flannery O'Connor

> "Drive Carefully. The life you save may be your own."

The old woman and her daughter were sitting on their porch when Mr. Shiftlet came up their road for the first time. The old woman slid to the edge of her chair and leaned forward, shading her eyes from the piercing sunset with her hand. The daughter could not see far in front of her and continued to play with her fingers. Although the old woman lived in this desolate spot with only her daughter and she had never seen Mr. Shiftlet before, she could tell, even from a distance, that he was a tramp and no one to be afraid of. His left coat sleeve was folded up to show there was only half an arm in it and his gaunt figure <u>listed</u> slightly to the side as if the breeze were pushing him. He had on a black town suit and a brown felt hat that was turned up in the front and down in the back and he carried a tin tool box by a handle. He came on, at an amble, up her road, his face turned toward the sun which appeared to be balancing itself on the peak of a small mountain.

The old woman didn't change her position until he was almost into her yard; then she rose with one hand fisted on her hip. The daughter, a large girl in a short blue organdy dress, saw him all at once and jumped up and began to stamp and point and make excited speechless sounds.

Mr. Shiftlet stopped just inside the yard and set his box on the ground and tipped his hat at her as if she were not in the least afflicted; then he turned toward the old woman and swung the hat all the way off. He had long black slick hair that hung flat from a part in the middle to beyond the tips of his ears on either side. His face descended in forehead for more than half its length and ended suddenly with his features just balanced over a jutting steel-trap jaw. He seemed to be a young man but he had a look of composed dissatisfaction as if he understood life thoroughly.

> He seemed to be a young man but he had a look of composed dissatisfaction as if he understood life thoroughly.

"Good evening," the old woman said. She was about the size of a cedar fence post and she had a man's gray hat pulled down low over her head.

The tramp stood looking at her and didn't answer. He turned his back and faced the sunset. He swung both his whole and his short arm up slowly so that they indicated an expanse of sky and his figure formed a crooked cross. The old woman watched him with her arms folded across her chest as if she were the owner of the sun, and the daughter watched, her head thrust forward and her fat helpless hands hanging at the wrists. She had long pink-gold hair and eyes as blue as a peacock's neck.

He held the pose for almost fifty seconds and then he picked up his box and came on to the porch and dropped down on the bottom step. "Lady," he said in a firm nasal voice, "I'd give a fortune to live where I could see me a sun do that every evening."

"Does it every evening," the old woman said and sat back down. The daughter sat down too and watched him with a cautious sly look as if he were a bird that had come up very close. He leaned to one side, rooting[1] in his pants pocket, and in a second he brought out a package of chewing gum and offered her a piece. She took it and unpeeled it and began to chew without taking her eyes off him. He offered the old woman a piece but she only raised her upper lip to indicate she had no teeth.

Mr. Shiftlet's pale sharp glance had already passed over everything in the yard—the pump near the corner of the house and the big fig tree that three or four chickens were preparing to roost in—and had moved to a shed where he saw the square rusted back of an automobile. "You ladies drive?" he asked.

"That car ain't run in fifteen year," the old woman said. "The day my husband died, it quit running."

"Nothing is like it used to be, lady," he said. "The world is almost rotten."

"That's right," the old woman said. "You from around here?"

"Name Tom T. Shiftlet," he murmured, looking at the tires.

---

1. **root.** Dig

list (list) *v.*, tilt to one side

"I'm pleased to meet you," the old woman said. "Name Lucynell Crater and daughter Lucynell Crater. What you doing around here, Mr. Shiftlet?"

He judged the car to be about a 1928 or '29 Ford. "Lady," he said, and turned and gave her his full attention, "lemme tell you something. There's one of these doctors in Atlanta that's taken a knife and cut the human heart— the human heart," he repeated, leaning forward, "out of a man's chest and held it in his hand," and he held his hand out, palm up, as if it were slightly weighted with the human heart, "and studied it like it was a day-old chicken, and lady," he said, allowing a long significant pause in which his head slid forward and his clay-colored eyes brightened, "he don't know no more about it than you or me."

"That's right," the old woman said.

"Why, if he was to take that knife and cut into every corner of it, he still wouldn't know no more than you or me. What you want to bet?"

"Nothing," the old woman said wisely. "Where you come from, Mr. Shiftlet?"

He didn't answer. He reached into his pocket and brought out a sack of tobacco and a package of cigarette papers and rolled himself a cigarette, expertly with one hand, and attached it in a hanging position to his upper lip. Then he took a box of wooden matches from his pocket and struck one on his shoe. He held the burning match as if he were studying the mystery of flame while it traveled dangerously toward his skin. The daughter began to make loud noises and to point to his hand and shake her finger at him, but when the flame was just before touching him, he leaned down with his hand cupped over it as if he were going to set fire to his nose and lit the cigarette.

He flipped away the dead match and blew a stream of gray into the evening. A sly look came over his face. "Lady," he said, "nowadays, people'll do anything anyways. I can tell you my name is Tom T. Shiftlet and I come from Tarwater, Tennessee, but you never have seen me before: how you know I ain't lying? How you know my name ain't Aaron Sparks, lady, and I come from Singleberry, Georgia, or how you know it's not George Speeds and I come from Lucy, Alabama, or how you know I ain't Thompson Bright from Toolafalls, Mississippi?"

"I don't know nothing about you," the old woman muttered, irked.

"Lady," he said, "people don't care how they lie. Maybe the best I can tell you is, I'm a man; but listen lady," he said and paused and made his tone more <u>ominous</u> still, "what is a man?"

The old woman began to gum a seed. "What you carry in that tin box, Mr. Shiftlet?" she asked.

om • i • nous (ŏ′ mə nəs) *adj.,* foreshadowing evil or menace

"Tools," he said, put back. "I'm a carpenter."

"Well, if you come out here to work, I'll be able to feed you and give you a place to sleep but I can't pay. I'll tell you that before you begin," she said.

There was no answer at once and no particular expression on his face. He leaned back against the two-by-four that helped support the porch roof. "Lady," he said slowly, "there's some men that some things mean more to them than money." The old woman rocked without comment and the daughter watched the trigger that moved up and down in his neck. He told the old woman then that all most people were interested in was money, but he asked what a man was made for. He asked her if a man was made for money, or what. He asked her what she thought she was made for but she didn't answer, she only sat rocking and wondered if a one-armed man could put a new roof on her garden house. He asked a lot of questions that she didn't answer. He told her that he was twenty-eight years old and had lived a varied life. He had been a gospel singer, a foreman on the railroad, an assistant in an undertaking parlor,[2] and he had come over the radio for three months with Uncle Roy and his Red Creek Wranglers. He said he had fought and bled in the Arm Service of his country and visited every foreign land and that everywhere he had seen people that didn't care if they did a thing one way or another. He said he hadn't been raised thataway.

> Everywhere he had seen people that didn't care if they did a thing one way or another.

A fat yellow moon appeared in the branches of the fig tree as if it were going to roost there with the chickens. He said that a man had to escape to the country to see the world whole and that he wished he lived in a desolate place like this where he could see the sun go down every evening like God made it to do.

"Are you married or are you single?" the old woman asked.

There was a long silence. "Lady," he asked finally, "where would you find you an innocent woman today? I wouldn't have any of this trash I could just pick up."

The daughter was leaning very far down, hanging her head almost between her knees, watching him through a triangular door she had made in her overturned hair; and she suddenly fell in a heap on the floor and began to whimper. Mr. Shiftlet straightened her out and helped her get back in the chair.

"Is she your baby girl?" he asked.

"My only," the old woman said, "and she's the sweetest girl in the world. I wouldn't give her up for nothing on earth. She's smart too. She can sweep the floor, cook, wash, feed the chickens, and hoe. I wouldn't give her up for a casket of jewels."

"No," he said kindly, "don't ever let any man take her away from you."

"Any man come after her," the old woman said, "I'll have to stay around the place."

Mr. Shiftlet's eye in the darkness was focused on a part of the automobile bumper that glittered in the distance. "Lady," he said, jerking his short arm up as if he could point with it to her house and yard and pump, "there ain't a broken thing on this plantation that I couldn't fix for you, one-arm jackleg[3] or not. I'm a man," he said with a <u>sullen</u> dignity, "even if I ain't a whole one. I got," he said, tapping his knuckles on the floor to emphasize the immensity of what he was going to say, "a moral intelligence!" and his face pierced out of the darkness into a shaft of doorlight and he

---

2. **undertaking parlor.** Funeral home
3. **jackleg.** One who is not properly trained or competent for a job

sul • len (su′ lən) *adj.*, gloomily or resentfully silent

He had his razor and a can of water on a crate that served him as a bedside table and he put up a piece of mirror against the back glass and kept his coat neatly on a hanger that he hung over one of the windows.

In the evenings he sat on the steps and talked while the old woman and Lucynell rocked violently in their chairs on either side of him. The old woman's three mountains were black against the dark blue sky and were visited off and on by various planets and by the moon after it had left the chickens.

stared at her as if he were astonished himself at this impossible truth.

The old woman was not impressed with the phrase. "I told you you could hang around and work for food," she said, "if you don't mind sleeping in that car yonder."

"Why listen, Lady," he said with a grin of delight, "the monks of old slept in their coffins!"

"They wasn't as advanced as we are," the old woman said.

T he next morning he began on the roof of the garden house while Lucynell, the daughter, sat on a rock and watched him work. He had not been around a week before the change he had made in the place was apparent. He had patched the front and back steps, built a new hog pen, restored a fence, and taught Lucynell, who was completely deaf and had never said a word in her life, to say the word "bird." The big rosy-faced girl followed him everywhere, saying "Burrttddt ddbirrrttdt," and clapping her hands. The old woman watched from a distance, secretly pleased. She was <u>ravenous</u> for a son-in-law.

Mr. Shiftlet slept on the hard narrow back seat of the car with his feet out the side window.

Mr. Shiftlet pointed out that the reason he had improved this plantation was because he had taken a personal interest in it. He said he was even going to make the automobile run.

He had raised the hood and studied the mechanism and he said he could tell that the car had been built in the days when cars were really built. You take now, he said, one man puts in one bolt and another man puts in another bolt and another man puts in another bolt so that it's a man for a bolt. That's why you have to pay so much for a car: you're paying all those men. Now if you didn't have to pay but one man, you could get you a cheaper car and one that had had a personal interest taken in it, and it would be a better car. The old woman agreed with him that this was so.

Mr. Shiftlet said that the trouble with the world was that nobody cared, or stopped and took any trouble. He said he never would have been able to teach Lucynell to say a word if he hadn't cared and stopped long enough.

rav • en • ous (ra′ və nəs) *adj.,* eager or greedy for food, satisfaction, or gratification

"Teach her to say something else," the old woman said.

"What you want her to say next?" Mr. Shift-let asked.

The old woman's smile was broad and toothless and suggestive. "Teach her to say 'sugarpie,'" she said.

Mr. Shiftlet already knew what was on her mind.

The next day he began to <u>tinker</u> with the automobile and that evening he told her that if she would buy a fan belt, he would be able to make the car run.

The old woman said she would give him the money. "You see that girl yonder?" she asked, pointing to Lucynell who was sitting on the floor a foot away, watching him, her eyes blue even in the dark. "If it was ever a man wanted to take her away, I would say, 'No man on earth is going to take that sweet girl of mine away from me!' but if he was to say, 'Lady, I don't want to take her away, I want her right here,' I would say, 'Mister, I don't blame you none. I wouldn't pass up a chance to live in a permanent place and get the sweetest girl in the world myself. You ain't no fool,' I would say."

> "No man on earth is going to take that sweet girl of mine away from me!"

"How old is she?" Mr. Shiftlet asked casually.

"Fifteen, sixteen," the old woman said. The girl was nearly thirty but because of her innocence it was impossible to guess.

"It would be a good idea to paint it too," Mr. Shiftlet remarked. "You don't want it to rust out."

"We'll see about that later," the old woman said.

The next day he walked into town and returned with the parts he needed and a can of gasoline. Late in the afternoon, terrible noises issued from the shed and the old woman rushed out of the house, thinking Lucynell was somewhere having a fit. Lucynell was sitting on a chicken crate, stamping her feet and screaming, "Burrddtttt! bddurrddtttt!" but her fuss was drowned out by the car. With a volley of blasts it emereged from the shed, moving in a fierce and stately way. Mr. Shiftlet was in the driver's seat, sitting very erect. He had an expression of serious modesty on his face as if he had just raised the dead.

That night, rocking on the porch, the old woman began her business at once. "You want you an innocent woman, don't you?" she asked sympathetically. "You don't want none of this trash."

"No'm, I don't," Mr. Shiftlet said.

"One that can't talk," she continued, "can't sass you back or use foul language. That's the kind for you to have. Right there," and she pointed to Lucynell sitting cross-legged in her chair, holding both feet in her hands.

"That's right," he admitted. "She wouldn't give me any trouble."

"Saturday," the old woman said, "you and her and me can drive into town and get married."

Mr. Shiftlet eased his position on the steps.

"I can't get married right now," he said. "Everything you want to do takes money and I ain't got any."

"What you need with money?" she asked.

"It takes money," he said. "Some people'll do anything anyhow these days, but the way I think, I wouldn't marry no woman that I couldn't take on a trip like she was somebody. I mean take her to a hotel and treat her. I wouldn't marry the Duchesser Windsor,"[4] he

---

4. **Duchesser Windsor.** Duchess of Windsor, the title given to Wallis Warfield Simpson when she married Edward, Duke of Windsor; he abdicated the British throne to marry her in 1937.

---

tin • ker (tiŋ′ kər) v., repair, adjust, or work with something in an unskilled or experimental manner

said firmly, "unless I could take her to a hotel and give her something good to eat.

"I was raised thataway and there ain't a thing I can do about it. My old mother taught me how to do."

"Lucynell don't even know what a hotel is," the old woman muttered. "Listen here, Mr. Shiftlet," she said, sliding forward in her chair, "you'd be getting a permanent house and a deep well and the most innocent girl in the world. You don't need no money. Lemme tell you something: there ain't any place in the world for a poor disabled friendless drifting man."

The ugly words settled in Mr. Shiftlet's head like a group of buzzards in the top of a tree. He didn't answer at once. He rolled himself a cigarette and lit it and then he said in an even voice, "Lady, a man is divided into two parts, body and spirit."

The old woman clamped her gums together.

"A body and a spirit," he repeated. "The body, lady, is like a house: it don't go anywhere; but the spirit, lady, is like a automobile: always on the move, always . . ."

"Listen, Mr. Shiftlet," she said, "my well never goes dry and my house is always warm in the winter and there's no mortgage on a thing about this place. You can go to the courthouse and see for yourself. And yonder under that shed is a fine automobile." She laid the bait carefully. "You can have it painted by Saturday. I'll pay for the paint."

In the darkness, Mr. Shiftlet's smile stretched like a weary snake waking up by a fire. After a second he recalled himself and said, "I'm only saying a man's spirit means more to him than anything else. I would have to take my wife off for the weekend without no regards at all for cost. I got to follow where my spirit says to go."

"I'll give you fifteen dollars for a weekend trip," the old woman said in a crabbed[5] voice. "That's the best I can do."

"That wouldn't hardly pay for more than the gas and the hotel," he said. "It wouldn't feed her."

"Seventeen-fifty," the old woman said. "That's all I got so it isn't any use you trying to milk me. You can take a lunch."

Mr. Shiftlet was deeply hurt by the word "milk." He didn't doubt that she had more money sewed up in her mattress but he had already told her he was not interested in her money. "I'll make that do," he said and rose and walked off without treating with her further.

On Saturday the three of them drove into town in the car that the paint had barely dried on and Mr. Shiftlet and Lucynell were married in the Ordinary's[6] office while the old woman witnessed. As they came out of the courthouse, Mr. Shiftlet began twisting his neck in his collar. He looked <u>morose</u> and bitter as if he had been insulted while someone held him. "That didn't satisfy me none," he said. "That was just something a woman in an office did, nothing but paper work and blood tests. What do they know about my blood? If they was to take my heart and cut it out," he said, "they wouldn't know a thing about me. It didn't satisfy me at all."

---

5. **crabbed.** Forbiddingly gloomy; ill tempered
6. **Ordinary.** Official of the court

mo • rose (mə rōs´) *adj.,* having a sullen and gloomy disposition

"It satisfied the law," the old woman said sharply.

"The law," Mr. Shiftlet said and spit. "It's the law that don't satisfy me."

He had painted the car dark green with a yellow band around it just under the windows. The three of them climbed in the front seat and the old woman said, "Don't Lucynell look pretty? Looks like a baby doll." Lucynell was dressed up in a white dress that her mother had uprooted from a trunk and there was a Panama hat on her head with a bunch of red wooden cherries on the brim. Every now and then her <u>placid</u> expression was changed by a sly isolated little thought like a shoot of green in the desert. "You got a prize!" the old woman said.

Mr. Shiftlet didn't even look at her.

They drove back to the house to let the old woman off and pick up the lunch. When they were ready to leave, she stood staring in the window of the car, with her fingers clenched around the glass. Tears began to seep sideways out of her eyes and run along the dirty creases in her face. "I ain't ever been parted with her for two days before," she said.

Mr. Shiftlet started the motor.

"And I wouldn't let no man have her but you because I seen you would do right. Goodby, Sugarbaby," she said, clutching at the sleeve of the white dress. Lucynell looked straight at her and didn't seem to see her there at all. Mr. Shiftlet eased the car forward so that she had to move her hands.

The early afternoon was clear and open and surrounded by pale blue sky. Although the car would go only thirty miles an hour, Mr. Shiftlet imagined a terrific climb and dip and swerve that went entirely to his head so that he forgot his morning bitterness. He had always wanted an automobile but he had never been able to afford one before. He drove very fast because he wanted to make Mobile by nightfall.

Occasionally he stopped his thoughts long enough to look at Lucynell in the seat beside him. She had eaten the lunch as soon as they were out of the yard and now she was pull-ing the cherries off the hat one by one and throwing them out the window. He became depressed in spite of the car. He had driven about a hundred miles when he decided that she must be hungry again and at the next small town they came to, he stopped in front of an aluminum-painted eating place called The Hot Spot and took her in and ordered her a plate of ham and grits. The ride had made her sleepy and as soon as she got up on the stool, she rested her head on the counter and shut her eyes. There was no one in The Hot Spot but Mr. Shiftlet and the boy behind the counter, a pale youth with a greasy rag hung over his shoulder. Before he could dish up the food, she was snoring gently.

"Give it to her when she wakes up," Mr. Shiftlet said. "I'll pay for it now."

The boy bent over her and stared at the long pink-gold hair and the half-shut sleeping eyes. Then he looked up and stared at Mr. Shiftlet. "She looks like an angel of Gawd," he murmured.

"Hitch-hiker," Mr. Shiftlet explained. "I can't wait. I got to make Tuscaloosa."

The boy bent over again and very carefully touched his finger to a strand of the golden hair and Mr. Shiftlet left.

He was more depressed than ever as he drove on by himself. The late afternoon had grown hot and <u>sultry</u> and the country had flattened out. Deep in the sky a storm was preparing very slowly and without thunder as if it meant to drain every drop of air from the earth before it broke. There were times when Mr. Shiftlet preferred not to be alone. He felt too that a man with a car had a responsibility to others and he kept his eye out for a hitch-hiker. Occasionally he saw a sign that warned: "Drive carefully. The life you save may be your own."

---

pla • cid (plaʹ sid) *adj.*, calm or free of disturbance
sul • try (sulʹ trē) *adj.*, very hot and humid

The narrow road dropped off on either side into dry fields and here and there a shack or a filling station stood in a clearing. The sun began to set directly in front of the automobile. It was a reddening ball that through his windshield was slightly flat on the bottom and top. He saw a boy in overalls and a gray hat standing on the edge of the road and he slowed the car down and stopped in front of him. The boy didn't have his hand raised to thumb the ride, he was only standing there, but he had a small cardboard suitcase and his hat was set on his head in a way to indicate that he had left somewhere for good. "Son," Mr. Shiftlet said, "I see you want a ride."

The boy didn't say he did or he didn't but he opened the door of the car and got in, and Mr. Shiftlet started driving again. The child held the suitcase on his lap and folded his arms on top of it. He turned his head and looked out the window away from Mr. Shiftlet. Mr. Shiftlet felt oppressed. "Son," he said after a minute, "I got the best old mother in the world so I reckon you only got the second best."

The boy gave him a quick dark glance and then turned his face back out the window.

"It's nothing so sweet," Mr. Shiftlet continued, "as a boy's mother. She taught him his first prayers at her knee, she give him love when no other would, she told him what was right and what wasn't, and she seen that he done the right thing.

"Son," he said, "I never rued[7] a day in my life like the one I rued when I left that old mother of mine."

The boy shifted in his seat but he didn't look at Mr. Shiftlet. He unfolded his arms and put one hand on the door handle.

"My mother was a angel of Gawd," Mr. Shiftlet said in a very strained voice. "He took her from heaven and giver to me and I left her." His eyes were instantly clouded over with a mist of tears. The car was barely moving.

The boy turned angrily in the seat. "You go to the devil!" he cried. "My old woman is a flea bag and yours is a stinking pole cat!"[8] and with that he flung the door open and jumped out with his suitcase into the ditch.

Mr. Shiftlet was so shocked that for about a hundred feet he drove along slowly with the door still open. A cloud, the exact color of the boy's hat and shaped like a turnip, had descended over the sun, and another, worse looking, crouched behind the car. Mr. Shiftlet felt that the rottenness of the world was about to engulf him. He raised his arm and let it fall again to his breast. "Oh Lord!" he prayed. "Break forth and wash the slime from this earth!"

The turnip continued slowly to descend. After a few minutes there was a <u>guffawing</u> peal of thunder from behind and fantastic raindrops, like tin-can tops, crashed over the rear of Mr. Shiftlet's car. Very quickly he stepped on the gas and with his stump sticking out the window he raced the galloping shower into Mobile. ❖

---

7. **rued.** Felt remorse or regret
8. **pole cat.** Skunk

> **guf • faw • ing** (gə fô´ iŋ) *adj.,* laughing loudly and coarsely

MIRRORS & **W**INDOWS

Mr. Shiftlet tells the old woman, "Nothing is like it used to be, lady." Has society changed for the better or the worse? Do people today have more or less integrity than people from years past?

Refer to Text ▶ ▶ ▶ ▶ ▶ **Reason with Text**

1a. What things can the old woman observe about Mr. Shiftlet the first time she sees him?	**1b.** Explain why the old woman's initial observations led her to believe that Mr. Shiftlet is "no one to be afraid of."	**Understand** Find meaning
2a. What does Mr. Shiftlet look at during his conversations with the old woman?	**2b.** Explain why Mr. Shiftlet wants to marry Lucynell.	**Apply** Use information
3a. List the statements Mr. Shiftlet makes about the world and the honesty and integrity of the people in it.	**3b.** How does Mr. Shiftlet portray himself? Compare and contrast his portrayal with his actions.	**Analyze** Take things apart
4a. What is Mr. Shiftlet's opinion of most single women of the day? What kind of woman do he and old Lucynell agree would make a good wife?	**4b.** Place each character in this story on a continuum from good to evil.	**Evaluate** Make judgments
5a. How does Mr. Shiftlet feel when he leaves Lucynell behind at The Hot Spot?	**5b.** Does Flannery O'Connor believe human nature is by nature good or evil? What do you believe and why?	**Create** Bring ideas together

Analyze Literature

Characterization and Dialect

Explain O'Connor's use of direct versus indirect characterization techniques. Which character does the reader know most about? Least about?

Identify several examples of dialect within the story. How does O'Connor use dialect to develop characters? What does the use of dialect reveal about the place, time, and social standing of the characters?

Extend the Text

Writing Options
Creative Writing Write a song that includes the story's title. The lyrics may or may not be based on the story itself, but they should reflect what the story suggests about human nature.

Expository Writing Write an essay analyzing the complexities of the character of Mr. Shiftlet. Organize the analysis in terms of the direct and indirect characterization techniques, devoting a paragraph to each.

Speaking and Listening
Practice Nonverbal Communication With a partner, play the roles of Mr. Shiftlet and old Lucynell in the first section of the story, where they meet each other. Develop your interpretation of the character using nonverbal communication such as gestures and facial expressions, and consider the character's motives and personality.

Media Literacy
Create a Newspaper Advertisement Imagine that you are old Lucynell and want a hired hand to make some repairs at your farm. Write a newspaper advertisement in which you specify the tasks that need to be done and explain your method of payment. Review the Classified Ads section of your local newspaper to get ideas and learn about the abbreviations often used in these ads.

 Go to **www.mirrorsandwindows.com** for more.

1. What is Mr. Shiftlet's main complaint about how most people live?

  A. They disrespect or ignore people with disabilities like his own.

  B. They automatically distrust other people.

  C. They are too lazy to do things properly.

  D. They are uncaring and lack morals.

  E. They manipulate other people for their own benefit.

2. How is old Lucynell guilty of manipulation?

  A. She tries to play up the attributes of her daughter, who otherwise would not receive any attention from men.

  B. She refuses to pay for Mr. Shiftlet's work, even though it's later revealed she had the money to do so.

  C. She knows Mr. Shiftlet wants the car but pushes him to marry her daughter to get it.

  D. She really wants someone else to take care of Lucynell but declares instead that she will not let her daughter go.

  E. She is not guilty of manipulation; only Mr. Shiftlet is.

3. Which of the following statements best explains why Mr. Shiftlet picks up a hitchhiker after he abandons Lucynell?

  A. He is looking for someone else to con out of money.

  B. He feels a bit guilty and is looking for someone to whom he may confess.

  C. He wants to show off his fancy car, into which he put so much work.

  D. He wants to make up for abandoning Lucynell by being nice to someone else.

  E. He feels lonely and thinks drivers are responsible for helping people who need a ride.

4. Which of the following best describes the theme of "The Life You Save May Be Your Own"?

  A. You should not trust strangers with the things you value.

  B. People look out for their own interests, even if it involves doing something questionable or illegal.

  C. People with disadvantages are not properly cared for or respected by society.

  D. Even the biggest sinner can be redeemed by performing good acts.

  E. It is impossible to avoid trouble.

5. After marrying Lucynell, Mr. Shiftlet is described as being in a *morose* mood. What does that mean?

  A. He is very pleased with his new marriage.

  B. He feels gloomy about having had to marry Lucynell to get the car.

  C. He is angry about the circumstances of the wedding.

  D. He feels nervous about this new change in his life.

  E. He is eagerly anticipating the next step in his plan to get rid of Lucynell.

6. Which sentence best exemplifies Southern Gothic writing?

  A. "His left coat sleeve was folded up to show there was only half an arm in it and his gaunt figure listed slightly to the side as if the breeze were pushing him."

  B. "He came up, at an amble, up her road, his face turned toward the sun which appeared to be balancing itself on the peak of a small mountain."

  C. "A fat yellow moon appeared in the branches of the fig tree as if it were going to roost there with the chickens."

  D. "With a volley of blasts it emerged from the shed, moving in a fierce and stately way."

  E. "'That's all I got so it isn't any use you trying to milk me.'"

7. Constructed Response: Describe the characterization techniques O'Connor uses to create the characters in the story. Use examples from the text to support your description.

8. Constructed Response: Explain the meaning of the title "The Life You Save May Be Your Own." It is featured in the story as a sign Mr. Shiftlet sees as he drives away, but why did O'Connor likely choose it for the title of the story? Use evidence from the text to support your ideas.

The Magic Barrel

A Short Story by Bernard Malamud

Build Background

Cultural Context Bernard Malamud's **"The Magic Barrel"** appeared in a short story collection of the same name published in 1958. Like many of Malamud's stories, it portrays the Jewish experience in the United States but in universal terms that transcend ethnic definition. "The Magic Barrel" is a story about the Jewish tradition of matchmaking, or arranging marriages.

In Jewish culture, the *shadchan,* or matchmaker, has played a highly significant role since biblical times. Families of every social class and economic status historically trusted this esteemed community member to find suitable mates for their children. However, as the concept of romantic love became the norm and opportunities for socialization increased, the shadchan's role became less and less valuable. Many Jews began to see matchmaking less as a divine calling and more as a business—and a sometimes less than ethical one. The value of a shadchan has since made something of a comeback among members of Orthodox Jewish communities, who today often employ private marriage brokers to make them a match.

Reader's Context When have you obtained help to attain a goal? Was getting help a good idea? Why or why not?

Meet the Author

Bernard Malamud (1914–1986) was born in Brooklyn, New York, to Russian Jewish immigrants. Educated at the City College of New York and Columbia University, where he earned his bachelor's and master's degrees, Malamud taught high school and then college English. In the wake of World War II, however, he began to focus on something more personal: Jewish history, tradition, and identity.

Malamud's works commonly employ literary conventions drawn from earlier Jewish literature. His first novel, *The Natural* (1952), a fable about a baseball player gifted with miraculous powers, deals with the nature of heroic figures. *The Fixer* (1966), which won the National Book Award and the Pulitzer Prize, tells the story of a Jewish handyman unjustly imprisoned for the murder of a Christian boy in Czarist Russia. His most celebrated collection of short stories, *The Magic Barrel* (1958), received the National Book Award and earned him a Ford Fellowship. Malamud once said the most important task of the writer is "to recapture his image as human being as each of us in his secret heart knows it to be."

Analyze Literature

Motivation and Antihero
A **motivation** is a force that moves a character to think, feel, or behave in a certain way.

An **antihero** is a central character who lacks all the qualities traditionally associated with heroes. An antihero may lack beauty, courage, grace, intelligence, or moral scruples. Antiheroes are common figures in modern fiction and drama.

Set Purpose

Different people may have a wide range of motivations to marry. Keep track of how Leo Finkle's motivation changes as the story progresses. In addition, make a cluster chart to list the characteristics that classify Leo Finkle as an antihero.

Preview Vocabulary

inherently, 848
menagerie, 848
ascetic, 848
trepidation, 853
nuptial, 853
profusion, 854
machination, 854
abjectly, 855
exasperating, 857
haggard, 859

Wedding, 1918. Marc Chagall.
Gosudarstrennaja Tretjakovsk Galerja, Moscow, Russia.

The Magic Barrel

by Bernard Malamud

"Believe me, if I was looking now for a bride, I would marry a widow."

Not long ago there lived in uptown New York, in a small, almost meager room, though crowded with books, Leo Finkle, a rabbinical student at the Yeshiva University.[1] Finkle, after six years of study, was to be ordained in June and had been advised by an acquaintance that he might find it easier to win himself a congregation if he were married. Since he had no present prospects of marriage, after two tormented days of turning it over in his mind,

he called in Pinye Salzman, a marriage broker whose two-line advertisement he had read in the *Forward.*[2]

The matchmaker appeared one night out of the dark fourth-floor hallway of the graystone rooming house where Finkle lived, grasping a

---

1. **Yeshiva University.** University in New York City offering both theological and secular courses
2. ***Forward.*** *The Jewish Daily Forward,* a New York City newspaper written in the Yiddish language

black, strapped portfolio that had been worn thin with use. Salzman, who had been long in the business, was of slight but dignified build, wearing an old hat, and an overcoat too short and tight for him. He smelled frankly of fish, which he loved to eat, and although he was missing a few teeth, his presence was not displeasing, because of an amiable manner curiously contrasted with mournful eyes. His voice, his lips, his wisp of beard, his bony fingers were animated, but give him a moment of repose and his mild blue eyes revealed a depth of sadness, a characteristic that put Leo a little at ease although the situation, for him, was <u>inherently</u> tense.

He thought it the better part of trial and error . . . to call in an experienced person to advise him on these matters.

He at once informed Salzman why he had asked him to come, explaining that his home was in Cleveland, and that but for his parents, who had married comparatively late in life, he was alone in the world. He had for six years devoted himself almost entirely to his studies, as a result of which, understandably, he had found himself without time for a social life and the company of young women. Therefore he thought it the better part of trial and error—of embarrassing fumbling—to call in an experienced person to advise him on these matters. He remarked in passing that the function of the marriage broker was ancient and honorable, highly approved in the Jewish community, because it made practical the necessary without hindering joy. Moreover, his own parents had been brought together by a matchmaker. They had made, if not a financially profitable marriage—since neither had possessed any worldly goods to speak of—at least a successful

one in the sense of their everlasting devotion to each other. Salzman listened in embarrassed surprise, sensing a sort of apology. Later, however, he experienced a glow of pride in his work, an emotion that had left him years ago, and he heartily approved of Finkle.

The two went to their business. Leo had led Salzman to the only clear place in the room, a table near a window that overlooked the lamp-lit city. He seated himself at the matchmaker's side but facing him, attempting by an act of will to suppress the unpleasant tickle in his throat. Salzman eagerly unstrapped his portfolio and removed a loose rubber band from a thin packet of much-handled cards. As he flipped through them, a gesture and sound that physically hurt Leo, the student pretended not to see and gazed steadfastly out the window. Although it was still February, winter was on its last legs, signs of which he had for the first time in years begun to notice. He now observed the round white moon, moving high in the sky through a cloud <u>menagerie</u>, and watched with half-open mouth as it penetrated a huge hen, and dropped out of her like an egg laying itself. Salzman, though pretending through eyeglasses he had just slipped on, to be engaged in scanning the writing on the cards, stole occasional glances at the young man's distinguished face, noting with pleasure the long, severe scholar's nose, brown eyes heavy with learning, sensitive yet <u>ascetic</u> lips, and a certain, almost hollow quality of the dark cheeks. He gazed around at shelves upon shelves of books and let out a soft, contented sigh.

When Leo's eyes fell upon the cards, he counted six spread out in Salzman's hand.

"So few?" he asked in disappointment.

"You wouldn't believe me how much cards I got in my office," Salzman replied. "The

---

in • her • ent • ly (in hār′ ənt lē) *adv.,* characteristically; naturally

me • nag • er • ie (mə na′ jə rē) *n.,* collection of wild or exotic animals

as • ce • tic (ə set′ ik) *adj.,* self-denying; severe

Marc Chagall

Marc Chagall (1887–1985) was a Jewish artist who was born in Vitebsk, Russia (now Belarus), but spent much of his life in France. He moved to St. Petersburg, Russia, in 1907 to pursue a career in art.

Life during this period was extremely difficult for Russian Jews, however. There were severe restrictions on where Jews could live and how many could pursue higher education. Additionally, violent *pogroms* (a Russian word meaning "to wreak havoc") against Jewish communities left thousands of innocent people severely injured or dead.

Given this environment, Chagall moved to Paris in 1910 and contributed many seminal paintings to the Parisian artistic community. He felt a strong longing for his homeland, however, and moved back to eastern Europe to participate in the Bolshevik Revolution of 1917. The Soviets named Chagall a Commissar of Art, but he quickly fell out of favor with the delicate political atmosphere there and returned to Paris in 1923.

Chagall's paintings combine elements of *Cubism* (a method that focuses on the use of space and geometric shapes) and *Surrealism* (a method that depicts ethereal, dreamlike images). His works often reflect happy childhood memories of his Jewish upbringing, as revealed in rustic scenes of Jewish villages and traditional Jewish symbols such as cows and fiddlers.

Critical Viewing Chagall once commented, "In our life there is a single color, as on an artist's palette, which provides the meaning of life and art. It is the color of love." Look at Chagall's painting *Wedding* on page 847. How is his use of color significant? Notice the details surrounding the central image of the couple. What do these details represent? How are Malamud's story and Chagall's painting connected in terms of subject matter and mood?

---

drawers are already filled to the top, so I keep them now in a barrel, but is every girl good for a new rabbi?"

Leo blushed at this, regretting all he had revealed of himself in a curriculum vitae[3] he had sent to Salzman. He had thought it best to acquaint him with his strict standards and specifications, but in having done so, he felt he had told the marriage broker more than was absolutely necessary.

He hesitantly inquired, "Do you keep photographs of your clients on file?"

"First comes family, amount of dowry, also what kind promises," Salzman replied, unbuttoning his tight coat and settling himself in the chair. "After come pictures, rabbi."

"Call me Mr. Finkle. I'm not yet a rabbi." Salzman said he would, but instead called him doctor, which he changed to rabbi when Leo was not listening too attentively.

Salzman adjusted his horn-rimmed spectacles, gently cleared his throat and read in an eager voice the contents of the top card:

"Sophie P. Twenty four years. Widow one year. No children. Educated high school and two years college. Father promises eight thousand dollars. Has wonderful wholesale business. Also real estate. On the mother's side comes teachers, also one actor. Well known on Second Avenue."

Leo gazed up in surprise. "Did you say a widow?"

"A widow don't mean spoiled, rabbi. She lived with her husband maybe four months. He was a sick boy she made a mistake to marry him."

"Marrying a widow has never entered my mind."

---

3. **curriculum vitae.** Summary of one's personal history and professional qualifications; a résumé

"This is because you have no experience. A widow, especially if she is young and healthy like this girl, is a wonderful person to marry. She will be thankful to you the rest of her life. Believe me, if I was looking now for a bride, I would marry a widow."

Leo reflected, then shook his head.

Salzman hunched his shoulders in an almost imperceptible gesture of disappointment. He placed the card down on the wooden table and began to read another:

"Lily H. High school teacher. Regular. Not a substitute. Has savings and new Dodge car. Lived in Paris one year. Father is successful dentist thirty-five years. Interested in professional man. Well Americanized family. Wonderful opportunity."

"I knew her personally," said Salzman. "I wish you could see this girl. She is a doll. Also very intelligent. All day you could talk to her about books and theater and what not. She also knows current events."

"I don't believe you mentioned her age?"

"Her age?" Salzman said, raising his brows. "Her age is thirty-two years."

Leo said after a while, "I'm afraid that seems a little too old."

Salzman let out a laugh. "So how old are you, rabbi?"

"Twenty-seven."

"So what is the difference, tell me, between twenty-seven and thirty-two? My own wife is seven years older than me. So what did I suffer?—Nothing. If Rothschild's[4] daughter wants to marry you, would you say on account her age, no?"

"Yes," Leo said dryly.

Salzman shook off the no in the yes. "Five years don't mean a thing. I give you my word that when you will live with her for one week you will forget her age. What does it mean five years—that she lived more and knows more than somebody who is younger? On this girl, God bless her, years are not wasted. Each one that it comes makes better the bargain."

"What subjects does she teach in high school?"

"Languages. If you heard the way she speaks French, you will think it is music. I am in the business twenty-five years, and I recommend her with my whole heart. Believe me, I know what I'm talking, rabbi."

"What's on the next card?" Leo said abruptly.

Salzman reluctantly turned up the third card:

"Ruth K. Nineteen years. Honor student. Father offers thirteen thousand cash to the right bridegroom. He is a medical doctor. Stomach specialist with marvelous practice. Brother in law owns own garment business. Particular people."

Salzman looked as if he had read his trump card.

"Did you say nineteen?" Leo asked with interest.

"On the dot."

"Is she attractive?" He blushed. "Pretty?"

Salzman kissed his finger tips. "A little doll. On this I give you my word. Let me call the

---

4. **Rothschild's.** The Rothschilds were once a wealthy Jewish family of international bankers and business leaders.

father tonight and you will see what means pretty."

But Leo was troubled. "You're sure she's that young?"

"This I am positive. The father will show you the birth certificate."

"Are you positive there isn't something wrong with her?" Leo insisted.

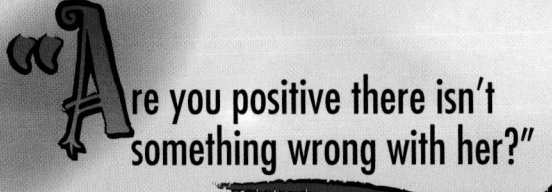

"Are you positive there isn't something wrong with her?"

"Who says there is wrong?"

"I don't understand why an American girl her age should go to a marriage broker."

A smile spread over Salzman's face.

"So for the same reason you went, she comes." Leo flushed. "I am pressed for time."

Salzman, realizing he had been tactless, quickly explained. "The father came, not her. He wants she should have the best, so he looks around himself. When we will locate the right boy he will introduce him and encourage. This makes a better marriage than if a young girl without experience takes for herself. I don't have to tell you this."

"But don't you think this young girl believes in love?" Leo spoke uneasily.

Salzman was about to guffaw but caught himself and said soberly, "Love comes with the right person, not before."

Leo parted dry lips but did not speak. Noticing that Salzman had snatched a glance at the next card, he cleverly asked, "How is her health?"

"Perfect," Salzman said, breathing with difficulty. "Of course, she is a little lame on her right foot from an auto accident that it happened to her when she was twelve years, but nobody notices on account she is so brilliant and also beautiful."

Leo got up heavily and went to the window. He felt curiously bitter and upbraided himself for having called in the marriage broker. Finally, he shook his head.

"Why not?" Salzman persisted, the pitch of his voice rising.

"Because I detest stomach specialists."

"So what do you care what is his business? After you marry her do you need him? Who says he must come every Friday night in your house?"

Ashamed of the way the talk was going, Leo dismissed Salzman, who went home with heavy, melancholy eyes.

Though he had felt only relief at the marriage broker's departure, Leo was in low spirits the next day. He explained it as arising from Salzman's failure to produce a suitable bride for him. He did not care for his type of clientele. But when Leo found himself hesitating whether to seek out another matchmaker, one more polished than Pinye, he wondered if it could be—his protestations to the contrary, and although he honored his father and mother—that he did not, in essence, care for the matchmaking institution? This thought he quickly put out of mind yet found himself still upset. All day he ran around in the woods—missed an important appointment, forgot to give out his laundry, walked out of a Broadway cafeteria without paying and had to run back with the ticket in his hand; had even not recognized his landlady in the street when she passed with a friend and courteously called out, "A good evening to you, Doctor Finkle." By nightfall, however, he had regained sufficient calm to sink his nose into a book and there found peace from his thoughts.

Almost at once there came a knock on the door. Before Leo could say enter, Salzman, commercial cupid, was standing in the room. His face was gray and meager, his expression hungry, and he looked as if he would expire on his feet. Yet the marriage broker managed, by some trick of the muscles, to display a broad smile.

"So good evening. I am invited?"

Leo nodded, disturbed to see him again, yet unwilling to ask the man to leave.

Beaming still, Salzman laid his portfolio on the table. "Rabbi, I got for you tonight good news."

"I've asked you not to call me rabbi. I'm still a student."

"Your worries are finished. I have for you a first-class bride."

"Your worries are finished. I have for you a first-class bride."

"Leave me in peace concerning this subject," Leo pretended lack of interest.

"The world will dance at your wedding."

"Please, Mr. Salzman, no more."

"But first must come back my strength," Salzman said weakly. He fumbled with the portfolio straps and took out of the leather case an oily paper bag, from which he extracted a hard, seeded roll and a small, smoked white fish. With a quick motion of his hand he stripped the fish out of its skin and began ravenously to chew. "All day in a rush," he muttered.

Leo watched him eat.

"A sliced tomato you have maybe?" Salzman hesitantly inquired.

"No."

The marriage broker shut his eyes and ate. When he had finished he carefully cleaned up the crumbs and rolled up the remains of the fish, in the paper bag. His spectacled eyes roamed the room until he discovered, amid some piles of books, a one-burner gas stove. Lifting his hat he humbly asked, "A glass tea you got, rabbi?"

Conscience-stricken, Leo rose and brewed the tea. He served it with a chunk of lemon and two cubes of lump sugar, delighting Salzman.

After he had drunk his tea, Salzman's strength and good spirits were restored.

"So tell me, rabbi," he said amiably, "you considered some more the three clients I mentioned yesterday?"

"There was no need to consider."

"Why not?"

"None of them suits me."

"What then suits you?"

Leo let it pass because he could give only a confused answer.

Without waiting for a reply, Salzman asked, "You remember this girl I talked to you—the high school teacher?"

"Age thirty-two?"

But, surprisingly, Salzman's face lit in a smile. "Age twenty-nine."

Leo shot him a look. "Reduced from thirty-two?"

"A mistake," Salzman avowed. "I talked today with the dentist. He took me to his safety deposit box and showed me the birth certificate. She was twenty-nine years last August. They made her a party in the mountains where she went for her vacation. When her father spoke to me the first time I forgot to write the age and I told you thirty-two, but now I remember this was a different client, a widow."

"The same one you told me about? I thought she was twenty-four?"

"A different. Am I responsible that the world is filled with widows?"

"No, but I'm not interested in them, nor for that matter, in school teachers."

Salzman pulled his clasped hands to his breast. Looking at the ceiling he devoutly exclaimed, "Yiddishe kinder,[5] what can I say to somebody that he is not interested in high school teachers? So what then you are interested?"

Leo flushed but controlled himself.

"In what else will you be interested," Salzman went on, "if you not interested in this fine girl that she speaks four languages and has personally in the bank ten thousand dollars? Also her father guarantees further twelve thousand. Also she has a new car, wonderful clothes, talks on all subjects, and she will give you a first-class home and children. How near do we come in our life to paradise?"

"If she's so wonderful, why wasn't she married ten years ago?"

"Why?" said Salzman with a heavy laugh.

"—Why? Because she is *partikiler*.[6] This is why. She wants the *best*."

Leo was silent, amused at how he had entangled himself. But Salzman had aroused his interest in Lily H., and he began seriously to consider calling on her. When the marriage broker observed how intently Leo's mind was at work on the facts he had supplied, he felt certain they would soon come to an agreement.

Late Saturday afternoon, conscious of Salzman, Leo Finkle walked with Lily Hirschorn along Riverside Drive. He walked briskly and erectly, wearing with distinction the black fedora he had that morning taken with <u>trepidation</u> out of the dusty hat box on his closet shelf, and the heavy black Saturday coat he had thoroughly whisked clean. Leo also owned a walking stick, a present from a distant relative, but quickly put temptation aside and did not use it. Lily, petite and not unpretty, had on something signifying the approach of spring. She was au courant,[7] animatedly, with all sorts of subjects, and he weighed her words and found her surprisingly sound—score another for Salzman, whom he uneasily sensed to be somewhere around, hiding perhaps high in a tree along the street, flashing the lady signals with a pocket mirror; or perhaps a cloven-hoofed Pan,[8] piping <u>nuptial</u> ditties as he danced his invisible way before them, strewing wild buds on the walk and purple grapes in their path, symbolizing fruit of a union, though there was of course still none.

Lily startled Leo by remarking, "I was thinking of Mr. Salzman, a curious figure, wouldn't you say?"

---

5. **Yiddishe kinder.** [Yiddish] Jewish children; Salzman is both calling Leo a child and lamenting the loss of the more traditional values Leo's parents' generation held.
6. *partikiler.* Particular; having high standards
7. **au courant.** [French] In keeping with the times; up to date
8. **Pan.** Greek god of fields, forests, wild animals, flocks, and shepherds, represented as a man with the legs of a goat who plays a flutelike instrument

---

trep • i • da • tion (treˈ pə dāˊ shən) *n.,* anxiety; nervousness

nup • tial (nupˊ shəl) *adj.,* concerning marriage or a wedding

Not certain what to answer, he nodded.

She bravely went on, blushing, "I for one am grateful for his introducing us. Aren't you?"

He courteously replied, "I am."

"I mean," she said with a little laugh—and it was all in good taste, or at least gave the effect of being not in bad—"do you mind that we came together so?"

He was not displeased with her honesty, recognizing that she meant to set the relationship aright, and understanding that it took a certain amount of experience in life, and courage, to want to do it quite that way. One had to have some sort of past to make that kind of beginning.

He said that he did not mind. Salzman's function was traditional and honorable—valuable for what it might achieve, which, he pointed out, was frequently nothing.

> **S**alzman's function was traditional and honorable—valuable for what it might achieve.

Lily agreed with a sigh. They walked on for a while and she said after a long silence, again with a nervous laugh, "Would you mind if I asked you something a little bit personal? Frankly, I find the subject fascinating." Although Leo shrugged, she went on half embarrassedly, "How was it that you came to your calling? I mean was it a sudden passionate inspiration?"

Leo, after a time, slowly replied, "I was always interested in the Law."

"You saw revealed in it the presence of the Highest?"

He nodded and changed the subject. "I understand that you spent a little time in Paris, Miss Hirschorn?"

"Oh, did Mr. Salzman tell you, Rabbi Finkle?" Leo winced but she went on, "It was ages ago and almost forgotten. I remember I had to return for my sister's wedding."

And Lily would not be put off. "When," she asked in a trembly voice, "did you become enamored of God?"

He stared at her. Then it came to him that she was talking not about Leo Finkle, but of a total stranger, some mystical figure, perhaps even passionate prophet that Salzman had dreamed up for her—no relation to the living or dead. Leo trembled with rage and weakness. The trickster had obviously sold her a bill of goods, just as he had him, who'd expected to become acquainted with a young lady of twenty-nine, only to behold, the moment he laid eyes upon her strained and anxious face, a woman past thirty-five and aging rapidly. Only his self control had kept him this long in her presence.

"I am not," he said gravely, "a talented religious person," and in seeking words to go on, found himself possessed by shame and fear. "I think," he said in a strained manner, "that I came to God not because I loved Him, but because I did not."

This confession he spoke harshly because its unexpectedness shook him.

Lily wilted. Leo saw a <u>profusion</u> of loaves of bread go flying like ducks high over his head, not unlike the winged loaves by which he had counted himself to sleep last night. Mercifully, then, it snowed, which he would not put past Salzman's <u>machinations</u>.

He was infuriated with the marriage broker and swore he would throw him out of the room the minute he reappeared. But Salzman did not come that night, and when Leo's anger had subsided, an unaccountable despair grew in its place. At first he thought this was caused

---

pro • fu • sion (prō fyü´ zhən) *n.*, large number; abundance
mach • i • na • tion (ma' kə nā´ shən) *n.*, clever plot or scheme

by his disappointment in Lily, but before long it became evident that he had involved himself with Salzman without a true knowledge of his own intent. He gradually realized—with an emptiness that seized him with six hands—that he had called in the broker to find him a bride because he was incapable of doing it himself. This terrifying insight he had derived as a result of his meeting and conversation with Lily Hirschorn. Her probing questions had somehow irritated him into revealing—to himself more than her—the true nature of his relationship to God, and from that it had come upon him, with shocking force, that apart from his parents, he had never loved anyone. Or perhaps it went the other way, that he did not love God so well as he might, because he had not loved man. It seemed to Leo that his whole life stood starkly revealed and he saw himself for the first time as he truly was—unloved and loveless. This bitter but somehow not fully unexpected revelation brought him to a point of panic, controlled only by extraordinary effort. He covered his face with his hands and cried.

> He gradually realized . . . that he had called in the broker to find him a bride because he was incapable of doing it himself.

The week that followed was the worst of his life. He did not eat and lost weight. His beard darkened and grew ragged. He stopped attending seminars and almost never opened a book. He seriously considering leaving the Yeshiva, although he was deeply troubled at the thought of the loss of all his years of study—saw them like pages torn from a book, strewn over the city—and at the devastating effect of this decision upon his parents. But he had lived without knowledge of himself, and never in the

Five Books[9] and all the Commentaries—mea culpa[10]—had the truth been revealed to him. He did not know where to turn, and in all this desolating loneliness there was no *to whom*, although he often thought of Lily but not once could bring himself to go downstairs and make the call. He became touchy and irritable, especially with his landlady, who asked him all manner of personal questions; on the other hand, sensing his own disagreeableness, he waylaid her on the stairs and apologized <u>abjectly</u>, until mortified, she ran from him. Out of this, however, he drew the consolation that he was a Jew and that a Jew suffered. But gradually, as the long and terrible week drew to a close, he regained his composure and some idea of purpose in life: to go on as planned. Although he was imperfect, the ideal was not. As for his quest of a bride, the thought of continuing afflicted him with anxiety and heartburn, yet perhaps with this new knowledge of himself he would be more successful than in the past. Perhaps love would now come to him and a bride to that love. And for this sanctified seeking who needed a Salzman?

The marriage broker, a skeleton with haunted eyes, returned that very night. He looked, withal, the picture of frustrated expectancy—as if he had steadfastly waited the week at Miss Lily Hirschorn's side for a telephone call that never came.

Casually coughing, Salzman came immediately to the point: "So how did you like her?"

Leo's anger rose and he could not refrain from chiding the matchmaker: "Why did you lie to me, Salzman?"

Salzman's pale face went dead white, the world had snowed on him.

---

9. **Five Books.** The Pentateuch, or Five Books of Moses, consists of Genesis, Exodus, Leviticus, Numbers, and Deuteronomy.
10. **mea culpa.** [Latin] "I am to blame."

> **ab • ject • ly** (abʹ jekt lē) *adv.*, miserably; in a manner showing hopelessness or resignation

"Did you not state that she was twenty-nine?" Leo insisted.

"I gave you my word—"

"She was thirty-five, if a day. *At least* thirty-five."

"Of this don't be too sure. Her father told me—"

"Never mind. The worst of it was that you lied to her."

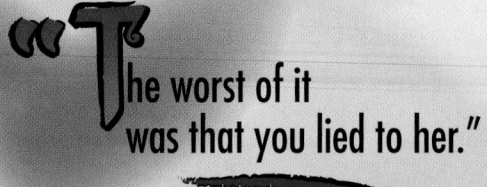
"The worst of it was that you lied to her."

"How did I lie to her, tell me?"

"You told her things about me that weren't true. You made me out to be more, consequently less than I am. She had in mind a totally different person, a sort of semimystical Wonder Rabbi."

"All I said, you was a religious man."

"I can imagine."

Salzman sighed. "This is my weakness that I have," he confessed. "My wife says to me I shouldn't be a salesman, but when I have two fine people that they would be wonderful to be married, I am so happy that I talk too much." He smiled wanly. "This is why Salzman is a poor man."

Leo's anger left him. "Well, Salzman, I'm afraid that's all."

The marriage broker fastened hungry eyes on him.

"You don't want any more a bride?"

"I do," said Leo, "but I have decided to seek her in a different way. I am no longer interested in an arranged marriage. To be frank, I now admit the necessity of premarital love. That is, I want to be in love with the one I marry."

"Love?" said Salzman, astounded. After a moment he remarked, "For us, our love is our life, not for the ladies. In the ghetto they—"

"I know, I know," said Leo. "I've thought of it often. Love, I have said to myself, should be a by-product of living and worship rather than

its own end. Yet for myself I find it necessary to establish the level of my need and fulfill it."

Salzman shrugged but answered, "Listen, rabbi, if you want love, this I can find for you also. I have such beautiful clients that you will love them the minute your eyes will see them."

Leo smiled unhappily. "I'm afraid you don't understand."

But Salzman hastily unstrapped his portfolio and withdrew a manila packet from it.

"Pictures," he said, quickly laying the envelope on the table.

Leo called after him to take the pictures away, but as if on the wings of the wind, Salzman had disappeared.

March came. Leo had returned to his regular routine. Although he felt not quite himself yet—lacked energy—he was making plans for a more active social life. Of course it would cost something, but he was an expert in cutting corners; and when there were no corners left he would make circles rounder. All the while Salzman's pictures had lain on the table, gathering dust. Occasionally as Leo sat studying, or enjoying a cup of tea, his eyes fell on the manila envelope, but he never opened it.

The days went by and no social life to speak of developed with a member of the opposite sex—it was difficult, given the circumstances of his situation. One morning Leo toiled up the stairs to his room and stared out the window at the city. Although the day was bright his view of it was dark. For some time he watched people in the street below hurrying along and then turned with a heavy heart to his little room. On the table was the packet. With a sudden relentless gesture he tore it open. For a half-hour he stood by the table in a state of excitement, examining the photographs of the ladies Salzman had included. Finally, with a deep sigh he put them down. There were six, of varying degrees of attractiveness, but look at them long enough and they all became Lily Hirschorn: all past their prime, all starved behind bright smiles, not a true personality in the lot. Life, despite their frantic

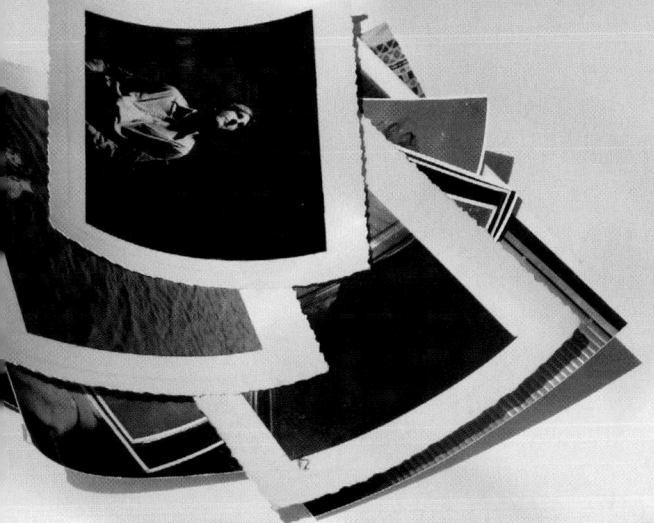

yoohooings, had passed them by; they were pictures in a briefcase that stank of fish. After a while, however, as Leo attempted to return the photographs into the envelope, he found in it another, a snapshot of the type taken by a machine for a quarter. He gazed at it a moment and let out a cry.

Her face deeply moved him. Why, he could at first not say. It gave him the impression of youth—spring flowers, yet age—a sense of having been used to the bone, wasted; this came from the eyes, which were hauntingly familiar yet absolutely strange. He had a vivid impression that he had met her before, but try as he might he could not place her although he could almost recall her name, as if he had read it in her own handwriting. No, this couldn't be; he would have remembered her. It was not, he affirmed, that she had an extraordinary beauty—no, though her face was attractive enough; it was that *something* about her moved him. Feature for feature, even some of the ladies of the photographs could do better; but she leaped forth to his heart—had *lived* or wanted to—more than just wanted, perhaps regretted how she had lived—had somehow deeply suffered. It could be seen in the depths of those reluctant eyes, and from the way the light enclosed and shone from her, and within her, opening realms of possibility: this was her own. Her he desired. His head ached and eyes narrowed with the intensity of his gazing, then as if an obscure fog had blown up in the mind,

he experienced fear of her and was aware that he had received an impression, somehow, of evil. He shuddered, saying softly, it is thus with us all. Leo brewed some tea in a small pot and sat sipping it without sugar, to calm himself. But before he had finished drinking, again with excitement he examined the face and found it good: good for Leo Finkle. Only such a one could understand him and help him seek whatever he was seeking. She might, perhaps, love him. How she had happened to be among the discards in Salzman's barrel he could never guess, but he knew he must urgently go find her.

How she had happened to be among the discards in Salzman's barrel he could never guess.

Leo rushed downstairs, grabbed up the Bronx telephone book, and searched for Salzman's home address. He was not listed, nor was his office. Neither was he in the Manhattan book. But Leo remembered having written down the address on a slip of paper after he had read Salzman's advertisement in the "personals" column of the *Forward.* He ran up to his room and tore through his papers, without luck. It was <u>exasperating</u>. Just when he needed the matchmaker he was nowhere to be found. Fortunately Leo remembered to look in his wallet. There on a card he found his name written and a Bronx address. No phone number was listed, the reason—Leo now recalled—he had originally communicated with Salzman by letter. He got on his coat, put a hat on over his skull cap and hurried to the subway station. All the way to the far end of the Bronx he sat on the edge of his seat. He was more than once tempted to take out the picture and see if

ex • as • per • at • ing (eg zas´ pʉr āt' iŋ) *adj.,* irritating; annoying

the girl's face was as he remembered it, but he refrained, allowing the snapshot to remain in his inside coat pocket, content to have her so close. When the train pulled into the station he was waiting at the door and bolted out. He quickly located the street Salzman had advertised.

The building he sought was less than a block from the subway, but it was not an office building, nor even a loft, nor a store in which one could rent office space. It was a very old tenement house. Leo found Salzman's name in pencil on a soiled tag under the bell and climbed three dark flights to his apartment. When he knocked, the door was opened by a thin, asthmatic, gray-haired woman, in felt slippers.

"Yes?" she said, expecting nothing. She listened without listening. He could have sworn he had seen her, too, before but knew it was an illusion.

"Salzman—does he live here? Pinye Salzman," he said, "the matchmaker?"

She stared at him a long minute. "Of course."

He felt embarrassed. "Is he in?"

"No." Her mouth, though left open, offered nothing more.

"The matter is urgent. Can you tell me where his office is?"

"In the air." She pointed upward.

"You mean he has no office?" Leo asked.

"In his socks."

He peered into the apartment. It was sunless and dingy, one large room divided by a half-open curtain, beyond which he could see a sagging metal bed. The near side of a room was crowded with rickety chairs, old bureaus, a three-legged table, racks of cooking utensils, and all the apparatus of a kitchen. But there was no sign of Salzman or his magic barrel, probably also a figment of the imagination. An odor of frying fish made Leo weak to the knees.

"Where is he?" he insisted. "I've got to see your husband."

At length she answered, "So who knows where he is? Every time he thinks a new

thought he runs to a different place. Go home, he will find you."

"Tell him Leo Finkle."

She gave no sign she had heard.

He walked downstairs, depressed.

But Salzman, breathless, stood waiting at his door.

Leo was astounded and overjoyed. "How did you get here before me?"

"I rushed."

"Come inside."

They entered. Leo fixed tea, and a sardine sandwich for Salzman. As they were drinking he reached behind him for the packet of pictures and handed them to the marriage broker.

Salzman put down his glass and said expectantly, "You found somebody you like?"

"Not among these."

The marriage broker turned away.

"Here is the one I want." Leo held forth the snapshot.

Salzman slipped on his glasses and took the picture into his trembling hand. He turned ghastly and let out a groan.

"What's the matter?" cried Leo.

"Excuse me. Was an accident this picture. She isn't for you."

Salzman frantically shoved the manila packet into his portfolio. He thrust the snapshot into his pocket and fled down the stairs.

Leo, after momentary paralysis, gave chase and cornered the marriage broker in the vestibule. The landlady made hysterical outcries but neither of them listened.

"Give me back the picture, Salzman."

"No." The pain in his eyes was terrible.

"Tell me who she is then."

"This I can't tell you. Excuse me."

He made to depart, but Leo, forgetting himself, seized the matchmaker by his tight coat and shook him frenziedly.

"Please," sighed Salzman. "*Please.*"

Leo ashamedly let him go. "Tell me who she is," he begged. "It's very important for me to know."

"She is not for you. She is a wild one—wild, without shame. This is not a bride for a rabbi."

"What do you mean wild?"

"Like an animal. Like a dog. For her to be poor was a sin. This is why to me she is dead now."

"In God's name, what do you mean?"

"Her I can't introduce to you," Salzman said.

"Why are you so excited?"

"Why, he asks," Salzman said, bursting into tears. "This is my baby, my Stella, she should burn in hell."

Leo hurried up to bed and hid under the covers. Under the covers he thought his life through. Although he soon fell asleep he could not sleep her out of his mind. He woke, beating his breast. Though he prayed to be rid of her, his prayers went unanswered. Through days of torment he endlessly struggled not to love her; fearing success, he escaped it. He then concluded to convert her to goodness, himself to God. The idea alternately nauseated and exalted him.

He perhaps did not know that he had come to a final decision until he encountered Salzman in a Broadway cafeteria. He was sitting alone at a rear table, sucking the bony remains of a fish. The marriage broker appeared <u>haggard</u>, and transparent to the point of vanishing.

Salzman looked up at first without recognizing him. Leo had grown a pointed beard and his eyes were weighted with wisdom.

"Salzman," he said, "love has at last come to my heart."

"Who can love from a picture?" mocked the marriage broker.

"It is not impossible."

"If you can love her, then you can love anybody. Let me show you some new clients that they just sent me their photographs. One is a little doll.

"Just her I want," Leo murmured.

"Don't be a fool, doctor. Don't bother with her."

"Put me in touch with her, Salzman," Leo said humbly. "Perhaps I can be of service."

Salzman had stopped eating and Leo understood with emotion that it was now arranged.

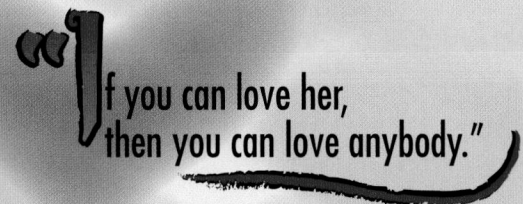

"If you can love her, then you can love anybody."

Leaving the cafeteria, he was, however, afflicted by a tormenting suspicion that Salzman had planned it all to happen this way.

Leo was informed by letter that she would meet him on a certain corner, and she was there one spring night, waiting under a street lamp. He appeared, carrying a small bouquet of violets and rosebuds. Stella stood by the lamppost, smoking. She wore white with red shoes, which fitted his expectations, although in a troubled moment he had imagined the dress red, and only the shoes white. She waited uneasily and shyly. From afar he saw that her eyes—clearly her father's—were filled with desperate innocence. He pictured, in her, his own redemption. Violins and lit candles revolved in the sky. Leo ran forward with flowers outthrust.

Around the corner, Salzman, leaning against a wall, chanted prayers for the dead. ❖

hag • gard (hăg´ ərd) adj., having a wasted or exhausted look

Arranged marriages are still common in many of the world's traditional societies. What would be the benefits of having a spouse chosen for you? What would be the drawbacks?

Refer to Text ▶ ▶ ▶ ▶ ▶ Reason with Text

1a. What part of Salzman's client profiles does Finkle want to see? How does Salzman respond?	**1b.** Infer why physical appearance is the last thing Salzman has his clients consider.	**Understand** Find meaning
2a. List the women Salzman initially suggests as potential brides. What characteristics do they have? Which one does Finkle actually meet?	**2b.** After talking to Lily Hirschorn, Finkle suspects Salzman has lied to both of them. Describe a case of "false advertising" that you or someone you know has experienced.	**Apply** Use information
3a. Recall what Finkle finds among the photographs that Salzman leaves behind.	**3b.** What emotions within Finkle does the photograph touch? What elements in the photo contribute to this effect?	**Analyze** Take things apart
4a. Where does Finkle go after finding the photograph of the intriguing young woman?	**4b.** Decide whether Finkle's impulsive actions are reasonable.	**Evaluate** Make judgments
5a. Early in the story, how does Leo justify his use of a marriage broker's services? What couple serves as his example of a marriage broker's success?	**5b.** Research the matchmaking traditions of another culture. Which tradition seems the more humane and workable to you?	**Create** Bring ideas together

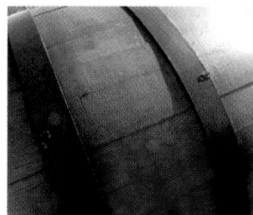

Analyze Literature

Motivation and Antihero

What was Finkle's initial motivation for calling on Salzman? What motivates him to seek out Salzman near the end of the story?

Review your cluster chart listing characteristics that make Finkle an antihero. What characteristics contradict the antihero profile?

Extend the Text

Writing Options

Creative Writing Write an epilogue to "The Magic Barrel" in which you let readers know the fates of Leo, Stella, and Salzman. Your epilogue might include short-term events (for example, the rest of the story's last scene), long-term events (what happens months or years later), or both.

Expository Writing Malamud's short stories and novels tend to share a few basic elements. Review some of these on the Before Reading page. Then write a one-page literary analysis in which you explain how "The Magic Barrel" is a typical Malamud story.

Collaborative Learning

Debate a Topic Research the practice of matchmaking in several different cultures. Establish two teams and pre-pare a debate on the topic. One team will argue the benefits of modern matchmaking, and the other will argue its drawbacks. After the debate, discuss which argument was more persuasive and why.

Media Literacy

Create a Movie Poster Imagine that "The Magic Barrel" is being produced as a film. With a partner, create a poster to advertise the film. It should include the names of the actors starring as Finkle and Salzman, as well as a graphic and a tagline that capture the meaning of the story. Present your poster to the class, explaining why you chose the elements you did.

 Go to **www.mirrorsandwindows.com** for more.

Understand the Concept

Hyphens, ellipsis points (or *ellipses* plural), and italics are commonly used grammatical tools that serve distinct purposes.

Hyphens are short dashes (-) used to connect elements in some compound words and expressions.

EXAMPLES
great-aunts
horror-struck
sixty-two
first-class
over-the-counter
two-year-old

See the Vocabulary & Spelling workshop on page 994 for more on compound words.

An **ellipsis** is a series of three spread points, or periods, used to signify a pause or incomplete thought.

EXAMPLE
He drifted off to sleep, knowing he was safe . . . for now . . .

An ellipsis also is used to indicate that words have been eliminated from within quoted text. When the eliminated words occur between complete sentences, the first sentence ends with a period and the ellipsis follows.

EXAMPLE
In his speech, the mayor said, "Providing citizens with a safe place to live is my primary goal. . . . I will focus my administration on achieving that goal."

In contrast to hyphens and ellipses, which are forms of punctuation, **italics** is a type of print, or *font*. This slanted type is used to emphasize specific words and to identify foreign words and phrases. In narrative writing, italic type often is used denote a character's thoughts.

EXAMPLES
I *knew* I had seen you somewhere before!

Despite her *mea culpa,* we were still angry with her.

Could he possibly be interested in me? she wondered.

Apply the Skill

Identify the Need for Hyphens, Ellipses, and Italics

In each of the following sentences, identify where a hyphen, ellipsis, and/or italic type is needed. Use a dictionary, if necessary.

1. In traditional Jewish communities, a matchmaker called a shadchan was hired to find suitable mates for young people.
2. As romantic love became the norm, matchmaking was considered less of a valuable *service* and more of a business.
3. Salzman lies and tells Leo that Lily is only twenty nine years old, but she is really in her mid thirties.
4. When Salzman calls on yiddisher kinder (Jewish children), he is simultaneously recognizing Finkle's inexperience and the loss of traditional values.
5. At several points in the story, Leo wonders, Will I ever find a wife?
6. When Leo and Stella have children, they could tell them the story of how they met by starting with "Once upon a time in New York City."

Use Hyphens, Ellipses, and Italics Effectively
Write a short fictionalized account of an event in your life. Incorporate ellipses and italics. You may want to include dialogue to help you do this most naturally. Use at least two compound words or expressions requiring hyphens.

Elegy for Jane
An Elegy by Theodore Roethke

Build Background

Literary Context **"Elegy for Jane"** first appeared in 1953 in Theodore Roethke's Pulitzer Prize–winning poetry collection *The Waking*. It is one of several elegies, or poems of mourning, written by Roethke. The subject of "Elegy for Jane" is a student of the poet's who was killed after falling from a horse. The use of natural imagery in the poem, especially images of birds and plants, is common in Roethke's work, as is the theme of loss.

Reader's Context Remember a time when you lost someone or something very important to you. What are your strongest images of that person or thing?

Meet the Author

Theodore Roethke (1908–1963) grew up in Saginaw, Michigan. A sensitive, sickly child, he spent his childhood outdoors and developed a reverence for nature—specifically, greenhouses. His father and uncle owned these structures, which later appeared as a frequent subject in his collection *The Lost Son and Other Poems.* He once wrote that the greenhouse "is . . . my symbol for the whole of life, a womb, a heaven-on-earth." At fifteen, Roethke became head of the household when his father died. His relationship with his father, coupled with his profound loss, became common writing themes.

After earning a bachelor's degree from the University of Michigan and doing graduate work at both Michigan and Harvard, Roethke taught English at various universities, including twenty-five years at the University of Washington in Seattle. There, he became well known among students for his public readings. A year after Roethke's death, an annual poetry-reading series was established in his honor.

Roethke's first book, *Open House* (1941), was reviewed by British poet W. H. Auden, who said Roethke had the ability to transform personal humiliation into something beautiful. The volume introduced the rich musicality and bitter wit that would characterize his work. Subsequent writings—including 227 notebooks of unpublished poetic ideas, journals, and essays found after Roethke's death—explored the relationship between humanity and nature as well as the struggle for meaning and happiness in life. Roethke's large presence, quirky behavior, and authentic writing endeared him to his students, fellow writers, and critics and made him a foremost writer of the twentieth century.

Analyze Literature

Elegy and Imagery
An **elegy** is poem of mourning, usually about someone who has died.

Imagery is the language used to create word pictures, or images. A writer may create images by literally describing something (descriptive language) or by using elements such as metaphor or personification (figurative language).

Set Purpose

As noted earlier, the concept of loss is found in much of Roethke's work, including several elegies. Identify what qualities make this poem an elegy. Determine the feelings the speaker has for Jane, his student. Also determine what techniques Roethke uses most frequently to create imagery. Create a two-column chart to record the uses of descriptive versus figurative language.

Preview Vocabulary

tendril, 863
console, 863

Elegy for Jane

by Theodore Roethke

I remember the neckcurls, limp and damp as <u>tendrils</u>;
And her quick look, a sidelong pickerel[1] smile;
And how, once startled into talk, the light
    syllables leaped for her,
And she balanced in the delight of her thought,

5 A wren, happy, tail into the wind,
Her song trembling the twigs and small branches.
The shade sang with her;
The leaves, their whispers turned to kissing;
And the mold sang in the bleached valleys under
    the rose.

10 Oh, when she was sad, she cast herself down
    into such a pure depth,
Even a father could not find her;
Scraping her cheek against straw;
Stirring the clearest water.

My sparrow, you are not here,
15 Waiting like a fern, making a spiny shadow.
The sides of wet stones cannot <u>console</u> me,
Nor the moss, wound with the last light.

If only I could nudge you from this sleep,
My maimed darling, my skittery[2] pigeon.
20 Over this damp grave I speak the words of my love:
I, with no rights in this matter,
Neither father nor lover. ❖

---

1. **pickerel.** Large-eyed like a pickerel, a type of fish
2. **skittery.** Coy; easily frightened

ten • dril (ten′ drəl) *n.,* something that curls in a spiral
con • sole (kən sōl′) *v.,* comfort

Where would you seek consolation after the death of a loved one?

Refer to Text ▶ ▶ ▶ ▶ ▶ Reason with Text

Refer to Text	Reason with Text	
1a. What effect does the wren's song have?	**1b.** Estimate the impact Jane had on people.	**Understand** Find meaning
2a. What emotion of Jane's is described in the second stanza?	**2b.** What picture do the first and second stanzas together paint of Jane?	**Apply** Use information
3a. Why is the speaker inconsolable?	**3b.** Compare and contrast the last three lines of the first stanza with the last three lines of the final stanza. Consider line length and tone.	**Analyze** Take things apart
4a. What words does the speaker utter over the damp grave?	**4b.** Argue whether the speaker has the right to speak about his love for Jane, even if he is outside her family.	**Evaluate** Make judgments
5a. What men in Jane's life does the speaker imply would have the right to express their love for her?	**5b.** What emotions do you associate with relationships such as friend, co-worker, and parent? How does the relationship define a person's rights to certain feelings?	**Create** Bring ideas together

Analyze Literature

Elegy and Imagery

If this poem were untitled, at what point would you guess it's an elegy? At what point would you be certain? Discuss the characteristics that make this poem an elegy.

Review the chart you created of types of images: descriptive versus figurative. Which type was more common? Identify one example of *metaphor* (one thing written about as if it were another) and one example of *personification* (a nonliving thing or idea described as having human characteristics).

Extend the Text

Writing Options

Creative Writing Choose one line from "Elegy for Jane," and use it as the first line of a short story. Change the punctuation as needed to form a complete sentence or thought. Remember that while Roethke's use of a certain phrase may be figurative, it may be literal in your story.

Narrative Writing Write a biographical essay about Roethke, focusing on one aspect of his life. For example, you might choose his childhood, his college days, or his popularity as a teacher and public reader.

Collaborative Learning

Bring Imagery to Life "Elegy for Jane" contains detailed imagery appealing to several senses, including sight, sound, and touch. With two classmates, create an audio or visual representation of a single image from the poem. For example, you might sketch or paint an image of Jane or make a video or audio recording of something described. Set up a display of the representations within your school.

Critical Literacy

Participate in a Panel Discussion The speaker in "Elegy for Jane" makes clear that his relationship with Jane is not romantic or parental, but he never specifies anything more. Initiate a panel discussion in which three people share their thoughts on this topic. Have another person serve as mediator, ensuring each person has a chance to speak and respond.

 Go to **www.mirrorsandwindows.com** for more.

One Art

A Lyric Poem by Elizabeth Bishop

Build Background

Literary Context Included in Elizabeth Bishop's 1977 collection *Geography III*, **"One Art"** addresses the poet's personal losses and underscores life's lack of permanence. Bishop's stoic tone reminds readers that loss is inevitable and that perseverance is necessary to master "the art of losing."

"One Art" is a **villanelle:** a nineteen-line poem consisting of **tercets** (three-line stanzas) that follow a specific rhyming pattern. Working within this two-rhyme pattern, Bishop achieved the controlled, emotional effect she wanted after two weeks of writing and seventeen different drafts. Spending just two weeks on a poem was uncharacteristic of Bishop. She wrote slowly, publishing her collections approximately every ten years and producing only about a hundred poems in her lifetime.

Reader's Context Whom or what of value have you lost? How can experiencing loss change your priorities in life?

Meet the Author

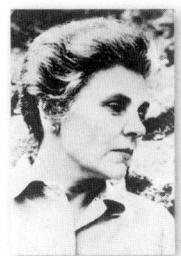

Elizabeth Bishop (1911–1979), who was born in Worcester, Massachusetts, spent her early years in upheaval. After her father's death and her mother's hospitalization four years later, Bishop was shuffled among relatives. Ultimately, she was sent to live with her grandparents in Nova Scotia, Canada, a place that provided a nurturing environment and fond memories. However, the remnants of those early childhood experiences can be seen in the voice of her poetry, which reveals deliberate, understated emotion.

Bishop pursued her love of literature and writing at Vassar College. After graduation, she lived abroad, traveling around Europe and Africa before settling in Brazil for sixteen years. After the death of her closest Brazilian friend, Bishop returned to the United States to teach at Harvard in the 1970s.

Bishop's writing was shaped by two prominent poets: Marianne Moore and Robert Lowell (see Units 5 and 8, respectively). She found a mentor in Moore, who encouraged and guided her career. Her lifelong friendship with Lowell was bound by their shared sense of loneliness and isolation. Lowell's influence can also be seen in the subtle details about nature Bishop includes in her poetry. Her writing style that emerged was reserved and spare, reflecting her belief that "something needn't be large to be good."

Although the volume of Bishop's poetry is slim, she received many awards, including the 1956 Pulitzer Prize for the combined collection *Poems: North and South—A Cold Spring* and the 1969 National Book Award for *Complete Poems.*

Analyze Literature

Tone and Rhyme Scheme
The **tone** of a literary work is the implied emotional attitude toward the reader or the subject.

The **rhyme scheme** is a pattern of end rhymes, or rhymes at the ends of lines of verse.

Set Purpose

"One Art" reflects Bishop's belief that "something needn't be large to be good" in that it does not dramatize the feelings of the speaker. How does the speaker feel about losing things in the first part of the poem? How does that attitude change throughout the poem? Examine Bishop's choice of words, along with other literary devices, to create tone. In addition, examine the rhyme scheme in this poem, which is a villanelle. Evaluate how closely Bishop follows the pattern of end rhymes for this poetic form.

Preview Vocabulary

intent, 866
vast, 866

One Art

by Elizabeth Bishop

The art of losing isn't hard to master;
so many things seem filled with the <u>intent</u>
to be lost that their loss is no disaster.

Lose something every day. Accept the fluster
5   of lost door keys, the hour badly spent.
The art of losing isn't hard to master.

Then practice losing farther, losing faster:
places, and names, and where it was you meant
to travel. None of these will bring disaster.

10 I lost my mother's watch. And look! my last, or
next-to-last, of three loved houses went.
The art of losing isn't hard to master.

I lost two cities, lovely ones. And, <u>vaster</u>,
some realms I owned, two rivers, a continent.
15 I miss them, but it wasn't a disaster.

—Even losing you (the joking voice, a gesture
I love) I shan't have lied. It's evident
the art of losing's not too hard to master
though it may look like (*Write* it!) like disaster. ❖

---

in • tent (in tent´) *n.,* purpose; plan
vast (vast) *adj.,* large; immense

The speaker advises the reader to "lose something every day," suggesting that experiencing loss makes it easier to accept. Do you agree that people get used to experiencing loss? Does loss become less painful the more you experience it?

Refer to Text ▶ ▶ ▶ ▶ ▶   Reason with Text

1a. What things does the speaker lose?

1b. Explain why the loss of "so many things" is considered "no disaster" in the first stanza.

Understand
Find meaning

2a. What is the speaker's advice on how to handle loss?

2b. Why does the speaker give this advice? Does it really apply to all of these situations?

Apply
Use information

3a. Compare the types of things the speaker describes losing in the second two stanzas with those in the last three.

3b. Detect what is happening as the speaker continues to talk about loss. What might he or she consider the greatest loss of all?

Analyze
Take things apart

4a. Indicate how the repeated line is altered in the last stanza.

4b. Evaluate whether the speaker sincerely feels that "the art of losing isn't hard to master."

Evaluate
Make judgments

5a. What about the "you" in the poem does the speaker miss?

5b. Develop a list of questions you would ask the speaker after having read his or her ideas about loss.

Create
Bring ideas together

Analyze Literature

Tone and Rhyme Scheme

What is the tone in the first few stanzas of the poem? Where does it start to change? How does Bishop indicate that the initial tone may not be what the speaker actually feels?

What is the rhyme scheme of this poem? What is the true rhyme scheme of a villanelle? Where does Bishop vary from this pattern? Discuss why she might have done so.

Extend the Text

Writing Options

Creative Writing Using "One Art" as a model, write a villanelle describing a loss of your own. Before you begin, review the general definition of *villanelle* and carefully examine the poem to identify Bishop's rhyme scheme.

Expository Writing Conduct some basic research about Elizabeth Bishop's personal life. Then write a one-page critical analysis in which you explore how "One Art" may be autobiographical. Infer the meanings of details such as the "three loved houses," "two cities," "two rivers," "a continent," and the identity of "you."

Lifelong Learning

Make a Villanelle Collection Create a collection of villanelles, such as "Do not go gentle into that good night," by Dylan Thomas. Write a brief introduction to each poem, including information on the poet, the subject, and the time period in which it was written. Analyze how closely each poem follows the standard form. Share your collection with classmates.

Media Literacy

Make a Lost-and-Found Presentation In recent years, collections have been made that research items left behind at war memorials, airport security, and lost-and-found departments. Do research to learn how these collections are displayed. Then with a small group, get permission from your school, church, or other organization to examine and photograph (or sketch) the items in the lost-and-found. For each item, consider who the owner might have been and how it got lost.

 Go to **www.mirrorsandwindows.com** for more.

Farewell to a Traveler

by Gabriela Mistral

Gabriela Mistral (1889–1957) well understood sorrow and loss, a fact that ironically helped make her a literary legend. Born Lucila Godoy y Alcayaga (she later took a name derived from the names of poets Gabriele D'Annunzio and Frédéric Mistral), the Chilean-born Mistral was abandoned by her father at age three. In 1909, at age twenty, she experienced another profound loss with the death of a close friend. The effect of this tragedy became increasingly apparent in her work. In 1945, Mistral became the first Latin American woman to win the Nobel Prize for literature. "What the soul is to the body," she once stated, "so is the artist to his people."

The poem **"Farewell to a Traveler"** was published in *Selected Poems of Gabriela Mistral*, a 1957 collection translated and edited by Mistral's American secretary, Doris Dana. The poem incorporates the maternal theme typical of many of Mistral's works.

May the same vagabond[1] wave
that takes you, return you.
May the road not entwine itself
about your neck like a serpent.
5 May it take you and carry you, but at last leave you.

May those on your path who see you
take joy of you as of a festival.
But don't be retained
behind walls or bolts
10 by a false mother, a false son.

Guard against the rise of foreign accents;
defend your laughter, your cry.
May the sun not weather your forehead
or exposure hoarsen your voice,
15 or tricks of carnival or commerce
close your open hand.

No one told you to go.
No one hastens your return.
But shoals[2] of fish teem,[3]
20 calling to their fishermen.

We had you at our table
like a tall silver pitcher.
Listening to you by the fireside
we called you "breast of oven."

---

1. **vagabond.** Moving around aimlessly; wandering
2. **shoals.** Crowds; large numbers
3. **teem.** To be present in large numbers, nearly to overflowing

Sailboats off a Rocky Coast, 1864. William Stanley Haseltine.
Brooklyn Museum, Brooklyn, New York.

25 Beneath palm trees or tamarinth,[4]
    waking or sleeping, whole or broken,
    may the Archangel Raphael[5] go by your side,
    may your island of palm trees cast fronded[6] shadows
    on your clothing, and kiss your face.

30 Rise then, and leap
    like a dolphin to the waves.
    May the way home, like a gadfly,[7]
    sting you, goad[8] you, and conquer.

    Come back, son, for our sake,
35 we who are stones of thresholds,
    and never again boatsmen or calkers[9]
    since we broke our oars
    and buried our boats.

---

4. **tamarinth.** Plural reference to the tamarind, a type of tropical tree
5. **Archangel Raphael.** St. Raphael, one of the seven archangels of God
   described in scripture, is the patron saint of travelers.
6. **fronded.** Reference to "frond," a palm or other large leaf
7. **gadfly.** Any stinging or biting fly
8. **goad.** To cause to move or take action
9. **calkers.** Variant of *caulker,* someone who seals a surface (as of a boat)
   against leakage

On the coast, our backs curved to the night,
40 we will light fires for you
should you forget the bay.
The tide will set you on the sand
like an alga[10] or a child
and we will all cry aloud
45 for joy, for joy.

In a round, in a ring, in a knot,
laughing and crying, we will teach
our forgetful one to speak again
when your old expression breaks forth on your face
50 and our names burst again from your mouth. ❖

---

10. **alga.** Singular form of *algae*, a type of seaweed

 **MIRRORS & WINDOWS** Think about a time you had to say good-bye to someone. How did you deal with the departure? Were you angry or hurt, understanding and supportive, or some of both?

Refer and Reason

1. Identify sections of the poem where the speaker advises or expresses what he or she wishes for the traveler. What fears or concerns of the speaker's do these sections seem to indicate?

2. What literary technique does Mistral use to describe most concepts in the poem? Argue what is effective or ineffective about the poet's use of this technique.

3. Imagine that ten years have passed. Predict whether the traveler will have returned by this point. Discuss what might have made him return or prevented him from ever doing so.

Writing Options

1. In the voice of the traveler, write a diary entry in which you express the emotions of leaving your home and family for something new. Before you begin, choose a time for the entry. For example, maybe the traveler has just embarked on his journey or maybe he has just decided to go.

2. Is the traveler literally the speaker's son? Write a paragraph in which you analyze the speaker's attitude toward the traveler. Frame your paragraph in terms of how you believe the two are related.

 Go to **www.mirrorsandwindows.com** for more.

ONCE MORE TO THE LAKE

by E. B. White

Elwyn Brooks (E. B.) White (1899–1985), born in Mount Vernon, New York, is most famous for his children's novels *Stuart Little* (1945) and *Charlotte's Web* (1954), which together won him the Laura Ingalls Wilder Medal for children's literature. White's name also is frequently attached to that of his former professor William Strunk Jr. as co-writer and editor of *The Elements of Style,* a legendary writers' guide that still is widely used today.

In addition, White was one of the most popular essayists for the *New Yorker* and *Harper's Magazine.* In 1978, he won a Pulitzer Prize for his body of work. His essay **"Once More to the Lake,"** first published in *Harper's Magazine* in 1941, describes his experience of returning as an adult to the vacation spot he had visited frequently as a child. He notes how the passage of time has been different for the lake and for him.

One summer, along about 1904, my father rented a camp on a lake in Maine and took us all there for the month of August. We all got ringworm from some kittens and had to rub Pond's Extract on our arms and legs night and morning, and my father rolled over in a canoe with all his clothes on; but outside of that the vacation was a success and from then on none of us ever thought there was any place in the world like that lake in Maine. We returned summer after summer— always on August 1st for one month. I have since become a salt-water man, but sometimes in summer there are days when the restlessness of the tides and the fearful cold of the sea water and the incessant[1] wind which blows across the afternoon and into the evening make me wish for the placidity[2] of a lake in the woods. A few weeks ago this feeling got so strong I bought myself a couple of bass hooks and a spinner and returned to the lake where we used to go, for a week's fishing and to revisit old haunts.

I took along my son, who had never had any fresh water up his nose and who had seen lily pads only from train windows. On the journey over to the lake I began to wonder what it would be like. I wondered how time would have marred this unique, this holy spot—the coves and streams, the hills that the sun set behind, the camps and the paths behind the camps. I was sure that the tarred road would have found it out and I wondered in what other ways it would be desolated.

---

1. **incessant.** Endless; constant
2. **placidity.** Calmness

It is strange how much you can remember about places like that once you allow your mind to return into the grooves which lead back. You remember one thing, and that suddenly reminds you of another thing. I guess I remembered clearest of all the early mornings, when the lake was cool and motionless, remembered how the bedroom smelled of the lumber it was made of and of the wet woods whose scent entered through the screen. The partitions in the camp were thin and did not extend clear to the top of the rooms, and as I was always the first up I would dress softly so as not to wake the others, and sneak out into the sweet outdoors and start out in the canoe, keeping close along the shore in the long shadows of the pines. I remembered being very careful never to rub my paddle against the gunwale[3] for fear of disturbing the stillness of the cathedral.

The lake had never been what you would call a wild lake. There were cottages sprinkled around the shores, and it was in farming although the shores of the lake were quite heavily wooded. Some of the cottages were owned by nearby farmers, and you would live at the shore and eat your meals at the farmhouse. That's what our family did. But although it wasn't wild, it was a fairly large and undisturbed lake and there were places in it which, to a child at least, seemed infinitely remote and primeval.[4]

I was right about the tar: it led to within half a mile of the shore. But when I got back there, with my boy, and we settled into a camp near a farmhouse and into the kind of summertime I had known, I could tell that it was going to be pretty much the same as it had been before—I knew it, lying in bed the first morning, smelling the bedroom, and hearing

Salmon Fishing on the Dee, c. 1850–1900. Joseph Farquharson.

the boy sneak quietly out and go off along the shore in a boat. I began to sustain the illusion that he was I, and therefore, by simple transposition, that I was my father. This sensation persisted, kept cropping up all the time we were there. It was not an entirely new feeling, but in this setting it grew much stronger. I seemed to be living a dual existence. I would be in the middle of some simple act, I would be picking up a bait box or laying down a table fork, or I would be saying something, and suddenly it would be not I but my father who was saying the words or making the gesture. It gave me a creepy sensation.

We went fishing the first morning. I felt the same damp moss covering the worms in the bait can, and saw the dragonfly alight on the tip of my rod as it hovered a few inches from the surface of the water. It was the arrival of this fly that convinced me beyond any doubt that everything was as it always had been, that the years were a mirage and there had been no years. The small waves were the same, chucking the rowboat under the chin as we fished at anchor, and the boat was the same

3. **gunwale.** Upper edge of a boat's side
4. **primeval.** Ancient

boat, the same color green and the ribs broken in the same places, and under the floor-boards the same freshwater leavings and debris—the dead helgramite,[5] the wisps of moss, the rusty discarded fishhook, the dried blood from yesterday's catch. We stared silently at the tips of our rods, at the dragonflies that came and wells. I lowered the tip of mine into the water, tentatively, pensively[6] dislodging the fly, which darted two feet away, poised, darted two feet back, and came to rest again a little farther up the rod. There had been no years between the ducking of this dragonfly and the other one—the one that was part of memory. I looked at the boy, who was silently watching his fly, and it was my hands that held his rod, my eyes watching. I felt dizzy and didn't know which rod I was at the end of.

> I LOOKED AT THE BOY, WHO WAS SILENTLY WATCHING HIS FLY, AND IT WAS MY HANDS THAT HELD HIS ROD, MY EYES WATCHING.

We caught two bass, hauling them in briskly as though they were mackerel, pulling them over the side of the boat in a businesslike manner without any landing net, and stunning them with a blow on the back of the head. When we got back for a swim before lunch, the lake was exactly where we had left it, the same number of inches from the dock, and there was only the merest suggestion of a breeze. This seemed an utterly enchanted sea, this lake you could leave to its own devices for a few hours and come back to, and find that it had not stirred, this constant and trustworthy body of water. In the shallows, the dark, water-soaked sticks and twigs, smooth and old, were undulating[7] in clusters on the bottom against the clean ribbed sand, and the track of the mussel was plain. A school of minnows swam by, each minnow with its small, individual shadow, doubling the attendance, so clear and sharp in the sunlight. Some of the other campers were in swimming, along the shore, one of them with a cake of soap, and the water felt thin and clear and insubstantial. Over the years there had been this person with the cake of soap, this cultist, and here he was. There had been no years.

Up to the farmhouse to dinner through the teeming, dusty field, the road under our sneakers was only a two-track road. The middle track was missing, the one with the marks of the hooves and the splotches of dried, flaky manure. There had always been three tracks to choose from in choosing which track to walk in; now the choice was narrowed down to two. For a moment I missed terribly the middle alternative. But the way led past the tennis court, and something about the way it lay there in the sun reassured me; the tape had loosened along the backline, the alleys were green with plantains and other weeds, and the net (installed in June and removed in September) sagged in the dry noon, and the whole place steamed with midday heat and hunger and emptiness. There was a choice of pie for dessert, and one was blueberry and one was apple, and the waitresses were the same country girls, there having been no passage of time, only the illusion of it as in a dropped curtain—the waitresses were still fifteen; their hair had been washed, that was the only difference—they had been to the movies and seen the pretty girls with the clean hair.

Summertime, oh summertime, pattern of life indelible,[8] the fade proof lake, the woods unshatterable, the pasture with the sweet fern and the juniper forever and ever, summer without end; this was the background, and the life along the shore was the design, the cottages with their innocent and tranquil design, their tiny docks with the flagpole and the American

---

5. **helgramite.** Insect often used as fishing bait
6. **tentatively, pensively.** Hesitantly, thoughtfully
7. **undulating.** Moving in waves
8. **indelible.** Unable to be erased

flag floating against the white clouds in the blue sky, the little paths over the roots of the trees leading from camp to camp and the paths leading back to the outhouses and the can of lime for sprinkling, and at the souvenir counters at the store the miniature birch-bark canoes and the post cards that showed things looking a little better than they looked. This was the American family at play, escaping the city heat, wondering whether the newcomers at the camp at the head of the cove were "common" or "nice," wondering whether it was true that the people who drove up for Sunday dinner at the farmhouse were turned away because there wasn't enough chicken.

It seemed to me, as I kept remembering all this, that those times and those summers had been infinitely precious and worth saving. There had been jollity and peace and goodness. The arriving (at the beginning of August) had been so big a business in itself, at the railway station the farm wagon drawn up, the first smell of the pine-laden air, the first glimpse of the smiling farmer, and the great importance of the trunks and your father's enormous author-

ity in such matters, and the feel of the wagon under you for the long ten-mile haul, and at the top of the last long hill catching the first view of the lake after eleven months of not seeing this cherished body of water. The shouts and cries of the other campers when they saw you, and the trunks to be unpacked, to give up their rich burden. (Arriving was less exciting nowadays, when you sneaked up in your car and parked it under a tree near the camp and took out the bags and in five minutes it was all over, no fuss, no loud wonderful fuss about trunks.)

Peace and goodness and jollity. The only thing that was wrong now, really, was the sound of the place, an unfamiliar nervous sound of the outboard motors. This was the note that jarred, the one thing that would sometimes break the illusion and set the years moving. In those other summertimes, all motors were inboard; and when they were at a little distance, the noise they made was a sedative, an ingredient of summer sleep. They were one-cylinder and two-cylinder engines, and some were make-and-break and some were jump-spark, but they all made a sleepy sound across the lake. The one-lungers throbbed and fluttered, and the twin-cylinder ones purred and purred, and that was a quiet sound too. But now the campers all had outboards. In the daytime, in the hot mornings, these motors made a petulant,[9] irritable sound; at night, in the still evening when the afterglow lit the

---

9. **petulant.** Rude

water, they whined about one's ears like mosquitoes. My boy loved our rented outboard, and his great desire was to achieve single-handed mastery over it, and authority, and he soon learned the trick of choking it a little (but not too much), and the adjustment of the needle valve. Watching him I would remember the things you could do with the old one-cylinder engine with the heavy flywheel, how you could have it eating out of your hand if you got really close to it spiritually. Motor boats in those days didn't have clutches, and you would make a landing by shutting off the motor at the proper time and coasting in with a dead rudder. But there was a way of reversing them, if you learned the trick, by cutting the switch and putting it on again exactly on the final dying revolution of the flywheel, so that it would kick back against compression and begin reversing. Approaching a dock in a strong following breeze, it was difficult to slow up sufficiently by the ordinary coasting method, and if a boy felt he had complete mastery over his motor, he was tempted to keep it running beyond its time and then reverse it a few feet from the dock. It took a cool nerve, because if you threw the switch a twentieth of a second too soon you would catch the flywheel when it still had speed enough to go up past center, and the boat would leap ahead, charging bull-fashion at the dock.

> MY BOY LOVED OUR RENTED OUTBOARD, AND HIS GREAT DESIRE WAS TO ACHIEVE SINGLE-HANDED MASTERY OVER IT, AND AUTHORITY.

We had a good week at the camp. The bass were biting well and the sun shone endlessly, day after day. We would be tired at night and lie down in the accumulated heat of the little bedrooms after the long hot day and the breeze would stir almost imperceptibly outside and the smell of the swamp drift in through the rusty screens. Sleep would come easily and in the morning the red squirrel would be on the roof, tapping out his gay routine. I kept remembering everything, lying in bed in the mornings—the small steamboat that had a long rounded stern like the lip of a Ubangi,[10] and how quietly she ran on the moonlight sails, when the older boys played their mandolins and the girls sang and we ate doughnuts dipped in sugar, and how sweet the music was on the water in the shining night, and what it had felt like to think about girls then. After breakfast we would go up to the store and the things were in the same place—the minnows in a bottle, the plugs and spinners disarranged and pawed over by the youngsters from the boys' camp, the fig newtons and the Beeman's gum. Outside, the road was tarred and cars stood in front of the store. Inside, all was just as it had always been, except there was more Coca Cola and not so much Moxie and root beer and birch beer and sarsaparilla. We would walk out with a bottle of pop apiece and sometimes the pop would backfire up our noses and hurt. We explored the streams, quietly, where the turtles slid off the sunny logs and dug their way into the soft bottom; and we lay on the town wharf and fed worms to the tame bass. Everywhere we went I had trouble making out which was I, the one walking at my side, the one walking in my pants.

One afternoon while we were there at that lake a thunderstorm came up. It was like the revival of an old melodrama that I had seen long ago with childish awe. The second-act climax of the drama of the electrical disturbance over a lake in America had not changed in any important respect. This was the big scene, still the big scene. The whole thing was so familiar, the first feeling of oppression and heat and a general air around camp of not wanting to go very far away. In mid-afternoon (it was all the

---

10. **Ubangi.** Member of a cultural group in the country of Chad where the women pierce their lips to insert wooden disks that elongate their lips

same) a curious darkening of the sky, and a lull in everything that had made life tick; and then the way the boats suddenly swung the other way at their moorings with the coming of a breeze out of the new quarter, and the premonitory[11] rumble. Then the kettle drum, then the snare, then the bass drum and cymbals, then crackling light against the dark, and the gods grinning and licking their chops in the hills. Afterward the calm, the rain steadily rustling in the calm lake, the return of light and hope and spirits, and the campers running out in joy and relief to go swimming in the rain, their bright cries perpetuating the deathless joke about how they were getting simply drenched, and the children screaming with delight at the new

sensation of bathing in the rain, and the joke about getting drenched linking the generations in a strong indestructible chain. And the comedian who waded in carrying an umbrella.

When the others went swimming my son said he was going in too. He pulled his dripping trunks from the line where they had hung all through the shower, and wrung them out. Languidly, and with no thought of going in, I watched him, his hard little body, skinny and bare, saw him wince slightly as he pulled up around his vitals the small, soggy, icy garment. As he buckled the swollen belt suddenly my groin felt the chill of death. ❖

_____

11. **premonitory.** Giving warning

What places do you remember fondly from childhood? Of the places you have revisited, how have they changed over time?

Refer and Reason

1. Identify the points at which White is uncertain whether he is his father or he is his son. What about these moments makes White go back in time?

2. How has technology and the passage of time affected the lake? Is White overly nostalgic about the "wonderful fuss about trunks" and the "ten-mile haul"? Explain.

3. What does White feel when his son prepares to go swimming? Describe how revisiting a place from your childhood might be as much about loss as it is about making new memories.

Writing Options

1. Write a series of three advertisements for rental cottages along White's lake that span several decades. Explain what attractions the lake has to offer to three different generations.

2. White is well known as co-author of *The Elements of Style*, a writers' guide. Select a paragraph from this essay and analyze his style, including paragraph construction, sentence length and structure, word choice, and so on.

 Go to **www.mirrorsandwindows.com** for more.

PART 2

Conflict and Conformity

The decade of the 1950s often is viewed with nostalgia as a time of well-being and opportunity. However, that perspective ignores the problems that had started to emerge in U.S. society, as not everyone fit happily into the mainstream image of an American or was allowed to pursue the American dream. To curb dissent, people often were encouraged to conform, creating a safe and happy community by being like everyone else. Disagreeing with the status quo was seen as suspicious, potentially dangerous, and sometimes even un-American.

That was the social and political environment that pervaded the McCarthy Era, when Senator Joseph McCarthy led a government "witch hunt" for suspected communists. The pressure to conform was immense, especially for people in government, entertainment, and other public positions. Novelist and playwright Arthur Miller found himself subject to government scrutiny and voiced his opposition in his play *The Crucible.*

In the mid-1950s, several landmark decisions by the U.S. Supreme Court focused the nation's attention on racial injustice and launched the Civil Rights movement. In *Brown v. Board of Education* in 1954, the Court outlawed the segregation of schools, a decision that marked the beginning of the end for the "separate but equal" argument. In 1955, the defiant action of a seamstress named Rosa Parks led to the Court ruling against segregation on buses. The injustice experienced by African Americans was reflected in the literature of the era, as well, including the work of writers Richard Wright and Naomi Long Madgett.

Conference at Night, 1949. Edward Hopper.
Wichita Art Museum, Wichita, Kansas.

The Drama Defined

A **drama,** or play, is a story told through characters played by actors. The **script,** or written form, is made up of *dialogue* spoken by the characters and *stage directions* that explain the setting and tell the actors how to give expression to emotions and physical movements.

Types of Drama

The two major types of drama are comedy and tragedy. A **comedy** is a lighthearted or humorous work that typically presents characters with limitations and misunderstandings. Standard elements of comedy include mistaken identities, word play, satire, and exaggerated characters and events.

A **tragedy** portrays the fall of a person of high status, such as king or god. It celebrates the courage and dignity of a *tragic hero,* the main character, in the face of inevitable doom. Sometimes the hero's fate is brought about by a *tragic flaw,* or personal weakness that brings about his or her fall.

Many dramas are predominantly comic or tragic but contain contrary or opposite elements. Comedies, for instance, often explore serious and tragic topics and themes. Conversely, tragedies often include humorous characters and events to create *comic relief,* or a break from the serious tone of the play.

Elements of the Drama

In a play, you will find many of the elements of fiction, such as character, theme, and plot, but you will also notice significant differences between the two genres. For instance, the author of a novel or short story can describe a person, object, or landscape for pages before a character utters a single word. The author of a play, or **playwright,** does not have this luxury. The **exposition,** or background information, and other commentary or description must be expressed by the characters through their dialogue and behavior.

Another important difference between a play and a work of fiction is that a play is meant to be performed and must create a visual picture on stage, or **spectacle.** As you read a play, examine how the playwright uses lighting and scenery to create mood, employs stage directions to direct the actors, and specifies the kinds of stage properties (props) to be used.

Act and Scene Division

A typical play is divided into acts and scenes. An **act** generally comprises several scenes. **Scene** breaks allow the dramatist to indicate a new time or place of action.

Stage Directions

Stage directions are notes included in a play that describe how something should be performed on stage. Such notes help the director to guide the actors as they translate words into performance. Stage directions indicate the writer's conception of setting, lighting, music, sound effects, entrances and exits, properties, and the movements of characters. Stage directions usually are printed in italic type and enclosed in brackets or parentheses.

Act 1 of Arthur Miller's *The Crucible* is prefaced by a fairly elaborate description of the **setting,** the time and place in which the play occurs. We learn that we are to be transported back to the Massachusetts of 1692. We are told that the Reverend Samuel Parris does his praying in the small bedchamber of his daughter, where the sun passing through a "narrow window" and a candle provide the only illumination of the scene.

Stage directions also may describe the physical traits of characters. For instance, the stage direction for the elderly character Giles Corey says he is "knotted with muscle, canny, inquisitive, and still powerful."

Another type of stage direction tells actors how a line or speech is to be delivered and how they are to convey the action. **Action** refers to how the characters move or behave. Many playwrights carefully indicate how actors should enter and exit the stage, pitch their voices, and make physical gestures.

Character

A **character** is an individual who takes part in the action of a literary work. Just as in fiction, the main character, or **protagonist,** is the most important character in a drama and is in conflict with the **antagonist.**

Characters can be classified in other ways, as well. *Major characters* play significant roles in a work, and *minor characters* play lesser roles. Whereas the major characters take part in the central conflict of the work, minor characters usually serve to fulfill a specific function. Such a character might play the part of a **foil,** a character whose traits contrast with and therefore highlight the traits of another character. As you read *The Crucible,* think about the relationship between the characters John Proctor and John Hale.

Another classification identifies static versus dynamic characters. A *static character* is one who does not change during the course of the play, and a *dynamic character* is one who does change. Tituba and Abigail Williams are examples of static characters, while John and Elizabeth Proctor are dynamic characters.

Irony

Irony is a difference between appearance and reality. There are three types of irony: (1) *dramatic irony* is when something is known by the reader or audience but unknown to the characters; (2) *verbal irony* is when a character says one thing but means another; and (3) *irony of situation* is when an event occurs that violates the expectations of the characters, the reader, or the audience.

All three types of irony are present in *The Crucible.* The central dramatic irony, of course, is that

Miller has given us a play about witch trials set in a superstitious age, with modern audiences knowing that witches do not exist. You will notice many instances of verbal irony. In the court scene of Act 3, the Reverend Parris tells the judge, "We are here, Your Honor, precisely to discover what no one has ever seen." In doing so, he unwittingly sums up the hoax that lies at the heart of the play. *The Crucible* also abounds with instances of situational irony, as when the virtuous and humane characters, Rebecca Nurse and Elizabeth Proctor, are arrested.

Dialogue

Dialogue is a conversation between two or more characters. If you have ever watched a dramatic television program, movie, or play, you know that most of what you learn about characters is based on what they say and do or from what others say about them.

In addition to dialogue, the playwright can use any of several literary devices to reveal a character's thoughts and motivations. In a **monologue,** a character speaks aloud or directly addresses the audience or another character in the play. In a **soliloquy,** a character is alone on stage, speaking his or her thoughts. In an **aside,** a character literally turns to the audience and comments on the situation, a device that may have a humorous effect.

HOW TO READ

Drama

Read the script aloud. A play is meant to be performed. Hearing the words spoken will help you better understand dialogue that relates characters' feelings or descriptions of events and settings.

Visualize. Try to picture the elements described by stage directions, such as props, costumes, and lighting. If the stage directions contain only minimal information, imagine how you would stage the play if you were producing it.

Use the organization of the text. Plays usually are divided into acts and scenes. Each scene change indicates a change in time or place. Make note of these changes to track when and where events take place.

Make inferences. It generally is not possible in a drama to provide lengthy exposition. Such explanatory information must come from the stage directions and characters' dialogue. Beyond that, you can make inferences about characters' motivations and other details.

Arthur Miller

> *"Drama is akin to the other inventions of man in that it ought to help us to know more, and not merely to spend our feelings."*

Arthur Miller (1915–2005) was born in New York City to Jewish immigrant parents. During his youth, his father's garment manufacturing business failed as part of the general economic downturn known as the Great Depression. This failure had a permanent impact on Miller, who went on to write great plays on themes related to social and political justice.

After graduating from high school, Miller worked at a local bakery and for his father to earn money for college. He attended the University of Michigan, initially studying journalism before trying his hand at writing drama. He changed his major to English after winning the Avery Hopwood Award for a play he wrote in six days.

Following graduation, Miller returned to New York as a freelance writer. Although his first play opened to disappointing reviews, his second, *All My Sons,* was a Broadway hit. This was followed only two years later by his most famous and acclaimed work, *Death of a Salesman* (1949), which earned Miller both a Pulitzer Prize and a Drama Critics Circle Award. In telling the story of the tragic downfall of its title character, partially as a result of his willingness to do anything for the "almighty dollar," the play serves as a classic exposé of the consequences of hypocrisy and greed. Miller's popularity continued with *The Crucible* (1952) and *A View from the Bridge* (1955), both of which examine themes of accusation, betrayal, and mistrust.

Although Miller's career declined somewhat in the 1960s and 1970s, he experienced a comeback with the 1991 productions of his plays *The Ride Down Mount Morgan* and *The Last Yankee.* Their success started something of a Miller revival on Broadway, as some of his earlier works returned to the stage. In addition to his scripts for live theater, Miller has written screenplays, including the script for *The Misfits,* a film that starred his second wife, Marilyn Monroe, and the script for *The Crucible,* which starred Daniel Day Lewis.

Among the many Americans to whom Arthur Miller's name is synonymous with drama may be the playwright himself. As he once said, "You specialize in something until one day you find it is specializing in you."

Noted Works

All My Sons (1947)	*The Price* (1968)
Death of a Salesman (1949)	*Timebends* (autobiography, 1987)
The Crucible (1952)	*Broken Glass* (1994)
The Misfits (screenplay, 1961)	

The Crucible, Act 1

A Drama by Arthur Miller

Build Background

Historical Context In 1692, a series of trials was held in Salem, Massachusetts, of persons accused of witchcraft. A number of people in the community and surrounding area had developed a disease resembling epilepsy, and suspicions arose that the afflictions might be the work of witches.

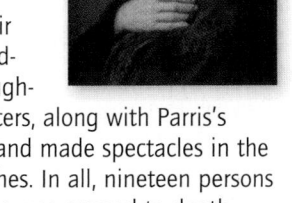

The governor of the colony of Massachusetts, Sir William Phips, began court proceedings. The proceedings were inflamed by accusations made by the daughters of a Salem minister named Parris. These daughters, along with Parris's niece Abigail, acted as though possessed by spirits and made spectacles in the courtroom during examinations of the accused witches. In all, nineteen persons were hanged as a result of the trials, and one person was pressed to death. Many others were imprisoned and tortured.

Various theories have been offered as to the cause of the hysteria, from Puritan zealotry to mob mentality. Recent research has shown that contamination of the rye grain called *ergot* may have played a major role. The symptoms of ergot poisoning include seizures, itching, diarrhea, vomiting, partial loss of sight, and hallucinations—all symptoms experienced by residents of Salem at that time.

Literary Context Arthur Miller became interested in the Salem witch trials during the McCarthy Era of the 1950s, a time when a similar "witch hunt" occurred in the United States, this one for suspected communists and other radicals in public office and the entertainment industry. Miller's classic, if somewhat controversial, play explores the psychology of mob hysteria and guilt by association. Although *The Crucible* opened on Broadway in January 1953, it did not receive the attention and critical acclaim it still enjoys today until its off-Broadway revival in 1957.

Reader's Context When have you felt social pressure to do something you knew was wrong? What did you decide to do?

Analyze Literature

Stage Directions and Dialogue
Stage directions are notes included in a play for the purpose of describing how something should be performed on stage. Stage directions describe setting, lighting, music, sound effects, entrances and exits, properties, and the movements of characters. They usually are printed in italics and may be enclosed in brackets or parentheses.

Dialogue is conversation between two or more characters.

Set Purpose

As you read Act 1 of *The Crucible,* make a simple chart listing the different kinds of details Miller provides in stage directions. Also identify three examples of dialogue that contain stage directions. For instance, early in Act 1, Abigail announces that Susanna Walcott has arrived and Parris says "Let her come." Their exchange directs another character to enter the drama.

Preview Vocabulary

predilection, 884
rankle, 884
ingratiating, 885
dissemble, 886
abomination, 887
calumny, 893
inculcation, 899
propitiation, 900
discomfit, 903
licentious, 903

THE CRUCIBLE[1]

by Arthur Miller

THE CAST
(in order of appearance)

REVEREND PARRIS	Fred Stewart
BETTY PARRIS	Janet Alexander
TITUBA	Jacqueline Andre
ABIGAIL WILLIAMS	Madeleine Sherwood
SUSANNA WALCOTT	Barbara Stanton
MRS. ANN PUTNAM	Jane Hoffman
THOMAS PUTNAM	Raymond Bramley
MERCY LEWIS	Dorothy Joliffe
MARY WARREN	Jennie Egan
JOHN PROCTOR	Arthur Kennedy
REBECCA NURSE	Jean Adair
GILES COREY	Joseph Sweeney
REVEREND JOHN HALE	E. G. Marshall
ELIZABETH PROCTOR	Beatrice Straight
FRANCIS NURSE	Graham Velsey
EZEKIEL CHEEVER	Don McHenry
MARSHAL HERRICK	George Mitchell
JUDGE HATHORNE	Philip Coolidge
DEPUTY GOVERNOR DANFORTH	Walter Hampden
SARAH GOOD	Adele Fortin
HOPKINS	Donald Marye

A NOTE ON THE HISTORICAL ACCURACY OF THIS PLAY

This play is not history in the sense in which the word is used by the academic historian. Dramatic purposes have sometimes required many characters to be fused into one; the number of girls involved in the "crying-out" has been reduced; Abigail's age has been raised; while there were several judges of almost equal authority, I have symbolized them all in Hathorne and Danforth. However, I believe that the reader will discover here the essential nature of one of the strangest and most awful chapters in human history. The fate of each character is exactly that of his historical model, and there is no one in the drama who did not play a similar—and in some cases exactly the same—role in history.

As for the characters of the persons, little is known about most of them excepting what may be surmised from a few letters, the trial record, certain broadsides written at the time, and references to their conduct in sources of varying reliability. They may therefore be taken as creations of my own, drawn to the best of my ability in conformity with their known behavior, except as indicated in the commentary I have written for this text.

---

1. **Crucible.** Situation in which multiple forces interact and cause change

Old Man in Prayer,
c. 1629–1630.
Workshop of
Rembrandt van Rijn.

Act 1: An Overture

A small upper bedroom in the home of Reverend Samuel Parris, Salem, Massachusetts, in the spring of the year 1692.

There is a narrow window at the left. Through its leaded panes the morning sunlight streams. A candle still burns near the bed, which is at the right. A chest, a chair, and a small table are the other furnishings. At the back a door opens on the landing of the stairway to the ground floor. The room gives off an air of clean spareness. The roof rafters are exposed, and the wood colors are raw and unmellowed.

As the curtain rises, Reverend Parris is discovered kneeling beside the bed, evidently in prayer. His daughter, Betty Parris, aged ten, is lying on the bed, inert.

At the time of these events Parris was in his middle forties. In history he cut a villainous path, and there is very little good to be said

for him. He believed he was being persecuted wherever he went, despite his best efforts to win people and God to his side. In meeting, he felt insulted if someone rose to shut the door without first asking his permission. He was a widower with no interest in children, or talent with them. He regarded them as young adults, and until this strange crisis he, like the rest of Salem, never conceived that the children were anything but thankful for being permitted to walk straight, eyes slightly lowered, arms at the sides, and mouths shut until bidden to speak.

His house stood in the "town"—but we today would hardly call it a village. The meeting house was nearby, and from this point outward—toward the bay or inland—there were a few small-windowed, dark houses snuggling against the raw Massachusetts winter. Salem had been established hardly forty years before. To the European world the whole province was a barbaric frontier inhabited by a sect of fanatics who, nevertheless, were shipping out products of slowly increasing quantity and value.

No one can really know what their lives were like. They had no novelists—and would not have permitted anyone to read a novel if one were handy. Their creed forbade anything resembling a theater or "vain enjoyment." They did not celebrate Christmas, and a holiday from work meant only that they must concentrate even more upon prayer.

Which is not to say that nothing broke into this strict and somber way of life. When a new farmhouse was built, friends assembled to "raise the roof," and there would be special foods cooked and probably some potent cider passed around. There was a good supply of ne'er-do-wells in Salem, who dallied at the shovelboard in Bridget Bishop's tavern. Probably more than the creed, hard work kept the morals of the place from spoiling, for the people were forced to fight the land like heroes for every grain of corn, and no man had very much time for fooling around.

That there were some jokers, however, is indicated by the practice of appointing a two-man patrol whose duty was to "walk forth in the time of God's worship to take notice of such as either lye about the meeting house, without attending to the word and ordinances, or that lye at home or in the fields without giving good account thereof, and to take the names of such persons, and to present them to the magistrates, whereby they may be accordingly proceeded against." This <u>predilection</u> for minding other people's business was time-honored among the people of Salem, and it undoubtedly created many of the suspicions which were to feed the coming madness. It was also, in my opinion, one of the things that a John Proctor would rebel against, for the time of the armed camp had almost passed, and since the country was reasonably—although

not wholly—safe, the old disciplines were beginning to <u>rankle</u>. But, as in all such matters, the issue was not clear-cut, for danger was still a possibility, and in unity still lay the best promise of safety.

The edge of the wilderness was close by. The American continent stretched endlessly west, and it was full of mystery for them. It stood, dark and threatening, over their shoulders night and day, for out of it Indian tribes marauded from time to time, and Reverend Parris had parishioners who had lost relatives to these heathen.[2]

The parochial[3] snobbery of these people was partly responsible for their failure to convert the Indians. Probably they also preferred to take land from heathens rather than from fellow Christians. At any rate, very few Indians were converted, and the Salem folk believed that the virgin forest was the Devil's last preserve, his home base and the citadel of his final stand. To the best of their knowledge the American forest was the last place on earth that was not paying homage to God.

For these reasons, among others, they carried about an air of innate resistance, even of persecution. Their fathers had, of course, been persecuted in England. So now they and their church found it necessary to deny any other sect its freedom, lest their New Jerusalem[4] be defiled and corrupted by wrong ways and deceitful ideas.

They believed, in short, that they held in their steady hands the candle that would light the world. We have inherited this belief, and it has helped and hurt us. It helped them with

They believed . . . they held in their steady hands the candle that would light the world.

---

2. **heathen.** Unreligious or uncivilized person
3. **parochial.** Narrow-minded; intolerant
4. **New Jerusalem.** New capital of Christianity, like the ancient holy city in Israel

---

pred • i • lec • tion (preꞏ də lekʹ shən) *n.,* established preference for, or bias toward, something
ran • kle (rāŋʹ kʹl) *v.,* cause anger or bitterness

the discipline it gave them. They were a dedicated folk, by and large, and they had to be to survive the life they had chosen or been born into in this country.

The proof of their belief's value to them may be taken from the opposite character of the first Jamestown settlement, farther south, in Virginia. The Englishmen who landed there were motivated mainly by a hunt for profit. They had thought to pick off the wealth of the new country and then return rich to England. They were a band of individualists, and a much more <u>ingratiating</u> group than the Massachusetts men. But Virginia destroyed them. Massachusetts tried to kill off the Puritans, but they combined; they set up a communal society which, in the beginning, was little more than an armed camp with an autocratic and very devoted leadership. It was, however, an autocracy by consent, for they were united from top to bottom by a commonly held ideology whose perpetuation was the reason and justification for all their sufferings. So their self-denial, their purposefulness, their suspicion of all vain pursuits, their hard-handed justice, were altogether perfect instruments for the conquest of this space so antagonistic to man.

But the people of Salem in 1692 were not quite the dedicated folk that arrived on the *Mayflower*. A vast differentiation had taken place, and in their own time a revolution had unseated the royal government and substituted a junta[5] which was at this moment in power. The times, to their eyes, must have been out of joint, and to the common folk must have seemed as insoluble and complicated as do ours today. It is not hard to see how easily many could have been led to believe that the time of confusion had been brought upon them by deep and darkling forces. No hint of such speculation appears on the court record, but

Witches' Hill, Salem Village.

social disorder in any age breeds such mystical suspicions, and when, as in Salem, wonders are brought forth from below the social surface, it is too much to expect people to hold back very long from laying on the victims with all the force of their frustrations.

The Salem tragedy, which is about to begin in these pages, developed from a paradox. It is a paradox in whose grip we still live, and there is no prospect yet that we will discover its resolution. Simply, it was this: for good purposes, even high purposes, the people of Salem developed a theocracy, a combine of state and religious power whose function was to keep the community together, and to prevent any kind of disunity that might open it to destruction by material or ideological enemies. It was forged for a necessary purpose and accomplished that purpose. But all organization is and must be grounded on the idea of exclusion and prohibition, just as two objects cannot occupy the same space. Evidently the time came in New

---

5. **junta.** Group controlling a government, especially after a seizure of power

---

in • gra • ti • at • ing (in grā′ shē āt′ iŋ) *adj.*, given to deliberate efforts to gain favorable acceptance

England when the repressions of order were heavier than seemed warranted by the dangers against which the order was organized. The witch-hunt was a perverse manifestation of the panic which set in among all classes when the balance began to turn toward greater individual freedom.

When one rises above the individual villainy displayed, one can only pity them all, just as we shall be pitied someday. It is still impossible for man to organize his social life without repressions, and the balance has yet to be struck between order and freedom.

The witch-hunt was not, however, a mere repression. It was also, and as importantly, a long overdue opportunity for everyone so inclined to express publicly his guilt and sins, under the cover of accusations against the victims. It suddenly became possible—and patriotic and holy—for a man to say that Martha Corey had come into his bedroom at night, and that, while his wife was sleeping at his side, Martha laid herself down on his chest and "nearly suffocated him." Of course it was her spirit only, but his satisfaction at confessing himself was no lighter than if it had been Martha herself. One could not ordinarily speak such things in public.

Long-held hatreds of neighbors could now be openly expressed, and vengeance taken, despite the Bible's charitable injunctions. Land-lust which had been expressed by constant bickering over boundaries and deeds, could now be elevated to the arena of morality; one could cry witch against one's neighbor and feel perfectly justified in the bargain. Old scores could be settled on a plane of heavenly combat between Lucifer[6] and the Lord; suspicions and the envy of the miserable toward the happy could and did burst out in the general revenge.

Reverend Parris is praying now, and, though we cannot hear his words, a sense of his confusion hangs about him. He mumbles, then seems about to weep; then he weeps, then prays again; but his daughter does not stir on the bed.

The door opens, and his Negro slave enters. Tituba is in her forties. Parris brought her with him from Barbados,[7] where he spent some years as a merchant before entering the ministry. She enters as one does who can no longer bear to be barred from the sight of her beloved, but she is also very frightened because her slave sense has warned her that, as always, trouble in this house eventually lands on her back.

TITUBA, *already taking a step backward:* My Betty be hearty soon?

PARRIS: Out of here!

TITUBA, *backing to the door:* My Betty not goin' die . . .

PARRIS, *scrambling to his feet in a fury:* Out of my sight! She is gone. Out of my—He is overcome with sobs. He clamps his teeth against them and closes the door and leans against it, exhausted. Oh, my God! God help me! Quaking with fear, mumbling to himself through his sobs, he goes to the bed and gently takes Betty's hand. Betty. Child. Dear child. Will you wake, will you open up your eyes! Betty, little one . . .

He is bending to kneel again when his niece, Abigail Williams, seventeen, enters—a strikingly beautiful girl, an orphan, with an endless capacity for dissembling. Now she is all worry and apprehension and propriety.

ABIGAIL: Uncle? He looks to her. Susanna Walcott's here from Doctor Griggs.

PARRIS: Oh? Let her come, let her come.

ABIGAIL, *leaning out the door to call to Susanna, who is down the hall a few steps:* Come in, Susanna.

Susanna Walcott, a little younger than Abigail, a nervous, hurried girl, enters.

---

6. **Lucifer.** The devil; Satan
7. **Barbados.** Island in the British West Indies that was a center for the slave trade

dis • sem • ble (də sem′ b′l) *v.,* put on a false appearance

PARRIS, *eagerly:* What does the doctor say, child?

SUSANNA, *craning around Parris to get a look at Betty:* He bid me come and tell you, reverend sir, that he cannot discover no medicine for it in his books.

PARRIS: Then he must search on.

SUSANNA: Aye, sir, he have been searchin' his books since he left you, sir. But he bid me tell you, that you might look to unnatural things for the cause of it.

PARRIS, *his eyes going wide:* No—no. There be no unnatural cause here. Tell him I have sent for Reverend Hale of Beverly, and Mr. Hale will surely confirm that. Let him look to medicine and put out all thought of unnatural causes here. There be none.

SUSANNA: Aye, sir. He bid me tell you. *She turns to go.*

ABIGAIL: Speak nothin' of it in the village, Susanna.

PARRIS: Go directly home and speak nothing of unnatural causes.

SUSANNA: Aye, sir. I pray for her. *She goes out.*

ABIGAIL: Uncle, the rumor of witchcraft is all about; I think you'd best go down and deny it yourself. The parlor's packed with people, sir. I'll sit with her.

PARRIS, *pressed, turns on her:* And what shall I say to them? That my daughter and my niece I discovered dancing like heathen in the forest?

ABIGAIL: Uncle, we did dance; let you tell them I confessed it—and I'll be whipped if I must be. But they're speakin' of witchcraft. Betty's not witched.

PARRIS: Abigail, I cannot go before the congregation when I know you have not opened with me. What did you do with her in the forest?

ABIGAIL: We did dance, uncle, and when you leaped out of the bush so suddenly, Betty was frightened and then she fainted. And there's the whole of it.

PARRIS: Child. Sit you down.

ABIGAIL, *quavering, as she sits:* I would never hurt Betty. I love her dearly.

PARRIS: Now look you, child, your punishment will come in its time. But if you trafficked with spirits in the forest I must know it now, for surely my enemies will, and they will ruin me with it.

ABIGAIL: But we never conjured spirits.

PARRIS: Then why can she not move herself since midnight? This child is desperate! *Abigail lowers her eyes.* It must come out—my enemies will bring it out. Let me know what you done there. Abigail, do you understand that I have many enemies?

ABIGAIL: I have heard of it, uncle.

PARRIS: There is a faction that is sworn to drive me from my pulpit. Do you understand that?

ABIGAIL: I think so, sir.

PARRIS: Now then, in the midst of such disruption, my own household is discovered to be the very center of some obscene practice. Abominations are done in the forest—

ABIGAIL: It were sport, uncle!

PARRIS, *pointing at Betty:* You call this sport? *She lowers her eyes. He pleads:* Abigail, if you know something that may help the doctor, for God's sake tell it to me. *She is silent.* I saw Tituba waving her arms over the fire when I came on you. Why was she doing that? And I heard a screeching and gibberish coming from her mouth. She were swaying like a dumb beast over that fire!

ABIGAIL: She always sings her Barbados songs, and we dance.

PARRIS: I cannot blink what I saw, Abigail, for my enemies will not blink it. I saw a dress lying on the grass.

---

abom • i • na • tion (a bŏ′ mə nā′ shən) *n.,* something worthy of hatred or disgust

A scene from the 1996 film version of *The Crucible.*

ABIGAIL, *innocently:* A dress?

PARRIS—*it is very hard to say:* Aye, a dress. And I thought I saw—someone naked running through the trees!

ABIGAIL, *in terror:* No one was naked! You mistake yourself, uncle!

PARRIS, *with anger:* I saw it! *He moves from her. Then, resolved:* Now tell me true, Abigail. And I pray you feel the weight of truth upon you, for now my ministry's at stake, my ministry and perhaps your cousin's life. Whatever abomination you have done, give me all of it now, for I dare not be taken unaware when I go before them down there.

ABIGAIL: There is nothin' more. I swear it, uncle.

PARRIS—*he studies her, then nods, half convinced:* Abigail, I have fought here three long years to bend these stiff-necked people to me, and now, just now when some good respect is rising for me in the parish, you compromise my very character. I have given you a home, child, I have put clothes upon your back—now give me upright answer. Your name in the town—it is entirely white, is it not?

ABIGAIL, *with an edge of resentment:* Why, I am sure it is, sir. There be no blush about my name.

PARRIS, *to the point:* Abigail, is there any other cause than you have told me, for your being

> "Your name in the town — it is entirely white, is it not?"

discharged from Goody Proctor's service? I have heard it said, and I tell you as I heard it, that she comes so rarely to the church this year for she will not sit so close to something soiled. What that remark?

Abigail: She hates me, uncle, she must, for I would not be her slave. It's a bitter woman, a lying, cold, sniveling woman, and I will not work for such a woman!

Parris: She may be. And yet it has troubled me that you are now seven month out of their house, and in all this time no other family has ever called for your service.

Abigail: They want slaves, not such as I. Let them send to Barbados for that. I will not black my face for any of them! *With ill-concealed resentment at him:* Do you begrudge my bed, uncle?

Parris: No—no.

Abigail, *in a temper:* My name is good in the village! I will not have it said my name is soiled! Goody Proctor is a gossiping liar!

Enter Mrs. Ann Putnam. She is a twisted soul of forty-five, a death-ridden woman, haunted by dreams.

Parris, *as soon as the door begins to open:* No—no, I cannot have anyone. *He sees her, and a certain deference springs into him, although his worry remains.* Why, Goody Putnam, come in.

Mrs. Putnam, *full of breath, shiny-eyed:* It is a marvel. It is surely a stroke of hell upon you.

Parris: No, Goody Putnam, it is—

Mrs. Putnam, *glancing at Betty:* How high did she fly, how high?

Parris: No, no, she never flew—

Mrs. Putnam, *very pleased with it:* Why, it's sure she did. Mr. Collins saw her goin' over Ingersoll's barn, and come down light as bird, he says!

Parris: Now, look you, Goody Putnam, she never—*Enter Thomas Putnam, a well-to-do, hard-handed landowner, near fifty.* Oh, good morning, Mr. Putnam.

Putnam: It is a providence[8] the thing is out now! It is a providence. *He goes directly to the bed.*

Parris: What's out, sir, what's—?

Mrs. Putnam goes to the bed.

Putnam, *looking down at Betty:* Why, *her* eyes is closed! Look you, Ann.

Mrs. Putnam: Why, that's strange. *To Parris:* Ours is open.

Parris, *shocked:* Your Ruth is sick?

Mrs. Putnam, *with vicious certainty:* I'd not call it sick; the Devil's touch is heavier than sick. It's death, y'know, it's death drivin' into them, forked and hoofed.

Parris: Oh, pray not! Why, how does Ruth ail?

Mrs. Putnam: She ails as she must—she never waked this morning, but her eyes open and she walks, and hears naught, sees naught, and cannot eat. Her soul is taken, surely.

Parris is struck.

Putnam, *as though for further details:* They say you've sent for Reverend Hale of Beverly?

Parris, *with dwindling conviction now:* A precaution only. He has much experience in all demonic arts, and I—

Mrs. Putnam: He has indeed; and found a witch in Beverly last year, and let you remember that.

Parris: Now, Goody Ann, they only thought that were a witch, and I am certain there be no element of witchcraft here.

Putnam: No witchcraft! Now look you, Mr. Parris—

Parris: Thomas, Thomas, I pray you, leap not to witchcraft. I know that you—you least of all, Thomas, would ever wish so disastrous a charge laid upon me. We cannot leap to witchcraft. They will howl me out of Salem for such corruption in my house.

---

8. **providence.** Guidance or care from God

A word about Thomas Putnam. He was a man with many grievances, at least one of which appears justified. Some time before, his wife's brother-in-law, James Bayley, had been turned down as minister of Salem. Bayley had all the qualifications, and a two-thirds vote into the bargain, but a faction stopped his acceptance, for reasons that are not clear.

Thomas Putnam was the eldest son of the richest man in the village. He had fought the Indians at Narragansett, and was deeply interested in parish affairs. He undoubtedly felt it poor payment that the village should so blatantly disregard his candidate for one of its more important offices, especially since he regarded himself as the intellectual superior of most of the people around him.

His vindictive nature was demonstrated long before the witchcraft began. A former Salem minister, George Burroughs, had had to borrow money to pay for his wife's funeral, and, since the parish was remiss in his salary, he was soon bankrupt. Thomas and his brother John had Burroughs jailed for debts the man did not owe. The incident is important only in that Burroughs succeeded in becoming minister where Bayley, Thomas Putnam's brother-in-law, had been rejected; the motif of resentment is clear here. Thomas Putnam felt that his own name and the honor of his family had been smirched by the village, and he meant to right matters however he could.

Another reason to believe him a deeply embittered man was his attempt to break his father's will, which left a disproportionate amount to a stepbrother. As with every other public cause in which he tried to force his way, he failed in this.

So it is not surprising to find that so many accusations against people are in the handwriting of Thomas Putnam, or that his name is so often found as a witness corroborating the super-natural testimony, or that his daughter led the crying-out at the most opportune junctures of the trials, especially when— But we'll speak of that when we come to it.

PUTNAM—*at the moment he is intent upon getting Parris, for whom he has only contempt, to move toward the abyss:* Mr. Parris, I have taken your part in all contention here, and I would continue; but I cannot if you hold back in this. There are hurtful, vengeful spirits layin' hands on these children.

PARRIS: But, Thomas, you cannot—

PUTNAM: Ann! Tell Mr. Parris what you have done.

MRS. PUTNAM: Reverend Parris, I have laid seven babies unbaptized in the earth. Believe me, sir, you never saw more hearty babies born. And yet, each would wither in my arms the very night of their birth. I have spoke nothin', but my heart has clamored intimations. And now, this year, my Ruth, my only— I see her turning strange. A secret child she has become this year, and shrivels like a sucking mouth were pullin' on her life too. And so I thought to send her to your Tituba—

PARRIS: To Tituba! What may Tituba—?

MRS. PUTNAM: Tituba knows how to speak to the dead, Mr. Parris.

PARRIS: Goody Ann, it is a formidable sin to conjure up the dead!

MRS. PUTNAM: I take it on my soul, but who else may surely tell us what person murdered my babies?

PARRIS, *horrified:* Woman!

MRS. PUTNAM: They were murdered, Mr. Parris! And mark this proof! Mark it! Last night my Ruth were ever so close to their little spirits; I know it, sir. For how else is she struck dumb now except some power of darkness would stop her mouth? It is a marvelous sign, Mr. Parris!

> "There are hurtful, vengeful spirits layin' hands on these children."

PUTNAM: Don't you understand it, sir? There is a murdering witch among us, bound to keep herself in the dark. *Parris turns to Betty, a frantic terror rising in him.* Let your enemies make of it what they will, you cannot blink it more.

PARRIS, *to Abigail:* Then you were conjuring spirits last night.

ABIGAIL, *whispering:* Not I, sir—Tituba and Ruth.

PARRIS, *turns now, with new fear, and goes to Betty, looks down at her, and then, gazing off:* Oh, Abigail, what proper payment for my charity! Now I am undone.

PUTNAM: You are not undone! Let you take hold here. Wait for no one to charge you—declare it yourself. You have discovered witchcraft—

PARRIS: In my house? In my house, Thomas? They will topple me with this! They will make of it a—

Enter Mercy Lewis, the Putnams' servant, a fat, sly, merciless girl of eighteen.

MERCY: Your pardons. I only thought to see how Betty is.

PUTNAM: Why aren't you home? Who's with Ruth?

MERCY: Her grandma come. She's improved a little, I think—she give a powerful sneeze before.

MRS. PUTNAM: Ah, there's a sign of life!

MERCY: I'd fear no more, Goody Putnam. It were a grand sneeze; another like it will shake her wits together, I'm sure. *She goes to the bed to look.*

PARRIS: Will you leave me now, Thomas? I would pray a while alone.

ABIGAIL: Uncle, you've prayed since midnight. Why do you not go down and—

PARRIS: No—no. *To Putnam:* I have no answer for that crowd. I'll wait till Mr. Hale arrives. *To get Mrs. Putnam to leave:* If you will, Goody Ann . . .

PUTNAM: Now look you, sir. Let you strike out against the Devil, and the village will bless you

for it! Come down, speak to them—pray with them. They're thirsting for your word, Mister! Surely you'll pray with them.

PARRIS, *swayed:* I'll lead them in a psalm, but let you say nothing of witchcraft yet. I will not discuss it. The cause is yet unknown. I have had enough contention since I came; I want no more.

MRS. PUTNAM: Mercy, you go home to Ruth, d'y'hear?

MERCY: Aye, mum.

Mrs. Putnam goes out.

PARRIS, *to Abigail:* If she starts for the window, cry for me at once.

ABIGAIL: I will, uncle.

PARRIS, *to Putnam:* There is a terrible power in her arms today. *He goes out with Putnam.*

ABIGAIL, *with hushed trepidation:* How is Ruth sick?

MERCY: It's weirdish, I know not—she seems to walk like a dead one since last night.

ABIGAIL—*she turns at once and goes to Betty, and now, with fear in her voice:* Betty? *Betty doesn't move. She shakes her.* Now stop this! Betty! Sit up now! *Betty doesn't stir. Mercy comes over.*

MERCY: Have you tried beatin' her? I gave Ruth a good one and it waked her for a minute. Here, let me have her.

ABIGAIL, *holding Mercy back:* No, he'll be comin' up. Listen, now; if they be questioning us, tell them we danced—I told him as much already.

MERCY: Aye. And what more?

ABIGAIL: He knows Tituba conjured Ruth's sisters to come out of the grave.

MERCY: And what more?

ABIGAIL: He saw you naked.

MERCY, *clapping her hands together with a frightened laugh:* Oh, Jesus!

Enter Mary Warren, breathless. She is seventeen, a subservient, naïve, lonely girl.

MARY WARREN: What'll we do? The village is out! I just come from the farm; the whole country's talkin' witchcraft! They'll be callin' us witches, Abby!

MERCY, *pointing and looking at Mary Warren:* She means to tell, I know it.

MARY WARREN: Abby, we've got to tell. Witchery's a hangin' error, a hangin' like they done in Boston two year ago! We must tell the truth, Abby! You'll only be whipped for dancin', and the other things!

ABIGAIL: Oh, *we'll* be whipped!

MARY WARREN: I never done none of it, Abby. I only looked!

MERCY, *moving menacingly toward Mary:* Oh, you're a great one for lookin', aren't you, Mary Warren? What a grand peeping courage you have!

Betty, on the bed, whimpers. Abigail turns to her at once.

ABIGAIL: Betty? *She goes to Betty.* Now, Betty, dear, wake up now. It's Abigail. *She sits Betty up and furiously shakes her.* I'll beat you, Betty! *Betty whimpers.* My, you seem improving. I talked to your papa and I told him everything. So there's nothing to—

BETTY—*she darts off the bed, frightened of Abigail, and flattens herself against the wall:* I want my mama!

ABIGAIL, *with alarm, as she cautiously approaches Betty:* What ails you, Betty? Your mama's dead and buried.

BETTY: I'll fly to Mama. Let me fly! *She raises her arms as though to fly, and streaks for the window, gets one leg out.*

ABIGAIL, *pulling her away from the window:* I told him everything; he knows now, he knows everything we—

BETTY: You drank blood, Abby! You didn't tell him that!

ABIGAIL: Betty, you never say that again! You will never—

BETTY: You did, you did! You drank a charm to kill John Proctor's wife! You drank a charm to kill Goody Proctor!

ABIGAIL, *smashing her across the face:* Shut it! Now shut it!

BETTY, *collapsing on the bed:* Mama. Mama! *She dissolves into sobs.*

ABIGAIL: Now look you. All of you. We danced. And Tituba conjured Ruth Putnam's dead sisters. And that is all. And mark this. Let either of you breathe a word, or the edge of a word, about the other things, and I will come to you in the black of some terrible night and I will bring a pointy reckoning that will shudder you. And you know I can do it; I saw Indians smash my dear parents' heads on the pillow next to mine, and I have seen some reddish work done at night, and I can make you wish you had never seen the sun go down! *She goes to Betty and roughly sits her up.* Now, you—sit up and stop this! *But Betty collapses in her hands and lies inert on the bed.*

"I have seen some reddish work done at night, and I can make you wish you had never seen the sun go down!"

MARY WARREN, *with hysterical fright:* What's got her? *Abigail stares in fright at Betty.* Abby, she's going to die! It's a sin to conjure, and we—

ABIGAIL, *starting for Mary:* I say shut it, Mary Warren!

Enter John Proctor. On seeing him, Mary Warren leaps in fright.

Proctor was a farmer in his middle thirties. He need not have been a partisan of any faction in the town, but there is evidence to suggest that he had a sharp and biting way with hypocrites. He was the kind of man—powerful of body, even-tempered, and not easily led—who cannot refuse support to partisans without drawing their deepest resentment. In Proctor's presence a fool felt his foolishness instantly—

Salem witchcraft.

and a Proctor is always marked for <u>calumny</u> therefore.

But as we shall see, the steady manner he displays does not spring from an untroubled soul. He is a sinner, a sinner not only against the moral fashion of the time, but against his own vision of decent conduct. These people had no ritual for the washing away of sins. It is another trait we inherited from them, and it has helped to discipline us as well as to breed hypocrisy among us. Proctor, respected and even feared in Salem, has come to regard himself as a kind of fraud. But no hint of this has yet appeared on the surface, and as he enters from the crowded parlor below it is a man in his prime we see, with a quiet confidence and an unexpressed, hidden force. Mary Warren, his servant, can barely speak for embarrassment and fear.

MARY WARREN: Oh! I'm just going home, Mr. Proctor.

PROCTOR: Be you foolish, Mary Warren? Be you deaf? I forbid you leave the house, did I not? Why shall I pay you? I am looking for you more often than my cows!

MARY WARREN: I only come to see the great doings in the world.

PROCTOR: I'll show you a great doin' on your arse one of these days. Now get you home; my wife is waitin' with your work! *Trying to retain a shred of dignity, she goes slowly out.*

MERCY LEWIS, *both afraid of him and strangely titillated:* I'd best be off. I have my Ruth to watch. Good morning, Mr. Proctor.

Mercy sidles out. Since Proctor's entrance, Abigail has stood as though on tip-toe, absorbing his presence, wide-eyed. He glances at her, then goes to Betty on the bed.

ABIGAIL: Gah! I'd almost forgot how strong you are, John Proctor!

PROCTOR, *looking at Abigail now, the faintest suggestion of a knowing smile on his face:* What's this mischief here?

ABIGAIL, *with a nervous laugh:* Oh, she's only gone silly somehow.

PROCTOR: The road past my house is a pilgrimage to Salem all morning. The town's mumbling witchcraft.

ABIGAIL: Oh, posh! *Winningly she comes a little closer, with a confidential, wicked air.* We were dancin' in the woods last night, and my uncle leaped in on us. She took fright, is all.

PROCTOR, *his smile widening:* Ah, you're wicked yet, aren't y'! *A trill of expectant laughter escapes her, and she dares come closer, feverishly looking into his eyes.* You'll be clapped in the stocks before you're twenty.[9]

He takes a step to go, and she springs into his path.

ABIGAIL: Give me a word, John. A soft word. *Her concentrated desire destroys his smile.*

PROCTOR: No, no, Abby. That's done with.

ABIGAIL, *tauntingly:* You come five mile to see a silly girl fly? I know you better.

PROCTOR, *setting her firmly out of his path:* I come to see what mischief your uncle's brewin'

---

9. **You'll be clapped in the stocks before you're twenty.** *Stocks* refers to a wooden device in which, during colonial times, a person would be locked as a form of punishment.

---

cal • um • ny (kal´ um nē) *n.,* attempt to harm a person's reputation through deliberate misrepresentation

now. *With final emphasis:* Put it out of mind, Abby.

ABIGAIL, *grasping his hand before he can release her:* John—I am waitin' for you every night.

PROCTOR: Abby, I never give you hope to wait for me.

ABIGAIL, *now beginning to anger—she can't believe it:* I have something better than hope, I think!

PROCTOR: Abby, you'll put it out of mind. I'll not be comin' for you more.

ABIGAIL: You're surely sportin'[10] with me.

PROCTOR: You know me better.

ABIGAIL: I know how you clutched my back behind your house and sweated like a stallion whenever I come near! Or did I dream that? It's she put me out, you cannot pretend it were you. I saw your face when she put me out, and you loved me then and you do now!

PROCTOR: Abby, that's a wild thing to say—

ABIGAIL: A wild thing may say wild things. But not so wild, I think. I have seen you since she put me out; I have seen you nights.

PROCTOR: I have hardly stepped off my farm this seven month.

ABIGAIL: I have a sense for heat, John, and yours has drawn me to my window, and I have seen you looking up, burning in your loneliness. Do you tell me you've never looked up at my window?

PROCTOR: I may have looked up.

ABIGAIL, *now softening:* And you must. You are no wintry man. I know you, John. I *know* you. *She is weeping.* I cannot sleep for dreamin'; I cannot dream but I wake and walk about the house as though I'd find you comin' through some door. *She clutches him desperately.*

PROCTOR, *gently pressing her from him, with great sympathy but firmly.* Child—

ABIGAIL, *with a flash of anger:* How do you call me child!

PROCTOR: Abby, I may think of you softly from time to time. But I will cut off my hand before I'll ever reach for you again. Wipe it out of mind. We never touched, Abby.

ABIGAIL: Aye, but we did.

PROCTOR: Aye, but we did not.

ABIGAIL, *with a bitter anger:* Oh, I marvel how such a strong man may let such a sickly wife be—

PROCTOR, *angered—at himself as well:* You'll speak nothin' of Elizabeth!

ABIGAIL: She is blackening my name in the village! She is telling lies about me! She is a cold, sniveling woman, and you bend to her! Let her turn you like a—

PROCTOR, *shaking her:* Do you look for whippin'?

A psalm is heard being sung below.

ABIGAIL, *in tears:* I look for John Proctor that took me from my sleep and put knowledge in my heart! I never knew what pretense Salem was, I never knew the lying lessons I was taught by all these Christian women and their covenanted[11] men! And now you bid me tear the light out of my eyes? I will not, I cannot! You loved me, John Proctor, and whatever sin it is, you love me yet! *He turns abruptly to go out. She rushes to him.* John, pity me, pity me!

The words "going up to Jesus" are heard in the psalm, and Betty claps her ears suddenly and whines loudly.

ABIGAIL: Betty? *She hurries to Betty, who is now sitting up and screaming. Proctor goes to Betty as Abigail is trying to pull her hands down, calling "Betty!"*

PROCTOR, *growing unnerved:* What's she doing? Girl, what ails you? Stop that wailing!

The singing has stopped in the midst of this, and now Parris rushes in.

---

10. **sportin'.** *Sporting,* used to mean "kidding"
11. **covenanted.** Committed by way of a pledge or contract

PARRIS: What happened? What are you doing to her? Betty! *He rushes to the bed, crying, "Betty, Betty!" Mrs. Putnam enters, feverish with curiosity, and with her Thomas Putnam and Mercy Lewis. Parris, at the bed, keeps lightly slapping Betty's face, while she moans and tries to get up.*

ABIGAIL: She heard you singin' and suddenly she's up and screamin'.

MRS. PUTNAM: The psalm! The psalm! She cannot bear to hear the Lord's name!

PARRIS: No, God forbid. Mercy, run to the doctor! Tell him what's happened here! *Mercy Lewis rushes out.*

MRS. PUTNAM: Mark it for a sign, mark it!

Rebecca Nurse, seventy-two, enters. She is white-haired, leaning upon her walking-stick.

PUTNAM, *pointing at the whimpering Betty:* That is a notorious sign of witchcraft afoot, Goody Nurse, a prodigious[12] sign!

MRS. PUTNAM: My mother told me that! When they cannot bear to hear the name of—

PARRIS, *trembling:* Rebecca, Rebecca, go to her, we're lost. She suddenly cannot bear to hear the Lord's—

Giles Corey, eighty-three, enters. He is knotted with muscle, canny, inquisitive and still powerful.

REBECCA: There is hard sickness here, Giles Corey, so please to keep the quiet.

GILES: I've not said a word. No one here can testify I've said a word. Is she going to fly again? I hear she flies.

PUTNAM: Man, be quiet now!

Everything is quiet. Rebecca walks across the room to the bed. Gentleness exudes from her. Betty is quietly whimpering, eyes shut. Rebecca simply stands over the child, who gradually quiets.

And while they are so absorbed, we may put a word in for Rebecca. Rebecca was the wife of Francis Nurse, who, from all accounts, was one of those men for whom both sides of the argument had to have respect. He was called upon to arbitrate disputes as though he were an unofficial judge, and Rebecca also enjoyed the high opinion most people had for him. By the time of the delusion, they had three hundred acres, and their children were settled in separate homesteads within the same estate. However, Francis had originally rented the land, and one theory has it that, as he gradually paid for it and raised his social status, there were those who resented his rise.

Another suggestion to explain the systematic campaign against Rebecca, and inferentially against Francis, is the land war he fought with his neighbors, one of whom was a Putnam. This squabble grew to the proportions of a battle in the woods between partisans of both sides, and it is said to have lasted for two days. As for Rebecca herself, the general opinion of her character was so high that to explain how anyone dared cry her out for a witch—and more, how adults could bring themselves to lay hands on her—we must look to the fields and boundaries of that time.

As we have seen, Thomas Putnam's man for the Salem ministry was Bayley. The Nurse clan had been in the faction that prevented Bayley's taking office. In addition, certain families allied to the Nurses by blood or friendship, and whose farms were contiguous with the Nurse farm or close to it, combined to break away from the Salem town authority and set up Topsfield, a new and independent entity whose existence was resented by old Salemites.

That the guiding hand behind the outcry was Putnam's is indicated by the fact that, as soon as it began, this Topsfield-Nurse faction absented themselves from church in protest

> "The psalm! The psalm! She cannot bear to hear the Lord's name!"

---

12. **prodigious.** Serving as an omen

and disbelief. It was Edward and Jonathan Putnam who signed the first complaint against Rebecca; and Thomas Putnam's little daughter was the one who fell into a fit at the hearing and pointed to Rebecca as her attacker. To top it all, Mrs. Putnam—who is now staring at the bewitched child on the bed—soon accused Rebecca's spirit of "tempting her to iniquity,"[13] a charge that had more truth in it than Mrs. Putnam could know.

MRS. PUTNAM, *astonished:* What have you done?

Rebecca, in thought, now leaves the bedside and sits.

PARRIS, *wondrous and relieved:* What do you make of it, Rebecca?

PUTNAM, *eagerly:* Goody Nurse, will you go to my Ruth and see if you can wake her?

REBECCA, *sitting:* I think she'll wake in time. Pray calm yourselves. I have eleven children, and I am twenty-six times a grandma, and I have seen them all through their silly seasons, and when it come on them they will run the Devil bowlegged keeping up with their mischief. I think she'll wake when she tires of it. A child's spirit is like a child, you can never catch it by running after it; you must stand still, and, for love, it will soon itself come back.

PROCTOR: Aye, that's the truth of it, Rebecca.

MRS. PUTNAM: This is no silly season, Rebecca. My Ruth is bewildered, Rebecca; she cannot eat.

REBECCA: Perhaps she is not hungered yet. *To Parris:* I hope you are not decided to go in search of loose spirits, Mr. Parris. I've heard promise of that outside.

PARRIS: A wide opinion's running in the parish that the Devil may be among us, and I would satisfy them that they are wrong.

PROCTOR: Then let you come out and call them wrong. Did you consult the wardens before you called this minister to look for devils?

PARRIS: He is not coming to look for devils!

PROCTOR: Then what's he coming for?

PUTNAM: There be children dyin' in the village, Mister!

PROCTOR: I seen none dyin'. This society will not be a bag to swing around your head, Mr. Putnam. *To Parris:* Did you call a meeting before you—?

PUTNAM: I am sick of meetings; cannot the man turn his head without he have a meeting?

PROCTOR: He may turn his head, but not to Hell!

REBECCA: Pray, John, be calm. *Pause. He defers to her.* Mr. Parris, I think you'd best send Reverend Hale back as soon as he come. This will set us all to arguin' again in the society, and we thought to have peace this year. I think we ought rely on the doctor now, and good prayer.

MRS. PUTNAM: Rebecca, the doctor's baffled!

REBECCA: If so he is, then let us go to God for the cause of it. There is prodigious danger in the seeking of loose spirits. I fear it, I fear it. Let us rather blame ourselves and—

PUTNAM: How may we blame ourselves? I am one of nine sons; the Putnam seed have peopled this province. And yet I have but one child left of eight—and now she shrivels!

REBECCA: I cannot fathom that.

MRS. PUTNAM, *with a growing edge of sarcasm:* But I must! You think it God's work you should never lose a child, nor grandchild either, and I bury all but one? There are wheels within wheels in this village, and fires within fires!

PUTNAM, *to Parris:* When Reverend Hale comes, you will proceed to look for signs of witchcraft here.

PROCTOR, *to Putnam:* You cannot command Mr. Parris. We vote by name in this society, not by acreage.

PUTNAM: I never heard you worried so on this society, Mr. Proctor. I do not think I saw you at Sabbath meeting since snow flew.

---

13. **iniquity.** Particularly evil sin

PROCTOR: I have trouble enough without I come five mile to hear him preach only hellfire and bloody damnation. Take it to heart, Mr. Parris. There are many others who stay away from church these days because you hardly ever mention God any more.

PARRIS, *now aroused:* Why, that's a drastic charge!

REBECCA: It's somewhat true; there are many that quail[14] to bring their children—

PARRIS: I do not preach for children, Rebecca. It is not the children who are unmindful of their obligations toward this ministry.

REBECCA: Are there really those unmindful?

PARRIS: I should say the better half of Salem village—

PUTNAM: And more than that!

PARRIS: Where is my wood? My contract provides I be supplied with all my firewood. I am waiting since November for a stick, and even in November I had to show my frostbitten hands like some London beggar!

GILES: You are allowed six pound a year to buy your wood, Mr. Parris.

PARRIS: I regard that six pound as part of my salary. I am paid little enough without I spend six pound on firewood.

PROCTOR: Sixty, plus six for firewood—

PARRIS: The salary is sixty-six pound, Mr. Proctor! I am not some preaching farmer with a book under my arm; I am a graduate of Harvard College.

GILES: Aye, and well instructed in arithmetic!

PARRIS: Mr. Corey, you will look far for a man of my kind at sixty pound a year! I am not used to this poverty; I left a thrifty business in the Barbados to serve the Lord. I do not fathom it, why am I persecuted here? I cannot offer one proposition but there be a howling riot of argument. I have often wondered if the Devil be in it somewhere; I cannot understand you people otherwise.

PROCTOR: Mr. Parris, you are the first minister ever did demand the deed to this house—

PARRIS: Man! Don't a minister deserve a house to live in?

PROCTOR: To live in, yes. But to ask ownership is like you shall own the meeting house itself; the last meeting I were at you spoke so long on deeds and mortgages I thought it were an auction.

PARRIS: I want a mark of confidence, is all! I am your third preacher in seven years. I do not wish to be put out like the cat whenever some majority feels the whim. You people seem not to comprehend that a minister is the Lord's man in the parish; a minister is not to be so lightly crossed and contradicted—

PUTNAM: Aye!

PARRIS: There is either obedience or the church will burn like Hell is burning!

PROCTOR: Can you speak one minute without we land in Hell again? I am sick of Hell!

PARRIS: It is not for you to say what is good for you to hear!

PROCTOR: I may speak my heart, I think!

PARRIS, *in a fury:* What, are we Quakers?[15] We are not Quakers here yet, Mr. Proctor. And you may tell that to your followers!

PROCTOR: My followers!

PARRIS—*now he's out with it:* There is a party in this church. I am not blind; there is a faction and a party.

PROCTOR: Against you?

PUTNAM: Against him and all authority!

PROCTOR: Why, then I must find it and join it.

There is shock among the others.

REBECCA: He does not mean that.

PUTNAM: He confessed it now!

---

14. **quail.** Draw back in fear
15. **Quakers.** Members of a Christian group formed in mid-seventeenth-century England who do not believe in ordained ministry or religious rites

PROCTOR: I mean it solemnly, Rebecca; I like not the smell of this "authority."

REBECCA: No, you cannot break charity with your minister. You are another kind, John. Clasp his hand, make your peace.

PROCTOR: I have a crop to sow and lumber to drag home. *He goes angrily to the door and turns to Corey with a smile.* What say you, Giles, let's find the party. He says there's a party.

GILES: I've changed my opinion of this man, John. Mr. Parris, I beg your pardon. I never thought you had so much iron in you.

PARRIS, *surprised:* Why, thank you, Giles!

GILES: It suggests to the mind what the trouble be among us all these years. *To all:* Think on it. Wherefore is everybody suing everybody else? Think on it now, it's a deep thing, and dark as a pit. I have been six time in court this year—

PROCTOR, *familiarly, with warmth, although he knows he is approaching the edge of Giles' tolerance with this:* Is it the Devil's fault that a man cannot say you good morning without you clap him for defamation? You're old, Giles, and you're not hearin' so well as you did.

GILES—*he cannot be crossed:* John Proctor, I have only last month collected four pound damages for you publicly sayin' I burned the roof off your house, and I—

PROCTOR, *laughing:* I never said no such thing, but I've paid you for it, so I hope I can call you deaf without charge. Now come along, Giles, and help me drag my lumber home.

PUTNAM: A moment, Mr. Proctor. What lumber is that you're draggin', if I may ask you?

PROCTOR: My lumber. From out my forest by the riverside.

PUTNAM: Why, we are surely gone wild this year. What anarchy is this? That tract is in my bounds, it's in my bounds, Mr. Proctor.

PROCTOR, In your bounds! *Indicating Rebecca:* I bought that tract from Goody Nurse's husband five months ago.

PUTNAM: He had no right to sell it. It stands clear in my grandfather's will that all the land between the river and—

PROCTOR: Your grandfather had a habit of willing land that never belonged to him, if I may say it plain.

GILES: That's God's truth; he nearly willed away my north pasture but he knew I'd break his fingers before he'd set his name to it. Let's get your lumber home, John. I feel a sudden will to work coming on.

PUTNAM: You load one oak of mine and you'll fight to drag it home!

GILES: Aye, and we'll win too, Putnam—this fool and I. Come on! *He turns to Proctor and starts out.*

PUTNAM: I'll have my men on you, Corey! I'll clap a writ[16] on you!

Enter Reverend John Hale of Beverly.

Mr. Hale is nearing forty, a tight-skinned, eager-eyed intellectual. This is a beloved errand for him; on being called here to ascertain witchcraft, he felt the pride of the specialist whose unique knowledge has at last been publicly called for. Like almost all men of learning, he spent a good deal of his time pondering the invisible world, especially since he had himself encountered a witch in his parish not long before. That woman, however, turned into a mere pest under his searching scrutiny, and the child she had allegedly been afflicting recovered her normal behavior after Hale had given her his kindness and a few days of rest in his own house. However, that experience never raised a doubt in his mind as to the reality of the underworld or the existence of Lucifer's many-faced lieutenants. And his belief is not to his discredit. Better minds than Hale's were— and still are—convinced that there is a society of spirits beyond our ken. One cannot help noting that one of his lines has never yet raised a laugh in any audience that has seen this play;

---

16. **writ.** Written order

it is his assurance that "We cannot look to superstition in this. The Devil is precise." Evidently we are not quite certain even now whether diabolism[17] is holy and not to be scoffed at. And it is no accident that we should be so bemused.[18]

Like Reverend Hale and the others on this stage, we conceive the Devil as a necessary part of a respectable view of cosmology.[19] Ours is a divided empire in which certain ideas and emotions and actions are of God, and their opposites are of Lucifer. It is as impossible for most men to conceive of a morality without sin as of an earth without "sky." Since 1692 a great but superficial change has wiped out God's beard and the Devil's horns, but the world is still gripped between two diametrically opposed absolutes. The concept of unity, in which positive and negative are attributes of the same force, in which good and evil are relative, ever-changing, and always joined to the same phenomenon—such a concept is still reserved to the physical sciences and to the few who have grasped the history of ideas. When it is recalled that until the Christian era the underworld was never regarded as a hostile area, that all gods were useful and essentially friendly to man despite occasional lapses; when we see the steady and methodical <u>inculcation</u> into humanity of the idea of man's worthlessness—until redeemed—the necessity of the Devil may become evident as a weapon, a weapon designed and used time and time again in every age to whip men into a surrender to a particular church or church-state.

Our difficulty in believing the—for want of a better word—political inspiration of the Devil is due in great part to the fact that he is called up and damned not only by our social antagonists but by our own side, whatever it may be. The Catholic Church, through its

Satan and sorcerer (1626).

Inquisition,[20] is famous for cultivating Lucifer as the arch-fiend, but the Church's enemies relied no less upon the Old Boy to keep the human mind enthralled. Luther[21] was himself accused of alliance with Hell, and he in turn accused his enemies. To complicate matters further, he believed that he had had contact with the Devil and had argued theology with him. I am not surprised at this, for at my own university a professor of history—a Lutheran, by the way—used to assemble his graduate students, draw the shades, and commune in the classroom with Erasmus.[22] He was never, to my knowledge, officially scoffed at for this, the reason being that the university officials, like most

17. **diabolism.** Dealings with the devil; devil worship
18. **bemused.** Confused
19. **cosmology.** Branch of science dealing with the nature of the universe
20. **Inquisition.** Former Roman Catholic process in which suspected or accused nonbelievers were tried
21. **Luther.** Martin Luther (1483–1546), a German monk who led the Protestant Reformation of the Christian church
22. **Erasmus.** Desiderius Erasmus (1466?–1536), a Dutch scholar who published editions of classical Greek and Latin works and early Christian writings; he also was a Humanist who spoke out against religious warfare and intolerance.

in • cul • ca • tion (in' kul kā´ shən) *n.,* teaching imparted through frequent repetition

of us, are the children of a history which still sucks at the Devil's teats. At this writing, only England has held back before the temptations of contemporary diabolism. In the countries of the Communist ideology, all resistance of any import is linked to the totally malign capitalist succubi,[23] and in America any man who is not reactionary in his views is open to the charge of alliance with the Red hell. Political opposition, thereby, is given an inhumane overlay which then justifies the abrogation[24] of all normally applied customs of civilized intercourse. A political policy is equated with moral right, and opposition to it with diabolical malevolence. Once such an equation is effectively made, society becomes a congeries of plots and counterplots, and the main role of government changes from that of the arbiter to that of the scourge of God.

The results of this process are no different now from what they ever were, except sometimes in the degree of cruelty inflicted, and not always even in that department. Normally the actions and deeds of a man were all that society felt comfortable in judging. The secret intent of an action was left to the ministers, priests, and rabbis to deal with. When diabolism rises, however, actions are the least important manifests of the true nature of a man. The Devil, as Reverend Hale said, is a wily one, and, until an hour before he fell, even God thought him beautiful in Heaven.

The analogy, however, seems to falter when one considers that, while there were no witches then, there are Communists and capitalists now, and in each camp there is certain proof that spies of each side are at work undermining the other. But this is a snobbish objection and not at all warranted by the facts. I have no doubt that people *were* communing with, and even worshiping, the Devil in Salem, and if the whole truth could be known in this case, as it is in others, we should discover a regular and conventionalized propitiation of the dark spirit. One certain evidence of this is the confession of Tituba, the slave of Reverend Parris, and another is the behavior of the children who were known to have indulged in sorceries with her.

There are accounts of similar *klatches* in Europe, where the daughters of the towns would assemble at night and, sometimes with fetishes, sometimes with a selected young man, give themselves to love, with some bastardly results. The Church, sharp-eyed as it must be when gods long dead are brought to life, condemned these orgies as witchcraft and interpreted them rightly, as a resurgence of the Dionysiac[25] forces it had crushed long before. Sex, sin, and the Devil were early linked, and so they continued to be in Salem, and are today. From all accounts there are no more puritanical mores in the world than those enforced by the Communists in Russia, where women's fashions, for instance, are as prudent and all-covering as any American Baptist would desire. The divorce laws lay a tremendous responsibility on the father for the care of his children. Even the laxity of divorce regulations in the early years of the revolution was undoubtedly a revulsion from the nineteenth-century Victorian immobility of marriage and the consequent hypocrisy that developed from it. If for no other reasons, a state so powerful, so jealous of the uniformity of its citizens, cannot long tolerate the atomization[26] of the family. And yet, in American eyes at least, there remains the conviction that

A political policy is equated with moral right, and opposition to it with diabolical malevolence.

---

23. **succubi.** [Latin] Plural form of *succubus*, an evil spirit in female form that assaults men in their sleep
24. **abrogation.** Breaking; stopping
25. **Dionysiac.** Devoted to the worship of Dionysus, the Greek god of wine
26. **atomization.** Splintering; dividing

pro • pi • ti • a • tion (prō pi shē ā´ shən) *n.,* act of pacifying or appeasing

the Russian attitude toward women is lascivi-ous.[27] It is the Devil working again, just as he is working within the Slav who is shocked at the very idea of a woman's disrobing herself in a burlesque show. Our opposites are always robed in sexual sin, and it is from this uncon-scious conviction that demonology gains both its attractive sensuality and its capacity to infu-riate and frighten.

Coming into Salem now, Reverend Hale conceives of himself much as a young doctor on his first call. His painfully acquired armory of symptoms, catchwords, and diagnostic pro-cedures is now to be put to use at last. The road from Beverly is unusually busy this morn-ing, and he has passed a hundred rumors that make him smile at the ignorance of the yeo-manry[28] in this most precise science. He feels himself allied with the best minds of Europe—kings, philosophers, scientists, and ecclesiasts of all churches. His goal is light, goodness and its preservation, and he knows the exaltation of the blessed whose intelligence, sharpened by minute examinations of enormous tracts, is finally called upon to face what may be a bloody fight with the Fiend[29] himself.

He appears loaded down with half a dozen heavy books.

HALE: Pray you, someone take these!

PARRIS, *delighted:* Mr. Hale! Oh! it's good to see you again! *Taking some books:* My, they're heavy!

HALE, *setting down his books:* They must be; they are weighted with authority.

PARRIS, *a little scared:* Well, you do come prepared!

HALE: We shall need hard study if it comes to tracking down the Old Boy. *Noticing Rebecca:* You cannot be Rebecca Nurse?

REBECCA: I am, sir. Do you know me?

HALE: It's strange how I knew you, but I sup-pose you look as such a good soul should. We have all heard of your great charities in Beverly.

PARRIS: Do you know this gentleman? Mr. Thomas Putnam. And his good wife Ann.

HALE: Putnam! I had not expected such distin-guished company, sir.

PUTNAM, *pleased:* It does not seem to help us today, Mr. Hale. We look to you to come to our house and save our child.

HALE: Your child ails too?

MRS. PUTNAM: Her soul, her soul seems flown away. She sleeps and yet she walks . . .

PUTNAM: She cannot eat.

HALE: Cannot eat! *Thinks on it. Then, to Proc-tor and Giles Corey:* Do you men have afflicted children?

PARRIS: No, no, these are farmers. John Proctor—

GILES COREY: He don't believe in witches.

PROCTOR, *to Hale:* I never spoke on witches one way or the other. Will you come, Giles?

GILES: No—no, John, I think not. I have some few queer questions of my own to ask this fellow.

PROCTOR: I've heard you to be a sensible man, Mr. Hale. I hope you'll leave some of it in Salem.

Proctor goes. Hale stands embarrassed for an instant.

PARRIS, *quickly:* Will you look at my daugh-ter, sir? *Leads Hale to the bed.* She has tried to leap out the window; we discovered her this morning on the highroad, waving her arms as though she'd fly.

HALE, *narrowing his eyes:* Tries to fly.

PUTNAM: She cannot bear to hear the Lord's name, Mr. Hale; that's a sure sign of witchcraft afloat.

HALE, *holding up his hands:* No, no. Now let me instruct you. We cannot look to superstition in

---

27. **lascivious.** Full of lust
28. **yeomanry.** Middle-class landowners, who hold little property compared to the gentry
29. **Fiend.** Reference to the devil

this. The Devil is precise; the marks of his presence are definite as stone, and I must tell you all that I shall not proceed unless you are prepared to believe me if I should find no bruise of Hell upon her.

PARRIS: It is agreed, sir—it is agreed—we will abide by your judgment.

HALE: Good then, *He goes to the bed, looks down at Betty. To Parris:* Now, sir, what were your first warning of this strangeness?

PARRIS: Why, sir—I discovered her—*indicating Abigail*—and my niece and ten or twelve of the other girls, dancing in the forest last night.

HALE, *surprised:* You permit dancing?

PARRIS: No, no, it were secret—

MRS. PUTNAM, *unable to wait:* Mr. Parris's slave has knowledge of conjurin', sir.

PARRIS, *to Mrs. Putnam:* We cannot be sure of that, Goody Ann—

MRS. PUTNAM, *frightened, very softly:* I know it, sir. I sent my child—she should learn from Tituba who murdered her sisters.

REBECCA, *horrified:* Goody Ann! You sent a child to conjure up the dead?

MRS. PUTNAM: Let God blame me, not you, not you, Rebecca! I'll not have you judging me any more! *To Hale:* Is it a natural work to lose seven children before they live a day?

PARRIS: Sssh!

Rebecca, with great pain, turns her face away. There is a pause.

HALE: Seven dead in childbirth.

MRS. PUTNAM, *softly:* Aye. *Her voice breaks; she looks up at him. Silence. Hale is impressed. Parris looks to him. He goes to his books, opens one, turns pages, then reads. All wait, avidly.*

PARRIS, *hushed:* What book is that?

MRS. PUTNAM: What's there, sir?

HALE, *with a tasty love of intellectual pursuit:* Here is all the invisible world, caught, defined, and calculated. In these books the Devil stands stripped of all his brute disguises. Here are all your familiar spirits—your incubi[30] and succubi; your witches that go by land, by air, and by sea; your wizards of the night and of the day. Have no fear now—we shall find him out if he has come among us, and I mean to crush him utterly if he has shown his face! *He starts for the bed.*

REBECCA: Will it hurt the child, sir?

HALE: I cannot tell. If she is truly in the Devil's grip we may have to rip and tear to get her free.

REBECCA: I think I'll go, then. I am too old for this. *She rises.*

PARRIS, *striving for conviction:* Why, Rebecca, we may open up the boil of all our troubles today!

REBECCA: Let us hope for that. I go to God for you, sir.

PARRIS, *with trepidation—and resentment:* I hope you do not mean we go to Satan here! *Slight pause.*

REBECCA: I wish I knew. *She goes out; they feel resentful of her note of moral superiority.*

PUTNAM, *abruptly:* Come, Mr. Hale, let's get on. Sit you here.

GILES: Mr. Hale, I have always wanted to ask a learned man—what signifies the readin' of strange books?

HALE: What books?

GILES: I cannot tell; she hides them.

HALE: Who does this?

> "We cannot look to superstition in this. The Devil is precise."

---

30. **incubi.** [Latin] Plural form of *incubus,* an evil spirit that violates women in their sleep

GILES: Martha, my wife. I have waked at night many a time and found her in a corner, readin' of a book. Now what do you make of that?

HALE: Why, that's not necessarily—

GILES: It discomfits me! Last night—mark this—I tried and tried and could not say my prayers. And then she close her book and walks out of the house, and suddenly—mark this—I could pray again!

Old Giles must be spoken for, if only because his fate was to be so remarkable and so different from that of all the others. He was in his early eighties at this time, and was the most comical hero in the history. No man has ever been blamed for so much. If a cow was missed, the first thought was to look for her around Corey's house; a fire blazing up at night brought suspicion of arson to his door. He didn't give a hoot for public opinion, and only in his last years— after he had married Martha—did he bother much with the church. That she stopped his prayer is very probable, but he forgot to say that he'd only recently learned any prayers and it didn't take much to make him stumble over them. He was a crank and a nuisance, but withal a deeply innocent and brave man. In court, once, he was asked if it were true that he had been frightened by the strange behavior of a hog and had then said he knew it to be the Devil in an animal's shape. "What frighted you?" he was asked. He forgot everything but the word "frighted," and instantly replied, "I do not know that I ever spoke that word in my life."

HALE: Ah! The stoppage of prayer—that is strange. I'll speak further on that with you.

GILES: I'm not sayin' she's touched the Devil, now, but I'd admire to know what books she reads and why she hides them. She'll not answer me, y' see.

HALE: Aye, we'll discuss it. *To all:* Now mark me, if the Devil is in her you will witness some frightful wonders in this room, so please to keep your wits about you. Mr. Putnam, stand close in case she flies. Now, Betty, dear, will you sit up? *Putnam comes in closer, ready-handed. Hale sits Betty up, but she hangs limp in his hands.* Hmmm. *He observes her carefully. The others watch breathlessly.* Can you hear me? I am John Hale, minister of Beverly. I have come to help you, dear. Do you remember my two little girls in Beverly? *She does not stir in his hands.*

PARRIS, *in fright:* How can it be the Devil? Why would he choose my house to strike? We have all manner of licentious people in the village!

HALE: What victory would the Devil have to win a soul already bad? It is the best the Devil wants, and who is better than the minister?

GILES: That's deep, Mr. Parris, deep, deep!

PARRIS, *with resolution now:* Betty! Answer Mr. Hale! Betty!

HALE: Does someone afflict you, child? It need not be a woman, mind you, or a man. Perhaps some bird invisible to others comes to you—perhaps a pig, a mouse, or any beast at all. Is there some figure bids you fly? *The child remains limp in his hands. In silence he lays her back on the pillow. Now, holding out his hands toward her, he intones:* In nomine Domini Sabaoth sui filiique ite ad infernos.[31] *She does not stir. He turns to Abigail, his eyes narrowing.* Abigail, what sort of dancing were you doing with her in the forest?

> "It is the best the Devil wants, and who is better than the minister?"

---

31. **In nomine . . . infernos.** [Latin] "In the name of the Lord of Hosts and His Son get thee to the lower world." Reverend Hale is commanding any evil spirits possessing Betty to leave her body and return to the underworld.

dis • com • fit (dis kumˊ fit) *v.,* confuse; disconcert
li • cen • tious (lə senˊ shəs) *adj.,* lacking morals

Tituba's powers.

ABIGAIL: Why—common dancing is all.

PARRIS: I think I ought to say that I—I saw a kettle in the grass where they were dancing.

ABIGAIL: That were only soup.

HALE: What sort of soup were in this kettle, Abigail?

ABIGAIL: Why, it were beans—and lentils, I think, and—

HALE: Mr. Parris, you did not notice, did you, any living thing in the kettle? A mouse, perhaps, a spider, a frog—?

PARRIS, *fearfully:* I—do believe there were some movement—in the soup.

ABIGAIL: That jumped in, we never put it in!

HALE, *quickly:* What jumped in?

ABIGAIL: Why, a very little frog jumped—

PARRIS: A frog, Abby!

HALE, *grasping Abigail:* Abigail, it may be your cousin is dying. Did you call the Devil last night?

ABIGAIL: I never called him! Tituba, Tituba . . .

PARRIS, *blanched:* She called the Devil?

HALE: I should like to speak with Tituba.

PARRIS: Goody Ann, will you bring her up? *Mrs. Putnam exits.*

HALE: How did she call him?

ABIGAIL: I know not—she spoke Barbados.

HALE: Did you feel any strangeness when she called him? A sudden cold wind, perhaps? A trembling below the ground?

ABIGAIL: I didn't see no Devil! *Shaking Betty:* Betty, wake up. Betty! Betty!

HALE: You cannot evade me, Abigail. Did your cousin drink any of the brew in that kettle?

ABIGAIL: She never drank it!

HALE: Did you drink it?

ABIGAIL: No, sir!

HALE: Did Tituba ask you to drink it?

ABIGAIL: She tried, but I refused.

HALE: Why are you concealing? Have you sold yourself to Lucifer?

ABIGAIL: I never sold myself! I'm a good girl! I'm a proper girl!

Mrs. Putnam enters with Tituba, and instantly Abigail points at Tituba.

ABIGAIL: She made me do it! She made Betty do it!

TITUBA, *shocked and angry:* Abby!

ABIGAIL: She makes me drink blood!

PARRIS: Blood!!

MRS. PUTNAM: My baby's blood?

TITUBA: No, no, chicken blood. I give she chicken blood!

HALE: Woman, have you enlisted these children for the Devil?

TITUBA: No, no, sir, I don't truck with no Devil!

HALE: Why can she not wake? Are you silencing this child?

TITUBA: I love me Betty!

HALE: You have sent your spirit out upon this child, have you not? Are you gathering souls for the Devil?

ABIGAIL: She sends her spirit on me in church; she makes me laugh at prayer!

PARRIS: She have often laughed at prayer!

ABIGAIL: She comes to me every night to go and drink blood!

TITUBA: You beg *me* to conjure! She beg *me* make charm—

ABIGAIL: Don't lie! *To Hale:* She comes to me while I sleep; she's always making me dream corruptions!

TITUBA: Why you say that, Abby?

ABIGAIL: Sometimes I wake and find myself standing in the open doorway and not a stitch on my body! I always hear her laughing in my sleep. I hear her singing her Barbados songs and tempting me with—

TITUBA: Mister Reverend, I never—

HALE, *resolved now:* Tituba, I want you to wake this child.

TITUBA: I have no power on this child, sir.

HALE: You most certainly do, and you will free her from it now! When did you compact with the Devil?

TITUBA: I don't compact with no Devil!

PARRIS: You will confess yourself or I will take you out and whip you to your death, Tituba!

PUTNAM: This woman must be hanged! She must be taken and hanged!

TITUBA, *terrified, falls to her knees:* No, no, don't hang Tituba! I tell him I don't desire to work for him, sir.

PARRIS: The Devil?

HALE: Then you saw him! *Tituba weeps.* Now Tituba, I know that when we bind ourselves to Hell it is very hard to break with it. We are going to help you tear yourself free—

TITUBA, *frightened by the coming process:* Mister Reverend, I do believe somebody else be witchin' these children.

HALE: Who?

TITUBA: I don't know, sir, but the Devil got him numerous witches.

HALE: Does he! *It is a clue.* Tituba, look into my eyes. Come, look into me. *She raises her eyes to his fearfully.* You would be a good Christian woman, would you not, Tituba?

TITUBA: Aye, sir, a good Christian woman.

HALE: And you love these little children?

TITUBA: Oh, yes, sir, I don't desire to hurt little children.

HALE: And you love God, Tituba?

TITUBA: I love God with all my bein'.

HALE: Now, in God's holy name—

TITUBA: Bless Him. Bless Him. *She is rocking on her knees, sobbing in terror.*

HALE: And to His glory—

TITUBA: Eternal glory. Bless Him—bless God . . .

HALE: Open yourself, Tituba—open yourself and let God's holy light shine on you.

TITUBA: Oh, bless the Lord.

HALE: When the Devil comes to you does he ever come—with another person? *She stares up into his face.* Perhaps another person in the village? Someone you know.

PARRIS: Who came with him?

PUTNAM: Sarah Good? Did you ever see Sarah Good with him? Or Osburn?

PARRIS: Was it man or woman came with him?

TITUBA: Man or woman. Was—was woman.

PARRIS: What woman? A woman, you said. What woman?

TITUBA: It was black dark, and I—

PARRIS: You could see him, why could you not see her?

TITUBA: Well, they was always talking; they was always runnin' round and carryin' on—

PARRIS: You mean out of Salem? Salem witches?

TITUBA: I believe so, yes, sir.

Now Hale takes her hand. She is surprised.

HALE: Tituba. You must have no fear to tell us who they are, do you understand? We will protect you. The Devil can never overcome a minister. You know that, do you not?

TITUBA—*she kisses Hale's hand:* Aye, sir, oh, I do.

HALE: You have confessed yourself to witchcraft, and that speaks a wish to come to Heaven's side. And we will bless you, Tituba.

TITUBA, *deeply relieved:* Oh, God bless you, Mr. Hale!

HALE, *with rising exaltation:* You are God's instrument put in our hands to discover the Devil's agents among us. You are selected, Tituba, you are chosen to help us cleanse our village. So speak utterly, Tituba, turn your back on him and face God—face God, Tituba, and God will protect you.

TITUBA, *joining with him:* Oh, God, protect Tituba!

HALE, *kindly:* Who came to you with the Devil? Two? Three? Four? How many?

Tituba pants and begins rocking back and forth again, staring ahead.

TITUBA: There was four. There was four.

PARRIS, *pressing in on her:* Who? Who? Their names, their names!

TITUBA, *suddenly bursting out:* Oh, how many times he bid me kill you, Mr. Parris!

PARRIS: Kill me!

TITUBA, *in a fury:* He say Mr. Parris must be kill! Mr. Parris no goodly man, Mr. Parris mean man and no gentle man, and he bid me rise out of my bed and cut your throat! *They gasp.* But I tell him "No! I don't hate that man. I don't want kill that man." But he say, "You work for me, Tituba, and I make you free! I give you pretty dress to wear, and put you way high up in the air, and you gone fly back to Barbados!" And I say, "You lie, Devil, you lie!" And then he come one stormy night to me, and he say, "Look! I have *white* people belong to me." And I look—and there was Goody Good.

PARRIS: Sarah Good!

Tituba, *rocking and weeping:* Aye, sir, and Goody Osburn.

Mrs. Putnam: I knew it! Goody Osburn were midwife[32] to me three times. I begged you, Thomas, did I not? I begged him not to call Osburn because I feared her. My babies always shriveled in her hands!

Hale: Take courage, you must give us all their names. How can you bear to see this child suffering? Look at her, Tituba. *He is indicating Betty on the bed.* Look at her God-given innocence; her soul is so tender; we must protect her, Tituba; the Devil is out and preying on her like a beast upon the flesh of the pure lamb. God will bless you for your help.

Abigail rises, staring as though inspired, and cries out.

Abigail: I want to open myself! *They turn to her, startled. She is enraptured, as though in a pearly light.* I want the light of God, I want the sweet love of Jesus! I danced for the Devil; I saw him; I wrote in his book; I go back to Jesus; I kiss His hand. I saw Sarah Good with the Devil! I saw Goody Osburn with the Devil! I saw Bridget Bishop with the Devil!

As she is speaking, Betty is rising from the bed, a fever in her eyes, and picks up the chant.

Betty, *staring too:* I saw George Jacobs with the Devil! I saw Goody Howe with the Devil!

Parris: She speaks! *He rushes to embrace Betty.* She speaks!

Hale: Glory to God! It is broken, they are free!

Betty, *calling out hysterically and with great relief:* I saw Martha Bellows with the Devil!

Abigail: I saw Goody Sibber with the Devil! *It is rising to a great glee.*

Putnam: The marshal, I'll call the marshal!

Parris is shouting a prayer of thanksgiving.

Betty: I saw Alice Barrow with the Devil!

The curtain begins to fall.

Hale, *as Putnam goes out:* Let the marshal bring irons!

Abigail: I saw Goody Hawkins with the Devil!

Betty: I saw Goody Bibber with the Devil!

Abigail: I saw Goody Booth with the Devil!

On their ecstatic cries the curtain falls. ❖

---

32. **midwife.** Woman who delivers babies; today, midwives are medically trained.

MIRRORS & WINDOWS Afraid that his reputation and ministry will be ruined, Reverend Parris insists that no one mention anything about witchcraft in the village. Think of a modern-day example of a cover-up. In today's world, is it possible to prevent the truth from being revealed?

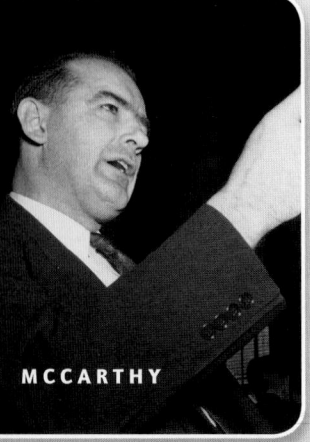
Primary Source Connection

When the 1996 film version of *The Crucible* opened in theaters, Arthur Miller reflected on what audiences of the 1990s may not have realized—the reasons he created the drama. He expressed his thoughts and reminiscence in the essay **"Why I Wrote 'The Crucible': An Artist's Answer to Politics,"** which appeared in the *New Yorker* magazine in October 1996.

In the essay, Miller described how the 1950s accusations of communist ties among leaders in government and entertainment were little more than a witch hunt—fear and paranoia that had spun out of control and infringed on civil liberties. He acknowledges the evolution of the play's interpretation, suggesting that its message and meaning are subject to changing times.

from WHY I WROTE "THE CRUCIBLE"

by Arthur Miller

As I watched "The Crucible" taking shape as a movie over much of the past year, the sheer depth of time that it represents for me kept returning to mind. As those powerful actors blossomed on the screen, and the children and the horses, the crowds and the wagons, I thought again about how I came to cook all this up nearly fifty years ago, in an America almost nobody I know seems to remember clearly. In a way, there is a biting irony in this film's having been made by a Hollywood studio, something unimaginable in the fifties. But there they are—Daniel Day-Lewis (John Proctor) scything his sea-bordered field, Joan Allen (Elizabeth) lying pregnant in the frigid jail, Winona Ryder (Abigail) stealing her minister-uncle's money, majestic Paul Scofield (Judge Danforth) and his righteous empathy with the Devil-possessed children, and all of them looking as inevitable as rain.

I remember those years—they formed "The Crucible" 's skeleton—but I have lost the dead weight of the fear I had then. Fear doesn't travel well; just as it can warp judgment, its absence can diminish memory's truth. What terrifies one generation is likely to bring only a puzzled smile to the next. I remember how in 1964, only twenty years after the war, Harold Clurman, the director of "Incident at Vichy," showed the cast a film of a Hitler speech, hoping to give them a sense of the Nazi period in which my play took place. They watched as Hitler, facing a vast stadium full of adoring people, went up on his toes in ecstasy, hands clasped under his chin, a sublimely self-gratified grin on his face, his body swivelling rather cutely, and they giggled at his overacting.

Likewise, films of Senator Joseph McCarthy are rather unsettling—if you remember the fear he once spread. Buzzing his truculent[1] sidewalk brawler's snarl through the hairs in his nose, squinting through his cat's eyes and sneering

---

1. **truculent.** Cruel; scathing

like a villain, he comes across now as nearly comical, a self-aware performer keeping a straight face as he does his juicy threat-shtick.

McCarthy's power to stir fears of creeping Communism was not entirely based on illusion, of course; the paranoid, real or pretended, always secretes its pearl around a grain of fact. From being our wartime ally, the Soviet Union rapidly became an expanding empire. In 1949, Mao Zedong took power in China. Western Europe also seemed ready to become Red—especially Italy, where the Communist Party was the largest outside Russia, and was growing. Capitalism, in the opinion of many, myself included, had nothing more to say, its final poisoned bloom having been Italian and German Fascism. McCarthy—brash and ill-mannered but to many authentic and true—boiled it all down to what anyone could understand: we had "lost China" and would soon lose Europe as well, because the State Department—staffed, of course, under Democratic Presidents—was full of treasonous pro-Soviet intellectuals. It was as simple as that.

If our losing China seemed the equivalent of a flea's losing an elephant, it was still a phrase—and a conviction—that one did not dare to question; to do so was to risk drawing suspicion on oneself. Indeed, the State Department proceeded to hound and fire the officers who knew China, its language, and its opaque culture—a move that suggested the practitioners of sympathetic magic who wring the neck of a doll in order to make a distant enemy's head drop off. There was magic all around; the politics of alien conspiracy soon dominated political discourse and bid fair to wipe out any other issue. How could one deal with such enormities in a play?

"The Crucible" was an act of desperation. Much of my desperation branched out, I suppose, from a typical Depression-era trauma—the blow struck on the mind by the rise of

European Fascism and the brutal anti-Semitism it had brought to power. But by 1950, when I began to think of writing about the hunt for Reds in America, I was motivated in some great part by the paralysis that had set in among many liberals who, despite their discomfort with the inquisitors' violations of civil rights, were fearful, and with good reason, of being identified as covert Communists if they should protest too strongly.

In any play, however trivial, there has to be a still point of moral reference against which to gauge the action. In our lives, in the late nineteen-forties and early nineteen-fifties, no such point existed anymore. The left could not look straight at the Soviet Union's abrogations of human rights. The anti-Communist liberals could not acknowledge the violations of those rights by congressional committees. The far right, meanwhile, was licking up all the cream. The days of "J'accuse"[2] were gone, for anyone needs to feel right to declare someone else wrong. Gradually, all the old political and moral reality had melted like a Dali watch. Nobody but a fanatic, it seemed, could really say all that he believed.

President Truman was among the first to have to deal with the dilemma, and his way of resolving itself having to trim his sails before the howling gale on the right turned out to be momentous. At first, he was outraged at the allegation of widespread Communist infiltration of the government and called the charge of "coddling Communists" a red herring[3] dragged in by the Republicans to bring down the Democrats. But such was the gathering power of raw belief in the great Soviet plot that Truman soon felt it necessary to institute loyalty boards of his own.

> Fear doesn't travel well; just as it can warp judgment, its absence can diminish memory's truth.

2. **"J'accuse."** [French] "I accuse"; a bitter and often public denunciation
3. **red herring.** Distraction to draw attention away from the real issue

The Red hunt,[4] led by the House Committee on Un-American Activities and by McCarthy, was becoming the dominating fixation of the American psyche. It reached Hollywood when the studios, after first resisting, agreed to submit artists' names to the House Committee for "clearing" before employing them. This unleashed a veritable holy terror among actors, directors, and others, from Party[5] members to those who had had the merest brush with a front organization.[6]

The Soviet plot was the hub of a great wheel of causation; the plot justified the crushing of all nuance, all the shadings that a realistic judgment of reality requires. Even worse was the feeling that our sensitivity to this onslaught on our liberties was passing from us—indeed, from me. In "Timebends," my autobiography, I recalled the time I'd written a screenplay ("The Hook") about union corruption on the Brooklyn waterfront. Harry Cohn, the head of Columbia Pictures, did something that would once have been considered unthinkable: he showed my script to the F.B.I. Cohn then asked me to take the gangsters in my script, who were threatening and murdering their opponents, and simply change them to Communists. When I declined to commit this idiocy (Joe Ryan, the head of the longshoremen's union, was soon to go to Sing Sing for racketeering), I got a wire from Cohn saying, "The minute we try to make the script pro-American you pull out." By then—it was 1951—I had come to accept this terribly serious insanity as routine, but there was an element of the marvellous in it which I longed to put on the stage. . . .

"The Crucible" took me about a year to write. With its five sets and a cast of twenty-one, it never occurred to me that it would take a brave man to produce it on Broadway, especially given the prevailing climate, but Kermit Bloomgarden[7] never faltered. Well before the play opened, a strange tension had begun to build. Only two years earlier, the "Death of a Salesman" touring company had played to a thin crowd in Peoria, Illinois, having been boycotted nearly to death by the American Legion and the Jaycees.[8] Before that, the Catholic War Veterans had prevailed upon the Army not to allow its theatrical groups to perform, first, "All My Sons," and then any play of mine, in occupied Europe. The Dramatists Guild refused to protest attacks on a new play by Sean O'Casey, a self-declared Communist, which forced its producer to cancel his option. I knew of two suicides by actors depressed by upcoming investigation, and every day seemed to bring news of people exiling themselves to Europe: Charlie Chaplin, the director Joseph Losey, Jules Dassin, the harmonica virtuoso Larry Adler, Donald Ogden Stewart, one of the most sought-after screenwriters in Hollywood, and Sam Wanamaker, who would lead the successful campaign to rebuild the Old Globe Theatre on the Thames.[9]

On opening night, January 22, 1953, I knew that the atmosphere would be pretty hostile. The coldness of the crowd was not a surprise; Broadway audiences were not famous for loving history lessons, which is what they made of the play. It seems to me entirely appropriate that on the day the play opened, a newspaper headline read "ALL 13 REDS GUILTY"—a story about American Communists who faced

> Even worse was the feeling that our sensitivity to this onslaught on our liberties was passing from us.

---

4. **Red hunt.** Search for communists and communist sympathizers
5. **Party.** Communist political party
6. **front organization.** Organization set up and controlled by another organization, often to conceal the activities of the parent organization; front organizations often are set up by intelligence agencies, religious groups, political movements, and terrorist groups.
7. **Kermit Bloomgarden.** American producer of dramatic and musical plays
8. **American Legion and the Jaycees.** Two public service organizations
9. **Sam Wanamaker . . . on the Thames.** In 1970, American actor Sam Wanamaker began a fund to rebuild London's Old Globe Theatre, which had been torn down in 1644, near its original spot on the south side of the River Thames.

prison for "conspiring to teach and advocate the duty and necessity of forcible overthrow of government." Meanwhile, the remoteness of the production was guaranteed by the director, Jed Harris, who insisted that this was a classic requiring the actors to face front, never each other. The critics were not swept away. "Arthur Miller is a problem playwright in both senses of the word," wrote Walter Kerr of the *Herald Tribune,* who called the play "a step backward into mechanical parable."[10] The *Times* was not much kinder, saying, "There is too much excitement and not enough emotion in 'The Crucible.'" But the play's future would turn out quite differently.

About a year later, a new production, one with younger, less accomplished actors, working in the Martinique Hotel ballroom, played with the fervor that the script and the times required, and "The Crucible" became a hit. The play stumbled into history, and today, I am told, it is one of the most heavily demanded trade-fiction paperbacks in this country; the Bantam and Penguin editions have sold more than six million copies. I don't think there has been a week in the past forty-odd years when it hasn't been on a stage somewhere in the world. Nor is the new screen version the first. Jean-Paul Sartre,[11] in his Marxist phase, wrote a French film adaptation that blamed the tragedy on the rich landowners conspiring to persecute the poor. (In truth, most of those who were hanged in Salem were people of substance, and two or three were very large landowners.)

It is only a slight exaggeration to say that, especially in Latin America, "The Crucible" starts getting produced wherever a political coup[12] appears imminent, or a dictatorial regime has just been over-thrown. From Argentina to Chile to Greece, Czechoslovakia, China, and a dozen other places, the play seems to present the same primeval structure of human sacrifice to the furies of fanaticism and paranoia that goes on repeating itself forever as though imbedded in the brain of social man.

I am not sure what "The Crucible" is telling people now, but I know that its paranoid center is still pumping out the same darkly attractive warning that it did in the fifties. For some, the play seems to be about the dilemma of relying on the testimony of small children accusing adults of sexual abuse, something I'd not have dreamed of forty years ago. For others, it may simply be a fascination with the outbreak of paranoia that suffuses[13] the play—the blind panic that, in our age, often seems to sit at the dim edges of consciousness. Certainly its political implications are the central issue for many people; the Salem interrogations turn out to be eerily exact models of those yet to come in Stalin's Russia, Pinochet's Chile, Mao's China, and other regimes. (Nien Cheng, the author of "Life and Death in Shang-hai," has told me that she could hardly believe that a non-Chinese—someone who had not experienced the Cultural Revolution—had written the play.) But below its concerns with justice the play evokes a lethal brew of illicit sexuality, fear of the supernatural, and political manipulation, a combination not unfamiliar these days. The film, by reaching the broad American audience as no play ever can, may well unearth still other connections to those buried public terrors that Salem first announced on this continent.

One thing more—something wonderful in the old sense of that word. I recall the weeks I spent reading testimony by the tome,[14] commentaries, broadsides, confessions, and accusations. And always the crucial damning event was the signing of one's name in "the Devil's book." This Faustian[15] agreement to hand over one's soul to the dreaded Lord of Darkness was the ultimate insult to God. But what were these new inductees supposed to have *done*

---

10. **parable.** Short story, usually fictional, meant to demonstrate a moral principle
11. **Jean-Paul Sartre.** French novelist and playwright associated with Existentialism
12. **political coup.** Sudden, forceful overthrow of a government; also *coup d'etat*
13. **suffuses.** Spreads throughout; fills
14. **tome.** Large book, typically academic in content
15. **Faustian.** Relating to the story of Faust, who strikes a bargain with the devil for gain in the present without regard for the future price of eternal damnation

once they'd signed on? Nobody seems even to have thought to ask. But, of course, actions are as irrelevant during cultural and religious wars as they are in nightmares. The thing at issue is buried intentions—the secret allegiances of the alienated hearts always the main threat to the theocratic mind, as well as its immemorial quarry.[16] ❖

---

16. **quarry.** Something hunted or pursued

Review Questions

1. Approximately how much time had passed between the production of the stage version of *The Crucible* and the film version? Identify the "biting irony" of the movie being made by a Hollywood studio.

2. What does Miller mean when he asserts that "fear doesn't travel well"? Analyze the reason *The Crucible* still has meaning for people even decades after the McCarthy Era.

3. Identify what Miller states is the main threat to a totalitarian or theocratic regime. Explain why this play seems popular in places where political turmoil is present.

TEXT $\xleftrightarrow{TO}$ TEXT CONNECTION

More than forty years after presenting *The Crucible* to Americans, Arthur Miller decided to publicly explain his reasons for doing so. The release of his essay clearly coincided with the release of the Hollywood version of the drama. But why else might Miller have chosen the mid-1990s to publish such an essay? Whom do you think the article may have interested most?

POLITICAL CONNECTION

Blacklisting in Hollywood

McCarthyism affected nearly every business and interest group in the United States, including the entertainment industry. Individuals associated with liberal organizations often were fired from their jobs and prevented from gaining further employment. The policy of refusing to hire or terminating someone whose opinions or associations are considered socially or politically unacceptable is called *blacklisting*.

Hollywood blacklisting started in 1947, when a group of ten screenwriters, producers, and directors refused to testify before the House Un-American Activities Committee (HUAC). This group, who would become known as the Hollywood Ten, was believed to include a number of communists and communist sympathizers.

Even though membership in this political party was not illegal, Congress pressured the film industry to ban the Hollywood Ten from employment. In response, film industry officials released a press notice announcing that these individuals would be blacklisted until they took a pledge against communism. Other individuals were banned, as well, even some who had sworn they were not communists. From 1947 to 1960, Hollywood blacklisted more than three hundred screenwriters, actors, directors, and producers.

Blacklisting efforts began to erode in 1957, when television show host John Henry Faulk sued his union for spreading incorrect information about his politics. By 1958, blacklisted screenwriters began to reappear in television and movie credits. Two years later, Dalton Trumbo, who had been the most prominent member of the Hollywood Ten, received a co-writing credit for the film *Spartacus*. Trumbo's re-emergence spelled the end of the blacklisting era in Hollywood.

Refer to Text ▶ ▶ ▶ ▶ ▶ **Reason with Text**

1a. To the residents of Salem in 1692, what was the key to maintaining a safe and orderly society? What kind of government did they establish?

1b. Explain how the community's structure and philosophies have led to its falling apart.

Understand
Find meaning

2a. What information is Reverend Parris trying to get from Abigail? What is Abigail's insistent response?

2b. Why does Parris suspect that Abigail may be hiding something? Would he be as suspicious if she were his own daughter? Explain.

Apply
Use information

3a. According to Abigail, who wanted her dismissed as the Proctors' servant? Why?

3b. What mixed emotions does John have on seeing Abigail again? Support your answer with examples.

Analyze
Take things apart

4a. In "Why I Wrote 'The Crucible,'" to which twentieth-century individuals and groups does Miller say he compares the alleged witches of Salem?

4b. Do you agree or disagree with Miller's analogy? How much of his reasoning seems based on opinion versus fact? What generalizations does he make?

Evaluate
Make judgments

5a. Identify the characters that enter and exit the room where Betty Parris lies. What interest or motive does each character have?

5b. Compare and contrast the characters' motives. Whose motives are essentially pure, whose are self-serving or underhanded, and whose fit both these descriptions?

Create
Bring ideas together

Analyze Literature

Stage Directions and Dialogue

What kinds of details does Miller provide in stage directions? For instance, what is the setting of the play? What details does Miller provide about characters' appearance, emotions, movements, and so on?

How does Miller use dialogue to present stage directions? What other information about characters is revealed through dialogue?

Extend the Text

Writing Options

Creative Writing Imagine that you are Reverend Parris. Write a sermon you might deliver to your congregation about how to recognize whether a witness is telling the truth about an accused witch.

Expository Writing Consider how the extended commentary about rigid, fear-ridden Puritan society, together with specific stage directions, sheds light on the unfolding action of Act 1. Write a one-paragraph analysis of what the commentary adds to the play, knowing that much of that information would not be known to the audience.

Media Literacy

Research Mob Hysteria Investigate the phenomenon of mob hysteria. What different theories explain its origins? Why does it become difficult, if not impossible, for one individual to stand up to a mob? Support your answers using real-life instances of mob hysteria.

Collaborative Learning

Understand Scapegoating Explore the concept of *scapegoating,* in which one person is made to take the blame for the wrongdoing of a group of people. Why does the New England community in *The Crucible* perceive a need for a scapegoat? Is scapegoating still practiced in some form in contemporary cultures?

 Go to **www.mirrorsandwindows.com** for more.

The Crucible, Act 2

A Drama by Arthur Miller

Build Background

Historical Context In Act 2 of *The Crucible,* the witch trial becomes increasingly hysterical. Abigail and her friends begin accusing other townspeople to serve their personal agendas. As arrests become more frequent, John Hale visits the Proctors to test their religious integrity. Although Hale directed the investigation in Act 1, he expresses surprise and skepticism over some of the arrests that occur in Act 2. At this point in the play, it becomes clear that he has lost control over the proceedings.

Although Miller's play is based on actual historical figures and events, he altered certain details to serve his dramatic purposes. For instance, as he explains at the beginning of Act 1 in "A Note on the Historical Accuracy of the Play" (see page 882), he reduced the number of characters in the drama by creating composite figures, "fusing" the traits of actual individuals. For instance, the various judges involved in the Salem witch trials are represented in the play by only two, Hathorne and Danforth.

The character John Hale bears a fairly close resemblance to the actual figure. Historical documents show that the real Hale dedicated much of his youth to learning about witchcraft and played a major role in prosecuting accused witches during the 1692 trials. However, when his wife, Sarah, fell under scrutiny, he became disillusioned and ended his participation in the trials. Five years later, he wrote a book entitled *A Modest Inquiry into the Nature of Witchcraft* that condemned the accusers' ulterior motives and panicked conclusions.

Another more central figure in the Salem witch trials, Judge Samuel

Judge Samuel Sewall (1652–1730).

Sewall, also regretted his involvement years later. As the newly appointed Justice of the Superior Court, Sewall presided over the trials and sentenced the condemned individuals. Five years later, Sewall publicly recanted the guilty verdicts and begged for forgiveness. Despite admitting this grievous error, Sewall remained a high-level judge for the rest of his life. He also became involved in humanitarian movements to free the slaves and to defend Native American rights.

Reader's Context When you have made up your mind about something, what does it take to change your opinion?

Analyze Literature

Characterization and Allusion
Characterization is the act of creating or describing a character. *Indirect techniques* include showing what characters say, do, or think and showing what other characters say or think about them. The *direct technique* involves describing a character's physical features and personality.

An **allusion** is a reference to a well-known person, event, object, or work from history or literature.

Set Purpose

In Act 2, we learn from Hale's facial expressions and words—two means of indirect characterization—that he doubts the accusations against the Proctors. As you read, find other examples of indirect and direct characterization. Also make note of the allusions in Act 2, such as Elizabeth's biblical allusion to the parting of the Red Sea, and consider their significance.

Preview Vocabulary

loftily, 918
ameliorate, 919
deference, 922
evade, 923
pious, 923

Liam Neeson and Laura Linney perform as John and Elizabeth Proctor during a 2002 New York stage production of *The Crucible.*

Act 2

The common room of Proctor's house, eight days later.

At the right is a door opening on the fields outside. A fireplace is at the left, and behind it a stairway leading upstairs. It is the low, dark, and rather long living room of the time. As the curtain rises, the room is empty. From above, Elizabeth is heard softly singing to the children. Presently the door opens and John Proctor enters, carrying his gun. He glances about the room as he comes toward the fireplace, then halts for an instant as he hears her singing. He continues on to the fireplace, leans the gun against the wall as he swings a pot out of the fire and smells it. Then he lifts out the ladle and tastes. He is not quite pleased. He reaches to a cupboard, takes a pinch of salt, and drops it into the pot. As he is tasting again, her footsteps are heard on the stair. He swings the pot into the fireplace and goes to a basin and washes his hands and face. Elizabeth enters.

ELIZABETH: What keeps you so late? It's almost dark.

PROCTOR: I were planting far out to the forest edge.

ELIZABETH: Oh, you're done then.

PROCTOR: Aye, the farm is seeded. The boys asleep?

ELIZABETH: They will be soon. *And she goes to the fireplace, proceeds to ladle up stew in a dish.*

PROCTOR: Pray now for a fair summer.

ELIZABETH: Aye.

PROCTOR: Are you well today?

ELIZABETH: I am. *She brings the plate to the table, and, indicating the food:* It is a rabbit.

PROCTOR, *going to the table:* Oh, is it! In Jonathan's trap?

ELIZABETH: No, she walked into the house this afternoon; I found her sittin' in the corner like she come to visit.

PROCTOR: Oh, that's a good sign walkin' in.

ELIZABETH: Pray God. It hurt my heart to strip her, poor rabbit. *She sits and watches him taste it.*

PROCTOR: It's well seasoned.

ELIZABETH, *blushing with pleasure:* I took great care. She's tender?

PROCTOR: Aye. *He eats. She watches him.* I think we'll see green fields soon. It's warm as blood beneath the clods.[1]

ELIZABETH: That's well.

Proctor eats, then looks up.

PROCTOR: If the crop is good I'll buy George Jacobs' heifer.[2] How would that please you?

ELIZABETH: Aye, it would.

PROCTOR, *with a grin:* I mean to please you, Elizabeth.

ELIZABETH—*it is hard to say:* I know it, John.

He gets up, goes to her, kisses her. She receives it. With a certain disappointment he returns to the table.

PROCTOR, *as gently as he can:* Cider?

ELIZABETH, *with a sense of reprimanding herself for having forgot:* Aye! *She gets up and goes and pours a glass for him. He now arches his back.*

PROCTOR: This farm's a continent when you go foot by foot droppin' seeds in it.

ELIZABETH, *coming with the cider:* It must be.

PROCTOR—*he drinks a long draught, then, putting the glass down:* You ought to bring some flowers in the house.

ELIZABETH: Oh! I forgot! I will tomorrow.

PROCTOR: It's winter in here yet. On Sunday let you come with me, and we'll walk the farm together; I never see such a load of flowers on the earth. *With good feeling he goes and looks up at the sky through the open doorway.* Lilacs have

Italian woodcut showing the practice of "witch dipping" in the early seventeenth century.

a purple smell. Lilac is the smell of nightfall, I think. Massachusetts is a beauty in the spring!

ELIZABETH: Aye, it is.

There is a pause. She is watching him from the table as he stands there absorbing the night. It is as though she would speak but cannot. Instead, now, she takes up his plate and glass and fork and goes with them to the basin. Her back is turned to him. He turns to her and watches her. A sense of their separation rises.

PROCTOR: I think you're sad again. Are you?

ELIZABETH—*she doesn't want friction, and yet she must:* You come so late I thought you'd gone to Salem this afternoon.

PROCTOR: Why? I have no business in Salem.

ELIZABETH: You did speak of going, earlier this week.

PROCTOR—*he knows what she means:* I thought better of it since.

---

1. **clods.** Lumps of earth
2. **heifer.** Young cow

ELIZABETH: Mary Warren's there today.

PROCTOR: Why'd you let her? You heard me forbid her to go to Salem any more!

ELIZABETH: I couldn't stop her.

PROCTOR, *holding back a full condemnation of her:* It is a fault, it is a fault, Elizabeth—you're the mistress here, not Mary Warren.

ELIZABETH: She frightened all my strength away.

PROCTOR: How may that mouse frighten you, Elizabeth? You—

ELIZABETH: It is a mouse no more. I forbid her go, and she raises up her chin like the daughter of a prince and says to me, "I must go to Salem, Goody Proctor; I am an official of the court!"

PROCTOR: Court! What court?

ELIZABETH: Aye, it is a proper court they have now. They've sent four judges out of Boston, she says, weighty magistrates of the General Court, and at the head sits the Deputy Governor of the Province.

PROCTOR, *astonished:* Why, she's mad.

ELIZABETH: I would to God she were. There be fourteen people in the jail now, she says. *Proctor simply looks at her, unable to grasp it.* And they'll be tried, and the court have power to hang them too, she says.

PROCTOR, *scoffing, but without conviction:* Ah, they'd never hang—

ELIZABETH: The Deputy Governor promise hangin' if they'll not confess, John. The town's gone wild, I think. She speak of Abigail, and I thought she were a saint, to hear her. Abigail brings the other girls into the court, and where she walks the crowd will part like the sea for Israel.[3] And folks are brought before them, and if they scream and howl and fall to the floor—the person's clapped in the jail for bewitchin' them.

"Where she walks the crowd will part like the sea for Israel."

PROCTOR, *wide-eyed:* Oh, it is a black mischief.

ELIZABETH: I think you must go to Salem, John. *He turns to her.* I think so. You must tell them it is a fraud.

PROCTOR, *thinking beyond this:* Aye, it is, it is surely.

ELIZABETH: Let you go to Ezekiel Cheever—he knows you well. And tell him what she said to you last week in her uncle's house. She said it had naught to do with witchcraft, did she not?

PROCTOR, *in thought:* Aye, she did, she did. *Now a pause.*

ELIZABETH, *quietly, fearing to anger him by prodding:* God forbid you keep that from the court, John. I think they must be told.

PROCTOR, *quietly, struggling with his thought:* Aye, they must, they must. It is a wonder they do believe her.

ELIZABETH: I would go to Salem now, John—let you go tonight.

PROCTOR: I'll think on it.

ELIZABETH, *with her courage now:* You cannot keep it, John.

PROCTOR, *angering:* I know I cannot keep it. I say I will think on it!

ELIZABETH, *hurt, and very coldly:* Good, then, let you think on it. *She stands and starts to walk out of the room.*

PROCTOR: I am only wondering how I may prove what she told me, Elizabeth. If the girl's a saint now, I think it is not easy to prove she's fraud, and the town gone so silly. She told it to me in a room alone—I have no proof for it.

ELIZABETH: You were alone with her?

PROCTOR, *stubbornly:* For a moment alone, aye.

---

3. **part like . . . Israel.** Reference to the biblical story of Moses parting the Red Sea to allow the Israelites to escape from Egypt

ELIZABETH: Why, then, it is not as you told me.

PROCTOR, *his anger rising:* For a moment, I say. The others come in soon after.

ELIZABETH, *quietly—she has suddenly lost all faith in him:* Do as you wish, then. *She starts to turn.*

PROCTOR: Woman. *She turns to him.* I'll not have your suspicion any more.

ELIZABETH, *a little <u>loftily</u>:* I have no—

PROCTOR: I'll not have it!

ELIZABETH: Then let you not earn it.

PROCTOR, *with a violent undertone:* You doubt me yet?

ELIZABETH, *with a smile, to keep her dignity:* John, if it were not Abigail that you must go to hurt, would you falter now? I think not.

PROCTOR: Now look you—

ELIZABETH: I see what I see, John.

PROCTOR, *with solemn warning:* You will not judge me more, Elizabeth. I have good reason to think before I charge fraud on Abigail, and I will think on it. Let you look to your own improvement before you go to judge your husband any more. I have forgot Abigail, and—

ELIZABETH: And I.

PROCTOR: Spare me! You forget nothin' and forgive nothin'. Learn charity, woman. I have gone tiptoe in this house all seven month since she is gone. I have not moved from there to there without I think to please you, and still an everlasting funeral marches round your heart. I cannot speak but I am doubted, every moment judged for lies, as though I come into a court when I come into this house!

ELIZABETH: John, you are not open with me. You saw her with a crowd, you said. Now you—

PROCTOR: I'll plead my honesty no more, Elizabeth.

ELIZABETH—*now she would justify herself:* John, I am only—

PROCTOR: No more! I should have roared you down when first you told me your suspicion. But I wilted, and, like a Christian, I confessed. Confessed! Some dream I had must have mistaken you for God that day. But you're not, you're not, and let you remember it! Let you look sometimes for the goodness in me, and judge me not.

ELIZABETH: I do not judge you. The magistrate sits in your heart that judges you. I never thought you but a good man, John—*with a smile*—only somewhat bewildered.

PROCTOR, *laughing bitterly:* Oh, Elizabeth, your justice would freeze beer! *He turns suddenly toward a sound outside. He starts for the door as Mary Warren enters. As soon as he sees her, he goes directly to her and grabs her by her cloak, furious.* How do you go to Salem when I forbid it? Do you mock me? *Shaking her:* I'll whip you if you dare leave this house again! *Strangely, she doesn't resist him but hangs limply by his grip.*

MARY WARREN: I am sick, I am sick, Mr. Proctor. Pray, pray, hurt me not. *Her strangeness throws him off, and her evident pallor[4] and weakness. He frees her.* My insides are all shuddery; I am in the proceedings all day, sir.

---

4. **pallor.** Pale complexion

> **loft · i · ly** (lôft´ ə lē) *adv.,* with a tone of superiority or self-pride

Proctor, *with draining anger—his curiosity is draining it:* And what of these proceedings here? When will you proceed to keep this house, as you are paid nine pound a year to do—and my wife not wholly well? *As though to compensate, Mary Warren goes to Elizabeth with a small rag doll.*

Mary Warren: I made a gift for you today, Goody Proctor. I had to sit long hours in a chair, and passed the time with sewing.

Elizabeth, *perplexed, looking at the doll:* Why, thank you, it's a fair poppet.[5]

Mary Warren, *with a trembling, decayed voice:* We must all love each other now, Goody Proctor.

Elizabeth, *amazed at her strangeness:* Aye, indeed, we must.

Mary Warren, *glancing at the room:* I'll get up early in the morning and clean the house. I must sleep now. *She turns and starts off.*

Proctor: Mary. *She halts.* Is it true? There be fourteen women arrested?

Mary Warren: No, sir. There be thirty-nine now—*She suddenly breaks off and sobs and sits down, exhausted.*

Elizabeth: Why, she's weepin'! What ails you, child?

Mary Warren: Goody Osburn—will hang! *There is a shocked pause, while she sobs.*

Proctor: Hang! *He calls into her face.* Hang, y'say?

Mary Warren, *through her weeping:* Aye.

Proctor: The Deputy Governor will permit it?

Mary Warren: He sentenced her. He must. *To ameliorate it:* But not Sarah Good. For Sarah Good confessed, y'see.

Proctor: Confessed! To what?

Mary Warren: That she—*in horror at the memory*—she sometimes made a compact with Lucifer, and wrote her name in his black book—with her blood—and bound herself to torment Christians till God's thrown down—and we all must worship Hell forevermore.

Pause.

Proctor: But—surely you know what a jabberer she is. Did you tell them that?

Mary Warren: Mr. Proctor, in open court she near to choked us all to death.

Proctor: How, choked you?

Mary Warren: She sent her spirit out.

Elizabeth: Oh, Mary, Mary, surely you—

Mary Warren, *with an indignant edge:* She tried to kill me many times, Goody Proctor!

Elizabeth: Why, I never heard you mention that before.

Mary Warren: I never knew it before. I never knew anything before. When she come into the court I say to myself, I must not accuse this woman, for she sleep in ditches, and so very old and poor. But then—then she sit there, denying and denying, and I feel a misty coldness climbin' up my back, and the skin on my skull begin to creep, and I feel a clamp around my neck and I cannot breathe air; and then—*entranced*—I hear a voice, a screamin' voice, and it were my voice—and all at once I remember everything she done to me!

Proctor: Why? What did she do to you?

Mary Warren, *like one awakened to a marvelous secret insight:* So many time, Mr. Proctor, she come to this very door, beggin' bread and a cup of cider—and mark this: whenever I turned her away empty, she *mumbled.*

> "I feel a misty coldness climbin' up my back, and the skin on my skull begin to creep."

---

5. **poppet.** Old English term for *doll*

ame • li • o • rate (ä me´ lē ōr āt) *v.,* make better or more tolerable

ELIZABETH: Mumbled! She may mumble if she's hungry.

MARY WARREN: But *what* does she mumble? You must remember, Goody Proctor. Last month—a Monday, I think—she walked away, and I thought my guts would burst for two days after. Do you remember it?

ELIZABETH: Why—I do, I think, but—

MARY WARREN: And so I told that to Judge Hathorne, and he asks her so. "Goody Osburn," says he, "what curse do you mumble that this girl must fall sick after turning you away?" And then she replies—*mimicking an old crone[6]*—Why, your excellence, no curse at all. I only say my commandments; I hope I may say my commandments," says she!

ELIZABETH: And that's an upright answer.

MARY WARREN: Aye, but then Judge Hathorne say, "Recite for us your commandments!"—*leaning avidly toward them*—and of all the ten she could not say a single one. She never knew no commandments, and they had her in a flat lie!

PROCTOR: And so condemned her?

MARY WARREN, *now a little strained, seeing his stubborn doubt:* Why, they must when she condemned herself.

PROCTOR: But the proof, the proof!

MARY WARREN, *with greater impatience with him:* I told you the proof. It's hard proof, hard as rock, the judges said.

PROCTOR—*he pauses an instant, then:* You will not go to court again, Mary Warren.

MARY WARREN: I must tell you, sir, I will be gone every day now. I am amazed you do not see what weighty work we do.

PROCTOR: What work you do! It's strange work for a Christian girl to hang old women!

MARY WARREN: But, Mr. Proctor, they will not hang them if they confess. Sarah Good will only sit in jail some time—*recalling*—and here's a wonder for you; think on this. Goody Good is pregnant!

ELIZABETH: Pregnant! Are they mad? The woman's near to sixty!

MARY WARREN: They had Doctor Griggs examine her, and she's full to the brim. And smokin' a pipe all these years, and no husband either! But she's safe, thank God, for they'll not hurt the innocent child. But be that not a marvel? You must see it, sir, it's God's work we do. So I'll be gone every day for some time. I'm—I am an official of the court, they say, and I—*She has been edging toward offstage.*

PROCTOR: I'll official you! *He strides to the mantel, takes down the whip hanging there.*

MARY WARREN, *terrified, but coming erect, striving for her authority:* I'll not stand whipping any more!

ELIZABETH, *hurriedly, as Proctor approaches:* Mary, promise now you'll stay at home—

MARY WARREN, *backing from him, but keeping her erect posture, striving, striving for her way:* The Devil's loose in Salem, Mr. Proctor; we must discover where he's hiding!

PROCTOR: I'll whip the Devil out of you! *With whip raised he reaches out for her, and she streaks away and yells.*

MARY WARREN, *pointing at Elizabeth:* I saved her life today!

Silence. His whip comes down.

ELIZABETH, *softly:* I am accused?

MARY WARREN, *quaking:* Somewhat mentioned. But I said I never see no sign you ever sent your spirit out to hurt no one, and seeing I do live so closely with you, they dismissed it.

ELIZABETH: Who accused me?

"The Devil's loose in Salem, Mr. Proctor; we must discover where he's hiding!"

---

6. **crone.** Withered old woman

MARY WARREN: I am bound by law, I cannot tell it. *To Proctor:* I only hope you'll not be so sarcastical no more. Four judges and the King's deputy sat to dinner with us but an hour ago. I—I would have you speak civilly to me, from this out.

PROCTOR, *in horror, muttering in disgust at her:* Go to bed.

MARY WARREN, *with a stamp of her foot:* I'll not be ordered to bed no more, Mr. Proctor! I am eighteen and a woman, however single!

PROCTOR: Do you wish to sit up? Then sit up.

MARY WARREN: I wish to go to bed!

PROCTOR, *in anger:* Good night, then!

MARY WARREN: Good night. *Dissatisfied, uncertain of herself, she goes out. Wide-eyed, both Proctor and Elizabeth stand staring.*

ELIZABETH, *quietly:* Oh, the noose, the noose is up!

PROCTOR: There'll be no noose.

ELIZABETH: She wants me dead. I knew all week it would come to this!

PROCTOR, *without conviction:* They dismissed it. You heard her say—

ELIZABETH: And what of tomorrow? She will cry me out until they take me!

PROCTOR: Sit you down.

ELIZABETH: She wants me dead, John, you know it!

PROCTOR: I say sit down! *She sits, trembling. He speaks quietly, trying to keep his wits.* Now we must be wise, Elizabeth.

ELIZABETH, *with sarcasm, and a sense of being lost:* Oh, indeed, indeed!

PROCTOR: Fear nothing. I'll find Ezekiel Cheever. I'll tell him she said it were all sport.

John Proctor (Daniel Day-Lewis) confronts Abigail Williams (Winona Ryder) in the 1996 film version of *The Crucible.*

ELIZABETH: John, with so many in the jail, more than Cheever's help is needed now, I think. Would you favor me with this? Go to Abigail.

PROCTOR, *his soul hardening as he senses:* . . . . What have I to say to Abigail?

ELIZABETH, *delicately:* John—grant me this. You have a faulty understanding of young girls. There is a promise made in any bed—

PROCTOR, *striving against his anger:* What promise!

ELIZABETH: Spoke or silent, a promise is surely made. And she may dote on it now—I am sure she does—and thinks to kill me, then to take my place.

Proctor's anger is rising; he cannot speak.

ELIZABETH: It is her dearest hope, John, I know it. There be a thousand names; why does she call mine? There be a certain danger in calling such a name—I am no Goody Good that sleeps in ditches, nor Osburn, drunk and half-witted. She'd dare not call out such a farmer's wife but there be monstrous profit in it. She thinks to take my place, John.

PROCTOR: She cannot think it! *He knows it is true.*

ELIZABETH, "reasonably": John, have you ever shown her somewhat of contempt? She cannot pass you in the church but you will blush—

PROCTOR: I may blush for my sin.

ELIZABETH: I think she sees another meaning in that blush.

PROCTOR: And what see you? What see you, Elizabeth?

ELIZABETH, "conceding": I think you be somewhat ashamed, for I am there, and she so close.

PROCTOR: When will you know me, woman? Were I stone I would have cracked for shame this seven month!

ELIZABETH: Then go and tell her she's a whore. Whatever promise she may sense—break it, John, break it.

PROCTOR, between his teeth: Good, then. I'll go. He starts for his rifle.

ELIZABETH, trembling, fearfully: Oh, how unwillingly!

PROCTOR, turning on her, rifle in hand: I will curse her hotter than the oldest cinder in hell. But pray, begrudge me not my anger!

ELIZABETH: Your anger! I only ask you—

PROCTOR: Woman, am I so base? Do you truly think me base?

ELIZABETH: I never called you base.

PROCTOR: Then how do you charge me with such a promise? The promise that a stallion gives a mare I gave that girl![7]

ELIZABETH: Then why do you anger with me when I bid you break it?

PROCTOR: Because it speaks deceit, and I am honest! But I'll plead no more! I see now your spirit twists around the single error of my life, and I will never tear it free!

ELIZABETH, crying out: You'll tear it free—when you come to know that I will be your only wife, or no wife at all! She has an arrow in you yet, John Proctor, and you know it well!

Quite suddenly, as though from the air, a figure appears in the doorway. They start slightly. It is Mr. Hale. He is different now—drawn a little, and there is a quality of <u>deference</u>, even of guilt, about his manner now.

HALE: Good evening.

PROCTOR, still in his shock: Why, Mr. Hale! Good evening to you, sir. Come in, come in.

HALE, to Elizabeth: I hope I do not startle you.

ELIZABETH: No, no, it's only that I heard no horse—

HALE: You are Goodwife Proctor.

PROCTOR: Aye; Elizabeth.

HALE—he nods, then: I hope you're not off to bed yet.

PROCTOR, setting down his gun: No, no. Hale comes further into the room. And Proctor, to explain his nervousness: We are not used to visitors after dark, but you're welcome here. Will you sit you down, sir?

HALE: I will. He sits. Let you sit, Goodwife Proctor. She does, never letting him out of her sight. There is a pause as Hale looks about the room.

PROCTOR, to break the silence: Will you drink cider, Mr. Hale?

HALE: No, it rebels my stomach; I have some further traveling yet tonight. Sit you down, sir. Proctor sits. I will not keep you long, but I have some business with you.

PROCTOR: Business of the court?

HALE: No—no, I come of my own, without the court's authority. Hear me. He wets his lips. I know not if you are aware, but your wife's name is—mentioned in the court.

---

7. **The promise that a stallion gives a mare . . .** Proctor is implying that his relationship with Abigail was no more romantic or meaningful than that between a male and a female horse.

def • er • ence (def´ ə rənts) *n.*, respect or esteem for an elder or superior

PROCTOR: We know it, sir. Our Mary Warren told us. We are entirely amazed.

HALE: I am a stranger here, as you know. And in my ignorance I find it hard to draw a clear opinion of them that come accused before the court. And so this afternoon, and now tonight, I go from house to house—I come now from Rebecca Nurse's house and—

ELIZABETH, *shocked:* Rebecca's charged!

HALE: God forbid such a one be charged. She is, however—mentioned somewhat.

ELIZABETH, *with an attempt at a laugh:* You will never believe, I hope, that Rebecca trafficked with the Devil.

HALE: Woman, it is possible.

PROCTOR, *taken aback:* Surely you cannot think so.

HALE: This is a strange time, Mister. No man may longer doubt the powers of the dark are gathered in monstrous attack upon this village. There is too much evidence now to deny it. You will agree, sir?

PROCTOR, *evading:* I—have no knowledge in that line. But it's hard to think so <u>pious</u> a woman be secretly a Devil's bitch after seventy year of such good prayer.

HALE: Aye. But the Devil is a wily one, you cannot deny it. However, she is far from accused, and I know she will not be. *Pause.* I thought, sir, to put some questions as to the Christian character of this house, if you'll permit me.

PROCTOR, *coldly, resentful:* Why, we—have no fear of questions, sir.

HALE: Good, then. *He makes himself more comfortable.* In the book of record that Mr. Parris keeps, I note that you are rarely in the church on Sabbath Day.[8]

PROCTOR: No, sir, you are mistaken.

HALE: Twenty-six time in seventeen month, sir. I must call that rare. Will you tell me why you are so absent?

PROCTOR: Mr. Hale, I never knew I must account to that man for I come to church or stay at home. My wife were sick this winter.

HALE: So I am told. But you, Mister, why could you not come alone?

PROCTOR: I surely did come when I could, and when I could not I prayed in this house.

HALE: Mr. Proctor, your house is not a church; your theology must tell you that.

PROCTOR: It does, sir, it does; and it tells me that a minister may pray to God without he have golden candlesticks upon the altar.

HALE: What golden candlesticks?

PROCTOR: Since we built the church there were pewter candlesticks upon the altar; Francis Nurse made them, y'know, and a sweeter hand never touched the metal. But Parris came, and for twenty week he preach nothin' but golden candlesticks until he had them. I labor the earth from dawn of day to blink of night, and I tell you true, when I look to heaven and see my money glaring at his elbows—it hurt my prayer, sir, it hurt my prayer. I think, sometimes, the man dreams cathedrals, not clapboard meetin' houses.

HALE—*he thinks, then:* And yet, Mister, a Christian on Sabbath Day must be in church. *Pause.* Tell me—you have three children?

PROCTOR: Aye. Boys.

HALE: How comes it that only two are baptized?

PROCTOR—*he starts to speak, then stops, then, as though unable to restrain this:* I like it not that Mr. Parris should lay his hand upon my baby. I see no light of God in that man. I'll not conceal it.

---

8. **Sabbath Day.** In Christianity, Sunday, a day of rest and worship

---

evade (ē vād´) *v.,* avoid answering directly
pi • ous (pī´ əs) *adj.,* devoted to divine worship; religious

HALE: I must say it, Mr. Proctor; that is not for you to decide. The man's ordained, therefore the light of God is in him.

PROCTOR, *flushed with resentment but trying to smile:* What's your suspicion, Mr. Hale?

HALE: No, no, I have no—

PROCTOR: I nailed the roof upon the church, I hung the door—

HALE: Oh, did you! That's a good sign, then.

PROCTOR: It may be I have been too quick to bring the man to book, but you cannot think we ever desired the destruction of religion. I think that's in your mind, is it not?

HALE, *not altogether giving way:* I—have—there is a softness in your record, sir, a softness.

ELIZABETH: I think, maybe, we have been too hard with Mr. Parris, I think so. But sure we never loved the Devil here.

HALE—*he nods, deliberating this. Then, with the voice of one administering a secret test:* Do you know your Commandments, Elizabeth?

ELIZABETH, *without hesitation, even eagerly:* I surely do. There be no mark of blame upon my life, Mr. Hale. I am a convenanted Christian woman.

HALE: And you, Mister?

PROCTOR, *a trifle unsteadily:* I—am sure I do, sir.

HALE—*he glances at her open face, then at John, then:* Let you repeat them, if you will.

PROCTOR: The Commandments.

HALE: Aye.

PROCTOR, *looking off, beginning to sweat:* Thou shalt not kill.

HALE: Aye.

PROCTOR, *counting on his fingers:* Thou shalt not steal. Thou shalt not covet thy neighbor's goods, nor make unto thee any graven image. Thou shalt not take the name of the Lord in vain; thou shalt have no other gods before me. *With some hesitation:* Thou shalt remember the Sabbath Day and keep it holy. *Pause. Then:* Thou shalt honor thy father and mother. Thou shalt not bear false witness. *He is stuck. He counts back on his fingers, knowing one is missing.* Thou shalt not make unto thee any graven image.

HALE: You have said that twice, sir.

PROCTOR, *lost:* Aye. *He is flailing for it.*

ELIZABETH, *delicately:* Adultery, John.

PROCTOR, *as though a secret arrow had pained his heart:* Aye. *Trying to grin it away—to Hale:* You see, sir, between the two of us we do know them all. *Hale only looks at Proctor, deep in his attempt to define this man. Proctor grows more uneasy.* I think it be a small fault.

HALE: Theology, sir, is a fortress; no crack in a fortress may be accounted small. *He rises;*

he seems worried now. He paces a little, in deep thought.

PROCTOR: There be no love for Satan in this house, Mister.

HALE: I pray it, I pray it dearly. *He looks to both of them, an attempt at a smile on his face, but his misgivings are clear.* Well, then—I'll bid you good night.

ELIZABETH, *unable to restrain herself:* Mr. Hale. *He turns.* I do think you are suspecting me somewhat? Are you not?

HALE, *obviously disturbed—and evasive:* Goody Proctor, I do not judge you. My duty is to add what I may to the godly wisdom of the court. I pray you both good health and good fortune. *To John:* Good night, sir. *He starts out.*

ELIZABETH, *with a note of desperation:* I think you must tell him, John.

HALE: What's that?

ELIZABETH, *restraining a call:* Will you tell him?

Slight pause. Hale looks questioningly at John.

PROCTOR, *with difficulty:* I—I have no witness and cannot prove it, except my word be taken. But I know the children's sickness had naught to do with witchcraft.

HALE, *stopped, struck:* Naught to do—?

PROCTOR: Mr. Parris discovered them sportin' in the woods. They were startled and took sick.

Pause.

HALE: Who told you this?

PROCTOR—*he hesitates, then:* Abigail Williams.

HALE: Abigail!

PROCTOR: Aye.

HALE, *his eyes wide:* Abigail Williams told you it had naught to do with witchcraft!

PROCTOR: She told me the day you came, sir.

HALE, *suspiciously:* Why—why did you keep this?

PROCTOR: I never knew until tonight that the world is gone daft with this nonsense.

HALE: Nonsense! Mister, I have myself examined Tituba, Sarah Good, and numerous others that have confessed to dealing with the Devil. They have *confessed* it.

PROCTOR: And why not, if they must hang for denyin' it? There are them that will swear to anything before they'll hang; have you never thought of that?

HALE: I have. I—I have indeed. *It is his own suspicion, but he resists it. He glances at Elizabeth, then at John.* And you—would you testify to this in court?

PROCTOR: I—had not reckoned with goin' into court. But if I must I will.

HALE: Do you falter here?

PROCTOR: I falter nothing, but I may wonder if my story will be credited in such a court. I do wonder on it, when such a steady-minded minister as you will suspicion such a woman that never lied, and cannot, and the world knows she cannot! I may falter somewhat, Mister; I am no fool.

HALE, *quietly—it has impressed him:* Proctor, let you open with me now, for I have a rumor that troubles me. It's said you hold no belief that there may even be witches in the world. Is that true, sir?

PROCTOR—*he knows this is critical, and is striving against his disgust with Hale and with himself for even answering:* I know not what I have said, I may have said it. I have wondered if there be witches in the world—although I cannot believe they come among us now.

HALE: Then you do not believe—

PROCTOR: I have no knowledge of it; the Bible speaks of witches, and I will not deny them.

HALE: And you, woman?

ELIZABETH: I—I cannot believe it.

HALE, *shocked:* You cannot!

PROCTOR: Elizabeth, you bewilder him!

ELIZABETH, *to Hale:* I cannot think the Devil may own a woman's soul, Mr. Hale, when she keeps an upright way, as I have. I am a good woman, I know it; and if you believe I may do only good work in the world, and yet be secretly bound to Satan, then I must tell you, sir, I do not believe it.

HALE: But, woman, you do believe there are witches in—

ELIZABETH: If you think that I am one, then I say there are none.

HALE: You surely do not fly against the Gospel, the Gospel—

PROCTOR: She believe in the Gospel, every word!

ELIZABETH: Question Abigail Williams about the Gospel, not myself!

Hale stares at her.

PROCTOR: She do not mean to doubt the Gospel, sir, you cannot think it. This be a Christian house, sir, a Christian house.

HALE: God keep you both; let the third child be quickly baptized, and go you without fail each Sunday in to Sabbath prayer; and keep a solemn, quiet way among you. I think—

Giles Corey appears in doorway.

GILES: John!

PROCTOR: Giles! What's the matter?

GILES: They take my wife.

Francis Nurse enters.

GILES: And his Rebecca!

PROCTOR, *to Francis:* Rebecca's in the *jail!*

FRANCES: Aye, Cheever come and take her in his wagon. We've only now come from the jail, and they'll not even let us in to see them.

ELIZABETH: They've surely gone wild now, Mr. Hale!

FRANCES, *going to Hale:* Reverend Hale! Can you not speak to the Deputy Governor? I'm sure he mistakes these people—

HALE: Pray calm yourself, Mr. Nurse.

FRANCES: My wife is the very brick and mortar of the church, Mr. Hale—*indicating Giles*—and Martha Corey, there cannot be a woman closer yet to God than Martha.

HALE: How is Rebecca charged, Mr. Nurse?

FRANCES, *with a mocking, half-hearted laugh:* For murder, she's charged! *Mockingly quoting the warrant:* "For the marvelous and supernatural murder of Goody Putnam's babies." What am I to do, Mr. Hale?

HALE, *he turns from Francis, deeply troubled, then:* Believe me, Mr. Nurse, if Rebecca Nurse be tainted, then nothing's left to stop the whole green world from burning. Let you rest upon the justice of the court; the court will send her home, I know it.

> "If you think that I am one, then I say there are none."

FRANCIS: You cannot mean she will be tried in court!

HALE, *pleading:* Nurse, though our hearts break, we cannot flinch; these are new times, sir. There is a misty plot afoot so subtle we should be criminal to cling to old respects and ancient friendships. I have seen too many frightful proofs in court—the Devil is alive in Salem, and we dare not quail to follow wherever the accusing finger points!

PROCTOR, *angered:* How may such a woman murder children?

HALE, *in great pain:* Man, remember, until an hour before the Devil fell, God thought him beautiful in Heaven.

GILES: I never said my wife were a witch, Mr. Hale; I only said she were reading books!

The recorded testimony of Abigail Williams against Elizabeth Proctor, dated May 31, 1692.

HALE: Mr. Corey, exactly what complaint were made on your wife?

GILES: That bloody mongrel Walcott charge her. Y'see, he buy a pig of my wife four or five year ago, and the pig died soon after. So he come dancin' in for his money back. So my Martha, she says to him, "Walcott, if you haven't the wit to feed a pig properly, you'll not live to own many," she says. Now he goes to court and claims that from that day to this he cannot keep a pig alive for more than four weeks because my Martha bewitch them with her books!

Enter Ezekiel Cheever. A shocked silence.

CHEEVER: Good evening to you, Proctor.

PROCTOR: Why, Mr. Cheever. Good evening.

CHEEVER: Good evening, all. Good evening, Mr. Hale.

PROCTOR: I hope you come not on business of the court.

CHEEVER: I do, Proctor, aye. I am clerk of the court now, y'know.

Enter Marshal Herrick, a man in his early thirties, who is somewhat shamefaced at the moment.

GILES: It's a pity, Ezekiel, that an honest tailor might have gone to Heaven must burn in Hell. You'll burn for this, do you know it?

CHEEVER: You know yourself I must do as I'm told. You surely know that, Giles. And I'd as lief you'd not be sending me to Hell. I like not the sound of it, I tell you; I like not the sound of it. *He fears Proctor, but starts to reach inside his coat.* Now believe me, Proctor, how heavy be the law, all its tonnage I do carry on my back tonight. *He takes out a warrant.* I have a warrant for your wife.

PROCTOR, *to Hale:* You said she were not charged!

HALE: I know nothin' of it. *To Cheever:* "When were she charged?

CHEEVER: I am given sixteen warrant tonight, sir, and she is one.

PROCTOR: Who charged her?

CHEEVER: Why, Abigail Williams charge her.

PROCTOR: On what proof, what proof?

CHEEVER, *looking about the room:* Mr. Proctor, I have little time. The court bid me search your house, but I like not to search a house. So will you hand me any poppets that your wife may keep here?

PROCTOR: Poppets?

ELIZABETH: I never kept no poppets, not since I were a girl.

CHEEVER, *embarrassed, glancing toward the mantel where sits Mary Warren's poppet:* I spy a poppet, Goody Proctor.

ELIZABETH: Oh! *Going for it:* Why, this is Mary's.

CHEEVER, *shyly:* Would you please to give it to me?

ELIZABETH, *handing it to him, asks Hale:* Has the court discovered a text in poppets now?

CHEEVER, *carefully holding the poppet:* Do you keep any others in this house?

PROCTOR: No, nor this one either till tonight. What signifies a poppet?

CHEEVER: Why, a poppet:—*he gingerly turns the poppet over*—a poppet may signify—Now, woman, will you please to come with me?

PROCTOR: She will not! *To Elizabeth:* Fetch Mary here.

CHEEVER, *ineptly reaching toward Elizabeth:* No, no, I am forbid to leave her from my sight.

PROCTOR, *pushing his arm away:* You'll leave her out of sight and out of mind, Mister. Fetch Mary, Elizabeth. *Elizabeth goes upstairs.*

HALE: What signifies a poppet, Mr. Cheever?

CHEEVER, *turning the poppet over in his hands:* Why, they say it may signify that she—*He has lifted the poppet's skirt, and his eyes widen in astonished fear.* Why, this, this—

PROCTOR, *reaching for the poppet:* What's there?

CHEEVER: Why—*he draws out a long needle from the poppet*—it is a needle! Herrick, Herrick, it is a needle!

Herrick comes toward him.

PROCTOR, *angrily, bewildered:* And what signifies a needle!

CHEEVER, *his hands shaking:* Why, this go hard with her, Proctor, this—I had my doubts, Proctor, I had my doubts, but here's calamity. *To Hale, showing the needle:* You see it, sir, it is a needle!

HALE: Why? What meanin' has it?

CHEEVER, *wide-eyed, trembling:* The girl, the Williams girl, Abigail Williams, sir. She sat to dinner in Reverend Parris's house tonight, and without word nor warnin' she falls to the floor. Like a struck beast, he says, and screamed a scream that a bull would weep to hear. And he goes to save her, and, stuck two inches in the flesh of her belly, he draw a needle out. And demandin' of her how she come to be so stabbed, she—*to Proctor now*—testify it were your wife's familiar spirit pushed it in.

PROCTOR: Why, she done it herself! *To Hale:* I hope you're not takin' this for proof, Mister!

Hale, struck by the proof, is silent.

CHEEVER: 'Tis hard proof! *To Hale:* I find here a poppet Goody Proctor keeps. I have found it, sir. And in the belly of the poppet a needle's stuck. I tell you true, Proctor, I never warranted to see such proof of Hell, and I bid you obstruct me not, for I—

Enter Elizabeth with Mary Warren. Proctor, seeing Mary Warren, draws her by the arm to Hale.

PROCTOR: Here now! Mary, how did this poppet come into my house?

MARY WARREN, *frightened for herself, her voice very small:* What poppet's that, sir?

PROCTOR, *impatiently, pointing at the doll in Cheever's hand:* This poppet, this poppet.

MARY WARREN, *evasively, looking at it:* Why, I—I think it is mine.

PROCTOR: It is your poppet, is it not?

MARY WARREN, *not understanding the direction of this:* It—is, sir.

PROCTOR: And how did it come into this house?

MARY WARREN, *glancing about at the avid faces:* Why—I made it in the court, sir, and—give it to Goody Proctor tonight.

PROCTOR, *to Hale:* Now, sir—do you have it?

HALE: Mary Warren, a needle have been found inside this poppet.

MARY WARREN, *bewildered:* Why, I meant no harm by it, sir.

PROCTOR, *quickly:* You stuck that needle in yourself?

MARY WARREN: I—I believe I did, sir, I—

PROCTOR, *to Hale:* What say you now?

HALE, *watching Mary Warren closely:* Child, you are certain this be your natural memory? May it be, perhaps, that someone conjures you even now to say this?

MARY WARREN: Conjures me? Why, no, sir, I am entirely myself, I think. Let you ask Susanna Walcott—she saw me sewin' it in court. *Or better still:* Ask Abby, Abby sat beside me when I made it.

PROCTOR, *to Hale, of Cheever:* Bid him begone. Your mind is surely settled now. Bid him out, Mr. Hale.

ELIZABETH: What signifies a needle?

HALE: Mary—you charge a cold and cruel murder on Abigail.

MARY WARREN: Murder! I charge no—

HALE: Abigail were stabbed tonight; a needle were found stuck into her belly—

ELIZABETH: And she charges me?

HALE: Aye.

ELIZABETH, *her breath knocked out:* Why—! The girl is murder! She must be ripped out of the world!

CHEEVER, *pointing at Elizabeth:* You've heard that, sir! Ripped out of the world! Herrick, you heard it!

PROCTOR, *suddenly snatching the warrant out of Cheever's hands:* Out with you.

CHEEVER: Proctor, you dare not touch the warrant.

PROCTOR, *ripping the warrant:* Out with you!

CHEEVER: You've ripped the Deputy Governor's warrant, man!

> "Now the little crazy children are jangling the keys of the kingdom, and common vengeance writes the law!"

PROCTOR: Damn the Deputy Governor! Out of my house!

HALE: Now, Proctor, Proctor!

PROCTOR: Get y'gone with them! You are a broken minister.

HALE: Proctor, if she is innocent, the court—

PROCTOR: If *she* is innocent! Why do you never wonder if Parris be innocent, or Abigail? Is the accuser always holy now? Were they born this morning as clean as God's fingers? I'll tell you what's walking Salem—vengeance is walking Salem. We are what we always were in Salem, but now the little crazy children are jangling the keys of the kingdom, and common vengeance writes the law! This warrant's vengeance! I'll not give my wife to vengeance!

ELIZABETH: I'll go, John—

PROCTOR: You will not go!

HERRICK: I have nine men outside. You cannot keep her. The law binds me, John, I cannot budge.

PROCTOR, *to Hale, ready to break him:* Will you see her taken?

HALE: Proctor, the court is just—

PROCTOR: Pontius Pilate![9] God will not let you wash your hands of this!

ELIZABETH: John—I think I must go with them. *He cannot bear to look at her.* Mary, there is bread enough for the morning; you will bake, in the afternoon. Help Mr. Proctor as you were his daughter—you owe me that, and much more. *She is fighting her weeping. To Proctor:* When the children wake, speak nothing of witchcraft—it will frighten them. *She cannot go on.*

PROCTOR: I will bring you home. I will bring you soon.

ELIZABETH: Oh, John, bring me soon!

PROCTOR: I will fall like an ocean on that court! Fear nothing, Elizabeth.

ELIZABETH, *with great fear:* I will fear nothing. *She looks about the room, as though to fix it in her mind.* Tell the children I have gone to visit someone sick.

She walks out the door, Herrick and Cheever behind her. For a moment, Proctor watches from the doorway. The clank of chain is heard.

PROCTOR: Herrick! Herrick, don't chain her! *He rushes out the door. From outside:* Damn you, man, you will not chain her! Off with them! I'll not have it! I will not have her chained!

There are other men's voices against his. Hale, in a fever of guilt and uncertainty, turns from the door to avoid the sight; Mary Warren bursts into tears and sits weeping. Giles Corey calls to Hale.

GILES: And yet silent, minister? It is fraud, you know it is fraud! What keeps you, man?

Proctor is half braced, half pushed into the room by two deputies and Herrick.

PROCTOR: I'll pay you, Herrick, I will surely pay you!

HERRICK, *panting:* In God's name, John, I cannot help myself. I must chain them all. Now let you keep inside this house till I am gone! *He goes out with his deputies.*

Proctor stands there, gulping air. Horses and a wagon creaking are heard.

HALE, *in great uncertainty:* Mr. Proctor—

PROCTOR: Out of my sight!

HALE: Charity, Proctor, charity. What I have heard in her favor, I will not fear to testify in court. God help me, I cannot judge her guilty or innocent—I know not. Only this consider: the world goes mad, and it profit nothing you should lay the cause to the vengeance of a little girl.

PROCTOR: You are a coward! Though you be ordained in God's own tears, you are a coward now!

HALE: Proctor, I cannot think God be provoked so grandly by such a petty cause. The jails are packed—our greatest judges sit in Salem now—and hangin's promised. Man, we must look to cause proportionate. Were there murder done, perhaps, and never brought to light? Abomination? Some secret blasphemy[10] that stinks to Heaven? Think on cause, man, and let you help me to discover it. For there's your way, believe it, there is your only way, when such confusion strikes upon the world. *He goes to Giles and Francis.* Let you counsel among yourselves; think on your village and what may have drawn from Heaven such thundering wrath upon you all. I shall pray God open up our eyes.

Hale goes out.

FRANCES, *struck by Hale's mood:* I never heard no murder done in Salem.

PROCTOR—*he has been reached by Hale's words:* Leave me, Francis, leave me.

GILES, *shaken:* John—tell me, are we lost?

---

9. **Pontius Pilate.** According to the Bible, the Roman official who ordered the crucifixion of Jesus Christ
10. **blasphemy.** Act of showing contempt for God

Proctor: Go home now, Giles. We'll speak on it tomorrow.

Giles: Let you think on it. We'll come early, eh?

Proctor: Aye. Go now, Giles.

Giles: Good night, then.

Giles Corey and Francis Nurse go out. After a moment:

Mary Warren, *in a fearful squeak of a voice:* Mr. Proctor, very likely they'll let her come home once they're given proper evidence.

Proctor: You're coming to the court with me, Mary. You will tell it in the court.

Mary Warren: I cannot charge murder on Abigail.

Proctor, *moving menacingly toward her:* You will tell the court how that poppet come here and who stuck the needle in.

Mary Warren: She'll kill me for sayin' that! *Proctor continues toward her.* Abby'll charge lechery on you, Mr. Proctor!

Proctor, *halting:* She's told you!

Mary Warren: I have known it, sir. She'll ruin you with it, I know she will.

Proctor, *hesitating, and with deep hatred of himself:* Good. Then her saintliness is done with.

Mary backs from him. We will slide together into our pit; you will tell the court what you know.

Mary Warren, *in terror:* I cannot, they'll turn on me—

Proctor strides and catches her, and she is repeating, "I cannot, I cannot!"

Proctor: My wife will never die for me! I will bring your guts into your mouth but that goodness will not die for me!

Mary Warren, *struggling to escape him:* I cannot do it, I cannot!

Proctor, *grasping her by the throat as though he would strangle her:* Make your peace with it! Now Hell and Heaven grapple on our backs, and all our old pretense is ripped away—make your peace! *He throws her to the floor, where she sobs, "I cannot, I cannot . . ." And now, half to himself, staring, and turning to the open door:* Peace. It is a providence, and no great change; we are only what we always were, but naked now. *He walks as though toward a great horror, facing the open sky.* Aye, naked! And the wind, God's icy wind, will blow!

And she is over and over again sobbing, "I cannot, I cannot, I cannot," as

THE CURTAIN FALLS ❖

Proctor points out that some people "will swear to anything before they'll hang." Recall a time when you wanted to stand up against an injustice but did not do anything. What kept you from acting on your belief?

Refer to Text ▷ ▷ ▶ ▶ ▶ **Reason with Text**

1a. What are the first topics John and Elizabeth Proctor discuss when John comes home?	**1b.** What does the nature of the couple's conversation suggest about their relationship?	**Understand** Find meaning
2a. According to Mary Warren, how did Goody Osburn "condemn herself" in court?	**2b.** Explain why the people of Salem might consider Goody Osburn's court experience as "hard proof" of her guilt.	**Apply** Use information
3a. Identify three bits of gossip Reverend Hale says he has heard about John Proctor.	**3b.** Infer what the people of Salem think about Proctor. How might their ideas lead them to support Abigail's accusation against Elizabeth?	**Analyze** Take things apart
4a. What does Mary Warren say when John Proctor questions her about the poppet on the mantel?	**4b.** Decide whether Mary is being completely truthful in her admission and explanation. Whom does Mary support: Abigail Williams or Elizabeth Proctor?	**Evaluate** Make judgments
5a. By the end of the scene, what evidence has been provided against Elizabeth Proctor? What facts may be in her favor?	**5b.** Predict Elizabeth's ultimate fate and how it will come about. Explain the factors on which you base your prediction.	**Create** Bring ideas together

Analyze Literature

Characterization and Allusion

Review the examples you found of direct and indirect characterization. Which method does Miller use most often? What do we learn about Reverend Hale through Miller's characterization of him? Discuss why this might be significant.

Explain the allusions in this act of the play, particularly those in reference to biblical figures and events. For instance, what does Elizabeth's allusion to the parting of the Red Sea suggest about Abigail's influence? What does John Proctor suggest by alluding to Pontius Pilate?

Extend the Text

Writing Options

Creative Writing Based on the questions asked so far and the information given about the behavior of witches, write a manual for Salem residents on how to identify witches. The tone of the manual should be ironic, as there really were not any witches in Salem.

Expository Writing Write a paragraph explaining the allusion in the title of Miller's play. Consider in what double sense the witch hunt is a crucible for the major characters in the drama.

Collaborative Learning

Perform a Scene Choose a scene from the play to perform with your classmates. Pay close attention to the stage directions that indicate tone of voice and movement. Make sure that all the performers understand their *blocking*, or movements on stage, as well as their lines.

Media Literacy

Practice Making Transcripts Much of what is known about the Salem witch trials comes from transcripts of the court proceedings. Go online to find the Salem transcripts or those from the McCarthy hearings (see pages 953–955). Review how a person's speech is recorded, including mistakes and restarts. Practice making a transcript of a segment of a television broadcast in which one or two people are interviewed.

 Go to **www.mirrorsandwindows.com** for more.

The Crucible, Act 3

A Drama by Arthur Miller

Build Background

Historical Context Act 3 of *The Crucible* opens in the Salem courtroom with Giles Corey accusing Thomas Putnam of intentionally deceiving the court. His claim is rejected, and Judges Danforth and Hathorne order his removal. The judges punish anyone who pleads for reason or refuses compliance, arguing that the condemned are attempting to thwart the court's efforts. At this point, it becomes clear that the courtroom is no longer operating as an institution of justice. The judges have transformed the investigation into a political campaign to increase their own power.

Literary scholars generally agree that Act 3 serves as an allusion to the congressional committees established in the late 1940s to investigate allegations of communism, which included the House Un-American Activities Committee (HUAC) and the Senate Internal Security Subcommittee (SISS). Like the Salem judges, the politicians heading these committees considered most of their targets guilty until proven innocent and generally relied on unsubstantiated evidence to pursue convictions. When accused individuals exercised their constitutional right to refuse questioning, they often were held in contempt of Congress and put in jail.

There are many similarities between Miller's depiction of the Salem judges and the individuals who fueled McCarthyism. Senator Joseph McCarthy, a conservative Republican senator from Wisconsin, was, like Judge Danforth, suspicious of learning and books. While he was the head of the Senate Permanent Subcommittee on Investigations (SPSI), McCarthy pressured libraries to remove certain titles from their shelves. When Senator Pat McCarran became chairman of the SISS, he asked defendants questions about their private lives that were only minimally related to their political beliefs. In Act 3 of Miller's play, the

Salem judges use the same tactic to intimidate their opponents.

Reader's Context

When you are accused of something that you didn't do, how do you typically react? What kind of argument do you make to try to convince others that you are innocent?

Analyze Literature

Irony and Mood

Irony is a difference between appearance and reality. The three types of irony are *dramatic irony*, in which something is known by the reader or audience but unknown to the characters; *verbal irony*, in which a character says one thing but means another; and *irony of situation*, in which an event occurs that violates the expectations of the characters, the reader, or the audience.

Mood, or atmosphere, is the emotion created in the reader by part or all of the work.

Set Purpose

Miller's play is replete with examples of dramatic and verbal irony. Consider, for instance, the irony in Danforth's claim "The pure in heart need no lawyers." As you read Act 3, record other examples of irony and identify each by type. Also trace the mood as it develops during the course of the act. At what point do you feel sympathetic? Angry?

Preview Vocabulary

contentious, 935
deposition, 936
prodigious, 941
effrontery, 942
confounded, 942
probity, 943
unperturbed, 950
gull, 951

Act 3

The vestry room[1] of the Salem meeting house, now serving as the anteroom[2] of the General Court.

As the curtain rises, the room is empty, but for sunlight pouring through two high windows in the back wall. The room is solemn, even forbidding. Heavy beams jut out, boards of random widths make up the walls. At the right are two doors leading into the meeting house proper, where the court is being held. At the left another door leads outside.

There is a plain bench at the left, and another at the right. In the center a rather long meeting table, with stools and a considerable armchair snugged up to it.

Through the partitioning wall at the right we hear a prosecutor's voice, Judge Hathorne's, asking a question; then a woman's voice, Martha Corey's, replying.

HATHORNE'S VOICE: Now, Martha Corey, there is abundant evidence in our hands to show that you have given yourself to the reading of fortunes. Do you deny it?

MARTHA COREY'S VOICE: I am innocent to a witch. I know not what a witch is.

HATHORNE'S VOICE: How do you know, then, that you are not a witch?

MARTHA COREY'S VOICE: If I were, I would know it.

HATHORNE'S VOICE: Why do you hurt these children?

MARTHA COREY'S VOICE: I do not hurt them. I scorn it!

---

1. **vestry room.** Room used to conduct church meetings
2. **anteroom.** Outer room that leads to another; waiting room

GILES' VOICE, *roaring:* I have evidence for the court!

Voices of townspeople rise in excitement.

DANFORTH'S VOICE: You will keep your seat!

GILES' VOICE: Thomas Putnam is reaching out for land!

DANFORTH'S VOICE: Remove that man, Marshal!

GILES' VOICE: You're hearing lies, lies!

A roaring goes up from the people.

HATHORNE'S VOICE: Arrest him, excellency!

GILES' VOICE: I have evidence. Why will you not hear my evidence?

The door opens and Giles is half carried into the vestry room by Herrick. Francis Nurse enters trailing behind Giles.

GILES: Hands off, damn you, let me go!

HERRICK: Giles, Giles!

GILES: Out of my way, Herrick! I bring evidence—

HERRICK: You cannot go in there, Giles; it's a court!

Enter Hale from the court.

HALE: Pray be calm a moment.

GILES: You, Mr. Hale, go in there and demand I speak.

HALE: A moment, sir, a moment.

GILES: They'll be hangin' my wife!

Judge Hathorne enters. He is in his sixties, a bitter, remorseless Salem judge.

HATHORNE: How do you dare come roarin' into this court! Are you gone daft, Corey?

GILES: You're not a Boston judge yet, Hathorne. You'll not call me daft!

Enter Deputy Governor Danforth and, behind him, Ezekiel Cheever and Parris. On his appearance, silence falls. Danforth is a grave man in his sixties, of some humor and sophistication that do not, however, interfere with an exact loyalty to his position and his cause. He comes down to Giles, who awaits his wrath.

DANFORTH, *looking directly at Giles:* Who is this man?

PARRIS: Giles Corey, sir, and a more <u>contentious</u>—

GILES, *to Parris:* I am asked the question, and I am old enough to answer it! *To Danforth, who impresses him and to whom he smiles through his strain:* My name is Corey, sir, Giles Corey. I have six hundred acres, and timber in addition. It is my wife you be condemning now. *He indicates the courtroom.*

DANFORTH: And how do you imagine to help her cause with such contemptuous riot? Now be gone. Your old age alone keeps you out of jail for this.

GILES, *beginning to plead:* They be tellin' lies about my wife, sir, I—

DANFORTH: Do you take it upon yourself to determine what this court shall believe and what it shall set aside?

GILES: Your Excellency, we mean no disrespect for—

DANFORTH: Disrespect indeed! It is disruption, Mister. This is the highest court of the supreme government of this province, do you know it?

GILES, *beginning to weep:* Your Excellency, I only said she were readin' books, sir, and they come and take her out of my house for—

DANFORTH, *mystified:* Books! What books?

GILES, *through helpless sobs:* It is my third wife, sir; I never had no wife that be so taken with books, and I thought to find the cause of it, d'y'see, but it were no witch I blamed her for. *He is openly weeping.* I have broke charity with the woman, I have broke charity with her. *He covers his face, ashamed. Danforth is respectfully silent.*

HALE: Excellency, he claims hard evidence for his wife's defense. I think that in all justice you must—

---

con • ten • tious (kən ten´ shəs) *adj.,* having a tendency to start arguments; belligerent

DANFORTH: Then let him submit his evidence in proper affidavit. You are certainly aware of our procedure here, Mr. Hale. *To Herrick:* Clear this room.

HERRICK: Come now, Giles. *He gently pushes Corey out.*

FRANCIS: We are desperate, sir; we come here three days now and cannot be heard.

DANFORTH: Who is this man?

FRANCIS: Francis Nurse, Your Excellency.

HALE: His wife's Rebecca that were condemned this morning.

DANFORTH: Indeed! I am amazed to find you in such uproar. I have only good report of your character, Mr. Nurse.

HATHORNE: I think they must both be arrested in contempt, sir.

DANFORTH, *to Francis:* Let you write your plea, and in due time I will—

FRANCIS: Excellency, we have proof for your eyes; God forbid you shut them to it. The girls, sir, the girls are frauds.

DANFORTH: What's that?

FRANCIS: We have proof of it, sir. They are all deceiving you.

Danforth is shocked, but studying Francis.

HATHORNE: This is contempt, sir, contempt!

DANFORTH: Peace, Judge Hathorne. Do you know who I am, Mr. Nurse?

FRANCIS: I surely do, sir, and I think you must be a wise judge to be what you are.

DANFORTH: And do you know that near to four hundred are in the jails from Marblehead to Lynn, and upon my signature?

FRANCIS: I—

DANFORTH: And seventy-two condemned to hang by that signature?

FRANCIS: Excellency, I never thought to say it to such a weighty judge, but you are deceived.

"The girls, sir, the girls are frauds."

Enter Giles Corey from left. All turn to see as he beckons in Mary Warren with Proctor. Mary is keeping her eyes to the ground; Proctor has her elbow as though she were near collapse.

PARRIS, *on seeing her, in shock:* Mary Warren! *He goes directly to bend close to her face.* What are you about here?

PROCTOR, *pressing Parris away from her with a gentle but firm motion of protectiveness:* She would speak with the Deputy Governor.

DANFORTH—*shocked by this, he turns to Herrick:* Did you not tell me Mary Warren were sick in bed?

HERRICK: She were, Your Honor. When I go to fetch her to the court last week, she said she were sick.

GILES: She has been strivin' with her soul all week, Your Honor; she comes now to tell the truth of this to you.

DANFORTH: Who is this?

PROCTOR: John Proctor, sir. Elizabeth Proctor is my wife.

PARRIS: Beware this man, Your Excellency, this man is mischief.

HALE, *excitedly:* I think you must hear the girl, sir, she—

DANFORTH, *who has become very interested in Mary Warren and only raises a hand toward Hale:* Peace. What would you tell us, Mary Warren?

Proctor looks at her, but she cannot speak.

PROCTOR: She never saw no spirits, sir.

DANFORTH, *with great alarm and surprise, to Mary:* Never saw no spirits!

GILES, *eagerly:* Never.

PROCTOR, *reaching into his jacket:* She has signed a <u>deposition</u>, sir—

---

de · po · si · tion (de pə zi´ shən) *n.,* recorded testimony taken under oath

Actors perform in the original 1953 Broadway production of *The Crucible.*

DANFORTH, *instantly:* No, no. I accept no depositions. *He is rapidly calculating this; he turns from her to Proctor.* Tell me, Mr. Proctor, have you given out this story in the village?

PROCTOR: We have not.

PARRIS: They've come to overthrow the court, sir! This man is—

DANFORTH: I pray you, Mr. Parris. Do you know, Mr. Proctor, that the entire contention of the state in these trials is that the voice of Heaven is speaking through the children?

PROCTOR: I know that, sir.

DANFORTH—*he thinks, staring at Proctor, then turns to Mary Warren:* And you, Mary Warren, how came you to cry out people for sending their spirits against you?

MARY WARREN: It were pretense, sir.

DANFORTH: I cannot hear you.

PROCTOR: It were pretense, she says.

DANFORTH: Ah? And the other girls? Susanna Walcott, and—the others? They are also pretending?

MARY WARREN: Aye, sir.

DANFORTH, *wide-eyed:* Indeed. *Pause. He is baffled by this. He turns to study Proctor's face.*

PARRIS, *in a sweat:* Excellency, you surely cannot think to let so vile a lie be spread in open court!

DANFORTH: Indeed not, but it strike hard upon me that she will dare come here with such a tale. Now, Mr. Proctor, before I decide whether I shall hear you or not, it is my duty to tell you this. We burn a hot fire here; it melts down all concealment.

PROCTOR: I know that, sir.

DANFORTH: Let me continue. I understand well, a husband's tenderness may drive him to extravagance in defense of a wife. Are you certain in your conscience, Mister, that your evidence is the truth?

PROCTOR: It is. And you will surely know it.

DANFORTH: And you thought to declare this revelation in the open court before the public?

PROCTOR: I thought I would, aye—with your permission.

DANFORTH, *his eyes narrowing:* Now, sir, what is your purpose in so doing?

PROCTOR: Why, I—I would free my wife, sir.

DANFORTH: There lurks nowhere in your heart, nor hidden in your spirit, any desire to undermine this court?

PROCTOR, *with the faintest faltering:* Why, no, sir.

CHEEVER—*he clears his throat, awakening:* I—Your Excellency.

DANFORTH: Mr. Cheever.

CHEEVER: I think it be my duty, sir—*Kindly, to Proctor:* You'll not deny it, John. *To Danforth:* When we come to take his wife, he damned the court and ripped your warrant.

PARRIS: Now you have it!

DANFORTH: He did that, Mr. Hale?

HALE—*he takes a breath:* Aye, he did.

PROCTOR: It were a temper, sir. I knew not what I did.

DANFORTH, *studying him:* Mr. Proctor.

PROCTOR: Aye, sir.

DANFORTH, *straight into his eyes:* Have you ever seen the Devil?

PROCTOR: No, sir.

DANFORTH: You are in all respects a Gospel Christian?

PROCTOR: I am, sir.

PARRIS: Such a Christian that will not come to church but once in a month!

DANFORTH, *restrained—he is curious:* Not come to church?

PROCTOR: I—I have no love for Mr. Parris. It is no secret. But God I surely love.

CHEEVER: He plow on Sunday, sir.

DANFORTH: Plow on Sunday!

CHEEVER, *apologetically:* I think it be evidence, John. I am an official of the court, I cannot keep it.

PROCTOR: I—I have once or twice plowed on Sunday. I have three children, sir, and until last year my land give little.

GILES: You'll find other Christians that do plow on Sunday if the truth be known.

HALE: Your Honor, I cannot think you may judge the man on such evidence.

DANFORTH: I judge nothing. *Pause. He keeps watching Proctor, who tries to meet his gaze.* I tell you straight, Mister—I have seen marvels in this court. I have seen people choked before my eyes by spirits; I have seen them stuck by pins and slashed by daggers. I have until this moment not the slightest reason to suspect that the children may be deceiving me. Do you understand my meaning?

PROCTOR: Excellency, does it not strike upon you that so many of these women have lived so long with such upright reputation, and—

PARRIS: Do you read the Gospel, Mr. Proctor?

PROCTOR: I read the Gospel.

PARRIS: I think not, or you should surely know that Cain were an upright man, and yet he did kill Abel.

PROCTOR: Aye, God tells us that. *To Danforth:* But who tells us Rebecca Nurse murdered seven babies by sending out her spirit on them? It is the children only, and this one will swear she lied to you.

Danforth considers, then beckons Hathorne to him. Hathorne leans in, and he speaks in his ear. Hathorne nods.

HATHORNE: Aye, she's the one.

DANFORTH: Mr. Proctor, this morning, your wife send me a claim in which she states that she is pregnant now.

PROCTOR: My wife pregnant!

DANFORTH: There be no sign of it—we have examined her body.

PROCTOR: But if she say she is pregnant, then she must be! That woman will never lie, Mr. Danforth.

DANFORTH: She will not?

PROCTOR: Never, sir, never.

DANFORTH: We have thought it too convenient to be credited. However, if I should tell you now that I will let her be kept another month; and if she begin to show her natural signs, you shall have her living yet another year until she is delivered—what say you to that? *John Proctor is struck silent.* Come now. You say your only purpose is to save your wife. Good, then, she is saved at least this year, and a year is long. What say you, sir? It is done now. *In conflict, Proctor glances at Francis and Giles.* Will you drop this charge?

PROCTOR: I—I think I cannot.

DANFORTH, *now an almost imperceptible hardness in his voice:* Then your purpose is somewhat larger.

PARRIS: He's come to overthrow this court, Your Honor!

PROCTOR: These are my friends. Their wives are also accused—

DANFORTH, *with a sudden briskness of manner:* I judge you not, sir. I am ready to hear your evidence.

PROCTOR: I come not to hurt the court; I only—

DANFORTH, *cutting him off:* Marshal, go into the court and bid Judge Stoughton and Judge Sewall declare recess for one hour. And let them go to the tavern, if they will. All witnesses and prisoners are to be kept in the building.

HERRICK: Aye, sir. *Very deferentially:* If I may say it, sir, I know this man all my life. It is a good man, sir.

DANFORTH—*it is the reflection on himself he resents:* I am sure of it, Marshal. *Herrick nods, then goes out.* Now, what deposition do you have for us, Mr. Proctor? And I beg you be clear, open as the sky, and honest.

PROCTOR, *as he takes out several papers:* I am no lawyer, so I'll—

DANFORTH: The pure in heart need no lawyers. Proceed as you will.

PROCTOR, *handing Danforth a paper:* Will you read this first, sir? It's a sort of testament. The people signing it declare their good opinion of Rebecca, and my wife, and Martha Corey. *Danforth looks down at the paper.*

PARRIS, *to enlist Danforth's sarcasm:* Their good opinion! *But Danforth goes on reading, and Proctor is heartened.*

PROCTOR: These are all landholding farmers, members of the church. *Delicately, trying to point out a paragraph:* If you'll notice, sir—they've known the women many years and never saw no sign they had dealings with the Devil.

Parris nervously moves over and reads over Danforth's shoulder.

"The pure in heart need no lawyers."

DANFORTH, *glancing down a long list:* How many names are here?

FRANCIS: Ninety-one, Your Excellency.

PARRIS, *sweating:* These people should be summoned. *Danforth looks up at him questioningly.* For questioning.

FRANCIS, *trembling with anger:* Mr. Danforth, I gave them all my word no harm would come to them for signing this.

PARRIS: This is a clear attack upon the court!

HALE, *to Parris, trying to contain himself:* Is every defense an attack upon the court? Can no one—?

PARRIS: All innocent and Christian people are happy for the courts in Salem! These people are gloomy for it. *To Danforth directly:* And I think you will want to know, from each and every one of them, what discontents them with you!

HATHORNE: I think they ought to be examined, sir.

DANFORTH: It is not necessarily an attack, I think. Yet—

FRANCIS: These are all covenanted Christians, sir.

DANFORTH: Then I am sure they may have nothing to fear. *Hands Cheever the paper.* Mr. Cheever, have warrants drawn for all of these—arrest for examination. *To Proctor:* Now, Mister, what other information do you have for us? *Francis is still standing, horrified.* You may sit, Mr. Nurse.

FRANCIS: I have brought trouble on these people; I have—

DANFORTH: No, old man, you have not hurt these people if they are of good conscience. But you must understand, sir, that a person is either with this court or he must be counted against it, there be no road between. This is a sharp time, now, a precise time—we live no longer in the dusky afternoon when evil mixed itself with good and befuddled the world. Now, by God's grace, the shining sun is up, and them that fear not light will surely praise it. I hope you will be one of those. *Mary Warren suddenly sobs.* She's not hearty, I see.

PROCTOR: No, she's not, sir. *To Mary, bending to her, holding her hand, quietly:* Now remember what the angel Raphael said to the boy Tobias.[3] Remember it.

MARY WARREN, *hardly audible:* Aye.

PROCTOR: "Do that which is good, and no harm shall come to thee."

MARY WARREN: Aye.

DANFORTH: Come, man, we wait you.

Marshal Herrick returns, and takes his post at the door.

GILES: John, my deposition, give him mine.

PROCTOR: Aye. *He hands Danforth another paper.* This is Mr. Corey's deposition.

DANFORTH: Oh? *He looks down at it. Now Hathorne comes behind him and reads with him.*

HATHORNE, *suspiciously:* What lawyer drew this, Corey?

GILES: You know I never hired a lawyer in my life, Hathorne.

DANFORTH, *finishing the reading:* It is very well phrased. My compliments. Mr. Parris, if Mr. Putnam is in the court, will you bring him in? *Hathorne takes the deposition, and walks to the window with it. Parris goes into the court.* You have no legal training, Mr. Corey?

GILES, *very pleased:* I have the best, sir—I am thirty-three time in court in my life. And always plaintiff, too.

DANFORTH: Oh, then you're much put-upon.

GILES: I am never put-upon; I know my rights, sir, and I will have them. You know, your father tried a case of mine—might be thirty-five year ago, I think.

DANFORTH: Indeed.

GILES: He never spoke to you of it?

DANFORTH: No, I cannot recall it.

GILES: That's strange, he give me nine pound damages. He were a fair judge, your father. Y'see, I had a white mare that time, and this fellow come to borrow the mare—*Enter Parris with Thomas Putnam. When he sees Putnam, Giles' ease goes; he is hard.* Aye, there he is.

DANFORTH: Mr. Putnam, I have here an accusation by Mr. Corey against you. He states that you coldly prompted your daughter to cry witchery upon George Jacobs that is now in jail.

PUTNAM: It is a lie.

DANFORTH, *turning to Giles:* Mr. Putnam states your charge is a lie. What say you to that?

GILES, *furious, his fists clenched:* A fart on Thomas Putnam, that is what I say to that!

---

3. **Now remember what the angel Raphael said to the boy Tobias.** The Old Testament's Book of Tobit tells the story of Tobit's son, Tobias, who cured his father's blindness by rubbing the elder man's eyes with bile from a fish. The Archangel Raphael, patron saint of travelers, had instructed him to do so.

DANFORTH: What proof do you submit for your charge, sir?

GILES: My proof is there! *Pointing to the paper.* If Jacobs hangs for a witch he forfeit up his property—that's law! And there is none but Putnam with the coin to buy so great a piece. This man is killing his neighbors for their land!

DANFORTH: But proof, sir, proof.

GILES, *pointing at his deposition:* The proof is there! I have it from an honest man who heard Putnam say it! The day his daughter cried out on Jacobs, he said she'd given him a fair gift of land.

HATHORNE: And the name of this man?

GILES, *taken aback:* What name?

HATHORNE: The man that give you this information.

GILES—*he hesitates, then:* Why, I—I cannot give you his name.

HATHORNE: And why not?

GILES—*he hesitates, then bursts out:* You know well why not! He'll lay in jail if I give his name!

HATHORNE: This is contempt of the court, Mr. Danforth!

DANFORTH, *to avoid that:* You will surely tell us the name.

GILES: I will not give you no name. I mentioned my wife's name once and I'll burn in Hell long enough for that. I stand mute.

DANFORTH: In that case, I have no choice but to arrest you for contempt of this court, do you know that?

GILES: This is a hearing; you cannot clap me for contempt of a hearing.

DANFORTH: Oh, it is a proper lawyer! Do you wish me to declare the court in full session here? Or will you give me good reply?

GILES, *faltering:* I cannot give you no name, sir, I cannot.

DANFORTH: You are a foolish old man. Mr. Cheever, begin the record. The court is now in session. I ask you, Mr. Corey—

PROCTOR, *breaking in:* Your Honor—he has the story in confidence, sir, and he—

PARRIS: The Devil lives on such confidences! *To Danforth:* Without confidences there could be no conspiracy, Your Honor!

HATHORNE: I think it must be broken, sir.

DANFORTH, *to Giles:* Old man, if your informant tells the truth let him come here openly like a decent man. But if he hide in anonymity I must know why. Now sir, the government and central church demand of you the name of him who reported Mr. Thomas Putnam a common murderer.

HALE: Excellency—

DANFORTH: Mr. Hale.

HALE: We cannot blink it more. There is a <u>prodigious</u> fear of this court in the country—

DANFORTH: Then there is a prodigious guilt in the country. Are *you* afraid to be questioned here?

HALE: I may only fear the Lord, sir, but there is fear in the country nevertheless.

DANFORTH, *angered now:* Reproach me not with the fear in the country; there is fear in the country because there is a moving plot to topple Christ in the country!

HALE: But it does not follow that everyone accused is part of it.

DANFORTH: No uncorrupted man may fear this court, Mr. Hale! None! *To Giles:* You are under arrest in contempt of this court. Now sit you down and take counsel with yourself, or you will be set in the jail until you decide to answer all questions.

Giles Corey makes a rush for Putnam. Proctor lunges and holds him.

PROCTOR: No, Giles!

GILES, *over Proctor's shoulder at Putnam:* I'll cut your throat, Putnam, I'll kill you yet!

---

pro • di • gious (prə di′ jəs) *adj.,* enormous; remarkable

PROCTOR, *forcing him into a chair:* Peace, Giles, peace. *Releasing him.* We'll prove ourselves. Now we will. *He starts to turn to Danforth.*

GILES: Say nothin' more, John. *Pointing at Danforth:* He's only playin' you! He means to hang us all!

Mary Warren bursts into sobs.

DANFORTH: This is a court of law, Mister. I'll have no <u>effrontery</u> here!

PROCTOR: Forgive him, sir, for his old age. Peace, Giles, we'll prove it all now. *He lifts up Mary's chin.* You cannot weep, Mary. Remember the angel, what he say to the boy. Hold to it, now; there is your rock. *Mary quiets. He takes out a paper, and turns to Danforth.* This is Mary Warren's deposition. I—I would ask you remember, sir, while you read it, that until two week ago she were no different than the other children are today. *He is speaking reasonably, restraining all his fears, his anger, his anxiety.* You saw her scream, she howled, she swore familiar spirits choked her; she even testified that Satan, in the form of women now in jail, tried to win her soul away, and then when she refused—

DANFORTH: We know all this.

PROCTOR: Aye, sir. She swears now that she never saw Satan; nor any spirit, vague or clear, that Satan may have sent to hurt her. And she declares her friends are lying now.

Proctor starts to hand Danforth the deposition, and Hale comes up to Danforth in a trembling state.

HALE: Excellency, a moment. I think this goes to the heart of the matter.

DANFORTH, *with deep misgivings:* It surely does.

HALE: I cannot say he is an honest man; I know him little. But in all justice, sir, a claim so weighty cannot be argued by a farmer. In God's name, sir, stop here; send him home and let him come again with a lawyer—

DANFORTH, *patiently:* Now look you, Mr. Hale—

Giles Corey on trial.

HALE: Excellency, I have signed seventy-two death warrants; I am a minister of the Lord, and I dare not take a life without there be a proof so immaculate no slightest qualm of conscience may doubt it.

DANFORTH: Mr. Hale, you surely do not doubt my justice.

HALE: I have this morning signed away the soul of Rebecca Nurse, Your Honor. I'll not conceal it, my hand shakes yet as with a wound! I pray you, sir, *this* argument let lawyers present to you.

DANFORTH: Mr. Hale, believe me; for a man of such terrible learning you are most bewildered—I hope you will forgive me. I have been thirty-two year at the bar, sir, and I should be <u>confounded</u> were I called upon to defend these people. Let you consider, now—*To Proctor and the others:* And I bid you all do likewise. In an ordinary crime, how does one defend the accused? One calls up witnesses to prove his

---

ef • fron • tery (e frun′ tər ē) *n.,* shameless boldness; gall
con • found • ed (kən foun′ dəd) *adj.,* baffled; frustrated

innocence. But witchcraft is *ipso facto*,[4] on its face and by its nature, an invisible crime, is it not? Therefore, who may possibly be witness to it? The witch and the victim. None other. Now we cannot hope the witch will accuse herself; granted? Therefore, we must rely upon her victims—and they do testify, the children certainly do testify. As for the witches, none will deny that we are most eager for all their confessions. Therefore, what is left for a lawyer to bring out? I think I have made my point. Have I not?

HALE: But this child claims the girls are not truthful, and if they are not—

DANFORTH: That is precisely what I am about to consider, sir. What more may you ask of me? Unless you doubt my probity?

HALE, *defeated:* I surely do not, sir. Let you consider it, then.

DANFORTH: And let you put your heart to rest. Her deposition, Mr. Proctor.

Proctor hands it to him, Hathorne rises, goes beside Danforth, and starts reading. Parris comes to his other side. Danforth looks at John Proctor, then proceeds to read. Hale gets up, finds position near the judge, reads too. Proctor glances at Giles. Francis prays silently, hands pressed together. Cheever waits placidly, the sublime official, dutiful. Mary Warren sobs once. John Proctor touches her head reassuringly. Presently Danforth lifts his eyes, stands up, takes out a kerchief and blows his nose. The others stand aside as he moves in thought toward the window.

PARRIS, *hardly able to contain his anger and fear:* I should like to question—

DANFORTH—*his first real outburst, in which his contempt for Parris is clear:* Mr. Parris, I bid you be silent! *He stands in silence, looking out the window. Now, having established that he will set the gait:* Mr. Cheever, will you go into the court and bring the children, here? *Cheever gets up and goes out upstage. Danforth now turns to Mary.* Mary Warren, how came you to this turnabout? Has Mr. Proctor threatened you for this deposition?

MARY WARREN: No, sir.

DANFORTH: Has he ever threatened you?

MARY WARREN, *weaker:* No, sir.

DANFORTH, *sensing a weakening:* Has he threatened you?

MARY WARREN: No, sir.

DANFORTH: Then you tell me that you sat in my court, callously lying, when you knew that people would hang by your evidence? *She does not answer.* Answer me!

MARY WARREN, *almost inaudibly:* I did, sir.

DANFORTH: How were you instructed in your life? Do you not know that God damns all liars? *She cannot speak.* Or is it now that you lie?

MARY WARREN: No, sir—I am with God now.

DANFORTH: You are with God now.

MARY WARREN: Aye, sir.

DANFORTH, *containing himself:* I will tell you this—you are either lying now, or you were lying in the court, and in either case you have committed perjury and you will go to jail for it. You cannot lightly say you lied, Mary. Do you know that?

MARY WARREN: I cannot lie no more. I am with God, I am with God.

But she breaks into sobs at the thought of it, and the right door opens, and enter Susanna Walcott, Mercy Lewis, Betty Parris, and finally Abigail. Cheever comes to Danforth.

CHEEVER: Ruth Putnam's not in the court, sir, nor the other children.

DANFORTH: These will be sufficient. Sit you down, children. *Silently they sit.* Your friend, Mary Warren, has given us a deposition. In which she swears that she never saw familiar spirits, apparitions, nor any manifest of the

---

4. **ipso facto.** [Latin] Literally, "by the fact itself"

> **pro • bi • ty** (prō′ bə tē) *n.,* honesty; uprightness

Devil. She claims as well that none of you have seen these things either. *Slight pause.* Now, children, this is a court of law. The law, based upon the Bible, and the Bible, writ by Almighty God, forbid the practice of witchcraft, and describe death as the penalty thereof. But likewise, children, the law and Bible damn all bearers of false witness. *Slight pause.* Now then. It does not escape me that this deposition may be devised to blind us; it may well be that Mary Warren has been conquered by Satan, who sends her here to distract our sacred purpose. If so, her neck will break for it. But if she speak true, I bid you now drop your guile and confess your pretense, for a quick confession will go easier with you. *Pause.* Abigail Williams, rise. *Abigail slowly rises.* Is there any truth in this?

ABIGAIL: No, sir.

DANFORTH—*he thinks, glances at Mary, then back to Abigail:* Children, a very auger[5] bit will now be turned into your souls until your honesty is proved. Will either of you change your positions now, or do you force me to hard questioning?

ABIGAIL: I have naught to change, sir. She lies.

DANFORTH, *to Mary:* You would still go on with this?

MARY WARREN, *faintly:* Aye, sir.

DANFORTH, *turning to Abigail:* A poppet were discovered in Mr. Proctor's house, stabbed by a needle. Mary Warren claims that you sat beside her in the court when she made it, and that you saw her make it and witnessed how she herself stuck her needle into it for safe-keeping. What say you to that?

ABIGAIL, *with a slight note of indignation:* It is a lie, sir.

DANFORTH, *after a slight pause:* While you worked for Mr. Proctor, did you see poppets in that house?

ABIGAIL: Goody Proctor always kept poppets.

PROCTOR: Your Honor, my wife never kept no poppets. Mary Warren confesses it was her poppet.

CHEEVER: Your Excellency.

DANFORTH: Mr. Cheever.

CHEEVER: When I spoke with Goody Proctor in that house, she said she never kept no poppets. But she said she did keep poppets when she were a girl.

PROCTOR: She has not been a girl these fifteen years, Your Honor.

HATHORNE: But a poppet will keep fifteen years, will it not?

PROCTOR: It will keep if it is kept, but Mary Warren swears she never saw no poppets in my house, nor anyone else.

PARRIS: Why could there not have been poppets hid where no one ever saw them?

> "There might also be a dragon with five legs in my house, but no one has ever seen it."

PROCTOR, *furious:* There might also be a dragon with five legs in my house, but no one has ever seen it.

PARRIS: We are here, Your Honor, precisely to discover what no one has ever seen.

PROCTOR: Mr. Danforth, what profit this girl to turn herself about? What may Mary Warren gain but hard questioning and worse?

DANFORTH: You are charging Abigail Williams with a marvelous cool plot to murder, do you understand that?

PROCTOR: I do, sir. I believe she means to murder.

DANFORTH, *pointing at Abigail, incredulously:* This child would murder your wife?

PROCTOR: It is not a child. Now hear me, sir. In the sight of the congregation she were twice this year put out of this meetin' house for laughter during prayer.

---

5. **auger.** Tool having a sharp, spiral structure used to bore holes

DANFORTH, *shocked, turning to Abigail:* What's this? Laughter during—!

PARRIS: Excellency, she were under Tituba's power at that time, but she is solemn now.

GILES: Aye, now she is solemn and goes to hang people!

DANFORTH: Quiet, man.

HATHORNE: Surely it have no bearing on the question, sir. He charges contemplation of murder.

DANFORTH: Aye. *He studies Abigail for a moment, then:* Continue, Mr. Proctor.

PROCTOR: Mary. Now tell the Governor how you danced in the woods.

PARRIS, *instantly:* Excellency, since I come to Salem this man is blackening my name. He—

DANFORTH: In a moment, sir. *To Mary Warren, sternly, and surprised:* What is this dancing?

MARY WARREN: I—*She glances at Abigail, who is staring down at her remorselessly. Then, appealing to Proctor:* Mr. Proctor—

PROCTOR, *taking it right up:* Abigail leads the girls to the woods, Your Honor, and they have danced there naked—

PARRIS: Your Honor, this—

PROCTOR, *at once:* Mr. Parris discovered them himself in the dead of night! There's the "child" she is!

DANFORTH—*it is growing into a nightmare, and he turns, astonished, to Parris:* Mr. Parris—

PARRIS: I can only say, sir, that I never found any of them naked, and this man is—

DANFORTH: But you discovered them dancing in the woods? *Eyes on Parris, he points at Abigail.* Abigail?

HALE: Excellency, when I first arrived from Beverly, Mr. Parris told me that.

DANFORTH: Do you deny it, Mr. Parris?

PARRIS: I do not, sir, but I never saw any of them naked.

DANFORTH: But she have *danced?*

PARRIS, *unwillingly:* Aye, sir.

Danforth, as though with new eyes, looks at Abigail.

HATHORNE: Excellency, will you permit me? *He points at Mary Warren.*

DANFORTH, *with great worry:* Pray, proceed.

HATHORNE: You say you never saw no spirits, Mary, were never threatened or afflicted by any manifest of the Devil or the Devil's agents.

MARY WARREN, *very faintly:* No, sir.

HATHORNE, *with a gleam of victory:* And yet, when people accused of witchery confronted you in court, you would faint, saying their spirits came out of their bodies and choked you—

MARY WARREN: That were pretense, sir.

DANFORTH: I cannot hear you.

MARY WARREN: Pretense, sir.

PARRIS: But you did turn cold, did you not? I myself picked you up many times, and your skin were icy. Mr. Danforth, you—

DANFORTH: I saw that many times.

PROCTOR: She only pretended to faint, Your Excellency. They're all marvelous pretenders.

HATHORNE: Then can she pretend to faint now?

PROCTOR: Now?

PARRIS: Why not? Now there are no spirits attacking her, for none in this room is accused of witchcraft. So let her turn herself cold now, let her pretend she is attacked now, let her faint. *He turns to Mary Warren.* Faint!

MARY WARREN: Faint?

PARRIS: Aye, faint. Prove to us how you pretended in the court so many times.

MARY WARREN, *looking to Proctor:* I—cannot faint now, sir.

PROCTOR, *alarmed, quietly:* Can you not pretend it?

MARY WARREN: I—*She looks about as though searching for the passion to faint.* I—have no sense of it now, I—

DANFORTH: Why? What is lacking now?

MARY WARREN: I—cannot tell, sir, I—

DANFORTH: Might it be that here we have no afflicting spirit loose, but in the court there were some?

MARY WARREN: I never saw no spirits.

PARRIS: Then see no spirits now, and prove to us that you can faint by your own will, as you claim.

MARY WARREN—*she stares, searching for the emotion of it, and then shakes her head:* I—cannot do it.

PARRIS: Then you will confess, will you not? It were attacking spirits made you faint!

MARY WARREN: No, sir, I—

PARRIS: Your Excellency, this is a trick to blind the court!

MARY WARREN: It's not a trick! *She stands.* I—I used to faint because I—I thought I saw spirits.

DANFORTH: *Thought* you saw them!

MARY WARREN: But I did not, Your Honor.

HATHORNE: How could you think you saw them unless you saw them?

MARY WARREN: I—I cannot tell how, but I did. I—I heard the other girls screaming, and you, Your Honor, you seemed to believe them, and I—It were only sport in the beginning, sir, but then the whole world cried spirits, spirits, and I—I promise you, Mr. Danforth, I only thought I saw them but I did not.

Danforth peers at her.

PARRIS, *smiling, but nervous because Danforth seems to be struck by Mary Warren's story:* Surely Your Excellency is not taken by this simple lie.

DANFORTH, *turning worriedly to Abigail:* Abigail. I bid you now search your heart and tell me this—and beware of it, child, to God every soul is precious and His vengeance is terrible on them that take life without cause. Is it possible, child, that the spirits you have seen are illusion only, some deception that may cross your mind when—

ABIGAIL: Why, this—this—is a base question, sir.

DANFORTH: Child, I would have you consider it—

ABIGAIL: I have been hurt, Mr. Danforth; I have seen my blood runnin' out! I have been near to murdered every day because I done my duty pointing out the Devil's people—and this is my reward? To be mistrusted, denied, questioned like a—

DANFORTH, *weakening:* Child, I do not mistrust you—

ABIGAIL, *in an open threat:* Let *you* beware, Mr. Danforth. Think you to be so mighty that the power of Hell may not turn *your* wits? Beware of it! There is—*Suddenly, from an accusatory attitude, her face turns, looking into the air above—it is truly frightened.*

DANFORTH, *apprehensively:* What is it, child?

ABIGAIL, *looking about in the air, clasping her arms about her as though cold:* I—I know not. A wind, a cold wind, has come. *Her eyes fall on Mary Warren.*

MARY WARREN, *terrified, pleading:* Abby!

MERCY LEWIS, *shivering:* Your Honor, I freeze!

PROCTOR: They're pretending!

HATHORNE, *touching Abigail's hand:* She is cold, Your Honor, touch her!

MERCY LEWIS, *through chattering teeth:* Mary, do you send this shadow on me?

MARY WARREN: Lord, save me!

SUSANNA WALCOTT: I freeze, I freeze!

ABIGAIL, *shivering visibly:* It is a wind, a wind!

MARY WARREN: Abby, don't do that!

DANFORTH, *himself engaged and entered by Abigail:* Mary Warren, do you witch her? I say to you, do you send your spirit out?

With a hysterical cry Mary Warren starts to run. Proctor catches her.

MARY WARREN, *almost collapsing:* Let me go, Mr. Proctor, I cannot, I cannot—

ABIGAIL, *crying to Heaven:* Oh, Heavenly Father, take away this shadow!

Without warning or hesitation, Proctor leaps at Abigail and, grabbing her by the hair, pulls her to her feet. She screams in pain. Danforth, astonished, cries, "What are you about?" and Hathorne and Parris call, "Take your hands off her!" and out of it all comes Proctor's roaring voice.

PROCTOR: How do you call Heaven! Whore! Whore!

Herrick breaks Proctor from her.

HERRICK: John!

DANFORTH: Man! Man, what do you—

PROCTOR, *breathless and in agony:* It is a whore!

DANFORTH, *dumfounded:* You charge—?

ABIGAIL: Mr. Danforth, he is lying!

PROCTOR: Mark her! Now she'll suck a scream to stab me with, but—

DANFORTH: You will prove this! This will not pass!

PROCTOR, *trembling, his life collapsing about him:* I have known her, sir. I have known her.

DANFORTH: You—you are a lecher?

FRANCIS, *horrified:* John, you cannot say such a—

PROCTOR: Oh, Francis, I wish you had some evil in you that you might know me! *To Danforth:* A man will not cast away his good name. You surely know that.

DANFORTH, *dumfounded:* In—in what time? In what place?

PROCTOR, *his voice about to break, and his shame great:* In the proper place—where my beasts are bedded. On the last night of my joy, some eight months past. She used to serve me in my house, sir. *He has to clamp his jaw to keep from weeping.* A man may think God sleeps, but God sees everything, I know it now. I beg you, sir, I beg you—see her what she is. My wife, my dear good wife, took this girl soon after, sir, and put her out on the highroad. And being what she is, a lump of vanity, sir —*He is being overcome. Excellency, forgive me, forgive me. Angrily against himself, he turns away from the Governor for a moment. Then, as though to cry out is his only means of speech left:* She thinks to dance with me on my wife's grave! And well she might, for I thought of her softly. God help me, I lusted, and there *is* a promise in such sweat. But it is a whore's vengeance, and you must see it; I set myself entirely in your hands. I know you must see it now.

DANFORTH, *blanched, in horror, turning to Abigail:* You deny every scrap and tittle of this?

ABIGAIL: If I must answer that, I will leave and I will not come back again!

Danforth seems unsteady.

PROCTOR: I have made a bell of my honor! I have rung the doom of my good name—you will believe me, Mr. Danforth! My wife is innocent, except she knew a whore when she saw one!

ABIGAIL, *stepping up to Danforth:* What look do you give me? *Danforth cannot speak.* I'll not have such looks! *She turns and starts for the door.*

DANFORTH: You will remain where you are! *Herrick steps into her path. She comes up short, fire in her eyes.* Mr. Parris, go into the court and bring Goodwife Proctor out.

PARRIS, *objecting:* Your Honor, this is all a—

DANFORTH, *sharply to Parris:* Bring her out! And tell her not one word of what's been spoken here. And let you knock before you enter. *Parris goes out.* Now we shall touch the bottom of this swamp. *To Proctor:* Your wife, you say, is an honest woman.

PROCTOR: In her life, sir, she have never lied. There are them that cannot sing, and them that

cannot weep—my wife cannot lie. I have paid much to learn it, sir.

DANFORTH: And when she put this girl out of your house, she put her out for a harlot?[6]

PROCTOR: Aye, sir.

DANFORTH: And knew her for a harlot?

PROCTOR: Aye, sir, she knew her for a harlot.

DANFORTH: Good then. *To Abigail:* And if she tell me, child, it were for harlotry, may God spread His mercy on you! *There is a knock. He calls to the door.* Hold! *To Abigail:* Turn your back. Turn your back. *To Proctor:* Do likewise. *Both turn their backs—Abigail with indignant slowness.* Now let neither of you turn to face Goody Proctor. No one in this room is to speak one word, or raise a gesture aye or nay. *He turns toward the door, calls:* Enter! *The door opens. Elizabeth enters with Parris. Parris leaves her. She stands alone, her eyes looking for Proctor. Mr. Cheever, report this testimony in all exactness. Are you ready?*

CHEEVER: Ready, sir.

DANFORTH: Come here, woman. *Elizabeth comes to him, glancing at Proctor's back.* Look at me only, not at your husband. In my eyes only.

ELIZABETH, *faintly:* Good, sir.

DANFORTH: We are given to understand that at one time you dismissed your servant, Abigail Williams.

ELIZABETH: That is true, sir.

DANFORTH: For what cause did you dismiss her? *Slight pause. Then Elizabeth tries to glance at Proctor.* You will look in my eyes only and not at your husband. The answer is in your memory and you need no help to give it to me. Why did you dismiss Abigail Williams?

> **"She thinks to dance with me on my wife's grave!"**

---

6. **harlot.** Prostitute

ELIZABETH, *not knowing what to say, sensing a situation, wetting her lips to stall for time:* She—dissatisfied me. *Pause.* And my husband.

DANFORTH: In what way dissatisfied you?

ELIZABETH: She were—*She glances at Proctor for a cue.*

DANFORTH: Woman, look at me! *Elizabeth does.* Were she slovenly? Lazy? What disturbance did she cause?

ELIZABETH: Your Honor, I—in that time I were sick. And I—My husband is a good and righteous man. He is never drunk as some are, nor wastin' his time at the shovelboard, but always at his work. But in my sickness—you see, sir, I were a long time sick after my last baby, and I thought I saw my husband somewhat turning from me. And this girl—*She turns to Abigail.*

DANFORTH: Look at me.

ELIZABETH: Aye, sir. Abigail Williams—*She breaks off.*

DANFORTH: What of Abigail Williams?

ELIZABETH: I came to think he fancied her. And so one night I lost my wits, I think, and put her out on the highroad.

DANFORTH: Your husband—did he indeed turn from you?

ELIZABETH, *in agony:* My husband—is a goodly man, sir.

DANFORTH: Then he did not turn from you.

ELIZABETH, *starting to glance at Proctor:* He—

DANFORTH, *reaches out and holds her face, then:* Look at me! To your own knowledge, has John Proctor ever committed the crime of lechery? *In a crisis of indecision she cannot speak.* Answer my question! Is your husband a lecher!

ELIZABETH, *faintly:* No, sir.

DANFORTH: Remove her, Marshal.

PROCTOR: Elizabeth, tell the truth!

DANFORTH: She has spoken. Remove her!

PROCTOR, *crying out:* Elizabeth, I have confessed it!

ELIZABETH: Oh, God! *The door closes behind her.*

PROCTOR: She only thought to save my name!

HALE: Excellency, it is a natural lie to tell; I beg you, stop now before another is condemned! I may shut my conscience to it no more—private vengeance is working through this testimony! From the beginning this man has struck me true. By my oath to Heaven, I believe him now, and I pray you call back his wife before we—

DANFORTH: She spoke nothing of lechery, and this man has lied!

HALE: I believe him! *Pointing at Abigail:* This girl has always struck me false! She has—

Abigail, with a weird, wild, chilling cry, screams up to the ceiling.

ABIGAIL: You will not! Begone! Begone, I say!

DANFORTH: What is it, child? *But Abigail, pointing with fear, is now raising up her frightened eyes, her awed face, toward the ceiling—the girls are doing the same—and now Hathorne, Hale, Putnam, Cheever, Herrick, and Danforth do the same.* What's there? *He lowers his eyes from the ceiling, and now he is frightened; there is real tension in his voice.* Child! *She is transfixed—with all the girls, she is whimpering open-mouthed, agape at the ceiling.* Girls! Why do you—?

MERCY LEWIS, *pointing:* It's on the beam! Behind the rafter!

DANFORTH, *looking up:* Where!

ABIGAIL: Why—? *She gulps.* Why do you come, yellow bird?

PROCTOR: Where's a bird? I see no bird!

ABIGAIL, *to the ceiling:* My face? My face?

PROCTOR: Mr. Hale—

DANFORTH: Be quiet!

PROCTOR, *to Hale:* Do you see a bird?

DANFORTH: Be quiet!!

ABIGAIL, *to the ceiling, in a genuine conversation with the "bird," as though trying to talk it out of attacking her:* But God made my face; you cannot want to tear my face. Envy is a deadly sin, Mary.

MARY WARREN, *on her feet with a spring, and horrified, pleading:* Abby!

ABIGAIL, <u>unperturbed</u>, *continuing to the "bird":* Oh, Mary, this is a black art to change your shape. No, I cannot, I cannot stop my mouth; it's God's work I do.

MARY WARREN: Abby, I'm *here!*

PROCTOR, *frantically:* They're pretending, Mr. Danforth!

ABIGAIL—*now she takes a backward step, as though in fear the bird will swoop down momentarily:* Oh, please, Mary! Don't come down.

SUSANNA WALCOTT: Her claws, she's stretching her claws!

PROCTOR: Lies, lies.

ABIGAIL, *backing further, eyes still fixed above:* Mary, please don't hurt me!

MARY WARREN, *to Danforth:* I'm not hurting her!

DANFORTH, *to Mary Warren:* Why does she see this vision?

MARY WARREN: She sees nothin'!

ABIGAIL, *now staring full front as though hypnotized, and mimicking the exact tone of Mary Warren's cry:* She sees nothin'!

MARY WARREN, *pleading:* Abby, you mustn't!

ABIGAIL and **ALL THE GIRLS,** *all transfixed:* Abby, you mustn't!

MARY WARREN, *to all the girls:* I'm here, I'm here!

GIRLS: I'm here, I'm here!

DANFORTH, *horrified:* Mary Warren! Draw back your spirit out of them!

MARY WARREN: Mr. Danforth!

GIRLS, *cutting her off:* Mr. Danforth!

DANFORTH: Have you compacted with the Devil? Have you?

MARY WARREN: Never, never!

GIRLS: Never, never!

DANFORTH, *growing hysterical:* Why can they only repeat you?

PROCTOR: Give me a whip—I'll stop it!

MARY WARREN: They're sporting. They—!

GIRLS: They're sporting!

MARY WARREN, *turning on them all hysterically and stamping her feet:* Abby, stop it!

GIRLS, *stamping their feet:* Abby, stop it!

MARY WARREN: Stop it!

GIRLS: Stop it!

---

un • per • turbed (un pər tʉrbd′) *adj.,* not upset or concerned

MARY WARREN, *screaming it out at the top of her lungs, and raising her fists:* Stop it!!

GIRLS, *raising their fists:* Stop it!!

Mary Warren, utterly confounded, and becoming overwhelmed by Abigail's—and the girls'—utter conviction, starts to whimper, hands half raised, powerless, and all the girls begin whimpering exactly as she does.

DANFORTH: A little while ago you were afflicted. Now it seems you afflict others; where did you find this power?

MARY WARREN, *staring at Abigail:* I—have no power.

GIRLS: I have no power.

PROCTOR: They're <u>gulling</u> you, Mister!

DANFORTH: Why did you turn about this past two weeks? You have seen the Devil, have you not?

HALE, *indicating Abigail and the girls:* You cannot believe them!

MARY WARREN: I—

PROCTOR, *sensing her weakening:* Mary, God damns all liars!

DANFORTH, *pounding it into her:* You have seen the Devil, you have made compact with Lucifer, have you not?

PROCTOR: God damns liars, Mary!

Mary utters something unintelligible, staring at Abigail, who keeps watching the "bird" above.

DANFORTH: I cannot hear you. What do you say? *Mary utters again unintelligibly.* You will confess yourself or you will hang! *He turns her roughly to face him.* Do you know who I am? I say you will hang if you do not open with me!

PROCTOR: Mary, remember the angel Raphael— do that which is good and—

ABIGAIL, *pointing upward:* The wings! Her wings are spreading! Mary, please, don't, don't—!

HALE: I see nothing, Your Honor!

DANFORTH: Do you confess this power! *He is an inch from her face.* Speak!

ABIGAIL: She's going to come down! She's walking the beam!

DANFORTH: Will you speak!

MARY WARREN, *staring in horror:* I cannot!

GIRLS: I cannot!

PARRIS: Cast the Devil out! Look him in the face! Trample him! We'll save you, Mary, only stand fast against him and—

ABIGAIL, *looking up:* Look out! She's coming down!

She and all the girls run to one wall, shielding their eyes. And now, as though cornered, they let out a gigantic scream, and Mary, as though infected, opens her mouth and screams with them. Gradually Abigail and the girls leave off, until only Mary is left there, staring up at the "bird," screaming madly. All watch her, horrified by this evident fit. Proctor strides to her.

PROCTOR: Mary, tell the Governor what they— *He has hardly got a word out, when, seeing him coming for her, she rushes out of his reach, screaming in horror.*

MARY WARREN: Don't touch me—don't touch me! *At which the girls halt at the door.*

PROCTOR, *astonished:* Mary!

MARY WARREN, *pointing at Proctor:* You're the Devil's man!

He is stopped in his tracks.

PARRIS: Praise God!

GIRLS: Praise God!

PROCTOR, *numbed:* Mary, how—?

MARY WARREN: I'll not hang with you! I love God, I love God.

DANFORTH, *to Mary:* He bid you do the Devil's work?

MARY WARREN, *hysterically, indicating Proctor:* He come at me by night and every day to sign, to sign, to—

gull (gul) *v.,* deceive

DANFORTH: Sign what?

PARRIS: The Devil's book? He come with a book?

MARY WARREN, *hysterically, pointing at Proctor, fearful of him:* My name, he want my name. "I'll murder you," he says, "if my wife hangs! We must go and overthrow the court," he says!

Danforth's head jerks toward Proctor, shock and horror in his face.

PROCTOR, *turning, appealing to Hale:* Mr. Hale!

MARY WARREN, *her sobs beginning:* He wake me every night, his eyes were like coals and his fingers claw my neck, and I sign, I sign . . .

HALE: Excellency, this child's gone wild!

PROCTOR, *as Danforth's wide eyes pour on him:* Mary, Mary!

MARY WARREN, *screaming at him:* No, I love God; I go your way no more. I love God, I bless God. *Sobbing, she rushes to Abigail.* Abby, Abby, I'll never hurt you more! *They all watch, as Abigail, out of her infinite charity, reaches out and draws the sobbing Mary to her, and then looks up to Danforth.*

DANFORTH, *to Proctor:* What are you? *Proctor is beyond speech in his anger.* You are combined with anti-Christ, are you not? I have seen your power; you will not deny it! What say you. Mister?

HALE: Excellency—

DANFORTH: I will have nothing from you, Mr. Hale! *To Proctor:* Will you confess yourself befouled with Hell, or do you keep that black allegiance yet? What say you?

PROCTOR, *his mind wild, breathless:* I say—I say—God is dead!

PARRIS: Hear it, hear it!

PROCTOR—*he laughs insanely, then:* A fire, a fire is burning! I hear the boot of Lucifer, I see his filthy face! And it is my face, and yours, Danforth! For them that quail to bring men out of ignorance, as I have quailed, and as you quail now when you know in all your black hearts that this be fraud—God damns our kind especially, and we will burn, we will burn together!

DANFORTH: Marshal! Take him and Corey with him to the jail!

HALE, *starting across to the door:* I denounce these proceedings!

PROCTOR: You are pulling Heaven down and raising up a whore!

HALE: I denounce these proceedings, I quit this court! *He slams the door to the outside behind him.*

DANFORTH, *calling to him in a fury:* Mr. Hale! Mr. Hale!

THE CURTAIN FALLS ❖

MIRRORS & WINDOWS Danforth tells Francis Nurse that "a person is either with this court or he must be counted against it, there be no road between." In most conflicts, is it possible to remain neutral and not take sides?

COHN

MCCARTHY

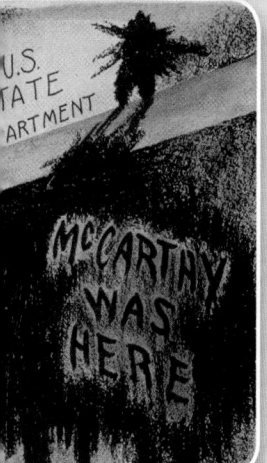

Informational Text Connection

The name Senator Joseph R. McCarthy is nearly synonymous with anticommunism. McCarthy, a U.S. Senator from 1946 to 1954, chaired the Senate's subcommittee on investigations. In this role, he aggressively pursued individuals within political departments and high-profile industries whom he believed were involved in communism.

The Army Signal Corps took particular exception to being interrogated, leading to a series of public hearings known as the **Army-McCarthy hearings.** As the investigation wore on, people began to see McCarthy's questioning as badgering and his claims as unfounded. His censure for conduct unbecoming a senator in December 1954 ended the brief historical period known as the McCarthy Era. This hearing transcript presents the actual dialogue between McCarthy and Special Counsel for the Army Joseph N. Welch.

Senate Hearings
McCarthy-Welch Exchange:
"Have You No Sense of Decency?"

McCarthy: (Mr. Chairman) . . . in view of Mr. Welch's request that the information be given once we know of anyone who might be performing any work for the Communist Party, I think we should tell him that he has in his law firm a young man named Fisher whom he recommended, incidentally, to do the work on this Committee, who has been, for a number of years, a member of an organization which is named, oh, years and years ago, as the legal bulwark[1] of the Communist Party, an organization which always springs to the defense of anyone who dares to expose Communists.

Knowing that, Mr. Welch, I just felt that I had a duty to respond to your *urgent* request that "before sundown," when we know of anyone serving the Communist cause we let

the agency know. Now, we're now letting you know that your man did belong to this organization for either three or four years, belonged to it long after he was out of law school. And I have hesitated bringing that up, but I have been rather bored with your phony requests to Mr. Cohn here, that he, *personally,* get every Communist out of Government before sundown. Whether you knew that he was a member of that Communist organization or not, I don't know. I assume you did not, Mr. Welch, because I get the impression that while you are quite an actor, you play for a laugh, I don't think you have any conception of the danger of

---

1. **bulwark.** Strong protection or defense, usually referring to a physical structure

the Communist Party. I don't think you, your-self, would ever knowingly aid the Communist cause. I think you're unknowingly aiding it when you try to burlesque[2] this hearing in which we're attempting to bring out the facts.

Welch: Mr. Chairman . . .

Mundt: The Chair may say that he has no rec-ognition or no memory of Mr. Welch recom-mending either Mr. Fisher or anybody else as counsel for this Committee.

McCarthy: I refer to the record, Mr. Chairman . . . to the news story on that.

Welch: Mr. Chairman. Under these circum-stances, I must myself have something appro-aching a personal privilege.

Mundt: You may have, sir—

Welch: Senator McCarthy, I did not know, Senator—Senator, sometimes you say may I have your attention—

McCarthy: I'm listening . . .

Welch: May I have your attention?

McCarthy: I can listen with one ear and talk with—

Welch: No, this time, sir, I want you to listen with both. Senator McCarthy, I think until this moment—

McCarthy: —Good. Just a minute. Jim, Jim, will you get the news story to the effect that this man belongs to the—to this Communist front organization . . .

Welch: I will tell you that he belonged to it.

McCarthy: Jim, will you get the citation, one of the citations showing that this was the legal arm of the Communist Party, and the length of time that he belonged, and the fact that he was recommended by Mr. Welch. I think that should be in the record . . .

Welch: Senator, you won't need anything in the record when I finish telling you this. Until this moment, Senator, I think I never

really gauged your cruelty, or your reckless-ness. Fred Fisher is a young man who went to the Harvard Law School and came into my firm and is starting what looks to be a brilliant career with us. When I decided to work for this Committee, I asked Jim St. Clair, who sits on my right, to be my first assistant. I said to Jim, "Pick somebody in the firm to work under you that you would like." He chose Fred Fisher, and they came down on an afternoon plane. That night, when we had taken a little stab at trying to see what the case is about, Fred Fisher and Jim St. Clair and I went to dinner together. I then said to these two young men, "Boys, I don't know anything about you, except I've always liked you, but if there's anything funny in the life of either one of you that would hurt anybody in this case, you speak up quick."

And Fred Fisher said, "Mr. Welch, when I was in the law school, and for a period of months after, I belonged to the Lawyers' Guild," as you have suggested, Senator. He went on to say, "I am Secretary of the Young Republican's League in Newton with the son of [the] Mas-sachusetts governor, and I have the respect and admiration of my community, and I'm sure I have the respect and admiration of the twenty-five lawyers or so in Hale & Dorr." And I said, "Fred, I just don't think I'm going to ask you to work on the case. If I do, one of these days that will come out, and go over national television, and it will just hurt like the dickens." And so, Senator, I asked him to go back to Boston. Little did I dream you could be so reckless and so cruel as to do an injury to that lad. It is, I regret to say, equally true that I fear he shall always bear a scar needlessly inflicted by you. If it were in my *power* to forgive you for your reck-less cruelty, I would do so. I like to think I'm a gentle man, but your forgiveness will have to come from someone other than me.

McCarthy: Mr. Chairman, may I say that Mr. Welch talks about this being cruel and reck-less. He was just baiting. He has been baiting

2. **burlesque.** Mock

Mr. Cohn here for hours, requesting that Mr. Cohn before sundown get out of any department of the government anyone who is serving the Communist cause. Now, I just give this man's record and I want to say, Mr. Welch, that it had been labeled long before he became a member, as early as 1944—

Welch: Senator, may we not drop this? We know he belonged to the Lawyers' Guild.

McCarthy: Let me finish . . .

Welch: And Mr. Cohn nods his head at me. I did you, I think, no personal injury, Mr. Cohn?

Cohn: No, sir.

Welch: I meant to do you no personal injury.

Cohn: No, sir.

Welch: And if I did, I beg your pardon. Let us not assassinate this lad further, Senator.

McCarthy: Let's, let's—

Welch: You've done enough. Have you no sense of decency, sir, at long last? Have you left no sense of decency?

McCarthy: I know this hurts you, Mr. Welch.

Welch: I'll say it hurts!

McCarthy: Mr. Chairman, as a point of personal privilege, I'd like to finish this.

Welch: Senator, I think it hurts you, too, sir.

McCarthy: I'd like to finish this. I know Mr. Cohn would rather not have me go into this. I intend to, however, and Mr. Welch talks about any "sense of decency." I have heard you and everyone else talk so much about laying the truth upon the table. But when I heard the completely phony Mr. Welch, I've been listening now for a long time, he's saying, now "before sundown" you must get these people "out of government." So I just want you to have it very clear, very clear that you were not so serious about that when you tried to recommend this man for this Committee.

Welch: Mr. McCarthy, I will not discuss this further with you. You have sat within six feet of me and could ask—could have asked me about Fred Fisher. You have seen fit to bring it out, and if there is a God in heaven, it will do neither you nor your cause any good. I will not discuss it further. I will not ask, Mr. Cohn, any more witnesses. You, Mr. Chairman, may, if you will, call the next witness. ❖

Review Questions

1. What fact does McCarthy say Welch should know? Summarize the irony of the alleged situation involving Fred Fisher.

2. Name the "reckless cruelty" of which Welch accuses McCarthy. Do you agree or disagree with Welch's labeling of McCarthy's actions? If you disagree, how would you describe what McCarthy is doing?

3. What final comment does Welch make about McCarthy's questioning him about Fred Fisher? What was the outcome of the exchange between McCarthy and Welch? Research others who appeared before McCarthy during these hearings, and describe the outcome for one of them.

TEXT ^{TO} TEXT CONNECTION

As described in the hearing transcript, Joseph Welch said he advised Fred Fisher to return to Boston, rather than serve on the investigations committee. What led to this advice? How does this situation seem to parallel Reverend Parris's prohibiting talk of witchcraft in the village (see Act 1, pages 886–887)?

Refer to Text ▶ ▶ ▶ ▶ ▶ **Reason with Text**

1a. What charge does Giles Corey make against Thomas Putnam? What evidence does he cite? What problem does the court have with this evidence?

1b. What possible bias might you infer from the court's reaction to Corey's charge and the evidence cited? Why might the court hold such a bias?

Understand
Find meaning

2a. What does John Proctor break down and confess in open court? What does he say is Abigail's motive for accusing his wife of witchcraft?

2b. How is what happens to John at the end of Act 3 an example of situational irony for Abigail?

Apply
Use information

3a. What does Abigail claim to see on the beam and blame on Mary? What does she say is "a deadly sin"?

3b. Analyze what Abigail's claims suggest about her, about Mary, and about the relationship between the two of them.

Analyze
Take things apart

4a. What pressures are put on Mary to denounce Proctor? What does Mary ultimately do?

4b. Evaluate whether Mary's actions are justifiable.

Evaluate
Make judgments

5a. Define the method of questioning Danforth uses with Mary. Explain using examples from the selection.

5b. Would such a method of questioning be acceptable in a court of law today? What is the weakness of this strategy?

Create
Bring ideas together

Analyze Literature

Irony and Mood
Review the examples and types of irony you found in reading Act 3. Explain the irony behind Elizabeth Proctor defending her husband's good name with a so-called white lie. What type of irony is this?

How does the mood of the drama change throughout Act 3? What different emotions did you experience as a reader? How does Miller achieve these shifts in mood?

Extend the Text

Writing Options
Creative Writing Write an address, or speech, to the jury, as though you were John Proctor. Defend yourself and refute the evidence that has been presented against you.

Expository Writing Write an essay analyzing Miller's tone and use of irony to create mood in Act 3 of *The Crucible*. Your audience is a friend who has not read the play.

Critical Literacy
Study the Judicial System Using the Internet or library as a resource, locate a news or magazine article about someone who was wrongly accused and perhaps convicted of a crime. What evidence was offered against him or her?

Did the person seem guilty beyond a reasonable doubt? How was he or she ultimately proven innocent?

Collaborative Learning
Research Famous Trials Form groups of at least four members. Have half the members research the Salem witch trials and the other half research the McCarthy hearings. Answer these questions: How did the event originate? What motivated the instigators as well as those who subsequently supported the event? Did anyone speak out against the instigators? What happened to them? As a whole group, share your findings about the two events.

 Go to **www.mirrorsandwindows.com** for more.

The Crucible, Act 4

A Drama by Arthur Miller

Build Background

Historical Context Act 4 begins during the fall of 1692, a few months after the end of Act 3. Reverend John Hale returns to Salem and discovers that, even though the trials are over, Judges Danforth and Hathorne continue to exercise their authoritarian rule over the people of Salem. The town's productivity has declined sharply, and its discontented citizenry are close to rebellion. Nonetheless, the judges deny any wrongdoing and will not release the prisoners who refuse to confess. Hathorne and Danforth both believe they must maintain the pretense of their beliefs to preserve their legal authority.

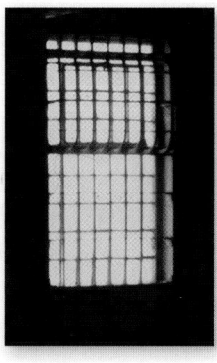

Historically, the first organized effort to end the Salem witch trials also began in the fall of 1692. On October 3, Salem minister Increase Mather published a treatise entitled "Cases of Conscience Concerning Evil Spirits." Within it, he wrote, "It were better that ten suspected witches should escape, than that one innocent person should be condemned." Shortly after this, the Reverend Francis Dane petitioned the governor of Massachusetts and implored him to release those who had been wrongly convicted. This public scrutiny prompted a new trial, which subsequently freed all those who remained imprisoned in May 1693.

Some of the worst offenders in the witch trials, such as Ann Putnam and Judge Samuel Sewall, publicly apologized for pursuing false convictions. However, Judge Hathorne and many of the other main participants in the trials

denied having any reason to be sorry. Hathorne's famous great-grandson, writer Nathaniel Hawthorne, was so embarrassed by his ancestor's zealotry that he changed the spelling of his last name once he became an established author.

Reader's Context

When you have spoken out against something you felt was wrong, how have you expressed your ideas? How did the problem get resolved?

Analyze Literature

Theme
A **theme** is a central message or perception about life revealed through a literary work. A *stated theme* is presented directly, whereas an *implied theme* must be inferred. A *universal theme* is a message about life than can be understood by people of most cultures.

Set Purpose

As Arthur Miller describes in the essay "Why I Wrote 'The Crucible'" (see pages 908–912), he wrote his play in the era of McCarthyism, when the fear of communism gripped Americans. As you read the last act, consider why Miller wrote the play about the Salem witch trials. Determine the various themes of the play and whether they are stated or implied. Which of these are universal themes?

Preview Vocabulary

conciliatory, 962
beguile, 962
adamant, 962
cleave, 963
penitence, 969

Act 4

A cell in Salem jail, that fall.

At the back is a high barred window; near it, a great, heavy door. Along the walls are two benches.

The place is in darkness but for the moonlight seeping through the bars. It appears empty. Presently footsteps are heard coming down a corridor beyond the wall, keys rattle, and the door swings open. Marshal Herrick enters with a lantern.

He is nearly drunk, and heavy-footed. He goes to a bench and nudges a bundle of rags lying on it.

HERRICK: Sarah, wake up! Sarah Good! *He then crosses to the other bench.*

SARAH GOOD, *rising in her rags:* Oh, Majesty! Comin', comin'! Tituba, he's here, His Majesty's come!

HERRICK: Go to the north cell; this place is wanted now. He *hangs his lantern on the wall. Tituba sits up.*

TITUBA: That don't look to me like His Majesty; look to me like the marshal.

HERRICK, *taking out a flask:* Get along with you now, clear this place. He *drinks, and Sarah Good comes and peers up into his face.*

SARAH GOOD: Oh, is it you, Marshal! I thought sure you be the Devil comin' for us. Could I have a sip of cider for me goin'-away?

HERRICK, *handing her the flask:* And where are you off to, Sarah?

TITUBA, *as Sarah drinks:* We goin' to Barbados, soon the Devil gits here with the feathers and the wings.

HERRICK: Oh? A happy voyage to you.

SARAH GOOD: A pair of bluebirds wingin' southerly, the two of us! Oh, it be a grand transformation, Marshal! *She raises the flask to drink again.*

HERRICK, *taking the flask from her lips:* You'd best give me that or you'll never rise off the ground. Come along now.

TITUBA: I'll speak to him for you, if you desires to come along, Marshal.

HERRICK: I'd not refuse it, Tituba; it's the proper morning to fly into Hell.

TITUBA: Oh, it be no Hell in Barbados. Devil, him be pleasure-man in Barbados, him be singin' and dancin' in Barbados. It's you folks— you riles him up 'round here; it be too cold 'round here for that Old Boy. He freeze his soul in Massachusetts, but in Barbados he just as sweet and—*A bellowing cow is heard, and Tituba leaps up and calls to the window:* Aye, sir! That's him, Sarah!

SARAH GOOD: I'm here, Majesty! *They hurriedly pick up their rags as Hopkins, a guard, enters.*

HOPKINS: The Deputy Governor's arrived.

HERRICK, *grabbing Tituba:* Come along, come along.

TITUBA, *resisting him:* No, he comin' for me. I goin' home!

HERRICK, *pulling her to the door:* That's not Satan, just a poor old cow with a hatful of milk. Come along now, out with you!

TITUBA, *calling to the window:* Take me home, Devil! Take me home!

SARAH GOOD, *following the shouting Tituba out:* Tell him I'm goin', Tituba! Now you tell him Sarah Good is goin' too!

In the corridor outside Tituba calls on—"Take me home, Devil; Devil take me home!" and Hopkins' voice orders her to move on. Herrick returns and begins to push old rags and straw into a corner. Hearing footsteps, he turns, and enter Danforth and Judge Hathorne. They are in greatcoats and wear hats against the bitter cold. They are followed in by Cheever, who carries a dispatch case and a flat wooden box containing his writing materials.

HERRICK: Good morning, Excellency.

DANFORTH: Where is Mr. Parris?

HERRICK: I'll fetch him. *He starts for the door.*

DANFORTH: Marshal. *Herrick stops.* When did Reverend Hale arrive?

HERRICK: It were toward midnight, I think.

DANFORTH, *suspiciously:* What is he about here?

HERRICK: He goes among them that will hang, sir. And he prays with them. He sits with Goody Nurse now. And Mr. Parris with him.

DANFORTH: Indeed. That man have no authority to enter here, Marshal. Why have you let him in?

HERRICK: Why, Mr. Parris command me, sir. I cannot deny him.

DANFORTH: Are you drunk, Marshal?

HERRICK: No, sir; it is a bitter night, and I have no fire here.

DANFORTH, *containing his anger:* Fetch Mr. Parris.

HERRICK: Aye, sir.

DANFORTH: There is a prodigious stench in this place.

HERRICK: I have only now cleared the people out for you.

DANFORTH: Beware hard drink, Marshal.

HERRICK: Aye, sir. *He waits an instant for further orders. But Danforth, in dissatisfaction, turns his back on him, and Herrick goes out. There is a pause. Danforth stands in thought.*

HATHORNE: Let you question Hale, Excellency; I should not be surprised he have been preaching in Andover lately.

DANFORTH: We'll come to that; speak nothing of Andover. Parris prays with him. That's strange. *He blows on his hands, moves toward the window. and looks out.*

HATHORNE: Excellency, I wonder if it be wise to let Mr. Parris so continuously with the prisoners. *Danforth turns to him, interested.* I think sometimes, the man has a mad look these days.

DANFORTH: Mad?

HATHORNE: I met him yesterday coming out of his house, and I bid him good morning—and he wept and went his way. I think it is not well the village sees him so unsteady.

DANFORTH: Perhaps he have some sorrow.

CHEEVER, *stamping his feet against the cold:* I think it be the cows, sir.

DANFORTH: Cows?

CHEEVER: There be so many cows wanderin' the highroads, now their masters are in the jails, and much disagreement who they will belong to now. I know Mr. Parris be arguin' with farmers all yesterday—there is great contention, sir, about the cows. Contention make him weep, sir; it were always a man that weep for contention. *He turns, as do Hathorne and Danforth, hearing someone coming up the corridor. Danforth raises his head as Parris enters. He is gaunt, frightened, and sweating in his greatcoat.*

PARRIS, *to Danforth, instantly:* Oh, good morning, sir, thank you for coming, I beg your pardon wakin' you so early. Good morning, Judge Hathorne.

DANFORTH: Reverend Hale have no right to enter this—

PARRIS: Excellency, a moment. *He hurries back and shuts the door.*

HATHORNE: Do you leave him alone with the prisoners?

DANFORTH: What's his business here?

PARRIS, *prayerfully holding up his hands:* Excellency, hear me. It is a providence. Reverend Hale has returned to bring Rebecca Nurse to God.

DANFORTH, *surprised:* He bids her confess?

PARRIS, *sitting:* Hear me. Rebecca have not given me a word this three month since she came. Now she sits with him, and her sister and Martha Corey and two or three others, and he pleads with them, confess their crimes and save their lives.

DANFORTH: Why—this is indeed a providence. And they soften, they soften?

PARRIS: Not yet, not yet. But I thought to summon you, sir, that we might think on whether it be not wise, to—*He dares not say it.* I had thought to put a question, sir, and I hope you will not—

DANFORTH: Mr. Parris, be plain, what troubles you?

PARRIS: There is news, sir, that the court—the court must reckon with. My niece, sir, my niece—I believe she has vanished.

DANFORTH: Vanished!

> "My niece, sir, my niece—I believe she has vanished."

PARRIS: I had thought to advise you of it earlier in the week, but—

DANFORTH: Why? How long is she gone?

PARRIS: This be the third night. You see, sir, she told me she would stay a night with Mercy Lewis. And next day, when she does not return, I send to Mr. Lewis to inquire. Mercy told him she would sleep in *my* house for a night.

DANFORTH: They are both gone?!

PARRIS, *in fear of him:* They are, sir.

DANFORTH, *alarmed:* I will send a party for them. Where may they be?

PARRIS: Excellency, I think they be aboard a ship. *Danforth stands agape.* My daughter tells me how she heard them speaking of ships last week, and tonight I discover my—my strongbox is broke into. *He presses his fingers against his eyes to keep back tears.*

HATHORNE, *astonished:* She have robbed you?

PARRIS: Thirty-one pound is gone. I am penniless. *He covers his face and sobs.*

DANFORTH: Mr. Parris, you are a brainless man! *He walks in thought, deeply worried.*

PARRIS: Excellency, it profit nothing you should blame me. I cannot think they would run off except they fear to keep in Salem any more. *He is pleading.* Mark it, sir, Abigail had close knowledge of the town, and since the news of Andover has broken here—

DANFORTH: Andover is remedied. The court returns there on Friday, and will resume examinations.

PARRIS: I am sure of it, sir. But the rumor here speaks rebellion in Andover, and it—

DANFORTH: There is no rebellion in Andover!

Martha Corey in jail.

PARRIS: I tell you what is said here, sir. Andover have thrown out the court, they say, and will have no part of witchcraft. There be a faction here, feeding on that news, and I tell you true, sir, I fear there will be riot here.

HATHORNE: Riot! Why at every execution I have seen naught but high satisfaction in the town.

PARRIS: Judge Hathorne—it were another sort that hanged till now. Rebecca Nurse is no Bridget that lived three year with Bishop before she married him. John Proctor is not Isaac Ward that drank his family to ruin. *To Danforth:* I would to God it were not so, Excellency, but these people have great weight yet in the town. Let Rebecca stand upon the gibbet[1] and send up some righteous prayer, and I fear she'll wake a vengeance on you.

HATHORNE: Excellency, she is condemned a witch. The court have—

DANFORTH, *in deep concern, raising a hand to Hathorne:* Pray you. *To Parris:* How do you propose, then?

PARRIS: Excellency, I would postpone these hangin's for a time.

DANFORTH: There will be no postponement.

PARRIS: Now Mr. Hale's returned, there is hope, I think—for if he bring even one of these to God, that confession surely damns the others in the public eye, and none may doubt more that they are all linked to Hell. This way, unconfessed and claiming innocence, doubts are multiplied, many honest people will weep for them, and our good purpose is lost in their tears.

DANFORTH, *after thinking a moment, then going to Cheever:* Give me the list.

Cheever opens the dispatch case, searches.

PARRIS: It cannot be forgot, sir, that when I summoned the congregation for John Proctor's excommunication there were hardly thirty people come to hear it. That speak a discontent, I think, and—

DANFORTH, *studying the list:* There will be no postponement.

PARRIS: Excellency—

---

1. **gibbet.** Structure used for hanging people; gallows

DANFORTH: Now, sir—which of these in your opinion may be brought to God? I will myself strive with him till dawn. *He hands the list to Parris, who merely glances at it.*

PARRIS: There is not sufficient time till dawn.

DANFORTH: I shall do my utmost. Which of them do you have hope for?

PARRIS, *not even glancing at the list now, and in a quavering voice, quietly:* Excellency— a dagger—*He chokes up.*

DANFORTH: What do you say?

PARRIS: Tonight, when I open my door to leave my house—a dagger clattered to the ground. *Silence. Danforth absorbs this. Now Parris cries out:* You cannot hang this sort. There is danger for me. I dare not step outside at night!

Reverend Hale enters. They look at him for an instant in silence. He is steeped in sorrow, exhausted, and more direct than he ever was.

DANFORTH: Accept my congratulations, Reverend Hale; we are gladdened to see you returned to your good work.

"While I speak God's law, I will not crack its voice with whimpering."

HALE, *coming to Danforth now:* You must pardon them. They will not budge.

Herrick enters, waits.

DANFORTH, <u>conciliatory</u>: You misunderstand, sir; I cannot pardon these when twelve are already hanged for the same crime. It is not just.

PARRIS, *with failing heart:* Rebecca will not confess?

HALE: The sun will rise in a few minutes. Excellency, I must have more time.

DANFORTH: Now hear me, and <u>beguile</u> yourselves no more. I will not receive a single plea for pardon or postponement. Them that will not confess will hang. Twelve are already executed; the names of these seven are given out, and the village expects to see them die this morning. Postponement now speaks a floundering on my part; reprieve or pardon must cast doubt upon the guilt of them that died till now. While I speak God's law, I will not crack its voice with whimpering. If retaliation is your fear, know this—I should hang ten thousand that dared to rise against the law, and an ocean of salt tears could not melt the resolution of the statutes. Now draw yourselves up like men and help me, as you are bound by Heaven to do. Have you spoken with them all, Mr. Hale?

HALE: All but Proctor. He is in the dungeon.

DANFORTH, *to Herrick:* What's Proctor's way now?

HERRICK: He sits like some great bird; you'd not know he lived except he will take food from time to time.

DANFORTH, *after thinking a moment:* His wife— his wife must be well on with child now.

HERRICK: She is, sir.

DANFORTH: What think you, Mr. Parris? You have closer knowledge of this man; might her presence soften him?

PARRIS: It is possible, sir. He have not laid eyes on her these three months. I should summon her.

DANFORTH, *to Herrick:* Is he yet <u>adamant</u>? Has he struck at you again?

HERRICK: He cannot, sir, he is chained to the wall now.

DANFORTH, *after thinking on it:* Fetch Goody Proctor to me. Then let you bring him up.

HERRICK: Aye, sir. *Herrick goes. There is silence.*

HALE: Excellency, if you postpone a week and publish to the town that you are striving for

con • cil • i • a • to • ry (kən sil´ ē ə tō rē) *adj.,* with an aim to please in order to gain something
be • guile (bə gīl´) *v.,* deceive by trickery
ad • a • mant (a´ də mənt) *adj.,* unyielding; insisting on maintaining a position

their confessions, that speak mercy on your part, not faltering.

DANFORTH: Mr. Hale, as God have not empowered me like Joshua to stop this sun from rising,[2] so I cannot withhold from them the perfection of their punishment.

HALE, *harder now:* If you think God wills you to raise rebellion, Mr. Danforth, you are mistaken!

DANFORTH, *instantly:* You have heard rebellion spoken in the town?

HALE: Excellency, there are orphans wandering from house to house; abandoned cattle bellow on the highroads, the stink of rotting crops hangs everywhere, and no man knows when the harlots' cry will end his life—and you wonder yet if rebellion's spoke? Better you should marvel how they do not burn your province!

DANFORTH: Mr. Hale, have you preached in Andover this month?

HALE: Thank God they have no need of me in Andover.

DANFORTH: You baffle me, sir. Why have you returned here?

HALE: Why, it is all simple. I come to do the Devil's work. I come to counsel Christians they should belie themselves. *His sarcasm collapses.* There is blood on my head! Can you not see the blood on my head!!

PARRIS: Hush! *For he has heard footsteps. They all face the door. Herrick enters with Elizabeth. Her wrists are linked by heavy chain, which Herrick now removes. Her clothes are dirty; her face is pale and gaunt. Herrick goes out.*

DANFORTH, *very politely:* Goody Proctor. *She is silent.* I hope you are hearty?

ELIZABETH, *as a warning reminder:* I am yet six month before my time.

DANFORTH: Pray be at your ease, we come not for your life. We— *uncertain how to plead, for he is not accustomed to it.* Mr. Hale, will you speak with the woman?

HALE: Goody Proctor, your husband is marked to hang this morning.

Pause.

ELIZABETH, *quietly:* I have heard it.

HALE: You know, do you not, that I have no connection with the court? *She seems to doubt it.* I come of my own, Goody Proctor. I would save your husband's life, for if he is taken I count myself his murderer. Do you understand me?

ELIZABETH: What do you want of me?

HALE: Goody Proctor, I have gone this three month like our Lord into the wilderness. I have sought a Christian way, for damnation's doubled on a minister who counsels men to lie.

HATHORNE: It is no lie, you cannot speak of lies.

HALE: It is a lie! They are innocent!

DANFORTH: I'll hear no more of that!

HALE, *continuing to Elizabeth:* Let you not mistake your duty as I mistook my own. I came into this village like a bridegroom to his beloved, bearing gifts of high religion; the very crowns of holy law I brought, and what I touched with my bright confidence, it died; and where I turned the eye of my great faith, blood flowed up. Beware, Goody Proctor— cleave to no faith when faith brings blood. It is mistaken law that leads you to sacrifice. Life, woman, life is God's most

> **"Beware, Goody Proctor—cleave to no faith when faith brings blood."**

---

2. **God have not empowered me like Joshua to stop this sun from rising.** In the Old Testament's Book of Joshua, Joshua commands the Lord to keep the sun from rising until the Israelites have defeated the Amorites in battle. According to the scripture, the sun and moon then "stood still in the midst of heaven, and did not hasten to go down for about a whole day" (Joshua 10:12–14).

cleave (klēv) *v.,* adhere to loyally

precious gift; no principle, however glorious, may justify the taking of it. I beg you, woman, prevail upon your husband to confess. Let him give his lie. Quail not before God's judgment in this, for it may well be God damns a liar less than he that throws his life away for pride. Will you plead with him? I cannot think he will listen to another.

ELIZABETH, *quietly:* I think that be the Devil's argument.

HALE, *with a climactic desperation:* Woman, before the laws of God we are as swine! We cannot read His will!

ELIZABETH: I cannot dispute with you, sir; I lack learning for it.

DANFORTH, *going to her:* Goody Proctor, you are not summoned here for disputation. Be there no wifely tenderness within you? He will die with the sunrise. Your husband. Do you understand it? *She only looks at him.* What say you? Will you contend with him? *She is silent.* Are you stone? I tell you true, woman, had I no other proof of your unnatural life, your dry eyes now would be sufficient evidence that you delivered up your soul to Hell! A very ape would weep at such calamity! Have the Devil dried up any tear of pity in you? *She is silent.* Take her out. It profit nothing she should speak to him!

ELIZABETH, *quietly:* Let me speak with him, Excellency.

PARRIS, *with hope:* You'll strive with him? *She hesitates.*

DANFORTH: Will you plead for his confession or will you not?

ELIZABETH: I promise nothing. Let me speak with him.

A sound—the sibilance[3] of dragging feet on stone. They turn. A pause. Herrick enters with John

John Proctor (George C. Scott) and Elizabeth Proctor (Colleen Dewhurst) say their final goodbyes in the 1967 television production of *The Crucible.*

Proctor. His wrists are chained. He is another man, bearded, filthy, his eyes misty as though webs had overgrown them. He halts inside the doorway, his eye caught by the sight of Elizabeth. The emotion flowing between them prevents anyone from speaking for an instant. Now Hale, visibly affected, goes to Danforth and speaks quietly.

HALE: Pray, leave them, Excellency.

DANFORTH, *pressing Hale impatiently aside:* Mr. Proctor, you have been notified, have you not? *Proctor is silent, staring at Elizabeth.* I see light in the sky, Mister; let you counsel with your wife, and may God help you turn your back on Hell. *Proctor is silent, staring at Elizabeth.*

HALE, *quietly:* Excellency, let—

Danforth brushes past Hale and walks out. Hale follows. Cheever stands and follows, Hathorne behind. Herrick goes. Parris, from a safe distance, offers:

PARRIS: If you desire a cup of cider, Mr. Proctor, I am sure I—*Proctor turns an icy stare at him, and he breaks off. Parris raises his palms toward Proctor.* God lead you now. *Parris goes out.*

---

3. **sibilance.** Sound quality resembling the sound of an *s* or *sh*

Alone. Proctor walks to her, halts. It is as though they stood in a spinning world. It is beyond sorrow, above it. He reaches out his hand as though toward an embodiment not quite real, and as he touches her, a strange soft sound, half laughter, half amazement, comes from his throat. He pats her hand. She covers his hand with hers. And then, weak, he sits. Then she sits, facing him.

PROCTOR: The child?

ELIZABETH: It grows.

PROCTOR: There is no word of the boys?

ELIZABETH: They're well. Rebecca's Samuel keeps them.

PROCTOR: You have not seen them?

ELIZABETH: I have not. *She catches a weakening in herself and downs it.*

PROCTOR: You are a—marvel, Elizabeth.

ELIZABETH: You—have been tortured?

PROCTOR: Aye. *Pause. She will not let herself be drowned in the sea that threatens her.* They come for my life now.

ELIZABETH: I know it.

Pause.

PROCTOR: None—have yet confessed?

ELIZABETH: There be many confessed.

PROCTOR: Who are they?

ELIZABETH: There be a hundred or more, they say. Goody Ballard is one; Isaiah Goodkind is one. There be many.

PROCTOR: Rebecca?

ELIZABETH: Not Rebecca. She is one foot in Heaven now; naught may hurt her more.

PROCTOR: And Giles?

ELIZABETH: You have not heard of it?

PROCTOR: I hear nothin', where I am kept.

ELIZABETH: Giles is dead.

He looks at her incredulously.

PROCTOR: When were he hanged?

ELIZABETH, *quietly, factually:* He were not hanged. He would not answer aye or nay to his indictment; for if he denied the charge they'd hang him surely, and auction out his property. So he stand mute, and died Christian under the law. And so his sons will have his farm. It is the law, for he could not be condemned a wizard without he answer the indictment, aye or nay.

PROCTOR: Then how does he die?

ELIZABETH, *gently:* They press him, John.

PROCTOR: Press?

ELIZABETH: Great stones they lay upon his chest until he plead aye or nay. *With a tender smile for the old man:* They say he give them but two words. "More weight," he says. And died.

PROCTOR, *numbed—a thread to weave into his agony:* "More weight."

ELIZABETH: Aye. It were a fearsome man, Giles Corey.

Pause.

PROCTOR, *with great force of will, but not quite looking at her:* I have been thinking I would confess to them, Elizabeth. *She shows nothing.* What say you? If I give them that?

ELIZABETH: I cannot judge you, John.

Pause.

PROCTOR, *simply—a pure question:* What would you have me do?

ELIZABETH: As you will, I would have it. *Slight pause.* I want you living, John. That's sure.

PROCTOR—*he pauses, then with a flailing of hope:* Giles' wife? Have she confessed?

ELIZABETH: She will not.

Pause.

PROCTOR: It is a pretense, Elizabeth.

ELIZABETH: What is?

PROCTOR: I cannot mount the gibbet like a saint. It is a fraud. I am not that man. *She is silent.* My honesty is broke, Elizabeth; I am no good man. Nothing's spoiled by giving them this lie that were not rotten long before.

ELIZABETH: And yet you've not confessed till now. That speak goodness in you.

PROCTOR: Spite only keeps me silent. It is hard to give a lie to dogs. *Pause, for the first time he turns directly to her.* I would have your forgiveness, Elizabeth.

ELIZABETH: It is not for me to give, John, I am—

PROCTOR: I'd have you see some honesty in it. Let them that never lied die now to keep their souls. It is pretense for me, a vanity that will not blind God nor keep my children out of the wind. *Pause.* What say you?

ELIZABETH, *upon a heaving sob that always threatens:* John, it come to naught that I should forgive you, if you'll not forgive yourself. *Now he turns away a little, in great agony.* It is not my soul, John, it is yours. *He stands, as though in physical pain, slowly rising to his feet with a great immortal longing to find his answer. It is difficult to say, and she is on the verge of tears.* Only be sure of this, for I know it now: Whatever you will do, it is a good man does it. *He turns his doubting, searching gaze upon her.* I have read my heart this three month, John. *Pause.* I have sins of my own to count. It needs a cold wife to prompt lechery.

PROCTOR, *in great pain:* Enough, enough—

ELIZABETH, *now pouring out her heart:* Better you should know me!

PROCTOR: I will not hear it! I know you!

ELIZABETH: You take my sins upon you, John—

PROCTOR, *in agony:* No, I take my own, my own!

ELIZABETH: John, I counted myself so plain, so poorly made, no honest love could come to

me! Suspicion kissed you when I did; I never knew how I should say my love. It were a cold house I kept! *In fright, she swerves, as Hathorne enters.*

HATHORNE: What say you, Proctor? The sun is soon up.

Proctor, his chest heaving, stares, turns to Elizabeth. She comes to him as though to plead, her voice quaking.

ELIZABETH: Do what you will. But let none be your judge. There be no higher judge under Heaven than Proctor is! Forgive me, forgive me, John—I never knew such goodness in the world! *She covers her face, weeping.*

Proctor turns from her to Hathorne; he is off the earth, his voice hollow.

PROCTOR: I want my life.

HATHORNE, *electrified, surprised:* You'll confess yourself?

PROCTOR: I will have my life.

HATHORNE, *with a mystical tone:* God be praised! It is a providence! *He rushes out the door, and his voice is heard calling down the corridor:* He will confess! Proctor will confess!

PROCTOR, *with a cry, as he strides to the door:* Why do you cry it? *In great pain he turns back to her.* It is evil, is it not? It is evil.

ELIZABETH, *in terror, weeping:* I cannot judge you, John, I cannot!

PROCTOR: Then who will judge me? *Suddenly clasping his hands:* God in Heaven, what is John Proctor, what is John Proctor? *He moves as an animal, and a fury is riding in him, a tantalized search.* I think it is honest, I think so; I am no saint. *As though she had denied this he calls*

> "Nothing's spoiled by giving them this lie that were not rotten long before."

angrily at her: Let Rebecca go like a saint; for me it is fraud!

Voices are heard in the hall, speaking together in suppressed excitement.

ELIZABETH: I am not your judge, I cannot be. *As though giving him release:* Do as you will, do as you will!

PROCTOR: Would you give them such a lie? Say it. Would you ever give them this? *She cannot answer.* You would not; if tongs of fire were singeing you you would not! It is evil. Good, then—it is evil, and I do it!

Hathorne enters with Danforth, and, with them, Cheever, Parris, and Hale. It is a businesslike, rapid entrance, as though the ice had been broken.

DANFORTH, *with great relief and gratitude:* Praise to God, man, praise to God; you shall be blessed in Heaven for this. *Cheever has hurried to the bench with pen, ink, and paper. Proctor watches him.* Now then, let us have it. Are you ready, Mr. Cheever?

PROCTOR, *with a cold, cold horror at their efficiency:* Why must it be written?

DANFORTH: Why, for the good instruction of the village, Mister; this we shall post upon the church door! *To Parris, urgently:* Where is the marshal?

PARRIS—*he runs to the door and calls down the corridor:* Marshal! Hurry!

DANFORTH: Now, then, Mister, will you speak slowly, and directly to the point, for Mr. Cheever's sake. *He is on record now, and is really dictating to Cheever, who writes.* Mr. Proctor, have you seen the Devil in your life? *Proctor's jaws lock.* Come, man, there is light in the sky; the town waits at the scaffold; I would give out this news. Did you see the Devil?

PROCTOR: I did.

PARRIS: Praise God!

DANFORTH: And when he come to you, what were his demand? *Proctor is silent. Danforth helps.* Did he bid you to do his work upon the earth?

PROCTOR: He did.

DANFORTH: And you bound yourself to his service? *Danforth turns, as Rebecca Nurse enters, with Herrick helping to support her. She is barely able to walk.* Come in, come in, woman!

REBECCA, *brightening as she sees Proctor:* Ah, John! You are well, then, eh?

Proctor turns his face to the wall.

DANFORTH: Courage, man, courage—let her witness your good example that she may come to God herself. Now hear it, Goody Nurse! Say on, Mr. Proctor. Did you bind yourself to the Devil's service?

REBECCA, *astonished:* Why, John!

PROCTOR, *through his teeth, his face turned from Rebecca:* I did.

DANFORTH: Now, woman, you surely see it profit nothin' to keep this conspiracy any further. Will you confess yourself with him?

REBECCA: Oh, John—God send his mercy on you!

DANFORTH: I say, will you confess yourself, Goody Nurse?

REBECCA: Why, it is a lie, it is a lie; how may I damn myself? I cannot, I cannot.

DANFORTH: Mr. Proctor. When the Devil came to you did you see Rebecca Nurse in his company? *Proctor is silent.* Come, man, take courage—did you ever see her with the Devil?

PROCTOR, *almost inaudibly:* No.

Danforth, now sensing trouble, glances at John and goes to the table, and picks up a sheet—the list of condemned.

DANFORTH: Did you ever see her sister, Mary Easty, with the Devil?

PROCTOR: No, I did not.

DANFORTH, *his eyes narrow on Proctor:* Did you ever see Martha Corey with the Devil?

PROCTOR: I did not.

DANFORTH, *realizing, slowly putting the sheet down:* Did you ever see anyone with the Devil?

PROCTOR: I did not.

DANFORTH: Proctor, you mistake me. I am not empowered to trade your life for a lie. You have most certainly seen some person with the Devil. *Proctor is silent.* Mr. Proctor, a score of people have already testified they saw this woman with the Devil.

PROCTOR: Then it is proved. Why must I say it?

DANFORTH: Why "must" you say it! Why, you should rejoice to say it if your soul is truly purged of any love for Hell!

PROCTOR: They think to go like saints. I like not to spoil their names.

DANFORTH, *inquiring, incredulous:* Mr. Proctor, do you think they go like saints?

PROCTOR, *evading:* This woman never thought she done the Devil's work.

DANFORTH: Look you, sir. I think you mistake your duty here. It matters nothing what she thought—she is convicted of the unnatural murder of children, and you for sending your spirit out upon Mary Warren. Your soul alone is the issue here, Mister, and you will prove its whiteness or you cannot live in a Christian country. Will you tell me now what persons conspired with you in the Devil's company? *Proctor is silent.* To your knowledge was Rebecca Nurse ever—

PROCTOR: I speak my own sins; I cannot judge another. *Crying out, with hatred:* I have no tongue for it.

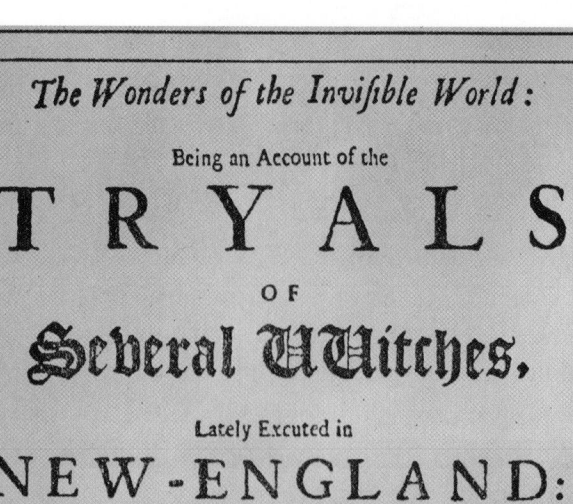

Cotton Mather, a prominent Puritan minister at the time of the Salem witch hunt, recounted the trials in this book, *The Wonders of the Invisible World* (1693). Although Mather did not play an official role in the trials, he warned the Boston public of the evils of witchcraft in his sermons and writings, thus promoting hysteria. In his book, Mather defended the trials as part of the Puritan mission to root out evil in the New World.

HALE, *quickly to Danforth:* Excellency, it is enough he confess himself. Let him sign it, let him sign it.

PARRIS, *feverishly:* It is a great service, sir. It is a weighty name; it will strike the village that Proctor confess. I beg you, let him sign it. The sun is up, Excellency!

DANFORTH—*he considers; then with dissatisfaction:* Come, then, sign your testimony. *To Cheever:* Give it to him. *Cheever goes to Proctor, the con-*

fession and a pen in hand. Come, man, sign it.

PROCTOR, *after glancing at the confession:* You have all witnessed it—it is enough.

DANFORTH: You will not sign it?

PROCTOR: You have all witnessed it; what more is needed?

DANFORTH: Do you sport with me? You will sign your name or it is no confession, Mister! *His breast heaving with agonized breathing, Proctor now lays the paper down and signs his name.*

PARRIS: Praise be to the Lord!

Proctor has just finished signing when Danforth reaches for the paper. But Proctor snatches it up, and now a wild terror is rising in him, and a boundless anger.

DANFORTH, *perplexed, but politely extending his hand:* If you please, sir.

PROCTOR: No.

DANFORTH, *as though Proctor did not understand:* Mr. Proctor, I must have—

PROCTOR: No, no. I have signed it. You have seen me. It is done! You have no need for this.

PARRIS: Proctor, the village must have proof that—

PROCTOR: Damn the village! I confess to God, and God has seen my name on this! It is enough!

DANFORTH: No, sir, it is—

PROCTOR: You came to save my soul, did you not? Here! I have confessed myself; it is enough!

DANFORTH: You have not con—

PROCTOR: I have confessed myself! Is there no good <u>penitence</u> but it be public? God does not need my name nailed upon the church! God sees my name; God knows how black my sins are! It is enough!

DANFORTH: Mr. Proctor—

PROCTOR: You will not use me! I am no Sarah Good or Tituba, I am John Proctor! You will

not use me! It is no part of salvation that you should use me!

DANFORTH: I do not wish to—

PROCTOR: I have three children—how may I teach them to walk like men in the world, and I sold my friends?

DANFORTH: You have not sold your friends—

PROCTOR: Beguile me not! I blacken all of them when this is nailed to the church the very day they hang for silence!

DANFORTH: Mr. Proctor, I must have good and legal proof that you—

PROCTOR: You are the high court, your word is good enough! Tell them I confessed myself; say Proctor broke his knees and wept like a woman; say what you will, but my name cannot—

DANFORTH, *with suspicion:* It is the same, is it not? If I report it or you sign to it?

PROCTOR—*he knows it is insane:* No, it is not the same! What others say and what I sign to is not the same!

DANFORTH: Why? Do you mean to deny this confession when you are free?

PROCTOR: I mean to deny nothing!

DANFORTH: Then explain to me, Mr. Proctor, why you will not let—

PROCTOR, *with a cry of his whole soul:* Because it is my name! Because I cannot have another in my life! Because I lie and sign myself to lies! Because I am not worth the dust on the feet of them that hang! How may I live without my name? I have given you my soul; leave me my name!

DANFORTH, *pointing at the confession in Proctor's hand:* Is that document a lie? If it is a lie I will not accept it! What say you? I will not deal in lies, Mister! *Proctor is motionless.* You will give me your honest confession in my hand, or I

---

pen • i • tence (pen´ ə tents) *n.*, humble remorse for wrongdoing

cannot keep you from the rope. *Proctor does not reply.* Which way do you go, Mister?

His breast heaving, his eyes staring, Proctor tears the paper and crumples it, and he is weeping in fury, but erect.

DANFORTH: Marshal!

PARRIS, *hysterically, as though the tearing paper were his life:* Proctor, Proctor!

HALE: Man, you will hang! You cannot!

PROCTOR, *his eyes full of tears:* I can. And there's your first marvel, that I can. You have made your magic now, for now I do think I see some shred of goodness in John Proctor. Not enough to weave a banner with, but white enough to keep it from such dogs. *Elizabeth, in a burst of terror, rushes to him and weeps against his hand.* Give them no tear! Tears pleasure them! Show honor now, show a stony heart and sink them with it! *He has lifted her, and kisses her now with great passion.*

REBECCA: Let you fear nothing! Another judgment waits us all!

DANFORTH: Hang them high over the town! Who weeps for these, weeps for corruption! *He sweeps out past them. Herrick starts to lead Rebecca, who almost collapses, but Proctor catches her, and she glances up at him apologetically.*

REBECCA: I've had no breakfast.

HERRICK: Come, man. *Herrick escorts them out, Hathorne and Cheever behind them. Elizabeth stands staring at the empty doorway.*

PARRIS, *in deadly fear, to Elizabeth:* Go to him, Goody Proctor! There is yet time!

From outside a drumroll strikes the air. Parris is startled. Elizabeth jerks about toward the window.

PARRIS: Go to him! *He rushes out the door, as though to hold back his fate.* Proctor! Proctor!

Again, a short burst of drums.

HALE: Woman, plead with him! *He starts to rush out the door, and then goes back to her.* Woman! It is pride, it is vanity. *She avoids his eyes, and moves to the window. He drops to his knees.* Be his helper! What profit him to bleed? Shall the dust praise him? Shall the worms declare his truth? Go to him, take his shame away!

ELIZABETH, *supporting herself against collapse, grips the bars of the window, and with a cry:* He have his goodness now. God forbid I take it from him!

The final drumroll crashes, then heightens violently. Hale weeps in frantic prayer, and the new sun is pouring in upon her face, and the drums rattle like bones in the morning air.

THE CURTAIN FALLS ❖

John Proctor refuses to sign a false confession about working with the devil, even if it will mean saving his life. When have you chosen to suffer the consequences of being truthful rather than hide behind dishonesty?

Refer to Text ▶ ▶ ▶ ▶ ▶   Reason with Text

1a. What reason does Cheever give Danforth for Parris's being emotionally troubled?

1b. Relate the situation he describes to what is happening to Salem as a community.

Understand
Find meaning

2a. Why is Parris afraid a riot will break out over the recent executions?

2b. What does Parris's explanation suggest about the justice system in Salem? On what basis are people truly judged?

Apply
Use information

3a. What does Danforth do in an attempt to obtain John Proctor's confession?

3b. Identify the speaking lines of Elizabeth that indicate her inner conflict over John's situation. What is causing this conflict?

Analyze
Take things apart

4a. After verbally confessing, what does John Proctor argue against doing?

4b. Do you agree or disagree with Proctor's reasoning in this matter. If you were a Salem resident, would how you learned of Proctor's confession make a difference?

Evaluate
Make judgments

5a. State what happens to John Proctor. How do you know this has happened?

5b. Summarize what you know about four of the play's main characters by the end of the play.

Create
Bring ideas together

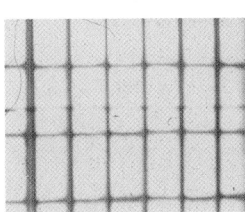

Analyze Literature

Theme

In Act 4, Reverend Hale directly states an important theme when he tells Elizabeth, "Cleave to no faith when faith brings blood." What other themes did you identify in *The Crucible*? Which are stated and which are implied? Write a sentence stating what you believe is the primary theme of the play. Is it a universal theme?

Extend the Text

Writing Options

Creative Writing Choose a character from *The Crucible,* and write a narrative account of the play's events from his or her point of view. You might summarize the entire play or focus on a single event or day. Read your account aloud to the class, and see how long it takes for someone to guess the character who is narrating the story.

Expository Writing Create study notes about one act from the play, including a summary and an analysis of characters, setting, plot, theme, and other major elements. Give your notes to a classmate. Have him or her verbally quiz you on the act, basing questions on your notes.

Media Literacy

Compare Visual Interpretations Several film adaptations of *The Crucible* have been produced since the play first appeared on stage in 1953. View one of the film versions. Then write an essay in which you analyze how the filmmaker's visual interpretation compares with your own as you read the play.

Collaborative Learning

Re-Enact a Witch Trial While *The Crucible* is a work of fiction, it is based on events that actually happened more than three hundred years ago. Learn more about the real Salem witch trials by doing an Internet search for the trial transcripts. Re-enact a scene from the trial, casting class members as the defendant, the judge, lawyers, witnesses, and family members.

 Go to **www.mirrorsandwindows.com** for more.

A critic using the political lens sees the literary text, first and foremost, as a political document. According to the theory of **political criticism,** a work cannot be viewed clearly unless it is placed in its cultural context. The critic then studies the relationship of the text to social and economic class. Specifically, the political critic asks questions such as What does this text (or author) assume about the key issues of class, race/ethnicity, and power? and Does this text support or challenge the existing power structure? The ideology of the author and the historical position of the literary work are given far more importance than, say, the structure or form of the work.

Overview of Political Criticism

Political criticism—the reading of a text through the lens of politics and culture—became popular in the 1920s with the Frankfurt school, a group of social theorists and philosophers based at the University of Frankfurt in Germany. The group formed in direct response to *fascism,* a repressive form of government that threatened to dominate Europe in the 1930s and led to World War II.

Political criticism, sometimes called *cultural Marxism* or *Marxist criticism* (in reference to economic and political philosopher Karl Marx [1818–1883]), enjoyed a revival in the 1960s, an era of radical social change. This was the period in which the Vietnam War sparked fierce debate and many young people protested the rigidity of traditional institutions. Anti-establishment critics applied the political lens to literature and, in doing so, broadened its scope. The traditional canon of American and British literature was re-evaluated, and new voices were heard from women, minority, and Third World writers.

Application of Political Criticism

When Arthur Miller's *The Crucible* is studied through the political lens, its major theme instantly becomes apparent. Miller wrote his play in 1953, when hearings were being conducted by congressional committees to root out supposed traitors to the nation. In 1950, Senator Joseph McCarthy declared that he had a list of names of Americans who were either "red" (communist) or accused of antisocial behavior. With this announcement, the hunt was on; anticommunist hysteria reached its peak in the early 1950s.

As you review *The Crucible,* consider how the following elements are interpreted according to the theory of political criticism.

Setting and Mood

The setting of the drama—Salem, Massachusetts, in 1692—establishes the mood that pervades *The Crucible.* Consider how the author depicts the atmosphere of this rural New England colony in Act 1:

> The edge of the wilderness was close by. The American continent stretched endlessly west, and it was full of mystery for them. It stood, dark and threatening, over their shoulders night and day, for out of it Indian tribes marauded from time to time, and Reverend Parris had parishioners who had lost relatives to these heathen.

❏ **Analyze** Consider how Miller juxtaposes the religious parish folk with the Native Americans. Which details give the impression that the Reverend Parris and his congregation are under attack? How do the details of the setting establish the mood and foreshadow the unfolding themes of persecution and religious zealotry?

Tone and Viewpoint

The author's tone and viewpoint are spelled out in the Overture of Act 1. Miller's explanation of the events that follow establishes his attitude toward the righteous people who seek to drive the "witches" out of Salem Village:

> Evidently the time came in New England when the repressions of order were heavier than seemed warranted by the dangers against which the order was organized. The witch-hunt was a perverse manifestation of the panic which set in among all classes when the balance began to turn toward greater individual freedom.

MILLER   MCCARTHY

❏ **Analyze** How does the fact that Miller wrote his play in the United States of the 1950s create an ironic tone? How would you summarize the author's viewpoint, based on this excerpt from the play?

Characterization

Now consider the characters that set the witch trials into motion. Reverend Hale comes to examine Betty, the daughter of Reverend Parris, who is apparently inhabited by an evil spirit. Hale's religious orthodoxy soon conquers even his protective impulses toward this apparently afflicted child and her teenage cohorts. Hale uses the language of the theocracy, the ruling class of New England.

In his quest for truth, Hale cross-examines the West Indian slave Tituba, servant to the Parris household and interpreter of the "evil" that lies in the forest. Tituba at first protests that she is innocent of witchcraft but soon senses a danger to herself and appears to recant (Act 1):

> TITUBA, *frightened by the coming process:* Mister Reverend, I do believe somebody else be witchin' these children.
>
> HALE: Who?
>
> TITUBA: I don't know, sir, but the Devil got him numerous witches.
>
> HALE: Does he! *It is a clue.* Tituba, look into my eyes. Come, look into me. *She raises her eyes to his fearfully.* You would be a good Christian woman, would you not, Tituba?
>
> TITUBA: Aye, sir, a good Christian woman.

❏ **Analyze** Karl Marx wrote about the class structure that perpetuates the ideology and lifestyle of the ruling class and keeps the underclass in a position of powerlessness. How does the language of each character reveal his or her social class? How does Hale use his position of power to turn Tituba into a witness for the prosecution?

Motivation and Class Conflict

The character of John Proctor can be understood by placing him in his social and economic context. Proctor is an independent farmer, a member of Salem's middle class. He does not belong to the lordly theocracy or the lowly class of servants and hired hands. Because he relies on the respect he has earned within the community, Proctor misjudges the temper of the times and gravely underrates the power of the clergy. When he exclaims "I like not the smell of this 'authority'" (Act 1), Proctor dares to question the men at the top of the class hierarchy.

Of course, Proctor has an internal, as well as an external, conflict. He becomes a man struggling to redeem his character after a moral lapse. If he cannot redeem his name with the truth, he believes, for a time, that he can do so with a lie. Ultimately, he will stand with Rebecca Nurse, the good woman who will not swear to falsehood under oath.

❏ **Analyze** Consider how Proctor's animosity toward Hale and the established clergy makes him Miller's spokesperson. How does Proctor struggle against persecution and, in doing so, become the hero of the drama?

WRITING ABOUT

Political Criticism

Write an essay that answers this question: How does the historical period in which the play was written determine how Arthur Miller depicts the Salem witch trials in *The Crucible?* Use details from the play to illustrate the concepts of persecution and resistance.

1. What is John Proctor's main reason for not attending church under the leadership of the Reverend Parris?
   A. Proctor is too busy clearing his land to travel the five miles to church.
   B. Proctor has a guilty conscience over his relationship with Abigail.
   C. The Parris family claims that part of Proctor's land is their own, which angers Proctor.
   D. Proctor is not a religious man and does not believe in God.
   E. Proctor thinks Parris talks too much about money, mortgages, and hell.

2. Abigail Williams is described as a "strikingly beautiful girl, an orphan, with an endless capacity for dissembling." What does *dissembling* mean?
   A. causing arguments
   B. appearing different from one time to the next
   C. putting on false appearances about one's behavior
   D. being analytical
   E. charming people with one's behavior and mannerisms

3. What does John Proctor believe is the underlying cause of hysteria in Salem?
   A. God's wrath about his sin
   B. vengeance
   C. illness from bad grain
   D. too much religion
   E. people not knowing the Commandments

4. As stated by Judge Danforth, why are only the victims and the accused allowed to testify?
   A. The courtroom will be too crowded if others are allowed to testify.
   B. The only witnesses to witchcraft are the victims and the witch, so no one else is needed.
   C. The character and motives of the other townspeople have been called into question.
   D. The crowds may influence the children who have been afflicted.
   E. Lawyers do not act upon the will of God.

5. In Act 4, what reason does Judge Danforth give for refusing to reprieve or pardon those who will not confess?
   A. Doing so will make people doubt whether those who were executed actually were guilty.
   B. He has evidence that they signed a pact with the devil.
   C. The remaining condemned people might stir up a rebellion in Salem.
   D. Doing so will call his authority as a judge into question.
   E. Doing so would be akin to defying the word of God.

6. Why does Reverend Hale state that he has returned to Salem to "do the Devil's work"?
   A. He has been infected by the witchcraft and wants to claim more souls for the devil.
   B. He has renounced his religion; therefore, anything he does is against God.
   C. He is trying to get the accused to lie and say they are witches to save their lives.
   D. He is following through with the court's decision, even though he no longer believes in it.
   E. He is in a state of spiritual confusion and does not know what he is doing.

7. In the Overture to *The Crucible*, Miller writes: "The Salem tragedy, which is about to begin in these pages, developed from a paradox. It is a paradox in whose grip we still live, and there is no prospect yet that we will discover its resolution." What are the two elements in this *paradox*, or seemingly contradictory statement?
   A. good and evil
   B. war and peace
   C. order and freedom
   D. humans and nature
   E. Christianity and heathenism

8. **Constructed Response:** Evaluate how the concept of goodness is used in *The Crucible*. For instance, compare and contrast John Proctor's idea of what makes a good person with that of Reverend Parris or Judge Danforth. Use evidence from the text to support your answer.

9. **Constructed Response:** Analyze the similarities between the Salem witch trials, as shown in *The Crucible*, and the McCarthy hearings, as excerpted in this unit. Consider the questioning style, the motivations, and the effect these trials had on the community or nation. Support your analysis with examples from the text.

Understand the Concept

Most people know the basic rules of **capitalization,** such as capitalizing the first word of a sentence. Less well known are the rules for capitalizing **proper nouns,** the names of specific persons, places, and things. Here are some common categories of proper nouns:

Specific people's names Arthur Miller, John Proctor

Titles used with names Judge Danforth, Senator Joseph McCarthy *but* the judge, the senator

Names of specific groups and organizations the Senate, the Communist Party, the U.S. Army *but* the army

Names of specific places Salem, Massachusetts, the Atlantic Ocean *but* the ocean

Names of countries, continents, and geographic regions the United States, North America, New England, the East Coast (*Names of directions are not capitalized:* east)

Names of days of the week, months, and holidays Monday, January, Martin Luther King Jr. Day (*Names of seasons are not capitalized:* winter)

Names of historical events, eras, and cultural movements World War II, the Cold War, the Civil Rights movement

Names of religious groups and terms the Puritans, Christians, God, the Bible

Titles of works of art and literature da Vinci's *Mona Lisa,* Miller's *The Crucible* (capitalize the first and last word and all important words)

Names of specific products and companies Coke, Microsoft Word, Apple Computer *but* personal computer

Another category of capitalized words is **proper adjectives,** which are descriptive words formed from proper nouns. Many proper adjectives are formed from the names of countries and continents, such as *American* and *European,* and others are formed from the names of historical figures, such as *Jeffersonian* (for Thomas Jefferson) and *Victorian* (for Queen Victoria). A trend toward less capitalization, however, has resulted in not capitalizing proper adjectives such as *congressional, senatorial,* and *biblical.*

Apply the Skill

Identify Capitalization Errors

Identify at least one capitalization error introduced in each of the following speaking lines from *The Crucible.*

1. Susanna walcott's here from doctor Griggs.
2. She always sings her Barbados Songs, and we dance.
3. I come to see what mischief your Uncle's brewin' now.
4. And yet, mister, a christian on Sabbath Day must be in church.
5. The law, based upon the Bible, and the bible, writ by Almighty God, forbid the practice of witchcraft, and describe death as the penalty thereof.

Fix Capitalization Errors

Most of the capitalization has been removed from the following paragraph. Rewrite the paragraph on your own paper, using three short underlines to indicate each letter that should be capitalized. (As you may know, three underlines is the proofreading mark for capitalization.)

> Many people learned about the tragedy at salem from seeing or reading arthur miller's play *the crucible.* To create the drama, the playwright investigated the judicial system of puritan society in seventeenth-century massachusetts. According to a protestant minister, the events began when betty parris and abigail williams displayed epileptic fits, perhaps during the winter of 1692. For the next fifteen months or so, more than 150 individuals were tried. The proceedings ended in may 1693.

Use Capitalized Words Correctly

Write an encyclopedia entry on a historical event that took place in your community or state. Focus on different types of proper nouns and adjectives, including as many capitalized words as possible without compromising readability. Review the guidelines at the beginning of this workshop before you begin.

from **Black Boy**

An Autobiography by Richard Wright

Build Background

Literary Context Richard Wright's autobiography, **Black Boy,** is considered by many literary critics to be his most important work. This narrative follows young Wright's journey from childhood to young adulthood in the segregated South.

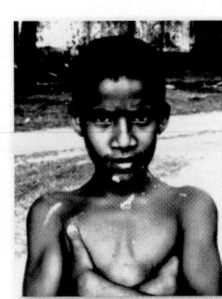

Through reading, Wright was able to escape the restraints of poverty and oppression. Borrowing books from Memphis's whites-only library by forging a note from a white patron, Wright read such prominent authors as H. L. Mencken and Sinclair Lewis, who gave him "a sense of life itself," a world of ideas outside his own.

In the following excerpt, Wright seeks refuge in fiction, much to the dismay of his grandmother, and discovers the power of words.

Reader's Context What story, poem, or novel have you read that made you want to read other selections by the same author? What about the work made you feel this way?

Meet the Author

Richard Wright (1908–1960) was born on a farm near Natchez, Mississippi. His childhood was characterized by poverty, emotional neglect, and frequent relocation. His father, an illiterate sharecropper, left the family in 1914, and for a time, Wright and his brother stayed in an orphanage. His mother was a schoolteacher but was unable to work due to frequent illness. Thus, Wright and his family were forced to depend on relatives.

Wright's schooling was erratic, but he enjoyed learning and graduated valedictorian of his ninth-grade class. An avid writer, he realized that to pursue this vocation, he would have to move North, where an African American could explore freedom of expression. At age nineteen, Wright moved to Chicago and worked for the Federal Writers' Project. His concern with the roots of racial oppression led him to become involved in social and political activism.

In 1937, Wright moved to New York to become editor of the *Daily Worker,* a radical newspaper. Shortly thereafter, he published his first short story collection, *Uncle Tom's Children* (1938), which portrayed the oppression of African Americans in the South. With the financial support of a Guggenheim fellowship, Wright completed *Native Son* (1940), one of the first best sellers written by an African American. Buoyed by its success, he completed *Black Boy* in 1945.

Analyze Literature

Purpose and Theme
A writer's **purpose** is his or her goal. The four common purposes are to inform or explain; to portray a person, place, object, or event; to convince people of a position; and to tell a story.

A **theme** is a central message about life revealed through a literary work. A *universal theme* is a message about life that can be understood by people of most cultures.

Set Purpose

Wright's firsthand observations of racial oppression made him a powerful voice in the literary world. As you read this excerpt from his autobiography, determine his purpose or purposes for writing. What did he intend to achieve? Also determine the main theme of the excerpt. Consider whether it is a universal theme, one to which most people can relate.

Preview Vocabulary

evasively, 977
apprehension, 977
endow, 977
dupe, 977
enthralled, 978
baleful, 978
intrigue, 978
deception, 978
elicit, 978
decipher, 978

from
Black Boy

by Richard Wright

*I had tasted what to me was life,
and I would have more of it,
somehow someway.*

Black Ghetto, c. 1968–1970. David C. Driskell. Fisk University, Nashville, Tennessee.

To help support the household my grandmother boarded a colored schoolteacher, Ella, a young woman with so remote and dreamy and silent a manner that I was as much afraid of her as I was attracted to her. I had long wanted to ask her to tell me about the books that she was always reading, but could never quite summon enough courage to do so. One afternoon I found her sitting alone upon the front porch reading.

"Ella," I begged, "please tell me what you are reading."

"It's just a book," she said <u>evasively</u>, looking about with <u>apprehension</u>.

"But what's it about?" I asked.

"Your grandmother wouldn't like it if I talked to you about novels," she told me.

I detected a note of sympathy in her voice.

"I don't care," I said loudly and bravely.

"Shhh—You mustn't say things like that," she said.

"But I want to know."

"When you grow up, you'll read books and know what's in them," she explained.

"But I want to know now."

She thought a while, then closed the book. "Come here," she said.

I sat at her feet and lifted my face to hers.

"Once upon a time there was an old, old man named Bluebeard," she began in a low voice.

She whispered to me the story of *Bluebeard and His Seven Wives* and I ceased to see the porch, the sunshine, her face, everything. As her words fell upon my new ears, I <u>endowed</u> them with a reality that welled up from somewhere within me. She told how Bluebeard had <u>duped</u> and married his seven wives, how he had loved and slain them, how he had hanged them up by their hair in a dark closet. The tale made the world around me be, throb, live. As she spoke,

---

eva • sive • ly (ē vā′ siv lē) *adv.,* in a manner intended to evade or avoid
ap • pre • hen • sion (a′ prē hen′ shən) *n.,* suspicion or fear
en • dow (en dou′) *v.,* provide with something freely or naturally
dupe (düp) *v.,* deceive by underhanded means; trick

reality changed, the look of things altered, and the world became peopled with magical presences. My sense of life deepened and the feel of things was different, somehow. Enchanted and <u>enthralled</u>, I stopped her constantly to ask for details. My imagination blazed. The sensations the story aroused in me were never to leave me. When she was about to finish, when my interest was keenest, when I was lost to the world around me, Granny stepped briskly onto the porch.

"You stop that, you evil gal!" she shouted. "I want none of that Devil stuff in my house!"

Her voice jarred me so that I gasped. For a moment I did not know what was happening.

"I'm sorry, Mrs. Wilson," Ella stammered, rising. "But he asked me—"

"He's just a foolish child and you know it!" Granny blazed.

Ella bowed her head and went into the house.

"But, Granny, she didn't finish," I protested, knowing that I should have kept quiet.

She bared her teeth and slapped me across my mouth with the back of her hand.

"You shut your mouth," she hissed. "You don't know what you're talking about!"

"But I want to hear what happened!" I wailed, dodging another blow that I thought was coming.

"That's the Devil's work!" she shouted.

My grandmother was as nearly white as a Negro can get without being white, which means that she was white. The sagging flesh of her face quivered; her eyes, large, dark, deep-set, wide apart, glared at me. Her lips narrowed to a line. Her high forehead wrinkled. When she was angry her eyelids drooped halfway down over her pupils, giving her a <u>baleful</u> aspect.

"But I liked the story," I told her.

"You're going to burn in hell," she said with such furious conviction that for a moment I believed her.

Not to know the end of the tale filled me with a sense of emptiness, loss. I hungered for the sharp, frightening, breathtaking, almost painful excitement that the story had given me, and I vowed that as soon as I was old enough I would buy all the novels there were and read them to feed that thirst for violence that was in me, for <u>intrigue</u>, for plotting, for secrecy, for bloody murders. So profoundly responsive a chord had the tale struck in me that the threats of my mother and grandmother had no effect whatsoever. They read my insistence as mere obstinacy, as foolishness, something that would quickly pass; and they had no notion how desperately serious the tale had made me. They could not have known that Ella's whispered story of <u>deception</u> and murder had been the first experience in my life that had <u>elicited</u> from me a total emotional response. No words or punishment could have possibly made me doubt. I had tasted what to me was life, and I would have more of it, somehow someway. I realized that they could not understand what I was feeling and I kept quiet. But when no one was looking I would slip into Ella's room and steal a book and take it back of the barn and try to read it. Usually I could not <u>decipher</u> enough words to make the story have meaning. I burned to learn to read novels and I tortured my mother into telling me the meaning of every strange word I saw, not because the word itself had any value, but because it was the gateway to a forbidden and enchanting land. ❖

MIRRORS & WINDOWS

Wright says that hearing the story of Bluebeard was the first experience in his life that had elicited a "total emotional response." When have you experienced a total emotional response to a work of art, literature, or music?

Refer to Text ▶ ▶ ▶ ▶ ▶ Reason with Text

1a. Describe Ella's manner.	**1b.** What does the young Wright find fascinating about Ella?	**Understand** Find meaning
2a. Who interrupts Ella's reading of the story? Why?	**2b.** What kinds of stories will the grandmother allow Wright to read?	**Apply** Use information
3a. Identify early signs that Wright would grow up to be a writer.	**3b.** Infer why Wright was not affected by the threats of his grandmother and mother.	**Analyze** Take things apart
4a. Why does Wright slip into Ella's room when no one is looking?	**4b.** Argue whether Wright's behavior is understandable. How else could he have explored the world of fiction?	**Evaluate** Make judgments
5a. What does Wright's grandmother call the story Ella was reading?	**5b.** Imagine you are Wright's grandmother. Describe your feelings when you catch Ella telling your grandson a story. What are you afraid of? What do you want for his future?	**Create** Bring ideas together

Analyze Literature

Purpose and Theme

In writing his autobiography, one of Wright's purposes was to tell a story. Therefore, *Black Boy* is an example of narrative writing. What other purposes might the author have had? Support your answer with details from the text.

What is the primary theme of this excerpt? Is it a universal theme? Again, explain using details from the text. What additional themes seem apparent to you?

Extend the Text

Writing Options

Creative Writing Many autobiographies are so engaging that they read like works of fiction. Rewrite the opening paragraphs of the excerpt as part of a novel based on Wright's youth. Write in the third person, change names and other key details, and alter the events in some way. Your intended audience is young adult readers.

Narrative Writing Write a one-page personal essay describing your relationship with reading. You might focus on a single aspect of this relationship, such as when or how you learned to read, or you might discuss what you most or least like to read. Exchange essays with a classmate and offer feedback.

Collaborative Learning

Perform Reader's Theater With three other students, choose a scene from the excerpt from *Black Boy* and adapt it for the stage by developing a script for a short skit. You can convert dialogue from the text into speaking lines, or if your chosen scene is narrative, you can develop it with speaking lines and other new details. Assign roles within your group, and perform your skit for the class.

Media Literacy

Create a Public Service Announcement Imagine that you are involved in an organization that promotes literacy. Write a television script for a thirty-second public service announcement (PSA) about the benefits of reading. The left side of the script should be the audio (what the voice-over will say), and the right side should list corresponding visuals. If possible, actually produce your PSA using the video and computer technology available to you.

 Go to **www.mirrorsandwindows.com** for more.

Midway

A Lyric Poem by Naomi Long Madgett

Build Background

Literary Context **"Midway,"** a poem by Naomi Long Madgett, first was published in 1959 in *Freedomways*, a journal featuring the voices of African-American writers. The nature and power of the poem's message seemed a perfect representation of the journal's mission to promote the creative expression of African-American ideas. Over its twenty-five-year history, *Freedomways* featured works by both historic and contemporary writers, including W. E. B. Du Bois, Alice Walker, and Nikki Giovanni, among others.

Historical Context Madgett wrote "Midway" shortly after the U.S. Supreme Court's 1954 desegregation ruling in *Brown v. Board of Education,* which gave her and other leaders of the Civil Rights movement the sense that racial justice was within reach. The historic ruling, according to Madgett, "led to the determination of Black people to move forward and never again accept the status quo."

Reader's Context When have you fought for something you believed you deserved? What steps did you take to get it?

Meet the Author

Naomi Long Madgett (b. 1923) was born Naomi Cornelia Long in Norfolk, Virginia, and spent her early years in New Jersey, where she was the only girl in her neighborhood. She often expressed her loneliness by writing poetry, receiving encouragement from her parents but rejection at her integrated school.

Positive change came when Madgett's family relocated to St. Louis in 1937. There, the young poet flourished in her all-black school, where students were taught to take pride in African-American achievements. Madgett published her first book of poetry, *Songs to a Phantom Nightingale,* days after graduating high school.

Madgett entered Virginia State College in 1945 and received a bachelor of arts degree. Soon after, she married and moved with her husband to Detroit, where she taught in the city's public schools while continuing to write and publish. Madgett served as an English professor at Eastern Michigan University from 1968 to 1984 and founded Lotus Press, a leading publisher of black literature, in 1972.

Madgett has written nine poetry collections and earned numerous awards, including the American Book Award (1993) and an honorary doctorate of fine arts degree (1994). She was named Detroit's poet laureate in 2001. Her autobiography, *Pilgrim Journey,* traces her evolution as a poet. Madgett continues to encourage fledgling African-American poets by conferring the Naomi Long Madgett Poetry Award, established in 1993.

Analyze Literature

Tone, Rhythm, and Meter
Tone is the emotional attitude toward the reader or toward the subject implied by a literary work—for instance, playful or ironic, sarcastic or sincere, hopeful or pessimistic.

Rhythm is the pattern of beats or stresses in a line of verse or prose. A regular rhythmic pattern in a poem is called a **meter,** which is determined by the number of stresses in each line.

Set Purpose

In three short stanzas, Madgett's poem expresses the spirit of an entire era. Consider how she captures that spirit in the tone of the poem. Write down three words that describe the tone, and analyze whether the tone changes in the poem. In addition, analyze the rhythm Madgett creates in "Midway." Is there a regular rhythmic pattern, or meter? Read the poem out loud to hear the rhythm.

Preview Vocabulary

bough, 981
abhor, 981
deride, 981
loom, 981

Midway

by Naomi Long Madgett

I've come this far to freedom and I won't turn back
I'm climbing to the highway from my old dirt track
>   I'm coming and I'm going
>   And I'm stretching and I'm growing
And I'll reap what I've been sowing[1] or my skin's not black

I've prayed and slaved and waited and I've sung my song
You've bled me and you've starved me but I've still grown strong
>   You've lashed me and you've treed me[2]
>   And you've everything but freed me
But in time you'll know you need me and it won't be long.

I've seen the daylight breaking high above the <u>bough</u>
I've found my destination and I've made my vow;
>   so whether you <u>abhor</u> me
>   Or <u>deride</u> me or ignore me
Mighty mountains <u>loom</u> before me and I won't stop now. ❖

---

1. **And I'll reap . . . sowing.** Literally, to gather what you have planted; "reap what you sow" often is used to mean receiving the rewards or consequences of something you have worked for or made happen.
2. **You've bled me . . . and you've treed me.** References to methods of cruel treatment of slaves by their owners, including whipping and tying them to trees

> **bough** (bou) *n.*, main branch of a tree
> **ab • hor** (əb hôr´) *v.*, feel disgust toward; hate
> **de • ride** (də rīd´) *v.*, laugh at; ridicule
> **loom** (lüm) *v.*, appear in excessively large form

MIRRORS & WINDOWS

Not even "mighty mountains" will stop the speaker from pursuit of her goal. What makes people keep going even in the face of defeat and hardship?

WARREN

Informational Text Connection

Named for one of its plaintiffs, Oliver Brown, the **U.S. Supreme Court case** known as ***Brown v. Board of Education of Topeka*** (1954) outlawed the segregation of black and white schoolchildren in Kansas, Delaware, South Carolina, Virginia, and Washington, DC. The case forced the Court to revisit the decision made fifty-eight years earlier in *Plessy v. Ferguson,* which upheld the idea of "separate but equal." In that case, the Court had ruled that as long as physical accommodations were reasonable, having separate facilities for blacks and whites did not violate the Fourteenth Amendment, which granted equal rights to all U.S. citizens.

The first part of the selection presents the case made in *Brown v. Board of Education,* arguing that "the 'separate but equal' doctrine . . . has no place in the field of public education." The second part of the selection is the decision of the U.S. Supreme Court, written by Chief Justice Earl Warren.

Syllabus
SUPREME COURT OF THE UNITED STATES

347 U.S. 483

Brown v. Board of Education of Topeka

APPEAL FROM THE UNITED STATES DISTRICT COURT FOR THE DISTRICT OF KANSAS

No. 1. Argued: Argued December 9, 1952
Reargued December 8, 1953—Decided: Decided May 17, 1954

Segregation of white and Negro children in the public schools of a State solely on the basis of race, pursuant to state laws permitting or requiring such segregation, denies to Negro children the equal protection of the laws guaranteed by the Fourteenth Amendment—even though the physical facilities and other "tangible" factors of white and Negro schools may be equal. Pp. 486–496.(a) The history of the Fourteenth Amendment is inconclusive as to its intended effect on public education. Pp. 489–490.(b) The question presented in these cases must be determined not on the basis of conditions existing when the Fourteenth Amendment was adopted, but in the light of the full development of public education and its present place in American life throughout the Nation.

Pp. 492–493.(c) Where a State has undertaken to provide an opportunity for an education in its public schools, such an opportunity is a right which must be made available to all on equal terms. P. 493.(d) Segregation of children in public schools solely on the basis of race deprives children of the minority group of equal educational opportunities, even though the physical facilities and other "tangible" factors may be equal. Pp. 493–494.(e) The "separate but equal" doctrine adopted in *Plessy v. Ferguson,* 163 U.S. 537, has no place in the field of public education. P. 495.(f) The cases are restored to the docket for further argument on specified questions relating to the forms of the decrees. Pp. 495–496.

Warren, C. J., Opinion of the Court
SUPREME COURT OF THE UNITED STATES

347 U.S. 483

Brown v. Board of Education of Topeka

APPEAL FROM THE UNITED STATES DISTRICT COURT
FOR THE DISTRICT OF KANSAS

No. 1. Argued: Argued December 9, 1952
Reargued December 8, 1953—Decided: Decide May 17, 1954

Mr. Chief Justice Warren delivered the opinion of the Court. . . .

Today, education is perhaps the most important function of state and local governments. Compulsory school attendance laws and the great expenditures for education both demonstrate our recognition of the importance of education to our democratic society. It is required in the performance of our most basic public responsibilities, even service in the armed forces. It is the very foundation of good citizenship. Today it is a principal instrument in awakening the child to cultural values, in preparing him for later professional training, and in helping him adjust normally to his environment. In these days, it is doubtful that any child may reasonably be expected to succeed in life if he is denied the opportunity of an education. Such an opportunity, where the state has undertaken to provide it, is a right which must be made available to all on equal terms.

We come then to the question presented: Does segregation of children in public schools solely on the basis of race, even though the physical facilities and other "tangible" factors may be equal, deprive the children of the minority group of equal educational opportunities? We believe that it does. . . .

We conclude that, in the field of public education, the doctrine of "separate but equal" has no place. Separate educational facilities are inherently unequal. Therefore, we hold that the plaintiffs and others similarly situated for whom the actions have been brought are, by reason of the segregation complained of, deprived of the equal protection of the laws guaranteed by the Fourteenth Amendment. ❖

Review Questions

1. What is the Court's position on segregation in public schools? Analyze the evidence the Court provides to support its position. What else, if anything, could the Court's opinion have stated?

2. According to Chief Justice Warren, why is providing public education important in a democratic society? Evaluate whether Warren's argument is still valid today.

3. On what basis must an answer to the question of segregation *not* be determined? What must be considered instead? List significant legal developments affecting U.S. public education that have been made since the 1954 ruling in *Brown v. Board of Education*. Consider both court decisions and laws that have been passed.

TEXT $\xleftrightarrow{\text{TO}}$ TEXT CONNECTION

Naomi Long Madgett was unhappy at her integrated school in New Jersey but fared much better at the all-black school in St. Louis. Considering Madgett's experience, what potential new problems might *Brown v. Board of Education* have presented? What might have been the root of these problems?

Refer to Text ▷ ▷ ▷ ▶ ▶	**Reason with Text**	
1a. In "Midway," to where does the speaker say she is climbing and from where has she come?	**1b.** Explain what each type of road means to the speaker. Why is she "climbing" to get from one to the other?	**Understand** Find meaning
2a. What does the speaker say she will do or her "skin's not black"?	**2b.** Emulate the speaker's confidence in making a similar declaration about yourself—for example, "I will pass this test or frogs don't jump."	**Apply** Use information
3a. According to the second stanza, what has been done to the speaker?	**3b.** Who is *you* in this poem? Infer the speaker's purpose in addressing *you*.	**Analyze** Take things apart
4a. What does the speaker say will happen in time?	**4b.** Predict whether what the speaker suggests will come true. How might *you* eventually need the speaker?	**Evaluate** Make judgments
5a. Describe what the speaker has seen. What now "looms" before her?	**5b.** The speaker refers to elements of nature to express her hopeful view of the future. How else could this view be expressed?	**Create** Bring ideas together

Analyze Literature

Tone, Rhythm, and Meter

Review the words you chose to describe the tone of the poem. Are they all similar, or do they describe different tones? Identify specific points where the tone was most clear to you, as well as points where the tone seemed to change.

What is the regular rhythm, or meter, in "Midway"? How does this use of meter contribute to the feeling of the poem? Would the poem be as effective if it lacked regular rhythm?

Extend the Text

Writing Options

Creative Writing Write a one-page cover letter to Naomi Long Madgett expressing your interest in a job opening as a clerical assistant at her publishing house, Lotus Press. Briefly summarize why you would be the best candidate for the job, and explain your strong interest in working for her.

Expository Writing The title "Midway" never is referenced or explained in the poem. Look up *midway* in a dictionary. How does its definition relate to the poem? Write a paragraph explaining the possible reasons Madgett believed this word captured the essence of her work.

Lifelong Learning

Create a Civil Rights Time Line Research events in the Civil Rights movement that occurred in the months and years following the 1954 *Brown v. Board of Education* ruling. Create an illustrated time line spanning at least twenty years that shows names, dates, places, and other key details associated with the movement.

Collaborative Learning

Share Speeches Research with a partner the various honors Naomi Long Madgett has received, and choose one to research. Then, as Madgett, write a speech accepting your chosen award or honor. Read your completed speech to your partner. Then listen critically as he or she does the same. Compare and contrast the speeches in terms of theme, style, tone, length, and other aspects.

 Go to **www.mirrorsandwindows.com** for more.

from
Quiet **Strength**

by Rosa Parks

In 1955, **Rosa Parks** (1913–2005), an African-American seamstress from Tuskegee, Alabama, secured a place in U.S.  history when she was arrested for refusing to relinquish her bus seat to a white passenger. Her act of defiance prompted a yearlong bus boycott in Montgomery, Alabama, which ended in 1956 when the U.S. Supreme Court declared segregation on buses unconstitutional.

Soon after the bus boycott, Parks and her husband, Raymond, became active in the National Association for the Advancement of Colored People (NAACP). Following her husband's death in 1977, Parks founded the Rosa and Raymond Institute for Self-Development to better the lives of youth. A recipient of both the Presidential Medal of Freedom (1996) and a Congressional Gold Medal (1999), Parks stated, "I think the American Dream should be to have a good life, and to live well, and to be a good citizen. I think that should apply to all of us."

In this excerpt from her autobiography, *Quiet Strength,* Parks reflects on the early days of the Civil Rights movement and her involvement in the Montgomery bus boycott.

After the 1954 Supreme Court ruling on *Brown v. Board of Education,* which designated separate-but-equal schools for children unlawful, a few people felt optimistic that things would get better. The laws were changed, but the heart of America remained unchanged.

One day I noticed a little child whose mother was taking him to one of the integrated schools. From the nervous look on his face I could tell he did not want to go to that white school, and his mother, she did not know what was going to happen. It was not easy for a small child to walk into a place of merely token integration, where a multitude of white persons had always been taught there should be racial segregation.

Despite the banning of separate schools for the races, most people did not react too favorably. They were more indifferent than interested. It was not easy, you see, because the pattern had existed so long. There were still separate elevators and fountains for white and colored people. I used them as little as possible.

The more I became involved with the NAACP, the more I learned of discrimination and acts of violence against blacks, such as lynchings,[1] rapes, and unsolved murders. And the more I learned about these incidents, the more I felt I could no longer passively sit by and accept the Jim Crow laws.[2] A better day had to come.

---

1. **lynchings.** Hangings, usually conducted by a mob of people
2. **Jim Crow laws.** Common name for segregation laws in effect between the 1870s and 1950s. *Jim Crow* refers to the name of a routine ("Jump Jim Crow") performed at minstrel shows, comedic musical acts that often mocked African Americans.

The custom for getting on the bus for black persons in Montgomery in 1955 was to pay at the front door, get off the bus, and then re-enter through the back door to find a seat. On the buses, if white persons got on, the colored would move back if the white section was filled. Black people could not sit in the same row with white people. They could not even sit across the aisle from each other. Some customs were humiliating, and this one was intolerable since we were the majority of the ridership.

On Thursday evening, December 1, I was riding the bus home from work. A white man got on, and the driver looked our way and said, "Let me have those seats." It did not seem proper, particularly for a woman to give her seat to a man. All the passengers paid ten cents, just as he did. When more whites boarded the bus, the driver, J. P. Blake, ordered the blacks in the fifth row, the first row of the colored section (the row I was sitting in), to move to the rear. Bus drivers then had police powers, under both municipal and state laws, to enforce racial segregation. However, we were sitting in the section designated for colored.

At first none of us moved.

"Y'all better make it light on yourselves and let me have those seats," Blake said.

Then three of the blacks in my row got up, but I stayed in my seat and slid closer to the window. I do not remember being frightened. But I sure did not believe I would "make it light" on myself by standing up. Our mistreatment was just not right, and I was tired of it.

Rosa Parks riding the bus in Montgomery, Alabama, on December 21, 1956, the day the U.S. Supreme Court ruled that segregation on city buses was unconstitutional.

The more we gave in, the worse they treated us. I kept thinking about my mother and my grandparents, and how strong they were. I knew there was a possibility of being mistreated, but an opportunity was being given to me to do what I had asked of others.

I knew someone had to take the first step. So I made up my mind not to move. Blake asked me if I was going to stand up.

The more **we gave in,** the **worse they treated us.**

"No. I am not," I answered.

Blake said that he would have to call the police. I said, "Go ahead." In less than five minutes, two policemen came, and the driver pointed me out. He said that he wanted the seat and that I would not stand up.

"Why do you push us around?" I said to one of the policemen.

"I don't know," he answered, "but the law is the law and you're under arrest."

◆ ◆ ◆

I did not get on the bus to get arrested; I got on the bus to go home. Getting arrested was one of the worst days in my life. It was not a happy experience. Since I have always been a strong believer in God, I knew that He was with me, and only He could get me through the next step.

I had no idea that history was being made. I was just tired of giving in. Somehow, I felt that what I did was right by standing up to that bus driver. I did not think about the consequences. I knew that I could have been lynched, manhandled,[3] or beaten when the police came. I chose not to move. When I made that decision, I knew that I had the strength of my ancestors with me.

There were other people on the bus whom I knew. But when I was arrested, not one of them came to my defense. I felt very much alone. One man who knew me did not even go by my house to tell my husband I had been arrested. Everyone just went on their way.

In jail I felt even more alone. For a moment, as I sat in that little room with bars, before I was moved to a cell with two other women, I felt that I had been deserted. But I did not cry. I said a silent prayer and waited.

Later that evening, to my great relief, I was released. It is strange: after the arrest, I never did reach the breaking point of shedding tears. The next day, I returned to work. It was pouring down rain, so I called a cab. The young man at work was so surprised to see me. He thought I would be too nervous and shaken to go back to work.

Three days later I was found guilty and ordered to pay a ten-dollar fine plus four dollars in court costs. The case was later appealed with the help of one of my attorneys, Fred Gray, and I did not have to pay anything.

It is funny to me how people came to believe that the reason that I did not move from my seat was that my feet were tired. I did not hear this until I moved to Detroit in 1957. My feet were not tired, but *I* was tired—tired of unfair treatment. I also heard later that Mother Pollard, one of the marchers in Montgomery, said that my feet were tired but my soul was rested. She was right about my soul.

On Monday, December 5, the day I went to court, the Montgomery Improvement Association (MIA) was formed to start the bus boycott. It is sad, in a way, to think about what we had to go through to get to that point. We, as a people, all felt discouraged with our situation, but we had not been united enough to conquer it. Now, the fearfulness and bitterness was turning into power.

Now, the **fearfulness** and **bitterness** was turning into power.

So the people started organizing, protesting, and walking. Many thousands were willing to sacrifice the comfort and convenience of riding the bus. This was the modern mass movement we needed. I suppose they were showing sympathy for a person who had been mistreated. It was not just my arrest that year. Many African-Americans, including Emmet Till, had been killed or beaten for racist reasons. I was the third woman in Montgomery to be arrested on a bus. We reached the point where we simply had to take action.

◆ ◆ ◆

Nearly a year later the segregated-bus ordinance was declared unconstitutional by the U.S.

---

3. **manhandled.** Treated roughly

Supreme Court. One day after the boycott ended, I rode a nonsegregated bus for the first time.

A month after the boycott began, I lost my twenty-five-dollar-a-week job when the now-defunct Montgomery Fair department store closed its tailor shop. I was given no indication from the store that my boycott activities were the reason I lost my job. People always wanted to say it was because of my involvement in the boycott.

I cannot say this is true. I do not like to form in my mind something I do not have any proof of.

Four decades later I am still uncomfortable with the credit given to me for starting the bus boycott. Many people do not know the whole truth; I would like them to know I was not the only person involved. I was just one of many who fought for freedom. And many others around me began to *want* to fight for their rights as well.

At that time, the Reverend Martin Luther King Jr. was emerging on the scene. He once said, "If you will protest courageously and yet with dignity and Christian love, when the history books are written in future generations, the historians will have to pause and say: there lived a great people—a black people—who injected new meaning and dignity into the veins of civilization." It was these words that guided many of us as we faced the trials and tribulations of fighting for our rights. ❖

Why do people go along with things they know are wrong? What does it take to defy expectation or tradition?

Refer and Reason

1. How does Parks describe her experience of being arrested? Based on her account, did she feel any sense of regret while in jail? Explain your answer.

2. According to Parks, why were "many thousands . . . willing to sacrifice" riding the bus? Do you agree with Parks's opinion on what motivated the people who joined the boycott? Suggest other reasons people might have had for joining the boycott.

3. Identify two misconceptions Parks says the public has long held about her experience. How might such misconceptions have begun? Why did so many people believe them?

Writing Options

1. Imagine going back in time and meeting Rosa Parks. What would you want to learn from her? Prepare a list of five to ten interview questions you would ask.

2. You are the mayor of Montgomery during the 1955 bus boycott. Prepare a position statement to be read at an upcoming meeting to discuss how to handle the boycott. State your position on the matter, supporting it with solid, fact-based reasons.

 Go to **www.mirrorsandwindows.com** for more.

In the 1950s, a small group of writers banded together to support one another in their innovative approach to literature and life. That group, which included writers Jack Kerouac, Allen Ginsberg, William S. Burroughs, and Lawrence Ferlinghetti, felt constrained by the rules of what was acceptable in both society and literature. They felt worn out, or "beat down," by the dictates of the so-called establishment, the moral and legal authority created by mainstream culture, government, and education. The **Beats,** as they came to be known, redefined what it meant to be a poet or writer and what it meant to be alive.

The members of the Beat generation, often called *beatniks,* were considered by many to be "bohemian libertines" or "counter-cultural subversives." Their radical culture of relaxed rebellion was portrayed in Kerouac's *On the Road* (1957), a fictional travel journal about friends traversing North America. Many Beat writers settled in San Francisco, where Ferlinghetti's City Lights bookstore became a hub of literary exploration. It attracted poets such as Gary Snyder, whose intense interests in nature and Zen Buddhism influenced the other Beats and subsequently larger portions of U.S. culture.

Despite the Beats' preference for "keeping it cool" and maintaining a low profile, the movement made several lasting impressions on the world of literature. Ginsberg's *Howl* (1956) and Burroughs's *Naked Lunch* (1959) helped change attitudes and policies about what legally could be published after both works were subjected to obscenity trials. The Beat writers also inspired future protests against the establishment, including the Vietnam War protests of the 1960s.

Twin Pines with Family Car, 2000. Mary Iverson.

from On the Road

A Novel by Jack Kerouac

Build Background

Literary Context Jack Kerouac's **On the Road** (1957) generally is considered the quintessential representation of life inside the Beat movement. Kerouac, the man who reportedly coined the term *Beat,* wrote this fictional travel journal in just three weeks on a single scroll of paper 120 feet long. Largely autobiographical, the story covers the travels of Dean Moriarty (a pseudonym for Kerouac's friend Neal Cassady) and Sal Paradise (Kerouac) as they travel to Chicago, San Francisco, Mexico, and places in between. The excerpts that follow describe two episodes from early in the trip, during which Sal rides a bus and hitchhikes from the East Coast to mid-America.

Publication of *On the Road* in 1957 drew immediate and widespread public attention. The *New York Times* praised the book as "the most beautifully executed, the clearest and most important utterance" of the Beat generation. In 2005, *Time* magazine included *On the Road* on its list of the best English-language novels.

Reader's Context Describe the last time you did something adventurous and carefree. What emotions did you feel? What risks were involved?

Meet the Author

Jack Kerouac (1922–1969) was born Jean Louis Lebris de Kerouac in Lowell, Massachusetts, to parents of French-Canadian descent. The youngest Kerouac was a bright and serious child. The devastating loss of his nine-year-old brother, followed by the failure of his father's printing business during the Great Depression, contributed to Kerouac's need to find deeper meaning in what seemed an otherwise joyless life.

Although Kerouac began creating stories at an early age, his athletic talent was what earned him a full scholarship to Columbia University in New York City. Injury, interpersonal conflicts, and disinterest in structured education soon ended his college career and brought his life to a crossroads. He briefly served in the U.S. Merchant Marine before returning to the Columbia vicinity, where he met fellow future beatniks William S. Burroughs and Allen Ginsberg, among others.

Kerouac eventually translated the journals he had kept during his adventures with these friends into a series of popular novels, including *On the Road* (1957), *Big Sur* (1958), and *The Dharma Bums* (1962). Kerouac, whose style echoed that of writer Thomas Wolfe, also published several unrelated novels and six poetry collections. The voice that inspired a generation, Kerouac died at age forty-seven.

Analyze Literature

Narrator and Diction

A **narrator** is a character or speaker who tells a story. The writer's choice of narrator is important in determining the amount and type of information readers are given in the story.

Diction, when applied to writing, refers to the author's choice of words. Much of a writer's style is determined by his or her diction.

Set Purpose

Sal Paradise, the narrator of *On the Road* who chronicles his cross-country trip by way of public transportation and hitchhiking, is believed to be Kerouac's alter ego. As you read, develop a brief profile of Sal and evaluate his effectiveness as a narrator. Also evaluate what seems to be Kerouac's preferred style of speaking. Record two or three examples of diction that illustrate the writer's style.

Preview Vocabulary

disperse, 992
sultry, 992

Arrested Vehicle (Fat Seats), 1970. John Salt.

from

ON THE ROAD

by Jack Kerouac

We lean forward to the next crazy venture beneath the skies.

It was an ordinary bus trip with crying babies and hot sun, and countryfolk getting on at one Penn town after another, till we got on the plain of Ohio and really rolled, up by Ashtabula and straight across Indiana in the night. I arrived in Chi quite early in the morning,[1] got a room in the Y, and went to bed with a very few dollars in my pocket. I dug Chicago after a good day's sleep.

The wind from Lake Michigan, bop at the Loop, long walks around South Halsted and North Clark,[2] and one long walk after midnight into the jungles, where a cruising car followed

---

1. **one Penn town . . . early in the morning.** In his characteristic diction, the narrator describes his westward trip from Pennsylvania ("Penn") to Chicago ("Chi"), during which he traveled through Ashtabula, Ohio.
2. **Lake Michigan . . . North Clark.** References to areas of interest in Chicago

me as a suspicious character. At this time, 1947, bop was going like mad all over America. The fellows at the Loop blew, but with a tired air, because bop was somewhere between its Charlie Parker Ornithology period and another period that began with Miles Davis.[3] And as I sat there listening to that sound of the night which bop has come to represent for all of us, my friends from one end of the country to the other and how they were really all in the same vast backyard doing something so frantic and rushing-about. And for the first time in my life, the following afternoon, I went into the West. It was a warm and beautiful day for hitchhiking. To get out of the impossible complexities of Chicago traffic I took a bus to Joliet, Illinois, went by the Joliet pen,[4] stationed myself just outside town after a walk through its leafy rickety streets behind, and pointed my way. All the way from New York to Joliet by bus, and I had spent more than half my money. . . .

W hat is that feeling when you're driving away from people and they recede on the plain till you see their specks <u>dispersing</u>?—it's the too-huge world vaulting us, and it's good-by. But we lean forward to the next crazy venture beneath the skies.

We wheeled through the <u>sultry</u> old light of Algiers, back on the ferry, back toward the mud-splashed, crabbed old ships across the river, back on Canal,[5] and out; on a two-lane highway to Baton Rouge in purple darkness; swung west there, crossed the Mississippi at a place called Port Allen. Port Allen—where the river's all rain and roses in a misty pinpoint darkness and where we swung around a circular drive in yellow foglight and suddenly

saw the great black body below a bridge and crossed eternity again. What is the Mississippi River?—a washed clod in the rainy night, a soft plopping from drooping Missouri banks, a dissolving, a riding of the tide down the eternal waterbed, a contribution to brown foams, a voyaging past endless vales and trees and levees, down along, down along, by Memphis, Greenville, Eudora, Vicksburg, Natchez, Port Allen, and Port Orleans, and Port of the Deltas, by Potash, Venice,[6] and the Night's Great Gulf, and out.

With the radio on to a mystery program, and as I looked out the window and saw a sign that said USE COOPER'S PAINT and I said, "Okay, I will." We rolled across the hoodwink night of the Louisiana plains—Lawtell, Eunice, Kinder, and De Quincy, western rickety towns becoming more bayou-like[7] as we reached the Sabine. In Old Opelousas I went into a grocery store to buy bread and cheese while Dean[8] saw to gas and oil. It was just a shack; I could hear the family eating supper in the back. I waited a minute; they went on talking. I took bread and cheese and slipped out the door. We had barely enough money to make Frisco.[9] . . . ❖

---

3. **fellows at the Loop . . . Davis.** "Bop," or "be-bop," is a style of music made popular in the 1940s by jazz greats such as Charlie Parker and Miles Davis. *Ornithology* was the name of one of Parker's best-known recordings.
4. **Joliet pen.** Joliet Penitentiary, a prison
5. **Algiers . . . Canal.** *Algiers*—a neighborhood in New Orleans; *Canal*—a street with a ferry crossing in New Orleans
6. **Memphis . . . Venice.** Towns along the Mississippi River
7. **bayou-like.** Like a marsh or swampy body of water
8. **Dean.** Dean is a frequent travel companion of Sal's and another of the major characters.
9. **Frisco.** San Francisco, California

---

dis • perse (dis pʉrs´) *v.,* spread or break apart
sul • try (sul´ trē) *adj.,* hot and humid

Finding himself alone in a strange hotel room, far from home, the narrator says he momentarily did not know who he was. How do you define yourself? What values or beliefs are at the core of your identity?

Refer to Text ▶ ▶ ▶ ▶ ▶   Reason with Text

1a. At the start of the first excerpt, how far has the narrator traveled by bus?

1b. Explain why the narrator now must hitch-hike. How does he feel about that?

Understand
Find meaning

2a. Name the geographic locations the narrator sees in these excerpts.

2b. Based on the narrator's brief descriptions, what can you infer about each location?

Apply
Use information

3a. How does the narrator describe the Mississippi River?

3b. How does he seem to feel about the Mississippi? How does he relate to it?

Analyze
Take things apart

4a. At the end of the second excerpt, what does the narrator take from the store?

4b. Determine why he steals these things. What do these excerpts reveal about the narrator's lifestyle?

Evaluate
Make judgments

5a. Identify details that indicate the narrator's conflicting feelings about the United States.

5b. List eight to ten symbols of the United States, and organize them into categories of objects, ideas, people, places, and other. Which category contains the most entries?

Create
Bring ideas together

Analyze Literature

Narrator and Diction
What can you infer about the narrator based on the information he provides? Is he an effective narrator for this travel narrative? How would the story have been different if told in the third person, rather than by the subject himself?

Review the words and phrases you recorded. Use them to characterize Kerouac's written style. How does his style fit the subject about which he's writing?

Extend the Text

Writing Options
Creative Writing Rewrite one of the excerpts from *On the Road* as a free-verse poem, the form that characterizes most Beat poetry. As the narrator, you might take the reader through your entire trip, or you might focus on a specific stop along the journey. Remember that free verse does not follow any specific pattern of rhyme, meter, or organization.

Narrative Writing Write your own narrative about a recent trip you took. It might be as major as an overseas vacation or as simple as your drive to school this morning. Model the narrative after *On the Road* in terms of writing style, tone, narration, and degree of detail.

Media Literacy
Create a Be-Bop Website Research the history and importance of "be-bop," a style of jazz music made popular in the 1940s, including its association with the Beat movement. Then draft a plan for a website about be-bop. Decide whether the site will serve as an introduction to the general public or be geared more toward jazz enthusiasts.

Critical Literacy
Communicate in "Beat Speak" Research words, phrases, and other conversational elements typically used among the Beat generation. For example, the narrator in *On the Road* "dug" (liked) Chicago. With a partner, create a dialogue using "Beat speak" to present to the class. Then repeat the exercise using more formal, traditional language to convey the same information. Compare and contrast the two dialogues.

 Go to **www.mirrorsandwindows.com** for more.

Understand the Concept

In *On the Road,* Jack Kerouac's use of words such as *countryfolk, hitchhiking,* and *foglight* demonstrates the modern trend toward creating **compound words,** in which two or more words are joined to create a single meaning. **Compound nouns** that are written as one word, with no space or punctuation, are called *closed compounds.* In other compound nouns, the words are joined with a hyphen, as in *runner-up* and *ten-year-old,* or left open, as in *master builder* and *high school.*

Perhaps the most commonly used compounds are **compound adjectives,** such as *part-time, two-lane,* and *follow-up.* Many compound adjectives are hyphenated, but others are closed, such as *childproof* and *trustworthy.* Common types of hyphenated adjective compounds include the following:

Ages a ten-year-old child, the twenty- to thirty-year-old group

Numbered ranks or positions the first-place winner, the second-to-last row, a third-floor room

Centuries or eras nineteenth-century history, space-age technology

Adjectives + nouns a small-town girl, middle-class status, high-level officials

Nouns + adjectives an interest-free loan, user-friendly software, a top-heavy load

Nouns + gerunds the decision-making process, mountain-climbing gear

Multiword phrases over-the-counter medicine, a matter-of-fact approach

By joining words to form compound adjectives, writers can create specific, unique descriptors, often with subtle shades of meaning. For instance, in *On the Road,* Kerouac describes the feeling of driving away and leaving behind a place or person using the expression "the too-huge world." In portraying the Mississippi River on a rainy evening, he describes the drops of moisture hanging in the night air as "a misty pinpoint darkness."

Compounds that are created for specific instances and used infrequently are called *temporary compounds.* Compounds that become accepted into everyday usage are called *permanent compounds* and appear in the dictionary.

Apply the Skill

Exercise A

Copy the following sentences on a sheet of paper. For each sentence, underline each compound noun once and each compound adjective twice. Be sure to look for open, closed, and hyphenated compounds.

1. *On the Road* is a fictional narrative about the cross-continent travels of several friends.
2. Kerouac's well-known book is based on his real-life experiences in the early 1950s.
3. In writing about a late-night adventure in Chicago, the narrator describes himself as a suspicious-looking character.
4. The cash-strapped narrator resorts at one point to stealing food from a small roadside store.
5. When *On the Road* was published in 1957, it became a best seller and brought Kerouac overnight success.

Exercise B

Review the compound adjectives you identified in the sentences in Exercise A. For each one, suggest another word or phrase that could be used in its place. For example, in the first sentence, the compound *cross-continent* could be replaced by *across the continent* or *North American.* Explain any difference in meaning between the replacement and the original compound. Also think about how not using compound adjectives affects the written style.

> ### SPELLING PRACTICE
>
> **Compound Words**
>
> Compounds that become accepted into regular use, called *permanent compounds,* often are written as one word, or *closed.* Review this list of closed compounds from *On the Road.*
>
> | | |
> |---|---|
> | afternoon | hitchhiking |
> | backyard | hometown |
> | baseball | midnight |
> | cornfields | Midwest |
> | countryside | myself |
> | crossroads | railroad |
> | downtown | roadside |
> | footsteps | sawdust |
> | halfway | |

A Supermarket in California

A Lyric Poem by Allen Ginsberg

Build Background

Literary Context Allen Ginsberg's **"A Supermarket in California"** is another classic representation of Beat literature. Written in 1955, it expresses the Beat generation's despair over the loss of American ideals they believed was occurring with the rise of commercialism and conformity.

The poem also represents the Beats' breaking with traditional poetic forms and using free verse and stream-of-consciousness writing. Some literary scholars regard "A Supermarket in California" as a *prose poem:* a work exhibiting the irregular, conversational qualities of prose along with certain elements of poetry, such as repetition and a sense of rhythm.

Reader's Context What do you consider American ideals? How would losing them affect American society?

Meet the Author

Allen Ginsberg (1926–1997), one of the leaders of the Beat movement, was born in Newark, New Jersey, and grew up in nearby Paterson. His parents, Louis and Naomi Ginsberg, were involved in New York's literary world and various progressive political causes. Both of these associations would influence young Allen, who started keeping journals in childhood.

In 1943, Ginsberg was accepted at Columbia University, where, after a brief involvement in the Merchant Marine, he ultimately earned a bachelor's degree. There, he met Jack Kerouac and other comrades, who would play key roles in the rest of his life and career. Around this time, Ginsberg also met fellow Paterson resident poet William Carlos Williams (see Unit 5), who would become a lifelong mentor.

Ginsberg was introduced to the poetry scene after moving to San Francisco in 1954. He soon was a major part of it, stirring controversy with a reading of his lengthy free-verse poem *Howl* at the famous Six Gallery. The explicit nature of this poem brought legal charges of obscenity when it was published in *Howl and Other Poems* in 1956. Later publications included the collections *Kaddish and Other Poems* (1961), *Planet News* (1968), and *America: Poems of These States* (1973), which won the National Book Award.

Although Kerouac is credited with having named the Beat movement, Ginsberg may have best defined its core philosophy. He once wrote, "Since art is merely and ultimately self-expressive, we conclude that the fullest art, the most individual, uninfluenced, unrepressed, uninhibited expression of art is true expression and the true art."

Analyze Literature

Free Verse and Allusion
Free verse is poetry that does not use regular rhyme, meter, or stanza division. It may contain irregular line breaks and sentence fragments and tends to mimic the rhythm of ordinary speech.

An **allusion** is a reference to a well-known person, event, object, or work from history or literature.

Set Purpose

Ginsberg learned to write poetry using traditional forms and conventions, but he found his voice writing free verse. As you read "A Supermarket in California," identify the characteristics of free verse that it demonstrates. Also identify the allusions the speaker makes to the pioneer of free verse, nineteenth-century poet Walt Whitman. In addition to these references to Whitman, what other allusions can you find?

Preview Vocabulary

enumeration, 996
odyssey, 997

A Supermarket in California

by Allen Ginsberg

What thoughts I have of you tonight, Walt Whitman, for I walked down the sidestreets under the trees with a headache self-conscious looking at the full moon.

In my hungry fatigue, and shopping for images, I went into
5   the neon fruit supermarket, dreaming of your <u>enumerations</u>!

What peaches and what penumbras![1] Whole families shopping at night! Aisles full of husbands! Wives in the avocados, babies in the tomatoes!—and you, García Lorca,[2] what were you doing down by the watermelons?

---

1. **penumbras.** Darkened or obscured areas. The speaker is pairing these with brightly colored fruit in a cheerily lit store for the purpose of irony.
2. **García Lorca.** Federico García Lorca (1898–1936), a progressive Spanish poet and playwright who wrote "Ode to Walt Whitman" and once attended Columbia University

---

enu • mer • a • tion (ē nü′ mər ā′ shən) *n.,* list of one thing after another

10   I saw you, Walt Whitman, childless, lonely old grubber,[3] poking among the meats in the refrigerator and eyeing the grocery boys.

      I heard you asking questions of each: Who killed the pork chops? What price bananas? Are you my Angel?

15   I wandered in and out of the brilliant stacks of cans following you, and followed in my imagination by the store detective.

      We strode down the open corridors together in our solitary fancy tasting artichokes, possessing every frozen delicacy, and never passing the cashier.

20   Where are we going, Walt Whitman? The doors close in an hour. Which way does your beard point tonight?

      (I touch your book and dream of our <u>odyssey</u> in the supermarket and feel absurd.)

      Will we walk all night through solitary streets? The trees add
25 shade to shade, lights out in the houses, we'll both be lonely.

      Will we stroll dreaming of the lost America of love past blue automobiles in driveways, home to our silent cottage?

      Ah, dear father, graybeard, lonely old courage-teacher, what America did you have when Charon quit poling his ferry and
30 you got out on a smoking bank and stood watching the boat disappear on the black waters of Lethe?[4] ❖

---

3. **childless, lonely old grubber.** Walt Whitman never married and had no children, although his being lonely may also refer to his intense individualism. A *grubber* is someone who is digging for something hard to obtain—in this case, both satisfactory grocery items and realization of dreams for society.

4. **what America . . . black waters of Lethe.** In Greek mythology, *Charon* ferried dead people across a river to Hades. The waters of Lethe, one of many rivers flowing through the mythological Hades, are said to cause people who drink from them to forget the past.

odys • sey (ô´ dis ē) *n.,* long, eventful voyage or quest

MIRRORS & WINDOWS   An old adage says that "Misery loves company." When you are unhappy, would you rather be alone or with other people?

Refer to Text ▶ ▶ ▶ ▶ ▶	Reason with Text	
1a. What types of patrons does the speaker observe shopping in the supermarket?	**1b.** Describe the speaker's attitude toward these people.	**Understand** Find meaning
2a. List the things the speaker observes Walt Whitman doing in the supermarket.	**2b.** What type of store patron does Whitman seem to be? Explain.	**Apply** Use information
3a. Compare and contrast the supermarket's environment with the environment just outside it.	**3b.** Infer what each of these worlds might represent to the speaker. In which is he most comfortable?	**Analyze** Take things apart
4a. In the last stanza, what does the speaker consider doing with Whitman?	**4b.** Evaluate the speaker. What kind of person is he? What kind of life does he have? Support your answer with details from the poem.	**Evaluate** Make judgments
5a. In the last line, how does the speaker address Whitman?	**5b.** Propose whether the speaker is being critical, complimentary, or both. Explain why he feels this way about Whitman.	**Create** Bring ideas together

Analyze Literature

Free Verse and Allusion
What characteristics of free verse does this poem demonstrate? How has Ginsberg portrayed the rhythms of everyday speech? How is the use of free verse appropriate to the subject and theme of the poem?

What allusions does the speaker make to Walt Whitman? In particular, what physical feature does the speaker mention twice? What significance might this feature have for the speaker? What other allusions did you find in the poem, and what does each mean?

Extend the Text

Writing Options
Creative Writing Write a dialogue between Allen Ginsberg and Walt Whitman (see Unit 3), in which they discuss the modern-day United States. Have them discuss how things have changed since Whitman's time, particularly in terms of the loss of traditional values and ideals.

Expository Writing Ginsberg, Federico García Lorca, Pablo Neruda, and several other poets have written poems about Walt Whitman. Write a paragraph explaining why Whitman has influenced so many poets. You might begin by researching similarities among these individuals.

Collaborative Learning
Discuss Poetic Questions "A Supermarket in California" contains a variety of questions. In a group with three or four classmates, discuss at least two questions from the poem. What literal and/or figurative meanings does each question seem to have? Is the question rhetorical, or does the speaker actually seek an answer?

Media Literacy
Research Artistic Tributes Writers, composers, and visual artists traditionally have expressed their appreciation of others' work by creating tributes. Many examples can be found in the recording industry, in particular. In "Vincent," singer/songwriter Don McLean pays tribute to troubled artist Vincent van Gogh. The song "Abraham, Martin and John," made popular by singer Dion, honors three civil rights icons. Choose one of these or another musical, poetic, or visual tribute to present to your class. Explain its meaning in detail.

 Go to **www.mirrorsandwindows.com** for more.

Understand the Concept

One of the ways words enter a language is through **borrowing,** or integrating words from other languages. Some words are integrated in slightly adapted forms, forming blends or composites of two languages. Others are integrated intact, with no change to the spelling or pronunciation; they are called *loan words.*

The United States' history of immigration and resettlement is reflected in the variety of words that have been integrated into American English. Some words have been borrowed outright from other languages, and others have been adapted for use in English. Here is a sampling of the many words English has borrowed from languages all over the world:

apartheid (Afrikaans)
assassin (Arabic)
bazaar (Persian)
corgi (Welsh)
cruise (Dutch)
curry (Tamil)
gong (Malay and Java)
guru (Hindi)
hula (Hawaiian)
karaoke (Japanese)
ketchup (Malay)
kiosk (Turkish)
mamba (Zulu)
perestroika (Russian)
saga (Old Norse)
sauna (Finnish)
sauerkraut (German)
taboo (Tongan)
tattoo (Tahitian)

(See also the discussion of Native American borrowed words in the Vocabulary & Spelling workshop in Unit 8, page 1113.)

To identify borrowed words, look them up in a dictionary. Most dictionaries provide a word's **etymology,** or origin and history, along with its pronunciation, definition, and forms.

Apply the Skill

Exercise A

Choose five words from the previous list. Locate each word in a dictionary to be sure you understand its meaning, and then use it in a sentence. Also record the etymology of each word, identifying its language of origin. Try to determine whether any of the words have changed in form or spelling from the original.

Exercise B

Identify at least one borrowed word in each of the following fragments from "A Supermarket in California." In your notebook, write the word (or words) and its general etymology.

1. In my hungry fatigue, and shopping for images, I went into the neon fruit supermarket, dreaming of your enumerations!
2. Aisles full of husbands! Wives in the avocados, babies in the tomatoes!
3. I heard you asking questions of each: Who killed the pork chops? What price bananas? Are you my Angel?
4. We strode down the open corridors together in our solitary fancy tasting artichokes, possessing every frozen delicacy, and never passing the cashier.
5. I touch your book and dream of our odyssey in the supermarket and feel absurd.

SPELLING PRACTICE

Borrowed Words

Most writers use borrowed words without knowledge of their origins. Review the following list of borrowed words from Ginsberg's "A Supermarket in California" to make sure you are familiar with the spellings, including the plural forms. Also try to determine from which language each word was borrowed.

absurd	cashier
artichokes	corridors
automobiles	fatigue
avocados	odyssey
bananas	tomatoes

Riprap

Pine Tree Tops

Lyric Poems by Gary Snyder

Build Background

Literary Context Included in Gary Snyder's first poetry collection, **"Riprap"** likens language and poetry to *riprap:* stones and other materials placed on a mountain trail to stabilize the surface and provide sure footing, particularly for horses. The written word, Snyder suggests, provides sure footing for humans as they navigate an ever-changing world.

In **"Pine Tree Tops,"** which is from Snyder's 1974 collection *Turtle Island*, the poet questions humankind's appreciation of the magnificence of nature. The poem's assonance (repetition of vowel sounds), beautiful imagery, and hushed mood all contribute to Snyder's reverent message.

Reader's Context What aspects of nature most fascinate you? What parallels can you make between them and details of your own life?

Meet the Author

Gary Snyder (b. 1930), a poet and environmentalist, was born in San Francisco but spent most of his childhood in the Pacific Northwest. Living in this region gave him an appreciation for nature and Native American culture, two frequent motifs in his writing.

When Snyder was seven, he had an accident that led to a four-month confinement, during which he immersed himself in library books. He once said in an interview, "At the end of four months, I had read more than most kids do by the time they're eighteen. And I didn't stop."

This love of reading and interest in culture led Snyder to earn a dual degree in literature and anthropology from Reed College. After graduating in 1950, he moved back to San Francisco, where he studied Asian languages at the University of California, Berkeley, and began writing poetry. His friendships with novelist Jack Kerouac and poet Allen Ginsberg, members of the Beat generation, led Snyder to become involved in this literary movement.

Snyder later spent several years in Japan, living under the teachings of Zen Buddhism. There, he published his first two books, *Riprap and Cold Mountain Poems* (1958) and *Myths and Texts* (1960), both of which draw on his life in the Pacific Northwest wilderness. His volume *Turtle Island* won the 1975 Pulitzer Prize for poetry. Snyder's writings reflect his belief in humanity's connectedness with nature—that "nature is not a place to visit, it is home." His work with environmental groups led to his recognition as a Living Legend in the Ecology Hall of Fame.

Analyze Literature

Concrete Language and Abstract Language
Concrete language comprises words and phrases that specifically name or describe something. Concrete words and phrases engage the five senses. *Buffalo, geranium, storm,* and *heron* are examples of concrete terms.

Abstract language refers to words and phrases that cannot be directly perceived by the senses. *Freedom, love, integrity, honesty,* and *loyalty* are examples of abstract words.

Set Purpose

As you read "Riprap" and "Pine Tree Tops," notice Snyder's use of concrete versus abstract language. Record examples of each in a simple two-column chart. Also evaluate when or why he seems to use each type of language. In particular, how does Snyder use concrete language to convey abstract ideas?

Preview Vocabulary

sediment, 1001

Riprap

by Gary Snyder

Lay down these words
Before your mind like rocks.
   placed solid, by hands
In choice of place, set
5   Before the body of the mind
   in space and time:
Solidity of bark, leaf or wall
   riprap of things:
Cobble[1] of milky way,
10   straying planets,
These poems, people,
   lost ponies with
Dragging saddles—
   and rocky sure-foot trails.
15 The worlds like an endless
   four-dimensional
Game of Go.
   ants and pebbles
In the thin loam,[2] each rock a word
20   a creek-washed stone
Granite: ingrained
   with torment of fire and weight
Crystal and <u>sediment</u> linked hot
   all change, in thoughts,
25 As well as things. ❖

---

1. **Cobble.** Cobblestones; rocks naturally larger than pebbles but smaller than boulders; often used in paving
2. **loam.** Type of soil consisting of a blend of sand, silt, and clay

sed • i • ment (sed′ ə mənt) *n.*, materials left or washed up by moving water

MIRRORS & WINDOWS

Who or what in your life keeps you grounded and "sure-footed," particularly when you are feeling troubled or uncertain?

PINE TREE TOPS

by Gary Snyder

In the blue night
frost haze, the sky glows
with the moon
pine tree tops
bend snow-blue, fade
into sky, frost, starlight.
The creak of boots.
Rabbit tracks, deer tracks,
what do we know.

MIRRORS & WINDOWS

Think of a natural environment around where you live. What are its main features? In how much detail can you describe them?

Refer to Text ▶ ▶ ▶ ▶ ▶	Reason with Text	
1a. In "Riprap," where does the speaker want the reader to "lay down these words"? How should they be "placed"?	**1b.** Summarize what the speaker is saying about each person's individual "riprap."	**Understand** Find meaning
2a. During what general time of day does "Pine Tree Tops" take place? In what likely season?	**2b.** How might the speaker have described the same scene at another time of day or year?	**Apply** Use information
3a. In "Riprap," what words and phrases does Snyder use to describe people?	**3b.** What can you infer about the poet's general philosophies about life and humanity?	**Analyze** Take things apart
4a. What question does the speaker ask in "Pine Tree Tops"?	**4b.** Evaluate what the speaker is implying about human beings. Do you agree with this implication? Explain.	**Evaluate** Make judgments
5a. What general environment does each poem seem to describe?	**5b.** Imagine the scenario that inspired Snyder to write one of the poems. Describe it in detail, and explain why the poet was there.	**Create** Bring ideas together

Analyze Literature

Concrete Language and Abstract Language

Review your chart of examples of concrete and abstract language. Evaluate how Snyder uses each type of language. For instance, in "Riprap," he uses many concrete words and phrases figuratively, not literally. What is the effect of using concrete examples from nature to portray abstract ideas?

Extend the Text

Writing Options

Creative Writing In his poems, Snyder draws attention to the smallest aspects of nature, such as the sound of one person walking outside on a quiet evening. Write a poem of your own that describes a quality or experience in nature that often goes unnoticed. If possible, get inspiration by actually observing or experiencing your chosen subject.

Expository Writing Write a comparison-and-contrast essay in which you compare "Riprap" or "Pine Tree Tops" with another poem by a Beat writer featured in this unit. Focus on form, style, language, and imagery, explaining how each poet uses these elements to convey his intended message.

Lifelong Learning

Research the Influence of Place on Poetry Each of the works by Beat movement authors has indicated one or more geographical locations with significant personal meaning, positive or negative. Choose three well-known poets not associated with the Beat movement whose works clearly were influenced by meaningful places in their lives. Write an essay on the role of place in popular poetry, supporting your analysis with examples from specific poems by your chosen poets.

Collaborative Learning

Hold a Snyder Fest Ever since his breakout book *Riprap* was published, Gary Snyder has had a loyal following of literary enthusiasts. Celebrate his place in the poetic world by selecting a variety of his works to read to an audience. Your event may involve a few classmates reading to the rest of the class or a presentation for another class or the school. Invite questions after each reading.

 Go to **www.mirrorsandwindows.com** for more.

1. In which of the following lines from "Riprap" does the speaker describe the human condition?
   A. "like rocks. placed solid"
   B. "an endless four-dimensional game of Go"
   C. "ants and pebbles in the thin loam"
   D. "lost ponies with dragging saddles"
   E. "torment of fire and weight"

2. In "Riprap," the line "In the thin loam, each rock a word" is an example of
   A. setting.
   B. simile.
   C. metaphor.
   D. personification.
   E. description.

3. Which of the following words is closest in meaning to the word *sediment,* as used in the line "Crystal and sediment linked hot" in "Riprap"?
   A. a type of rock
   B. tender feelings
   C. anger toward something
   D. sand
   E. residue

4. Which of the following excerpts from "Riprap" is an example of alliteration?
   A. "Lay down these words"
   B. "Before your mind like rocks"
   C. "Solidity of bark, leaf or wall / riprap of things"
   D. "These poems, people, / lost ponies"
   E. "Granite: ingrained / with torment of fire and weight"

5. In "Pine Tree Tops," what signs of human existence are present?
   A. footprints in the snow
   B. a voice heard on the wind
   C. the creaking sound of boots
   D. a road through the pines
   E. There are no signs of human existence in the poem.

6. Which of the following is evidence of the season in "Pine Tree Tops"?
   A. "frost haze"
   B. "pine tree tops / bend snow-blue"
   C. "The creak of boots"
   D. "Rabbit tracks, deer tracks"
   E. All provide evidence of the season.

7. Which of the following statements best describes the theme conveyed in both poems?
   A. The objects and events in nature are real, but human nature often is confused and lost.
   B. Human beings are but a small part of a vast universe.
   C. The things people think are solid and real are only imagined.
   D. Nature is poetry if only people would listen.
   E. The issues of space and time are irrelevant to the solid objects of nature.

8. Constructed Response: Analyze how Snyder uses concrete language to convey abstract ideas in his poems. Consider, in particular, his use of images from nature. Use specific examples from the poems to illustrate your points.

9. Constructed Response: Argue whether Snyder's poems are typical of Beat poetry. Support your argument using at least three characteristics of "Riprap" and "Pine Tree Tops."

TEST-TAKING TIP

If you have trouble answering a sentence-completion question, determine what part of speech is missing from the sentence. For instance, if a verb is missing, then eliminate from consideration all answer options that are not verbs. Doing so will narrow the range of options, helping you identify the correct answer or at least increasing your chances of guessing correctly.

Constantly risking absurdity

by Lawrence Ferlinghetti

Lawrence Ferlinghetti (b. 1919) was born in Yonkers, New York, and attended Mount Hermon School. After earning a bachelor's degree from the University of North Carolina at Chapel Hill, he served in the U.S. Navy during World War II, participating in both the Normandy invasion and the U.S. occupation of Japan. After the war, Ferlinghetti earned a master's degree at Columbia University and a doctoral degree from the Sorbonne in Paris.

In 1951, Ferlinghetti settled in San Francisco, and over the next few years, he started a magazine, a bookstore, and a publishing company called *City Lights,* named after a Charlie Chaplin movie. The magazine would be short lived, but the success of the bookstore and publishing house helped establish Ferlinghetti as a central figure in the Beat movement (see the Literary Connection on page 1007).

In **"Constantly risking absurdity,"** published in the 1958 collection *A Coney Island of the Mind,* Ferlinghetti uses the metaphor of a tightrope acrobat to ponder his own profession. His other poetry collections include *Starting from San Francisco* (1967) and *How to Paint Sunlight* (2001).

Constantly risking absurdity
                    and death
          whenever he performs
                    above the heads
5   of his audience
     the poet like an acrobat
                    climbs on rime[1]
                         to a high wire of his own making
     and balancing on eyebeams[2]
10   above a sea of faces
          paces his way
                    to the other side of day
     performing entrechats[3]
                    and sleight-of-foot tricks
15 and other high theatrics
                    and all without mistaking
          any thing
                    for what it may not be

---

1. **rime.** Alternate spelling of *rhyme*
2. **eyebeams.** Glances of the eye
3. **entrechats.** In ballet, leaps straight upward, during which the dancer beats his or her calves together

Aerial Act, 1940. Louis Schanker.
Smithsonian American Art Museum, Washington, DC.

> For he's the super realist
> 20   who must perforce[4] perceive
>   taut[5] truth
>   before the taking of each stance or step
>   in his supposed advance
>   toward that still higher perch
> 25 where Beauty stands and waits
>   with gravity
>   to start her death-defying leap
>   And he
>   a little charleychaplin[6] man
> 30   who may or may not catch
>   her fair eternal form
>   spreadeagled in the empty air
>   of existence ❖

---

4. **perforce.** Necessarily
5. **taut.** Tightly drawn
6. **Charley Chaplin.** Sir Charles Spencer (1889–1977), also known as Charlie Chaplin;
   English comic actor known for his portrayal of a duck-toed hobo in tattered evening dress

Are you a risk taker? What would you risk to try to achieve something that may or may not succeed?

LITERARY CONNECTION

City Lights Publishing and Bookstore

Intent on making alternative literature available, Lawrence Ferlinghetti founded the City Lights bookstore in San Francisco's historic North Beach neighborhood in 1953 and established the publishing house two years later. For more than fifty years, patrons have been able to browse the City Lights bookshelves and find literature unavailable in mainstream bookstores. Similarly, City Lights Publishing has produced projects deemed too odd or controversial for corporate publishers.

One of the most controversial works—a collection of poetry containing Allen Ginsberg's *Howl*—was published in 1956, just one year after City Lights Publishing opened its doors. The book drew the attention of censors and resulted in Ferlinghetti's being arrested for violating obscenity ordinances. Prominent professors, writers, and literary critics spoke on behalf of the publisher, and he ultimately was acquitted of any wrongdoing.

Somewhat ironically, the obscenity trial raised the credibility of City Lights within the intellectual community. The bookstore became an important meeting place for writers and artists, many of whom also presented their works in readings and other performances. In fact, the walls of the store are adorned with colorful tile patterns and artworks painted by Ferlinghetti and other local artists. In 2001, San Francisco designated the building a landmark, citing its architectural, cultural, and historical importance.

Still in operation, the City Lights bookstore is one of the most successful independent bookstores in the United States. City Lights Publishing has more than one hundred titles in print and publishes about twelve new titles each year. A fiftieth anniversary celebration of Jack Kerouac's *On the Road* was planned for 2007.

Quiet Strength: The Faith, the Hope, and the Heart of a Woman Who Changed a Nation by Rosa Parks with Gregory J. Reed

Rosa Parks did not intend to become an icon of the Civil Rights movement, but she devoted her life to ending discrimination and creating opportunities for people who had been oppressed. Aptly named, her autobiography reflects the deep religious faith and commitment to freedom that guided her life.

A Sand County Almanac by Aldo Leopold

When *A Sand County Almanac* was published in 1949, most Americans were not thinking about the negative consequences that industrialization might have on the environment. Aldo Leopold challenged this lack of foresight with a collection of essays and sketches that praise the natural world and condemn those who would destroy it.

I've Got the Light of Freedom: The Organizing Tradition and the Mississippi Freedom Struggle by Charles M. Payne

Payne explores the early days of the Civil Rights movement, constructing his narrative around the grassroots organizers in Greenwood, Mississippi. Avoiding the dry prose typical of many historical accounts, Payne tells the life story of the movement's principal members using their own words and voices.

Homeward Bound: American Families in the Cold War Era by Elaine Tyler May

In this study of domestic life in the post–World War II United States, May examines the national policy of containing communism and its subsequent influence on the family. Interviews and testimonies from those who lived in the Cold War Era give readers a vivid sense of everyday life in this socially tumultuous period.

A Good Man Is Hard to Find and Other Stories by Flannery O'Connor

Although praised for their authentic Southern dialogue and depiction of rural working-class life, O'Connor's stories sometimes are criticized for their grotesqueness and violence. However, with the violence comes the opportunity for change. The grandmother in the title story understands her connection to the murderous misfit only as she faces death, and the landowner in "The Displaced Person" becomes an outsider herself through her complicity in a refugee worker's death.

Invisible Man by Ralph Waldo Ellison

Invisible Man was the only novel Ralph Ellison published, but its brilliance secured his legacy as a literary giant. The book's nameless protagonist journeys from the rural South to the urban North, struggling to overcome racism in all its forms. Full of challenging metaphors and literary allusions, this novel is considered by literary scholars among the twentieth century's finest.

You can improve your ability as both a listener and a speaker by developing your nonverbal communication skills. A key element of nonverbal communication is body language: the messages you send to people around you by your posture, facial expressions, hand gestures, and other actions.

It's important to be aware of the messages you send without saying a word. People often form positive or negative judgments of others based on body language alone. You should be conscious of the messages your posture, facial expressions, and gestures may suggest. Conversely, you should learn to interpret the body language of other people and what it conveys about your own communication.

People from different cultures may differ in what they consider appropriate body language. To Native Americans, for example, bowing your head while you listen to someone speak is considered a sign of respect. Among other peoples, lack of eye contact suggests shyness or weakness. When you meet someone from a culture whose customs are unfamiliar to you, recognize and respect the diversity of communication practices.

1. Be Conscious of Nonverbal Communication as a Listener

As an audience member at a speech or other oral presentation, keep in mind that your nonverbal communication affects both the speaker and other audience members. For example, if you slouch in your seat, move about restlessly, or read materials, the speaker may assume you are bored with the presentation.

Sending such a message, even without meaning to, can be doubly harmful. First, you may hurt the speaker's feelings with your apparent, if unintended, rudeness, and second, if the speaker is upset by your negative feedback, the rest of the speech may suffer. If you are having trouble hearing the speaker, send a polite signal—touch your ear, perhaps. Then during the question session after the presentation, ask for clarification of hard-to-understand information.

Some listeners may be tempted to engage in nonverbal communication with friends elsewhere in the audience by sending notes, waving, or making faces. Clearly, such behavior is unacceptable. If you must

leave the room while a speech is in progress, do so unobtrusively, without attracting attention.

2. Be Conscious of Nonverbal Communication as a Speaker

When you are the speaker, a key aspect of delivering your oral presentation is being aware of your nonverbal communication. Your posture, hand gestures, and facial expressions should support the information you are presenting and indicate that you are confident and respectful of your listeners.

Also be aware of the nonverbal communication of your listeners. Do they seem puzzled? Distracted? Bored? Learn to recognize signals that your audience is not following your presentation. If you suspect this is happening, restate your ideas in simpler language or change your style of delivery.

3. Role-Play to Learn Appropriate Nonverbal Communication

Working with groups of classmates, take turns role-playing the parts of listeners and speakers. Concentrate on your awareness of appropriate nonverbal communication. After each role-play session, discuss ways to improve nonverbal communication in a variety of speaking and listening situations.

SPEAKING & LISTENING RUBRIC

Your nonverbal communication skills will be evaluated on these elements:

❑ As a listener, you avoid sending nonverbal messages that may distract or insult the speaker. If you cannot follow what the speaker is saying, you wait until the question period to ask politely for clarification.

❑ As a speaker, you are conscious of your body language and how it communicates your knowledge of your subject, your confidence as a speaker, and your respect for the audience. If you sense that audience members are not following your presentation, perhaps due to misunderstanding or boredom, you use this feedback to change your delivery.

As you read and perhaps watched Arthur Miller's *The Crucible,* you undoubtedly formed an opinion about it. Perhaps the subject matter seemed foreign and the language dated, making it difficult for you to relate to the play. Maybe you had the opposite reaction, finding the message timeless and accurately portrayed.

Consciously or not, we judge every film and play we watch. We may become absorbed in the believable acting or distracted by an actor's absurd accent. We may find the cinematography gorgeously epic or the camera work jumpy.

We do much the same thing when we write a review but in a more conscious way. For this assignment, you will write a review of a film or play. Your review not only will critique the work but recommend to readers whether it is worth seeing.

> **Assignment** Plan, write, and revise a film or play review.
>
> **Purpose** To convince readers to see or avoid a certain movie or play
>
> **Audience** Someone who is undecided whether to watch the piece

❶ Prewrite

Select Your Topic
You may choose to review a film or play with which you are very familiar or a work entirely new to you. Another option is to focus on a specific aspect of a film or play, such as the performance of a particular actor or the authenticity of the production.

Create a list of five or six plays or films you might want to review, including both familiar and unfamiliar works. From the list, choose the film or play that interests you most.

Gather Information
To write an informed review, you will have to pay close attention as you watch the piece. If possible, take notes during the viewing to record supporting details for your analysis. (This will depend on whether you view the work in a theater or on a television or video monitor.) Also, view the work more than once, if you have the opportunity.

Use a chart like the one on page 1011 to organize your notes, keeping in mind your categories will differ depending on your focus.

Organize Your Ideas
Look over your chart. Do you have at least five distinct points to discuss? Is each supported with examples from the film or play?

Circle the three most complete points, and number them in the order you want them to appear in your review. If the film or play you are critiquing has a chronological structure, you might find it easiest to structure your review accordingly.

Write Your Thesis Statement
For this assignment, your recommendation will serve as your **thesis statement.** Using information from the Film/Play Review Chart, one student, Kelly, wrote this thesis about the character of Amanda, played by Joanne Woodward in a 1987 film version of *The Glass Menagerie:*

WOODWARD

> *Joanne Woodward in the role of Amanda is the most effective actor.*

Kelly later revised her thesis to offer her recommendation:

> *Joanne Woodward's compelling performance in the role of Amanda is what makes this movie worth seeing.*

WRITING RUBRIC

A successful film or play review has these elements:
- ❑ an introduction that provides some background on the film or play
- ❑ a thesis statement that clearly states the writer's stance on the piece
- ❑ a body that presents specific reasoning supported with examples from the film or play
- ❑ a conclusion that restates the writer's stance and brings the review to a close

Film/Play Review Chart: Joanne Woodward in <u>The Glass Menagerie</u>

	Point in Film	Voice	Actions/Facial Expressions	Interactions with Others
1	Early	Nagging Tom	Face shows complexity of Amanda's anger and disappointment	Provokes Tom to argue with her; continues nagging him as if can't help it
		Voice gets higher; Southern accent fluctuates depending on mood	Facial expersions show desperation and fear; gestures are exaggerated	Is afraid Tom will leave
2	Middle	Patience and frustration toward Laura heard in voice	Look in her eye when she communicates with Laura	Begs Tom to stay until Laura has husband
		Desperation with getting money ("Bless you" repeated)	Tension/distress shown on face in phone scene	Communicates with customers in desperate way; risks friendships
3	End	Annoyance with Laura heard in tone	Frustration seen in forehead lines	Trying to get Laura ready for Gentleman Caller
		Longing expressed in wistful speech	Eyes are glazed; has small smile	Tells stories about wanting to be desired by gentlemen

❷ Draft

Write your review by following this three-part framework: introduction, body, and conclusion.

Introduction Give a brief synopsis of your film or play to ground readers, and present your thesis statement.
Body Write one paragraph for each main point of your argument, and support each point with specific examples from the film or play.
Conclusion Re-emphasize your recommendation, and finish your review.

Draft Your Introduction

Your introduction should include a clear thesis statement that offers your recommendation. It also should provide a brief synopsis of the film or play to give readers who are unfamiliar with the work some basis for understanding what you write about it. Finally, your introduction should generate interest. Why will what you have to say interest readers?

The introduction that Kelly wrote during the Draft stage is shown in the first column on page 1013. In the first two sentences, Kelly gives some background information about the movie, and in the last sentence, she states her thesis. However, there are some crucial details missing. What else could Kelly do to give readers more of a context? How could she improve her thesis?

> ### What Great Writers Do
> In writing your review, take a clear stand and support it definitively. Follow the advice of Herbert Bayard Swopes, the first recipient of the Pulitzer Prize for reporting, who said, "I can't give you a sure-fire formula for success, but I can give you a formula for failure: try to please everybody all the time."

Draft Your Body

The body should state each point of your argument in a separate paragraph, supported by specific examples from the film or play. Use the arguments and reasoning you mapped out in the Prewrite stage.

Kelly began her review by describing an early scene in the movie. Look at the draft of her first body paragraph in the left-hand column on page 1013. Kelly also drafted two more body paragraphs, using specific examples from the film to back up her point in each.

Consider the three main points you circled on your Review Chart and the order in which you plan to present them. State each point as a topic sentence, and then develop it into a paragraph by adding evidence from the film or play. Each example should clearly relate to the argument you are making, as stated in your thesis.

Draft Your Conclusion

Finally, write the conclusion for your review. A good conclusion should do two things: (1) re-emphasize your recommendation without merely restating it and (2) bring discussion to a close. Look at the draft of Kelly's conclusion in the chart on page 1014. Does she do both these things in her conclusion?

❸ Revise

Evaluate Your Draft

Exchange reviews with a classmate and assess each other's work. If you exchange reviews with someone familiar with the work you reviewed, ask if he or she thinks you neglected to mention something that will help your argument. If he or she is unfamiliar with the work, determine if your review convinces him or her to see or avoid the film or play.

Begin by reviewing the content and organization of the review as a whole. Make sure the three parts of the review—the introduction, body, and conclusion—work together to prove the thesis. It should be obvious how each paragraph connects to the next and how each relates to the overall argument. Use the Revision Checklist below to help you evaluate. Write comments directly on the review.

Next, check the organization of each paragraph. Having clear topic sentences not only helps you as a writer to organize your thoughts, but it also helps orient your reader. Look at the chart on page 1013 and compare the first body paragraph of Kelly's first and revised drafts. Note how adding the topic sentence strengthens the paragraph.

Finally, check for sentence-level errors. Using the Revision Checklist, examine the draft to ensure you have followed the guidelines in the Grammar & Style

> ### REVISION CHECKLIST
>
> #### Content & Organization
> ❏ Does the introduction offer readers grounding details, such as brief background about the play or film?
> ❏ Is there an obvious thesis statement (your recommendation) in the introduction?
> ❏ Does each paragraph in the body work to prove the thesis?
> ❏ Does each body paragraph provide enough relevant, specific details from the film or play to support the argument?
> ❏ Does the conclusion reemphasize the recommendation and bring the review to a close?
>
> #### Grammar & Style
> ❏ Are hyphens, ellipses, and italics used correctly? (page 861)
> ❏ Are proper nouns and proper adjectives capitalized correctly? (page 975)

DRAFT STAGE		REVISE STAGE	
Introduction Tennessee Williams's drama *The Glass Menagerie* takes place entirely in a small apartment in St. Louis during the 1930s and features only four characters: Amanda Wingfield, a middle-aged woman; her grown son, Tom; her abnormally shy grown daughter, Laura; and a gentleman caller named Jim. In the 1987 film adaptation of the drama, Joanne Woodward in the role of Amanda is the most effective actor.	Provides brief synopsis for context States thesis	Tennessee Williams's drama *The Glass Menagerie* takes place entirely in a small apartment in St. Louis during the ~~1930s~~ Great Depression and features only four characters: Amanda Wingfield, a middle-aged woman; her grown son, Tom; her abnormally shy grown daughter, Laura; and a gentleman caller named Jim. In the 1987 film adaptation of the drama, directed by Paul Newman, these four roles are played by Joanne Woodward, John Malkovich, Karen Allen, and James Naughton. ~~Joanne~~ Woodward's compelling performance in the role of Amanda is ~~the most effective actor.~~ what makes the film worth seeing.	Adds significant detail Adds director's and actors' names for more context Revises thesis to include recommendation
Body Paragraph In a convincing early scene, Amanda provokes Tom to argue with her. He insults her and storms from the house. The next morning, Laura convinces him to apologize for his behavior. After the actors share a tense moment of silence, the audience wonders if Amanda and Tom will reach any understanding. Woodward also brings out the mother's fear that Tom will leave the family. As Amanda gets more desperate, her voice gets higher and she gestures wildly.	Includes details from the film Shows complexity of characters	Woodward's fine acting reveals the complexity of Amanda's character. Watching Woodward's facial expressions, the audience experiences Amanda's anger and disappointment. In a convincing early scene, Amanda provokes Tom to argue with her. ~~He insults her and storms from the house. The next morning, Laura convinces him to apologize for his behavior.~~ , as if she is testing his devotion. After the actors share a tense moment of silence, the audience wonders if Amanda and Tom will reach any understanding. In the next several scenes, Woodward ~~also~~ brings out the mother's fear that Tom will leave the family. As Amanda ~~gets more desperate, her voice gets higher and she gestures wildly.~~ 's desperation increases, her voice creeps higher and her gestures become less controlled.	Adds topic sentence Offers analysis; removes unnecessary summation Smoothes transition Improves diction; uses parallel structure Refocuses discussion on Woodward

DRAFT STAGE		REVISE STAGE	
Conclusion Through Woodward's skillful acting, the audience comes to know the real Amanda. She is a woman struggling to provide a life for her grown children while clinging to her own youth.	Recaps main idea of film to provide some closure	Through Woodward's skillful acting in *The Glass Menagerie*, the audience comes to know the real Amanda. ~~She is~~ a woman struggling to ~~provide a life for her grown children~~ live in the present while clinging to ~~her own youth~~ the past. This film version of Williams's famous play owes a great deal to Woodward's subtle handling of a complex role.	Restates title of film Rewords to create parallel structure Restates thesis and recommendation

workshops in this unit. Consider how the language could be improved. One way to do this is to replace vague and overused words with fresh, specific ones.

Revise for Content, Organization, and Style

Kelly reread her review and found that many things could be improved. Look at the chart on pages 1013–1014 (this time, the right-hand column) to see how she revised the three paragraphs you read earlier:

- **Introduction:** By adding more background details, Kelly was able to better ground her readers. She also clarified her thesis to include a recommendation.
- **Body:** Kelly eliminated the excess discussion of Tom's actions and refocused her analysis on Amanda/Woodward, more effectively proving her thesis.
- **Conclusion:** Adding her recommendation helped Kelly echo her thesis while providing better closure for her readers.

Review the notes you or your partner made on your draft. Apply pertinent comments as you revise your draft.

Proofread for Errors

While you can look for errors as you revise your essay, in this stage, you should concentrate on looking for errors that you might have missed or that were intro-duced in new material you added. Use proofreader's symbols to mark any errors you find.

Finally, print out a final draft and read it aloud before turning it in. Doing this will force you to slow down and catch errors you might otherwise overlook. Make these final corrections and changes.

Read Kelly's final draft on the next page. See how she worked through the three stages of the writing process: Prewrite, Draft, and Revise.

Writing Follow-Up

Publish and Present

- If anyone in your class wrote a review of the same film or play you did, discuss your analyses. What about the film or play did each of you like or dislike?
- Many newspapers' Arts & Entertainment sections contain reviews of films and plays. See if your local paper accepts critiques from amateur writers, and submit yours for publication.

Reflect

- Since writing your review, have you found yourself critiquing other movies or plays more overtly? How might this writing experience affect your appreciation of movies and plays in the future?

STUDENT MODEL

A Critique of Joanne Woodward in *The Glass Menagerie*
by Kelly McElroy

Tennessee Williams's drama *The Glass Menagerie* takes place entirely in a small apartment in St. Louis during the Great Depression and features only four characters: Amanda Wingfield, a middle-aged woman; her grown son, Tom; her abnormally shy grown daughter, Laura; and a gentleman caller named Jim. In the 1987 film adaptation of the drama, directed by Paul Newman, these four roles are played by Joanne Woodward, John Malkovich, Karen Allen, and James Naughton. Woodward's compelling performance in the role of Amanda is what makes the film worth seeing.

Woodward's fine acting reveals the complexity of Amanda's character. Watching Woodward's facial expressions, the audience experiences Amanda's anger and disappointment. In a convincing early scene, Amanda provokes Tom to argue with her, as if she is testing his devotion. After the actors share a tense moment of silence, the audience wonders if Amanda and Tom will reach any understanding. In the next several scenes, Woodward brings out the mother's fear that Tom will leave the family. As Amanda's desperation increases, her voice creeps higher and her gestures become less controlled.

One of Woodward's most skillful scenes occurs midway in the film, when Amanda attempts to earn money by selling magazine subscriptions over the phone. The audience seems to be spying on Amanda as she tries to coax customers into renewing. The women she calls are friendly acquaintances, and she puts their relationships at risk by asking for money. Woodward captures Amanda's desperation in the tears of relief she sheds and the repeated "Bless you's" she utters when one woman agrees to renew. Woodward also reveals Amanda's distress and embarrassment over this task in the tightness of her face when one woman hangs up on her.

Woodward's strong performance continues through the end of the film, when she portrays a mother eager for her daughter to have the comfortable life she somehow failed to secure for herself. In response to Amanda's nagging, Tom invites a co-worker to dinner as a potential suitor for Laura. As the climactic scene approaches, Amanda tells melancholy stories of her youth that captivate both Laura and the audience. Here again, Woodward transforms herself into Amanda. Her wistful voice, glazed eyes, and small smile all suggest her longing for the past, her "Blue Mountain days."

Through Woodward's skillful acting in *The Glass Menagerie*, the audience comes to know the real Amanda: a woman struggling to live in the present while clinging to the past. This film version of Williams's famous play owes a great deal to Woodward's subtle handling of a complex role.

The title of a review should reflect its purpose.

What grounding details about the drama are provided?

Locate the writer's thesis statement.

How does the topic sentence relate to the thesis?

What details from the film are provided to support the analysis?

What makes it clear that the analysis proceeds chronologically through the film?

A balance of analysis and summary are provided.

A summary of theme and restatement of thesis leaves readers with a sense of closure.

Reading Skills

Evaluate Point of View

The **point of view** is the vantage point, or perspective, from which a story is told—in other words, who is telling the story. Most works of fiction are written in first- or third-person point of view.

In **first-person point of view,** the narrator participates in or witnesses the story; this point of view is indicated by the use of words such as *I* and *we.* In **third-person point of view,** the narrator usually stands outside the action and observes; the narrator uses words such as *he, she, it,* and *they.* In some stories, the narrator's point of view is **limited.** This type of narrator can reveal only his or her private, internal thoughts or the thoughts of a single character. In other stories, the narrator's point of view is **omniscient,** or all knowing. This type of narrator can reveal the private, internal thoughts of all the characters.

Second-person point of view is found primarily in informative and persuasive writing. In text that provides directions, the word *you* is used either directly or implicitly in the imperative form—for example, *First,*
you connect part A with part B or *Begin by connecting part A with part B.* In an essay, the writer might address the audience to relate to them directly and be more persuasive—for example, *If you are patient, you eventually will benefit from these actions.*

Once you have identified what point of view the author is using, then you can evaluate how effective that perspective is. Consider what the author is able to relate using this point of view and how the work would be different if another point of view were used.

TEST-TAKING TIP

When answering multiple-choice questions on a timed test, don't spend too much time on any one question. Skip over difficult questions and plan on going back to answer them if time allows. To help you find these questions later, clearly mark them in some way. Then start from the beginning of the test and revisit these items in order, answering as many as you can in the time that's left.

Practice

Directions: Read the following passage. The questions that come after it will ask you to evaluate the point of view.

FICTION: This passage is from Ralph Ellison's novel *Invisible Man.*

When I reached the door of Mr. Emerson's office it occurred to me that perhaps I should have waited until the business of the day was under way, but I disregarded the
5 idea and went ahead. My being early would be, I hoped, an indication of both how badly I wanted work, and how promptly I would perform any assignment given me. Besides, wasn't there a saying that the first person of
10 the day to enter a business would get a bargain? . . .

He looked at me with a jerk of his head, his face beginning to twitch again.

"I suppose I've been evading the issue
15 again—as always. Look," he burst out impulsively. "Do you believe that two people, two strangers who have never seen one another before can speak with utter frankness and sincerity?"
20 "Sir?"

". . . What I mean is, do you believe it possible for us, the two of us, to throw off the mask of custom and manners that insulate man from man, and converse in naked
25 honesty and frankness?"

"I don't know what you mean exactly, sir," I said.

"Are you sure?"

"I . . ."

30   "Of course, of course. If I could only speak plainly! I'm confusing you. Such frankness just isn't possible because all our motives are impure. Forget what I just said. I'll try to put it this way—and remember 35 this, please . . ."

My head spun. He was addressing me, leaning forward confidentially, as though he'd known me for years, and I remembered something my grandfather had said long 40 ago: *Don't let no white man tell you his business, 'cause after he tells you he's liable to git shame he tole it to you and then he'll hate you. Fact is, he was hating you all the time . . .*

". . . I want to try to reveal a part of 45 reality that is most important to you—but I warn you, it's going to hurt. No, let me finish," he said, touching my knee lightly and quickly removing his hand as I shifted my position.

50   "What I want to do is done very seldom, and, to be honest, it wouldn't happen now if I hadn't sustained a series of impossible frustrations. You see—well, I'm a thwarted . . . Oh, . . . there I go again, thinking only of myself 55 . . . We're both frustrated, understand? Both of us, and I want to help you . . ."

Multiple Choice

1. In the first paragraph, the author uses which point of view?
   A. first-person
   B. second-person
   C. third-person limited
   D. third-person omniscient

2. This use of point of view makes the story
   F. more real and personal.
   G. shorter and simpler.
   H. less likely to be criticized.
   J. more broad in perspective.

3. Who is the narrator of this story?
   A. Mr. Emerson
   B. Mr. Ellison
   C. a nameless job interviewer
   D. a nameless job seeker

4. In lines 40–44, italic type is used to show
   F. a change in point of view.
   G. the author's memories.
   H. dialogue.
   J. the internal thoughts of the interviewer.

Constructed Response

5. Analyze the author's use of point of view. How would the story have been different if he had used another point of view?

Writing Skills

Stay on Task

While writing your essay, keep referring to your outline and be sure to follow it. If you think of another point to add while you are writing, you can add it. Likewise, if you think of a better organizational plan, you can follow it. In general, however, do not stray from your initial outline. It is easy to go off on a tangent, especially with a subject about which you have strong feelings, but you should refrain from doing so. Following your outline is the key to staying on task in a timed writing situation.

Also refer back to the writing prompt from time to time to ensure you stay on task. Look at the key words and phrases you underlined and any notes you made when analyzing the prompt. The topic stated in the prompt is the topic you are expected to address. Everything in your essay should somehow connect to the prompt and express your thesis in a clear, concise, and forceful way.

Finally, keep track of the time, but don't worry about it to the point that you are distracted from the task. Don't allow your attention to wander or look to see what others are doing.

> **TEST-TAKING TIP**
>
> When you practice for the essay section of a standardized test, don't limit yourself to writing. Read and evaluate sample essays to get a sense of what kind of writing earns a high score.

Practice

Timed Writing: 30 minutes

Benjamin Franklin wrote, "In this world nothing can be said to be certain, except death and taxes." Although this statement is intended to be witty, it also contains a great deal of truth. Life is full of uncertainty, and the lives of high school students may be more uncertain than most.

Some people feel stressed by not knowing what the future holds for them. They consider uncertainty bad. They may turn to fortune-tellers, tarot cards, and similar practices of predicting the future. Other people believe that the uncertainty inherent in life is not necessarily bad. In your opinion, is having uncertainty in life good or bad?

Assignment: In your essay, take a position on this question. You may write about either one of the perspectives given, or you may present a different perspective on this question. Use specific reasons and examples to support your position.

Revising and Editing Skills

Some standardized tests ask you to read a draft of an essay and answer questions about how to improve it. As you read the draft, watch for errors such as these:

- incorrect spellings
- disagreement between subject and verb; inconsistent verb tense; incorrect forms for irregular verbs; sentence fragments and run-ons; double negatives; and incorrect use of frequently confused words, such as *affect* and *effect*

- missing end marks, incorrect comma use, and lowercased proper nouns and proper adjectives
- unclear purpose, unclear main ideas, and lack of supporting details
- confusing order of ideas and missing transitions
- language that is inappropriate to the audience and purpose, and mood that is inappropriate for the purpose

After checking for errors, read each test question and decide which answer is best.

Practice

Directions: In the passage that follows, certain words and phrases are numbered and underlined. In the questions below the passage, alternatives are provided for each underlined word or phrase. In each case, choose the alternative that best expresses the idea, that is worded most consistently with the style and tone of the rest of the passage, or that makes the text correct according to the conventions of standard written English. If you think the original version is best, choose the first alternative, MAKE NO CHANGE. To indicate your answer, circle the letter of the chosen alternative.

(1) Just between <u>you and I, wouldn't it be great if we could see into the future?</u> (2) We would be <u>better prepared and less stressed, having</u> eliminated uncertainty. (3) On the other <u>hand, do we really want to know if something is going to end bad?</u> (4) Just as I don't read the last chapter of a book first or watch the end of a movie at the <u>beginning, neither do I want to know what's going to happen</u> to me.

Multiple Choice

1. A. MAKE NO CHANGE.
    B. you and I, wouldn't it be great if you could see into the future?
    C. you and I, wouldn't seeing into the future be great?
    D. you and me, wouldn't it be great if we could see into the future?

2. F. MAKE NO CHANGE.
    G. prepared better and less stressed, having
    H. better prepared, and less stressed, because of having
    J. better prepared and less stressed; if we

3. A. MAKE NO CHANGE.
    B. hand do we really want to know if something is going to end bad?
    C. hand, do we really want to know if something is going to end badly?
    D. hand, do we really want to know if some thing is going to end bad?

4. F. MAKE NO CHANGE.
    G. beginning neither do I want to know what's going to happen
    H. beginning, neither do I want to know whats going to happen
    J. beginning, nor do I want to know what's going to happen

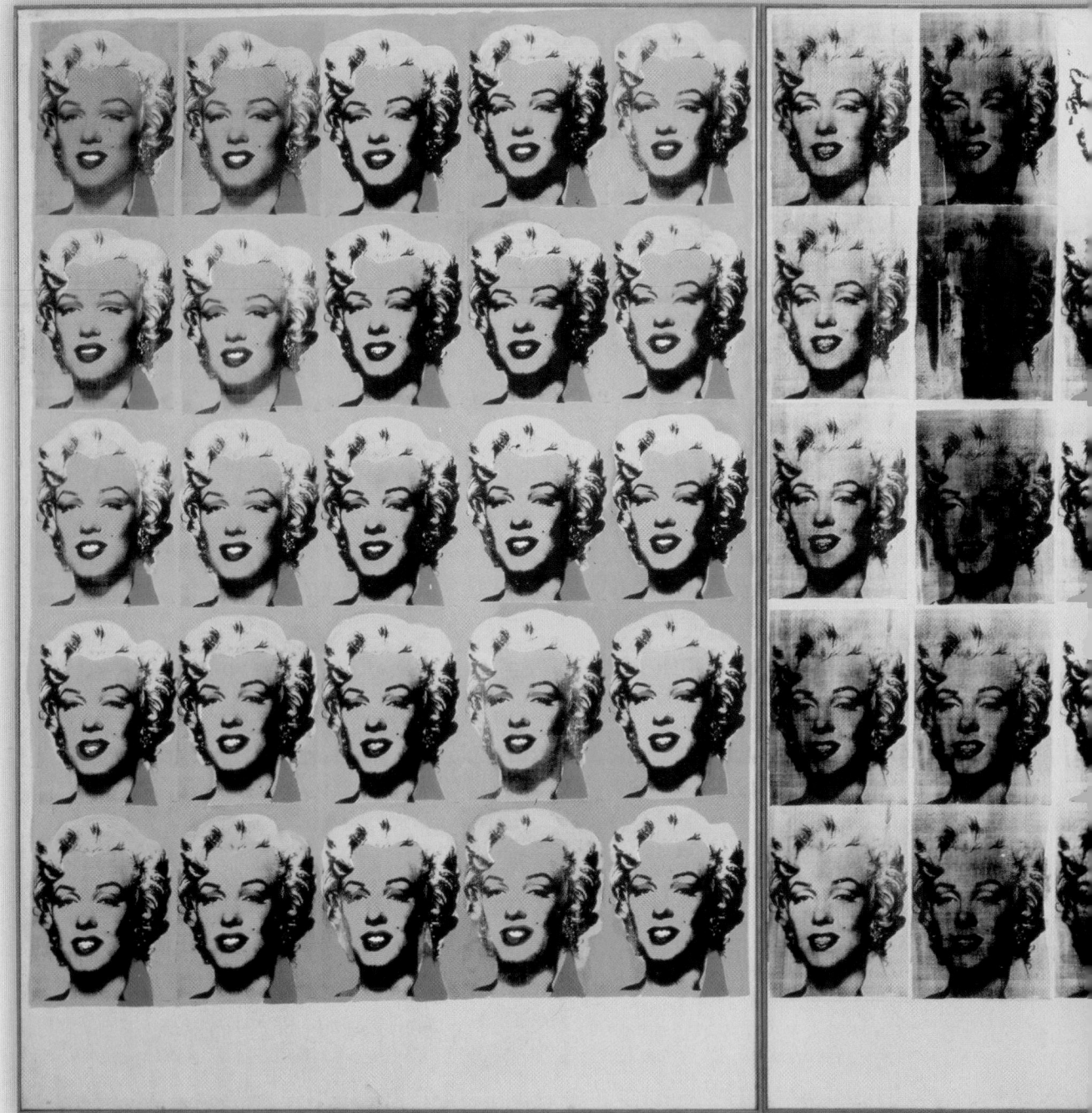

Marilyn Diptych, 1962. Andy Warhol.
Tate Gallery, London, England.

Early Contemporary

Unit 8

Era 1960–1980

1960

1965

AMERICAN LITERATURE AMERICAN LITERATURE AMERICAN LITERATURE AM

1960
Harper Lee publishes *To Kill a Mockingbird*

1961
Joseph Heller publishes *Catch-22*

1962
Ken Kesey publishes *One Flew Over the Cuckoo's Nest*

1962
Rachel Carson publishes *Silent Spring*

1963
Sylvia Plath's novel *The Bell Jar* is published posthumously

1963
Betty Friedan publishes *The Feminine Mystique*

1965
Malcolm X co-writes his autobiography with Alex Haley

MALCOLM X

1966
Truman Capote publishes *In Cold Blood*

1967
Bernard Malamud's *The Fixer* wins the Pulitzer Prize for fiction

1968
Tom Wolfe publishes *The Electric Kool-Aid Acid Test*

1969
Kurt Vonnegut publishes *Slaughterhouse Five*

AMERICAN HISTORY AMERICAN HISTORY AMERICAN HISTORY AMERICAN HIS

1961
John F. Kennedy becomes president

1963
Martin Luther King Jr. organizes the March on Washington and delivers his "I Have a Dream" speech

1963
Four children are killed when a bomb explodes in an African-American church in Birmingham, Alabama

1963
President John F. Kennedy is assassinated; Lyndon B. Johnson assumes office

1964
The Civil Rights Act of 1964 outlaws discrimination

1964
U.S. involvement in Vietnam formally begins with the Gulf of Tonkin incident

1967
Thurgood Marshall becomes the first African-American U.S. Supreme Court Justice

1968
Martin Luther King Jr. is assassinated, prompting riots across the country

1968
Senator Robert F. Kennedy is assassinated while campaigning for the presidency

1968
Richard Nixon is elected president

1969
The Cuyahoga River catches fire in Cleveland, Ohio, helping to spur the environmental movement

1969
Neil Armstrong becomes the first human to walk on the moon

WORLD HISTORY WORLD HISTORY WORLD HISTORY WORLD HISTORY WORL

1961
The Berlin Wall is built between East and West Germany

1961
The U.S.-led Bay of Pigs invasion fails to topple Fidel Castro's regime in Cuba

1962
The Soviet Union deploys nuclear missiles to Cuba, resulting in the Cuban Missile Crisis

1963
Soviet Astronaut Valentina Tereshkova becomes first woman in space

1965
The United States increases bombing of North Vietnam with Operation Rolling Thunder

1965
Mobutu Seko becomes dictator of the Democratic Republic of Congo and changes the country's name to Zaire

1968
Viet Cong soldiers launch the Tet Offensive

1968
Hundreds are killed in Mexico during the Tlatelolco massacre

1970

1975

ANGELOU

1970
Maya Angelou publishes
*I Know Why the Caged
Bird Sings*

1970
James Dickey publishes
Deliverance

1972
Hunter S. Thompson
publishes *Fear and
Loathing in Las Vegas*

1974
Carl Bernstein and Bob
Woodward publish *All the
President's Men*

1975
Edward Abbey publishes
The Monkey Wrench Gang

1976
Alex Haley publishes *Roots*

1976
Alice Walker publishes
Meridian

1978
Tim O'Brien's *Going After
Cacciato* wins the National
Book Award

1979
Tom Wolfe publishes
The Right Stuff

1970
President Richard Nixon
establishes the Environmental
Protection Agency (EPA)

1970
Four Kent State University
students are killed when the
Ohio National Guard tries to
break up a war protest

1972
Burglars are caught breaking
into the Democratic
National Headquarters at
the Watergate Hotel in
Washington, DC

1972
President Nixon is re-elected

1973
In *Roe v. Wade,* the U.S.
Supreme Court rules that
abortion is a constitutionally
protected medical procedure

1973
The Paris Peace Accords
formally put an end to
U.S. involvement in the
Vietnam War

1974
Nixon resigns from
the presidency and
is succeeded by
Gerald Ford

1976
Jimmy Carter is
elected president

1979
Iranian militants take over
the U.S. embassy in Tehran
and seize fifty-two American
hostages

1980
Ronald Reagan is elected
president, defeating
incumbent Jimmy Carter

CARTER

1970
The first Earth Day is held
on April 22

1971
Idi Amin seizes power in
Uganda, resulting in years of
internal violence and struggle

1972
Eleven Israeli athletes are
taken hostage and later
killed at the Olympic Games
in Munich, Germany

1973
Chilean President Salvador
Allende is assassinated

1975
The Soviet *Soyuz* and
U.S. *Apollo* spacecraft link
in space

1977
Fifteen countries, including
the United States and Soviet
Union, sign an agreement to
curb the spread of nuclear
weapons

1978
Israel and Egypt agree to
peace at the Camp David
Accords

1979
The Soviet Union invades
Afghanistan

1979
Revolutionary forces
under Ayatollah
Khomeini take
control of Iran
after the Shah
goes into exile

KHOMEINI

> ## "Man holds in his mortal hands the power to abolish all forms of human poverty and all forms of human life."
>
> —JOHN F. KENNEDY

The Turbulent Sixties

When John F. Kennedy defeated Richard Nixon in the 1960 presidential election, it seemed to many Americans that a new age had dawned. Kennedy pointed the nation toward a New Frontier and proposed a number of social and economic initiatives, including a sweeping civil rights bill and ambitious space exploration program.

In foreign policy, however, Kennedy continued the Cold War politics of the 1950s and supported a covert operation to invade Fidel Castro's Cuba. The Bay of Pigs invasion was launched in April 1961 by Cuban exiles of the former regime, who accused Castro of turning toward communism. The invasion failed, further escalating tension with the Soviets. In October 1962, when a U.S. spy plane detected Soviet missile sites in Cuba, Kennedy warned the Soviets to remove them or face war. For the thirteen days of the Cuban Missile Crisis, the threat of nuclear war was all too real.

These events led the Soviet Union, the United States, and Great Britain to negotiate the first of many treaties limiting the testing and use of nuclear arms. However, the arms race continued unabated, with each side following a policy of "mutually assured destruction" as it stockpiled weapons to deter the other side from making a first strike. Cold War tensions also led to construction of the Berlin Wall, which halted migration from East Germany (occupied by the Soviets) to West Germany (occupied by England, the United States, and France.)

Race Relations

Race relations had become a central issue in the United States following the 1954 U.S. Supreme Court decision ruling "separate but equal schools" unconstitutional and the 1955 Montgomery, Alabama, bus boycott, during which advocacy for civil rights turned into a nonviolent mass movement. The early 1960s saw protests in the forms of lunch counter sit-ins at segregated restaurants and so-called Freedom Rides on interstate buses to protest segregated public transportation in the South. In the summer of 1963, the March on Washington brought citizens of all backgrounds together to protest the nation's racism. Eighteen days later, a bomb exploded in an African-American church

Guards in position at a break in the Berlin Wall (1960).

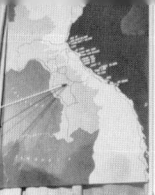

in Birmingham, Alabama, killing four girls attending a Sunday school class. Later that year, President Kennedy was assassinated in Dallas, Texas.

President Lyndon Johnson carried on his predecessor's civil rights policies. He pressed for passage of the Civil Rights Act of 1964, which protected against discrimination in accommodations and employment and tied federal education funding to school desegregation. The Voting Rights Act of 1965 followed, protecting against discrimination at the polls.

After defeating Barry Goldwater in the presidential election of 1964, Johnson initiated a legislative program designed to build the Great Society. He pushed his War on Poverty initiatives through Congress, including increased funding for housing, health care for the poor and elderly, education, and a major new agency, the Office of Economic Opportunity. Passage of the Great Society legislation initiated a political debate between advocates of increased domestic spending and supporters of greater defense spending that would continue into the next century.

"History will have to record that the greatest tragedy of this period of social transition was not the strident clamor of the bad people, but the appalling silence of the good people."

—MARTIN LUTHER KING JR.

NOTABLE NUMBERS

164 Race riots that broke out during the summer of 1967, causing 100 deaths and 2,000 injuries

500,000 Young people who flocked to Woodstock in 1969 to hear performers such as Jimi Hendrix, the Grateful Dead, and Janis Joplin

4 Kent State University students killed in 1970 when Ohio National Guardsmen fired into a crowd of antiwar demonstrators

444 Days fifty-two Americans were held hostage at the U.S. Embassy in Iran in 1979

Despite these successes, frustration with discrimination and poverty ignited major race riots in several U.S. cities, including the Watts neighborhood in Los Angeles in 1967. Following the assassinations of Martin Luther King Jr. and Senator Robert Kennedy in 1968, the nation was in a state of shock.

The Vietnam Conflict

Despite Johnson's domestic political accomplishments, he had a troubled presidency because of U.S. involvement in the Vietnam War. Previous presidents had supplied arms first to the French occupation and then arms and military advisers to the U.S.-supported successor regimes in South Vietnam. By the time Johnson assumed office in 1963, 16,000 U.S. advisers were in place, with some engaged in combat against the Viet Cong in the North.

Using a questionable set of circumstances in the Gulf of Tonkin, Johnson persuaded Congress to pass a resolution in 1964 authorizing a police action to defend American forces in the area. However, modern warfare, including saturation bombing and Agent Orange defoliation, did not defeat the North Vietnamese guerrillas in the coming years. As U.S. troop involvement and casualties escalated, so did Americans' opposition to the war, eventually leading to widespread antiwar demonstrations.

The demonstrations were connected to a larger counterculture rebellion among American youth born after the end of World War II, now dubbed the baby boomers. Growing up in the relatively prosperous 1950s, these youth rebelled against the nation's materialistic values and conformity and often expressed their dissatisfaction through music. The 1969 Woodstock Music and Art Fair drew members of the counterculture to a farm in upstate New York and became the event that signified the divide between generations.

Grassroots Movements

Although some of the extremes of the 1960s passed into oblivion, the Civil Rights movement and Vietnam War protests demonstrated the power of grassroots political organizing to bring about change. This

lesson was especially inspiring to those concerned about women's rights and the environment.

When a presidential commission reported on discrimination against women in the workplace, Congress responded with the Equal Pay Act in 1963. At the same time, Betty Friedan's *The Feminine Mystique* appeared, challenging the notion that women were content with their domestic roles. Friedan's book revived the women's movement and led to creation of the National Organization for Women (NOW) to push for women's rights. By 1972, women's advocacy had resulted in the Education Amendments Act, outlawing sexual discrimination in higher education, and passage of the Equal Rights Amendment (ERA) by Congress. However, the ERA was not ratified by the necessary thirty-eight states and thus failed to become law.

During the 1960s, public attitudes began to change toward industry's impact on the environment. In 1962, marine biologist Rachel Carson published *Silent Spring*, detailing the effects of commonly used toxic pesticides, such as DDT. In 1968, *Apollo 8* astronauts photographed the whole planet Earth while returning from their pioneering orbital flight around the moon. This image of Earth—small, fragile, beautiful, and unique—made an immediate impact on Americans and stirred interest in environmental issues. Thus, when Ohio's oil-covered Cuyahoga River caught fire in

1969, public reaction was intense. Ecology flags were waved along with peace signs, and millions of Americans joined in the first Earth Day on April 22, 1970. Congress listened, creating the Environmental Protection Agency in 1970 and passing the Clean Air Act, the Clean Water Act of 1972, and the Endangered Species Act of 1973.

Politics in the Seventies

In 1968, following a turbulent presidential campaign, Republican Richard Nixon was elected to the White House. While he fulfilled his election promise to withdraw troops from Vietnam, he launched an unsuccessful invasion of neighboring Cambodia in 1970. This act prompted Congress to resolve that the president could not extend the war without its approval. In 1973, a cease fire was reached with Vietnam, formally ending the war.

The Nixon administration pursued a policy of *détente,* or improved relations, with the Soviet Union, negotiating the first of a series of Strategic Arms Limitation Treaties (SALT). Relations with China also improved following the president's 1972 visit. Nixon's term came to an abrupt end, however, when he resigned following hearings on 1972 election improprieties, including the break-in at Democratic National Committee headquarters in the Watergate Hotel. Nixon was succeeded by his vice president, Gerald Ford.

Economic difficulties faced the Ford administration, including an Arab oil embargo during the Yom Kippur War that sent U.S. fuel prices soaring. When Ford cut government spending, the country spun into recession. Ford lost the 1976 election to Governor Jimmy Carter of Georgia. The Carter administration followed a policy of promoting human rights around the world and succeeded in bringing Israel and Egypt, traditional enemies in the Middle East, to the negotiating table. Energy conservation was a major issue for Carter, and Congress passed the National Energy Act at his urging. However, domestic economic troubles, coupled with the Iran hostage crisis, in which Islamic fundamentalists in Tehran, Iran, took over the American Embassy, led to Carter's defeat by Ronald Reagan in 1980.

The earth rising over the surface of the moon, as seen by the orbiting *Apollo 8* spacecraft.

The 1960s began with peace and prosperity, providing relief from the era of the Great Depression and World War II. However, tensions were rising on the global front over the threat of nuclear war and American involvement in Vietnam.

At his inauguration in January 1961, John F. Kennedy spoke about freedom and opportunity but also the nation's commitment to defending liberty worldwide. The Soviet Union, which had been an ally during World War II, increasingly was becoming a threat. The Cold War nearly became a nuclear war in 1962 during the Cuban Missile Crisis, when Soviet missile installations were detected in Cuba. The tensions and fears that arose from these events were expressed in literature such as Donald Barthelme's short story "Game." Poet William Stafford also wrote about nuclear arms and the dehumanizing effect of technology on humanity.

The United States' involvement in the Vietnam War, which lasted from 1961 to 1973, also was a catalyst for much literature of the period. The war was unpopular among Americans, and many protests, some violent, occurred across the country. The most potent Vietnam Era literature, however, came from those who served in the conflict and witnessed the death and destruction firsthand. Fiction writer Tim O'Brien and poet Yusef Komunyakaa reported their wartime experiences with chilling reality.

Whaam! 1963. Roy Lichtenstein. Tate Gallery, London, England.

Inaugural Address

A Speech by John F. Kennedy

Build Background

Historical Context When John F. Kennedy was elected President of the United States, he succeeded Dwight D. Eisenhower, a much-decorated World War II general. At the time of Kennedy's election, in November 1960, the nation was mostly peaceful and prosperous. Tensions existed, however, between North America and Western Europe, on one hand, and the communist-led Soviet Union and other Eastern European nations, on the other.

In his Inaugural Address, delivered on January 20, 1961, Kennedy spoke of the international conflicts and set the goals of his new administration. He also sought to establish himself as a forceful leader who, despite his youthful charm, could assert himself with the nation's adversaries in Moscow.

Reader's Context If you had listened to the Inaugural Address on January 20, 1961, what elements of the speech would have impressed you the most?

Meet the Author

John F. Kennedy (1917–1963), thirty-fifth president of the United States, was born in Brookline, Massachusetts, and earned his undergraduate degree at Harvard University in 1940. In World War II, Kennedy served as a torpedo boat commander and was honored for his bravery.

Kennedy's political career began soon after his return home to Massachusetts. In 1946, he was elected to the U.S. House of Representatives, and in 1953, he was elected to the Senate, where he served for eight years. That same year, Kennedy married Jacqueline Bouvier. In 1954–1955, while bedridden with a back injury, Kennedy wrote the Pulitzer Prize winner *Profiles in Courage,* which explored the moral actions of eight American leaders.

In 1960, Kennedy was elected president, the youngest person and the first and only Catholic to occupy the White House to date. Two years later, Kennedy faced a nuclear confrontation with what was then the Soviet Union in an incident known as the Cuban Missile Crisis. Although a compromise was reached, tensions persisted. The president also created the Peace Corps, an agency that sent Americans to Third World nations to teach, and he promoted civil rights legislation. On November 22, 1963, after less than three years in office, Kennedy was assassinated in Dallas, Texas. His body lies in Arlington National Cemetery.

Analyze Literature

Purpose and Repetition
A writer's or speaker's **purpose** is his or her aim, or goal. A work may have one or more of the following purposes: to inform, to describe, to persuade, and to narrate.

Repetition is the writer's intentional reuse of a sound, word, phrase, or sentence.

Set Purpose

Kennedy's inaugural is generally considered one of his most inspiring speeches and one of the most noted inaugural addresses. As you read it, determine what his chief purposes were in speaking to Americans and to the world. In addition, look for examples of Kennedy's oratorical style, such as his use of repetition.

Preview Vocabulary

temper, 1030
venture, 1030
asunder, 1030
subversion, 1031
sovereign, 1031
invective, 1031
civility, 1031
belabor, 1031
invoke, 1032
eradicate, 1032

Inaugural Address

by John F. Kennedy

And so, my fellow Americans: ask not what your country can do for you—ask what you can do for your country.

We observe today not a victory of party but a celebration of freedom—symbolizing an end as well as a beginning—signifying renewal as well as change. For I have sworn before you and Almighty God the same solemn oath our forebears[1] prescribed nearly a century and three-quarters ago.

The world is very different now. For man holds in his mortal hands the power to abolish all forms of human poverty and all forms of human life. And yet the same revolutionary

---

1. **forebears.** Ancestors; the reference is to the American colonists who defeated Britain and established the United States.

The Kennedy Assassination

On November 22, 1963, President John F. Kennedy visited Dallas, Texas, with his wife, Jacqueline. As they paraded through Dealey Plaza at 12:30 PM, three gunshots rang out from the Texas Book Depository. Two of the bullets struck Kennedy, killing him instantly.

One hour and twenty minutes after the attack, Dallas police apprehended Lee Harvey Oswald in a local movie theater. After reviewing his background, the police learned that Oswald was a former U.S. Marine who had temporarily defected to the Soviet Union. As authorities transferred their suspect from the local police station to the Dallas County Jail, a man named Jack Ruby emerged from the throng of reporters that had gathered outside and shot Oswald to death on national television.

Left with no explanation from the killer, many people began wondering whether Kennedy's death had been part of a national or international conspiracy. When Lyndon B. Johnson took office, he ordered a federal committee to investigate the assassination. Supreme Court Chief Justice Earl Warren directed the investigatory group, which became known as the Warren Commission. After interviewing hundreds of witnesses and reviewing thousands of documents, the Warren Commission released its report on September 24, 1964. It claimed that Oswald had acted alone in killing the president.

Years after the event, the Kennedy assassination remains a hotly debated topic. In 1978, the House Select Committee on Assassinations (HSCA) reviewed the Warren Commission's report and criticized its methods. HSCA's forensic scientists analyzed a sound recording of the gunshots and determined with near certainty that a fourth shot was fired, indicating the presence of a second gunman.

To quell conspiracy theorists, President George H. W. Bush signed into law the President John F. Kennedy Assassination Records Collection Act on October 26, 1992. It established a collection within the National Archives to house all government materials related to Kennedy's assassination. Even though some documents remain classified, the act declared that everything must become public by 2017.

---

beliefs for which our forebears fought are still at issue around the globe—the belief that the rights of man come not from the generosity of the state but from the hands of God.

We dare not forget today that we are the heirs of that first revolution. Let the word go forth from this time and place, to friend and foe alike, that the torch has been passed to a new generation of Americans—born in this century, <u>tempered</u> by war, disciplined by a hard and bitter peace, proud of our ancient heritage—and unwilling to witness or permit the slow undoing of those human rights to which this nation has always been committed, and to which we are committed today at home and around the world.

Let every nation know, whether it wishes us well or ill, that we shall pay any price, bear any burden, meet any hardship, support any friend, oppose any foe to assure the survival and the success of liberty.

This much we pledge—and more.

To those old allies whose cultural and spiritual origins we share, we pledge the loyalty of faithful friends. United, there is little we cannot do in a host of cooperative <u>ventures</u>. Divided, there is little we can do—for we dare not meet a powerful challenge at odds and split <u>asunder</u>.

To those new states whom we welcome to the ranks of the free, we pledge our word that one form of colonial control shall not have passed away merely to be replaced by a far more iron tyranny. We shall not always expect

---

tem • per (tem´ pər) v., toughen, as by difficult experiences
ven • ture (ven´ chər) n., risky or dangerous project
asun • der (ə sun´ dər) adv., separated in direction or position

to find them supporting our view. But we shall always hope to find them strongly supporting their own freedom—and to remember that, in the past, those who foolishly sought power by riding the back of the tiger ended up inside.

To those people in the huts and villages of half the globe struggling to break the bonds of mass misery, we pledge our best efforts to help them help themselves, for whatever period is required—not because the Communists may be doing it, not because we seek their votes, but because it is right. If a free society cannot help the many who are poor, it cannot save the few who are rich.

To our sister republics south of our border, we offer a special pledge—to convert our good words into good deeds—in a new alliance for progress—to assist free men and free governments in casting off the chains of poverty. But this peaceful revolution of hope cannot become the prey of hostile powers. Let all our neighbors know that we shall join with them to oppose aggression or <u>subversion</u> anywhere in the Americas. And let every other power know that this hemisphere intends to remain the master of its own house.

To that world assembly of <u>sovereign</u> states, the United Nations, our last best hope in an age where the instruments of war have far outpaced the instruments of peace, we renew our pledge of support—to prevent it from becoming merely a forum for <u>invective</u>—to strengthen its shield of the new and the weak—and to enlarge the area in which its writ may run.

Finally, to those nations who would make themselves our adversary, we offer not a pledge but a request—that both sides begin anew the quest for peace before the dark powers of destruction unleashed by science engulf all humanity in planned or accidental self-destruction. We dare not tempt them with weakness. For only when our arms are sufficient beyond doubt can we be certain beyond doubt that they will never be employed.

But neither can two great and powerful groups of nations take comfort from our present

Official portrait of President John F. Kennedy, created in 1970 by Aaron Shikler.

course—both sides overburdened by the cost of modern weapons, both rightly alarmed by the steady spread of the deadly atom, yet both racing to alter that uncertain balance of terror that stays the hand of mankind's final war.

So let us begin anew—remembering on both sides that <u>civility</u> is not a sign of weakness, and sincerity is always subject to proof. Let us never negotiate out of fear. But let us never fear to negotiate.

Let both sides explore what problems unite us instead of <u>belaboring</u> those problems which divide us.

sub • ver • sion (sub vur´ zhən) *n.*, systematic attempt to overthrow a government
sov • er • eign (säv´ ər in) *adj.*, independent
in • vec • tive (in vek´ tiv) *n.*, insulting or abusive language
ci • vil • i • ty (sə vil´ ə tē) *n.*, politeness
be • la • bor (bə lā´ bər) *v.*, spend too much time or effort on

Let both sides, for the first time, formulate serious and precise proposals for the inspection and control of arms—and bring the absolute power to destroy other nations under the absolute control of all nations.

Let both sides seek to <u>invoke</u> the wonders of science instead of its terrors. Together let us explore the stars, conquer the deserts, <u>eradicate</u> disease, tap the ocean depths, and encourage the arts and commerce.

Let both sides unite to heed in all corners of the earth the command of Isaiah—to "undo the heavy burdens . . . [and] let the oppressed go free."[2]

And if a beachhead[3] of cooperation may push back the jungle of suspicion, let both sides join in creating a new endeavor, not a new balance of power but a new world of law, where the strong are just and the weak secure and the peace preserved.

All this will not be finished in the first 100 days. Nor will it be finished in the first 1,000 days, nor in the life of this administration, nor even perhaps in our lifetime on this planet. But let us begin.

In your hands, my fellow citizens, more than mine, will rest the final success or failure of our course. Since this country was founded, each generation of Americans has been summoned to give testimony to its national loyalty. The graves of young Americans who answered the call to service surround the globe.

Now the trumpet summons us again—not as a call to bear arms, though arms we need— not as a call to battle, though embattled we are—but a call to bear the burden of a long twilight struggle, year in and year out, "rejoicing in hope, patient in tribulation"[4]—a struggle against the common enemies of man: tyranny, poverty, disease, and war itself.

Can we forge against these enemies a grand and global alliance, North and South, East and West, that can assure a more fruitful life for all mankind? Will you join in that historic effort?

In the long history of the world, only a few generations have been granted the role of defending freedom in its hour of maximum danger. I do not shrink from this responsibility —I welcome it. I do not believe that any of us would exchange places with any other people or any other generation. The energy, the faith, the devotion which we bring to this endeavor will light our country and all who serve it— and the glow from that fire can truly light the world.

And so, my fellow Americans: ask not what your country can do for you—ask what you can do for your country.

My fellow citizens of the world: ask not what America will do for you, but what together we can do for the freedom of man.

Finally, whether you are citizens of America or citizens of the world, ask of us here the same high standards of strength and sacrifice which we ask of you. With a good conscience our only sure reward, with history the final judge of our deeds, let us go forth to lead the land we love, asking His blessing and His help, but knowing that here on earth God's work must truly be our own. ❖

---

2. **"undo . . . free."** From the Bible, Isaiah 58:6
3. **beachhead.** Position gained as a secure starting point for an action
4. **"rejoicing . . . tribulation."** From the Bible, Romans 12:12

in • voke (in vōk´) v., call on for blessing, help, or inspiration
erad • i • cate (ē rad´ ə kāt) v., get rid of; wipe out; destroy

MIRRORS & WINDOWS

John F. Kennedy delivered his Inaugural Address in January 1961. Are the issues he spoke about still relevant today?

Refer to Text ▶ ▶ ▶ ▶ ▶   Reason with Text

1a. What is "that first revolution" of which today's generation is the heir?	**1b.** Discuss why Kennedy uses the image of a torch being passed.	**Understand** Find meaning
2a. Who is invited to join an "alliance for progress"?	**2b.** In the nineteenth century, U.S. opposition to European influence in Latin America was expressed in the Monroe Doctrine. What is Kennedy's likely policy toward that doctrine?	**Apply** Use information
3a. Identify the groups that Kennedy addresses in his speech.	**3b.** To which group does he speak the longest? In this section, what two contradictory issues does the speech attempt to balance?	**Analyze** Take things apart
4a. After World War II, a number of countries in Asia, Africa, and parts of Latin America gained independence from European colonial rule. What two promises does Kennedy make to these new nations?	**4b.** Decide whether Kennedy really wants to base his policies on what is right rather than on what the communists are doing.	**Evaluate** Make judgments
5a. According to Kennedy, what should citizens ask of their nation?	**5b.** What contributions might Americans make to their nation today?	**Create** Bring ideas together

Analyze Literature

Purpose and Repetition
What major purposes does Kennedy have in this speech? How well did he achieve them? Discuss which of these purposes seem aimed at his American audience and which seem aimed at his world audience.

In which passages does Kennedy use repetition to emphasize ideas or to provide unity? How effective are these passages? Why is repetition an effective oratorical technique?

Extend the Text

Writing Options
Creative Writing In the role of a White House media aide, prepare a press release summarizing the main points of another speech by Kennedy. Use library and Internet resources to locate an appropriate speech.

Expository Writing Find an inaugural address by a president since Kennedy. In a brief essay, describe the similarities and differences between the two speeches. Discuss not only the issues and topics mentioned in the speeches but also the style and tone.

Collaborative Learning
Design a Commemorative Coin With a small group, design a coin to honor John F. Kennedy. Research his family, presidency, writings, or legacy to choose photographs or illustrations with details that could be used for a commemorative disk. If the graphics cannot be downloaded legally, make sketches based on them. (Be sure to credit the photographer or artist.) Display your coin design.

Media Literacy
Develop a Time Line Show John Kennedy's achievements in historical context by preparing a time line of the literary and political milestones of his career. To begin, research dates and other key details; then decide which events to include on the time line.

 Go to **www.mirrorsandwindows.com** for more.

At the Bomb Testing Site
Traveling Through the Dark

Poems by William Stafford

Build Background

Literary Context These two selections by William Stafford explore humanity's effect on the natural world. In **"At the Bomb Testing Site,"** the reader views an atomic test area in the southwestern U.S. desert through the eyes of a lizard. The lizard's uncanny sense of danger of the consequences of technology reflects a common theme in Stafford's poetry. Published in *West of Your City* (1960), the poem was a response to the nuclear arms race between the United States and the Soviet Union.

"Traveling Through the Dark," which is possibly Stafford's best-known poem, is from a collection by the same title published in 1962. This volume of poetry won the National Book Award in 1963. "Traveling Through the Dark" is a narrative poem told from the perspective of a motorist stopping for a dead deer. It shows the collision, both literally and figuratively, between nature and technology.

Reader's Context Stafford once said in an interview, "Every poem I have ever written is a quiet protest poem." What other authors or poets have used their writing to call attention to humanity's intrusion on its environment?

Meet the Author

William Stafford (1914–1993) was born in Hutchinson, Kansas. Growing up, his family moved frequently so his father could find work. Young Stafford found work, as well, doing odd jobs to help with the family's finances during the Great Depression. This transient childhood made it difficult for Stafford to establish friendships, so books became a favorite companion.

Stafford attended the University of Kansas, graduating in 1937, and returned to the university to earn his master's degree in 1947. During World War II, Stafford was a *conscientious objector*, someone who was opposed to war on moral grounds. Instead of being sent overseas, he was assigned to the Civilian Public Service camps, where he performed soil conservation, road maintenance, and fire fighting. His book *Down in My Heart* (1948) is a memoir based on his experiences in the civilian service.

After receiving his doctorate degree from the University of Iowa in 1954, Stafford taught at Lewis and Clark College in Oregon and was named Oregon's Poet Laureate in 1975. Beginning in the 1960s, Stafford produced more than sixty books of prose and poetry and was named Consultant in Poetry to the Library of Congress in 1970. His prolific literary career was the result of his belief in writing a poem a day—even on the day he died.

Analyze Literature

Mood and Diction

Mood, or atmosphere, is the emotion created in the reader by a literary work.

Diction refers to the author's choice of words. A writer's choice of words is one of the primary characteristics of his or her written style.

Set Purpose

Stafford is well known for his ability to evoke a response, such as fear or delight, through the use of descriptive language and sensory details. As you read the two poems, look for startling images. Write down a word or two that describes the mood of each poem. Also consider how Stafford's diction helps create mood. Identify specific words and phrases from each poem that evoke a certain response.

At the Bomb Testing Site

by William Stafford

At noon in the desert a panting lizard
waited for history, its elbows tense,
watching the curve of a particular road
as if something might happen.

5 It was looking at something farther off
than people could see, an important scene
acted in stone for little selves
at the flute end of consequences.

There was just a continent without much on it
10 under a sky that never cared less.
Ready for a change, the elbows waited.
The hands gripped hard on the desert. ❖

MIRRORS & WINDOWS What is more important: protecting the environment or making economic and technological progress? Is it possible to do both?

Traveling Through the Dark

by William Stafford

Traveling through the dark I found a deer
dead on the edge of the Wilson River road.
It is usually best to roll them into the canyon:
that road is narrow; to swerve might make more dead.

5 By glow of the tail-light I stumbled back of the car
and stood by the heap, a doe, a recent killing:
she had stiffened already, almost cold.
I dragged her off; she was large in the belly.

My fingers touching her side brought me the reason—
10 her side was warm; her fawn lay there waiting.
alive, still, never to be born.
Beside that mountain road I hesitated.

The car aimed ahead its lowered parking lights;
under the hood purred the steady engine.
15 I stood in the glare of the warm exhaust turning red;
around our group I could hear the wilderness listen.

I thought hard for us all—my only swerving—,
then pushed her over the edge into the river. ❖

 **MIRRORS & WINDOWS**   If you were the driver in the poem, would you have hesitated? Would you be able to provide help in an emergency? What would be difficult for you?

Refer to Text ▶ ▶ ▶ ▶ ▶ Reason with Text

1a. In stanza 1 of the first poem, where is the lizard, and what is it waiting for?	**1b.** Explain why the speaker chose to have a lizard observe the bomb site.	**Understand** Find meaning
2a. What does the speaker in the second poem discover about the doe in stanza 3?	**2b.** Examine why the speaker hesitates in "Traveling Through the Dark."	**Apply** Use information
3a. In "At the Bomb Testing Site," what group is contrasted with "little selves"? Where are the selves said to be?	**3b.** Deduce who might be the "little selves." To what might "flute end of consequences" refer?	**Analyze** Take things apart
4a. Recall how the speaker handles the deer in the second poem.	**4b.** Why does the speaker act as he does in "Traveling Through the Dark"?	**Evaluate** Make judgments
5a. Do the poems use relatively familiar words or fairly difficult ones?	**5b.** Relate the main ideas of the poems. Cite details from each poem to support your answer.	**Create** Bring ideas together

Analyze Literature

Mood and Diction
What mood does Stafford create in each poem? What startling images and other details does he use to create that mood? How is the mood of each poem appropriate for its subject?

How do Stafford's word choices help create mood? Support your response with specific words and phrases from each poem. How would you characterize the diction in these poems?

Extend the Text

Writing Options
Creative Writing Write an advice column in response to a reader's letter about how to handle injured or dead animals on a road. Include in your response information about local laws concerning this situation; contact law enforcement agencies and the Department of Natural Resources.

Expository Writing Reading more than one work by a writer provides an opportunity to examine his or her work in some depth. Write a comparison and contrast essay on the two Stafford poems. Consider issues such as theme, diction, point of view, and sensory details and imagery.

Collaborative Learning
Illustrate a Poem Choose one of Stafford's poems to illustrate by creating a painting, drawing, photograph, sculpture, or other form. Focus on capturing details from the poem. With a partner or in a small group, display your artwork for others to enjoy.

Lifelong Learning
Prepare an Annotated Bibliography Nature is among the most frequent topics in poetry. Select one aspect of nature that interests you—for example, its fragility. Then conduct research to locate ten poems about the subject. For each poem, provide a brief *annotation*, or comment about the work that discusses its theme, mood, tone, and other interesting aspects. Organize the list of annotations alphabetically by writer.

 Go to **www.mirrorsandwindows.com** for more.

Ambush

A Short Story by Tim O'Brien

Build Background

Literary Context According to Tim O'Brien, "The best literature is always explorative. It's searching for answers and never finding them." This approach sums up his short story collection *The Things They Carried* (1990), stories about a platoon of Vietnam soldiers. In **"Ambush,"** a young girl asks her father if he ever killed anyone in the war. This tough question forces the narrator to relive a moment when he killed a man with a grenade. The narrator grapples with his past moral decision and his justification for it.

Historical Context Many characters in O'Brien's *The Things They Carried* are struggling with posttraumatic stress disorder (PTSD), a condition that often occurs after a traumatic incident. Soldiers who have witnessed wartime atrocities are particularly susceptible. The disorder came to the forefront after the Vietnam War, when at least 30 percent of returning soldiers, according to the National Institute of Mental Health, were diagnosed with similar signs and symptoms. These signs and symptoms include flashbacks, sleep disturbances, feelings of isolation and guilt, depression, anxiety, and angry outbursts. Physical problems may result, as well. Possible treatments include therapy and medication.

Reader's Context How do you handle a moral dilemma? What factors do you consider when making your decision?

Meet the Author

Tim O'Brien (b. 1946), a Vietnam War veteran, is best known for his fiction about the experiences of American soldiers in that conflict. Born in Austin, Minnesota, O'Brien received a bachelor's degree from Macalester College in Saint Paul. While there, he participated in war protests. Ironically, he was drafted into the army and considered fleeing to Canada to avoid serving but feared disapproval. During his year in Vietnam, he earned a Purple Heart, an award given to those injured or killed in military service. Later, O'Brien reflected on his decision to go to war and called it an act of cowardice.

During the early 1970s, O'Brien briefly attended Harvard and then worked as a *Washington Post* reporter until he began writing fiction full time. He once commented, "I believe in stories, in their incredible power to keep people alive, to keep the living alive, and the dead." O'Brien's wartime novel *Going After Cacciato* (1978) won the National Book Award. In his collection *The Things They Carried* (1990), O'Brien weaves reality and fiction to depict the physical and mental ravages of the Vietnam War. Other works by O'Brien include *If I Die in a Combat Zone, Box Me Up and Ship Me Home* (1973), *In the Lake of the Woods* (1994), *Tomcat in Love* (1998), and *July, July* (2002).

Analyze Literature

Realism and Climax
Realism is the attempt to achieve, in a work of art, an accurate portrayal of the world.

The **climax** is the high point of interest or suspense in the development of the plot.

Set Purpose

Like many other authors who have written about their wartime experiences, O'Brien creates a strong sense of Realism in his stories and novels. As you read "Ambush," consider how the narrator's style and the details he provides lend realism to the story. Also trace the plot and identify its high point of interest, or climax. How is this event a turning point or decisive moment?

Preview Vocabulary

ambush, 1040
platoon, 1040
watch, 1040
lob, 1041
peril, 1042

by Tim O'Brien

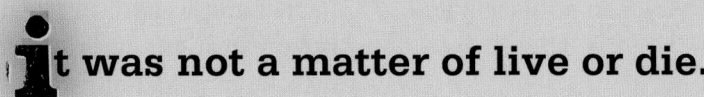

it was not a matter of live or die.

When she was nine, my daughter Kathleen asked if I had ever killed anyone. She knew about the war; she knew I'd been a soldier. "You keep writing these war stories," she said, "so I guess you must've killed somebody." It was a difficult moment, but I did what seemed right, which was to say, "Of course not," and then to take her onto my lap and hold her for a while. Someday, I hope, she'll ask again. But here I want to pretend she's a grown-up. I want to tell her exactly what happened, or what I remember happening, and then I want to say to her that as a little girl she was absolutely right. This is why I keep writing war stories:

He was a short, slender young man of about twenty. I was afraid of him—afraid of

Origins of the Vietnam War

In the late nineteenth century, France gained control of Vietnam, then known as Indochina, through a series of colonial wars. In 1945, communist revolutionary Ho Chi Minh organized resistance forces and established the Democratic Republic of Vietnam. France tried to regain control of Vietnam in 1946 and was supported in this effort by the United States, which feared the spread of communism in Asia.

During the Geneva Conference in 1954, the Vietnamese agreed to divide their country. The division was intended to be temporary, but a 1956 election to unify the two sectors never took place. North Vietnam became a socialist state and was controlled by Minh; South Vietnam became a noncommunist state and was led by U.S.-backed President Ngo Dinh Diem. Diem's violent regime was extremely unpopular, and masses of South Vietnamese defected to the North. Because of this, the U.S. government en-dorsed Diem's removal from office in 1963. This created a period of instability, which increased the number of communist insurgents in South Vietnam.

To avoid the collapse of the noncommunist government in South Vietnam, the United States began sending military personnel into the region in 1963. A few months later, after the alleged attack on U.S. ships in the Gulf of Tonkin, Congress voted to give President Lyndon Johnson full military control without a declaration of war. By 1965, more than 150,000 U.S. soldiers had been sent to Vietnam to fight the North's takeover of the South.

HO CHI MINH

Recognizing that they could not overpower the superior technology and weaponry of the U.S. military, the North Vietnamese focused instead on using their familiarity with the terrain and harsh environment to demoralize the opposition. This strategy was successful. In 1973, facing mounting casualties and criticism of U.S. involvement stateside, President Richard Nixon announced the gradual withdrawal of troops from Vietnam. Two years later, Saigon, the South Vietnamese capital, fell to the communists.

JOHNSON

---

something—and as he passed me on the trail I threw a grenade that exploded at his feet and killed him.

Or to go back:

Shortly after midnight we moved into the ambush site outside My Khe.[1] The whole platoon was there, spread out in the dense brush along the trail, and for five hours nothing at all happened. We were working in two-man teams—one man on guard while the other slept, switching off every two hours—and I remember it was still dark when Kiowa shook me awake for the final watch. The night was foggy and hot. For the first few moments I felt lost, not sure about directions, groping for my helmet and weapon. I reached out and found three grenades and lined them up in front of me; the pins had already been straightened for quick throwing. And then for maybe half an hour I kneeled there and waited. Very

---

1. **My Khe.** Village in Vietnam

---

am • bush (am´ bush) *n.*, trap in which a concealed soldier or soldiers lie in wait to attack by surprise

pla • toon (plä tün´) *n.*, subdivision of a military unit, normally consisting of sixteen to forty-four personnel

watch (wäch) *n.*, period of time during which a soldier stays awake to guard or protect his or her group

of what was happening in my stomach. I had already pulled the pin on a grenade. I had come up to a crouch. It was entirely automatic. I did not hate the young man; I did not see him as the enemy; I did not ponder issues of morality or politics or military duty. I crouched and kept my head low. I tried to swallow whatever was rising from my stomach, which tasted like lemonade, something fruity and sour. I was terrified. There were no thoughts about killing. The grenade was to make him go away—just evaporate—and I leaned back and felt my mind go empty and then felt it fill up again. I had already thrown the grenade before telling myself to throw it. The brush was thick and I had to <u>lob</u> it high, not aiming, and I remember the grenade seeming to freeze above me for an instant, as if a camera had clicked, and I remember ducking down and holding my breath and seeing little wisps of fog rise from the earth. The grenade bounced once and rolled across the trail. I did not hear it, but there must've been a sound, because the young man dropped his weapon and began to run, just two or three quick steps, then he hesitated, swiveling to his right, and he glanced down at the grenade and tried to cover his head but never did. It occurred to me then that he was about to die. I wanted to warn him. The grenade made a popping noise—not soft but not loud either—not what I'd expected—and there was a puff of dust and smoke—a small white puff—and the young man seemed to jerk upward as if pulled by invisible wires. He fell on his back. His rubber sandals had been blown off. There was no wind. He lay at the center of the trail, his right leg bent beneath him, his one eye shut, his other eye a huge star-shaped hole.

gradually, in tiny slivers, dawn began to break through the fog, and from my position in the brush I could see ten or fifteen meters up the trail. The mosquitoes were fierce. I remember slapping at them, wondering if I should wake up Kiowa and ask for some repellent, then thinking it was a bad idea, then looking up and seeing the young man come out of the fog. He wore black clothing and rubber sandals and a gray ammunition belt. His shoulders were slightly stooped, his head cocked to the side as if listening for something. He seemed at ease. He carried his weapon in one hand, muzzle down, moving without any hurry up the center of the trail. There was no sound at all—none that I can remember. In a way, it seemed, he was part of the morning fog, or my own imagination, but there was also the reality

lob (lŏb) *v.,* throw, hit, or propel easily or in a high arc

This statue, *The Three Soldiers,* was created in 1984 by sculptor Frederick Hart. It was placed only a few yards from the Vietnam Veteran's Memorial on the National Mall in Washington, DC, with the figures looking toward the memorial.

It was not a matter of live or die. There was no real peril. Almost certainly the young man would have passed by. And it will always be that way.

Later, I remember, Kiowa tried to tell me that the man would've died anyway. He told me that it was a good kill, that I was a soldier and this was a war, that I should shape up and stop staring and ask myself what the dead man would've done if things were reversed.

None of it mattered. The words seemed far too complicated. All I could do was gape at the fact of the young man's body.

Even now I haven't finished sorting it out. Sometimes I forgive myself, other times I don't.

In the ordinary hours of life I try not to dwell on it, but now and then, when I'm reading a newspaper or just sitting alone in a room, I'll look up and see the young man coming out of the morning fog. I'll watch him walk toward me, his shoulders slightly stooped, his head cocked to the side, and he'll pass within a few yards of me and suddenly smile at some secret thought and then continue up the trail to where it bends back into the fog. ❖

> **per • il** (pār´ ̍l) *n.,* exposure to risk of being injured, destroyed, or lost

MIRRORS & WINDOWS

In reflecting on what he did in the war, the narrator says, "Sometimes I forgive myself, other times I don't." Why might someone like a soldier, who acts on orders, feel guilty about what he or she has done?

Refer to Text ▶ ▶ ▶ ▶ ▶ Reason with Text

1a. How does the narrator respond when Kathleen says he must have killed someone in the war?

1b. Interpret why the narrator pretends, as he tells the story, that Kathleen is an adult.

Understand
Find meaning

2a. How does the narrator respond when Kiowa shakes him? What does the narrator emphasize about the weather?

2b. Suggest why the narrator provides these descriptions.

Apply
Use information

3a. How does the narrator describe the young man?

3b. How does the narrator's perception of the young man differ from his actual response to this soldier?

Analyze
Take things apart

4a. Indicate how Kiowa reacts to the incident.

4b. Do you agree with Kiowa's explanation of the incident? How would you respond to the narrator if you met or wrote to him?

Evaluate
Make judgments

5a. What does the narrator want to do as he watches the young man apparently reacting to a noise?

5b. List the details in the story that present an antiwar message.

Create
Bring ideas together

Analyze Literature

Realism and Climax

What elements of realism did you identify in reading "Ambush"? How would the story be different if the narrator had used a more formal, less conversational style and fewer naturalistic details? How is O'Brien's use of realism appropriate to his purpose in telling the story?

What is the climax of this story? What events lead up to this decisive moment, and what events follow it? In what ways is this a turning point?

Extend the Text

Writing Options

Creative Writing You are a war correspondent who observed the incident at My Khe. Write a brief newspaper article describing the event, organizing it according to the five Ws of reporting: *who, what, when, where,* and *why.* Fill in the details needed to make your report complete.

Persuasive Writing Should the draft be mandatory, requiring young men and women to serve in the military? Write a persuasive paragraph in response to this question.

Collaborative Learning

Conduct an Interview Working with a partner or a small group, interview a Vietnam veteran and write a summary of his or her experiences. If you are unable to locate a Vietnam veteran, contact a local chapter of the Veterans of Foreign Wars (VFW) or Vietnam Veterans of America. Quite often, these organizations will put you in touch with veterans who are willing to share their experiences.

Media Literacy

Review a Movie Several emotionally powerful films have been made about the Vietnam War. *Apocalypse Now* (1979) reveals the horrors of combat; *Forrest Gump* (1994) comments on the unpopularity of the war; and *Born on the Fourth of July* (1989) depicts the aftermath of the war. Watch a film that interests you, and write a one-page review that critiques the key subjects, events, or themes of the film. Recommend whether others should or should not view the film.

 Go to **www.mirrorsandwindows.com** for more.

1. Why does the narrator's daughter assume that he must have killed somebody?
   A. He is haunted by nightmares of the young man he killed.
   B. She has read stories about his platoon's military action.
   C. She found a picture of the young Vietnamese man that he killed.
   D. He keeps writing war stories that involve killing.
   E. She assumes that everyone in a war has killed someone.

2. Which of the following best explains why the narrator tells his story twice?
   A. The first version of the story contains inaccuracies.
   B. The first version of the story has been revised to make it less frightening to the nine-year-old daughter.
   C. The first version is short and factual, but it does not really explain the situation.
   D. The first version is how the narrator wishes the story had happened.
   E. The first version is the official military report.

3. How did the appearance of the young Vietnamese man strike the narrator?
   A. He seemed unreal or dreamlike.
   B. He seemed menacing.
   C. He seemed at ease.
   D. Both A and B
   E. Both A and C

4. The narrator says he had to lob the grenade. What does the word *lob* mean?
   A. to ready it by removing the pin
   B. to aim it with precision
   C. to throw it in a high arc
   D. to set it out in front of him in preparation
   E. to roll it through the dense brush

5. Which of the following is *not* true regarding the narrator's experience with the grenade?
   A. He aimed it at the young man's feet.
   B. He had thrown it before he told himself to throw it.
   C. He viewed it as a device to make the young man go away, not die.
   D. It made an unexpected popping sound.
   E. Time seemed to slow down in the moments after he threw it.

6. Which of the following lines from the story does *not* lend to the general atmosphere around the time of the killing?
   A. "The night was foggy and hot."
   B. "For the first few moments I felt lost."
   C. "The mosquitoes were fierce."
   D. "There was no sound at all—none that I can remember."
   E. "In a way, it seemed, he was part of the morning fog, or my own imagination."

7. The narrator and Kiowa react very differently to the killing. How does this show what different types of soldiers they are?
   A. Kiowa is proud of the narrator for the killing, but the narrator is ashamed.
   B. Kiowa sees the killing as a victory for their side, but the narrator takes it more seriously.
   C. Kiowa thinks the killing is insignificant in terms of the larger picture of the war, but the narrator feels it is significant to him.
   D. Kiowa thinks the man would have died anyway and the narrator was just doing his duty, but the narrator feels there were other options.
   E. Kiowa is upset that he was not part of the action, but the narrator is upset that the action happened at all.

8. Which word best describes how the narrator feels about the killing?
   A. haunted
   B. objective
   C. justified
   D. unconcerned
   E. proud

9. **Constructed Response:** Stories that emphasize the interior, subjective experiences of the characters are called *psychological fiction*. Explain how "Ambush" is an example of psychological fiction. What aspects of the story deal with mental disturbance or anguish? Support your response using details from the story.

10. **Constructed Response:** Describe the mood of "Ambush" and its effect on the reader. Also analyze how O'Brien creates mood using sensory details and descriptive language.

Understand the Concept

Sensory details are words and phrases that describe how things look, sound, smell, taste, and feel. Writers use sensory details to bring descriptions to life and help readers experience what they are describing. Good descriptive writing relies on sensory details to make it vivid and real.

For example, in "Ambush," Tim O'Brien uses sensory details to describe the eerie setting and create a sense of confusion and fear. He describes the night as being "foggy and hot" and how "very gradually, in tiny slivers, dawn began to break through the fog." In addition to these visual details, O'Brien provides details about sounds:

EXAMPLES

"The grenade made a popping noise—not soft but not loud either."

"There was no sound at all—none that I can remember."

O'Brien even describes the taste in the speaker's mouth as he prepares to throw the grenade, helping readers experience the man's anxiety and fear:

EXAMPLE

"I tried to swallow whatever was rising from my stomach, which tasted like lemonade, something fruity and sour."

Try to incorporate sensory details into your own writing to make it more clear, interesting, and believable. Choose details that are appropriate to your subject, purpose, and audience. For instance, in "Ambush," O'Brien describes the enemy by giving only basic visual details about his appearance and manner:

EXAMPLE

"He wore black clothing and rubber sandals and a gray ammunition belt. His shoulders were slightly stooped, his head cocked to the side as if listening for something. He seemed at ease. He carried his weapon in one hand, muzzle down, moving without any hurry up the center of the trail."

This description helps readers see the enemy as the speaker saw him: a stranger emerging from the fog. To give more details about, say, the enemy's facial features would make him seem more of an individual and less like a stranger and enemy.

Apply the Skill

Identify Sensory Details

On your own paper, draw a simple chart with columns that label the different senses: sight, sound, smell, taste, and touch. In each column, record the sensory details you identify in the following passage from "Ambush."

> The brush was thick and I had to lob [the grenade] high, not aiming, and I remember the grenade seeming to freeze above me for an instant, as if a camera had clicked, and I remember ducking down and holding my breath and seeing little wisps of fog rise from the earth. The grenade bounced once and rolled across the trail. I did not hear it, but there must've been a sound.

Create Sensory Details

For each of the following general settings and persons, provide three vivid sensory details. At least one of the three sensory details should describe a sound, smell, taste, or touch (that is, a detail other than sight).

1. Playground
2. Newborn baby
3. Urban street
4. Fast-food restaurant
5. Professional athlete (specify a sport)
6. Holiday parade

Camouflaging the Chimera
Monsoon Season

Lyric Poems by Yusef Komunyakaa

Build Background

Literary Context The setting of these poems by
Yusef Komunyakaa is the Vietnam War. In **"Camou-**
flaging the Chimera," the speaker is an American
soldier describing efforts to blend in with the landscape as he and his comrades prepare for a nighttime
ambush of the enemy, the Viet Cong. The speaker refers
to the Mekong River, a waterway that runs through
Vietnam, and to the animals and plants indigenous
(native) to Vietnam. The word *chimera* (kī mir´ ə) in
the poem's title is used in the traditional sense to refer to the fire-breathing
monster of Greek mythology. In modern usage, the word refers to a misleading
image or illusion.

The speaker in **"Monsoon Season"** also is a soldier. He is describing the
effects of the monsoon season, which lasts up to six months and brings 60
to 100 inches of rain to Vietnam. The rain disturbs the natural surroundings,
swelling the Mekong River and producing treacherous muddy conditions,
mosquito-ridden air, and medical ailments ranging from malaria to foot fungus.

Reader's Context Imagine being a soldier in Vietnam. How would the
climate and terrain compound the difficulties of being in a war?

Meet the Author

Yusef Komunyakaa (b. 1947) was born in Bogalusa, Louisiana, and longed to escape the segregated South. Unable
to check out books from the whites-only library, he read the
Bible—twice. After graduating from high school in 1965, he
enlisted in the army. His service as a Vietnam War correspondent for the military newspaper the *Southern Cross* earned
him a bronze star for valor. After the war, Komunyakaa earned a bachelor's
degree from the University of Colorado and two master's degrees: one from
Colorado State University and one from the University of California, Irvine.

Komunyakaa has published several poetry collections that reflect the
influence of contemporary African-American writers such as James Baldwin,
Gwendolyn Brooks, and Langston Hughes. His first publication to gain wide
acceptance was *Copacetic* (1984), a collection of poems noted for their jazz
rhythms and striking imagery. One of his most admired collections is *Dien Cai
Dau* (1988); the title, pronounced "dinky dow," means "crazy" in Vietnamese.
Neon Vernacular: New and Selected Poems (1993) won a Pulitzer Prize. More
recent collections include *Pleasure Dome* (2002). Komunyakaa has taught
creative writing at many universities and currently is a professor at New York
University.

Analyze Literature

Imagery and Simile
Imagery is the figurative or
descriptive language used to
create word pictures, or images.

A **simile** is a comparison of two
seemingly unlike things using
the word *like* or *as*.

Set Purpose

Komunyakaa is well known
for his creation of strong, vivid
images. His use of imagery to
portray the difficult conditions
soldiers faced in the Vietnam
War helps readers understand
their experience. As you read
"Camouflaging the Chimera"
and "Monsoon Season," record
specific images and what they
seem to mean. Also note Komunyakaa's use of similes, another
type of figurative language.
What comparison or com-
parisons does he make in
each poem?

Preview Vocabulary

refuge, 1048
foliage, 1049

Camouflaging the Chimera

by Yusef Komunyakaa

We tied branches to our helmets.
We painted our faces & rifles
with mud from a riverbank,

blades of grass hung from the pockets
5   of our tiger suits.[1] We wove
ourselves into the terrain,
content to be a hummingbird's target.

---

1. **tiger suits.** Camouflage uniforms with black and green stripes

We hugged bamboo & leaned
against a breeze off the river,
10 slow-dragging with ghosts

from Saigon to Bangkok,
with women left in doorways
reaching in from America.
We aimed at dark-hearted songbirds.

15 In our way station of shadows
rock apes[2] tried to blow our cover,
throwing stones at the sunset.
                    Chameleons

crawled our spines, changing from day
20 to night: green to gold,
gold to black. But we waited
till the moon touched metal,

till something almost broke
inside us. VC[3] struggled
25 with the hillside, like black silk[4]

wrestling iron through grass.
We weren't there. The river ran
through our bones. Small animals took refuge
against our bodies; we held our breath,

30 ready to spring the L-shaped
ambush, as a world revolved
under each man's eyelid. ❖

---

2. **rock apes.** Monkeys known to throw rocks at humans, often
   scaring soldiers into thinking the enemy was near
3. **VC.** Viet Cong, the enemy forces
4. **black silk.** Nighttime camouflage uniforms worn by the
   Viet Cong

ref • uge (re´ fyüj) *n.*, shelter; protection

MIRRORS & WINDOWS

If you were the soldier in the poem, what would you find most difficult about
what you were experiencing?

MONSOON SEASON

by Yusef Komunyakaa

A river shines in the jungle's
wet leaves. The rain's finally
let up but whenever wind shakes
the <u>foliage</u> it starts to fall.
5   The monsoon uncovers troubled
seasons we tried to forget.

fo • liage (fō´ lē ij) *n.*, collection of leaves, flowers,
and plants

Dead men slip through bad weather,
stamping their muddy boots to wake us,
their curses coming easier.
10 There's a bend in everything,
in elephant grass & flame trees,[1]
raindrops pelting the sand-bagged
bunker like a muted gong.
White phosphorus[2] washed from the air,
15 wind sways with violet myrtle,
beating it naked. Soaked to the bone,
jungle rot brings us down to earth.
We sit in our hooches[3]
with too much time,
20 where grounded choppers
can't fly out the wounded.
Somewhere nearby a frog
begs a snake.
I try counting droplets,
25 stars that aren't in the sky.
My poncho feels like a body bag.
I lose count. Red leaves
whirl by, the monsoon
unburying the dead. ❖

---

1. **elephant grass & flame trees.** Elephant grass, which
   is tall and broad, often is grown for animal feed. Flame
   trees have scarlet or yellow blossoms.
2. **white phosphorus.** Poisonous, flammable substance
   used in weapons in Vietnam
3. **hooches.** Slang for soldiers' primitive dwellings on base
   camp

MIRRORS & WINDOWS

The speaker says the soldiers have "too much time." What does this suggest about
the day-to-day life of a soldier? What does it suggest about war?

Refer to Text ▶ ▶ ▶ ▶ ▶ **Reason with Text**

1a. In stanzas 1–4 of "Camouflaging the Chimera," what are the soldiers doing to themselves and why? Whom do they imagine their enemy to be?

1b. Why do the soldiers imagine these attackers? Who will the actual attackers be?

Understand
Find meaning

2a. What does the speaker in "Monsoon Season" say the dead men do?

2b. Suggest what the description of the dead men indicates about the soldiers.

Apply
Use information

3a. In lines 14–16 of "Monsoon Season," what environmental damage do the rain and wind cause?

3b. Compare the weather's effect on the soldiers to its impact on the environment. How does the soldiers' awareness of what is happening to the jungle affect them?

Analyze
Take things apart

4a. In "Camouflaging the Chimera," when do the soldiers expect the VC to arrive? How do you know?

4b. Interpret what the speaker means when he says the soldiers "weren't there." What does he mean by "The river ran through our bones"?

Evaluate
Make judgments

5a. Identify references to nature in both poems. How does each speaker interact with his environment?

5b. What might the natural imagery in these poems say about the Vietnam War and the effects of war on nature in general?

Create
Bring ideas together

Analyze Literature

Imagery and Simile
What specific images did you find in each poem? What do they mean? Which images do you find especially moving or unusual? How does the use of imagery help create the tone of each poem?

Locate the similes in the two poems. What items are being compared and for what purpose or effect? How does the use of similes help create the tone of each poem?

Extend the Text

Writing Options
Creative Writing Imagine that you are a soldier in one of Komunyakaa's poems. Write a diary entry of your experiences during the events described in the poem.

Expository Writing Both Tim O'Brien and Yusef Komunyakaa are Vietnam veterans. How are O'Brien's story "Ambush" and Komunyakaa's poems alike and how are they different? Write a comparison-and-contrast essay in which you discuss the story and the poems.

Collaborative Learning
Communicate with a Vietnamese School With a group, write or e-mail the Vietnamese consulate in a nearby city or state to ask if it is possible to write

(in English) to students in a Vietnam school to learn more about their culture. If it is not possible, ask the consulate for materials about life in present-day Vietnam. Use them to create a classroom display of pictures and information.

Critical Literacy
Prepare an Explication of One of the Poems An *explication* is a detailed analysis of a literary work, in which you examine features such as diction, sentence structure, imagery, subject matter, emotional impact, musical quality, and point of view. Choose one of Komunyakaa's poems and prepare an explication, focusing on the literary device(s) you consider most appropriate.

 Go to **www.mirrorsandwindows.com** for more.

1. Which of the following is *not* one of the ways the soldiers in "Camouflaging the Chimera" tried to blend in with their surroundings?
   A. They put mud on their faces and guns.
   B. They attached tree branches to their helmets.
   C. They communicated with each other using bird calls.
   D. They hung grass from their pockets.
   E. They wore uniforms that blended into the jungle.

2. Which of the following lines from "Camouflaging the Chimera" best conveys the sense of waiting in the poem?
   A. "In our way station of shadows"
   B. "Chameleons crawled our spines, changing from day to night"
   C. "content to be a hummingbird's target"
   D. "the river, slow-dragging with ghosts"
   E. "like black silk wrestling iron through grass"

3. In "Camouflaging the Chimera," the speaker mentions small animals taking refuge. What does the word *refuge* mean?
   A. nourishment
   B. shelter
   C. risks
   D. rest
   E. heed of a warning

4. Which of the following is *not* a problem caused by the monsoon in "Monsoon Season"?
   A. The helicopters cannot fly the wounded soldiers out of the area.
   B. Many of the soldiers have jungle rot, a foot fungus.
   C. The soldiers are bored because they cannot move from their location.
   D. The sound of rain on their helmets gives away their location to the enemy.
   E. The rain uncovers and washes up dead bodies.

5. In what way is the monsoon "unburying the dead"?
   A. The break in fighting gives the soldiers time to think about their fallen comrades.
   B. The rain and wind uncover the soldiers who have been buried.
   C. The dampness causes the soldiers to hallucinate about the dead walking about.
   D. Both A and B
   E. Both B and C

6. Find the two similes in "Monsoon Season." What do they contribute to the poem?
   A. Both contribute to the violent imagery.
   B. Both contribute to the nature imagery.
   C. Both contribute to describing the soldiers' daily tasks.
   D. Both contribute to softening the tone.
   E. Both contribute to describing the environment and conditions of war.

7. Which somewhat surprising aspect of war do both poems illustrate?
   A. Weather and other elements of nature can work both for and against a military action.
   B. U.S. troops were not prepared to fight in a jungle setting.
   C. Periods of waiting and inaction are typical of warfare.
   D. Soldiers who are stationed overseas often imagine they are somewhere else.
   E. Soldiers may feel hopeless when they have time to think about the death and destruction around them.

8. **Constructed Response:** At the end of "Camouflaging the Chimera," the speaker states that "a world revolved under each man's eyelid." Explain the meaning of this line. Support your answer using evidence from the poem and what you know about Yusef Komunyakaa.

9. **Constructed Response:** Analyze Komunyakaa's use of natural imagery in "Camouflaging the Chimera" and "Monsoon Season." How does each speaker view nature? In what ways are their views similar and different? Support your analysis with examples from the poems.

TEST-TAKING TIP

Don't be alarmed if a test contains an essay or passage on a topic you know little or nothing about. Test writers intentionally include material that likely will be foreign to everyone taking the test. Doing so helps ensure test takers will start on an equal level of knowledge. Even though the topic may be unfamiliar, the text will contain all the information you need to know to answer the questions.

GAME

by Donald Barthelme

Donald Barthelme (1931–1989) was born in Philadelphia, Pennsylvania, and grew up in Houston, Texas. After being drafted into the military in 1953, he arrived in Korea on the day the fighting stopped.

Barthelme's literary career began in 1964 with publication of his first short story collection, *Come Back, Dr. Caligari.* In his career, Barthelme produced almost a dozen short story collections, four novels, and other works and was well known for his deviations from literary convention.

"Game" is an example of *Absurdist,* or *Surrealist,* literature, in which events may happen for no apparent reasons, characters may behave in unexpected or unexplainable ways, and the ordinary rules of living often seem not to apply. As you read the story, ask yourself who or what is more absurd: the characters and setting Barthelme has created or the arms race (or other unspecified project) that has placed the two men in a bare underground room.

IN THE BEGINNING
I took care to behave normally. So did Shotwell. Our behavior was painfully normal.

Shotwell keeps the jacks and the rubber ball in his attaché case and will not allow me to play with them. He plays with them, alone, sitting on the floor near the console[1] hour after hour, chanting "onesies, twosies, threesies, foursies" in a precise, well-modulated voice, not so loud as to be annoying, not so soft as to allow me to forget. I point out to Shotwell that two can derive more enjoyment from playing jacks than one, but he is not interested. I have asked repeatedly to be allowed to play by myself, but he simply shakes his head. "Why?" I ask. "They're mine," he says. And when he has finished, when he has sated[2] himself, back they go into the attaché case.

It is unfair but there is nothing I can do about it. I am aching to get my hands on them.

Shotwell and I watch the console. Shotwell and I live under the ground and watch the console. If certain events take place upon the console, we are to insert our keys in the appropriate locks and turn our keys. Shotwell has a key and I have a key. If we turn our keys simultaneously the bird flies, certain switches are activated and the bird flies. But the bird never flies. In one hundred thirty-three days the bird has not flown. Meanwhile Shotwell and I watch each other. We each wear a

---

1. **console.** Desk- or cabinet-like control panel
2. **sated.** Satisfied

.45 and if Shotwell behaves strangely I am supposed to shoot him. If I behave strangely Shotwell is supposed to shoot me. We watch the console and think about shooting each other and think about the bird. Shotwell's behavior with the jacks is strange. Is it strange? I do not know. Perhaps he is merely selfish . . . perhaps his character is flawed, perhaps his childhood was twisted. I do not know.

> ## PERHAPS HE IS MERELY SELFISH . . .
> perhaps his character is flawed, perhaps his childhood was twisted. I do not know.

Each of us wears a .45 and each of us is supposed to shoot the other if the other is behaving strangely. How strangely is strangely? I do not know. In addition to the .45 I have a .38 which Shotwell does not know about concealed in my attaché case, and Shotwell has a .25 caliber Beretta which I do not know about strapped to his right calf. Sometimes instead of watching the console I pointedly watch Shotwell's .45, but this is simply a ruse,[3] simply a maneuver, in reality I am watching his hand when it dangles in the vicinity of his right calf. If he decides I am behaving strangely he will shoot me not with the .45 but with the Beretta. Similarly, Shotwell pretends to watch my .45 but he is really watching my hand resting idly atop my attaché case, my hand resting idly atop my attaché case, my hand. My hand resting idly atop my attaché case.

In the beginning I took care to behave normally. So did Shotwell. Our behavior was painfully normal. Norms of politeness, consideration, speech, and personal habits were scrupulously observed. But then it became apparent that an error had been made, that our relief was not going to arrive. Owing to an oversight. Owing to an oversight we have been here

---

3. **ruse.** Deception or trick

for one hundred thirty-three days. When it became clear that an error had been made, that we were not to be relieved, the norms were relaxed. Definitions of normality were redrawn in the agreement of January 1, called by us, The Agreement. Uniform regulations were relaxed, and mealtimes are no longer rigorously scheduled. We eat when we are hungry and sleep when we are tired. Considerations of rank and precedence[4] were temporarily put aside, a handsome concession on the part of Shotwell, who is a captain, whereas I am only a first lieutenant. One of us watches the console at all times rather than two of us watching the console at all times, except when we are both on our feet. One of us watches the console at all times and if the bird flies then that one wakes the other and we turn our keys in the locks simultaneously and the bird flies. Our system involves a delay of perhaps twelve seconds but I do not care because I am not well, and Shotwell does not care because he is not himself. After the agreement was signed Shotwell produced the jacks and the rubber ball from his attaché case, and I began to write a series of descriptions of forms occurring in nature, such as a shell, a leaf, a stone, an animal. On the walls.

Shotwell plays jacks and I write descriptions of natural forms on the walls.

Shotwell is enrolled in a USAFI[5] course which leads to a master's degree in business administration from the University of Wisconsin (although we are not in Wisconsin, we are in Utah, Montana or Idaho). When we went down it was in either Utah, Montana or Idaho, I don't remember. We have been here for one hundred thirty-three days owing to an oversight. The pale green reinforced concrete walls sweat and the air conditioning zips on and off erratically and Shotwell reads *Introduction to Marketing* by Lassiter and Munk, making notes with a blue ballpoint pen. Shotwell is not himself but I do not know it, he presents a calm aspect and reads *Introduction to Marketing* and

makes his exemplary[6] notes with a blue ballpoint pen, meanwhile controlling the .38 in my attaché case with one-third of his attention. I am not well.

WE HAVE BEEN HERE
for one hundred thirty-three days owing to an oversight.

We have been here one hundred thirty-three days owing to an oversight. Although now we are not sure what is oversight, what is plan. Perhaps the plan is for us to stay here permanently, or if not permanently at least for a year, for three hundred sixty-five days. Or if not for a year for some number of days known to them and not known to us, such as two hundred days. Or perhaps they are observing our behavior in some way, sensors[7] of some kind, perhaps our behavior determines the number of days. It may be that they are pleased with us, with our behavior, not in every detail but in sum. Perhaps the whole thing is very successful, perhaps the whole thing is an experiment and the experiment is very successful. I do not know. But I suspect that the only way they can persuade sun-loving creatures into their pale green sweating reinforced concrete rooms under the ground is to say that the system is twelve hours on, twelve hours off. And then lock us below for some number of days known to them and not known to us. We eat well although the frozen enchiladas are damp when defrosted and the frozen devil's food cake is sour and untasty. We sleep uneasily and acrimoniously.[8] I hear Shotwell shouting in his sleep, objecting, denouncing, cursing sometimes, weeping sometimes, in his sleep. When Shotwell sleeps I try to pick the lock on

---

4. **precedence.** Order of importance
5. **USAFI.** United States Armed Forces Information, an agency that oversees instruction for members of the military
6. **exemplary.** Providing a model
7. **sensors.** Detection devices
8. **acrimoniously.** With bitterness

read what I have written? I do not know. I am aware that Shotwell regards my writing-behavior as a little strange. Yet it is no stranger than his jacks-behavior, or the day he appeared in black bathing trunks with the .25 caliber Beretta strapped to his right calf and stood over the console, trying to span with his two arms outstretched the distance between the locks. He could not do it, I had already tried, standing over the console with my two arms outstretched, the distance is too great. I was moved to comment but did not comment, comment would have provoked counter-comment, comment would have led God knows where. They had in their infinite patience, in their infinite foresight, in their infinite wisdom already imagined a man standing over the console with his two arms outstretched, trying to span with his two arms outstretched the distance between the locks.

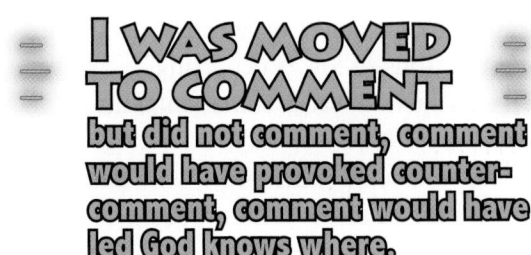

I WAS MOVED TO COMMENT but did not comment, comment would have provoked counter-comment, comment would have led God knows where.

his attaché case, so as to get at the jacks. Thus far I have been unsuccessful. Nor has Shotwell been successful in picking the locks on my attaché case so as to get at the .38. I have seen the marks on the shiny surface. I laughed, in the latrine, pale green walls sweating and the air conditioning whispering, in the latrine.

I write descriptions of natural forms on the walls, scratching them on the tile surface with a diamond. The diamond is a two and one-half carat solitaire I had in my attaché case when we went down. It was for Lucy. The south wall of the room containing the console is already covered. I have described a shell, a leaf, a stone, animals, a baseball bat. I am aware that the baseball bat is not a natural form. Yet I described it. "The baseball bat," I said, "is typically made of wood. It is typically one meter in length or a little longer, fat at one end, tapering to afford a comfortable grip at the other. The end with the handhold typically offers a slight rim, or lip, at the nether[9] extremity, to prevent slippage." My description of the baseball bat ran to 4500 words, all scratched with a diamond on the south wall. Does Shotwell

Shotwell is not himself. He has made certain overtures.[10] The burden of his message is not clear. It has something to do with the keys, with the locks. Shotwell is a strange person. He appears to be less affected by our situation than I. He goes about his business stolidly, watching the console, studying *Introduction to Marketing,* bouncing his rubber ball on the floor in a steady, rhythmical, conscientious manner. He appears to be less affected by our situation than I am. He is stolid. He says nothing. But he has

---

9. **nether.** Lower; bottom
10. **overtures.** Offers; advances

made certain overtures, certain overtures have been made. I am not sure that I understand them. They have something to do with the keys, with the locks. Shotwell has something in mind. Stolidly he shucks the shiny silver paper from the frozen enchiladas, stolidly he stuffs them into the electric oven. But he has something in mind. But there must be a quid pro quo.[11] I insist on a quid pro quo. I have something in mind.

I am not well. I do not know our target. They do not tell us for which city the bird is targeted. I do not know. That is planning. That is not my responsibility. My responsibility is to watch the console and when certain events take place upon the console, turn my key in the lock. Shotwell bounces the rubber ball on the floor in a steady, stolid, rhythmical manner. I am aching to get my hands on the ball, on the jacks. We have been here one hundred thirty-three days owing to an oversight. I write on the walls. Shotwell chants "onesies, twosies, threesies, foursies" in a precise, well-modulated voice. Now he cups the jacks and the rubber ball in his hands and rattles them suggestively. I do not know for which city the bird is targeted. Shotwell is not himself.

Sometimes I cannot sleep. Sometimes Shotwell cannot sleep. Sometimes when Shotwell cradles me in his arms and rocks me to sleep, singing Brahms' "Guten Abend, gute Nacht,"[12] or I cradle Shotwell in my arms and rock him to sleep, singing, I understand what it is Shotwell wishes me to do. At such moments we are very close. But only if he will give me the jacks. That is fair. There is something he wants me to do with my key, while he does something with his key. But only if he will give me my turn. That is fair. I am not well. ❖

---

11. **quid pro quo.** [Latin] "Something for something"; indicates an even exchange
12. **"Guten Abend, gute Nacht."** [German] "Good evening, good night"; from a work, often called a lullaby, by composer Johannes Brahms (1833–1897)

MIRRORS & **W**INDOWS

Shotwell and the narrator have been locked in the underground room for almost five months, "owing to an oversight." How do people behave when they feel trapped? Can they be considered rational?

Refer and Reason

1. What does the narrator say about the guns he and Shotwell have? What does this suggest about the men's behavior?

2. How do the narrator and Shotwell pass the time? Infer what these pastimes indicate about the two men's responses to being locked in the underground room.

3. How is the game a *metaphor* (a figure of speech in which one thing is spoken or written about as if it were another) of the men's difficulty? How is the game a metaphor of the nuclear arms race?

Writing Options

1. Write a sequel, or follow-up story, to Barthelme's "Game." Use your knowledge and imagination to continue the story, and add events and characters as appropriate. Share your work with a partner or a group.

2. Write a one-page character analysis of the narrator. Base your analysis on details from the story and what you can infer about his life before going underground.

Understand the Concept

A **comma** is a punctuation mark used to separate words and groups of words. Commas clarify meaning by showing the relationships among parts of a sentence.

For instance, one of the most common uses of commas is to separate items in a series. A *series* may comprise words, phrases, or clauses, as shown by these examples from Barthelme's short story "Game":

EXAMPLES

Words in a series Norms of *politeness, consideration, speech, and personal habits* were scrupulously observed.

Phrases in a series Now we are not sure *what is oversight, what is plan.*

Clauses in a series But then it became apparent *that an error had been made, that our relief was not going to arrive.*

A comma also is used to separate independent clauses (that is, complete sentences) in a compound sentence. The comma is added before the coordinating conjunction (*and, but, or, nor, yet, so,* or *for*) that joins the clauses.

EXAMPLE

I point out to Shotwell that two can derive more enjoyment from playing jacks than one, *but* he is not interested.

Finally, commas generally are used to set off introductory words, phrases, and clauses at the beginnings of sentences and subordinate words and phrases within sentences.

EXAMPLES

Introductory clause set off *If certain events take place upon the console,* we are to insert our keys in the appropriate locks and turn our keys.

Subordinate phrase set off It may be that they are pleased with us, *with our behavior,* not in every detail but in sum.

Apply the Skill

Identify Uses of Commas

In each of these sentences from "Game," identify how the comma is used in the sentence: to separate items in a series, to combine sentences, or to set off elements.

1. Sometimes instead of watching the console I pointedly watch Shotwell's .45, but this is simply a ruse.
2. I began to write a series of descriptions of forms occurring in nature, such as a shell, a leaf, a stone, an animal.
3. Considerations of rank and precedence were temporarily put aside, a handsome concession on the part of Shotwell, who is a captain, whereas I am only a first lieutenant.
4. The end with the handhold typically offers a slight rim, or lip, at the nether extremity, to prevent slippage.
5. Shotwell bounces the rubber ball on the floor in a steady, stolid, rhythmical manner.

Fix Errors in Comma Use

Copy the following sentences on a sheet of paper, adding or removing commas as needed for correct punctuation.

1. Author Donald Barthelme, was drafted into the military in 1953 early in the Cold War.
2. During his career Barthelme wrote four novels twelve collections of short stories and several other works.
3. His first short story collection, *Come Back, Dr. Caligari* was published in 1964.
4. The short story, "Game," is considered an example of Surrealist literature.
5. In Surrealist literature events have a dreamlike quality and characters behave in unusual ways.
6. The absurdity of the nuclear arms race, is captured in the characters, and setting, of Barthelme's short story.

Use Commas in Your Writing

Write a paragraph about a time you were bored. Why were you bored? What did you do to occupy yourself and pass the time? Provide enough details for the reader to understand the situation, and explain anything he or she might not understand. When you are finished, exchange paragraphs with a classmate and check each other's use of commas.

PART 2

Personal Challenges

On July 20, 1969, astronaut Neil Armstrong, commander of the *Apollo 11* mission, became the first human to walk on the moon. Americans celebrated Armstrong's self-described "giant leap for mankind" and enjoyed taking the lead in the world's space race. However, serious challenges faced Americans at home.

Social unrest over failings in civil rights began brewing in the early 1960s. Martin Luther King Jr. emerged as the leader of the Civil Rights movement in 1963 with his famous "I Have a Dream" speech, delivered during the March on Washington. In his "Letter from Birmingham Jail," King described African Americans' historical struggle for equality. Writers such as James Baldwin and Gwendolyn Brooks also portrayed African Americans' ongoing frustration with poverty and discrimination.

Multicultural issues emerged in the mid-1960s, as well, when changes in U.S. immigration policy initiated a surge of immigration and an increasingly diverse population. Writers from across the cultural spectrum, including Chinese American Maxine Hong Kingston, described the difficulties of fitting into modern-day America while trying to maintain their cultural heritage. Similarly, Native American writers such as N. Scott Momaday and Simon Ortiz asserted their cultural identity and the importance of preserving ancestral values and traditions.

Personal challenges on a more individual level often were the focus of two celebrated American writers of the era. Poet Richard Wilbur and essayist/fiction writer John Updike both explored coming-of-age and generational issues.

400 Years of Our People, 1994. Michael Escoffery. Private collection.

Letter from Birmingham Jail
A Letter by Martin Luther King Jr.

Build Background

Historical Context On April 12, 1963, Martin Luther King Jr. was jailed for disobeying a court order forbidding a group of African Americans from marching to downtown Birmingham, Alabama. Four days later, eight clergymen from Alabama, including bishops, ministers, and a rabbi, published a statement in a newspaper criticizing King for defying the law. At first, King had only scraps of the newspaper to write on, but he nonetheless drafted a response to the clerics. (He later obtained writing paper.) The long letter would become a statement of principle for the Civil Rights movement.

In the excerpt from the letter printed here, King says he feels compelled to employ civil disobedience to protest unjust measures. In other portions of the letter, King explains that nonviolent tactics, such as marches and boycotts, are a means of bringing supporters of segregation to the negotiating table. In response to his critics' observation that change takes time, he notes that African Americans have waited centuries for equality.

Reader's Context When, if ever, are people justified in breaking the law? Use examples to explain your answer.

Meet the Author

Martin Luther King Jr. (1929–1968) was born in Atlanta, Georgia, the son and grandson of Baptist ministers. He enrolled in Morehouse College when he was only fifteen. Later, at a seminary in Pennsylvania where he was preparing for the ministry, King was influenced by the nonviolent teachings of American Transcendentalist Henry David Thoreau (1817–1862) and Indian leader Mohandas Gandhi (1869–1948). King completed his education by earning a doctorate degree from Boston University in 1955.

The Southern Christian Leadership Conference (SCLC), an organization founded by King, served as a platform from which to speak on civil rights issues throughout the United States. As a civil rights leader, minister, and orator, he led protests across the South, advocating nonviolent civil disobedience to combat racism and discrimination. In 1964, King was awarded the Nobel Peace Prize, the youngest ever recipient, and he donated the $54,000 cash award to support the Civil Rights movement.

In 1968, while in Memphis, Tennessee, to show support for striking sanitation workers, King was assassinated.

Analyze Literature

Argument and Allusion
An **argument** is a form of persuasion that makes a case to an audience for accepting or rejecting a proposition or course of action.

An **allusion** is a reference to a well-known person, event, object, or work from history or literature.

Set Purpose

Many of Martin Luther King Jr.'s speeches and writings became statements of principle for the Civil Rights movement. As you read this excerpt from "Letter from Birmingham Jail," identify the arguments King makes and consider whether each is based primarily on religion or politics. Also identify the allusions King makes to support his ideas. Record these historical and literary references in a list.

Preview Vocabulary

cognizant, 1062
provincial, 1062
deplore, 1063
gainsay, 1063
moratorium, 1063
paradoxical, 1063
anarchy, 1065
scintillating, 1065

Letter from Birmingham JAIL

by Martin Luther King Jr.

One who breaks an unjust law must do so openly, lovingly, and with a willingness to accept the penalty.

April 16, 1963

MY DEAR FELLOW CLERGYMEN:

While confined here in the Birmingham city jail, I came across your recent statement calling my present activities "unwise and untimely." Seldom do I pause to answer criticism of my work and ideas. If I sought to answer all the criticisms that cross my desk, my secretaries would have little time for anything other than such correspondence in the course of the day, and I would have no time for constructive work. But since I feel that you are men of genuine good will and that your criticisms are sincerely set forth, I want to try to answer your

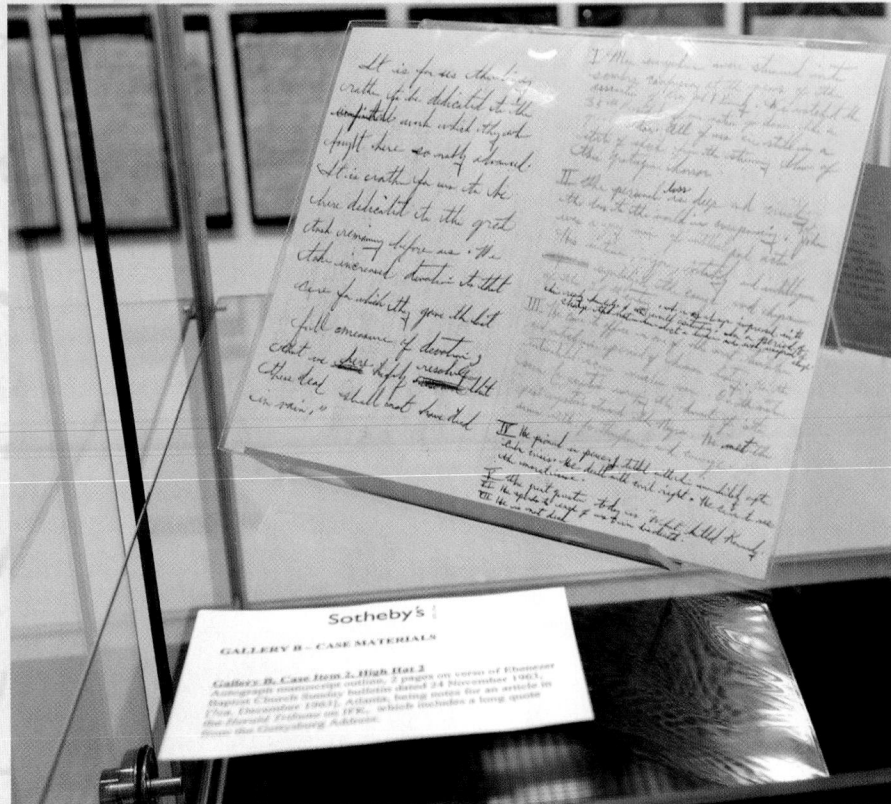
The handwritten text of King's letter.

But more basically, I am in Birmingham because injustice is here. Just as the prophets of the eighth century B.C. left their villages and carried their "thus saith the Lord" far beyond the boundaries of their home towns, and just as the Apostle Paul left his village of Tarsus and carried the gospel of Jesus Christ to the far corners of the Greco-Roman world, so am I compelled to carry the gospel of freedom beyond my own home town. Like Paul, I must constantly respond to the Macedonian call for aid.[1]

statements in what I hope will be patient and reasonable terms.

I think I should indicate why I am here in Birmingham, since you have been influenced by the view which argues against "outsiders coming in." I have the honor of serving as president of the Southern Christian Leadership Conference, an organization operating in every southern state, with headquarters in Atlanta, Georgia. We have some eighty-five affiliated organizations across the South, and one of them is the Alabama Christian Movement for Human Rights. Frequently we share staff, educational and financial resources with our affiliates. Several months ago the affiliate here in Birmingham asked us to be on call to engage in a nonviolent direct-action program if such were deemed necessary. We readily consented, and when the hour came we lived up to our promise. So I, along with several members of my staff, am here because I was invited here. I am here because I have organizational ties here.

Moreover, I am <u>cognizant</u> of the interrelatedness of all communities and states. I cannot sit idly by in Atlanta and not be concerned about what happens in Birmingham. Injustice anywhere is a threat to justice everywhere. We are caught in an inescapable network of mutuality, tied in a single garment of destiny. Whatever affects one directly, affects all indirectly. Never again can we afford to live with the narrow, <u>provincial</u> "outside agitator" idea. Anyone who lives inside the United States can never be considered an outsider anywhere within its bounds.

1. **Macedonian call for aid.** From the Bible, Acts 16: 9–10: "And a vision was showed to Paul in the night, which was a man of Macedonia standing and beseeching him and saying: Pass over into Macedonia and help us. And as soon as he had seen the vision, immediately we sought to go into Macedonia: being assured that God had called us to preach the gospel to them."

cog • ni • zant (kôg′ nə zənt) *adj.,* aware; knowledgeable
pro • vin • cial (prō vin′ chəl) *adj.,* having a simple or limited perspective

You <u>deplore</u> the demonstrations taking place in Birmingham. But your statement, I am sorry to say, fails to express a similar concern for the conditions that brought about the demonstrations. I am sure that none of you would want to rest content with the superficial kind of social analysis that deals merely with effects and does not grapple with underlying causes. It is unfortunate that demonstrations are taking place in Birmingham, but it is even more unfortunate that the city's white power structure left the Negro community with no alternative.

In any nonviolent campaign there are four basic steps: collection of the facts to determine whether injustices exist; negotiation; self-purification; and direct action. We have gone through all these steps in Birmingham. There can be no <u>gainsaying</u> the fact that racial injustice engulfs this community. Birmingham is probably the most thoroughly segregated city in the United States. Its ugly record of brutality is widely known. Negroes have experienced grossly unjust treatment in the courts. There have been more unsolved bombings of Negro homes and churches in Birmingham than in any other city in the nation. These are the hard, brutal facts of the case. On the basis of these conditions, Negro leaders sought to negotiate with the city fathers. But the latter consistently refused to engage in good-faith negotiation.

Then, last September, came the opportunity to talk with leaders of Birmingham's economic community. In the course of the negotiations, certain promises were made by the merchants—for example, to remove the store's humiliating racial signs. On the basis of these promises, the Reverend Fred Shuttlesworth and the leaders of the Alabama Christian Movement for Human Rights agreed to a <u>moratorium</u> on all demonstrations. As the weeks and months went by, we realized that we were the victims of a broken promise. A few signs, briefly removed, returned; the others remained.

As in so many past experiences, our hopes had been blasted, and the shadow of deep disappointment settled upon us. We had no alternative except to prepare for direct action, whereby we would present our very bodies as a means of laying our case before the conscience of the local and the national community. Mindful of the difficulties involved, we decided to undertake a process of self-purification. We began a series of workshops on nonviolence, and we repeatedly asked ourselves: "Are you able to accept blows without retaliating?" "Are you able to endure the ordeal of jail?" . . .

You express a great deal of anxiety over our willingness to break laws. This is certainly a legitimate concern. Since we so diligently urge people to obey the Supreme Court's decision of 1954 outlawing segregation in the public schools, at first glance it may seem rather <u>paradoxical</u> for us consciously to break laws. One may well ask: "How can you advocate breaking some laws and obeying others?" The answer lies in the fact that there are two types of laws: just and unjust. I would be the first to advocate obeying just laws. One has not only a legal but a moral responsibility to obey just laws. Conversely, one has a moral responsibility to disobey unjust laws. I would agree with St. Augustine that "an unjust law is no law at all."

One has a moral responsibility to disobey unjust laws.

Now, what is the difference between the two? How does one determine whether a law is just or unjust? A just law is a man-made code that squares with the moral law or the law of

---

de • plore (də plōr´) v., regret; consider unworthy
gain • say (gān´ sā) v., deny or declare untrue
mor • a • to • ri • um (mōr´ ə tōr´ ē um) n., authorized delay or suspension of activity
par • a • dox • i • cal (pār´ ə dôk´ sik´ l) adj., seemingly contradictory

KING

The King Assassination

On April 4, 1968, Dr. Martin Luther King Jr. was shot and killed while standing on the balcony of the Lorraine Motel in Memphis, Tennessee. He had gone to Memphis to support striking African-American sanitation workers. Immediately following his assassination, a wave of riots broke out in more than fifty cities across the United States.

Two months later, James Earl Ray, an escaped convict, was caught and charged with the killing; he confessed to the crime but recanted his confession three days later. Ray was tried and convicted, nonetheless, and sentenced to a ninety-nine-year prison term. He died in prison in 1998.

Some people, including members of King's family, do not believe Ray acted alone in the assassination. In 1999, a jury settled a wrongful death suit in favor of King's widow, Coretta Scott King.

The suit had been brought against Loyd Jowers, a Memphis restaurant owner, and "other unknown co-conspirators" who were alleged to have plotted to murder King. Upon delivering the verdict, the jury stated that "government agencies" also were involved in the assassination plot. In 2000, the U.S. Department of Justice completed an investigation into Jowers's claims of government and mafia involvement but did not find any evidence of a conspiracy.

The night before King's death, he gave his famous "I've been to the Mountaintop" speech, in which he stated his confidence in African Americans' reaching the "Promised Land." King declared: "I'm happy tonight; I'm not worried about anything; I'm not fearing any man. Mine eyes have seen the glory of the coming of the Lord."

God. An unjust law is a code that is out of harmony with the moral law. To put it in the terms of St. Thomas Aquinas[2] An unjust law is a human law that is not rooted in eternal law and natural law. Any law that uplifts human personality is just. Any law that degrades human personality is unjust. All segregation statutes are unjust because segregation distorts the soul and damages the personality. It gives the segregator a false sense of superiority and the segregated a false sense of inferiority. Segregation, to use the terminology of the Jewish philosopher Martin Buber,[3] substitutes an "I-it" relationship for an "I-thou" relationship and ends up relegating persons to the status of things. Hence segregation is not only politically, economically and sociologically unsound, it is morally wrong and sinful. Paul Tillich[4] said that sin is separation. Is not segregation an existential expression of man's tragic separation, his awful estrangement, his terrible sinfulness? Thus it is that I can urge men to obey the 1954 decision of the Supreme Court,[5] for it is

morally right; and I can urge them to disobey segregation ordinances, for they are morally wrong.

Let us consider a more concrete example of just and unjust laws. An unjust law is a code that a numerical or power majority group compels a minority group to obey but does not make binding on itself. This is *difference* made legal. By the same token, a just law is a code that a majority compels a minority to follow and that it is willing to follow itself. This is *sameness* made legal.

Let me give another explanation. A law is unjust if it is inflicted on a minority that, as a result of being denied the right to vote, had no

---

2. **St. Thomas Aquinas** (1226–1274). Italian theologian whose writings significantly influenced Catholicism
3. **Martin Buber** (1878–1965). German Jewish religious philosopher
4. **Paul Tillich** (1886–1965). German Protestant theologian
5. **1954 Supreme Court decision.** *Brown v. Board of Education*, in which the U.S. Supreme Court ruled that segregated public schools are unconstitutional.

part in enacting or devising the law. Who can say that the legislature of Alabama which set up that state's segregation laws was democratically elected? Throughout Alabama all sorts of devious methods are used to prevent Negroes from becoming registered voters, and there are some counties in which, even though Negroes constitute a majority of the population, not a single Negro is registered. Can any law enacted under such circumstances be considered democratically structured?

Sometimes a law is just on its face and unjust in its application. For instance, I have been arrested on a charge of parading without a permit. Now, there is nothing wrong in having an ordinance which requires a permit for a parade. But such an ordinance becomes unjust when it is used to maintain segregation and to deny citizens the First-Amendment privilege of peaceful assembly and protest.

> **Sometimes a law is just on its face and unjust in its application.**

I hope you are able to see the distinction I am trying to point out. In no sense do I advocate evading or defying the law, as would the rabid segregationist. That would lead to <u>anarchy</u>. One who breaks an unjust law must do so openly, lovingly, and with a willingness to accept the penalty. I submit that an individual who breaks a law that conscience tells him is unjust and who willingly accepts the penalty of imprisonment in order to arouse the conscience of the community over its injustice, is in reality expressing the highest respect for law. . . .

Never before have I written so long a letter. I'm afraid it is much too long to take your precious time. I can assure you that it would have been much shorter if I had been writing from a comfortable desk, but what else can one do when he is alone in a narrow jail cell, other than write long letters, think long thoughts and pray long prayers?

If I have said anything in this letter that overstates the truth and indicates an unreasonable impatience, I beg you to forgive me. If I have said anything that understates the truth and indicates my having a patience that allows me to settle for anything less than brotherhood, I beg God to forgive me.

I hope this letter finds you strong in the faith. I also hope that circumstances will soon make it possible for me to meet each of you, not as an integrationist or a civil rights leader but as a fellow clergyman and a Christian brother. Let us all hope that the dark clouds of racial prejudice will soon pass away and the deep fog of misunderstanding will be lifted from our fear-drenched communities, and in some not too distant tomorrow the radiant stars of love and brotherhood will shine over our great nation with all their <u>scintillating</u> beauty.

Yours for the cause of Peace and Brotherhood,

MARTIN LUTHER KING, JR. ❖

---

an • ar • chy (an´ är kē) *n.*, state of lawlessness
scin • til • lat • ing (sin´ til āt iŋ) *adj.*, sparkling

MIRRORS & WINDOWS

In describing the effects of discrimination, King says, "Whatever affects one directly, affects all indirectly." Do you think this is true? Do social issues ultimately affect everyone in a society?

ABERNATHY & KING

Informational Text Connection

In the 1960s, accounts of civil rights marches and other nonviolent demonstrations appeared regularly in newspapers and on television. The photographs and film clips of police in riot gear confronting peaceful demonstrators aroused anger among many Americans, including elected officials. Unfortunately, these clashes would become increasingly violent throughout the decade.

The article **"Dr. King Arrested at Birmingham"** appeared in the *New York Times* on April 13, 1963, one day after Martin Luther King Jr. was arrested. Written by **Foster Hailey,** a reporter on the scene, the article details the arrest of King and Ralph Abernathy, another civil rights leader who assumed leadership of the movement after King's assassination in 1968. King was jailed for eleven days following this arrest, during which time he wrote "Letter from Birmingham Jail."

Dr. King Arrested at Birmingham

by Foster Hailey

BIRMINGHAM, Ala., April 12—The Rev. Dr. Martin Luther King Jr. was arrested this afternoon when he defied a court injunction and led a march of Negroes toward the downtown section.

The marchers were halted after four and a half blocks—but not before more than a thousand shouting, singing Negroes had joined in the demonstration.

In addition to Dr. King, the Rev. Dr. Ralph D. Abernathy, secretary of the Southern Christian Leadership Conference, and more than 60 others were taken into custody. There was no violence. . . .

Safety Commissioner T. Eugene Connor, who directed the arrests, said Dr. King would be charged with violation of a city ordinance in parading without a permit and also with defying a state court injunction against demonstrations.

The penalty on conviction of the city charge is 180 days in jail and a fine of $100. Punishment for the injunction violation could be much more severe. The injunction was issued by Circuit Court Judge W. A. Jenkins

Wednesday night. Dr. King announced yesterday his intention to defy it. . . .

Today's march was the most widely advertised demonstration yet held and was viewed by larger groups of Negroes than any of the others. It was originally scheduled to start at noon from the Sixth Avenue Zion Hill Baptist Church, a small church at 14th Street and Sixth Avenue North, three blocks inside the main Negro section of the city.

It was 2:40 P.M., however, before Dr. King and the others emerged from the church doors and started east up Sixth Avenue, Dr. King and Dr. Abernathy were at the head of a procession of 40 or 50 marchers. They were dressed in blue jeans and blue cotton shirts to dramatize the efforts they have been making to bring about a Negro boycott of Easter buying at downtown white stores.

The march continued up Sixth Avenue to 17th Street, where police had sealed off a whole block, obviously hoping to trap the marchers there and keep onlookers back. It was at that corner that the only violence of the last 10 days occurred last Sunday when police dogs were used to drive back onlookers.

Instead of proceeding up Sixth Avenue toward City Hall, as the police had expected, the marchers turned south at the corner and marched on toward Fifth Avenue and the downtown business section.

'Stop Them There'

At Fifth Avenue they turned east again. The police, meanwhile, had re-deployed their forces and were waiting halfway down the block. As the head of the march passed behind some trucks at the entrance to a garage, Commissioner Connor told his forces "stop them there."

Two motorcycle patrolmen and two detectives grabbed Dr. King and Dr. Abernathy and hustled them into a police van a few steps away. The order of the marchers, which had started out two abreast, had been disrupted as eager onlookers joined in behind them and on either side. Thus police had difficulty trying to sort the marchers from spectators.

Most of the marchers, however, including Dr. Fulton, voluntarily stepped forward and lined up to enter other waiting police vans. . . .

There were shouts of anger from the several hundred Negroes who were in sight of the downtown arrests and who had been singing and clapping hands as they walked or ran alongside the marchers.

When police moved toward them and ordered them back west down Fifth Avenue most of them gave way freely. Three who stopped to argue with policemen were arrested.

The police quickly cleared the streets and sidewalks for two blocks and even moved onlookers out of a small park on 17th Street, but Mr. Connor ordered them to let the people in the park alone.

"Let them stay there and sing all they want to," he said.

When the demonstration started, Mr. Connor asked an onlooker what he thought of the parade, but without pausing for an answer, inquired:

"Was King in that bunch?"

Told that he was, Mr. Connor said:

"That's what he came down here for, to get arrested. Now he's got it."

What effect Dr. King's arrest will have on the campaign is problematical. His father and brother, the latter a clergyman at near-by Ensley, Ala., are still here and all the local leaders are now out of jail. . . .

Dr. King and the local leaders say that no matter who is arrested others will step forward to take their place. They say that the campaign will be continued until there is at least a beginning made in easing discrimination. ❖

Review Questions

1. Why are the marchers wearing blue jeans and blue cotton shirts? Infer what this choice of clothing indicates about the campaign for equality.

2. Which person on the scene does Hailey quote the most? Evaluate Hailey's coverage of this person. Does it seem objective and fair? Does he sympathize with one or the other side in this conflict?

3. What do King and local leaders say will happen if anyone is arrested? Explain why this policy is essential to the success of the movement. How would this policy become critical following King's assassination five years later?

TEXT $\xrightarrow{\text{TO}}$ TEXT CONNECTION

How are this newspaper account of King's arrest and King's letter to the clerics different in purpose and tone? How does reading an account of King's arrest help place his letter in perspective? How does reading Hailey's article make King's letter more powerful?

HISTORY CONNECTION

Malcolm X

While Martin Luther King Jr. was the most recognized figure of the Civil Rights movement, Malcolm X (1925–1965) was important to the movement, as well. He represented an alternative viewpoint and challenged Americans to consider more aggressive means to achieving equal rights.

Malcolm Little was born in Omaha, Nebraska, and moved to Boston at age eighteen, where he joined the criminal world. Three years later, in 1946, he was arrested for grand larceny and sent to a federal penitentiary. While in prison, Malcolm read every book available to him and converted to Islam. During his six years of incarceration, he transformed himself from a criminal into a minister and an intellectual. When he emerged from prison

in 1952, he changed his last name from *Little* to *X*, claiming that *Little* was a slave master's name. Malcolm X became minister of the largest mosque in Harlem and worked tirelessly to expand its membership.

Malcolm X became well known for his charisma and strong opinions about racism and discrimination. In contrast to Dr. King, Malcolm X did not believe peaceful coexistence was an effective means of achieving equality. He became a magnet for conflict in both the Civil Rights movement and Islam, and members of the media flocked to him in the hope of obtaining controversial quotes. Malcolm X was assassinated in 1965 while delivering a speech in New York City.

Refer to Text ▶ ▶ ▶ ▶ ▶   Reason with Text

1a. Why did members of the Southern Christian Leadership Conference (SCLC) in Atlanta travel to Birmingham?

1b. Explain King's statement that "Injustice anywhere is a threat to justice everywhere."

Understand
Find meaning

2a. Under what conditions might a protester be called an "outside agitator"?

2b. Suggest why "outside agitator" became a popular insult used by critics of the Civil Rights movement to condemn protestors.

Apply
Use information

3a. Identify the four basic steps in a nonviolent campaign.

3b. How does one step lead to the next?

Analyze
Take things apart

4a. According to King, how does St. Thomas Aquinas explain an unjust law?

4b. King gives both philosophical and concrete reasons for ending segregation. What does this suggest about his role as an advocate for civil rights?

Evaluate
Make judgments

5a. When does an undemocratically elected legislature pass unjust laws, from King's view?

5b. Propose how citizens can work to prevent the enactment of unjust laws.

Create
Bring ideas together

Analyze Literature

Argument and Allusion
What arguments does King make in responding to his critics? Which arguments are based on religious tenets, and which are based on politics? Why might King have decided to present both types of arguments? Are these arguments still relevant today? Explain.

Review the list of allusions you recorded. How is each one used to support or clarify King's stance? Is King's use of allusions effective? Why or why not?

Extend the Text

Writing Options
Creative Writing Write a letter to a government representative, such as a city council member or state legislator, stating your opinion on a public matter. Be sure to present a reasonable, well-supported argument and use respectful language. Use the Internet to find the official addresses of the representatives of your district.

Persuasive Writing An elderly friend has asked for your views on King's Birmingham letter. Write a brief analysis of the arguments King makes, identifying their strengths and weaknesses and explaining why you agree or disagree with them.

Collaborative Learning
Hold a Roundtable Discussion Working with a group, choose historical figures from the Civil Rights movement to portray in a *roundtable discussion,* a public conversation among people on both sides of an issue. Students can role-play King and his supporters, the clergy members who criticized him, Eugene Conner (see the newspaper article), Foster Hailey (the *Times* reporter), and ordinary citizens. Allow everyone in the discussion to speak and be heard.

Lifelong Learning
Prepare a Time Line With a partner or a group, prepare a time line of the events in the days leading up to the writing of King's letter. Then briefly describe how the eight clerics, the media, and the public reacted to the letter. Illustrate the time line and description with photographs from the Internet. (Credit the photographers as needed.)

 Go to **www.mirrorsandwindows.com** for more.

1. How does King defend his being in Birmingham when he is considered an "outsider" by his critics?
- **A.** He believes that what happens in Birmingham will affect people outside Birmingham, too.
- **B.** He has ties with the organizations in Birmingham that invited him there.
- **C.** He goes wherever there is injustice to fight.
- **D.** He states that any resident of the United States is not an outsider within its borders.
- **E.** All of the above

2. How does King differentiate between a just and an unjust law?
- **A.** A just law is created by or voted on by the people who will be affected by it.
- **B.** A just law conveys a sense of superiority to a group.
- **C.** A just law is binding to all people, not just the minority.
- **D.** Both A and C
- **E.** Both B and C

3. King writes that "One who breaks an unjust law must do it openly, lovingly." What does he mean by the word *lovingly?*
- **A.** in a gentle, tender way
- **B.** in a painstakingly careful way
- **C.** with respect for others and passion for a cause
- **D.** in a way that openly shows affection for someone
- **E.** with strictness, which may seem cruel but actually shows love

4. According to King, what action shows "the highest respect for law"?
- **A.** obeying all laws but arguing to change those that are unjust
- **B.** creating laws that uphold the dignity of all people
- **C.** breaking an unjust law and accepting the penalty in order to bring about change
- **D.** obeying only the laws with which you agree
- **E.** breaking an unjust law and refusing to accept the penalty

5. King suggests that it may seem paradoxical for his followers "consciously to break laws." What does *paradoxical* mean?
- **A.** unwise
- **B.** radical in concept
- **C.** defiantly bold
- **D.** self-serving
- **E.** seemingly contradictory

6. In the article about King's arrest, what did Commissioner Connor claim was King's reason for demonstrating?
- **A.** to encourage shoppers to boycott white-owned stores at Easter
- **B.** to protest the law that requires having a permit to parade
- **C.** to get arrested
- **D.** to campaign for an elected office on Birmingham's city council
- **E.** to commemorate the violence that had happened there ten days earlier

7. In King's letter, why does he allude to Paul of Tarsus?
- **A.** to compare himself to a figure from the Bible
- **B.** to remind those who will read the letter that he is a good Christian
- **C.** to make the point that Jesus would support his cause
- **D.** to give an example of someone else who traveled far to help people in need
- **E.** to compare the whites of Birmingham to biblical oppressors

8. Constructed Response: Analyze how King counters or responds to the arguments against his actions in "Letter from Birmingham Jail." In particular, explain how he structures his counterargument. Use examples from the text to support your explanation.

9. Constructed Response: Martin Luther King Jr. was inspired by Transcendentalist Henry David Thoreau, who advocated civil disobedience as a way to accomplish social and political change. Compare and contrast King's letter with Thoreau's essay *Civil Disobedience* (see Unit 2). Discuss three beliefs found in both selections.

TEST-TAKING TIP

Don't underestimate the importance of preparing your answer sheet according to guidelines. Specifically, be sure to use a number 2 graphite pencil, and avoid making extra marks or smudges on the answer sheet. In marking your answers, fill in the oval completely and verify that you mark the correct oval for each question. Remember that your answer sheet will be read by a machine, which may misinterpret stray marks or insufficiently shaded answers.

The Rockpile

A Short Story by James Baldwin

Build Background

Literary Context First published in 1965 in *Going to Meet the Man,* a collection of short stories, James Baldwin's **"The Rockpile"** draws on some of the same characters and events featured later in his 1953 novel *Go Tell It on the Mountain.* The characters, members of an African-American family in Depression-era Harlem, confront the issues that appear in various other Baldwin works: poverty, violence between African-American males, and the importance of religion in the African-American community.

The family in "The Rockpile" lives near "a mass of natural rock jutting out of the ground." Described as a favorite gathering spot for youth, the rockpile is a source of temptation and danger. As such, it symbolizes the physical and social problems faced by the family as well as the community.

Reader's Context How does the community in which you live influence your family? How does it influence you?

Meet the Author

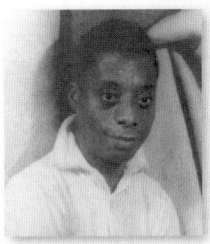

James Baldwin (1924–1987) was born in Harlem, the oldest of nine children in a poor family. His creativity and love of books emerged during childhood, and his teachers encouraged him to write. At age twelve, he published his first short story in a church newspaper. At fourteen, he became a minister, preaching in Harlem churches. He left the ministry after three years to pursue a career as a writer.

Hoping to distance himself from the racism he encountered in the United States, Baldwin moved to Paris, France, in 1948. There, he completed his first novel, the semiautobiographical *Go Tell It on the Mountain* (1953), which explored his life as a young minister. He described this novel as "the book I had to write if I was ever going to write anything else." In 1955, Baldwin published *Notes of a Native Son,* a collection of early poems, stories, and book reviews. Encouraged by developments in the Civil Rights movement, Baldwin returned to the United States in 1957. Four years later, he expressed his disappointment and disillusionment in a powerful collection of essays about race relations, *Nobody Knows My Name* (1961).

Although Baldwin's later literary output received less critical acclaim than his early works, he continued to write while dividing his time among the United States, France, and Turkey. Other acclaimed works include the novels *Tell Me How Long the Train's Been Gone* (1968) and *Just Above My Head* (1979), a collection of essays on civil rights called *The Fire Next Time* (1963), and a Broadway play, *Blues for Mr. Charlie* (1964).

Analyze Literature

Setting and Characterization

The **setting** is the time and place in which a story occurs, together with all the details used to create the sense of a particular time and place.

Characterization is the act of creating or describing a character. A writer may create characters using *indirect techniques,* by showing what they do, say, or think or by revealing what other characters say or think about them, or *direct techniques,* by describing characters' appearance and personality.

Set Purpose

Baldwin's choice of title clearly indicates the significance of the setting in this story. As you read it, think about why the rockpile is important. Identify the ways it both challenges and endangers those attracted to it. Also determine how each character's behavior somehow is tied to the rockpile. Determine what characterization techniques Baldwin uses to develop Roy, John, Elizabeth, and Gabriel.

Preview Vocabulary

decorously, 1073
latent, 1073
malevolence, 1079
perdition, 1079
propitiation, 1079

Harlem Street Scene, 1942. Jacob Lawrence. Private collection.

The Rockpile

by James Baldwin

Roy felt it to be his right, not to say his duty, to play there.

Across the street from their house, in an empty lot between two houses, stood the rockpile. It was a strange place to find a mass of natural rock jutting out of the ground; and someone, probably Aunt Florence, had once told them that the rock was there and could not be taken away because without it the subway cars underground would fly apart, killing all the people. This, touching on some natural mystery concerning the surface and the center of the earth, was far too intriguing an explanation to be challenged, and it invested the rockpile, moreover, with such mysterious importance that Roy felt it to be his right, not to say his duty, to play there.

Other boys were to be seen there each afternoon after school and all day Saturday and Sunday. They fought on the rockpile. Sure footed, dangerous, and reckless, they rushed each other and grappled on the heights, sometimes disappearing down the other side in a confusion of dust and screams and upended, flying feet. "It's a wonder they don't kill themselves," their mother said, watching sometimes from the fire escape. "You children stay away from there, you hear me?" Though she said "children" she was looking at Roy, where he sat beside John on the fire escape. "The good Lord knows," she continued, "I don't want you to come home bleeding like a hog every day the Lord sends." Roy shifted impatiently, and continued to stare at the street, as though in this gazing he might somehow acquire wings. John said nothing. He had not really been spoken to: he was afraid of the rockpile and of the boys who played there.

Each Saturday morning John and Roy sat on the fire escape and watched the forbidden street below. Sometimes their mother sat in the room behind them, sewing, or dressing their younger sister, or nursing the baby, Paul. The sun fell across them and across the fire escape with a high, benevolent indifference; below them, men and women, and boys and girls, sinners all, loitered; sometimes one of the church-members passed and saw them and waved. Then, for the moment that they waved decorously back, they were intimidated. They watched the saint, man or woman, until he or she had disappeared from sight. The passage of one of the redeemed made them consider,

however vacantly, the wickedness of the street, their own latent wickedness in sitting where they sat; and made them think of their father, who came home early on Saturdays and who would soon be turning this corner and entering the dark hall below them.

> He was afraid of the rockpile and of the boys who played there.

But until he came to end their freedom, they sat, watching and longing above the street. At the end of the street nearest their house was the bridge which spanned the Harlem River and led to a city called the Bronx; which was where Aunt Florence lived. Nevertheless, when they saw her coming, she did not come from the bridge, but from the opposite end of the street. This, weakly, to their minds, she explained by saying that she had taken the subway, not wishing to walk, and that, besides, she did not live in that section of the Bronx. Knowing that the Bronx was across the river, they did not believe this story ever, but, adopting toward her their father's attitude, assumed that she had just left some sinful place which she dared not name, as, for example, a movie palace.

In the summertime boys swam in the river, diving off the wooden dock, or wading in from the garbage-heavy bank. Once a boy, whose name was Richard, drowned in the river. His mother had not known where he was; she had even come to their house, to ask if he was

---

dec • o • rous • ly (dek´ ɐr əs lē) *adv.*, with good manners; politely

la • tent (lā´ tənt) *adj.*, hidden but likely to emerge at some time

and came rushing out of doors to stand in the gutter, watching. Then the small procession disappeared within the house which stood beside the rockpile. Then, *"Lord, Lord, Lord!"* cried Elizabeth, their mother, and slammed the window down.

One Saturday, an hour before his father would be coming home, Roy was wounded on the rockpile and brought screaming upstairs. He and John had been sitting on the fire escape and their mother had gone into the kitchen to sip tea with Sister McCandless. By and by Roy became bored and sat beside John in restless silence; and John began drawing into his schoolbook a newspaper advertisement which featured a new electric locomotive. Some friends of Roy passed beneath the fire escape and called him. Roy began to fidget, yelling down to them through the bars. Then a silence fell. John looked up. Roy stood looking at him.

"I'm going downstairs," he said.

"You better stay where you is, boy. You know Mama don't want you going downstairs."

"I be right *back.* She won't even know I'm gone, less you run and tell her."

"I ain't *got* to tell her. What's going to stop her from coming in here and looking out the window?"

"She's talking," Roy said. He started into the house.

"But Daddy's going to be home soon!"

"I be back before *that.* What you all the time got to be so *scared* for?" He was already in the house and he now turned, leaning on the windowsill, to swear impatiently, "I be back in *five* minutes."

there. Then, in the evening, at six o'clock, they had heard from the street a woman screaming and wailing; and they ran to the windows and looked out. Down the street came the woman, Richard's mother, screaming, her face raised to the sky and tears running down her face. A woman walked beside her, trying to make her quiet and trying to hold her up. Behind them walked a man, Richard's father, with Richard's body in his arms. There were two white policemen walking in the gutter, who did not seem to know what should be done. Richard's father and Richard were wet, and Richard's body lay across his father's arms like a cotton baby. The woman's screaming filled all the street; cars slowed down and the people in the cars stared; people opened their windows and looked out

John watched him sourly as he carefully unlocked the door and disappeared. In a moment he saw him on the sidewalk with his friends. He did not dare to go and tell his mother that Roy had left the fire escape because he had practically promised not to.

He started to shout, *Remember, you said five minutes!* but one of Roy's friends was looking up at the fire escape, John looked down at his schoolbook: he became engrossed again in the problem of the locomotive.

When he looked up again he did not know how much time had passed, but now there was a gang fight on the rockpile. Dozens of boys fought each other in the harsh sun: clambering up the rocks and battling hand to hand, scuffed shoes sliding on the slippery rock; filling the bright air with curses and jubilant cries. They filled the air, too, with flying weapons: stones, sticks, tin cans, garbage, whatever could be picked up and thrown. John watched in a kind of absent amazement—until he remembered that Roy was still downstairs, and that he was one of the boys on the rockpile. Then he was afraid; he could not see his brother among the figures in the sun; and he stood up, leaning over the fire-escape railing. Then Roy appeared from the other side of the rocks; John saw that his shirt was torn; he was laughing. He moved until he stood at the very top of the rockpile. Then, something, an empty tin can, flew out of the air and hit him on the forehead, just above the eye. Immediately, one side of Roy's face ran with blood, he fell and rolled on his face down the rocks. Then for a moment there was no movement at all, no sound, the sun, arrested, lay on the street and the sidewalk and the arrested[1] boys. Then someone screamed or shouted; boys began to run away, down the street, toward the bridge. The figure on the ground, having caught its breath and felt its own blood, began to shout. John cried, "Mama! Mama!" and ran inside.

"Don't fret, don't fret," panted Sister McCandless as they rushed down the dark, narrow, swaying stairs, "don't fret. Ain't a boy been born don't get his knocks every now and again. *Lord!*" they hurried into the sun. A man had picked Roy up and now walked slowly toward them. One or two boys sat silent on their stoops; at either end of the street there was a group of boys watching. "He ain't hurt bad," the man said, "wouldn't be making this kind of noise if he was hurt real bad."

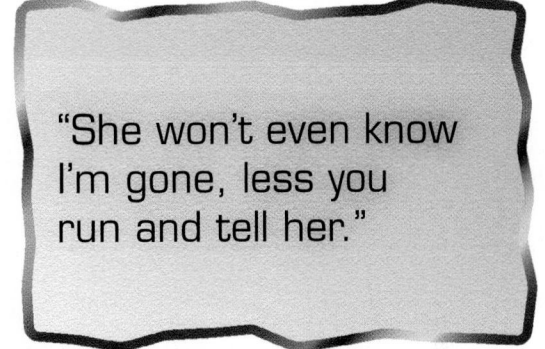

"She won't even know I'm gone, less you run and tell her."

Elizabeth, trembling, reached out to take Roy, but Sister McCandless, bigger, calmer, took him from the man and threw him over her shoulder as she once might have handled a sack of cotton. "God bless you," she said to the man, "God bless you, son." Roy was still screaming. Elizabeth stood behind Sister McCandless to stare at his bloody face.

"It's just a flesh wound," the man kept saying, "just broke the skin, that's all." They were moving across the sidewalk, toward the house. John, not now afraid of the staring boys, looked toward the corner to see if his father was yet in sight.

Upstairs, they hushed Roy's crying. They bathed the blood away, to find, just above the left eyebrow, the jagged, superficial scar. "Lord, have mercy," murmured Elizabeth, "another inch and it would've been his eye." And she looked with apprehension toward the clock. "Ain't it the truth," said Sister McCandless, busy with bandages and iodine.

---

1. **arrested.** Here, the word means "stopped."

"When did he go downstairs?" his mother asked at last.

Sister McCandless now sat fanning herself in the easy chair, at the head of the sofa where Roy lay, bound and silent. She paused for a moment to look sharply at John. John stood near the window, holding the newspaper advertisement and the drawing he had done.

"We was sitting on the fire escape," he said. "Some boys he knew called him."

"When?"

"He said he'd be back in five minutes."

"Why didn't you tell me he was downstairs?"

He looked at his hands, clasping his notebook, and did not answer.

"Boy," said Sister McCandless, "you hear your mother a-talking to you?"

He looked at his mother. He repeated:

"He said he'd be back in five minutes."

"He said he'd be back in five minutes," said Sister McCandless with scorn, "don't look to me like that's no right answer. You's the man of the house, you supposed to look after your baby brothers and sisters—you ain't supposed to let them run off and get half-killed. But I expect," she added, rising from the chair, dropping the cardboard fan, "your Daddy'll make you tell the truth. Your Ma's way too soft with you."

He did not look at her, but at the fan where it lay in the dark red, depressed seat where she had been. The fan advertised a pomade for the hair and showed a brown woman and her baby, both with glistening hair, smiling happily at each other.

"Honey," said Sister McCandless, "I got to be moving along. Maybe I drop in later tonight. I don't reckon you going to be at Tarry Service tonight?"

Tarry Service was the prayer meeting held every Saturday night at church to strengthen believers and prepare the church for the coming of the Holy Ghost on Sunday.

"I don't reckon," said Elizabeth. She stood up; she and Sister McCandless kissed each other on the cheek. "But you be sure to remember me in your prayers."

"I surely will do that." She paused, with her hand on the door knob, and looked down at Roy and laughed. "Poor little man," she said, "reckon he'll be content to sit on the fire escape *now*."

Elizabeth laughed with her. "It sure ought to be a lesson to him. You don't reckon," she asked nervously, still smiling, "he going to keep that scar, do you?"

"Lord, no," said Sister McCandless, "ain't nothing but a scratch. I declare, Sister Grimes, you worse than a child. Another couple of weeks and you won't be able to *see* no scar. No, you go on about your housework, honey, and thank the Lord it weren't no worse." She opened the door; they heard the sound of feet on the stairs. "I expect that's the Reverend," said Sister McCandless, placidly, "I *bet* he going to raise cain."[2]

"Maybe it's Florence," Elizabeth said. "Sometimes she get here about this time." They stood in the doorway, staring, while the steps reached the landing below and began again climbing to their floor. "No," said Elizabeth then, "that ain't her walk. That's Gabriel."

"Well, I'll just go on," said Sister McCandless, "and kind of prepare his mind." She pressed Elizabeth's hand as she spoke and started into the hall, leaving the door behind her slightly ajar. Elizabeth turned slowly back into the room. Roy did not open his eyes, or move; but she knew that he was not sleeping; he wished to delay until the last possible moment any contact with his father. John put his newspaper and his notebook on the table and stood, leaning on the table, staring at her.

"It wasn't my fault," he said. "I couldn't stop him from going downstairs."

"No," she said, "you ain't got nothing to worry about. You just tell your Daddy the truth."

He looked directly at her, and she turned to the window, staring into the street. What was Sister McCandless saying? Then from her bedroom she heard Delilah's thin wail and she turned, frowning, looking toward the bedroom and toward the still open door. She knew that John was watching her. Delilah continued to wail, she thought, angrily, *Now that girl's getting too big for that,* but she feared that Delilah would awaken Paul and she hurried into the bedroom. She tried to soothe Delilah back to sleep. Then she heard the front door open and close—too loud, Delilah raised her voice, with an exasperated sigh Elizabeth picked the child up. Her child and Gabriel's, her children and Gabriel's: Roy, Delilah, Paul. Only John was nameless and a stranger, living, unalterable testimony to his mother's days in sin.

"What happened?" Gabriel demanded. He stood, enormous, in the center of the room, his black lunchbox dangling from his hand,

staring at the sofa where Roy lay. John stood just before him, it seemed to her astonished vision just below him, beneath his fist, his heavy shoe.

The child stared at the man in fascination and terror—when a girl down home she had seen rabbits stand so paralyzed before the barking dog. She hurried past Gabriel to the sofa, feeling the weight of Delilah in her arms like the weight of a shield, and stood over Roy, saying:

"Now, ain't a thing to get upset about, Gabriel. This boy sneaked downstairs while I had my back turned and got hisself hurt a little. He's alright now."

> He wished to delay until the last possible moment any contact with his father.

Roy, as though in confirmation, now opened his eyes and looked gravely at his father. Gabriel dropped his lunchbox with a clatter and knelt by the sofa.

"How you feel, son? Tell your Daddy what happened?"

Roy opened his mouth to speak and then, relapsing into panic, began to cry. His father held him by the shoulder.

"You don't want to cry. You's Daddy's little man. Tell your Daddy what happened."

"He went downstairs," said Elizabeth, "where he didn't have no business to be, and got to fighting with them bad boys playing on the rockpile. That's what happened and it's a mercy it weren't nothing worse."

He looked up at her. "Can't you let this boy answer me for hisself?"

---

2. **raise cain.** Slang for "create a disturbance."

Ignoring this, she went on, more gently: "He got cut on the forehead, but it ain't nothing to worry about."

"You call a doctor? How you know it ain't nothing to worry about?"

"Is you got money to be throwing away on doctors? No, I ain't called no doctor. Ain't nothing wrong with my eyes that I can't tell whether he's hurt bad or not. He got a fright more'n anything else, and you ought to pray God it teaches him a lesson."

> "Can't you let this boy answer me for hisself?"

"You got a lot to say now," he said, "but I'll have *me* something to say in a minute. I'll be wanting to know when all this happened, what you was doing with your eyes *then*." He turned back to Roy, who had lain quietly sobbing eyes wide open and body held rigid: and who now, at his father's touch, remembered the height, the sharp, sliding rock beneath his feet, the sun, the explosion of the sun, his plunge into darkness and his salty blood; and recoiled, beginning to scream, as his father touched his forehead. "Hold still, hold still," crooned his father, shaking, "hold still. Don't cry. Daddy ain't going to hurt you, he just wants to see this bandage, see what they've done to his little man." But Roy continued to scream and would not be still and Gabriel dared not lift the bandage for fear of hurting him more. And he looked at Elizabeth in fury: "Can't you put that child down and help me with this boy? John, take your baby sister from your mother—don't look like neither of you got good sense."

John took Delilah and sat down with her in the easy chair. His mother bent over Roy, and held him still, while his father, carefully—but still Roy screamed—lifted the bandage and stared at the wound. Roy's sobs began to lessen. Gabriel readjusted the bandage. "You see," said Elizabeth, finally, "he ain't nowhere near dead."

"It sure ain't your fault that he ain't dead." He and Elizabeth considered each other for a moment in silence. "He came mightly close to losing an eye. Course, his eyes ain't as big as your'n, so I reckon you don't think it matters so much." At this her face hardened; he smiled. "Lord, have mercy," he said, "you think you ever going to learn to do right? Where was you when all this happened? Who let him go downstairs?"

"Ain't nobody let him go downstairs, he just went. He got a head just like his father, it got to be broken before it'll bow. I was in the kitchen."

"Where was Johnnie?"

"He was in here."

"Where?"

"He was on the fire escape."

"Didn't he know Roy was downstairs?"

"I reckon."

"What you mean, you reckon? He ain't got your big eyes for nothing, does he?" He looked over at John. "Boy, you see your brother go downstairs?"

"Gabriel, ain't no sense in trying to blame Johnnie. You know right well if you have trouble making Roy behave, he ain't going to listen to his brother. He don't hardly listen to me."

"How come you didn't tell your mother Roy was downstairs?"

John said nothing, staring at the blanket which covered Delilah.

"Boy, you hear me? You want me to take a strap to you?"

"No, you ain't," she said. "You ain't going to taken no strap to this boy, not today you ain't. Ain't a soul to blame for Roy's lying up there now but you—you because you done spoiled him so that he thinks he can do just anything and get away with it. I'm here to tell you that ain't no way to raise no child. You don't pray to the Lord to help you do better than you been doing, you going to live to shed bitter tears that the Lord didn't take his soul today." And she

> ## "I'm here to tell you that ain't no way to raise no child."

was trembling. She moved, unseeing, toward John and took Delilah from his arms. She looked back at Gabriel, who had risen, who stood near the sofa, staring at her. And she found in his face not fury alone, which would not have surprised her; but hatred so deep as to become insupportable in its lack of personality. His eyes were struck alive, unmoving, blind with <u>malevolence</u>—she felt, like the pull of the earth at her feet, his longing to witness her <u>perdition</u>. Again, as though it might be <u>propitiation</u>, she moved the child in her arms. And at this his eyes changed, he looked at Elizabeth, the mother of his children, the helpmeet given by the Lord. Then her eyes clouded; she moved to leave the room; her foot struck the lunchbox lying on the floor.

"John," she said, "pick up your father's lunchbox like a good boy."

She heard, behind her, his scrambling movement as he left the easy chair, the scrape and jangle of the lunchbox as he picked it up, bending his dark head near the toe of his father's heavy shoe. ❖

---

ma • lev • o • lence (mä le′ və lənts) *n.*, ill will; spite; hatred
per • di • tion (pʉr di′ shən) *n.*, destruction; damnation
pro • pi • ti • a • tion (prō pi′ shē ā′ shən) *n.*, atonement; act of making amends for wrongdoing

---

When have you been drawn to something that you knew was dangerous or forbidden? Why were you attracted to it?

MORRISON

Literature Connection

Toni Morrison (b. 1931) delivered this *eulogy,* or speech honoring the dead, at the memorial service for James Baldwin, in December 1987. One of many writers to speak at the service, Morrison spoke about her feelings of indebtedness to Baldwin, whom she described as a great influence on her style and subject matter.

A highly respected novelist, Morrison is best known for *The Bluest Eye* (1970), *Song of Solomon* (1977), and *Beloved* (1987). *Beloved* won the Pulitzer Prize for fiction in 1988 and was made into a film starring Oprah Winfrey ten years later. Morrison ran the writing program at Princeton University for nearly twenty years. In 1993, she was awarded the Nobel Prize for literature for her "visionary force and poetic import." In 2006, *Beloved* was selected by the *New York Times* as the best work of American fiction in the last twenty-five years.

from On James Baldwin
by Toni Morrison

Jimmy, there is too much to think about you, and too much to feel. The difficulty is your life refuses summation—it always did—and invites contemplation instead. Like many of us left here I thought I knew you. Now I discover that in your company it is myself I know. That is the astonishing gift of your art and your friendship: You gave us ourselves to think about, to cherish. We are like Hall Montana[1] watching "with new wonder" his brother saints, knowing the song he sang is us, "He is us."

I never heard a single command from you, yet the demands you made on me, the challenges you issued to me, were nevertheless unmistakable, even if unenforced: that I work and think at the top of my form, that I stand on moral ground but know that ground must be shored up by mercy, that "the world is before [me] and [I] need not take it or leave it as it was when [I] came in."

Well, the season was always Christmas with you there and, like one aspect of that scenario, you did not neglect to bring at least three gifts. You gave me a language to dwell in, a gift so perfect it seems my own invention. I have been thinking your spoken and written thoughts for so long I believed they were mine. I have been seeing the world through your eyes for so long, I believed that clear clear view was my own. Even now, even here, I need you to tell me what I am feeling and how to articulate it. So I have pored again through the 6,895 pages of

---

1. **Hall Montana.** Character in Baldwin's novel *Just Above My Head*

your published work to acknowledge the debt and thank you for the credit. No one possessed or inhabited language for me the way you did. You made American English honest—genuinely international. . . .

The second gift was your courage, which you let us share: the courage of one who could go as a stranger in the village and transform the distances between people into intimacy with the whole world; courage to understand that experience in ways that made it a personal revelation for each of us. It was you who gave us the courage to appropriate an alien, hostile, all-white geography because you had discovered that "this world [meaning history] is white no longer and it will never be white again." Yours was the courage to live life in and from its belly as well as beyond its edges, to see and say what it was, to recognize and identify evil but never fear or stand in awe of it. It is a courage that came from a ruthless intelligence married to a pity so profound it could convince anyone who cared to know that those who despised us "need the moral authority of their former slaves, who are the only people in the world who know anything about them and who may be indeed, the only people in the world who really care anything about them.". . .

The third gift was hard to fathom and even harder to accept. It was your tenderness—a tenderness so delicate I thought it could not last, but last it did and envelop me it did. In the midst of anger it tapped me lightly like the child in Tish's[2] womb. . . .

You knew, didn't you, how I needed your language and the mind that formed it? How I relied on your fierce courage to tame wildernesses for me? How strengthened I was by the certainty that came from knowing you would never hurt me? You knew, didn't you, how I loved your love? You knew. This then is no calamity. No. This is jubilee. "Our crown," you said, "has already been bought and paid for. All we have to do," you said, "is wear it."

And we do, Jimmy. You crowned us. ❖

---

2. **Tish's.** Reference to a character in Baldwin's novel *If Beale Street Could Talk*

Review Questions

1. According to Morrison, what is the "astonishing gift" of Baldwin's art and friendship? Describe the expectations that come with that gift.

2. What other "three gifts" does Morrison identify? Evaluate the value of each gift in her life.

3. Explain why Morrison reread all of Baldwin's published writing. What writers have inspired or comforted you? Explain why.

TEXT ^{TO} TEXT CONNECTION

How did Baldwin "tame wildernesses" in writing about racism and discrimination? Which of the qualities that Morrison admired in Baldwin's writing are evident in "The Rockpile"? What did Baldwin likely mean when he said, "Our crown has already been bought and paid for"?

Refer to Text ▶ ▶ ▶ ▶ ▶ Reason with Text

1a. According to Aunt Florence, why can't the rockpile be removed?

1b. State the real reason the rockpile can't be taken away.

Understand
Find meaning

2a. What has happened to the boy named Richard?

2b. Infer what this incident suggests about the neighborhood. What does it foreshadow, or hint, will happen later in the story?

Apply
Use information

3a. What does Sister McCandless assure Elizabeth about Roy's injury?

3b. Identify the more serious family problem that Roy's accident reveals.

Analyze
Take things apart

4a. Whom does Gabriel blame for the accident? Whom does Elizabeth blame?

4b. Why are the family members intent on blaming one another?

Evaluate
Make judgments

5a. What does Elizabeth's foot strike as she leaves the room? Where else in the story is this item mentioned? With what other item is it associated?

5b. Propose what the two objects symbolize. Why does Elizabeth ask John to pick up one of the items?

Create
Bring ideas together

Analyze Literature

Setting and Characterization

How is the rockpile both challenging and dangerous? How is it an essential feature of the story? Explain how the story would be different if the neighborhood did not have the rockpile.

How does the presence of the rockpile affect each character? How does Baldwin develop each character? What methods of characterization does he use? Discuss his use of direct versus indirect techniques.

Extend the Text

Writing Options

Creative Writing Think of a place you enjoyed when you were young, or imagine a place that children today might enjoy. Write a descriptive paragraph about this place, focusing on the qualities children would enjoy.

Expository Writing In developing characters, authors sometimes portray how one character's behavior affects the other characters. Analyze this cause-and-effect relationship among the characters in "The Rockpile." Choose Roy, John, Elizabeth, or Gabriel, and write an essay analyzing how his or her actions affect the other characters.

Collaborative Learning

Research the Civil Rights Movement With two or three classmates, research James Baldwin's participation in the Civil Rights movement, including his associations with leaders such as Martin Luther King Jr., Medgar Evans, and Malcolm X. As a group, prepare a chart showing how key events in the movement seemed to influence Baldwin's life and writing.

Media Literacy

Create an Art Exhibit Like their literary counterparts, African-American artists have produced fine work. Look on the Internet for legally downloadable reproductions of drawings and paintings by artists such as Jacob Lawrence. Choose several artists and write brief descriptions of one or two of each artist's works. If you are unable to obtain reproductions, prepare a brief catalog that provides the names of several artists and describes one or two of their works.

 Go to **www.mirrorsandwindows.com** for more.

Understand the Concept

A **colon** is a punctuation mark used to mean "note what follows." It can be used to introduce a series of items or a quotation. Observe how colons are used in these examples from James Baldwin's "The Rockpile":

EXAMPLES

To introduce a list They filled the air, too, with flying weapons: stones, sticks, tin cans, garbage, whatever could be picked up and thrown.

To introduce a quotation Ignoring this, she went on, more gently: "He got cut on the forehead, but it ain't nothing to worry about."

A colon also can be used between two independent clauses when the second clause explains or summarizes the first clause.

EXAMPLE

He had not really been spoken to: he was afraid of the rockpile and of the boys who played there.

A **semicolon** is used to join the independent clauses of a compound sentence if no coordinating conjunction is used (*and, but, so, or, nor, for,* and *yet*). Doing so adds emphasis to the second clause.

EXAMPLE

Then someone screamed or shouted; boys began to run away, down the street, toward the bridge.

A second use of semicolons is to separate the items in a series when the items themselves contain commas.

EXAMPLE

Then he was afraid; he could not see his brother among the figures in the sun; and he stood up, leaning over the fire-escape railing.

Apply the Skill

Identify Uses of Colons and Semicolons

For each of these sentences from "The Rockpile," identify the use of the colon (list, quotation, or explanation/summary) or semicolon (independent clauses or items in a series).

1. His mother had not known where he was; she had even come to their house, to ask if he was there.
2. John looked down at his schoolbook: he became engrossed again in the problem of the locomotive.
3. One or two boys sat silent on their stoops; at either end of the street there was a group of boys watching.
4. She opened the door; they heard the sound of feet on the stairs.
5. Her child and Gabriel's, her children and Gabriel's: Roy, Delilah, Paul.

Use Colons and Semicolons Correctly

For each of the following sentences, insert the proper punctuation, whether a colon or semicolon. You may need to change the capitalization of some words.

1. And he looked at Elizabeth in fury, "Can't you put that child down and help me with this boy?"
2. At this her face hardened, he smiled.
3. Then her eyes clouded, she moved to leave the room, her foot struck the lunchbox lying on the floor.
4. It was a strange place to find a mass of natural rock jutting out of the ground. And someone, probably Aunt Florence, had once told them that the rock was there and could not be taken away because without it the subway cars underground would fly apart.
5. The woman's screaming filled all the street, cars slowed down and the people in the cars stared, people opened their windows and looked out and came rushing out of doors to stand in the gutter, watching.

Use Colons and Semicolons in Your Writing

Write a paragraph about a time in your childhood when you took a risk or got hurt. Make sure to describe the scene well, using sensory details, and explain the relationships between the people involved. Use colons and semicolons to connect closely related ideas, to set off items in lists, and to emphasize important ideas and quotations.

The Memoir Defined

A **memoir** is a type of autobiography that focuses on one event or period in an individual's life. Memoirs often are based on individuals' memories of and reactions to historical events.

In some respects, it is difficult to distinguish the memoir from other forms of narrative. Like its close relative the **autobiography**, the memoir is rooted in fact. However, unlike the autobiography, the memoir need not be scrupulously exact. Real people can take on a fictive or symbolic status, and events need not be tied to an exact chronology. Instead, the memoir can be something of a stroll down memory lane, with the author stopping at various points of interest.

The scope of the memoir also distinguishes it from the autobiography. A memoir focuses on a particular period or series of related events. It is not intended to be comprehensive, and the reader does not go to it for the entire history of the author's life. The history that is included, however, must be considered revealing.

The memoir often is placed in the category of **literary nonfiction,** a hybrid form or genre sometimes referred to as *creative nonfiction* (see Unit 9, Understanding Literary Forms). The memoirist straddles the worlds of nonfiction and fiction, simultaneously playing the roles of essayist and storyteller. The writing may be straightforward and objective, or it may be lyrical and emotional in tone.

In sum, there are as many styles of memoir as there are memoirists. What these works share is an introspective quality, as the writer seeks to make meaning of a deeply personal and unforgettable experience. How the writer approaches that purpose varies widely, however.

In the following excerpt from Gwendolyn Brooks's memoir, *Report from Part One,* the author's first-person

> *"An autobiography may be largely fictional. . . . Everyone tends to remember what he wants to remember. Disagreeable facts are sometimes glossed over or repressed."*
>
> —J. A. CUDDON, *THE DICTIONARY OF LITERARY TERMS*

voice is strong and direct as she recounts her experiences as an awkward adolescent. The same clear voice characterizes the excerpt from *The Woman Warrior,* Maxine Hong Kingston's painful account of an episode in which she bullied a shy girl at school. N. Scott Momaday takes a more indirect approach in the excerpt from his memoir, *The Way to Rainy Mountain,* defining himself by way of a place, a beloved elder, and a tribal history, all of which have made him the person he is. The narrative voice in this memoir might as easily belong to fiction as nonfiction.

As you read these selections, consider how each writer approaches his or her subject. Analyze the literary elements of setting and mood, tone, narrative technique, figurative language, and theme.

Elements of the Memoir

Setting and Mood

The **setting** of a literary work is the time and place in which it occurs, together with all the details used to create a sense of a particular time and place. The **mood** is the emotion created in the reader by part or all of a literary work. In a memoir, these elements typically play a dominant role.

For Momaday, the setting of Rainy Mountain is associated with the memory of his late grandmother. His pilgrimage to this place is his way of honoring her and of understanding the experience of his ancestors. The mood of his memoir is one of nostalgia for a simpler and more natural way of life. In Brooks's memoir, it is the writer's bedroom, with its evocative old desk, that comprises the setting and establishes for the reader a sense of a private world of real loneliness and imagined grandeur.

Tone

Tone is the emotional attitude toward the reader or subject implied by a literary work. Consider Brooks's ingenuous, falsely naive tone as she exclaims, "Why, there were *oodles* of *other* writers! They, too, suffered, and had suffered." Brooks the grown woman and published author views her girlhood self from a pinnacle of achievement. She is slyly mocking yet showing compassion for the young Gwendolyn, who kept notebooks

BROOKS   **MOMADAY**   **KINGSTON**

about her undistinguished childhood while dreaming of future greatness.

Narrative Technique

Like a work of fiction, a memoir may include elements of **plot,** or a series of events related to a central conflict or struggle. In describing the clash between the Native American and dominant white cultures, Momaday provides **exposition,** introducing necessary background information. In the excerpt from Kingston's *The Woman Warrior,* the account reaches a **climax,** or high point of interest or suspense, when the writer tries to force a silent girl to speak. It then reaches a **resolution,** in which the central conflict is ended, or resolved.

The memoirist also uses **characterization** techniques to portray other people in the account—for instance, describing their appearance or behavior or revealing what others say or think about them. The use of **dialogue,** or conversation, is an effective characterization technique. Although the girl in Kingston's memoir never speaks, her reactions to the author's one-sided conversation reveal elements of her character.

Figurative Language

The author of a memoir, like the authors of fiction and poetry, can use **figurative language,** which is meant to be understood imaginatively instead of literally. Types of figurative language include hyperbole, metaphor, personification, simile, and understatement.

Unusual figures of speech help readers see things in new ways. For instance, Momaday characterizes the prairie home of the Kiowas as "an anvil's edge," employing a **metaphor,** a figure of speech in which one thing is spoken or written about as if it were another. In stating that "Houses are like sentinels in the plain, old keepers of the weather watch," he presents a **simile,** a comparison of two seemingly unlike things using the word *like* or *as.*

Theme

A **theme** is a central message or perception about life revealed through a literary work. Theme may be stated or implied. A *stated theme* is presented directly, whereas an *implied theme* must be inferred. A single work may reveal a number of themes, but one or two usually predominate.

For example, Momaday's memoir develops the theme of remembrance along with the themes of loss, cultural relativity, and kinship. The dominant themes in Kingston's memoir relate to oppression and submission, which the author allows to unfold with a minimum of editorializing. The memoirist's recollections can be shocking and painful as well as beautiful and inspiring.

HOW TO READ

A Memoir

Identify the author's purpose. The memoirist's primary purpose is to describe an event or period in his or her life, which is a combination of de-scriptive and narrative writing. Beyond that, the memoirist may have as a secondary purpose explanation (expository writing) or persuasion (persuasive writing).

Distinguish fact from opinion. Memoirs are based on factual information but not restricted to it. As you read, identify *facts,* statements that can be proven true or false. Look for gaps in

information and errors in sequence that reveal some reorganization or interpretation of the facts. Also distinguish facts from opinions, which express attitudes or desires.

Make inferences. Consider what information the memoirist does and does not provide. How might the passage of time have affected his or her perspective? Also look beyond the personal details of the account and infer what you can about the time and place in which it occurred.

"Exhaust the little moment. Soon it dies."

Gwendolyn Brooks (1917–2000) was born in Topeka, Kansas, and raised in what was known as the Bronzeville section of Chicago. Today, Bronzeville is considered a historic Chicago area for the so-called Black Metropolis, a city-within-the-city that became known for the cultural and entrepreneurial contributions of its largely African-American residents, such as Louis Armstrong (jazz musician), Bessie Coleman (first African-American woman pilot), and Ida B. Wells-Barnett (women's and civil rights activist). Brooks attended Wilson Junior College on Chicago's South Side.

As the selection from Brooks's memoir indicates, she began "rhyming" when she was seven but only started collecting poems in her notebooks when she was eleven. Her earliest works were published in the *Chicago Defender*, an African-American newspaper. Brooks later met writers James Weldon Johnson and Langston Hughes, who encouraged her to read modern poetry and write as much as possible. Her first book of poetry, *A Street in Bronzeville*, appeared in 1945. Five years later, Brooks received the Pulitzer Prize for her second volume of poetry, *Annie Allen* (1949), becoming the first African American to receive this prestigious award. Brooks's first two collections of poetry and her novel *Maude Martha* (1953) all draw on her experiences growing up in inner-city Chicago. Other works by Brooks include

The Bean Eaters (1960), a collection of poetry; *Bronzeville Boys and Girls* (1956), a children's book; and *Report from Part One* (1972), her memoir. *Winnie* (1988) is a book of poetry inspired by the South African leader Winnie Mandela, the former wife of Nelson Mandela, the antiapartheid activist who became president of the nation's first black majority government.

In 1962, President John F. Kennedy invited Brooks to read at a poetry festival held by the Library of Congress. Six years later, she was named Poet Laureate of the State of Illinois. She was appointed poetry consultant to the Library of Congress seven years after that, the first African-American woman to hold that position. In the late 1960s, Brooks became an active part of the Black Arts Movement, aimed at developing the voices of African Americans and promoting the black aesthetic. Her focus on the lives of people in Bronzeville made her the prominent figure in the Chicago School of that movement.

Brooks's final collection of poems, *In Montgomery* (2003), was published after her death. That same year, the Illinois State Library in the capital, Springfield, was renamed the Gwendolyn Brooks Illinois State Library in the poet's honor.

Noted Works

A Street in Bronzeville (1945)	*Report from Part One* (1972)
Annie Allen (1949)	*Winnie* (1988)
The Bean Eaters (1960)	*In Montgomery* (2003)

from Report from Part One

A Memoir by Gwendolyn Brooks

To Black Women
The Explorer

Lyric Poems by Gwendolyn Brooks

Build Background

Literary Context In the first selection by Gwendolyn Brooks, which is from her memoir, **Report from Part One** (1972), the author provides a good-natured account of her earliest efforts at writing and of the transition from childhood to young adulthood. Although the brief selection suggests that Brooks did not mind poking fun at herself, the reader understands that she took her work seriously.

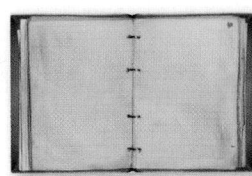

The second selection, the poem **"To Black Women,"** reflects issues from the Civil Rights movement of the late 1950s and 1960s. During this period, enormous strides were made toward racial and ethnic equality. A significant part of that movement was the call by activists such as Eldridge Cleaver, Bobby Seale, Huey Newton, and Malcolm X for Black Pride: pride in the traditions, history, and culture of African Americans. In poems like "To Black Women," Brooks reminds the world of her sisters' struggles, triumphs, and potential to achieve. The poem was published in the 1981 collection *To Disembark*.

The third selection, **"The Explorer,"** is a jagged narrative of a man walking through the halls of an apartment house, touching the "throbbing knobs" of door after door. He is looking for a "still spot in the noise," a quiet place where he can feel comfortable with himself. This poem reflects Brooks's awareness of the stresses of the modern world and her ability to use simple diction (word choices) to create dignity and evoke compassion. "The Explorer" first appeared in the 1987 collection *Blacks*.

South Side Street, Chicago, c. 1960.
Franklin McMahon.

Reader's Context If you were going to write a memoir about an event from your adolescence, what would it be? What details would you include, and what details would you leave out?

Analyze Literature

Theme and Parallelism

A **theme** is a central message or perception about life revealed through a literary work. A *stated theme* is presented directly, whereas an *implied theme* must be inferred by the reader from details in the work. A *universal theme* is a message about life that can be understood by people of most cultures.

Parallelism is a rhetorical technique in which the writer emphasizes the equal significance of two or more ideas by expressing them in the same grammatical form.

Set Purpose

Brooks's poetry is rich with themes about the human experience, particularly the struggles endured by women and people living in poverty. After you read each poem, write a sentence stating its theme. In reading all three selections, record examples of parallelism. Consider how its use affects your reading and understanding of each selection.

Preview Vocabulary

prevail, 1090
shrewd, 1090
wily, 1091

Report from Part One

by Gwendolyn Brooks

Somewhere in America, c. 1933–1934. Robert Brackman. Smithsonian American Art Museum, Washington, DC.

"Of course I would be a poet! Was a poet!"

IV

Dreamed a lot. As a little girl I dreamed freely, often on the top step of the back porch— morning, noon, sunset, deep twilight. I loved clouds, I loved red streaks in the sky. I loved the gold worlds I saw in the sky. Gods and little girls, angels and heroes and future lovers labored there, in misty glory or sharp grandeur.

I was writing all the time. My mother says I began rhyming at seven—but my notebooks date back to my eleventh year only. Careful rhymes. Lofty meditations.

FORGIVE AND FORGET
If others neglect you,
Forget; do not sigh,
For, after all, they'll select you,
In times by and by.
If their taunts cut and hurt you,
They are sure to regret.
And, if in time, they desert you,
Forgive and forget.

THE BUSY CLOCK

Clock, clock, tell the time,
Tell the time to me.
Magic, patient instrument,
That is never free.

Tick, tock, busy clock!
You've no time to play!
Bustling men and women
Need you all the day.

When I was thirteen I met, somehow, *Writer's Digest*.[1] A milestone. Why, there were *oodles* of *other* writers! They, too, suffered, and had suffered. They, too, ached for the want of the right word—reckoned with mean nouns, virtueless adjectives. They, too, sent Things out, got Things back. They, too, knew the coldness of editors, spent much money on stamps, waited, loud-hearted, for the postman.

My father provided me with a desk, an old desk given him "at McKinley's," a desk with many little compartments, with long drawers at the bottom, and a removable glass-protected shelf at the top, for books. Certainly up there, holding special delights for a writing-girl, were the Emily books, L. M. Montgomery's books about a Canadian girl who wrote, kept notebooks even as I kept notebooks, dreamed, reached. I loved the little adventures—yearning to meet their splendid creator. But who ever met an Author? Certainly there, also, to look down at me whenever I sat at the desk, was Paul Laurence Dunbar.[2] *"You,"* my mother had early announced, "are going to be the *lady* Paul Laurence Dunbar." I still own the Emily books and the "Complete Paul Laurence Dunbar."

Of course I would be a poet! *Was* a poet! Didn't I write a poem every day? Sometimes *two* poems?

And there were few large distractions. For I did not have an active social life. I went to few parties. I was uncomfortable at the parties. I danced the Charleston very well, but that was not what you did at parties!—besides, the Charleston could not stay in style forever. The one-step was all right, and the two-step—and I knew something about these. But you needed more, at those teen parties. You needed to be Fast. You needed to sashay, with loud laughter, into the mysteries of the "kissing games." "Post Office." "Kiss the Pilla." I remember being very glad, when interest in the "kissing games" finally died off. When they played "Post Office" I did not attract many letters. I was timid to the point of terror, silent, primly dressed. AND DARK. The boys did not mind telling me that *this* was the failing of failings.

At the age of fourteen I was fonder of paper dolls than of parties. I owned great numbers of them, organized governments, theaters, tournaments—planned wardrobes, coiffures, planned feasts—feasts inspired by Palmer Cox's "The Brownies in November."

I cannot say that, as a very young girl, I *Had Boy Friends.* Ida DeBroe *Had Boy Friends.* Rose Hurd and Eleanor Griffin and Rebecca Dorsey (so stylish and straight and cold) *Had Boy Friends. I "Wrote."* I spent most of my free time in my room, writing, reading, reflecting. I was always mooning over some little boy or other. I'd go to bed and dream of embracing and marrying Him, of becoming the mother of His one child, of being desperately loved by Him. The adored Gwendolyn. Sometimes—in my musings—the little boy would *fight* for the privilege of possessing—whom?—why, Gwendolyn, of course. ❖

---

1. **Writer's Digest.** Magazine offering advice to writers, especially ones not established in their profession
2. **Paul Laurence Dunbar.** Highly respected African-American poet (1872–1906)

MIRRORS & WINDOWS

When you were eleven, what did you want to be? Who or what made you interested in that career?

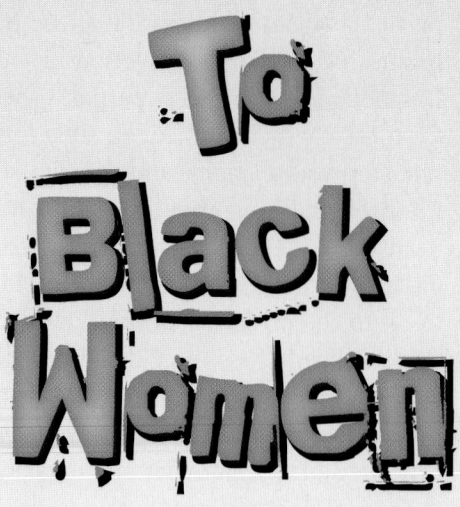

To Black Women

by Gwendolyn Brooks

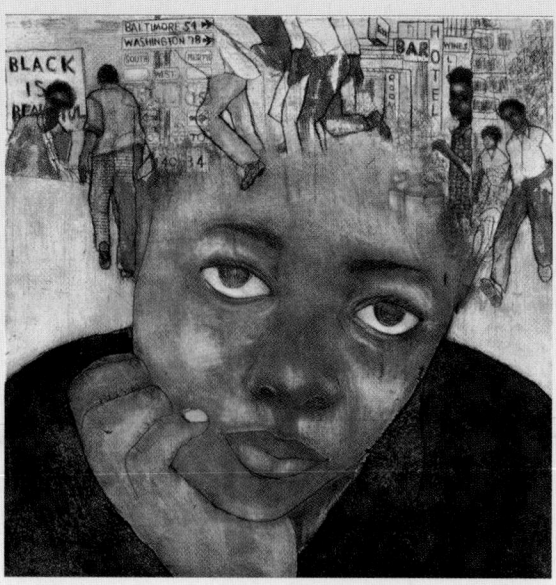

Gemini Etching, 1969. Lou Mills.

Sisters,
where there is cold silence—
no hallelujahs, no hurrahs at all, no handshakes,
no neon red or blue, no smiling faces—<u>prevail</u>.
5   Prevail across the editors[1] of the world!
who are obsessed, self-honeying and self-crowned
in the seduced arena.

It has been a
hard trudge, with fainting, bandaging and death.
10 There have been startling confrontations.
There have been tramplings. Tramplings
of monarchs[2] and of other men.

But there remain large countries in your eyes.
<u>Shrewd</u> sun.
15 The civil balance.
The listening secrets.

And you create and train your flowers still. ❖

---

1. **editors.** Those who accept and prepare written material for publication
2. **monarchs.** Person who rules over a kingdom or empire, such as a
   king or queen

> **pre • vail** (prē vāl´) *v.,* triumph
> **shrewd** (shrüd) *adj.,* having acute perception

How can the speaker in "To Black Women" be considered a role model to her
"sisters"? What qualities are important in a role model?

The Explorer

by Gwendolyn Brooks

Somehow to find a still spot in the noise
Was the frayed inner want, the winding, the frayed hope
Whose tatters he kept hunting through the din.
A satin peace somewhere.
5   A room of <u>wily</u> hush somewhere within.

So tipping down the scrambled halls he set
Vague hands on throbbing knobs. There were behind
Only spiraling, high human voices,
The scream of nervous affairs.
10   Wee griefs,
Grand griefs. And choices.

He feared most of all the choices, that cried to be taken.

There were no bourns.[1]
There were no quiet rooms. ❖

---

1. **bourns** Boundaries; limits.

wi • ly (wī´ lē) *adj.*, sly

The man in the poem "feared most of all the choices." How can having choices or making decisions be frightening or intimidating?

Refer to Text ▶ ▶ ▶ ▶ ▶ **Reason with Text**

1a. In paragraph 2 of Brooks's memoir, how does she describe what she wrote in her notebook?

1b. Describe the *tone,* or attitude, of Brooks's description of her early efforts as a writer.

Understand
Find meaning

2a. How does the speaker in "To Black Women" describe the "editors of the world"?

2b. After reading the passage from Brooks's memoir, suggest why the speaker in the poem singles out "editors." Why does she use such sharp language in lines 7–8?

Apply
Use information

3a. What does the man in "The Explorer" hear behind the "throbbing" doorknobs?

3b. Infer what these sounds indicate about the man's life.

Analyze
Take things apart

4a. Where does the speaker in "To Black Women" see hope for the sisters?

4b. Interpret lines 14–17. Are they hopeful or gloomy? Explain.

Evaluate
Make judgments

5a. In "To Black Women," who has experienced the "hard trudge," "confrontations," and "tramplings"? Who has been responsible for these acts?

5b. Summarize your impressions of Brooks's life, personality, and values, based on your reading of these three selections.

Create
Bring ideas together

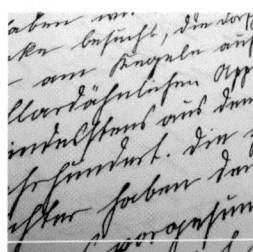

Analyze Literature

Theme and Parallelism

Review your statement of theme for each poem. Is the theme stated or implied? Could it be considered a universal theme? How are the themes of the two poems similar and different?

What examples of parallelism did you find in the three selections? What ideas are reinforced or emphasized by the use of parallel structure? How does its use affect the rhythm and sound of the language?

Extend the Text

Writing Options

Creative Writing Imagine you are a child's toy, book, or other cherished possession of a small boy or girl. Write a one-page make-believe memoir from the perspective of this beloved item, in which you describe your experiences with the child.

Expository Writing Visualize the setting of "The Explorer," and assume the role of the man tripping down the halls of the building. Then write a paragraph analyzing the role of setting, or environment, in the poem and what it might represent to the man in the poem.

Collaborative Learning

Celebrate African-American Women With a small group of classmates, plan a celebration of the works of African-American women poets. Write an introduction for each poet; then select one of her poems to share with the group or class. Explain the themes the poet writes about and how one or more are evidenced in the poem you selected.

Critical Literacy

Create a Display of Documents about Black Pride The Black Pride movement of the 1960s produced a number of documents, such as letters, statements of purpose, editorials, radio transcripts, and speeches. Locate some of these materials on the Internet or in books, and make copies of those that are legally reproducible. Display the materials and provide a summary of what each item represented in the Black Pride movement.

 Go to **www.mirrorsandwindows.com** for more.

from **The Woman Warrior**

A Memoir by Maxine Hong Kingston

Build Background

Cultural Context This excerpt from Maxine Hong Kingston's memoir, **_The Woman Warrior_** (1976), focuses on the author's difficulty growing up in two cultures: Chinese at home and American at school. Earlier in the memoir, Kingston writes: "At first it did not occur to me I was supposed to talk or to pass kindergarten. I talked at home and to one or two of the Chinese kids in class." She remembers that reading aloud was easier than talking, because she "did not have to make up what to say." In this excerpt, the author narrates an afternoon when, in the sixth grade, she confronts a Chinese-American classmate who could not or would not speak in school, other than to read aloud.

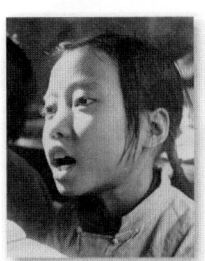

The Woman Warrior has been heralded by literary scholars as an honest portrayal of the immigrant experience in the United States. The memoir also has been recognized for its exploration of women's role in a patriarchal (male-dominated) culture. The book's title honors Fa Mu-lan, the celebrated "woman warrior" in Chinese history.

Reader's Context What challenges do immigrant students face in American schools?

Meet the Author

Maxine Hong Kingston (b. 1940) was born in Stockton, California, to parents who were Chinese immigrants. Her parents were well educated: Her father was a poet and scholar in China, and her mother was a midwife/doctor. Arriving separately in the United States, her parents found work in the laundry business. As a child, Kingston was enthralled by her mother's stories, which were steeped in Chinese folklore and told of ancestral adventures. This ritual storytelling, coupled with Kingston's own struggle to blend two cultures, laid the foundation for her writing.

A talented student, Kingston was awarded several scholarships and graduated in 1962 with a bachelor's degree in English from the University of California, Berkeley. There, she met her future husband. They subsequently moved to Hawaii, where Kingston taught at several universities. She later returned to Berkeley to teach creative writing.

Kingston's first book, _The Woman Warrior_ (1976), received the National Book Critics Circle Award for Nonfiction. Her next book, the novel _China Men_ (1980), won the National Book Award for Nonfiction. In 1997, President Bill Clinton awarded Kingston a National Humanities Medal and praised her as the writer who "brought the Asian-American experience to life . . . and inspired a new generation to make their own unique voices and experiences heard." More recent Kingston works include _To Be the Poet_ (2002) and _The Fifth Book of Peace_ (2003).

Analyze Literature

Motivation and Simile
Motivation is a force that causes a character to think, feel, or behave in a certain way.

A **simile** is a comparison of two seemingly unlike things using the word _like_ or _as_.

Set Purpose

This excerpt from Kingston's memoir reads like a short story in which she is one of the characters. As you read, think about Kingston's motivation. Specifically, why does she hate the quiet girl? Pay particular attention to Kingston's descriptions of the girl, which include several similes. Record the similes and identify the items being compared.

Preview Vocabulary

faltering, 1094
recluse, 1102

from The Woman Warrior

by Maxine Hong Kingston

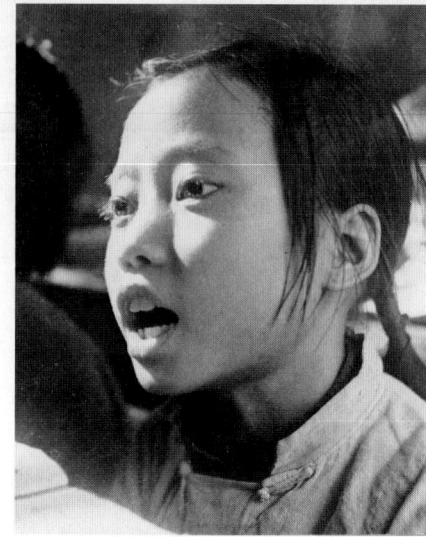

I hated the younger sister, the quiet one.

Normal Chinese women's voices are strong and bossy. We American-Chinese girls had to whisper to make ourselves American-feminine. Apparently we whispered even more softly than the Americans. Once a year the teachers referred my sister and me to speech therapy, but our voices would straighten out, unpredictably normal, for the therapists. Some of us gave up, shook our heads, and said nothing, not one word. Some of us could not even shake our heads. At times shaking my head no is more self-assertion than I can manage. Most of us eventually found some voice, however <u>faltering</u>. We invented an American-feminine speaking personality, except for that one girl who could not speak up even in Chinese school.

She was a year older than I and was in my class for twelve years. During all those years she read aloud but would not talk. Her older sister was usually beside her; their parents kept the older daughter back to protect the younger one. They were six and seven years old when they began school. Although I had flunked kindergarten, I was the same age as most other students in our class; my parents had probably lied about my age, so I had had a head start and came out even. My younger sister was in the class below me; we were normal ages and normally separated. The parents of the quiet girl, on

> **fal · ter · ing** (fäl´ tər iŋ) *adj.,* unsteady; wavering

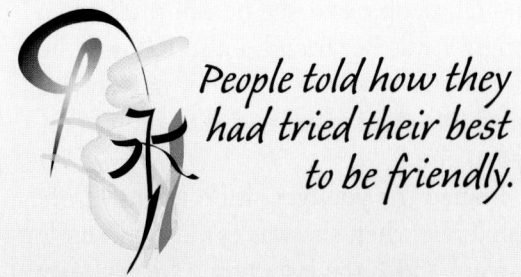

the other hand, protected both daughters. When it sprinkled, they kept them home from school. The girls did not work for a living the way we did. But in other ways we were the same.

We were similar in sports. We held the bat on our shoulders until we walked to first base. (You got a strike only when you actually struck at the ball.) Sometimes the pitcher wouldn't bother to throw to us. "Automatic walk," the other children would call, sending us on our way. By fourth or fifth grade, though, some of us would try to hit the ball. "Easy out," the other kids would say. I hit the ball a couple of times. Baseball was nice in that there was a definite spot to run to after hitting the ball. Basketball confused me because when I caught the ball I didn't know whom to throw it to. "Me. Me," the kids would be yelling. "Over here." Suddenly it would occur to me I hadn't memorized which ghosts[1] were on my team and which were on the other. When the kids said, "Automatic walk," the girl who was quieter than I kneeled with one end of the bat in

each hand and placed it carefully on the plate. Then she dusted her hands as she walked to first base, where she rubbed her hands softly, fingers spread. She always got tagged out before second base. She would whisper-read but not talk. Her whisper was as soft as if she had no muscles. She seemed to be breathing from a distance. I heard no anger or tension.

> *People told how they had tried their best to be friendly.*

I joined in at lunchtime when the other students, the Chinese too, talked about whether or not she was mute, although obviously she was not if she could read aloud.

---

1. **ghosts.** As a child, Kingston referred to people who were not American Chinese as "ghosts."

People told how *they* had tried *their* best to be friendly. *They* said hello, but if she refused to answer, well, they didn't see why they had to say hello anymore. She had no friends of her own but followed her sister everywhere, although people and she herself probably thought I was her friend. I also followed her sister about, who was fairly normal. She was almost two years older and read more than anyone else.

I hated the younger sister, the quiet one. I hated her when she was the last chosen for her team and I, the last chosen for my team. I hated her for her China doll hair cut. I hated her at music time for the wheezes that came out of her plastic flute.

One afternoon in the sixth grade (that year I was arrogant with talk, not knowing there were going to be high school dances and college seminars to set me back), I and my little

sister and the quiet girl and her big sister stayed late after school for some reason. The cement was cooling, and the tetherball poles made shadows across the gravel. The hooks at the rope ends were clinking against the poles. We shouldn't have been so late; there was laundry work to do and Chinese school to get to by 5:00. The last time we had stayed late, my mother had phoned the police and told them we had been kidnapped by bandits. The radio stations broadcast our descriptions. I had to get home before she did that again. But sometimes if you loitered long enough in the schoolyard, the other children would have gone home and you could play with the equipment before the office took it away. We were chasing one another through the playground and in and out of the basement, where the playroom and lavatory were. During air raid drills (it was during the Korean War, which you knew about because every day the front page of the newspaper printed a map of Korea with the top part red and going up and down like a window shade), we curled up in this basement. Now everyone was gone. The playroom was army green and had nothing in it but a long trough with drinking spigots in rows. Pipes across the ceiling led to the drinking fountains and to the toilets in the next room. When someone flushed you could hear the water and other matter, which the children named, running inside the big pipe above the drinking spigots. There was one playroom for girls next to the girls' lavatory and one playroom for boys next to the boys' lavatory. The stalls were open and the toilets had no lids, by which we knew that ghosts have no sense of shame or privacy.

Inside the playroom the lightbulbs in cages had already been turned off. Daylight came in x-patterns through the caging at the windows. I looked out and, seeing no one in the schoolyard, ran outside to climb the fire escape upside down, hanging on to the metal stairs with fingers and toes.

I did a flip off the fire escape and ran across the schoolyard. The day was a great eye, and it was not paying much attention to me now. I could disappear with the sun; I could turn quickly sideways and slip into a different world. It seemed I could run faster at this time, and by evening I would be able to fly. As the afternoon wore on we could run into the forbidden places—the boys' big yard, the boys' playroom. We could go into the boys' lavatory and look at the urinals. The only time during school hours I had crossed the boys' yard was when a flatbed truck with a giant thing covered with canvas and tied down with ropes had parked across the street. The children had told one another that it was a gorilla in captivity; we couldn't decide whether the sign said "Trail of the Gorilla" or "Trial of the Gorilla." The thing was as big as a house. The teachers couldn't stop us from hysterically rushing to the fence and clinging to the wire mesh. Now I ran across the boys' yard clear to the Cyclone fence and thought about the hair that I had seen sticking out of the canvas. It was going to be summer soon, so you could feel that freedom coming on too.

I ran back into the girls' yard, and there was the quiet sister all by herself. I ran past her, and she followed me into the girls' lavatory. My footsteps rang hard against cement and tile because of the taps I had nailed into my shoes. Her footsteps were soft, padding after me. There was no one in the lavatory but the two of us. I ran all around the rows of twenty-five open stalls to make sure of that. No sisters. I think we must have been playing hide-and-go-seek. She was not good at hiding by herself and usually followed her sister; they'd hide in the same place. They must have gotten separated. In this growing twilight, a child could hide and never be found.

I stopped abruptly in front of the sinks, and she came running toward me before she could stop herself, so that she almost collided with me. I walked closer. She backed away, puzzlement, then alarm in her eyes.

"You're going to talk," I said, my voice steady and normal, as it is when talking to the familiar, the weak, and the small. "I am going to make you talk, you sissy-girl." She stopped backing away and stood fixed.

She came running toward me before she could stop herself, so that she almost collided with me.

I looked into her face so I could hate it close up. She wore black bangs, and her cheeks were pink and white. She was baby soft. I thought that I could put my thumb on her nose and push it bonelessly in, indent her face. I could poke dimples into her cheeks. I could work her face around like dough. She stood still, and I did not want to look at her face anymore; I hated fragility. I walked around her, looked her up and down the way the Mexican and Negro girls did when they fought, so tough. I hated her weak neck, the way it did not support her head but let it droop; her head would fall backward. I stared at the curve of her nape. I wished I was able to see what my own neck looked like from the back and sides. I hoped it did not look like hers; I wanted a stout neck. I grew my hair long to hide it in case it was a flower-stem neck. I walked around to the front of her to hate her face some more.

I reached up and took the fatty part of her cheek, not dough, but meat, between my thumb and finger. This close, and I saw no pores. "Talk," I said. "Are you going to talk?" Her skin was fleshy, like squid out of which the glassy blades of bones had been pulled. I wanted tough skin, hard brown skin. I had callused my hands; I had scratched dirt to blacken the nails, which I cut straight across to make stubby fingers. I gave her face a squeeze. "Talk." When I let go, the pink rushed back into my white thumbprint on her skin. I walked around to her side. "Talk!" I shouted

Chinatowns

When the Chinese first began immigrating to different parts of the globe, they often encountered hostility toward their traditional cultural practices. In many cases, local authorities forced Chinese immigrants to live in subsections of their cities, creating communities called *Chinatowns*.

The first Chinatown was founded when the Ming Dynasty fell in the mid-1600s. Ming supporters fled to Nagasaki, Japan, and established a Chinese community that still thrives today. In the mid-1800s, the Chinese began immigrating to San Francisco during the California gold rush and established one of the most famous Chinatowns in the world. Other large Chinatowns exist in Bangkok, Thailand; Casablanca, Morocco; Paris, France; Sydney, Australia; and New York City and Las Vegas in the United States.

The entrance to a Chinatown usually is designated with a large gateway, or *paifang*. In many cases, the Chinese government has donated the *paifang* to support the local Chinese community. Another well-known feature of Chinatowns is the abundance and variety of food. Restaurants feature traditional regional cuisines, such as Cantonese, Hunan, and Szechuan, along with more Westernized dishes such as chop suey and chow mein.

Extensive Chinatown markets feature food, as well, often specializing in Asian teas, spices, aquatic life, and other items that may not be available outside China.

The Chinese New Year is celebrated in Chinatowns with festive parades, during which participants set off fireworks and gather under colorful lion and dragon puppets. For outsiders, events like these allow them to experience particular aspects of Chinese culture.

into the side of her head. Her straight hair hung, the same all these years, no ringlets or braids or permanents. I squeezed her other cheek. "Are you? Huh? Are you going to talk?" She tried to shake her head, but I had hold of her face. She had no muscles to jerk away. Her skin seemed to stretch. I let go in horror. What if it came away in my hand? "No, huh?" I said, rubbing the touch of her off my fingers. "Say 'No,' then," I said. I gave her another pinch and a twist. "Say 'No.'" She shook her head, her straight hair turning with her head, not swinging side to side like the pretty girls'. She was so neat. Her neatness bothered me. I hated the way she folded the wax paper from her lunch; she did not wad her brown paper bag and her

school papers. I hated her clothes—the blue pastel cardigan, the white blouse with the collar that lay flat over the cardigan, the homemade flat, cotton skirt she wore when everybody else was wearing flared skirts. I hated pastels; I would wear black always. I squeezed again, harder, even though her cheek had a weak rubbery feeling I did not like. I squeezed one cheek, then the other, back and forth until the tears ran out of her eyes as if I had pulled them out. "Stop crying," I said, but although she habitually followed me around, she did not obey. Her eyes dripped; her nose dripped. She wiped her eyes with her papery fingers. The skin on her hands and arms seemed powdery-dry, like tracing paper, onion skin. I hated her fingers. I could snap them like breadsticks. I pushed her hands down. "Say 'Hi,'" I said. "'Hi.' Like that. Say your name. Go ahead. Say it. Or are you stupid? You're so stupid, you don't know your own name, is that it? When I say, 'What's your name?' you just blurt it out, o.k.? What's your name?" Last year the whole class had laughed at a boy who couldn't fill out a form because he didn't know his father's name. The teacher sighed, exasperated, and was very sarcastic, "Don't you notice things? What does your mother call him?" she said. The class laughed at how dumb he was not to notice things. "She calls him father of me," he said. Even we laughed, although we knew that his mother did not call his father by name, and a son does not know his father's name. We laughed and were relieved that our parents had had the foresight to tell us some names we could give the teachers. "If you're not stupid," I said to the quiet girl, "what's your name?" She shook her head, and some hair caught in the tears; wet black hair stuck to the side of the pink and white face. I reached up (she was taller than I) and took a strand of hair. I pulled it. "Well, then, let's honk your hair," I said. "Honk. Honk." Then I pulled the other side— "ho-o-n-k"—a long pull; "ho-o-n-n-k"—a longer pull. I could see her little white ears, like white cutworms curled underneath the hair. "Talk!" I yelled into each cutworm.

I looked right at her. "I know you talk," I said. "I've heard you." Her eyebrows flew up. Something in those black eyes was startled, and I pursued it. "I was walking past your house when you didn't know I was there. I heard you yell in English and in Chinese. You weren't just talking. You were shouting. I heard you shout. You were saying, 'Where are you?' Say that again. Go ahead, just the way you did at home." I yanked harder on the hair, but steadily, not jerking. I did not want to pull it out. "Go ahead. Say, 'Where are you?' Say it loud enough for your sister to come. Call her. Make her come help you. Call her name. I'll stop if she comes. So call. Go ahead."

She shook her head, her mouth curved down, crying. I could see her tiny white teeth, baby teeth. I wanted to grow big strong yellow teeth. "You do have a tongue," I said. "So use it." I pulled the hair at her temples, pulled the tears out of her eyes. "Say, 'Ow,'" I said. "Just 'Ow.' Say, 'Let go.' Go ahead. Say it. I'll honk you again if you don't say, 'Let me alone.' Say, 'Leave me alone,' and I'll let you go. I will. I'll let go if you say it. You can stop this anytime you want to, you know. All you have to do is tell me to stop. Just say, 'Stop.' You're just asking for it, aren't you? You're just asking for another honk. Well then, I'll have to give you another honk. Say, 'Stop.'" But she didn't. I had to pull again and again.

Sounds did come out of her mouth, sobs, chokes, noises that were almost words. Snot ran out of her nose. She tried to wipe it on her hands, but there was too much of it. She used her sleeve. "You're disgusting," I told her. "Look at you, snot streaming down your nose, and you won't say a word to stop it. You're such a nothing." I moved behind her and pulled the hair growing out of her weak neck. I let go. I stood silent for a long time. Then I screamed, "Talk!" I would scare the words out of her. If she had had little bound feet, the toes twisted under the balls, I would have jumped up and landed on them—crunch!—stomped on them with my iron shoes. She cried hard, sobbing aloud. "Cry, 'Mama,'" I said. "Come on. Cry, 'Mama.' Say, 'Stop it.'"

I put my finger on her pointed chin. "I don't like you. I don't like the weak little toots you make on your flute. Wheeze. Wheeze. I don't like the way you don't swing at the

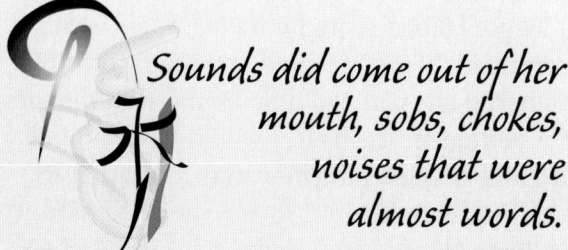

ball. I don't like the way you're the last one chosen. I don't like the way you can't make a fist for tetherball. Why don't you make a fist?

Sounds did come out of her mouth, sobs, chokes, noises that were almost words.

Come on. Get tough. Come on. Throw fists." I pushed at her long hands; they swung limply at her sides. Her fingers were so long, I thought maybe they had an extra joint. They couldn't

possibly make fists like other people's. "Make a fist," I said. "Come on. Just fold those fingers up; fingers on the inside, thumbs on the outside. Say something. Honk me back. You're so tall, and you let me pick on you.

"Would you like a hanky? I can't get you one with embroidery on it or crocheting along the edges, but I'll get you some toilet paper if you tell me to. Go ahead. Ask me. I'll get it for you if you ask." She did not stop crying. "Why don't you scream, 'Help'?" I suggested. "Say, 'Help.' Go ahead." She cried on. "O.K. O.K. Don't talk. Just scream, and I'll let you go. Won't that feel good? Go ahead. Like this." I screamed, not too loudly. My voice hit the tile and rang it as if I had thrown a rock at it.

The stalls opened wider and the toilets wider and darker. Shadows leaned at angles I had not seen before. It was very late. Maybe a janitor had locked me in with this girl for the night. Her black eyes blinked and stared, blinked and stared. I felt dizzy from hunger. We had been in this lavatory together forever. My mother would call the police again if I didn't bring my sister home soon. "I'll let you go if you say just one word," I said. "You can even say, 'a' or 'the,' and I'll let you go. Come on. Please." She didn't shake her head anymore, only cried steadily, so much water coming out of her. I could see the two duct holes where the tears welled out. Quarts of tears but no words. I grabbed her by the shoulder. I could feel bones. The light was coming in queerly through the frosted glass with the chicken wire embedded in it. Her crying was like an animal's—a seal's—and it echoed around the basement. "Do you want to stay here all night?" I asked. "Your mother is wondering what happened to her baby. You wouldn't want to have her mad at you. You'd better say something." I shook her shoulder. I pulled her hair again. I squeezed her face. "Come on! Talk! Talk! Talk!" She didn't seem to feel it anymore when I pulled her hair. "There's nobody here but you and me. This isn't a classroom or a playground or a crowd. I'm just one person. You can talk in front of one person. Don't make me pull harder and harder until you talk." But her hair seemed to stretch; she did not say a word. "I'm going to pull harder. Don't make me pull anymore, or your hair will come out and you're going to be bald. Do you want to be bald? You don't want to be bald, do you?"

Far away, coming from the edge of town, I heard whistles blow. The cannery was changing shifts, letting out the afternoon people, and still we were here at school. It was a sad sound—work done. The air was lonelier after the sound died.

"Why won't you talk?" I started to cry. What if I couldn't stop, and everyone would want to know what happened? "Now look

She didn't seem to feel it anymore when I pulled her hair.

what you've done," I scolded. "You're going to pay for this. I want to know why. And you're going to tell me why. You don't see I'm trying to help you out, do you? Do you want to be like this, dumb (do you know what dumb means?), your whole life? Don't you ever want to be a cheerleader? Or a pompon girl? What are you going to do for a living? Yeah, you're going to have to work because you can't be a housewife. Somebody has to marry you before you can be a housewife. And you, you are a plant. Do you know that? That's all you are if you don't talk. If you don't talk, you can't have a personality. You'll have no personality and no hair. You've got to let people know you have a personality and a brain. You think somebody is going to take care of you all your stupid life? You think you'll always have your big sister? You think somebody's going to marry you, is that it? Well, you're not the type that gets dates, let alone gets married. Nobody's going to notice you. And you have to talk for interviews, speak right up in front of the boss. Don't you know that? You're so dumb. Why do I waste my time on you?" Sniffling and snorting, I couldn't stop crying and talking at the same time. I kept wiping my nose on my arm, my sweater lost somewhere (probably not worn because my mother said to wear a sweater). It seemed as if I had spent my life in that basement, doing the worst thing I had yet done to another person. "I'm doing this for your own good," I said. "Don't you dare tell anyone I've been bad to you. Talk. Please talk."

I was getting dizzy from the air I was gulping. Her sobs and my sobs were bouncing wildly off the tile, sometimes together, sometimes alternating. "I don't understand why you won't say just one word," I cried, clenching my teeth. My knees were shaking, and I hung on to her hair to stand up. Another time I'd stayed too late, I had had to walk around two Negro kids who were bonking each other's head on the concrete. I went back later to see if the concrete had cracks in it. "Look. I'll give you something if you talk. I'll give you my pencil box. I'll buy you some candy. O.K.? What do you want? Tell me. Just say it, and I'll give it to you. Just say, 'yes,' or, 'O.K.,' or, 'Baby Ruth.'" But she didn't want anything.

I had stopped pinching her cheek because I did not like the feel of her skin. I would go crazy if it came away in my hands. "I skinned her," I would have to confess.

Suddenly I heard footsteps hurrying through the basement, and her sister ran into the lavatory calling her name. "Oh, there you are," I said. "We've been waiting for you. I was only trying to teach her to talk. She wouldn't cooperate, though." Her sister went into one of the stalls and got handfuls of toilet paper and wiped her off. Then we found my sister, and we walked home together. "Your family really ought to force her to speak," I advised all the way home. "You mustn't pamper her."

The world is sometimes just, and I spent the next eighteen months sick in bed with a mysterious illness. There was no pain and no symptoms, though the middle line in my left palm broke in two. Instead of starting junior high school, I lived like the Victorian <u>recluses</u> I read about. I had a rented hospital bed in the living room, where I watched soap operas on t.v., and my family cranked me up and down. I saw no one but my family, who took good care of me. I could have no visitors, no other relatives, no villagers. My bed was against the west window, and I watched the seasons change the peach tree. I had a bell to ring for help. I used a bedpan. It was the best year and a half of my life. Nothing happened.

> *The world is sometimes just, and I spent the next eighteen months sick in bed with a mysterious illness.*

But one day my mother, the doctor, said, "You're ready to get up today. It's time to get up and go to school." I walked about outside to get my legs working, leaning on a staff I cut from the peach tree. The sky and trees, the sun were immense—no longer framed by a window, no longer grayed with a fly screen. I sat down on the sidewalk in amazement—the night, the stars. But at school I had to figure out again how to talk. I met again the poor girl I had tormented. She had not changed. She wore the same clothes, hair cut, and manner as when we were in elementary school, no make-up on the pink and white face, while the other Asian girls were starting to tape their eyelids. She continued to be able to read aloud. But there was hardly any reading aloud anymore, less and less as we got into high school.

I was wrong about nobody taking care of her. Her sister became a clerk-typist and stayed unmarried. They lived with their mother and father. She did not have to leave the house except to go to the movies. She was supported. She was protected by her family, as they would normally have done in China if they could have afforded it, not sent off to school with strangers, ghosts, boys. ❖

> **re • cluse** (re´ klüs) *n.,* person who is withdrawn from society

MIRRORS & WINDOWS

As Kingston points out all the things she hates about the silent girl, she also stresses how much she does not want to be like the girl. What does the silent girl represent to the young Kingston? What does the adult Kingston recognize that the child did not?

Refer to Text ▶ ▶ ▶ ▶ ▶   Reason with Text

1a. Instead of speaking in their normal voices, what did the American-Chinese girls do to make themselves "American-feminine"?

1b. Based on how these girls speak, infer how they feel about being Chinese in an American school.

Understand
Find meaning

2a. Explain why Kingston and her sister were not supposed to have been so late to school.

2b. What does the sisters' after-school schedule suggest about some American-Chinese families in California in the 1940s?

Apply
Use information

3a. List Kingston's reasons for hating the silent girl.

3b. What deeper reason or reasons might explain Kingston's hate?

Analyze
Take things apart

4a. How long does Kingston say the afternoon seemed? How does she describe her reaction to her behavior in the basement?

4b. Judge why Kingston treats the girl so cruelly.

Evaluate
Make judgments

5a. How did Kingston spend the next eighteen months?

5b. Write a new ending for the story, in which Kingston attempts to explain her behavior to the girl.

Create
Bring ideas together

Analyze Literature

Motivation and Simile

Why does Kingston hate the girl? Why is she unable to stop harassing her? How does the girl's response (or lack of it) seem to increase Kingston's motivation? Discuss how the vivid description of the incident helps you understand Kingston's motivation.

How is the girl described? What similes are used? How does the use of similes help you understand Kingston's reaction to the girl?

Extend the Text

Writing Options
Creative Writing Imagine you are the silent girl. Write a journal entry describing the incident in the basement. Use vivid details to express your feelings and reactions. Try to use similes to convey your reaction.

Persuasive Writing Kingston says she wanted to make the silent girl talk for her own good. Write a brief response to the writer, supporting or criticizing her explanation. Use evidence from the selection to support your answer. Compare your response with that of a classmate.

Collaborative Learning
Role-Play a Counseling Session With a group of classmates, role-play a counseling session in which Kingston and other characters discuss the incident in the basement. Have students play the roles of Kingston and the silent girl, as well as a school counselor, the girl's parents, and Kingston's parents. After discussing the incident, determine what, if any, punishment Kingston should receive and what counseling the girl might need.

Critical Literacy
Review a Work by a Chinese-American Writer
Read a complete work by a Chinese-American writer (you might choose *The Woman Warrior*), and write a brief review of it for a literary magazine. In your review, address how the author deals with the issues of culture and culture clashes.

 Go to **www.mirrorsandwindows.com** for more.

1. According to Kingston, why do most of the American-Chinese girls whisper?
   A. They are embarrassed by their Chinese accents.
   B. They are unsure of their English-speaking skills.
   C. They do not want to draw attention to themselves.
   D. They want to have feminine voices like the other American girls.
   E. It is considered inappropriate in Chinese culture for girls to speak up.

2. What does Kingston enjoy about staying late after school?
   A. She gets the chance to confront the quiet girl.
   B. She has the freedom to do what she can't do during the school day.
   C. She can use the open toilet stalls with privacy.
   D. If she stays late enough, she can avoid going to Chinese school.
   E. She can hear the sound of the cannery whistle blowing.

3. In the line "Most of us eventually found some voice, however faltering," what does the word *faltering* mean?
   A. full of mistakes
   B. muted
   C. unsteady
   D. harsh
   E. unfamiliar

4. Which of the following statements best explains Kingston's hatred of the quiet girl?
   A. Kingston is active and strong, so she cannot understand why the girl is so quiet and weak.
   B. Kingston resents that the quiet girl does better than she does in school.
   C. Kingston is jealous that the quiet girl's family takes care of her, whereas she (Kingston) must take care of herself and her sister.
   D. Kingston thinks the quiet girl's family is too traditionally Chinese and thus critical of her own American-Chinese family.
   E. Kingston is afraid of being like the quiet girl: weak and unable to fit into American culture.

5. Toward the end of the scene in the bathroom, Kingston tells the quiet girl, "Look, I'll give you something if you talk." Why does she soften her treatment of the girl?
   A. She realizes she has been mean.
   B. She finally has heard the girl talk.
   C. She understands why the girl won't talk.
   D. She is desperate for the confrontation to end but can't back down.
   E. She is afraid that others will find out what she has done.

6. How does Kingston come to the conclusion that "the world is sometimes just"?
   A. Following the incident with the quiet girl, Kingston becomes sick and is bedridden for a long time.
   B. The quiet girl ends up having a comfortable life, despite being bullied by Kingston.
   C. Because the quiet girl does not speak in school, she is held back and ultimately is unsuccessful in life.
   D. School authorities learn about the incident and don't allow Kingston to return to school.
   E. The quiet girl's sister confronts Kingston and makes her ashamed of what she did.

7. What is notable about the fate of the quiet girl?
   A. Her life turned out exactly the way Kingston predicted.
   B. Her life turned out the way it probably would have in China if her parents had had enough money.
   C. She became successful at a job that requires a lot of speaking.
   D. She never was able to stand up to her parents or her sister.
   E. Her life became an example of the American dream.

8. **Constructed Response:** As noted earlier, this excerpt from Kingston's memoir reads very much like a short story. Analyze the plot by identifying the central conflict and discussing how it is developed and resolved. Also discuss the exposition, or background information, and why it is relevant to understanding what happens. Use details from the excerpt to support your analysis.

9. **Constructed Response:** Discuss Kingston's use of the word *normal* in this excerpt. What does she mean by *normal?* Why does she always use this word instead of providing variety, sometimes using *usual* or *typical?* Support your discussion using information from the text.

from **The Way to Rainy Mountain**

A Memoir by N. Scott Momaday

Build Background

Literary Context This nonfiction narrative is from N. Scott Momaday's memoir, **The Way to Rainy Mountain,** which was published in 1969. In this excerpt, Momaday tells the story of his Kiowa ancestors' migration from the mountains of Yellowstone to the Plains of Oklahoma, and he also traces his grandmother's life from childhood to old age. Using lyrical prose to describe the land the Kiowas have inhabited,

the author evokes his ancestral memories. *The Way to Rainy Mountain* also has special significance for Momaday because it was illustrated by his father.

Reader's Context What do you know about your family's history? What connection do you feel to your ancestors?

Meet the Author

N. Scott Momaday (b. 1934) grew up on Kiowa, Navajo, Apache, and Pueblo Indian reservations. His father was an artist, and his mother was a writer who encouraged her only child to write. Both parents taught on the Indian reservation where Momaday learned to live in two different cultures: the microcosm of the reservation and the multicultural world beyond.

After graduating with a bachelor's degree from the University of New Mexico in 1958, Momaday won a poetry fellowship to Stanford University, where he earned a master's degree in 1960 and a doctorate in 1963. He went on to teach writing and literature classes, including a course on American Indian literature, at several prestigious universities, including Columbia, Princeton, and Stanford, his alma mater.

In 1969, Momaday won the Pulitzer Prize for his first novel, *House Made of Dawn,* the story of a young Native American torn between his ancestral roots and twentieth-century mainstream society. His essay "The American Land Ethic," published in 1971, drew attention to Native Americans' tradition of respect for nature. This essay was followed by two volumes of poetry, *Angle of Geese and Other Poems* (1974) and *The Gourd Dancer* (1976). More recent works include *In the Presence of the Sun* (1991), *The Native Americans: Indian Country* (1993), and *In the Bear's House* (1999).

Momaday has devoted his life to teaching and writing about Native American folklore, history, and mythology. Describing his literary success, he has noted, "I simply kept my goal in mind and persisted. Perseverance is a large part of writing."

Analyze Literature

Narration and Description
Narration is a type of writing that tells a story or describes events. Narrative writing usually follows *chronological order,* or the order in which events occurred.

Description is a type of writing that portrays a person, object, or scene. Descriptive writing uses *sensory details:* words and phrases that describe how things look, sound, smell, taste, or feel.

Set Purpose

Momaday's narrative technique is somewhat unique in that he includes several stories within the larger story of his life. As you read, look for this layering of narratives and think about how the stories fit together. Distinguish these narrative passages from the descriptive passages in the memoir. Write down examples of the sensory details Momaday provides, particularly in describing places.

Preview Vocabulary

writhe, 1107
infirm, 1107
disposition, 1107
profusion, 1109
wean, 1109
tenuous, 1109
consummate, 1110
opaque, 1110
enmity, 1111
nocturnal, 1111

Kiowa Funeral, 1930. James Auchiah. California Academy of Sciences, San Francisco, California. (See detail on p. 1105.)

The Way to Rainy Mountain

by N. Scott Momaday

*Your imagination comes to life,
and this, you think,
is where creation was begun.*

A single knoll rises out of the plain in Oklahoma, north and west of the Wichita Range.[1] For my people, the Kiowas, it is an old landmark, and they gave it the name Rainy Mountain. The hardest weather in the world is there. Winter brings blizzards, hot tornadic winds arise in the spring, and in summer the prairie is an anvil's edge. The grass turns brittle and brown, and it cracks beneath your feet. There are green belts along the rivers and creeks, linear groves of hickory and pecan, willow and witch hazel. At a distance in July or

---

1. **Wichita Range.** Mountains in southwest Oklahoma

August the steaming foliage seems almost to writhe in fire. Great green and yellow grasshoppers are everywhere in the tall grass, popping up like corn to sting the flesh, and tortoises crawl about on the red earth, going nowhere in the plenty of time. Loneliness is an aspect of the land. All things in the plain are isolate; there is no confusion of objects in the eye, but *one* hill or *one* tree or *one* man. To look upon that landscape in the early morning, with the sun at your back, is to lose the sense of proportion. Your imagination comes to life, and this, you think, is where Creation was begun.

I returned to Rainy Mountain in July. My grandmother had died in the spring, and I wanted to be at her grave. She had lived to be very old and at last infirm. Her only living daughter was with her when she died, and I was told that in death her face was that of a child.

When she was born, the Kiowas were living the last great moment of their history.

I like to think of her as a child. When she was born, the Kiowas were living the last great moment of their history. For more than a hundred years they had controlled the open range from the Smoky Hill River to the Red, from the headwaters of the Canadian to the fork of the Arkansas and Cimarron.[2] In alliance with the Comanches,[3] they had ruled the whole of the southern Plains. War was their sacred business, and they were among the finest horsemen the world has ever known. But warfare for the Kiowas was preeminently a matter of disposition rather than of survival, and they never understood the grim, unrelenting advance of the U.S. Cavalry. When at last, divided and ill-provisioned, they were driven onto the Staked Plains[4] in the cold rains of autumn, they fell into panic.

In Palo Duro Canyon they abandoned their crucial stores to pillage[5] and had nothing then but their lives. In order to save themselves, they surrendered to the soldiers at Fort Sill and were imprisoned in the old stone corral that now stands as a military museum. My grandmother was spared the humiliation of those high gray walls by eight or ten years, but she must have known from birth the affliction of defeat, the dark brooding of old warriors.

Her name was Aho, and she belonged to the last culture to evolve in North America. Her forebears came down from the high country in western Montana nearly three centuries ago. They were a mountain people, a mysterious tribe of hunters whose language has never been positively classified in any major group. In the late seventeenth century they began a long migration to the south and east. It was a journey toward the dawn, and it led to a golden age. Along the way the Kiowas were befriended by the Crows,[6] who gave them the culture and religion of the Plains. They acquired horses, and their ancient nomadic spirit was suddenly free of the ground. They acquired Taime, the sacred Sun Dance doll, from that moment the object and symbol of their worship, and so shared in the divinity of the sun. Not least, they acquired the sense of destiny, therefore courage and pride. When they entered upon the southern Plains they had been transformed. No longer were they slaves to the simple necessity of survival; they were a lordly and dangerous society of fighters and thieves, hunters and priests of the sun. According to their origin

---

2. **Arkansas and Cimarron.** Two rivers that join in northeast Oklahoma
3. **Comanches.** Native peoples of the plains
4. **Staked Plains.** Plateau region in southeast New Mexico and west Texas
5. **pillage.** Something taken during looting or plundering, especially in war
6. **Crows.** Native peoples who lived between the Platte and the Yellowstone rivers

---

writhe (rīth) *v.*, twist as if struggling or in pain
in • firm (in furm´) *adj.*, feeble from age; sick
dis • po • si • tion (dis' pō zi´ shən) *n.*, general nature or character

James Auchiah

James Auchiah (1906–1974), a Kiowa artist, was born near Medicine Park, Oklahoma. The grandson of a medicine man and artist, he became interested in Kiowa mythology at an early age. This led to his eagerly exploring native legends and practicing painting them on canvas.

As Auchiah's artistic skills developed, he attracted attention from local art schools and galleries. Interest in Kiowa art grew, and others in the community were encouraged to develop their talents. By the 1920s, five Kiowa artists had attracted national attention, and their work was exhibited by the American Federation of Arts. The so-called Kiowa Five combined the Kiowa pictorial tradition with European methods of painting. Ironically, some museums that collected Native American artifacts rejected these artists' work, labeling it "unauthentic." Others saw Auchiah and his fellow artists as creating a modern Native American style.

As the last of the Kiowa Five, Auchiah exhibited his work widely around the United States and the world. He also was commissioned to paint

murals in public places, including several for the Public Works of Art project during the Great Depression. Auchiah returned to Oklahoma in 1940 to teach at the Riverside Indian School, where he encouraged students to celebrate their Kiowa heritage.

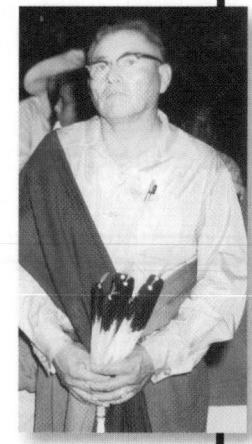

Critical Viewing Return to page 1106 and view *Kiowa Funeral* (1930), one of Auchiah's most famous paintings. Compare it to the Native American work of art on page 450 in Unit 4, *Battle of Little Big Horn* (c. 1890–1900), by Kicking Bear. What similarities and differences do you see between the works? What aspects of Auchiah's painting seem more European in style? Does this style difference compromise the authenticity of Auchiah's work? Why or why not?

---

myth, they entered the world through a hollow log. From one point of view, their migration was the fruit of an old prophecy, for indeed they emerged from a sunless world.

> **The immense landscape of the continental interior lay like memory in her blood.**

Although my grandmother lived out her long life in the shadow of Rainy Mountain, the immense landscape of the continental interior lay like memory in her blood. She could tell of the Crows, whom she had never seen, and of the Black Hills,[7] where she had never been. I wanted to see in reality what she had seen more perfectly in the mind's eye, and traveled fifteen hundred miles to begin my pilgrimage.

Yellowstone,[8] it seemed to me, was the top of the world, a region of deep lakes and dark timber, canyons and waterfalls. But, beautiful as it is, one might have the sense of confinement there. The skyline in all directions is close at hand, the high wall of the woods and deep cleavages of shade. There is a perfect freedom in the mountains, but it belongs to the eagle and the elk, the badger and the bear. The Kiowas reckoned their stature by the distance they could see, and they were bent and blind in the wilderness.

Descending eastward, the highland meadows are a stairway to the plain. In July the inland slope of the Rockies is luxuriant with

---

7. **Black Hills.** Mountains in South Dakota and Wyoming
8. **Yellowstone.** National park in Wyoming. The name is credited to the native peoples who lived in the area; the Yellowstone River has high cliffs of yellow rock in the northern area of the modern-day park.

flax and buckwheat, stonecrop and larkspur. The earth unfolds and the limit of the land recedes. Clusters of trees, and animals grazing far in the distance, cause the vision to reach away and wonder to build upon the mind. The sun follows a longer course in the day, and the sky is immense beyond all comparison. The great billowing clouds that sail upon it are the shadows that move upon the grain like water, dividing light. Farther down, in the land of the Crows and Blackfeet,[9] the plain is yellow. Sweet clover takes hold of the hills and bends upon itself to cover and seal the soil. There the Kiowas paused on their way; they had come to the place where they must change their lives. The sun is at home on the plains. Precisely there does it have the certain character of a god. When the Kiowas came to the land of the Crows, they could see the dark lees[10] of the hills at dawn across the Bighorn River,[11] the <u>profusion</u> of light on the grain shelves, the oldest deity ranging after the solstices.[12] Not yet would they veer southward to the caldron of the land that lay below; they must <u>wean</u> their blood from the northern winter and hold the mountains a while longer in their view. They bore Tai-me in procession to the east.

A dark mist lay over the Black Hills, and the land was like iron. At the top of a ridge I caught sight of Devil's Tower upthrust against the gray sky as if in the birth of time the core of the earth had broken through its crust and the motion of the world was begun. There are things in nature that engender an awful quiet in the heart of man; Devil's Tower is one of them. Two centuries ago, because they could not do otherwise, the Kiowas made a legend at the base of the rock. My grandmother said: *Eight children were there at play, seven sisters and their brother. Suddenly the boy was struck dumb; he trembled and began to run upon his hands and feet. His fingers became claws, and his body was covered with fur. Directly there was a bear where the boy had been. The sisters were terrified; they ran, and the bear after them. They came to the stump of a great tree, and the tree spoke to them.*

Devil's Tower, Wyoming.

It bade them climb upon it, and as they did so it began to rise into the air. The bear came to kill them, but they were just beyond its reach. It reared against the tree and scored the bark all around with its claws. The seven sisters were borne into the sky, and they became the stars of the Big Dipper.[13] From that moment, and so long as the legend lives, the Kiowas have kinsmen in the night sky. Whatever they were in the mountains, they could be no more. However <u>tenuous</u> their well-being, however much they had suffered and would suffer again, they had found a way out of the wilderness.

My grandmother had a reverence for the sun, a holy regard that now is all but gone out of mankind. There was a wariness in her, and an ancient awe. She was a Christian in her later years, but she had come a long way about, and she never forgot her birthright. As a child she had been to the Sun Dances; she had taken part in those annual rites, and by them she

---

9. **Blackfeet.** Native American confederacy of the Montana, Alberta, and Saskatchewan peoples
10. **lees.** Sheltered sides
11. **Bighorn River.** Waterway in northern Wyoming and southeastern Montana that flows north into the Yellowstone River
12. **solstices.** Times when events based on the position of the sun in summer cause the longest day and in winter the shortest day
13. **Big Dipper.** Seven main stars of the constellation Ursa Major, the "big bear," which form a shape like a dipper (water scooper)

---

pro • fu • sion (prō fyü´ zhən) *n.,* great quantity; abundance
wean (wēn) *v.,* free from dependence or custom
ten • u • ous (ten´ yü əs) *adj.,* flimsy; weak

had learned the restoration of her people in the presence of Tai-me. She was about seven when the last Kiowa Sun Dance was held in 1887 on the Washita River above Rainy Mountain Creek. The buffalo were gone. In order to <u>consummate</u> the ancient sacrifice—to impale the head of a buffalo bull upon the medicine tree—a delegation of old men journeyed into Texas, there to beg and barter for an animal from the Goodnight herd. She was ten when the Kiowas came together for the last time as a living Sun Dance culture. They could find no buffalo; they had to hang an old hide from the sacred tree. Before the dance could begin, a company of soldiers rode out from Fort Sill under orders to disperse the tribe. Forbidden without cause the essential act of their faith, having seen the wild herds slaughtered and left to rot upon the ground, the Kiowas backed away forever from the medicine tree. That was July 20, 1890, at the great bend of the Washita. My grandmother was there. Without bitterness, and for as long as she lived, she bore a vision of deicide.[14]

> # I never understood her prayers, but there was something inherently sad in the sound.

Now that I can have her only in memory, I see my grandmother in the several postures that were peculiar to her: standing at the wood stove on a winter morning and turning meat in a great iron skillet; sitting at the south window, bent above her beadwork, and afterwards, when her vision failed, looking down for a long time into the fold of her hands; going out upon a cane, very slowly as she did when the weight of age came upon her; praying. I remember her most often at prayer. She made long, rambling prayers out of suffering and hope, having seen many things. I was never sure that I had the right to hear, so exclusive were they of all mere custom and company. The last time I saw her she prayed standing by the side of her bed at night, naked

to the waist, the light of a kerosene lamp moving upon her dark skin. Her long, black hair, always drawn and braided in the day, lay upon her shoulders and against her breasts like a shawl. I do not speak Kiowa, and I never understood her prayers, but there was something inherently sad in the sound, some merest hesitation upon the syllables of sorrow. She began in a high and descending pitch, exhausting her breath to silence; then again and again—and always the same intensity of effort, of something that is, and is not, like urgency in the human voice. Transported so in the dancing light among the shadows of her room, she seemed beyond the reach of time. But that was illusion; I think I knew then that I should not see her again.

Houses are like sentinels in the plain, old keepers of the weather watch. There, in a very little while, wood takes on the appearance of great age. All colors wear soon away in the wind and rain, and then the wood is burned gray and the grain appears and the nails turn red with rust. The windowpanes are black and <u>opaque</u>; you imagine there is nothing within, and indeed there are many ghosts, bones given up to the land. They stand here and there against the sky, and you approach them for a longer time than you expect. They belong in the distance; it is their domain.

Once there was a lot of sound in my grandmother's house, a lot of coming and going, feasting and talk. The summers there were full of excitement and reunion. The Kiowas are a summer people; they abide the cold and keep to themselves, but when the season turns and the land becomes warm and vital they cannot hold still; an old love of going returns upon them. The aged visitors who came to my grandmother's house when I was a child were made of lean and leather, and they bore themselves

---

14. **deicide.** Act of killing a divine being or god

> **con • sum • mate** (kän´ sü māt) v., complete; finish
> **opaque** (ō pāk´) adj., not admitting light

A Kiowa named Elk Tongue with his daughter, A-ke-a (c. 1891).

upright. They wore great black hats and bright ample shirts that shook in the wind. They rubbed fat upon their hair and wound their braids with strips of colored cloth. Some of them painted their faces and carried the scars of old and cherished <u>enmities</u>. They were an old council of warlords, come to remind and be reminded of who they were. Their wives and daughters served them well. The women might indulge themselves; gossip was at once the mark and compensation of their servitude. They made loud and elaborate talk among themselves, full of jest and gesture, fright and false alarm. They went abroad in fringed and flowered shawls, bright beadwork and German silver. They were at home in the kitchen, and they prepared meals that were banquets.

There were frequent prayer meetings, and great <u>nocturnal</u> feasts. When I was a child I played with my cousins outside, where the lamplight fell upon the ground and the singing of the old people rose up around us and carried away into the darkness. There were a lot of good things to eat, a lot of laughter and surprise. And afterwards, when the quiet returned, I lay down with my grandmother and could hear the frogs away by the river and feel the motion of the air.

Now there is a funeral silence in the rooms, the endless wake of some final word. The walls have closed in upon my grandmother's house. When I returned to it in mourning, I saw for the first time in my life how small it was. It was late at night, and there was a white moon, nearly full. I sat for a long time on the stone steps by the kitchen door. From there I could see out across the land; I could see the long row of trees by the creek, the low light upon the rolling plains, and the stars of the Big Dipper. Once I looked at the moon and caught sight of a strange thing. A cricket had perched upon the handrail, only a few inches away from me. My line of vision was such that the creature filled the moon like a fossil. It had gone there, I thought, to live and die, for there, of all places, was its small definition made whole and eternal. A warm wind rose up and purled like the longing within me.

The next morning I awoke at dawn and went out on the dirt road to Rainy Mountain. It was already hot, and the grasshoppers began to fill the air. Still, it was early in the morning, and the birds sang out of the shadows. The long yellow grass on the mountain shone in the bright light, and a scissortail hied above the land. There, where it ought to be, at the end of a long and legendary way, was my grandmother's grave. Here and there on the dark stones were ancestral names. Looking back once, I saw the mountain and came away. ❖

en • mi • ty (en´ mi tē) *n.*, active and usually mutual hatred or ill will

noc • tur • nal (nôk tʉr´ nəl) *adj.*, of, relating to, or occurring at night

MIRRORS & WINDOWS

Momaday describes his people's ancestral lands with great reverence and affection. Think of a place that has special meaning for your family. What is its history? Why is it special?

Refer to Text ▶ ▶ ▶ ▶ ▶ Reason with Text

1a. What event occurred about ten years before Aho was born? What does Momaday think she must have experienced despite having missed this event?

1b. What significance does the Fort Still imprisonment have for Momaday?

Understand
Find meaning

2a. From where did Aho's forebears come some three hundred years ago?

2b. According to Momaday, why did the Kiowas descend from the mountains? Why did the sun have such an impact on them?

Apply
Use information

3a. Where is Aho's grave?

3b. Suggest why this location is appropriate.

Analyze
Take things apart

4a. What, in particular, does the narrator remember his grandmother doing?

4b. Interpret why Momaday was impressed with his grandmother's spirituality and reverence.

Evaluate
Make judgments

5a. What natural occurrence is explained by the legend or myth at the base of Devil's Tower?

5b. Summarize why myths such as this are significant to Native American peoples.

Create
Bring ideas together

Analyze Literature

Narration and Description

What different stories did you identify within the larger story of the memoir? How do these narratives fit together? How do they help you understand the experience of the Kiowas and other native peoples?

Reread the first paragraph, and write down the sensory details it contains. Why is it important for readers to visualize this place? Where else does Momaday use descriptive writing? How would the memoir be different without these highly descriptive passages?

Extend the Text

Writing Options
Creative Writing Create a brief myth of your own that explains how a natural object or event came to be. Imagine that you will read the myth aloud to a group of elementary school children, so choose language and style appropriate to your audience.

Expository Writing Through the use of vivid description, Momaday aims to make readers feel as though they are on Rainy Mountain. Write an essay in which you evaluate the effectiveness of the author's descriptions. Use details from the selection to support your evaluation.

Collaborative Learning
Develop an Anthology of Creation Myths Working with a partner or in a group, find four Native American *creation myths*, traditional stories that explain how

the world came to be. Choose myths from several Native American groups, such as those mentioned in Momaday's memoir and also in Unit 2 of this book. Compile the myths in a handmade book to share with classmates or others.

Lifelong Learning
Display Images of Native American Arts and Crafts Collect images of Native American pottery, weaving, and other artifacts from the Internet or books on Native American arts and crafts. (Be sure that reproduction or downloading of images is legal, and give credit to photographers and others.) Assemble the images you locate, and write a brief explanation of each artifact's origin and purpose.

 Go to **www.mirrorsandwindows.com** for more.

Understand the Concept

As noted elsewhere, English has borrowed words from many other languages, reflecting centuries of historical events and cultural influences. American English has borrowed heavily from the languages of Native American peoples, particularly a family of languages called *Algonquian*. Comprising about thirty different native languages, the Algonquian languages were spoken by Native Americans from the eastern United States across the Great Plains to the Rocky Mountains and into southern and eastern Canada.

These Native American peoples were the first to make contact with the Europeans who came to North America. Thus, many of the words incorporated from Native American languages refer to plants, animals, and foods that were unfamiliar to European settlers. The words *pecan* and *hickory*, which appear in *The Way to Rainy Mountain*, are examples. *Pecan* is a blend from French and the language of the Illinois tribe, and *hickory* is from the Virginia Algonquian group. Today, about one hundred fifty Algonquian words are in general use in the English language.

Some of the most common borrowed Native American words are place names. European settlers readily adopted the names of local lakes, rivers, ponds, and creeks. Four of the five Great Lakes have Native American names (*Lake Superior* is French), as do the United States' two largest rivers, the *Mississippi* and the *Missouri*. In fact, twenty-eight of the fifty U.S. states derive their names from Native American words. Eight of these names are Algonquian in origin: *Connecticut, Massachusetts, Illinois, Michigan, Mississippi, Missouri, Wisconsin,* and *Wyoming*.

Apply the Skill

Exercise A

Each of the following words comes from a Native American language. Use a dictionary or online source to learn more about the *etymology*, or origin, of each term. Identify which Native American language the word comes from and whether the word entered English through another language, such as Spanish or French. Be sure you know what each word means.

1. bayou
2. chipmunk
3. Michigan
4. moccasin
5. moose
6. Oklahoma
7. skunk
8. succotash
9. Tennessee
10. tomato

Exercise B

Make lists of the foods you have eaten at three meals this week (three lists in all). If you can, include information on how the foods were prepared (barbecued, grilled, sautéed, etc.). Look up the etymology of each food item and cooking method to see if it is a borrowed word.

SPELLING PRACTICE

Silent Letters

Silent letters can pose a problem in spelling unless you are familiar with the word or can recognize a common form. For instance, if you know that the *b* in the word *comb* is silent, then you will know how to pronounce *lamb* when you see it and may be able to remember to spell it with the silent letter. Group these words from *The Way to Rainy Mountain* according to the patterns of silent letters.

although	exhausting
autumn	fighters
bright	ought
business	slaughtered
caught	weight
climb	whole
daughter	whose
dumb	writhe

Hunger in New York City

A Lyric Poem by Simon Ortiz

Build Background

Cultural Context The poem **"Hunger in New York City,"** by Simon Ortiz, first appeared in *Pembroke Magazine* and later was published in a collection of poetry called *Going for the Rain* (1976). The poem explores the different types of hunger, or longing, experienced by a Native American far from his homeland.

Much of Ortiz's work addresses the ancient oral traditions of the Acoma tribe, which he learned at an early age. He once commented, "This early language from birth to six years of age in the Acoma family and community was the basis and source of all I would do later in poetry, short fiction, essay, and other work."

Reader's Context How can the word *hunger* mean more than the physical need or desire for food?

Meet the Author

Simon Ortiz (b. 1941) grew up in McCartys, an Acoma Pueblo village in New Mexico. There, he listened to Native American storytellers and learned to speak the Acoma dialect. As a youth, he attended an Indian boarding school, where he was forced to learn English to assimilate to the mainstream white culture. Ortiz turned to writing to alleviate his frustration in straddling two different cultures. He published his first poem in a school newspaper when he was eleven, and by the time he reached high school, he was determined to become a writer.

After graduating from high school, Ortiz worked briefly in the mining industry and then attended Fort Lewis College. He left to serve in the army for three years and then resumed his education at the University of New Mexico, earning his undergraduate degree in 1968. Ortiz attended the esteemed Writers' Workshop at the University of Iowa and received his master of fine arts degree in 1969. He went on to teach writing and Native American literature at several colleges, including his alma mater, the University of New Mexico. He currently is a professor at the University of Toronto in Ontario, Canada.

Regarded as one of the United States' most important Native American poets, Ortiz has been honored with several awards, including a Lifetime Achievement Award from the Native Writer's Circle of the Americas (1993). His poetry collections include *Going for the Rain* (1976), *A Good Journey* (1977), and *Fight Back* (1980). *Fightin': New and Collected Stories* was published in 1983.

Analyze Literature

Metaphor and Repetition
A **metaphor** is a figure of speech in which one thing is spoken or written about as if it were another. This figure of speech invites the reader to make a comparison between the writer's actual subject, the *tenor* of the metaphor, and another thing to which the subject is likened, the *vehicle* of the metaphor.

Repetition is a writer's intentional reuse of a sound, word, phrase, or sentence. Writers often use repetition to emphasize ideas or create a musical effect.

Set Purpose

One of the themes running through Native American literature is the sanctity of ancestral traditions and the obstacles native peoples face in preserving their ways of life. As you read, consider how Ortiz expresses that theme in "Hunger in New York City." What metaphor does he use to represent the longing for those traditions and ways of life? Also examine Ortiz's use of repetition. Write down examples of repeated words and phrases, and think about Ortiz's purpose in using them.

Hunger in New York City

by Simon Ortiz

Hunger crawls into you
from somewhere out of your muscles
or the concrete or the land
or the wind pushing you

5 It comes to you, asking
for food, words, wisdom, young memories
of places you ate at, drank cold spring water,
or held somebody's hand,
or home of the gentle, slow dances,
10 the songs, the strong gods, the world
you know.

That is, hunger searches you out.
It always asks you,
How are you, son? Where are you?
15 Have you eaten well?
Have you done what you as a person
of our people is supposed to do?

And the concrete of this city,
the oily wind, the blazing windows,
20 the shrieks of automation[1] cannot,
truly cannot, answer for that hunger
although I have hungered,
truthfully and honestly, for them
to feed myself with.

25 So I sang to myself quietly:
I am feeding myself
with the humble presence
of all around me;
I am feeding myself
30 with your soul, my mother earth;
make me cool and humble.
Bless me. ❖

---

1. **automation.** Processes operated by mechanical or electronic devices instead of human labor; industrialization; mechanization

MIRRORS & WINDOWS

If you had to leave home for a long time, what would you miss the most? What would make you homesick?

Refer to Text ▶ ▶ ▶ ▶ ▶ **Reason with Text**

1a. For what things does the speaker hunger?	**1b.** What does this hunger reveal about his old home and way of life?	**Understand** Find meaning
2a. How does the speaker describe the city? What is it unable to do?	**2b.** Generalize how he feels about this place.	**Apply** Use information
3a. Identify where Ortiz uses *personification*, portraying hunger as a human being.	**3b.** How does the use of personification help characterize the speaker's hunger?	**Analyze** Take things apart
4a. In stanza 3, what does hunger ask of the speaker?	**4b.** Interpret the meaning of the question in lines 16–17.	**Evaluate** Make judgments
5a. What does the speaker ask of "mother earth" in the last stanza?	**5b.** Advise the speaker on whether he should try to adapt to the city or move home.	**Create** Bring ideas together

Analyze Literature

Metaphor and Repetition

Identify the various types of hunger mentioned in the poem. For what is the speaker longing? What is the effect of using this word, which generally refers to a physical element of survival, as a metaphor for longing?

What examples of repetition did you find? What ideas does Ortiz emphasize by repeating these words and phrases? How does the use of repetition affect the sound of the poem?

Extend the Text

Writing Options

Creative Writing Think of something you have dreamed of doing, such as meeting a famous athlete, winning a talent contest, or appearing on a game show. Write a brief personal essay about making that dream come true. Start by explaining how your longing began, and then describe how you would fulfill the dream.

Persuasive Writing You would like your school or community to set up an exchange program that arranges for students to spend summers visiting other cultures; for instance, students from rural areas would visit urban areas. Write a letter to the school or local newspaper, explaining why such a program should be supported.

Collaborative Learning

Give an Oral Presentation With a partner or small group, locate one or more Native American legends or tales from the oral tradition and prepare a group reading of the work. If you prefer, turn the story into a brief play, with group members taking roles (including the role of narrator, if appropriate).

Critical Literacy

Hold a Group Discussion Many well-known authors have written poems about New York. Find and read one of these poems; then write a short summary of what viewpoint it presents about the city. Share your poem and summary with a group of classmates, and discuss the poets' differing opinions.

 Go to **www.mirrorsandwindows.com** for more.

The Writer
Boy at the Window

Lyric Poems by Richard Wilbur

Build Background

Literary Context The two selections by Richard Wilbur, "The Writer" and "Boy at the Window," develop an imaginative link between human consciousness and the natural world, between childhood preoccupation and adult observation.

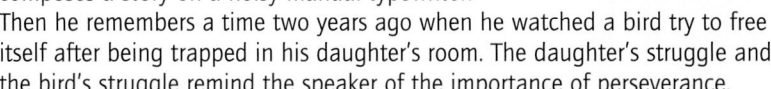

In **"The Writer,"** the speaker is at first amused by his daughter's concentration as she composes a story on a noisy manual typewriter. Then he remembers a time two years ago when he watched a bird try to free itself after being trapped in his daughter's room. The daughter's struggle and the bird's struggle remind the speaker of the importance of perseverance.

In **"Boy at the Window,"** the speaker describes a small boy's sadness as he looks at a snowman condemned to endure the wintry night. What the boy has yet to learn is that the frozen-water figure would melt if it joined him in the house. Like "The Writer," this poem uses compassion in examining the world from a young person's perspective. In addition, both poems examine some of the lessons learned in coming of age.

Reader's Context Think back to when you were eight or ten years old. What did you like about being that age? What didn't you like?

Meet the Author

Richard Wilbur (b. 1921) was born in New York City but grew up on a New Jersey farm, a place that fostered the appreciation of nature so evident in his poetry. He initially planned to become an artist like his father, but his love of words convinced him to pursue a writing career.

Wilbur attended Amherst College, where he was editor of the college newspaper and earned a bachelor of arts degree in 1942. After serving in the army during World War II, he studied at Harvard and received his master's degree in 1947. Wilbur has taught writing and literature at several prestigious universities, including Harvard, Wellesley, Smith, and Wesleyan.

Wilbur's writing style has been described as traditional verse with rhythmic precision and organization. His poems reflect a keen observation of nature and are rich in detail and imagery. His poetry collection *Things of This World* (1957) earned a Pulitzer Prize, as did *New and Collected Poems* (1989). More recent works include *Mayflies* (2000) and *Collected Poems, 1943–2004*. Wilbur also has worked as a dramatist. In addition to translating seventeenth-century French dramas, he wrote the lyrics for the Broadway production of *Candide*. Wilbur was named Poet Laureate of the United States in 1987.

Analyze Literature

Extended Metaphor and Personification
An **extended metaphor** is a point-by-point presentation of one thing as though it were another.

Personification is a figure of speech in which an animal, object, force of nature, or idea is described as if it were human.

Set Purpose

The link between the natural world and human experience is a theme found in much of Wilbur's poetry. As you read "The Writer," trace the extended metaphor he develops to portray the speaker's comprehension of his daughter's efforts. To what is the daughter's struggle to write being compared? In reading the second poem, "Boy at the Window," examine Wilbur's use of personification. Record examples of the snowman being described as if it is human. What brings the snowman to life, if only briefly?

The Writer

by Richard Wilbur

In her room at the prow[1] of the house
Where light breaks, and the windows are tossed with linden,[2]
My daughter is writing a story.

I pause in the stairwell, hearing
5   From her shut door a commotion of typewriter-keys
Like a chain hauled over a gunwale.[3]

---

1. **prow.** Front part of a ship
2. **linden.** Type of shade tree
3. **gunwale.** Upper edge of the side of a ship

Young as she is, the stuff
Of her life is a great cargo, and some of it heavy:
I wish her a lucky passage.

10   But now it is she who pauses,
As if to reject my thought and its easy figure.[4]
A stillness greatens, in which

The whole house seems to be thinking,
And then she is at it again with a bunched clamor
15   Of strokes, and again is silent.

I remember the dazed starling
Which was trapped in that very room, two years ago;
How we stole in, lifted a sash

And retreated, not to affright[5] it;
20   And how for a helpless hour, through the crack of the door,
We watched the sleek, wild, dark

And iridescent creature
Batter against the brilliance, drop like a glove
To the hard floor, or the desk-top,

25   And wait then, humped and bloody,
For the wits to try it again; and how our spirits
Rose when, suddenly sure,

It lifted off from a chair-back,
Beating a smooth course for the right window
30   And clearing the sill of the world.

It is always a matter, my darling,
Of life or death, as I had forgotten. I wish
What I wished you before, but harder. ❖

---

4. **figure.** Figure of speech
5. **affright.** Frighten or scare

MIRRORS & WINDOWS

The parent tells the child, "I wish what I wished you before, but harder." What do parents wish for their children? From what do parents want to protect their children?

Boy at the Window

by Richard Wilbur

Seeing the snowman standing all alone
In dusk and cold is more than he can bear.
The small boy weeps to hear the wind prepare
A night of gnashings and enormous moan.
5   His tearful sight can hardly reach to where
The pale-faced figure with bitumen[1] eyes
Returns him such a God-forsaken stare
As outcast Adam[2] gave to paradise.

The man of snow is, nonetheless, content,
10   Having no wish to go inside and die.
Still, he is moved to see the youngster cry.
Though frozen water is his element,
He melts enough to drop from one soft eye
A trickle of the purest rain, a tear
15   For the child at the bright pane surrounded by
Such warmth, such light, such love, and so much fear. ❖

---

1. **bitumen.** Resembling a kind of coal
2. **outcast Adam.** Refers to the expulsion of Adam and Eve from the Garden of
   Eden, in the Book of Genesis in the Bible. They were expelled for eating an
   apple from the tree of knowledge.

MIRRORS & WINDOWS

Think of a time from your childhood when you attributed human characteristics
to something nonhuman. Why do children tend to view the world in this way?

Refer to Text ▶ ▶ ▶ ▶ ▶	**Reason with Text**	
1a. Where is the speaker's daughter in "The Writer," and what does he hear her doing?	**1b.** What two unlike elements are compared in the simile in lines 5–6?	**Understand** Find meaning
2a. Describe how the snowman looks at the boy in lines 6–8 of "Boy at the Window."	**2b.** Relate the allusion to Adam in line 8 to this description.	**Apply** Use information
3a. In line 16 of "The Writer," what does the speaker remember?	**3b.** Contrast the speaker's feelings while watching the bird with his response to his daughter at the typewriter.	**Analyze** Take things apart
4a. In which lines of "Boy at the Window" does the speaker describe the snowman responding to the boy? How does the snowman respond?	**4b.** Argue whether the poem is effective in portraying the thoughts and feelings of a child.	**Evaluate** Make judgments
5a. In the last stanza of "The Writer," to whom is the speaker talking? In the last line of "Boy at the Window," what stark contrast is presented?	**5b.** Summarize the concept of youth and childhood presented in each poem.	**Create** Bring ideas together

Analyze Literature

Extended Metaphor and Personification

What is the extended metaphor in "The Writer"? How do the metaphors early in the poem develop the extended one? What does the extended metaphor suggest about the speaker's hopes for his daughter?

What details from "Boy at the Window" describe the snowman as human? What causes the snowman to come to life? What feeling do you have at the end of the poem?

Extend the Text

Writing Options

Creative Writing The snowman responds to the boy by shedding a tear. Acting as the snowman, write a poem to the boy (or to a girl, if you prefer). Respond to the child's fears and feelings for the snowman.

Expository Writing You are planning to read "The Writer" to members of a writers' group. To help the members appreciate the extended metaphor in the poem, prepare a one-page literary analysis, explaining what the bird's struggle for survival suggests about the writing process.

Lifelong Learning

Illustrate Wilbur's Images The description in "The Writer" of the trapped starling includes some striking images. Using the graphic medium of your choice—such as cartooning, drawing, painting, clay modeling, origami (paper folding), or photography—illustrate the bird's desperate attempt to escape. Work with a partner or a small group. Display the representations in your class. You also may add your own metaphorical representation of what the writing process seems like to you.

Collaborative Learning

Give a Reading of Wilbur's Poetry Many poems gain meaning and impact when they are read aloud. Select a few other poems by Wilbur, and deliver them in an oral presentation. Students can recite one poem on their own, or two students can share in the recitation of a poem. Discuss with the group where you think appropriate pauses and stresses should be added and how hearing and reading a poem allow different experiences of it.

 Go to **www.mirrorsandwindows.com** for more.

THE HANDSOMEST DROWNED MAN IN THE WORLD

by Gabriel García Márquez
Translated by Gregory Rabassa

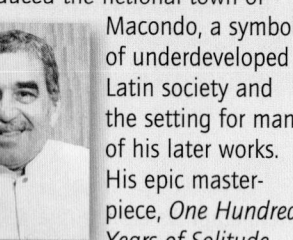

Gabriel García Márquez
(b. 1928) was born in Aracataca, Colombia. In his first book, García Márquez introduced the fictional town of Macondo, a symbol of underdeveloped Latin society and the setting for many of his later works. His epic masterpiece, *One Hundred Years of Solitude* (trans. 1970), has sold more copies around the world than any other work by a present-day Spanish-speaking author. In 1982, García Márquez was awarded the Nobel Prize for literature for his writing "in which the fantastic and the realistic are combined in a richly composed world of imagination, reflecting a continent's life and conflicts."

"The Handsomest Drowned Man in the World" is about a legendary character from Latin America. The story shows how transformations of the ordinary into the mythical take place. García Márquez is recognized as the master of **Magical Realism,** a kind of fiction that is primarily realistic but contains elements of fantasy.

The first children who saw the dark and slinky bulge approaching through the sea let themselves think it was an enemy ship. Then they saw it had no flags or masts and they thought it was a whale. But when it washed up on the beach, they removed the clumps of seaweed, the jellyfish tentacles, and the remains of fish and flotsam,[1] and only then did they see that it was a drowned man.

They had been playing with him all afternoon, burying him in the sand and digging him up again, when someone chanced to see them and spread the alarm in the village. The men who carried him to the nearest house noticed that he weighed more than any dead man they had ever known, almost as much as a horse, and they said to each other that maybe he'd been floating too long and the water had got into his bones. When they laid him on the floor they said he'd been taller than all other men because there was barely enough room for him in the house, but they thought that maybe the ability to keep on growing after death was part of the nature of certain drowned men. He had the smell of the sea about him and only his shape gave one to suppose that it was the corpse of a human being, because the skin was covered with a crust of mud and scales.

---

1. **flotsam.** Debris floating on the water

After the Hurricane, Bahamas, 1899. Winslow Homer. Art Institute of Chicago, Chicago, Illinois.

They did not even have to clean off his face to know that the dead man was a stranger. The village was made up of only twenty-odd wooden houses that had stone courtyards with no flowers and which were spread about on the end of a desertlike cape.[2] There was so little land that mothers always went about with the fear that the wind would carry off their children and the few dead that the years had caused among them had to be thrown off the cliffs. But the sea was calm and bountiful and all the men fit into seven boats. So when they found the drowned man they simply had to look at one another to see that they were all there. That night they did not go out to work at sea. While the men went to find out if any-one was missing in neighboring villages, the women stayed behind to care for the drowned man. They took the mud off with grass swabs, they removed the underwater stones entangled in his hair, and they scraped the crust off with tools used for scaling fish. As they were doing that they noticed that the vegetation on him came from faraway oceans and deep water and that his clothes were in tatters, as if he had sailed through labyrinths[3] of coral. They noticed too that he bore his death with pride, for he did not have the lonely look of other drowned men who came out of the sea or that haggard, needy look of men who drowned in rivers. But only when they finished cleaning him off did they become aware of the kind of man he was and it left them breathless. Not only was he the tallest, strongest, most virile, and best built man they had ever seen, but even though they were looking at him there was no room for him in their imagination.

> THEY DID NOT EVEN HAVE TO CLEAN OFF HIS FACE TO KNOW THAT THE DEAD MAN WAS A STRANGER.

2. **cape.** Piece of land jutting into a body of water
3. **labyrinths.** Complicated mazes

NOT ONLY WAS HE THE TALLEST, STRONGEST, MOST VIRILE, AND BEST BUILT MAN THEY HAD EVER SEEN, BUT EVEN THOUGH THEY WERE LOOKING AT HIM THERE WAS NO ROOM FOR HIM IN THEIR IMAGINATION.

They could not find a bed in the village large enough to lay him on nor was there a table solid enough to use for his wake. The tallest men's holiday pants would not fit him, nor the fattest ones' Sunday shirts, nor the shoes of the one with the biggest feet. Fascinated by his huge size and his beauty, the women then decided to make him some pants from a large piece of sail and a shirt from some bridal brabant linen[4] so that he could continue through his death with dignity. As they sewed, sitting in a circle and gazing at the corpse between stitches, it seemed to them that the wind had never been so steady nor the sea so restless as on that night and they supposed that the change had something to do with the dead man. They thought that if that magnificent man had lived in the village, his house would have had the widest doors, the highest ceiling, and the strongest floor, his bedstead would have been made from a midship frame held together by iron bolts, and his wife would have been the happiest woman. They thought that he would have had so much authority that he could have drawn fish out of the sea simply by calling their names and that he would have put so much work into his land that springs would have burst forth from among the rocks so that he would have been able to plant flowers on the cliffs. They secretly compared him to their own men, thinking that for all their lives theirs were incapable of doing what he could do in one night, and they ended up dismissing them deep in their hearts as the weakest, meanest, and most useless creatures on earth. They were wandering through that maze of fantasy when the oldest woman, who as the oldest had looked upon the drowned man with more compassion than passion, sighed:

"He has the face of someone called Esteban."[5]

It was true. Most of them had only to take another look at him to see that he could not have any other name. The more stubborn among them, who were the youngest, still lived for a few hours with the illusion that when they put his clothes on and he lay among the flowers in patent leather shoes his name might be Lautaro. But it was a vain illusion. There had not been enough canvas, the poorly cut and worse sewn pants were too tight, and the hidden strength of his heart popped the buttons on his shirt. After midnight the whistling of the wind died down and the sea fell into its Wednesday drowsiness. The silence put an end to any last doubts: he was Esteban. The women who had dressed him, who had combed his hair, had cut his nails and shaved him were unable to hold back a shudder of pity when they had to resign themselves to his being dragged along the ground. It was then that they understood how unhappy he must have been with that huge body since it bothered him even after death. They could see him in life, condemned to going through doors sideways, cracking his head on crossbeams, remaining on his feet during visits, not knowing what to do with his soft, pink, sea lion hands while the lady of the house looked for her most resistant chair and begged him, frightened to death, sit here, Esteban, please, and he, leaning against the wall, smiling, don't

---

4. **brabant linen.** Fabric from Brabant, a province on the border between Belgium and the Netherlands, known for its excellent textiles
5. **Esteban.** Spanish equivalent of the name Stephen

The Latin American Boom

BORGES

In the midtwentieth century, Latin American literature attracted widespread attention in the United States and Europe. This literary period, now called the *Latin American boom,* featured writers who were proud of their cultural heritage and frequently incorporated native folk traditions within their literature through Magical Realism. The work of Gabriel García Márquez is representative of this movement.

Argentine writer Jorge Luis Borges (pronounced "Boar-hayz") (1899–1986) often is cited as the founder of this movement in Latin American literature. He was born in Buenos Aires but spent much of his youth with his family in Europe, where his father received medical treatment for an eye condition that eventually blinded him. The family returned to Buenos Aires in 1921, and Borges began publishing poems and essays in literary journals. He would become well known to Western audiences for his short stories and fictional essays; however, he also was a famous literary critic and translator. Borges continued to write even after becoming blind late in life, like his father. His legacy is so influential that the Argentine government issued currency bearing his portrait in 1999.

Although the Latin American boom was dominated by men writers, a second generation of writers in the 1980s and 1990s included more women. Writers such as Laura Esquivel (b. 1950) and Isabel Allende (b. 1942) have written some of the most famous Latin American novels to date.

---

bother, ma'am, I'm fine where I am, his heels raw and his back roasted from having done the same thing so many times whenever he paid a visit, don't bother, ma'am, I'm fine where I am, just to avoid the embarrassment of breaking up the chair, and never knowing perhaps that the ones who said don't go, Esteban, at least wait till the coffee's ready, were the ones who later on would whisper the big boob finally left, how nice, the handsome fool has gone. That was what the women were thinking beside the body a little before dawn. Later, when they covered his face with a handkerchief so that the light would not bother him, he looked so forever dead, so defenseless, so much like their men that the first furrows[6] of tears opened in their hearts. It was one of the younger ones who began the weeping. The others, coming to, went from sighs to wails, and the more they sobbed the more they felt like weeping because the drowned man was becoming all the more Esteban for them, and so they wept so much, for he was the most destitute,[7] most peaceful, and most obliging man on earth, poor Esteban.

So when the men returned with the news that the drowned man was not from the neighboring villages either, the women felt an opening of jubilation in the midst of their tears.

"Praise the Lord," they sighed, "he's ours!"

The men thought the fuss was only womanish frivolity.[8] Fatigued because of the difficult night-time inquiries, all they wanted was to get rid of the bother of the newcomer once and for all before the sun grew strong on that arid, windless day. They improvised a litter[9] with the remains of foremasts and gaffs, tying it together with rigging so that it would bear the weight of the body until they reached the cliffs. They wanted to tie the anchor from a cargo ship to him so that he would sink easily into the deepest waves, where fish are blind and divers die of nostalgia, and bad currents would not bring him back to shore, as had happened with other

---

6. **furrows.** Narrow grooves; deep wrinkles
7. **destitute.** Abandoned; forsaken
8. **frivolity.** Merriment; lack of seriousness
9. **improvised a litter.** Made a makeshift, movable cot for moving injured or ill people

bodies. But the more they hurried, the more the women thought of ways to waste time. They walked about like startled hens, pecking with the sea charms on their breasts, some interfering on one side to put a scapular of the good wind[10] on the drowned man, some on the other side to put a wrist compass[11] on him, and after a great deal of *get away from there, woman, stay out of the way, look, you almost made me fall on top of the dead man,* the men began to feel mistrust in their livers and started grumbling about why so many main-altar decorations for a stranger, because no matter how many nails and holy water jars he had on him, the sharks would chew him all the same, but the women kept piling on their junk relics, running back and forth, stumbling, while they released in sighs what they did not in tears, so that the men finally exploded with *since when has there ever been such a fuss over a drifting corpse, a drowned nobody, a piece of cold Wednesday meat.* One of the women, mortified[12] by so much lack of care, then removed the handkerchief from the dead man's face and the men were left breathless too.

He was Esteban. It was not necessary to repeat it for them to recognize him. If they had been told Sir Walter Raleigh, even they might have been impressed with his gringo accent, the macaw on his shoulder, his cannibal-killing blunderbuss,[13] but there could be only one Esteban in the world and there he was, stretched out like a sperm whale, shoeless, wearing the pants of an undersized child, and with those stony nails that had to be cut with a knife. They only had to take the handkerchief off his face to see that he was ashamed, that it was not his fault that he was so big or so heavy or so handsome, and if he had known that this was going to happen, he would have looked for a more discreet[14] place to drown in, seriously, I even would have tied the anchor off a galleon around my neck and staggered off a cliff like someone who doesn't like things in order not to be upsetting people now with this Wednesday dead body, as you people say, in order not to be bothering anyone with this filthy piece

of cold meat that doesn't have anything to do with me. There was so much truth in his manner that even the most mistrustful men, the ones who felt the bitterness of endless nights at sea fearing that their women would tire of dreaming about them and begin to dream of drowned men, even they and others who were harder still shuddered in the marrow of their bones at Esteban's sincerity.

THEY ONLY HAD TO TAKE THE HANDKERCHIEF OFF HIS FACE TO SEE THAT HE WAS ASHAMED, THAT IT WAS NOT HIS FAULT THAT HE WAS SO BIG OR SO HEAVY OR SO HANDSOME.

That was how they came to hold the most splendid funeral they could conceive of for an abandoned drowned man. Some women who had gone to get flowers in the neighboring villages returned with other women who could not believe what they had been told, and those women went back for more flowers when they saw the dead man, and they brought more and more until there were so many flowers and so many people that it was hard to walk about. At the final moment it pained them to return him to the waters as an orphan and they chose a father and mother from among the best people, and aunts and uncles and cousins, so that through him all the inhabi-

---

10. **scapular of the good wind.** Garment with religious significance
11. **wrist compass.** Compass placed on the wrist for the purpose of directing the soul to God
12. **mortified.** Shamed; humiliated
13. **Sir Walter Raleigh . . . blunderbuss.** English navigator and diplomat (1552–1618). He is portrayed here as having an English accent, a tropical bird on his shoulder, and a blunderbuss, or old-fashioned gun with a large muzzle, accurate only at short range.
14. **discreet.** Inconspicuous
15. **kinsmen.** Relative; family member

tants of the village became kinsmen.[15] Some sailors who heard the weeping from a distance went off course and people heard of one who had himself tied to the mainmast, remembering ancient fables about sirens.[16] While they fought for the privilege of carrying him on their shoulders along the steep escarpment[17] by the cliffs, men and women became aware for the first time of the desolation of their streets, the dryness of their courtyards, the narrowness of their dreams as they faced the splendor and beauty of their drowned man. They let him go without an anchor so that he could come back if he wished and whenever he wished, and they all held their breath for the fraction of centuries the body took to fall into the abyss. They did not need to look at one another to realize that they were no longer all present, that they would never be. But they also knew that everything would be different from then on, that their houses would have wider doors, higher ceilings, and stronger floors so that Esteban's memory could go everywhere without bumping into beams and so that no one in the future would dare whisper the big boob finally died, too bad, the handsome fool has finally died, because they were going to paint their house fronts gay colors to make Esteban's memory eternal and they were going to break their backs digging for springs among the stones and planting flowers on the cliffs so that in future years at dawn the passengers on great liners would awaken, suffocated by the smell of gardens on the high seas, and the captain would have to come down from the bridge in his dress uniform, with his astrolabe,[18] his pole star, and his row of war medals and, pointing to the promontory of roses on the horizon, he would say in fourteen languages, look there, where the wind is so peaceful now that it's gone to sleep beneath the beds, over there, where the sun's so bright that sunflowers don't know which way to turn, yes, the over there, that's Esteban's village. ❖

---

16. **sirens.** Sea nymphs who lured sailors to their deaths
17. **escarpment.** Steep slope
18. **astrolabe.** Ancient navigational instrument

MIRRORS & WINDOWS

The villagers are so fascinated with the drowned man that they create an imaginary life for him. Why are people sometimes overly impressed by newcomers? How can a stranger take on larger-than-life qualities?

Refer and Reason

1. How do the men respond when one of the women uncovers Esteban's face? Contrast how the women and the men respond to Esteban after they have seen his face.

2. What do the villagers do to ensure that Esteban's memory will be kept alive? Argue whether they are justified in fussing so much over Esteban. What do their actions reveal about them?

3. Explain why the villagers drop Esteban's body into the sea without an anchor. Suggest how the story would have been different if a living stranger had come to the village. How might the men and the women have reacted?

Writing Options

1. Working in the style of Magical Realism, write a one-page narrative about a mysterious experience of your own. You might work with a partner to plan which parts of the story will be realistic and which will be fictional.

2. You have been invited by a reading group to discuss "The Handsomest Drowned Man in the World." Prepare by writing one paragraph that analyzes the story as a commentary on human nature. How are the villagers like many ordinary people in their response to Esteban?

Son

by John Updike

John Updike (b. 1932) grew up in Shillington, Pennsylvania, an area that became the setting for several of his stories. An avid reader and excellent student, he was encouraged to write by his mother, herself an aspiring writer.

Updike was awarded a scholarship to Harvard, where he graduated in 1954 with a degree in English. Shortly thereafter, he went to write for the *New Yorker,* which launched his career as a prominent twentieth-century writer. His first major success came in 1960 with the novel *Rabbit, Run.* In 1982, another novel in the *Rabbit* series, *Rabbit Is Rich,* won the Pulitzer Prize for fiction, the National Book Award, and the Critics Circle Award. Eight years later, he received a second Pulitzer for *Rabbit at Rest.* Most of Updike's works reflect his own middle-class upbringing in small-town America.

The short story **"Son"** has an unusual narrative structure. It looks back in time at four generations of unnamed fathers and sons (and a couple of mothers) in one family. As you read, note the links between the generations and the narrators.

He is often upstairs, when he has to be home. He prefers to be elsewhere. He is almost sixteen, though beardless still, a man's mind indignantly[1] captive in the frame of a child. I love touching him, but don't often dare. The other day, he had the flu, and a fever, and I gave him a back rub, marvelling at the symmetrical knit of muscle, the organic tension. He is high-strung. Yet his sleep is so solid he sweats like a stone in the wall of a well. He wishes for perfection. He would like to destroy us, for we are, variously, too fat, too jocular,[2] too sloppy, too affectionate, too grotesque and heedless[3] in our ways. His mother smokes too much. His younger brother chews with his mouth open. His older sister leaves unbuttoned the top button of her blouses. His younger sister tussles with the dogs, getting them overexcited, avoiding doing her homework. Everyone in the house talks nonsense. He would be a better father than his father. But time has tricked him, has made him a son. After a quarrel, if he cannot go outside and kick a ball, he retreats to a corner of the house and reclines on the beanbag chair in an attitude of strange—infantile or leonine—torpor.[4] We exhaust him, without meaning to. He takes an interest in the newspaper now, the front page as well as the sports, in this tiring year of 1973.

---

1. **indignantly.** With resentment or annoyance
2. **jocular.** Playful; joking
3. **heedless.** Careless; neglectful
4. **infantile or leonine—torpor.** *Infantile:* immature or childish; *leonine:* resembling a lion; *torpor:* state of inactivity or apathy

He is upstairs, writing a musical comedy. It is a Sunday in 1949. He has volunteered to prepare a high-school assembly program; people will sing. Songs of the time go through his head, as he scribbles new words. *Up in de mornin', down at de school, work like a debil for my grades.*[5] Below him, irksome voices grind on, like machines working their way through tunnels. His parents each want something from the other. "Marion, you don't understand that man like I do; he has a heart of gold." His father's charade is very complex: the world, which he fears, is used as a flail[6] on his wife. But from his cringing attitude he would seem to an outsider the one being flailed. With burning red face, the woman accepts the role of aggressor as penance for the fact, the incessant[7] shameful fact, that *he* has to wrestle with the world while she hides here, in solitude, at home. This is normal, but does not seem to them to be so. Only by convolution[8] have they arrived at the dominant/submissive relationship society has assigned them. For the man is maternally kind and with a smile hugs to himself his jewel, his certainty of being victimized; it is the mother whose tongue is sharp, who

sometimes strikes. "Well, he gets you out of the house, and I guess that's gold to you." His answer is "Duty calls," pronounced mincingly.[9] "The social contract is a balance of compromises." This will infuriate her, the son knows; as his heart thickens, the downstairs overflows with her hot voice. "*Don't* wear that smile at me! And *take* your hands off your hips; you look like a fairy!" Their son tries not to listen. When he does, visual details of the downstairs flood his mind: the two antagonists,[10] circling with their coffee cups; the shabby mismatched furniture; the hopeful books; the docile[11] framed photographs of the dead, docile and still like cowed[12] students. This matrix of pain that bore him—he feels he is floating above it, sprawled on the bed as on a cloud, stealing songs as they come into his head (*Across the hallway from the guidance room / Lives a French instructor called Mrs. Blum*), contemplating the view from the upstairs window (last summer's burdock stalks[13] like the beginnings of an alphabet, an apple tree holding three rotten apples as if pondering why they failed to fall), yearning for Monday, for the ride to school with his father, for the bell that calls him to

Their son tries not to listen. When he does, visual details of the downstairs flood his mind.

5. *Up in de mornin' . . . work like a debil for my grades.* This verse is mimicking a traditional spiritual.
6. **flail.** Device used to thrash or beat someone; consists of a staff or handle to which a shorter, free-swinging stick is attached
7. **incessant.** Constant; never ending
8. **convolution.** Complicated or difficult process
9. **mincingly.** In a crisp, distinct manner
10. **antagonists.** Competitors; enemies
11. **docile.** Meek; tame
12. **cowed.** Intimidated; frightened
13. **burdock stalks.** Long stems of a prickly herb plant

homeroom, for the excitements of class, for Broadway, for fame, for the cloud that will carry him away, out of this, out.

He returns from his paper-delivery route and finds a few Christmas presents for him on the kitchen table. I must guess at the year. 1913? Without opening them, he knocks them to the floor, puts his head on the table, and falls asleep. He must have been consciously dramatizing his plight:[14] his father was sick, money was scarce, he had to work, to win food for the family when he was still a child. In his dismissal of Christmas, he touched a nerve: his love of anarchy,[15] his distrust of the social contract. He treasured this moment of revolt; else why remember it, hoard[16] a memory so bitter, and confide it to his son many Christmases later? He had a teaching instinct, though he claimed that life miscast him as a schoolteacher. I suffered in his classes, feeling the confusion as a persecution of him, but now wonder if his rebellious heart did not court confusion, not as Communists do, to intrude their own order, but, more radical still, as an end pleasurable in itself, as truth's very body. Yet his handwriting (an old pink permission slip recently fluttered from a book where it had been marking a page for twenty years) was always considerately legible, and he was sitting up doing arithmetic the morning of the day he died.

And letters survive from that yet prior son, written in brown ink, in a tidy tame hand, home to his mother from the Missouri seminary where he was preparing for his vocation.[17] The dates are 1887, 1888, 1889. Nothing much happened: he missed New Jersey, and was teased at a church social for escorting a widow. He wanted to do the right thing, but the little sheets of faded penscript exhale a dispirited[18] calm, as if his heart already knew he would not make a successful minister, or live to be old. His son, my father, when old, drove hundreds of miles out of his way to visit the Missouri

town from which those letters had been sent. Strangely, the town had not changed; it looked just as he had imagined, from his father's descriptions: tall wooden houses, rain-soaked, stacked on a bluff. The town was a sepia[19] postcard mailed homesick home and preserved in an attic. My father cursed: his father's old sorrow bore him down into depression, into hatred of life. My mother claims his decline in health began at that moment.

He is wonderful to watch, playing soccer. Smaller than the others, my son leaps, heads, dribbles, feints,[20] passes. When a big boy knocks him down, he tumbles on the mud, in his green-and-black school uniform, in an ecstasy of falling. I am envious. Never for me the jaunty[21] pride of the school uniform, the solemn ritual of the coach's pep talk, the camaraderie of shook hands and slapped backsides, the shadow-striped hush of late afternoon and last quarter, the solemn vaulted universe of official combat, with its cheering mothers and referees exotic as zebras and the bespectacled[22] timekeeper alert with his claxon.[23] When the boy scores a goal, he runs into the arms of his teammates with upraised arms and his face alight as if blinded by triumph. They lift him from the earth in a union of muddy hugs. What spirit! What valor! What skill! His father, watching from the sidelines, inwardly registers only one complaint: he feels the boy, with his talent, should be more aggressive.

They drove across the Commonwealth of Pennsylvania to hear their son read

---

14. **plight.** Predicament; difficult situation
15. **anarchy.** Absence of government or order
16. **hoard.** Save; put aside
17. **vocation.** Calling; in this case, the ministry
18. **dispirited.** Depressed; discouraged
19. **sepia.** Brown colored, like an old photograph
20. **feints.** Moves so as to trick or deceive
21. **jaunty.** Spirited; lively
22. **bespectacled.** Wearing spectacles, or glasses
23. **claxon.** Loud horn

in Pittsburgh. But when their presence was announced to the audience, they did not stand; the applause groped[24] for them and died. My mother said afterwards she was afraid she might fall into the next row if she tried to stand in the dark. Next morning was sunny, and the three of us searched for the house where once they had lived. They had been happy there; I imagined, indeed, that I had been conceived there, just before the slope of the Depression[25] steepened and fear gripped my family. We found the library where she used to read Turgenev,[26] and the little park where the bums slept close as paving stones in the summer night; but their street kept eluding us, though we circled in the car. On foot, my mother found the tree. She claimed she recognized it, the sooty linden tree she would gaze into from their apartment windows. The branches, though thicker, had held their pattern. But the house itself, and the entire block, was gone. Stray bricks and rods of iron in the grass suggested that the demolition had been recent. We stood on the empty spot and laughed. They knew it was right, because the railroad tracks were the right distance away. In confirmation,[27] a long freight train pulled itself east around the curve, its great weight gliding as if on a river current; then a silver passenger train came gliding as effortlessly in the other direction. The curve of the tracks tipped the cars slightly toward us. The Golden Triangle,[28] gray and hazed, was off to our left, beyond a forest of bridges. We stood on the grassy rubble that morning, where something once had been, beside the tree still there, and were intensely happy. Why? We knew.

"'No,' Dad said to me, 'the Christian ministry isn't a job you choose, it's a vocation for which you got to receive a call.'[29] I could tell he wanted me to ask him. We never talked much, but we understood each other, we were both scared devils, not like you and the kid. I asked him, Had he ever received the call? He said No. He said No, he never had. Received the call. That was a terrible thing, for him to admit. And I was the one he told. As far as I knew he never admitted it to anybody, but he admitted it to me. He felt like hell about it, I could tell. That was all we ever said about it. That was enough."

24. **groped.** Fumbled; felt around for
25. **Depression.** Great Depression; economic downturn of the late 1920s and 1930s
26. **Turgenev.** Ivan Sergeyevich Turgenev (1818–1883); Russian novelist and playwright
27. **confirmation.** Evidence; verification
28. **Golden Triangle.** Central business district of Pittsburgh
29. **receive a call.** Experience the desire to become a minister

He has made his younger brother cry, and justice must be done. A father enforces justice. I corner the rat in our bedroom; he is holding a cardboard mailing tube like a sword. The challenge flares white-hot; I roll my weight toward him like a rock down a mountain, and knock the weapon from his hand. He smiles. Smiles! Because my facial expression is silly? Because he is glad that he can still be over-powered, and hence is still protected? Why? I do not hit him. We stand a second, father and son, and then as nimbly as on the soccer field he steps around me and out the door. He slams the door. He shouts obscenities in the hall, slams all the doors he can find on the way to his room. Our moment of smilingly shared silence was the moment of compression;[30] now the explosion. The whole house rocks with it. Downstairs, his siblings and mother come to me and offer advice and psychological analysis. I was too aggressive. He is spoiled. What they can never know, my grief alone to treasure, was

that lucid[31] many-sided second of his smiling and my relenting, before the world's wrathful[32] pantomime of power resumed.

As we huddle whispering about him, my son takes his revenge. In his room, he plays his guitar. He has greatly improved this winter; his hands getting bigger is the least of it. He has found in the guitar an escape. He plays the Romanza[33] wherein repeated notes, with a sliding like the heart's valves, let themselves fall along the scale:

The notes fall, so gently he bombs us, drops feathery notes down upon us, our visitor, our prisoner. ❖

---

30. **compression.** Pressure; tension
31. **lucid.** Clear; logical
32. **wrathful.** Furious; enraged
33. **Romanza.** Romantic musical selection

MIRRORS & WINDOWS

Generations of this family's history are revealed by the individual stories of the fathers and sons. What stories from your family members would give others insight into your family's history?

Refer and Reason

1. Trace the passage of time in the story. Do you find the unusual time frame effective or confusing in telling the story of this family? Explain.

2. How do the characters' social or psychological concerns vary with the shift in time? Relate this to how the tone of the story (that is, the author's attitude) changes.

3. Describe how the story would be different if told in chronological order, from the earliest incident (1880s) to the most recent. What other changes, besides chronology, would you make in the work? Why?

Writing Options

1. Updike's story "Son" may be a good candidate for adaptation to the screen. Working with a partner or small group, create a film script version of "Son." You can include narration with voice-over by the appropriate actors.

2. Some classmates have asked for help in following the shifts in narrator, or point of view, in "Son." Write a brief critique in which you discuss the effect of these shifts. Share your explanation with a partner or group for feedback.

In the 1950s and 1960s, readers of poetry saw a shift toward poems that seemed to reveal details about the emotions and private lives of the poets. The *I* in these poems was not just an invented speaker, formed to give a first-person perspective; rather, the speaker seemed to *be* the poet. Known as the Confessional poets, these writers approached poetry as an outlet for autobiographical expression. **Confessional poetry** is verse that describes, sometimes with painful explicitness, the private or personal affairs of the writer.

The primary poets of the Confessional movement were Robert Lowell, Anne Sexton, Sylvia Plath, John Berryman, and W. D. Snodgrass. Lowell was considered the leader of the movement, and his book *Life Studies* (1959), a collection of poetry, set the course for the movement. Both Sexton and Plath studied under him and acknowledged his influence on their writing.

Much Confessional poetry is about personal experiences with illness, depression, and family relationships and can be correlated with actual events in the poets' lives. Sexton is said to have started writing at the suggestion of her therapist to provide an outlet for her psychological struggles. Not all Confessional poetry can be interpreted as purely autobiographical, however. Biographers of Sylvia Plath found that she often created fictionalized versions of herself in her poetry.

The baring of the soul that the Confessional poets pioneered had a dramatic impact on American poetry. Its influences can be seen in the works of contemporary poets such as Sharon Olds and Marie Howe.

Poet's Currents, c. 1990s. Diptych by Gerrit Greve.

The Starry Night
A Lyric Poem by Anne Sexton

Build Background

Literary Context **"The Starry Night"** appeared in Anne Sexton's collection *All My Pretty Ones* (1962). The title of the collection is an allusion (reference) to Shakespeare's tragedy *Macbeth*—specifically, from Macduff's response to learning of the deaths of his wife and children.

The title of Sexton's poem, in turn, refers to a famous painting by Vincent van Gogh, which appears on the next page. Like Sexton, van Gogh experienced depression throughout his life; in the painter's case, the condition was intensified by a crisis of religious faith. The epigraph at the beginning of the poem is from one of the remarkable letters Vincent wrote to his brother Theo.

Reader's Context How can looking at a painting inspire a poet? What works of art, music, or literature have inspired you?

Meet the Author

Anne Sexton (1928–1974) was born in Newton, Massachusetts. Her well-to-do parents seemed to have little time to spend with their children and sent their somewhat rebellious daughter away to boarding school. Sexton went on to attend Garland Junior College in 1947 but left a year later to marry at age twenty. She and her husband had two children, after which Sexton suffered severe postpartum depression. This marked the start of her lifelong battle with depression.

At age twenty-eight, Sexton began writing as part of her psychiatric therapy. After attending a Boston University writing workshop taught by Robert Lowell, she recorded in her poems her intimate experiences with fear, anxiety, suffering, and confusion. She once said in an interview, "Poetry should be a shock to the senses. It should almost hurt."

Sexton's poems were published in several notable magazines, including the *New Yorker* and *Saturday Review*. Her first poetry collection, *To Bedlam and Part Way Back* (1960), described her recovery from an emotional breakdown. In 1967, Sexton received the Pulitzer Prize for her collection *Live or Die*. Her shockingly frank poems brought her literary fame but received mixed reactions from critics. The volume *Transformations* (1971) contains eerie retellings of fairy tales by the Brothers Grimm.

Tragically, Sexton succumbed to her depression in 1974. Two volumes of her poetry and a collection of personal letters were published after her death by her daughter Linda.

Analyze Literature

Epigraph and Myth

An **epigraph** is a quotation or motto used at the beginning of a literary work to help establish the work's theme or purpose.

A **myth** is a traditional story, rooted in a particular culture, which deals with gods, goddesses, and other supernatural beings, as well as human heroes. Myths often embody religious beliefs and values and explain natural phenomena.

Set Purpose

In the epigraph that opens "The Starry Night," Sexton quotes a letter written by Vincent van Gogh, in which he implies that painting the stars is a religious experience. Consider how this epigraph establishes the theme or purpose of the poem. Also consider Sexton's use of mythical elements, such as "a god." Make a simple two-column chart in which you record these elements and describe how they are used. For instance, the element "a god" is used to describe the moon.

The Starry Night, 1889. Vincent van Gogh.
Museum of Modern Art, New York, New York. (See detail on p. 1134.)

The Starry Night

by Anne Sexton

That does not keep me from having a terrible
need of—shall I say the word—religion.
Then I go out at night to paint the stars.

—*Vincent van Gogh*[1]
in a letter to his brother

The town does not exist
except where one black-haired tree slips
up like a drowned woman into the hot sky.
The town is silent. The night boils with eleven stars.
5   Oh starry starry night! This is how
I want to die.

---

1. **Vincent van Gogh** (1853–1890). Dutch artist, first of the great modern
Expressionist painters. The letter from which this passage was taken was
written while van Gogh was working on another painting of the night sky
called *Starry Night on the Rhône* (the Rhône is a river in France).

It moves. They are all alive.
Even the moon bulges in its orange irons
to push children, like a god, from its eye.
10 The old unseen serpent swallows up the stars.
Oh starry starry night! This is how
I want to die:

into that rushing beast of the night,
sucked up by that great dragon, to split
15 from my life with no flag,
no belly,
no cry. ❖

Countless artists and writers have found their inspiration in nature. What in nature has inspired you?

ART CONNECTION

Vincent van Gogh

Dutch painter Vincent van Gogh (1853–1890) was born in Groot-Zundert, a small village in the southern Netherlands, and grew up in a devoutly Catholic household. He attended school until age fifteen and then spent the next years of his life drifting among jobs as an art salesman, a low-level clerk, and eventually a preacher. When the clergy dismissed him for being overzealous in 1880, van Gogh decided to become a painter.

Six years later, van Gogh moved to Paris to live with his younger brother, Theo. Paris was home to many well-known artists at the time, including the famous Impressionists Claude Monet and Paul Gauguin, whom van Gogh befriended. They influenced his artistic style, transforming his use of the dark, moody colors of the Dutch Masters to a lighter, more colorful palette.

Self-Portrait, 1887. Vincent van Gogh. Art Institute of Chicago, Chicago, Illinois.

In the coming years, van Gogh became increasingly irrational and dysfunctional. He began to experience seizures, hallucinations, and paranoia. In 1888, following a crisis during which he sliced off the end of his left ear, the artist admitted himself to a psychiatric hospital in Saint-Rémy, France.

Van Gogh continued to paint while convalescing at Saint-Rémy, producing some of his most renowned work, including *The Starry Night* (1889). It was during this period that he developed the swirling colorful style for which he became famous.

Despite constant medical supervision, van Gogh's condition deteriorated. He died one year later at age thirty-seven. Even though he eventually became one of the most famous artists in history, van Gogh sold only one painting during his lifetime and did not receive critical acclaim until years after his death.

Critical Viewing Like van Gogh, Anne Sexton used art as a creative outlet to manage personal trauma. What qualities of the painting *The Starry Night* (see page 1135) might have appealed to Sexton? What qualities of the painting are reflected in Sexton's poem?

Refer to Text ▷ ▷ ▶ ▶ ▶ Reason with Text

1a. What "does not exist"? To what is the "one black-haired tree" compared?	**1b.** Describe who the "one black-haired tree" might represent. How can the town "not exist" yet be "silent"?	**Understand** Find meaning
2a. What are the moon and the stars doing in the poem?	**2b.** What image in the painting suggests the "night boils"?	**Apply** Use information
3a. Identify the main differences between the town and the sky.	**3b.** What is the speaker's attitude toward the town, on the one hand, and toward the tree and the night sky, on the other?	**Analyze** Take things apart
4a. According to the speaker, what figure will suck her up into "that rushing beast of the night"? To what image in stanza 2 does this figure correspond?	**4b.** The speaker wants to "split from [her] life with no flag, no belly, no cry." How does this passage suggest she has lost the will to live?	**Evaluate** Make judgments
5a. According to the epigraph, what motivated van Gogh to paint the stars?	**5b.** Propose what Sexton observed in the painting that inspired her to write the poem.	**Create** Bring ideas together

Analyze Literature

Epigraph and Myth
How does the epigraph by van Gogh relate to the theme or purpose of the poem? What religious experience does Sexton describe? Reflect on how Sexton has integrated the painting and van Gogh's statement into her verse. How does comparing the three works enrich your understanding of them?

What mythical elements does Sexton include in the poem? How is each used?

Extend the Text

Writing Options
Creative Writing As Vincent van Gogh, write a business letter to your art dealer saying you have completed the painting *The Starry Night* and would like to sell it. Describe the work in detail, and explain what inspired you to paint it.

Expository Writing Read several more of Sexton's poems, and choose one for analysis. Write an analytical paragraph explaining how she develops the poem's theme.

Collaborative Learning
Write a Paragraph or Poem Working with a partner or small group, locate several paintings you can legally download or photocopy. Choose one that you find inspi-

rational, and write a poem or paragraph that reflects your feelings. Discuss with classmates their experiences in using a painting as inspiration.

Media Literacy
Explore Outreach Programs Work with classmates to explore different types of community outreach programs—for example, programs in which students visit people in hospitals or nursing homes or go to schools to work as tutors. Write letters to the people in charge of these facilities and schools, asking whether your services would be helpful. Include a brief proposal for what services you would like to provide.

MW Go to **www.mirrorsandwindows.com** for more.

Understand the Concept

Celestial words are terms relating to heavenly bodies, including the stars, the sun, and the moon. For example, the word *stellar,* which means "of or relating to the stars," comes from the Latin *stella,* or "star." The word *stellar* also can be used to mean "outstanding," just as the word *star* can refer to someone noted for excellence.

Other words referring to stars and outer space begin with the prefixes *astr-* and *astro-,* which are from the Greek for "star." Words that begin with these prefixes include *astronomy, astrological, astronaut,* and *astral.* The word *astronomical* can be used to describe something related to astronomy or something tremendously large or great.

Words referring to the sun may have the prefix *heli-* or *helio-,* from the Greek for "sun." Examples include *heliocentric* and *heliotropism.* Other sun-related words come from the Latin noun *sol* or adjective *solaris;* a familiar example is the phrase *solar system.*

The Latin word *lunar* means both "of the moon" and "in the shape of a crescent moon." A *lunette,* for instance, is shaped like the moon. The words *lunacy* and *lunatic* originated in the now-discredited belief that insanity is influenced by the phases of the moon.

Apply the Skill

Exercise A
The following celestial terms are from Greek or Latin word parts. Use each word or phrase in a sentence that provides a context for its meaning. Consult a dictionary, if necessary, to clarify the word's definition and part of speech.

1. heliport
2. astrophysicist
3. solarium
4. lunar eclipse
5. astrology
6. lunate
7. astrolabe
8. solarize
9. heliocentric
10. solstice

Exercise B
Use each of the following word parts from Greek or Latin to create a new word. Then define the word. The first one has been done as an example.

1. helio + <u>phone</u> = heliophone
   Definition: two-way communication that works only in sunlight.
2. astro-
3. luna-
4. sol-
5. stella-

SPELLING PRACTICE

Commonly Misspelled Words

Many everyday words are commonly misspelled, including those listed below from "The Starry Night." Study the list and identify those words that you find troublesome. Identify a spelling rule or create a mnemonic device that will help you remember how to spell each word.

beast	paint
bulges	religion
children	serpent
drowned	silent
except	starry
night	swallows
orange	terrible

Morning Song
Mirror

Lyric Poems by Sylvia Plath

Build Background

Literary Context The first selection, **"Morning Song,"**
is about the birth of Sylvia Plath's daughter, Frieda, in
1960. Like much of Plath's work, this poem is highly personal and contains brilliant imagery. What might have
been a joyful poem of celebration, however, includes elements of sadness.

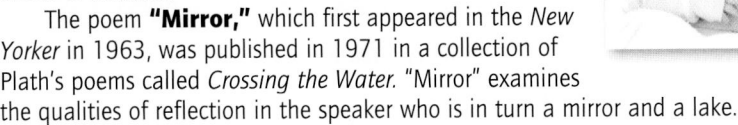

The poem **"Mirror,"** which first appeared in the *New
Yorker* in 1963, was published in 1971 in a collection of
Plath's poems called *Crossing the Water.* "Mirror" examines
the qualities of reflection in the speaker who is in turn a mirror and a lake.

Reader's Context British playwright George Bernard Shaw once said,
"You use a glass mirror to see your face; you use works of art to see yourself."
Explain what this means.

Meet the Author

Sylvia Plath (1932–1963) was born in Boston to well-educated
parents. Her passion for words as a child led to publication of her
first poem at age eight. By the time she had graduated from high
school, Plath's writing had appeared in *Seventeen* magazine, the
Christian Science Monitor, and the *Boston Globe.*

Plath continued her writing at Smith College. During her
junior year, she received a prize for fiction from *Mademoiselle*
magazine and spent the following summer as a guest editor
for the publication. After graduating from Smith in 1955, she was awarded a
Fulbright scholarship to Cambridge University in England, where she met and
married British poet Ted Hughes in 1956. They had two children and moved
from London to the English countryside. Feeling isolated in her rural surroundings, Plath battled loneliness and depression. She and her children moved back
to London two years later, where Plath succumbed to depression.

Plath's fame was achieved posthumously. In her short life, she had one
poetry volume published, *The Colossus and Other Poems* (1960). This collection
of personal poems reflects the influence of Confessional poet Robert Lowell,
whose teaching lectures Plath attended. Her works portray honest emotions
and reveal her own inner turmoil. At times, her writing style shows stark contrasts between childlike innocence and harsh truths, often seen in her use of
alliteration and bold imagery.

Plath's finest collection, *Ariel* (1968), was written in the last months of her
life. Other volumes include *Crossing the Water* (1971) and *Winter Trees* (1972),
which reveal a growing detachment from life. Her novel *The Bell Jar* (1963) is
a fictionalized account of the nervous breakdown she suffered while in college.

Analyze Literature

Speaker and Enjambment
The **speaker** is the person who
speaks in, or narrates, a poem—
the voice assumed by the writer.
The speaker and the writer of
a poem are not necessarily the
same person, however.

Enjambment is the act of
continuing a statement beyond
the end of a line. In contrast, an
end-stopped line is one in which
both the sense and the grammar are complete at the end
of the line.

Set Purpose

In studying works by Confessional poets, many readers
assume the speaker is the poet.
As you read these two poems
by Sylvia Plath, identify the
speaker in each one. Write down
details from the poem that suggest the speaker's identity. In
addition, examine Plath's use of
enjambed versus end-stopped
lines. Read each poem aloud
to hear the difference between
the two.

Preview Vocabulary

distil, 1140
effacement, 1140
preconception, 1141
agitation, 1141

Morning Song

by Sylvia Plath

Mother and Child, 1967. Alice Neel. Private collection.

Love set you going like a fat gold watch.
The midwife slapped your footsoles, and your bald cry
Took its place among the elements.

Our voices echo, magnifying your arrival. New statue.
5 In a drafty museum, your nakedness
Shadows our safety. We stand round blankly as walls.

I'm no more your mother
Than the cloud that <u>distils</u> a mirror to reflect its own slow
<u>Effacement</u> at the wind's hand.

10 All night your moth breath
Flickers among the flat pink roses. I wake to listen:
A far sea moves in my ear.

One cry, and I stumble from bed, cow-heavy and floral
In my Victorian nightgown.
15 Your mouth opens clean as a cat's. The window square

Whitens and swallows its dull stars. And now you try
Your handful of notes;
The clear vowels rise like balloons. ❖

---

dis • til (di stil´) *v.,* let fall in drops, like rain (also spelled *distill*)
ef • face • ment (e fās´ mənt) *n.,* disappearance or fading as if by wearing away

---

The word *bittersweet* is used to describe something that is both happy and sad.
When can a happy event, such as a birth or wedding, also have sad or troubling
consequences?

Mirror

by Sylvia Plath

I am silver and exact. I have no <u>preconceptions</u>.
Whatever I see I swallow immediately
Just as it is, unmisted by love or dislike.
I am not cruel, only truthful—
5   The eye of a little god, four-cornered.
Most of the time I meditate on[1] the opposite wall.
It is pink, with speckles. I have looked at it so long
I think it is a part of my heart. But it flickers.
Faces and darkness separate us over and over.

10 Now I am a lake. A woman bends over me,
Searching my reaches for what she really is.
Then she turns to those liars, the candles or the moon.
I see her back, and reflect it faithfully.
She rewards me with tears and an <u>agitation</u> of hands.
15 I am important to her. She comes and goes.
Each morning it is her face that replaces the darkness.
In me she has drowned a young girl, and in me an old woman
Rises toward her day after day, like a terrible fish. ❖

---

1. **meditate on.** Focus one's thoughts on; concentrate on

> **pre • con • cep • tion** (prē′ kən sep′ shən) *n.,* idea formed beforehand
> **ag • i • ta • tion** (a′ jə tā′ shən) *n.,* irregular, rapid, or violent movement or action

MIRRORS **&** **W**INDOWS   The mirror says that it is "not cruel, only truthful." How can the truth sometimes be cruel? Is honesty always the best policy?

Refer to Text ▶ ▶ ▶ ▶ ▶   Reason with Text

1a. In stanza 1 of "Morning Song," how does the baby respond when the midwife assisting at the birth slaps its tiny feet?

1b. Infer what the speaker means in stanza 2 by "In a drafty museum / your nakedness / Shadows our safety."

Understand
Find meaning

2a. In stanza 3 of "Morning Song," what does the cloud "distill"? What happens to the distilled object?

2b. What does the wind represent to the speaker?

Apply
Use information

3a. In stanza 2 of "Mirror," what has the speaker become?

3b. Analyze the change in the speaker's identity. What qualities have changed, and what qualities have remained the same?

Analyze
Take things apart

4a. In stanza 2 of "Mirror," with what does the woman "reward" the speaker?

4b. Describe what is ironic about this "reward."

Evaluate
Make judgments

5a. In the last line of "Morning Song," what simile does the speaker use to describe the baby's voice?

5b. Write another simile to describe the sound of a baby or young child's voice.

Create
Bring ideas together

Analyze Literature

Speaker and Enjambment

Who is the speaker in each poem? What details suggest each speaker's identity? In "Mirror," discuss how the speaker's identity shifts from stanza 1 to stanza 2. How does this shift relate to the theme of the poem?

What examples of enjambment did you find in "Morning Song"? In "Mirror"? How does the use of enjambed versus end-stopped lines affect your reading of the poem? How does it affect your understanding of the poem?

Extend the Text

Writing Options

Creative Writing Imagine that you are an advice columnist for a newspaper and have received a letter from someone who is frustrated with his or her age—for instance, a child who wants to be older or an elderly person who wants to be younger. Respond with some reassuring words about the stages of life and what each has to offer.

Expository Writing Write a comparison-and-contrast essay in which you discuss the differences and similarities between the speakers in Plath's poem. You may present your ideas point by point or analyze one poem at a time.

Collaborative Learning

Adapt a Novel Read a chapter or two from Sylvia Plath's novel *The Bell Jar.* Then with a small group, select a scene to adapt by presenting it on the stage. Use the author's ideas and words to develop a script. Create dialogue and stage directions as needed.

Media Literacy

Evaluate Age Discrimination In U.S. society, older people sometimes face age discrimination. For instance, older workers sometimes are forced out of jobs because it is assumed they cannot learn to use modern technology. Conduct research on age discrimination to learn how and when it happens and what legal rights people have. Present your findings on a poster or in a flier.

 Go to **www.mirrorsandwindows.com** for more.

1. In "Morning Song," what is the general tone of the speaker concerning the child?
   A. She is happy and fulfilled.
   B. She is protective and caring.
   C. She is resentful and a bit sad.
   D. She is somewhat stunned and distant but dutiful.
   E. She is scared but hopeful.

2. In "Morning Song," which of the following best expresses the meaning in the line "I'm no more your mother / Than the cloud that distils a mirror to reflect its own slow / Effacement at the wind's hand"?
   A. As she watches the child grow, she will notice herself fading away or growing older.
   B. She feels a connection to the child that is no stronger than a breeze.
   C. She sees herself within the child and thus cannot deny the bond.
   D. At times, she feels a strong bond with her child, but at other times, they seem like strangers.
   E. She sees how she has shaped the child, as well as how the child will come to shape her.

3. Which of the following is closest in meaning to the word *effacement?*
   A. reflection
   B. building up
   C. wearing away
   D. sharpening
   E. scattering

4. In line 1 of "Morning Song," the line "Love set you going like a fat gold watch" is an example of what type or types of figure of speech?
   A. personification
   B. metaphor
   C. simile
   D. Both A and B
   E. Both A and C

5. In "Mirror," why might the speaker be seen as cruel?
   A. The speaker distorts reality.
   B. The speaker reflects the truth without adornment.
   C. The speaker has drowned a young girl.
   D. The speaker does not comfort the woman when she is upset.
   E. The speaker often is covered in darkness.

6. Why does the woman in "Mirror" turn to candles or the moon?
   A. They are romantic.
   B. They give off light.
   C. They seem magical to her.
   D. They are older forms of light and reflection, compared to a mirror.
   E. Their light is more flattering.

7. Which of the following lines from the second stanza of "Mirror" is an example of personification?
   A. "Now I am a lake."
   B. "Then she turns to those liars, the candles or the moon."
   C. "Each morning it is her face that replaces the darkness."
   D. "In me she has drowned a young girl"
   E. "an old woman / Rises toward her day after day, like a terrible fish"

8. **Constructed Response:** Examine Plath's use of imagery in the poem "Mirror." What are the meanings of the images of the mirror and the lake? Use details from the poem to support your examination.

9. **Constructed Response:** Compare and contrast the speaker in "Morning Song" with the woman described in "Mirror." What might they have in common? How might they be different? Infer what Sylvia Plath might be suggesting about getting older.

> **TEST-TAKING TIP**
>
> If you are taking a test with a written portion, an essay judge will read your work and assign it a score—along with thousands of other essays. The judge will not have much time to read your work, so you should concentrate on constructing a clear, concise argument with a straightforward structure. Make your argument obvious, and support your claims with examples from the text that relate clearly to your argument.

Commander Lowell

by Robert Lowell

Robert Lowell (1917–1977), poet, playwright, and translator, was born in Boston, Massachusetts, to parents who traced their ancestry back to early New England families. He is best known for writing tightly patterned poems that incorporate traditional meter and rhyme, as well as autobiographical poetry structured in looser forms.

Lowell's poem **"Commander Lowell,"** a critical portrait of his father, appeared in an early collection called *Life Studies* (1959), which provided glimpses into Lowell's experiences as a child and noted their effect on his later life. Considered a landmark work in the Confessional poetry movement, Lowell's collection had an enormous influence on future poetry in the United States.

Lowell won the Pulitzer Prize for poetry in 1947 for his collection *Lord Weary's Castle,* in which rebellion is a dominant theme. He won a second Pulitzer in 1973 for *The Dolphin,* one of three volumes of poetry published that year.

There were no undesirables or girls in my set,
when I was a boy at Mattapoisett—[1]
only Mother, still her Father's daughter.
Her voice was still electric
5 with a hysterical, unmarried panic,
when she read to me from the Napoleon book.
Long-nosed Marie Louise
Hapsburg[2] in the frontispiece[3]
had a downright Boston bashfulness,
10 where she groveled[4] to Bonaparte, who scratched his navel,
and bolted his food—just my seven years tall!
And I, bristling and manic,
skulked[5] in the attic,
and got two hundred French generals by name,
15 from *A* to *V*—from Augereau to Vandamme.
I used to dope myself asleep,
naming those unpronounceables like sheep.

Having a naval officer
for my Father was nothing to shout
20 about to the summer colony at "Matt."[6]

---

1. **Mattapoisett.** Summer resort town in southeastern Massachusetts
2. **Marie Louise Hapsburg** (1791–1847). Second wife of Napoléon Bonaparte, military hero who ruled as emperor of France until his exile
3. **frontispiece.** Illustration preceding and usually facing the title page of a book
4. **groveled.** Acted or accepted being treated as if unworthy
5. **skulked.** Hid or concealed himself out of cowardice or fear
6. **"Matt."** Slang abbreviation for *Mattapoisett*

He wasn't at all "serious,"
when he showed up on the golf course,
wearing a blue serge jacket and numbly cut white ducks he'd
    bought
at a Pearl Harbor commissariat[7] . . .
25   and took four shots with his putter to sink his putt.
"Bob," they said, "golf's a game you really ought to know how
    to play,
if you play at all."
They wrote him off as "naval,"
naturally supposed his sport was sailing.
30   Poor Father, his training was engineering!
Cheerful and cowed[8]
among the seadogs[9] at the Sunday yacht club,
he was never one of the crowd.

"Anchors aweigh," Daddy boomed in his bathtub,
35   "Anchors aweigh,"
when Lever Brothers offered to pay
him double what the Navy paid.

---

7. **commissariat.** Military store that supplies food and other goods to the troops
8. **cowed.** Frightened; intimidated
9. **seadogs.** Experienced soldiers

I nagged for his dress sword with gold braid,
and cringed because Mother, new
40 caps on all her teeth, was born anew
at forty. With seamanlike celerity[10]
Father left the Navy,
and deeded Mother his property.

He was soon fired. Year after year,
45 he still hummed "Anchors aweigh" in the tub—
whenever he left a job,
he bought a smarter car.
Father's last employer
was Scudder, Stevens and Clark, Investment Advisors
50 himself his only client.
While Mother dragged to bed alone,
read Menninger,[11]
and grew more and more suspicious,
he grew defiant.
55 Night after night,
à la clarté déserte de sa lampe,[12]
he slid his ivory Annapolis[13] slide rule
across a pad of graphs—
piker speculations![14] In three years
60 he squandered sixty thousand dollars.

Smiling on all,
Father was once successful enough to be lost
in the mob of ruling-class Bostonians.

---

10. **celerity.** Quickness of motion or action
11. **Menninger.** Karl Menninger (1893–1966), American psychiatrist and author of
    The Human Mind and *Man Against Himself*
12. *à la clarté déserte de sa lampe.* [French] By the deserted light of the lamp
13. **Annapolis slide rule.** *Annapolis*—U.S. Naval Academy in Annapolis, Maryland.
    Slide rule—Manual device used for mathematical calculations.
14. **piker speculations.** Investments made with small amounts of money

65   As early as 1928,
    he owned a house converted to oil,
    and redecorated by the architect
    of St. Mark's School. . . . Its main effect
    was a drawing room, "longitudinal as Versailles,"[15]
70   its ceiling, roughened with oatmeal, was blue as the sea.
    And once
    nineteen, the youngest ensign[16] in his class,
    he was "the old man" of a gunboat on the Yangtze.[17] ❖

---

15. **"longitudinal as Versailles."** As long as the Palace of Versailles in France
16. **ensign.** Commissioned officer in the navy, ranking above a chief warrant officer and below a lieutenant junior grade
17. **Yangtze.** River in China that flows into the China Sea

The speaker describes his father as "Smiling on all." Do you think the father was happy? How much do children understand about their parents' failures and successes?

Refer and Reason

1. After leaving the navy, what does the father sing in the bathtub? What is ironic, or unexpected, about singing this song in the tub? Infer what the father's continued singing indicates about his life.

2. In the last stanza, where does the speaker suggest his father was a war hero? Do you feel greater sympathy toward the speaker or the father? Why?

3. After reading about Napoléon, what does the speaker memorize? Summarize what the implied connection between Napoléon (1769–1821) and the speaker's father, a minor figure in World War II, suggests about success and failure.

Writing Options

1. Imagine that Commander Lowell has just died. Write an obituary for him for the local newspaper. You might read several examples of obituaries in your local newspaper before you begin.

2. Select one of the *allusions* in this poem, or references to well-known persons, events, objects, or works from history or literature. Write a paragraph in which you discuss how knowing more about this reference can help readers appreciate the poem.

Going After Cacciato by Tim O'Brien

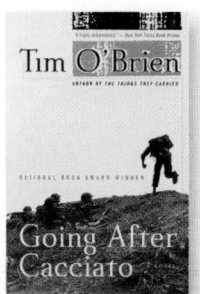

Regarded as the best fictional account of the Vietnam War, O'Brien's surreal novel alternates between a hallucinatory journey and memories of warfare. Cacciato decides to leave the war and walk the 8,600 miles to the Paris Peace Talks. Ordered after him, his squad follows a trail of chocolate M & Ms into the mountains. What happens from there is anyone's guess.

All the President's Men
by Carl Bernstein and Bob Woodward

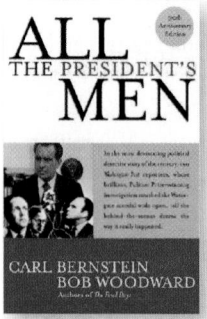

This thrilling narrative recounts the saga of the two *Washington Post* journalists primarily responsible for uncovering President Richard Nixon's involvement in the Watergate scandal and ultimately bringing about his resignation. Full of late-night calls and secret rendezvous, Woodward and Bernstein's investigation leads them through a labyrinth of suspicion and intrigue.

Profiles in Courage by John F. Kennedy

Described by its author as "a book about that most admirable of human virtues," *Profiles in Courage* tells the stories of eight U.S. senators who maintained their integrity in the face of overwhelming opposition. Written in 1954–1955, this Pulitzer Prize–winning book was reissued following Kennedy's assassination and included a foreword by his brother, Senator Robert F. Kennedy.

The Autobiography of Malcolm X
as told to Alex Haley

Shortly before being assassinated, Malcolm X dictated this autobiography to famous African-American writer Alex Haley. Published posthumously, the book has since become one of the most essential discourses on U.S. race relations. *Time* magazine named *The Autobiography* one of the ten most important nonfiction books of the twentieth century.

The Right Stuff by Tom Wolfe

Journalist Tom Wolfe portrays the rise of the first seven astronauts chosen for the U.S. space program. Through a combination of detailed research, interviews, and humorous anecdotes, Wolfe injects a human element into this landmark scientific event. The author's literary flair makes this book an enjoyable read, even for those with little scientific background.

Go Tell It on the Mountain
by James Baldwin

James Baldwin's semiautobiographical novel follows the life of a young boy growing up in Harlem. Throughout this narrative, Baldwin presents themes related to religion and family within the African-American community. Readers who enjoyed Baldwin's short story "The Rockpile" earlier in this unit will find the same characters developed further in this novel.

A good way to learn about effective oral presentations is to observe skilled, experienced speakers in action. For instance, you might be in the audience when a professional speaker, such as a politician running for office, visits your community. If you cannot attend a speech, you can watch one on television or listen to it on the radio.

Another way to sharpen your oral presentation skills is to read and analyze a well-known speech or address by a respected speaker. You might even try reciting such a speech yourself to get an idea of what it feels like to deliver a major address. If possible, obtain an audiotape or videotape of the speech. Use the following questions as guidelines in analyzing a prominent speech.

1. How Does the Message Fit the Occasion?

Find out the relevant information: What was the purpose of the speech? Where and when was it given? Who was the audience? Then, as you read the speech, identify its primary message. Was this message suitable to the purpose, location, and audience? For example, turn to President John F. Kennedy's Inaugural Address, given on January 20, 1961 (see pages 1029–1032). What is the primary message, and how does it, along with other features of the presentation, fit the historic occasion?

2. What Rhetorical Devices Does the Speaker Use, and How Effective Are They?

A *rhetorical device* is a technique a speaker or writer uses to achieve a particular effect, especially to influence listeners. Frequently used devices include *repetition* (usually of words and phrases) and *parallelism* (repetition of grammatical form, for emphasis).

When you analyze a speech, look for these and other rhetorical devices. Then consider the purpose and the effectiveness of the device. For example, where does Kennedy use repetition? Where does he use parallelism? Which ideas do these devices emphasize? Is their use effective? If you have an audiotape or videotape of the speech, what do you observe about Kennedy's delivery?

3. What Passages in the Speech Are Especially Memorable?

The most famous passage in Kennedy's Inaugural Address comes near the end, where he states "Ask not what your country can do for you—ask what you can do for your country." What makes these few words so powerful that they have become a verbal icon of modern U.S. history? What might Kennedy have had in mind when he spoke them? How did he expect his listeners to respond? What does the passage suggest about Kennedy's goals for his incoming presidency?

4. How Is the Speech Similar to or Different from Other Speeches of the Same Type?

Every U.S. president has given at least one inaugural address, so you might look for similarities and differences between Kennedy's speech, given in 1961, and those of other presidents. In making such a comparison, keep in mind two important points: (1) Each inaugural address reflects its era—in Kennedy's case, the Cold War period; and (2) the address reflects the political, social, and economic philosophy of the newly elected or re-elected president. How would you characterize Kennedy's views on the role of government? If you study another president's inaugural address, how would you characterize his views? How does each address reflect its era?

5. Where Can I Find Other Prominent Speeches to Analyze?

Check on the Internet or in a library for speeches by other effective orators—for example, Abraham Lincoln, Franklin D. Roosevelt, and Martin Luther King Jr.

SPEAKING & LISTENING RUBRIC

Your analysis of a prominent speech will be evaluated on these elements:

Research

❏ You locate a well-known speech or address by a prominent speaker.

Analysis

❏ You evaluate the speech as a reflection of its time, for its use of rhetorical devices, and for its likely listener response.

❏ If you obtain an audiotape or videotape, evaluate the speaker's delivery, as well.

Like a catchy song, a good descriptive poem draws in readers with its calculated rhythm and precise language. Because of a poem's typically short length, the diction, line breaks, stanza divisions, and punctuation all need to be decided carefully. These elements work together to create the overall tone and meaning.

For this assignment, you will write a descriptive poem that portrays an object in a way that conveys your feelings about it.

> **Assignment** Plan, write, and revise a descriptive poem.
>
> **Purpose** To express your feelings about an object
>
> **Audience** A new friend or classmate

❶ Prewrite

Select Your Topic
Make a list of five or six familiar objects. They can be items from nature or your everyday world. Then choose the one object to which you feel most connected.

Gather Information
To gather information, create a web or semantic map. Draw a circle and write your object inside it. Next, brainstorm about the object, surrounding the circle with related details of thoughts, feelings, and images.

Organize Your Ideas
Review your map or web. How do the images, feelings, and thoughts connect to each other? Try to identify a central idea, or *theme,* running through the diagram.

> **WRITING RUBRIC**
>
> A well-written descriptive poem has these qualities:
> - ❏ an opening stanza that presents an object and suggests one or more feelings
> - ❏ middle stanzas that effectively use rhythm and imagery to enhance meaning
> - ❏ a closing stanza that provides a satisfying finish

Highlight the details that best represent your connection to the object. Then consider the order in which they should appear. One option is to present the strongest or most obvious details first. Another option is to build the sense of the object gradually, saving the strongest details for the end. Number the details in the order you want them to appear in your poem.

Write Your Controlling Idea
Write a sentence summarizing the feeling or feelings your poem will express. This sentence, called the *controlling idea,* will not appear in your poem but will help you focus on your topic and purpose.

> ### What Great Writers Do
> If you are having trouble deciding on a topic, think about a person, event, or place that stirs your emotions. Robert Frost, who is perhaps Americans' best-loved poet, described 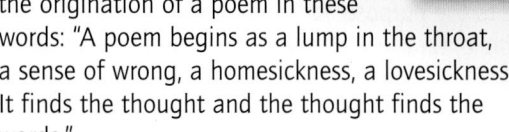 the origination of a poem in these words: "A poem begins as a lump in the throat, a sense of wrong, a homesickness, a lovesickness. It finds the thought and the thought finds the words."

❷ Draft

Write your poem by following this three-part framework: opening stanza, middle stanzas, and final stanza.

> **Opening stanza** Capture the reader's attention by presenting a specific object and feelings.
>
> **Middle stanzas** Use details to describe your object and feelings.
>
> **Final stanza** Leave readers with a strong final sense of your object and feelings.

The opening stanza should capture readers' interest and identify the object and your feelings about it.

The middle stanzas should describe the object, revealing details and reinforcing feelings about it. Review the details from your map or web and the

order in which you planned to present them. Group similar details to create stanzas that are logical and engaging.

Compose the final stanza with the goal of leaving readers with the same feeling or feelings for the object that you have.

③ Revise

Evaluate Your Draft

Evaluate your own poem, or exchange poems with a classmate and evaluate each other's. Consider which parts of the poem work well and which can be improved.

First, look at the content and organization. Make sure all the stanzas connect to the controlling idea and work together to express the intended feelings. Use the following Revision Checklist to help you evaluate. Note the needed changes directly on the draft.

Next, check for sentence- and word-level errors. Be sure you have applied the guidelines in the Grammar & Style workshops in this unit. Again, use the Revision Checklist to help you.

REVISION CHECKLIST

Content & Organization

❑ Does the opening stanza present the object in a way that suggests your feelings?

❑ Does each stanza continue to develop these feelings?

❑ Does each stanza contain appropriate word choices in terms of meaning and tone?

❑ Does the last stanza reinforce your feelings in a way that will satisfy readers?

Grammar & Style

❑ Have you used sensory details to portray how things look, sound, smell, taste, and feel? (page 1045)

❑ Have you used commas correctly? (page 1058)

❑ Have you used colons and semicolons correctly? (page 1083)

What Great Writers Do

In a poem, the quantity of words is not important. As Transcendentalist writer Ralph Waldo Emerson noted, "Poetry teaches the enormous force of a few words."

EMERSON

Revise for Content, Organization, and Style

Read the notes you or your partner made on your draft. Consider these comments as you revise your poem.

Proofread for Errors

Now look for remaining mistakes, using proofreader's symbols to mark any you find. To complete the poem, print out a final draft and read it aloud before turning it in. This will help you slow down to catch errors you might not otherwise see.

Writing Follow-Up

Publish and Present

● Read your poem at a poetry slam or other open reading, or hold your own poetry slam in your classroom.

● Draw or paint a picture to accompany your poem, and add your work to a classroom book of illustrated poems.

Reflect

● Poems often celebrate common things, identifying their quality or value. How has writing a poem about an object increased its value for you?

● How has writing your own poem made you appreciate the work of the poets you read in this unit or elsewhere?

Reading Skills

Analyze Literary Elements

Literary elements comprise the terms that label qualities of or techniques used in literature. Literary elements commonly found in various types of literature include the following:

Tone: the emotional attitude toward the reader or toward the subject implied by a literary work

Point of view: the vantage point, or perspective, from which the story is being told

Characterization: the act of creating or describing a character

Plot: the series of events related to a central conflict, or struggle; a plot typically introduces a conflict, develops it, and eventually resolves it

Foreshadowing: the technique of hinting at events that will occur later in a story

Theme: a central message or perception about life revealed through a literary work.

Allusion: a reference to a well-known person, place, event, or work of art, music, or literature.

The use of figurative language and imagery, symbolism, rhythm, and sound is most often associated with poetry, but these techniques can be found in other literary works, too. Some of the most common types of figurative language include these:

Simile: a comparison of two seemingly unlike things using the word *like* or *as*

Metaphor: a figure of speech in which one thing is spoken or written about as if it were another

Personification: describing or attributing human characteristics to an animal, thing, or idea

---

TEST-TAKING TIP

Don't let the unfamiliar wording of a test question throw you off and make you think you don't know the answer. One strategy is to reword the text so you better understand it; this can waste valuable time, however. Another strategy is to become familiar with the wording used in certain standardized tests. Do so well in advance of taking the test, so you don't have to spend time during the test analyzing and rewording questions.

Practice

Directions: Read the following passage. The questions that follow it ask you to analyze various literary elements.

FICTION: This passage is from the short story "Slump," by John Updike.

They say reflexes, the coach says reflexes, even the papers now are saying reflexes, but I don't think it's the reflexes so much—
last night, as a gag to cheer me up, the wife
5   walks into the bedroom wearing one of the kids' rubber gorilla masks and I was under the bed in six-tenths of a second, she had the stopwatch on me. It's that I can't see the ball the way I used to. It used to come float-
10 ing up with all seven continents showing, and the pitcher's thumbprint, and a grass

smooch or two, and the Spalding guarantee in ten-point san-serif, and *whop!* I could feel the sweet wood with the bat still cocked.
15 Now, I don't know, there's like a cloud around it, a sort of spiral vagueness, maybe the Van Allen belt, or maybe I lift my eye in the last second, planning how I'll round second base, or worrying which I do first,
20 tip my cap or slap the third-base coach's hand. You can't see a blind spot, Kierkegaard says, but in there now, between when the ball leaves the bleacher background and I can hear it plop all fat and satisfied in the
25 catcher's mitt, there's somehow just nothing, where there used to be a lot, everything in fact, because they're not keeping me around for my fielding, and already I see the afternoon tabloid has me down as trade bait.
30   The flutters don't come when they used to. It used to be, I'd back the convertible

out of the garage and watch the electric eye
put the door down again and drive in to the
stadium, and at about the bridge turnoff I'd
35 ease off grooving with the radio rock, and
then on the lot there'd be the kids waiting
to get a look and that would start the big
butterflies, and when the attendant would
take my car I'd want to shout *Stop, thief,* and
40 walking down that long cement corridor I'd
fantasize like I was going to the electric chair
and the locker room was some dream after
death, and I'd wonder why the suit fit, and
how these really immortal guys, that I recog-
45 nized from the bubble-gum cards I used to
collect, knew my name. *They* knew *me.* And
I'd go out and the stadium mumble would
scoop at me and the grass seemed too precious to walk on, like emeralds, and by the

50 time I got into the cage I couldn't remember
if I batted left or right.
    Now, heck, I move over the bridge sing-
ing along with the radio, and brush through
the kids at just the right speed, not so fast I
55 knock any of them down, and the attendant
knows his Labor Day tip is coming, and
we wink, and in the batting cage I own the
place, and take my cuts, and pop five or six
into the bullpen as easy as dropping dimes
60 down a sewer. But when the scoreboard
lights up, and I take those two steps up
from the dugout, the biggest two steps in a
ballplayer's life, and kneel in the circle, giving the crowd the old hawk profile, where
65 once the flutters would ease off, now they
dig down and begin.

Multiple Choice

1. The narrator's use of *I* in telling the story
   indicates that the point of view is
   A. first-person.
   B. third-person.
   C. third-person, limited.
   D. third-person, omniscient.
   E. first-person and third-person together.

2. In line 21, the reference to *Kierkegaard,* a
   nineteenth-century Danish philosopher,
   is an example of
   A. a metaphor.
   B. a simile.
   C. an allusion.
   D. characterization.
   E. personification.

3. In lines 24–25, the narrator describes hearing the baseball "plop all fat and satisfied in
   the catcher's mitt." This is an example of
   A. a metaphor.
   B. a simile.

   C. characterization.
   D. plot.
   E. personification.

4. In lines 48–49, the narrator describes the grass
   on the field as being "too precious to walk on,
   like emeralds." The descriptor "like emeralds"
   is an example of
   A. a metaphor.
   B. a simile.
   C. an allusion.
   D. plot.
   E. personification.

Constructed Response

5. In lines 25–27, the narrator says, "There's
   somehow just nothing, where there used to
   be a lot, everything in fact." Discuss this statement as it relates to the theme of the passage.

Writing Skills

Write a Good Conclusion

Because the conclusion is the last thing the reader (and thus the test scorer) will encounter, it is very important to the essay. In the conclusion, your goals are to bring together the main ideas and to create a sense of closure to the issue you raised in your thesis statement. Ask yourself "So what?" Why should someone want to read your essay? What idea or information do you want him or her to take away?

You can do this in any number of ways. Depending on your essay, some techniques might work better than others. There is, however, no one correct way of writing a good conclusion. Think about what will be effective for your essay when considering the following options:

- *Summarizing or restating your main points* is probably the easiest technique. The strength of this approach is that you leave the reader with a clear understanding of your main points. Try to use different, interesting, and strong words.

- *Making a generalization or linking your main idea to a broader issue* has the advantage of increasing the relevance of your subject. If you use this technique, be sure not to make too big a leap in generalizing.

- *Expanding on your main idea by connecting it to the reader's own interests* is similar to the previous technique but makes the subject of your essay seem even more relevant.

- *Calling on the reader to adopt a view or take an action* is a forceful way to end a persuasive essay. It is a plea or an order addressed directly to the reader.

TEST-TAKING TIP

Keep breathing during the test. This tip may sound ridiculous because breathing is so automatic. However, if you become stressed when taking a test, you might find yourself holding your breath from time to time or breathing erratically. Such improper breathing will impede your thinking. So, seriously, keep breathing!

Practice

Timed Writing: 25 minutes

Think carefully about the issue presented in the following excerpt and the assignment that follows it.

Being content generally is considered a good personal quality or goal. When people are asked to list what they want for themselves or others they care about, they often put *contentment* near the top of the list, just slightly under *happiness*.

In fact, the word *contentment* sometimes is used as a synonym for *happiness*. But are the two really the same? Does feeling content necessarily mean being happy? Can contentment instead mean being bored or lacking excitement and challenge?

Assignment: Is being content necessarily good? Plan and write an essay in which you develop your perspective on this issue. Support your position with reasoning and examples taken from your reading, studies, experience, or observations.

Revising and Editing Skills

As part of the Writing section, some standardized tests ask you to identify sentence errors. These errors deal with grammar, usage, word choice, idioms, and mechanics. Being able to find mistakes in what you have written is a required skill for writing well. Examples of common errors you should watch for include the following:

- incorrect spellings and capitalization
- dangling participles

- disagreement between subject and verb
- inconsistent verb tense
- incorrect forms of irregular verbs
- incorrect use of frequently confused words such as *between* and *among*
- double negatives
- adjective/adverb confusion
- incorrect or missing punctuation

Practice

Directions: In the following section, each item consists of a sentence containing a single error or no error. If there is no error, circle E, "No error." If there is an error, it occurs in one of the under- lined parts of the sentence. To indicate the error, circle the letter at the beginning of the incorrect underlined text. Do not circle more than one let- ter because no sentence contains more than one error.

Multiple Choice

1. Being contented means not thinking about what (A) should have been or feeling dis- satisfied about how things are (B) going, it means feeling (C) satisfied and not wanting things to be (D) any different. (E) No error

2. (A) Going to summer camp changed me for life, (B) the reason being that before I had been a loner, (C) never really feeling part of a team (D) or comfortable spending much time in groups. (E) No error

3. Global warming (A) is already having seri- ous (B) effects; in the (C) future, it is (D) expected to affect everyone and every- thing on the planet. (E) No error

4. I (A) can assure you that (B) to ensure your (C) well-being, both financial and emotional, you need (D) to insure your home. (E) No error

Clouds of Paris on the Third Offbeat, c. 1965–1985.
Friedensreich Hundertwasser. Private collection.

Contemporary Era

Unit 9

1980 to Present

Contemporary Era 1980 to Present

1980

1990

AMERICAN LITERATURE

1980
Norman Mailer wins the Pulitzer Prize for *The Executioner's Song*

1982
Alice Walker publishes *The Color Purple;* it wins the Pulitzer Prize in 1983

1984
David Mamet wins the Pulitzer Prize for *Glengarry Glen Ross*

1985
Larry McMurtry publishes *Lonesome Dove*

1987
Toni Morrison publishes *Beloved*

1989
Amy Tan publishes *The Joy Luck Club*

1990
Michael Crichton publishes *Jurassic Park*

1990
Playwright August Wilson wins the Pulitzer Prize for *The Piano Lesson*

1991
Jane Smiley publishes *A Thousand Acres*

1993
Annie Proulx wins the National Book Award for *The Shipping News*

1993
Toni Morrison wins the Nobel Prize for literature

1994
Louise Erdrich publishes *The Bingo Palace*

AMERICAN HISTORY

1983
Time magazine names the personal computer (PC) its Person of the Year

1983
Sally Ride becomes the first woman in space

1986
The *Challenger* space shuttle explodes, killing all seven astronauts aboard

1986
The Reagan administration sells weapons to Iran

1987
The New York Stock Exchange suffers its largest one-day loss in history

1989
The *Exxon Valdez* spills nearly eleven million gallons of oil in Alaska

1992
Riots break out in Los Angeles following the Rodney King trial

1993
New York's World Trade Center is bombed but remains intact

1993
Seventy-four members of the Branch Davidian religious sect are killed in Waco, Texas, following a standoff with federal agents

1993
President Clinton signs into law the North American Free Trade Agreement (NAFTA)

1994
The Hubble Space Telescope, launched in 1990, proves the existence of black holes

WORLD HISTORY

1981
The AIDS epidemic begins

1984
Eastern bloc countries boycott the Summer Olympics in Los Angeles

1984
Indian Prime Minister Indira Gandhi is assassinated

1986
A nuclear power plant melts down in Chernobyl, Ukraine

1989
The Berlin Wall is torn down, reuniting Germany

1989
The Tiananmen Square Protests in China result in violence between the Chinese government and political activists

1990
Iraq invades Kuwait, starting the first Gulf War

1991
The Soviet Union collapses, ending the Cold War

1992
The European Union (EU) is officially formed

1994
The apartheid government falls in South Africa; Nelson Mandela is elected president

1994
Hutu extremists kill more than one million Tutsi people in Rwanda

AMERICAN LITERATURE

1995
Judith Ortiz Cofer publishes *An Island Like You,* a collection of short stories

1996
Playwright Jonathan Larson is posthumously awarded the Pulitzer Prize and several Tony Awards for *Rent*

1997
Philip Roth publishes *American Pastoral*

WOLFE

1998
Tom Wolfe publishes *A Man in Full*

1999
Poet Shel Silverstein dies

2001
Michael Chabon wins the Pulitzer Prize for *The Amazing Adventures of Kavalier & Clay*

2003
Dan Brown publishes *The Da Vinci Code*

2006
James Frey's memoir, *A Million Little Pieces,* is proven to contain numerous fabrications

2007
The fiftieth anniversary is celebrated of publication of Jack Kerouac's *On the Road*

2007
Science fiction writer Ray Bradbury receives a special citation from the Pulitzer Board, celebrating his career

AMERICAN HISTORY

1995
Timothy McVeigh bombs the Alfred P. Murrah Federal Building in Oklahoma City

1997
The *Pathfinder* lands on Mars and begins returning data to the National Aeronautics and Space Administration (NASA)

1998
President Clinton is impeached for obstruction of justice but not removed from office

1999
American cyclist Lance Armstrong achieves the first of seven consecutive Tour de France wins

CLINTON

2000
George W. Bush is elected president; controversy erupts over voting results in Florida

2001
Al-Qaeda terrorists attack New York City and Washington, DC, on September 11, causing nearly 3,000 deaths

2003
The United States goes to war in Afghanistan in response to the 9-11 attack

2003
The United States goes to war in Iraq as part of its "war on terrorism"

2005
Hurricane Katrina devastates New Orleans and the Mississippi Delta

2006
The National Security Agency's warrantless wiretapping program is declared unconstitutional

WORLD HISTORY

1996
The Taliban gains control of Afghanistan

1997
Scottish researchers clone a sheep

SUHARTO

1997
Great Britain cedes Hong Kong to China

1998
The Kosovo War begins between North Atlantic Treaty Organization (NATO) troops and the former Yugoslavia

1998
Indonesian Prime Minister Suharto resigns from office following the East Asian financial crisis

2003
The Darfur conflict begins in Sudan between Arab militias and African rebels

2004
A major earthquake and resulting tsunamis devastate countries bordering the Indian Ocean

2004
The European Union (EU) expands to twenty-five nations

2006
North Korea announces its first nuclear weapons test

2007
Gordon Brown succeeds Tony Blair as British prime minister

"There is nothing wrong with America that cannot be cured by what is right with America."

—PRESIDENT BILL CLINTON

The Eighties

The decade opened with heated negotiations for the release of fifty-two U.S. hostages held in Iran since November 1979. President Carter's failure to secure their release contributed to his losing the 1980 presidential election to Ronald Reagan. Six years later, during the Iran-Contra hearings, Americans learned that officials in the Reagan administration had sent arms to Iran in exchange for the hostages and then used money from the sale to covertly support the Nicaraguan Contras in their fight against the Sandinista government.

Having inherited an ailing economy, Reagan pursued a conservative political agenda of lower taxes on corporations and the wealthy, reduced government regulation of industry, cuts in social programs, and increased military spending. This approach, which would become known as *Reaganomics,* was heralded as a way to spur economic growth. However, the national debt rose to an all-time high during the Reagan years.

Technological advances in the 1980s heralded the immense changes that average Americans would see in the coming years. The development of an efficient fiber optic cable allowed the transmission of information that could be translated into a picture or sound, making the 1980 Winter Olympics the first fiber optic television transmission. In 1981, the first personal computers (PCs) were offered to the public and the first commercial cellular phone system began operating in Chicago and Washington, DC.

By 1987, American farmers were caught in the worst depression in fifty years, and environmental quality declined as economic expansion became a priority. Chemical and nuclear accidents happened in Bhopal, India, and Chernobyl, Ukraine; disastrous oil spills occurred, including that of the *Exxon Valdez* in Alaska; and climate change accelerated worldwide. The United States was documented as the largest emitter of greenhouse gases, a concern tied to global warming and the depletion of the ozone layer.

Geopolitical Changes

Tensions flared between the United States and Soviet Union in 1981 over Solidarity, a Polish trade union, and again in 1984, when the Soviets led a boycott of the Summer Olympics in Los Angeles. Then in October 1987, an international stock market crash delivered

On March 24, 1989, the *Exxon Valdez* spilled more than eleven million gallons of oil in Prince William Sound, Alaska.

a crippling blow to the suffering economies of the Soviet Union's Eastern bloc nations. In 1989, the Soviet Union, no longer able to support the economies of communist regimes in other countries, announced it would no longer intervene in Eastern Europe. That policy allowed prodemocracy movements to successfully challenge communist governments in Poland, Czechoslovakia, and Romania. In addition, it brought about the fall of the Berlin Wall and the reunification of East and West Germany.

In 1991, the Soviet Union was transformed into the Commonwealth of Independent States and its armed forces were turned over to Boris Yeltsin, President of Russia. The Cold War had ended.

The Nineties

With the collapse of the Soviet Union, formerly independent ethnic groups reclaimed their sovereignty. This resurgence of ethnic identity led to ten years of Serbian terror within the former Yugoslavia, led by President Slobodan Milosevic. In the Middle East, Iraqi troops, commanded by dictator Saddam Hussein, invaded Kuwait in 1991 to seize its oil fields. The United States responded militarily with Operation Desert Storm, marking the first time a war was conducted almost entirely with high-tech weaponry.

In 1992, Bill Clinton claimed the presidency, beginning a two-term administration that saw renewed economic prosperity led by investment in technology. Clinton sought to reduce the budget deficit by cutting spending and raising taxes on the wealthy and corporations. However, his steps to control spiraling health care costs faltered.

Sadly, the 1990s also was a time of increasing violence. In 1995, a bomb ripped through the Murrah Federal Building in Oklahoma City, killing 168 people. Near the end of the decade, five mass shootings occurred on U.S. school grounds within two years.

Amazing developments in medicine and technology were made during the 1990s. With funding from the international Human Genome Project, scientists began mapping all of the genes on human DNA, dis-

covering new genes and the roles they play in disease. The shocking realization that AIDS (acquired immune deficiency syndrome) had spread rapidly throughout the world brought about significant developments in treatment, although no cure was discovered. In 1997, British researchers announced they had successfully cloned a lamb named Dolly from the single cell of an adult sheep. These developments, along with discussion of stem cell research, raised serious ethical questions about bioindustry that Americans continue to debate.

The 1990s brought increased awareness of environmental hazards, such as global warming and acid rain, and recognition that the world's most difficult problems were tied to the world population explosion. Progress was made with the 1992 United Nations Earth Summit, at which a treaty on biodiversity was negotiated.

One of the most significant developments during the decade was the availability of a vast amount of information and entertainment on the Internet. Although the hypertext transfer protocol (http) was invented in 1989, the World Wide Web did not open for public use until 1993. Soon users were zooming across

NOTABLE NUMBERS

- **2.5 million** Americans who were homeless in 1982 at the height of the worst recession in almost fifty years

- **3** Babies born per second worldwide in 1994, as the world's population exploded

- **2,973** People killed in the September 11, 2001, terrorist attacks

- **$81.2 billion** Cost of damage caused by Hurricane Katrina in 2005

- **1 billion** People with Internet access in 2007, up from 45 million in 1998

- **2,500** Scientists who contributed to a 2007 international report stating humans' likely contribution to global warming

> *"The Internet is becoming the town square for the global village of tomorrow."*
>
> — BILL GATES, FOUNDER/CHAIRMAN OF MICROSOFT

space on the so-called Information Superhighway using voice over Internet protocol (VoIP) to talk across continents. With the new millennium, Americans would be using computers to download audio to digital players, to share photos and video from digital cameras, and to participate in blogging and social networking websites. However, all new technologies would bring with them new concerns and legal challenges in the areas of copyright protection and personal privacy.

The New Millennium

Less than a year after taking office, President George W. Bush faced one of the most tragic events to occur

A New York firefighter views the site of the World Trade Center (September 12, 2001).

on American soil: the terrorist attacks of September 11, 2001. On that day, nineteen men hijacked four airplanes, flying two of them into the World Trade Center in New York City and one into the Pentagon in Washington, DC. Plans to fly the fourth plane into the White House were thwarted by a group of passengers who overtook the hijackers, causing the plane to crash in a field in Pennsylvania. In total, nearly three thousand people were killed. A terrorist group called Al-Qaeda, led by Osama bin Laden, claimed responsibility.

Shortly after the 9-11 attack, the United States declared a "war on terrorism" and sent troops to Afghanistan to attack the Taliban, a repressive regime that harbored bin Laden's terrorist training camp. The U.S. military deposed the Taliban but did not capture Osama bin Laden. With the assistance of the U.S. military, the new Iraqi government struggled to maintain control over a nation embroiled in civil war. Americans' growing discontent with the U.S. occupation of Iraq became one of the key issues in the 2008 presidential campaign.

In August 2005, a Category 5 hurricane named Katrina struck the southern United States, devastating the city of New Orleans and the Mississippi Delta region. The hurricane breached the levee system surrounding New Orleans, flooding the city and killing thousands. Charges that the federal government's response was inadequate prompted investigation into the role and readiness of the Federal Emergency Management Agency (FEMA). Rebuilding the city was slow, and many evacuated residents never returned to their damaged homes.

In the twenty-first century, as the United States becomes ever more ethnically diverse, new challenges confront policy makers. Debate over immigration has focused on issues of national security and economic and social policy. Critics of immigration point to lost jobs and strains on welfare and school systems, while supporters argue that immigrants' overall contribution to the U.S. economy significantly outweighs the costs of resettlement. Whatever policies are adopted in the future, the face of America will continue to change.

Early generations of Americans were expected to *assimilate,* or conform to mainstream social standards. American society was described as a "melting pot," in which people from all backgrounds blended by putting aside their unique cultural characteristics. As time went on, however, more people chose not only to acknowledge their cultural heritage but to embrace it. Today, American society is viewed less as a melting pot and more as a "quilt" or "tossed salad"—a collection of diverse elements that coexist to create a harmonious whole yet maintain their distinct characteristics.

The value of cultural heritage is a prominent theme in contemporary American literature. Many authors have expressed their sense of heritage by re-evaluating aspects of family history that may have been overlooked or undervalued in the past. Alice Walker, Louise Erdrich, Rita Dove, and Naomi Shihab Nye all portray the experiences of their cultures by writing about everyday family activities and events. These accounts of ordinary life reveal the extraordinary strength and endurance that women have demonstrated in preserving the family and maintaining cultural traditions.

Untitled, c. 1985. Romare Bearden. Art © Romare Bearden Foundation/Licensed by VAGA, New York, NY.

Other contemporary authors have examined the evolution of heritage that is part of the immigrant experience. Amy Tan, Judith Ortiz Cofer, Sandra Cisneros, and Julia Alvarez reveal the challenges faced by individuals living in two cultures: the culture of their homeland and that of mainstream America. The different, sometimes conflicting perspectives of immigrant parents and their children is a topic common to many of these writers. Poets Li-Young Lee, Garrett Hongo, and Yvonne Sapia consider heritage in terms of the parent-child relationship.

Alice Walker

> "No person is your friend who demands
> your silence, or denies your right to grow."

Alice Walker (b. 1944) was born in Eatonton, Georgia, the eighth child of sharecroppers who farmed land owned by an elderly woman. While still a child, Walker was blinded in one eye when her brother accidentally shot her in the face with a BB gun. Self-conscious about the scarring that resulted, she withdrew from others and turned to writing poetry to help her cope with her loneliness.

Despite her limited eyesight, Walker was able to pursue an education and became an excellent student. After spending two years at Spelman College in Atlanta, she transferred to Sarah Lawrence College in New York City. She had written her first book of poetry before earning a bachelor's degree in 1965. Walker also became active in the Civil Rights movement, working in Mississippi to help African Americans register to vote. She later wrote a novel, *Meridian* (1976), based on her experiences as an activist.

While employed at *Ms.,* a magazine that promotes women's rights, Walker introduced readers to the works of neglected African-American writer Zora Neale Hurston (see Unit 5). Walker also taught writing at several universities, including the women's college Wellesley, where she was the first person to teach a course on African-American women writers.

Walker may be most famous for her novel *The Color Purple* (1982), which won the Pulitzer Prize for fiction. This celebrated novel chronicles the experiences of an African-American community struggling against poverty and racism in a small Southern town. Director Steven Spielberg adapted the novel into a movie (1985), which was nominated for eleven Academy Awards. More recently, *The Color Purple* was produced as a popular Broadway play (2005).

Walker went on to write a number of novels, including *Now Is the Time to Open Your Heart* (2004). Her early short stories are collected in *You Can't Keep a Good Woman Down* (1982); *The Complete Stories* appeared in 1994. Between 1973 and 2003, Walker wrote seven volumes of poetry; in 2005, her *Collected Poems* was published. She is the author, as well, of several nonfiction works. Walker's writings reflect her desire to enlighten her readers on racial and gender equality as well as the importance of honoring ancestors—in particular, strong women.

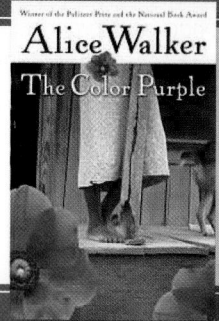

Noted Works

The Color Purple (1982)

You Can't Keep a Good Woman Down (1982)

The Temple of My Familiar (1989)

Anything We Love Can Be Saved (1997)

Absolute Trust in the Goodness of the Earth (2003)

Though We May Feel Alone
Dream

Lyric Poems by Alice Walker

My Mother's Blue Bowl

An Essay by Alice Walker

Build Background

Literary Context The following three selections by Alice Walker, two poems and an essay, focus on the writer's awareness of the presence in her life of her forebears, especially women. Although lesser known than her fiction, Walker's poetry is a study in contrasts. Her style is simple yet insightful, blunt yet compassionate, intimate yet universal. Typically, she writes in *free verse:* poetry that does not use regular rhyme, meter, or stanza division. It may contain irregular line breaks and sentence fragments and tends to mimic the rhythms of ordinary speech. Walker's essays often reflect her conversational style and her passion and determination to empower women to lead fulfilling lives.

"Though We May Feel Alone" is part of the poetry collection *Absolute Trust in the Goodness of the Earth* (2003). The poem suggests that the wisdom, strength, and encouragement of our ancestors can guide us in the modern world. Walker also suggests that the choices we make sometimes lead us astray and that if we "right ourselves," the journey will be rewarding.

The poem **"Dream"** celebrates Walker's mother, a woman whose faith and strength triumphed over adversity. Walker is inspired by her mother's dual identities—as a woman who tended to others' needs but yearned to loosen the bonds to pursue her own dreams. This poem also appears in the collection *Absolute Trust in the Goodness of the Earth*.

The essay **"My Mother's Blue Bowl"** first appeared in the magazine *Family Circle* in 1997. In the essay, Walker explains how her aging mother gradually gave away many of her possessions, which Walker describes as "light-

California Governor Arnold Schwarzenegger inducts Walker into the California Hall of Fame.

ening her load, permitting her worldly possessions to dwindle in significance." One of the items Walker asks to have is her mother's bright blue bowl. Although the bowl means little to her mother, for Walker, the bowl brings back childhood memories and reminds her of how her mother made their home a place of beauty and warmth despite their poverty.

Reader's Context How do our ancestors—parents, grandparents, and generations further removed—influence our thoughts and values?

Analyze Literature

Free Verse and Style
Free verse is poetry that does not use regular rhyme, meter, or stanza division.

Style refers to the manner in which a passage is spoken or written. A writer's style is characterized by elements such as word choice (*diction*), sentence structure and length, and other recurring features.

Set Purpose

As you read Walker's poems, identify the characteristics of free verse they demonstrate. Think about how the use of free verse is a feature of Walker's poetic style. As you read the essay, continue to think about Walker's written style. Identify the recurring features that lead many literary scholars to describe her style as *conversational* or *understated*.

Preview Vocabulary

subversive, 1169
serene, 1171
musing, 1171
solace, 1171
divestiture, 1171
marvel, 1171
cauldron, 1173
riotous, 1173
itinerant, 1173
rapaciously, 1173

Shotgun, Third Ward #1, 1966. John T. Biggers. Smithsonian American Art Museum, Washington, DC.
Art © John T. Biggers Estate/Licensed by VAGA, New York, NY/Estate represented by Michael Rosenfeld Gallery.

Though We May Feel Alone

by Alice Walker

Though we may feel
Alone
We never
Really are.
5   The ancestors
The one called
God
&
The one called
10   Death
Prominent
Among them
Rest on our
Shoulders
15   Always.

It is as if
We carried two
Birds' nests
Just below
20   Our ears;
In these
Like so many eggs
The ancestors
Sit.

<pre>
25   They ride along
          Overhearing
          Every conversation
          Every
          Thought
30   Watching everything
          We do.

          Fragile as eggs
          But tough
          Cookies
35   Too
          It does not matter
          To them
          If we lose our
          Way
40   On occasion
          That we become
          Lost
          Or fall down.

          Missteps are
45   Common
          On every path
          They've seen
          (& they've seen lots!).

          What matters to them
50   Is that
          We right ourselves
          Keep a better watch
          Over where we're going
          That they retain
55   The high view
          They like
          & what is most
          Crucial
          For helping us:
60   Balance. ❖
</pre>

Consider the question suggested by the title of this poem, "Though We May Feel Alone." Are we alone? Where do people find guidance in life?

Billie Holiday (1938).

by Alice Walker

Sometimes
When I dream
About
My mother
5   She is in

One of the
Shacks
Her art
Made
10   Radiant.

She might
Be lying
All in pink
Just
15   In
The doorway
Sunlight
Warm
Upon her
20   Singing.

In Life,
A Methodist
Then an
Atonal

<pre>
25   Jehovah's
            Witness
            My mother
            Did not
            Sing.

30   At least
            Not the
            <u>Subversive</u>
            Jazzy
            Melodies
35   She favors
            In
            My
            Dream.

            On my altar
40   For years
            Two women's
            Framed
            Faces
            Have inspired
45   Challenged
            Nourished me
            In every way:

    (Although I had not noticed, before my dream,
        their resemblance, as close as twins.)

50   One contained
            Righteous
            In her garden
            My mother;
            The other an Outlaw
55   In a smoky
            Nightclub
            Lady Day.[1] ❖
</pre>

---

1. **Lady Day.** Nickname of Billie Holiday (1915–1959), African-American jazz singer

> **sub • ver • sive** (sub vʉr´ siv) *adj.*, causing a corruption of morals or ideas

MIRRORS & WINDOWS

How might a child's image of his or her mother be different from the mother's image of herself?

Blue Bowl and Lily, 2007. Suzanne Koch.

My Mother's Blue Bowl

by Alice Walker

If there's anything you want, take it when you leave; it might not be here when you come back.

Visitors to my house are often served food—soup, potatoes, rice—in a large blue stoneware bowl, noticeably chipped at the rim. It is perhaps the most precious thing I own. It was given to me by my mother in her last healthy days. The days before a massive stroke laid her low and left her almost speechless. Those days when to visit her was to be drawn into a serene cocoon of memories and present-day musings and to rest there, in temporary retreat from the rest of the world, as if still an infant, nodding and secure at her breast.

For much of her life my mother longed, passionately longed, for a decent house. One with a yard that did not have to be cleared with an ax. One with a roof that kept out the rain. One with floors that you could not fall through. She longed for a beautiful house of wood or stone. Or of red brick, like the houses her many sisters and their husbands had. When I was thirteen she found such a house. Green-shuttered, white-walled. Breezy. With a lawn and a hedge and giant pecan trees. A porch swing. There her gardens flourished in spite of the shade, as did her youngest daughter, for whom she sacrificed her life doing hard labor in someone else's house, in order to afford peace and prettiness for her child, to whose grateful embrace she returned each night.

But, curiously, the minute I left home, at seventeen, to attend college, she abandoned the dream house and moved into the projects. Into a small, tight apartment of few breezes, in which I was never to feel comfortable, but that she declared suited her "to a T." I took solace in the fact that it was at least hugged by spacious lawn on one side, and by forest, out the back door, and that its isolated position at the end of the street meant she would have a measure of privacy.

Her move into the projects—the best housing poor black people in the South ever had, she would occasionally declare, even as my father struggled to adjust to the cramped rooms and hard, unforgiving qualities of brick—was, I now understand, a step in the direction of divestiture, lightening her load, permitting her worldly possessions to dwindle in significance and, well before she herself would turn to spirit, roll away from her.

She owned little, in fact. A bed, a dresser, some chairs. A set of living-room furniture. A set of kitchen furniture. A bed and wardrobe (given to her years before, when I was a teenager, by one of her more prosperous sisters). Her flowers: everywhere, inside the house and outside. Planted in anything she managed to get her green hands on, including old suitcases and abandoned shoes. She recycled everything, effortlessly. And gradually she had only a small amount of stuff—mostly stuff her children gave her: nightgowns, perfume, a microwave—to recycle or to use.

Each time I visited her I marveled at the modesty of her desires. She appeared to have hardly any, beyond a thirst for a Pepsi-Cola or a hunger for a piece of fried chicken or fish. On every visit I noticed that more and more of what I remembered of her possessions seemed to be missing. One day I commented on this.

Taking a deep breath, sighing, and following both with a beaming big smile, which lit up her face, the room, and my heart, she said: Yes, it's all going. I don't need it anymore. If there's

se • rene (sə rēn´) *adj.,* calm
mus • ing (myüz´ iŋ) *n.,* reflection or meditation
so • lace (sä´ ləs) *n.,* comfort; consolation
di • ves • ti • ture (dī ves´ tə chür´) *n.,* act of disposing of or freeing oneself of something
mar • vel (mär´ vəl) *v.,* become filled with surprise, wonder, or curiosity

anything you want, take it when you leave; it might not be here when you come back.

The dishes my mother and father used daily had come from my house; I had sent them years before, when I moved from Mississippi to New York. Neither the plates nor the silver matched entirely, but it was all beautiful in her eyes. There were numerous paper items, used in the microwave, and stacks of plastic plates and cups, used by the scores of children from the neighborhood who continued throughout her life to come and go. But there was nothing there for me to want.

One day, however, looking for a jar into which to pour leftover iced tea, I found myself probing deep into the wilderness of the overstuffed, airless pantry. Into the land of the old-fashioned, the outmoded, the outdated. The humble and the obsolete. There was a smoothing iron, a churn. A butter press. And two large bowls.

One was cream and rose with a blue stripe. The other was a deep, vivid blue.

May I have this bowl, Mama, I asked, looking at her and at the blue bowl with delight.

You can have both of them, she said, barely acknowledging them, and continuing to put leftover food away.

I held the bowls on my lap for the rest of the evening, while she watched a TV program about cops and criminals that I found too horrifying to follow.

Before leaving the room I kissed her on the forehead and asked if I could get anything for her from the kitchen; then I went off to bed. The striped bowl I placed on a chair beside the door, so I could look at it from where I lay. The blue bowl I placed in the bed with me.

In giving me these gifts, my mother had done a number of astonishing things, in her typically offhand way. She had taught me a lesson about letting go of possessions—easily,

In winter my mother's riotous flowers would be absent, and the shack stood revealed for what it was.

Slogging through sleet and wind to the sagging front door, thankful that our house was too far from the road to be seen clearly from the school bus, I always felt a wave of embarrassment and misery. But then I would open the door. And there inside would be my mother's winter flowers: a glowing fire in the fireplace, colorful handmade quilts on all our beds, paintings and drawings of flowers and fruits and yes, of Jesus, given to her by who knows whom—and, most of all, there in the center of the rough-hewn table, which in the tiny kitchen almost touched the rusty wood-burning stove, stood the big blue bowl, full of whatever was the most tasty thing on earth.

There was my mother herself. Glowing. Her teeth sparkling. Her eyes twinkling. As if she lived in a castle and her favorite princes and princesses had just dropped by to visit.

The blue bowl stood there, seemingly full forever, no matter how deeply or <u>rapaciously</u> we dipped, as if it had no bottom. And she dipped up soup. Dipped up lima beans. Dipped up stew. Forked out potatoes. Spooned out rice and peas and corn. And in the light and warmth that was *Her,* we dined.

Thank you, Mama ❖

without emphasis or regret—and she had given me a symbol of what she herself represented in my life.

For the blue bowl especially was a <u>cauldron</u> of memories. Of cold, harsh, wintry days, when my brothers and sister and I trudged home from school burdened down by the silence of frigidity of our long trek from the main road, down the hill to our shabby-looking house. More rundown than any of our classmates' houses. In winter my mother's <u>riotous</u> flowers would be absent, and the shack stood revealed for what it was. A gray, decaying, too small barrack meant to house the <u>itinerant</u> tenant workers on a prosperous white man's farm.

---

caul • dron (kôl´ drən) *n.,* large pot or kettle
ri • ot • ous (rī´ ə təs) *adj.,* abundant; enthusiastic
itin • er • ant (ī ti´ nə rənt) *adj.,* traveling from place to place
ra • pa • cious • ly (rə pā´ shəs lē) *adv.,* with excessive hunger or desire

---

The blue bowl brought back warm childhood memories for Walker. What object from your past evokes these kinds of memories for you?

Refer to Text ▶ ▶ ▶ ▶ ▶ **Reason with Text**

1a. Name the two ancestors the speaker identifies by name in "Though We May Feel Alone."	**1b.** How can each of these figures be considered an ancestor?	**Understand** Find meaning
2a. In stanza 5 of "Dream," what is on the speaker's "altar," or place of significance?	**2b.** The mother did not sing, so to whom does "her" refer in line 19? In stanza 5, what does the reference to the two women stress about the speaker?	**Apply** Use information
3a. In "My Mother's Blue Bowl," why does Walker's mother leave her "dream house" and move to the projects?	**3b.** Analyze Walker's mother's reasons for downsizing and parting with her possessions. What lesson does Walker learn from her?	**Analyze** Take things apart
4a. In "Though We May Feel Alone," what do the ancestors think is most important in helping the individual?	**4b.** Judge the effectiveness of the simile comparing *ancestors* to *eggs* in lines 22–24 and 32.	**Evaluate** Make judgments
5a. In "My Mother's Blue Bowl," how did Walker feel as a child about her family's first house on the farm, both inside and outside?	**5b.** Explain how Walker's mother taught her children the value of having beauty and creativity despite being poor.	**Create** Bring ideas together

Analyze Literature

Free Verse and Style

What characteristics of free verse did you identify in Walker's poems? How does her use of free verse fit the topics and themes of her poems? Discuss how your understanding and appreciation of the poems would be different if Walker followed poetic conventions such as rhyme and meter.

What recurring features characterize Walker's written style, both poetry and prose? Consider, for instance, her use of sentence fragments. What words would you use to describe her style? Evaluate the effectiveness of her style in writing about her heritage.

Extend the Text

Writing Options

Creative Writing Review the characteristics of free verse and other qualities of Walker's style. Then write a poem imitating that style on a subject of interest to you. Share your work with one or more classmates.

Expository Writing At a meeting of the Literature and History Club, you will present a brief analysis of how Walker incorporates in her work real and imagined historical events and individuals. Write an analytical paragraph discussing the significance of the past in the selections.

Collaborative Learning

Create Recycled Heirlooms Walker's mother "recycled everything, effortlessly" in making planters for her

flowers. With a group, plan how old toys, jewelry, china, and other items can be used in new ways to make either a functional object, such as a planter, or a piece of art.

Media Literacy

Prepare a Transcript for a Documentary Conduct a survey of people on the street or at school by asking the question What is art? Take careful notes on the responses you receive so you can later prepare a transcript of the information. Share with the class a summary of your findings.

 Go to **www.mirrorsandwindows.com** for more.

1. In "Though We May Feel Alone," what is the ancestors' greatest concern?
   A. whether we do things according to tradition
   B. that we have pure thoughts and live virtuous lives
   C. that we respect the presence of Death and God
   D. that we learn from our errors and keep moving ahead
   E. that they always have a place in our lives

2. In "Though We May Feel Alone," the description of the ancestors as being "fragile as eggs" is an example of
   A. irony.
   B. a metaphor.
   C. a simile.
   D. personification.
   E. characterization.

3. In stanza 5 of "Dream," what is implied by Walker's reference to "On my altar"?
   A. her sense of irony about her mother's life
   B. her commitment to religious values
   C. her appreciation for jazz music
   D. her memories of her childhood home
   E. her sense of respect and devotion for her mother

4. Which of the following statements about "Dream" is correct?
   A. The speaker's mother was a good singer.
   B. The speaker had not seen the resemblance between her mother and Billie Holiday until her dream.
   C. The speaker's mother was famous, but she also saw her mother's quiet side at home.
   D. The speaker became interested in Billie Holiday because her mother was a fan of jazz.
   E. None of the above

5. In "Dream," the speaker says that in her dream, her mother sings "subversive jazzy melodies." What does the word *subversive* mean?
   A. dangerous
   B. corrupting
   C. experimental
   D. cheerful
   E. soulful

6. In "My Mother's Blue Bowl," why is Walker surprised by her mother's decision to move to an apartment in the projects?
   A. She did not think her mother could afford to do so.
   B. She had not realized that caring for a garden and yard had become too much work for her mother.
   C. She had always heard her mother say that she hated the projects.
   D. She knew her father did not want to move.
   E. An apartment in the projects was smaller and less comfortable than the home Walker's mother left.

7. When Walker states that her mother's move to the projects was "a step in the direction of *divestiture*," what does the word *divestiture* mean?
   A. getting rid of
   B. increasing diversity
   C. personal investment
   D. independence
   E. relaxation

8. To Walker, the blue bowl represents
   A. shame over her family's poverty.
   B. her mother's spirituality.
   C. the warmth and generosity of her mother's love.
   D. overcoming the poverty she experienced as a child.
   E. her mother's artistry.

9. **Constructed Response:** Compare and contrast the description of the mother in the poem "Dream" with that of the mother in the essay "My Mother's Blue Bowl." Argue whether the mother in the poem is Alice Walker's real mother, given what you know about her from the essay. Support your analysis with details from both selections.

10. **Constructed Response:** Describe how Walker values small instances of beauty and creativity, as suggested in both her essay and her poems. Use evidence from the texts to support your answer.

Understand the Concept

Whether writing an essay or a research paper, you should use information from other sources to lend credibility to your ideas. Understanding how to include this information is essential to writing a paper that not only demonstrates its validity by citing other sources but also avoids **plagiarism,** which is using others' information without crediting them.

One of the ways to incorporate this information in your paper is to use **quotations,** repeating the exact words and punctuation from another source. In selecting quotations, look for statements that are particularly well expressed and that are made by recognized authorities on the topic. (See the Grammar & Style workshop about summarizing and paraphrasing on page 1269.)

To distinguish quoted text from your own writing, the convention is to enclose the text within quotation marks. Follow this guideline if the quotation will run fewer than three printed lines in your paper. For a longer quotation, set off the text by indenting it five letter spaces from the left margin and adding blank line spaces above and below the indented block. The indenting indicates that the passage is a quote, so quotation marks are not needed.

Finally, be sure to identify the source of the quotation in the sentence in which it appears or that introduces it. This is particularly important if you are using quotes from more than one source. To cite sources in a research paper, cite the author and page number, as well. (See the Grammar & Style workshop about documentation on page 1270.)

Note the language and punctuation used to introduce the quotes in these short and long examples:

EXAMPLES

Short quotation In her essay "My Mother's Blue Bowl," Walker states, "She had taught me a lesson about letting go of possessions—easily, without emphasis or regret."

Long quotation In her essay "My Mother's Blue Bowl," Walker describes how she realized over time that her mother had increasingly fewer possessions:

> Each time I visited her I marveled at the modesty of her desires. She appeared to have hardly any, beyond a thirst for a Pepsi-Cola or a hunger for a piece of fried chicken or fish. On every visit I noticed that more and more of what I remembered of her possessions seemed to be missing.

If only a fragment of a quotation is used, embed it in your own sentence and start it with a lowercase letter:

EXAMPLE

Fragment quoted Walker recalls returning home in the winter to see "the big blue bowl, full of whatever was the most tasty thing on earth."

Apply the Skill

Improve the Use of Quotations

Rewrite each of the following sentences to correctly use the quoted text, which is underlined. Consider the capitalization and use of punctuation (commas and quotation marks) in quoting either a fragment or an entire sentence, as indicated.

1. **Sentence quoted** In the essay "My Mother's Blue Bowl," Walker explains, <u>For much of her life my mother longed, passionately longed, for a decent house</u>.

2. **Fragment quoted** When Walker was thirteen, her mother, <u>Found such a house</u>.

3. **Fragment quoted** A few years later, when Walker went away to college, her mother <u>abandoned the dream house and moved into the projects</u>.

4. **Sentence quoted** Walker recalls how her mother gave away her possessions. She writes <u>On every visit I noticed that more and more of what I remembered of her possessions seemed to be missing</u>.

5. **Fragment quoted** Walker was pleased to get her mother's blue bowl, describing it as, <u>Perhaps the most precious thing I own</u>.

Use Quotations in Your Writing

When you have gathered your sources for an essay or paper, write down or highlight phrases and sentences worthy of quoting. Remember to introduce the source, give page numbers if necessary, and use quotation marks and other punctuation appropriately. Integrate each quotation within your own writing by setting the context for it and explaining it, if needed.

The Names of Women

An Essay by Louise Erdrich

Build Background

Cultural Context Louise Erdrich is a member of the Turtle Mountain Band of Chippewa Indians, although she calls herself a "mixed-blood descendant," having grown up in the mainstream white culture while preserving her Native American ties. **"The Names of Women,"** an essay from *The Bingo Palace* (1994), explains how the Anishinabe (ä nish' ə nä´ bā), Erdrich's maternal ancestors, named women according to their distinctive traits. Later on, many Anishinabe married French settlers and took the names of Christian saints.

Note that the Anishinabe are known as *Chippewa* in the United States and as *Ojibwe* in Canada.

Reader's Context How does an individual's name become part of his or her identity? How can changing one's name alter this identity?

Meet the Author

Louise Erdrich (b. 1954) was born in Little Falls, Minnesota, but grew up in Wahpeton, North Dakota. The oldest of seven children, Erdrich is of mixed heritage: Her mother was from French and Ojibwe parentage, and her father was German American. Her parents were both teachers and fostered creative writing and storytelling in their daughter. Erdrich also was exposed to her mother's ancestral language, Ojibwemowin, through her family's storytelling, motivating her to preserve this folklore in her later works.

Erdrich pursued her love of writing while attending Dartmouth College from 1972 to 1976. Three years later, she completed her master's degree at Johns Hopkins. She has worked as an editor of *The Circle,* a Native American newspaper, but admittedly has learned important life lessons from her experiences as a waitress, lifeguard, prison teacher, and farm worker.

By age thirty-one, Erdrich had published *Jacklight,* a poetry collection, and *Love Medicine* (1984), a novel that won the National Book Critics Circle Award and established her name. This poetic novel weaves together a series of stories about two Native American families over fifty years. Erdrich's non-chronological plot is reminiscent of the work of William Faulkner, one of her writing influences.

Later works have included the novels *The Beet Queen* (1986), *The Antelope Wife* (1998), and *The Painted Drum* (2005); a collection of verse called *Original Fire: Selected and New Poems* (2003); and the nonfiction volume *The Blue Jay's Dance: A Birthyear* (1995). Erdrich continues to write and is the owner of BirchBark Books, a Minneapolis bookstore that features Native American literature and gifts.

Analyze Literature

Purpose and Catalog
A writer's **purpose** is his or her aim, or goal. Writers usually have one or more of the following purposes: to inform; to portray a person, place, object, or event; to persuade; or to tell a story.

A **catalog** is a list of people, places, or objects.

Set Purpose

Like Alice Walker, Louise Erdrich explores her heritage through the lives of her women ancestors. As you read, determine Erdrich's purpose or purposes in writing. Also consider the many women's names she provides. Make a list of the names, and record what each suggests about the woman it identifies.

Preview Vocabulary

decimate, 1178
presumptuous, 1179
undeviating, 1179
novel, 1180
slough, 1181

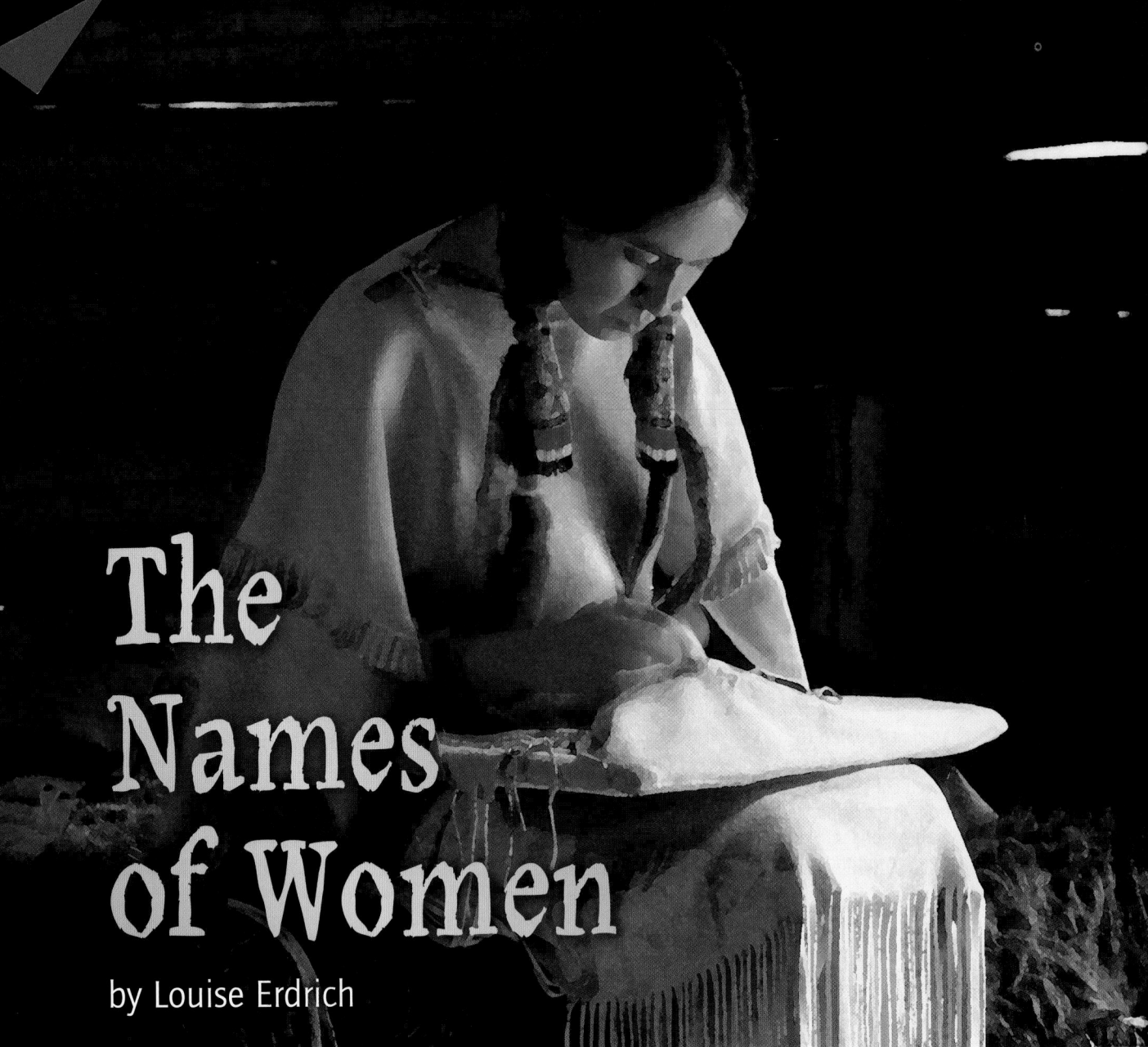

The Names of Women

by Louise Erdrich

These names tell stories, or half stories, if only we listen closely.

Ikwe is the word for woman in the language of the Anishinabe, my mother's people, whose descendants, mixed with and married to French trappers and farmers, are the Michifs of the Turtle Mountain Reservation in North Dakota. Every Anishinabe *Ikwe*, every mixed-blood descendant like me, who can trace her way back a generation or two, is the daughter of a mystery. The history of the woodland Anishinabe—<u>decimated</u> by disease, fighting Plains Indians tribes to the west and squeezed

> **dec • i • mate** (des´ ə māt) *v.*, reduce drastically

by European settlers to the east—is much like most other Native American stories, a confusion of loss, a tale of absences, of a culture that was blown apart and changed so radically in such a short time that only the names survive.

And yet, those names.

The names of the first women whose existence is recorded on the rolls of the Turtle Mountain Reservation, in 1892, reveal as much as we can ever recapture of their personalities, complex natures and relationships. These names tell stories, or half stories, if only we listen closely.

There once were women named *Standing Strong, Fish Bones, Different Thunder.* There once was a girl called *Yellow Straps.* Imagine what it was like to pick berries with *Sky Coming Down,* to walk through a storm with *Lightning Proof.* Surely, she was struck and lived, but what about the person next to her? People always avoided *Steps Over Truth,* when they wanted a straight answer, and *I Hear,* when they wanted to keep a secret. *Glittering* put coal on her face and watched for enemies at night. The woman named *Standing Across* could see things moving far across the lake. The old ladies gossiped about *Playing Around,* but no one dared say anything to her face. *Ice* was good at gambling. *Shining One Side* loved to sit and talk to *Opposite the Sky.* They both knew *Sounding Feather, Exhausted Wind* and *Green Cloud,* daughter of *Seeing Iron. Center of the Sky* was a widow. *Rabbit, Prairie Chicken* and *Daylight* were all little girls. *She Tramp* could make great distance in a day of walking. *Cross Lightning* had a powerful smile. When *Setting Wind* and *Gentle Woman Standing* sang together the whole tribe listened. *Stop the Day* got her name when at her shout the afternoon went still. *Log* was strong, *Cloud Touching Bottom* weak and consumptive.[1] *Mirage* married *Wind.* Everyone loved *Musical Cloud,* but children hid from *Dressed in Stone. Lying Down Grass* had such a gentle voice and touch, but no one dared to cross *She Black of Heart.*

We can imagine something of these women from their names. Anishinabe historian Basil

Glittering put coal on her face and watched for enemies at night.

Johnston notes that 'such was the mystique and force of a name that it was considered <u>presumptuous</u> and unbecoming, even vain, for a person to utter his own name. It was the custom for a third person, if present, to utter the name of the person to be identified. Seldom, if ever, did either husband or wife speak the name of the other in public.'

Shortly after the first tribal roll, the practice of renaming became an ecclesiastical exercise, and, as a result, most women in the next two generations bear the names of saints particularly beloved by the French. *She Knows the Bear* became Marie. *Sloping Cloud* was christened Jeanne. *Taking Care of the Day* and *Yellow Day Woman* turned into Catherines. Identities are altogether lost. The daughters of my own ancestors, *Kwayzancheewin—Acts Like a Boy* and *Striped Earth Woman*—go unrecorded, and no hint or reflection of their individual natures comes to light through the scattershot records of those times, although they must have been genetically tough in order to survive: there were epidemics of typhoid, flu, measles and other diseases that winnowed the tribe each winter. They had to have grown up sensible, hard-working, <u>undeviating</u> in their attention to their tasks. They had to have been lucky. And if very lucky, they acquired carts.

---

1. **consumptive.** Having tuberculosis or other tissue-weakening disease

---

pre • sump • tu • ous (prē zump´ chü əs) *adj.,* taking liberties; overstepping bounds
un • de • vi • at • ing (un dē´ vē āt iŋ) *adj.,* unchanging; persistent

Anishinabe Creation Myth

Most cultures have a *creation myth,* or a story that defines its beginnings. Erdrich's forebears, the Anishinabe, believe that their tribal name means "original people." They point to the Great Spirit Gitchi Manitou as the creator of the world and all those living in it.

The Anishinabe believe that Gitchi Manitou sent a character named Nanabozho to Earth to name each plant and animal and to act as a liaison between spirits and human beings. Nanabozho is uniquely situated to handle this responsibility, since his mother was human and his father was a spirit from the West named E-bangshimog. Characters that are half-mortal and half-immortal are a common feature of many mythologies around the globe. For example, the Greek heroes Hercules

and Achilles both share this trait with Nanabozho. In some stories, Nanabozho embodies the trickster archetype by taking on a rabbit form. To pay homage to her ancestral folklore, Erdrich created several characters in her writings that embody the characteristics of this mythological creature.

(See Unit 1, Understanding Literary Forms, for more information about Native American mythology and other literature from the oral tradition.)

I t is no small thing that both of my great-grandmothers were known as women with carts.

The first was Elise Eliza McCloud, the great-granddaughter of *Striped Earth Woman.* The buggy she owned was somewhat grander than a cart. In her photograph, Elise Eliza gazes straight ahead, intent, elevated in her pride. Perhaps she and her daughter Justine, both wearing reshaped felt fedoras, were on their way to the train that would take them from Rugby, North Dakota, to Grand Forks, and back again. Back and forth across the upper tier of the plains, they peddled their handworked tourist items—dangling moccasin brooches and little beaded hats, or, in the summer, the wild berries, plums and nuts that they had gathered from the wooded hills. Of Elise Eliza's industry there remains in the family only an intricately beaded pair of buffalo horns and a piece of real furniture, a 'high-boy,' an object once regarded with some awe, a prize she won for selling the most merchandise from a manufacturer's catalogue.

The owner of the other cart, Virginia Grandbois, died when I was nine years old: she was a fearsome and fascinating presence, an old woman seated like an icon behind the door of my grandparents' house. Forty years before I was born, she was photographed on her way to fetch drinking water at the reservation well. In the picture she is seated high, the reins in her fingers connected to a couple of shaggy fetlocked draft ponies. The barrel she will fill stands behind her. She wears a man's sweater and an expression of vast self-pleasure. She might have been saying *Kaygoh,* a warning, to calm the horses. She might have been speaking to whomever it was who held the camera, still a <u>novel</u> luxury.

Virginia Grandbois was known to smell of flowers. In spite of the potato picking, water hauling, field and housework, she found the time and will to dust her face with pale powder, in order to look more French. She was the great-great-granddaughter of the daughter of the principal leader of the *A-waus-e,* the Bullhead clan, a woman whose real name

nov • el (nô´ v'l) *adj.,* new; unheard of

was never recorded but who, on marrying a Frenchman, was 'recreated' as Madame Cadotte. It was Madame Cadotte who acted as a liaison[2] between her Ojibway relatives and her husband so that, even when French influence waned in the region, Jean-Baptiste Cadotte stayed on as the only trader of importance, the last governor of the fort at Sault St. Marie.

By the time I knew Virginia Grandbois, however, her mind had darkened, and her body deepened, shrunk, turned to bones and leather. She did not live in the present or in any known time at all. Periodically, she would awaken from dim and unknown dreams to find herself seated behind the door in her daughter's house. She then cried out for her cart and her horses. When they did not materialize, Virginia Grandbois rose with great energy and purpose. Then she walked towards her house, taking the straightest line.

She wanted her own place back, the place she had made, not her daughter's, not anyone else's.

That house, long sold and gone, lay over one hundred miles due east and still Virginia Grandbois charged ahead, no matter what lay in her path—fences, <u>sloughs</u>, woods, the yards of other families. She wanted home, to get home, to be home. She wanted her own place back, the place she had made, not her daughter's, not anyone else's. Hers. There was no substitute, no kindness, no reality that would change her mind. She had to be tied to the chair, and the chair to the wall, and still there was no reasoning with Virginia Grandbois. Her entire life, her hard-won personality, boiled down in the end to one stubborn, fixed, desperate idea.

I started with the same idea—this urge to get home, even if I must walk straight across the world. Only, for me, the urge to walk is the urge to write. Like my great-grandmother's house, there is no home for me to get to. A mixed-blood, raised in the Sugarbeet Capital, educated on the Eastern seaboard, married in a tiny New England village, living now on a ridge directly across from the Swan Range in the Rocky Mountains, my home is a collection of homes, of wells in which the quiet of experience shales away into sweet bedrock.

Elise Eliza pieced the quilt my mother slept under, a patchwork of shirts, pants, other worn-out scraps, bordered with small rinsed and pressed Bull Durham sacks.[3] As if in another time and place, although it is only the dim barrel of a four-year-old's memory, I see myself lying wrapped under smoky quilts and dank green army blankets in the house in which my mother was born. In the fragrance of tobacco, some smoked in home-rolled cigarettes, some offered to the Manitous[4] whose presence still was honored, I dream myself home. Beneath the rafters, shadowed with bunches of plants and torn calendars, in the nest of a sagging bed, I listen to mice rustle and the scratch of an owl's claws as it paces the shingles.

Elise Eliza's daughter-in-law, my grandmother Mary LeFavor, kept that house of hand-hewed and stacked beams, mudded between. She managed to shore it up and keep it standing by stuffing every new crack with disposable diapers. Having used and reused cloth to diaper her own children, my grandmother washed and hung to dry the paper and plastic diapers

---

2. **liaison** (lē ā´ zôn). Mediator, or person who helps two sides communicate
3. **Bull Durham sacks.** Large bags that had contained a brand of tobacco
4. **Manitous.** Supernatural forces that the Anishinabe people believe are present in the natural world

> **slough** (slü) *n.*, deep, muddy place

Ojibwe hand drum.

I am affected by the change of seasons. Here is a time when plants consolidate their tonic and drop seed, when animals store energy and grow thick fur. As for me, I start keeping longer hours, writing more, working harder, though I am obviously not a creature of a traditional Anishinabe culture. I was not raised speaking the old language, or adhering to the cycle of religious ceremonies that govern the Anishinabe spiritual relationship to the land and the moral order within human configurations. As the wedding of many backgrounds, I am free to do what simply feels right.

As the wedding of many backgrounds, I am free to do what simply feels right.

that her granddaughters bought for her great-grandchildren. When their plastic-paper shredded, she gathered them carefully together and one day, on a summer visit, I woke early to find her tamping the rolled stuff carefully into the cracked walls of that old house.

I t is autumn in the Plains, and in the little sloughs ducks land, and mudhens, whose flesh always tastes greasy and charred. Snow is coming soon, and after its first fall there will be a short, false warmth that brings out the sweet-sour odor of highbush cranberries. As a descendant of the women who skinned buffalo and tanned and smoked the hides, of women who pounded berries with the dried meat to make winter food, who made tea from willow bark and rosehips, who gathered snakeroot,

My mother knits, sews, cans, dries food and preserves it. She knows how to gather tea, berries, snare rabbits, milk cows and churn butter. She can grow squash and melons from seeds she gathered the fall before. She is, as were the women who came before me, a repository of all of the homely virtues, and I am the first in a long line who has not saved the autumn's harvest in birch bark *makuks* and skin bags and in a cellar dry and cold with dust. I am the first who scratches the ground for pleasure, not survival, and grows flowers instead of potatoes. I record rather than practise the arts that filled the hands and days of my mother and her mother, and all the mothers going back into the shadows, when women wore names that told us who they were. ❖

MIRRORS & WINDOWS

Erdrich describes her women ancestors as "[wearing] names that told us who they were." What can a name reveal about a person? How are contemporary names different from the traditional names of past generations?

Refer to Text ▶ ▶ ▶ ▶ ▶ **Reason with Text**

1a. What caused the decimation of the Anishinabe in the late 1800s and early 1900s?

1b. Explain why the speaker says that "every mixed-blood descendant like me . . . is the daughter of mystery."

Understand
Find meaning

2a. What does Erdrich say the names tell us "if only we listen closely"?

2b. How does Erdrich "listen closely"? Is her account of her ancestors a historical one?

Apply
Use information

3a. With which of her ancestors does Erdrich identify most? How are they alike?

3b. Describe the difference between the two women's notions of home.

Analyze
Take things apart

4a. How many women ancestors does Erdrich list and describe?

4b. Evaluate her likely purpose in providing this catalog.

Evaluate
Make judgments

5a. Identify an example of interaction between the traditional culture and the mainstream.

5b. What do these interactions suggest about the future of native peoples?

Create
Bring ideas together

Analyze Literature

Purpose and Catalog

Discuss Erdrich's purpose or purposes in writing this essay. What seems to be her primary purpose? What purposes seems secondary? Explain your answers.

Review the catalog of names in the essay. What does each name suggest about the woman it identifies? What do these names suggest about the Anishinabe? Why might the tribal roll of names be among the few records to have survived?

Extend the Text

Writing Options

Creative Writing Think of an elderly relative or friend (even one who is no longer living), or imagine such a person. Then create a brief profile of his or her personality, appearance, and other traits. If possible, describe the person's *foibles*, or minor flaws, as well as positive qualities.

Expository Writing Write a one-paragraph summary of Erdrich's essay in which you focus on her primary purpose in writing. Clarify her primary aim or goal as a writer—what she intended readers to take away from the essay.

Collaborative Learning

Provide Names That Explain Choose five friends or family members and give them names that explain or describe something about them, such as their hobbies and interests, their work, or their positive and negative qualities. Work with a partner and, if possible, select people you both know. After you have assigned the names, exchange papers and see whether you agree with one another's choices. If you wish, illustrate each person on your list.

Media Literacy

Publicize Ways to Live in Harmony with Nature Louise Erdrich notes that she is the first in her family not to follow some of the "homey virtues" of her female ancestors. Working with a group, make a list of ways people in your community can live more in harmony with nature. For example, perhaps local families could grow vegetables in a community garden. Then publicize your list on a poster board or in a flier.

 Go to **www.mirrorsandwindows.com** for more.

Daughter of Invention

A Short Story by Julia Alvarez

Build Background

Literary Context "Daughter of Invention" is one of fifteen interconnected stories that form Julia Alvarez's first novel, *How the García Girls Lost Their Accents* (1991). The work relates the experiences of four sisters who have emigrated from the Dominican Republic to New York City. The stories are told in backward chronological order, from 1989 to 1956, a few years before the family permanently left the Dominican Republic.

This selection focuses on the García girls' mother, Laura, and one of her daughters, Yolanda (Yoyo), in their efforts to assimilate into mainstream American culture. Ironically, an obstacle to their assimilation is Carlos, Yoyo's father, who has mixed feelings about his daughter's emerging independence. Carlos comes to realize that his wife and daughter's need to reinvent themselves stems from their desire for acceptance, not their abandonment of cultural values and traditions.

Reader's Context How can straddling two cultures create tension among immigrant family members? What interventions can help manage these misunderstandings?

Meet the Author

Julia Alvarez (b. 1950) was born in New York City but spent the first decade of her life in her family's native homeland, the Dominican Republic. The Alvarez family returned to the United States when Julia was ten to escape the repressive dictatorship of General Rafael Trujillo. Alvarez grew up in a culture in which oral storytelling was important—a tradition that runs through her stories. As a young girl learning a new language, she was an avid reader and paid particular attention to the nuances of words. By the time she was a teenager, she knew she wanted to be a writer.

In 1971, Alvarez earned a bachelor's degree from Middlebury College in Vermont, and she later earned a master's degree from Syracuse University. She has taught writing and poetry at all grade levels but eventually returned to her alma mater, Middlebury College, as a writer-in-residence and adviser to Latino students.

Alvarez's essays, poems, and stories have been published in the *New Yorker, Allure,* and *Hispanic Magazine,* and she has written many novels, including *In the Time of the Butterflies* (1994), *Yo!* (1997), *Before We Were Free* (2002), and *Saving the World* (2006). Her book *Something to Declare* (1998) contains twenty-four personal essays on her experiences as an immigrant and a writer.

Analyze Literature

Conflict and Cliché
A **conflict** is a struggle between two forces in a literary work. In an *external conflict,* the main character struggles against another character, the forces of nature, society, or fate. In an *internal conflict,* the main character struggles against an element within himself or herself.

A **cliché** is an overused or unoriginal expression, such as "quiet as a mouse."

Set Purpose

In her writing, Alvarez explores the themes of belonging and identity that result from living in two cultures. As you read, identify the conflicts that arise from the family members' different experiences and perspectives on assimilation. Identify each conflict as external or internal. In addition, consider the use of clichés, particularly by the mother, Laura, who often misquotes well-known but stale sayings.

Preview Vocabulary

cursory, 1187
poignant, 1187
labyrinth, 1187
communal, 1187
prodigious, 1189
plagiarist, 1190
noncommittal, 1191
florid, 1191
expurgate, 1191
sibyl, 1193

Daughter of INVENTION

by Julia Alvarez

Woman with Medallion, 1997. Matias Morales.
Private collection.

"This is America, Papi, America!"

For a period after they arrived in this country, Laura García tried to invent something. Her ideas always came after the sightseeing visits she took with her daughters to department stores to see the wonders of this new country. On his free Sundays, Carlos carted the girls off to the Statue of Liberty or the Brooklyn Bridge or Rockefeller Center, but as far as Laura was concerned, these were men's wonders. Down in housewares were the true treasures women were after.

Laura and her daughters would take the escalator, marveling at the moving staircase, she teasing them that this might be the ladder Jacob saw with angels moving up and down to heaven. The moment they lingered by a display, a perky saleslady approached, no doubt thinking a young mother with four girls in

Yoyo was sure her mother had drawn a picture of a man's you-know-what; she showed her sisters her find, and with coy, posed faces they inquired of their mother what she was up to. *Ay,* that was one of her failures, she explained to them, a child's double-compartment drinking glass with an outsized, built-in straw.

Her daughters would seek her out at night when she seemed to have a moment to talk to them: they were having trouble at school or they wanted her to persuade their father to give them permission to go into the city or to a shopping mall or a movie—in broad daylight, Mami! Laura would wave them out of her room. "The problem with you girls . . ." The problem boiled down to the fact that they wanted to become Americans and their father—and their mother, too, at first—would have none of it.

"You girls are going to drive me crazy!" she threatened, if they kept nagging. "When I end up in Bellevue,[1] you'll be safely sorry!"

She spoke in English when she argued with them. And her English was a mishmash of mixed-up idioms and sayings that showed she was "green behind the ears," as she called it.

If her husband insisted she speak in Spanish to the girls so they wouldn't forget their native tongue, she'd snap, "When in Rome, do unto the Romans."

Yoyo, the Big Mouth, had become the spokesman for her sisters, and she stood her ground in that bedroom. "We're not going to that school anymore, Mami!"

"You have to." Her eyes would widen with worry. "In this country, it is against the law not to go to school. You want us to get thrown out?"

"You want us to get killed? Those kids were throwing stones today!"

tow fit the perfect profile for the new refrigerator with automatic defrost or the heavy duty washing machine with the prewash soak cycle. Laura paid close attention during the demonstrations, asking intelligent questions, but at the last minute saying she would talk it over with her husband. On the drive home, try as they might, her daughters could not engage their mother in conversation, for inspired by what she had just seen, Laura had begun inventing.

She never put anything actual on paper until she had settled her house down at night. On his side of the bed her husband would be conked out for an hour already, his Spanish newspaper draped over his chest, his glasses propped up on his bedside table, looking out eerily at the darkened room like a disembodied bodyguard. In her lighted corner, pillows propped behind her, Laura sat up inventing. On her lap lay one of those innumerable pads of paper her husband brought home from his office, compliments of some pharmaceutical company, advertising tranquilizers or antibiotics or skin cream. She would be working on a sketch of something familiar but drawn at such close range so she could attach a special nozzle or handier handle, the thing looked peculiar. Her daughters would giggle over the odd doodles they found in kitchen drawers or on the back shelf of the downstairs toilet. Once

---

1. **Bellevue.** Well-known psychiatric hospital in New York City

"Sticks and stones don't break bones," she chanted. Yoyo could tell, though, by the look on her face, it was as if one of those stones the kids had aimed at her daughters had hit her. But she always pretended they were at fault. "What did you do to provoke them? It takes two to tangle, you know."

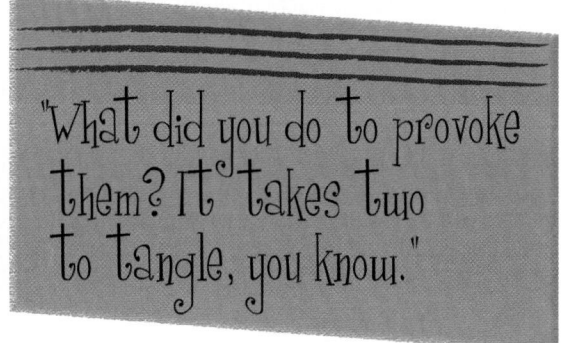

"What did you do to provoke them? It takes two to tangle, you know."

"Thanks, thanks a lot, Mom!" Yoyo stormed out of that room and into her own. Her daughters never called her *Mom* except when they wanted her to feel how much she had failed them in this country. She was a good enough Mami, fussing and scolding and giving advice, but a terrible girlfriend parent, a real failure of a Mom.

Back she went to her pencil and pad, scribbling and tsking and tearing off sheets, finally giving up, and taking up her *New York Times*. Some nights, though, if she got a good idea, she rushed into Yoyo's room, a flushed look on her face, her tablet of paper in her hand, a <u>cursory</u> knock on the door she'd just thrown open. "Do I have something to show you, Cuquita!"

This was Yoyo's time to herself, after she finished her homework, while her sisters were still downstairs watching TV in the basement. Hunched over her small desk, the overhead light turned off, her desk lamp <u>poignantly</u> lighting only her paper, the rest of the room in warm, soft, uncreated darkness, she wrote her secret poems in her new language.

"You're going to ruin your eyes!" Laura began, snapping on the overly bright overhead light, scaring off whatever shy passion Yoyo, with the blue thread of her writing, had just begun coaxing out of a <u>labyrinth</u> of feelings.

"Oh, Mami!" Yoyo cried out, her eyes blinking up at her mother. "I'm writing."

"*Ay*, Cuquita." That was her <u>communal</u> pet name for whoever was in her favor. "Cuquita, when I make a million, I'll buy you your very own typewriter." (Yoyo had been nagging her mother for one just like the one her father had bought to do his order forms at home.) "Gravy on the turkey" was what she called it when someone was buttering her up. She buttered and poured. "I'll hire you your very own typist."

Down she plopped on the bed and held out her pad. "Take a guess, Cuquita?" Yoyo studied the rough sketch a moment. Soap sprayed from the nozzle head of a shower when you turned the knob a certain way? Instant coffee with creamer already mixed in? Time-released water capsules for your potted plants when you were away? A keychain with a timer that would go off when your parking meter was about to expire? (The ticking would help you find your keys easily if you mislaid them.) The famous one, famous only in hindsight, was the stick person dragging a square by a rope—a suitcase with wheels? "Oh, of course," Yoyo said, humoring her. "What every household needs: a shower like a car wash, keys ticking like a bomb, luggage on a leash!" By now, it had become something of a family joke, their Thomas Edison Mami, their Benjamin Franklin Mom.

Her face fell. "Come on now! Use your head." One more wrong guess, and she'd show Yoyo, pointing with her pencil to the different highlights of this incredible new wonder.

---

cur • so • ry (kŭr´ sər ē) *adj.*, rapidly and often inadequately performed or done
poi • gnant • ly (poi´ nyənt lē) *adv.*, in a manner that deeply affects the emotions
lab • y • rinth (la´ bə rinth) *n.*, maze
com • mu • nal (kə myü´ n'l) *adj.*, participated in, shared, or used by members of a group or a community

President Trujillo of the Dominican Republic

Rafael Trujillo (1891–1961) was dictator of the Dominican Republic from 1930 to 1938 and again from 1942 to 1952. While in power, he gained control over every aspect of Dominican life. For instance, he changed the name of the country's capital from Santo Domingo to Ciudad Trujillo (Trujillo City). He also assumed control of privately owned plantations and businesses, amassing a huge fortune for himself and his family.

Trujillo was able to stay in power by forming a secret police to suppress his opponents. The Servi-cio de Inteligencia Militar (SIM) not only gathered information about suspected opponents but also tortured and killed thousands of people. In 1937, Trujillo ordered the massacre of twenty thousand black Haitians who had settled in the Dominican Republic. In addition, he masterminded the failed assassination of the president of Venezuela.

Despite Trujillo's corruption and human rights violations, some Dominicans supported the dictator because his strict control over the country allowed the economy to expand. Advances in public health care, education, road systems, technology, and industry all occurred during Trujillo's rule.

"Remember that time we took the car to Bear Mountain, and we re-ah-lized that we had forgotten to pack an opener with our pick-a-nick?" (Her daughters kept correcting her, but she insisted this was how it should be said.) "When we were ready to eat we didn't have any way to open the refreshments cans?" (This before flip-top lids, which she claimed had crossed her mind.) "You know what this is now?" Yoyo shook her head. "Is a car bumper, but see this part is a removable can opener. So simple and yet so necessary, eh?"

"Yeah, Mami. You should patent it." Yoyo shrugged as her mother tore off the scratch paper and folded it, carefully, corner to cor-ner, as if she were going to save it. But then, she tossed it in the wastebasket on her way out of the room and gave a little laugh like a disclaimer. "It's half of one or two dozen of another."

None of her daughters was very encourag-ing. They resented her spending time on those dumb inventions. Here they were trying to fit in America among Americans; they needed help figuring out who they were, why the Irish kids whose grandparents had been micks were calling them spics. Why had they come to this country in the first place? Important, crucial, final things, and here was their own mother, who didn't have a second to help them puzzle any of this out, inventing gadgets to make life easier for the American Moms.

Sometimes Yoyo challenged her. "Why, Mami? Why do it? You're never going to make money. The Americans have already thought of everything, you know that."

"Maybe not. Maybe, just maybe, there's something they've missed that's important. With patience and calm, even a burro can climb a palm." This last was one of her many Dominican sayings she had imported into her scrambled English.

"But what's the point?" Yoyo persisted.

"Point, point, does everything need a point? Why do you write poems?"

Yoyo had to admit it was her mother who had the point there. Still, in the hierarchy of things, a poem seemed much more important than a potty that played music when a toilet-training toddler went in its bowl.

They talked about it among themselves, the four girls, as they often did now about the many puzzling things in this new country.

"Better she reinvents the wheel than be on our cases all the time," the oldest, Carla, observed. In the close quarters of an American nuclear family, their mother's <u>prodigious</u> energy was becoming a real drain on their self-determination. Let her have a project. What harm could she do, and besides, she needed that acknowledgement. It had come to her automatically in the old country from being a de la Torre. "García de la Torre," Laura would enunciate carefully, giving her maiden as well as married name when they first arrived. But the blank smiles had never heard of her name. She would show them. She would prove to these Americans what a smart woman could do with a pencil and pad.

> She would prove to these Americans what a smart woman could do with a pencil and pad.

She had a near miss once. Every night, she liked to read *The New York Times* in bed before turning off her light, to see what the Americans were up to. One night, she let out a yelp to wake up her husband beside her. He sat bolt upright, reaching for his glasses which in his haste, he knocked across the room. "*¿Qué pasa? ¿Qué pasa?*" What is wrong? There was terror in his voice, the same fear she'd heard in the Dominican Republic before they left. They had been watched there; he was followed. They could not talk, of course, though they had whispered to each other in fear at night in the dark bed. Now in America, he was safe, a success even; his Centro de Medicina in the Bronx was thronged with the sick and the homesick yearning to go home again. But in dreams, he went back to those awful days and long nights, and his wife's screams confirmed his secret fear: they had not gotten away after all; the SIM[2] had come for them at last.

"*Ay*, Cuco! Remember how I showed you that suitcase with little wheels so we should not have to carry those heavy bags when we traveled? Someone stole my idea and made a million!" She shook the paper in his face. "See, see! This man was no *bobo*! He didn't put all his pokers on a back burner. I kept telling you, one of these days my ship would pass me by in the night!" She wagged her finger at her husband and daughters, laughing all the while, one of those eerie laughs crazy people in movies laugh. The four girls had congregated in her room. They eyed their mother and each other. Perhaps they were all thinking the same thing, wouldn't it be weird and sad if Mami did end up in Bellevue?

"*¡Ya, ya!*" She waved them out of her room at last. "There is no use trying to drink spilt milk, that's for sure."

It was the suitcase rollers that stopped Laura's hand; she had weathervaned a minor brainstorm. And yet, this <u>plagiarist</u> had gotten all the credit, and the money. What use was it trying to compete with the Americans: they would always have the head start. It was their country, after all. Best stick close to home. She cast her sights about—her daughters ducked—and found her husband's office in need. Several days a week, dressed professionally in a white smock with a little name tag pinned on the

---

2. **SIM.** Servicio de Inteligencia Militar, the Dominican Republic's secret military police

> **pro • di • gious** (prō di´ jəs) *adj.,* causing amazement or wonder
> **pla • gia • rist** (plā´ jə rist) *n.,* someone who takes credit for the ideas or work of another person

nation. At first she didn't want to and then she couldn't seem to write that speech. She should have thought of it as "a great honor," as her father called it. But she was mortified. She still had a slight accent, and she did not like to speak in public, subjecting herself to her classmates' ridicule. It also took no great figuring to see that to deliver a eulogy for a convent full of crazy, old, overweight nuns was no way to endear herself to her peers.

lapel, a shopping bag full of cleaning materials and rags, she rode with her husband in his car to the Bronx. On the way, she organized the glove compartment or took off the address stickers from the magazines for the waiting room because she had read somewhere how by means of these stickers drug addict patients found out where doctors lived and burglarized their homes looking for syringes. At night, she did the books, filling in columns with how much money they had made that day. Who had time to be inventing silly things!

She did take up her pencil and pad one last time. But it was to help one of her daughters out. In ninth grade, Yoyo was chosen by her English teacher, Sister Mary Joseph, to deliver the Teacher's Day address at the school assembly. Back in the Dominican Republic growing up, Yoyo had been a terrible student. No one could ever get her to sit down to a book. But in New York, she needed to settle somewhere, and since the natives were unfriendly, and the country inhospitable, she took root in the language. By high school, the nuns were reading her stories and compositions out loud in English class.

But the spectre of delivering a speech brownnosing the teachers jammed her imagi-

But she didn't know how to get out of it. Night after night, she sat at her desk, hoping to polish off some quick, <u>noncommittal</u> little speech. But she couldn't get anything down.

The weekend before the assembly Monday morning Yoyo went into a panic. Her mother would just have to call in tomorrow and say Yoyo was in the hospital, in a coma.

Laura tried to calm her down. "Just remember how Mister Lincoln couldn't think of anything to say at the Gettysburg, but then, bang! *Four score and once upon a time ago,*" she began reciting. "Something is going to come if you just relax. You'll see, like the Americans say, *Necessity is the daughter of invention.* I'll help you."

That weekend, her mother turned all her energy towards helping Yoyo write her speech. "Please, Mami, just leave me alone, please," Yoyo pleaded with her. But Yoyo would get rid of the goose only to have to contend with the gander. Her father kept poking his head in the door just to see if Yoyo had "fulfilled your obligations," a phrase he had used when the girls were younger and he'd check to see whether

---

non • com • mit • tal (nôn kə mit´ 'l) *adj.,* giving no clear indication of attitude or feeling

they had gone to the bathroom before a car trip. Several times that weekend around the supper table, he recited his own high school valedictorian speech. He gave Yoyo pointers on delivery, notes on the great orators and their tricks. (Humbleness and praise and falling silent with great emotion were his favorites.)

Laura sat across the table, the only one who seemed to be listening to him. Yoyo and her sisters were forgetting a lot of their Spanish, and their father's formal, <u>florid</u> diction was hard to understand. But Laura smiled softly to herself, and turned the lazy Susan at the center of the table around and around as if it were the prime mover, the first gear of her attention.

That Sunday evening, Yoyo was reading some poetry to get herself inspired: Whitman's poems in an old book with an engraved cover her father had picked up in a thrift shop next to his office. *I celebrate myself and sing myself. . . . He most honors my style who learns under it to destroy the teacher.* The poet's words shocked and thrilled her. She had gotten used to the nuns, a literature of appropriate sentiments, poems with a message, <u>expurgated</u> texts. But here was a flesh and blood man, belching and laughing and sweating in poems. *Who touches this book touches a man.*

When Yoyo was done, she read over her words, and her eyes filled. She finally sounded like herself in English!

That night, at last, she started to write, recklessly, three, five pages, looking up once only to see her father passing by the hall on tiptoe. When Yoyo was done, she read over her words, and her eyes filled. She finally sounded like herself in English!

As soon as she had finished that first draft, she called her mother to her room. Laura listened attentively while Yoyo read the speech out loud, and in the end, her eyes were glistening too. Her face was soft and warm and proud. "*Ay,* Yoyo, you are going to be the one to bring our name to the headlights in this country! That is a beautiful, beautiful speech I want for your father to hear it before he goes to sleep. Then I will type it for you, all right?"

Down the hall they went, mother and daughter, faces flushed with accomplishment. Into the master bedroom where Carlos was propped up on his pillows, still awake, reading the Dominican papers, already days old. Now that the dictatorship had been toppled, he had become interested in his country's fate again. The interim government was going to hold the first free elections in thirty years. History was in the making, freedom and hope were in the air again! There was still some question in his mind whether or not he might move his family back. But Laura had gotten used to the life here. She did not want to go back to the old country where, de la Torre or not, she was only a wife and a mother (and a failed one at that, since she had never provided the required son). Better an independent nobody than a high-class houseslave. She did not come straight out and disagree with her husband's plans. Instead, she fussed with him about reading the papers in bed, soiling their sheets with those poorly printed, foreign tabloids. "*The Times* is not that bad!" she'd claim if her husband tried to humor her by saying they shared the same dirty habit.

The minute Carlos saw his wife and daughter filing in, he put his paper down, and his face brightened as if at long last his wife had delivered the son, and that was the news she was bringing him. His teeth were already grinning from the glass of water next to his bedside

---

flor • id (flôr´ id) *adj.,* flowery or overly elaborate in style
ex • pur • gate (eks´ pər gāt) *v.,* remove objectionable parts from a work before publication or presentation

lamp, so he lisped when he said, "Eh-speech, eh-speech!"

"It is so beautiful, Cuco," Laura coached him, turning the sound on his TV off. She sat down at the foot of the bed. Yoyo stood before both of them, blocking their view of the soldiers in helicopters landing amid silenced gun reports and explosions. A few weeks ago it had been the shores of the Dominican Republic. Now it was the jungles of Southeast Asia they were saving. Her mother gave her the nod to begin reading.

Yoyo didn't need much encouragement. She put her nose to the fire, as her mother would have said, and read from start to finish without looking up. When she concluded, she was a little embarrassed at the pride she took in her own words. She pretended to quibble with a phrase or two, then looked questioningly to her mother. Laura's face was radiant. Yoyo turned to share her pride with her father.

The expression on his face shocked both mother and daughter. Carlos's toothless mouth had collapsed into a dark zero. His eyes bored into Yoyo, then shifted to Laura. In barely audible Spanish, as if secret microphones or informers were all about, he whispered to his wife, "You will permit her to read *that?*"

> The expression on his face shocked both mother and daughter.

Laura's eyebrows shot up, her mouth fell open. In the old country, any whisper of a challenge to authority could bring the secret police in their black V.W.'s. But this was America. People could say what they thought. "What is wrong with her speech?" Laura questioned him.

"What ees wrrrong with her eh-speech?" Carlos wagged his head at her. His anger was always more frightening in his broken English. As if he had mutilated the language in his fury—and now there was nothing to stand between them and his raw, dumb anger. "What is wrong? I will tell you what is wrong. It show no gratitude. It is boastful. *I celebrate myself? The best student learns to destroy the teacher?*" He mocked Yoyo's plagiarized words. "That is insubordinate. It is improper. It is disrespecting of her teachers—" In his anger he had forgotten his fear of lurking spies: each wrong he voiced was a decibel higher than the last outrage. Finally, he shouted at Yoyo, "As your father, I forbid you to make that eh-speech!"

Laura leapt to her feet, a sign that *she* was about to deliver her own speech. She was a small woman, and she spoke all her pronouncements standing up, either for more projection or as a carry-over from her girlhood in convent schools where one asked for, and literally, took the floor in order to speak. She stood by Yoyo's side, shoulder to shoulder. They looked down at Carlos. "That is no tone of voice—" she began.

But now, Carlos was truly furious. It was bad enough that his daughter was rebelling, but here was his own wife joining forces with her. Soon he would be surrounded by a houseful of independent American women. He too leapt from the bed, throwing off his covers. The Spanish newspapers flew across the room. He snatched the speech out of Yoyo's hands, held it before the girl's wide eyes, a vengeful, mad look in his own, and then once, twice, three, four, countless times, he tore the speech into shreds.

"Are you crazy?" Laura lunged at him. "Have you gone mad? That is her speech for tomorrow you have torn up!"

"Have *you* gone mad?" He shook her away. "You were going to let her read that . . . that insult to her teachers?"

"Insult to her teachers!" Laura's face had crumpled up like a piece of paper. On it was written a love note to her husband, an unhappy,

For the rest of his life, he would be haunted by blood in the streets and late night disappearances. Even after all these years, he cringed if a black Volkswagen passed him on the street. He feared anyone in uniform: the meter maid giving out parking tickets, a museum guard approaching to tell him not to get too close to his favorite Goya.[3]

On her knees, Yoyo thought of the worst thing she could say to her father. She gathered a handful of scraps, stood up, and hurled them in his face. In a low, ugly whisper, she pronounced Trujillo's hated nickname: "Chapita![4] You're just another Chapita!"

It took Yoyo's father only a moment to register the loathsome nickname before he came after her. Down the halls they raced, but Yoyo was quicker than he and made it into her room just in time to lock the door as her father threw his weight against it. He called down curses on her head, ordered her on his authority as her father to open that door! He throttled that doorknob, but all to no avail. Her mother's love of gadgets saved Yoyo's hide that night. Laura had hired a locksmith to install good locks on all the bedroom doors after the house had been broken into once while they were away. Now if burglars broke in again, and the family were at home, there would be a second round of locks for the thieves to contend with.

haunted man. "This is America, Papi, America! You are not in a savage country anymore!"

Meanwhile, Yoyo was on her knees, weeping wildly, collecting all the little pieces of her speech, hoping that she could put it back together before the assembly tomorrow morning. But not even a <u>sibyl</u> could have made sense of those tiny scraps of paper. All hope was lost. "He broke it, he broke it," Yoyo moaned as she picked up a handful of pieces.

Probably, if she had thought a moment about it, she would not have done what she did next. She would have realized her father had lost brothers and friends to the dictator Trujillo.

---

3. **Goya.** Francisco José de Goya y Lucientes (1746–1828), Spanish painter
4. **Chapita.** [Spanish] Slang for "bottle cap"; nickname for General Trujillo because as a child he collected the scalloped lids of soda bottles. He hated this nickname so much, however, that when he became dictator, he banished the word from the language.

sib • yl (sib´ 'l) *n.,* fortune teller or female prophet

"Lolo," she said, trying to calm him down. "Don't you ruin my new locks."

Finally he did calm down, his anger spent. Yoyo heard their footsteps retreating down the hall. Their door clicked shut. Then, muffled voices, her mother's rising in anger, in persuasion, her father's deeper murmurs of explanation and self-defense. The house fell silent a moment, before Yoyo heard, far off, the gun blasts and explosions, the serious, self-important voices of newscasters reporting their TV war.

A little while later, there was a quiet knock at Yoyo's door, followed by a tentative attempt at the door knob. "Cuquita?" her mother whispered. "Open up, Cuquita."

"Go away," Yoyo wailed, but they both knew she was glad her mother was there, and needed only a moment's protest to save face.

Together they concocted a speech: two brief pages of stale compliments and the polite commonplaces on teachers, a speech wrought by necessity and without much invention by mother and daughter late into the night on one of the pads of paper Laura had once used for her own inventions. After it was drafted, Laura typed it up while Yoyo stood by, correcting her mother's misnomers and mis-sayings.

Yoyo came home the next day with the success story of the assembly. The nuns had been flattered, the audience had stood up and given "our devoted teachers a standing ovation," what Laura had suggested they do at the end of the speech.

She clapped her hands together as Yoyo recreated the moment. "I stole that from your father's speech, remember? Remember how he put that in at the end?" She quoted him in Spanish, then translated for Yoyo into English.

That night, Yoyo watched him from the upstairs hall window, where she'd retreated the minute she heard his car pull up in front of the house. Slowly, her father came up the driveway, a grim expression on his face as he grappled with a large, heavy cardboard box. At the front door, he set the package down carefully and patted all his pockets for his house keys. (If only he'd had Laura's ticking key chain!) Yoyo heard the snapping open of locks downstairs. She listened as he struggled to maneuver the box through the narrow doorway. He called her name several times, but she did not answer him.

"My daughter, your father, he love you very much," he explained from the bottom of the stairs. "He just want to protect you." Finally, her mother came up and pleaded with Yoyo to go down and reconcile with him. "Your father did not mean to harm. You must pardon him. Always it is better to let bygones be forgotten, no?"

Downstairs, Yoyo found her father setting up a brand new electric typewriter on the kitchen table. It was even better than her mother's. He had outdone himself with all the extra features: a plastic carrying case with Yoyo's initials decaled below the handle, a brace to lift the paper upright while she typed, an erase cartridge, an automatic margin tab, a plastic hood like a toaster cover to keep the dust away. Not even her mother could have invented such a machine!

But Laura's inventing days were over just as Yoyo's were starting up with her school-wide success. Rather than the rolling suitcase everyone else in the family remembers, Yoyo thinks of the speech her mother wrote as her last invention. It was as if, after that, her mother had passed on to Yoyo her pencil and pad and said, "Okay, Cuquita, here's the buck. You give it a shot." ❖

Yoyo admits finding it difficult to understand how her father's past has affected his values and outlook on life. What do you find hard to understand about one or both of your parents? What do they find hard to understand about you?

Refer to Text ▶ ▶ ▶ ▶ ▶ Reason with Text

1a. What do Laura and Yoyo like to do in their spare time?	**1b.** Infer what each person's choice of pastimes says about her.	**Understand** Find meaning
2a. What does Laura promise she will buy for Yoyo when she becomes rich?	**2b.** What later event does the mention of the typewriter foreshadow? What is the significance of this event?	**Apply** Use information
3a. Identify the famous author who inspires Yoyo to write her speech for Teacher's Day. What most appeals to Yoyo about his work?	**3b.** Why is Carlos angry when he reads Yoyo's speech? How does the second speech differ from the first?	**Analyze** Take things apart
4a. State the name Yoyo calls Carlos after he tears up her speech.	**4b.** What was particularly insulting about Yoyo's name-calling?	**Evaluate** Make judgments
5a. Where does the story refer to the cliché "Necessity is the mother of invention"?	**5b.** Propose why Alvarez used an alternative of this saying as the title of her story.	**Create** Bring ideas together

Analyze Literature

Conflict and Cliché

What conflicts are faced by members of the Alvarez family? How does Yoyo handle the external and internal conflicts she faces? How do her mother and father address the conflicts they face? Discuss how these conflicts relate to the story's theme.

What does Laura's frequent misuse of clichés suggest about her character's ambitions and limitations? How does her misusing these stale sayings add humor to the story?

Extend the Text

Writing Options

Creative Writing Suppose you are Yoyo and your cousin from the Dominican Republic is coming to visit. Write an e-mail message, explaining what he or she can expect during the trip. Explain what activities you have planned along with any cultural differences you think you should describe to your cousin.

Descriptive Writing Write a two-page character analysis of Yoyo; Laura, her mother; or Carlos, her father. Include information on the character's motivation and the conflicts he or she experiences in the story.

Collaborative Learning

Exploring Context With a partner or small group, research what conditions were like in the Dominican

Republic under the dictator Trujillo. Use the History Connection box on page 1188 to identify possible topics to explore. Present your findings in a one-page summary.

Critical Literacy

Draw Inspiration from a Poem Yoyo is inspired by these lines from Walt Whitman's *Song of Myself:* "I celebrate myself and sing myself. . . . He most honors my style who learns under it to destroy the teacher. . . . Who touches this book touches a man." Write Yoyo's Teacher's Day address in response to these lines from Whitman's poem. If possible, deliver the speech to your classmates. (See Unit 3 for more information about Whitman.)

 Go to **www.mirrorsandwindows.com** for more.

What Is Supposed to Happen

A Lyric Poem by Naomi Shihab Nye

Build Background

Literary Context **"What Is Supposed to Happen"** originally appeared in Naomi Shihab Nye's collection *Red Suitcase* (1994). The title of the poem suggests the speaker's wistful realization that parents cannot stop the natural process of a child growing up and gaining independence. This simple but eloquent example of free verse expresses the complex emotions of a common experience.

Reader's Context What emotions might parents feel upon watching their child grow from infancy to independence?

Meet the Author

Naomi Shihab Nye (b. 1952) was born in St. Louis, Missouri, to a Palestinian father and an American mother. She began writing poetry when she was six, and by age seven, she was a published poet. Growing up, Nye was a voracious reader and a diligent recorder of her experiences—two activities that she carried into adulthood and that are reflected in her poetry's diction. She once recalled, "I went to school and came home to find words waiting for me. . . . I played with words, stacking and rearranging them."

When she was fourteen, Nye's family moved to Jerusalem to live near her father's relatives, but they returned to the United States when the Six-Day War erupted. The family settled in San Antonio, Texas, where Nye attended Trinity University and graduated in 1974 with a bachelor of arts degree in English and world religions. She began her writing career shortly thereafter and published her first poetry collection, *Different Ways to Pray,* in 1980.

Nye's multicultural perspective permeates her more than twenty volumes of poetry, including *Fuel* (1998), *19 Variations of Gazelle: Poems of the Middle East* (2002), and *You & Yours* (2006). She also has written two young adult novels and several children's books. Her passion for multicultural understanding and tolerance led her to edit *This Same Sky: A Collection of Poems from Around the World,* a volume containing poems from 129 writers representing 68 nations.

Nye has traveled across the United States and abroad to promote artistic diversity and international goodwill. For that reason, she calls herself a "wandering poet." She has won four Pushcart Prizes and a Guggenheim Fellowship. Nye continues to write and believes in the power of words to build bridges among cultures.

Analyze Literature

Speaker and Metaphor
The **speaker** is the character who speaks in, or narrates, a poem—the voice assumed by the writer. The speaker and the writer of a poem are not necessarily the same person, however.

A **metaphor** is a figure of speech in which one thing is spoken or written about as if it were another.

Set Purpose

Nye's free-verse poetry reflects her ability to make the ordinary seem extraordinary. "What Is Supposed to Happen" describes an ordinary experience of parenting. Identify the speaker describing this experience and what feelings she expresses. Also make note of the metaphors Nye uses to express the child's development. What do these metaphors suggest?

What Is Supposed to Happen

by Naomi Shihab Nye

When you were small,
we watched you sleeping,
waves of breath
filling your chest.
5 Sometimes we hid behind
the wall of baby, soft cradle
of baby needs.
I loved carrying you between
my own body and the world.

10 Now you are sharpening pencils,
entering the forest of
lunch boxes, little desks.
People I never saw before
call out your name
15 and you wave.

This loss I feel,
this shrinking,
as your field of roses
grows and grows. . . .

20 Now I understand history.
Now I understand my mother's ancient eyes. ❖

MIRRORS & WINDOWS

The mother speaking in this poem feels a sense of loss over her child's growing up. Why do parents sometimes have difficulty watching their children grow up? How might the experience be different for mothers versus fathers?

Refer to Text ▷ ▷ ▷ ▷ ▷	Reason with Text	
1a. As the parents watched the baby sleeping, what did they observe?	**1b.** Infer what lines 5–7 indicate about the speaker's feelings toward parenthood.	**Understand** Find meaning
2a. How did the speaker like to carry the baby?	**2b.** How is the physical act of carrying the baby also symbolic of the parent's role?	**Apply** Use information
3a. At what point does the speaker observe a change in the child's behavior?	**3b.** Identify the people the speaker has "never [seen] before." What do they represent to her?	**Analyze** Take things apart
4a. What contrast does the speaker present in stanza 3?	**4b.** What is the metaphor in stanza 3? Judge its effectiveness in conveying the speaker's feelings about the child.	**Evaluate** Make judgments
5a. In the last two lines, what two things does the speaker say she understands?	**5b.** Suggest what the speaker means by these lines.	**Create** Bring ideas together

Analyze Literature

Speaker and Metaphor

Who is the speaker in "What Is Supposed to Happen"? What feelings is she expressing about being a parent? What does the title indicate about her feelings?

List the metaphors Nye uses to describe the child's development. For each metaphor, identify the tenor and the vehicle. What do these choices of metaphor reveal?

Extend the Text

Writing Options

Creative Writing The speaker in Nye's poem seems to have gained a new understanding of her mother now that she is a mother herself. Write a personal letter from the speaker to her mother, explaining what the younger woman understands now about being a parent and how she arrived at that knowledge.

Expository Writing Stanza 2 uses striking images to portray its setting without actually naming it. Write a one-paragraph *explication,* or careful analysis of the text, that discusses the effectiveness of the images in stanza 2.

Collaborative Learning

Create a Pamphlet for Parents With two or three classmates, create a pamphlet for new parents entitled *Safety First for Children.* To find useful safety tips, such as keeping household cleaning products away from children, consult sources from the Red Cross and parenting organi-

zations. Check both library and online sources. If possible, illustrate the pamphlet. As a group, discuss ways of distributing the pamphlet.

Lifelong Learning

Display Pictures of Equipment for Children A wide range of equipment has been produced in recent years for carrying, holding, and transporting children. Using library and online sources, research the development of car seats, strollers, high chairs, and the like. Determine what issues, in addition to safety, have led to improvements in these products. Reproduce photographs and drawings and display them, along with captions you write, in the classroom. Provide credit, where needed, to photographers, artists, and other originators of the images you reproduce.

 Go to **www.mirrorsandwindows.com** for more.

The Latin Deli: An Ars Poetica

A Lyric Poem by Judith Ortiz Cofer

Build Background

Cultural Context In **"The Latin Deli: An Ars Poet-ica,"** Judith Ortiz Cofer portrays a saleswoman at the counter of a *bodega,* or grocery store catering to Hispanic customers. What the store offers shoppers, however, is more than plantains (banana-like fruits) and *jamón y queso* (hä mōn´ ē kä´ sō) (ham and cheese). In addition to shopping lists, immigrants from Latin America bring with them memories of Puerto Rico or the simple hope of striking it rich in the United States. Perhaps most important, they feel at ease in a place where their first language *is* the language.

Literary Context The subtitle of Cofer's poem, "An Ars Poetica," means "The Art of Poetry." The Roman poet Horace (c. 65–8 BCE) wrote an essay called "Ars Poetica," in which he addressed concepts such as the relationship between style and subject and the need for poems to be brief in length but lasting in meaning. Other poets also have attempted to describe their theory of their art, including Archibald MacLeish and Marianne Moore in Unit 5.

Reader's Context Why might immigrants be attracted to a neighborhood shop even if the merchandise is available for less money at a chain store?

Meet the Author

Judith Ortiz Cofer (b. 1952) was born in Hormigueros, Puerto Rico, and emigrated with her family to Paterson, New Jersey, when she was about four. Later, the family moved to Augusta, Georgia. Cofer earned a bachelor's degree at Augusta College and then a master's degree from Florida Atlantic University. She has taught English and creative writing at the University of Georgia for many years.

From her grandmother in Puerto Rico, Cofer learned the art of storytelling. As in the poem printed here, Cofer often depicts immigrants who feel ambivalent about having settled in the United States. They may experience homesickness or guilt at leaving loved ones behind, but they also may be determined to be successful in their new life.

This selection is from *The Latin Deli* (1993), a collection of poetry, short fiction, and personal narrative. Other works by Cofer include the novels *The Line of the Sun* (1989) and *The Meaning of Consuelo* (2003) and the collections *Reaching for the Mainland and Selected New Poems* (1995) and *Woman in Front of the Sun: On Becoming a Writer* (2000).

Analyze Literature

Tone and Theme

Tone is the emotional attitude toward the reader or toward the subject, such as playful, sarcastic, or sincere. Tone may be revealed by such elements as word choice (*diction*), sentence structure, and images.

The **theme** is a central message or perception about life revealed through a literary work. A *stated theme* is presented directly, whereas an *implied theme* must be inferred. A *universal theme* is a message about life that can be understood by people of most cultures.

Set Purpose

Although Cofer writes about the experiences of Puerto Ricans, immigrants from many countries can relate to what she describes. As you read "The Latin Deli," think about the attitude Cofer portrays about those experiences. Analyze how she achieves that tone through her diction and vivid use of sensory details. Consider, too, what central message Cofer presents in this poem. Is that theme stated or implied? Is it a universal theme?

The Latin Deli
An Ars Poetica

by Judith Ortiz Cofer

Presiding over a formica counter,
plastic Mother and Child magnetized
to the top of an ancient register,
the heady mix of smells from the open bins
5   of dried codfish, the green plantains
hanging in stalks like votive offerings,[1]
she is the Patroness of Exiles,
a woman of no-age who was never pretty,
who spends her days selling canned memories

---

1. **votive offerings.** Sacrifices offered in devotion or to fulfill a promise

10   while listening to the Puerto Ricans complain
        that it would be cheaper to fly to San Juan
        than to buy a pound of Bustelo coffee here,
        and to Cubans perfecting their speech
        of a "glorious return" to Havana—where no one
15   has been allowed to die and nothing to change until then;
        to Mexicans who pass through, talking lyrically
        of *dólares* to be made in El Norte—

                                all wanting the comfort
        of spoken Spanish, to gaze upon the family portrait
20   of her plain wide face, her ample bosom
        resting on her plump arms, her look of maternal interest
        as they speak to her and each other
        of their dreams and their disillusions—
        how she smiles understanding,
25   when they walk down the narrow aisles of her store
        reading the labels of packages aloud, as if
        they were the names of lost lovers: *Suspiros,*[2]
        Merengues,[3] the stale candy of everyone's childhood.

                                She spends her days
30   slicing *jamón y queso*[4] and wrapping it in wax paper
        tied with string: plain ham and cheese
        that would cost less at the A&P, but it would not satisfy
        the hunger of the fragile old man lost in the folds
        of his winter coat, who brings her lists of items
35   that he reads to her like poetry, or the others,
        whose needs she must divine,[5] conjuring up products
        from places that now exist only in their hearts—
        closed ports she must trade with. ❖

---

2. **Suspiros** (sü spe´ rōs). [Spanish] Small sponge cakes
3. **Merengues** (mā rāŋ´ gās). [Spanish] Sweets made of meringue; baked mixture of egg
        whites and sugar
4. **jamón y queso** (hä mōn´ ē kā´ sō). [Spanish] Ham and cheese
5. **divine.** Perceive or discover

MIRRORS & WINDOWS   The native countries of the immigrants "now exist only in their hearts." If you
        moved to another country, what would you miss the most about your home?

Refer to Text  Reason with Text

1a. Identify the person described in lines 1–28. What is her job? What title does the speaker give her?

1b. What does the title suggest about this person's job? Infer why the speaker refers to her by this title rather than her name.

Understand
Find meaning

2a. List the references to well-known cultural items from the world of commerce.

2b. What do these cultural references suggest about the store's customers?

Apply
Use information

3a. According to the speaker, what is the difference between *jamón y queso* and ham and cheese?

3b. Compare and contrast the two foods from the perspective of the customers.

Analyze
Take things apart

4a. Describe what the customers do as they walk down the aisles of the store.

4b. Why must the saleswoman "divine" what some customers are looking for?

Evaluate
Make judgments

5a. Quote two lines or phrases that suggest the customers think of the saleswoman as a substitute mother.

5b. Explain how the deli represents a *microcosm* (miniature version) of the Latin American community in the United States.

Create
Bring ideas together

Analyze Literature

Tone and Theme

Choose one or two words to describe the tone of "Latin Deli." How does Cofer create that tone through her diction, descriptive details, cultural references, and so on? What does this tone suggest about the immigrant experience?

Write a sentence stating the theme of the poem. Is the theme stated or implied? Discuss whether it is a universal theme, one to which most people can relate. Also discuss how the tone of the poem helps portray this theme.

Extend the Text

Writing Options

Creative Writing Although there is no dialogue in the poem, there are implied conversations. Based on these unstated discussions, write a brief script of a conversation between the saleswoman and one or two customers. Use the conversation to reveal the poem's theme. Exchange scripts with a partner to compare themes.

Descriptive Writing Think of a place you know well, whether similar to or different from the bodega. Using vivid sensory details, write a descriptive paragraph that helps make readers feel they are there. If possible, visit the place and record the sights, sounds, and smells that define it.

Collaborative Learning

Make an Oral History Collection Working with a small group, invite recent or long-ago immigrants to

discuss their experiences with you. Have group members take turns interviewing and recording notes of the conversations. If possible, videotape the interviews. When all the interviews have been completed, transcribe the conversations (or type up the notes) to create an oral history collection.

Lifelong Learning

Volunteer as an English Language Tutor School-children who are recent immigrants or have not had the opportunity to improve their English skills can benefit from tutoring. With a group of classmates, set up a program in which you work with younger students to coach them in English language skills. (Be sure to obtain permission from the students' school before implementing your program.)

 Go to **www.mirrorsandwindows.com** for more.

Wingfoot Lake

A Lyric Poem by Rita Dove

Build Background

Literary Context **"Wingfoot Lake"** is from a poetry collection by Rita Dove called *Thomas and Beulah,* a series of narrative poems that show the life journey of a married couple from 1924 to 1963. Loosely based on the lives of Dove's grandparents, this Pulitzer Prize–winning book is divided into two sequences: "Mandolin," devoted to Thomas, and "Canary in Bloom," devoted to Beulah. The selection that follows examines Beulah's life after the death of her husband.

Historical Context In "Wingfoot Lake," Beulah alludes to the Civil Rights march of August 28, 1963, comparing the movement of the marchers through Washington, DC, to "a crow's wing [that] moved slowly through the white streets of government." This historic march drew 250,000 protesters, including Dr. Martin Luther King Jr., whose "I Have a Dream" speech garnered worldwide attention.

Reader's Context Why might an older African American who experienced segregation be afraid of an event like a Civil Rights march that many others find hopeful?

Meet the Author

Rita Dove (b. 1952) was born in Akron, Ohio, to parents who valued education and reading. At an early age, she began writing plays and stories. When a high school teacher took her to a local writers' conference, Dove started thinking of writing as a career. A high school Presidential Scholar in 1970, Dove went on to graduate from Miami University in Ohio. Four years later, she won a Fulbright Scholarship to study in West Germany and later attended graduate school at the University of Iowa Writers' Workshop, where she earned a master's degree in 1977.

Although Dove has written short stories, a novel, and a play, she is best known for her lyrical, free-verse poetry. Her poetry collections include *The Yellow House on the Corner* (1980), *Grace Notes* (1989), *Mother Love* (1995), and *On the Bus with Rosa Parks* (1999). In 1993, Dove became the first African American to be appointed Poet Laureate of the United States.

Dove has accomplished her goal "to bring poetry into everyday discourse." Her verse has been incorporated into music and was featured in the Steven Spielberg documentary *The Unfinished Journey.* She also has shared the works of other poets in her weekly column for the *Washington Post.* Dove was named the 2004 Poet Laureate of Virginia and Chancellor of the Academy of American Poets in 2006. She has taught creative writing at the University of Virginia, in Charlottesville, for the past fourteen years.

Analyze Literature

Characterization and Allusion

Characterization is the act of creating or describing a character. Writers create characters using *indirect characterization* techniques, showing what a character is like and allowing readers to judge him or her, and the *direct characterization* technique, telling what the character is like.

An **allusion** is a reference to a well-known person, place, event, or work of art, music, or literature.

Set Purpose

In *Thomas and Beulah,* Rita Dove's series of narrative poems about her grandparents, readers come to know these individuals and understand the history they have lived. As you read "Wingfoot Lake," record the details Dove reveals about her grandmother, Beulah. Identify which details are presented using direct versus indirect characterization techniques. In addition, be alert to the allusions Dove makes to events such as the famous march on Washington.

Church Picnic, 1998. Faith Ringgold. High Museum, Atlanta, Georgia.

Wingfoot Lake
(Independence Day, 1964)
by Rita Dove

On her 36th birthday, Thomas had shown her
her first swimming pool. It had been
his favorite color, exactly—just
so much of it, the swimmers' white arms jutting
5   into the chevrons[1] of high society.
She had rolled up her window
and told him to drive on, fast.

---

1. **chevrons.** Sleeve badges, often V-shaped, sewn onto military
   uniforms. *Chevrons of high society* refers to symbols designating a privi-
   leged group of people.

Now this *act of mercy:* four daughters
dragging her to their husbands' company picnic,
10 white families on one side and them
on the other, unpacking the same
squeeze bottles of Heinz,² the same
waxy beef patties and Salem potato chip bags.
So he was dead for the first time
15 on Fourth of July—ten years ago

had been harder, waiting for something to happen,
and ten years before that, the girls
like young horses eyeing the track.
Last August she stood alone for hours
20 in front of the T.V. set
as a crow's wing moved slowly through
the white streets of government.
That brave swimming

scared her, like Joanna saying
25 *Mother, we're Afro-Americans now!*
What did she know about Africa?
Were there lakes like this one
with a rowboat pushed under the pier?
Or Thomas' Great Mississippi
30 with its sullen³ silks? (There was
the Nile but the Nile belonged

to God.) Where she came from
was the past, 12 miles into town
where nobody had locked their back door,
35 and Goodyear⁴ hadn't begun to dream of a park
under the company symbol, a white foot
sprouting two small wings. ❖

---

2. **Heinz.** Brand of ketchup
3. **sullen.** In referring to the Mississippi River, the word probably means
   both "slow moving" and "somber in color or sound."
4. **Goodyear.** Tire company that has the logo (marketing symbol) of a
   winged foot

Think of a grandparent or another elderly person you know. What event or
experience from the past seems to have shaped his or her life?

Refer to Text ▶ ▶ ▶ ▶ ▶ Reason with Text

1a. How does Beulah respond when Thomas points to the first swimming pool she has ever seen?

1b. Explain what Beulah's response indicates about her feelings toward the pool and the people using it.

Understand
Find meaning

2a. On what day is the company picnic? What did Beulah watch on TV "last August"?

2b. What does the metaphor "crow's wing moved slowly" suggest was happening? Why are the "streets of government" said to be "white"?

Apply
Use information

3a. Name the two things that scare Beulah.

3b. Suggest why she is afraid of these things.

Analyze
Take things apart

4a. What does the speaker call an "act of mercy"?

4b. Interpret the significance or meaning of this event to Beulah.

Evaluate
Make judgments

5a. What does the daughter Joanna say to Beulah?

5b. Imagine that you are Joanna. What do you think of your mother's attitude toward racial issues?

Create
Bring ideas together

Analyze Literature

Characterization and Allusion

Review the details you recorded about Beulah. Which are presented using direct characterization? Which are presented using indirect techniques? By the end of the poem, what is your impression of Beulah?

What allusions did you find in this poem, and what does each mean? For instance, why is it significant that the poem takes place on Independence Day? What does the reference to a park bearing the Goodyear logo (a white winged foot) indicate about opportunities in corporate America?

Extend the Text

Writing Options

Creative Writing Create a one-page journal entry about an incident of discrimination of which you are aware—for instance, one based on race/ethnicity, gender, religion, or disability. The incident might be a personal experience, an event you witnessed, or something you read or heard about in the media.

Descriptive Writing Imagine that you have been invited to appear on a talk show about the Civil Rights struggles of the 1960s. To prepare for your appearance, write a brief character sketch of Beulah. Use the sketch to reveal attitudes toward Civil Rights and discrimination.

Collaborative Learning

Prepare a Time Line With a partner or in a group, read the remaining poems in Dove's collection *Thomas*

and Beulah. Divide the poems so one or more students read the section on Thomas and one or more read the section on Beulah. Together, make a time line chronicling events in the couple's lives. Be sure to include the Civil Rights march and the Fourth of July picnic.

Lifelong Learning

Display Memorabilia Using library or Internet sources, find images of memorabilia from the 1960s: household items, souvenirs, decorative objects, movie reviews, and similar materials that highlight the culture of the time. Make photocopies of the images you collect. (Be sure you reproduce the images legally and provide credit where appropriate.) For each item, prepare a caption that explains how the artifact was used.

 Go to **www.mirrorsandwindows.com** for more.

Mother Tongue

An Essay by Amy Tan

Build Background

Cultural Context In the essay **"Mother Tongue,"** first published in 1990, Amy Tan describes her Chinese-born mother's version of English and how friends, businesspeople, and even doctors reacted to what sometimes is called "broken English." In the essay, Tan suggests that there are many "Englishes" and that all nuances of the language offer richness and eloquence. In addition, she scolds native speakers, saying that "imperfect expression does not mean imperfect thoughts."

Reader's Context How can a person's ability to use language determine what opportunities and successes he or she will have in life?

Meet the Author

Amy Tan (b. 1952) was born in Oakland, California, to Chinese immigrant parents. Although Mandarin Chinese was her first language, she was encouraged to learn English to assimilate into mainstream culture. Her relationship with her parents (especially her mother) was strained growing up, partly due to Tan's rebellious nature and partly due to her parents' high expectations of her. The young Tan pursued her favorite activities: reading and writing.

When Tan was fourteen, her father and one of her brothers both died from brain tumors within a year's time. Tan's mother took her and her surviving brother to Switzerland, where Tan finished high school. In defiance of her mother and her language aptitude test scores, Tan earned a bachelor's degree in English and linguistics from San Jose State University in California in 1972 and stayed on to finish her master's degree in linguistics a year later.

Tan began her writing career as a partner in a business-writing company but later decided to look for a more creative outlet. After an emotional mother-daughter trip to China, Tan wrote her first book, *The Joy Luck Club* (1989), a series of narratives examining the relationships between Chinese-American daughters and their immigrant mothers. The book was a best seller and was made into a film in 1993. Tan's other works include the novels *The Kitchen God's Wife* (1991), *The Bonesetter's Daughter* (2001), and *Saving Fish from Drowning* (2005); the nonfiction collection *The Opposite of Fate: A Book of Musings* (2003); and two children's books.

Tan currently is an editor for the *Los Angeles Times* Sunday magazine and continues to write and lecture about her craft. She also is a member of the Rock Bottom Remainders, a rock band that raises money for literacy and First Amendment rights groups.

Analyze Literature

Thesis and Voice

A **thesis** is a main idea that is presented and supported in a work of nonfiction.

Voice is the way a writer uses language to reflect his or her unique personality and attitude toward the topic, form, and audience.

Set Purpose

Tan's "Mother Tongue" was selected as a Best American Essay in 1991, a year after it was published. As you read this outstanding essay, determine the author's thesis. What does she say about the power of language and the ability to use it? What personal experiences and observations does she provide to support her thesis? Also analyze Tan's written voice. Record details from the essay that give insights into her personality and attitude toward the topic.

Preview Vocabulary

evoke, 1208
belie, 1210
impeccable, 1211
benign, 1212

MOTHER TONGUE

by Amy Tan

> **When I was growing up, my mother's "limited" English limited my perception of her.**

I am not a scholar of English or literature. I cannot give you much more than personal opinions on the English language and its variations in this country or others.

I am a writer. And by that definition, I am someone who has always loved language. I am fascinated by language in daily life. I spend a great deal of my time thinking about the power of language—the way it can <u>evoke</u> an emotion,

evoke (ē vōk´) v., bring to mind

a visual image, a complex idea, or a simple truth. Language is the tool of my trade. And I use them all—all the Englishes I grew up with.

Recently, I was made keenly aware of the different Englishes I do use. I was giving a talk to a large group of people, the same talk I had already given to half a dozen other groups. The nature of the talk was about my writing, my life, and my book, *The Joy Luck Club*. The talk was going along well enough, until I remembered one major difference that made the whole talk sound wrong. My mother was in the room. And it was perhaps the first time she had heard me give a lengthy speech, using the kind of English I have never used with her. I was saying things like, "The intersection of memory upon imagination" and "There is an aspect of my fiction that relates to thus-and-thus"—a speech filled with carefully wrought grammatical phrases, burdened, it suddenly seemed to me, with nominalized forms,[1] past perfect tenses, conditional phrases, all the forms of standard English that I had learned in school and through books, the forms of English I did not use at home with my mother.

> It has become our language of intimacy, a different sort of English that relates to family talk, the language I grew up with.

Just last week, I was walking down the street with my mother, and I again found myself conscious of the English I was using, the English I do use with her. We were talking about the price of new and used furniture and I heard myself saying this; "Not waste money that way." My husband was with us as well, and he didn't notice any switch in my English. And then I realized why. It's because over the twenty years we've been together I've often used that same kind of English with him,

and sometimes he even uses it with me. It has become our language of intimacy, a different sort of English that relates to family talk, the language I grew up with.

So you'll have some idea of what this family talk I heard sounds like, I'll quote what my mother said during a recent conversation which I videotaped and then transcribed. During this conversation my mother was talking about a political gangster in Shanghai who had the same last name as her family's, Du, and how the gangster in his early years wanted to be adopted by her family, which was rich by comparison. Later, the gangster became more powerful, far richer than my mother's family, and one day showed up at my mother's wedding to pay his respects. Here's what she said in part:

"Du Yusong having business like fruit stand. Like off the street kind. He is Du like Du Zong—but not Tsung-ming Island people. The local people call putong, the river east side, he belong to that side local people. That man want to ask Du Zong father take him in like become own family. Du Zong father wasn't look down on him, but didn't take seriously, until that man big like become a mafia. Now important person, very hard to inviting him. Chinese way, came only to show respect, don't stay for dinner. Respect for making big celebration, he shows up. Mean gives lots of respect. Chinese custom. Chinese social life that way. If too important won't have to stay too long. He come to my wedding. I didn't see, I heard it. I gone to boy's side, they have YMCA dinner. Chinese age I was nineteen."

You should know that my mother's expressive command of English <u>belies</u> how much she actually understands. She reads the *Forbes* report, listens to *Wall Street Week,* converses daily with her stockbroker, reads all of Shirley MacLaine's books[2] with ease—all kinds of

---

1. **nominalized forms.** Nouns made from other parts of speech
2. **Shirley MacLaine's books.** The film actress has written on the subject of reincarnation.

> **be • lie** (bə lī´) *v.,* give a false impression of

The Chinese Language

Chinese is among the world's most widely spoken languages. In China alone, nearly one billion people speak one of the dialects of the language. Mandarin is the most common dialect.

One of the qualities that distinguishes spoken Chinese is that the meanings of particular sounds depend on slight differences in *tone,* or pitch. In Mandarin Chinese, for example, the word *yao* can be uttered in four different tones, ranging from high to low. Not only does each tone have its own meaning, but the four meanings are unrelated. The word *yao* can mean "waist," "to shake," "to bite," and "to want," depending on the tone in which it's spoken. Another quality of Mandarin Chinese is that many words are *monosyllabic,* having only one syllable. Many words also end in a vowel or one of a small number of consonants.

Written Chinese uses a set of characters known as *hànzi.* Originally based on pictures of animals, people, and objects, these characters have been altered to the extent that they no longer resemble what they initially represented. Each character represents a syllable of spoken language and has a specific meaning. Characters can be used individu-ally or in combina-tion, which means there is no finite number of *hànzi* characters. To read a Chinese newspaper, a person would need to know about three thou-sand characters. To read literature and more technical works would require knowledge of at least nine thousand characters.

Until recently, Chinese words were represented in English using a system called the *Wade-Giles method.* For instance, before the 1980s, people in the English-speaking world referred to the capital of the People's Republic of China as *Peking,* accord-ing to the Wade-Giles spelling. However, in the last several decades, *pinyin* has become the preferred representational system. Today, the capital city commonly is known as *Beijing.*

---

things I can't begin to understand. Yet some of my friends tell me they understand 50 per-cent of what my mother says. Some say they understand 80 to 90 percent. Some say they understand none of it, as if she were speaking pure Chinese. But to me, my mother's En-glish is perfectly clear, perfectly natural. It's my mother tongue. Her language, as I hear it, is vivid, direct, full of observation and imagery. That was the language that helped shape the way I saw things, expressed things, made sense of the world.

Lately, I've been giving more thought to the kind of English my mother speaks. Like others, I have described it to people as "broken" or "fractured" English. But I wince when I say that. It has always bothered me that I can think of no way to describe it other than "broken," as if it were damaged and needed to be fixed, as if it lacked a certain wholeness and soundness. I've heard other terms used, "limited English," for example. But they seem just as bad, as if everything is limited, including people's percep-tions of the limited English speaker.

I know this for a fact, because when I was growing up, my mother's "limited" English limited my perception of her. I was ashamed of her English. I believed that her English reflected the quality of what she had to say. That is, because she expressed them imper-fectly her thoughts were imperfect. And I had plenty of empirical[3] evidence to support me: the fact that people in department stores, at banks, and at restaurants did not take her seriously, did not give her good service, pretended not to understand her, or even acted as if they did not hear her.

My mother has long realized the limitations of her English as well. When I was fifteen, she used to have me call people on the phone to pretend I was she. In this guise, I was forced to ask for information or even to complain and yell at people who had been rude to her. One time it was a call to her stockbroker in New York. She had cashed out her small portfolio and it just so happened we were going to go to New York the next week, our very first trip outside California. I had to get on the phone and say in an adolescent voice that was not very convincing, "This is Mrs. Tan."

> **My mother has long realized the limitations of her English as well.**

And my mother was standing in the back whispering loudly, "Why he don't send me check, already two weeks late. So mad he lie to me, losing me money."

And then I said in perfect English, "Yes, I'm getting rather concerned. You had agreed to send the check two weeks ago, but it hasn't arrived."

Then she began to talk more loudly. "What he want, I come to New York tell him front of his boss, you cheating me?" And I was trying to calm her down, make her be quiet, while telling the stockbroker, "I can't tolerate any more excuses. If I don't receive the check immediately, I am going to have to speak to your manager when I'm in New York next week." And sure enough, the following week there we were

in front of this astonished stockbroker, and I was sitting there red-faced and quiet, and my mother, the real Mrs. Tan, was shouting at his boss in her <u>impeccable</u> broken English.

We used a similar routine just five days ago, for a situation that was far less humorous. My mother had gone to the hospital for an appointment, to find out about a <u>benign</u> brain tumor a CAT scan had revealed a month ago. She said she had spoken very good English, her best English, no mistakes. Still, she said, the hospital did not apologize when they said they had lost the CAT scan and she had come for nothing. She said they did not seem to have any sympathy when she told them she was anxious to know the exact diagnosis, since her husband and son had both died of brain tumors. She said they would not give her any more information until the next time and she would have to make another appointment for that. So she said she would not leave until the doctor called her daughter. She wouldn't budge. And when the doctor finally called her daughter, me, who spoke in perfect English—lo and behold—we had assurances the CAT scan would be found, promises that a conference call on Monday would be held, and apologies for any suffering my mother had gone through for a most regrettable mistake.

I think my mother's English almost had an effect on limiting my possibilities in life as well. Sociologists and linguists probably will tell you that a person's developing language skills are more influenced by peers. But I do think that the language spoken in the family, especially in immigrant families which are more insular, plays a large role in shaping the language of the child. And I believe that it affected my results

---

3. **empirical.** Based on experience and observation

---

im • pec • cable (im pek´ ə b'l) *adj.*, without error
be • nign (bə nīn´) *adj.*, harmless; not cancerous

on achievement tests, IQ tests, and the SAT. While my English skills were never judged as poor, compared to math, English could not be considered my strong suit. In grade school I did moderately well, getting perhaps B's, sometimes B-pluses, in English and scoring perhaps in the sixtieth or seventieth percentile on achievement tests. But those scores were not good enough to override the opinion that my true abilities lay in math and science, because in those areas I achieved A's and scored in the ninetieth percentile or higher.

This was understandable. Math is precise; there is only one correct answer. Whereas, for me at least, the answers on English tests were always a judgment call, a matter of opinion and personal experience. Those tests were con-structed around items like fill-in-the-blank

sentence completion, such as, "Even though Tom was _____, Mary thought he was _____." And the correct answer always seemed to be the most bland combinations of thoughts, for example, "Even though Tom was shy, Mary thought he was charming," with the grammatical structure "even though" limiting the correct answer to some sort of semantic opposites,[4] so you wouldn't get answers like, "Even though Tom was foolish, Mary thought he was ridiculous." Well, according to my mother, there were very few limitations as to what Tom could have been and what Mary might have thought of him. So I never did well on tests like that.

---

4. **semantic opposites.** Antonyms; words opposite in meaning

The same was true with word analogies, pairs of words in which you were supposed to find some sort of logical, semantic relationship—for example, "*Sunset* is to *nightfall* as _____ is to _____." And here you would be presented with a list of four possible pairs, one of which showed the same kind of relationship: *red* is to *stoplight, bus* is to *arrival, chills* is to *fever, yawn* is to *boring.* Well, I could never think that way. I knew what the tests were asking, but I could not block out of my mind the images already created by the first pair, "sunset is to nightfall"—and I would see a burst of colors against a darkening sky, the moon rising, the lowering of a curtain of stars. And all the other pairs of words—red, bus, stoplight, boring—just threw up a mass of confusing images, making it impossible for me to sort out something as logical as saying: "A sunset precedes nightfall" is the same as "a chill precedes a fever." The only way I would have gotten that answer right would have been to imagine an associative[5] situation, for example, my being disobedient and staying out past sunset, catching a chill at night, which turns into feverish pneumonia as punishment, which indeed did happen to me.

I have been thinking about all this lately, about my mother's English, about achievement tests. Because lately I've been asked, as a writer, why there are not more Asian Americans represented in American literature. Why are there few Asian Americans enrolled in creative writing programs? Why do so many Chinese students go into engineering? Well, these are broad sociological questions I can't begin to answer. But I have noticed in surveys—in fact, just last week—that Asian students, as a whole, always do significantly better on math achievement tests than in English. And this makes me think that there are other Asian-American students whose English spoken in the home might also be described as "broken" or "limited." And perhaps they also have teachers who are steering them away from writing

and into math and science, which is what happened to me.

Fortunately, I happen to be rebellious in nature and enjoy the challenge of disproving assumptions made about me. I became an English major my first year in college, after being enrolled as pre-med. I started writing nonfiction as a freelancer the week after I was told by my former boss that writing was my worst skill and I should hone my talents toward account management.

> I happen to be rebellious in nature and enjoy the challenge of disproving assumptions made about me.

But it wasn't until 1985 that I finally began to write fiction. And at first I wrote using what I thought to be wittily crafted sentences, sentences that would finally prove I had mastery over the English language. Here's an example from the first draft of a story that later made its way into *The Joy Luck Club,* but without this line: "That was my mental quandary in its nascent state."[6] A terrible line, which I can barely pronounce.

Fortunately, for reasons I won't get into today, I later decided I should envision a reader for the stories I would write. And the reader I decided upon was my mother, because these were stories about mothers. So with this reader in mind—and in fact she did read my early drafts—I began to write stories using all the Englishes I grew up with: the English I spoke to my mother, which for lack of a better term might be described as "simple"; the English she used with me, which for lack of

---

5. **associative.** Indicating a link between one thought and another
6. **quandary in its nascent state.** Uncertainty at its beginning

a better term might be described as "broken"; my translation of her Chinese, which could certainly be described as "watered down"; and what I imagined to be her translation of her Chinese if she could speak in perfect English, her internal language, and for that I sought to preserve the essence, but neither an English nor a Chinese structure. I wanted to capture what language ability tests can never reveal: her intent, her passion, her imagery, the rhythms of her speech and the nature of her thoughts.

Apart from what any critic had to say about my writing, I knew I had succeeded where it counted when my mother finished reading my book and gave me her verdict: "So easy to read." ❖

MIRRORS & WINDOWS

Tan writes, "I happen to be rebellious in nature and enjoy the challenge of disproving assumptions made about me." What do people assume about you? Are they right or wrong?

Refer to Text ▶ ▶ ▶ ▶ ▶ **Reason with Text**

1a. Why does Tan give a paragraph-long example of her mother's English?	**1b.** Explain how Tan feels about her own use of the English "she grew up with."	**Understand** Find meaning
2a. What evidence does Tan give that her mother understands English much better than her spoken language indicates?	**2b.** The term *mother tongue* means a person's native language. How does Tan's use of the term differ from this commonly used meaning?	**Apply** Use information
3a. What English tests were the most troublesome for Tan?	**3b.** Analyze why Tan was able to translate her mother's English yet scored more poorly on English tests than math tests.	**Analyze** Take things apart
4a. According to Tan, what group of people is presumed to have the most influence on a young person's developing language skills?	**4b.** Argue for or against Tan's opinion that children's language development is influenced more by the family, especially in immigrant families.	**Evaluate** Make judgments
5a. Describe the voice Tan originally planned to use when she began writing fiction.	**5b.** Suggest why Tan imagined her mother as the intended reader when she was writing *The Joy Luck Club*.	**Create** Bring ideas together

Analyze Literature

Thesis and Voice
Write a sentence stating Tan's central message, or thesis. What information does she provide to support her beliefs about the power and influence of language? Evaluate how well she supports her thesis in this essay.

Review the details you recorded that give insights into Tan's personality and attitude toward her topic. What did you learn about Amy Tan? How would you characterize her written voice?

Extend the Text

Writing Options

Creative Writing You would like to apply for a summer job with a newspaper. The editor has asked for a sample of your writing to be titled "The Role of Language in My Life." Write a one-page personal essay on the subject.

Expository Writing Imagine that Mrs. Tan has asked you to explain how her English is similar to and different from standard English. Write a brief comparison-and-contrast essay in which you discuss the two Englishes.

Collaborative Learning

Research Language Acquisition in Children Do Internet or library research on the topic of how children learn language. Working with a group, have each member explore specific theories of language development—

for example, the theory of psychologist Jean Piaget (1896–1980). Then collaborate to prepare a chart identifying the major theories of language acquisition.

Media Literacy

Conduct a Survey on Language Access Find out whether non-English speakers in your community have access to translators and interpreters. Work with a group to conduct a small-scale survey of government sites (such as city hall, the parks board, or the department of motor vehicles) and professional offices (doctors, dentists, and lawyers). Contact organizations such as these, asking politely whether translators are available to people who need help communicating across language barriers. Present your findings to the class.

 Go to **www.mirrorsandwindows.com** for more.

What does it mean to study *society?* Society is both the larger group and the individuals who comprise it. Such a group is not fixed but rather in constant flux.

This also is true of the works of art in which a society is reflected. As seen through the sociological lens, a literary text is part of a cultural process. It cannot be seen apart from the values and rules that govern the society at large. However, just as the social structure keeps changing and evolving, so do the expectations or attitudes of authors and readers. **Sociological criticism** is sensitive to how a work of art both mirrors and influences society.

> *"[People] grow used to everything except to living in a society which has not their own manners."*
>
> —ALEXIS DE TOCQUEVILLE, NINETEENTH-CENTURY HISTORIAN

Overview of Sociological Criticism

A sociological reading of literature proposes to discover the mind-set and behavior of the individuals and groups a text portrays. At the same time, such a reading recognizes the power of the text to reshape social expectations.

Sociological literary criticism overlaps with political criticism in some ways (see Unit 7, pages 972–973). Both study a text for what it reveals about economic and social class. Sociological criticism is less rigid than political criticism, however, and looks at a text from a variety of perspectives. The sociological critic asks questions such as Who is the writer? Who is the audience for this text? How does the work reflect on the society it depicts? What is the writer's political and social agenda?

Such questions are especially relevant today. In fact, sociological criticism is most pertinent when literature asks profound questions about the society it depicts. The very act of raising such issues can be seen as a form of political and social action.

There is a clear historical basis for modern sociological criticism. In the late-nineteenth century, novelists and intellectuals began responding directly to the pressures of industrialized life. The relationship of the individual to new economic and social structures was addressed in novels by authors such as Mark Twain, Theodore Dreiser, and Upton Sinclair. It seemed as though society finally had become aware of itself and that writers were at the forefront of this social consciousness.

The field of modern sociology also has its roots in this rapidly changing era. In the United States, a new breed of social scientists began studying social patterns and structures. They paid particular attention to industrialization, urbanization (the movement of people to the cities), the growing immigrant population, and the emergence of a leisure class. Contemporary sociological theory continues to follow social trends and patterns, and literary theory keeps pace with these changes.

Application of Sociological Criticism

Some works lend themselves particularly well to sociological analysis. Consider Amy Tan's memoir of an immigrant Chinese mother who spoke so-called broken English. As you study "Mother Tongue," notice the following elements.

Author's Voice and Tone

Tan defines herself as "someone who has always loved language," but her identity as a Chinese American is complicated by the question of which language to speak: the language of her Chinese family or the language of mainstream American culture. Notice how language and identity come together in her description of this scene:

> Recently, I was made keenly aware of the different Englishes I do use. I was giving a talk to a large group of people, the same talk I had already given to half a dozen other groups. The nature of the talk was about my writing, my life, and my book, *The Joy Luck Club.* The talk was going along well enough, until I remembered one major difference that made the whole talk sound wrong. My mother was

TAN

in the room. And it was perhaps the first time she had heard me give a lengthy speech, using the kind of English I have never used with her. I was saying things like, "The intersection of memory upon imagination" and "There is an aspect of my fiction that relates to thus-and-thus-"—a speech filled with carefully wrought grammatical phrases, burdened, it suddenly seemed to me, with nominalized forms, past perfect tenses, conditional phrases, all the forms of standard English that I had learned in school and through books, the forms of English I did not use at home with my mother.

❏ **Analyze** Tan suggests that her life as her mother's child has been affected by a lifelong unease with the problem of language. How is her formal English "burdened"? What does this choice of verb reveal about Tan's views of language? How would you describe her tone in this passage?

Conflict and Identity

Next, examine the language of Tan's mother and how it appears to limit her. The author's use of dialogue shows a keen awareness of Mrs. Tan's problem. It's a problem of culture and class, as Tan has long since recognized. Her mother is victimized because she uses so-called broken, or nonstandard, English. In this instance, the author is forced to intervene on her mother's behalf so that Mrs. Tan will be treated fairly in a financial transaction:

> And my mother was standing in the back whispering loudly, "Why he don't send me the check, already two weeks late. So mad he lie to me, losing me money."
>
> And then I said in perfect English, "Yes, I'm getting rather concerned. You had agreed to send me the check two weeks ago, but it hasn't arrived."

❏ **Analyze** In what sense is Tan's mother, an intelligent and well-read person, in conflict with the values and unspoken rules of her adopted homeland?

Consider why the stockbroker fails to respond to her demand for better service. How does the use of formal, mainstream language appear to resolve the situation? What does this suggest about how immigrants are treated in U.S. society?

Characterization and Theme

Tan reflects that her mother's social and educational limitations easily could have had a similar effect on her own future. Notice how she offers what is, in fact, a sociological interpretation of a significant trend in the education of Asian-American students:

> Why are there few Asian Americans enrolled in creative writing programs? Why do so many Chinese students go into engineering? Well, these are broad sociological questions I can't begin to answer. But I have noticed in surveys—in fact, just last week—that Asian students, on the whole, always do significantly better on math achievement tests than in English. And this makes me think that there are other Asian-American students whose English spoken in the home might also be described as "broken" or "limited." And perhaps they also have teachers who are steering them away from writing and into math and science, which is what happened to me.

❏ **Analyze** How does the author generalize from her own experience to the experience of an entire population? Does she seem to believe that this situation is normal or acceptable? Which details indicate that Tan believes Asian-American students are being stereotyped and denied a broad choice of careers?

WRITING ABOUT

Sociological Criticism

Write an essay that answers this question: What is Amy Tan's political and social agenda in writing "Mother Tongue"? Use details from the essay to explore how personal experience and social realities can become the basis for a social commentary.

Straw Into Gold: The Metamorphosis of the Everyday

An Essay by Sandra Cisneros

Build Background

Literary Context In **"Straw Into Gold: The Metamorphosis of the Everyday,"** Sandra Cisneros offers insights into her past to show how she has pursued opportunities, even when faced with obstacles. The title of the essay alludes to the fairy tale "Rumpelstiltskin," in which a young woman is ordered to spin straw into gold. Although the task seems impossible, she succeeds. The essay's subtitle, "The Metamorphosis of the Everyday," refers to how Cisneros has taken her everyday experiences and spun them into rich stories. A *metamorphosis* is a change in form or appearance—in this case, Cisneros's growth as a writer.

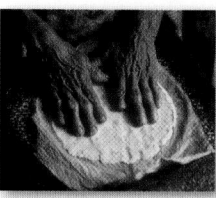

Reader's Context How do you approach a task that seems impossible? Are you inspired by the challenge or intimidated by the prospect of failure?

Meet the Author

Sandra Cisneros (b. 1954) was born in Chicago to a Mexican father and a Mexican-American (Chicana) mother. One of seven children, she grew up in poverty. Her family moved frequently between Mexico City and Chicago's *barrio,* home to the poorest Chicano families. This transient lifestyle made it difficult for Cisneros to make friends, so she buried herself in books. In high school, she was editor of the literary magazine, an experience that kindled her love for writing.

Cisneros attended Loyola University in Chicago and graduated in 1976 with an English degree. Her writing skills blossomed at the prestigious University of Iowa Writers' Workshop, where she completed her master's degree in 1978.

Cisneros returned to Chicago and began her first book, *The House on Mango Street* (1983), a series of narratives told by a girl growing up in a Chicago *barrio.* These writings reflect Cisneros's belief that stories should spring from a writer's own experiences. In addition to writing about her Chicana upbringing, Cisneros is known for her strong feminine characters.

Cisneros's works include the poetry collections *Bad Boys* (1980), *The Rodrigo Poems* (1985), *My Wicked Wicked Ways* (1987), and *Loose Woman* (1994) and the novel *Caramelo* (2002). She has been awarded two National Endowment for the Arts grants and a MacArthur, or "genius" grant, which is given to someone who has excelled in the arts or sciences. Cisneros currently lives in San Antonio, Texas, where she conducts workshops at the Guadalupe Cultural Arts Center and works on an autobiographical essay collection entitled *Writing in My Pajamas.*

Analyze Literature

Essay and Metaphor
An **essay** is a short nonfiction work that presents a single main idea, or *thesis,* about a particular topic. An essay can be *expository* (informative), *persuasive,* or *personal,* depending on the author's subject and purpose.

A **metaphor** is a figure of speech in which one thing is written about as if it were another. A metaphor invites readers to compare the writer's actual subject, the *tenor* of the metaphor, with something to which the subject is likened, the *vehicle* of the metaphor.

Set Purpose

Cisneros once said, "I have to understand what my strengths and limitations are, and work from a true place." Keep this philosophy in mind as you read "Straw Into Gold." Determine what type of essay it is, and record the details that lead you to this conclusion. Also consider Cisneros's use of the "straw into gold" metaphor. If the task of turning straw into gold is the vehicle of the metaphor, then what is the tenor?

Preview Vocabulary

subsist, 1219
intuitively, 1220
taboo, 1221
nomadic, 1221
nostalgia, 1221

Straw Into Gold

The Metamorphosis[1] of the Everyday

by Sandra Cisneros

**I've done all kinds of things
I didn't think I could do since then.**

When I was living in an artists' colony in the south of France, some fellow Latin-Americans who taught at the university in Aix-en-Provence[2] invited me to share a home-cooked meal with them. I had been living abroad almost a year then on an NEA[3] grant, <u>subsisting</u> mainly on French bread and lentils while in France so that my money could last longer. So when the invitation to dinner arrived, I accepted without hesitation. Especially since they had promised Mexican food.

What I didn't realize when they made this invitation was that I was supposed to be involved in preparing this meal. I guess they

---

1. **Metamorphosis.** Change in physical or other form
2. **Aix-en-Provence** (ā′ zô[n] prō vôns′). City in southeastern France
3. **NEA.** National Endowment for the Arts, an organization that funds artists and writers

> **sub • sist** (sub sist′) v., exist; have the necessities of life; nourish oneself

to get my graduate degree. How was I to start? There were rules involved here, unlike writing a poem or story, which I did <u>intuitively</u>. There was a step-by-step process needed and I had better know it. I felt as if making tortillas, or writing a critical paper for that matter, were tasks so impossible I wanted to break down into tears.

Somehow though, I managed to make those tortillas—crooked and burnt, but edible nonetheless. My hosts were absolutely ignorant when it came to Mexican food; they thought my tortillas were delicious. (I'm glad my mama wasn't there.) Thinking back and looking at the photograph documenting the three of us consuming those lopsided circles I am amazed. Just as I am amazed I could finish my MFA exam (lopsided and crooked, but finished all the same). Didn't think I could do it. But I did.

I've managed to do a lot of things in my life I didn't think I was capable of and which many others didn't think me capable of either.

Especially because I am a woman, a Latina, an only daughter in a family of six men. My father would've liked to have seen me married long ago. In our culture, men and women

assumed I knew how to cook Mexican food because I was Mexican. They wanted specifically tortillas, though I'd never made a tortilla in my life.

It's true I had witnessed my mother rolling the little armies of dough into perfect circles, but my mother's family is from Guanajuato,[4] *provinciales,*[5] country folk. They only know how to make flour tortillas. My father's family, on the other hand, is chilango,[6] from Mexico City. We ate corn tortillas but we didn't make them. Someone was sent to the corner tortilleria to buy some. I'd never seen anybody make corn tortillas. Ever.

Well, somehow my Latino hosts had gotten a hold of a packet of corn flour, and this is what they tossed my way with orders to produce tortillas. *Asi como sea.* Any ol' way, they said and went back to their cooking.

Why did I feel like the woman in the fairy tale who was locked in a room and ordered to spin straw into gold? I had the same sick feeling when I was required to write my critical essay for my MFA[7] exam—the only piece of noncreative writing necessary in order

---

4. **Guanajuato** (gwä' nä hwä' tō). City and state in central Mexico
5. *provinciales* (prō vēn sē äl' äs). [Spanish] Country dwellers; provincials
6. *chilango* (chē läŋ' gō). [Spanish] Native of Mexico City
7. **MFA.** Master of Fine Arts

in • tu • i • tive • ly (in tü' it iv lē) *adv.,* through intuition; without having to think about it or be taught how to do it

don't leave their father's house except by way of marriage. I crossed my father's threshold with nothing carrying me but my own two feet. A woman whom no one came for and no one chased away.

To make matters worse, I had left before any of my six brothers had ventured away from home. I had broken a terrible <u>taboo</u>. Somehow, looking back at photos of myself as a child, I wonder if I was aware of having begun already my own quiet war.

I like to think that somehow my family, my Mexicanness, my poverty all had something to do with shaping me into a writer. I like to think my parents were preparing me all along for my life as an artist even though they didn't know it. From my father I inherited a love of wandering. He was born in Mexico City but as a young man he traveled into the U.S. vagabonding. He eventually was drafted and thus became a citizen. Some of the stories he has told about his first months in the U.S. with little or no English surface in my stories in *The House on Mango Street* as well as others I have in mind to write in the future. From him I inherited a sappy heart. (He still cries when he watches the Mexican soaps—especially if they deal with children who have forsaken their parents.)

> ## I like to think that somehow my family, my Mexicanness, my poverty all had something to do with shaping me into a writer.

My mother was born like me—in Chicago but of Mexican descent. It would be her tough, street-wise voice that would haunt all my stories and poems. An amazing woman who loves to draw and read books and can sing an opera. A smart cookie.

When I was a little girl we traveled to Mexico City so much I thought my grandparents' house on La Fortuna, Number 12, was home. It was the only constant in our <u>nomadic</u> ramblings from one Chicago flat to another. The house on Destiny Street, Number 12, in the colonia Tepeyac,[8] would be perhaps the only home I knew, and that <u>nostalgia</u> for a home would be a theme that would obsess me.

My brothers also figured greatly in my art. Especially the oldest two; I grew up in their shadows. Henry, the second oldest and my favorite, appears often in poems I have written and in stories which at times only borrow his nickname, Kiki. He played a major role in my childhood. We were bunkbed mates. We were co-conspirators. We were pals. Until my oldest brother came back from studying in Mexico and left me odd-woman-out for always.

What would my teachers say if they knew I was a writer? Who would've guessed it? I wasn't a very bright student. I didn't much like school because we moved so much and I was always new and funny-looking. In my fifth-grade report card, I have nothing but an avalanche of C's and D's, but I don't remember being that stupid. I was good at art and I read plenty of library books and Kiki laughed at all my jokes. At home I was fine, but at school I never opened my mouth except when the teacher called on me, the first time I'd speak all day.

When I think how I see myself, it would have to be at age eleven. I know I'm thirty-two on the outside, but inside I'm eleven. I'm

---

8. **colonia Tepeyac.** Neighborhood in Mexico City

---

ta • boo (ta bü´) *n.,* something forbidden because of social custom or for protection
no • ma • dic (nō ma´ dik) *adj.,* roaming from place to place aimlessly
nos • tal • gia (nä stal´ jä) *n.,* state of sentimental longing, often for the past; homesickness

César Chávez

When Cisneros uses the Spanish words *Chicano* and *Chicana* in her essay, she is referring to Americans of Mexican descent (men and women, respectively). This terminology evolved from the Mexican-American labor and farm demonstrations of the 1960s, when workers tried to forge a distinct political and ethnic identity for themselves. César Chávez (1927–1993) was the principal organizer of those demonstrations and today is considered one of the United States' greatest civil rights leaders.

Chávez was born in 1927 outside Yuma, Arizona, to a family of Mexican-American migrant workers. He graduated from eighth grade in 1942 but could not attend high school because he needed to help support his impoverished family. While working as a farm laborer, he grew discontented with the poor treatment he and his Mexican-American co-workers received. The farm workers earned such low wages they could not maintain a proper standard of living. Additionally, their work exposed them to harsh pesticides and forced them to operate dangerous equipment.

Intent on improving these conditions, Chávez began working as a labor organizer in California in the early 1950s. He registered workers to vote, orchestrated mass boycotts, and conducted strikes. He became famous for his hunger strikes, during which he would fast for weeks to advocate a wage increase or pesticide ban. Through his tireless crusading, Chávez instituted a wave of legislative and internal reforms that greatly benefited the Mexican-American farm laborers working in California. In 1962, he founded the organization that would become his legacy, the National Farm Workers Association (now known as the United Farm Workers of America), which continues to protect the rights of farm laborers.

In 1993, President Bill Clinton awarded Chávez the Presidential Medal of Freedom posthumously. Chávez also has been recognized by the U.S. Postal Service with a commemorative stamp bearing his portrait, and numerous cities, including California's state capital, Sacramento, have dedicated parks, street names, libraries, and elementary schools in his honor. Today, California celebrates Chávez's birthday as a state holiday and closes all government offices.

the girl in the picture with skinny arms and a crumpled shirt and crooked hair. I didn't like school because all they saw was the outside me. School was lots of rules and sitting with your hands folded and being very afraid all the time. I liked looking out the window and thinking. I liked staring at the girl across the way writing her name over and over again in red ink. I wondered why the boy with the dirty collar in front of me didn't have a mama who took better care of him.

I think my mama and papa did the best they could to keep us warm and clean and never hungry. We had birthday and graduation parties and things like that, but there was another hunger that had to be fed. There was a hunger I didn't even have a name for. Was this when I began writing?

In 1966 we moved into a house, a real one, our first real home. This meant we didn't have to change schools and be the new kids on the block every couple of years. We could make friends and not be afraid we'd have to say goodbye to them and start all over. My brothers and the flock of boys they brought home would become important characters eventually for my stories—Louie and his cousins, Meme

Ortiz and his dog with two names, one in English and one in Spanish.

My mother flourished in her own home. She took books out of the library and taught herself to garden, producing flowers so envied we had to put a lock on the gate to keep out the midnight flower thieves. My mother is still gardening to this day.

This was the period in my life, that slippery age when you are both child and woman and neither, I was to record in *The House on Mango Street*. I was still shy. I was a girl who couldn't come out of her shell.

I was still shy. I was a girl who couldn't come out of her shell.

How was I to know I would be recording and documenting the women who sat their sadness on an elbow and stared out a window? It would be the city streets of Chicago I would later record, but from a child's eye.

I've done all kinds of things I didn't think I could do since then. I've gone to a prestigious university, studied with famous writers and taken away an MFA degree. I've taught poetry in the schools in Illinois and Texas. I've gotten an NEA grant and run away with it as far as my courage would take me. I've seen the bleached and bitter mountains of the Peloponnesus.[9] I've lived on a Greek island. I've been to Venice[10] twice. In Rapallo, I met Ilona[11] once and

forever and took her sad heart with me across the south of France and into Spain.

I've lived in Yugoslavia. I've been to the famous Nice[12] flower market behind the opera house. I've lived in a village in the pre-Alps[13] and witnessed the daily parade of promenaders.[14]

I've moved since Europe to the strange and wonderful country of Texas, land of polaroid-blue skies and big bugs. I met a mayor with my last name. I met famous Chicana/o artists and writers and *políticos*.[15]

Texas is another chapter in my life. It brought with it the Dobie-Paisano Fellowship, a six-month residency on a 265-acre ranch. But most important Texas brought Mexico back to me.

Sitting at my favorite people-watching spot, the snaky Woolworth's counter across the street from the Alamo,[16] I can't think of anything else I'd rather be than a writer. I've traveled and lectured from Cape Cod to San Francisco, to Spain, Yugoslavia, Greece, Mexico, France, Italy, and finally today to Seguin, Texas. Along the way there is straw for the taking. With a little imagination, it can be spun into gold. ❖

---

9. **Peloponnesus.** Peninsula at the southern tip of Greece
10. **Venice.** City in Italy on the Mediterranean Sea
11. **Rapallo . . . Ilona.** *Rapallo*—a resort city in Italy; *Ilona*—a reference to a woman also featured in Cisneros's poem "A Letter to Ilona from the South of France"
12. **Nice** (nēs). Port city and summer vacation spot in the south of France
13. **pre-Alps.** Foothills of the Alps, a mountain range in south central Europe
14. **promenaders.** People strolling in a public space, often a plaza
15. **políticos.** [Spanish] Politicians
16. **Alamo.** Structure in San Antonio, the site of a siege on Texas revolutionaries by Mexican troops in 1836

 **MIRRORS & WINDOWS** What have you done that you didn't think you could do? Did the experience motivate you to try new things?

Refer to Text ▷ ▷ ▶ ▶ ▶ **Reason with Text**

1a. Why did Cisneros's friends in Aix-en-Provence assume she could make corn tortillas?	**1b.** Why did Cisneros accept the challenge rather than admit she didn't know how to make corn tortillas?

Understand
Find meaning

2a. Identify the two taboos that Cisneros, as a Latina, broke.	**2b.** How might breaking the taboos have helped Cisneros later turn "straw into gold"?

Apply
Use information

3a. Why did Cisneros's teachers expect so little from her? Why didn't she expect to succeed as an adult?	**3b.** Suggest why Cisneros received low grades even though she considered herself intelligent. Why was the family's move to a house a turning point in her life?

Analyze
Take things apart

4a. What does Cisneros say she inherited from her father? How did she benefit from his experiences?	**4b.** Judge how Cisneros's traveling probably helped her when she felt challenged to "turn straw into gold."

Evaluate
Make judgments

5a. What is Cisneros referring to when she says that people at school saw only "the outside me"?	**5b.** Why do people sometimes respond to each other based on what is "outside"? Explain what harm such a response can cause.

Create
Bring ideas together

Analyze Literature

Essay and Metaphor
What type of essay is "Straw Into Gold": expository, persuasive, or personal? What led you to this conclusion? Support your answer with details from the essay.

Explain the "straw into gold" metaphor, identifying both the vehicle and the tenor. What does the task of turning straw into gold represent? Evaluate whether this is an effective metaphor, given Cisneros's purpose in writing the essay.

Extend the Text

Writing Options
Creative Writing List five questions you would like to ask Sandra Cisneros about her life and writing. Then for each question, write a sentence or two explaining why you want to ask it. Research Cisneros's life to identify topics for specific questions.

Narrative Writing Read or recollect a fairy tale, myth, or similar story. Then develop an analogy from the story, as Cisneros does, for use in describing a challenge, success, or other significant event in your life. (If you prefer, describe an imaginary event rather than a real one.)

Collaborative Learning
Learn about NEA Grants Visit the website of the National Endowment for the Arts (NEA) to learn about high school students who have been awarded grants (funding) for literacy training projects. With a partner, conduct research to determine who is eligible for such grants, what kinds of projects are appropriate, and how and when to submit a grant proposal. Summarize your findings in a step-by-step explanation of the granting process.

Lifelong Learning
Develop a Student Itinerary Develop an *itinerary*, or detailed travel plan, for a summer trip to a foreign country. Select a country and several locations within it that you and several friends can visit. Recommend transportation, housing, restaurants, and places of interest, such as museums and wildlife preserves.

 Go to **www.mirrorsandwindows.com** for more.

1. Why doesn't Cisneros know how to make corn tortillas?
   A. She has never been much of a cook.
   B. Although her friends assume she is Mexican, in fact she is not.
   C. Her mother only knew about flour tortillas; the family bought corn tortillas.
   D. She spent much of her youth writing stories and poems instead of helping her mother in the kitchen.
   E. Growing up in Chicago, she wanted to distance herself from her Latina background.

2. Why was moving out of her parents' house considered a taboo?
   A. She moved out on her own and was not married.
   B. She was expected to stay home and take care of her parents.
   C. Her older brothers had not yet moved out.
   D. Both A and B
   E. Both A and C

3. Why does Cisneros likely provide so many details and include several foreign terms in her essay?
   A. to boast about her knowledge and accomplishments
   B. to contrast how different cultures regard heritage
   C. to demonstrate why Latinas have had such difficulty being successful
   D. to help readers better understand what her life has been like
   E. to contrast her life with that of the girl in "Rumpelstiltskin"

4. Why didn't Cisneros like school?
   A. She wasn't very smart.
   B. Her family moved often, so she was always a new student.
   C. She got into trouble for talking too much.
   D. She was embarrassed by her accent, so she didn't participate much.
   E. The other children were not very nice to her.

5. How did Cisneros's personality contribute to her becoming a writer?
   A. She was shy and writing was a way to express herself.
   B. She always cherished her past, and writing provided a way to record past events.
   C. She was very observant, so writing served as a sort of written photograph.
   D. She was imaginative and writing allowed her to create new worlds.
   E. She often was lonely, so she created characters with which to interact.

6. Someone who lives a *nomadic* lifestyle does what?
   A. reminisces frequently
   B. raises his or her own vegetables
   C. moves from place to place
   D. doesn't depend on others
   E. makes the best of every situation

7. What is the theme, or central message, of "Straw Into Gold"?
   A. People create obstacles for those who are different from them.
   B. You can achieve your goals in spite of or because of the obstacles you face.
   C. You should make the best of every situation.
   D. The best writers often have had difficult childhoods.
   E. Writing is a way to escape your circumstances and reinvent yourself.

8. Constructed Response: Cisneros states that although she had enough to eat as a child, she still had "another hunger that had to be fed." What was that other hunger? What might have given Cisneros her drive and ambition? Describe how Cisneros became an author, citing examples from the essay.

9. Constructed Response: Explain Cisneros's choice of the title and subtitle "Straw Into Gold: The Metamorphosis of the Everyday." What do the straw and gold symbolize? How did the author turn "straw into gold"? Use evidence from the text to support your answer.

TEST-TAKING TIP

If it often takes you a long time to read the text in the critical-reading section of a test, try reading the questions before you read the text. Doing so will help you to identify the specific details required to answer the questions. Moreover, you will block out unnecessary details and save yourself valuable time for completing later parts of the section.

One of the most confusing things about the English language is that some words sound alike but are spelled differently and have different functions and meanings. For instance, many people have trouble distinguishing among *there, their,* and *they're* and *to, too,* and *two*. These kinds of words, which are called **homophones,** often are misused by writers who substitute one word for another.

Two commonly confused homophones are *accept* and *except.* These words usually are pronounced the same, yet they are different parts of speech and have different meanings. *Accept* is a verb that means "to consent to" or "to understand." *Except* is a preposition that means "other than" or "not including." These sentences from "Straw Into Gold," by Sandra Cisneros, show the correct uses of the homophones *accept* and *except:*

> **EXAMPLES**
>
> So when the invitation to dinner arrived, I *accepted* without hesitation.
>
> In our culture, men and women don't leave their father's house *except* by way of marriage.

Here are some other sets of homophones that are commonly confused in writing:

affect (verb): change
effect (noun): result
capital (adjective): important
capitol (noun): center of government
cite (verb): refer to
site or *sight* (noun): location *or* vision

coarse (adjective): rough
course (noun): class *or* route
passed (verb): moved beyond
past (adjective): before now
peace (noun): calm; harmony
piece (noun): part
plain (adjective): basic; simple
plane (noun): flat surface *or* airplane
presence (noun): being there
presents (noun): gifts
principle (noun): belief
principal (noun *or* adjective): leader *or* primary
threw (verb): tossed
through (preposition): from end to end

To help you remember the difference between homophones, try developing *mnemonic devices,* which are mental associations. For instance, many people remember that *principal* means "leader," such as the leader of a school, by using the phrase "Your *principal* is your *pal.*"

Always check your homework for homophone errors, especially your essays. The spell-check feature on your computer may not catch these kinds of errors.

Apply the Skill

Identify the Correct Homophones

In each of the following sentences, determine whether the words in italics are used correctly. If they are not, rewrite the sentence.

1. *Who's* book is this? You should *right your* name in it in case you lose it.
2. Bertran could not decide *whether* to *except* the job offer.
3. *Too* many customers *passed* by the door of Dina's store instead of entering.
4. The medication's *effect* on the *patience* may be lessened by lowering the dosage.
5. The author makes an *illusion* to Greek mythology and *cites* Homer as his influence.

SPELLING PRACTICE

Words with Double Consonants

Many people have trouble spelling words with double consonants, such as *quarrel* and *occur.* To help you spell these words, think about how they are pronounced. Usually, the consonant is doubled at the point where the word is stressed. In the word *cinnamon,* for instance, the stress is on the first syllable, *cin-,* so the *n* is doubled. The *m* is not doubled, however. Determine in how many cases this rule holds true for these words from "Straw Into Gold."

accepted	marriage
appears	necessary
arrived	slippery
assumed	supposed
carrying	terrible
collar	village
fellowship	witnessed
impossible	written
little	

Thinking Back

by Claribel Alegría
Translated by D. J. Flakoll

Claribel Alegría (b. 1924) was born in Estelí, Nicaragua, but spent most of her early years in El Salvador. She later came to the United States and earned a bachelor's degree from George Washington University. Upon returning to her homeland in 1985, she participated in the reconstruction of Nicaragua after the overthrow of dictator Somoza.

Alegría has been involved in nonviolent resistance movements throughout her life and is considered part of the literary movement popular in Central America in the 1950s and 1960s called *La Generación Comprometida*, or the *Committed Generation*. Her first literary work appeared in 1948, and she has published nearly twenty more since then. She lives in Managua, the capital of Nicaragua.

Alegría's poem **"Thinking Back"** was published in a collection called *Fugues* in 1959. (The English translation is reprinted here.) In it, the speaker examines events from her past, including her bold decision to be a poet.

Alone at last
with no masks
no faces spying on me
alone with my past
5 my present
that soon will be my past.
Memories murmur
in all the corners
my once quick hands
10 have turned to spiders
cautiously they advance
across the lined face
rejecting disguises
sneering at mirrors.
15 With these same tremorous hands
that can scarcely hold a glass
I'd rather now paw through the baubles
of my early parties.
The kite of my first love soars upward.
20 I was nine years old
and my heart leapt
in hot
and cold waves.

Later
25 at fourteen
I discovered poetry
and I swore to follow it
to pursue it.
My aunts looked at me
30 with mocking features.
I was afraid
for the first time
I felt threatened
and began to build
35 rainbow parasols
to protect myself
from the stinging hail. ❖

Crossing the Spider Web, c. 1800s. Victor Hugo.
Maison Victor Hugo, Musée de la Ville de Paris, Paris, France.

What sorts of things from childhood do people feel compelled to keep? What reminders of your childhood do you have?

Refer and Reason

1. Why is the description of the speaker's hands as spiders an appropriate *metaphor,* or figurative comparison? Infer what the metaphor reveals about her.

2. Why do the speaker's aunts respond "with mocking features" when she swears to pursue poetry? How does the speaker respond?

3. At the end of the poem, with what does the speaker intend to protect herself from "the stinging hail"? What is paradoxical (contradictory) about this image? Interpret what the image means.

Writing Options

1. Rewrite the poem as though it were a personal essay expressing the same ideas. Decide who the speaker is and where he or she is in life. Then describe his or her motivation to start examining the past.

2. Translating poetry from one language to another usually presents more challenges than translating prose. Write a paragraph explaining why one task likely is more difficult than the other.

 Go to **www.mirrorsandwindows.com** for more.

A Story

by Li-Young Lee

Li-Young Lee (b. 1957) was born in Jakarta, Indonesia. After his parents were forced to flee China, Lee and his family wandered through Hong Kong, Macau, and Japan until they finally settled in the United States. Of these early travels from place to place, Lee has said, "I feel as if [my family's] experience may be no more than an outward manifestation of a homelessness that people in general feel."

Marked by celebration, intimacy, passion, and sadness, Lee's poetry often draws on stories, many about his father, who was a professor before becoming a Presbyterian minister. **"A Story"** is about a father who is afraid of disappointing his son because he cannot think of a new story to tell him. As you read the poem, consider how it suggests the differing needs and desires of parents and children.

Sad is the man who is asked for a story
and can't come up with one.

His five-year-old son waits in his lap.
Not the same story, Baba. A new one.
5 The man rubs his chin, scratches his ear.

In a room full of books in a world
of stories, he can recall
not one, and soon, he thinks, the boy
will give up on his father.

10 Already the man lives far ahead, he sees
the day this boy will go. *Don't go!*
Hear the alligator story! The angel story once more!
You love the spider story. You laugh at the spider.
Let me tell it!

15 But the boy is packing his shirts,
he is looking for his keys. *Are you a god,*
the man screams, *that I sit mute before you?*
Am I a god that I should never disappoint?

But the boy is here. *Please, Baba, a story?*
20 It is an emotional rather than logical equation,
an earthly rather than heavenly one,
which posits[1] that a boy's supplications[2]
and a father's love add up to silence. ❖

---

1. **posits.** Assumes or claims as true
2. **supplications.** Humble requests or pleas

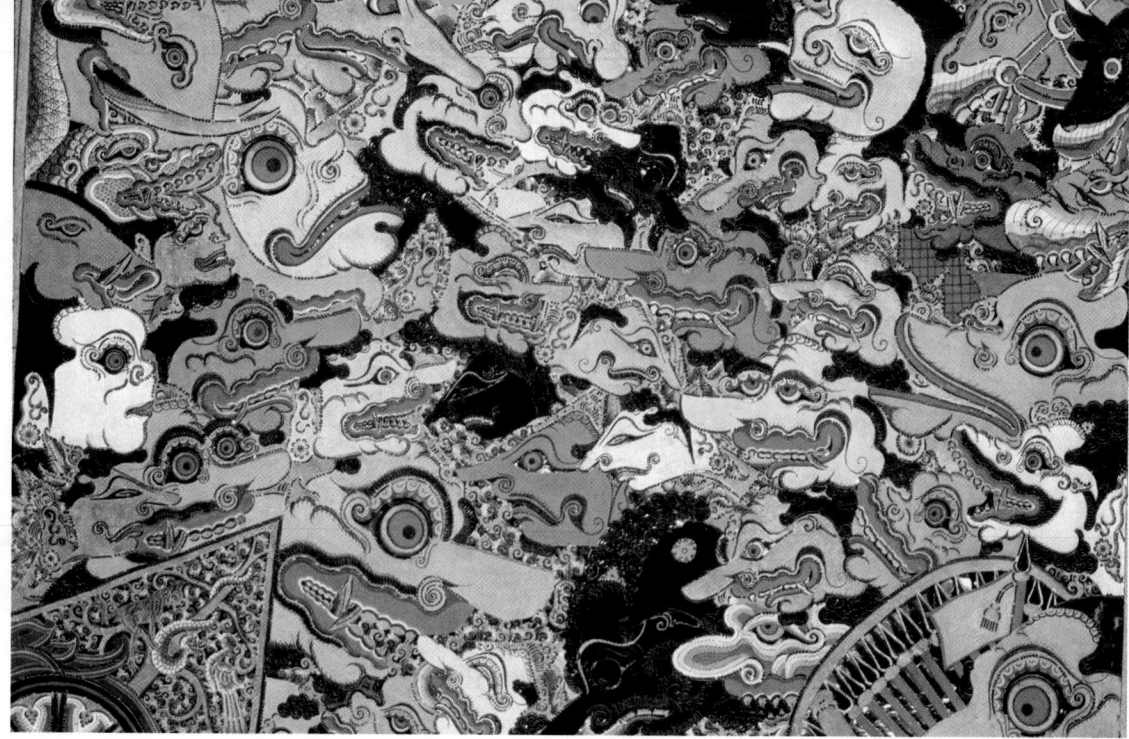

Group of Indonesian *Wayang Kulit* puppets.

The father worries that his son will "give up" on him if he runs out of stories. Why do parents and children grow apart? What can they do not to grow apart?

Refer and Reason

1. Describe the setting of the poem and the people involved. Infer the importance of storytelling to their relationship.

2. In stanzas 4 and 5, what is the father envisioning? What does he realize about his son, himself, and their relationship?

3. How does the tone, or emotional attitude, of stanza 6 differ from that of stanza 5? Interpret what the change in tone suggests about the father's feelings.

Writing Options

1. Imagine that you have promised to tell a young child a story that also is a poem. First, select a story, such as a fairy tale or myth, or create one of your own. Then rewrite the story as a narrative poem, using rhythm, rhyme, alliteration, and other poetic effects to create action and suspense.

2. With two or three classmates, create a *bibliography* (list of books) of ten popular books for young children (say, five- and six-year-olds). Look for information provided by organizations such as the American Library Association (ALA) that review and recommend outstanding children's books. For each book you choose, provide the author, date, and publication information along with a short summary.

Go to **www.mirrorsandwindows.com** for more.

What For

by Garrett Hongo

Japanese-American writer **Garrett Hongo** (b. 1951) was born in Hawaii but grew up in Los Angeles. His credentials include a bachelor's degree from Pomona College in California and a master's degree. from the University of California, Irvine.

Hongo's two poetry collections, *Yellow Light* (1982) and *The River of Heaven* (1988), both contain works rich in imagery and reflective of Asian-American culture and experiences. His use of repetition provides a framework for his narrative poetry and adds lyricism to his diction. Hongo's writing talent has earned him Guggenheim and National Endowment for the Arts Fellowships. He currently teaches at the University of Oregon, Eugene.

In the poem **"What For,"** which is included in the collection *Yellow Light,* the speaker fondly recalls his boyhood memories of his grandparents and his hard-working father. Writing from the perspective of a six-year-old, Hongo juxtaposes the traditional Japanese culture of his ancestors with the postwar industrialization experienced by his father.

At six I lived for spells:
how a few Hawaiian words could call
up the rain, could hymn like the sea
in the long swirl of chambers
5   curling in the nautilus of a shell,
how Amida's[1] ballads of the Buddhaland
in the drone of the priest's liturgy
could conjure money from the poor
and give them nothing but mantras,[2]
10 the strange syllables that healed desire.

I lived for stories about the war
my grandfather told over *hana* cards,[3]
slapping them down on the mats
with a sharp Japanese *kiai.*[4]

15 I lived for songs my grandmother sang
stirring curry into a thick stew,
weaving a calligraphy of Kannon's love[5]
into grass mats and straw sandals.

---

1. **Amida's.** Among the Pure Land sect of Buddhism in Eastern Asia, Amida was worshipped as a savior.
2. **mantras.** Words said again and again in chants or prayers
3. ***hana* cards.** Flower-patterned cards that players match in a popular Japanese card game
4. ***kiai.*** [Japanese] Sound made when the *hana* cards are slapped down
5. **Kannon's love.** Element in Buddhist belief

I lived for the red volcano dirt
staining my toes, the salt residue
of surf and sea wind in my hair,
the arc of a flat stone skipping
in the hollow trough of a wave.

I lived a child's world, waited
for my father to drag himself home,
dusted with blasts of sand, powdered rock,
and the strange ash of raw cement,
his deafness made worse by the clang
of pneumatic drills, sore in his bones
from the buckings of a jackhammer.
He'd hand me a scarred lunchpail,
let me unlace the hightop G.I. boots,[6]
call him the new name I'd invented
that day in school, write it for him
on his newspaper. He'd rub my face
with hands that felt like gravel roads,
tell me to move, go play, and then he'd
walk to the laundry sink to scrub,
rinse the dirt of his long day
from a face brown and grained as koa wood.[7]

6. **G.I. boots.** Army boots
7. **koa wood.** Wood from the acacia tree, native to Hawaii

I wanted to take away the pain
in his legs, the swelling in his joints,
give him back his hearing,
clear and rare as crystal chimes,
45   the fins of glass that wrinkled
and sparked the air with their sound.

I wanted to heal the sores that work
and war had sent to him,
let him play catch in the backyard
50   with me, tossing a tennis ball
past papaya trees without the shoulders
of pain shrugging back his arms. ❖

MIRRORS & WINDOWS — What is your earliest memory of realizing that your parent or parents experienced hurt or disappointment? How do children make sense of the feelings and actions of the adults around them?

Refer and Reason

1. About what subjects does the boy like to hear stories? Infer how culture is transmitted from one generation to the next through storytelling.

2. According to the boy, what does the father look and feel like when he comes home? Why does the boy likely remember these details from his childhood?

3. What would the boy like to be able to do for his father? Suggest the kind of life the boy envisions himself having as an adult.

Writing Options

1. Write a poem about what you "lived for" when you were a young child. Include sensory details of sight, sound, touch, taste, and smell to make your descriptions vivid.

2. Write a paragraph in which you explain the title of Hongo's poem. What tone, or emotional attitude, does the title "What For" convey? Evaluate how well the title fits the topic and tone of the poem.

 Go to **www.mirrorsandwindows.com** for more.

Defining the Grateful Gesture

by Yvonne Sapia

Yvonne Sapia (b. 1946) was born in New York City to Puerto Rican parents but was raised in Florida. She has earned a bachelor's degree from Florida Atlantic University, a master's degree from the University of Florida, and a doctorate degree from Florida State University. She also has been awarded a National Endowment for the Arts Fellowship.

Sapia writes about the struggle of immigrants to embrace a different culture yet maintain their own identity. Her works include two poetry collections, *The Fertile Crescent* (1983) and *Valentino's Hair* (1987), and the novel *DiMaggia Dreams* (2006). She currently teaches English at Lake City Community College in Florida.

"Defining the Grateful Gesture," from *Valentino's Hair,* demonstrates Sapia's conversational tone and narrative writing style. In this poem, she writes about her mother, who is bothered by her children's lack of gratitude for the meals she has prepared.

According to our mother,
when she was a child
what was placed before her
for dinner was not a feast,
5 but she would eat it
to gain back the strength
taken from her by long hot days
of working in her mother's house
and helping her father make
10 candy in the family kitchen.
No idle passenger
travelling through life was she.

And that's why she resolved
to tell stories about
15 the appreciation for satisfied hunger.
When we would sit down
for our evening meal
of arroz con pollo
or frijoles negros con plátanos[1]

---

1. **arroz con pollo** (ä rōz´ kōn pō´ yō) **or frijoles negros con plátanos** (frē hō´ lās nā´ grōs kōn plä´ tä nōs). [Spanish] *Arroz con pollo*—rice with chicken; *frijoles negros con plátanos*—black beans with plantains

Series: Balconies, Image of Short Love in Guatemala, 1991.
Pedro Pablo Oliva.

20   she would expect us
to be reverent to the sources
of our undeserved nourishment,
and to strike a thankful pose
before each lift of the fork
25   or swirl of the spoon.

For the dishes she prepared
we were ungrateful,
she would say, and repeat
her archetypal tale about the Perez
30   brothers from her girlhood town of Ponce,
who looked like ripe mangoes,
their cheeks rosed despite poverty.

My mother would then tell us about the day
she saw Mrs. Perez searching
35   the neighborhood garbage,
picking out with a missionary's care

the edible potato peels, the plantain skins,
the shafts of old celery to take
home to her muchachos[2]
40 who required more food
than she could afford.

Although my brothers and I never
quite mastered the ritual
of obedience our mother craved,
45 and as supplicants[3] failed
to feed her with our worthiness,
we'd sit like solemn loaves of bread,
sighing over the white plates
with a sense of realization, or relief,
50 guilty about possessing appetite. ❖

---

2. **muchachos** (mü chä´ chōs). [Spanish] Boys
3. **supplicants.** People who make humble requests or pleas

 **MIRRORS & WINDOWS**

Why do parents tell their children stories about the hardships they faced growing up?
What stories have your parents told you? What stories might you tell your children?

Refer and Reason

1. Describe the type of childhood the speaker's mother had. Infer from the tone of poem the speaker's attitude toward her mother's stories.

2. How does the speaker's mother describe the appearance of the Perez brothers? What does the speaker point out is ironic about this description?

3. Why cannot the speaker and her own brothers master "the ritual of obedience" (lines 43–44) their mother wants? What do the last two lines suggest about the children's attitudes toward eating?

Writing Options

1. Imagine that you have been invited for dinner with the speaker's family. How will you respond if the subject of gratitude comes up? Prepare a brief dialogue of an imagined dinner-table conversation—what you and the family members might say on the subject.

2. Write a paragraph explaining how Sapia uses images of food in this poem. How does referring to specific types of food add to the meaning of the poem?

 Go to **www.mirrorsandwindows.com** for more.

PART 2

Contemporary America

The diversity that characterizes Americans themselves also characterizes contemporary American culture. Americans enjoy foods, fashions, arts, and sports from around the world. Yet when asked to describe American culture, many people would list such hallmarks as jazz and baseball, fast food and malls, wide open spaces and crowded city streets.

Several of these topics are explored by poets Donald Hall and Billy Collins, both known for their straightforward, accessible writing style. Many of Hall's poems are about life in rural New England, baseball as an American tradition, and love and loss in the context of the family. Collins's work explores a broad range of subjects but in innovative, often humorous ways. For instance, he writes about humans'

connection to music—jazz, in particular—in a poem about a man walking down the busy streets of New York listening to a compact disc.

In contrast to the noise and crowds of New York's streets, the vast emptiness and stillness of the Great Plains is the subject of nonfiction works by Ian Frazier and Kathleen Norris. Both authors recognize that, despite most Americans' tendency to overlook this region of the country, it was the birthplace of much of what is considered the American character. In other works of nonfiction, Eric Schlosser and Joan Didion examine the impact of two prominent fixtures in contemporary America: fast food and shopping malls. These writers raise questions about the homogenization of culture occurring through the impulses of convenience and comfort.

In the final selection in the unit, novelist and essayist Anna Quindlen uses the metaphor of a quilt to describe how diverse elements of U.S. society coexist, although at times under strain. Quindlen suggests that the terrorist attacks of September 11 may have served to unify Americans, if only briefly.

Atlanta, c. 1980–2000. Mark McMahon.

Literary Nonfiction Defined

As the name suggests, **literary nonfiction,** sometimes referred to as *creative nonfiction,* is a hybrid genre. Works in this category are *nonfiction* in the sense that they are fact-based accounts of actual events, people, and places. However, they are *literary* in their exploration of universal themes and use of techniques common to fiction and poetry.

By most accounts, literary nonfiction originated with the works of several American journalists during the 1940s. In *Let Us Now Praise Famous Men,* journalist James Agee, with photographer Walker Evans, portrayed the conditions of white sharecroppers in the Depression South. In a second landmark work, John Hersey interviewed Japanese survivors of the atomic bomb and recounted their stories in *Hiroshima.* (Excerpts from Agee's and Hersey's books appear in Unit 6.)

A number of essayists, fiction writers, and playwrights also have explored the genre of literary nonfiction. Truman Capote, Norman Mailer, E. B. White, Hunter S. Thompson, Calvin Trillin, Barbara Ehrenreich, and Joan Didion are among the most well-recognized writers of this genre.

Types of Literary Nonfiction

Among the most common types of literary nonfiction are literary journalism, memoir, nature writing, and travel writing.

Literary Journalism

The literary journalist goes well beyond basic reporting, fleshing out the story with meticulous detail, as Eric Schlosser does in "Throughput," an excerpt from his book *Fast Food Nation*. This type of journalist also interprets and evaluates the story, providing commentary in addition to description.

Memoir

A **memoir** is a type of autobiography that focuses on one incident or period in an individual's life. Memoirs often are based on memories of and reactions to historical events. As such, memoirs typically are rooted in fact but not restricted to it. (See the Understanding Literary Forms in Unit 8, pages 1084–1085, for a discussion of the memoir.)

Nature Writing

Nature writing is based on close observation of the natural world as it shapes and illuminates the human experience. It combines elements of science, natural philosophy, and sometimes memoir. Most important, it grows out of minute personal observation of landscapes and living things. Consider how Kathleen Norris lovingly describes the Dakota plains and then speculates, "Maybe seeing the Plains is like seeing an icon: what seems stern and almost empty is merely open, a door into some simple and holy state."

Travel Writing

Evocative travel writing recreates a sense of place and in doing so informs readers about a particular region and its inhabitants, history, culture, and uniqueness. For instance, the Great Plains that Ian Frazier portrays is much more than a geographical region to be documented with facts. Rather, it is a place the writer has entered imaginatively, a wild land under a sky "which farmers have cursed and blasted with dynamite barrages and prodded with hydrogen balloons and seeded with silver-iodide crystals and prayed to in churches every day for months at a time, for rain."

Elements of Literary Nonfiction

In line with its hybrid nature, literary nonfiction shares some of the formal elements of the essay, as well as the novel, the short story, and the poem.

Thesis

Works of literary nonfiction often are compared to or even described as **essays,** short nonfiction works that present a single main idea, or **thesis,** about a particular topic. The writer typically builds this central statement into the introduction, announcing his or her intent. For instance, in the first paragraph of "On the Mall," Didion states that malls "are toy garden cities in which no one lives but everyone consumes, profound equalizers, the perfect fusion of the profit motive and the egalitarian ideal."

FRAZIER · **NORRIS** · **DIDION** · **SCHLOSSER**

In some cases, however, the thesis is presented later in the work, even near the end. In "Throughput," Schlosser waits until the final paragraph before stating that "the stance of the fast food industry on issues involving employee training, the minimum wage, labor unions, and overtime pay strongly suggests that its motives in hiring the young, the poor, and the handicapped are hardly altruistic."

Purpose

As indicated by the variety of types of literary nonfiction, writers in this genre may have any of several **purposes,** or aims. They may intend to inform or explain (*expository writing*); to portray a person, place, object, or event (*descriptive writing*); to convince people to accept a position (*persuasive writing*); or to tell a story (*narrative writing*).

For instance, Frazier's purpose in *Great Plains* is primarily descriptive, as he offers natural observations about the region. Even so, he incorporates elements of exposition and narrative in relating the history and geography of the land and even persuasion in suggesting that "the Great Plains are like a sheet Americans screened their dreams on for a while and then largely forgot about." In "Throughput," Schlosser begins with the story of a teen worker (narration) and goes on to explain hiring practices and operations in

the fast food industry (exposition). He presents this information, however, to build to an indictment of the industry, revealing his primary purpose as persuasion.

Figurative Language

To help readers see common things in new ways, writers of every genre employ **figurative language,** which is intended to be understood imaginatively rather than literally. Consider Norris's use of **personification** in describing sunflowers as if they were people: "Acres of sunflowers brighten the land in summer, their heads alert, expectant. By fall they droop like sad children, waiting patiently for the first frost and harvest." Notice her use of **simile,** as well, in which she uses the connector *like* to compare the sunflowers to "sad children."

Fictional Elements

As modern storytellers, writers of literary nonfiction often employ the elements of fiction, such as **plot, character,** and **dialogue.** Works of the memoir subtype, in particular, tend to display the qualities of a short story or novel. Didion presents herself as something of a character in "On the Mall," revealing details of her own personal story in the context of chronicling the history of the mall.

HOW TO READ

Literary Nonfiction

Find the main idea. Identify the writer's thesis, or main idea, and then examine the information the writer provides to support that thesis. Evaluate how effectively the writer conveys his or her central idea.

Identify the author's purpose. Try to distinguish the writer's primary purpose from secondary goals. Determine in what ways he or she wanted to affect readers.

Distinguish fact from opinion. As you read, identify *facts,* statements that can be proven

true or false. Distinguish facts from *opinions,* which express attitudes or desires. You can disagree with an opinion but not prove it right or wrong.

Recognize bias. Consider whether the writer's interpretation or evaluation of the topic is fair and balanced. Bias can be evident in what the writer says directly or in the details he or she leaves out.

from **Great Plains**

Literary Nonfiction by Ian Frazier

Seeing, from **Dakota: A Spiritual Geography**

Literary Nonfiction by Kathleen Norris

Build Background

Literary Context In the 1980s, Ian Frazier drove an old van more than 25,000 miles throughout the Great Plains to get a firsthand account of its history and inhabitants. His tales of adventure and witty observations are recorded in **Great Plains,** from which this excerpt is taken. Frazier writes about the vastness of the Plains and the difficulty of establishing its boundaries. He wryly points out that cross-country travelers view the Plains as a medial stretch, not as a destination.

Kathleen Norris's **"Seeing,"** a chapter from her book *Dakota: A Spiritual Geography*, paints the harsh yet sublime landscape of South Dakota and its influence on the human spirit. She describes Dakota as "my spiritual geography, the place where I've wrestled my story out of the circumstances of landscape and inheritance." Norris finds quiet contemplation in this rugged, unyielding environment.

Reader's Context What type of landscape is your "spiritual geography"? Are you most at home in the mountains, at the beach, on the prairie, or somewhere else?

Meet the Authors

Ian Frazier (b. 1951) grew up in Ohio and later attended Harvard University, where he wrote for the renowned humor magazine the *Harvard Lampoon.* After graduating in 1973, he continued to write for several notable publications, including *Atlantic Monthly* and the *New Yorker.* Known for his humorous observations and matter-of-fact style, Frazier also has researched and written first-person narratives on the outdoors and on U.S. history. His books include *Great Plains* (1989), *Family* (1994), *Coyote v. Acme* (1996), and *On the Rez* (1999).

Kathleen Norris (b. 1947) was born in Washington, DC, but raised in Hawaii. After graduating in 1969 from Bennington College in Vermont, she moved to New York City, where she worked for the American Academy of Poets and published several successful poetry collections. Four years later, she had grown tired of big-city life and moved to her grandmother's farm in South Dakota. The desolation of the Plains, coupled with her residence in a Benedictine monastery, instilled in Norris the concept of community, both social and spiritual. She shared her insights on simple living in her nonfiction books *Dakota: A Spiritual Geography* (1993), *The Cloister Walk* (1996), and *Amazing Grace: A Vocabulary of Faith* (1998).

Compare Literature

Description and Tone
A **description** is a picture in words. Descriptive writing includes *sensory details*—words and phrases that describe how things look, sound, smell, taste, or feel.

Tone is the emotional attitude toward the reader or subject implied in a literary work.

Set Purpose

Although Frazier and Norris both write about the Great Plains, they take different approaches to the topic. As you read each essay, record the details the author provides to describe this region of the country. In particular, note each author's use of sensory details about nature. Also consider the tone of each essay. Think of a word or two that identifies each author's attitude toward the subject.

Preview Vocabulary

quell, 1241
balk, 1244
inherent, 1247
prosaic, 1247
amicably, 1247
icon, 1247
indigenous, 1248

from Great Plains
by Ian Frazier

Just where the Great Plains begin and end is not always certain.

A way to the Great Plains of America, to that immense Western short-grass prairie now mostly plowed under! Away to the still-empty land beyond newsstands and malls and velvet restaurant ropes! Away to the headwaters of the Missouri, now <u>quelled</u> by many impoundment dams, and to the headwaters of the Platte, and to the almost invisible headwaters of the slurped-up Arkansas! Away to the land where TV used to set its most popular dramas, but not anymore! Away to the land beyond the hundredth meridian of longitude,[1] where

---

1. **hundredth meridian of longitude.** One of the imaginary lines along the Earth, running from the North Pole to South Pole and used in designating locations on the globe

quell (kwel) *v.*, subdue; calm

sometimes it rains and sometimes it doesn't, where agriculture stops and does a double take! Away to the skies of sparrow hawks sitting on telephone wires, thinking of mice and flaring their tail feathers suddenly, like a card trick! Away to the air shaft of the continent, where weather fronts from two hemispheres meet, and the wind blows almost all the time! Away to the fields of wheat and milo and sudan grass and flax and alfalfa and nothing! Away to parts of Montana and North Dakota and South Dakota and Wyoming and Nebraska and Kansas and Colorado and New Mexico and Oklahoma and Texas! Away to the high plains rolling in waves to the rising final chord of the Rocky Mountains!

A discount airplane ticket from New York City to the middle of the Great Plains—to Dodge City, Kansas, say, which once called itself Queen of the Cowtowns—costs about $420, round trip. A discount ticket over the plains—to the mountains, to Salt Lake City, to Seattle, to Los Angeles—is much cheaper. Today, most travellers who see the plains do it from thirty thousand feet. A person who wanted to go from New York to California overland in 1849, with the Gold Rush, could take a passenger ship to Baltimore, the B & O Railroad to Cumberland, Maryland, a stagecoach over the Allegheny Mountains to the Monongahela River, a steamboat to Pittsburgh, another steamboat down the Ohio to the Mississippi to St. Louis, another from St. Louis up the Missouri to Independence or St. Joseph or Council Bluffs, and an ox-drawn wagon west from there. If you left the East in early April, you might be on the plains by mid-May, and across by the Fourth of July. Today, if you leave Kennedy Airport in a 747 for Los Angeles just after breakfast, you will be over the plains by lunch. If you lean across the orthopedist from Beverly Hills who specializes in break-dancing injuries and who is in the window seat returning from his appearance on *Good Morning*

America, you will see that the regular squares of cropland below you have begun to falter, that the country is for great distances bare and puckered by dry watercourses, that big green circles have begun to appear, and that often long, narrow rectangles of green alternate with equal rectangles of brown.

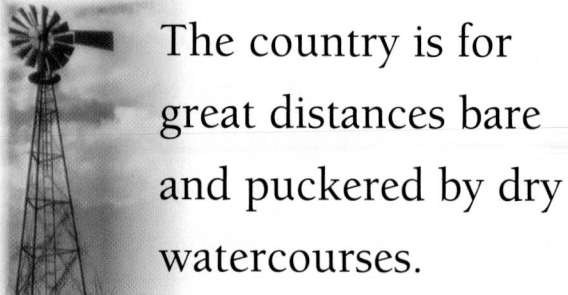

The country is for great distances bare and puckered by dry watercourses.

Chances are, nothing in the seat pocket in front of you will mention that those green circles are fields watered by central-pivot irrigation, where a wheeled span of irrigation pipe as much as a quarter mile long makes a slow circuit, like the hand of a clock. If you ask the flight attendant about those green and brown rectangles, chances are he or she will not say that in the spring of 1885 a wheat farmer on the Canadian plains named Angus Mackay was unable to plant a field which had already been plowed when his hands left to help suppress a rebellion of frontiersmen of French and Indian ancestry against the Dominion of Canada, and so he left the field fallow, cultivating it occasionally to kill the weeds; that when he planted it the following year, it weathered a drought to produce thirty-five bushels of wheat per acre, thirty-three bushels more than continuously cropped land; that the practice he had initiated, called summer fallow, was an effective way to conserve moisture in the soil in a semi-arid climate, and many other farmers adopted it; that the one problem with summer fallow was the tendency of fields with no crop cover sometimes to dry up and blow away; that in 1918 two other Canadian farmers, Leonard and Arie

Koole, experimented successfully with crops planted in narrow sections at right angles to the prevailing winds, to protect sections of fallow ground in between; and that this refinement, called strip farming, turned out to be the best way to raise wheat on the northern plains.

Crossing high and fast above the plains, headed elsewhere, you are doing what rain clouds tend to do. You are in a sky which farmers have cursed and blasted with dynamite barrages and prodded with hydrogen balloons and seeded with silver-iodide crystals and prayed to in churches every day for months at a time, for rain. Usually the clouds wait to rain until they are farther west or east—over the Rockies, or the Midwest. Probably, as you look out the airplane window, you will see the sun. On the plains, sunshine is dependable. Most of the buildings on the plains have roofs of galvanized metal. As dawn comes up, and the line of sunlight crosses the land, the roofs of barns and equipment sheds and grain silos and Department of Agriculture extension stations and grain elevators and Air Force barracks and house trailers and pipe warehouses and cafes and roadside-table shelters start to tick and pop in scattered unison, all the way from Canada to Texas.

The Great Plains are about 2,500 miles long, and about 600 miles across at their widest point. The area they cover roughly parallels the Rocky Mountains, which make their western boundary. Although they extend from the Southwestern United States well into Canada, no single state or province lies entirely within them. North to south, the states of the Great Plains are:

Montana	North Dakota
	South Dakota
Wyoming	Nebraska
Colorado	Kansas
New Mexico	Oklahoma
Texas	

The Great Plains include the eastern part of the first column, the western part of the second column, some of west Texas, and all of the Texas panhandle. In Canada, they include southern Alberta, Saskatchewan, and Manitoba. They are five hundred to a thousand miles inland from the Pacific Ocean, and over a thousand miles inland from the Atlantic. The Texas plains are about five hundred miles from the Gulf of Mexico.

Just where the Great Plains begin and end is not always certain. To the west, they sometimes continue past the Rocky Mountain front through gentle foothills all the way to the Continental Divide. To the north, flatlands stretch past the Arctic Circle, but the open prairie has

RING LITERATURE COMPARING LITERATURE COMPARING LITERATURE COMPARING

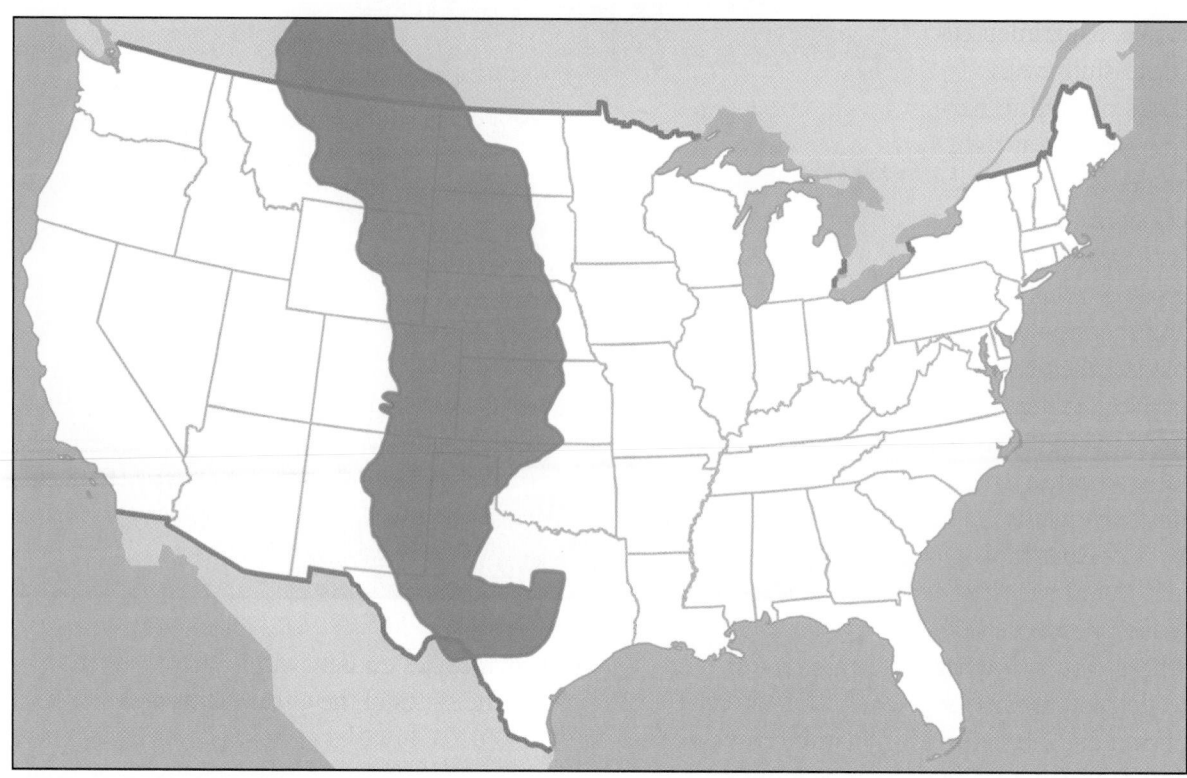
The region of the United States comprising the Great Plains.

given way to boreal pine forests long before that. In the Southwest, a change from semi-arid grassland to true desert is sudden in some places, slow in others. Of all the Great Plains boundaries, the eastern one is the hardest to fix. Many geographers and botanists have said that the Great Plains begin at the hundredth meridian, because that is the approximate limit of twenty-inch annual rainfall. Before Europeans came, it was more or less where the tall grasses of the East stopped and the Western short grasses started. (The hundredth meridian is the eastern line of the Texas panhandle; a map of the lower forty-eight states folds in half a little bit to the right of it.) Since the same amount of rain never falls two years in a row, this eastern boundary always changes. Sometimes it happens to coincide at certain points with the Missouri River; the eastern side of the river will be green and lush, and the western side will be a tan and dusty cowboy-movie set. Farmers can't grow corn, or raise dairy cattle,

or do much European-style agriculture at all on sub-twenty-inch rainfall, and when they first moved out onto the Great Plains, they sometimes had difficulty borrowing money. Many banks and insurance companies had a policy of not lending money for the purposes of agriculture west of the hundredth meridian. So, whether or not the rain stopped exactly at the hundredth meridian, at one time lots of Eastern loan officers did. If you were beyond their help, you knew you were on the Great Plains.

It makes sense that traditional finance would <u>balk</u> there, because the Great Plains don't exactly qualify as real estate. In fact, the Great Plains are probably better described in terms of the many things they aren't. They aren't woodlands; their subsoil doesn't have enough moisture for tree roots. You can go a long way out there without seeing a single tree. They

balk (bôk) v., stop and refuse to continue

aren't mountains (although they contain the Black Hills in South Dakota and the Bearpaw Mountains in Montana and the Cypress Hills in Canada), and they aren't Land of a Thousand Lakes (although they used to have many sweetwater springs, and hundreds of rivers and streams, and an underground aquifer the volume of Lake Huron), and they aren't standard farmland (although they export two-thirds of the world's wheat, and could export more). And although they have suffered droughts about every twenty years since white people first settled there, and millions of acres have gone to blowing sand, and although Zebulon Pike, who happened to pick a route that led through the sandhills region when he explored for the government in 1806–7, compared the Great Plains to the deserts of Africa, and although the members of a later expedition, in 1819–20, agreed with Pike, and published a map with the words "Great Desert" across the southern plains, and although a popular atlas of 1822 extended the label over more territory and in another edition changed it to "Great American Desert," and although that appeared in the middle of North America on maps and globes for fifty years afterwards, and generations of geography students wondered about it and dreamed of going there, the Great Plains are not a desert.

White people did not consider moving onto the Great Plains in any numbers until after the Civil War. When they did, railroad promoters, governors of empty Western states, syndicates[2] with land to sell, emigration societies, scientists, pretend scientists, politicians in crowded Eastern states, U.S. Geological Survey officials, Walt Whitman, *The New York Times, The New York Tribune,* all loudly advertised the Great Plains as a garden spot. The idea of the

The Great Plains don't exactly qualify as real estate.

Great American Desert came in for much scoffing and debunking. Strangely, the Great Plains greened up with good rains several times just as another wave of homeseekers was about to go there. People thought they'd harvest a couple of good crops and pay off their starting costs and be in business. In the 1870s and '90s, and in 1918–24, and, most spectacularly, in the 1930s, drought knocked parts of these waves back. Since their days as a Great Desert, the Great Plains have also been the Frontier (supposedly of such importance in the formation of the American character), the "newer garden of creation" (Whitman's phrase), the Breadbasket of the World, the Dust Bowl, Vanishing Rural America. The Great Plains are like a sheet Americans screened their dreams on for a while and then largely forgot about. Since 1930, two-thirds of the counties on the Great Plains have lost population. About fifteen years ago,[3] the Great Plains reappeared, briefly, as part of the New Energy Frontier. The Great Plains contain more than fifty percent of America's coal reserves. When we finally do run out of oil, somebody will probably think up yet another name for the Great Plains. ❖

---

2. **syndicates.** Groups of businesses working together on a project, often for the purpose of controlling prices
3. **fifteen years ago.** The book containing this excerpt was published in 1989.

MIRRORS & **W**INDOWS   The Great Plains have been misunderstood and unappreciated throughout history, according to Frazier. What does this suggest about American values and priorities?

Seeing
from
Dakota: A Spiritual Geography

by Kathleen Norris

The midwestern landscape is abstract, and our response to
the geology of the region might be similar to our response
to the contemporary walls of paint in museums.
We are forced to live in our eye.
—Michael Martone

Abba Bessarion, at the point of death, said, "The monk
ought to be like the Cherubim and the Seraphim: all eye."
—*The Desert Christian*

The emptiness is full of small things.

Once, when I was describing to a friend from Syracuse, New York, a place on the plains that I love, a ridge above a glacial moraine[1] with a view of almost fifty miles, she asked, "But what is there to see?"

The answer, of course, is nothing. Land, sky, and the everchanging light. Except for a few signs of human presence—power and telephone lines, an occasional farm building, the glint of a paved road in the distance—it's like looking at the ocean.

The landscape of western Dakota is not as abstract as the flats of Kansas, but it presents a similar challenge to the eye that appreciates the vertical definition of mountains or skyscrapers; that defines beauty in terms of the spectacular or the busy: hills, trees, buildings, highways, people. We seem empty by comparison.

Here, the eye learns to appreciate slight variations, the possibilities <u>inherent</u> in emptiness. It sees that the emptiness is full of small things, like grasshoppers in their samurai[2] armor clicking and jumping as you pass. This empty land is full of grasses: sedges, switch grass, needlegrass, wheatgrass. Brome can grow waist-high by early summer. Fields of wheat, rye, oats, barley, flax, alfalfa. Acres of sunflowers brighten the land in summer, their heads alert, expectant. By fall they droop like sad children, waiting patiently for the first frost and harvest.

In spring it is a joy to discover, amid snow and mud and pale, withered grass, the delicate lavender of pasqueflower blooming on a ridge with a southern exposure. There is variety in the emptiness; the most <u>prosaic</u> pasture might contain hundreds of different wildflowers along with sage, yucca, and prairie cactus. Coulees[3] harbor chokecherry, buffalo berry, and gooseberry bushes in their gentle folds, along with groves of silvery cottonwoods and Russian olive. Lone junipers often grow on exposed hillsides.

This seemingly empty land is busy with inhabitants. Low to the ground are bullsnakes, rattlers, mice, gophers, moles, grouse, prairie chickens, and pheasant. Prairie dogs are more noticeable, as they denude the landscape with their villages. Badgers and skunk lumber[4] busily through the grass. Jackrabbits, weasels, and foxes are quicker, but the great runners of the Plains are the coyote, antelope, and deer. Meadowlarks, killdeer, blackbirds, lark buntings, crows, and seagulls dart above the fields, and a large variety of hawks, eagles, and vultures glide above it all, hunting for prey.

Along with the largeness of the visible—too much horizon, too much sky—this land's essential indifference to the human can be unnerving. We had a visitor, a friend from back East who flew into Bismarck and started a two-week visit by photographing the highway on the way to Lemmon; "Look how far you can see!" he kept exclaiming, trying to capture the whole of it in his camera lens. He seemed relieved to find a few trees in town and in our yard, and did not relish going back out into open country.

One night he called a woman friend from a phone booth on Main Street and asked her to marry him. After less than a week, he decided to cut his visit short and get off the Plains. He and his fiancée broke off the engagement, mutually and <u>amicably</u>, not long after he got

---

1. **moraine.** Accumulation of earth and stones carried and finally deposited by a glacier
2. **samurai.** Relating to or like a medieval Japanese warrior
3. **Coulees.** Usually small or shallow ravines
4. **lumber.** Move clumsily

> **in • her • ent** (in hār´ ənt) *adj.,* belonging by nature or habit
> **pro • sa • ic** (prō zā´ ik) *adj.,* dull; unimaginative
> **am • i • ca • bly** (am´ ik ə blē) *adv.,* in a friendly or peaceful manner

home to Boston. The proposal had been a symptom of "Plains fever."

A person is forced inward by the spareness of what is outward and visible in all this land and sky. The beauty of the Plains is like that of an <u>icon</u>; it does not give an inch to sentiment or romance. The flow of the land, with its odd twists and buttes, is like the flow of Gregorian chant[5] that rises and falls beyond melody, beyond reason or human expectation, but perfectly.

Maybe seeing the Plains is like seeing an icon: what seems stern and almost empty is merely open, a door into some simple and holy state.

Not long ago, at a difficult time in my life, when my husband was recovering from surgery, I attended a drum ceremony with a Native American friend. Men and boys gathered around the sacred drum and sang a song to bless it. Their singing was high-pitched, repetitive, solemn, and loud. As they approached the song's end, drumming louder and louder, I realized that the music was also restorative; my two-day headache was gone, my troubles no longer seemed so burdensome.

I wondered how this loud, shrill, holy music, the <u>indigenous</u> song of those who have truly seen the Plains, could be so restful, while the Gregorian chant that I am just learning to sing can be so quiet, and yet as stirring as any drum. Put it down to ecstasy. ❖

---

5. **Gregorian chant.** Religious singing performed during Roman Catholic mass, with origins in the Middle Ages; characterized by an unmeasured, single-voice line

icon (ī´ kän) *n.,* symbolic religious image
in • dig • e • nous (in dij´ ə nəs) *adj.,* having originated in and being produced, growing, living, or occurring naturally in a particular region or environment

Why might an empty landscape be unsettling to some people yet restorative to others? With which group would you agree?

Literature Connection

Ted Kooser (b. 1939) was born in Ames, Iowa, and has remained close to his midwestern roots. After earning a bachelor's degree from Iowa State University and a master's degree from the University of Nebraska, he began a lifelong career in the insurance business. Yearning for a creative outlet, he arose early each day to write poetry.

Kooser's poems have been collected in *One World at a Time* (1985), *Weather Central* (1994), and *Delights & Shadows* (2004), which won the 2005 Pulitzer Prize. Upon being appointed U.S. Poet Laureate in 2004, he made it his mission to make poetry accessible to everyone. His clear, precise writing style and observations about everyday people and places echo that philosophy. Kooser currently is an English professor at the University of Nebraska–Lincoln.

"So This Is Nebraska," from the collection *Flying at Night* (2005), portrays the quiet, slow pace of the Midwest. Kooser uses vivid imagery to capture an ordinary summer afternoon outing.

So This Is Nebraska

by Ted Kooser

The gravel road rides with a slow gallop
over the fields, the telephone lines
streaming behind, its billow of dust
full of the sparks of redwing blackbirds.

5   On either side, those dear old ladies,
the loosening barns, their little windows
dulled by cataracts of hay and cobwebs
hide broken tractors under their skirts.

So this is Nebraska. A Sunday
10 afternoon; July. Driving along
with your hand out squeezing the air,
a meadowlark waiting on every post.

COMPARING LITERATURE COMPARING LITERATURE COMPARING LITERATURE COMPARING

Behind a shelterbelt of cedars,
top-deep in hollyhocks, pollen and bees,
15 a pickup kicks its fenders off
and settles back to read the clouds.

You feel like that; you feel like letting
your tires go flat, like letting the mice
build a nest in your muffler, like being
20 no more than a truck in the weeds,

clucking with chickens or sticky with honey
or holding a skinny old man in your lap
while he watches the road, waiting
for someone to wave to. You feel like

25 waving. You feel like stopping the car
and dancing around on the road. You wave
instead and leave your hand out gliding
larklike over the wheat, over the houses. ❖

Review Questions

1. What is happening in the poem? What activity does it describe? Explain how this relates to the title of the poem, which also is stated in line 9.

2. What are the "dear old ladies" described in line 5? How does the speaker seem to feel about the landscape, based on this use of personification?

3. In the last several stanzas, what does "you" feel like doing? What does "you" do instead? Summarize how a person's environment can affect his or her perspective on what's important in life.

TEXT $\xleftrightarrow{\text{TO}}$ TEXT CONNECTION

Compare and contrast the images used to portray the Plains in "So This Is Nebraska" with those in Frazier's *Great Plains* and Norris's "Seeing." Also compare and contrast tone across the three selections. Write a sentence stating each writer's perspective on the Great Plains.

Refer to Text ▶ ▶ ▶ ▶ ▶   Reason with Text

1a. In Frazier's selection, what end punctuation mark is used repeatedly in paragraph 1?

1b. Interpret why Frazier uses this punctuation. How might this be considered ironic, given the topic?

Understand
Find meaning

2a. In "Seeing," how does Norris respond to the friend who asks what there is to see in the Plains?

2b. Relate Norris's short initial response to the more elaborate explanation she provides. What does this contrast suggest?

Apply
Use information

3a. In "Seeing," what happens to the man who has "Plains fever"? In *Great Plains,* how long did it take someone to cross the United States in 1849 versus 1989?

3b. Point out what each of these references suggests about the purpose of the selection in which it appears.

Analyze
Take things apart

4a. Which selection is written in first-person point of view, and which is written in third-person point of view?

4b. How does the difference in point of view influence your response to the selections?

Evaluate
Make judgments

5a. Identify the primary feature shared by the Frazier and Norris selections.

5b. How would each author respond to the other's work? Write their possible responses.

Create
Bring ideas together

Compare Literature

Description and Tone
How would you compare the two authors' approaches to description in *Great Plains* and "Seeing"? What sensory details does each provide to enhance his or her description?

What similarities and differences do you find in the tone of the two essays? Infer each author's attitude about the Great Plains.

Extend the Text

Writing Options
Creative Writing Write a one-page *travelogue* (discussion of travel) about a trip you have taken or one you would like to take. Include sensory details to make your description come alive for your readers. If possible, include graphics, such as photos and drawings, of your real or imaginary trip.

Expository Writing Write a comparison-and-contrast essay discussing tone in the selections by Norris and Frazier. In your conclusion, state which essay you found more appealing or more convincing.

Collaborative Learning
Create a Visitors' Brochure of the Great Plains
With two or three classmates, collect information that would be useful in planning a trip to one area of the Great Plains—how to get there, what to see, where to stay, and so on. The group should select one area of the region on which to focus. Provide photos in your brochure.

Critical Literacy
Prepare an Annotated Bibliography With a partner or a group, prepare an *annotated bibliography* of books (novels, nonfiction, and poetry), magazine and newspaper articles, and other published materials on the subject of the Great Plains. For each item in the list, write an *annotation,* or brief note on what the work has to offer, how to find it, or other useful information.

 Go to **www.mirrorsandwindows.com** for more.

1. According to Ian Frazier in *Great Plains,* how do most people today see the Plains?
   A. on television shows
   B. when flying over them
   C. by driving across the United States
   D. by cross-country train
   E. in the movies

2. Which of the following is closest in meaning to the word *quell,* which is used to describe the Missouri River in *Great Plains?*
   A. to stir up
   B. to subdue
   C. to confuse
   D. to describe
   E. to eliminate

3. What is the "Plains fever" that Kathleen Norris mentions in "Seeing" from *Dakota?*
   A. the strong desire to get married so as not be alone
   B. the temporary blindness that occurs from looking at a vast landscape too long
   C. the peacefulness that comes from hearing sacred drum songs
   D. the feeling of being surrounded by small creatures
   E. the sense of fear that comes from realizing the land's indifference to humans

4. How is one's vision challenged on the Dakota Plains, according to Norris?
   A. The eyes must learn to appreciate subtlety and small things.
   B. There is so much sky that the sun can be very glaring.
   C. The eyes need to adjust to seeing the spectacular and the busy.
   D. One has to adjust to seeing nothing in the vast landscape.
   E. There is too much to take in all at once.

5. Norris writes, "The most *prosaic* pasture might contain hundreds of different wildflowers." What does the word *prosaic* mean in this sentence?
   A. bountiful
   B. ordinary
   C. varied
   D. large
   E. peaceful

6. Which of the following best describes the mood of Ted Kooser's "So This Is Nebraska"?
   A. carefree
   B. bored
   C. amazed
   D. hurried
   E. hopeful

7. In Kooser's poem, the line "a pickup kicks its fenders off / and settles back to read the clouds" is an example of what literary device?
   A. metaphor
   B. simile
   C. personification
   D. characterization
   E. description

8. What is most significant about the title "So This Is Nebraska"?
   A. its meter
   B. its use of sensory details
   C. its conversational tone
   D. its contrast to the subject of the poem itself
   E. its use of *Nebraska* as a metaphor

9. **Constructed Response:** Analyze the topic of *seeing* in the excerpt from Kathleen Norris's *Dakota.* How is the idea of seeing related to the Great Plains? Consider not just the physical act of seeing but also the idea of seeing in a philosophical or spiritual sense. Use details from the excerpt to support your analysis.

10. **Constructed Response:** Describe the significance of the Great Plains based on how this region is described in the selections by Frazier, Norris, and Kooser. How might others disagree with the authors' perspectives? Cite evidence from the texts to support your explanation.

TEST-TAKING TIP

If an essay passage or test question contains a word for which you don't know the meaning, try to decipher it. Familiarize yourself with the meanings of common prefixes and suffixes. For example, knowing that the prefix *hyper-* means "over the normal amount" will help you infer with reasonable certainty that *hypersensitive* means "overly sensitive."

Understand the Concept

Learning some common rules will help improve both your spelling and your ability to proofread for common spelling errors. One useful set of spelling rules applies to **affixes,** or the prefixes and suffixes that are added to change the functions and meanings of words. When a **prefix** is added to a word, the spelling of the word usually does not change:

EXAMPLES

un- + cooperative = uncooperative

pre- + existence = preexistence

Adding a **suffix** to a word may or may not change the spelling, depending on the suffix. Adding the suffix -ment, -ness, or -ly generally does not change the spelling:

EXAMPLES

establish + -ment = establishment

aware + -ness = awareness

decorative + -ly = decoratively

Adding suffixes to words that end in y is more complicated. When the y follows a vowel, the y usually is left in place when a suffix is added. When the y follows a consonant, however, the y becomes an i:

EXAMPLES

employ + -ment = employment

happy + -ness = happiness

Adding suffixes to words ending with a silent e also can be complicated. When a suffix beginning with a vowel is added, the final e usually is dropped from the word. When a suffix beginning with a consonant is added, the e usually stays in place:

EXAMPLES

receptive + -ity = receptivity

conclusive + -ly = conclusively

Notice how the word *usually* or *generally* is included in many of these supposed rules. In fact, there are few absolute rules in spelling English words. Knowing common patterns, such as those described here, will help make you a better speller. In addition, you should become familiar with commonly misspelled words and look for them in proofreading your writing.

Here is a list of words that high school students often misspell:

acknowledgment	fulfill	occurrence
anonymous	guidance	parallel
beautiful	hypocrite	pastime
beginning	independent	permanent
calendar	influential	privilege
committee	judgment	referred
definitely	license	receipt
discipline	mischievous	schedule
embarrass	misspell	separate
enthusiastically	naïve	surprise
existence	necessity	tomorrow
fascinating	occasionally	vehicle

Apply the Skill

Exercise A

Choose ten words from the preceding list or your own list of troublesome spelling words. For each word, make up a saying or image to help you remember the correct spelling. For example, the saying "There is *a rat* in sep*arate*" can help remind you that *separate* is spelled with *ar*, not *er*. These kinds of memory helpers are called *mnemonic* (the initial *m* is silent) *devices.* Here are some more examples:

EXAMPLES

Station**e**ry includes l**e**tt**e**rs and **e**nvelop**e**s.

You are station**a**ry when you st**a**nd in pl**a**ce.

Exercise B

In each of the following groups of words, identify the correctly spelled word. Use a dictionary for help.

1. concede, conceed, consede
2. unecessary, unnecessary, unneccessary
3. relieved, releived, releeved
4. disatisfied, disatisfyed, dissatisfied
5. sincerly, sincerely, sinserely
6. cheerilly, cherrily, cheerily
7. occaisonaly, ocaissonally, occasionally
8. rearranged, rearanged, reearanged
9. fullfillment, fulfillment, fulfilment
10. enbarassed, embarrased, embarrassed

Throughput, from Fast Food Nation

Literary Nonfiction by Eric Schlosser

Build Background

Cultural Context In the mid-1990s, journalist Eric Schlosser, a self-acknowledged consumer of fast food, pitched an idea for an article to *Rolling Stone* magazine: to examine the success behind fast food chains. In the two-part article that followed, published in 1998, Schlosser exposed unsanitary food conditions, horrific slaughterhouse practices, and unfavorable hiring practices. In addition, he criticized the fast food industry's negative effects on the United States' health, economy, environment, and culture.

In 2001, Schlosser expanded his findings into the best-selling book *Fast Food Nation: The Dark Side of the All-American Meal.* **"Throughput,"** an excerpt from that book, introduces one young worker at a fast food chain but then broadens its focus to consider two key issues: the common hiring of inexperienced teenagers to work for low wages and workplace routines that tightly control employees.

Reader's Context Should high schools ban the selling or promotion of fast food on school property and at school events? Explain.

Meet the Author

Eric Schlosser (b. 1959) was born in New York City but spent part of his childhood in Los Angeles, where his father was president of the NBC network. Schlosser earned a bachelor's degree in American history from Princeton University in 1981 and later earned a graduate degree in British Imperial history from Oxford University.

After struggling as a novelist and playwright, Schlosser found his niche as an investigative journalist. In 1996, he was hired as a correspondent for *Atlantic Monthly,* and his writing also has been featured in *Rolling Stone, Vanity Fair,* and the *New Yorker.* Known for his meticulous research and straightforward writing style, Schlosser has received several journalism awards, including a National Magazine Award and the Sidney Hillman Foundation Award for Reporting.

Schlosser's scathing report on the fast food industry in *Fast Food Nation* established him as a prominent investigative journalist. In 2006, he co-authored a book aimed at the largest consumer of fast food: children. *Chew on This: Everything You Don't Want to Know About Fast Food* (2006) exposes the marketing techniques fast food chains use to cater to children. Schlosser currently is writing a book about the U.S. prison system.

Analyze Literature

Persuasion and Thesis Persuasion, or *persuasive writing,* is intended to change or influence the way a reader thinks or feels about a particular issue or idea.

The **thesis** is the main idea presented and supported in a work of nonfiction.

Set Purpose

Schlosser once said, "A lot of what I write about is what people on some level don't want to hear about. But it's also what people need to know." As you read this excerpt from *Fast Food Nation,* consider how the author intends to influence how you feel or what you think about fast food restaurants. Identify Schlosser's thesis, or main idea. Then record examples of the evidence he provides to prove that idea.

Preview Vocabulary

ethos, 1257
altruistic, 1259

THROUGHPUT

from *Fast Food Nation*

by Eric Schlosser

The fast food industry now employs some of the most disadvantaged members of American society.

Every Saturday Elisa Zamot gets up at 5:15 in the morning. It's a struggle, and her head feels groggy as she steps into the shower. Her little sisters, Cookie and Sabrina, are fast asleep in their beds. By 5:30, Elisa's showered, done her hair, and put on her McDonald's uniform. She's sixteen, bright-eyed and olive-skinned, pretty and petite, ready for another day of work. Elisa's mother usually drives her the half-mile or so to the restaurant, but sometimes Elisa walks, leaving home before the sun rises. Her family's modest townhouse sits beside a busy highway on the south side of Colorado Springs, in a largely poor and working-class neighborhood. Throughout the day, sounds of traffic fill the house, the steady whoosh of passing cars. But when Elisa heads for work, the streets are quiet, the sky's still dark, and the lights are out in the small houses and rental apartments along the road.

When Elisa arrives at McDonald's, the manager unlocks the door and lets her in. Sometimes the husband-and-wife cleaning crew are just finishing up. More often, it's just Elisa and the manager in the restaurant, surrounded by an empty parking lot. For the next hour or so, the two of them get everything ready. They turn on the ovens and grills. They go downstairs into the basement and get food and supplies for the morning shift. They get the paper cups, wrappers, cardboard containers, and packets of condiments. They step into the big freezer and get the frozen bacon, the frozen pancakes, and the frozen cinnamon rolls. They get the frozen hash browns, the frozen biscuits, the frozen McMuffins. They get the cartons of scrambled egg mix and orange juice mix. They bring the food upstairs and start preparing it before any customers appear, thawing some things in the microwave and cooking other things on the grill. They put the cooked food in special cabinets to keep it warm.

After seven hours of standing at a cash register, her feet hurt. She's wiped out.

The restaurant opens for business at seven o'clock, and for the next hour or so, Elisa and the manager hold down the fort, handling all the orders. As the place starts to get busy, other employees arrive. Elisa works behind the counter. She takes orders and hands food to customers from breakfast through lunch. When she finally walks home, after seven hours of standing at a cash register, her feet hurt. She's wiped out. She comes through the front door, flops onto the living room couch, and turns on the TV. And the next morning she gets up at 5:15 again and starts the same routine.

Up and down Academy Boulevard, along South Nevada, Circle Drive, and Woodman Road, teenagers like Elisa run the fast food restaurants of Colorado Springs. Fast food kitchens often seem like a scene from *Bugsy Malone,* a film in which all the actors are children pretending to be adults. No other industry in the United States has a workforce so dominated by adolescents. About two-thirds of the nation's fast food workers are under the age of twenty. Teenagers open the fast food outlets in the morning, close them at night, and keep them going at all hours in between. Even the managers and assistant managers are sometimes in their late teens. Unlike Olympic gymnastics— an activity in which teenagers consistently perform at a higher level than adults—there's nothing about the work in a fast food kitchen that requires young employees. Instead of relying upon a small, stable, well-paid, and well-trained workforce, the fast food industry seeks out part-time, unskilled workers who are willing to accept low pay. Teenagers have been the perfect candidates for these jobs, not only because they are less expensive to hire than adults, but also because their youthful inexperience makes them easier to control.

The labor practices of the fast food industry have their origins in the assembly line systems adopted by American manufacturers in the early twentieth century. Business historian Alfred D. Chandler has argued that a high rate of "throughput" was the most important aspect of these mass production systems. A factory's throughput is the speed and volume of its flow—a much more crucial measurement, according to Chandler, than the number of workers it employs or the value of its machinery. With innovative technology and the proper organization, a small number of work-

Beef Production

Most people—whether they buy chopped meat at a grocery store and flip their burgers at home or buy meat patties piled high on buns at a fast food outlet—have little knowledge of where the meat comes from. Popular breeds of cattle, including Herefords, Beef Shorthorn, Aberdeen Angus, and Highland, originally were bred in England and Scotland. As settlers from Great Britain took up life in other parts of the world, they brought their livestock with them. In fact, the three biggest beef-producing nations today—the United States, Argentina, and Australia—had no cattle before the 1800s. Other countries noted for prime steaks are Canada and Japan.

There is a great deal of debate over what to feed cattle and how that feed affects the meat people eat. Nutritionists tend to associate eating red meat with heart disease. However, studies have shown that Argentines have a much lower rate

of heart disease than Americans do, even though they consume more beef per capita. Some scientists attribute this difference to the diet of Argentine cattle, which consists primarily of grass, the cow's natural food source. In contrast, most American cattle eat corn, which is not a natural part of the bovine diet. When cows eat corn, their meat includes higher levels of fat and sodium, both of which relate directly to heart disease. Given these findings, agriculturalists are starting to condemn corn-fed beef as unhealthy and biologically careless.

---

ers can produce an enormous amount of goods cheaply. Throughput is all about increasing the speed of assembly, about doing things faster in order to make more.

Although the McDonald brothers had never encountered the term "throughput" or studied "scientific management," they instinctively grasped the underlying principles and applied them in the Speedee Service System. The restaurant operating scheme they developed has been widely adopted and refined over the past half century. The <u>ethos</u> of the assembly line remains at its core. The fast food industry's obsession with throughput has altered the way millions of Americans work, turned commercial kitchens into small factories, and changed familiar foods into commodities that are manufactured.

At Burger King restaurants, frozen hamburger patties are placed on a conveyer belt and emerge from a broiler ninety seconds later fully cooked. The ovens at Pizza Hut

and at Domino's also use conveyer belts to ensure standardized cooking times. The ovens at McDonald's look like commercial laundry presses, with big steel hoods that swing down and grill hamburgers on both sides at once. The burgers, chicken, french fries, and buns are all frozen when they arrive at a McDonald's. The shakes and sodas begin as syrup. At Taco Bell restaurants the food is "assembled," not prepared. The guacamole[1] isn't made by workers in the kitchen; it's made at a factory in Michoacán, Mexico, then frozen and shipped north. The chain's taco meat arrives frozen and precooked in vacuum-sealed plastic bags. The

---

1. **guacamole** (gwä′ kə mō′ lā). Mashed and seasoned avocado, usually served as a dip

> **ethos** (ē′ thōs) *n.*, guiding belief or principle of a group or institution

beans are dehydrated and look like brownish corn flakes. The cooking process is fairly simple. "Everything's add water," a Taco Bell employee told me. "Just add hot water."

Although Richard and Mac McDonald introduced the division of labor to the restaurant business, it was a McDonald's executive named Fred Turner who created a production system of unusual thoroughness and attention to detail. In 1958, Turner put together an operations and training manual for the company that was seventy-five pages long, specifying how almost everything should be done. Hamburgers were always to be placed on the grill in six neat rows; french fries had to be exactly 0.28 inches thick. The McDonald's operations manual today has ten times the number of pages and weighs about four pounds. Known within the company as "the Bible," it contains precise instructions on how various appliances should be used, how each item on the menu should look, and how

employees should greet customers. Operators who disobey these rules can lose their franchises.[2] Cooking instructions are not only printed in the manual, they are often designed into the machines. A McDonald's kitchen is full of buzzers and flashing lights that tell employees what to do.

> *Operators who disobey these rules can lose their franchises.*

At the front counter, computerized cash registers issue their own commands. Once an order has been placed, buttons light up and suggest other menu items that can be added. Workers at the counter are told to increase

---

2. **franchises.** Licensed outlets of a business

the size of an order by recommending special promotions, pushing dessert, pointing out the financial logic behind the purchase of a larger drink. While doing so, they are instructed to be upbeat and friendly. "Smile with a greeting and make a positive first impression," a Burger King training manual suggests. "Show them you are GLAD TO SEE THEM. Include eye contact with the cheerful greeting."

The strict regimentation at fast food restaurants creates standardized products. It increases the throughput. And it gives fast food companies an enormous amount of power over their employees. "When management determines exactly how every task is to be done . . . and can impose its own rules about pace, output, quality, and technique," the sociologist Robin Leidner has noted, "[it] makes workers increasingly interchangeable." The management no longer depends upon the talents or skills of its workers—those things are built into the operating system and machines. Jobs that have been "de-skilled" can be filled cheaply. The need to retain any individual worker is greatly reduced by the ease with which he or she can be replaced.

Teenagers have long provided the fast food industry with the bulk of its workforce. The industry's rapid growth coincided with the baby-boom expansion of that age group. Teenagers were in many ways the ideal candidates for these low-paying jobs. Since most teenagers still lived at home, they could afford to work for wages too low to support an adult, and until recently, their limited skills attracted few other employers. A job at a fast food restaurant became an American rite of passage, a first job soon left behind for better things. The flexible terms of employment in the fast food industry also attracted housewives who needed extra income. As the number of baby-boom teenagers declined, the fast food chains began to hire other marginalized workers: recent immigrants, the elderly, and the handicapped.

Teenagers have long provided the fast food industry with the bulk of its workforce.

English is now the second language of at least one-sixth of the nation's restaurant workers, and about one-third of that group speak no English at all. The proportion of fast food workers who cannot speak English is even higher. Many know only the names of the items on the menu; they speak "McDonald's English."

The fast food industry now employs some of the most disadvantaged members of American society. It often teaches basic job skills—such as getting to work on time—to people who can barely read, whose lives have been chaotic or shut off from the mainstream. Many individual franchisees are genuinely concerned about the well-being of their workers. But the stance of the fast food industry on issues involving employee training, the minimum wage, labor unions, and overtime pay strongly suggests that its motives in hiring the young, the poor, and the handicapped are hardly <u>altruistic</u>. ❖

al • tru • ist • ic (ăl′ trü is′ tik) *adj.*, motivated by unselfish concern for the welfare of others

MIRRORS & WINDOWS Does the standardization of procedures and products at fast food restaurants make workers more or less productive?

Refer to Text ▶ ▶ ▶ ▶ ▶	Reason with Text	
1a. List the tasks Elisa and her manager do to get the restaurant ready to open each morning.	**1b.** Summarize what Elisa's daily life is like outside work.	**Understand** Find meaning
2a. What types of employees does the fast food industry want to hire? What qualities do they have?	**2b.** Why is this type of employee well suited to standardized procedures and products?	**Apply** Use information
3a. Define the term *throughput,* as used in the selection.	**3b.** How did applying the throughput philosophy change traditional work practices in the fast food industry?	**Analyze** Take things apart
4a. In what ways does the fast food industry control its workers?	**4b.** Describe how the throughput system might affect employees in both the short and long term.	**Evaluate** Make judgments
5a. According to Schlosser, what is the fast food industry's stance on employee issues?	**5b.** Suggest reforms that would help the fast food industry be a better employer.	**Create** Bring ideas together

Analyze Literature

Persuasion and Thesis
What would Schlosser like you to think or feel about the fast food industry? What is his thesis, or main idea? Where is it stated? What evidence does Schlosser provide to try to persuade you? What evidence is more or less convincing? Why?

Extend the Text

Writing Options
Creative Writing Imagine that you are Elisa, just home from the fast food restaurant where you work. Write a journal entry about a typical day at your job, describing the things you did, problems you might have had, interactions with customers or co-workers, and so on. Also describe how you feel about your job and your future work prospects.

Persuasive Writing As a member of a book club that has read *Fast Food Nation,* you need to prepare for discussion of how workers are treated in the fast food industry. Write a paragraph in which you agree or disagree with Schlosser's assertions about throughput and its effects on the hiring and treatment of workers. Use evidence from the selection to support your opinion.

Collaborative Learning
Develop a Time Line Learn about the history of the fast food industry by doing brief research on the Internet or in the library. (Other chapters in *Fast Food Nation* may provide useful information.) Then create a time line of the major events in the industry's growth and development. If you would like, illustrate the time line with cartoons, sketches, or original artwork.

Critical Literacy
Write an Editorial Write a guest editorial for your school newspaper or a community paper in which you present your opinion on the fast food industry's policy of hiring large numbers of teenage workers. Support your opinion by including information you obtain from interviews of teenage fast food workers and managers. Include quotations from these interviews in your editorial.

 Go to **www.mirrorsandwindows.com** for more.

On the Mall
Literary Nonfiction by Joan Didion

Build Background

Literary Context In **"On the Mall,"** Joan Didion examines consumerism in the United States. Calling the years after World War II "a peculiar and visionary time," the author sees shopping malls as symbolic of those postwar years, a time when Americans believed that social and moral progress was unlimited and that conditions could only improve. On this subject, Didion has said, "When we start deceiving ourselves into thinking not that we want something or need something, not that it is a pragmatic necessity for us to have it, but that it is a moral imperative that we have it, then is when we join the fashionable madmen, and then is when the thin whine of hysteria is heard in the land, and then is when we are in bad trouble." The selection was published in 1979, in Didion's collection of essays *The White Album*.

Reader's Context How would you describe the shopping centers or malls with which you are familiar? How does each have a culture, or character, of its own?

Meet the Author

Joan Didion (b. 1934) is an acclaimed novelist, screenwriter, and journalist. Born in Sacramento, California, Didion graduated from the University of California, Berkeley. After winning a contest for young writers, she worked as an editor at *Vogue* magazine. Her first novel, *Run River*, was published in 1963. Later novels include *A Book of Common Prayer* (1977) and *The Last Thing He Wanted* (1996), both of which comment on American cultural and political attitudes.

Didion is known for her spare and precise language and for her exploration of the desolate cultural landscape of the contemporary United States. She has been called the "finest woman prose stylist writing in English today." In her nonfiction works, including magazine articles and essays, Didion writes in the first person, blending her experiences with factual information to evoke a personal vision of her subject. Her essay collections *Slouching Towards Bethlehem* (1968) and *The White Album* (1979) contain essays about life in California in the 1960s.

In 2005, Didion's book-length essay *The Year of Magical Thinking* was published. The work narrates the year following the death of Didion's husband, John Gregory Dunne. While Didion was grieving for Dunne, their daughter, thirty-nine-year-old Quintana, was dangerously ill and died before the book's release. The work received the National Book Award for nonfiction.

Analyze Literature

Purpose and Irony
Purpose is the writer's aim, or goal, such as to inform or explain (*expository writing*); to portray a person, place, object, or event (*descriptive writing*); to convince readers to accept a position (*persuasive writing*); and to tell a story (*narrative writing*).

Irony is the difference between appearance and reality.

Set Purpose

As discussed in Understanding Literary Forms (pages 1238–1239), writers of literary nonfiction can have any of several purposes. As you read "On the Mall," determine Didion's purpose or purposes in writing. List details from the selection that illustrate each purpose you identify. Also look for instances of irony as you read. For instance, what is ironic about the names of the malls listed in the first paragraph?

Preview Vocabulary

fusion, 1262
egalitarian, 1262
enigmatic, 1263
recondite, 1266
impenetrable, 1266
vehemently, 1266

On the Mall

by Joan Didion

They made something of nothing. They gambled and sometimes lost. They staked the past to seize the future.

They float on the landscape like pyramids to the boom years, all those Plazas and Malls and Esplanades. All those Squares and Fairs. All those Towns and Dales, all those Villages, all those Forests and Parks and Lands. Stonestown. Hillsdale. Valley Fair, Mayfair, Northgate, Southgate, Eastgate, Westgate. Gulfgate. They are toy garden cities in which no one lives but everyone consumes, profound equalizers, the perfect <u>fusion</u> of the profit motive and the <u>egalitarian</u> ideal, and to hear their names is to recall words and phrases no

> **fu • sion** (fyü´ zhən) *n.,* merging of distinct elements into a unified whole
>
> **egal • i • tar • i • an** (ē gal´ ə tãr´ ē ən) *adj.,* asserting a belief in human equality, especially in terms of social, political, and economic rights

longer quite current. Baby Boom. Consumer Explosion. Leisure Revolution. Do-It-Yourself Revolution. Backyard Revolution. Suburbia. "The Shopping Center," the Urban Land Institute could pronounce in 1957, "is today's extraordinary retail business evolvement. . . . The automobile accounts for suburbia, and suburbia accounts for the shopping center."

It was a peculiar and visionary time, those years after World War II to which all the Malls and Towns and Dales stand as climate-controlled monuments. Even the word "automobile," as in "the automobile accounts for suburbia and suburbia accounts for the shopping center," no longer carries the particular freight it once did: as a child in the late Forties in California I recall reading and believing that the "freedom of movement" afforded by the automobile was "America's fifth freedom."[1] The trend was up. The solution was in sight. The frontier had been reinvented, and its shape was the subdivision,[2] that new free land on which all settlers could recast their lives *tabula rasa.*[3] For one perishable moment there the American idea seemed about to achieve itself, via F.H.A.[4] housing and the acquisition of major appliances, and a certain <u>enigmatic</u> glamour attached to the architects of this newfound land. They made something of nothing. They gambled and sometimes lost. They staked the past to seize the future. I have difficulty now imagining a childhood in which a man named Jere Strizek, the developer of Town and Country Village outside Sacramento (143,000 square feet gross floor area, 68 stores, 1000 parking spaces, the Urban Land Institute's "prototype[5] for centers using heavy timber and tile construction for informality"), could materialize as a role model, but I had such a childhood, just after World War II, in Sacramento. I never met or even saw Jere Strizek, but at the age of 12 I imagined him a kind of frontiersman, a romantic and revolutionary spirit, and in the indigenous grain[6] he was.

I suppose James B. Douglas and David D. Bohannon were too.

> ## The frontier had been reinvented, and its shape was the subdivision.

I first heard of James B. Douglas and David D. Bohannon not when I was 12 but a dozen years later, when I was living in New York, working for *Vogue,* and taking, by correspondence, a University of California Extension course in shopping-center theory. This did not seem to me eccentric at the time. I remember sitting on the cool floor in Irving Penn's[7] studio and reading, in *The Community Builders Handbook,* advice from James B. Douglas on shopping-center financing. I recall staying late in my pale-blue office on the twentieth floor of the Graybar Building to memorize David D. Bohannon's parking ratios. My "real" life was to sit in this office and describe life as it was lived in Djakarta and Caneel Bay and in the great châteaux of the Loire Valley,[8] but my dream life was to put together a Class-A regional shopping center with three full-line department stores as major tenants.

---

1. **"America's fifth freedom."** In 1941, President Franklin D. Roosevelt spoke about the "four freedoms" for all people of the world: freedom of speech, freedom of religion, freedom from want, and freedom from fear.
2. **subdivision.** Previously rural, unowned land surveyed and divided into lots for sale
3. *tabula rasa.* [Latin] Clean slate; anything in its original and pure state
4. **F.H.A.** Federal Housing Administration, a federal agency that provides programs to support first-time and low-income homeowners
5. **prototype.** Standard on which other things are modeled; the first working model of its type
6. **in the indigenous grain.** In the American way
7. **Irving Penn.** Photographer for *Vogue*
8. **Djakarta . . . Loire Valley.** *Djakarta*—Alternate spelling of Jakarta, the capital of Indonesia; *Caneel Bay*—Luxury resort in the Virgin Islands; *châteaux* [French]—Castles; *Loire Valley*—Region in France

---

en • ig • ma • tic (en' ig ma´ tik) *adj.,* mysterious; hard to explain

center game: I would lease warehouses in, say, Queens, and offer Manhattan delicatessens the opportunity to sell competitively by buying cooperatively, from my trucks. I see a few wrinkles in this scheme now (the words "concrete overcoat" come to mind), but I did not then. In fact I planned to run it right out of the pale-blue office.

James B. Douglas and David D. Bohannon. In 1950 James B. Douglas had opened Northgate, in Seattle, the first regional center to combine a pedestrian mall with an underground truck tunnel. In 1954 David D. Bohannon had opened Hillsdale, a forty-acre regional center on the peninsula south of San Francisco. That is the only solid bio I have on James B. Douglas and David D. Bohannon to this day, but many of their opinions are engraved on my memory. David D. Bohannon believed in preserving the integrity of the shopping center by not cutting up the site with any dedicated roads. David D. Bohannon believed that architectural setbacks in a center looked "pretty on paper" but caused "customer resistance." James B. Douglas advised that a small-loan office could prosper in a center only if it were placed away from foot traffic, since people who want small loans do not want to be observed getting them. I do not now recall whether it was James B. Douglas or David D. Bohannon or someone else altogether who passed along this hint on how to paint the lines around the parking spaces (actually this is called "striping the lot," and the spaces are "stalls"): make each space a foot wider than it need be—ten feet, say, instead of nine—when the center first opens and busi-

That I was perhaps the only person I knew in New York, let alone on the Condé Nast[9] floors of the Graybar Building, to have memorized the distinctions among "A," "B," and "C" shopping centers did not occur to me (the defining distinction, as long as I have your attention, is that an "A," or "regional," center has as its major tenant a full-line department store which carries major appliances; a "B," or "community," center has as its major tenant a junior department store which does not carry major appliances; and a "C," or "neighborhood," center has as its major tenant only a supermarket): my interest in shopping centers was in no way casual. I did want to build them. I wanted to build them because I had fallen into the habit of writing fiction, and I had it in my head that a couple of good centers might support this habit less taxingly than a pale-blue office at *Vogue.* I had even devised an original scheme by which I planned to gain enough capital and credibility to enter the shopping-

9. **Condé Nast.** Company that publishes magazines, including *Vogue*

Evolution of the Mall

The first shopping centers were open marketplaces, often in the central plaza of a town or urban area, where farmers and craftspeople sold their goods. While markets like this still exist all over the world, enclosed malls developed in the United States around the middle of the twentieth century and became commonplace within twenty years.

Today, some Americans are critical of the wide-spread expansion of malls and shopping centers, for several reasons. One is that malls tend to house only corporate-owned chain stores and restaurants, which means they draw money away from older and smaller local businesses. Given this trend, malls nationwide are nearly identical in terms of the products and services they offer.

Another criticism of malls is leveled at the structures themselves. Because architects typically prioritize function over aesthetics when they build malls, they create structures characterized by large parking garages, wide expanses of concrete, and unattractive buildings. Most people do not want to live near structures like these, which results in declining property values. Problems with traffic congestion and crime around malls further contribute to this problem.

The ongoing expansion of suburbia and resulting development of new malls has caused some malls to go out of business, particularly older ones. When this happens, the space often sits abandoned for years before it is renovated or demolished. The large size and generally poor construction of the typical mall makes it difficult to adapt to new purposes.

A current trend in the evolution of malls is to make them entertainment destinations, offering not only a full spectrum of stores and restaurants but also indoor parks complete with rides, pools and slides, skating rinks, and other attractions. Hotels and convention centers are being built adjacent to and even attached to malls to encourage visitors to take extended trips. This approach underlies much of the success of the largest mall in the United States, the Mall of America (MOA), in Bloomington, Minnesota, which draws forty million visitors a year.

ness is slow. By this single stroke the developer achieves a couple of important objectives, the appearance of a popular center and the illusion of easy parking, and no one will really notice when business picks up and the spaces shrink.

Nor do I recall who first solved what was once a crucial center dilemma: the placement of the major tenant vis à vis[10] the parking lot. The dilemma was that the major tenant—the draw, the raison d'être[11] for the financing, the Sears, the Macy's, the May Company—wanted its customer to walk directly from car to store.

The smaller tenants, on the other hand, wanted that same customer to *pass their stores* on the way from the car to, say, Macy's. The solution to this conflict of interests was actually very simple: *two major tenants,* one at each end of a mall. This is called "anchoring the mall," and represents seminal[12] work in shopping center theory. One thing you will note about

10. **vis á vis** (vēs´ ä vē'). [French] In relation to
11. **raison d'être** (rā´ zō(n) detr´). [French] Reason for being
12. **seminal.** Planting the seeds for later development; creative; original

shopping-center theory is that you could have thought of it yourself, and a course in it will go a long way toward dispelling the notion that business proceeds from mysteries too <u>recondite</u> for you and me.

A few aspects of shopping-center theory do in fact remain <u>impenetrable</u> to me. I have no idea why the Community Builders' Council ranks "Restaurant" as deserving a Number One (or "Hot Spot") location but exiles "Chinese Restaurant" to a Number Three, out there with "Power and Light Office" and "Christian Science Reading Room." Nor do I know why the Council approves of enlivening a mall with "small animals" but specifically, <u>vehemently</u>, and with no further explanation, excludes "monkeys." If I had a center I would have monkeys, and Chinese restaurants, and

Mylar[13] kites and bands of small girls playing tambourine.

A few years ago at a party I met a woman from Detroit who told me that the Joyce Carol Oates novel with which she identified most closely was *Wonderland*.

I asked her why.

"Because," she said, "my husband has a branch there."

---

13. **Mylar.** Polyester made in thin but durable sheets; used in some helium balloons

> **re • con • dite** (rə kän´ dīt) *adj.*, difficult or impossible for the average person to understand; deep
>
> **im • pen • e • tra • ble** (im pen´ ə trə b'l) *adj.*, unable to be comprehended or penetrated
>
> **ve • hem • ent • ly** (vē´ hə mənt lē) *adv.*, with force or intensity

I did not understand.

"In Wonderland the center," the woman said patiently. "My husband has a branch in Wonderland."

I have never visited Wonderland but imagine it to have bands of small girls playing tambourine.

A few facts about shopping centers. The "biggest" center in the United States is generally agreed to be Woodfield, outside Chicago, a "super" regional or "leviathan"[14] two-million-square-foot center with four major tenants.

The "first" shopping center in the United States is generally agreed to be Country Club Plaza in Kansas City, built in the twenties. There were some other earlier centers, notably Edward H. Bouton's 1907 Roland Park in Baltimore, Hugh Prather's 1931 Highland Park Shopping Village in Dallas, and Hugh Potter's 1937 River Oaks in Houston, but the developer of Country Club Plaza, J. C. Nichols, is referred to with ritual frequency in the literature of shopping centers, usually as "pioneering J. C. Nichols" or "J. C. Nichols, father of the center as we know it."

Those are some facts I know about shopping centers because I still want to be Jere Strizek or James B. Douglas or David D. Bohannon. Here are some facts I know about shopping centers because I never will be Jere Strizek or James B. Douglas or David D. Bohannon: a good center in which to spend the day if you wake feeling low in Oxnard, California, is The Esplanade, major tenants the May Company and Sears. A good center in which to spend the day if you wake feeling low in Biloxi, Mississippi, is Edgewater Plaza, major tenant Godchaux's. Ala Moana in Honolulu is larger than The Esplanade in Oxnard, and The Esplanade in Oxnard is larger than Edgewater Plaza in

Biloxi. Ala Moana has carp pools. The Esplanade and Edgewater Plaza do not.

These marginal distinctions to one side, Ala Moana, The Esplanade, and Edgewater Plaza are the same place, which is precisely their role not only as equalizers but in the sedation[15] of anxiety. In each of them one moves for a while in an aqueous[16] suspension not only of light but of judgment, not only of judgment but "personality." One meets no acquaintances at The Esplanade. One gets no telephone calls at Edgewater Plaza. "It's a hard place to run in to for a pair of stockings," a friend complained to me recently of Ala Moana, and I knew that she was not yet ready to surrender her ego to the idea of the center. The last time I went to Ala Moana it was to buy *The New York Times*. Because *The New York Times* was not in, I sat on the mall for a while and ate caramel corn. In the end I bought not *The New York Times* but two straw hats at Liberty House, four bottles of nail enamel at Woolworth's, and a toaster, on sale at Sears. In the literature of shopping centers these would be described as impulse purchases, but the impulse here was obscure. I do not wear hats, nor do I like caramel corn. I do not use nail enamel. Yet flying back across the Pacific I regretted only the toaster. ❖

---

14. **"leviathan."** Gigantic and frightening
15. **sedation.** Creation of a relaxed state, especially by sedatives; a type of medication
16. **aqueous.** Of, relating to, or resembling water

MIRRORS & WINDOWS

Didion uses the term "shopping-center theory" to label the principles that explain why malls are successful. What do you think makes a mall successful?

Refer to Text ▶ ▶ ▶ ▶ ▶ **Reason with Text**

1a. To which era are the shopping malls "monuments"?	**1b.** Summarize the relationship among automobiles, suburbia, and shopping malls.	**Understand** Find meaning
2a. In the postwar era, what became the "fifth freedom"?	**2b.** What is ironic about Didion's "fifth freedom," considering the nature of the original four freedoms?	**Apply** Use information
3a. According to Didion, malls are the fusion of what two values or ideals?	**3b.** Explain how malls are particularly American, given this fusion.	**Analyze** Take things apart
4a. What was Didion's "dream life" when she worked at *Vogue* magazine?	**4b.** Argue whether Didion is being serious or ironic in saying that she thought about developing a mall.	**Evaluate** Make judgments
5a. What does Didion say about the items she purchased in Hawaii when the *New York Times* was not available?	**5b.** Write about how shopping malls and shoppers have changed since Didion wrote this essay in 1979.	**Create** Bring ideas together

Analyze Literature

Purpose and Irony

What purposes did Didion have in writing "On the Mall"? What seems to have been her primary purpose? Provide evidence from the selection to support your answer.

Discuss Didion's use of irony in this selection. For instance, what is ironic about the names of the malls? How does Didion's use of irony relate to her purposes in writing?

Extend the Text

Writing Options

Creative Writing Write a thirty-second radio advertisement to promote an area mall. In your effort to persuade shoppers to come to the mall, appeal to the psychology of consumerism. Consider what the mall has to offer a variety of consumers.

Descriptive Writing Joan Didion reveals a good deal about herself in her discussion of malls, both through her distinct written *voice*, or personality, and her inclusion of details from her life. Write a one-page character sketch of Didion, citing details from the selection that portray her.

Collaborative Learning

Design a Mall With a small group, plan a shopping mall for your area. First, decide which stores and other attractions to include, and then figure out how to arrange them. For example, should similar kinds of stores be grouped in one area, or should they be scattered to encourage shoppers to walk around the mall? Map out your plan, using a large sheet of paper to show each level of the mall. Include a directory of stores and other facilities, and color-code or number them on the map.

Media Literacy

Hold a Discussion on Urban Sprawl Suburban planning, as it was practiced in the postwar United States, has been widely criticized as creating urban sprawl. In small groups, research the controversy surrounding the development of suburbs. Look into the environmental, economic, and cultural effects of urban sprawl. Find articles both against and in support of suburban development. Discuss the issue of urban sprawl as a class.

 Go to **www.mirrorsandwindows.com** for more.

Understand the Concept

In addition to using quotations to support your own ideas in an essay or report, you also can incorporate information from other sources by summarizing and paraphrasing. Developing these research skills will help you write a paper that demonstrates its validity by citing other sources and that also avoids **plagiarism,** which is using others' information or writing without crediting them.

Summarizing involves identifying the main point of a story, essay, or article. When you summarize, you condense the information, stating the general idea in your own words but leaving out the details. For instance, the second paragraph of Didion's "On the Mall" can be summarized in these two sentences:

EXAMPLE

The post–World War II era brought forth a new prosperity, represented by the automobile and the emergence of suburbia. Developers created shopping malls for Americans to enjoy their success and pursue the American dream.

When you **paraphrase** information, you essentially translate it, restating the text in your own words but maintaining the level of detail in the original. Consider this paraphrase of the first sentence in the same paragraph from Didion's essay:

EXAMPLES

Original sentence It was a peculiar and visionary time, those years after World War II to which all the Malls and Towns and Dales stand as climate-controlled monuments.

Paraphrase The many malls built after World War II are representative of the values of this unique and future-focused period in American history.

Notice that in the paraphrase, words are substituted and phrases are rearranged and simplified. The ideas being conveyed and the general level of detail are the same as in the original, however.

Summarizing is appropriate for incorporating information from sources that provide general or background information. Paraphrasing is appropriate for incorporating detailed information, such as facts and descriptions. Paraphrasing generally is preferable to quoting because you record the information in your own words. Doing so makes it easier to incorporate the information with the rest of your writing.

Whether you quote, paraphrase, or summarize information, you must document the original source of that information. (See the workshop on documentation on the following page.)

Apply the Skill

Use Summary

Write a two- or three-sentence summary of the sixth paragraph of Didion's "On the Mall," which begins "James B. Douglas and David D. Bohanon." Then exchange papers with a classmate to check that you have not missed the main ideas or included too many details.

Use Paraphrase

Paraphrase these sentences from Didion's essay. Again, exchange work with a classmate to get feedback on your accuracy.

1. "They are toy garden cities in which no one lives but everyone consumes, profound equalizers, the perfect fusion of the profit motive and the egalitarian ideal, and to hear their names is to recall words and phrases no longer quite current."
2. "I never met or even saw Jere Strizek, but at the age of 12 I imagined him a kind of frontiersman, a romantic and revolutionary spirit, and in the indigenous grain he was."
3. "One thing you will note about shopping-center theory is that you could have thought of it yourself, and a course in it will go a long way toward dispelling the notion that business proceeds from mysteries too recondite for you and me."
4. "The 'first' shopping center in the United States is generally agreed to be Country Club Plaza in Kansas City, built in the twenties."
5. "The developer of Country Club Plaza, J. C. Nichols, is referred to with ritual frequency in the literature of shopping centers, usually as 'pioneering J. C. Nichols' or 'J. C. Nichols, father of the center as we know it.'"

Understand the Concept

Many subject areas have their own systems of **documentation,** or citing sources. In English, the system is that of the Modern Language Association (MLA). MLA style has two components: (1) abbreviated citations of sources within the text of the paper and (2) a full listing of sources at the end of the paper.

To cite sources within the text, use **parenthetical citation**, in which a brief form of the source is provided in parentheses. Provide the author's last name and the page or pages that contain the information you are using. If you mention the author's name in your text, cite only the page or pages in parentheses.

To avoid plagiarism, cite sources for all the information you use from others' work. Follow these examples for citing information you quote, paraphrase, or summarize in your paper:

EXAMPLES

Quotation "It was a peculiar and visionary time, those years after World War II" (Didion 1263).

Paraphrase In her essay "On the Mall," Joan Didion describes the years after World War II as marked by an optimistic desire for progress and development (1263).

Summary Joan Didion's essay "On the Mall" relates the history and development of the American mall (1262-67).

The second component of MLA documentation is the **bibliography,** or list of sources. Called *Works Cited,* this list should include all the sources you cite in your paper arranged in alphabetical order.

Here are some examples of the information provided for common types of sources:

Book
Author name. *Title*. Place of Publication: Publisher, Year.
Smith, John. *The Science Behind Global Warming.* New York: Hutton House, 2007.

Article in scholarly journal
Author name. "Title of Article." *Journal* Volume number (Year): Pages.
Jones, Markesa. "Alternative Fuel Advancements." *Science Studies* 26 (2006): 1012-43.

Article in magazine
Author name. "Title." *Magazine* Date: Pages.
Singh, Rajiv. "Reducing Your Carbon Footprint." *Young Scientist* 22 April 2007: 34-41.

Website
Website name. Editor name (if available). Date of publication or last update. Name of sponsoring organization. Date accessed site <URL>.
GreenGuardian.com. 10 Jan. 2007. Solid Waste Management Coordinating Board. 27 May 2007 <http://www.greenguardian.com>.

See the *MLA Handbook for Writers of Research Papers* for additional examples of types of sources as well as complete Works Cited lists.

Apply the Skill

Identify and Use Correct Parenthetical Citation
For each of the following sentences, decide whether the parenthetical citation is correct. Rewrite the sentences that contain citation errors in correct form.

1. According to Didion, "The frontier had been reinvented, and its shape was the subdivision, that new free land on which all settlers could recast their lives *tabula rasa*" (Didion 1263).
2. Putting major stores at the ends or corners of a mall forces customers to pass by many small stores on their way back and forth (Didion 1266).
3. People in malls seem to move "in an aqueous suspension not only of light but of judgment, not only of judgment but 'personality'" (1267).
4. To attract shoppers to a new mall, developers recommend painting lines to create parking spaces that are bigger than normal. (Didion, p. 1265)
5. Throughout "On the Mall," Didion includes her own personal experiences with and reflections on malls (1262-67).

Create a Works Cited List
On a subject of your choosing, find one of each kind of source mentioned previously and write a Works Cited entry for it. Then compile the sources in a single Works Cited list.

Man Listening to Disc
The Blues

Lyric Poems by Billy Collins

Build Background

Cultural Context The following two poems by Billy Collins are about the appeal of jazz and the blues. In **"Man Listening to Disc,"** the speaker feels an intimate link to the players in the jazz combo he is listening to while he maneuvers through the crowded New York streets. The musicians the speaker mentions are well-known jazz performers whose improvisational style is playful and unconventional, much like Collins's poetry.

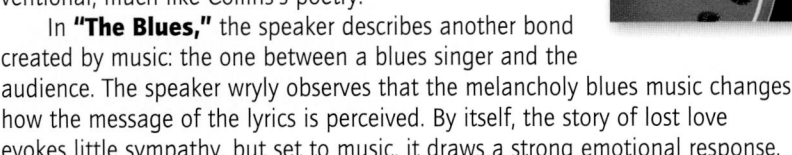

In **"The Blues,"** the speaker describes another bond created by music: the one between a blues singer and the audience. The speaker wryly observes that the melancholy blues music changes how the message of the lyrics is perceived. By itself, the story of lost love evokes little sympathy, but set to music, it draws a strong emotional response.

Reader's Context What do people respond to in music?

Meet the Author

Billy Collins (b. 1941) was born in New York City. An only child, he started writing "observational poems" at an early age and enjoyed reading contemporary poems in his father's *Poetry* magazine. His literary interests led him to pursue an English degree at the College of the Holy Cross in Massachusetts. After graduating in 1963, he attended the University of California, Riverside, where he earned a master's degree in 1965 and a doctorate in 1971.

As a budding poet, Collins wrote obscure, somewhat Confessional poetry. Upon realizing that poetry does not have to be complicated to be insightful, he adopted the simple, humorous, playful style for which he is known.

Collins's poems have appeared in *Poetry* magazine, *Harper's,* and the *New Yorker*. His collections include *Video Poems* (1980), *Questions about Angels* (1991), and *The Trouble with Poetry and Other Poems* (2005). He has received fellowships from the Guggenheim Foundation and the National Endowment for the Arts, and in 2001, he was named U.S. Poet Laureate. In that role, he spoke out against pretentious poets who equate a poem's value with its complexity, and he established *Poetry 180,* a collection of poems, one for each school day, to be read by high school students.

Collins is a Professor of English at Lehman College and a visiting writer at Sarah Lawrence College in New York. He performs poetry readings around the world and on National Public Radio.

Analyze Literature

Diction and Rhythm
Diction refers to the author's choice of words.

Rhythm is the pattern of beats or stresses in a line of verse, which can be regular or irregular.

Set Purpose

Collins's belief that poetry does not have to be complex to have substance is reflected clearly in his works. As you read his poems, think about the words he chooses. How does Collins's diction contribute to his easygoing style? Also analyze the rhythm in these selections. Determine whether each poem has a regular or irregular rhythm. Read the poems out loud to hear and feel the rhythm.

Preview Vocabulary

profusion, 1272
suffuse, 1272
unwieldy, 1273
cumbersome, 1273
aggregation, 1274
ardent, 1275
beseeching, 1275
acute, 1275

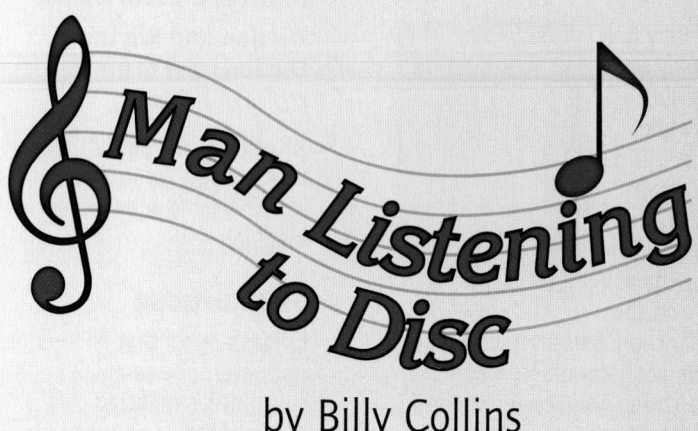
Man Listening to Disc

by Billy Collins

Thelonious Monk (c. 1950s).

This is not bad—
ambling along 44th Street[1]
with Sonny Rollins[2] for company,
his music flowing through the soft calipers
5   of these earphones,

as if he were right beside me
on this clear day in March,
the pavement sparkling with sunlight,
pigeons fluttering off the curb,
10 nodding over a <u>profusion</u> of bread crumbs.

---

1. **44th Street.** Starting here, the speaker walks through one of the busiest areas of Manhattan.
2. **Sonny Rollins** (b. 1930). Jazz tenor saxophone player

pro • fu • sion (prō fyü´ zhən) *n.*, great amount or number

In fact, I would say
my delight at being <u>suffused</u>
with phrases from his saxophone—
some like honey, some like vinegar—
15   is surpassed only by my gratitude

to Tommy Potter[3] for taking the time
to join us on this breezy afternoon
with his most <u>unwieldy</u> bass
and to the esteemed Arthur Taylor[4]
20   who is somehow managing to navigate

this crowd with his <u>cumbersome</u> drums.
And I bow deeply to Thelonious Monk[5]
for figuring out a way
to motorize—or whatever—his huge piano
25   so he could be with us today.

The music is loud yet so confidential
I cannot help feeling even more
like the center of the universe
than usual as I walk along to a rapid
30   little version of "The Way You Look Tonight,"[6]

and all I can say to my fellow pedestrians,
to the woman in the white sweater,
the man in the tan raincoat and the heavy glasses,
who mistake themselves for the center of the universe—
35   all I can say is watch your step

---

3. **Tommy Potter** (1918–1988). Jazz string bass player
4. **Arthur Taylor** (1929–1995). Jazz drummer
5. **Thelonious Monk** (1917–1982). Jazz pianist and composer
6. **"The Way You Look Tonight."** A composition by Jerome Kern and Dorothy
   Fields from the musical *Swing Time*, which won the Academy Award for best
   song in 1936. This piece is considered a jazz standard and has been recorded
   by many well-known artists.

suf • fuse (sə fyüz´) *v.*, spread through; fill
un • wieldy (un wēld´ ē) *adj.*, not easy to carry or handle
cum • ber • some (kum´ bər sum) *adj.*, hard to move or carry due to bulk
   or heaviness

because the five of us, instruments and all,
are about to angle over
to the south side of the street
and then, in our own tightly knit way,
40   turn the corner at Sixth Avenue.

And if any of you are curious
about where this <u>aggregation</u>,
this whole battery-powered crew,
is headed, let us just say
45   that the real center of the universe,

the only true point of view,
is full of the hope that he,
the hub of the cosmos
with his hair blown sideways,
50   will eventually make it all the way downtown. ❖

ag • gre • ga • tion (aˈ grə gāˊ shən) *n.,* group or collection

MIRRORS & **W**INDOWS
Listening to music makes the speaker feel "like the center of the universe." How does music affect your outlook or mood? Do you listen to specific songs or artists when you are in certain moods?

by Billy Collins

Red Hot Blues, 1998. Patti Mollica.
Private collection.

Much of what is said here
must be said twice,
a reminder that no one
takes an immediate interest in the pain of others.

5 Nobody will listen, it would seem,
if you simply admit
your baby left you early this morning
she didn't even stop to say good-bye.

But if you sing it again
10 with the help of the band
which will now lift you to a higher,
more <u>ardent</u> and <u>beseeching</u> key,

people will not only listen;
they will shift to the sympathetic
15 edges of their chairs,
moved to such <u>acute</u> anticipation

---

ar • dent (är´ dənt) *adj.,* passionate
be • seech • ing (bē sēch´ iŋ) *adj.,* begging or imploring
acute (ä kyüt´) *adj.,* sharp

by that chord and the delay that follows,
they will not be able to sleep
unless you release with one finger
20   a scream from the throat of your guitar

and turn your head back to the microphone
to let them know
you're a hard-hearted man
but that woman's sure going to make you cry. ❖

How does putting words to music make them more powerful? What does this say about the purpose of music? What does music bring to people's lives?

MUSIC CONNECTION

History of the Blues

The musical genre known as *the blues* emerged during the late nineteenth century from African-American communities in the lower Mississippi Delta. The music evolved in large part from slave spirituals, which were rooted in West and Central African musical traditions. The mournful, or "blue," melody and lyrics of this music expressed the discontent African Americans felt toward life in the Deep South, where the oppressive legacy of slavery was still prevalent.

The most common form of early blues music was the *twelve-bar blues,* in which one verse comprises twelve measures (or bars) divided into three lines. The words usually are the same in the first two lines but change in the third, creating an *aab* pattern. Often, a problem is stated or a question is asked in lines 1 and 2, and it is answered in line 3. Blues music also has a characteristic three-chord pattern, which is repeated throughout the song.

The twelve-bar blues was made popular in the late 1800s by singers such as Ma Rainey, Bessie Smith, W. C. Handy, and Charley Patton, who were accompanied by acoustic instruments such as the guitar, banjo, and harmonica. Later musicians adapted this simple form to create several other musical genres. For instance, in New Orleans, early jazz artists played the twelve-bar blues on traditional instruments such as the clarinet, trumpet, and trombone.

The blues spread with the Great Migration in the early 1900s, when many African-American musicians moved to large northern cities. Artists such as Muddy Waters and Howlin' Wolf played the blues using electric guitars, basses, and pianos. Their sound influenced a new musical genre called *rock 'n roll,* which applied faster rhythms and more commercially appealing lyrics to the electrified blues form. Because of this, nearly every jazz and rock 'n roll artist has paid musical homage to the blues, directly or indirectly.

Refer to Text ▷ ▶ ▶ ▶ ▶ Reason with Text

1a. In "Man Listening to Disc," whom does the speaker say he has for company as he walks down the street? What is his "companion" doing?	**1b.** Identify the words and phrases the speaker uses to suggest that the musicians actually are with him.	**Understand** Find meaning
2a. In "The Blues," how will the audience respond if the singer admits his baby has left him without even saying good-bye?	**2b.** How is blues music well suited to the topics of love and loss?	**Apply** Use information
3a. In stanza 6 of "Man Listening to Disc," whom does the speaker say is "the center of the universe"? In stanza 7, whom does he say "mistake themselves for the center of the universe"?	**3b.** Analyze what the speaker means by this contrast.	**Analyze** Take things apart
4a. In stanza 6 of "The Blues," what does the speaker say the singer should do?	**4b.** Identify the most and least important parts of the performance for the speaker.	**Evaluate** Make judgments
5a. In "Man Listening to Disc," where does the speaker say he is going?	**5b.** Explain the apparent contradiction between the speaker's self-description as "the hub of the cosmos" and his modest goal.	**Create** Bring ideas together

Analyze Literature

Diction and Rhythm

Describe Collins's diction in terms of its difficulty or complexity. Provide examples from the poems to support your description. How does Collins's choice of words contribute to his easygoing style?

How would you characterize the rhythm in Collins's poems? Does each poem have a regular or irregular rhythm? Again, provide details from the poems. How does the rhythm suit Collins's style?

Extend the Text

Writing Options

Creative Writing You have been invited to a *poetry slam,* a gathering in which participants read poems they have written. For the slam, write a poem about your favorite type of music or piece of music. Create rhythm in the poem by imitating the music you have in mind.

Expository Writing Music has a place in almost every culture. Choose a non-Western society (that is, a culture outside Europe and North America) and do simple research to learn about one type of music that is part of its culture. Summarize your findings in a paragraph.

Collaborative Learning

Create a Music Video With a group, create a music video that provides a visual representation of a song of your choosing. Some members of the group can write or select the music and lyrics, others can sing or play instruments, and still others can operate the camera. If you do not have the equipment to perform or record the song, then present a live performance with appropriate visual representation.

Media Literacy

Prepare a Public Service Announcement Some child psychologists suggest that babies who listen to classical music later may excel as students. Conduct research on the subject and, based on your findings, prepare a public service announcement (PSA) to be distributed to radio stations, local newspapers, and other media outlets in your area.

 Go to **www.mirrorsandwindows.com** for more.

Donald Hall

"The life we live eludes us as we live it."

Donald Hall (b. 1928) was born in New Haven, Connecticut, but spent many summers on his grandparents' farm in New Hampshire. He grew up in what he called a "literary household," in which poetry was read, recited, and discussed. He began writing at age twelve, and at age sixteen, he published his first poem.

Hall earned a bachelor's degree from Harvard University in 1951 and a second degree in literature from Oxford University in 1953. While at Oxford, he was awarded the university's prestigious Newdigate Prize, given to the best poem written in English. That poem, "Exiles," was included in his first collection, *Exiles and Marriages* (1955).

Hall taught at the University of Michigan, Ann Arbor, beginning in 1957 and divided his time between teaching and writing. While there, he met poet Jane Kenyon, whom he married in 1972. A few years later, the couple moved to Hall's grandparents' former homestead, Eagle Pond Farm, to focus on writing. Hall wrote short stories, plays, and essays, but poetry remained his first love.

Among Hall's fifteen poetry collections are *The Town of Hill* (1975); *The One Day* (1988), which won the National Book Critics Circle Award; *The Museum of Clear Ideas* (1996); and *White Apples and the Taste of Stone: Selected Poems, 1946–2006* (2006). His prose collections include *To Read Literature* (1980), *Fathers Playing Catch with Sons: Essays on Sport (Mostly Baseball)* (1985), and *Seasons at Eagle Pond* (1987).

Hall has received two Guggenheim fellowships and was named New Hampshire's Poet Laureate in 1984 and U.S. Poet Laureate in 2006, stepping down from that post in 2007. Committed to the craft of writing poetry, Hall admittedly is his worst critic, saying "I don't publish anything I haven't worked over 100 times." His writing style has been described as straightforward and sincere, and his subjects include rural New England, baseball, and love and loss.

In 1989, Hall was diagnosed with colon cancer. Sadly, while he was recovering, his wife developed leukemia and died in 1995. To express his anguish, Hall wrote *Without: Poems* (1998), a two-part collection that focuses on Kenyon's illness and death as well as Hall's grief and life after her death.

Hall continues to write at his farm and frequently performs poetry readings around the United States. He also is a writer-in-residence at Bennington College in Vermont.

Noted Works

Ox-Cart Man (children's book, 1979 Caldecott winner)

The Happy Man (1986)

The One Day (1988)

Without: Poems (1998)

The Painted Bed (2002)

White Apples and the Taste of Stone: Selected Poems 1946–2006 (2006)

Couplet: Old-Timers' Day, Fenway Park, 1 May 1982
Letter in Autumn

Lyric Poems by Donald Hall

Build Background

Literary Context Donald Hall has referred to baseball as "the preferred sport of American poets," and his love for the game is evident in several of his poems and prose works. This first selection, **"Couplet: Old-Timers' Day, Fenway Park, 1 May 1982,"** is part of Hall's latest poetry collection, *White Apples and the Taste of Stone: Selected Poems 1946–2006.* The poem captures the reunion of several former Boston Red Sox players as they play a nostalgic baseball game in their home stadium, Fenway Park.

The main title "Couplet" is ironic. The word **couplet** means two successive lines of poetry that rhyme; however, this poem is written in free verse with no rhyming pattern. Perhaps the couplet Hall had in mind was the juxtaposition of the aging athlete whose glory days were long past with the young athlete whose quickness and prowess on the diamond make him comparable to Achilles, the famed Greek warrior. This is a fitting analogy, as both "number nine" and Achilles fell from glory after being betrayed by their bodies.

The second poem, **"Letter in Autumn,"** is from the same collection. In this selection, Hall addresses a letter to his wife, poet Jane Kenyon, who died shortly before the poem was written. The poem is a kind of **elegy,** or poem of mourning, yet it contains many everyday references to the couple's life together: the names of family members and Gus the dog, a baseball game at the Kingdome stadium near Seattle, and Kenyon's scattered personal items at the farmhouse they shared. The intimate tone of this poem reveals Hall's loving relationship with his wife of twenty-three years, as well as his struggle with the heartache and sorrow he has felt since her passing. Hall finds comfort in the memories of their life together.

Reader's Context How do you handle loss? What helps you find comfort in difficult times?

Fenway Park in Boston, Massachusetts, opened on April 20, 1912, and is still the home of the Red Sox (1912).

Analyze Literature
Symbol and Mood
A **symbol** is anything that stands for or represents both itself and something else. A *conventional symbol* is one with traditional, widely recognized associations, such as doves to represent peace. A *personal,* or *idiosyncratic symbol* is one that assumes its secondary meaning because of the special way the writer uses it.

Mood, or atmosphere, is the emotion created in the reader by part or all of a literary work. The writer can evoke an emotional response in the reader by using descriptive language and sensory details.

Set Purpose
In the quote at the start of the Author Focus on the previous page, Hall suggests that life has meaning beyond the obvious or apparent. Consider how that notion might apply to his poetry, as well—particularly his use of symbols. As you read each poem, list the symbols you find, and note whether each is conventional or personal. Also consider the mood in each poem and how Hall uses sensory details and descriptions to create it.

Preview Vocabulary
armature, 1283
cadence, 1283

COUPLET

Old-Timers' Day, Fenway Park, 1 May 1982

by Donald Hall

When the tall puffy
figure wearing number
nine starts
late for the fly ball,
5 laboring forward
like a lame truckhorse
startled by a gartersnake,
—this old fellow
whose body we remember
10 as sleek and nervous
as a filly's—

and barely catches it
in his glove's
tip, we rise
15 and applaud weeping:
On a green field
we observe the ruin
of even the bravest
body, as Odysseus[1]
20 wept to glimpse
among shades the shadow
of Achilles.[2] ❖

---

1. **Odysseus.** In Greek mythology, an elderly hero who survives the Trojan War; known for his skills as a tactician, orator, and leader
2. **Achilles.** In Greek mythology, a young hero who dies after being wounded in the Trojan War; known for his physical prowess and daring, brash personality

MIRRORS & WINDOWS Why are professional athletes often revered as heroes? Are they good role models?

Autumn, Sussex, c. 1800s. Hercules Brabazon.
Victoria and Albert Museum, London, England.

Letter in Autumn

by Donald Hall

This first October of your death
I sit in my blue chair
looking out at late afternoon's
western light suffusing
5   its goldenrod yellow over
the barn's unpainted boards—
here where I sat each fall
watching you pull your summer's
garden up.

10   Yesterday
I cleaned out your Saab
to sell it. The dozen tapes
I mailed to Caroline.
I collected hairpins and hair ties.
15   In the Hill's Balsam[1] tin
where you kept silver for tolls
I found your collection
of slips from fortune cookies:
YOU ARE A FANTASTIC PERSON!
20   YOU ARE ONE OF THOSE PEOPLE
WHO GOES PLACES IN THEIR LIFE!

As I slept last night:
You leap from our compartment
in an underground railroad yard
25   and I follow; behind us the train
clatters and sways; I turn
and turn again to see you tugging
at a gold bugle welded
to a freight car; then you vanish
30   into the pitchy clanking dark.

Here I sit in my blue chair
not exactly watching Seattle
beat Denver in the Kingdome.[2]
Last autumn above Pill Hill
35   we looked from the eleventh floor
down at Puget Sound,[3]

---

1. **Hill's Balsam.** Line of cough-relief products that includes lozenges that come in a metal box, or tin
2. **Kingdome.** Indoor sports stadium in Seattle; home to the area's professional baseball, football, and basketball teams from 1976 to 2000, when it was demolished
3. **Pill Hill . . . Puget Sound.** *Pill Hill* is a nickname for the First Hill neighborhood in Seattle; the nickname comes from the many medical facilities in the area. *Puget Sound* is the body of water that connects Seattle with the Pacific Ocean, some fifty miles away; it is an estuary, where saltwater from the ocean mixes with freshwater from rainfall and runoff.

at Seattle's skyline,
and at the Kingdome scaffolded
for repair. From your armature

40 of tubes, you asked, "Perkins,[4]
am I going to live?"

                    When you died
in April, baseball took up
its cadences again

45 under the indoor ballpark's
patched and recovered ceiling.
You would have admired
the Mariners,[5] still hanging on
in October, like blue asters

50 surviving frost.

                    Sometimes
when I start to cry,
I wave it off: "I just
did that." When Andrew[6]

55 wearing a dark suit and necktie
telephones from his desk,
he cannot keep from crying.
When Philippa[7] weeps,
Allison at seven announces,

60 "The river is flowing."

---

4. **Perkins.** Hall's nickname
5. **Mariners.** Seattle's professional baseball team
6. **Andrew.** Hall's son by a previous marriage
7. **Philippa.** Hall's daughter by a previous marriage

arm • a • ture (ärm´ ə chər) *n.*, framework or
    defensive structure
ca • dence (kā´ dənts) *n.*, rhythmic motion or
    sequence

Gus[8] no longer searches for you,
but when Alice or Joyce[9] comes calling
he dances and sings. He brings us
one of your white slippers
65   from the bedroom.

        I cannot discard
your jeans or lotions or T-shirts.
I cannot disturb your tumbles
of scarves and floppy hats.
70   Lost unfinished things remain
on your desk, in your purse
or Shaker basket. Under a cushion
I discover your silver thimble.
Today when the telephone rang
75   I thought it was you.

At night when I go to bed
Gus drowses on the floor beside me.
I sleep where we lived and died
in the painted Victorian bed
80   under the tiny lights
you strung on the headboard
when you brought me home
from the hospital four years ago.
The lights still burned last April
85   early on a Saturday morning
while you died.

        At your grave
I find tribute: chrysanthemums,
cosmos, a pumpkin, and a poem
90   by a woman who "never knew you"
who asks, "Can you hear me Jane?"
There is an apple and a
heart-shaped pebble.

---

8. **Gus.** Hall and Kenyon's beloved dog
9. **Alice or Joyce.** Alice Mattison and Joyce Peseroff,
   friends of Jane Kenyon who helped finalize the
   volume of her work published after her death

> Looking south
> 95 from your stone, I gaze at the file
>   of eight enormous sugarmaples
>   that rage and flare in dark noon,
>   the air grainy with mist
>   like the rain of Seattle's winter.
> 100 The trees go on burning
>   without ravage of loss or disorder.
>   I wish you were that birch
>   rising from the clump behind you,
>   and I the gray oak alongside. ❖

MIRRORS & WINDOWS Many of the speaker's memories of his wife are associated with specific items, events, and times of year. Of whom do you have memories like this? Are these kinds of memories painful or comforting?

LITERARY CONNECTION

The U.S. Poet Laureate

In 1937, the U.S. Library of Congress followed in the tradition of Great Britain by creating the position of Poet Laureate to raise public awareness and appreciation of poetry. Each year, the Librarian of Congress appoints a Poet Laureate after consulting with literary critics and former laureates, and the honored individual generally fills the position from October to May.

The Poet Laureate receives a stipend of $35,000, which is intended for use in creating and supporting public poetry projects. However, few restrictions are imposed on how or where the money can be used, allowing each laureate to pursue his or her unique goals. For example, Joseph Brodsky, who served as Poet Laureate during 1991–1992, installed poetry in airports, supermarkets, and other public areas, whereas Gwendolyn Brooks (1985–1986) focused on encouraging elementary-age children to write poetry. In addition to these

projects, the Poet Laureate also holds public readings of his or her work and arranges for other poets to do the same.

In addition to Donald Hall, who served as Poet Laureate during 2006–2007, many of the poets featured in this book have served in this position: Robert Lowell (1947–1948), Elizabeth Bishop (1949–1950), William Carlos Williams (1952), Randall Jarrell (1956–1958), Robert Frost (1958–1959), William Stafford (1970–1971), Gwendolyn Brooks (1985–1986), Richard Wilbur (1987–1988), Rita Dove (1993–1995), Billy Collins (2001–2003), and Ted Kooser (2004–2006).

KENYON

Literature Connection

Jane Kenyon (1947–1995) was born in Ann Arbor, Michigan, and graduated from the University of Michigan. While there, she met and married writer and poet Donald Hall. Their marital and creative union was celebrated in Bill Moyers's Emmy Award–winning documentary *A Life Together* (1993). Kenyon's poetry reflects their intimate relationship, cherished farm life, and struggles with mortality. She is known for her simple, introspective verse and use of sensory details.

   "Let Evening Come" was first published in 1990 in a collection by the same title. The poem addresses the quiet acceptance of nature's cycle and the assurance that comfort can be found even in loss. Although the poem's inspiration was her husband's battle with cancer, its meaning became all too clear for Kenyon when she was diagnosed with leukemia soon thereafter.

Let Evening Come
by Jane Kenyon

Let the light of late afternoon
shine through chinks[1] in the barn, moving
up the bales as the sun moves down.

Let the cricket take up chafing[2]
5   as a woman takes up her needles
and her yarn. Let evening come.

---

1. **chinks.** Slits; openings
2. **chafing.** Rubbing together, as in the cricket's forewings,
   which produces a sound

Let dew collect on the hoe abandoned
in long grass. Let the stars appear
and the moon disclose her silver horn.

10 Let the fox go back to its sandy den.
Let the wind die down. Let the shed
go black inside. Let evening come.

To the bottle in the ditch, to the scoop
in the oats, to air in the lung
15 let evening come.

Let it come, as it will, and don't
be afraid. God does not leave us
comfortless, so let evening come. ❖

Review Questions

1. In stanza 2, to what does the speaker compare the cricket? Describe the mood created by this comparison.

2. Identify the word and phrase repeated in the poem. Explain how Kenyon's use of repetition affects the tone and general message of the poem.

3. List the physical objects the speaker mentions or describes. How does Kenyon use them to convey a sense of life on the farm? What might she be suggesting about life in general?

TEXT ^{TO} TEXT CONNECTION

Sometimes the speaker of a poem is the poet himself or herself, but sometimes the speaker is a voice assumed by the poet. What seems to be the case for "Let Evening Come" and for "Letter in Autumn"? Use details from each poem to support your analysis of the speaker.

Refer to Text ▶ ▶ ▶ ▶ ▶ Reason with Text

1a. In stanza 1 of "Couplet," what *simile,* or comparison using *like* or *as,* does the speaker use to describe the player's "laboring forward"?

1b. Explain what this simile suggests about the player.

Understand
Find meaning

2a. In stanzas 2 and 8 of "Letter in Autumn," what task does the speaker describe doing?

2b. How do the speaker's feelings about doing this task seem to change from stanza 2 to 8? What might explain this change?

Apply
Use information

3a. Describe how others are reacting to the death of the person the speaker is talking to in "Letter in Autumn"?

3b. Infer whether these people and pets bring comfort or sadness to the speaker.

Analyze
Take things apart

4a. In "Couplet," what is Odysseus's reaction to seeing the "shadow of Achilles"?

4b. Evaluate the effectiveness of the analogy between Odysseus's response to Achilles and the fans' reaction to player nine.

Evaluate
Make judgments

5a. In the final stanza of "Letter in Autumn," what does the speaker wish?

5b. Explain what the trees symbolize to the speaker.

Create
Bring ideas together

Analyze Literature

Symbol and Mood
What symbols did you find in each poem? Which are conventional, and which are personal? How does Hall use symbols to create meaning in each poem?

Describe the mood of each poem using one or two words. What sensory details and descriptions contribute to this mood? How are the two poems similar and different in mood?

Extend the Text

Writing Options
Creative Writing "Couplet" depicts baseball fans' response to a moment that is both exciting and sad. Write a one-paragraph description of an experience, real or imaginary, that evokes conflicting emotions. Use sensory details to describe the experience and how you feel about it.

Expository Writing Mood is a significant element in the poems by Hall and Kenyon. Write a comparison-and-contrast essay that examines how mood is created in these poems and how it affects your understanding and appreciation of the selections.

Collaborative Learning
Prepare a Tourist Map of Baseball Stadiums
With several classmates, research five or more of the United States' best-known baseball stadiums, such as Yankee Stadium, Fenway Park, Camden Yards, Wrigley Field, and any others you prefer. Write a short description of the history and features of each stadium. Then prepare a map showing where the stadiums are located.

Critical Literacy
Write a Poem Eliciting an Emotional Response
Connect with others emotionally by writing a poem that expresses your feelings about a real or imaginary event, place, or person. Begin by deciding on a topic and identifying the emotions you associate with it. Then write the poem, relating your feelings in a way others will find believable, touching, even comforting. Exchange poems with a partner, and discuss how effectively your works elicit the desired emotional response.

 Go to **www.mirrorsandwindows.com** for more.

1. Why might Hall have chosen the title "Couplet"?
  A. It essentially is a love poem.
  B. It emphasizes the baseball theme.
  C. It is a couplet in the modern poetic sense.
  D. It deals with the past and the present.
  E. It contrasts with the reference to Odysseus.

2. In "Couplet," why do the spectators "applaud weeping" when the baseball player catches the ball?
  A. The player has made the final out, winning the game for the home team.
  B. The crowd is impressed with the player's remarkable athletic ability.
  C. Given the player's age, it is harder for him to do now what he used to do with ease.
  D. The crowd remembers those who have died in war whom the player is representing.
  E. The player made a good catch, but the team still lost the game.

3. In "Couplet," the line "laboring forward / like a lame truckhorse / startled by a gartersnake" is an example of
  A. a metaphor.
  B. personification.
  C. irony.
  D. characterization.
  E. a simile.

4. What is the purpose of the allusion to Odysseus and Achilles at the end of "Couplet"?
  A. to compare classic mythological heroes to modern-day sports figures
  B. to sound more poetic
  C. to suggest that the ballplayer is Greek
  D. to give the poem a serious, thought-provoking ending
  E. to show the irony of modern heroes being sport figures, not warriors

5. In "Letter in Autumn," which of the following is the strongest indicator that the speaker's grief is still quite strong?
  A. He has cleaned out his deceased wife's car.
  B. When the phone rings, he thinks it's his wife.
  C. He cannot bring himself to get rid of her personal possessions.
  D. He has kept the lights on the headboard of the bed in which she died.
  E. He allows their dog to sleep on the floor beside him.

6. Each of the following can be deduced about the speaker's deceased wife except what?
  A. She enjoyed gardening.
  B. She often wore casual, fun clothes.
  C. She could sew.
  D. She was somewhat famous.
  E. Her death was unexpected.

7. Which of the following best describes the tone of "Let Evening Come"?
  A. bored
  B. ominous
  C. grateful
  D. regretful
  E. comforting

8. Which of the following most likely explains what is meant by "evening" in the Kenyon poem?
  A. disease
  B. blindness
  C. aging and death
  D. poverty
  E. boredom

9. Constructed Response: Discuss what Hall and Kenyon seem to appreciate about their lives, as portrayed in their poems. Do they appreciate the same things? Are the things they appreciate valued by most people? Cite evidence from the poems to support your discussion.

10. Constructed Response: Compare and contrast the themes about aging and death presented in these three poems. In each poem, is growing old portrayed in positive or negative terms? Is the notion of dying presented as comforting or frightening? Again, use details from the selections to support your analysis.

Learning to Love AMERICA

by Shirley Geok-lin Lim

Shirley Geok-lin Lim (b. 1944) was born in Melaka (also known as Malacca), in peninsular Malaysia, and came to the United States in the 1960s. She has taught English at the University of Hong Kong and the University of California, Santa Barbara. Her first collection of poems, *Crossing the Peninsula* (1980), won the Commonwealth Poetry Prize. In 1996, Lim published her memoirs in *Among the White Moon Faces,* which won the 1997 American Book Award. Lim also has written a number of scholarly works and a novel, *Joss and Gold* (2001).

Lim's poem **"Learning to Love America"** is from the collection *What the Fortune Teller Didn't Say* (1998). As you read the list of reasons "to love America," consider how the speaker feels about making the United States her home. What does the title suggest about the speaker's attitude?

because it has no pure products

because the Pacific Ocean sweeps along the coastline
because the water of the ocean is cold
and because land is better than ocean

5   because I say we rather than they

because I live in California
I have eaten fresh artichokes
and jacarandas bloom in April and May

because my senses have caught up with my body
10   my breath with the air it swallows
my hunger with my mouth

because I walk barefoot in my house

because I have nursed my son at my breast
because he is a strong American boy
15   because I have seen his eyes redden when he is asked who he is
because he answers I don't know

because to have a son is to have a country
because my son will bury me here
because countries are in our blood and we bleed them

20   because it is late and too late to change my mind
because it is time. ❖

The speaker says that "countries are in our blood and we bleed them." Is this a patriotic poem? What is your definition of *patriotism?*

Refer and Reason

1. What doesn't America have, according to the speaker? Infer why this is important to her.

2. Where in America does the speaker live? Summarize what she likes about living in this region of the country.

3. What does the speaker reveal about her son? How does having a child affect her sense of belonging or heritage?

Writing Options

1. Write your own version of this poem, describing how you feel about living in your city, town, state, or country. Include specific details about the place itself and the feelings and ideas you associate with it. Convey not only what you like but also what you have come to appreciate or accept about the place.

2. Write a paragraph discussing Lim's use of repetition in the poem. What does it suggest about the speaker's feelings? How does it contribute to the rhythm and sound of the poem?

 Go to **www.mirrorsandwindows.com** for more.

A Quilt of a Country

by Anna Quindlen

Anna Quindlen (b. 1952), a Philadelphia native, entered the field of journalism in 1974 after graduating from Barnard College. In 1977, she began a nearly twenty-year career at the *New York Times,* during which she would become one of only three women ever to be an op-ed (opinion-editorial) columnist for the prestigious paper. That column, "Public and Private," earned her a Pulitzer Prize for commentary in 1992. Quindlen left the *Times* in 1995 to be a full-time novelist and has published five best-selling novels. She also writes a biweekly column of social commentary for *Newsweek* magazine called "The Last Word."

"A Quilt of a Country" appeared in *Loud and Clear* (2004), one of several collections of Quindlen's newspaper and magazine columns. In this piece, Quindlen uses the metaphor of a quilt to discuss the diverse nature of the United States and suggests that the disaster of September 11, 2001, served, at least briefly, as a unifying event among Americans.

September 2001

America is an Improbable Idea. A mongrel nation built of ever-changing disparate parts, it is held together by a notion, the notion that all men are created equal, though everyone knows that most men consider themselves better than someone. "Of all the nations in the world, the United States was built in nobody's image," the historian Daniel Boorstin wrote. That's because it was built of bits and pieces that seem discordant,[1] like the crazy quilts that have been one of its great folk art forms, velvet and calico and checks and brocades.

Out of many, one. That is the ideal.

The reality is often quite different, a great national striving consisting frequently of failure. Many of the oft-told stories of the most pluralistic nation on earth are stories not of tolerance, but of bigotry. Slavery and sweatshops, the burning of crosses and the ostracism[2] of the other. Children learn in social studies class and in the news of the lynching of blacks, the denial of

Out of many, one. That is the ideal.

---

1. **discordant.** Showing lack of unity or harmony
2. **ostracism.** Exclusion of certain people or groups from certain privileges or social acceptance

Observers peruse the NAMES Project AIDS Memorial Quilt on the Mall in Washington, DC.

rights to women, the murders of gay men. It is difficult to know how to persuade them that this amounts to "crown thy good with brotherhood," that amid all the failures is something spectacularly successful. Perhaps they understand it at this moment, when enormous tragedy, as it so often does, demands a time of reflection on enormous blessings.

This is a nation founded on a conundrum,[3] what Mario Cuomo[4] has characterized as "community added to individualism." These two are our defining ideals; they are also in constant conflict. Historians today bemoan the ascendancy of a kind of prideful apartheid[5] in America, saying that the clinging to ethnicity, in background and custom, has undermined the concept of unity. These historians must have forgotten the past, or have gilded it. The New York of my children is no more Balkanized,[6]

probably less so, than the Philadelphia of my father, in which Jewish boys would walk several blocks out of their way to avoid the Irish divide of Chester Avenue. (I was the product of a mixed marriage, across barely bridgeable lines: an Italian girl, an Irish boy. How quaint it seems now, how incendiary[7] then.) The Brooklyn of Francie Nolan's famous tree,[8] the Newark of which Portnoy complained,[9] even

3. **conundrum.** Riddle; difficult question to answer
4. **Mario Cuomo.** Governor of New York (1983–1995)
5. **apartheid.** System of legalized discrimination against blacks in South Africa; segregation
6. **Balkanized.** Broken up into hostile units. The word comes from the Balkan Peninsula in southeastern Europe, which was divided into small states after World War I.
7. **incendiary.** Flammable; likely to lead to hostility
8. **Francie Nolan's famous tree.** Allusion to the novel *A Tree Grows in Brooklyn* (1943), by Betty Smith
9. **Portnoy complained.** Allusion to the novel *Portnoy's Complaint* (1969), by Philip Roth, about a Jewish family in Newark, New Jersey

Other countries with such divisions have in fact divided into new nations with new names, but not this one.

the uninflected WASP suburbs of Cheever's characters:[10] They are ghettos, pure and simple. Do the Cambodians and the Mexicans in California coexist less easily today than did the Irish and Italians of Massachusetts a century ago? You know the answer.

What is the point of this splintered whole? What is the point of a nation in which Arab cabbies chauffeur Jewish passengers through the streets of New York—and in which Jewish cabbies chauffeur Arab passengers, too, and yet speak in theory of hatred, one for the other? What is the point of a nation in which one part seems to be always on the verge of fisticuffs with another, blacks and whites, gays and straights, left and right, Pole and Chinese and Puerto Rican and Slovenian? Other countries with such divisions have in fact divided into new nations with new names, but not this one, impossibly interwoven even in its hostilities.

Once these disparate parts were held together by a common enemy, by the fault lines of world wars and the electrified fence of communism. With the end of the cold war, there was the creeping concern that without a focus for hatred and distrust, a sense of national identity would evaporate, that the left side of the hyphen—African-American, Mexican-American, Irish-American—would overwhelm the right. And slow-growing domestic traumas like economic unrest and increasing crime seemed more likely to emphasize division than community. Today the citizens of the United States have come together once more because of armed conflict and enemy attack. Terrorism has led to devastation—and unity.

Yet even in 1994, the overwhelming majority of those surveyed by the National Opinion Research Center agreed with this statement: "The U.S. is a unique country that stands for something special in the world." One of the things that it stands for is this vexing notion that a great nation can consist entirely of refugees from other nations, that people of different, even warring religions and cultures can live, if not side by side, then on either side of the country's Chester Avenues. Faced with this diversity there is little point in trying to isolate anything remotely resembling a national character, but there are two strains of behavior that, however tenuously,[11] abet[12] the concept of unity.

There is that Calvinist[13] undercurrent in the American psyche that loves the difficult, the demanding, that sees mastering the impossible, whether it be prairie or subway, as a test of character, and so glories in the struggle of this fractured coalescing.[14] And there is a grudging fairness among the citizens of the United

---

10. **WASP suburbs of Cheever's characters.** Allusion to the novels and stories by John Cheever (1912–1982), whose works focused on white Anglo-Saxon Protestants (WASPs)
11. **tenuously.** Without strength
12. **abet.** Help to accomplish
13. **Calvinist.** Referring to the religious teachings of French theologian and reformer John Calvin (1509–1564)
14. **coalescing.** Act of unifying or bringing together

States that eventually leads most to admit that, no matter what the English-only advocates try to suggest, the new immigrants are not so different from our own parents or grandparents. Leonel Castillo, former director of the Immigration and Naturalization Service and himself the grandson of Mexican immigrants, once told the writer Studs Terkel[15] proudly, "The old neighborhood Ma-Pa stores are still around. They are not Italian or Jewish or Eastern European any more. Ma and Pa are now Korean, Vietnamese, Iraqi, Jordanian, Latin American. They live in the store. They work seven days a week. Their kids are doing well in school. They're making it. Sound familiar?"

Tolerance is the word used most often when this kind of coexistence succeeds, but tolerance is a vanilla pudding word, standing for little more than the allowance of letting others live unremarked and unmolested. Pride seems excessive, given the American willingness to endlessly complain about them, them being whoever is new, different, unknown, or currently under suspicion. But patriotism is partly taking pride in this unlikely ability to throw all of us together in a country that across its length and breadth is as different as a dozen countries, and still be able to call it by one name. When photographs of the faces of all of those who died in the World Trade Center destruction are assembled in one place, it will be possible to trace in the skin color, the shape of the eyes and the noses, the texture of the hair, a map of the world. These are the representatives of a mongrel nation that somehow, at times like this, has one spirit. Like many improbable ideas, when it actually works, it's a wonder. ❖

---

15. **Studs Terkel** (b. 1912). Author, historian, and broadcaster

Quindlen describes the 9/11 terrorist attacks as leading to both "devastation" and "unity." Why do tragedies often bring people together? How can that sense of unity be retained after a tragedy has passed?

Refer and Reason

1. In what ways is the United States a "mongrel nation"? Explain why the metaphor of a quilt is more appropriate than the metaphor of a "melting pot" for describing contemporary American society.

2. Identify the "two strains of behavior" that help unify Americans, despite their clear differences. How do most Americans feel about immigrants, according to Quindlen?

3. What does the word *tolerance* mean, according to Quindlen? Explain how Quindlen relates *tolerance* to *patriotism*.

Writing Options

1. Create your own metaphor to characterize a group of people, perhaps in your school, neighborhood, or city or town. Write a one-page extended metaphor, in which you make a point-by-point comparison of a group of people with something else.

2. Quindlen offers a definition of patriotism near the end of the selection. Write a paragraph that defines this word from your perspective.

 Go to **www.mirrorsandwindows.com** for more.

Beloved by Toni Morrison

Toni Morrison's most famous novel begins in the years following the Civil War, when a mysterious and childlike stranger called "Beloved" appears on the doorstep of an emancipated family. Beloved quickly endears herself to Sethe, the family's matriarch, but a series of strange events bordering on the supernatural make other family members wary of the stranger's presence.

I Dream a World: Portraits of Black Women Who Changed America
by Brian Lanker

In this book, Pulitzer Prize–winning photographer Brian Lanker compiles his portraits of seventy-five African-American women, adding testimonies about their achievements. Lanker's subjects range from award-winning authors and law professors to single mothers and working-class heroines. This book functions as an art collection, a U.S. history textbook, and a poignant social commentary.

A People's History of the United States: 1492–Present by Howard Zinn

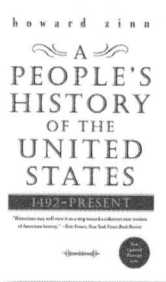

Historian Howard Zinn believes that U.S. history often is presented from an elite vantage point. In A People's History, Zinn recounts the United States' historical narrative through the eyes of those it traditionally has disinherited: African Americans, women, Native Americans, and the working class. Zinn's approach to studying history has reinvented the way Americans study the past and look toward the future.

A Prayer for Owen Meany
by John Irving

John Irving's heart-warming slapstick novel begins when the diminutive Owen Meany inadvertently kills his best friend's mother with a stray fly ball. Determined to redeem himself, Meany dedicates his life to achieving a goal that becomes clear at the end of the story. The journey along the way makes this an unforgettable story.

Fast Food Nation: The Dark Side of the All-American Meal by Eric Schlosser

Investigative journalist Eric Schlosser uncovers the social, biological, and political implications of the fast food industry in his book Fast Food Nation, which followed from a two-part article published in 1998 in Rolling Stone magazine. Based on three years of research, Schlosser's exposé exposed unsanitary food conditions, horrific slaughterhouse practices, and unfavorable hiring practices.

Into Thin Air: A Personal Account of the Mt. Everest Disaster
by Jon Krakauer

Mountaineer Jon Krakauer reveals the truth behind his fateful 1996 climb of Mount Everest, in which eight of his fellow climbers died and many others were critically injured. Thoroughly researched and skillfully written, Krakauer's narrative recreates the brutal conditions of the climb without being sensational or condemnatory. In addition, Krakauer raises thought-provoking questions about human nature and behavior in a crisis.

A common reason for giving a speech is to present an argument. In doing so, the speaker makes a case to the audience to accept or reject a proposition or course of action. For example, when political candidates give speeches, their goal is to convince voters to agree with their positions and elect them.

For your own persuasive speech, select a topic such as a school or community issue. Then develop an argument on the topic, gather details in support of the argument, and deliver a convincing speech. Your purpose in delivering a persuasive speech is the same as that in writing a persuasive essay: to convince others of your point of view. Keep that similarity in mind as you complete this workshop (see also the following Writing Workshop).

1. Prepare an Argument on a School or Community Issue

What school or community issues are of particular interest or concern to you? Maybe your school needs to update classroom technology, or maybe the city council needs to enhance the local road system to improve safety. Brainstorm a list of five or six topics for consideration. You might review the school or city newspaper for ideas.

In choosing a topic, remember that you must be able to support your view with convincing evidence, such as details, facts, opinions from authoritative people, and so on. Also, your argument should be of interest to your listeners, regardless of whether they agree with your position. Avoid choosing a topic that may have limited appeal.

2. Gather Information and Organize Your Presentation

After you have decided on a topic for your argument, locate supporting evidence. You already may know some relevant facts and details if your topic is one that has interested you for some time. Other evidence may be available from school or community media, such as newspaper, radio, and television reports.

As you gather evidence, evaluate its accuracy and objectivity. For instance, the information provided in editorials and political statements might help you understand different viewpoints on a topic, but it may well be biased or even incorrect. Look for current, accurate evidence from well-established organizations and individuals.

Organize the evidence in the way that will make your argument most convincing. Presenting your strongest piece of evidence last will ensure that you leave your audience with a strong sense of your argument.

Next, prepare a set of notes that follow your organizational plan (see Speaking & Listening Workshop, Unit 2). Also prepare visual aids such as photographs and charts that may help audience members grasp your argument (see Unit 5).

3. Practice Your Delivery

How you present yourself to your audience will determine in part whether they accept your proposition. Even listeners who agree with the ideas a speaker presents may be distracted or put off by a speaker's unconfident body language, such as lack of eye contact and slouching or nervous posture (see Unit 7). Similarly, a speaker whose voice sounds faint or otherwise uncertain will not be persuasive.

The more you practice your delivery, the more at ease you will feel in persuading listeners to accept your argument. Include your note cards and visual aids when you practice so you will learn to use them comfortably and confidently.

To get feedback about your presentation, practice in front of a mirror, ask a friend or family member to be your audience, or audiotape or videotape your delivery. As you practice, you may find you need to clarify your argument, strengthen your evidence, or make other changes.

SPEAKING & LISTENING RUBRIC

Your presentation will be evaluated on these elements:

Content

- ❏ You have formed an argument about a school or community issue.
- ❏ You have gathered and organized adequate supporting evidence.
- ❏ You have prepared notes and useful visual aids.

Delivery & Presentation

- ❏ Your body language and spoken manner convey confidence and authority.
- ❏ Your notes and visual aids are well handled and coordinated with your delivery.

As described in many of the selections in this unit, immigrants face a number of challenges when they come to live in the United States, such as learning to speak English and adapting to American life while maintaining their native cultural identity. The topic of immigration also generates discussion, even controversy, about social and political issues such as national security, citizenship, the economy, and public education.

In this assignment, you will write a research paper stating an argument about some aspect of contemporary immigration to the United States. You should defend your argument using information gathered from research and document your sources using Modern Language Association (MLA) format.

The fact that you are making an argument and supporting it with evidence makes the research paper a form of persuasive writing. In this sense, a research paper is different from an informational report, which presents information about a topic but does not take a stand on it.

Assignment Plan, write, and revise a research paper that presents an argument about immigration

Purpose To convince readers of your viewpoint

Audience Someone who disagrees with your viewpoint or has no opinion on the topic

---

WRITING RUBRIC

A successful research paper has these qualities:

- ❏ an introduction that generates interest and provides a context for the topic
- ❏ a thesis statement that clearly expresses the writer's argument about the issue
- ❏ a body that supports the thesis with detailed evidence gathered from research
- ❏ a conclusion that restates the thesis and makes a recommendation or call to action

❶ Prewrite

Select Your Topic

The general topic of your research paper—contemporary U.S. immigration—already has been decided for you. That likely will be the case for many of the research papers you write in high school and college. Whatever the general topic, you should narrow it further by identifying a more specific and thus manageable aspect about which to research and write.

Consider a few of the issues about immigration and the arguments surrounding them. Look through newspapers and magazines for ideas. Pay attention to discussions of immigration on television and radio programs. Do some key-word searches online. Talk to someone who has immigrated to the United States about his or her experience. Consider your own experience, if relevant. Narrow your focus to a specific aspect of contemporary immigration.

What Great Writers Do

Your purpose in writing a research paper is not to solve a problem. Rather, it is to become informed about a topic and make an argument that you can defend to others. As Friedrich Dürrenmatt, a twentieth-century Swiss author and dramatist, noted, "A writer doesn't solve problems. He allows them to emerge."

Gather Information

Begin your research by gathering background information on your topic. Although you already may have an opinion you plan to argue, look for information about all sides of the issue. Familiarizing yourself with the full range of perspectives on your topic will help you cover it completely and address opposing views when you write your paper.

Proceed from gathering general background to gathering increasingly specific information about your topic. Move from general sources, such as encyclopedias and popular magazines, to books and journals that focus more specifically on your topic. This should be a natural progression as you learn increasingly more about your topic.

As you begin research, develop a system for recording notes and tracking sources. Possible note-taking systems include writing information in a research notebook, entering it into your computer, and recording it on note cards. Whatever system you use, make sure it is flexible enough to allow you to access and organize the information later. Experienced researchers record information in small amounts on single pages in a notebook or computer file or on individual note cards.

> Tan, Amy   1
>   "Mother Tongue."
>   Mirrors & Windows
>   St. Paul, MN: EMC Publishing, 2008
>   pp. 1208-14
>   English classroom

What Great Writers Do

Writers from Mark Twain to H. G. Wells have commented on the misuse of statistical information. One common error is to use statistics out of context, presenting only the numbers that support the argument and ignoring inconsistent or contradictory information. Doing so makes it possible to prove almost any point with statistics. As stated by contemporary journalist Gregg Easterbrook, "Torture numbers, and they'll confess to anything."

BRANDEIS

Another common error is to use statistics that are from unreliable sources or based on questionable methods of research. Early twentieth-century Supreme Court Justice Louis D. Brandeis offered this example of the misuse of averages: "A man may have six meals one day and none the next, making an average of three meals per day, but that is not a good way to live."

Also keep track of the sources you consult in your research. Use the time-tested method of preparing a **working bibliography,** in which you record all the information needed to prepare the bibliography entry for each source. That information usually includes the author's first and last names, the title of the work, the details of its publication, and the page numbers. Record the information for each source on a separate note card, or keep a running list of sources in a note-book or computer file. You will use the information from your working bibliography later in preparing the final Works Cited list for your paper.

Many writers find it helpful to include several other details in the working bibliography. For instance, numbering the sources will help you keep track of what information came from which source (see example above). Assign a number to each new source you review, and then add that number to all the cards or pages of notes you take from that source. Another useful detail to record for each print source is where you found it—for instance, your school or local library. For a book from a library collection, include the call number, which identifies where the book is stored. Taking the time to record these details while you conduct research can save you valuable time later should you need to follow up on source information.

It is critical to put this note-taking/source-tracking system in place at the start of your research. Otherwise, you may waste considerable time later when you try to organize your information and write your paper. It is difficult, if not impossible, to retrace your steps and find missing source information.

Write Your Thesis Statement

You may have a good idea of the argument you plan to make when you start doing research. If not, gathering background information should help you develop a tentative argument. Use that argument to guide the direction you follow in your research. As noted earlier, your research should gather increasingly specific information from professional sources. The more focused your research becomes, the more focused and definitive your argument will become.

As you near completion of your research, fine-tune your argument by writing a **thesis statement.** Your thesis should be a sentence stating the specific argument you plan to prove in your research paper. That means you must be able to support the thesis using the information you gathered in your research. As you work on your thesis statement, evaluate your notes and do additional research to fill in any gaps in your support material.

One student, Nancy, began research with the idea of arguing that U.S. public schools should deliver instruction to all students in English. She changed her focus after background research revealed the benefits of immigrant students using their native language in the classroom. After conducting further research into the benefits of native language use, Nancy wrote this thesis statement:

Using native language in the classroom is necessary for immigrant students' academic success.

Organize Your Ideas

With your thesis in mind, organize the information you have gathered by creating an outline. This will serve as the blueprint or for writing the draft of your paper.

Begin by making a simple list of possible main points for your paper. Review your notes to look for recurring ideas or patterns. Try to identify three to five key ideas that can be supported by your research. For instance, Nancy realized she had gathered a lot of information about English language learners' difficulty learning academic content in English-only classrooms. She also had a lot of notes about these students becoming discouraged in school and losing their motivation for learning. By reviewing her notes further, she came up with several more general ideas. She recorded her ideas in the list shown at the top of the next column.

Next, review the ideas you have listed against your thesis statement. Determine whether each idea can be offered as evidence or proof of the thesis, and eliminate any ideas that cannot. In reviewing the points on her list, Nancy determined that discussing students' family and cultural identity was somewhat unrelated to her thesis about academic success, so she crossed it off the list. She also determined that her point about immigrants having functional language skills was off target and eliminated it from the list.

TOPIC: Native language use in the classroom

THESIS: Using native language in the classroom is necessary for immigrant students' academic success.

2 Using native language helps students feel secure in classroom

~~Using native language supports students' family and cultural identity~~

1 Having limited English skills hurts academic performance

3 Using native language enhances critical-thinking skills

~~Most immigrants have only functional English language skills~~

Finally, construct a **formal outline** of the body of your research paper. Follow the format shown below, which includes four levels of information. Each of the main ideas you identified should label a major division of the outline, as indicated with a roman numeral. Develop each main idea by adding subpoints, which are illustrated with examples and then specific details, as shown in the sample.

Remember the rule for outlining that "If you have an A, you must have a B." The logic underlying this rule is that it is impossible to divide something into just one subpart. Add subpoints to your outline only if you can create two or more under any given point.

Review your notes carefully to match the information with points in your outline. Again, make sure you can support every point you plan to make. Look for gaps in your notes and fill them in by doing additional research.

I. First main idea
  A. First subpoint
  B. Second subpoint
    1. First example
    2. Second example
      a. First detail
      b. Second detail

---

❷ Draft

Write your paper by following this three-part framework: Introduction, Body, and Conclusion.

Introduction Draw readers in by creating interest and providing context; then present your thesis statement.

Body Write at least one paragraph supporting each main idea of your argument.

Conclusion Restate your thesis and provide closure, perhaps issuing a call to action or recommendation.

Draft Your Introduction

The introduction to a research paper should draw readers in by introducing the topic with an interesting quote, shocking fact, or revealing anecdote. The introduction also should put the topic in a context to which readers can relate. Providing context gives readers a reason for wanting to know more. Finally, the introduction should include a thesis statement that presents the main argument to be made in the paper.

Draft Your Body

Devote at least one body paragraph to each main idea you offer in support of your argument. State that main idea in the topic sentence of the paragraph, and then explain it using the subpoints, examples, and details you recorded on your outline. Follow your outline as closely as possible as you draft your paper; make notes about any topics or points you may need to check on or expand.

Use the information you gathered in note taking accurately and with purpose. Avoid committing **plagiarism,** which is using others' information without crediting them. Follow these general guidelines for quoting, summarizing, and paraphrasing:

- **Quoting** involves repeating the exact words and punctuation from the original source. In selecting quotations to use in your paper, look for statements that are particularly well expressed and are made by recognized authorities on your topic.
- **Paraphrasing** is essentially translating information, restating the text in your own words but

maintaining the level of detail in the original. Paraphrasing is appropriate for incorporating details into your paper, such as facts and descriptions. Paraphrasing generally is preferable to quoting because you record the information in your own words..

- **Summarizing** involves stating the main idea of a source. When you summarize, you condense the information, presenting the main idea but leaving out the details. Summarizing is appropriate for incorporating information from sources that provide general or background information.

What Great Writers Do

Many writers make the mistake of using too many quotations in their work. Doing so makes it difficult to achieve a strong, consistent written style because the work is, in fact, a mixture of many people's writing. Overusing quotations may also imply that the writer is unable to state his or her own ideas and so repeats the ideas of others. Follow the advice of Transcendentalist writer Ralph Waldo Emerson, who wrote, "Stay at home in your mind. Don't recite other people's opinions. . . . Tell me what you know."

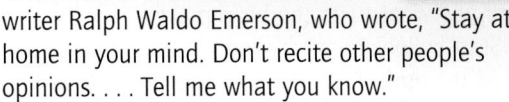
EMERSON

This does not mean you should never use quotations. Rather, use them with purpose, choosing expressions that are clever, eloquent, or simply well put. Use quotations to support your own ideas, not replace them. The originator of the essay, Renaissance French writer Michel de Montaigne, stated, "I quote others only in order the better to express myself."

As you write your draft, be sure to include the sources of the information you use within the body of the paper. To avoid plagiarism, you should cite sources for all the information you use from others' work, whether quoted, paraphrased, or summarized. Follow the **documentation** style of the Modern Language Association (MLA).

To cite sources within the text, use **parenthetical citation,** in which you add an abbreviated source reference in parentheses following the information from the source. Provide the author's last name and the page or pages that contain the information you are using. If you mention the author's name in your text, cite only the page or pages in parentheses.

Draft Your Conclusion

Finally, draft the conclusion for your research paper. A good conclusion should do two things: (1) restate the thesis and (2) wrap up the discussion, often by providing a recommendation or call to action.

Draft Your Works Cited Page

The final page of your research paper should provide a list of all the sources cited within it. Called *Works Cited,* this list should present the sources in alphabetical order. See the *MLA Handbook for Writers of Research Papers* for examples of types of sources as well as complete Works Cited lists.

❸ Revise

Evaluate Your Draft

Evaluate your own research paper, or exchange papers with a classmate and evaluate each other's work. Think carefully about what parts of the paper are sound and what parts can be improved.

Start by looking at the content and organization. Review the draft against the outline from which it was written. Make sure the body paragraphs work together to prove the thesis statement. Each main idea should be supported with subpoints, examples, and details, and information from researched sources should be documented. Review the Grammar & Style workshops in this unit to confirm the correct use of quotations, paraphrases, and summaries and to ensure the documentation style is correct.

Also review the introduction and conclusion to ensure you start and end the paper well. In a longer work such as a research paper, your introduction and conclusion may be somewhat more detailed and thus longer than in a shorter work, such as an essay.

Use the Revision Checklist above to help you evaluate the draft. Make notes directly on the paper about changes to be made.

REVISION CHECKLIST

Content & Organization

- ❏ Does the introduction draw readers in and provide a context for the topic?
- ❏ Does the thesis statement present a clear argument?
- ❏ Does each paragraph in the body state a main idea that connects to the thesis?
- ❏ Is the main idea in each body paragraph developed with supporting information?
- ❏ Is all information from researched sources properly documented using MLA format?
- ❏ Does the conclusion restate the main argument of the paper and bring it to a close by making a recommendation or call to action?

Grammar & Style

- ❏ Do you use quotations accurately and in appropriate instances? (see page 1176)
- ❏ Do you paraphrase and summarize information correctly and in appropriate instances? (see page 1269)
- ❏ Do you follow correct MLA style in your intext source citations and Works Cited list? (see page 1270)

Revise for Content, Organization, and Style

Nancy read over the draft of her research paper and found a number of things to improve:

- **Introduction:** To draw readers into her essay, Nancy added a short paragraph containing a quotation from Amy Tan's essay "Mother Tongue"; she also provided a parenthetical source citation. Nancy used Tan's mother as an example of the difficulties many immigrants experience because of having limited language skills.
- **Body:** After reviewing the body of her paper against her outline, Nancy decided to break up some long paragraphs. She created two paragraphs for several of her main ideas, breaking out the sub-

points (the A's and B's in her outline). Nancy also added the credentials for several of the people she quoted—for example, noting that Jim Cummins is an expert on language acquisition. Doing so highlighted these people's expertise and indicated why they were being quoted.

- **Conclusion:** Nancy felt that her paper ended too abruptly, without making any recommendation or call to action. She added several sentences focusing on the benefits associated with bilingual education and ended by recommending adoption of this educational model.

Read over the comments you or your partner made on your draft. Make appropriate changes as you revise your research paper.

Proofread for Errors

The purpose of proofreading is to check for remaining errors. Use proofreader's symbols to mark any errors you find. To complete the assignment, print out a final draft and read it aloud before turning it in. Doing so will allow you to catch any remaining errors.

Read Nancy's final draft on the next several pages. Note how she worked through the three stages of the writing process: Prewrite, Draft, and Revise.

A Note About the Student Model

The sample shown on the next few pages is intended to illustrate the basic elements of a research paper but in a condensed or abbreviated manner. The sample is considerably shorter than most research papers. See the bracketed notations within the body of the paper that indicate where additional examples and details normally would be provided.

In writing your own research paper, be sure to meet the length requirement identified by your instructor. Also be aware of any requirements for including a specific number or certain types of sources in your Works Cited list.

Writing Follow-Up

Publish & Present

- Explore your classmates' different viewpoints on the many issues associated with immigration. Hold debates on the topics students have written about in their research papers. Try to reach some consensus on what should be done to resolve current problems or prevent future ones.

- Submit your research paper to an online forum that discusses immigration issues.

Reflect

- How have your feelings on immigration changed since completing your research paper? Explain your answer.

- What kinds of programs and services for immigrants are in place in your school and community? What else could be done to help immigrants' transition to American society?

STUDENT MODEL

An Argument for Using Native Language in the Classroom
by Nancy Robinson

In the essay "Mother Tongue," Amy Tan describes the limited English skills of her mother, a Chinese immigrant, noting that "my mother had long realized the limitations of her English" (Tan 1211). Tan goes on to describe how her mother had to compensate for these limitations throughout her life.

How does the quotation draw readers into the paper?

This is the experience of many immigrants to the United States, who struggle to learn a new language while adapting to life in a new country. Immigrant children have the opportunity to learn English in the public schools, but educators do not agree on the best approach to teaching them. Some advocate total immersion in an English-only classroom, while others contend that students should be allowed to use their native language at least while they develop English language skills. Using native language in the classroom is necessary for immigrant students' academic success.

What context is provided for the topic? Why will readers want to know more?

What is the thesis statement?

Students who cannot speak English well enough to participate in the classroom will suffer academically. Teachers report that when students are not allowed to use their native language, they often repeat what they have heard without actually understanding the concepts (Dahlberg 11). Doing so affects their ability to learn not only English but content in other subject areas, as well. [Add examples and details]

What is the main idea of this paragraph? What support information is paraphrased and documented?

Results from standardized tests demonstrate that many English language learners lag behind their peers in academic achievement (Leonard and Rivera 212-13). [Add examples and details]

Students who are allowed to use their native language in the classroom feel a greater sense of security, which enhances their ability to learn. Third-grade teacher Debbie Walsh, who teaches in a bilingual program in Miami, Florida, strongly believes that "children need to know they can ask for help, explain problems, say how they feel, and so on" (*Teacher Talk*). For many children, doing so requires using their native language, at least early on. [Add examples and details]

What is the main idea of this paragraph? Does it relate clearly to the thesis statement?

Students who are discouraged from speaking their native language may feel personally rejected. According to Professor Jim Cummins, an expert on language acquisition, "When [students] feel this rejection, they are much less likely to participate actively and confidently in classroom instruction" (Cummins). It follows that students who do not or cannot participate in the classroom will lose their motivation for learning (Dahlberg 12). [Add examples and details]

Evaluate the use of the quotation here. What type of source is "Cummins"?

Allowing students to use their native language also enhances their critical-thinking skills, further boosting their academic achievement. Again quoting Cummins, "Bilingual children may develop more flexibility in their thinking as a result of processing information through two different languages" (Cummins). Research involving elementary-age students has shown that when children continue to develop skills in two or more languages, they have broader language skills and a better understanding of how to use language effectively (Leonard and Rivera 214-15). [**Add examples and details**]

Conversely, children who do not have regular opportunities to use their native language can lose their ability to speak it within two or three years of starting school (Cummins). [**Add examples and details**]

Allowing immigrant students to use their native language in the classroom is key to their academic success. Not only does native language use support students in developing English language skills and learning academic content, but it also gives them the confidence and motivation to participate in the classroom community. The critical-thinking abilities that have been proven to result from speaking multiple languages should encourage educators nationwide to adopt a bilingual model of education. Native and nonnative English speakers alike would benefit from that approach to instruction.

> What examples and details might be provided about the research mentioned?
>
> Where is the thesis restated?
>
> What recommendation or call to action is made?

Works Cited

Cummins, Jim. "Bilingual Children's Mother Tongue: Why Is It Important for Education?" 2003. 4 May 2008 <http://www.iteachilearn.com/cummins/mother.htm>.

Dahlberg, Joan S. "Pros and Cons of the English-Only (EO) Classroom." *ESL Journal* 29.2 (2006): 10-15.

Leonard, Martin, and Hector Rivera. "Language Skills and Achievement in the Content Areas." *English Teachers Journal* 65 (2004): 211-15. *ETJ Online.* 8 May 2008 <http://www.etj.com/leonard_rivera.htm>.

Tan, Amy. "Mother Tongue." *Mirrors & Windows: Connecting with Literature, American Tradition.* St. Paul, MN: EMC Publishing, 2008. 1208-14.

Teacher Talk. Ed. Debbie Walsh. 2007. 4 May 2008 <http://www.ttalk.org>.

> In what order are the sources arranged?
>
> What types of sources are included in this list?

Reading Skills

Evaluate an Argument

As explained in the previous workshops, an **argument** is a form of persuasion that makes a case for accepting or rejecting a proposition or course of action. To be a skilled reader, you need to know how to evaluate the argument an author is making. To do so, ask yourself these questions:

- Is the argument valid? That is, is it reasonable and logical? If not, where is the problem?
- Are the premises on which the argument is based true? Can you find cases in which the premises are not true?
- Is the author credible? Does he or she seem knowledgeable about the subject? Is he or she ethical and fair? Does the author connect with the audience? Does this connection seem positive, or do you feel manipulated by the author's approach?
- How much evidence does the author provide to support his or her position? What types of evidence does the author provide: mostly facts or mostly opinions? Does the author rely heavily on personal experience?
- Are the argument and support presented in a convincing way? What strategies does the author use? How effective are they?
- Is there a balance between reason and emotion? Does the author try to appeal to your sense of right and wrong, common feelings of nostalgia or pity, or the desire to be popular?
- Does the argument stay focused and on track, or does it wander? Does the author present irrelevant or vague issues to cover up some weakness in the argument and support?

TEST-TAKING TIP

When you take the reading comprehension section of a test, scan the questions about the passage before you actually read it. Doing so will help you identify particular topics to look for when reading. Then as you read the passage, make note of where you find these topics so you can refer back to them in answering the questions.

Practice

Directions: Read the following passage. The questions that come after it will ask you to evaluate the argument.

NONFICTION: This excerpt is from Daniel J. Boorstin's essay "Why I Am Optimistic About America."

You ask what is the basis for my optimism. With a Europe in disarray in a century plagued by two murderous World Wars, by genocides without precedent—the
5   German-Nazi massacre of six million and the Stalin-Soviet massacre of 30 million—how can I speak so hopefully about the American future?
One answer is very personal. I was
10   raised and went to public school in the 1920s in Tulsa, Okla., which then called itself "The Oil Capital of the World," but could perhaps have been called "The Optimism Capital of the World." . . .
15   My father was one of the most enthusiastic "boosters," and the growing city seemed to justify his extravagant optimism. I came to sympathize with that American frontier newspaperman who was attacked
20   for reporting as facts the mythic marvels of his upstart pioneer village—including its impressive hotel and prosperous Main Street. In America, he said, it was not fair to object to the rosy reports of community
25   boosters simply because they had "not yet gone through the formality of taking place." I suppose I have never been cured of my distinctively American Oklahoma optimism, bred in the bone and confirmed by the real
30   history of Tulsa.

Another reason for my optimism is in American history. The exhilarating features of our history and culture have in the past been captured in the idea of "American
35 Exceptionalism." This is a long word for a simple idea: the traditional belief that the United States is a very special place, unique in crucial ways. American Exceptionalism is a name too for a cosmopolitan, optimistic
40 and humanistic view of history—that the modern world, while profiting from the European inheritance, need not be imprisoned in Old World molds. And, therefore, that the future of the United States and of its
45 people need not be governed by the same expectations or plagued by the same problems that had afflicted people elsewhere.

How have we lost sight of this beacon? We have been seduced by the rise of
50 our country as a "superpower." For while power is quantitative, the uniqueness of the

United States is not merely quantitative. We have suffered, too, from the consequences of our freedom. Totalitarian societies exagger-
55 ate their virtues. But free societies like ours somehow seize the temptation to exaggerate their vices. The negativism of our press and television reporting are, of course, the best evidence of our freedom to scrutinize our-
60 selves. Far better this than the chauvinism of self-righteousness which has been the death of totalitarian empires in our time.

Yet we must never forget that, while to the Old World we were the Unexpected
65 Land, we have ever since been the Land of the Unexpected. The main features of the culture of our United States are just what the wise men of Europe, looking at their own past, could not have conjured up. A short list of
70 the American surprises includes what we have done here with four basic elements of culture—religion, language, law, and wealth. . . .

Multiple Choice

1. What is the thesis, or main idea, presented in this essay?
   A. People have different opinions on what is good and bad about the United States.
   B. The United States has surprised the world by what it has accomplished.
   C. There are many reasons to be optimistic about the United States' future.
   D. The United States has made advances in the areas of religion, language, law, and wealth.

2. What is the main purpose of the introductory paragraph?
   F. to describe the state of the world
   G. to acknowledge reasons for pessimism
   H. to establish the author's knowledge of world events
   J. to let readers know the time period in which this essay was written

3. Boorstin does all of the following *except* what to engage readers?
   A. addresses readers in a familiar way
   B. evokes fear to get readers to take his side
   C. includes an anecdote and details to which readers probably can relate
   D. appeals to emotions such as nostalgia and pride in the United States

4. This essay is different from many essays because
   F. it provides few facts as supporting evidence.
   G. it uses personal experience as evidence.
   H. it does not directly state a thesis.
   J. it evokes emotions in the audience.

Constructed Response

5. Evaluate one piece of evidence the author provides to support his thesis. Does it effectively support his position? Explain.

Writing Skills

Prepare for the Test

Take advantage of all the resources available to help you prepare for the test. A variety of test-prep study guides and Internet sites are available for most standardized tests, including the ACT, SAT, and Advancement Placement (AP) tests. These resources usually provide test-taking tips specific to the particular test. They also explain policies about scoring (such as whether points are deducted for wrong answers) and contain samples of questions and responses from various sections of the test.

Although these materials may be useful, reviewing them will not provide real practice in test taking. The best way to prepare for a test is to write practice essays in response to sample prompts. Only by practicing writing will you learn how to function in a timed situation. With practice, you will become accustomed to the time you should spend on each step in writing an essay. With enough practice, you will develop a built-in clock of sorts, so you will not need to check the time so often in an actual testing situation.

In preparing for the test, also think of all the things about test taking that make you feel anxious. Then think about ways to eliminate or reduce each source of stress. When you feel prepared, you will feel more in charge and less stressed. You will then be better able to stay focused and put forth your best effort.

TEST-TAKING TIP

When you reread what you have written, take a critical stance. Try to distance yourself and look at your writing objectively. Consider whether it will make sense to the reader. Don't assume that someone who is familiar with the topic will be able to infer what you mean if you don't clearly state it.

Practice

Timed Writing: 30 minutes

Some people are optimistic about the future of where they live. Based on their city's or state's history and the values of the people in the area, these optimists are confident of success. Others are pessimistic, contending that the future does not look bright at all. They point to serious social and economic problems and question the city's or state's ability to overcome them. Are you optimistic or pessimistic about the future of where you live?

In your essay, take a position on this question. You may write about either one of the two perspectives given, or you may present a different perspective on this question. Use specific reasons and examples to support your position.

Revising and Editing Skills

Some standardized tests ask you to read a draft of an essay and answer questions about how to improve it. As you read the draft, watch for errors such as these:

- incorrect spellings
- disagreement between subject and verb; inconsistent verb tense; incorrect forms for irregular verbs; sentence fragments and run-ons; double negatives; and incorrect use of frequently confused words, such as *affect* and *effect*

- missing end marks, incorrect comma use, and low-ercased proper nouns and proper adjectives
- unclear purpose, unclear main ideas, and lack of supporting details
- confusing order of ideas and missing transitions
- language that is inappropriate to the audience and purpose, and mood that is inappropriate for the purpose

After checking for errors, read each test question and decide which answer is best.

Practice

Directions: In the passage that follows, certain words and phrases are numbered and underlined. In the questions below the passage, alternatives are provided for each underlined word or phrase. In each case, choose the alternative that best expresses the idea, that is worded most consistently with the style and tone of the rest of the passage, or that makes the text correct according to the conventions of standard written English. If you think the original version is best, choose the first alternative, "MAKE NO CHANGE." To indicate your answer, circle the letter of the chosen alternative.

(1) I live in Amherst Massachusetts, and from what I have seen, the future here looks bright. (2) There is a lot of opportunities in this area, and its atmosphere is stimulating. (3) Most of the people I know have great dreams for the future; more importantly, they have the ability and motivation to attain they're goals. (4) Not only will they get what they want for themselves, they also may make the world an over all better place.

Multiple Choice

1. A. MAKE NO CHANGE.
   B. Amherst, Massachusetts, and from what I have seen, the future here looks bright.
   C. Amherst Massachusetts and, from what I have seen, the future here looks bright.
   D. Amherst Massachusetts, and from what I have seen, the future here looks brightly.

2. F. MAKE NO CHANGE.
   G. There is a lot of opportunities in this area, and it's
   H. Theirs a lot of opportunities in this area, and its
   J. There are a lot of opportunities in this area, and its

3. A. MAKE NO CHANGE.
   B. future, more importantly, they have the ability and motivation to attain they're
   C. future; more important, they have the ability and motivation to attain they're
   D. future; more important, they have the ability and motivation to attain their

4. F. MAKE NO CHANGE.
   G. themselves; they also may make the world an over all
   H. themselves, but they also may make the world an overall
   J. themselves, they also may make the world an over all

Language Arts Handbook

1 Reading Strategies & Skills

1.1 The Reading Process

The reading process begins before you actually start to read. All readers use a reading process, even if they don't think about it. By becoming aware of this process, you can become a more effective reader. The reading process can be broken down into three stages: before reading, during reading, and after reading.

BEFORE READING | DURING READING | AFTER READING

BUILD BACKGROUND

- Think about the **context** you as a reader bring to the selection based on your knowledge and experiences. What do you know about the topic? What do you want to know?

SET PURPOSE

- **Preview** the text to set a purpose for reading.

Skim the first few paragraphs and glance through the selection to figure out what it's about and who the main characters are. What can you learn from the art or photos?

USE READING SKILLS

- Apply **reading skills** such as determining the author's purpose, analyzing text structure, and previewing new vocabulary.

BEFORE READING | DURING READING | AFTER READING

USE READING STRATEGIES

- **Ask questions** about things that seem unusual or interesting, like why a character might have behaved in an unexpected way.
- **Visualize** by forming pictures in your mind to help you see the characters or actions.
- **Make predictions** about what's going to happen next. As you read, gather more clues that will either confirm or change your predictions.
- **Make inferences,** or educated guesses, about what is not stated directly. Things may be implied or hinted at, or they may be left out altogether.

- **Clarify** your understanding of what you read by rereading any difficult parts.

ANALYZE LITERATURE

- Determine what **literary elements** stand out as you read the selection. Ask whether the characters are engaging and lifelike. Determine if there is a strong central conflict or theme.

MAKE CONNECTIONS

- Notice where there are **connections** between the story and your life or the world beyond the story. Be aware of feelings or thoughts you have while reading the story.

BEFORE READING | DURING READING | AFTER READING

REFER TO TEXT

- Think about the facts. **Remember details** like characters' names, locations or settings, and any other things that you can recall.
- Determine the **sequence of events** or the order in which things happened.
- **Reread** the story to pick up any details you may have missed the first time around.
- Try to **summarize** the story in a sentence or two based on the events.

REASON WITH TEXT

- **Analyze** the text by breaking down information into smaller pieces and figuring out how those pieces fit into the story as a whole. Your knowledge of literary tools can help you analyze the author's technique.
- **Evaluate** the text. **Synthesize** and **draw conclusions** by bringing together what you have read and using it to make a decision or form an opinion. Decide if you agree with the author's views.

Framework for Reading

BEFORE READING

ASK YOURSELF

- [ ] What's my purpose for reading this?
- [ ] What is this going to be about?
- [ ] How is this information organized?
- [ ] What do I already know about the topic?
- [ ] How can I apply this information to my life?

DURING READING

ASK YOURSELF

- [ ] What is the best way to accomplish my purpose for reading?
- [ ] What do I want or need to find out while I'm reading?
- [ ] What is the essential information presented here?
- [ ] What is the importance of what I am reading?
- [ ] Do I understand what I just read?
- [ ] What can I do to make the meaning more clear?

AFTER READING

ASK YOURSELF

- [ ] What did I learn from what I have read?
- [ ] What is still confusing?
- [ ] What do I need to remember from my reading?
- [ ] What effect did this text have on me?
- [ ] What else do I want to know about this topic?

1.2 Using Reading Strategies

Reading actively means thinking about what you are reading as you read it. A **reading strategy,** or plan, helps you read actively and get more from your reading. The following strategies can be applied at each stage of the reading process: before, during, and after reading.

Reading Strategies

- Build Background
- Set Purpose
- Ask Questions
- Visualize
- Make Predictions
- Make Inferences
- Clarify
- Make Connections

1.3 Using Reading Skills

Using the following skills as you read helps you to become an independent, thoughtful, and active reader who can accomplish tasks evaluated on tests, particularly standardized tests.

Reading Skills

- Identify Author's Purpose and Approach
- Skim and Scan
- Find the Main Idea
- Determine Importance of Details
- Understand Literary Elements
- Meaning of Words
- Use Context Clues
- Take Notes
- Analyze Text Organization
- Identify Sequence of Events
- Compare and Contrast
- Evaluate Cause and Effect
- Classify and Reorganize Information
- Distinguish Fact from Opinion
- Identify Multiple Levels of Meaning
- Interpret Visual Aids
- Monitor Comprehension
- Summarize
- Draw Conclusions

2 Vocabulary & Spelling

2.1 Using Context Clues

You can often figure out the meaning of an unfamiliar word by using context clues. Context clues, or hints you gather from the words and sentences around the unfamiliar word, prevent you from having to look up every unknown word in the dictionary. The types of context clues include comparison, contrast, restatement, examples, and cause and effect. Refer to the Vocabulary & Spelling workshop, Context Clues, on page 435 for more instuction.

2.2 Word Parts

Many words are formed by adding prefixes and suffixes to main word parts called base words (if they can stand alone) or word roots (if they can't). A prefix is a letter or group of letters added to the beginning of a word to change its meaning. A suffix is a letter or group of letters added to the end of a word to change its meaning.

Word Part	Definition	Example
base word	main word part that can stand alone	form
word root	main word part that can't stand alone	struc
prefix	letter or group of letters added to the beginning of the word	pre–
suffix	letter or group of letters added to the end of the word	–tion

Refer to the Vocabulary & Spelling Workshop, Word Parts, on page 85 for more instruction.

2.3 Using a Dictionary

When you can't figure out a word using the strategies already described, or when the word is important to the meaning of the text and you want to make sure you have it right, use a dictionary. There are many parts to a dictionary entry. Study the following sample. Then read the explanations of each part of an entry below.

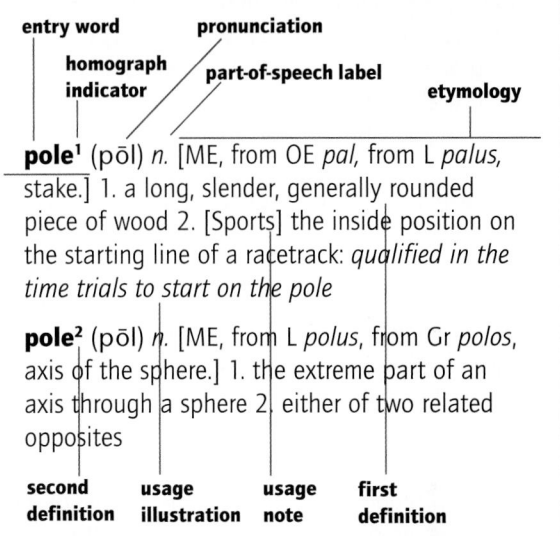

The **pronunciation** is given immediately after the entry word. The dictionary's table of contents will tell you where you can find a complete key to pronunciation symbols. In some dictionaries, a simplified pronunciation key is provided at the bottom of each page.

An abbreviation of the **part of speech** usually follows the pronunciation. This label tells how the word can be used. If a word can be used as more than one part of speech, a separate entry is provided for each part of speech.

An **etymology** is the history of the word. In the first entry, the word *pole* can be traced back through Middle English (ME) and Old English (OE) to the Latin (L) word *palus,* which means "stake." In the second entry, the word *pole* can be traced back through Middle English to the Latin word *polus,* which comes from the Greek (Gr) word *polos,* meaning "axis of the sphere."

Sometimes the entry will include a list of **synonyms,** or words that have the same or very similar meanings. The entry may also include a **usage illustration,** which is an example of how the word is used in context.

2.4 Understanding Multiple Meanings

Each definition in the entry gives a different meaning of the word. When a word has more than one meaning, the different definitions are numbered. The first definition in an entry is the most common meaning of the word, but you will have to choose the meaning that fits the context in which you have found the word. Try substituting each definition for the word until you find the one that makes the most sense. If you come across a word that doesn't seem to make sense in context, consider whether that word might have another, lesser known meaning. Can the word be used as more than one part of speech, for example, as either a noun or a verb? Does it have a broader meaning than the one that comes to your mind? For example, a line from *The Odyssey* reads "he gave me seven shining talents." The most common meaning of *talent* is "special skill or ability," but that doesn't fit here. Consulting the footnote at the bottom of the page, you would discover that the word *talent* can also refer to a type of old coin.

Keep in mind that some words not only have multiple meanings but also different pronunciations. Words that are spelled the same but are pronounced differently are called **homographs.**

2.5 Spelling

SPELLING RULES

Always check your writing for spelling errors, and try to recognize the words that give you more trouble than others. Use a dictionary when you find you have misspelled a word. Keep a list in a notebook of words that are difficult for you to spell. Write the words several times until you have memorized the correct spelling. Break down the word into syllables and carefully pronounce each individual syllable.

Some spelling problems occur when adding prefixes or suffixes to words or when making nouns plural. Other spelling problems occur when words follow certain patterns, such as those containing *ie/ei*. The following spelling rules can help you spell many words correctly.

SPELLING PATTERNS

The ie/ei Spelling Pattern

A word spelled with the letters *i* and *e* and has a long *e* sound is usually spelled *ie* except after the letter *c.*

EXAMPLES

belief	conceive
piece	receive
field	deceit

EXCEPTIONS

leisure	either

Use *ei* when the sound is not long *e.*

EXAMPLES

forfeit	surfeit	foreign	height

EXCEPTIONS

science	mischief	sieve

If the vowel combination has a long *a* sound (as in *eight*), always spell it with *ei.*

EXAMPLES

weight	vein	reign

When two vowels are pronounced separately in a word, spell them in the order of their pronunciation.

EXAMPLES

siesta	patio	diode	transient

The "Seed" Sound Pattern

The "seed" ending sound has three spellings: *–sede,* *–ceed,* and *–cede.*

EXAMPLES

Only one word ends in *–sede: supersede*

Three words end in *–ceed: proceed, succeed, exceed*

All other words end in *–cede: accede, concede, recede, precede, secede*

Silent Letters

Some spelling problems result from letters written but not heard when a word is spoken. Becoming familiar with the patterns in letter combinations containing silent letters will help you identify other words that fit the patterns.

- Silent *b* usually occurs with *m*.

EXAMPLES

dumb   bomb   climb   lamb

- Silent *b* also appears in *debt* and *doubt*.

- Silent *c* often appears with *s*.

EXAMPLES

scissors   scent   scenic   science

- Silent *g* often appears with *n*.

EXAMPLES

design   resign   gnome   foreign

- Silent *gh* often appears at the end of a word, either alone or in combination with *t (–ght)*.

EXAMPLES

fright   freight   sought   wrought

- Silent *h* appears at the beginning of some words.

EXAMPLES

hourly   heir   honestly   honor

- Silent *h* also appears in a few other words, as in *rhythm* and *ghost*.

- Silent *k* occurs with *n*.

EXAMPLES

knack   knight   knot   kneecap
knapsack

- Silent *n* occurs with *m* at the end of some words.

EXAMPLES

condemn   solemn   column   autumn

- Silent *p* occurs with *s* at the beginning of some words.

EXAMPLES

psyche   psychosis   psaltery   psoriasis

- Silent *s* occurs with *l* in some words.

EXAMPLES

island   islet   aisle

- Silent *t* occurs with *s* in a few words.

EXAMPLES

listen   hasten   nestle

- Silent *w* occurs at the beginnings of some words.

EXAMPLES

wreak   wrong   wraith   wrapper

- Silent *w* also occurs with *s* in a few words, such as *sword* and *answer*.

Letter Combinations

Some letter combinations have a different pronunciation when combined and can cause spelling problems.

- The letters *ph* produce the *f* sound.

EXAMPLES

sphinx   photograph   alphanumeric
phosphate

- The letters *gh* produce the *f* sound usually at the end of a word. (Otherwise, they are silent.)

EXAMPLES

cough   enough   neigh   weigh

- The letter combination *tch* sounds the same as *ch*.

EXAMPLES

sketch   pitch   snitch   hatch
such   hunch   grouch   torch

If the letters *c* and *g* have soft sounds (of *s* and *j*), they will usually be followed by *e, i,* or *y*.

EXAMPLES

cyclone	giant
circle	gyroscope
cent	region
regent	outrageous

If the letters *c* and *g* have hard sounds (of *k* and *g*), they will usually be followed by *a, o,* or *u*.

EXAMPLES

candid	gasket
congeal	engorge
convey	garland
conjugate	argument
cunning	gun

Numerals

Spell out numbers of *one hundred* or less and all numbers rounded to hundreds. Larger round numbers such as *seven thousand* or *three million* should also be spelled out.

EXAMPLES

Joe Morgan hit more than **twenty** home runs and stole at least **thirty** bases in the same season **four** times in his career.

Joe DiMaggio was the first baseball player to receive an annual salary of more than **a hundred thousand** dollars.

Use a hyphen to separate compound numbers from twenty-one through ninety-nine.

EXAMPLES

forty-two birds
seventy-four candles
one hundred soldiers
sixty thousand dollars

Use a hyphen in a fraction used as a modifier, but not in a fraction used as a noun.

EXAMPLES

The glass is **two-fifths full** of water.

After an hour, I had mowed **three fourths** of the backyard.

Use Arabic numerals for numbers greater than one hundred that are not rounded numbers.

EXAMPLES

Our company sent out **493,745** mailings in just **145** days this year.

My uncle boasted that he has read **1,323** books thus far in his life.

If a number appears at the beginning of a sentence, spell it out or rewrite the sentence.

EXAMPLES

incorrect
356 years ago, my ancestors moved to North America.
correct
Three hundred fifty-six years ago, my ancestors moved to North America.
correct
My ancestors moved to North America **356** years ago.

Use words to write the time unless you are writing the exact time (including the abbreviation AM or PM). When the word *o'clock* is used for time of day, express the number in words.

EXAMPLES

Our meeting will start at **a quarter after ten.**

At **eight-thirty,** the show will begin.

I was born at **5:22 PM** on a Monday.

You have until **three o'clock** to finish the proposal.

Use numerals to express dates, street numbers, room numbers, apartment numbers, telephone numbers, page numbers, exact amounts of money, scores, and percentages. Spell out the word *percent.* Round dollar or cent amounts of only a few words may be expressed in words.

EXAMPLES

May 27, 1962
(402) 555-1725
5219 Perret Street
pages 49–73
seventy cents
three hundred dollars
Apartment 655
38 percent
$1.6 billion (or $1,600,000,000)
$2,634

When you write a date, do not add *–st, –nd,* or *–th.*

EXAMPLES

incorrect
August 17th, 1968   November 5th
correct
August 17, 1968   November 5 or the
                      fifth of November

COMMON SPELLING ERRORS

Pronunciation is not always a reliable guide for spelling because words are not always spelled the way they are pronounced. However, by paying attention to both letters that spell sounds and letters that are silent, you can improve some aspects of your spelling. Always check a dictionary for the correct pronunciations and spellings of words that are new to your experience.

Extra Syllables

Sometimes people misspell a word because they include an extra syllable. For example, *arthritis* is easily misspelled if it is pronounced *artheritis,* with four syllables instead of three. Pay close attention to the number of syllables in these words.

EXAMPLES

two syllables

foundry   carriage   lonely

three syllables

privilege   boundary   separate

Omitted Sounds

Sometimes people misspell a word because they do not sound one or more letters when pronouncing the word. Be sure to include the underlined letters of these words even if you don't pronounce them.

EXAMPLES

barb<u>a</u>rous   can<u>d</u>idate   drown<u>e</u>d

gra<u>t</u>itude   gov<u>er</u>nor   groc<u>e</u>ry

literature   soph<u>o</u>more   quan<u>ti</u>ty

mischi<u>e</u>vous

Homophones

Words that have the same pronunciation but different spellings and meanings are called **homophones.** An incorrect choice can be confusing to your readers. Knowing the spelling and meaning of these groups of words will improve your spelling.

EXAMPLES

allowed/aloud   compliment/complement

sole/soul   alter/altar

hear/here   some/sum

ascent/assent   lead/led

threw/through   bear/bare

night/knight   wait/weight

brake/break   pair/pear

weak/week   buy/bye/by

peace/piece   who's/whose

capital/capitol   plain/plane

coarse/course   site/sight/cite

Commonly Confused Words

Some other groups of words are not homophones, but they are similar enough in sound and spelling to create confusion. Knowing the spelling and meaning of these groups of words will also improve your spelling.

EXAMPLES

access/excess   farther/further

nauseous/nauseated   accept/except

formally/formerly   passed/past

alternate/alternative   literal/literally

principle/principal   desert/dessert

loose/lose   stationary/stationery

3 Grammar & Style

3.1 The Sentence

THE SENTENCE

In the English language, the sentence is the basic unit of meaning. A **sentence** is a group of words that expresses a complete thought. Every sentence has two basic parts: a subject and a predicate. The **subject** tells whom or what the sentence is about. The **predicate** tells information about the subject.

EXAMPLE

> **sentence**
> The experienced detective **[subject]** |
> asked the suspect several questions **[predicate].**

FUNCTIONS OF SENTENCES

There are four different kinds of sentences: *declarative, interrogative, imperative,* and *exclamatory*. Each kind of sentence has a different purpose. You can vary the tone and mood of your writing by using the four different sentence types.

- A **declarative sentence** makes a statement. It ends with a period.

EXAMPLE

> Samantha is in the backyard trying to repair the lawnmower.

- An **interrogative sentence** asks a question. It ends with a question mark.

EXAMPLE

> Will she be joining you for supper later tonight?

- An **imperative sentence** gives an order or makes a request. It ends with a period or an exclamation point. An imperative sentence has an understood subject, most often *you*.

EXAMPLES

> (You) Please take a glass of lemonade to her.
> (You) Don't touch that sharp blade!

- An **exclamatory sentence** expresses strong feeling. It ends with an exclamation point.

EXAMPLE

> Samantha is a wizard at fixing lawnmowers!

SIMPLE AND COMPLETE SUBJECTS AND PREDICATES

In a sentence, the **simple subject** is the key word or words in the subject. The simple subject is usually a noun or a pronoun and does not include any modifiers. The **complete subject** includes the simple subject and all the words that modify it.

The **simple predicate** is the key verb or verb phrase that tells what the subject does, has, or is. The **complete predicate** includes the verb and all the words that modify it.

In the following sentence, a vertical line separates the complete subject and complete predicate. The simple subject is underlined once. The simple predicate is underlined twice.

EXAMPLE

> Bright orange <u>tongues</u> of flame **[complete subject]** |
> <u>danced</u> erratically in the center of the clearing **[complete predicate].**

Sometimes, the simple subject is also the complete subject, and the simple predicate or verb is also the complete predicate.

EXAMPLE

> <u>Falcons</u> | <u>swooped</u>.

To find the simple subject and simple predicate in a sentence, first break the sentence into its two basic parts: complete subject and complete predicate. Then, identify the simple predicate by asking yourself, "What is the action of this sentence?" Finally, identify the simple subject by asking yourself, "Who or what is performing the action?" In the following sentences, the complete predicate is in parentheses. The simple predicate, or verb, appears in boldface.

EXAMPLES

> **one-word verb**
> Your friend on the track team (**runs** swiftly.)
> **two-word verb**
> Your friend on the track team (**will run** swiftly in this race.)
> **three-word verb**
> All season long, your friend on the track team (**has been running** swiftly.)

four-word verb

If he hadn't twisted his ankle last week, your friend on the track team (**would have been running** swiftly today.)

COMPOUND SUBJECTS AND PREDICATES

A sentence may have more than one subject or predicate. A **compound subject** has two or more simple subjects that have the same predicate. The subjects are joined by the conjunction *and, or,* or *but.*

A **compound predicate** has two or more simple predicates, or verbs, that share the same subject. The verbs are connected by the conjunction *and, or,* or *but.*

EXAMPLES

compound subject

Pamela and Else | read their books in the library.

compound predicate

Four maniacal crows | watched and waited while I washed the car.

The conjunctions *either* and *or* and *neither* and *nor* can also join compound subjects or predicates.

EXAMPLES

compound subject

Either Peter *or* Paul | sings the national anthem before each game.
Neither yesterday *nor* today | seemed like a good time to start the project.

compound predicate

Her dogs | *either* heard *or* smelled the intruder in the basement.
The police inspector | *neither* visited *nor* called last night.

A sentence may also have a compound subject and a compound predicate.

EXAMPLE

compound subject and compound predicate

Mandy and Eric | grilled the hamburgers and made the coleslaw.

SENTENCE STRUCTURES

A **simple sentence** consists of one independent clause and no subordinate clauses. It may have a compound subject and a compound predicate. It may

also have any number of phrases. A simple sentence is sometimes called an independent clause because it can stand by itself.

EXAMPLES

Three bears emerged from the forest.

They spotted the campers and the hikers and decided to pay a visit.

The three bears enjoyed eating the campers' fish, sandwiches, and candy bars.

A **compound sentence** consists of two sentences joined by a semicolon or by a coordinating conjunction and a comma. Each part of the compound sentence has its own subject and verb. The most common coordinating conjunctions are *and, or, nor, for, but, so,* and *yet.*

EXAMPLES

Feeding bears is dangerous and unwise, **for** it creates larger problems in the long run.

Our zoo is home to two panda bears**;** they were originally captured in Asia.

A **complex sentence** consists of one independent clause and one or more subordinate clauses. The subordinate clauses in the examples below are underlined.

EXAMPLES

When you finish your report, remember to print it out on paper that contains 25 percent cotton fiber.

Jim will water the lawn after he returns home from the baseball game.

If you combine a compound sentence and a complex sentence, you form a **compound-complex sentence.** This kind of sentence must have two or more independent clauses and at least one subordinate clause. In the following examples, the subordinate clauses are underlined.

EXAMPLES

Rabbits, which like to nibble on the flowers, often visit my garden early in the morning, or they wait until early evening when the dog is inside the house.

Larry enthusiastically leaps out of bed each morning after his alarm clock rings, yet he often feels sleepy in the afternoon.

3.2 The Parts of Speech

IDENTIFYING THE PARTS OF SPEECH

Each word in a sentence performs a basic function or task. Words perform four basic tasks: they name, modify, express action or state of being, or link.

There are eight different parts of speech. Each part of speech is defined in the following chart.

Part of Speech	Definition	Example
noun	A **noun** names a person, place, thing, or idea.	**Apples, oranges,** and **potato chips** were the only **items** on the **list.**
pronoun	A **pronoun** is used in place of a noun.	Fanny whispered to **her** friend as **they** waited for **their** new teacher.
verb	A **verb** expresses action or a state of being.	Playful fox cubs **tumbled** out of the den and **chased** one another across the field.
adjective	An **adjective** modifies a noun or pronoun. The most common adjectives are the articles *a, an,* and *the.*	**Tattered** curtains hung in the **dark** windows of the **gray, sagging** house.
adverb	An **adverb** modifies a verb, an adjective, or another adverb.	**Sharply** turning to the left, the bicyclist **nearly** caused an accident.
preposition	A **preposition** shows the relationship between its object—a noun or a pronoun—and another word in a sentence. Common prepositions include *after, around, at, behind, beside, off, through, until, upon,* and *with.*	**During** winter, we often sit **by** the fireplace **in** the evening.
conjunction	A **conjunction** joins words or groups of words. Common conjunctions are *and, but, for, nor, or, so,* and *yet.*	**Neither** Grant **nor** Felix felt tired after two miles, **so** they ran another mile.
interjection	An **interjection** is a word used to express emotion. Common interjections are *oh, ah, well, hey,* and *wow.*	**Wow!** Did you see the dive he took from the high jump?

3.3 Nouns

NOUNS

A **noun** is a part of speech that names a person, place, idea, or thing. In this unit, you'll learn about the different kinds of nouns and what they name.

Types of Nouns	Definition	Example
common noun	names a person, place, idea, or thing	mother, garage, plan, flower
proper noun	names a specific person, place, or thing; begins with capital letter	John Adams, New York City, Monroe Doctrine
concrete noun	names a thing that can be touched, seen, heard, smelled, or tasted	ruler, mirror, giggle, garbage, banana
abstract noun	names an idea, a theory, a concept, or a feeling	approval, philosophy, faith, communism
singular noun	names one person, place, idea, or thing	governor, tree, thought, shoe
plural noun	names more than one thing	governors, trees, thoughts, shoes
possessive noun	shows ownership or possession of things or qualities	Jan's, Mrs. Wilson's, women's, intern's
compound noun	made up of two or more words	staircase, picnic table, brother-in-law
collective noun	names group	organization, platoon, team

GRAMMAR & STYLE

3.4 Pronouns

PRONOUNS

A **pronoun** is used in place of a noun. Sometimes a pronoun refers to a specific person or thing.

Pronouns can help your writing flow more smoothly. Without pronouns, your writing can sound awkward and repetitive.

The most commonly used pronouns are *personal pronouns, reflexive and intensive pronouns, demonstrative pronouns, indefinite pronouns, interrogative pronouns*, and *relative pronouns.*

Types of Pronouns	Definition	Examples
personal pronoun	used in place of the name of a person or thing	I, me, we, us, he, she, it, him, her, you, they, them
indefinite pronoun	points out a person, place, or thing, but not a specific or definite one	one, someone, anything, other, all, few, nobody
reflexive pronoun	refers back to a noun previously used; adds –self and –selves to other pronoun forms	myself, herself, yourself, themselves, ourselves
intensive pronoun	emphasizes a noun or a pronoun	me myself, he himself, you yourself, they themselves, we ourselves
interrogative pronoun	asks a question	who, whose, whom, what, which
demonstrative pronoun	points out a specific person, place, idea, or thing	this, these, that, those
relative pronoun	introduces an adjective clause	that, which, who, whose, whom
singular pronoun	used in place of the name of one person or thing	I, me, you, he, she, it, him, her
plural pronoun	used in place of more than one person or thing	we, us, you, they, them
possessive pronoun	shows ownership or possession	mine, yours, his, hers, ours, theirs

PRONOUNS AND ANTECEDENTS

The word that a pronoun stands for is called its **antecedent.** The antecedent clarifies the meaning of the pronoun. The pronoun may appear in the same sentence as its antecedent or in a following sentence.

EXAMPLES

number

singular	**Robert Frost** wrote many poems. "Stopping by Woods on a Snowy Evening" is perhaps **his** most well-known poem.
plural	The visiting **poets** were asked if **they** would give a reading on Saturday night.

gender

masculine	**Robert Frost** was born in California, but **he** was raised in Massachusetts and New Hampshire.
feminine	**Toni Morrison** begins **her** writing day before dawn.
neutral	The **poem** is titled "Birches," and **it** is one of my favorites.

PRONOUN CASES

Personal pronouns take on different forms—called *cases*—depending on how they are used in sentences. Personal pronouns can be used as subjects, direct objects, indirect objects, and objects of prepositions. In the English language, there are three case forms for personal pronouns: *nominative, objective,* and *possessive*. The following chart organizes personal pronouns by case, number, and person.

Personal Pronouns

	Nominative Case	Objective Case	Possessive Case
Singular			
first person	I	me	my, mine
second person	you	you	your, yours
third person	he, she, it	him, her, it	his, her, hers, its
Plural			
first person	we	us	our, ours
second person	you	you	your, yours
third person	they	them	their, theirs

Indefinite Pronouns

An **indefinite pronoun** points out a person, place, or thing, but not a particular or definite one. The indefinite pronouns are listed below.

Singular	Plural	Singular or Plural
another	both	all
anybody	few	any
anyone	many	more
anything	others	most
each	several	none
each other		some
either		
everybody		
everyone		
everything		
much		
neither		
nobody		
no one		
nothing		
one		
one another		
somebody		
someone		
something		

③⑤ Verbs

VERBS — PREDICATES

Every sentence can be divided into two parts: the **subject** and the **predicate.** The following sentence is divided between the complete subject and the complete predicate.

EXAMPLE

The tardy **student** | **raced** through the maze of hallways to class.

The subject of a sentence names whom or what the sentence is about. The predicate tells what the subject does, is, or has. A **verb** is the predicate without any complements, linkers, or modifiers. In other words, the verb is the simple predicate.

Verbs are the **expressers** of the English language. Verbs are used to express action or a state of being. They tell whether the action is completed, continuing, or will happen in the future. Verbs also express all kinds of conditions for the action. Verbs in the English language can be from one to four words long. When a main verb is preceded by one or more helping verbs, it is called a **verb phrase.**

EXAMPLES

Lauren **volunteers** at the food pantry.

Lauren **is volunteering** at the food pantry.

Lauren **has been volunteering** at the food pantry.

Lauren **might have been volunteering** at the food pantry.

The following chart lists the different types of verbs and their functions, along with examples of how they are used.

Type of Verb	Definition	Examples
action verb	names an action	howl, wobble, skitter, flutter, fly
helping verb	helps a main verb express action or a state of being	My dogs will howl when a siren sounds. A butterfly has been fluttering above the daisies.
linking verb	connects a noun with another noun, pronoun, or adjective that describes or identifies it; the most common linking verbs are formed from the verb *to be*	The butterfly is a monarch. It seems to float in the breeze.
transitive verb	has a direct object	The scientist remembered the secret code.
intransitive verb	does not have a direct object	My brother snores.
irregular verb	has a different past tense form and spelling	forget/forgot think/thought write/wrote

VERB TENSES

The Simple Tenses

Verbs have different forms, called **tenses,** which are used to tell the time in which an action takes place. The **simple tenses** of the verb are **present, past,** and **future.**

The **present tense** tells that an action happens now—in present time.

EXAMPLES

present tense singular
The short-order cook **flips** pancakes on the grill.

present tense plural
The short-order cooks **flip** pancakes on the grill.

The **past tense** tells that an action happened in the past—prior to the present time. The past tense of a regular verb is formed by adding *—d* or *—ed* to the present verb form.

EXAMPLES

past tense singular
The short-order cook **flipped** pancakes on the grill.

past tense plural
The short-order cooks **flipped** pancakes on the grill.

The **future tense** tells that an action will happen in the future. The future tense is formed by adding the word *will* or *shall* before the present verb form.

EXAMPLES

future tense singular
The short order cook **will (shall) flip** pancakes on the grill.

future tense plural
The short-order cooks **will (shall) flip** pancakes on the grill.

The Perfect Tenses

The **perfect tenses** of verbs also express present, past, and future time, but they show that the action continued and was completed over a period of time or that the action will be completed in the present or future. The perfect tense is formed by using *has, have,* or *had* with the past participle.

EXAMPLES

present perfect singular
Vincent **has watered** the garden. The garden **has been watered** by Vincent.

present perfect plural
Vincent and Lena **have watered** the garden. (have or has + past participle)

past perfect singular
Vincent **had watered** the garden yesterday. The garden **had been watered** yesterday by Vincent.

past perfect plural
Vincent and Lena **had watered** the garden yesterday. (had + past participle)

future perfect singular
Vincent **will have watered** the garden by now.

future perfect plural
Vincent and Lena **will have watered** the garden by now. (will have or shall have + past participle)

THE PROGRESSIVE AND EMPHATIC VERB FORMS

Each of the six tenses has another form called the progressive form. The **progressive form** of a verb is used to express continuing action or state of being. The progressive form is made of the appropriate tense of the verb *be* and the present participle of a verb.

EXAMPLES

present progressive
I **am singing.** He **is singing.** They **are singing.**

past progressive
I **was singing.** They **were singing.**

future progressive
I **will (shall) be singing.**

present perfect progressive
He **has been singing.** They **have been singing.**

past perfect progressive
I **had been singing.**

future perfect progressive
I **will (shall) have been singing.**

The **emphatic form** of a verb is used to express emphasis. Only the present and past tenses have the emphatic form.

EXAMPLES

present emphatic
I **do try** to be punctual.
It **does matter** to me.

past emphatic
I **did clean** my room.

3.6 Complements

COMPLEMENTS FOR ACTION VERBS

A sentence must have a subject and a verb to communicate its basic meaning. In the following sentences, the subject and verb express the total concept. There is no receiver of the verb's action.

EXAMPLES

The girls shopped.

Sandra seldom shouts.

The thunder boomed.

Many sentences that include action verbs, however, need an additional word or group of words to complete the meaning.

EXAMPLES

The musicians tuned.

The musicians tuned their instruments.

The group of words *The musicians tuned* contains a subject *(musicians)* and a verb *(tuned)*. Although the group of words may be considered a sentence, it does not express a complete thought. The word *instruments* completes the meaning expressed by the verb *tuned*. Therefore, *instruments* is called a **complement** or a completing word. The *completers* for action verbs are **direct objects** and **indirect objects.**

Direct Objects

A **direct object** receives the action in the sentence. It usually answers the question *what?* or *whom?* To find the direct object, find the action verb in the sentence. Then ask *what?* or *whom?* about the verb.

EXAMPLES

Sam **drove Jilly** to her mother's house. (*Drove* is the action verb. Whom did Sam drive? *Jilly* is the direct object.)

The coach **blew** her **whistle**. (*Blew* is the action verb. What did the coach blow? *Whistle* is the direct object.)

Remember to use object pronouns for a direct object.

singular me, you, him, her, it
plural us, you, them

EXAMPLES

Adam invited **us** to the party.

My dog follows **me** everywhere.

Indirect Objects

Sometimes the direct object is received by someone or something. This receiver is called the **indirect object.** It comes before the direct object and tells *to whom* the action is directed or *for whom* the action is performed. Only verbs that have direct objects can have indirect objects.

EXAMPLE

Lorelei **gave** the **teacher** her project. (*Gave* is the action verb. *Project* is the direct object because it tells what Lorelei gave. *Teacher* is an indirect object. It tells to whom Lorelei gave her project.)

To identify the indirect object: (1) Look for a noun or a pronoun that precedes the direct object. (2) Determine whether the word you think is a direct object seems to be the understood object of the preposition *to* or *for*.

COMPLEMENTS FOR LINKING VERBS

A **linking verb** connects a subject with a noun, a pronoun, or an adjective that describes it or identifies it. Linking verbs do not express action. Instead, they express state of being and need a noun, a pronoun or an adjective to complete the sentence meaning.

In each of the following sentences, the subject and verb would not be complete without the words that follow them.

EXAMPLES

Franklin D. Roosevelt **was** a popular president.

He **seemed** trustworthy and reliable.

Most linking verbs are forms of the verb *to be*, including *am, are, is, was,* and *been*. Other words that can be used as linking verbs include *appear, feel, grow, smell, taste, seem, sound, look, stay, feel, remain,* and *become*. When *to be* verbs are part of an action verb, they are helpers.

PREDICATE NOUNS AND PREDICATE PRONOUNS

A **predicate noun** is a noun that completes a sentence that uses a form of the verb *to be*. Similarly, a **predicate pronoun** is a pronoun that completes a sentence that uses a form of the verb *to be*. In fact, the relationship between the subject and the predicate noun or pronoun is so close that the sentence usually suggests an equation. Such sentences can often be reordered without changing the meaning.

EXAMPLES

> **predicate noun**
> Jacinta was the first girl to play on the boys' baseball team. (Jacinta = girl)
>
> The first girl to play on the boys' baseball team was Jacinta. (girl = Jacinta)
>
> **predicate pronoun**
> The friend who took me bowling was you. (friend = you)
>
> You were the friend who took me bowling. (You = friend)

To find a predicate noun or pronoun, ask the same question you would ask to find a direct object.

EXAMPLES

> My aunt is a great **chef.** (My aunt is a what? *Chef* is the predicate noun that renames or identifies *aunt,* the subject of the sentence.)
>
> The first contestant will probably be **you.** (The first contestant will be who? *You* is the predicate pronoun that renames or identifies contestant, the subject of the sentence.)
>
> The ticket taker at the booth was **she.** (Think: She was the ticket taker at the booth.)
>
> The leaders of the hike were Sara and **he.** (Think: Sara and he were the leaders of the hike.)

PREDICATE ADJECTIVES

A **predicate adjective** completes a sentence by modifying, or describing, the subject of a sentence. To find a predicate adjective, ask the same question you would ask to find a direct object.

EXAMPLE

> Your directions were **precise.** (Your directions were what? *Precise* is the predicate adjective that describes *directions,* the subject of the sentence.)

3.7 Modifiers

ADJECTIVES AND ADVERBS

Adjectives and adverbs—two kinds of **modifiers**—add meaning to nouns, adjectives, verbs, and adverbs. An **adjective** modifies a noun or a pronoun. An **adverb** modifies a verb, an adjective, or another adverb.

EXAMPLES

> **adjective**
> The **yellow** roses have rambled up the **wooden** trellis onto the roof.
> (*Yellow* modifies the noun *roses; wooden* modifies the noun *trellis.*)
>
> **adverb**
> The roses are **too** thorny to be trimmed.
> (*Too* modifies the adjective *thorny.*)
>
> The roses have grown **very** slowly, but they bloom **profusely** every spring.
> (*Very* modifies the adverb *slowly; profusely* modifies the verb *bloom.*)

To determine whether a modifier is an adjective or an adverb, you can follow these steps.
1. Look at the word that is modified.
2. Ask yourself, "Is this modified word a noun or a pronoun?" If the answer is yes, the modifier is an adjective. If the answer is no, the modifier is an adverb.

In the following example, the word *balloonist* is modified by the word *daring*. The word *balloonist* is a noun, so the word *daring* is an adjective.

EXAMPLE

> The **daring balloonist** traveled around the world.

In the next example, the word *landed* is modified by the word *safely*. The word *landed* is a verb; therefore, the word *safely* is an adverb.

EXAMPLE

> After surviving a storm at sea, the balloonist **landed safely** in Australia.

3.8 Prepositions and Conjunctions

PREPOSITIONS AND CONJUNCTIONS

Prepositions and conjunctions are the linkers of the English language. They are used to join words and phrases to the rest of a sentence. They also show the relationships between ideas. Prepositions and conjunctions help writers vary their sentences by connecting sentence parts in different ways.

A **preposition** is used to show how its object, a noun or a pronoun, is related to other words in the sentence. Some commonly used prepositions include *above, after, against, among, around, at, behind, beneath, beside, between, down, for, from, in, on, off, toward, through, to, until, upon,* and *with.*

EXAMPLES

A bright beacon led them safely **to** the shore.

He placed the book **beside** the bed.

A **conjunction** is a word used to link related words, groups of words, or sentences. Like a preposition, a conjunction shows the relationship between the words it links. Some of the most commonly used conjunctions are *and, but, for, nor, or, yet, so, if, after, because, before, although, unless, while,* and *when.* Some conjunctions are used in pairs, such as *both/and, neither/nor,* and *not only/but also.*

EXAMPLES

We went out for dinner **and** a movie on Saturday night.

They played poorly **because** they did not warm up before the game.

Neither I **nor** my brother inherited our mother's red hair.

Certain words can function as either conjunctions or prepositions. There are two important differences between a word used as a preposition and one used as a conjunction.

1. A preposition is always followed by an *object,* but a conjunction is not.

EXAMPLES

preposition
You may have a turn **after** your sister. (The noun *sister* is the object of the preposition *after.*)

conjunction
After you arrived, we had a wonderful time. (*After* is not followed by an object. It introduces a group of words, or clause, that depends on the rest of the sentence for meaning.)

2. A preposition introduces a prepositional phrase that connects parts of a sentence. A conjunction connects words or groups of words (clauses containing a subject and verb).

EXAMPLES

preposition
I never eat breakfast **before** exercising. (*Before* introduces the prepositional phrase *before exercising.*)

conjunction
Put on sunscreen **before** the swim meet begins. (*Before* introduces a clause, that is, a subject and verb, that modifies *put,* telling when to put on the sunscreen.)

3.9 Interjections

An **interjection** is a part of speech that expresses feeling, such as surprise, joy, relief, urgency, pain, or anger. Common interjections include *ah, aha, alas, bravo, dear me, goodness, great, ha, help, hey, hooray, hush, indeed, mercy, of course, oh, oops, ouch, phooey, really, say, see, ugh,* and *whew.*

EXAMPLES

Hey, that's not fair!

Goodness, you don't need to get so upset.

Hush! You'll wake the baby.

Why, of course! Please do join us for dinner.

Interjections actually indicate different degrees of emotion. They may express intense or sudden emotion, as in *Wow! That was unexpected.* Notice that the strong expression of emotion stands alone in the sentence and is followed by an exclamation point. Interjections can also express mild emotion, as in *Well, that is the best we could do.* In this sentence, the interjection is part of the sentence and is set off only with a comma. Even when interjections are part of a sentence, they do not relate grammatically to the rest of the sentence.

3.10 Phrases

A **phrase** is a group of words used as a single part of speech. A phrase lacks a subject, a verb, or both; therefore, it cannot be a sentence. There are three common kinds of phrases: prepositional phrases, verbal phrases, and appositive phrases.

PREPOSITIONAL PHRASES

A **prepositional phrase** consists of a preposition, its object, and any modifiers of that object. A prepositional phrase adds information to a sentence by relating its object to another word in the sentence. It may function as an adjective or an adverb.

EXAMPLES

adjectives

Sue planned a party **with music and dancing.** (The prepositional phrase *with music and dancing* tells what kind of party Sue planned. The phrase is used as an adjective, modifying the noun *party.*)

She found the CDs and tapes in a box **under her bed.** (The prepositional phrase *under her bed* tells in which box Sue found the CDs and tapes. The phrase is used as an adjective, modifying the object of the prepositional phrase *in a box.*)

adverbs

Albert struggled **into his jacket.** (The prepositional phrase *into his jacket* tells how Albert struggled. The phrase is used as an adverb, modifying the verb *struggled.*)

My friend is generous **with her time.** (The prepositional phrase *with her time* tells how the friend is generous. The phrase is used as an adverb, modifying the adjective *generous.*)

Use prepositional phrases to create sentence variety. When every sentence in a paragraph starts with its subject, the rhythm of the sentences becomes boring. Revise your sentences, where it is appropriate, to start some with prepositional phrases.

EXAMPLE

Chad stacked sandbags **for nearly eight hours.**

For nearly eight hours, Chad stacked sandbags.

3.11 Common Usage Problems

INCORRECT USE OF APOSTROPHES

Use an apostrophe to replace letters that have been left out in a contraction.

EXAMPLES

that's = that is
aren't = are not
we'll = we will

Use an apostrophe to show possession.

Singular Nouns

Use an apostrophe and an *s* (*'s*) to form the possessive of a singular noun, even if it ends in *s, x,* or *z.*

EXAMPLES

storm's damage
Chris's guitar
Max's spoon
jazz's history

Plural Nouns

Use an apostrophe and an *s* (*'s*) to form the possessive of a plural noun that does not end in *s.*

EXAMPLES

geese's flight
women's conference

Use an apostrophe alone to form the possessive of a plural noun that ends in *s.*

EXAMPLES

dolphins' migration
wheels' hubcaps

Do not add an apostrophe or *'s* to possessive personal pronouns: *mine, yours, his, hers, its, ours,* or *theirs.* They already show ownership.

EXAMPLES

His homework is finished; **mine** is not done yet.

The red house on the corner is **theirs.**

DOUBLE NEGATIVES

A **double negative** is the use of two negative words together when only one is needed. Correct double negatives by removing one of the negative words or by replacing one of the negative words with a positive word.

EXAMPLES

double negative
They can't hardly afford the plane tickets.

corrected sentence
They can hardly afford the plane tickets.
They can't afford the plane tickets.

double negative
Cassidy hasn't never read *The Call of the Wild.*

corrected sentence
Cassidy hasn't ever read *The Call of the Wild.*
Cassidy has never read *The Call of the Wild.*

DANGLING AND MISPLACED MODIFIERS

Place modifying phrases and clauses as close as possible to the words they modify; otherwise, your sentences may be unclear or unintentionally humorous.

A **dangling modifier** has nothing to modify because the word it would logically modify is not present in the sentence. In the following sentence, the modifying phrase has no logical object. The sentence says that a spider was reading.

EXAMPLE

Reading in his rocking chair, a spider was spotted on the wall.

You can eliminate dangling modifiers by rewriting the sentence so that an appropriate word is provided for the modifier to modify. You can also expand a dangling phrase into a full subordinate clause.

EXAMPLES

Reading in his rocking chair, he spotted a spider on the wall.

While Frank was reading in his rocking chair, he spotted a spider on the wall.

A **misplaced modifier** is located too far from the word it should modify.

EXAMPLE

Jennifer arrived home after the two-week training session on Friday.

You can revise a misplaced modifier by moving it closer to the word it modifies.

EXAMPLES

Jennifer arrived home on Friday after the two-week training session.

On Friday, Jennifer arrived home after the two-week training session.

SPLIT INFINITIVES

An infinitive, the base verb combined with *to,* should not be split under most circumstances. Infinitives such as *to save, to teach,* and *to hold* should not be interrupted by adverbs or other sentence components.

EXAMPLES

nonstandard
I began to seriously think about becoming a vegetarian.

standard
I began to think seriously about becoming a vegetarian.

In some cases, a modifier sounds awkward if it does not split the infinitive. In these situations, it may be best to reword the sentence to eliminate splitting the infinitive. In certain cases, you may want to use a split infinitive to clarify the meaning of the sentence.

Punctuation Reference Chart

Punctuation	Function	Examples
End Marks	tell the reader where a sentence ends and show the purpose of the sentence; periods are also used for abbreviations.	Our next-door neighbor is Mrs**.** Ryan**.**
Periods	with **declarative** sentences	The weather forecast predicts rain tonight**.**
	with **abbreviations**	
	personal names	**N.** Scott Momaday, **W. W.** Jacobs, Ursula **K.** Le Guin
	titles	**Mr.** Bruce Webber, **Mrs.** Harriet Cline, **Ms.** Steinem, **Dr.** Duvall, **Sen.** Hillary Clinton, **Gov.** George Pataki, **Capt.** Horatio Hornblower, **Prof.** Klaus
	business names	Tip Top Roofing **Co.**, Green **Bros.** Landscaping, Gigantic **Corp.**
	addresses	Oak **Dr.**, Grand **Blvd.**, Main **St.**, Kennedy **Pkwy.**, Prudential **Bldg.**
	geographical terms	Kensington, **Conn.**, San Francisco, **Calif.**, Canberra, **Aus.**
	time	2 **hrs.** 15 **min.**, **Thurs.** morning, **Jan.** 20, 21st **cent.**
	units of measurement	3 **tbsp.** olive oil 1/2 **c.** peanut butter 8 **oz.** milk 5 **ft.** 4 **in.** 20 **lbs.**
	exceptions: metric measurements, state names in postal addresses, or directional elements	**metric measurements** cc, ml, km, g, L **state postal codes** MN, WI, IA, NE, CA, NY **compass points** N, NW, S, SE
Question Marks	with **interrogative** sentences	May I have another serving of spaghetti**?**
Exclamation Points	with **exclamatory** sentences	Hey, be careful**!**
Commas	to separate words or groups of words within a sentence; to tell the reader to pause at certain spots in the sentence	Casey was confident he could hit a home run**,** but he struck out.
	to separate items in a series	The magician's costume included a **silk scarf, black satin hat,** and **magic wand.**
	to combine sentences using *and, but, or, nor, yet, so,* or *for*	An infestation of beetles threatened the summer squash and zucchini crops, **yet** the sturdy plants thrived. I'll apply an organic insecticide, **or** I'll ignore the garden pest problem.
	after an introductory word, phrase, or clause	**Surprisingly,** fashions from the 1970s are making a comeback. **Frayed and tight-fitting,** denim bellbottoms remain a fashion hit.

Punctuation	Function	Examples
	to set off words or phrases that interrupt sentences	Harpers Ferry**, a town in northeastern West Virginia,** was the site of John Brown's raid in 1859. The violent raid**, however,** frightened people in the North and South. **An abolitionist leader,** Brown was captured during the raid and later executed.
	between two or more adjectives that modify the same noun and that could be joined by *and*	A **warm,** [and] **spicy** aroma enticed us to enter the kitchen. Steaming bowls of chili satisfied the **tired,** [and] **hungry** travelers.
	to set off names used in direct address	**Olivia,** the zinnias and daisies need to be watered. Please remember to turn off the back porch light**, John.**
	to separate parts of a date	The United States Stock Exchange collapsed on October **28, 1929.** The stock market crash in October 1929 precipitated a severe economic crisis.
	to separate items in addresses	Gabriel García Márquez was born in **Aracataca, Colombia.** My brother will be moving to **1960 Jasmine Avenue, Liberty, Missouri 64068.**
Semicolons	to join two closely related sentences	It was a beautiful summer morning**;** we took advantage of it by going on a picnic.
	to join the independent clauses of a compound sentence if no coordinating conjunction is used	Marjory Stoneman Douglas was a pioneer conservationist. She formed a vigorous grassroots campaign to protect and restore the Everglades. Marjory Stoneman Douglas was a pioneer conservationist**;** she formed a vigorous grassroots campaign to protect and restore the Everglades.
	between independent clauses joined by a conjunction if either clause contains commas	Douglas was a writer, editor, publisher, and tireless advocate for the protection of the Everglades**;** and President Clinton awarded her the Medal of Freedom in 1993 for her work.
	between items in a series if the items contain commas	Members of Friends of the Everglades **wrote petitions; contacted local groups, political organizations, and governmental agencies; and gathered public support** for the restoration of the Everglades.
	between independent clauses joined by a conjunctive adverb or a transitional phrase	**conjunctive adverb** Starting in 1948, the Central and Southern Florida Project ditched and drained the Everglades**; consequently,** the four million acre wetland was reduced by half. **transitional phrase** Douglas knew that restoration of the Everglades would be a daunting task**; in other words,** she knew that it would take the combined efforts of local, state, and federal groups working in unison.
Colons	to mean "note what follows"	Make sure you have all your paperwork in order**:** passport, visa, and tickets.
	to introduce a list of items	*The Tragedy of Romeo and Juliet* explores **these dominant themes:** civil strife, revenge, love, and fate. The main characters in the play are **as follows:** Romeo, Juliet, Paris, Mercutio, Tybalt, and Friar Lawrence. The role of Juliet has been played by **the following actresses:** Norma Shearer, Susan Shentall, and Olivia Hussey.

Punctuation	Function	Examples
	to introduce a long or formal statement or a quotation	Shakespeare's prologue to *Romeo and Juliet* begins with **these memorable lines:** Two households, both alike in dignity, In fair Verona, where we lay our scene, From ancient grudge break to new mutiny, Where civil blood makes civil hands unclean. John Dryden made **the following remark about Shakespeare:** "He was the man who of all modern, and perhaps ancient poets, had the largest and most comprehensive soul." Nearly everyone recognizes **this line by Shakespeare:** "All the world's a stage."
	between two independent clauses when the second clause explains or summarizes the first clause	Shakespeare deserves the greatest of praise**:** his work has influenced and inspired millions of people over the centuries. For Romeo and Juliet, their love is star-crossed**:** If they tell their feuding parents of their love, they will be forbidden from seeing each other. On the other hand, by keeping their love secret, they follow a path that leads, tragically, to their deaths.
	between numbers that tell hours and minutes, after the greeting in a business letter, and between chapter and verse of religious works	Our English class meets Tuesdays and Thursdays from **9:00** AM to **10:00** AM Dear Juliet**:** Please meet me on the balcony at midnight. Ecclesiastes **3:1–8**
	not after a verb, between a preposition and its object(s), or after *because* or *as*	**after a verb** **incorrect** Three of Shakespeare's most famous plays are: *Romeo and Juliet, Macbeth,* and *Hamlet.* **correct** These are three of Shakespeare's most famous plays: *Romeo and Juliet, Macbeth,* and *Hamlet.* **between a preposition and its object(s)** **incorrect** I have seen performances of Shakespeare's plays in: London, New York, and Chicago. **correct** I have seen performances of Shakespeare's plays in the following cities: London, New York, and Chicago. **after *because* or *as*** **incorrect** Shakespeare was a great playwright because: he had an extraordinary skill in depicting human nature and the universal struggles all people experience. **correct** Shakespeare was a great playwright because he had an extraordinary skill in depicting human nature and the universal struggles all people experience.
Ellipsis Points	to show that material from a quotation or a quoted passage has been left out	"Doing something does not require discipline**...**it creates its own discipline."
	if material is left out at the beginning of a sentence or passage	**...**The very thought of hard work makes me queasy.
	if material is left out in the middle of a sentence	The very thought**...**makes me queasy.
	if material is left out at the end of a sentence	It's hard work, doing something with your life**....**I'd rather die in peace. Here we are, all equal and alike and none of us much to write home about**....**

Punctuation	Function	Examples
Apostrophes	to form the possessive case of a singular or plural noun	the **window's** ledge, **Carlos's** father, **jazz's** beginnings, **wolves'** howls, twenty-five **cents'** worth, **countries'** treaties, **students'** textbooks
	to show joint or separate ownership	**Zack and Josh's** experiment, **Lisa and Randall's** cabin, **Sarah's** and **Jason's** schedules, **Steve's** and **John's** trumpets
	to form the possessive of an indefinite pronoun	**anyone's** guess, **each other's** notes, **everybody's** dream
	to form a contraction to show where letters, words, or numerals have been omitted	**I'm** = I am **you're** = you are **she's** = she is **o'clock** = of the clock **they're** = they are
	to form the possessive of only the last word in a compound noun, such as the name of an organization or a business	brother-in-**law's** sense of humor; Teller, Teller, and **Teller's** law firm; Volunteer Nursing **Association's** office
	to form the possessive of an acronym	**NASA's** flight plan, **NATO's** alliances, **UNICEF's** contributions
	to form the plural of letters, numerals, and words referred to as words	two **A's**, **ABC's**, three **7's**, twelve **yes's**
	to show the missing numbers in a date	drought of **'02**, class of **'06**
Underlining and Italics	with titles of books, plays, long poems, periodicals, works of art, movies, radio and television series, videos, computer games, comic strips, and long musical works and recordings	**books:** *To Kill a Mockingbird, Silent Spring, Black Elk Speaks* **plays:** *The Tragedy of Romeo and Juliet, The Monsters Are Due on Maple Street* **long poems:** *Metamorphoses, The Odyssey* **periodicals:** *Sports Illustrated, Wall Street Journal, The Old Farmer's Almanac* **works of art:** *The Acrobat, In the Sky, The Teacup* **movies:** *Il Postino, North by Northwest, Cast Away* **radio/television series:** *Fresh Air, West Wing, Friends, Animal Planet* **videos:** *Yoga for Strength, Cooking with Julia, Wizard of Oz* **computer games:** *Empire Earth, Age of Wonders II* **comic strips:** *Zits, Foxtrot, Overboard* **long musical works/recordings:** *Requiem, Death and the Maiden, La Traviata*
	with the names of trains, ships, aircraft, and spacecraft	**trains:** *Sunset Limited* **ships:** *Titanic* **aircraft:** *Air Force One* **spacecraft:** *Apollo 13*
	with words, letters, symbols, and numerals referred to as such	The word *filigree* has a Latin root. People in western New York pronounce the letter *a* with a harsh, flat sound. The children learned that the symbol *+* is used in addition. Your phone number ends with four *7*'s.
	to set off foreign words or phrases that are not common in English	Did you know the word *amor* means "love"? The first Italian words I learned were *ciao* and *pronto*.
	to place emphasis on a word	Why is the soup *blue*? You're not going to borrow *my* car.

Punctuation	Function	Examples
Quotation Marks	at the beginning and end of a direct quotation	"Do you want to ride together to the concert?" asked Margaret. "Don't wait for me," sighed Lillian. "I'm running late as usual."
	to enclose the titles of short works such as short stories, poems, articles, essays, parts of books and periodicals, songs, and episodes of TV series	**short stories:** "Gwilan's Harp," "Everyday Use" **poems:** "Hanging Fire," "Mirror" **articles:** "Where Stars Are Born," "Ghost of Everest" **essays:** "Thinking Like a Mountain," "It's Not Talent; It's Just Work" **parts of books:** "The Obligation to Endure," "Best Sky Sights of the Next Century" **songs:** "At the Fair," "Johnny's Garden" **episodes of TV series:** "The Black Vera Wang," "Isaac and Ishmael"
	to set off slang, technical terms, unusual expressions, invented words, and dictionary definitions	We nicknamed our dog **"Monkey"** because he moves quickly and loves to play tricks. My mother says that **"groovy"** and **"cool"** were the slang words of her generation. Did you know that the word *incident* means **"a definite, distinct occurrence"**?
Hyphens	to make a compound word or compound expression	**compound nouns:** great-grandfather Schaefer, great-uncle Tom **compound adjectives used before a noun:** best-known novel, down-to-earth actor, real-life adventure **compound numbers:** ninety-nine years, twenty-five cents **spelled-out fractions:** one-half inch, three-fourths cup
	to divide an already hyphenated word at the hyphen	Finally, after much coaxing, our **great-grandfather** told his stories.
	to divide a word only between syllables	**incorrect:** After hiking in the woods, the novice ca-mpers became tired and hungry. **correct:** After hiking in the woods, the novice **camp-ers** became tired and hungry.
	with the prefixes *all-, ex-, great-, half-* and *self*, and with all prefixes before a proper noun or proper adjective	**all**-purpose, **ex**-husband, **pre**-Industrial age, **great**-grandparent, **half**-baked, **self**-expression
	with the suffixes *-free, -elect,* and *-style*	fragrance-**free** detergent, mayor-**elect** Kingston, Southern-**style** hospitality
Dashes	to show a sudden break or change in thought	"I say it did," replied the other. "There was no thought about it; I had just—What's the matter?"
	to mean *namely, that is,* or *in other words*	Our puppy knows only two commands—*sit* and *stay*. The hotel rates were surprisingly reasonable—less than a hundred dollars—for a double room.
Parentheses and Brackets	around material added to a sentence but not considered of major importance	Toni Cade Bambara (1939–1995) grew up in Harlem and Brooklyn, New York. The Taj Mahal (a majestic site!) is one man's tribute of love to his departed, beloved wife. More grocery stores are stocking natural food ingredients (for example, whole grains, soy products, and dried fruits).

Punctuation	Function	Examples
	to punctuate a parenthetical sentence contained within another sentence.	When the quilt is dry (it shouldn't take long), please fold it and put it in the linen closet. The piping-hot funnel cakes (they were covered with powdered sugar!) just melted in our mouths. The vitamin tablets (aren't you supposed to take one every morning?) provide high doses of vitamins A and E.
	to enclose words or phrases that interrupt the sentence and are not considered essential to meaning.	They took pasta salad and fruit (how could we have forgotten dessert?) to the summer concert.
	to enclose information that explains or clarifies a detail in quoted material	A literary critic praised the author's new book, "She [Martha Grimes] never fails to delight her devoted fans with witty dialogue, elegant prose, and a cast of characters we'd like to consider our friends." Another literary critic wrote, "[Martha] Grimes is the queen of the mystery genre."

4 Writing

4.1 The Writing Process

All writers—whether they are beginning writers, famous published writers, or somewhere in between—go through a process that leads to a complete piece of writing. The specifics of each writer's process may be unique, but for every writer, writing is a series of steps or stages.

The Writing Process

Stage	Tasks
1. Prewriting	Plan your writing: choose a topic, audience, purpose, and form; gather ideas; arrange them logically.
2. Drafting	Get your ideas down on paper.
3. Revising	Evaluate, or judge, the writing piece and suggest ways to improve it. Judging your own writing is called self-evaluation. Judging a classmate's writing is called peer evaluation.
	Work to improve the content, organization, and expression of your ideas.
	Proofread your writing for errors in spelling, grammar, capitalization, and punctuation. Correct these errors, make a final copy of your paper, and proofread it again.
Writing Follow-Up: Publish and Present	Share your work with an audience.
Reflect	Think through the writing process to determine what you learned as a writer, what you accomplished, and what you would like to strengthen the next time you write.

1 PREWRITE

In the prewriting stage of the writing process, you decide on a purpose, audience, topic, and form. You also begin to discover your voice and gather and organize ideas.

Prewriting Plan

Set Your Purpose	A **purpose,** or aim, is the goal that you want your writing to accomplish.
Identify Your Audience	An **audience** is the person or group of people intended to read what you write.
Find Your Voice	**Voice** is the quality of a work that tells you that one person wrote it.
Select Your Topic	A **topic** is simply something to write about. For example, you might write about a sports hero or about a cultural event in your community.
Select a Writing Form	A **form** is a kind of writing. For example, you might write a paragraph, an essay, a short story, a poem, or a news article.

Purpose and Mode of Writing

When you choose your mode and form of writing, think about what purpose or aim you are trying to accomplish. Your purpose for writing might be to inform, to tell a story, to describe something, or to convince others to see your viewpoint. Your writing might have more than one purpose. For example, a piece of writing might inform your readers about an important event while persuading them to respond in a specific way.

Mode of Writing	Purpose	Form
expository	to inform	news article, research report
narrative	to express thoughts or ideas, or to tell a story	personal account, memoir, short story
descriptive	to portray a person, place, object, or event	travel brochure, personal profile, poem
persuasive	to convince people to accept a position and respond in some way	editorial, petition, political speech

Gather Ideas

After you have identified your purpose, audience, topic, and form, the next step in the prewriting stage is to gather ideas. There are many ways to gather ideas for writing.

- **Brainstorm** When you **brainstorm,** you think of as many ideas as you can, as quickly as you can, without stopping to evaluate or criticize them. Anything goes—no idea should be rejected in the brainstorming stage.
- **Freewrite. Freewriting** is simply taking a pencil and paper and writing whatever comes into your mind. Try to write for several minutes without stopping and without worrying about spelling, grammar, usage, or mechanics.

- **Question** Ask the **reporting questions** *who, what, where, when, why,* and *how* about your topic. This questioning strategy is especially useful for gathering information about an event or for planning a story.
- **Create a Graphic Organizer** A good way to gather information is to create a **graphic organizer,** such as a Cluster Chart, Venn Diagram, Sensory Details Chart, Time Line, Story Map, or Pro-and-Con Chart. For examples, see the Language Arts Handbook, section 1, Reading Strategies and Skills, page 1029.

Write Your Thesis Statement

One way to start organizing your writing, especially if you are writing an informative or persuasive essay, is to identify the main idea of what you want to say. Present this idea in the form of a sentence or two called a thesis statement. A **thesis statement** is simply a sentence that presents the main idea or the position you will take in your essay.

Example thesis for a persuasive essay

The development at Rice Creek Farm should be stopped because it will destroy one of the best natural areas near the city.

Example thesis for an informative essay

Wilma Rudolph was an athlete who succeeded in the elite sport of tennis before the world was willing to recognize her.

Methods of Organization

The ideas in your writing should be ordered and linked in a logical and easily understandable way. You can organize your writing in the following ways:

Methods of Organization	
Chronological Order	Events are given in the order they occur.
Order of Importance	Details are given in order of importance or familiarity.
Comparison-and-Contrast Order	Similarities and differences of two things are listed.
Cause-and-Effect Order	One or more causes are presented followed by one or more effects.

To link your ideas, use connective words and phrases. In informational or persuasive writing, *for example, as a result, finally, therefore,* and *in fact* are common

connectives. In narrative and descriptive writing, words like *first, then, suddenly, above, beyond, in the distance,* and *there* are common connectives. In comparison-contrast organization, common phrases include *similarly, on the other hand,* and *in contrast.* In cause-and-effect organization, linkers include *one cause, another effect, as a result, consequently, finally,* and *therefore.*

Create an Outline An **outline** is an excellent framework for highlighting main ideas and supporting details. To create a rough outline, simply list your main ideas in some logical order. Under each main idea, list the supporting details set off by dashes.

EXAMPLE

What Is Drama?
Definition of Drama
—Tells a story
—Uses actors to play characters
—Uses a stage, properties, lights, costumes, makeup, and special effects
Types of Drama
—Tragedy
    —Definition: A play in which the main character meets a negative fate
    —Examples: *Antigone, Romeo and Juliet, Death of a Salesman*
—Comedy
    —Definition: A play in which the main character meets a positive fate
    —Examples: *A Midsummer Night's Dream, Cyrano de Bergerac, The Odd Couple*

2 DRAFT

After you have gathered your information and organized it, the next step in writing is to produce a draft. A **draft** is simply an early attempt at writing a paper. Different writers approach drafting in different ways. Some prefer to work slowly and carefully, perfecting each part as they go. Others prefer to write a discovery draft, getting all their ideas down on paper in rough form and then going back over those ideas to shape and focus them. When writing a discovery draft, you do not focus on spelling, grammar, usage, and mechanics. You can take care of those details during revision.

Draft Your Introduction

The purpose of an introduction is to capture your reader's attention and establish what you want to say. An effective introduction can start with a quotation, a question, an anecdote, an intriguing fact, or a description that hooks the reader to keep reading. An effective introduction can open with a quotation, question, anecdote, fact, or description.

EXAMPLES

"That's one small step for man, one giant leap for mankind." With these words, Neil Armstrong signaled his success as the first man to set foot on the moon...

What would it be like if all the birds in the world suddenly stopped their singing?

Draft Your Body

When writing the body of an essay, refer to your outline. Each heading in your outline will become the main idea of one of your paragraphs. To move smoothly from one idea to another, use transitional words or phrases. As you draft, include evidence from documented sources to support the ideas that you present. This evidence can be paraphrased, summarized, or quoted directly. For information on proper documentation, see the Language Arts Handbook 5.6, Documenting Sources, page 1101.

Draft Your Conclusion

In the conclusion, bring together the main ideas you included in the body of your essay and create a sense of closure to the issue you raised in your thesis. There is no single right way to conclude a piece of writing. Possibilities include:

- Making a generalization
- Restating the thesis and major supporting ideas in different words
- Summarizing the points made in the rest of the essay
- Drawing a lesson or moral
- Calling on the reader to adopt a view or take an action
- Expanding on your thesis or main idea by connecting it to the reader's own interests
- Linking your thesis to a larger issue or concern

3 REVISE

Evaluate Your Draft

Self- and Peer Evaluation When you evaluate something, you examine it carefully to find its strengths and weaknesses. Evaluating your own writing is called **self-evaluation.** A **peer evalua-**

tion is an evaluation of a piece of writing done by classmates, or peers. The following tips can help you to become a helpful peer reader, to learn to give and receive criticism, and to improve your writing.

Tips for evaluating writing

- **Check for content** Is the content, including the main idea, clear? Have any important details been left out? Do unimportant or unrelated details confuse the main point? Are the main idea and supporting details clearly connected to one another?
- **Check for organization** Are the ideas in the written work presented in a logical order?
- **Check the style and language** Is the language appropriately formal or informal? Is the tone appropriate for the audience and purpose? Have any key or unfamiliar terms been defined?

Tips for delivering helpful criticism

- **Be focused** Concentrate on content, organization, and style. At this point, do not focus on proofreading matters such as spelling and punctuation; they can be corrected during the proofreading stage.
- **Be positive** Respect the writer's feelings and genuine writing efforts. Tell the writer what you like about his or her work. Answer the writer's questions in a positive manner, tactfully presenting any changes you are suggesting.
- **Be specific** Give the writer concrete ideas for improving his or her work.

Tips for benefiting from helpful criticism

- **Tell your peer evaluator your specific concerns and questions.** If you are unsure whether you've clearly presented an idea, ask the evaluator how he or she might restate the idea.
- **Ask questions to clarify comments that your evaluator makes.** When you ask for clarification, you make sure you understand your evaluator's comments.
- **Accept your evaluator's comments graciously.** Criticism can be helpful, but you don't have to use any or all of the suggestions.

Revise for Content, Organization, and Style

After identifying weaknesses in a draft through self-evaluation and peer evaluation, the next step is to revise the draft. Here are four basic ways to improve meaning and content:

- **Adding or Expanding** Sometimes writing can be improved by adding details, examples, or transitions to connect ideas. Often a single added adjective, for example, can make a piece of writing clearer or more vivid.

  draft Wind whistled through the park.

  revised The **bone-chilling** wind whistled through the park.

- **Cutting or Condensing** Often writing can be improved by cutting unnecessary or unrelated material.

  draft Will was firmly determined to find the structure of the DNA molecule.

  revised Will was determined to find the structure of the DNA molecule.

- **Replacing** Sometimes weak writing can be made stronger through more concrete, more vivid, or more precise details.

  draft Several things had been bothering Tanya.

  revised Several personal problems had been bothering Tanya.

- **Moving** Often you can improve the organization of your writing by moving part of it so that related ideas appear near one another.

After you've revised the draft, ask yourself a series of questions. Think of these questions as your "revision checklist."

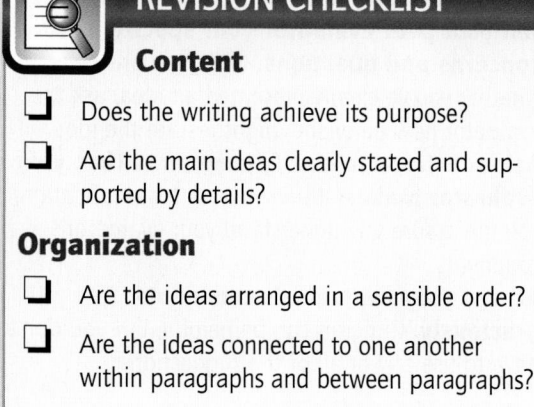

REVISION CHECKLIST

Content

❑ Does the writing achieve its purpose?

❑ Are the main ideas clearly stated and supported by details?

Organization

❑ Are the ideas arranged in a sensible order?

❑ Are the ideas connected to one another within paragraphs and between paragraphs?

Style

❑ Is the language appropriate to the audience and purpose?

❑ Is the mood appropriate to the purpose of the writing?

Proofread for Errors

When you proofread your writing, you read it through to look for errors and to mark corrections. When you mark corrections, use the standard proofreading symbols as shown in the following chart.

Proofreader's Symbols

Symbol and Example	Meaning of Symbol
The very first time	Delete (cut) this material.
dog's life	Insert (add) something that is missing.
George	Replace this letter or word.
All the horses king's	Move this word to where the arrow points.
french toast	Capitalize this letter.
the vice-President	Lowercase this letter.
housse	Take out this letter and close up space.
book keeper	Close up space.
gebril	Change the order of these letters.
end. "Watch out," she yelled.	Begin a new paragraph.
Love conquers all.	Put a period here.
Welcome friends.	Put a comma here.
Get the stopwatch	Put a space here.
Dear Madam:	Put a colon here.
She walked he rode.	Put a semicolon here.
name-brand products	Put a hyphen here.
cats meow	Put an apostrophe here.
cat's cradle stet	Let it stand. (Leave as it is.)

After you have revised your draft, make a clean copy of it and proofread it for errors in spelling, grammar, and punctuation. Use the following proofreading checklist.

WRITING

Proofreading Checklist

Spelling

❑ Are all words, including names, spelled correctly?

Grammar

❑ Does each verb agree with its subject?

❑ Are verb tenses consistent and correct?

❑ Are irregular verbs formed correctly?

❑ Are there any sentence fragments or run-ons?

❑ Have double negatives been avoided?

❑ Have frequently confused words, such as affect and effect, been used correctly?

Punctuation

❑ Does every sentence end with an end mark?

❑ Are commas used correctly?

❑ Do all proper nouns and proper adjectives begin with capital letters?

Prepare Your Final Manuscript

After proofreading your draft, you will prepare your final manuscript. Follow the guidelines given by your teacher or the guidelines provided here. After preparing a final manuscript according to these guidelines, proofread it one last time for errors.

Guidelines for Final Manuscript Preparation

- Keyboard your manuscript using a typewriter or word processor, or write it neatly using blue or black ink.
- Double-space your writing.
- Use one side of the paper.
- Leave one-inch margins on all sides of the text.
- Indent the first line of each paragraph.
- Make a cover sheet listing the title of the work, your name, the date, and the class.
- In the upper right-hand corner of the first page, put your name, class, and date. On every page after the first, include the page number in the heading, as follows:

EXAMPLE

Sharon Turner
English 9
March 25, 2009
p. 2

WRITING FOLLOW-UP

Publish and Present

Some writing is done just for oneself—journal writing, for example. Most writing, however, is meant to be shared with others. Here are several ways in which you can publish your writing or present it to others:

- Submit your work to a local publication, such as a school literary magazine, school newspaper, or community newspaper.
- Submit your work to a regional or national publication.
- Enter your work in a contest.
- Read your work aloud to classmates, friends, or family members.
- Collaborate with other students to prepare a publication—a brochure, online literary magazine, anthology, or newspaper.
- Prepare a poster or bulletin board, perhaps in collaboration with other students, to display your writing.
- Make your own book by typing or word processing the pages and binding them together.
- Hold an oral reading of student writing as a class or school-wide project.
- Share your writing with other students in a small writers' group.

Reflect

After you've completed your writing, think through the writing process to determine what you learned as a writer, what you learned about your topic, how the writing process worked or didn't work for you, and what skills you would like to strengthen.

Reflection can be done on a self-evaluation form, in small-group discussion, or simply in silent reflection. By keeping a journal, however, you'll be able to keep track of your writing experience and pinpoint ways to make the writing process work better for you. Here are some questions to ask as you reflect on the writing process and yourself as a writer:

- Which part of the writing process did I enjoy most and least? Why? Which part of the writing process was most difficult? least difficult? Why?

- What would I change about my approach to the writing process next time?
- What have I learned in writing about this topic?
- What have I learned by using this form?
- How have I developed as a writer while writing this piece?
- What strengths have I discovered in my work?
- What aspects of my writing do I want to strengthen? How can I strengthen them?

4.2 Modes and Purposes of Writing

Types of writing generally fall within four main classifications or modes: expository, narrative, descriptive, and persuasive. Each of these modes has a specific purpose. See the Mode of Writing Chart on page 1089.

Expository Writing

The purpose of **expository writing** is to inform, to present or explain an idea or a process. News articles and research reports are examples of informative expository writing. One function of expository writing is to define, since a definition explains what something is. Another function of expository writing is to analyze and interpret. For example, a book review is writing that analyzes and interprets a piece of literature to inform an audience about its worth. Similarly, a movie review evaluates and judges for its viewing audience how well a movie accomplishes its purpose.

Narrative Writing

Narrative writing tells a story or relates a series of events. It can be used to entertain, to make a point, or to introduce a topic. Narrating an event involves the dimension of action over time.

Narratives are often used in essays, reports, and other nonfiction forms because stories are entertaining and fun to read. Just as important, they are a good way to make a point. Biographies, autobiographies, and family histories are also forms of narrative writing.

Descriptive Writing

The purpose of **descriptive writing** is to entertain, enrich, and enlighten by using a form such as fiction or poetry to share a perspective. Descriptive writing is used to describe something, to set a scene, to create a mood, to appeal to the reader's senses. Descriptive writing is often creative and uses visual and other sensual details, emotional responses, and imagery. Poems, short stories, and plays are examples of descriptive writing.

Persuasive Writing

The purpose of **persuasive writing** is to persuade readers or listeners to respond in some way, such as to agree with a position, change a view on an issue, reach an agreement, or perform an action. Examples of persuasive writing are editorials, petitions, political speeches, and essays.

5 Research & Documentation

5.1 Critical Thinking Skills

In literature and informational texts, some things are stated as facts *(literal)* and other things are inferred or implied by the author *(inferential)*. We use **critical thinking skills** to fully understand and interpret what we read. There are six basic levels of understanding, or *cognitive domains,* which are listed below: The categories can be thought of as degrees of difficulty. That is, the first one must be mastered before the next one can take place. We apply these skills as we read a text.

Levels of Critical Thinking		
Refer to Text	**Remember**	**Recall facts:** Retrieve information presented in the text
Reason with Text	**Understand**	**Find meaning:** Interpret and explain ideas or concepts
	Apply	**Use information:** Utilize knowledge in another situation
	Analyze	**Take things apart:** Break down details to explore interpretations and relationships
	Evaluate	**Make judgments:** Justify a decision or course of action
	Create	**Bring ideas together:** Synthesize understanding to generate new ideas, products, or ways of viewing things

The paired **Refer to Text/Reason with Text** questions following the selections in this textbook are broken down into *literal* questions that refer directly to the facts in the text (Refer to Text) followed by inferential questions that ask you to apply higher levels of thinking to interpret the text (Reason with Text).

5.2 Research Skills

Learning is a lifelong process, one that extends far beyond school. Both in school and on your own, it is important to remember that your learning and growth are up to you. One good way to become an independent lifelong learner is to master research skills. Research is the process of gathering ideas and information. One of the best resources for research is the library.

How Library Materials Are Organized

Each book in a library is assigned a unique number, called a call number. The call number is printed on the spine (edge) of each book. The numbers serve to classify books as well as to help the library keep track of them. Libraries commonly use one of two systems for classifying books. Most school and public libraries use the Dewey Decimal System.

Dewey Decimal System	
Call Numbers	**Subjects**
000–099	Reference and General Works
100–199	Philosophy, Psychology
200–299	Religion
300–399	Social Studies
400–499	Language
500–599	Science, Mathematics
600–699	Technology
700–799	Arts
800–899	Literature
900–999	History, Geography, Biography[1]

1. Biographies (920s) are arranged alphabetically by the name of the person whose life is treated in each biography.

Most college libraries use the Library of Congress Classification System or the LC system, shown on the following page.

Library of Congress System

Call Numbers	Subjects
A	Reference and General Works
B–BJ	Philosophy, Psychology
BK–BX	Religion
C–DF	History
G	Geography, Autobiography, Recreation
H	Social Sciences
J	Political Science
K	Law
L	Education
M	Music
N	Fine Arts
P	Language, Literature
Q	Science, Mathematics
R	Medicine
S	Agriculture
T	Technology
U	Military Science
V	Naval Science
Z	Bibliography, Library Science

Internet Libraries It is also possible to visit the Internet Public library online at **http://www.ipl. org/.** The Internet Public Library is the first public library online of the Internet. This site provides library services to the Internet community by finding, evaluating, selecting, organizing, describing, and creating quality information resources; teaches what librarians have to contribute in a digital environment; and promotes the importance of libraries.

Computerized Catalogs Many libraries today use computerized catalogs. Systems differ from library to library, but most involve using a computer terminal to search through the library's collection. You can usually search by author, title, subject, or key word.

Using Reference Works

Most libraries have an assortment of reference works in which knowledge is collected and organized so that you can find it easily. Usually, reference works cannot be checked out of the library. Reference works that that may assist you in your research include dictionaries, thesauruses, almanacs, yearbooks, atlases, and encyclopedias.

Primary and Secondary Sources

Primary sources are the original unedited materials created by someone directly involved in an event or speaking directly for a group. They may include first-hand documents such as diaries, interviews, works of fiction, artwork, court records, research reports, speeches, letters, surveys, and so on.

Secondary sources offer commentary or analysis of events, ideas, or primary sources. They are often written significantly later and may provide historical context or attempt to describe or explain primary sources. Examples of secondary sources include dictionaries, encyclopedias, textbooks, and books and articles that interpret or review original works.

	Primary Source	Secondary Source
Art	Painting	Article critiquing the artist's technique
History	Prisoner's diary	Book about World War II internment camps
Literature	Poem	Literary criticism on a particular form of poetry
Science	Research report	Analysis of results

5.3 Internet Research

The Internet is an enormous collection of computer networks that can open a whole new world of information. With just a couple of keystrokes, you can access libraries, government agencies, high schools and universities, nonprofit and educational organizations, museums, user groups, and individuals around the world.

Keep in mind that the Internet is not regulated and everything you read online may not be verified or accurate. Confirm facts from the Internet against another source. In addition, to become a good judge of Internet materials, do the following:

- **Consider the domain name of the resource.** Be sure to check out the sites you use to see if they are commercial (.com or .firm), educational (.edu), governmental (.gov), or organizational (.org or .net). Ask yourself questions like these: What bias might a commercial site have that would influence its presentation of information? Is the site sponsored by a special-interest group that slants or spins information to its advantage?

Key to Internet Domains

.com	commercial entity
.edu	educational institution
.firm	business entity
.gov	government agency or department
.org or .net	organization

- **Consider the author's qualifications.** Regardless of the source, ask these questions: Is the author named? What expertise does he or she have? Can I locate other online information about this person? Evaluate the quality of information.
- **How accurate is the information?** Does it appear to be reliable and without errors? Is the information given without bias?
- **Check the date posted.** Is the information timely? When was the site last updated?

Search Tools

A number of popular and free search engines allow you to find topics of interest. Keep in mind that each service uses slightly different methods of searching, so you may get different results using the same key words.

All the Web	http://www.alltheweb.com
AltaVista	http://www.altavista.com
Go	http://www.go.com
Yahoo	http://www.yahoo.com
Excite	http://www.excite.com
HotBot	http://www.hotbot.com
WebCrawler	http://www.webcrawler.com
Google	http://www.google.com

Search Tips

- To make searching easier, less time consuming, and more directed, narrow your subject to a key word or a group of key words. These key words are your search terms. Key search connectors, or Boolean commands, can help you limit or expand the scope of your topic.

- AND (or +) narrows a search by retrieving documents that include both terms—for example: Ulysses Grant AND Vicksburg.

- OR broadens a search by retrieving documents that include any of the terms—for example: Ulysses Grant OR Vicksburg OR Civil War.

- NOT narrows a search by excluding documents containing certain words—for example: Ulysses Grant NOT Civil War.

- If applicable, limit your search by specifying a geographical area by using the word *near*—for example, golf courses near Boulder, Colorado.
- When entering a group of key words, present them in order, from the most important to the least important key word.
- If the terms of your search are not leading you to the information you need, try using synonyms. For example, if you were looking for information about how to care for your garden, you might use these terms: *compost, pest control,* and *watering*.
- Avoid opening the link to every page in your results list. Search engines typically present pages in descending order of relevancy or importance. The most useful pages will be located at the top of the list. However, skimming the text of lower order sites may give you ideas for other key words.
- If you're not getting the desired results, check your input. Common search mistakes include misspelling search terms and mistyping URLs. Remember that URLs must be typed exactly as they appear, using the exact capital or lowercase letters, spacing, and punctuation.

For information on citing Internet sources, see the Language Arts Handbook 5.6, Documenting Sources.

5.4 Media Literacy

The term **media,** in most applications, is used as a plural of *medium,* which means a channel or system of communication, information, or entertainment. *Mass media* refers specifically to means of communication, such as newspapers, radio, or television, which are designed to reach the mass of the people. *Journalism* is the gathering, evaluating, and disseminating, through various media, of news and facts of current interest. Originally, journalism encompassed only such printed matter as newspapers and periodicals. Today, however, it includes other media used to distribute news, such as radio, television, documentary or newsreel films, the Internet, and computer news services.

5.5 Evaluating Sources

To conduct your research efficiently, you need to evaluate your sources and set priorities among them. Ideally, a source will be:

- **Unbiased.** When an author has a personal stake in what people think about a subject, he or she may withhold or distort information. Investigate the author's background to see if she or he is liable to be biased. Using loaded language and overlooking obvious counterarguments are signs of author bias.

- **Authoritative.** An authoritative source is reliable and trustworthy. An author's reputation, especially among others who conduct research in the same field, is a sign of authority. Likewise, periodicals and publishers acquire reputations for responsible or poor editing and research.
- **Timely.** Information about many subjects changes rapidly. An astronomy text published last year may already be out of date. In other fields — for instance, algebra — older texts may be perfectly adequate. Consult with your teacher and your librarian to decide how current your sources must be.
- **Available.** Borrowing through interlibrary loan, tracing a book that is missing, or recalling a book that has been checked out to another person takes time. Make sure to allow enough time for these materials.
- **Appropriate for your level.** Find sources that present useful information that you can understand. Materials written for "young people" may be too simple to be helpful. Books written for experts may presume knowledge that you do not have. Struggling with a difficult text is often worth the effort, but if you do so, monitor your time and stay on schedule.

5.6 Documenting Sources

As you use your research in your writing, you must document your sources of information.
- Credit the sources of all ideas and facts that you use.
- Credit original ideas or facts that are expressed in text, tables, charts, and other graphic information.
- Credit all artistic property, including works of literature, song lyrics, and ideas.

Keeping a Research Journal A research journal is a notebook, electronic file, or other means to track the information you find as you conduct research. A research journal can include the following:
- A list of questions you want to research. (Such questions can be an excellent source of writing topics.)

EXAMPLES

How did the Vietnam Veterans Memorial come to be? Why is it one of the most visited memorials in America?

Where can I find more artwork by Faith Ringgold?

Why was Transcendentalism such an important literary movement in America but not in Europe?

As you conduct your research, rely on your research journal as a place to take notes on the sources you find and your evaluation of them. Keeping a research journal can be an invaluable way to track your research and to take notes.

Avoiding Plagiarizing Plagiarism is taking someone else's words or thoughts and presenting them as your own. Plagiarism is a very serious problem and has been the downfall of many students and professionals. Whenever you use someone else's writing to help you with a paper or a speech, you must be careful either to **paraphrase,** put the ideas in your own words; **summarize** the main ideas; or to use **quotation marks.** In any case, you must document your sources and give credit to the person whose ideas you are using. As you do research, make sure to include paraphrases, summaries, and direct quotations in your notes.

Citing Sources

The following chart shows the correct form for citing different types of bibliography entries, following the *Modern Language Association (MLA) Handbook for Writers of Research Papers.*

MLA Forms for Works Cited	
Book	Douglass, Frederick. *Escape from Slavery: The Boyhood of Frederick Douglass in His Own Words.* New York: Alfred A. Knopf, 1994.
Magazine article	Reston, James, Jr. "Orion: Where Stars Are Born." *National Geographic* Dec. 1995: 90-101.
Encyclopedia entry	"Lewis and Clark Expedition." *Encyclopedia Americana.* Jackson, Donald. 1995 ed.
Interview	Campbell, Silas. Personal interview. 6 Feb. 2007.
Film	*The Big Heat.* Dir. Fritz Lang. Perf. Glenn Ford and Gloria Grahame. Screenplay by Sidney Boehm. Columbia, 1953.

Citing Internet Sources

To document Internet sources, use your research journal to record each site you visit (see the Language Arts Handbook, 5.3 Internet Research, page 1342) or make bibliography cards as you search. An Internet source entry should include the following general pieces of information:

- Name of the author, if available, last name first, followed by a period.
- Title of the source, document, file, or page in quotation marks, followed by a period.
- If available, the information about the print publication, followed by a period.
- Name of the database or online source, in italics, and followed by a period.
- The date the website was last updated, followed by a period.
- The name of the institution or organization associated with the website, followed by a period.
- Date the source was accessed (day, month, year).
- Electronic address, enclosed in angle brackets (< >), followed by a period. MLA style suggests that writers avoid showing network and e-mail addresses as underlined hyperlinks. Note that when line length forces you to break a Web address, always break it after a slash mark.

The *MLA Handbook for Writers of Research Papers* acknowledges that all source tracking information on the Internet may not be obtainable. Therefore, the manual recommends that if you cannot find some of this information, you should cite what is available.

EXAMPLE INTERNET CITATIONS

Armstrong, Mark. "That's 'Sir' Mick Jagger to You." E! Online. 17 June 2002. E! Online, Inc. 17 June 2003 <http://www.eonline.com/ News/Items/0,1,10110,00.html>.

For sites with no name of the database or online source:

Chachich, Mike. "Letters from Japan Vol 1" 30 Mar. 1994. 17 June 2003 <http://www .chachich.com/cgi-bin/catlfj?1>.

For sites with no author:

"The Science Behind the Sod." *MSU News Bulletin.* 13 June 2002. Michigan State University. 17 June 2003 <http://www .newsbulletin.msu.edu/june13/sod.html>.

For an e-mail message:

Daniel Akaka (senator@akaka.senate.gov). "Oceanic Exploration Grant." E-mail to Joseph Biden (senator@biden.senate.gov). 17 June 2003.

Parenthetical Documentation

Parenthetical documentation is currently the most widely used form of documentation. To use this method to document the source of a quotation or an idea, you place a brief note identifying the source in parentheses immediately after the borrowed material. This type of note is called a parenthetical citation, and the act of placing such a note is called citing a source.

The first part of a parenthetical citation refers the reader to a source in your List of Works Cited or Works Consulted. For the reader's ease in finding the source in your bibliography, you must cite the work according to how it is listed in the bibliography.

EXAMPLE PARENTHETICAL CITATIONS

For works listed by title, use an abbreviated title.

Sample bibliographic entry
"History." *Encyclopedia Britannica: Macropædia.* 1992 ed.

Sample citation
Historians go through three stages in textual criticism ("History" 615).

For works listed by author or editor, use the author's or editor's last name.

Sample bibliographic entry
Brown, Dee. *Bury My Heart at Wounded Knee: An Indian History of the American West.* New York: Holt, 1970.

Sample citation
"Big Eyes Schurz agreed to the arrest" (Brown 364).

When the listed name or title is stated in the text, cite only the page number.

Brown states that Big Eyes Schurz agreed to it (364).

For works of multiple volumes, use a colon after the volume number.

Sample bibliographic entry
Pepys, Samuel. *The Diary of Samuel Pepys.* Eds. Robert Latham and William Matthews. 10 vols. Berkeley: University of California Press, 1972.

Sample citation
On the last day of 1665, Pepys took the occasion of the new year to reflect, but not to celebrate (6: 341-42).

For works quoted in secondary sources, use the abbreviation "qtd. in."

Sample citation
According to R. Bentley, "reason and the facts outweigh a hundred manuscripts" (qtd. in "History" 615).

For classic works that are available in various editions, give the page number from the edition you are using, followed by a semicolon; then identify the section of the work to help people with other editions find the reference.

Footnotes and Endnotes

In addition to parenthetical documentation, footnoting and endnoting are two other accepted methods.

Footnotes Instead of putting citations in parentheses within the text, you can place them at the bottom or foot of the page; hence the term *footnote*. In this system, a number or symbol is placed in the text where the parenthetical citation would otherwise be, and a matching number or symbol at the bottom of the page identifies the citation. This textbook, for example, uses numbered footnotes in its literature selections to define obscure words and to provide background information.

Endnotes Many books use endnotes instead of footnotes. Endnotes are like footnotes in that a number or symbol is placed within the text, but the matching citations are compiled at the end of the book, chapter, or article rather than at the foot of the page. Footnote and endnote entries begin with the author's (or editor's) name in its usual order (first name, then last) and include publication information and a page reference.

EXAMPLE FOOTNOTE OR ENDNOTE CITATIONS

Book with one author
[1]Jean Paul-Sartre, *Being and Nothingness* (New York: The Citadel Press, 1966) 149-51.

Book with one editor and no single author
[2]Shannon Ravenel, ed., *New Stories from the South: The Year's Best, 1992* (Chapel Hill, NC: Algonquin Books, 1992) 305.

Magazine article
[3]Andrew Gore, "Road Test: The Apple Powerbook," *MacUser,* Dec. 1996: 72.

6.1 Workplace and Consumer Documents

Applied English is English in the world of work or business, or *practical* English. Entering a new school, writing a professional letter, applying for a job, reading an instructional manual—these are but a few of the many situations you may encounter that involve **workplace and consumer documents.** You can apply English skills to many real-world situations, using your reading, writing, speaking, and listening abilities to help you be successful in any field or occupation you choose to pursue.

6.2 Writing a Step-by-Step Procedure

A **step-by-step procedure** is a how-to or process piece that uses directions to teach someone something new. Written procedures include textual information and sometimes graphics. Spoken procedures can be given as oral demonstrations. They can include textual and graphic information and other props. Examples of step-by-step procedures include an oral demonstration of how to saddle a horse; instructions on how to treat a sprained ankle; a video showing how to do the perfect lay-up in basketball; and an interactive Internet site allowing the user to design and send a bouquet of flowers.

Guidelines for Writing a Step-by-Step Procedure

- Demonstrate the steps. If you are showing how to make something, create several different samples to show each step of the procedure. For example, if you are showing how to make a wooden basket, you might want to display the raw materials, the started basket, the basket halfway finished, and then the finished product.
- Be prepared. The best way to prevent problems is to anticipate and plan for them. Rehearse an oral demonstration several times. If you are preparing the procedure in written form, go through your directions as if you knew nothing about the process. Anticipate what it would be like to learn this procedure for the first time. See if you can follow your own directions, or have a friend work through the procedure and offer suggestions for improvement.

- Acknowledge mistakes. If you are sharing a procedure "live" as an oral demonstration and you can't talk around or correct a mistake, tell your audience what has gone wrong, and why. If you handle the situation in a calm, direct way, the audience may also learn from your mistake.
- Know your topic. The better you know it, the better you will be able to teach others.

6.3 Writing a Business Letter

A **business letter** is usually addressed to someone you do not know personally. Therefore, a formal tone is appropriate for such a letter. Following appropriate form is especially important when writing business letters. If you follow the correct form and avoid errors in spelling, grammar, usage, and mechanics, your letter will sound professional and make a good impression. Above the salutation, a business letter should contain the name and title of the person to whom you are writing and the name and address of that person's company or organization (see the model on the following page).

One common form for a business letter is the block form. In the **block form,** each part of the letter begins at the left margin. The parts are separated by line spaces.

Begin the salutation with the word *Dear,* followed by the courtesy or professional title used in the inside address, such as Ms., Mr., or Dr., and a colon. If you are not writing to a specific person, you may use a general salutation such as *Dear Sir or Madam.*

In the body of your letter, use a polite, formal tone and standard English. Make your points clearly, in as few words as possible.

End with a standard closing such as *Sincerely, Yours truly,* or *Respectfully yours.* Capitalize only the first word of the closing. Type your full name below the closing, leaving three or four blank lines for your signature. Sign your name below the closing in blue or black ink (never in red or green). Proofread your letter before you send it. Poor spelling, grammar, or punctuation can ruin an otherwise well-written business letter.

Guidelines for Writing a Business Letter

- Outline your main points before you begin.
- Word process your letter, if at all possible. Type or print it on clean 8 1/2" x 11" white or off-white paper. Use only one side of the paper.
- Use the block form or another standard business letter form.
- Single space, leaving a blank line between each part, including paragraphs.
- Use a standard salutation and a standard closing.
- Stick to the subject. State your main idea clearly at the beginning of the letter. Keep the letter brief and informative.

- Check your spelling, grammar, usage, and punctuation carefully.

6.4 Application Letter

One of the most frequently used types of business letters is an **application letter,** which you would write to apply to a school or for a job. In an application letter, it is important to emphasize your knowledge about the business and the skills that you can bring to the position. The following is an example of a letter written to the owner of a dive shop to apply for a summer job.

EXAMPLE APPLICATION LETTER

498 Blue Key Rd.
Charleston, SC 02716

May 3, 2008

Mr. Davy Jones, Owner
Deep Sea Divers, Inc.
73 Ocean St.
Charleston, SC 02716

Dear Mr. Jones:

Please consider me for a position as a part-time clerk in your store for the coming summer. I understand that in the summer your business increases considerably and that you might need a conscientious, hardworking clerk. I can offer you considerable knowledge of snorkeling and diving equipment and experience working in a retail shop.

I will be available for work three days per week between June 1 and August 12. I am enclosing a résumé and references. Please contact me if you wish to set up an interview.

Sincerely,

Jorge Alvarez
Jorge Alvarez

6.5 Writing a Résumé

A **résumé** is a summary of a job applicant's career objectives, previous employment experience, and education. Its purpose is to help the applicant obtain the job he or she seeks. A résumé should be accompanied by a cover letter to the employer (see 6.4 Application Letter). Many helpful books and articles are available in libraries and bookstores on writing a résumé. Here are some guidelines.

Guidelines for Writing a Résumé

- Keep your information brief—to one page if possible. The goal of the résumé is to give a potential employer a quick snapshot of your skills and abilities.

- Include all vital contact information—name, address, phone number, and e-mail address, if applicable—at the top of the page.
- Use headings to summarize information regarding job or career objective, education, work experience, skills, extracurricular activities, awards (if applicable), and references. Note that work experience should be listed starting with your most recent job and working backward.
- Key or type your résumé on white or off-white paper. Proofread it carefully for any errors; all facts must be accurate as well. Make it as neat as possible.
- You may list references, or simply state that they are available on request.

EXAMPLE RÉSUMÉ

Pat Mizos
5555 Elm Street
Anytown, NY 20111
(212) 555-5555

Objective:
To gain employment working in a summer camp program for children

Education:
Orchard High School, 2008 graduate

Major area of study: College preparatory, with concentration in science and physical education classes

Grade point average: 3.5 (B+)

Work experience:

Summer 2007	Summer youth counselor, Anytown Parks and Recreation Department
Summer 2006	Dishwasher, The Lobster Shack, Anytown, NY

Skills:
Intermediate level Spanish (3 years in high school)
Beginning level American Sign Language (1 semester at Anytown Vocational School)
Certified in CPR

Extracurricular Activities:
Swim team, tennis team, youth hot-line crisis volunteer

References:
Available on request.

6.6 Writing a Memo

In businesses, schools, and other organizations, employees, students, and others often communicate by means of *memoranda,* or **memos.** For example, the director of a school drama club might write a memo to the editor of the student newspaper announcing tryouts for a new play. Some memos will be more informal than others. If you know the person to whom you are writing well or if the memo has only a social function such as announcing a party, the tone can be fairly informal. Most memos, however, have a fairly formal tone. A memo begins with a header. Often this header contains the word *memorandum* (the singular form of memoranda) and the following words and abbreviations:

TO:
FR: (from)
DT: (date)
RE: (regarding)
cc: (copy)

In the following example, Jack Hart, the president of the drama club at Wheaton High School, wishes to have the upcoming tryouts for his club's production of *Oklahoma!* announced in the school newspaper. He decides to write a memo to the editor of the paper, Lisa Lowry.

EXAMPLE MEMORANDUM

MEMORANDUM
TO: Lisa Lowry
FR: Jack Hart
RE: Tryouts for the spring production of *Oklahoma!*
DT: February 12, 2008
cc: Ms. Wise

Please include the following announcement in the upcoming issue of the *Wheaton Crier:* Tryouts for the Wheaton Drama Club's spring production of *Oklahoma!* will be held on Friday, February 26, at 6:00 p.m. in the Wheaton High School Auditorium. Students interested in performing in this musical should come to the auditorium at that time prepared to deliver a monologue less than two minutes long and to sing one song from the musical. Copies of the music and lyrics can be obtained from the sponsor of the Wheaton Drama Club, Ms. Wise. For additional information, please contact Ms. Wise or any member of the Drama Club.

Thank you.

6.7 Writing a Proposal

A **proposal** outlines a project that a person wants to complete. It presents a summary of an idea, the reasons why the idea is important, and an outline of how the project would be carried out. Because the proposal audience is people who can help carry out the proposal, a proposal is both informative and persuasive.

EXAMPLES

- You want funding for an art project that would benefit your community.

- Your student council proposes a clothing drive for disaster relief.

- You and a group of your friends want to help organize a summer program for teens your age.

Proposal: To host a Community Arts Day at the park behind Jordan High School that would allow high school artists to try new art forms and to exhibit their works.

Rationale: The art students at Jordan High School have shown there is a lot of talent here worth sharing. A Community Arts Day would let everyone interested get involved, and build school and community pride. Art students could lead others through simple art projects, and people could learn new things. At the end, the art could be displayed in an art fair at the community park. Artwork and refreshments could be sold, with all proceeds going to the Jordan High School Art Scholarship.

Schedule/Preparation Outline

Present proposal to School Pride Committee	April 1
Meet with art students to organize event	April 6-15
Contact area businesses for donations	April 6-15
Advertise event and sell tickets	April 16-25
Have practice day to make sure art activities work	April 20
Hold Community Arts Day	April 26

BUDGET

Expenses

Posters, mailings, tickets	$30
Art supplies	$200
Refreshments	$75

Note: Expenses will be less if we ask area businesses to help sponsor event.

Total estimated expenses	$305

Income

Ticket sales (Estimated 150 tickets sold @ $3 each)	$450
Refreshment sales	$100
Earnings from art sold at exhibit	$200
Total estimated income	$750
Net proceeds	$445

Note: All proceeds will be donated to the Jordan High School Art Scholarship Fund.

Guidelines for Writing a Proposal

- Keep the tone positive, courteous, and respectful.
- State your proposal and rationale briefly and clearly.
- Give your audience all necessary information. A proposal with specific details makes it clear what you want approved, and why your audience—often a committee or someone in authority—should approve it.
- Use standard, formal English.
- Format your proposal with headings, lists, and schedules to make your proposed project easy to understand and approve.

6.8 Writing a Press Release

A **press release** is an informative piece intended for publication in local news media. A press release is usually written to promote an upcoming event or to inform the community of a recent event that promotes, or strengthens, an individual or organization.

EXAMPLES

- a brief notice from the choir director telling the community of the upcoming spring concert

- an informative piece by the district public information officer announcing that your school's art instructor has been named the state Teacher of the Year

Guidelines for Writing a Press Release

- Know your purpose. What do you want your audience to know from reading your piece?
- Use the 5 *Ws* and an *H*—*who, what, where, why, when,* and *how*—questioning strategy to convey the important information at the beginning of your story.
- Keep the press release brief. Local media are more likely to publish or broadcast your piece if it is short and to the point.
- Include contact information such as your name, phone number, and times you can be reached. Make this information available to the media representative or, if applicable, to the reading public.
- Type your press release using conventional manuscript form. Make sure the text is double-spaced and that you leave margins of at least an inch on all sides of the page.
- At the beginning of the press release, key the day's date and the date the information is to be released. (You can type "For immediate release" or designate the date you would like the press release to be printed in the newspaper.)
- At the end of the press release, key the word "END."
- Check a previous newspaper for deadline information or call the newspaper office to make sure you get your material there on time. Address the press release to the editor.

6.9 Writing a Public Service Announcement

A **public service announcement,** or **PSA,** is a brief, informative article intended to be helpful to the community. PSAs are written by nonprofit organizations and concerned citizens for print in local newspapers, for broadcast by television and radio stations, and for publication on the Internet.

EXAMPLES

- an article by the American Cancer Society outlining early warning signs of cancer

- an announcement promoting Safety Week

- an informative piece telling coastal residents what to do during a hurricane

Guidelines for Writing a Public Service Announcement

- Know your purpose. What do you want your audience to know from reading or hearing your piece?
- State your information as objectively as possible.
- As with most informative writing, use the 5 *Ws* and an *H*—*who, what, where, why, when,* and *how*—questioning strategy to get your important information at the beginning of your story.
- Keep your announcement brief. Local media are more likely to publish or broadcast your piece if it is short and to the point.
- Include contact information in case the media representative has any questions. You might also include contact information in the PSA itself.
- Key or type your PSA in conventional manuscript form. Make sure the text is double-spaced and that you leave margins of at least an inch on all sides of the page.
- At the end of the PSA, key "END" to designate the end of the announcement.
- Be aware of print and broadcast deadlines and make sure your material is sent on time.

7.1 Verbal and Nonverbal Communication

Human beings use both verbal and nonverbal communication to convey meaning and exchange ideas. When a person expresses meaning through words, he or she is using verbal communication. When a person expresses meaning without using words, for example by standing up straight or shaking his or her head, he or she is using nonverbal communication. When we speak to another person, we usually think that the meaning of what we say comes chiefly from the words we use. However, as much as sixty percent of the meaning of a message may be communicated nonverbally.

Elements of Verbal Communication

Element	Description	Guidelines for Speakers
Volume	Loudness or softness	Vary your volume, but make sure that you can be heard.
Melody, Pitch	Highness or lowness	Vary your pitch. Avoid speaking in a monotone (at a single pitch).
Pace	Speed	Vary the speed of your delivery to suit what you are saying.
Tone	Emotional quality	Suit your tone to your message, and vary it appropriately as you speak.
Enunciation	Clearness with which words are spoken	When speaking before a group, pronounce your words more precisely than you would in ordinary conversation.

Elements of Nonverbal Communication

Element	Description	Guidelines for Speakers
Eye contact	Looking audience members in the eye	Make eye contact regularly with people in your audience. Try to include all audience members.
Facial expression	Using your face to show your emotions	Use expressions to emphasize your message — raised eyebrows for a question, pursed lips for concentration, eyebrows lowered for anger, and so on.
Gesture	Meaningful motions of the arms and hands	Use gestures to emphasize points. Be careful, however, not to overuse gestures. Too many can be distracting.
Posture	Position of the body	Keep your spine straight and head high, but avoid appearing stiff. Stand with your arms and legs slightly open, except when adopting other postures to express particular emotions.
Proximity	Distance from audience	Keep the right amount of distance between yourself and the audience. You should be a comfortable distance away, but not so far away that the audience cannot hear you.

7.2 Listening Skills

Learning to listen well is essential not only for success in personal life but also for success in school and, later, on the job. It is estimated that high school and college students spend over half their waking time listening to others, yet most people are rather poor listeners.

Active Versus Passive Listening

Active listening requires skill and concentration. The mind of a good listener is focused on what a speaker is trying to communicate. In other words, an effective listener is an active listener. Ineffective listeners view listening as a passive activity, something that simply "happens" without any effort on their part. **Passive listening** is nothing more than hearing sounds. This type of listening can cause misunderstanding and miscommunication.

ADAPTING LISTENING SKILLS

Just as different situations require different types of listening, different tasks or goals may also require different listening strategies and skills.
- **Listening for comprehension** means listening for information or ideas communicated by other people. For example, you are listening for comprehension when you try to understand directions to a friend's house or your teacher's explanation of how

to conduct a classroom debate.

- **Listening critically** means listening to a message in order to comprehend and evaluate it. When listening for comprehension, you usually assume that the information presented is true. Critical listening, on the other hand, includes **comprehending and judging** the arguments and appeals in a message in order to decide whether to accept or reject them. Critical listening is most useful when you encounter a persuasive message such as a sales pitch, advertisement, campaign speech, or news editorial.

- **Listening to learn vocabulary** involves a very different kind of listening because the focus is on learning new words and how to use them properly. For instance, you have a conversation with someone who has a more advanced vocabulary and use this as an opportunity to learn new words. The key to listening in order to learn vocabulary is to **pay attention to how words are used in context.** Sometimes it is possible to figure out what an unfamiliar word means based simply on how the word is used in a sentence.

- **Listening for appreciation** means listening purely for enjoyment or entertainment. You might listen appreciatively to a singer, a comedian, a storyteller, an acting company, or a humorous speaker. Appreciation is a very individual matter and there are no rules about how to appreciate something. However, as with all forms of listening, listening for appreciation requires attention and concentration.

7.3 Collaborative Learning and Communication

Collaboration is the act of working with one or more other people to achieve a goal. Many common learning situations involve collaboration.

- Participating in a small-group discussion
- Doing a small-group project
- Tutoring another student or being tutored
- Doing peer evaluation

Guidelines for Group Discussion

- **Listen actively.** Maintain eye contact with the speakers. Make notes on what they say. Mentally translate what they say into your own words. Think

critically about whether you agree or disagree with each speaker, and why.

- **Be polite.** Wait for your turn to speak. Do not interrupt others. If your discussion has a group leader, ask to be recognized before speaking by raising your hand.

- **Participate in the discussion.** At appropriate times, make your own comments or ask questions of other speakers.

- **Stick to the discussion topic.** Do not introduce unrelated or irrelevant ideas.

- **Assign roles.** For a formal dicussion, choose a group leader to guide the discussion and a secretary to record the minutes (the main ideas and proposals made by group members). Also draw up an agenda before the discussion, listing items to be discussed.

Guidelines for Projects

- **Choose a group leader** to conduct the meetings of your project group.

- **Set a goal** for the group. This goal should be some specific outcome or set of outcomes that you want to bring about.

- **Make a list of tasks** that need to be performed.

- **Make a schedule** for completing the tasks, including dates and times for completion of each task.

- **Make an assignment sheet.** Assign certain tasks to particular group members. Be fair in distributing the work to be done.

- **Set times for future meetings.** You might want to schedule meetings to evaluate your progress toward your goal as well as meetings to actually carry out specific tasks.

- **Meet to evaluate** your overall success when the project is completed. Also look at the individual contributions of each group member.

7.4 Asking and Answering Questions

There are many situations in which you will find it useful to ask questions of a speaker, or in which you will be asked questions about a presentation. Often a formal speech or presentation will be followed by a question-and-answer period. Keep the following guidelines in mind when asking or answering questions.

Guidelines for Asking and Answering Questions

- **Wait to be recognized.** In most cases, it is appropriate to raise your hand if you have a question and to wait for the speaker or moderator to call on you.
- **Make questions clear and direct.** The longer your question, the less chance a speaker will understand it. Make your questions short and to the point.
- **Do not debate or argue.** If you disagree with a speaker, the question-and-answer period is not the time to hash out an argument. Ask to speak with the speaker privately after the presentation is over, or agree on a later time and place to meet.
- **Do not take others' time.** Be courteous to other audience members and allow them time to ask questions. If you have a follow-up question, ask the speaker if you may proceed with your follow up.
- **Do not give a speech.** Sometimes audience members are more interested in expressing their own opinion than in asking the speaker a question. Do not give in to the temptation to present a speech of your own.
- **Come prepared for a question-and-answer period.** Although you can never predict the exact questions that people will ask you, you can anticipate many questions that are likely to be asked. Rehearse aloud your answers to the most difficult questions.
- **Be patient.** It may take some time for audience members to formulate questions in response to your speech. Give the audience a moment to do so. Don't run back to your seat the minute your speech is over, or if there is an awkward pause after you invite questions.
- **Be direct and succinct.** Be sure to answer the question directly as it has been asked, and to provide a short but clear answer.

7.5 Conducting an Interview

In an interview, you meet with someone and ask him or her questions. Interviewing experts is an excellent way to gain information about a particular topic. For example, if you are interested in writing about the art of making pottery, you might interview an art teacher, a professional potter, or the owner of a ceramics shop.

When planning an interview, you should do some background research on your subject and think carefully about questions you would like to ask. Write out a list of questions, including some about the person's background as well as about your topic. Other questions might occur to you as the interview proceeds, but it is best to be prepared. For guidelines on being a good listener, see Language Arts Handbook 7.2, Listening Skills, page 1111. Guidelines for interviewing appear on the following page:

Guidelines for Conducting an Interview

- **Set up a time in advance.** Don't just try to work questions into a regular conversation. Set aside time to meet in a quiet place where both you and the person you are interviewing can focus on the interview.
- **Explain the purpose** of the interview. Be sure the person you are interviewing knows what you want to find out and why you need to know it. This will help him or her to answer your questions in a way that is more useful and helpful to you.
- **Ask mostly open-ended questions.** These are questions that allow the person you are interviewing to express a personal point of view. They cannot be answered with a simple "yes" or "no" nor a brief statement of fact. The following are all examples of open-ended questions:

  "Why did you become a professional potter?"
  "What is the most challenging thing about owning your own ceramics shop?"
  "What advice would you give to a beginning potter?"

  One of the most valuable questions to ask at the end of the interview is, "What would you like to add that I haven't asked about?" This can provide some of the most interesting or vital information of all.
- **Tape-record the interview** (if possible). Then you can review the interview at your leisure. Be sure to ask the person you are interviewing whether or not you can tape-record the session. If the person refuses, accept his or her decision.
- **Take notes** during the interview, whether or not you are also tape-recording it. Write down the main points and some key words to help you remember details. Record the person's most important statements word for word.
- **Clarify spelling and get permission** for quotations. Be sure to get the correct spelling of the person's name and to ask permission to quote his or her statements.

- **End the interview on time.** Do not extend the interview beyond the time limits of your appointment. The person you are interviewing has been courteous enough to give you his or her time. Return this courtesy by ending the interview on time, thanking the person for his or her help, and leaving.
- **Write up the results** of the interview as soon as possible after you conduct it. Over time, what seemed like a very clear note may become unclear or confusing. If you are unclear of something important that the person said, contact him or her and ask for clarification.
- Send a thank-you note to the person you interviewed as a follow-up.

7.6 Public Speaking

The fear of speaking in public, although quite common and quite strong in some people, can be overcome by preparing a speech thoroughly and practicing positive thinking and relaxation. Learning how to give a speech is a valuable skill, one that you most likely will find much opportunity to use in the future.

The nature of a speech, whether formal or informal, is usually determined by the situation or context in which it is presented. **Formal speeches** usually call for a greater degree of preparation, might require special attire such as a suit or dress, and are often presented to larger groups who attend specifically to hear the presentation. A formal speech situation might exist when presenting an assigned speech to classmates, giving a presentation to a community group or organization, or presenting a speech at an awards ceremony. **Informal speeches** are more casual and might include telling a story among friends, giving a pep talk to your team at halftime, or presenting a toast at the dinner table.

Types of Speeches

The following are four common types of speeches:
- **Extemporaneous:** a speech in which the speaker refers to notes occasionally and that has a specific purpose and message. An example would be a speech given at a city council meeting.
- **Informative:** a speech used to share new and useful information with the audience. Informative speeches are based on fact, not opinion. Examples would include a speech on how to do something or a speech about an event.

- **Persuasive:** a speech used to convince the audience to side with an opinion and adopt a plan. The speaker tries to persuade the audience to believe something, do something, or change their behavior. Persuasive speeches use facts and research to support, analyze, and sell an opinion and plan. Martin Luther King's famous "I Have a Dream" speech and Nelson Mandela's "Glory and Hope" speech are examples of persuasive speeches.
- **Commemorative:** a speech that honors an individual for outstanding accomplishments and exemplary character. Examples would be a speech honoring a historical figure, leader, teacher, athlete, relative, or celebrity.

Guidelines for Giving a Speech

A speech should always include a beginning, a middle, and an end. The **beginning,** or introduction, of your speech should spark the audience's interest, present your central idea, and briefly preview your main points. The **middle,** or body, of your speech should expand upon each of your main points in order to support the central idea. The **end,** or conclusion, of your speech should be memorable and should give your audience a sense of completion.

- **Be sincere and enthusiastic.** Feel what you are speaking about. Apathy is infectious and will quickly spread to your audience.
- **Maintain good but relaxed posture.** Don't slouch or lean. It's fine to move around a bit; it releases normal nervous tension. Keep your hands free to gesture naturally instead of holding on to note cards, props, or the podium so much that you will "tie up" your hands.
- **Speak slowly.** Oral communication is more difficult than written language and visual images for audiences to process and understand. Practice pausing. Don't be afraid of silence. Focus on communicating with the audience. By looking for feedback from the audience, you will be able to pace yourself appropriately.
- **Maintain genuine eye contact.** Treat the audience as individuals, not as a mass of people. Look at individual faces.
- **Speak in a genuine, relaxed, conversational tone.** Don't act or stiffen up. Just be yourself.
- **Communicate.** Focus on conveying your message, not "getting through" the speech. Focus on communicating with the audience, not speaking at or to it.

- **Use strategic pauses.** Pause briefly before proceeding to the next major point, before direct quotations, and to allow important or more complex bits of information to sink in.
- **Remain confident and composed.** Remember that listeners are generally "for you" while you are speaking, and signs of nervousness are usually undetectable. To overcome initial nervousness, take two or three deep breaths as you are stepping up to speak.

7.7 Oral Interpretation

Oral interpretation is the process of presenting a dramatic reading of a literary work or group of works. The presentation should be sufficiently dramatic to convey to the audience a sense of the particular qualities of the work. Here are the steps you need to follow to prepare and present an oral interpretation:

Guidelines for Oral Interpretation

1. **Choose a cutting,** which may be a single piece; a selection from a single piece; or several short, related pieces on a single topic or theme.
2. **Write** the introduction and any necessary transitions. The introduction should mention the name of each piece, the author, and, if appropriate, the translator. It should also present the overall topic or theme of the interpretation. Transitions should introduce and connect the parts of the interpretation.
3. **Rehearse,** using appropriate variations in volume, pitch, pace, stress, tone, gestures, facial expressions, and body language. If your cutting contains different voices (a narrator's voice and characters' voices, for example), distinguish them. Try to make your verbal and nonverbal expression mirror what the piece is saying. However, avoid movement—that's for drama. Practice in front of an audience or mirror, or use a video camera or tape recorder.
4. **Present** your oral interpretation. Before actually presenting your interpretation, relax and adopt a confident attitude. If you begin to feel stage fright, try to concentrate on the work you are presenting and the audience, not on yourself.

Interpreting Poetry

Here are some additional considerations as you prepare to interpret a poem. The way you prepare your interpretation of a poem will depend on whether the poem you have chosen is a lyric poem, a narrative poem, or a dramatic poem.

- A **lyric poem** has a single speaker who reports his or her own emotions.
- A **narrative poem** tells a story. Usually a narrative poem has lines belonging to the narrator, or person who is telling the story. The narrator may or may not take part in the action.
- A **dramatic poem** contains characters who speak. A dramatic poem may be lyrical, in which characters simply report emotions, or narrative, which tells a story. A dramatic monologue presents a single speaker at a moment of crisis or self-revelation and may be either lyrical or narrative.

Before attempting to dramatize any poem, read through the poem carefully several times. Make sure that you understand it well. To check your understanding, try to paraphrase the poem, or restate its ideas, line by line, in your own words.

7.8 Telling a Story

A story or narrative is a series of events linked together in some meaningful fashion. We use narratives constantly in our daily lives: to make a journal entry, to tell a joke, to report a news story, to recount a historical event, to record a laboratory experiment, and so on. When creating a narrative, consider all of the following elements:

Guidelines for Storytelling

- **Decide on your purpose.** Every story has a point or purpose. It may be simply to entertain or to share a personal experience, but it may have a moral or lesson.
- **Select a focus.** The focus for your narrative will depend largely on your purpose in telling it.
- **Choose your point of view.** The storyteller or narrator determines the point of view from which the story will be told. You can choose to speak in the *first person,* either as a direct participant in the events or as an observer (real or imagined) who witnessed the events firsthand, or in the *third person* voice to achieve greater objectivity.
- **Determine sequence of events.** The sequence of events refers to the order in which they are presented. Although it might seem obvious that stories should "begin at the beginning," this is not always the best approach. Some narratives begin with the turning point of the story to create

a sense of drama and to capture the listeners' interest. Others begin at the end of the story and present the events leading up to this point in hindsight. Wherever you choose to begin the story, your narrative should present events in a logical fashion and establish a clear sense of direction for your listeners.

- **Determine duration of events.** Duration refers to how long something lasts. Everyone has experienced an event that seemed to last for hours, when in reality it only took minutes to occur. A good storyteller can likewise manipulate the duration of events in order to affect the way listeners experience them.

- **Select details carefully.** Make them consistent with your focus and make sure they are necessary to your purpose. A well-constructed story should flow smoothly, and should not get bogged down by irrelevant or unnecessary detail. Details can also establish the tone and style of the story and affect how listeners react to the events being described.

- **Choose characters.** All stories include characters who need to be developed so that they become real for listeners. Try to provide your listeners with vivid, concrete descriptions of the mental and physical qualities of important characters in the story. Remember that listeners need to understand and relate to the characters in order to appreciate their behavior.

- **Create dialogue.** Although it is possible to tell a story in which the characters do not speak directly, conversation and dialogue help to add life to a story. As with detail, dialogue should be used carefully. It is important that dialogue sound authentic, relate to the main action of the story, and advance the narrative.

7.9 Participating in a Debate

A debate is a contest in which two people or groups of people defend opposite sides of a proposition in an attempt to convince a judge or an audience to agree with their views. Propositions are statements of fact, value, or policy that usually begin with the word "resolved." The following are examples of typical propositions for debate:

RESOLVED   That lie detector tests are inaccurate. (proposition of fact)

RESOLVED   That imagination is more important than knowledge. (proposition of value)

RESOLVED   That Congress should prohibit the sale of handguns to private citizens. (proposition of policy)

The two sides in a debate are usually called the affirmative and the negative. The affirmative takes the "pro" side of the debate and argues in favor of the proposition, whereas the negative takes the "con" side and argues against the proposition. Using a single proposition to focus the debate ensures that the two sides argue or clash over a common topic. This allows the participants in the debate to develop their logic and ability to argue their positions persuasively.

Guidelines for Participating in a Debate

- **Be prepared.** In a debate, it will never be possible to anticipate all the arguments your opponent might make. However, by conducting careful and thorough research on both sides of the issue, you should be able to prepare for the most likely arguments you will encounter. You can prepare briefs or notes on particular issues in advance of the debate to save yourself preparation time during the debate.

- **Be organized.** Because a debate involves several speeches that concern the same basic arguments or issues, it is important that you remain organized during the debate. When attacking or refuting an opponent's argument, or when advancing or defending your own argument, be sure to follow a logical organizational pattern to avoid confusing the audience or the other team.

- **Take notes** by turning a long sheet of paper sideways. Draw one column for each speaker, taking notes on each speech going down one column, and recording notes about a particular argument or issue across the page as it is discussed in each successive speech.

- **Be audience-centered.** In arguing with your opponent, it is easy to forget the goal of the debate: to persuade your audience that your side of the issue is correct.

- **Prepare in advance** for the most likely arguments your opponents, will raise. Use time sparingly to organize your materials and think of responses to unanticipated arguments. Save time for the end of the debate, during rebuttal speeches, when it will be more valuable.

7.10 Preparing a Multimedia Presentation

Whether you use a simple overhead projector and transparencies or a PowerPoint presentation that involves graphics, video, and sound, multimedia technology can add an important visual element to a presentation. Consider the following guidelines to create a multimedia presentation:

Guidelines for a Multimedia Presentation

- **Use effective audiovisuals** that enhance understanding. The multimedia elements should add to the verbal elements, not distract from them. Be sure the content of the presentation is understandable, and that the amount of information—both verbal and visual—will not overwhelm audience members.
- **Make sure the presentation is clearly audible and visible.** Video clips or graphics may appear blurry on a projection screen or may not be visible to audience members in the back or on the sides of the room. Audio clips may sound muffled or may echo in a larger room or a room with different acoustics. When creating a multimedia presenta-

tion, be sure the presentation can be easily seen and heard from all parts of the room.

- **Become familiar with the equipment.** Well before the presentation, be sure you know how to operate the equipment you will need, that you know how to troubleshoot if the equipment malfunctions, and that the equipment you will use during the presentation is the same as that which you practiced with.
- **Check the room** to be sure it can accommodate your needs. Once you know where you will make your presentation, be sure the necessary electrical outlets and extension cords are available, that lights can be dimmed or turned off as needed, that the room can accommodate the equipment you will use, and so on.
- **Rehearse with the equipment.** Make sure that you can operate the equipment while speaking at the same time. Be sure that the multimedia elements are coordinated with other parts of your presentation. If you will need to turn the lights off in the room, make sure you can operate the equipment in the dark and can still see your note cards.

8.1 Preparing for Tests

Tests are a common part of school life. You take tests in your classes to show what you have learned in each class. In addition, you might have to take one or more standardized tests each year. Standardized tests measure your skills against local, state, or national standards and may determine whether you graduate, what kind of job you can get, or which college you can attend. Learning test-taking strategies will help you succeed on the tests you are required to take.

The following guidelines will help you to prepare for and take tests on the material you have covered in class.

Preparing for a Test
- **Know what will be covered on the test.** If you have questions about what will be covered, ask your teacher.
- **Make a study plan** to allow yourself time to go over the material. Avoid last-minute cramming.
- **Review the subject matter.** Use the graphic organizers and notes you made as you read as well as notes you took in class. Review any study questions given by your teacher.
- **Make lists** of important names, dates, definitions, or events. Ask a friend or family member to quiz you on them.
- **Try to predict questions** that may be on the test. Make sure you can answer them.
- **Get plenty of sleep** the night before the test. Eat a nutritious breakfast on the morning of the test.

Taking a Test
- **Survey the test** to see how long it is and what types of questions are included.
- **Read all directions and questions carefully.** Make sure you know exactly what to do.
- **Plan your time.** Answer easy questions first. Allow extra time for complicated questions. If a question seems too difficult, skip it and go back to it later. Work quickly, but do not rush.
- **Save time for review.** Once you have finished, look back over the test. Double-check your answers, but do not change answers too readily. Your first responses are often correct.

8.2 Strategies for Taking Standardized Tests

Standardized tests are given to large groups of students in a school district, a state, or a country. Statewide tests measure how well students are meeting the learning standards the state has set. Other tests, such as the SAT (Scholastic Aptitude Test) or ACT (American College Test), are used to help determine admission to colleges and universities. Others must be taken to enter certain careers. These tests are designed to measure overall ability or skills acquired so far. Learning how to take standardized tests will help you to achieve your goals.

You can get better at answering standardized test questions by practicing the types of questions that will be on the test. Use the Test Practice Workshop questions in this book and other sample questions your teacher gives you to practice. Think aloud with a partner or small group about how you would answer each question. Notice how other students tackle the questions and learn from what they do.

In addition, remember these points:
- **Rule out some choices** when you are not sure of the answer. Then guess from the remaining possibilities.
- **Skip questions that seem too difficult** and go back to them later. Be aware, however, that most tests allow you to go back only within a section.
- **Follow instructions exactly.** The test monitor will read instructions to you, and instructions may also be printed in your test booklet. Make sure you know what to do.

8.3 Answering Objective Questions

An **objective question** has a single correct answer. The following chart describes the kinds of questions you may see on objective tests. It also gives you strategies for tackling each kind of question.

Description	Guidelines
True/False You are given a statement and asked to tell whether the statement is true or false.	• If any part of a statement is false, then the statement is false. • Words like *all, always, never,* and *every* often appear in false statements. • Words like *some, usually, often,* and *most* often appear in true statements. • If you do not know the answer, guess. You have a 50/50 chance of being right.
Matching You are asked to match items in one column with items in another column.	• Check the directions. See if each item is used only once. Also check to see if some are not used at all. • Read all items before starting. • Match those items you know first. • Cross out items as you match them.
Short Answer You are asked to answer the question with a word, phrase, or sentence.	• Read the directions to find out if you are required to answer in complete sentences. • Use correct spelling, grammar, punctuation, and capitalization. • If you cannot think of the answer, move on. Something in another question might remind you of the answer.

8.4 Answering Multiple-Choice Questions

On many standardized tests, questions are multiple choice and have a single correct answer. The guidelines below will help you answer these kinds of questions effectively.

- **Read each question carefully.** Pay special attention to any words that are bolded, italicized, written in all capital letters, or otherwise emphasized.
- **Read all choices** before selecting an answer.
- **Eliminate** any answers that do not make sense, that disagree with what you remember from reading a passage, or that seem too extreme. Also, if two answers have exactly the same meaning, you can eliminate both.
- **Beware of distractors.** These are incorrect answers that look attractive because they are partially correct. They might contain a common misunderstanding, or they might apply the right information in the wrong way. Distractors are based on common mistakes students make.
- **Fill in circles completely** on your answer sheet when you have selected your answer.

8.5 Answering Reading Comprehension Questions

Reading comprehension questions ask you to read a passage and answer questions about it. These questions measure how well you perform the essential reading skills. Many of the Reading Assessment questions that follow each literature selection in this book are reading comprehension questions. Use them to help you learn how to answer these types of questions correctly. Work through each question with a partner using a "think aloud." Say out loud how you are figuring out the answer. Talk about how you can eliminate incorrect answers and determine the correct choice. You may want to make notes as you eliminate answers. By practicing this thinking process with a partner, you will be more prepared to use it silently when you have to take a standardized test.

The following steps will help you answer the reading comprehension questions on standardized tests.

- **Preview the passage and questions** and predict what the text will be about.
- **Use the reading strategies** you have learned to read the passage. Mark the text and make notes in the margins.
- **Reread the first question carefully.** Make sure you know exactly what it is asking.
- **Read the answers.** If you are sure of the answer, select it and move on. If not, go on to the next step.
- **Scan the passage** to look for key words related to the question. When you find a key word, slow down and read carefully.
- **Answer the question** and go on to the next one. Answer each question in this way.

8.6 Answering Synonym and Antonym Questions

Synonym or antonym questions give you a word and ask you to select the word that has the same meaning (for a synonym) or the opposite meaning (for an antonym). You must select the best answer even if none is exactly correct. For this type of question, you should consider all the choices to see which is best. Always notice whether you are looking for a synonym or an antonym. You will usually find both among the answers.

8.7 Answering Sentence Completion Questions

Sentence completion questions present you with a sentence that has one or two words missing. You must select the word or pair of words that best completes the sentence. The key to questions with two words missing is to make sure that both parts of the answer you have selected work well in the sentence.

8.8 Answering Constructed-Response Questions

In addition to multiple-choice questions, many standardized tests include **constructed-response questions** that require you to write essay answers in the test booklet. Constructed-response questions might ask you to identify key ideas or examples from the text by writing a sentence about each. In other cases, you will be asked to write a paragraph in response to a question about the selection and to use specific details from the passage to support your answer.

Other constructed-response questions ask you to apply information or ideas from a text in a new way. Another question might ask you to use information from the text in a particular imaginary situation. As you answer these questions, remember that you are being evaluated based on your understanding of the text. Although these questions may offer opportunities to be creative, you should still include ideas, details, and examples from the passage you have just read.

The following tips will help you answer constructed-response questions effectively:

- **Skim the questions first.** Predict what the passage will be about.
- **Use reading strategies** as you read. Underline information that relates to the questions and make notes. After you have finished reading, you can decide which of the details you have gathered to use in your answers.
- **List the most important points** to include in each answer. Use the margins of your test booklet or a piece of scrap paper.
- **Number the points** you have listed to show the order in which they should be included.
- **Draft your answer to fit** in the space provided. Include as much detail as possible in the space you have.
- **Revise and proofread** your answers as you have time.

8.9 Answering Essay Questions

An essay question asks you to write an answer that shows what you know about a particular subject. A simplified writing process like the one below will help you tackle questions like this.

1. Analyze the Question

Essay questions contain clues about what is expected of you. Sometimes you will find key words that will help you determine exactly what is being asked. See the chart below for some typical key words and their meanings.

Key Words for Essay Questions	
analyze; identify	break into parts, and describe the parts and how they are related
compare	tell how two or more subjects are similar; in some cases, also mention how they are different
contrast	tell how two or more subjects are different from each other
describe	give enough facts about or qualities of a subject to make it clear to someone who is unfamiliar with it
discuss	provide an overview and analysis; use details for support
evaluate; argue	judge an idea or concept, telling whether you think it is good or bad, or whether you agree or disagree with it
explain	make a subject clearer, providing supporting details and examples
interpret	tell the meaning and importance of an event or concept
justify	explain or give reasons for decisions; be persuasive
prove	provide factual evidence or reasons for a statement
summarize	state only the main points of an event, concept, or debate

2. Plan Your Answer

As soon as the essay prompt is clear to you, collect and organize your thoughts about it. First, gather ideas using whatever method is most comfortable for you. If you don't immediately have ideas, try freewriting for five minutes. When you **freewrite,** you write whatever comes into your head without letting your hand stop moving. You might also gather ideas in a cluster chart like the one on the following page. Then, organize the ideas you came up with. A simple outline or chart can help.

Name of Character or Topic

question. Then follow your organizational plan to provide support for your thesis. Devote one paragraph to each major point of support for your thesis. Use plenty of details as evidence for each point. Write quickly and keep moving. Don't spend too much time on any single paragraph, but try to make your answer as complete as possible. End your essay with a concluding sentence that sums up your major points.

4. Revise Your Answer

Make sure you have answered all parts of the question and included everything you were asked to include. Check to see that you have supplied enough details to support your thesis. Check for errors in grammar, spelling, punctuation, and paragraph breaks. Make corrections to your answer.

3. Write Your Answer

Start with a clear thesis statement in your opening paragraph. Your **thesis statement** is a single sentence that sums up your answer to the essay

ABRIDGMENT. An **abridgment** is a shortened version of a work. When doing an abridgment, an editor attempts to preserve the most significant elements of the original. The travel narrative *A Journey Through Texas,* by Álvar Núñez Cabeza de Vaca, is an abridgment (Unit 1).

ABSTRACT LANGUAGE. Abstract language refers to words and phrases that cannot be directly perceived by the senses. *Freedom, love, integrity, honesty,* and *loyalty* are examples of abstract terms. The opposite of *abstract,* in this sense, is *concrete.* Gary Snyder's poem "Riprap" contains examples of both abstract and concrete language (Unit 7). *See also* Concrete Language.

ACT. *See* Drama.

ALLEGORY. An **allegory** is a work in which the characters, events, or settings symbolize, or represent, something else. The fiction of Nathaniel Hawthorne (Unit 2), in which characters, objects, and events often represent moral qualities or circumstances, is highly allegorical.

ALLITERATION. Alliteration is the repetition of initial consonant sounds in consecutive or slightly separated words. Although alliteration usually refers to sounds at the beginnings of words, it can also be used to refer to sounds within words. Walt Whitman's "By the Bivouac's Fitful Flame" makes effective use of alliteration (Unit 3).

ALLUSION. An **allusion** is a reference to a well-known person, place, event, or work of art, music, or literature. In *Walden* (Unit 2), Henry David Thoreau makes allusions to many literary sources, including the Bible and Virgil's *Aeneid*.

AMPLIFICATION. *See* Elaboration.

ANALOGY. An **analogy** is a comparison of two things that are alike in some ways but otherwise quite different. Often, an analogy explains or describes something unfamiliar by comparing it to something more familiar. In the sermon "Sinners in the Hands of an Angry God," Jonathan Edwards uses the analogy of holding a spider or insect over the fire to describe God holding sinners over hell (Unit 1).

ANAPEST. *See* Meter.

ANECDOTE. An **anecdote** is a usually short account of an interesting, amusing, or biographical incident. Anecdotes sometimes are used in nonfiction writing as examples to help support an idea or opinion.

ANTAGONIST. An **antagonist** is a character or force in a literary work that is in conflict with a main character, or protagonist. In Robert Frost's "Mending Wall," the speaker's neighbor can be considered an antagonist. *See* Character.

ANTIHERO. An **antihero** is a central character who lacks all the qualities traditionally associated with heroes. An antihero may be lacking in beauty, courage, grace, intelligence, or moral scruples. Antiheroes are common figures in modern fiction and drama. The character of Leo Finkle in Bernard Malamud's short story "The Magic Barrel" is an antihero (Unit 7).

APHORISM. An **aphorism** is a short saying that makes an often witty observation about life. Examples of aphorisms by Benjamin Franklin include "The early bird catches the worm" and "Time is money" (Unit 1).

ARCHETYPE. An **archetype** is a type of character, image, theme, symbol, plot, or other element that has appeared in the literature of the world from ancient times until today. For example, the story of a quest or journey, in which someone sets, experiences adventure and danger, and becomes wiser, may be considered archetypal. In Eudora Welty's short story "A Worn Path," the protagonist, Phoenix Jackson, makes an archetypal journey (Unit 6).

ARGUMENT. An **argument** is a form of persuasion that makes a case to an audience for accepting or rejecting a proposition or course of action. *See* Persuasion.

ASSONANCE. Assonance is the repetition of vowel sounds in stressed syllables that end with different consonant sounds. An example is the repetition in Emily Dickinson's "Because I could not stop for Death" of the long *a* sound: "We passed the fields of Gazing Grain —" (Unit 3).

ATMOSPHERE. *See* Mood.

AUTOBIOGRAPHY. An **autobiography** is the story of a person's life written by that person. Richard Wright's autobiography is entitled *Black Boy* (Unit 7). *See* Memoir.

BALLAD. A **ballad** is a poem that tells a story and is written in four- to six-line stanzas, usually meant to be sung. Most ballads have regular rhythms and rhyme schemes and feature a refrain, or repetition of lines.

BEATS. The **Beats** were a group of writers from the 1950s and early 1960s who expressed their feelings of being constrained by the rules of what was acceptable in both society and literature. They felt worn out, or "beat down," by the dictates of the so-called establishment, the moral and legal authority created by mainstream culture, government, and education. Primary Beat writers included Jack Kerouac, Allen Ginsberg, William S. Burroughs, Gary Snyder, and Lawrence Ferlinghetti (Unit 7, Part 3).

BIOGRAPHICAL-HISTORICAL CRITICISM. **Biographical-historical criticism** is a theory of literary criticism that examines the writer's life and look for ways in which his or her work is tied to the historical period and culture in which it was created. Much of the writing of Mark Twain can be examined from this literary perspective (see Understanding Literary Criticism, Unit 4).

BIOGRAPHY. A **biography** is the story of a person's life, told by someone other than that person. Doris Kearns Goodwin has written a number of biographies, including *No Ordinary Time,* which is about Franklin Delano Roosevelt (Unit 6).

BLANK VERSE. **Blank verse** is unrhymed poetry written in iambic pentameter. William Cullen Bryant's poem "Thanatopsis" is written in blank verse (Unit 2). *See* Meter.

CAESURA (si zyür´ ə) A **caesura** is a major pause in a line of poetry, as in the following line from T. S. Eliot's "The Love Song of J. Alfred Prufrock": Let us go then, || you and I," (Unit 5).

CATALOG. A **catalog** is a list of people or things. In the essay "The Names of Women," Louise Erdrich catalogs the names of her female ancestors (Unit 9).

CHARACTER. A **character** is an individual that takes part in the action of a literary work. A character is usually a person but also may be a personified plant, animal, object, or imaginary creature. The main character, or *protagonist,* is the most important character in the work and is in conflict with the *antagonist.* Characters also can be classified in other ways. *Major characters* play significant roles in a work, and *minor characters* play lesser roles. A *flat character* shows only one quality, or character trait. A *round character* shows the multiple character traits of a real person. A *static character* does not change during the course of the action, whereas a *dynamic character* does change. *See* Characterization *and* Motivation.

CHARACTERIZATION. **Characterization** is the act of creating or describing a character. Writers create characters using three major techniques: showing what characters say, do, or think; showing what other characters say or think about them; and describing what physical features, dress, and personality the characters display. The first two methods are examples of *indirect characterization,* in which the writer *shows* what a character is like and allows the reader to judge the character. The third technique is considered *direct characterization,* in which the writer *tells* what the character is like. *See* Character.

CHRONOLOGICAL ORDER. **Chronological order** is the arrangement of details in order of their occurrence. It is the primary method of organization used in narrative writing and also is common in nonfiction writing that describes processes, events, and cause-and-effect relationships.

CLASSICISM. **Classicism** is a collection of ideas about literature and art derived from the study of works by the ancient Greeks and Romans. Definitions of what constitutes the Classical style differ, but most agree that it encompasses beauty, reason, restraint, self-control, simplicity, tradition, and unity. Classicism is most often contrasted with Romanticism and Realism. *See* Romanticism *and* Realism.

CLICHÉ. A **cliché** is an overused or unoriginal expression such as "quiet as a mouse" or "couch potato." Most clichés originate as vivid, colorful expressions but soon lose their appeal because of overuse. In Julia Alvarez's short story "The Daughter of Invention," the mother is prone to misusing clichés (Unit 9).

CLIMAX. The **climax** is the high point of interest and suspense in a literary work. The term also is sometimes used to describe the turning point of the action in a story or play—the point at which the rising action ends and the falling action begins. *See* Plot.

COMEDY. A **comedy** is any lighthearted or humorous literary work with a happy ending, especially a drama. Comedy is often contrasted with *tragedy,* in which the hero meets an unhappy fate. Comedies typically show characters with human limitations, faults, and misunderstandings. The action in a comedy usually progresses from initial order to a humorous misunderstanding or confusion and back to order again. Standard elements of comedy include mistaken identities, word play, satire, and exaggerated characters and events. *See* Drama *and* Tragedy.

CONCRETE LANGUAGE. Concrete language comprises words and phrases that specifically name or describe something. Concrete words or phrases engage the five senses. *Buffalo, geranium, storm,* and *heron* are examples of concrete terms. Gary Snyder's poem "Riprap" contains examples of both concrete and abstract language (Unit 7). *See* Abstract Language.

CONFESSIONAL POETRY. Confessional poetry is verse that describes, sometimes with painful explicitness, the private or personal affairs of the writer. Contemporary Confessional poets include Sylvia Plath, Anne Sexton, and Robert Lowell (Unit 8, Part 3).

CONFLICT. A conflict, or *crisis,* is a struggle between two forces in a literary work. A plot introduces a conflict, develops it, and eventually resolves it. There are two types of conflict. In an *external conflict*, the main character struggles against another character, against the forces of nature, against society or social norms, or against fate. In an *internal conflict*, the main character struggles against some element within himself or herself. In Jack London's short story "To Build a Fire," the nameless man faces an external conflict in his struggle against nature and fate. *See* Plot.

CONNOTATION. The connotation of a word is the set of ideas or emotional associations it suggests, in addition to its actual meaning. For example, the word *economical* has a positive connotation, whereas the word *cheap* has a negative connotation, even though both words refer to low cost. *See* Denotation.

CONSONANCE. Consonance is the repetition of consonant sounds at the ends of words or accented syllables, as in *wind* and *sound*. In Ralph Waldo Emerson's poem "Concord Hymn," the repetition of *d* sounds in line 4 (*fired, heard, round, world*) illustrates consonance (Unit 2).

COUPLET. A couplet is two lines of verse that rhyme. A *closed couplet* is a pair of rhyming lines that present a complete statement. A pair of rhyming iambic pentameter lines also is known as a *heroic couplet*. These lines from Anne Bradstreet's poem "To My Dear and Loving Husband" provide an example: "If ever two were one, then surely we. / If ever man were loved by wife, then thee;" (Unit 1).

CRISIS. *See* Conflict.

DACTYL. *See* Meter.

DENOTATION. The **denotation** of a word is its dictionary meaning without any emotional associations. For example, the words *dirt* and *soil* have the same denotation. However, *dirt* has a negative connotation of uncleanliness, whereas *soil* does not. *See* Connotation.

DÉNOUEMENT. *See* Plot.

DESCRIPTION. A **description** is a picture in words. *Descriptive writing* is used to portray a character, object, or scene. Descriptions include *sensory details:* words and phrases that describe how things look, sound, smell, taste, or feel.

DIALECT. A **dialect** is a version of a language spoken by the people of a particular place, time, or social group. A *regional dialect* is one spoken in a particular place. A *social dialect* is one spoken by members of a particular social group or class. Writers often use dialect to give their works a realistic flavor, as does Mark Twain in "The Notorious Jumping Frog of Calaveras County" (Unit 4).

DIALOGUE. Dialogue is conversation between two or more people or characters. Dramas are made up of dialogue and stage directions. Fictional works are made up of dialogue, narration, and description. When dialogue is included in fiction or nonfiction, the speaker's words are usually enclosed in quotation marks.

DICTION. Diction, when applied to writing, refers to the author's choice of words. Much of a writer's style is determined by his or her diction, the types of words that he or she chooses. Jack Kerouac's informal diction in *On the Road* is a key element of his written style (Unit 7). *See* Style.

DRAMA. A **drama** is a story told through characters played by actors. Dramas are divided into segments called *acts*. The script of a drama is made up of dialogue spoken by the characters and stage directions. Because it is meant to be performed before an audience, drama features elements such as lighting, costumes, makeup, properties, set pieces, music, sound effects, and the movements and expressions of actors. Two major types of drama are comedy and tragedy. Arthur Miller's *The Crucible* is one of the most significant American dramas (Understanding Literary Forms, Unit 7). *See* Comedy; Dialogue; Stage Directions; *and* Tragedy.

DRAMATIC IRONY. *See* Irony.

DRAMATIC MONOLOGUE. A **dramatic monologue** is a poem written in the form of a speech of a single character to an imaginary audience. A modern example of a dramatic monologue is T. S. Eliot's "The Love Song of J. Alfred Prufrock" (Unit 5). *See* Soliloquy.

DRAMATIC POEM. A **dramatic poem** relies heavily on dramatic elements such as *monologue* (speech by a single character) and *dialogue* (conversation involving two or more characters). Often, dramatic poems tell stories. Types of dramatic poetry include the dramatic monologue and the soliloquy. Edgar Lee Masters's "Lucinda Matlock" and "Petit, the Poet" are both examples of dramatic poems (Unit 5). *See* Dialogue; Dramatic Monologue; *and* Soliloquy.

ELABORATION. **Elaboration,** or amplification, is a writing technique in which a subject is introduced and then expanded on by means of repetition with slight changes, the addition of details, or similar devices. Walt Whitman uses elaboration in "Song of Myself" when the speaker responds to the question "What is the grass?" with a series of possibilities, each beginning with the phrase "I guess" (Unit 3).

ELEGY. An **elegy** is a poem of mourning, usually about someone who has died. Theodore Roethke's "Elegy for Jane" is an example of an elegy (Unit 7).

ENJAMBMENT. **Enjambment** is the act of continuing a statement beyond the end of a line. In contrast, an *end-stopped line* is a line of verse in which both the sense and the grammar are complete at the end of the line. Sylvia Plath's "Morning Song" makes effective use of enjambment (Unit 8).

ENLIGHTENMENT. The **Enlightenment** was an eighteenth-century philosophical movement characterized by belief in reason, the scientific method, and the perfectibility of people and society. Thinkers of the Enlightenment Era, or Age of Reason, believed that the universe was governed by discoverable, rational principles. By extension, they believed that people could, through the application of reason, discover truths relating to the conduct of life or of society. Leading American thinkers of the Enlightenment included Patrick Henry, Benjamin Franklin, and Thomas Jefferson (Unit 1). *See* Neoclassicism.

EPIC. An **epic** is a long story, often told in verse, involving heroes and gods. Grand in length and scope, an epic provides a portrait of an entire culture—the legends, beliefs, values, laws, arts, and ways of life of a people. Famous epic poems include Homer's *The Odyssey* and *The Iliad*, Virgil's *Aeneid*, Dante's *The Divine Comedy*, the anonymous Old English *Beowulf*, and John Milton's *Paradise Lost*.

EPIGRAM. An **epigram** is a short, often witty, saying. An example of an epigram is Benjamin Franklin's "Three may keep a secret, if two of them are dead" (Unit 1).

EPIGRAPH. An **epigraph** is a quotation or motto used at the beginning of a literary work to help establish the work's theme or purpose. Anne Sexton begins "The Starry Night" with an epigraph from a letter written by painter Vincent van Gogh (Unit 8).

EPITHET. An **epithet** is a characteristic word or phrase used alongside the name of a person, place, or thing. *Spring, the season of new beginnings,* is an example. Some epithets are so familiar that they can be used in place of a name. For example, the epithet "Freer of Slaves" can be used in place of "Abraham Lincoln."

ESSAY. An **essay** is a short nonfiction work that presents a single main idea, or *thesis,* about a particular topic. There are three general types of essays, each defined by its purpose. An *expository,* or *informative, essay* explores a topic with the goal of informing or enlightening the reader. A *persuasive essay* aims to persuade the reader to accept a certain point of view. A *personal essay* explores a topic related to the life or interests of the writer. Personal essays are characterized by an intimate and informal style or tone. Among the most famous American essayists are Ralph Waldo Emerson and Henry David Thoreau (Understanding Literary Forms, Unit 2).

EXPOSITION. In a plot, the **exposition** provides background information, often about the characters, setting, or conflict. *See* Expository Writing *and* Plot.

EXPOSITORY WRITING. **Expository writing** is the type of writing that aims to inform or explain. An essay that explores a topic with the goal of informing or enlightening reader is considered expository. *See* Essay.

EXPRESSIONISM. **Expressionism** was a twentieth-century movement in literature and art that reacted against Realism. Expressionists exaggerated the elements of the artistic medium itself to express their ideas and feelings. *See* Realism.

EXTENDED METAPHOR. An **extended metaphor** is a point-by-point presentation of one thing as though it were another. The description is meant as an implied comparison, inviting the reader to associate the thing being described with something that is quite different from it. Emily Dickinson's "Because I could not stop for Death—"is an extended metaphor, in which Death is characterized as a carriage driver and the speaker of the poem as his passenger (Unit 3).

FABLE. A **fable** is a brief story, often with animal characters, told to express a moral. Famous fables include those of Aesop and Jean de La Fontaine. Fables are part of the oral tradition of many cultures (Understanding Literary Forms, Unit 1).

FALLING ACTION. *See* Plot.

FARCE. A **farce** is a type of comedy that depends heavily on so-called low humor and improbable, exaggerated, extreme situations and characters.

FEET. *See* Meter.

FICTION. A work of **fiction** tells an invented or imaginary story. The primary forms of fiction are the novel and short story (see Understanding Literary Forms, Units 5 and 7, respectively). *See* Novel *and* Short Story.

FIGURATIVE LANGUAGE. **Figurative language** is writing or speech meant to be understood imaginatively instead of literally. Many writers, especially poets, use figurative language to help readers see things in new ways. Types of figurative language, or **figures of speech,** include *hyperbole, metaphor, personification, simile,* and *understatement. See each of these terms.*

FIGURES OF SPEECH. *See* Figurative Language.

FIRESIDE POETS. The **Fireside poets,** who wrote during the early to mid-1800s, were the first Americans to receive the same literary recognition and popularity of European poets of the day. Included in this group were Henry Wadsworth Longfellow, John Greenleaf Whittier, Oliver Wendell Holmes, and James Russell Lowell. The label *Fireside* described readers sitting in front of the family hearth, enjoying an evening of reading (Unit 2, Part 1).

FLASHBACK. A **flashback** interrupts the chronological sequence of a literary work and presents an event that occurred earlier. Writers use flashbacks most often to provide background information about characters or situations. Ambrose Bierce uses flashbacks to enter the mind of Peyton Farquhar in the short story "An Occurrence at Owl Creek Bridge" (Unit 3).

FOIL. A **foil** is a character whose traits contrast with and therefore highlight the traits of another character. The husky dog in Jack London's "To Build a Fire" can be considered a foil to the nameless man.

FOLK TALE. A **folk tale** is a brief story passed by word of mouth from generation to generation. Folk tales are part of the oral tradition of many cultures (Understanding Literary Forms, Unit 1).

FOOT. *See* Meter.

FORESHADOWING. **Foreshadowing** is the technique of hinting at events that will occur later in a story. Edgar Allan Poe foreshadows many of the developments in the short story "The Fall of the House of Usher" (Unit 2).

FRAME TALE. A **frame tale** is a story that provides a means for telling another story or group of stories. Mark Twain's "The Notorious Jumping Frog of Calaveras County" is written as a frame tale (Unit 4).

FREE VERSE. **Free verse** is poetry that does not use regular rhyme, meter, or stanza division. Free verse may contain irregular line breaks and sentence fragments and tends to mimic the rhythms of ordinary speech. Walt Whitman is generally considered to have pioneered the use of free verse (Unit 3). Much contemporary poetry is written in free verse.

GENRE. A **genre** (zhän′ rə) is one of the types or categories into which literary works are divided. Major genres of literature include fiction, nonfiction, poetry, and drama. *See* Drama; Fiction; Nonfiction; *and* Poetry.

GOTHIC FICTION. **Gothic fiction** is a style of fiction characterized by the use of medieval settings, a murky atmosphere of horror and gloom, and grotesque, mysterious, or violent incidents. Essential to Gothic fiction is a setting that evokes strong feelings of foreboding or anticipation. Many of Edgar Allan Poe's stories, including "The Fall of the House of Usher," are representative of Gothic fiction (Unit 2). Elements of Gothic fiction can also be found in the work of southern writers such as William Faulkner (Unit 6) and Flannery O'Connor (Unit 7).

HARLEM RENAISSANCE. The **Harlem Renaissance** was a period of intense creative activity among African-American writers and other artists living in Harlem in New York City during the 1920s. Major writers of the Harlem Renaissance included Arna Bontemps, Countee Cullen, Langston Hughes, Claude McKay, and Jean Toomer (Unit 5, Part 3).

HYPERBOLE. A **hyperbole** (hī pür´ bə lē¹) is a deliberate exaggeration made for effect. Anne Bradstreet uses hyperbole in "To My Dear and Loving Husband" when she writes "My love is such that rivers cannot quench, / Nor ought but love from thee, give recompense" (Unit 1).

IAMB. *See* Meter.

IAMBIC PENTAMETER. *See* Meter.

IMAGERY. **Imagery** is the figurative or descriptive language used to create word pictures, or images. *See* Description *and* Figurative Language.

IMAGISM. **Imagism** was a literary movement of the early twentieth century in which poets attempted to present single moments of sensory perception without reference to the emotions or opinions of the author, narrator, or speaker. Ezra Pound is often considered the founder of the Imagist movement. His poem "In a Station of the Metro" demonstrates Imagism (Unit 5).

INTERNAL MONOLOGUE. An **internal monologue** presents the private sensations, thoughts, and emotions of a character. The reader is allowed to step inside the character's mind and overhear what is going on in there. Which characters' internal states can be revealed in a work of fiction depends on the point of view from which the work is told. *See* Point of View.

IRONY. **Irony** is the difference between appearance and reality. There are three types of irony: *dramatic irony*, in which something is known by the reader or audience but unknown to the characters; *verbal irony*, in which a writer or character says one thing but means another; and *irony of situation*, in which an event occurs that violates the expectations of the characters, the reader, or the audience.

LEGEND. A **legend** is a story passed down over the generations that is often based on real events or characters from the past. Unlike myths, legends usually are considered to be historical; however, they may contain elements that are fantastic or unverifiable. Legends are part of the oral tradition of many cultures (Understanding Literary Forms, Unit 1).

LITERARY NONFICTION. Works of **literary nonfiction** are fact-based accounts of actual events, people, and places that explore universal themes and use techniques common to fiction and poetry. James Agee's *Let Us Now Praise Famous Men* and Randall Jarrell's *Hiroshima* are considered two of the earliest works of literary nonfiction (Unit 6). Contemporary writers of literary nonfiction include Ian Frazier, Kathleen Norris, Eric Schlosser, and Joan Didion (Understanding Literary Forms, Unit 9).

LOCAL COLOR. *See* Regionalism.

LYRIC POEM. A **lyric poem** is a highly musical type of poetry that expresses the emotions of a speaker. Lyric poems often are contrasted with narrative poems, which have storytelling as their main purpose. Walt Whitman and Emily Dickinson are two of the most recognized American lyric poets (Unit 3, Part 2). *See* Narrative Poem.

MAGICAL REALISM. **Magical Realism** is a kind of fiction that is, for the most part, realistic but contains elements of fantasy. It originated in the works of Latin American writers of the 1960s and reflects the fact that Latin American culture often accepts what Europeans would consider "fantastic occurrences" as part of everyday life. *Black Elk Speaks,* by Nicholas Black Elk and John G. Reinhardt, contains elements of Magical Realism (Unit 4).

MEMOIR. A **memoir** is a type of autobiography that focuses on one incident or period in a person's life. Memoirs often are based on a person's memories of and reactions to historical events. N. Scott Momaday's *The Way to Rainy Mountain* and Maxine Hong Kingston's *The Woman Warrior* are examples of memoirs (Understanding Literary Forms, Unit 8). *See* Autobiography *and* Biography.

METAPHOR. A **metaphor** is a figure of speech in which one thing is spoken or written about as if it were another. This figure of speech invites the reader to make a comparison between the writer's actual subject, the *tenor* of the metaphor, and another thing to which the subject is likened, the *vehicle* of the metaphor. In his essay "Self-Reliance," Ralph Waldo Emerson uses this metaphor: "Society is a joint-stock company." The tenor of the metaphor is *society,* and the vehicle of the metaphor is *joint-stock company* (Unit 2). *See* Figurative Language.

METER. **Meter** is a regular rhythmic pattern in poetry, as determined by the number of beats, or stresses, in each line. Stressed and unstressed syllables are divided into rhythmical units called *feet*. Feet commonly used in English poetry are as follow:

iamb (iambic): an unstressed syllable followed by a stressed syllable, as in the word *in**sist***

trochee (trochaic): a stressed syllable followed by an unstressed syllable, as in ***free**dom*

anapest (anapestic): two unstressed syllables followed by one stressed syllable, as in *unim-**pressed***

dactyl (dactylic): one stressed syllables followed by two unstressed syllable, as in ***fe**verish*

spondee (spondaic): two stressed syllables, as in ***baseball***

Terms used to describe the number of feet in a line include the following:

monometer for a one-foot line
dimeter for a two-foot line
trimeter for a three-foot line
tetrameter for a four-foot line
pentameter for a five-foot line
hexameter (or *Alexandrine*) for a six-foot line
heptameter for a seven-foot line
octameter for an eight-foot line

A complete description of the meter of a line includes both the term for the type of foot used most often in the line and the term for the number of feet in the line. The most common English meters are *iambic tetrameter* and *iambic pentameter*. The following are examples of these two meters:

Iambic Tetrameter

˘ / ˘ / ˘ / ˘ /
O slow | ly, slow | ly rose | she up

Iambic Pentameter

˘ / ˘ / ˘ / ˘ / ˘ /
The cur | few tolls | the knell | of part | ing day

MODERNISM. **Modernism** was an artistic and literary movement of the early twentieth century that was characterized by a rejection of the artistic conventions of the past. As such, it was a response to the perceived breakdown of modern culture. Significant Modernist writers included poets Ezra Pound and T. S. Eliot and novelists F. Scott Fitzgerald and Ernest Hemingway (Unit 5).

MOOD. **Mood**, or atmosphere, is the emotion created in the reader by part or all of a literary work. The writer can evoke in the reader an emotional response—such as fear, discomfort, longing, or anticipation—by using descriptive language and sensory details. *See* Description *and* Sensory Details.

MOTIVATION. A **motivation** is a force that moves a character to think, feel, or behave in a certain way. In Ambrose Bierce's "An Occurrence at Owl Creek Bridge," the main character is motivated by a desire to save his own life by escaping from his captors (Unit 3). *See* Character.

MYTH. A **myth** is a traditional story, rooted in a particular culture, that deals with gods, goddesses, and other supernatural beings, as well as human heroes. Myths often embody religious beliefs and values and explain natural phenomena. Every early culture has produced its own myths. Examples of myths include the Osage and Navajo creation myths (Unit 1). Myths are part of the oral tradition of many cultures (Understanding Literary Forms, Unit 1).

NARRATION. **Narration** is a type of writing that tells a story or describes events.

NARRATIVE. A **narrative** is a story or told in fiction, nonfiction, poetry, or drama. A narrative is usually told in *chronological order*, or in order in which events occurred. Álvar Núñez Cabeza de Vaca's *A Journey Through Texas* is an example of a narrative (Unit 1). *See* Chronological Order *and* Narrative Poem.

NARRATIVE POEM. A **narrative poem** is one that tells a story. Edgar Allan Poe's "The Raven" is a well-known narrative poem (Unit 2).

NARRATOR. A **narrator** is a character or speaker who tells a story. The writer's choice of narrator is important to the story and determines how much and what kind of information readers will be given about events and other characters. The narrator in a work of fiction may be a major or minor character or simply someone who witnessed or heard about the events being related. The narrator in F. Scott Fitzgerald's *The Great Gatsby* is Nick Carraway, Gatsby's neighbor (Unit 5). *See* Point of View *and* Speaker.

NATURALISM. **Naturalism** was a literary movement of the late nineteenth and early twentieth centuries that saw actions and events as resulting inevitably from biological or natural forces or from forces in the environment. Generally, these forces are deemed beyond the comprehension or control of the characters subjected to them. Jack London's short story "To Build a Fire" and Stephen Crane's poem "A Man Said to the Universe" both represent the Naturalistic perspective (Unit 4).

NEOCLASSICISM. Neoclassicism was a revival during the European Enlightenment of the eighteenth century of the ideals of art and literature derived from the Greek and Roman classics. These ideals included respect for authority and tradition, austerity, clarity, conservatism, decorum, economy, grace, imitation of natural order, harmony, moderation, proportion, reason, restraint, self-control, simplicity, tradition, wit, and unity. Neoclassical literature was witty and socially astute but tended toward excessive didacticism and an excessive distrust of invention and imagination. Among American writers, Benjamin Franklin best reflects the Neoclassical spirit of urbane rationality (Unit 1). *See* Classicism *and* Romanticism.

NONFICTION. Nonfiction is prose writing about real events. Essays, autobiographies, biographies, and news articles are all types of nonfiction. *See* Prose.

NOVEL. A **novel** is a long work of fiction. Often, a novel has an involved plot, many characters, and numerous settings. Among the most famous American novelists are F. Scott Fitzgerald and Ernest Hemingway (Understanding Literary Forms, Unit 5).

OCTAVE. An **octave** is an eight-line stanza of poetry. A Petrarchan sonnet begins with an octave. *See* Meter *and* Sonnet.

ODE. An **ode** is a lyric poem on a serious theme, usually with varying line lengths and complex stanzas. Pablo Neruda's "Ode to Walt Whitman" expresses the poet's gratitude to his mentor and contains literary allusions to specific Whitman poems (Unit 3).

OMNISCIENT POINT OF VIEW. *See* Narrator *and* Point of View.

ONOMATOPOEIA. Onomatopoeia (än' ō mat' ō pē´ ə) is the use of words or phrases that sound like the things to which they refer. Examples of onomatopoeia include words such as *buzz, click,* and *pop.* Walt Whitman's "Beat! Beat! Drums!" demonstrates the use of onomatopoeia (Unit 3).

ORAL TRADITION. The **oral tradition** is the passing of a work, idea, or custom by word of mouth from generation to generation. Common works found in the oral traditions of peoples around the world include folk tales, fables, fairy tales, tall tales, nursery rhymes, proverbs, legends, myths, parables, riddles, charms, spells, and ballads. Early Native American works belong to the oral tradition (Understanding Literary Forms, Unit 1). *See* Folk Tale *and* Myth.

ORATORY. Oratory is the art of public speaking. It involves studying the skills necessary to be an eloquent, persuasive speaker. Patrick Henry is recognized as an outstanding American orator (Unit 1). *See* Rhetoric.

OXYMORON. An **oxymoron** is a statement that contradicts itself. Words such as *bittersweet* and *pianoforte* (literally, "soft-loud") are oxymorons.

PARABLE. A **parable** is a brief story told to teach a moral lesson. The most famous parables are those told by Jesus in the Bible.

PARADOX. A **paradox** is a seemingly contradictory statement, idea, or event that may actually be true. Some paradoxes present unresolvable contradictory ideas. An example of such a paradox is the statement "This sentence is a lie." If the sentence is true, then it is false; if it is false, then it is true. In Anne Bradstreet's "To My Dear and Loving Husband," the line "That when we live no more, we may live ever" is paradoxical (Unit 1). *See* Irony *and* Oxymoron.

PARALLELISM. Parallelism is a rhetorical device in which a writer emphasizes the equal value or weight of two or more ideas by expressing them in the same grammatical form. Thomas Jefferson uses parallelism in the Declaration of Independence in citing his list of grievances against King George, starting each grievance with "He has" (Unit 1). *See* Rhetorical Device.

PARODY. A **parody** is a literary work that closely imitates the style of another work for humorous purposes. Parodies often exaggerate elements of the original work to create a comic effect. In the indented stanzas of "Do not weep, maiden, for war is kind," Stephen Crane subtly parodies overly dramatic patriotic speeches (Unit 3).

PERSONIFICATION. Personification is a type of figurative language in which an animal, thing, force of nature, or idea is described as if it were human or given human characteristics. In the poem "The Tide Rises, the Tide Falls," Henry Wadsworth Longfellow personifies waves, describing them as having "soft, white hands" (Unit 2).

PERSUASION. Persuasion, or *persuasive writing,* is intended to change or influence the way a reader thinks or feels about a particular issue or idea. Many essays and works of literary nonfiction have a persuasive purpose, including Eric Schlosser's "Throughput," from *Fast Food Nation* (Unit 9).

PETRARCHAN SONNET. *See* Sonnet.

PLAIN STYLE. The **plain style** of writing uses uncomplicated sentences and precise words to produce clear, simple statements. This type of writing often was used by Puritan writers such as Anne Bradstreet and Edward Taylor, who opposed unnecessary ornamentation in both the religious and secular aspects of life (Unit 1).

PLOT. A **plot** is the series of events related to a central conflict, or struggle. A plot typically introduces a conflict, develops it, and eventually resolves it. A plot often contains the following elements, although it may not include all of them and they may not appear in precisely this order:

- The **exposition,** or introduction, sets the tone or mood, introduces the characters and setting, and provides necessary background information.
- In the **rising action,** the conflict is developed and intensified.
- The **climax,** or *crisis,* is the high point of interest or suspense.
- The **falling action** consists of all the events that follow the climax.
- The **resolution,** or *dénouement* (dā' nü män´), is the point at which the central conflict is ended, or resolved.

See Conflict; Exposition; *and* Resolution.

POETRY. Poetry, a major genre of literature, is characterized by imaginative language that is carefully chosen and arranged to communicate experiences, thoughts, and emotions. Poetry differs from prose in that it compresses meaning into fewer words and often uses meter, rhyme, and imagery. Poetry usually is arranged in lines and stanzas, as opposed to sentences and paragraphs, and can be more free in the ordering of words and use of punctuation. Types of poetry include narrative, dramatic, and lyric (Understanding Literary Forms, Unit 3). *See* Dramatic Poem; Imagery; Lyric Poem; Meter; Narrative Poem; Prose; *and* Rhyme.

POINT OF VIEW. The **point of view** is the vantage point, or perspective, from which a story is told—in other words, who is telling the story. In *first-person point of view,* the story is told by someone who participates in or witnesses the action; this person, called the *narrator,* uses words such as *I* and *we* in telling the story. In *third-person point of view,* the narrator usually stands outside the action and observes; the narrator uses words such as *he, she, it,* and *they.* In a *limited point of view,* the thoughts of only the narrator or a single character are revealed. In an *omniscient point of view,* the thoughts of all the characters are revealed. *See* Narrator.

POLITICAL CRITICISM. Political criticism is a theory of literary criticism that suggests a work cannot be viewed clearly unless it is placed in its cultural context; the critic then studies the relationship of the text to social and economic class. The ideology of the author and the historical position of the literary work are given far more importance than, say, the structure or form of the work (Understanding Literary Criticism, Unit 7).

PRIMARY SOURCE. A **primary source** is direct evidence, or proof that comes straight from the individual or individuals involved in an event or activity. Primary sources include official documents as well as firsthand accounts such as diaries, letters, photographs, and paintings produced by participants or witnesses. *See* Source.

PROSE. Prose is the broad term used to describe all writing that is not drama or poetry, including fiction and nonfiction. Types of prose include novels, short stories, essays, and news stories. Most biographies, autobiographies, and letters are written in prose. *See* Drama; Fiction; Nonfiction; Poetry.

PROTAGONIST. The **protagonist** is the main character of a literary work. *See* Antagonist *and* Character.

PSYCHOLOGICAL CRITICISM. Psychological criticism is a theory of literary criticism that suggests a literary text is a storehouse of symbols. The critic applying this theory examines literary elements such as setting, character, conflict, and figurative language using psychoanalytical concepts such as the unconscious, the Oedipal complex, and archetypes. Psychological criticism is rooted in the work of Sigmund Freud and Carl Jung, two nineteenth-century Europeans who created the frame of reference for modern psychology (Understanding Literary Criticism, Unit 2).

PURPOSE. A writer's **purpose** is his or her aim, or goal. A writer usually has one or more of the following purposes: to inform or explain (*expository writing*); to portray a person, place, object, or event (*descriptive writing*); to convince people to accept a position and respond in some way (*persuasive writing*); and to tell a story (*narrative writing*).

QUATRAIN. A **quatrain** is a stanza of poetry containing four lines. *See* Stanza.

READER-RESPONSE CRITICISM. **Reader-response criticism** is a theory of literary criticism that suggests the reader creates the meaning of a text by reading and responding to it. As the reader delves into a literary work, he or she is engaged in a creative process that takes in the text and extends its significance in countless directions (Understanding Literary Criticism, Unit 5).

REALISM. **Realism** is the philosophy that works of art should accurately portray reality. The theory that the purpose of art is to imitate life is at least as old as Aristotle. The term *Realism* also is applied to American literature and painting of the late nineteenth century, which was a reaction to Romanticism and emphasized details of ordinary life. American Realist writers include Bret Harte, Henry James, and Mark Twain. *See* Romanticism.

REFRAIN. A **refrain** is a line or group of lines repeated in a poem or song. Many ballads contain refrains.

REGIONALISM. In art and literature, **Regionalism** is characterized by works that are set in a particular geographical region. The details used to create a particular regional setting often are called *local color.* Much American literature deals with the people and ways of life of particular regions of the country, such as New York City, the western frontier, or a small town in the South or New England. Fiction writer Willa Cather is often considered a Regionalist writer, as are poets Robert Frost and Carl Sandburg (Unit 5).

REPETITION. **Repetition** is a writer's intentional reuse of a sound, word, phrase, or sentence. Writers often use repetition, which is a rhetorical device, to emphasize ideas or, especially in poetry, to create a musical

effect. Presidents Franklin Delano Roosevelt (Unit 6) and John F. Kennedy (Unit 8) used repetition effectively in some of their most famous addresses. *See* Rhetorical Device.

RESOLUTION. The **resolution,** or *dénouement* (dā' nü män´), is the point at which the central conflict of the plot is ended, or resolved. *See* Plot.

RHETORIC. **Rhetoric** is the art of speaking or writing effectively. It involves studying how language affects an audience. Rhetoric also sometimes is defined as "the art of persuasion." *See* Persuasion.

RHETORICAL DEVICE. A **rhetorical device** is a technique used by a speaker or writer to achieve a particular effect, especially to persuade or influence. Common rhetorical devices include parallelism, repetition, and rhetorical questions. *See* Parallelism; Repetition; *and* Rhetorical Question.

RHETORICAL QUESTION. A **rhetorical question** is one asked for effect but not meant to be answered because the answer is clear from the context. Patrick Henry, in his Speech in the Virginia Convention, poses a series of rhetorical questions (Unit 1).

RHYME. **Rhyme** is the repetition of sounds at the ends of words. Types of rhyme include the following:

> *end rhyme,* the use of rhyming words at the ends of lines
> *internal rhyme,* the use of rhyming words within lines
> *exact rhyme,* in which the rhyming words end with the same sound or sounds, as in *moon* and *June*
> *slant rhyme,* in which the rhyming sounds are similar but not identical, as in *rave* and *rove*
> *sight rhyme,* in which the words are spelled similarly but pronounced differently, as in *lost* and *ghost*

RHYME SCHEME. A **rhyme scheme** is a pattern of end rhymes, or rhymes at the ends of lines of verse. The rhyme scheme of a poem is designated by letters, with matching letters signifying matching sounds. *See* Rhyme.

RHYTHM. **Rhythm** is the pattern of beats or stresses in a line of verse or prose. Rhythm can be regular or irregular. A regular rhythmic pattern in a poem is called a *meter. See* Meter.

RISING ACTION. *See* Plot.

ROMANTICISM. Romanticism was a literary and artistic movement of the eighteenth and nineteenth centuries that placed value on emotion or imagination over reason, the individual over society, nature and wildness over human works, the country over the city, common people over the ruling class, and freedom over control or authority. Transcendentalism was a particularly American form of Romanticism (Unit 2, Part 2). *See* Transcendentalism.

SATIRE. Satire is humorous writing or speech intended to point out human errors, falsehoods, foibles, or failings. It is written for the purpose of reforming human behavior or human institutions.

SCANSION. Scansion is the art of analyzing poetry to determine its meter. *See* Meter.

SENSORY DETAILS. Sensory details are words and phrases that describe how things look, sound, smell, taste, or feel. The use of sensory details is a key quality of descriptive writing. In the poem "Chicago," Carl Sandburg uses sensory details to capture the character of the city. *See* Description.

SESTET. A **sestet** is a stanza with six lines, such as the second part of a Petrarchan, or Italian, sonnet. See Meter *and* Sonnet.

SETTING. The **setting** of a literary work is the time and place in which it occurs, together with all the details used to create a sense of a particular time and place. Writers create setting by various means. In drama, the setting often is revealed by the stage set and the costumes, although it may be revealed through what the characters say about their environs. In fiction, setting is most often revealed by means of description of elements such as landscape, scenery, buildings, furniture, clothing, the weather, and the season. Setting also can be revealed by how characters talk and behave.

SHORT STORY. A **short story** is brief work of fiction. A short story is carefully crafted to develop a plot, characters, setting, mood, and theme, all within relatively few pages. Some of the earliest American writers of short stories were Nathaniel Hawthorne, Washington Irving, and Edgar Allan Poe (Unit 2). Southern Renaissance writers such as William Faulkner, Katherine Anne Porter, Eudora Welty, and Tennessee Williams also popularized the genre (Understanding Literary Forms, Unit 6). *See* Fiction.

SIMILE. A **simile** is a comparison of two seemingly unlike things using the word *like* or *as.* In the poem "Camouflaging the Chimera," Yusef Komunyakaa describes the enemy with this simile: "VC struggled with the hillside, like black silk wrestling iron through grass" (Unit 8).

SLANT RHYME. In **slant rhyme,** sounds are similar but not exact, as in *world/boiled* and *bear/bore.* Emily Dickinson uses slant rhyme in "Much Madness is divinest sense"—for instance, "sense" and "madness"; "eye" and "majority" (Unit 3). *See* Rhyme.

SOCIOLOGICAL CRITICISM. Sociological criticism is a theory of literary criticism that suggests a literary text cannot be seen apart from the values and rules that govern the society at large. However, just as the social structure keeps changing and evolving, so do the expectations or attitudes of authors and readers (Understanding Literary Criticism, Unit 9).

SOLILOQUY. A **soliloquy** is a speech delivered by a lone character in a drama that reveals his or her thoughts and feelings.

SONNET. A **sonnet** is a fourteen-line poem, usually in iambic pentameter, that follows one of a number of different rhyme schemes. The *English, Elizabethan,* or *Shakespearean* sonnet is divided into four parts: three quatrains and a final couplet. The rhyme scheme of such a sonnet is *abab cdcd efef gg.* "Sonnet XXX," by Edna St. Vincent Millay, is an example of an English sonnet (Unit 5). The *Italian,* or *Petrarchan,* sonnet is divided into two parts: an octave and a sestet. The rhyme scheme of the octave is *abbaabba.* The rhyme scheme of the sestet can be *cdecde, cdcdcd,* or *cdedce.* *See* Rhyme Scheme *and* Stanza.

SOURCE. A **source** is evidence of an event, idea, or development. *See* Primary Source.

SOUTHERN RENAISSANCE. The **Southern Renaissance** movement of the 1930s and 1940s marked a deliberate break from the region's traditional literary aesthetic. Southern Renaissance writers such as William Faulkner, Katherine Anne Porter, and Tennessee Williams revealed the beauty and grace of Southern culture without condoning the racism and cruelty it had endorsed. In addition, they experimented with such as stream-of-consciousness writing and complex narratives (Unit 6, Part 2). *See* Stream-of-Consciousness Writing.

SPEAKER. The **speaker** is the character who speaks in, or narrates, a poem—the voice assumed by the writer. The speaker and the writer of a poem are not necessarily the same person. The indecisive, middle-aged J. Alfred Prufrock is the speaker in T. S. Eliot's "The Love Song of J. Alfred Prufrock" (Unit 5). In Carl Sandburg's "Grass," the grass is the speaker (Unit 5). *See* Narrator.

SPEECH. A **speech** is a public communication or expression of thought in spoken words. The purpose of a speech is often to inform an audience about a given subject or to persuade them to a particular point of view (Understanding Literary Forms, Unit 4).

STAGE DIRECTIONS. **Stage directions** are notes included in a play, in addition to the dialogue, for the purpose of describing how something should be performed on stage. Stage directions describe setting, lighting, music, sound effects, entrances and exits, properties, and the movements of characters. These directions usually are printed in italics and enclosed in brackets or parentheses. Playwright Arthur Miller is known for his extensive stage directions (Unit 7).

STANZA. A **stanza** is a group of lines in a poem. The following are common types of stanzas:

two-line stanza	couplet
three-line stanza	triplet or tercet
four-line stanza	quatrain
five-line stanza	quintain
six-line stanza	sestet
seven-line stanza	heptastich
eight-line stanza	octave

STREAM-OF-CONSCIOUSNESS WRITING. **Stream-of-consciousness writing** attempts to present the flow of feelings, thoughts, and impressions within the minds of characters. Modern American masters of stream-of-consciousness writing include William Faulkner and Katherine Anne Porter. An example of stream-of-consciousness writing is Porter's "The Jilting of Granny Weatherall" (Unit 6).

STYLE. **Style** refers to the manner in which something is said or written. A writer's style is characterized by elements such as word choice (or *diction*), sentence structure and length, and other recurring features that distinguish his or her work from that of another. One way to think of a writer's style is as his or her written personality.

SUSPENSE. **Suspense** is a feeling of expectation, anxiousness, or curiosity created by questions raised in the mind of a reader or viewer. The high point of interest and suspense in a literary work is called the *climax. See* Climax.

SYMBOL. A **symbol** is anything that stands for or represents both itself and something else. Writers use two types of symbols. A *conventional symbol* is one with traditional, widely recognized associations. Such symbols include doves for peace; the color green for jealousy; winter, evening, or night for old age; wind for change or inspiration. A *personal,* or *idiosyncratic, symbol* is one that assumes its secondary meaning because of the special way the writer uses it. In "Song of Myself," Walt Whitman uses *grass* as a personal symbol for the beauty and value of simple, lowly things (Unit 3).

TALL TALE. A **tall tale** is a story, often lighthearted or humorous, that contains highly exaggerated, unrealistic elements. Mark Twain's "The Notorious Jumping Frog of Calaveras County" is an example of a tall tale (Unit 4).

THEME. A **theme** is a central message or perception about life revealed through a literary work. A *stated theme* is presented directly, whereas an *implied theme* must be inferred. Most works of fiction do not have a stated theme but rather several implied themes. A *universal theme* is a message about life that can be understood by people of most cultures.

THESIS. A **thesis** is a main idea presented and supported in a work of nonfiction. *See* Nonfiction.

TONE. **Tone** is the emotional attitude toward the reader or toward the subject implied by a literary work. Tone may be revealed by such elements as word choice (*diction*), sentence structure, and use of imagery. Examples of tone include familiar, ironic, playful, sarcastic, serious, and sincere.

TRAGEDY. A **tragedy** is a work of literature, particularly a drama, that tells the story of the fall of a person of high status. It celebrates the courage and dignity of a *tragic hero,* or the main character in a tragedy, in the face of inevitable doom. Sometimes that doom is made inevitable by a *tragic flaw,* or personal weakness that brings about a fall, in the hero. Today, the term *tragedy* is used more loosely to mean any work that has a sad ending. *See* Comedy *and* Drama.

TRANSCENDENTALISM. As a variation of European Romanticism, **Transcendentalism** was rooted in the belief in a realm of spiritual or transcendent truths beyond what humans can know through their senses. Placing oneself in a natural environment was believed to increase the ability to attain transcendent thought. Transcendentalists exalted the spiritual and the individual over the material and conventional. The Transcendentalist movement, which developed in the Boston area in the mid-1800s, attracted many of the leading intellectuals of the day, including Henry David Thoreau, Ralph Waldo Emerson, Bronson Alcott, and Margaret Fuller (Unit 2, Part 2).

VERNACULAR. The **vernacular** is the speech of the common people. The term *vernacular* often is used loosely today to refer to dialogue or to writing in general that uses colloquial, dialectical, or slang expressions. Jack Kerouac and the other Beat writers used vernacular language in their works (Unit 7, Part 3). *See* Dialogue.

VILLANELLE. A **villanelle** is a complex and intricate nineteen-line form of French verse. The rhyme scheme is *aba aba aba aba abaa*. Line 1 is repeated as lines 6, 12, and 18. Line 3 is repeated as lines 9, 15, and 19. Line 1 and 3 appear as a rhymed couplet at the end of the poem. Elizabeth Bishop's poem "One Art" is an example of a villanelle (Unit 6).

VOICE. **Voice** comprises the writer's use of language to reflect his or her unique personality and attitude toward the topic, form, and audience. A writer expresses his or her voice through tone, word choice, and sentence structure.

Glossary of Vocabulary Words

A

ab • di • cate (ab´ də kāt) *v.*, give up a right or a responsibility

abey • ance (ä bā´ yents) *n.*, temporary inactivity

ab • hor (əb hōr´) *v.*, feel disgust toward; hate; shrink from in disgust

abide (ə bīd´) *v.*, accept; tolerate

abode (ä bōd´) *n.*, where one lives or stays; home

ab • ject • ly (ab´ jekt lē) *adv.*, miserably; in a manner showing hopelessness or resignation

abom • i • na • tion (a bô' mə nā´ shən) *n.*, something worthy of hatred or disgust

ac • cliv • i • ty (ə kliv´ ə tē) *n.*, upward slope

ac • qui • esce (a kwē es´) *v.*, agree without protest

acute (ä kyüt´) *adj.*, sharp

ad • a • mant (a´ də mənt) *adj.*, unyielding; insisting on maintaining a position

aes • thet • ics (as thet´ ik) *n.*, set of principles, often related to appearance

af • fec • tions (ä fek´ shənz) *n.*, emotions

af • flic • ted (ə flik´ təd) *adj.*, suffering from an illness or other painful physical condition

ag • grand • ize (ə grand´ īz) *v.*, increase one's power and wealth

ag • gre • ga • tion (a' grə gā´ shən) *n.*, group or collection

ag • i • ta • tion (a' jə tā´ shən) *n.*, appreciable motion or disturbance; irregular, rapid, or violent movement or action

al • be • it (əl bē´ it) *conj.*, even though

al • leged (ə lejd´) *adj.*, accused but not proven or convinced

al • tru • ist • ic (äl' trü is´ tik) *adj.*, motivated by unselfish concern for the welfare of others

am • bush (am´ bùsh) *n.*, trap in which a concealed soldier or soldiers lie in wait to attack by surprise

ame • li • o • rate (ä me´ lē ōr āt) *v.*, make better or more tolerable

am • i • ca • bly (am´ ik ə blē) *adv.*, in a friendly or peaceful manner

an • ar • chy (an´ är kē) *n.*, state of lawlessness

an • guished (āŋ´ gwisht) *adj.*, extremely anxious; tormented

an • ni • hi • late (an nī´ il āt) *v.*, destroy

ap • a • thet • i • cal • ly (a´ pə the´ tik lē) *adv.*, without emotion

ap • a • thy (a´ pə thē) *n.*, lack of interest or concern; indifference

ap • par • el (ä pār´ 'l) *n.*, clothing

ap • pa • ri • tion (a pə ri´ shən) *n.*, ghost, specter, or phantom

ap • pend (ə pend´) *v.*, attach or affix

ap • pre • hen • sion (a' prē hen´ shən) *n.*, anxiety; dread; suspicion or fear

ar • dent (är´ dənt) *adj.*, passionate

ar • du • ous (är´ jü əs) *adj.*, difficult; hard to accomplish or achieve

arm • a • ture (ärm´ ə chər) *n.*, framework or defensive structure

ar • rant (är´ ənt) *adj.*, extreme

ar • ray (ə rā´) *v.*, dress somebody in particular clothes; arrange something for display

as • cer • tain (a sʉr tān´) *v.*, determine

as • ce • tic (ə set´ ik) *adj.*, self-denying; severe

as • cribe (ə skrīb´) *v.*, assign; attribute

as • sail (ə sāl´) *v.*, attack vigorously with words or actions

as • sent (ə sent´) *v.*, agree

as • sert (ä sʉrt´) *v.*, declare; affirm

as • sur • ance (ä shʉr´ ənts) *n.*, confidence in ability or status

asun • der (ə sun´ dər) *adv.*, separated in direction or position

au • dac • i • ty (ô da´ sə tē) *n.*, boldness; daring

au • gust (ä´ gəst) *adj.*, majestic, noble, and impressive

avail (ä vāl´) *v.*, be of use or advantage

aver • sion (ä vʉr´ shən) *n.*, strong dislike

avert (ä vʉrt´) *v.*, turn away; prevent

B

bale • ful (bāl´ f'l) *adj.*, sinister

balk (bôk) *v.*, stop and refuse to continue

bar • rack (bär´ ək) *n.,* shed for temporary dwelling

base (bās) *adj.,* of low place or position

be • guile (bə gīl´) *v.,* deceive by trickery

be • guil • ing (bə gī´ liŋ) *adj.,* charming; leading by deception

be • la • bor (bə lā´ bər) *v.,* spend too much time or effort on

be • lie (bə lī´) *v.,* give a false impression of

bel • li • cose (bel´ ə kōs) *adj.,* hostile; eager to fight

be • nign (bə nīn´) *adj.,* harmless; not cancerous

be • seech (bi sēch´) *v.,* beg; plead

be • seech • ing (bē sēch´ iŋ) *adj.,* begging or imploring

bi • son (bī´ s'n) *n.,* type of mammal having a shaggy mane, short, curved horns, and humped back; commonly referred to as the American buffalo

blight (blīt) *n.,* anything that destroys or prevents growth

blithe (blī<u>th</u>) *adj.,* happy, blissful

bough (bou) *n.,* main branch of a tree

brack • en (brak´ ən) *n.,* large, coarse, weedy ferns occurring in meadows and woods

brusque • ness (brusk´ nes) *n.,* abrupt or blunt manner

C

ca • dence (kā´ dənts) *n.,* rhythmic motion or sequence

ca • la • mi • ty (kə lam´ ə tē) *n.,* disaster

cal • low (ka´ lō) *adj.,* lacking adult sophistication

cal • um • ny (kal´ um nē) *n.,* attempt to harm a person's reputation through deliberate misrepresentation

ca • vort (kə vōrt´) *v.,* leap about; prance

caul • dron (kôl´ drən) *n.,* large pot or kettle

cir • cum • vent (sʉr kum vent´) *v.,* outwit, get around

ci • vil • i • ty (sə vil´ ə tē) *n.,* gentleness, politeness; civilized manner

cleave (klēv) *v.,* adhere to loyally

clod (kläd) *n.,* lump, often of earth or clay

cog • ni • zant (kôg´ nə zənt) *adj.,* aware; knowledgeable

com • mu • nal (kə myü´ n'l) *adj.,* participated in, shared, or used by members of a group or a community

com • mun • ion (kə myü´ nyən) *n.,* act of sharing thoughts and actions

com • pla • cent (kəm plā´ sənt) *adj.,* being unconcerned or self-satisfied

con • ceit (kən sēt´) *n.,* idea, thought; personal opinion

con • cil • i • a • to • ry (kən sil´ ē ə tō rē) *adj.,* with an aim to please in order to gain something

con • found • ed (kən foun´ dəd) *adj.,* baffled; frustrated

con • jec • ture (kən jek´ chər) *n.,* prediction based on guesswork

con • se • crate (kän´ sə krāt) *v.,* make or declare sacred

con • sole (kən sōl´) *v.,* comfort

con • spic • u • ous (kən spik´ yü əs) *adj.,* easily seen

con • sti • tu • tion (kän' stə tü´ shən) *n.,* physical makeup of a person

con • sum • mate (kän´ sü māt) *v.,* complete; finish

con • tempt (kən tempt´) *n.,* strong dislike, lack of respect

con • temp • tu • ous (kən temp´ chü əs) *adj.,* demon-strating a strong dislike or lack of respect

con • tend • er (kən ten´ dər) *n.,* one who strives or fights in competition

con • ten • tious (kən ten´ shəs) *adj.,* having a tendency to start arguments; belligerent

con • triv • ance (kən trī´ vəns) *n.,* invention; clever plan

con • viv • i • al (kən vē´ vē əl) *adj.,* relating to feasting, drinking, and good company

cor • pu • lent (kōr´ pyü lənt) *adj.,* obese

cra • ven (krā´ vən) *n.,* coward

crim • soned (krim´ sənd) *v.,* reddened

cum • ber • some (kum´ bər sum) *adj.,* hard to move or carry due to bulk or heaviness

cur • so • ry (kʉr´ sər ē) *adj.,* rapidly and often inadequately performed or done

cyn • ic • al (sin´ ə k'l) *adj.,* mocking or scornful

D

de • cep • tion (dē sep´ shən) *n.,* act of misleading by a false appearance or statement

dec • i • mate (des´ ə māt) *v.,* reduce drastically

de • ci • pher (dē sī´ fər) *v.,* make out the meaning of

dec • o • rous • ly (dek´ ʉr əs lē) *adv.,* with good manners; politely

def • er • ence (def´ ə rənts) *n.,* respect or esteem for an elder or superior

def • er • en • tial (def' ər en´ ch'l) *adj.,* respectful

de • fraud (də fräd´) *v.,* take someone's money or property dishonestly; to cheat

de • gen • er • ate (dē jen´ ʉr ət) *adj.,* having sunk to a lower level of quality or being

de • mur (di mər´) *v.,* disagree

de • plor • a • ble (di plōr´ ə bəl) *adj.,* wretched; awful

de • plore (də plōr´) *v.,* regret; consider unworthy

de • po • si • tion (de pə zi´ shən) *n.,* recorded testimony taken under oath

de • ride (də rīd´) *v.,* laugh at; ridicule

de • riv • a • tive (də riv´ ə tiv) *adj.,* based on something else; imitative

des • ul • to • ry (de səl´ tōr ē) *adj.,* irregular; uneven

di • gress (dī gres´) *v.,* deviate from the main topic in speaking or writing

di • lap • i • dat • ed (də lap´ ə dā təd) *adj.,* falling to pieces or into disrepair

di • late (dī´ lāt) *v.,* become larger or wider

dil • i • gent • ly (dil´ ə jənt lē) *adv.,* painstakingly; industriously

di • shev • el • ment (di shev´ 'l mənt) *n.,* disorderliness

di • vest (dī vest´) *v.,* strip; cast off

di • ves • ti • ture (dī ves´ tə chùr') *n.,* act of disposing of or freeing oneself of something

dis • cern • ing (di sərn´ iŋ) *adj.,* critical

dis • com • fit (dis kum´ fit) *v.,* confuse; disconcert

dis • con • so • late (dis kôn´ sə lət) *adj.,* saddened; not capable of being consoled

dis • dain (dis dān´) *v.,* treat as unworthy

dis • fran • chised (dis fran´ chīzd) *adj.,* deprived of legal rights, particularly voting

dis • perse (dis pʉrs´) *v.,* spread or break apart

dis • po • si • tion (dis pə zi´ shən) *n.,* one's customary frame of mind; general nature or character

dis • sem • ble (də sem´ b'l) *v.,* put on a false appearance

dis • til (di stil´) *v.,* let fall in drops, like rain (also spelled *distill*)

dod • der • ing (dä´ də riŋ) *adj.,* senile; feeble

dole • ful (dōl´ fəl) *adj.,* full of or causing sorrow or sadness

dupe (düp) *v.,* deceive by underhanded means; trick

dwin • dle (dwin´ d'l) *v.,* languish; fade

E

ear • nest (ʉr´ nəst) *adj.,* serious; sincere

ef • face (ə fās´) *v.,* erase; wipe out; eliminate

ef • face • ment (e fās´ mənt) *n.,* disappearance or fading as if by wearing away

ef • fec • tu • al (i fek´ chə[wə]l) *adj.,* effective

ef • fi • gy (ef´ ə gē) *n.,* image or representation of a person

ef • fron • tery (e frun´ tər ē) *n.,* shameless boldness; gall

egal • i • tar • i • an (ē gal' ə tār´ ē ən) *adj.,* asserting a belief in human equality, especially in terms of social, political, and economic rights

elic • it (ē lis´ it) *v.,* draw forth or bring out

em • bel • lish • ment (em bel´ ish mənt) *n.,* act or process of making beautiful with ornamentation

em • bra • sure (em brā´ zhər) *n.,* slanted opening in a wall that increases the firing angle of a gun

em • ploy (em ploi´) *n.,* use

en • com • pass (in kəm´ pəs) *v.,* include; enclose

en • cum • brance (ən kum´ brəns) *n.,* hindrance; burden

en • deav • or (in de´ vər) *v.,* attempt

en • dow (en dou´) *v.,* provide with something freely or naturally

en • ig • ma • tic (en' ig ma´ tik) *adj.,* mysterious; hard to explain

en • mi • ty (en´ mi tē) *n.,* active and usually mutual hatred or ill will

en • sue (en sü´) *v.*, come afterward; follow immediately

en • thralled (in thräld´) *adj.*, spellbound; mesmerized

en • treat (en trēt´) *v.*, beg; ask earnestly

en • treaty (en trē´ tē) *n.*, earnest request; plea; act of asking urgently

enu • mer • a • tion (ē nü' mər ā´ shən) *n.*, list of one thing after another

equa • nim • i • ty (e kwä nim´ ə tē) *n.*, evenness of temper; quality of remaining calm

equi • vo • cal (e kwiv´ ə k'l) *adj.*, able to be understood in more than one way

erad • i • cate (ē rad´ ə kāt) *v.*, get rid of; wipe out; destroy

er • ro • ne • ous (i rōn´ ē əs) *adj.*, incorrect or based on an incorrect assumption

es • the • tic (es the´ tik) *adj.*, pleasing in appearance

ethe • re • al (ē thē´ rē 'l) *adj.*, heavenly; delicate and refined

ethos (ē´ thōs) *n.*, guiding belief or principle of a group or institution

evade (ē vād´) *v.*, avoid answering directly

eva • sive • ly (ē vā´ siv lē) *adv.*, in a manner intended to evade or avoid

evince (ē vins´) *v.*, show plainly

evoke (ē vōk´) *v.*, bring to mind

ex • as • per • at • ing (eg zas´ pʉr āt' iŋ) *adj.*, irritating; annoying

ex • hil • a • ra • tion (eks iľ ə rā´ shən) *n.*, joy and excitement

ex • hor • ter (ig zôrt´ ər) *n.*, one who urges earnestly by advice or warning

ex • pe • di • ent (eks pē´ dē 'nt) *n.*, temporary means to an end

ex • pend (ik spend´) *v.*, use for a specific purpose

ex • pur • gate (eks´ pər gāt) *v.*, remove objectionable parts from a work before publication or presentation

ex • tem • po • rize (eks tem p ´ ə rīz) *v.*, contrive in a makeshift way to meet a pressing need

ex • trem • i • ty (eks trem´ ə tē) *n.*, state of extreme necessity or danger

F

fal • ter • ing (fäl´ tər iŋ) *adj.*, unsteady; wavering

fas • cist (fa´ shist) *n.*, member of an oppressive political movement

fawn • ing (fän´ iŋ) *adj.*, showing affection with flattery or in a cringing manner

fee • ble (fē´ bl) *adj.*, weak

feign (fān) *v.*, pretend; dissemble

fe • lo • ni • ous (fə lōn´ ē əs) *adj.*, of a criminal

fis • sure (fi´ zhər) *n.*, long, narrow, deep cleft or crack

flor • id (flōr´ id) *adj.*, flowery or overly elaborate in style

fluc • tu • ate (fluk´ chü āt) *v.*, change or vary continuously

foe (fō) *n.*, enemy or adversary

fo • liage (fō´ lē ij) *n.*, collection of leaves, flowers, and plants

for • lorn (fər lôrn´) *adj.*, sad and lonely due to isolation or desertion

for • mi • da • ble (fōr mid´ ə b'l) *adj.*, overwhelming

for • mu • lat • ed (fōr´ myü lā təd) *adj.*, systematical; precise

for • ti • tude (fōr´ tə tüd) *n.*, strength of mind that enables a person to accomplish a goal

freight • ed (frā´ təd) *v.*, loaded

fur • row (fʉr´ ō) *n.*, narrow rut or groove

fu • sion (fyü´ zhən) *n.*, merging of distinct elements into a unified whole

G

gain • say (gān´ sā) *v.*, deny or declare untrue

gar • ment (gär´ mənt) *n.*, any article of clothing

gar • ru • lous (gār´ ə ləs) *adj.*, talking a lot or too much

gaunt (gônt) *adj.*, excessively thin and angular

ges • tic • u • late (jes tik´ yü lāt') *v.*, make gestures with hands or arms

glut • ton • y (glut´ tən ē) *n.*, habit or act of eating too much

grudge (grudj) *v.*, allow or give something reluctantly; be envious or resentful

guf • faw • ing (gə fô´ iŋ) *adj.*, laughing loudly and coarsely

guile (gīl) *n.*, secretiveness, sneakiness

guile • less (gīl´ ləs) *adj.*, without deceit

gull (gul) *v.*, deceive

gul • ly (gʉ´ lē) *n.*, channel or hollow worn by running water

H

hag • gard (hāg ´ ərd) *adj.*, having a wasted or exhausted look

har • bor (här´ bər) *v.*, serve as, or provide, a place of protection

haugh • ty (hô´ tē) *adj.*, disdainfully or contemptuously proud

he • do • nis • tic (hē də nis´ tik) *adj.*, relating to or characterized by pleasure

hoary (hōr´ ē) *adj.*, having white or gray hair

ho • mo • ge • ne • i • ty (hō´ mō jə nā´ ə tē) *n.*, quality of being the same or similar in nature

husky (hus´ kē) *adj.*, solid; burly; strong

I

icon (ī´ kän) *n.*, symbolic religious image

ig • no • rant (ig´ nʉr ənt) *adj.*, unaware

im • pal • pa • ble (im pal´ pə b'l) *adj.*, that which cannot be felt by touching

im • pec • cable (im pek´ ə b'l) *adj.*, without error

im • pen • e • tra • ble (im pen´ ə trə b'l) *adj.*, unable to be comprehended or penetrated

im • per • a • tive (im pār´ ə tiv) *adj.*, absolutely necessary

im • pe • ri • al • ly (im pēr´ ē əl ē) *adv.*, grandly or majestically

im • pe • ri • ous (im pir´ ē əs) *adj.*, intensely compelling

im • pet • u • ous (im pet´ chü əs) *adj.*, here, forceful; violent

im • ple • ment (im´ plə mənt) *n.*, tool; utensil

im • por • tu • ni • ty (im´ pōr tü´ nə tē) *n.*, persistent demand

in • cen • di • ary (in sen´ dē ār ē) *adj.*, relating to or involving deliberate burning of property

in • cense (in sens´) *v.*, make very angry

in • ces • sant (in ses´ ənt) *adj.*, continuing or following without interruption

in • ces • sant • ly (in ses´ ənt lē) *adv.*, continuing for a long time without stopping

in • co • her ent (in´ kō här´ ənt) *adj.*, unclear; not understandable

in • cul • ca • tion (in´ kul kā´ shən) *n.*, teaching imparted through frequent repetition

in • dict • ment (in dīt´ mənt) *n.*, state of being charged with a crime or offense

in • dif • fer • ence (in di´ frənts) *n.*, quality or state of being impartial or disinterested

in • dig • e • nous (in dij´ ə nəs) *adj.*, having originated in and being produced, growing, living, or occurring naturally in a particular region or environment

in • duce (in düs´) *v.*, persuade

in • ef • fec • tu • al (i nə fek´ chə[wə]l) *adj.*, not powerful enough to achieve the desired effect; inadequate

in • es • ti • ma • ble (in es´ tə mä b'l) *adj.*, that which cannot be measured

in • ev • i • ta • ble (i ne´ və tə bəl) *adj.*, incapable of being avoided or evaded

in • fa • my (in´ fə mē) *n.*, evil reputation brought about by something grossly criminal, shocking, or brutal

in • fi • del (in´ fə del) *n.*, person who does not believe in a particular religion

in • fin • i • tes • i • mal (in´ fin ə tes´ ə mäl) *adj.*, immeasurably or incalculably small

in • firm (in fʉrm´) *adj.*, feeble from age; sick

in • gra • ti • at • ing (in grā´ shē āt´ iŋ) *adj.*, given to deliberate efforts to gain favorable acceptance

in • her • ent (in här´ ənt) *adj.*, belonging by nature or habit

in • her • ent • ly (in här´ ənt lē) *adv.*, characteristically; naturally

in • nu • en • do (in´ yü en´ dō) *n.*, indirect remark or gesture with a suggestion of impropriety

in • nu • mer • a • ble (i nü´ mʉr ə b'l) *adj.*, too many to count

in • or • di • nate (in ōr´ di nət) *adj.*, excessive; beyond reasonable limits

in • sen • si • ble (in sen´ sə bəl) *adj.*, lacking sensation; unaware

in • sid • i • ous (in sid´ ē əs) *adj.*, deceitful; sly; crafty

in • sip • id (in sip´ əd) *adj.*, without flavor

in • so • lence (in´ sə lənts) *n.*, disrespectfulness

in • sur • gent (in sʉr´ jənt) *adj.*, revolting against an established government

in • sur • rec • tion (in sʉr rek´ shən) *n.*, uprising, rebellion

in • tent (in tent´) *n.*, purpose; plan

in • ter • mi • na • ble (in tʉr´ min ə bl´) *adj.*, without, or apparently without, end

in • ter • mi • na • bly (in tʉr´ min ə blē) *adv.*, endlessly

in • ter • mit • tent (in tʉr mit´ ənt) *adj.*, coming and going at intervals; not continuous

in • trigue (in´ trēg) *n.*, secret scheme

in • trin • sic (in trinz´ ək) *adj.*, belonging to the essential nature or constitution of a thing

in • tu • i • tive • ly (in tü´ it iv lē) *adv.*, through intuition; without having to think about it or be taught how to do it

in • vec • tive (in vek´ tiv) *n.*, insulting or abusive language

in • vi • o • late (in vī´ ə lət) *adj.*, sacred

in • voke (in vōk´) *v.*, call on for blessing, help, or inspiration

itin • er • ant (ī ti´ nə rənt') *adj.*, traveling from place to place

J

jilt (jilt) *v.*, reject; cast off

joc • u • lar • i • ty (jôk' yü lār´ ə tē) *n.*, humor; joking

jux • ta • po • si • tion (juks' tə pō zi´ shən) *n.*, state of being side by side

L

lab • y • rinth (la´ bə rinth) *n.*, maze

lapse (laps) *n.*, discontinuation; passing away

lash (lash) *v.*, strike hard with great force

la • tent (lā´ tənt) *adj.*, hidden but likely to emerge at some time

li • cen • tious (lə sen´ shəs) *adj.*, lacking morals

lim • ber (lim´ bər) *adj.*, having a supple and resilient quality

lin • ger (liŋ´ gər) *v.*, remain or stay longer than usual

lin • guist (liŋ´ gwist) *n.*, specialist in the science of language

list (list) *v.*, tilt to one side

loath • some (lō<u>th</u>´ səm) *adj.*, disgusting

lob (lôb) *v.*, throw, hit, or propel easily or in a high arc

loft • i • ly (lôft´ ə lē) *adv.*, with a tone of superiority or self-pride

loom (lüm) *v.*, appear in excessively large form

lu • di • crous (lü´ di krəs) *adj.*, absurd; ridiculous

M

mach • i • na • tion (ma' kə nā´ shən) *n.*, clever plot or scheme

mag • na • nim • i • ty (mag' nə nim´ ə tē) *n.*, state of being above pettiness

ma • lev • o • lence (mä le´ və lənts) *n.*, ill will; spite; hatred

ma • lice (ma´ lis) *n.*, active ill will; evil intent; desire to cause pain or injury to another

ma • lign (mə līn´) *adj.*, malicious; evil

ma • lin • ger (mə liŋ´ gər) *v.*, pretend illness

man • i • fest (man´ ə fest) *adj.*, noticeable

man • i • fold (man´ i fōld) *adv.*, many times; a great deal

mar • tial (mär´ shəl) *adj.*, warlike; relating to the military

mar • vel (mär´ vəl) *v.*, become filled with surprise, wonder, or curiosity

ma • son (mā´ sən) *n.*, a skilled worker in brick and stone

me • nag • er • ie (mə na´ jə rē) *n.*, collection of wild or exotic animals

mol • li • fy (môl´ ə fī) *v.*, soothe the temper of

moon (mün) *v.*, behave in a dreamy abstracted manner

mor • a • to • ri • um (mōr' ə tōr´ ē um) *n.*, authorized delay or suspension of activity

mo • rose (mə rōs´) *adj.*, having a sullen and gloomy disposition

mus • ing (myüz´ iŋ) *n.*, reflection or meditation

my • ri • ad (mīr´ ē əd) *adj.*, of a varied nature

mys • ti • fic • a • tion (mis tə fi kā´ shən) *n.*, act of making something mysterious or hard to explain

N

noc • tur • nal (nôk tʉr´ nəl) *adj.*, of, relating to, or occurring at night

no • ma • dic (nō ma´ dik) *adj.*, roaming from place to place aimlessly

non • cha • lance (nôn shə läns´) *n.*, state of being seemingly unconcerned; coolness

non • com • mit • tal (nôn kə mit´ 'l) *adj.*, giving no clear indication of attitude or feeling

nos • tal • gia (nä stal´ jä) *n.*, state of sentimental longing, often for the past; homesickness

nov • el (nô´ v'l) *adj.*, new; unheard of

nov • el • ty (nä´ vəl tē) *n.*, something new or unusual

nu • cle • us (nü´ klē əs) *n.*, core; central part

nup • tial (nup´ shəl) *adj.*, concerning marriage or a wedding

O

obei • sance (ō bā´ səns) *n.*, gesture of respect

ob • dur • ate (ôb´ dʉr ət) *adj.*, unsympathetic; hardened

ob • lit • er • ate (ô bli´ tʉr āt) *v.*, wipe away; erase

ob • sti • nate (äb´ stə nət), *adj.*, stubborn; not easily changed

ob • tuse (ôb tüs´) *adj.*, slow to understand or perceive; insensitive

odi • ous (ō´ dē əs) *adj.*, arousing or deserving hatred

odys • sey (ô´ dis ē) *n.*, long, eventful voyage or quest

of • fen • sive (ō fen´ siv) *n.*, attack

ol • i • gar • chy (ä´ lə gär' kē) *n.*, government in which a small group exercises control, especially for corrupt and selfish purposes

om • i • nous (ô´ mə nəs) *adj.*, foreshadowing evil or menace

on • slaught (än´ slôt) *n.*, especially fierce attack

opaque (ō pāk´) *adj.*, not admitting light

or • nery (ōr´ nər ē) *adj.*, having an ugly or mean disposition

os • cil • la • tion (äs' ə lā´ shən) *n.*, act of swinging back and forth

os • ten • ta • tion (ô sten tā´ shən) *n.*, showiness, often intended to attract attention

os • ten • ta • tious • ly (ôs ten tā´ shəs lē) *adv.*, so as to attract attention

over • ture (ōv´ rə chʉr) *n.*, musical introduction to an opera or other large musical work

P

pall (pôl) *n.*, covering that obscures or cloaks gloomily

pal • pa • ble (pal´ pə b'l) *adj.*, easily perceived; obvious; clear; able to be touched or felt

par • a • dox • i • cal (pār' ə dôk´ sik 'l) *adj.*, seemingly contradictory

par • ley (pär´ lē) *n.*, conference with an enemy

par • si • mo • ny (pär´ sə mō' nē) *n.*, stinginess

pa • tri • arch (pā´ trē ärk) *n.*, father; ruler; founder

pen • du • lum (pen´ jə lum) *n.*, object suspended from a fixed point that swings freely back and forth; commonly used to regulate movement, as in a clock

pen • i • tence (pen´ ə tents) *n.*, humble remorse for wrongdoing

pen • sive (pen´ səv) *adj.*, expressing deep thoughtfulness, often mixed with sadness

per • di • tion (pʉr di´ shən) *n.*, destruction; damnation

per • emp • to • ri • ly (pʉr emp´ tər ə lē) *adv.*, in a commanding manner

per • en • ni • al (pʉr en´ ē 'l) *adj.*, repeated every year

per • il (pār´ 'l) *n.*, exposure to risk of being injured, destroyed, or lost

per • ish (pār´ ish) *v.*, die

per • pe • tu • i • ty (pʉr' pə tü´ ə tē) *n.*, eternity

per • se • vere (pʉr sə vēr´) *v.*, continue in spite of difficulty; persist

pet • ri • fied (pe´ trə fīd) *adj.*, turned to stone

phi • lan • thro • py (fə lan´ thrō pē) *n.*, act or gift of dispensing aid or funds set aside for humanitarian purposes

pic • tur • esque (pik´ chər resk´) *adj.*, resembling a picture; charming or quaint

pil • fer (pil´ fʊr) *v.*, steal

pil • grim • age (pil´ grə mij) *n.*, journey to a sacred place

pi • ous (pī´ əs) *adj.*, devoted to divine worship; religious

pique (pēk) *v.*, irritate; provoke

pla • cid (pla´ sid) *adj.*, calm or free of disturbance

pla • gia • rist (plā´ jə rist) *n.*, someone who takes credit for the ideas or work of another person

pla • toon (plä tün´) *n.*, subdivision of a military unit, normally consisting of sixteen to forty-four personnel

poi • gnant (poi´ nyənt) *adj.*, sharp; painful

poi • gnant • ly (poi´ nyənt lē) *adv.*, in a manner that deeply affects the emotions

poise (poiz) *n.*, balance; self-control

pomp • ous (päm´ pəs) *adj.*, showing great self-importance; arrogant

pos • ter • i • ty (pô tär´ ə tē) *n.*, all future generations

pre • car • i • ous (prə kär´ ē əs) *adj.*, dangerous

pre • car • i • ous • ness (prə kär´ ē əs nəs) *n.*, uncertainty; danger

pre • cip • i • tous (prē sip´ ə təs) *adj.*, steep

pre • con • cep • tion (prē' kən sep´ shən) *n.*, idea formed beforehand

pred • i • lec • tion (pre də lek´ shən) *n.*, established preference for, or bias toward, something

pre • dis • pos • ing (prē[dəs pōz´ iŋ) *adj.*, making likely to happen

pre • dom • i • nate (prē dô´ mi nāt) *v.*, have authority or influence over

pre • lude (prā´ lüd) *n.*, first movement of an opera; introduction

pre • med • i • tat • ed (prē me´ də tā təd) *adj.*, characterized by willful intent and a degree of forethought and planning

pre • sume (prē züm´) *v.*, dare; venture; take upon oneself

pre • sump • tu • ous (prē zump´ chü əs) *adj.*, taking liberties; overstepping bounds

pre • vail (prē vāl´) *v.*, triumph

prev • a • lent (pre´ və lənt) *adj.*, widespread

pro • bi • ty (prō´ bə tē) *n.*, honesty; uprightness

pro • cure (prō kyür´) *v.*, obtain by any means; acquire

prod • i • gal • i • ty (prô' də gal´ ə tē) *n.*, excess; waste

pro • di • gious (prə di´ jəs) *adj.*, enormous; remarkable; monstrous; causing amazement or wonder

pro • fane (prō fān´) *adj.*, blasphemous, irreverent; not devoted to religion or religious ends

prof • li • gate (prôf´ li gət) *adj.*, wildly extravagant

pro • fu • sion (prō fyü´ zhən) *n.*, large number; abundance

pro • lif • ic (prə li´ fik) *adj.*, creating abundant growth

prom • i • nence (prôm´ ə nents) *n.*, conspicuousness

pro • pi • ti • ate (prō pi´ shē āt) *v.*, gain, as someone's goodwill, by treating agreeably

pro • pi • ti • a • tion (prō pi shē ā´ shən) *n.*, act of pacifying or appeasing; making amends for wrongdoing

pro • sa • ic (prō zā´ ik) *adj.*, dull; unimaginative

pro • vin • cial (prō vin´ chəl) *adj.*, having a simple or limited perspective

pro • voked (prə vōkt´) *adj.*, made very angry; irritated; annoyed

pru • dence (prü´ dəns) *n.*, sense; care; caution

Q

quad • ru • ped (kwä´ drü ped) *n.*, animal, especially a mammal, with four feet

quell (kwel) *v.*, subdue; calm

quer • u • lous (kwär´ yə ləs) *adj.*, full of complaint

quiv • er • ing (kwiv´ ər iŋ) *n.*, shaking or moving characterized by a slight trembling motion

R

ran • kle (rāŋˊ k'l) *v.*, cause anger or bitterness

ra • pa • cious • ly (rə pāˊ shəs lē) *adv.*, with excessive hunger or desire

rap • tur • ous (rapˊ chʉr əs) *adj.*, full of joy or pleasure

rav • ag • es (raˊ və jəz) *n.*, damaging effects of something

rav • en • ous (raˊ və nəs) *adj.*, eager or greedy for food, satisfaction, or gratification

ra • vine (rä vēnˊ) *n.*, small, narrow, steep-sided valley larger than a gully and smaller than a canyon

re • cluse (reˊ klüs) *n.*, person who is withdrawn from society

rec • om • pense (rekˊ əm pens) *n.*, reward; payment

re • con • dite (rə känˊ dīt) *adj.*, difficult or impossible for the average person to understand; deep

rec • ti • lin • e • ar (rek' tə linˊ ē ər) *adj.*, moving or forming a straight line

re • deem (ri dēmˊ) *v.*, fulfill; restore

re • dress (rə dresˊ) *n.*, compensation or satisfaction, as for a wrong done

ref • uge (reˊ fyüj) *n.*, shelter; protection

ref • use (reˊ fyüs) *n.*, worthless materials; garbage

re • it • er • ate (rē iˊ tər āt) *v.*, repeat

rem • nant (remˊ nənt) *n.*, remainder

re • mon • strate (rə mänˊ strāt) *v.*, demonstrate

rend (rend) *v.*, tear apart

re • nowned (rə noundˊ) *adj.*, famous

re • pose (rə pōzˊ) *n.*, rest

re • proach (rə prōchˊ) *n.*, blaming or reproving; rebuke

re • pug • nant (rē pugˊ nənt) *adj.*, exciting distaste or aversion.

re • sig • na • tion (re zig nāˊ shən) *n.*, submissiveness; patient acceptance

re • so • lute (re zō lütˊ) *adj.*, strong in purpose; unyielding

re • spec • tive (rə spekˊ tiv) *adj.*, as relates individually to each of two or more persons or things

rev • er • en • tial (rev' ər enˊ ch'l) *adj.*, showing a feeling of deep respect, love, and awe

re • vert (rə vʉrtˊ) *v.*, return to a former practice or state

ri • ot • ous (rīˊ ə təs) *adj.*, abundant; enthusiastic

ro • bust (rō bustˊ) *adj.*, full of health and strength; vigorous

rouse (rowz) *v.*, become stirred

rum • mage (rumˊ əj) *v.*, search through thoroughly; ransack

ruth • less (rüthˊ ləs) *adj.*, cruel; without mercy

S

sanc • ti • ty (sāŋkˊ tə tē) *n.*, holiness

sat • u • rate (saˊ chʉr āt) *v.*, thoroughly soak

scar • ci • ty (skerˊ sə tē) *n.*, insufficient amount

scin • til • lat • ing (sinˊ til āt iŋ) *adj.*, sparkling

scoff • ing (skäfˊ iŋ) *n.*, showing disrespect; mocking

score (skōr) *n.*, set of twenty

scourge (skʉrj) *n.*, cause of widespread suffering

se • date • ly (sə dātˊ lē) *adv.*, with a quiet, steady pace

sed • i • ment (sedˊ ə mənt) *n.*, materials left or washed up by moving water

sep • ul • cher (sepˊ əl kʉr) *n.*, vault for burial

se • rene (sə rēnˊ) *adj.*, calm

shrewd (shrüd) *adj.*, having acute perception

sib • yl (sib' 'l) *n.*, fortune teller or female prophet

sin • gu • lar (siŋˊ gyü lʉr) *adj.*, unusual; strange

sire (sīr') *n.*, father or forefather

slough (slü) *n.*, deep, muddy place

so • lace (säˊ ləs) *n.*, comfort; consolation

so • lic • i • ta • tion (sô li' si tāˊ shən) *n.*, entreaty; petition; request

sor • rel (sôrˊ əl) *adj.*, light reddish-brown

sov • er • eign (sävˊ ər in) *adj.*, independent; above or superior to all others

spe • cious (spēˊ shəs) *adj.*, false; misleading

spec • u • late (spekˊ yü lāt) *v.*, take a risk in business, with the hope of making a profit

stal • wart (stälˊ wʉrt) *adj.*, brave; hardy

su • per • flu • ous (sü pʉrˊ flü əs) *adj.*, excessive; unnecessary

sub • due (sub düˊ) *v.*, overcome; control; reduce

sub • ju • gate (subˊ jə gāt) *v.*, conquer or subdue

sub • ju • ga • tion (sub jə gā' shən) *n.,* take-over; enslavement

sub • lime (sə blīm´) *adj.,* grand or exalted

sub • mis • sion (sub mi´ shən) *n.,* act of yielding; surrendering

sub • sist (sub sist´) *v.,* exist; have the necessities of life; nourish oneself

sub • tle (sut´ l) *adj.,* slight and not obvious

sub • ver • sion (sub vʉr´ zhən) *n.,* systematic attempt to overthrow a government

sub • ver • sive (sub vʉr´ siv) *adj.,* causing a corruption of morals or ideas

suf • fice (sə fīs´) *v.,* be enough; be sufficient or adequate

suf • fuse (sə fyüz´) *v.,* spread through; fill

sul • len (su´ lən) *adj.,* gloomily or resentfully silent

sul • try (sul´ trē) *adj.,* hot and humid

sur • cease (sʉr sēs´) *n.,* relief (from); end

sur • mise (sər mīz´) *v.,* infer; make a guess

sus • cep • ti • bil • i • ty (sə sep tə bi´ lə tē) *n.,* sensitivity

sym • me • try (sim´ ə trē) *n.,* beauty of form arising from balanced proportion

T

ta • boo (ta bü´) *n.,* something forbidden because of social custom or for protection

tar • ry (tār´ ē) *v.,* stay longer; linger

te • di • ous (tē´ dē əs) *adj.,* long and tiresome

teem • ing (tēm´ iŋ) *adj.,* overflowing; abounding

te • mer • i • ty (tə mār´ ə tē) *n.,* recklessness

tem • per (tem´ pər) *v.,* toughen, as by difficult experiences

tem • per • ance (tem´ pʉr əns) *n.,* moderation, restraint

tem • pest (tem´ pəst) *n.,* violent storm

ten • dril (ten´ drəl) *n.,* something that curls in a spiral

ten • u • ous (ten´ yü əs) *adj.,* flimsy; weak

ter • rain (tə rān´) *n.,* ground seen in terms of its features or physical nature; territory in this context

theo • log • i • cal (thē ō lä´ jik 'l) *adj.,* of or relating to theology, or the study of religious faith, practice, and experience

tin • ker (tiŋ´ kər) *v.,* repair, adjust, or work with something in an unskilled or experimental manner

tran • quil (traŋ´ kwil) *adj.,* peaceful

tran • si • ent (tran´ zē ənt) *adj.,* not permanent; temporary

treach • ery (tre´ chə rē) *n.,* violation of allegiance or trust

trea • ty (trē´ tē) *n.,* formal agreement between two or more nations

trem • u • lous • ly (trəm yə ləs lē) *adv.,* in a trembling or quivering manner

trep • i • da • tion (tre' pə dā´ shən) *n.,* anxiety; nervousness

triv • i • al • i • ty (triv' ē al´ ə tē) *n.,* something insignificant

tu • mul • tu • ous • ly (tü môl´ chü əs lē) *adv.,* wildly

U

ubi • qui • ty (yü bi´ kwə tē) *n.,* state of seeming to be everywhere

un • bound • ing (un baůnd´ iŋ) *adj.,* without limit or restraint

un • daunt • ed (un dän´ ted) *adj.,* firm in the face of danger; unafraid

un • de • vi • at • ing (un dē´ vē āt iŋ) *adj.,* unchanging; persistent

un • du • la • tion (un' jə lā´ shən) *n.,* rising and falling in waves

un • err • ing (un ār´ iŋ) *adj.,* free from error; certain

un • per • turbed (un pər tʉrbd´) *adj.,* not upset or concerned

un • re • quit • ed (un' rē kwīt´ əd) *adj.,* not rewarded or paid for

un • scru • pu • lous (un skrü´ pyü ləs) *adj.,* lacking moral principles

un • ut • ter • a • ble (ən ə´ tə rə bəl) *adj.,* beyond description or expression

un • wieldy (un wēld´ ē) *adj.,* not easy to carry or handle

usur • pa • tion (yü' sʉr pā´ shən) *n.,* unlawful or violent taking of power

V

vac • u • ous (vak´ yü əs) *adj.*, lacking intelligence

vag • a • bond (vāg´ ə bänd) *n.*, wandering, idle, disreputable, or shiftless person

val • id (va´ ləd) *adj.*, sound; just

va • lor (va´ lər) *n.*, bravery

van • quished (vaŋ´ kwish) *adj.*, conquered or defeated

var • nished (vär´ nisht) *adj.*, decorated; adorned

vast (vast) *adj.*, large; immense

ve • hem • ent • ly (vē´ hə mənt lē) *adv.*, with force or intensity

ven • er • a • ble (ven´ ɥr ə b´l) *adj.*, worthy of respect by reason of age and dignity

ven • ture (ven´ chər) *n.*, risky or dangerous project

vig • or (vig´ ər) *n.*, active physical or mental force or strength; intensity

vile (vīl) *adj.*, offensive

vin • di • cate (vin´ də kāt) *v.*, prove correct

vir • u • lent (vēr´ ə lənt) *adj.*, malignant, bitterly hostile

vol • a • tile (väl´ ə tīl) *adj.*, unstable; likely to change without warning

vo • li • tion (vō li´ shən) *n.*, choice or decision made

W

wan • ton (wän´ tən) *adj.*, unrestrained; merciless

watch (wäch) *n.*, period of time during which a soldier stays awake to guard or protect his or her group

wean (wēn) *v.*, free from dependence or custom

wi • ly (wī´ lē) *adj.*, sly

writhe (rī<u>th</u>) *v.*, twist as if struggling or in pain

X

xe • no • pho • bic (zē' nō fō´ bik) *adj.*, fearful of or showing hatred toward foreigners

Arte Publico Press. "The Latin Deli: An Ars Poetica" by Judith Ortiz Cofer from *The Americas Review,* Vol. 19, No. 1, 1991. Used by permission of Arte Publico Press, University of Houston.

James Baldwin Estate. "The Rockpile" by James Baldwin. Copyright © 1965 by James Baldwin. Collected in *Going to Meet the Man.* Copyright © renewed. Published by Vintage Books. Used by arrangement with the James Baldwin Estate.

Elizabeth Barnett. "Sonnet XXX" from *Fatal Interview* by Edna St. Vincent Millay. Copyright © 1931, 1958 by Edna St. Vincent Millay and Norma Millay Ellis. All rights reserved. Used by permission of Elizabeth Barnett, literary executor.

Beacon Press. "Death of Edgar Allan Poe" from *New Voices of Hispanic America* by Darwin Flakoll. Copyright © 1962 by Darwin J. Flakoll and Claribel A. Flakoll. Reprinted by permission of Beacon Press, Boston.

Susan Bergholz Literary Services. "Daughter of Invention" from *How the Garcia Girls Lost Their Accents.* Copyright © 1991 by Julia Alvarez. Published by Plume, an imprint of The Penguin Group (USA), and originally in hardcover by Algonquin Books of Chapel Hill. Reprinted by permission of Susan Bergholz Literary Services, New York. All rights reserved. "Straw into Gold: The Metamorphosis of the Everyday." Copyright © 1987 by Sandra Cisneros. First published in *The Texas Observer,* September 1987. Reprinted by permission of Susan Bergholz Literary Services, New York. All rights reserved.

BOA Editions, Ltd. "A Story" by Li-Young Lee from *The City in Which I Love You,* 1990. Reprinted by permission of BOA Editions, Ltd. "What Is Supposed to Happen" from *Red Suitcase: Poems* by Naomi Shihab Nye. Copyright © 1994 BOA Editions, Ltd. Reprinted by permission of BOA Editions, Ltd.

Georges Borchardt, Inc. "The Watch" from *One Generation After* by Elie Wiesel. English translation © 1965, 1967, 1970 by Elie Wiesel. Reprinted by permission of Georges Borchardt, Inc., on behalf of Elirion Associates.

Brooks Permissions. From *Report from Part One* by Gwendolyn Brooks, 1972. Reprinted by consent of Brooks Permissions. "The Explorer" and "To Black Women" from *Blacks* by Gwendolyn Brooks. Copyright © 1987. Reprinted by consent of Brooks Permissions.

Collins & Brown Ltd. "Coyote and the Earth Monster" from *Native American Myths* by Diana Ferguson. Copyright © 2001 Collins & Brown Ltd. Used by permission.

Curbstone Press. "Pasando Revista/Thinking Back" from *Fugues* (Curbstone Press, 1993) by Claribel Alegría. English translation by D. J. Flakoll. Reprinted with the permission of Curbstone Press. Distributed by Consortium.

Sandra Dijkstra Literary Agency. "Mother Tongue" by Amy Tan. Copyright © 1990 by Amy Tan. First appeared in *The Threepenny Review,* Fall 1990. Reprinted by permission of the author and the Sandra Dijkstra Literary Agency.

Rita Dove. "Wingfoot Lake" from *Thomas and Beulah,* Carnegie Mellon University Press. Copyright © 1986 by Rita Dove. Reprinted by permission of the author.

Faber and Faber Ltd. "The Love Song of J. Alfred Prufrock" from *Collected Poems 1909–1962* by T. S. Eliot. Reprinted by permission of Faber and Faber Ltd.

Farrar, Straus and Giroux, LLC. "Commander Lowell" from *Life Studies* by Robert Lowell. Copyright © 1959 by Robert Lowell. Copyright © renewed 1987 by Harriet Lowell, Sheridan Lowell, and Caroline Lowell. Reprinted by permission of Farrar, Straus and Giroux, LLC. "Death of the Ball Turret Gunner" from *The Complete Poems by Randall Jarrell.* Copyright © 1969, renewed 1997 by Mary von S. Jarrell. Reprinted by permission of Farrar, Straus and Giroux, LLC. Excerpt from *Great Plains* by Ian Frazier. Copyright © 1989 by Ian Frazier. Reprinted by permission of Farrar, Straus and Giroux, LLC. "On the Mall" from *The White Album* by Joan Didion. Copyright © 1979 by Joan Didion. Reprinted by permission of Farrar, Straus and Giroux, LLC. "One Art" from *The Complete Poems 1927–1979* by Elizabeth Bishop. Copyright © 1979, 1983 by Alice Helen Methfessel. Reprinted by permission of Farrar, Straus and Giroux, LLC. "The Magic Barrel" from *The Magic Barrel* by Bernard Malamud. Copyright © 1950, 1958, renewed 1977, 1986 by Bernard Malamud. Reprinted by permission of Farrar, Straus and Giroux, LLC. Excerpts from "When the Negro Was in Vogue"

LITERARY ACKNOWLEDGMENTS

by permission of Random House, Inc. "Dream" and "Though We May Feel Alone" from *Absolute Trust in the Goodness of the Earth: New Poems* by Alice Walker. Copyright © 2002 by Alice Walker. Used by permission of Random House, Inc. "Elegy for Jane" from *The Collected Poems of Theodore Roethke* by Theodore Roethke. Copyright © 1950 by Theodore Roethke. Used by permission of Doubleday, a division of Random House, Inc. "A Noiseless Flash" from *Hiroshima* by John Hersey. Copyright © 1946 and renewed 1974 by John Hersey. Used by permission of Alfred A. Knopf, a division of Random House, Inc. "I, too, sing America" and "The Negro Speaks of Rivers" from *The Collected Poems of Langston Hughes* by Langston Hughes. Copyright © 1994 by The Estate of Langston Hughes. Used by permission of Alfred A. Knopf, a division of Random House, Inc. "Is Phoenix Jackson's Grandson Really Dead?" from *The Eye of the Story* by Eudora Welty. Copyright © 1978 by Eudora Welty. "My Mother's Blue Bowl" by Alice Walker from *Anything We Love Can Be Saved*. Copyright © 1997 by Alice Walker. Reprinted by permission of Random House. Used by permission of Random House, Inc. From *Of Plymouth Plantation 1620–1647* by William Bradford, edited by Samuel Eliot Morison, Copyright © 1952 by Samuel Eliot Morison and renewed 1980 by Emily M. Beck. Used by permission of Alfred A. Knopf, a division of Random House, Inc. From "The Slump" from *Museums and Women and Other Stories* by John Updike. Copyright © 1972 by John Updike. Used by permission of Alfred A. Knopf, a division of Random House, Inc. "Son" by John Updike from *Problems and Other Stories* by John Updike. Copyright © 1972, 1973, 1974, 1975, 1976, 1977, 1978, 1979 by John Updike. Used by permission of Alfred A. Knopf, a division of Random House, Inc. From *The Woman Warrior* by Maxine Hong Kingston. Copyright © 1975, 1976 by Maxine Hong Kingston. Used by permission of Alfred A. Knopf, a division of Random House, Inc. "Upon Receiving the Nobel Prize for Literature, 1950" from *Essays, Speeches, Letters* by William Faulkner, edited by James B. Meriwether. Copyright © 1950 by William Faulkner. Used by permission of Random House, Inc.

Yvonne Sapia. "Defining the Grateful Gesture" from *Valentino's Hair* by Yvonne Sapia. Copyright © 1987 by Yvonne Sapia. Reprinted by permission of the author.

Seaver Books. "Prayer to the Pacific" by Leslie Marmon Silko. Copyright © 1981 by Leslie Marmon Silko. Reprinted from *Storyteller* by Leslie Marmon

Silko, published by Seaver Books, New York, NY. Used by permission.

Shoemaker & Hoard. "Riprap" from *Riprap and Cold Mountain Poems*. Copyright © 2004 by Gary Snyder. Reprinted by permission of Shoemaker & Hoard.

Greg Simon. "Ode to Walt Whitman" from *The Poetry of Pablo Neruda* by Pablo Neruda, translated by Greg Simon. Copyright © 2003 by Greg Simon. Used by permission of the translator.

Simon & Schuster, Inc. From Chapter 3 from *The Great Gatsby* by F. Scott Fitzgerald. Copyright © 1925 by Charles Scribner's Sons. Copyright renewed 1953 by Frances Scott Fitzgerald Lanahan. Reprinted with the permission of Scribner, an imprint of Simon & Schuster Adult Publishing Group. From Chapter 26 from *For Whom the Bell Tolls* by Ernest Hemingway. Copyright © 1940 by Ernest Hemingway. Copyright renewed © 1968 by Mary Hemingway. Reprinted with the permission of Scribner, an imprint of Simon & Schuster Adult Publishing Group. From Chapter 18 from *The Sun Also Rises* by Ernest Hemingway. Copyright © 1926 by Charles Scribner's Sons. Copyright renewed 1954 by Ernest Hemingway. Reprinted with permission of Scribner, an imprint of Simon & Schuster Adult Publishing Group. From *No Ordinary Time: Franklin and Eleanor Roosevelt: The Home Front in World War II* by Doris Kearns Goodwin. Copyright © 1994 by Doris Kearns Goodwin. Reprinted by permission of Simon & Schuster. "Poetry" from *The Collected Poems of Marianne Moore* by Marianne Moore. Copyright © 1935 by Marianne Moore. Copyright renewed © 1963 by Marianne Moore and T. S. Eliot. Reprinted with the permission of Scribner, an imprint of Simon & Schuster Adult Publishing Group.

Sterling Lord Literistic, Inc. "Man Listening to Disc" by Billy Collins, originally appeared in *The Atlantic Monthly*. Copyright © by Billy Collins. Reprinted by permission of Sll/Sterling Lord Literistic, Inc.

Sunstone Press. "Song of the Sky Loom" from *Songs of the Tewa* appears courtesy of Sunstone Press, Box 2321, Santa Fe, NM 87504-2321. Reprinted by permission of Sunstone Press.

Syracuse University Press. Excerpt from *Parker on the Iroquis*, edited by William N. Fenton (Syracuse University Press, Syracuse, NY, 1968). Reprinted by permission.

Tilbury House, Publishers. "Once More to the Lake" from *One Man's Meat* by E. B. White. Text copyright © 1941 by E. B. White. Copyright renewed. Reprinted by permission of Tilbury House, Publishers, Gardiner, Maine.

University of California Press. From *Songs of Gold Mountain: Cantonese Rhymes from San Francisco Chinatown* by Marlon K. Hom. Copyright © 1987 University of California Press. Used by permission of the University of California Press and the author.

University of Nebraska Press. From *Black Elk Speaks: Being the Life Story of a Holy Man of the Oglala Sioux* by John G. Neihardt. Copyright © 1932, 1959, 1972 by John G. Neihardt. © 1961 by the John G. Neihardt Trust. © 2000 by the University of Nebraska Press. Used by permission of the University of Nebraska Press.

University of New Mexico Press. "The Way to Rainy Mountain" from *The Way to Rainy Mountain* by N. Scott Momaday, 1969. Reprinted by permission of the University of New Mexico Press.

University of Pittsburgh Press. "The Blues" from *The Art of Drowning* by Billy Collins. Copyright © 1995. Reprinted by permission of the University of Pittsburgh Press. "So This Is Nebraska" from *Flying at Night: Poems 1965–1985* by Ted Kooser. Copyright © 2005. Reprinted by permission of the University of Pittsburgh Press.

University of Texas Press. "The Son" from *The Decapitated Chicken and Other Stories* by Horacio Quiroga, translated by Margaret Sayers Peden. Copyright © 1976 by the University of Texas Press. By permission of the University of Texas Press.

University of Virginia Press. "A Man Said to the Universe" and "Do not weep, maiden, for war is kind" by Stephen Crane. Edited by Fredson Bowers from *The Works of Stephen Crane.* Copyright © 1975. University of Virginia Press. Used by permission. "We Wear the Mask" by Paul Lawrence Dunbar from *The Collected Poetry of Paul Lawrence Dunbar* edited by Joanne Braxton. Reprinted with permission of the University of Virginia Press.

Eliot Weinberger. "Ars Poetica" from *Altazor: A Voyage in a Parachute* by Vicente Huidobro (1919), translated by Eliot Weinberger, 1963. Used by permission.

Wesleyan University Press. "Camouflaging the Chimera" and "Monsoon Season" by Yusef Komunyakaa from *Pleasure Dome* (Wesleyan University Press, 2001). Copyright © Yusef Komunyakaa 2001 and reprinted by permission of Wesleyan University Press. "The Last Wolverine" by James Dickey from *Poems 1957–1967* (Wesleyan University Press, 1978). Copyright © 1978 by James Dickey and reprinted by permission of Wesleyan University Press. *www.wesleyan.edu/wespress*. "What For" by Garrett Hongo from *Yellow Light.* Copyright © 1982 by Garrett Hongo. Reprinted by permission of Wesleyan University Press.

West End Press. "Learning to Love America" by Shirley Geok-lin Lim. Used by permission of West End Press.

Writers House. Excerpts from "Martin Luther King's Letter from Birmingham Jail" by Martin Luther King. Reprinted by arrangement with the Estate of Martin Luther King Jr., c/o Writers House as agent for the proprietor, New York, NY. Copyright © 1963 Martin Luther King Jr. Copyright © renewed 1991 Coretta Scott King.

The Wylie Agency, Inc. "Game" from *Unspeakable Practices, Unnatural Acts* by Donald Barthelme. Copyright © 1968 by Donald Barthelme. Reprinted by permission of The Wylie Agency. "The Names of Women" by Louise Erdrich. First printed in *Granta* 41, Autumn 1992. Copyright © 1992 by Louise Erdrich. Reprinted by permission of The Wylie Agency.

Yale University Press. From "Sinners in the Hands of an Angry God" by Jonathan Edwards from *Images or Shadows of Divine Things* (The Works of Jonathan Edwards). Used by permission of Yale University Press.

Zondervan. Taken from *Quiet Strength* by Rosa L. Parks with Gregory J. Reed. Copyright © 1994 by Rosa L. Parks. Used by permission of Zondervan.

Art and Photo Credits

Cover (top left) © Minnesota Historical Society/ CORBIS; (top right) Michael K. Nichols/National Geographic/Getty Images; (bottom left) © Tetra Images/Tetra Images/Corbis; (bottom right) © Alexandra Day/Corbis; (spine) © Tetra Images/Tetra Images/Corbis; **viii** (all) Library of Congress; **x** (top) Library of Congress; **xi** (top) © Bettmann/CORBIS; **xii** (bottom) © Mick Roessler/Corbis; **xv** (middle) © Christina Richards/Corbis; (bottom) © Francis G. Mayer/CORBIS; **xvi** (top) Library of Congress; **xvii** © Raymond Gehman/CORBIS; **xix** (top) The Granger Collection, New York; **xx** (bottom) © Sandro Vannini/ CORBIS; **xxii** (top) Library of Congress; (bottom) National Archives; **xxiv** (bottom) © Julie Dennis Brothers/CORBIS; **xxvii** (top) alptraum/www.stockxpert.com; (bottom) © G. Baden/zefa/Corbis

Unit 1

1 © PoodlesRock/CORBIS; **2** (top left) © CORBIS; **3** (middle left) Library of Congress; (middle right) Library of Congress; (top right) Library of Congress; **4** (middle) Library of Congress; (middle right) Library of Congress; **5** (banner–all) Library of Congress; (bottom left) The Granger Collection, New York; **6** (all) Library of Congress; **7** © Karl Weatherly/CORBIS; **9** (top left) © Catherine Karnow/CORBIS; (top right) Library of Congress; **10** (top) The Art Archive/Gift of the Coe Foundation/Buffalo Bill Historical Center, Cody, Wyoming/37.64; (bottom) © Layne Kennedy/CORBIS; **11** The Art Archive/Gift of the Coe Foundation/ Buffalo Bill Historical Center, Cody, Wyoming/37.64; **13** Courtesy of NASA; **15** (top) © Collier Campbell Lifeworks/CORBIS; (bottom) © Erich Schlegel/Dallas Morning News/CORBIS; **16** © Collier Campbell Lifeworks/CORBIS; **17** (top left) © Christopher Felver/ CORBIS; (middle left) © Darrell Gulin/CORBIS; (bottom left) © AINACO/CORBIS; **25** No Nee Yeath Tan no Ton, King of the Generath, 1710 (oil on canvas), Verelst, Johannes or Jan (b.1648-fl.1719)/ Private Collection/The Bridgeman Art Library; **27** © Francis G. Mayer/CORBIS; **28** (bottom) The Granger Collection, New York; **29** (top) © George H. H. Huey/CORBIS; **31** © CORBIS; **34** (top) The Granger Collection, New York; (bottom) © Bettmann/CORBIS; **35, 37** The Granger Collection, New York; **40** © Bettmann/CORBIS; **42** The Granger Collection, New

York; **46** (top) © Burstein Collection/CORBIS; (bottom) The Granger Collection, New York; **47** © Burstein Collection/CORBIS; **50** (top) © Bettmann/CORBIS; (bottom) The Granger Collection, New York; **51** © Bettmann/CORBIS; **54** (all) The Granger Collection, New York; **55** Smithsonian American Art Museum, Washington, DC/Art Resource, NY; **57-58** (all) The Granger Collection, New York; **62** Library of Congress; **63** © Bettmann/CORBIS; **64** © CORBIS; **66** Library of Congress; **67** The Granger Collection, New York; **69** © Francis G. Mayer/CORBIS; **70** Library of Congress; **71** (top) © Bettmann/CORBIS; (bottom) Library of Congress; **72** © Bettmann/CORBIS; **74** © MIMS R/ CORBIS SYGMA; **75** Library of Congress; **76** (top left) © Bettmann/CORBIS; (bottom left) The Granger Collection, New York; (middle left) © CORBIS; **77** The Granger Collection, New York; **80** (top) The Granger Collection, New York; (bottom) Library of Congress; **81** The Granger Collection, New York; **86-87** (all) Library of Congress; **88** © Bettmann/CORBIS; **92** (top) The Granger Collection, New York; (bottom) Library of Congress; **93-95** (all) The Granger Collection, New York; **97** (top left) Library of Congress; (middle right) Library of Congress; **101** The Granger Collection, New York; **102** © Bettmann/CORBIS; **104** The Granger Collection, New York; **105** Scala/Art Resource, NY; **106** © Christie's Images/CORBIS; **107** The Granger Collection, New York; **108** Book cover from *Founding Mothers* by Cokie Roberts. Copyright © 2004 by Cokie Roberts. Reprinted by permission of HarperCollins Publishers. Book cover from *A People's History of the American Revolution: How Common People Shaped the Fight for Independence* by Ray Raphael. Reprinted by permission of The New Press. Book cover from *The Interesting Narrative of the Life of Olaudah Equiano, or Gustavus Vassa, the African, Written by Himself* by Olaudah Equiano, edited by Werner Sollors. Copyright © 2001 by W.W. Norton & Company, Inc. Reprinted by permission of W.W. Norton & Company, Inc. Book cover from *Dearest Friend: A Life of Abigail Adams* by Lynne Withey. Reprinted by permission of The Free Press. Book cover from *Four Voyages by Christopher Columbus.* Reprinted by permission of Penguin Group (USA) Inc. Book cover from *American Indian Myths and Legends* selected and edited by Richard Erdoes and Alfonso Ortiz. Reprinted by permission of Random House, Inc.; **112** (all) Library of Congress

Unit 2

120–121 © Burstein Collection/CORBIS; **122** (top left) Library of Congress; (top right) Library of Congress; (middle) Library of Congress; **123** (top left) Library of Congress; (bottom left) Library of Congress; (top right) Library of Congress; **124** (top left) Library of Congress; (middle) Library of Congress; (top right) Library of Congress; (bottom left) © Bettmann/CORBIS; **125** (top left) The Granger Collection, New York; (top middle left) Library of Congress; (top middle) Library of Congress; (top middle right) Library of Congress; (top right) Library of Congress; **126** (all) Library of Congress; **127** © Archivo Iconografico, S.A./CORBIS; **128** (top) © Francis G. Mayer/CORBIS; (bottom) Library of Congress; **129** © Francis G. Mayer/CORBIS; **131** Library of Congress; **136** (top) © Bettmann/CORBIS; (bottom) Library of Congress; **137** © Bettmann/CORBIS; **139** (top) © Brooklyn Museum/CORBIS; (bottom) Library of Congress; **140** © Brooklyn Museum/CORBIS; **142** (top) Snark/Art Resource, NY; (bottom) Library of Congress; **143** Snark/Art Resource, NY; **144** Erich Lessing/Art Resource, NY; **148** Library of Congress; **149** © Christie's Images/SuperStock; **150** Library of Congress; **151** © Philadelphia Museum of Art/CORBIS; **153** © Brooklyn Museum/ CORBIS; **155** (all), **156** Library of Congress; **157** (bottom), **158, 162** © Michael P. Gadomski/SuperStock; **165** (top) The Granger Collection, New York; **165** (bottom) © Kevin Fleming/CORBIS; **166** The Granger Collection, New York; **168** (all) Library of Congress; **169** (top) © Mick Roessler/CORBIS; (bottom) © Lee Snider/Photo Images/CORBIS; **170** © Mick Roessler/CORBIS; **173** Library of Congress; **176** © David Muench/CORBIS; **179** (left) Time & Life Pictures/Getty Images; **184, 185** © Playboy Archive/CORBIS; **186, 190** The Granger Collection, New York; **195** Library of Congress; **197** © Christie's Images/CORBIS; **198** (top) © SuperStock, Inc./SuperStock; (bottom) Library of Congress; **199** © SuperStock, Inc./SuperStock; **201** The Granger Collection, New York; **202, 205** © Bettmann/CORBIS; **207** © The Corcoran Gallery of Art/CORBIS; **210** (bottom left) The Granger Collection, New York; (bottom right) Library of Congress; **211** (top) © David Sandberg/Taxi/Getty Creative; (bottom) Illustration for 'The Raven', by Edgar Allen Poe, 1875 (litho), Manet, Edouard (1832-83)/On Loan to the Hamburg Kunsthalle, Hamburg, Germany,/The Bridgeman Art Library; **212** © David Sandberg/Taxi/Getty Creative; **215** The Granger Collection, New York; **216** © Brooklyn Museum/CORBIS; **217** (top left), **221** (bottom), **225** The Granger Collection, New York; **227** © Images.com/CORBIS; **232** © agefotostock/SuperStock; **234** Scala/Art Resource, NY; **239** (left) Library of Congress; (middle) © Hulton-Deutsch Collection/CORBIS; (right) © Hulton-Deutsch Collection/CORBIS; **243, 244** Library of Congress; **245** The Art Archive/Musée Carnavalet Paris/Dagli Orti (A); **246** Time & Life Pictures/Getty Images; **249** Library of Congress; **251** © Pascal Deloche/Godong/CORBIS; **254** Library of Congress; **255** © Bettmann/CORBIS; **256** Clore Collection, Tate Gallery, London/Art Resource, NY; **260** Book cover from *Great Short Works of Herman Melville,* edited by Warner Berthoff. Introduction, headnotes, bibliography, and chronology copyright © 1970 by Warner Berthoff. Reprinted by permission of HarperCollins Publishers. Montana Historical Society. Image "Lewis and Clark at Three Forks" by E.S. Paxon on the Book cover from *Undaunted Courage by Stephen Ambrose.* Reprinted by permission of Simon & Schuster and Montana Historical Society. Book cover from *American Women Poets of the Nineteenth Century: An Anthology (*American Women Writers Series) by Cheryl Walker. Reprinted by permission of Rutgers University Press. Book cover from *Last of the Mohicans* by James Fenimore Cooper. Reprinted by permission of Penguin Group (USA) Inc. Book cover *The Essential Writings of Ralph Waldo Emerson* by Ralph Waldo Emerson, copyright © 2000. Used by permission of Modern Library, a division of Random House, Inc.; **262** © Eric Fougere/VIP Images/CORBIS

Unit 3

268–269 The Metropolitan Museum of Art, gift of Mrs. William F. Milton, 1923 (23.77.1). Image © The Metropolitan Museum of Art; **270** (all) Library of Congress; **271** (top left) Library of Congress; (top right) Library of Congress; (middle left) Library of Congress; (middle right) Library of Congress; (bottom left) Coldimages/www.stockxpert.com; **272** (all) Library of Congress; **273** (banner) Library of Congress; (bottom left) The Granger Collection, New York; **274** (all) Library of Congress; **275** © Minnesota Historical Society/CORBIS; **276** (top) Property of the Westervelt Company and displayed in The Westervelt-Warner Museum of American Art in Tuscaloosa, AL.; **276** (bottom) Library of Congress; **277** Property of the Westervelt Company and displayed in The Westervelt-Warner Museum of American Art in Tuscaloosa, AL.;

278 © CORBIS; 281 (top left) Library of Congress; (middle left) © Kelly-Mooney Photography/Corbis; (top middle left) Library of Congress; (top middle right) © Pach Brothers/CORBIS; (top right) Library of Congress; 282 © Bettmann/CORBIS; 283 Library of Congress; 286 (top) © Medford Historical Society Collection/CORBIS; (bottom) Library of Congress; 287 © Medford Historical Society Collection/CORBIS; 290 Library of Congress; 297–298 (all) Library of Congress; 299 (middle left) Library of Congress; (middle) Library of Congress; (middle right) Library of Congress; (top right) Library of Congress; (bottom left) Library of Congress; 300 The Granger Collection, New York; 302 The Granger Collection, New York; 305 (top) Library of Congress; (middle) Library of Congress; (bottom) The Granger Collection, New York; 306 Library of Congress; 307 (bottom left) Library of Congress; (top middle), Library of Congress; 309 Library of Congress; 311 Smithsonian American Art Museum, Washington, DC/Art Resource, NY; 312 © Bettmann/CORBIS; 315 © Christie's Images/ CORBIS; 317 (left) Library of Congress; (right) © Bettmann/CORBIS; 318 (left) The Pierpont Morgan Library/Art Resource, NY; (right) Library of Congress; 319 Library of Congress; 320 © Christina Richards/ CORBIS; 322 (top) Library of Congress; (middle) Library of Congress; (bottom) © CORBIS; 325 (top) Boy Sitting on the Grass, c.1882 (oil on canvas), Seurat, Georges Pierre (1859-91)/Art Gallery and Museum, Kelvingrove, Glasgow, Scotland, © Glasgow City Council (Museums); 325 (bottom) © SuperStock, Inc./SuperStock; 326 Boy Sitting on the Grass, c.1882 (oil on canvas), Seurat, Georges Pierre (1859-91)/Art Gallery and Museum, Kelvingrove, Glasgow, Scotland, © Glasgow City Council (Museums).; 329 Photo by jeffclow/www.stocxpert.com; 335 (top) © Minnesota Historical Society/CORBIS; (bottom) Library of Congress; 336 © Francis G. Mayer/CORBIS; 337 © Minnesota Historical Society/CORBIS; 339 (top left) © Bettmann/CORBIS; (bottom left) © Hulton-Deutsch Collection/CORBIS; 339 (middle left) The Granger Collection, New York; (middle) The Granger Collection, New York; (middle right) The Granger Collection, New York; (top right) The Granger Collection, New York; 340 The Granger Collection, New York; 341 (all) Library of Congress; 342 Library of Congress; 344 © Bettmann/CORBIS; 345 Art: © Banco de México Trust/© 2008 Banco de México. Diego Rivera & Frida Kahlo Museums Trust. Av. Cinco de Mayo No. 2, Col. Centro, Del. Cuauhtémoc 06059, México, D.F./Photo: Bridgeman-Giraudon/Art Resource, NY; 348 Library of

Congress; 349 (top) © Fine Art Photographic Library/ CORBIS; 349 (bottom) Amherst College Archives and Special Collections. Used by permission of the Trustees of Amherst College.; 350 © 2008 Salvador Dali, Gala-Salvador Dali Foundation/Artists Rights Society (ARS), New York. Photo: © Christie's Images; 352 © Fine Art Photographic Library/CORBIS; 354 The Granger Collection, New York; 355 (top left) © James Marshall/CORBIS; (middle left) © Hulton-Deutsch Collection/CORBIS; (middle right) © Bettmann/ CORBIS; (bottom left) The Granger Collection, New York; (top right) © Lake County Museum/CORBIS; 360 Book cover from *His Promised Land: The Autobiography of John P. Parker, Former Slave and Conductor on the Underground Railroad* by John P. Parker, edited by Stuart Seely Sprague. Reprinted by permission of W.W. Norton & Company, Inc.. Book cover from *The Civil War: An Illustrated History* by Geoffrey C. Ward and others. Reprinted by permission of Random House, Inc. Book cover from *The Belle of Amherst: A Play Based on the Life of Emily Dickinson* by William Luce. Reprinted by permission of the author. Book cover from *Bleeding Kansas: Contested Liberty in the Civil War Era* by Nicole Etcheson. Reprinted by permission of University Press of Kansas. Book cover from *Complete Poems* by Walt Whitman. Reproduced by permission of Penguin Group (UK) Ltd. Book cover from *The Killer Angels* by Michael Shaara, copyright © 1974 and renewed 2002. Used by permission of Ballantine Books, a division of Random House, Inc.

Unit 4

372–373 © Burstein Collection/CORBIS; 374 (top left) The Granger Collection, New York; (top right) Library of Congress; (middle left) Library of Congress; (middle right) Photo by jamesgroup/www.stockxpert. com; 375 (top left) Library of Congress; (top middle) Library of Congress; (top right) Bettmann/CORBIS; (middle right) Library of Congress; (bottom right) Library of Congress; 376 (banner, all) Library of Congress; (bottom right) © Bettmann/CORBIS; 377 (all) Library of Congress; 378 (all) Library of Congress; 379 © Geoffrey Clements/CORBIS; 380 (left) The Granger Collection, New York; (right) Library of Congress; 381 (top) The Granger Collection, New York; (bottom) © CORBIS; 382 The Granger Collection, New York; 384 The Granger Collection, New York; 385 Library of Congress; 387 (top right) Library of Congress; (middle right) © CORBIS; 393 (top)

Collected Poems of William Carlos William, Vol. 2: 1939–1962 edited by Christopher MacGowan. Used courtesy of New Directions Publishing Corporation.; (right) Library of Congress; **570** Smithsonian American Art Museum, Washington, DC/Art Resource, NY; **572** © Francis G. Mayer/CORBIS; **575** (top) © Alexander Burkatovski/CORBIS; (bottom) © Bettmann/CORBIS; **576** © Alexander Burkatovski/CORBIS; **579** © Fine Art Photographic Library/CORBIS; **583** © Bettmann/CORBIS; **584** (top) © SuperStock, Inc./SuperStock; (middle, bottom) Library of Congress; **585** © 2008 Artists Rights Society (ARS), New York/ADAGP, Paris/Succession Marcel Duchamp. Photo: © SuperStock, Inc./SuperStock**; 587** © SuperStock, Inc./SuperStock; **590** © SuperStock, Inc./SuperStock; **591** The Granger Collection, New York; **592, 593** (top) © Bettmann/CORBIS; **595** © Francis G. Mayer/CORBIS; **596** (bottom) Library of Congress; **597** Hirshhorn Museum, Washington DC. Gift of Joseph H. Hirshhorn Foundation, 1966.; **600** © Peter M. Fisher/CORBIS; **602** © Burstein Collection/CORBIS; **607** (bottom) Library of Congress; **608** Stone City, Iowa, c.1930. Grant Wood. Joslyn Museum, Omaha, Nebraska. Art © Estate of Grant Wood/Licensed by VAGA, New York, NY. Photo: © SuperStock, Inc./SuperStock; **609** (left) © Bettmann/CORBIS; (right) American Gothic, 1930. Grant Wood. Art Institute of Chicago, Chicago, Illinois. Art © Estate of Grant Wood/Licensed by VAGA, New York, NY. Photo: © SuperStock, Inc./SuperStock; **610** © Kirsten Soderlind/CORBIS; **612** Library of Congress; **613** © Fine Art Photographic Library/CORBIS; **614** © Fine Art Photographic Library/CORBIS; **616** (middle left, bottom left) Library of Congress; **617** © Culver Pictures Inc./Superstock; **618** © Sandro Vannini/CORBIS; **620** © Burstein Collection/CORBIS; **622** Bridgeman-Giraudon/Art Resource, NY; **627** (top) © Underwood & Underwood/CORBIS; (bottom) Library of Congress; **628** © Underwood & Underwood/CORBIS; **637** Library of Congress; **639** © 2008 The Jacob and Gwendolyn Lawrence Foundation, Seattle/Artists Rights Society (ARS), New York. Photo: The Jacob and Gwendolyn Lawrence Foundation/Art Resource, NY**; 640, 641** Library of Congress; **642** From the collection of the Indiana State Museum and Historic Sites; **644** National Portrait Gallery, Smithsonian Institution/Art Resource, NY; **645** (middle right) Library of Congress; (top left) Library of Congress; (middle) Library of Congress; (bottom) Library of Congress; **649** © Christie's Images/CORBIS; **650** Smithsonian American Art Museum, Washington, DC/Art Resource, NY; **651** (all) Smithsonian American Art Museum, Washington, DC/Art Resource, NY; **654** Library of Congress; **657, 658** © Thom Lang/CORBIS; **659** (bottom left) The Granger Collection, New York; (middle left) © Rudy Sulgan/CORBIS; (middle right) Library of Congress; **660** © Bettmann/CORBIS; **662** © Thom Lang/CORBIS; **664** Library of Congress; **665** Smithsonian American Art Museum, Washington, DC/Art Resource, NY; **666** © Bettmann/CORBIS; **667** Smithsonian American Art Museum, Washington, DC/Art Resource, NY; **668** Library of Congress; **669** © Brooklyn Museum/CORBIS; **672** The Granger Collection, New York; **674** Book cover from *The Saint Paul Stories of F. Scott Fitzgerald* by F. Scott Fitzgerald, introduced by Patricia Hampl and Dave Page. Reprinted by permission of Borealis Books. Book cover from *Classic Fiction of the Harlem Renaissance*, edited by William L. Andrews (1994). Used by permission of Oxford University Press, Inc. Book cover from *In Our Time* by Ernest Hemingway. Reprinted by permission of Simon & Schuster, Inc. Book cover *The Autobiography of Mother Jones* by Mary Harris Jones. Reprinted by permission of Dover Publications. Book cover from *Main Street* by Sinclair Lewis. Reprinted by permission of Penguin Group (USA) Inc.Reprinted by permission of Dover Publications

Unit 6

686–687 © SuperStock, Inc./SuperStock; **688** (top left) Library of Congress; (top right) Library of Congress; (middle left) National Archives; **689** (bottom left) Library of Congress; (top left) © Bettmann/CORBIS; (top right) © Bettmann/CORBIS; (middle left) © Bettmann/CORBIS; (bottom) Library of Congress; **690** (all) Library of Congress; **691** (all) Library of Congress; **692** (left) Library of Congress; **692** (middle left) Library of Congress; (middle) Library of Congress**;** (middle righ) Library of Congress; (right) National Archives; (bottom left) © Corbis; **693** Mabel and the Goat, 1961. Thomas Hart Benton**.** Art © Thomas Hart Benton and Rita P. Benton Testamentary Trusts/UMB Bank Trustee/Licensed by VAGA, New York, NY. Photo: © Burstein Collection/CORBIS; **694** (top) Library of Congress; (middle) © John Springer Collection/CORBIS; (bottom) Library of Congress; **695** Library of Congress; **696** Library of Congress; **698** Library of Congress; **699** Library of Congress; **700** Library of Congress; **702** (left) The Granger Collection, New York; (right) © Bettmann/CORBIS; **703** (top left) © CORBIS; **704** © CORBIS; **706** (top) © Bettmann/CORBIS; (bottom) © Horace Bristol/CORBIS; **707**

Unit 8

(top left) © David J. & Janice L. Frent Collection/ CORBIS; (middle left) Library of Congress; (top right) © Douglas Kent Hall/ZUMA/CORBIS; **1026** (top left) © Bettmann/CORBIS; (middle left) Courtesy of Photofest; (middle) Library of Congress; (middle right) Library of Congress; (top right) Library of Congress; (bottom left) Courtesy of NASA; **1027** Art © Estate of Roy Lichtenstein. Photo: Tate Gallery London/Art Resource, NY; **1028** (top) © Bettmann/CORBIS; **1028** (bottom) Library of Congress; **1029** © Bettmann/ CORBIS; **1030** Library of Congress; **1031** © Geoffrey Clements/CORBIS; **1033** Library of Congress; **1034** Lewis and Clark College; **1036** © Richard Hamilton Smith/CORBIS; **1037** © Richard Hamilton Smith/ CORBIS; **1038** (bottom) Jerry Bauer; **1039** © Henri Bureau/Sygma/CORBIS; **1040** © Bettmann/ CORBIS; **1041** © Tim Page/CORBIS; **1042** Richard McCulley; **1046** (top) © Wolfgang Kaehler/CORBIS; (bottom) Time & Life Pictures/Getty Images; **1047** © Wolfgang Kaehler/CORBIS; **1048** © Wolfgang Kaehler/CORBIS; **1049** © Bettmann/CORBIS; **1051** © Wolfgang Kaehler/CORBIS; **1053** Mariana Cook; **1054** © G. Baden/zefa/CORBIS; **1056** © Images. com/CORBIS; **1059** © 2008 Michael Escoffery/ Artists Rights Society (ARS), New York. Photo: Michael Escoffery/Art Resource, NY; **1060** (top) © Bettmann/ CORBIS; (bottom) Library of Congress; **1061** © Bettmann/CORBIS; **1062** Stephen Chernin/Stringer/ Getty Images; **1066** (top right) Library of Congress; (middle left) © Flip Schulke/CORBIS; (middle right) © Bettmann/CORBIS; **1069** Library of Congress; **1071** (top) Photo by Luminis/www.stockexpert.com; (bottom) Library of Congress; **1072** © 2008 The Jacob and Gwendolyn Lawrence Foundation, Seattle/Artists Rights Society (ARS), New York. Photo: The Jacob and Gwendolyn Lawrence Foundation/Art Resource, NY; **1074** Photo by Gregory Runyan; **1076** © Rainer Eggers/zefa/CORBIS; **1078** Photo by Luminis/www. stockexpert.com; **1080** (middle right) © Christopher Felver/CORBIS; (right) Library of Congress; **1085** (left) © Bettmann/CORBIS; (middle) © Christopher Felver/CORBIS; **1086** Library of Congress; **1087** (top) Scyza/www.stockexpert.com; (bottom) © Franklin McMahon/CORBIS; **1088** Smithsonian American Art Museum, Washington, DC/Art Resource, NY; **1090** Evan-Tibbs Collection. Washington, DC; **1091** © Phil Schermeister/CORBIS; **1093** (top) Library of Congress; (bottom) © Christopher Felver/CORBIS; **1094** Library of Congress; **1095** © Richard Berenholtz/CORBIS; **1098** Photo by Jacqueline Munoz; **1100** Photo by Sam LeVan; **1103** Photo by Janet Goulden; **1105** (top) California Academy of Sciences, The Ruth & Charles

Elkus Collection, catalog # CAS 0370-1248; (bottom) © Christopher Felver/Corbis; **1106** California Academy of Sciences, The Ruth & Charles Elkus Collection, catalog # CAS 0370-1248; **1108** Research Division of the Oklahoma Historical Society; **1109** alptraum/www.stockxpert.com; **1111** Library of Congress; **1112** alptraum/www.stockxpert.com; **1114** (bottom) Photo by Alison Freese; **1117** (bottom) © Oscar White/CORBIS; **1122** © Bettmann/CORBIS; **1123** Art Institute of Chicago, Chicago, Illinois; **1125** © Sophie Bassouls/CORBIS SYGMA; **1128** © Christopher Felver/CORBIS; **1129** © Brooke Fasani/ CORBIS; **1133** © Gerrit Greve/CORBIS; **1134** (top) Painting housed in the Museum of Modern Art, New York; (bottom) Library of Congress; **1139** (top) Photo by George Crux; (bottom) © Bettmann/CORBIS; **1140** Private Collection © The Estate of Alice Neel; **1141** © Envision/CORBIS; **1142** © ENVISION/CORBIS; **1144** © Oscar White/CORBIS; **1145** © CORBIS; **1148** Book cover *Going After Cocciato* by Tim O' Brien. Copyright © 1975, 1976, 1977, 1978 by Tim O' Brien. Reprinted by permission of Dell Publishing, a division of Random House, Inc.; Book cover *All the President's Men* by Bob Woodward and Carl Bernstein. Reprinted by permission of Wendell Minor.; Book cover from *Profiles in Courage* by John F. Kennedy. Copyright © 1955, 1961 by John F. Kennedy. Copyright renewed © 1983, 1984, 1989 by Jacqueline Kennedy Onassis. Forward copyright © 1964 by Robert F. Kennedy. Reprinted by permission of HarperCollins Publishers.; Book cover *The Autobiography of Malcolm X* by Malcolm X and Alex Haley. Copyright © 1964 by Random House, Inc. Used by permission of Random House, Inc.; Book cover from *The Right Stuff* by Tom Wolfe. Used by permission of Bantam Books, a division of Random House, Inc.; Book cover from *Go Tell it On the Mountain* by James Baldwin. Used by permission of Doubleday, a division of Random House, Inc.; **1150—1151** Library of Congress

---

Unit 9

1156—1157 © Christie's Images/CORBIS; **1158** (middle left) Striker77s/www.stockexpert.com; (middle right) Library of Congress; (bottom left) Photo by Stasi Albert; **1159** (top left) © Lynn Goldsmith/CORBIS; **1160** (middle right) Library of Congress; (top right) Enderbirer/www.stockexpert.com; (bottom) National Oceanic and Atmospheric Administration; **1161** (middle right) © Peter Turnley/CORBIS; (top right) Photo by Trish Parisy; **1162** (top left) Irochka/www.

stockexpert.com; (middle left) Library of Congress; (top right) Photo by David Lat; **1163** Art © Romare Bearden Foundation/Licensed by VAGA, New York/Photo: © Christie's Images/CORBIS; **1164** (bottom left) Harcourt, Inc. Book cover The Color Purple by Alice Walker. Copyright © 1982 by Alice Walker. Reprinted by permission of Harcourt, Inc.; (bottom right) © Roger Ressmeyer/CORBIS; **1165** (top) Painting by Suzanne Koch; (bottom) © Kimberly White/Reuters/Corbis; **1166** Smithsonian American Art Museum, Washington, DC/Art Resource, NY; **1168** © Underwood & Underwood/CORBIS; **1170** Painting by Suzanne Koch; **1172–1173** © Jeremy Cockayne/Arcaid/Corbis; **1174** © Jeremy Cockayne/Arcaid/Corbis; **1177** (top right) © Lowell Georgia/CORBIS; (bottom) © Louise Erdrich, reprinted with permission of The Wylie Agency, Inc.; **1178** © Lowell Georgia/CORBIS; **1182** © Burstein Collection/CORBIS; **1183** © Burstein Collection/CORBIS; **1184** (top) Photo by Marcin Sokolowski; (bottom) Daniel Cima; **1185** © Matias Morales; **1188** © Bettmann/CORBIS; **1190** Photo by Marcin Sokolowski; **1193** © Rudy Sulgan/Corbis; **1196** (top) © Najlah Feanny/Corbis; (bottom) © Ha Lam Photography; **1197** © Najlah Feanny/Corbis; **1198** Photo by Marja Flick-Buijs; **1199** (top) © L. Clarke/Corbis; (bottom) The University of Georgia Press; **1200** © L. Clarke/Corbis; **1202** © L. Clarke/Corbis; **1203** (top) Jonathan M.; (bottom) © Christopher Felver/CORBIS; **1204** © 1998 Faith Ringgold; **1206** Photo by Jonathan M.; **1207** (top) © Roger Allyn Lee/SuperStock; (bottom) © Christopher Felver/CORBIS; **1208** © Roger Allyn Lee/SuperStock; **1217** © Christopher Felver/CORBIS; **1218** (top) © Robert van der Hilst/CORBIS; (bottom) Getty Images; **1219** © Robert van der Hilst/CORBIS; **1220** © Steph Fowler/Brand X/Corbis; **1222** (left) © Hulton-Deutsch Collection/CORBIS; (right) © Bob Sacha/Corbis; **1227** AFP/Getty Images; **1228** Maison de Victor Hugo/Musee de la Ville de Paris/Giraudon/Art Resource, NY; **1229** William Abranowitz/A+C Anthology; **1230** © Lindsay Hebberd/CORBIS; **1231–1233** (background) © Lowell Georgia/

CORBIS; **1235** © Christie's Images/CORBIS; **1237** © Franklin McMahon/CORBIS; **1239** (top left) Getty Images; (middle left) David Dwyer; (middle right) © Christopher Felver/CORBIS; (right) AP Wide World Photos; **1240** (top) © Reed Kaestner/CORBIS; (middle) Getty Images; (bottom) David Dwyer; **1241** © Reed Kaestner/CORBIS; **1243** © Ron Chapple/Corbis; **1254** (top) John Evans; (bottom) Getty Images; **1255** © Gaetan Bally/Keystone/Corbis; **1257** Photo by Luann Johnson; **1258** © Robert Wallis/Corbis; **1260** Greg Olsen; **1261** (bottom) © Christopher Felver/CORBIS; **1264** Photo by Paul Szustka; **1265** © David Sailors; **1268** Photo by Paul Szustka; **1271** (bottom) © Christopher Felver/CORBIS; **1272** © Mosaic Images/CORBIS; **1274** © Alan Schein Photography/CORBIS; **1275** © Patti Mollica/SuperStock; **1278** Photo by Linden Frederick; **1279** (bottom) MLB Photos via Getty Images; **1281** Victoria & Albert Museum, London/Art Resource, NY; **1286** (top, middle left) William Abranowitz. Courtesy of Graywolf Press; **1288** John Evans; **1292** Getty Images; **1293** © Hisham Ibrahim/Corbis; **1296** Book cover from *Beloved* by Toni Morrison, copyright © 1987 by Toni Morrison. Used by permission of Alfred A. Knopf, a division of Random House, Inc.; Book cover from *A Prayer for Owen Meany* by John Irving. Copyright © 1990. Used by permission of Ballantine Books, a division of Random House, Inc.; Book cover from *I Dream a World: Portraits of Black Women Who Changed America* by Brian Lanker. Reprinted by permission of Harry N. Abrams, Inc.; Book cover from *Fast Food Nation* by Eric Schlosser. Copyright © 2002, 2001 by Eric Schlosser. Reprinted by permission of Houghton Mifflin Company.; Book cover from *A People's History of the United States: 1942-Present* by Howard Zinn. Copyright © 1980 by Howard Zinn. Reprinted by permission of HarperCollins Publishers.; Book cover from *Into Thin Air* by Jon Krakauer. Copyright © 1997 by Jon Krakauer. Used by permission of Villard Books, a division of Random House, Inc.; **1299** © Bettmann/CORBIS; **1300** © CORBIS

Index of Skills

Vocabulary & Spelling

Grammar & Style

Research & Documentation

Index of Humanities Topics

INDEX OF HUMANITIES TOPICS

Index of Titles and Authors

For Your Reading List